Light on Masonry

Also from Westphalia Press
westphaliapress.org

Brethren: Behold Your Supreme Council: Bio-Bibliographical Dictionary of the SGIG and Deputies of the Supreme Council, 33°

A Study in American Freemasonry

ESOTERIKA by Albert Pike: The Symbolism of the Blue Degrees of Freemasonry

Ancient Mysteries and Modern Masonry: The Collected Writings of Jewel P. Lightfoot

Essay on The Mysteries and the True Object of The Brotherhood of Freemasons

James Hoban's Secret Society

Female Emancipation and Masonic Membership: An Essential Collection

The Rosicrucian Philosophy in Questions and Answers

Freemasonry, Heir to the Enlightenment

Grand Crosses of the Court of Honour: Concise Scottish Rite Biographical Dictionary

Masonic Myths and Legends

A Radical In The East

Brought to Light: The Mysterious George Washington Masonic Cave

Worlds of Print: The Moral Imagination of an Informed Citizenry, 1734 to 1839

History of the Grand Orient of Italy

Why Thirty-Three?: Searching for Masonic Origins

A Place in the Lodge: Dr. Rob Morris, Freemasonry and the Order of the Eastern Star

The Great Transformation: Scottish Freemasonry 1725-1810

The 33 Principles Every Mason Should Live By: The True Meaning of Being a Mason

Masonic Regularity and Recognition: A Global Issue

Getting the Third Degree: Fraternalism, Freemasonry and History

Dudley Wright: Writer, Truthseeker & Freemason

Freemasonry: A French View

LIGHT ON MASONRY

The History and Rituals of America's
Most Important Masonic Exposé

David Bernard

ARTURO DE HOYOS, 33°, K.Y.C.H.
Past Master, McAllen Lodge No. 1110, A.F.&A.M. of Texas
Grand Archivist & Grand Historian, Supreme Council, 33°, S.J.

Westphalia Press
An imprint of Policy Studies Organization

Light on Masonry: The History and Rituals of America's Most Important Masonic Exposé

All Rights Reserved © 2024 by Policy Studies Organization

Westphalia Press
An imprint of Policy Studies Organization
1527 New Hampshire Ave NW
Washington, DC 20036
info@ipsonet.org

ISBN: 978-1-63391-956-3

Designed by Elizabeth A. W. McCarthy and Arturo de Hoyos

Layout by Elizabeth A. W. McCarthy and S. Brent Morris

Cover design by Jeffrey Barnes
jbarnesbook.design

Daniel Gutierrez-Sandoval, Executive Director
Policy Studies Organization & Westphalia Press

For Bro∴ Ronald C. Radatz
"A true and trusty friend"

A NOTE ON THE CONTENTS OF THIS BOOK

This book is not a study of present-day Masonic ritual. The rituals included herein represent pre–1831 Freemasonry. They do not take into account the tremendous ritual revisions which occurred following the post–1842 revival of the Fraternity in America.

David Bernard's *Light on Masonry: A Collection of All the Most Important Documents on the Subject of Speculative Free Masonry* (Utica, New York: William Williams, 1829) was the most important exposé ever published on American soil. A hostile work, it purported to print the rituals used by most American Masonic organizations almost 200 years ago. As will be demonstrated in the introduction, a good deal of the text was authentic. On the other hand, "infamous interpolations" were also made to some of the texts. The result is that, by exercising caution, we may learn a great deal about early American Masonry.

This study includes a facsimile reprint the fifth edition of *Light on Masonry*. Although all five of the original editions were available to me, I selected the fifth edition because it was the most well-organized, used the best type, and had the finest layout of all editions; it was also the most complete edition ever published. Of more particular interest to members of the Scottish Rite, it was the only edition to include Giles F. Yates's ca. 1823–27 revision of the Ineffable Degrees of the Lodge of Perfection.

March 13, 2008　　　　　　　　　　　　　　　　　　Arturo de Hoyos, 33°
House of the Temple　　　　　　　　*Grand Archivist and Grand Historian*
Washington, D.C.　　　　　　　　　　　　　　Supreme Council, 33°, S∴J∴

CONTENTS

A Note On The Contents Of This Book vi
Illustrations viii
Introduction 9
    The Masonic Exposé 10
    Masonic Origins 11
Exposures of Craft Masonry 13
    Early Masonic Craft Exposés, 1696–1730 13
    English Masonic Craft Exposés, 1760–69 18
    French Masonic Craft Exposés, 1737–51 19
Exposures of "High Degree" Masonry 20
    French Haut Grades *Exposés, 1763–85* 21
    An English High Grade Exposé 22
Pre-1826 American Masonic Exposés 24
    Daniel Parker's Masonic Tablet 28
The William Morgan Affair 34
    Morgan as an Itinerant Lecturer 34
    Morgan's Exposé 36
    Martin Smith's Bogus Exposé 38
    Mary Hanlon's Revelations 38
    David Bernard, the Man and the Freemason 42
    Exit Freemasonry 45
    A Revelation of Free Masonry 46
Light on Masonry 49
    Whence Came the Rituals? 56
    A Reverend "Black Coat" 57
    O Tempora! O Mores! 61
    Whiting's Betrayal Confirmed 63
    An Untempered Response 66
    Whiting's Feeble anti-Masonry 69
    Homage to Whiting 71
    Light on Masonry – *An Overview of its Contents* 74
    Neither a Jot nor a Tittle Shall Pass 80
    No Honor Among Thieves 86
Appendix 1 91
Appendix 2 97
Appendix 3 135
Appendix 4 167
Appendix 5 199
Notes 206
The Facsimile 217

ILLUSTRATIONS

1. Daniel Parker's *Masonic Tablet* (1822) 31
2. Smith's and Rohr's *The Free Mason's Instructor* (1812) 32
3. The signature of William Morgan, besmeared with ink
   and his Mark Master Mason Jewel 37
4. Mary Hanlon's *Revelations in Masonry* (1827) 39
5. The Reverend David Bernard 41
6. Giles F. Yates, 33°, Sublime Grand Master 43
7. Letter of J. J. J. Gourgas, Aug. 6, 1829, to Moses Holbrook 65
8. Illustration from *Le tombeau de Jacques Molai* (1797) 75
9. Genealogy of the S.R. rituals exposed in *Light on Masonry* 79
10. Knight of the East and West, ritual of ca. 1825 81
11. "Mysterious ladder" of the Knight Kadosh Degree 84
12. Secret Master, ritual of 1827 87

INTRODUCTION

"There are no secrets that time does not reveal."
—Narcissus, in Jean Racine, *Britannicus*, act 4, sc. 4 (1669)

"The treason is good, but the traitor is detestable."
—Spanish proverb, Miguel de Cervantes, *Don Quixote* (1605)[1]

"To David Bernard perhaps more than to any other man, the world is indebted for the revelation of the most execrable mysteries of Masonry."
—John Quincy Adams, *Letters on the Masonic Institution* (1847)

L IGHT ON MASONRY was the first great exposure of Masonic ritual published on American soil. I use the word "great" deliberately and in its most literal sense, for the book is both massive in size and impressive in content. In scope and substance it outshadowed and overpowered its predecessors, as it also easily negated the need for any real competition. It was the grandest and most successful of the many exposés published during the anti-Masonic period which swept America from 1826–42.

This fascinating, terrible, and turbulent period in American history seemingly erupted from nowhere like a virtual powder keg, hidden just beneath the surface of polite American society. And when it exploded its shock and report shook the fabric and foundations of the social order, disrupting the day-to-day life of untold thousands, Mason and non–Mason alike, laying waste to the innocence of the Fraternity which boasted many of the Founding Fathers within its fellowship. The frenzy which ensued affected the development of the young nation, and effected the creation of the first "third party" in American national politics (the "Anti-Masonic Party").

Men, who had been previously esteemed as the leaders of American society, risked becoming outcasts, accused of membership in a dangerous, treasonous, and even murderous society. The Fraternity's image as a temple of virtue was razed to the ground and transformed almost overnight. No more was it the "handmaid of religion"; it was now denounced as the "anti–Christ" at pulpits across the Country. In a panic to escape the mark of the Beast, men of every class—politicians, farmers, bankers—abandoned their once beloved society of men "who can best work and best agree," until Freemasonry across the United States teetered on the point of extinction.

The spark which ignited this catastrophic event was the abduction and presumed murder of a single man, William Morgan of Batavia, New York, following his boast that he had prepared an exposure of Masonic ritual for publication. Morgan's disappearance aroused a type of fervor which is difficult to imagine today, but has been accurately compared with the both the Colonial witch hunts of New England, and the "Red scare" of the McCarthy Era. The public outcry and outrage over Morgan's disappearance dealt a near-fatal blow to the Fraternity, and almost 200 years later he is still touted as a "martyr" by anti-Masons.

All socio-political movements benefit from a constitution, a manifesto, or a position paper, and the anti-Masons found theirs in *Light on Masonry*, a work which became so important that it was dubbed "the anti-Masonic Bible." Yet, surprisingly (to me at least), none of the many published studies of anti-Masonry focused with any detail on the book or its origins. In addition to boasting the most complete exposé of Masonic ritual ever published, it contained much additional material, including anti-Masonic committee reports and open letters from seceding Masons. Its author, or rather compiler, was the thirty year-old Rev. David Bernard (Figure 5), a man who was catapulted from obscurity to become America's most (in)famous anti-Mason. Notwithstanding the disappearance of Morgan, the attempted suppression of his exposé and its subsequent publication under the title *Illustrations of Masonry by one of the fraternity* (1826),[2] it is unlikely that anti-Masonry could have reached its zenith without Bernard or his book. And, as with that *other* Bible—which was also thumped upon pulpits in condemnation of the Fraternity—a study into the origins of Bernard's book yields surprises.

The Masonic Exposé

A great secret of Masonic historians is that many of us have a love affair with ritual exposures. Like other affairs of the heart, it is exciting, but it may also be a love–hate relationship. On the one hand, they are the product of betrayal and are *ipso facto* suspect. On the other hand, they present the *possibility* of authenticity and may teach us a great deal about the evolution of the ritual. Authenticity may be disproved, partially verified, or even wholly confirmed, in a number of ways. For example, a suspect text may be compared with genuine texts (should they exist) of the same period, or we may rely upon the testimony of contemporary witnesses (weighed against motive). In many cases, however, the authors or compilers of the Masonic exposures are anonymous or pseudonymous, forcing the historian to perform a variety of investigative techniques.

During the "Morgan episode" the desire for exposures was so great that they assumed diverse forms. Public exhibitions of the initiation ceremonies were per-

INTRODUCTION.

formed on stage by former members; straightforward printed exposés flooded the market and could be purchased at virtually any bookseller; anti-Masonic almanacs appeared which, month to month, included crude woodcuts depicting the modes of recognition; serial descriptions of the "evils and mysteries" of the Fraternity were published in anti-Masonic newspapers; the records of State legislatures included testimony describing the "terrible" initiation ceremonies, obligations and penalties; small printed leaflets and cards (similar to baseball cards) had caricatures of Masons in various unflattering postures. The atmosphere was ripe for the opportunist. In a notable instance the public's prurient interests and gullibility were rewarded with the publication of a completely bogus Masonic exposé, bearing all the hallmarks of authenticity. This was the environment into which *Light on Masonry* was born and which it helped maintain.

As we shall see, the origins of Bernard's rituals were partially known during his lifetime, but his own limited understanding of Masonry resulted in a confused report, at best. His book was reprinted numerous times, and pilfered even more, but the origins of many of its rituals were enigmatic to modern Masonic scholars. Readers of *Heredom* volume 1 (1992) may recall S. Brent Morris's premiere article, "Why Thirty-three?" which posed thirty-three unanswered questions relative to the Scottish Rite. His eighth query was, "What is the source of the 'Degrees' in Bernard's *Light on Masonry*?" Unable to resist a ritual mystery I subsequently answered the question and shared my findings with my late friend and posthumous Mackey Scholar, Kent L. Walgren.[3] I belatedly followed his advice and published the results of my study in *Heredom* volume 12 (2004).[4] The present introduction enlarges upon my previous exposition.

Masonic Origins

Freemasonry's rituals are not its only mystery. In fact, the question of Masonic origins has excited as much controversy—and as many heated debates—among its friends as its "secrets" have among its enemies. Though an investigation into Freemasonry's beginnings is beyond the scope of this introduction, some background information will help in understanding the evolution of Craft ritual.

Investigators are pretty well divided into two schools of thought: (1) the "authentic school," which, relying on the discipline of historical research, advocates a "transition theory" back to the operative stonemasons of Scotland and England, and (2) the "romantic school," which believes that Masonic legends, symbolism, and circumstantial evidence point to a number of other possible origins. Among the most popular "romantic" notions of origin are (a) Solomon's Temple, (b) the medieval Knights Templar, suppressed by Pope Clement V and King Philip the Fair of France, (c) the Hermeticists and/or Rosicrucians, (d) the Essenes, a Jewish sect which existed about two millennia ago, and (e) the ancient Egyptians.

LIGHT ON MASONRY.

The authentic school readily admits that Freemasonry's symbols and legends *borrow* from a wide range of traditions, but historians are quick to note that this eclecticism should not obscure the society's true origins. Rather, there is compelling, overwhelming and substantive evidence that the Masonic lodge, including its private ceremonies of admission, was a byproduct of the operative stonemasons by the late sixteenth century.[5]

In early days a lodge (*luge*, *lodg*, etc.) was a temporary structure, erected near the operative mason's building site, where he could rest and refresh himself from the day's labors. In time it evolved into something far greater. It has been suggested that King James III of Scotland's elevation of Robert Cochrane, once the King's "Master Mason" and architect of the great hall of Stirling Castle, increased respect among gentleman for the profession of masonry. Be that as it may, there is direct evidence that the Scottish lodges, which were established by royal degree, subsequently developed into social organizations providing mutual benefit to the early members.

William Schaw, appointed "Master of the Works" for life by James VI, in 1583, played a significant role in the early development of Freemasonry. His issue of the first and second "Schaw Statutes" in Scotland in 1598 and 1599 introduced many concepts which continue today. These statutes were founded on the "Old Charges" or "Gothic Consitutions," a collection of documents entailing the mason's code of conduct, his regulations, and a traditional history. The two earliest known copies of these constitutions are the *Regius MS.* (ca. 1390) and the *Cooke MS.* (ca. 1400).[6] These constitutions form the basis of government for modern Masonic Grand Lodges. The Schaw Statutes enlarged the idea of the lodge to encompass a broader territorial jurisdiction, and defined a hierarchy of "wardenis, dekynis, and maisteris in all thingis concerning thair craft." Lodges were to be presided over by a "Wardene generall," while William Schaw presided over all the Masonic lodges in his Country, as grand masters do throughout most of the world today (although the United States has fifty-one Grand Lodges). It is important to note that both before and after the institution of the lodge system masons continued as members of the incorporated trade guilds. Lodges operated in parallel to, and sometimes in competition with, these incorporations.

Admittance to the lodge was not a right afforded to all masons; rather, admission to this fellowship was a privilege conferred by a ceremonial induction. Initiation to the society included (1) a prayer, (2) a description of the seven liberal arts or sciences, (3) the recital of the Craft's traditional "history," (4) a reading from the Old Charges, (5) the administration of an oath or obligation of secrecy, and (6) the communication of the "Mason Word"—a term embodying the sum of the private modes of recognition (the catechism, words, grips, and signs).[7] The earliest evidence for the Mason Word dates to 1630, and it was viewed by

INTRODUCTION.

non-Masons with suspicion. The ability of Masons to communicate by nonverbal means was regarded as a mysterious power and may have contributed to rumors of Freemasonry's ties to esotericism.[8] However, some writers have correctly noted the second Schaw Statute's promotion of an "esoteric" method of learning. It ordained that "ye warden of ye lug of Kilwynning ... tak tryall of ye airt of memorie and science yrof." The "art of memory" is a mental exercise employing abstract images and architectural features to create a mental map which assisted memory.[9]

By the 1640s persons who were not stonemasons were initiated and became non-operative "masons." The initiation of non-operative gentlemen, and the conferral of the Mason Word, is the *sine qua non* of modern Speculative Freemasonry. It is important to note that there is still much to be learned about the origins of Masonry. Although Scotland played an indubitable and vital role in the formation of speculative Masonry, there remain enigmas to be solved on the English side. For example, all known copies of the Old Charges are of English origin. These documents predate Scottish Masonic traditions by 200 years. How did they develop, and under what circumstances? We do not yet know.

EXPOSURES OF CRAFT MASONRY

Early Masonic Craft Exposés, 1696–1730

The ridicule of Freemasonry, and the betrayal of its secrets, was more than a century-old practice when the American anti-Masonic movement began. The earliest known attack on the Fraternity was a leaflet addressed to the citizens of London in 1698 (shown on the next page in facsimile).[10] Its arguments laid the groundwork for further attacks, and its language anticipated that of the organized anti-Masonic movement which was to follow in the New World.

When the Grand Lodge of England was founded in 1717, speculative Freemasonry consisted of only two degrees: 1°, Entered Apprentice, and 2°, Fellow Craft. Contemporary allusions to "Masters" simply referred to senior Fellow Crafts. The 3°, Master Mason—an addition to the original system—became the first "high degree," and is not known to have been conferred prior to 1725.[11]

Modern Masonic scholarship includes a corpus of literature which analyzes the earliest descriptions of Masonic ritual and its subsequent development. Among the most important studies in this genre is Douglas Knoop, G. P. Jones, and Douglas Hamer's study, *The Early Masonic Catechisms* (Manchester University Press, 1943; Quatuor Coronati Lodge No. 2076, 1963). The editors transcribed and analyzed the following sixteen documents (nine in manuscript, seven in print), dating from 1696 to 1730.

TO ALL GODLY PEOPLE,
in the Citie of
LONDON.

HAving thought it needful to warn you of the Mischiefs and Evils practised in the Sight of God by those called Freed Masons, I say take Care left their Ceremonies and secret Swearings take hold of you; and be wary that none cause you to err from Godliness. For this devllish Sect of Men are Meeters in secret which swear against all without their Following. They are the Anti Christ which was to come leading Men from Fear of God. For how should Men meet in secret Places and with secret Signs taking care that none observe them to do the work of God; are not these the Ways of Evil-doers?

Knowing how that God obferveth privilly them that sit in Darkness they shall be smitten and the Secrets of their hearts layed bare. Mingle not among this corrupt People left you be found so at the World's Conflagration.

Set forth as a Warning to this Christian Generation by *M. Winter*, and Printed by *R. Sare* at Gray's Inn-gate at *Holbourn*.

1698,

INTRODUCTION.

MANUSCRIPT DOCUMENTS

1. *Edinburgh Register House MS.*	1696
2. *Chetwood Crawley MS.*	ca. 1700
3. *Sloane MS.*	ca. 1700
4. *Dumphries No. 4 MS.*	ca. 1710
5. *Trinity College, Dublin, MS.*	1711
6. *Wilkinson MS.*	1724–30
7. *Institution of Free Masons*	ca. 1725
8. *Graham MS.*	1726
9. *Chesham MS.*	ca. 1740
10. *Essex MS.*	ca. 1750

PRINTED DOCUMENTS

11. *A Mason's Examination*	1723
12. *The Grand Mystery of Free-Masons Discover'd*	1724
13. *The Whole Institutions of Free-Masons Opened*	1725
14. *The Grand Mystery Laid Open*	1726
15. *A Mason's Confession*	? 1725 (printed 1755)
16. *The Mystery of Free-Masonry*	1730
17. *Masonry Dissected*	1730

The earliest of these documents, the *Edinburgh Register House MS. 1696*, is not believed to have been an exposé, but was probably used as an *aide–mémoire*. Thus, it may preserve an authentic catechism used by early Freemasons. Its text, which follows below *in extenso*, is the earliest "complete" description of Masonic ceremony known, and provides insights into the early two-degree system.

[*Edinburgh Register House MS. 1696*]

SOME QUESTIONES THAT MASONS USE TO PUT TO THOSE WHO HAVE Y^e WORD BEFORE THEY WILL ACKNOWLEDGE THEM

Quest. 1. Are you a mason. Answer yes

Q: 2. How shall I know it? Ans: you shall know it in time and place convenient. Remark the forsd answer is only to be made when there is company present who are not masons But if there be no such company by, you should answer by signes tokens and other points of my entrie

Q: 3. What is the first point? Ans: Tell me the first point ile tell you the second, The first is to heill and conceall, second, under no less pain, which is then· cutting of your throat, For you most make that sign, when you say that

LIGHT ON MASONRY.

Q: 4   Where wes you entered? An: At the honourable lodge.
Q 5   What makes a true and perfect lodge? An: seven masters, five entered apprentices, A dayes Journey from a burroughs town without bark of dog or crow of cock
Q 6   Does no less make a true and perfect lodge, An: yes five masons and three entered apprentices &c.
Q 7   Does no less. An: The more the merrier the fewer the better chear
Q 8   What is the name of your lodge An: Kilwinning.
Q 9   How stands your lodge An east and west as the temple of jerusalem.
Q 10 Where wes the first lodge. An: in the porch of Solomons Temple
Q: 11. Are there any lights in your lodge An yes three the north east. s w, and eastern passage The one denotes the master mason, the other the warden The third the setter croft.
Q: 12 Are there any jewells in your lodge An Yes three, Perpend Esler a Square pavement and a broad ovall.
Q 13 where shall I find the key of your lodge, yes [? = Ans] Three foot and an half from the lodge door under a perpend esler, and a green divot. But under the lap of my liver where all my secrets of my heart lie.
Q: 14 Which is the key of your lodge. An: a wed hung tongue.
Q 15 where lies the key. Ans: In the bone box.
       After the masons have examined you by all or some of these Questions and that you have answered them exactly and mad the signes, they will acknowledge you, but not a master mason or fellow croft but only as as [? = an] apprentice, soe they will say I see you have been in the Kitchine but I know not if you have been in the hall, Ans I have been in the hall as weel as in the kitchine.
Quest 1 Are you a fellow craft Ans yes.
Quest 2 How many points of the fellowship are ther Ans fyve viz foot to foot Knee to Kn[ee] Heart to Heart, Hand to Hand and ear to ear. Then make the sign of fellowship and shake hand and you will be acknowledged a true mason. The words are in the I of the Kings Ch 7, v, 21, and in 2 chr: ch 3 verse last.

THE FORME OF GIVING THE MASON WORD

Imprimis you are to take the person to take the word upon his knees and after a great mar y ceremonies to frighten him you make him take up the bible and laying his right hand on it you are to conjure him, to sec[r]ecie, By threatning that if [he] shall break his oath the sun in the firmament will be a witness agst him and all the company then present, which will be an occasion of his damnation and that likewise the masons will be sure to murder him, Then after he hes promised secrecie They give him the oath a[s] follows

INTRODUCTION.

By god himself and you shall answer to god when you shall stand nakd before him, at the great day, you shall not reveal any pairt of what you shall hear or see at this time whither by word nor write nor put it in wryte at any time nor draw it with the point of a sword, or any other instrument upon the snow or sand, nor shall you speak of it but with an entered mason, so help you god.

After he hes taken the oath he is removed out of the company, with the youngest mason, where after he is sufficiently frighted with 1000 ridicolous postures and grimmaces, He is to learn from the sd mason the manner of makeing his due guard whis [? = which] is the signe and the postures and words of his entrie which are as follows

ffirst when he enters again into the company he must make a ridiculous bow, then the signe and say God bless the honourable company. Then putting off his hat after a very foolish manner only to be demonstrated then (as the rest of the signes are likewise) he sayes the words of his entrie which are as follows

Here come I the youngest and last entered apprentice As I am sworn by God and St Jhon by the Square and compass, and common judge to attend my masters service at the honourable lodge, from munday in the morning till saturday at night and to keep the Keyes therof, under no less pain then haveing my tongue cut out under my chin and of being buried, within the flood mark where no man shall know, then he makes the sign again with drawing his hand under his chin alongst his throat which denotes that it be cut out in caise he break his word.

Then all the mason present whisper amongst themselves the word beginning at the youngest till it come to the master mason who gives the word to the entered apprentice.

Now it is to be remarked that all the signes and words as yet spoken of are only what belong to the entered apprentice, But to be a master mason or fellow craft there is more to be done which after follows. ffirst all the prentices are to be removed out of the company and none suffered to stay but masters.

Then he who is to be admitted a member of fellowship is putt again to his knees, and gets the oat[h] administrated to him of new afterwards he must go out of the company with the youngest mason to learn the postures and signes of fellowship, then comeing in again, He makes the masters sign, and sayes the same words of entrie as the app[rent]ice did only leaving out the com[m]on Judge then the masons whisper the word among themselves begginning at the youngest as formerly afterwards the youngest mason must advance and put himself into the posture he is to receive the word and sayes to the eldest mason in whispering

The worthy masters and honourable company greet you weel, greet you weel, greet I you weel.

Then the master gives him the word and gripes his hand after the masons way, which is all that is to be done to make him a perfect mason

[*Endorsement*]

LIGHT ON MASONRY.

Some Questiones Anent the mason word 1696

The early ritual descriptions and exposés reveal increasingly complex developments which reached a summit with Samuel Prichard's *Masonry Dissected* (1730). Pritchard, who claimed he was a Mason, produced a 32–page pamphlet which was in a completely different class than its predecessors; it was the most important of the early exposés and provides the earliest known description of the Master Mason Degree and the Hiramic legend. Its text was meticulously analyzed and reprinted in facsimile by Masonic scholar Harry Carr.[11]

English Masonic Craft Exposés, 1760–69

Masonry Dissected had all the success for which the author could have hoped. Between 1730 and 1760 it dominated the market, and no new English exposés appeared. However, beginning in the latter year a new series of exposés appeared, one of which later exerted a tremendous influence on the development of Masonic ritual in the United States.

English Exposés, 1760–69

1.	*The Three Distinct Knocks*	1760
2.	*A Master–Key to Free–Masonry*	1760
3.	*Jachin and Boaz*	1762
4.	*Hiram, or The Grand Master–Key*	1746
5.	*Shibboleth*	1765
6.	*Solomon in All His Glory*	1766
7.	*Mahhabone*	1766
8.	*The Free-Mason Stripped Naked*	1769

These new exposés were as different from *Masonry Dissected* as it was from its predecessors. For instance, they added an additional level of complexity which included a symbolic interpretation of the working tools (earlier symbolism is vague at best). The two most important exposés in this group were *The Three Distinct Knocks* (*TDK*) and *Jachin and Boaz* (*J&B*), which respectively purported to reveal the rituals used by the "Moderns" and "Antients," two rival Grand Lodges then operating in England. The texts of these exposés have been analyzed and reprinted by Harry Carr and A. C. F. Jackson.[13] In *TDK*, for example, we discover the first evidence of passwords being used in an English ritual, although they appeared seventeen years earlier in the French book *L'Ordre des Franc–Maçons Trahi* (1745).

Ritual historians have long recognized that the authors of Masonic exposés plagiarized from each other. *TDK* supplied much of the text for *J&B*, and these two, in turn, provided the ceremonies described in *Hiram*, as well as much of

INTRODUCTION.

the text of *Shibboleth*, although the latter was also supplemented by material from *L'Ordre des Franc–Maçons Trahi*. A. C. F. Jackson observed that Thomas Wilson's *Solomon in All His Glory* "is nothing more than a translation of the French exposure *Le Maçon Démasqué* of 1751."[14] Thus, the French borrowed from the English, who returned the favor and borrowed from the French. The result of this mutual theft was the creation of texts that are interesting to read, but that are unreliable guides to lodge practices, as they presented a type of Masonry which never really existed.

French Masonic Craft Exposés, 1737–51

The following list demonstrates the frequency with which French publications appeared. Not surprisingly, the first of these was a translation of Prichard's remarkable work, *Masonry Dissected*.

French Exposés, 1737–51

1. *Réception d'un Frey–Maçon* 1737
   (Reception of a Free-Mason)
2. *La Réception Mystérieuse* 1738
   (The Mysterious Reception)
3. *Le Secret des Franc-Maçons* 1742
   (The Secret of the Free-Mason)
4. *Le Catéchime des Francs–Maçons* 1744
   (The Catechism of the Free-Masons)
5. *La Franc–Maçonne* 1744
   (The Free-Mason)
6. *Le Parfait Maçon* 1744
   (The Perfect Mason)
7. *Le Sceau Rompu* 1745
   (The Broken Seal)
8. *L'Ordre des Franc–Maçons Trahi* 1745
   (The Order of Free-Masons Betrayed)
9. *Les Francs–Maçons Ecrasés* 1747
   (The Free-Masons Crushed)
10. *La Désolation des Entrepreneurs Modernes du Temple de Jerusalem* 1747
    (The Desolation of the Modern Builders of the Temple of Jerusalem)
11. *L'Anti–Maçon* 1748
    (The anti-Mason)

12. *Le Maçon Démasqué* 1751
    (The Mason Unmasked)

Happily, English-speaking students of ritual may study this collection, it having been translated and analyzed by Harry Carr in his book *The Early French Exposures* (1971).[15] Of the foregoing exposures *Le Parfait Maçon* has particular relevance to the development of high degree Freemasonry. In the section "Secret des maçons ecossaise" (Secret of the Scottish Masons) it introduces a direct ancestor of the high degrees:

> It is said among the Masons, that there are still several degrees above that of the masters, of which I have just spoken; some say there are six in all, & others go up to seven. Those called *Escossais* [*Scottish*] *Masons* claim that they form the fourth grade. As this Masonry, different from the others in many ways, is beginning to become known in France, the Public will not be annoyed is I relate what I have read about it ... which seems to give the *Escossais* a degree of superiority above the Apprentices. Fellows, & ordinary Masters.
>
> Instead of weeping over the ruin of the temple of Solomon, as their brethren do, the *Escossais* are concerned with rebuilding it.
>
> Everyone knows that after seventy years of captivity in Babylon, the Great Cyrus permitted the Israelites to rebuild the temple & the City of Jerusalem; that Zerubabel, of the House of David, was appointed by him [Cyrus] the Chief & leader of that people for their return to the Holy City; that the first stone of the temple was laid during the reign of Cyrus, but that it was not completed until the sixth year of that of Darius, King of the Persians.
>
> It is from this great event that the *Escossais* derive the epoch of their institution, & although they are later than the other Masons by several centuries, they consider themselves of a superior grade.

If this theme seems somewhat familiar, it should. Members of the Scottish Rite will recognize a part of it as surviving in the Rite's 15°, Knight of the East, and 16°, Prince of Jerusalem. As one of the oldest high degree themes, it is not surprising to find it in other Masonic systems as well, including the American York Rite (Illustrious Order of the Red Cross), the Knight Masons of Ireland (Knight of the East), and the English Allied Masonic Degrees (Red Cross of Babylon).

EXPOSURES OF "HIGH DEGREE" MASONRY

As noted, the birth of "high degree" Freemasonry was heralded by the creation of the Master Masons Degree in 1725, just eight short years after the organization of the premiere Grand Lodge. Other high degrees followed suit and emerged within eight years of the appearance of the Master Masons Degree. As early as 1733 a manuscript referred to a "Scotch Masons' Lodge," and a year later it was men-

INTRODUCTION.

tioned again in a printed list of Masonic Bodies. It is important to note that the early designations "Scots," "Scotch," and "Scottish" refer to a *type* of Freemasonry practiced, rather than to native Scotsmen. Thus, we read that from 1733–40 a "Scotch Master Masons" Degree was being conferred on "normal" Master Masons, and by 1734–35 more degrees were invented, two of which were "Excellent Mason" and "Grand Mason." These early "Scotch" (or Scottish) degrees are ancestors of the Scottish Rite in both name and tradition, and represent a type of Masonry almost as old as the Master Masons Degree itself.[16] Next to the Master Masons Degree, "Scottish Masonry" is the oldest high-degree Masonry known, reaching back even further than Royal Arch Masonry.

FRENCH *HAUT GRADES* EXPOSÉS, 1763–85
- *Conversations Allégoriques, Organisées par la Sagesse* [Allegorical Conversations, Organized by the Wise] (1763).[17] This work, by Érasme Pincemaille, was the first exposé of the high degrees. It included the catechisms for the following degrees, several of which were destined to become a part of the Scottish Rite.

1. *Maîtres Parfaits*	(Perfect Masters)
2. *Maîtres Irlandois*	(Irish Masters)
3. *Maîtres Anglois*	(English Masters)
4. *Maîtres Élus*	(Elected Masters)
5. *Maîtres Élus de l'Inconnu*	(Elected Masters of the Unknown)
6. *Maîtres Élus des Quinze*	(Elected Masters of the Fifteen)
7. *Maîtres Illustres*	(Illustrious Masters)
8. *Écossois*	(Scot)
9. *Sublimes Écossois*	(Sublime Scot)
10. *Parfait Maîtres Angloisi*	(Perfect English Masters)

- *Les Plus Secrets Mystères des Hauts Grades de la Maçonnerie Dévoilés* [The Most Secret Mysteries of the High Degrees of Masonry Unveiled] (1766), by Monsieur (or Chevalier) de Bérage, soon followed Pincemaille's work and proved to be extremely popular; it was reprinted many times and included rituals of the following seven degrees:

1. *Parfaits Maçon Élu*	(Perfect Elect Mason)
2. *Élu de P.*	(Elect of P[erignan])
3. *Élu des 15*	(Elect of 15)
4. *Petit Architecte*	(Minor Architect)
5. *Grand Architecte*	(Grand Architect)
6. *Chevalier de l'épée et de*	(Knight of the Sword and of

  Rose-Croix.   Rose Croix)
 7. *Noachite ou Chevalier Prussien* (Noachite or Prussian Knight)
• ***Recueil Précieux de la Maçonnerie Adonhiramite*** [The Precious Collection of Adonhiramite Masonry] (1781; enl. ed., 1785), by Louis Guillemain de Saint-Victor, printed the ritual of the "Adonhiramite Rite," as well as those of the androgynous *La Vraie Maçonnerie d'Adoption* [The True Masonry of Adoption].

  1. *Apprenti*   (Apprentice)
  2. *Compagnon*   (Fellow Craft)
  3. *Maître*   (Master Mason)
  4. *Maitre Parfait*   (Perfect Master)
  5. *Premier Elu, ou L'Elu des Neuf* (First Elect, or Elect of Nine)
  6. *Second Elu nommé*   (Second Elect, called
   Elu de Pérignan.   Elect of Perignan)
  7. *Troisiéme Elu nommé*   (Third Elect, called
   Elu des Quinze.   Elect of Fifteen)
  8. *Petit Architecte*   (Minor Architect)
  9. *Grand Archirecte, ou*   (Grand Architect, or
   Compagnon Écossois   Scottish Fellow Craft)
 10. *Maître Écossois*   (Scottish Master)
 11. *Chevalier de l'Épée surnommé* (Knight of the Sword, surnamed
   Chevalier de l'Orient ou de l'Aigle Knight of the East, or of the Eagle)
 12. *Chevalier Rose-Croix*   (Knight Rose Croix)
 13. *Noachite, ou Chevalier Prussien* (Noachite, or Prussian Knight)
 15. *Apprentissage*   (Apprentice)
 16. *Compagnonage*   (Companion)
 17. *Maîtrese*   (Mistress)
 18. *Maîtrese Parfaite*   (Perfect Mistress)

  As we shall later see, some of the French exposés would provide an important contribution to *Light on Masonry*, and the inclusion of some of their ceremonies would play an even more direct role than the English collection.

An English High Grade Exposé
• ***Manual of Freemasonry*** (1825). This was the most complete exposé of Freemasonry published in England. It was prepared (perhaps predictably) by Richard Carlile, the infamous freethinker, advocate of social reform, and champion for freedom of the press. His work, which was first published serially in *The Republican*,[18] included much extraneous and irrelevant commentary, the bulk of which

INTRODUCTION.

was omitted when printed as a stand alone volume in 1845. Its ritual contents included the following degrees:
1. *Entered Apprentice*
2. *Fellow Craft*
3. *Master Mason*
4. *Past Master's Degree*
5. *Royal Arch Masonry*
6. *Knights Templar*
7. *Mark Man*
8. *Mark Master*
9. *Architect's Degree*
10. *Grand Architect*
11. *Scotch Master or Superintendent*
12. *Secret Master* [or, *Secret Provost and Levitical Order of Priesthood*]
13. *Perfect Master*
14. *Intimate Secretary, Obtained by Curiosity, or English Master's Degree*
15. *Intendent of the Buildings, or Master in Israel*
16. *Past Master*
17. *Excellent Masons*
18. *Super-Excellent Masons*
19. *Nine Elected Knights* [or, *Sublime Knights Elected*]
20. *Elect of Nine*
21. *Second Elect of Nine, or Perignon*
22. *Third Elect, or Elect of Fifteen*
23. *Priestly Order of Israel, or Provost and Judge*
24. *Provost and Judge, or Irish Master*
25. *Noahites or Prussian Knights*
26. *Red Cross Sword of Babylon*
27. *Knights of the Sword of the East*
28. *Red Cross of Rome and Constantine*
29. *Knights of the White Eagle or Pelican*
30. *Rosicrucian, or Ne Plus Ultra Degree*

Carlile's *Manual of Freemasonry* is of particular interest to students of the development of English Masonic ritual. It appeared just twelve years after the rival "Antients" and "Moderns" Grand Lodges reconciled and formed the current United Grand Lodge of England (UGLE). Soon thereafter, the UGLE organized a "Lodge of Reconciliation," which was tasked with producing a ritual to incorporate material from the former rivals. The work was performed between 1814 and 1816. Although the Lodge of Reconciliation did not produce an "official" ritual, to be promulgated throughout the UGLE's jurisdiction, it seems to have produced an "acceptable" one that forms the basis for most of the rituals used throughout the United Kingdom today. Individual English lodges are free to practice the ritual of their choice (a variety exist), as long as they incorporate certain essentials.

In *A Commentary on the Freemasonic Ritual* (1947, rev. 1973), Dr. E. H. Cartwright, explained that while Carlile's publication was unquestionably a "'spurious ritual' ... there is no doubt that in some points it does present the contemporary practice of regular Lodges and provides useful evidence...." This is important because Carlile's *Manual* offers the earliest description of post-union ritual. A fair degree of reliability may be assumed—at least in the Craft Degrees—because his text bears an uncanny resemblance to the "Emulation" and "Stability" rituals, both of which claim to exemplify the ritual of the Lodge of Reconciliation.[19] Carlile's ritual sources included the works of such prominent English Masons as William Preston, William Finch, Samuel Hemming, and Waller Rodwell Wright.

PRE-1826 AMERICAN MASONIC EXPOSÉS

As early as 1832 it was naïvely asserted, "The first revelation of Masonry in this country, was made by William Morgan."[20] On the contrary, both exposés (works intended for the public) and ritual guides (aids to the Fraternity) had been printed just shy of 100 years before Morgan's work.

AMERICAN EXPOSÉS, 1730–1822

1. *The Mystery of Free-Masonry*	1730
2. *Masonry Dissected*	1749/50
3. *Hiram: Or the Grand Master-Key*	1768
4. *Jachin and Boaz*	1774–1825
5. *Recueil Précieux de la Maçonnerie Adonhiramite*	1812
6. *4ème Grade sous le Titre de Maître-Parfait*	1812
7. *The Free Mason's Instructor*	1812
8. *The Masonic Tablet*	1822

Each of these will be discussed briefly below. Notably, the first exposé published in America was printed by a man now deemed one of America's most distinguished Masons.

• ***The Mystery of Free-Masonry* (1730).**[21] This anonymous and brief exposé of a Craft initiation, originally published in London in 1730,[22] was slightly reedited, and republished by Benjamin Franklin in his *Pennsylvania Gazette* a scant year before he himself joined St. John's Lodge, which met at Tun Tavern in Philadel-

INTRODUCTION.

phia. The text, which appears entirely in catechistical form, reveals a primitive state of Masonic ritual.

The Mystery of *Free-Masonry*.

Question, ARE you a Mason? *Answer*, I am. *Q*. How shall I know you are a Mason? *A*. By Signs, Tokens, and Points of my Enterance. *Q*. How was you made? *A*. Neither naked nor cloathed, standing or lying, but in due Form. *Q*. Give me a Sign? *A*. Every Square is a Sign; but the most Solemn is the Right-hand upon the Left-breast, the Arm hanging down, a little extended from the Body. *Q*. Give me a Letter? *A*. B. O. A. Z. *(When this Question is ask'd you are to give the Letter* B. *The Querist will say* O. *you* A. *he* Z.*)* *Q*. Give me another? *A*. J. A. C. H. I. N. *(Alternately as* Boaz. *N.B.* Boaz *and* Jachin *were two Pillars in* Solomon's *Porch.* I Kings, vii. 21.*)* *Q*. To what Lodge do you belong? *A*. The Holy Lodge of St. John. *Q*. How is it seated? *A*. East and West, as all other Temples are. *Q*. Where was you enter'd? *A*. In a Just and Perfect Lodge. *Q*. What makes a Just and Perfect Lodge? *A*. A Master, two Wardens, and four Fellows, with Square, Compass, and Common Gudge. (N.B. *One of them must be a Working Mason.*) *Q*. Where was you made? *A*. In the Valley of Jehosaphat, behind a Rush Bush, where a Dog was never heard to bark, nor a Cock to crow, or elsewhere. *Q*. Where was the first Lodge kept? *A*. In Solomon's Porch, the Pillars were call'd Jachin and Boaz. *Q*. How many Orders be there in Architecture? *A*. There be five, Tuscan, Dorick, Ionick, Corinthian, and Composite or Roman. *Q*. How many Points be there in the Fellowship? *A*. There be five, 1st Foot to Foot, 2d Knee to Knee, 3d Hand to Hand, 4th Heart to Heart, and 5th Ear to Ear. *Q*. How do Masons take their Place in Work? *A*. The Master's Place East, the Warden's East, and the Fellows the Eastern Passage. *Q*. How many precious Jewels be there in Masonry? *A*. Three, the Master, Wardens, and Fellows. *Q*. Whence comes the Pattern of an Arch? *A*. From the Rainbow. *Q*. Is there a Key for your Lodge? *A*. Yes, there is. *Q*. Where is it kept? *A*. In an Ivory Box, between my Tongue and my Teeth, or under the Lap of my Liver, where the Secrets of my Heart are. *Q*. Is there a Chain to your Key? *A*. Yes, there is. *Q*. How long is it? *A*. As long as from my Tongue to my Heart. *Q*. Where does the Key of the Working-Lodge lie? *A*. It lies upon the Right-hand, from the Door two Feet and a half, under a Green Turf, or under a Square Ashler. *Q*. Where does the Master Mason set his Mark upon the Work. *A*. Upon the South-East Corner. *Q*. Have you been in the Kitchen? (N.B. *You shall know an Enter'd Apprentice by this Question.*) *A*. Yes, I have. *Q*. Did you ever dine in the Hall? (N.B. *A Brother Mason by this Question.*) *A*. Yes, I did. *Q*. How old are you? *A*. Under 5, or under 7, which you will. (N.B. *When you are first made a Mason, you are only entered Apprentice; and till you are made a Master, or, as they call it, pass'd the Master's Part, you are only an enter'd Apprentice, and consequently must answer under 7; for if you say above, they will expect the Master's Word and Signs.* Note, *There is not one Mason in an Hundred that will be at the Expence to pass the Master's Part, except it be for Interest.*) *Q*. How was you admitted? (N.B. *Some will ask what was that Form after the third Question and Answer above.*) *A*. When I came to the first Door, a Man with a drawn Sword asked me, If I had any Weapons? I answer'd, No. Upon which he let me pass by him into a dark Entry; there two Wardens took me under each Arm, and conducted me from Darkness into Light, passing thro' two Rows of the Brotherhood, who stood mute, to the upper End of the Room, from whence the Master went down the Outside of one of the Rows, and touching a young Brother on the Shoulder, said, who have we here? To which he answer'd, A Gentleman who desires to be admitted a Member of the Society. Upon which he came up again, and asked me, If I came there thro' my own Desire, or at the Request or Desire of another? I said, My own. He then told me, If I would become a Brother of their Society, I must take the Oath administered on that Occasion. To which assenting, a Square was laid on the Ground, in which they made me kneel bareknee'd, and giving a Compass into my Right-Hand, I set the Point to my Left-Breast, and my Left-Arm hanging down. The Words of the Oath I can't remember, but the Purport was as follows:

I Solemnly protest and swear, in the Presence of Almighty God, and this Society, that I will not, by Word of Mouth or Signs, discover any Secrets which shall be communicated to me this Night, or at any time hereafter: That I will not write, carve, engrave, or cause to be written, carved, or engraven the same, either upon Paper, Copper, Brass, Wood, or Stone, or any Moveable or Immoveable, or any other way discover the same, to any but a Brother or Fellow Craft, under no less Penalty than having my Heart pluck'd thro' the Pap of my Left-Breast, my Tongue by the Roots from the Roof of my Mouth, my Body to be burnt, and my Ashes to be scatter'd abroad in- the Wind, whereby I may be lost to the Remembrance of a Brother.

After which I was cloathed. (N.B. *The Cloathing is putting on the Apron and Gloves.*) Q. How was the Master cloathed? A. In a Yellow Jacket and Blue Pair of Breeches. (N.B. *The Master is not otherwise cloathed than common; the Question and Answer are only emblematical, the Yellow Jacket, the Compasses, and the Blue Breeches, the Steel Points.*) Q. What was you doing while the Oath was tendering? A. I was kneeling bare-knee'd betwixt the Bible and the Square, taking the solemn Oath of a Mason. (Note, *There's a Bible put in the Right-Hand, and the Square under the Right-Elbow.*)

- *Masonry Dissected* (1749/50).[23] This was perhaps the most important of the early exposés of the Craft Degrees, and was originally published in London in 1730. This 32 page pamphlet was the first document to describe the Master Mason's Degree and played a tremendous role in stabilizing the Masonic ritual as practiced in England. Like *The Mystery of Free-Masonry*, its ritual text was entirely catechetical.
- *Hiram: Or the Grand Master-Key* (1768).[24] An exposé of the Craft Degrees originally published in London in 1764. It also included some of the Constitutions and Charges, as well as additional material.
- *Jachin and Boaz* (1774–1825). This revelation of the English "Antients" Grand Lodge ritual was first published in 1762. It was reprinted twenty-six times in the United States between the years 1774 and 1825, and was popular enough to warrant a Spanish edition in 1822.[25] Prior to the publication of Morgan's work, it was the most important exposé published on American soil, and greatly aided

INTRODUCTION.

ritual uniformity. In May 1828 ex–Mason Solomon Southwick (editor of the anti-Masonic newspaper *The National Observer*), stated that Thomas Smith Webb, the "father" of American Craft ritual, held a copy of *Jachin and Boaz* in his hands while teaching him and other young Masons their work (this accounts for the strong similarities between it and the "model Webb work"). Southwick wrote that he had

> obtained possession of a printed copy of the very identical edition of JACHIN AND BOAZ, out of which he was himself taught the first three degrees of Masonry, by the late Thomas S. Webb, author of the Masonic Monitor, and during his lifetime regarded by the fraternity as an infallible oracle, in their *"sublime"* mysteries. This copy is—(what Jachin and Boaz was before free masons mutilated and palmed it off as Morgan's book)—a complete view of the first three degrees.... *Henry C. Spencer*, of this city, the partner in business of Thomas S. Webb—but no Mason—printed and sold it slyly to such young *Noodles* as I myself then was—and Mr. Webb lectured them from it, as he did me, in the old Master's (afterwards Union, or Temple) Lodge, in North Pearl Street.[26]

Southwick's remarks might be misread to mean that Spencer reprinted *Jachin and Boaz*, but he and Webb only co-published *The Freemason's Monitor* (1797).[27]

- *Recueil Précieux de la Maçonnerie Adonhiramite* (1812).[28] Originally published in Paris in 1783, with a ritual of several degrees, this American version of *Recueil Précieux* contained only the catechism of the First Degree, with the ceremony of opening and closing the lodge. It was likely prepared for French-speaking Philadelphia Masons.
- *4ème Grade sous le Titre de Maître-Parfait* (1812).[29] This catechism of the Perfect Master Degree was also likely prepared for the above-mentioned French-speaking Philadelphia Masons.
- *The Free Mason's Instructor* (1812).[30] This text, prepared by Bro. Smith Allison, was published under the name of its sales agent, Bro. John A. Rohr, self-styled "Worshipful Master of Philadelphia Union Mark Lodge No. 1" (not recognized as a regular Mark Lodge in Pennsylvania).[31] The text was in plain English, but with the secret work abbreviated and/or missing. Its catechism of the Craft Degrees was based on the revisions of William Finch, the English ritualist. The ostensible purpose for printing the work was "to let every Brother know the true Ancient system." After its publication the Grand Lodge of Pennsylvania summoned Smith and Rohr to justify their actions. After an investigation they were ordered "[to] be reprimanded in Open Grand Lodge by the R.W. Grand Master, and make open Acknowledgement and recantation of their misconduct." Allison submitted and was reprimanded, while Rohr refused to appear before the Grand Lodge. He was expelled.[32]
- *The Masonic Tablet* (1822).[33] This work was America's first "cipher ritual," and was published in editions with the Craft and/or the Chapter Degree rituals. Its author and distributor was the Rev. Daniel Parker, High Priest elect of Mount

LIGHT ON MASONRY.

Horeb Chapter No. 75, Kingston, New York. Because Parker's work parallels Morgan's in location, scope and time, it is treated in more detail below.

DANIEL PARKER'S *MASONIC TABLET*

Exposés and guides published in the United States prior to 1822 actually represented either English or French workings. The Rev. Daniel Parker's *Masonic Tablet* was the first to print a uniquely American ritual, which it did by employing a simple cipher. The ritual was available in three versions—Craft, Chapter, or both. The cipher utilized five tactics to conceal the ritual: (1) letter and/or number substitution, (2) omission of letters, (3) inclusion of meaningless letters between backward brackets, numbers and punctuation marks, (4) spelling words backwards, and (5) inclusion of simple foreign words.

Lacking a title page, it is sometimes referred to as the "Ast ritual"—an allusion to the first line on the document. The heading of the first page of the Craft Ritual reads ":Ast SC PE's L," which deciphers as "[Fir]st S[e]c[tion] E[ntered] [A]p[prentice]'s L[ecture]," and the Chapter page begins "TP OS TCL," meaning "P[as]t [Master']s L[e]ct[ure]." I have decrypted a portion of the first catechism below, so that it may be compared with *The Mystery of Free-Masonry* (1730), as well as with the Morgan's text, which was reproduced by Bernard. The original *Masonic Tablet* runs the text together; but it is here broken apart into sentences for ease of comparison.

MASONIC TABLET – CIPHER TEXT	MASONIC TABLET – PLAIN TEXT
:Ast SC PE's L	**First Section Entered Apprentice's Lecture**
1. FM whnc cm u]oviz[sa na PE]gmz[	From whence came you as an Entered Apprentice?
2. fm]gp[e g f h st jn t j]mqz[rsa]pq[lm	From the lodge of holy St. John at Jerusalem.
5 wt cm u hr o d]mpq[	What came you here to do?
8 o lrn o sbdu ym psns nd mprv flsm n ysm	To learn to subdue my passions and improve myself in Masonry.
3 tn u r a]vs[n i prsm	Then you are a Mason I presume?
4 I m os tkn nd cptd mg brs nd swlf	I am so taken and accepted among Brothers and Fellows.
7 hw d u no urslf]pmz[o b a n	How do you know yourself to be a Mason?
6 y hvg bn ftn trd]cma[nv dnd nd m wlng o b trd gn	By having been often tried, never denied and my willingness to be tried again.
3 wt mks u a n	What makes you a Mason?
2 ym obn	My obligation.
1 hw shl I no u o b a n	How shall I know you to be a Mason?
4 y a crtn sn nkt drw nd e prft stnp f ym ntnc	By a certain sign, token, word, and the perfect points of my entrance.
1 wt r sns	What are signs?
2 rt slgna, sltnzrh, nd srlcdnprp.	Right angles, horizontals, and perpendiculars.

INTRODUCTION.

The *Masonic Tablet* must have gratified some Masons while simultaneously angering others. However it was received, Charles T. McClenachan reported the negative response of the Grand Lodge of New York.

> A Communication was received from Kingston Lodge, No. 20, informing the Grand Lodge that a printed work, as a help to the memory, called the "Masonic Tablet," was being advertised and sold by the Rev. Daniel Parker, to whom the Grand Secretary had written, condemning the same. The Communication of the Grand Secretary was approved by the Grand Lodge, which added that it decidedly condemned the use of all books or manuscripts, the support or tendency of which was to elucidate and explain Freemasonry.[34]

Because the *Masonic Tablet* included the rituals of Capitular Masonry, the Grand Chapter of Royal Arch Masons of the State of New York also had cause to investigate the matter. The detailed reports of the Grand Chapter, which describe Parker's odyssey, reveal that he was afforded due process when his troubles began in February 1823.

> A complaint was made by Comp. LIVINGSTON BILLINGS against Comp. DANIEL PARKER, P∴H∴P∴ of a Chapter under the jurisdiction of this Grand Chapter, which was referred to a Committee, which reported as follows:
>
> It appears to your Committee that, within the last year, Comp. PARKER, has procured to be published and had offered publicly for sale, certain printed pamphlets purporting to be the lectures on the several degrees in masonry. Your Committee are of opinion that such publication is a violation of every principle of masonry, and subversive of the best interests thereof. Your Committee have prepared resolutions which they deem proper to be adopted in the premises, which they beg leave to submit.
>
> 1. *Resolved*, That the Grand Secretary cite the said DANIEL PARKER to appear before the Grand Chapter on the first day of the nest annual meeting, to show cause why he should not be expelled for unmasonic conduct in the premises. And further, that the Grand Secretary furnish said PARKER with a copy of these resolutions.
>
> 2. *Resolved*, That it shall not be lawful for any Companion or Brother under the jurisdiction of this Grand Chapter, to write, print, or publish, or cause to be written, printed, or published, any book or books, or anything on the subject of masonry, without the permission and approbation of the Grand Council.
>
> 3. *Resolved*, That the Grand Secretary transmit a copy of these resolutions to every Subordinate Chapter under the jurisdiction of this Grand Chapter, and a like copy to each Grand Chapter in the United States.
>
> L. Billings,
>
> B. Chamberlain.[35]

The following year (February 5, 1824) the committee reported.

"The Committee appointed to investigate the case of Comp. DANIEL PARKER, High Priest elect of a subordinate Chapter at Kingston, reported as follows:
That they have given the subject that attention which the circumstances under which they were compelled to act would permit. It is with deep regret that your Committee are compelled to state their conviction, that the said Comp. DANIEL PARKER, by a series of reprehensible conduct as a Mason, has rendered himself a dangerous member of our fraternity and wholly undeserving of its benefits, its honors, or its confidence. It has satisfactorily appeared to your Committee, after a patient examination of a number of brethren, some of whom occupy and adorn the highest stations in the gift of then order, that Comp. PARKER has not only expressly violated one of the most important of our Masonic obligations, by printing and publishing, or causing to be printed and published, a work calculated to expose some of the mysteries which bind together and preserve our fraternity; but, in order to find a more ready and profitable market, he has added to his perfidy a series of falsehoods in regard to the opinions of his work entertained by some of our most eminent officers. * * * * With these facts before them, the Committee cannot hesitate as to the course that ought to be pursued. Comp. PARKER cannot be allowed, while laboring under charges or imputations like these, to mingle in fellowship with our brethren—much less to preside as the head of a subordinate Chapter, whose motto is "Holiness to the Lord." Your Committee therefore recommend the adoption of the following resolutions:

Resolved, That Comp. DANIEL PARKER, recently elected High Priest of MOUNT HOREB CHAPTER, No. 75, at Kingston, be, and he is hereby suspended, not only as the presiding officer of said Chapter, but as a member of our fraternity.

Resolved, That the aforesaid DANIEL PARKER be cited to appear before this Grand Chapter on the first day of its session, to be held in February, 1825, to show cause, if any he has, why he should not be expelled.

Resolved, That the Grand Secretary, under the direction of the Grand Council, be instructed to prepare charges and specifications, upon which the foregoing report and resolutions are founded, and serve a copy of the same upon the said DANIEL PARKER.

All of which is respectfully submitted,
By order of the Committee,
WILLIAM L. STONE,
Chairman.[36]

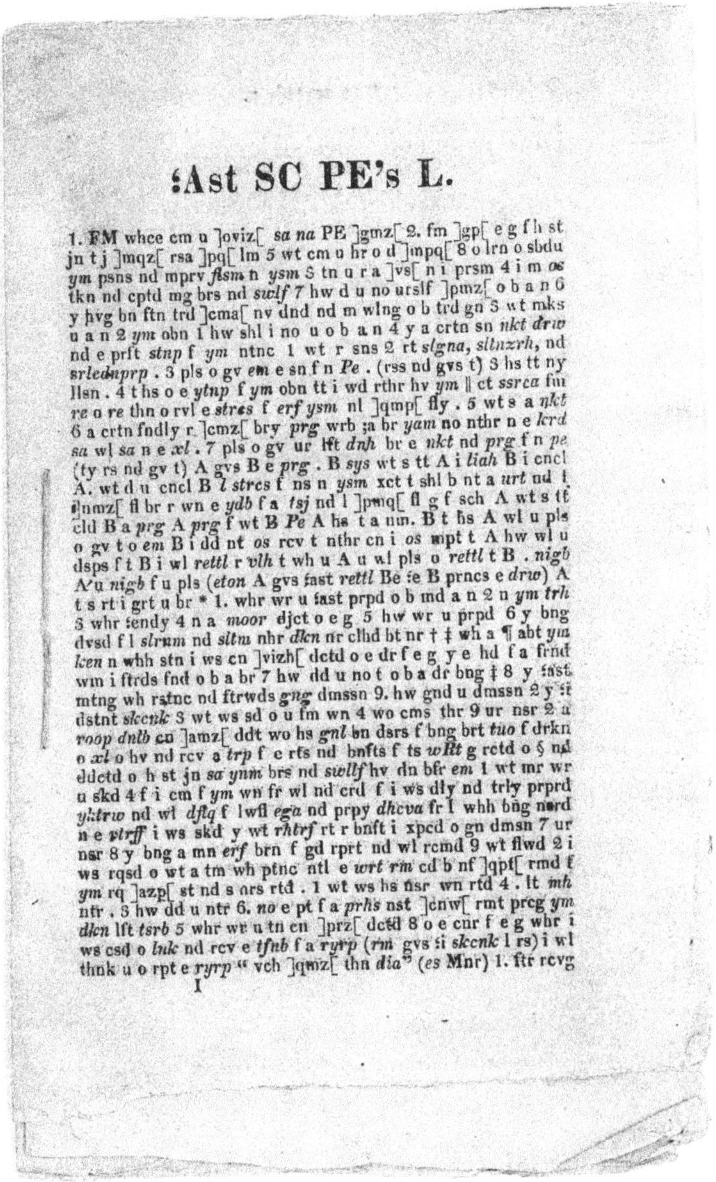
:Ast SC PE's L.

1. FM whce cm u]oviz[sa na PE]gmz[2. fm]gp[e g f h st jn t j]mqz[rsa]pq[lm 5 wt cm u hr o d]mpq[8 o lrn o sbdu ym psns nd mprv fism n ysm 3 tn u r a]vs[n i prsm 4 i m os tkn nd cptd mg brs nd swlf 7 hw d u no urslf]pmz[o b a n 6 y hvg bn ftn trd]cma[nv dnd nd m wlng o b trd gn 3 wt mks u a n 2 ym obn 1 hw shl i no u o b a n 4 y a crtn sn nkt drw nd e prft stnp f ym ntnc 1 wt r sns 2 rt slgna, sltnzrh, nd srledaprp . 3 pls o gv em e sn f n Pe . (rss nd gvs t) 3 hs tt ny llsn . 4 t hs o e ytnp f ym obn tt i wd rthr hv ym ‖ ct ssrca fm re o re thn o rvl e strcs f erf ysm nl]qmp[fly . 5 wt s a nkt 6 a crtn fndly r]cmz[bry prg wrb ;a br yam no nthr n e krd sa wl sa n e xl . 7 pls o gv ur lft dnh br e nkt nd prg f n pe (ty rs nd gv t) A gvs B e prg . B sys wt s tt A i liah B i cncl A. wt d u cncl B l strcs f ns n ysm xct t shl b nt a urt nd t dnmz[fl br r wn e ydb f a tsj nd l]pmq[fl g f sch A wt s tt cld B a prg A prg f wt B Pe A hs t a nm. B t hs A wl u pls o gv t o em B i dd nt os rcv t nthr cn i os mpt t A hw wl u dsps f t B i wl rettl r vlh t wh u A u wl pls o rettl t B . nigb A'u nigb f u pls (eton A gvs fast rettl Be :e B prncs e drw) A t s rt i grt u br * 1. whr wr u fast prpd o b md a n 2 u ym trh 3 whr fendy 4 n a moor djct o e g 5 hw wr u prpd 6 y bng dvsd f l slrum nd sltm nhr dlcn nr clhd bt nr † ‡ wh a ¶ abt ym kcn n whh stn i ws cn]vizh[dctd o e dr f e g y e hd f a frnd wm i ftrds fnd o b a br 7 hw dd u no t o b a dr bng ‡ 8 y fast mtng wh rstnc nd ftrwds gng dmssn 9. hw gnd u dmssn 2 y :t dstnt skcnk 3 wt ws sd o u fm wn 4 wo cms thr 9 ur nsr 2 u roop dnlb cn]amz[ddt wo hs gnl bn dsrs f bng brt tuo f drkn o xl o hv nd rcv a trp f e rfs nd bnfts f ts wRt g rctd o § nd ddctd o h st jn sa ynm brs nd swllf hv dn bfr em 1 wt mr wr u skd 4 f i cm f ym wn fr wl nd crd f i ws dly nd trly prprd yltrw nd wl dflq f lwfl ega nd prpy dhcva fr l whh bng nerd n e vlrff i ws skd y wt rhtrf rt r bnft i xpcd o gn dmsn 7 ur nsr 8 y bng a mn erf brn f gd rprt nd wl rcmd 9 wt flwd 2 i ws rqsd o wt a tm wh ptnc ntl e wrt rm cd b nf]qpt[rmd f ym rq]azp[st nd s ors rtd . 1 wt ws hs nsr wn rtd 4 . lt mh ntr . 3 hw dd u ntr 6. no e pt f a prhs nst]cnw[rmt preg ym dlcn lft tsrb 5 whr wr u tn cn]prz[dctd 8 o e cnr f e g whr i ws csd o lnk nd rcv e tfnb f a ryrp (rm gvs :i skcnk l rs) i wl thnk u o rpt e ryrp " vch]qmz[thn dia" (es Mnr) 1. ftr rcvg

I

Figure 1. The Reverend Daniel Parker's *Masonic Tablet* (New York, 1822), or "Ast Ritual," was both the first publication ever of a uniquely American Masonic ritual, and the first American cipher ritual. This copy is the only known example of the first edition.

LECTURES ON FREE MASONRY.

FIRST SECTION. FIRST DEGREE.

AS Free and Accepted Masons, where did you and I first m—t?
Upon the L—.
Where hope to p—t?—Upon the Sq—.
Why m—, and p—, in this peculiar manner?
As Masons, we ought always to m— upon the L—, so as to be enabled to p—t upon the S— with all mankind; but more especially with a Brother Mason.
From whence came you? From the w—.
Where do you direct your course? To the E—.
What induced you to leave the W— to go to the E—?
In search of the M—, and from him to gain instruction.
Who are you that want instruction?
A Free and A— M—.
What sort of men ought F— and A— M— to be?
Free men born of a free woman; brother to a king; fellow to a prince; and companion to a b—, if a Mason and a worthy man.
Why so free born?
It treats of that grand festival which *Abraham* made at the weaning of his son *Isaac*. When *Sarah* saw *Ishmael*, the son of *Hagar*, the Egyptian bond-woman, teazing and perplexing her son, she remonstrated with *Abraham*, saying, put away that bond-woman and her son, for such as they shall not inherit with the free-born; she speaking as being endowed by divine inspiration, well knowing that from *Isaac's* loins would spring a great and mighty people, such as would serve the Lord with Freedom, F and Z, and she fearing if they were brought up together, *Isaac* might imbibe some of *Ishmael's* slavish principles, it being generally remarked that the minds of slaves are much more contaminated than the free-born.
Why those equalities amongst Masons?
We are all equal by creation, but more so by the strength of our masonic Ob——
Generally speaking as a Mason, from whence came you?
From the Holy Lodge of St. John.
What recommendation have you brought?
The recommendation I brought from the Holy Lodge of St. John is to g—t your W—p well.
Any other recommendation?
*A hearty good wish to all B—s and F—s.
What is our peculiar province as Masons?
To learn to rule and subdue our passions, and make a zealous but prudent progres in the noble science of Masonry.
By this I presume you are a M—.
I am, R. W. Sir, so ta— and **** amongst brothers and fellows.
How shall I know that? By S. T—, and perfect P— of E—
What are S—?
All S—sL—s and P—s, are true and proper S—s to know a M— by.
What are T—s?
Certain regular and friendly G—s which enables us to know a brother Mason in the D—, as well as the L—.

Figure 2. Bro. Smith Allison's and Bro. John A. Rohr's *The Free Mason's Instructor* (Philadelphia, 1812) was an unauthorized *aide-mémoire* based on the rituals of William Finch. Allison submitted to the Grand Lodge of Pennsylvania and was reprimanded; Rohr refused and was expelled.

INTRODUCTION.

A family illness prevented Parker from attending the February 1825 meeting. At the meeting of February 8, 1826, while Parker served as High Priest of Mount Horeb Chapter, it was reported:

> That the Grand High Priest has had an interview with Comp. PARKER on the subject of his tracts, as he calls them, and by referring to a letter from the said PARKER, which accompanies this report, dated Jan. 30th, 1826, to Comp. AMES, it will be perceived that he admits the substance of the charges against him, and justifies his conduct. The Grand Chapter will therein discover the reasons which he urges in his defence. The Grand Council are in possession of his tract with explanations, which it is unnecessary to detail in this report.

The report was received and referred to a select committee. On February 10, 1826, the committee reported:

> That they deemed the publication of the tract alluded to in said charges and which the said PARKER, in the letter accompanying the report, admits he has published, a direct violation of the long established usages of the fraternity. The Committee have also perused the letter in which the said PARKER justifies the said publication, and cannot forebear giving it as their decided opinion that the language it contains is highly indecorous and insulting to the Grand Council; and that said Comp. Parker ought to be suspended or expelled from all participation in the benefits of masonry.
>
> Whereupon, it was
>
> *Resolved*, that DANIEL PARKER, High Priest of MOUNT HOREB CHAPTER, No. 75, be and he is hereby expelled from this Grand Chapter, and from all the communication with the Chapter and mark Lodges under the jurisdiction of the same.[97]

Parker's conduct, which was deemed "reprehensible," resulted in his expulsion from the Fraternity only a few months before Morgan disappeared. In a letter to John Quincy Adams, William L. Stone, author of *Letters on Masonry and Anti-Masonry* (1832), cited Parker's case in reference to the so-called Masonic "penalties" to demonstrate that expulsion is the only true penalty of the Fraternity.

> The truth is, that a simple expulsion from a lodge, or chapter, with a public advertisement of the fact, is the only penalty, for any offence, which the Masons, previously to the Morgan outrage, have ever, to my knowledge, considered themselves authorized to inflict. As an illustration of this assertion, I may perhaps be excused for stating a case in point. No longer than the year 1824,—only two years before the Morgan outrage—I myself introduced a resolution into the Grand Chapter, requiring the Grand Priest of a subordinate chapter to show cause why he should not be expelled. The accusation was the same as that for which Morgan died, viz: the writing and revealing of Masonic secrets. The charge was investigated, *and he was expelled*. He is

yet a living witness that his throat was not cut across, nor his tongue torn out by its roots, nor his body buried in the rough sands of the sea.[38]

It is not known if there were any bitter feelings on Parker's part, but Stone noted that *someone*, who resembles Rev. Parker, met with William Morgan at a hotel. If true, Morgan may have been influenced by the *Masonic Tablet*:

> He [Morgan] was at a Masonic hotel in this city, for a short time, in the course of that year, and was often closeted with a man of considerable talents, and some scholarship, who had been expelled from the fraternity the preceding year, for a breach of his Masonic faith, in writing and exhibiting certain Masonic matters that were then supposed to be unwritten. Parts of his manuscripts had been shown by Morgan to his friends....[39]

THE WILLIAM MORGAN AFFAIR

But for the disappearance of William Morgan (see frontispiece of facsimile) in September 1826, and the controversy which followed, both he and David Bernard would likely have passed through American history without notice. Although the definitive study of the anti-Masonic episode has yet to be written, the Morgan affair has been sufficiently examined in other works, so that I need only offer the briefest review here.[40]

William Morgan was born in Culpepper County, Virginia on August 7, 1774. Often referred to as "Captain Morgan," he may have fought under General Andrew Jackson at the Battle of New Orleans in 1815.[41] In 1819 he married Lucinda Pendelton, and in 1821 they moved to Upper Canada where he worked as a brewer. After a fire destroyed his business he was reduced to poverty, whence he commenced work as a stonemason. He thus worked in the environs of Rochester and Batavia, New York. While in the area he began attending local Masonic lodges, and he may have claimed to have been made a Mason in Canada, where the ceremonies and initiation rituals differed. Indeed, no evidence of his initiation or "regularity" (Masonic legitimacy) has been discovered. It is possible that he had studied an exposé, such as the oft-reprinted *Jachin and Boaz* (which, it will be recalled, resembled the Webb-workings), and he may thus have been admitted into the Lodge after passing a "Tiler's examination" (a simple test of the signs, tokens and passwords).

Morgan as an Itinerant Lecturer

Morgan, who was able to memorize the rituals, gained a reputation as a "bright Mason," and apparently acted as an itinerant lecturer in the Craft Degrees. Itinerant or traveling lecturers (called "degree peddlers" by their detractors) helped support themselves by selling or conferring Masonic degrees. Although they con-

INTRODUCTION.

tributed both to the spread of Freemasonry and to the uniformity of the rituals, they were sometimes viewed with suspicion.

Today, most American Masons look upon Thomas Smith Webb, Jeremy L. Cross, Benjamin Gleason, John Barney, and John Snow as great promoters of the Fraternity, but their contemporaries sometimes held different opinions. Today, Jeremy L. Cross is remembered, and even revered, as the author of *The True Masonic Chart, or Hieroglyphic Monitor* (1819),[42] the first Masonic monitor to include illustrations. During his lifetime, however (and in spite of the official positions he held), some high degree Masons were suspicious and wary of him. For example, Dr. Moses Holbrook, Grand Commander of the Scottish Rite's Southern Supreme Council wrote, "Jeremy L. Cross & all the whole traveling Caravan of wandering Lecturers, never extended the nor propagated any knowled[g]e of the *science* of Freemasonry, though they may have made their fortunes by their labors & publications."[43] Holbrook's criticisms were not reserved for "rivals." He also noted that Comte Alexandre François de Grasse-Tilly, founder of the Scottish Rite in France, Italy, Spain, and Belgium, reputedly made his living "by making Masons clandestinely."[44] If de Grasse-Tilly's culpability is debatable, there are straightforward examples of opportunists, such as Dr. James H. C. Miller, a struggling physician who sought Masonic charity while peddling his chivalric "Order of the Holy Cross." Miller's system was eventually condemned, and eventually disappeared from the Masonic scene (although its rituals, which were exposed by Bernard, were scavenged by other systems, including the prestigious Red Cross of Constantine).[45]

In spite of concerns, many Masons were sympathetic to the itinerant lecturers, and some local lodges were all too happy to employ an "expert," as Robert Morris explained in *William Morgan; or Political Anti-Masonry* (1883):

> [William Morgan] became a regular visitor and soon picked up a superficial acquaintance with the ceremonies of the Order. Traveling from place to place, in his vocation as journeyman bricklayer, he timed his stay at each place to cover the regular and called meetings of the Lodges, which were then almost as numerous in western New York as now, and he made it a point to attend them. The Lodges were full of work at every meeting, candidates were initiated, passed and raised, and the Lodges soon found use for a Brother whose voice was loud and sonorous, who displayed an easy manner as one who had mixed much with mankind, who could sit up all night if need be, to finish the whole work at hand, and who at the festive board could sing his song with the best, offer his toast, and also, drink his glass with the merriest....
>
> These peculiar gifts of William Morgan, his physical endurance, strong voice, dramatic style and social disposition, caused him, after a while, to be in demand. Lodges, learning that he had a job of bricklaying in the vicinity, would invite him to assist them in their labors. He learned to handle the Senior Deacon's rod expertly. The lengthy utterances of the Fellowcraft Degree which few learn, he memorized and delivered with emphasis and

effect. In return for this his Brethren paid his hotel bills and often contributed sums for the support of his family. In one instance where he remained several days, and gave the Lodge more than ordinary assistance, an appropriation of ten dollars was made him.[46]

Morgan's Exposé

No one knows for certain the cause of Morgan's disaffection and treachery. Reduced to desperate circumstances he may have succumbed to the "gnaw of poverty," which has tempted even good men to commit dishonorable acts; or perhaps he was angered that his personal intemperate habits ("he was a hard drinker"[47]) caused the lodge door to close to his face. Richard Carlile, an English freethinker and champion for a free press, contended that his own exposé of Freemasonry (first published in 1825 while a prisoner in Dorchester jail), induced Morgan to write his own.[48] An oft-repeated story asserts that because Morgan's Masonic regularity could not be ascertained, his signature on the records of his Royal Arch Chapter (dated May 31, 1825) was besmeared with ink.[49] This smear presumably stained his reputation as well and embittered him to the Fraternity. However, Stone's aforementioned *Letters on Masonry and Anti-Masonry* states that Morgan may have been working on his book several months earlier: "Morgan had commenced writing something upon the subject of Freemasonry, for what purpose it is not known, as early as the winter or spring of 1825."[50] The full title of Morgan's work was to be *Illustrations of Masonry, by one of the fraternity, who has devoted thirty years to the subject*. In selecting his title Morgan mimicked one of the most renowned Masonic works, William Preston's *Illustrations of Masonry* (London, 1772),[51] a guidebook used by English-speaking Freemasons on both sides of the Atlantic.

Most historians accept that Morgan and his intended publisher, David Cade Miller (a 1°, Entered Apprentice Mason who never advanced), encountered a series of obstacles and misfortunes connected with their venture. Among these were intimidation, an attempt to burn down the printing house, an offer to buy the manuscripts, and the theft of said manuscripts. The abduction and alleged murder of Morgan (drowned in the Niagara) was but the final *coup* in an ill conceived—and unsuccessful—attempt to halt publication. The resulting fury delivered such a blow to the Fraternity that it only began to recover about 1842, although the aftershock of the Morgan Affair still agitates anti-Masons today.

Considering the similarities between Daniel Parker's and William Morgan's offenses we may well ask, *what was their material difference?* And why would Morgan's intended work have outraged the Fraternity any more than Parker's? The difference, I suggest, was motive. Because Parker valued his membership in the Fraternity he enciphered the *Masonic Tablet* which he intended as nothing more than an *aide-mémoire* for his Brethren. *William Morgan, on the other hand, was a "cowan."* He had never been initiated into Masonry, and his entire Masonic experience was built upon deception. This stood in stark contrast with the principles

INTRODUCTION.

Figure 3. The signature of William Morgan, signed May 31, 1825, on the bylaws of the Royal Arch Chapter at Leroy, New York, was besmeared with ink. It appears with a redrawn facsimile in Rob Morris, *William Morgan; or Political Anti-Masonry* (New York, 1883). Below is the Mark Master Mason jewel of William Morgan, redrawn from a tracing made by the late Kent L. Walgren from a Mark Book in a private collection.

of Masonry, which Morgan himself repeated: "Truth is a divine attribute, and the foundation of every virtue. To be good and true are the first lessons we are taught in Masonry" (see facsimile, pp. 34–35). Embittered toward the Craft and influenced by mercenary motives, he intended his own work as a purely commercial venture. He unwisely boasted that he would not only expose the Craft rituals, *but the hitherto unpublished American Royal Arch Chapter Degrees in plain English*. Early American Masons would have viewed Morgan's treachery much more gravely than Parker's indiscretion. Rob Morris explained:

> When, therefore, it was announced that William Morgan was about to expose the mysteries of Masonry to the profane world, a general feeling of

wrath animated the Craft. Ashamed of the patronage they had extended to him, wounded in pocket and reputation for cherishing so base a man, ridiculed by wives and daughters for their associations with so unworthy a character, the indignation of the Brethren was sufficiently hot to call out threats and violent speeches from the more imprudent, and inward searchings of heart from all.

But how much worse the matter when it was discovered (about March, 1826) that Morgan had never been made a Mason. They had cherished an imposter in their bosoms. The man to whom they had communicated their Masonic esotery was under no obligations binding him to keep it secret ... for he was neither a non–affiliating Mason nor a seceding Mason—*he was not a Mason at all.*[52]

Martin Smith's Bogus Exposé

In spite of Morgan's disappearance his work was published with its exposition of the three Craft Degrees rituals, but the text ended abruptly following an unfulfilled promise to reveal the higher grades ("I shall now proceed with the Mark Master's degree...."). This deficiency, coupled with the excitement over Morgan's disappearance and his supposed murder, created a market for Masonic exposés. Bibliographer Kent L. Walgren lists twenty-three editions of Morgan's exposé published in just a year and a half following his disappearance. Many of these imprints were pirated editions, with none of their proceeds benefiting Morgan's business partner, David Cade Miller, or his widow, Lucinda Pendleton Morgan. With the public's interests aroused for further unveilings of the mysteries of Masonry, they were also ripe for a clever deception. The most successful delusion was *The Second Part; or, a Key to the Higher Degrees of Freemasonry ... By a Member of the Craft* (Cincinnati, 1827).[53] This book mimicked an exposé, but presented completely bogus and contrived rituals of the Chapter Degrees of Mark Master, Past Master, Most Excellent Master, and Royal Arch Mason.

The author's ruse included a preface which offered his reasons for exposing the degrees, and expressed concern for the supposed dangers which awaited him, should his identity ever be discovered. Of course, no secrets were actually revealed. Rather, the spurious rituals were built around authentic extracts from real ritual monitors. In this way a curious non-Mason could "verify" the authenticity of the ritual by referring to a Freemasons' monitor. This clever ploy evidently worked well enough, evinced by its reprinting in Cincinnati about 1850, and New York about 1860.[54] The copyright to the original edition was filed by a "Levi Smith," but Walgren discovered evidence that it was actually written by "Martin Smith." It is not known which name is authentic, or if Levi and Martin Smith were relatives.

Mary Hanlon's Revelations

The first attempt at an authentic *haut grade* exposure published in the United States was Mary Hanlon's *Revelations in Masonry, Made by a Late Member of the*

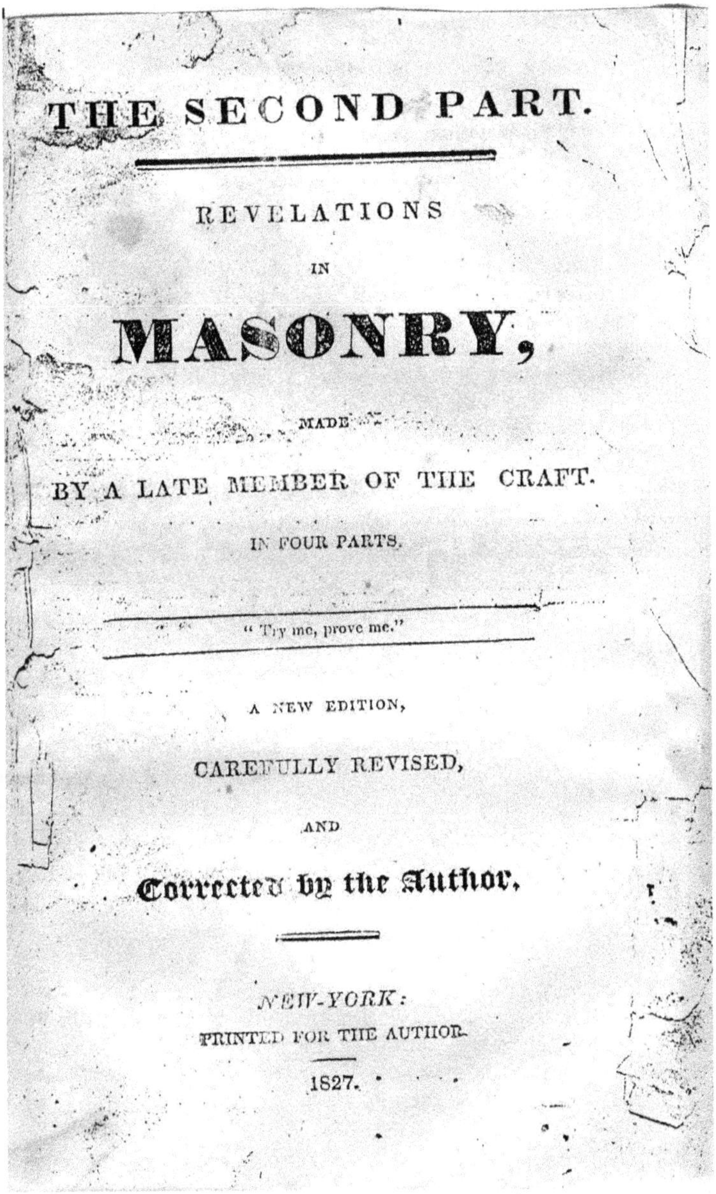

INTRODUCTION.

THE SECOND PART.

REVELATIONS

IN

MASONRY,

MADE

BY A LATE MEMBER OF THE CRAFT.

IN FOUR PARTS.

"Try me, prove me."

A NEW EDITION,

CAREFULLY REVISED,

AND

𝕮𝖔𝖗𝖗𝖊𝖈𝖙𝖊𝖉 𝖇𝖞 𝖙𝖍𝖊 𝕬𝖚𝖙𝖍𝖔𝖗,

NEW-YORK:
PRINTED FOR THE AUTHOR.
1827.

Figure 4. Mary Hanlon's *Revelations in Masonry, Made by a Late Member of the Craft, in Four Parts* (New York, 1827) was the first attempt to expose high grade Masonry in the United States. Its contents were actually plagiarized from an English exposé.

Craft, in Four Parts (1827).⁵⁵ This work is sometimes referred to as a "Four Part Morgan," because most bound copies included Morgan's *Illustrations of Masonry* as the first of its four parts (although some editions substituted a reprint of *Jachin and Boaz*). Hanlon's publication contained the following high grade initiations:

> *The Second Part.* Architect's Degree; Grand Architect; Scotch Master or Superintendant; Secret Master; Perfect Master; Intimate Secretary; Intendant of the Buildings, or Master in Israel.
> *The Third Part.* Nine Elected Knights, or Sublime Knights Elected; Knights of the White Eagle or Pelican; Knights of the Eagle.
> *The Fourth Part.* Rosicrucian or Ne Plus Ultra; Recapitulation of the following degrees: Grand Architect; Scotch Master or Superintendant; Secret Master; Perfect Master; Intimate Secretary, or English Master; Nine Elected Knights, or Sublime Knights Elected; Intendant Knights of the White Eagle or Pelican; Rosicrucian.

Its impressive contents notwithstanding, *all* of the above ritual material was plagiarized from Richard Carlile's aforementioned exposé of Freemasonry recently published in *The Republican* (London, 1825).⁵⁶ Hanlon's secret was relatively safe because few Americans would have been aware of Carlile's work. Although Hanlon's *Revelations in Masonry* enjoyed only modest success, it succeeded in attracting the attention of high-degree Masons. The leaders of the two American Scottish Rite Supreme Councils enjoyed an ongoing correspondence and readily shared information. John James Joseph Gourgas, Grand Secretary General of the Supreme Council, 33°, for the Northern District and Jurisdiction of the United States of America (later, "Northern Masonic Jurisdiction, U.S.A."), purchased a copy for Dr. Moses Holbrook, Grand Commander of the Supreme Council at Charleston, South Carolina (the "Southern Jurisdiction"), which Holbrook acknowledged receiving in a letter of August 22, 1827. In a curious way Holbrook's comment regarding the Hanlon's exposure reveals more about his own state of mind than they did about the publication.

> I think Mary Hanlon's "Revelations" will be of real service to the good cause—for in Nonsense, her pamphlets excel Morgan—I hope some bean will run away with her & get married so as to give her 4 pamphlets an equal chance with Morgan who by the way—if he has been murdered—has met his fate from David Cade Miller & Co's investigations—I think Morgan yet lives.⁵⁷

If Holbrook believed that the "revelations" were over, he would soon witness an unveiling of apocalyptic proportions. Unknown to him at the time the fate of Freemasonry for the next sixteen years was about to travel by manuscript into the hands of a young member of Holbrook's own beloved Scottish Rite.

INTRODUCTION.

Figure 5. The Reverend David Bernard, later in life. Frontispiece to *Light on Masonry, by Eld. David Bernard. Revised Edition, with an Appendix Revealing the Mysteries of Odd Fellowship By a Member of the Craft*. Eleventh Edition (Dayton, Ohio, 1870).

LIGHT ON MASONRY.

DAVID BERNARD, THE MAN AND THE FREEMASON
For all the popularity he enjoyed, Rev. David Bernard was reticent to speak about himself. However, a few brief autobiographical remarks, collated from accounts published when he was in his seventiess, provide some details about his life.[58] He was born on Christmas Eve, 1798, in Utica, Oneida County, New York, and spent most of his early life there, working in clerkships and teaching school. He read law with Felix Grundy (who was appointed Attorney General of the United States by Martin Van Buren in 1838) and was also a student at Columbian College, in Washington, D.C. (a predecessor of George Washington University). Bernard was baptized in Utica, where he was also licensed to preach.

Craft Masonry. On May 15, 1822, when he was twenty-three years old, Bernard was made a Mason in Utica Lodge No. 270. The Master of his lodge was Ezra S. Cozier, one of the most active Masons in New York State.[59] (To his undoubted chagrin, Cozier was elected Deputy Grand Master of the General Grand Encampment of Knights Templar the same year Bernard published *Light on Masonry*.) Bernard said he was influenced to join the Fraternity by both friends and his eldest brother, whom he described as "a high mason."[60] After his disaffection Bernard claimed he had only attended a few lodge meetings. According to a letter published in 1828 (hereafter cited in full), he was not impressed with the initiation ceremonies, rather stating that he was "completely disgusted."

Royal Arch Chapter. Despite his disappointment with Craft Masonry, Bernard says that he joined (date unknown) the Royal Arch Chapter "at Union Village, Washington County," New York, although it was probably Washington Chapter No. 49, in Greenwich. Again dissatisfied, Bernard stated that he found the ceremonies "a piece with the others."

Encampment (Masonic Knighthood). According to Dr. Daniel White, of Covington, New York, Bernard petitioned for the degrees of Knighthood in Rochester, New York, but his petition was rejected. At this period the Grand Encampment of Knights Templar of New York was in its infancy, and no Encampment is recorded under its jurisdiction at Rochester. However, it may have been one of the independent bodies operating under what the Grand Encampment called the "old system."

Scottish Rite. In September 1826 Giles Fonda Yates, 33°, Sublime Grand Master of "Delta Lodge of Perfection," in Schenectady, New York, communicated the first three degrees of "Ineffable and Sublime Masonry" (4°, Secret Master, 5°, Perfect Master, and 6°, Intimate Secretary) to Bernard, who was then twenty-seven years old. Bernard stated that he took the "higher degrees of Masonry" at the suggestion of his friend Rev. Nathan N. Whiting, who served as both Deputy Grand Master of Delta Lodge of Perfection and Deputy of the Albany Consistory of Sublime Princes of the Royal Secret.[61] In a letter Yates wrote to J. J. J. Gourgas on February 5, 1828, he confirmed Bernard's reception of these Degrees, "One of

INTRODUCTION.

Figure 6. Giles F. Yates, 33°, Sublime Grand Master of "Delta Lodge of Perfection," communicated the first three degrees of the Lodge of Perfection to Bernard in 1826. Yates's deputy, Rev. N. N. Whiting, betrayed Masonry and loaned Bernard the Scottish Rite's rituals. Yates remained faithful to Freemasonry, and became Grand Commander of the Supreme Council, 33°, Northern Masonic Jurisdiction, in 1851. From *Proceedings of the Forty-fifth Council of Deliberation* (New York, 1914).

our Sublime Brethren a Baptist *Clergyman* named Bernard, (only an Intimate Secretary) has denounced & renounced Masonry."[62] Confirming his former standing, Bernard identified himself as an "Intimate Secretary" on the "Declaration of Independence from the Masonic Institution" (adopted July 4, 1828, at Le Roy, New York), and on the title page of *Light on Masonry* he touted himself as "Once an Intimate Secretary in the Lodge of Perfection...."

Bernard Exaggerates his Masonic Standing. It is a matter of curiosity that Bernard, who was supposedly "completely disgusted" from the beginning of his Masonic career in 1822, continued to take degrees up to the very month of Morgan's disappearance in 1826. Early in his anti-Masonic career Bernard correctly represented his former Masonic status. His published "renunciation" stated, "I have taken ten degrees in speculative Freemasonry, and was the *first Royal Arch Mason*, with the exception of Wm. Morgan, that ever denounced the institution as corrupt to my knowledge."[63] (In fact, Morgan did not denounce Freemasonry "as corrupt"; he simply exposed its rituals.) As detailed above, the ten degrees taken by Bernard were the three Craft Degrees, the four Chapter Degrees, and the first three degrees in the Lodge of Perfection. However, on September 16, 1830, when he attended the United States Anti-Masonic Convention, Bernard misrepresented his standing by claiming *all eleven* Degrees of the Lodge of Perfection. He there signed himself as "David Bernard, *Grand Elect, Perfect, and Sublime Mason*. Delegate from New York."[64] This was no simple misunderstanding of titles; Bernard had already published both the text of "The Degree of Perfection or Grand Elect Perfect and Sublime Mason" and a chart which identified it as the Fourteenth Degree. This exaggerated claim would be repeated throughout his life. In November 1870 he told the New York Antimasonic convention that he had received "the eleven ineffable degrees ... in Schenectady, N.Y.,"[65] and as late as 1874 he referred to himself as "Elder David Bernard, Grand Elect Perfect and Sublime Mason."[66] Even a late reprint of *Light on Masonry* stated, "It will be recollected that Elder Bernard had taken fifteen degrees in Masonry before he seceded."[67] (Rev. Bernard's exaggerated claims set a precedent for later anti-Masons. A recent example is the late Rev. James D. Shaw, an ex–Mason who falsely promoted himself as a Past Master and a Thirty-third Degree Mason.[68])

At this early period it was customary to verbally "communicate" the Scottish Rite Degrees a few at a time, rather than to "confer" them in dramatic form. It is possible that Bernard justified his false claim on the grounds that he *may* have been elected to receive the eleven Ineffable Degrees. Or, perhaps Bernard had taken a generic obligation to "keep the secrets of the Lodge of Perfection" on the presumption that he would thereafter receive the other degrees piecemeal, but this is unproven. What is known, however, is that after receiving the three degrees Whiting mailed Bernard an enciphered letter containing their "modes of recognition," i.e., the signs, tokens and words. Following its reception Bernard responded that he had enough of Masonry, and that there was no need to send anything else. It is thus only demonstrable that he received the three lowest degrees of the Lodge of Perfection, and that he was initially content to claim nothing more.

EXIT FREEMASONRY

It was probably in August 1826, some five weeks prior to Morgan's abduction, that Bernard learned from a fellow Mason, the Rev. E. M. Spencer, pastor of First Baptist Church in Middlebury, Genessee County, that Morgan was preparing his exposé.[69] Bernard claimed that "several weeks" before the abduction he was some 250 miles from Batavia when he "heard masons of high standing converse upon the subject of his [Morgan's] abduction." On his return home he met with Elder John G. Stearns, who sold him a copy of his book, *An Inquiry into the Nature and Tendency of Speculative Free-Masonry*.[70] Although Stearns was a Mason, his work was critical of the Fraternity's quasi-religious character. At this time Bernard also learned of Morgan's disappearance and presumed murder. He showed Stearns's work to another Mason, who later purchased a copy of his own. Greatly influenced by the book, Bernard remarked that he could find "no fault in it." After his study of Stearn's work he began to "converse freely upon the principles of the institution with Masons, and others."

About this time a "special" lodge meeting was called in Covington, where Bernard was a member. He attended the meeting and the subject of Morgan's disappearance was brought up. Bernard says that he critically addressed the lodge in relation to Morgan's treatment and was answered with accusations relative to his own activities and his use of Stearns's book. Although he did not say how the meeting ended, his recital concluded with a vitriolic denunciation and renunciation of Freemasonry.

> The next regular meeting of the lodge I attended, being requested by the Master, at the above named special meeting, and here a scene passed which I shall never forget. If ever a poor mortal was abused I was. Dr. Daniel White was one of the foremost, in treating me shamefully. Here I did not know what to do; I rather thought there would be warm work, I therefore kept perfectly cool, as I can abundantly prove, and nothing passed my lips but what I am willing should be repeated a thousand times. I then and there declared some of my then principal objections to Freemasonry. They were not removed. I finally told them to take their own course, such were my views, and if they chose they could expel me. It has been said that I begged them not to do it, but this is false and I can prove it. I told them I did not ask them to expel me, but they could take their own course. I finally left them hoping and praying that they would forever disown me as I did them....
>
> I trust I am a true friend to all men. But I am a decided enemy to Freemasonry, and it is because, from a thorough investigation of its principles before and since I left it, I fully believe that it is not only the most abominable but also the most dangerous institution that ever was imposed upon

man; it is anti-republican and anti-christian. It is somewhat imposing owing to its borrowed garments, but this renders it more dangerous, for like the wily serpent, it lures but to destroy. Man never invented, hell never devised, wicked men and devils never palmed upon the public a more *foolish, corrupt, awful, soul destroying and Heaven daring institution, than Speculative Freemasonry! It may truly be said to be* HELL'S MASTER-PIECE....

I solemnly renounce all fealty to Masonry, and do most earnestly beseech my brethren in Christ Jesus, of every name, to come out and bear unequivocal testimony against them....[71]

Following his departure from the fraternity, Bernard quickly united himself with the growing body of anti-Masons in New York and became a ready and eager adviser to his new *compagnons d'armes*. He later boasted proudly that he not only purchased the very first copy of Morgan's *Illustrations of Masonry* sold (cost $1), but that he also vouched for the accuracy of the exposé, telling the printers to "go ahead" with their work.

I went to Batavia to obtain Captain Morgan's book, and calling at Col. D. C. Miller's office, where it was printed, I found the doors locked and the office guarded by pistols and muskets and cannon all loaded and the inmates ready for defence.

The office had been attacked and fired and they were on the look out for another Masonic raid.

Mr. Scranton, the deputy sheriff, introduced me to the printers and the door flew open at my approach. My position on the subject of Masonry had reached Batavia, and they were glad to see me. They asked me into the office and requested me to examine a copy of the "Illustrations of Masonry" by Morgan. Not a copy of it had been issued from the office. I gave the work sufficient attention as to be confident that Morgan was a bright Mason and had made a correct expose of Masonry. I purchased the copy I had examined and Mr. Scranton paid for it. The dollar for the book was sent to Mrs. Morgan with a message that it was for the first copy sold, and that it had been examined by Elder Bernard, a Royal Arch Mason, and found to be all right. And I said to the printers, "It is all right; go ahead."

This was the first copy of the work which cost Wm. Morgan his life. And you have a transcript of that book by Morgan with the typographical errors all corrected in *Light on Masonry*. It is Morgan's revelation as he wrote the degrees in Batavia, and they are as I received them in the lodge in Utica, and as Colonel William Williams for me in Utica published them.[72]

A Revelation of Free Masonry

Bernard's first significant anti-Masonic act was to serve as Secretary of the "Convention of Seceding Free Masons," held in the village of Le Roy, Genesee County, New York, on February 19–20, 1828. During the convention "a committee of fifteen [Seceding Masons was] appointed to prepare the several Degrees, above that of Master [Mason], for publication."[73] The convention's plan to expose these "higher

INTRODUCTION.

degrees," was published in several New York newspapers, and attracted the attention Giles F. Yates who, it will be recalled, had communicated the three lowest degrees of the Lodge of Perfection to Bernard.

In a letter of April 10, 1828 Gourgas wrote to Holbrook and forwarded copies of three anti-Masonic newspapers which had been loaned to him by Yates. In his letter Gourgas also quoted from two letters written by Yates, which informed him that David Bernard was a 6°, Intimate Secretary member of Delta Lodge of Perfection at Schenectady. Yates feared Bernard's treachery was "common" and noted the intent of seceding Masons to publish "all the degrees of Masonry." Gourgas related to Holbrook:

> You will observe the name *one* "David Bernard"—of whom Br. Y[ates]. writes me 5th February thus—
> "one of our sublime Brethren a Baptist clergyman named 'Bernard' (only an Intimate Secretary) has denounced and renounced Masonry; My conscience is clear as to the part I took in his initiation—his character then was perfectly fair and he was a regular R[oyal]. A[rch]. (modern) Renunciations in the western part of this state are common & I fear treachery is as common. The first step having been taken, many with *Jesuitical* morality absolve themselves from their obligations—and Pray who are they that have denounced Masonry? Vagabonds who have been supported on its charity, and Priests who have been admitted *gratis*—as to those gratis initiations I set my face fully against them."
> He writes me again on the 24th March thus—
> "The Morgan excitement still rages—the degrees of Mark to R[oyal]. A[rch]. are published and you will see by one of the 3 newspapers I send you, that a number of masons have met & will meet again on some future occasion for the purpose of *publishing all* the degrees of Masonry i.e. as many as they can get hold of; in this business they have made some progress already."[74]

As Yates obtained further details he apprised Gourgas of continuing anti-Masonic developments; on June 9, 1828, he wrote:

> You have seen by the anti papers, I presume, that the antis intend on the 4th of July next to have a *grand* meeting at Le Roy & to publish to the world what they will pretend to be the *secrets* of the Ch[apter]∴ & Encampment Degrees &c. <It will prove to be> "Montes parturient, nascetur ridiculus mus." "The mountains laboured & brought forth a —— mouse [*sic*]."[75]

On July 4 the "committee of fifteen" appointed by the Convention of Seceding Free Masons reassembled when the collated degrees were read through.[76] Three weeks later Yates reported to Gourgas that "the *only* degrees to be published under the sanction of the seceders at Le Roy are from Mark Master to & including the R[oyal]. A[rch]. & the degrees of Red Cross Templar, Malta, Holy Sepulchre,

Christian Mark &c. There are some degrees known which Southwick will publish on his own responsibility."[77]

The Le Roy Convention's work was approved and published under the title *A Revelation of Free Masonry, as Published to the World by a Convention of Seceding Masons*.[78] The book begins with a "Report of the Publishing Committee" which disingenuously asserted the exposure was prepared for Freemasons as "a book of reference." More useful today, however, are the statements revealing the origins of the exposed rituals.

Report of the Publishing Committee

THE Committee appointed by the Convention of Seceding Masons, at Le Roy, on the 4th of July, to superintend the printing of this Revelation, now present to the world, the SECRETS OF FREE MASONRY, as derived from the most authentic sources.

There is such a diversity of *"work,"* as the Craft term it, in the different Chapters, that the Committee's duties have been necessarily arduous, but this work is according to the best authorities which they have been able to consult. There may be verbal and immaterial variations in this work, but all the essentials of Free Masonry have been strictly preserved. The Committee desired to present a work to the public that will stand the severest scrutiny of the Fraternity, and even become a book of reference for the *Craft themselves*, should they attempt, hereafter, to continue their operations. No expense or labour, to make this a perfect Revelation of Free Masonry, has been spared.

The Degrees which form this work, were obtained from the following sources, and have been faithfully revised and corrected by those whom the Fraternity would distinguish as *bright* Masons. We add our own testimony in favour of their correctness. The three first Degrees, viz:—Mark Master, Past Master, and Most Excellent Master, were compiled by Capt. WILLIAM MORGAN, author of *"Illustrations of Masonry,"* the manuscripts of which, in his own handwriting, were politely furnished by his widow, and are in possession of the Committee. The truth of these Degrees are presumed to be abundantly established, having been sealed with the blood of the author! Capt. MORGAN also prepared the Royal Arch Degree for publication, but that was basely stolen from him by the conspirators, and sent by a special messenger to the General Grand Chapter. Col. KNAP, of Washington City, was Chairman of the Committee to whom the manuscript was referred, and Col. STONE, of New-York, says the messenger was directed to return the manuscript—but this has never been done. As this Degree is represented by Masons as *"indescribably more august and important than all which precede it, and is the summit and perfection of Ancient masonry,"* it was thought advisable to obtain it as given by the General Grand Lecturer of the United States. Accordingly a companion was dispatched to reside in the vicinity of that Lecturer, (Jeremy L. Cross,) who attended his Lectures until the entire Degree was accurately written out. The Royal Arch Degree, therefore, is given as it is taught by the primum moble of Free Masonry.

INTRODUCTION.

The Degrees of the Encampment are copied directly from the manuscript furnished by the officer sent by the Grand Encampment to install Genesee Encampment, No. 10. This manuscript was left to instruct the officers of the new Encampment in their duties. The charter of this Encampment has been returned, since the abduction of Capt. Morgan, and its members have revealed its secrets. The Degrees of the Ancient Council of the Trinity are also copied from a manuscript left at the formation of a Council in Le Roy.

The Committee submit the result of their labours without comment. The public have, in the following pages, genuine Free Masonry, as it exists and is practiced throughout the world. In renouncing its principles and revealing its mysteries, Seceding Masons have discharged a duty which they owed to themselves and their country, and they look to the impartial reader and an enlightened, free people, for protection against the "VENGEANCE" which they have incurred from those who support the Institution in the spirit of its obligations, *"right or wrong."*

SOLOMON SOUTHWICK,
DAVID BERNARD,
RICHARD HOLLISTER,
WILLARD SMITH,
HERBERT A. READ,
JOHN HASKALL,
SAMUEL D. GREENE.

Soon after the publication of *A Revelation of Free Masonry*, Samuel B. Bradley, a Freemason from Greece, Monroe County, New York, wrote to Yates and alerted him that the exposition was both available and accurate. Yates, in turn, passed the news to Gourgas and added his own lament that the rituals had ever been distributed in manuscript.

> Bradley writes me that he has read the revelations of the higher Δs [degrees] as they are termed, and says that it is from *official MSS.* that the degrees of Templar & Cross are published. Bradley is a Templar under the old European system & never received the degree of the cross.... I may be wrong, but I sometimes think that a fundamental principle has been long violated in committing the mysteries of the higher degrees to writing.[79]

LIGHT ON MASONRY

Although *A Revelation of Free Masonry* was extremely accurate, there remained further degrees which escaped. In spite of this, it successfully exposed most of the rituals then practiced by American Freemasons. However, there remained others that were more exotic, if lesser known, including the Ineffable Degrees

Bernard had received in Schenectady. Bernard soon began working on another exposure which, when published, would make him America's foremost anti-Mason. On August 29, 1828, Albany's *National Observer* announced:

> ELDER BERNARD'S WORK—We solicit the attention of our readers to the work of Elder Bernard, of which the Prospectus will be found in our columns of this day. No man has suffered more for his attachment to the best of causes, than Elder Bernard. Every species of calumny has been heaped upon him. But he has talents, firmness and energy of character. His book will be an invaluable compilation.[80]

The prospectus, which is reproduced below, detailed a work unlike anything which had been published in America.

PROPOSALS
For Publishing a Book, Entitled
LIGHT ON MASONRY,
A collection of Documents on the subject of
SPECULATIVE FREE-MASONRY:

EMBRACING all the degrees on Masonry, from an Entered Apprentice to the Thrice Illustrious Order of the Cross, as published by Capt. William Morgan, the martyr; and the Convention of Seceding Masons, held at Le Roy, July 4th and 5th 1828.

COMPILED BY
ELDER DAVID BERNARD,
OF WARSAW, GEN. CO., N.Y.

Once an Intimate Secretary in the Lodge of Perfection.

"For there is nothing covered that shall not be revealed; and nothing hid, that shall not be known."

"And what ye hear in the ear, that preach ye upon the house tops."

—JESUS CHRIST.

The above work in addition to all the Degrees of Masonry, from an entered apprentice, to the Thrice Illustrious Order of the Cross; will contain the SIGNS, GRIPS and PASS WORDS, of a number of the Ineffable degrees, as conferred in the "Lodge of Perfection" and the following very interesting and important Documents:

1st. Result of a Convention of the Saratoga Baptist Association, containing *Fifteen Reasons* for their disfellowshipping Free masonry.

2nd, Report of the Western Committees, appointed by the people in the counties of Genessee, Livingston, Ontario, Monroe and Niagara, with an Appendix, being a *Narrative of Facts*, in relation to the abduction and murder of Capt. William Morgan, &c. &c., &c.

INTRODUCTION.

3d, TRIALS *of Masonic Conspirators*, who confessed themselves *Guilty* of Kidnapping Capt. William Morgan.

4th, PROCEEDINGS of the Convention of Seceding Masons, held at Le Roy, Feb. 19 and 20, 1828.

5th, PROCEEDINGS of the Anti Masonic Convention of the Twelve Western counties of New-York, held at Le Roy, March 5th and 7th 1828, including thetir very able address to the people of the state of New-York.

5th, [*sic*] IMPORTANT EXTRACTS from the proceedings of the Legislature of New York, relative to the Masonic Outrages, committed Sept. 1826, including the Speech of the Hon. Mr. Crary before the Senate.

7th, PROCEEDINGS of the Convention of Seceding Masons held at Le Roy, July 4th, and 5th, 1828, including important Extracts from the *Masterly Oration* of Solomon Southwick Esq. delivered to that body and the *Oration* of Herbert A. Read Esq; a Seceding Knight Templar, pronounced at Le Roy, July 4th, 1828, to an Assembly of about 10,000 persons.

8th, PROCEEDINGS of the Anti-Masonic New York State Convention, held at Utica, August 4th and 5th 1828.

9th, AN ADDRESS to all Honest Masons in 8 numbers by a Seceding Knight Templar.

10th, A CANDID APPEAL to professors of Religion on the subject of Speculative Freemasonry by R. B. Hotchkin, Ruling Elder in the 1st Presbyterian Church, in Le Roy.

11th, RENUNCIATIONS of Freemasonry, by Seceding Masons.

12th, THE GREAT QUESTIONS ANSWERED, "If Freemasonry be so great an evil, why have the great and good men united with and continued to countenance the Institution so long?" by a Seeding [*sic*] Mason.

13th, MASONS JUSTIFIED in breaking their Masonic Oaths, and publishing the secrets of the order to the world? by a Seceding Mason.

14th FACTS not included in the above Documents proving the truth of Morgan's *Abduction and Murder*, and the awful corruption of the Masonic Institution NOTES, and *Critical Remarks* on the whole work by the Compiler and Publisher, &c &c. &c.

A moment's reflection will convince the candid that the above work is greatly needed. Many parts of this state (N.Y.) and a great part of the United States, are yet in darkness as it relates to the recent *Masonic Outrages*, and the secret mysteries, and abominations of Freemasonry; Ant it is not only important that the *Light* on this subject should be spread throughout the Union, but it is necessary for the good of posterity, that the facts now in possession should be secured in such a manner as not to be easily mutilated and destroyed.

RESOLUTION of an Anti-Masonic Convention of Genessee County, held at Bethany July 23, 1828, in favour of the above work. "WHEREAS the title and Prospectus of a book entitled "LIGHT ON MASONRY &c. &c. has been read to this Convention; Therefore, *resolved*, that for the advancement of Light and Truth, in the great and holy cause of Anti-Masonry, and for the good of future generations, we deem it of the highest importance that such

LIGHT ON MASONRY.

a work be published, and from our knowledge of the talents, character, intelligence, and zeal of Elder David Bernard, we believe him to be eminently qualified for such an undertaking: we therefore *solicit* him to persevere in the work without delay, as *such* a work is worthy of then patronage of the friends of liberty and religion, throughout the whole civilized world.

ROBERT EARLL, Jr. *President.*

CEPHAS A. SMITH, *Secretary.*

RESOLUTION of an Anti Masonic New York State Convention held at Utica August 4th, 1828, in favour of the above work, "WHEREAS the Title and prospectus of a Book entitled "LIGHT ON MASONRY &c. by Elder David Bernard, has been read to this Convention, and entertaining the fullest confidence in the integrity, zeal and ability of the compiler; and being deeply impressed with the importance of the proposed publication, to the cause of Truth and Justice: Therefore, Resolved, that we recommend the Compiler to proceed without delay in the publication of his Book; and we recommend it to the attention and patronage of all the friends of truth and the cause of Civil Liberty throughout the whole civilized world.

JAMES HAWKS, *President.*

THOMS. C. GREEN,
SETH A. ABBEY, } *Secretaries.*

The above work will contain 600 pages duodecimo, printed with a fair type, on good paper, and full bound. Prince to Subscribers, 1 50

The $1.50 subscription price was about $30 in today's money—a very fair charge for a leather-bound book of this size. The above prospectus represented this new work as different from *A Revelation of Free Masonry* in two important regards. First, it promised a number (though not all) of the Ineffable degrees, and second, it would include important non-ritual documents. The title, *Light on Masonry*, made mockery of Masonic ritual, in which candidates seek "light." It will be remembered that William Morgan copied his title from a well-known Masonic guide book, and Bernard may have intended something similar. The subtitle, "Documents on ... Speculative Free-Masonry," is similar to an earlier Masonic work, Joseph M'Cosh's *Documents upon Sublime Masonry* (1823), a book known to Bernard and used by him without credit.[81] Bernard selected William Williams of Albany as his publisher, who had previously printed Stearn's *An Inquiry into the Nature and Tendency of Speculative Free-Masonry* (the book which initiated Bernard's criticism of the Fraternity).

Bernard had a good sense of self-promotion and received a fair amount of press coverage. His letters to private citizens were reprinted in newspapers, and provided some hint as to the source of the rituals to come.

INTRODUCTION.

> The first three degrees are fairly and fully before the public as written by Capt. Morgan. The book is entitled "Illustrations of Masonry," &c. The four degrees which are conferred in the Royal Arch Chapter are also all and fully before the public, as revealed by the Le Roy Convention, July 4 and 5, 1828. All the foregoing I *know* from my *own* knowledge to be *correct and full*. The five degrees conferred in the Grand Encampment of Knights Templars, are, I believe, revealed by the same convention, and are now published to the world. These last degrees I have never taken; but from the evidence in my possession of their truth, I as much believe they are correct, as I believe there is such a place as London or New Orleans. Some of the gentlemen who revealed these degrees I know, and I have the fullest confidence in their veracity. They were members of the encampment at Le Roy, and withdrew.... The exposures made on the 19th of February, so far as the Royal Arch degree, are in substance correct. By comparing what was revealed the 4th of July, you will see there is a trifling difference, but nothing essential. The *last* is *most* correct. We had more time of the last, and made it more perfect. The *whole* of the first twelve degrees are, then, now before the world. All of masonry which had not been revealed by Morgan, was revealed by the convention of the 4th of July, of which they had knowledge, excepting some degrees in the Lodge of Perfection, of which I had possession. These were, however, of the same character with the others, and will soon appear, with many more degrees of a higher order, which I have obtained from the *highest authority*, in all, *forty-two degrees*. My book is now in press at Utica, and will contain 600 pages, full bound, for $1, 50.[82]

Although the Le Roy Convention had already published most of the Masonic degrees known at the time, the prurient appeal of *Light on Masonry* was its promise to unveil even more, including some (though not all) of the Ineffable Degrees conferred in the Lodge of Perfection. But what of the "degrees of a higher order ... obtained from the *highest authority*?" Statements such as this gave well-informed Masons reason to suspect that Bernard had somehow obtained the rituals of the Scottish Rite. Again, Samuel B. Bradley expressed his concerns to Giles F. Yates, who quoted them in a letter of January 12, 1829.

> "The Light of Δy [Masonry] by Bernard is not yet published. Giddens told me it will *not come out till the spring*, & that it will be mostly a collection of Documents. He says however that it will contain the grips & words of about 40 Δs [degrees] (perhaps the Ineffable? which have hitherto wonderfully escaped)."[83]

Bradley's informant, who lived just eight miles away in Rochester, was Edward Giddins, the author of a series of anti-Masonic almanacs, as well as *An Account of the Savage Treatment of Captain William Morgan, in Fort Niagara, who was Subsequently Murdered by the Masons, and Sunk in Lake Ontario, for Publishing the Secrets of Masonry* (1828).[84] Eager to promote the anti-Masonic cause, newspapers trumpeted Bernard's forthcoming exposé.

LIGHT ON MASONRY.

THE SECRETS OF MASONRY

The Rev. David Bernard thus writes concerning his intended publication, disclosing the secrets of masonry. Mr. Bernard is a seceding mason, who has taken all the degrees of masonry and knighthood that are conferred in this country.

Ed. Free Press.

Extract from a letter from the Rev. David Bernard.

"You speak of my book, it is now in the press a Utica, and it will contain all of 600 pages, printed on excellent paper, and well bound. As to matter, sir, it will embrace, in addition to all the most important documents in relation to the recent Masonic outrages committed in this country, doings of the legislature of this state, proceedings of conventions, orations, essays, &c. on the subject of free masonry; together with all the degrees of the institution, amounting to *forty-two!* Three as written by Capt. Wm. Morgan, the martyr; nine as revealed by the convention at Le Roy, and thirty of a still higher order. The highest conferred in Europe and America, as obtained by me from the highest authority; I know them to be correct. These degrees are of vast importance to the glorious cause in which we are engaged, and will much enhance the value of my publication, though not the price. I am determined to sell for only one dollar and fifty cents, what masons have sold at one hundred and fifty dollars. As to the nature of the upper degrees, I can only say in this communication, that the folly, wickedness and awful blasphemy, which they contain, could not be fully described in one or one hundred letters."[85]

On February 20, 1829 Bernard wrote that *Light on Masonry* would be out in April, and in the same letter he did not miss an opportunity to take potshots at the Fraternity, calling it the "Beast" with a "cloven foot" which had "worshippers in disguise." Misinterpreting the symbolism of the old 28°, Knight of the Sun, he alleged Freemasonry taught its members "that in order to be perfect, they must 'crush the serpent of ignorance,' (the Christian Religion.)."[86] Bernard's next newspaper announcement listed the specific degrees which were to be exposed. As seen below, he was able to acquire most of the degrees conferred by the Supreme Councils.

SECRETS OF MASONRY.

It may be recollected that a committee was raised at the Le Roy Convention, to publish to the world the several degrees of masonry in their possession. The following doings of this committee are interesting, as informing the reader of the result of their labors.

At a meeting of the Publishing Committee of seceding masons, held at Le Roy, Dec. 11, 1828, John Hascall, Esq. chairman, and Samuel D. Greene, secretary, the following resolutions were passed unanimously—

Resolved, That the degrees of Freemasonry, of which the following names are a list, were presented for our inspection by Elder David Bernard, and are about to be published in his work, entitled, "*Light on Masonry;*" from their

INTRODUCTION.

striking similarity and connection with the lower degrees of which we have a perfect knowledge; and from the very high and undoubted authority from which they were obtained, are true and genuine; that we consider them a very important acquisition to the cause of Anti-Masonry, and that Elder Bernard has our unqualified approbation in publishing them to the world.

LIST OF DEGREES

Given in the Sublime Grand Lodge of Perfection.

1st.	Secret Master.
2d.	Perfect Master.
3d.	Intimate Secretary.
4th.	Provost and Judge.
5th.	Intendant of the Buildings.
6th.	Elected Knights of 9.
7th.	Illustrious Elected of 15.
8th.	Sublime Knights Elected.
9th.	Grand Master Architect.
10th.	Knights of the Ninth Arch.
11th.	Perfection.

Given by the Council of Grand Inspectors
Who are SOVEREIGNS of Masonry.

12th.	Knight of the East and West.
13th.	Sovereign Prince of Rose Croix de Heredon.
14th.	Grand Pontiff.
15th.	Grand Master of all Symbolic Lodges.
16th.	Grand Patriarch; Knights of the Royal Arch.
17th.	Chief of the Tabernacle.
18th.	Prince of the Tabernacle.
19th.	Prince of Mercy.
20th.	Knights of the Brazen Serpent.
21st.	Sovereign or Commander of the Temple of Jerusalem.
22d.	Knight of the Sun.
23d.	Knight of the Kadosh.

Sublime French Degrees.

24th.	Elect of Perigran.
25th.	Sub Architect.
26th.	Grand Architect.
27th.	Scotch Master.
28th.	Knight of the East.
29th.	Knight of the Rose Cross.
30th.	Prussian Knight.

JOHN HASKALL, *Ch'n*

LIGHT ON MASONRY.

S. D. Greene, *Sec'y*.[87]

WHENCE CAME THE RITUALS?
Inasmuch as Bernard had only received the first three degrees of the Lodge of Perfection, he must have obtained copies of the Supreme Council's higher degree rituals from someone else. On the basis of the newspaper advertisement above, Bernard's informant would have been a 30°, Knight of Kadosh, or possibly even higher. The prime suspect, on what must have been a short list of potential traitors, was John Barker, 33°, a member of the Supreme Council at Charleston. Barker was sometimes called the Supreme Council's "deputy," but was more often referred to as its "agent"—a term which is not Masonic, but was used to imply the limited powers he exercised.

A native of Connecticut, Barker was a gifted ritualist who traveled as an itinerant lecturer. He was admitted to the Supreme Council on May 13, 1823, and actively disseminated the Scottish Rite, establishing Masonic bodies from Alabama and Georgia to Ohio and New York. As a true "traveling man" he had been extremely useful to the Supreme Council in resolving problems. For example, when James Cushman, the first Grand Lecturer of the Grand Lodge of Virginia, and Jeremy L. Cross, author of *The True Masonic Chart* (1819), somehow obtained a Thirty-third Degree manuscript ritual, Barker met with them, secured the manuscript, obligated them to secrecy, and conferred on them the Thirty-third Degree. This made them the first known "Honorary Members" in the history of the Supreme Council.[88] An even more important act occurred on October 25, 1825, when Barker conferred the Thirty-third Degree on Giles F. Yates[89] and provided him with copies of the rituals used by Supreme Council at Charleston.

In spite of his services, Barker had been an occasional thorn in the side of the Supreme Council at Charleston. Contributing to the negative reputation of itinerant lecturers, he supplemented his income by selling copies of the Scottish Rite's rituals to Masonic bodies and individual Masons. Sometimes the manuscripts he provided were less than useful. Barker's lax attitude, a disregard for formality, and his failure to send timely reports to the Supreme Council at Charleston gave them grave cause for concern. In December 1828 Holbrook wrote:

> I have just heard that Br Barker has arrived at his residence in Wallingford in Connecticut—He has made no returns of his journey west of the mountains—his last letter was early in October 1827—and all his powers as our Deputy are by his neglect null and void—and as this Sup[reme]. Counc[il]. is now situated, I am positive he cannot get it renewed—it was always void in your state—so if you hear of his meddling—it is without any authority whatever—but he has neglected to write to us—and has made a great deal of money so report says—[90]

INTRODUCTION.

Gourgas likewise expressed his misgivings about Barker in his letter to Holbrook on April 25, 1829.

> Do you not feel uneasy as to the conduct of ... B[arke]r – ? – to say the least, it appears to me strange & doubtful in the extreme *"en complete opposition à tous ses sermons et promesse de soumission, sujétion et obeisance à ses supérieurs, & d'exécuter et faire exécuter les lois, statuts et réglements &c"*—at the very short visit I received once from him, He appeared more like a man in a great hurry, on some business errand, than one who cared ~~for~~ to ~~impart & receive~~ information, understood much what he was about or the importance of it—You, who naturally must know him more particularly as to his moral qualities may judge better, but with present impressions and appearances—I fear very much all will not go right—& I think it would be wise, *the sooner the better* to put it out of his power, to make any more money—by withdrawing all such materials as ~~have~~ he has been entrusted with.[91]

If they lacked positive assurance Gourgas and Holbrook would soon have confirmation that financial gain and security were especially strong incentives to abandon Freemasonry, when one's livelihood was intertwined with the growing anti-Masonic movement.

A Reverend "Black Coat"

The Reverend Nathan N. Whiting was a member of Tyrian Mark Lodge No. 66, under the jurisdiction of the Grand Chapter Royal Arch Masons, New York, and served as a representative to the Grand Chapter in 1821.[92] As noted earlier, he was also second-in-command to Giles F. Yates in both Schenectady's Delta Lodge of Perfection and the Albany Consistory of Sublime Princes of the Royal Secret.

Rev. Whiting was a man of considerable talents and strong religious convictions. A *koiné* Greek scholar, he would later publish his own translation of the New Testament under the title *The Good News of Our Lord Jesus, the Anointed* (1849),[93] and become a member of the American Bible Union (comprised primarily of Baptists), which organized to revise the English Bible.[94] As "brothers in Christ" the Reverends Bernard and Whiting formed a strong friendship in 1823, and it was Whiting who suggested that Bernard take the "higher degrees of Masonry." As will be seen, Bernard returned the favor by convincing Whiting to withdraw from the Fraternity. Whiting's disaffection occurred before the end of 1827 and, although he did not officially ask for a demission until 1828, he assisted Bernard by providing a certificate to accompany the following letter Bernard published in the *Batavia Advocate*.

> It may not be amiss here to observe, that I have taken ten degrees in "Sublime Freemasonry," and was the *first Royal Arch Mason*, with the exception of Wm. Morgan, that ever denounced the institution as corrupt, to my knowledge. This is one reason, no doubt, why the fraternity have been so inveterate against me. Another is, a story was circulated, about the time I

left them, that I was writing against the institution: and it was all important, for the safekeeping of the craft, that the confidence the public had in my integrity should be shaken.

As I have frequently been asked why I continued with the institution so long, and as this has been brought up by many to impeach my honesty in renouncing it; it may not be improper to give a very brief statement of facts, as touching my connexion with masonry. About the time I commenced preaching the Gospel of Christ, my eldest brother (now dead) a high mason, gave me to understand that masonry was a good thing, and very important to one who attempted to preach the Gospel. This was the language also of some others in whom I thought I could place confidence; and no doubt I was influenced, in a considerable degree, to receive the obligations. In taking the three first degrees, I visited the lodge twice or thrice. I was completely disgusted with the *ceremonies* of the degrees, but thought there were principles in the institution that were good. These, however, I did not then examine; and so little did think of the matter, I did not visit a lodge for nearly two years subsequent, and then I did it in hopes as I was informed, of finding something more valuable than I had in the first degrees. I then went to a Chapter, and in one afternoon and evening received four degrees more; and as I found these to be of a piece with the others, I did not again visit a lodge or chapter until I came to Covington. Being frequently requested by the masons in Covington, I occasionally went to the lodge for a few minutes, although I could see nothing in the institution worthy of my attention. I thought from the high standing of some of its votaries, both in the political and religious world, together with the high claims to antiquity, morality and benevolence, it must be of importance; and that it was owing, in a great measure, to my ignorance of its principles, that I thought so lightly of it. Viewing the subject in this light, I have, in a few instances spoken in its favor: and under these impressions, I was induced, one year ago last Sept. when in Schenectady, to take upon me all the degrees conferred in the lodge of perfection, being eleven.—These degrees were to be sent to me by mail three of which I received after I arrived home, and the rest *I would not receive* and wrote to my correspondent *not to send them*, as I had got enough of masonry. In this thing the masons have said that *I lied*, stating not only that *I had applied for the degrees* and *could not obtain them*, but also, that *such a thing as receiving degrees by letter could not be affected.*

For proof of the above fact, I refer the reader who may suspect my integrity, to Elder N. N. Whiting of Vernon, one of the highest masons in the state, who is the gentleman that sent me the degrees; and if further proof is required, I have the letter containing the degrees, and will show it to any mason or any man, who disputes my word, if he will call at my home. I also insert Elder N. N. Whiting's certificate which I have just received, which must forever settle the point on this subject.

Vernon, Dec. 5, 1827

"I certify, at the request of Elder D. Bernard, that I was present when he received from Giles F. Yates, Esq. of the City of Schenectady, a Grand Inspector of the 33d degree, and agent for the Sup. G. Council of the 33d sitting in

INTRODUCTION.

> Charleston, S. Carolina. That by the order of said Yates, I communicated to said Bernard a letter pr. mail, written partly in hieroglyphics, describing the words, pass-words, signs of two or three of the first three degrees, That soon after, said Bernard informed me by letter, that it was not necessary that I should transmit the rest of the words, &c. of the ineffable degrees.
>
> N. N. WHITING.
>
> Now I ask who has *lied*, those who have asserted that I "applied for degrees and could not obtain them," and that "I never received such degrees in the aforesaid manner," or myself? Let the people judge.[95]

Yates was probably not aware of Bernard's influence when he learned of Whiting's decision to withdraw from Freemasonry. However this may be, Yates did not fear his former first officer would publicly renounce the Fraternity:

> Br. Whiting at Vernon Oneida Co. Matters with him have come to this pass. He must either give up masonry, or lose his place as a Baptist clergyman, on which & which *alone*, he depends for his *daily bread*. He wished to satisfy the demands of his Baptist brethren, although intolerant, bigotted & persecuting. He has as much regard for masonry as ever, yet he begs an honorable dismission, upon showing which his brethren will be satisfied. Br. W. has always conducted worthily, evinced great zeal in the mas[onic]. cause & done much to build it up, but he lives in a contaminated atmosphere. I should be sorry to have his name added to the *growing* list of those who renounce masonry *publickly* but I do not fear such a result.[96]

Yates resisted granting Whiting a demission, asserting in his letter of April 4, 1828 that he did not possess the authority to do so, since the Consistory could not meet for business.

> This morning I received your letter requesting me to send you a dismission in form from the Consistory of the 32d degree &c and that I should do this in my capacity as a Grand Inspector of the 33 &c & representative of the Sup∴ Council at Charleston So. Car.
>
> You know that the charter for the Consistory to be located at Albany, was granted by said Supreme Council to five or six persons including yourself, and that circumstances have prevented us from doing any thing as a body since the receipt of the Charter in the fall of 1824. You know too, that afterwards on account of our location, it was deemed proper by said Sup∴ Council to transfer their jurisdiction over our Consistory, to the Sup∴ Council at New=York. To effectuate this object, and also that the interests of the *Southern* Sup∴ Council, and of our Consistory might be promoted, they thought it expedient to appoint a representative in the *Northern* Sup∴ Council, and as I was the presiding officer of the Consistory, this appointment fell upon me. I could not however act as such representative, without first receiving the degree of Grand Inspector of the 33d &c, which I accordingly received shortly after.

> From what I have already said, and also from what follows, you will perceive that it is not in my power, to grant you a dismission from the Consistory in my capacity as a Grand Inspector, for the simple reason that I have not the authority so to do. My powers as an Inspector are circumscribed. A Gr. Inspector has no individual power within a jurisdiction or district already lawfully and consitutionally occupied, except that of general inspection. The powers anciently possessed by Inspectors in this district were annulled 5th Augt 1813, upon the establishment of the Sup∴ Council at New York, for the Northern Jurisdiction of the United States of America. In addition to the power of general inspection, he an Inspector may exercise such further & other powers as may be granted him by a special patent to that effect by the Grand & Sup∴ Council under which he hails, and to which he is amenable for all his acts. — On the 6th Sep = 1826, the Sup∴ Council at New York wrote to the Sup∴ Council at Charleston as follows. "Your request to have us recognize Il∴ Br∴ Giles F. Yates of Schenectady as your representative near our Sup∴ Council, is accepted with pleasure satisfaction. ++++ But as to admitting or recognizing him, or any other brother as your agent in the State of New York, is totally impossible. Besides Besides permit us to say that the word "*Agent*" is a term unknown in freemasonry."
>
> As to granting you, or any other worthy brother a dismission there can be no objection. A worthy mason applying to a Lodge or any other masonic body, of which he is a member, upon applying for dismission, I take it, such dismission may should be granted as of course, no man is made a Mason against his will & no man should be curtained or retained as a member of any Masonic body against his will. But you must receive your dismission from the Consistory when in Session. But here is a difficulty, th or rather there are several difficulties. The authority of our cons[istory]∴ has never yet been legally confirmed. We hardly be said to be as yet completely organized. The members reside in different parts of the State & one S. Solomon has even moved to Canada; so that a meeting cannot be had without great inconvenience & expence which the circumstances of your case do not seem to require.[97]

Although he approved of Yates's response, Grand Secretary Gourgas thought it was perhaps a better course to grant Whiting his demit, and take pains to retrieve all the manuscript rituals in his possession:

> Your answer to a Rev.ᵈ Gentleman is very good & correct—but I think you might write to your Illˢ∴ Bⁿ∴ & agree to grant him *at once* the object of his wish—on condition however of his giving up & surrendering to you, *all* M.S.S. papers & documents he may have in his possession relating to such things—if he is attached & truly sincere he cannot refuse it —the sooner done the better.[98]

Readily acceding to the cautious counsel of Grand Secretary J. J. J. Gourgas, Yates quickly moved to recover the rituals. He replied three days later that Whiting had returned the ritual manuscripts held in his possession and had been granted his demit, "The Rev: Br∴ of whom I spoke in my last, has given up his MSS. & I gave

INTRODUCTION.

a certificate (which will answer his purpose) as presiding officer of the G[rand]. Consistory of S[ublime]. P[rinces]. [of the] R[oyal]. S[ecret]."[99] With his faith in Rev. Whiting yet unshaken, Yates assured Gourgas a week later, "It is farthest from Br. W[hiting]'s wishes or intentions to withdraw from masonry."[100]

O TEMPORA! O MORES!
Yates's faith was soon to be tested. Two months before the Le Roy Convention of July 4–5, 1828 he—like many other Masons—was concerned with rumors of forthcoming exposures. Yet he endeavored to mollify any concerns Gourgas may have held in regard to the Scottish Rite's rituals: "I now can assure you that there are not half a dozen masons in this State *out* of the City of New York that know any thing about the sublime degrees except what they have received from Br. Barker & myself."[101] Unfortunately, Whiting was one of the few who *did* know about the Sublime Degrees and he, like his friend Bernard, quickly enrolled among the anti-Masonic ranks. When Yates finally learned of Whiting's defection he dashed a note off to Gourgas on Christmas Day, 1828. Yates's frustration is evident as he pondered his former friend's betrayal. The painful realization that his erstwhile confidant and deputy was now aiding the enemy evoked from Yates the exasperation of Marcus Tullius Cicero's *Oratio Catilinam Prima*.

> I have not heard or seen any thing of Br. N. N. Whiting for some time, & the last accounts from him were not very favor[able]. From a paragraph in the newspaper I send herewith, y[ou] will perceive that he is about (together with sundry other *black-coats* to join the antimasonic ranks. Well, let him go—we can do without him. I have lately seen a new prospectus of Bernard's "Light on ∆y" [Masonry] in which he proposes to give a revelation (as he terms it) of some of the Sub[lime] ∴ ∆s [Degrees] & also some French ∆s [Degrees], making in all *42* ∆s [degrees] which he pretends to reveal. No doubt the publication of his work has been postponed in order to enable him to make these additions to it. I am anxious to see what sort of a book he will publish & expect to receive some copies as soon as published. Could it be possible that W[hiting]. has assisted him??!!! O! tempora, o! mores!!![102]

I suspect that Yates's disappointment resulted from stronger ties than simple friendship and the bonds of fraternity. While investigating the history of Schenectady County I discovered that Yates and Whiting were related by marriage. Whiting's wife was Jane Helen Fonda, who was the daughter of Jellis A. Fonda and Elizabeth Yates; her great-grandfather was Jellis Fonda, patriarch of Schenectady's Fonda clan. Giles Fonda Yates was the son of John R. Yates and Margaret Fonda; his great-grandfather was the very same Jellis Fonda. The Yates and Fonda families had a long history of intermarriage in the Schenectady area since about year 1700.[103]

In a January 15, 1829, letter Yates informed Gourgas about Whiting's disaffection and raised suspicions about his recent request to borrow the rituals of the 17°,

Knight of the East and West, and 28°, Knight of the Sun, two of the degrees controlled by the Supreme Councils. Yates added that Whiting may already have copies of the Ineffable Degrees, but he assured Gourgas that nobody else had seen the higher degree rituals or been admitted beyond the 16°, Prince of Jerusalem.

> The resolutions passed by N. N. W[hiting]. & his Baptist Brethren I have lately seen, they are in the following words.
> "Resolved that we relinquish our connexion with the Masonic institution. Resolved that we advise all our Brethren who are masons to act in accordance with the above resolution. 'Blessed are peace makers for they shall be called the children of God.'"
> "Resolved that we entreat all our churches to treat masonic Brethren with mildness and pursue peaceable & persuasive measures. 'Charity suffereth long and is kind.'"
> On the receipt of the MSS. sent by Br. Barker, W[hiting]. looked over them cursorily, and requested the loan of the ∆s [Degrees] of Kt. of E[ast]. & W[est]. & K[night]∴ of the sun (I believe those were the only ones) to peruse, which request was granted. You may remember the time I wrote you my *suspicions* respecting his conduct. At that time I requested him per letter to return me those MSS. alledging that I wished to have them Examined by your Supreme Council &c. He returned them to me promptly. I do not know that he has any other MSS unless perhaps of the Ineffable ∆s [Degrees]. It is some time ago, but if I remember right, he took a copy for his own use of those ∆s [Degrees] as they came to our hands *previous* to our having any communication with the Charleston Sup[reme]. Council. I had not turned my attention to the study of the Sub[lime].∴ ∆s [Degrees] more than a few months, before I became more & more convinced of the propriety & great expediency of having some check devised, or rule established to prevent every ∆ [Mason] admitted to the ∆s [Degrees] from taking copies of the MSS. for their own use. Accordingly on the establishment of our G[rand]. Council of P[rinces]. of Jer[usalem]. I had a clause in the ob[ligation]∴ ~~that~~ of every G[rand]. Master Elect of a Lodge of Perf[ection]∴ not to suffer or permit any ∆ [Mason] even of the grade of G[rand]. E[lect]. P[erfect]. & S[ublime]. M[ason]. to peruse any part of the "Directory" (as we termed it) much less make a copy of it, & to hand over to his *successor* in office such Directory. By this means no [Mason] obtained a copy of the MSS of the Inef[fable]∴ ∆s [Degrees] except a Prince of Jer[usalem]. who was actually presiding over a Lodge of Perfection. As to the ∆s [Degrees] above prince we have admitted *not a single individual* to the ∆s [Degrees] much less has any one seen the MSS we have & which you have seen in full & I know not of the existence of a single MS. belonging to any person connected with me in the formation of our Consistory, except as above stated respecting W[hiting].[104]

INTRODUCTION.

WHITING'S BETRAYAL CONFIRMED

The copyright for *Light on Masonry* was filed on April 13, 1829, and the book was released before the end of the month. Within days of its public sale Gourgas sent a "confidential" letter to Yates, requesting a copy of Bernard's new book and a couple more copies of the "revelations" (it is unclear whether he meant Mary Hanlon's or the Le Roy Convention's exposé), "Oblige ᵐᵉ to send me again *two* more of the "revelations"—and *one* of Bernard's light—as early as you can conveniently procure them."[105] Yates responded that he would comply with the request as soon as possible.[106]

As requested, Yates purchased and sent the two exposés to Gourgas who studied them intently. Because he was a keen student of ritual, familiar with both manuscript and printed texts, it was not difficult for Gourgas to deduce the source of Bernard's Scottish Rite exposure. Disquieted by what he discovered, on August 6 Gourgas mailed a letter to Holbrook which, because of its sensitive nature, was partially encrypted (the deciphered text is **bolded**; see Figure 7).

> I presume you have ~~seen~~ ᵖᵉʳᵘˢᵉᵈ *cinq cent pages* **David Bernards Light on Masonry** lately published containing the whole **33—Sublime Degrees at full length** from **your Charleston—M-S-S—sent—to—Albany since —** 1825—"verbatim et literatum"—Comment in any shape on such despicable **Reverend** caracters as B[ernard] and **Whiting** would be useless—the more so as in spite of all such worthless contemptible beings—[107]

Awareness that Bernard had obtained and exposed the Southern Jurisdiction's rituals created something of a dilemma. Yates had already admitted he was "anxious" to see what kind of book Bernard would produce, but now that it had been published Whiting's culpability was indisputable. It must have been upsetting for Yates to admit that Rev. Whiting—his friend, relative by marriage, and former deputy—had violated his solemn obligations of loyalty and secrecy. If Yates felt betrayed, he may also have worried that others would wonder how the security breach occurred, and may even lay the ultimate blame at his own feet, since he was the custodian of the rituals. Certainly, there were but few people who *could* be blamed, in light of the fact that Yates had already acknowledged to Gourgas that nobody but he and Whiting had seen the rituals they received from Barker in 1825.

In a weak attempt to divert attention and culpability from himself Yates dashed off a desperate letter to Gourgas on September 4, 1829, which was nothing but obfuscation. He began his missive by casually stating that he had "nothing in particular to communicate," but it soon becomes apparent that he has *much* to communicate, as he "protests too much." First, he delivered a litany of possible sources for the exposed rituals. Next, and in spite of the evidence he cited in his January 15, 1829, letter, Yates asserted that Whiting had no intentions of renouncing Masonry. Then Yates then pointed an unsteady finger at John Barker, agent of

LIGHT ON MASONRY.

the Supreme Council at Charleston, as the possible traitor. And finally, Yates suggested that *Light on Masonry* should just be ignored, since it would most likely be unsuccessful. Whatever gifts Yates possessed, it is evident that prophesy was not among them. By the end of the year, *Light on Masonry* would be reprinted in four improved and enlarged editions.

> Having an opportunity to send you a line by private hand, I thought I would avail myself of it, although I have nothing in particular to communicate.
>
> *Before I had* read L[*ight on Masonry*] (having only cast my eyes over it before sending to you) I expressed an opinion to you that I presumed it consisted of translations from some Fr[ench] T[ile]r. This my opinion was based partly upon the fact that some extracts from the work published in the papers, (I believe I send you a few numbers e.g. *the Boston Press* &^{c}) were materially different from any *mss* I had ever seen, & also upon the fact that it appeared to treat of certain Fr[ench] ∴ ∆s [Degrees], which I had never seen any there, till I saw them in the T[ile]r you sent me and some of them in "Maconnerie Adoniramique" a Book I have owned since the year 1823—or 1824 purchased at Albany—
>
> Since I have read L[*ight on Masonry*] I have been induced to change my opinion in part, and since the receipt of your letter to me to examine & compare as far as I could. The following is the result. The Inef[fable] ∴ ∆s [degrees] vary much from the Ch[arleston] mss. especially the R[oyal]. A[rch]. Which in the latter is nearly twice as long as in L[*ight on Masonry*] —The K[nigh]t of E[ast] is an exact translation from Mac∴ Adon∴ and so is R[ose] + [Croix] in L[*ight on Masonry*] so is chev[alier] Prus[sien] & so are the ∆s [degrees] termed *French* ∆s [Degrees]. In the R[ose]. + [Croix] there is an ode introduced which I *think* I saw in Barker's ms. Those papers after you had perused them were boxed up & returned to B[arke]r and I cannot of course have acces to them but as you have read them, no doubt more attentively than I did, you are a better judge than I can be with respect to the other ∆s. [Degrees] K[nigh]t. of S[word]. & K[night]. of E[ast]. & W[est]. are the only ms. That were out of my hands as I stated in a former letter during the whole period I had them in my custody, except at the commencement of our Consistory business say in the year 1825–1826 It is possible, and I now think not unlikely that copies were made or at least abstracts—at first perhaps only for private use, but afterwards converted to another use where treachery entered the heart of two Rev^d—Judasses—W[hiting] denies however having renounced ∆y [Masonry] or having any concern with Ber[nar]d—at least he did some time ago & I have not communicated with him of late—he seems rather to decline it correspondence, and I feel no disposition to urge it, or to have any cultivate any more acquaintance with him. There are certain passages in L[*ight on Masonry*] which I *am assured* could *only* have been procured from the MSS of Barker. It never occurred to me before but is it not possible that *he* is concerned? But it is of no consequence. As Hudibras says—or one of his followers.
>
> "The more you stir a stagnant pot,
>
> "The more of stench it doth emit."

INTRODUCTION.

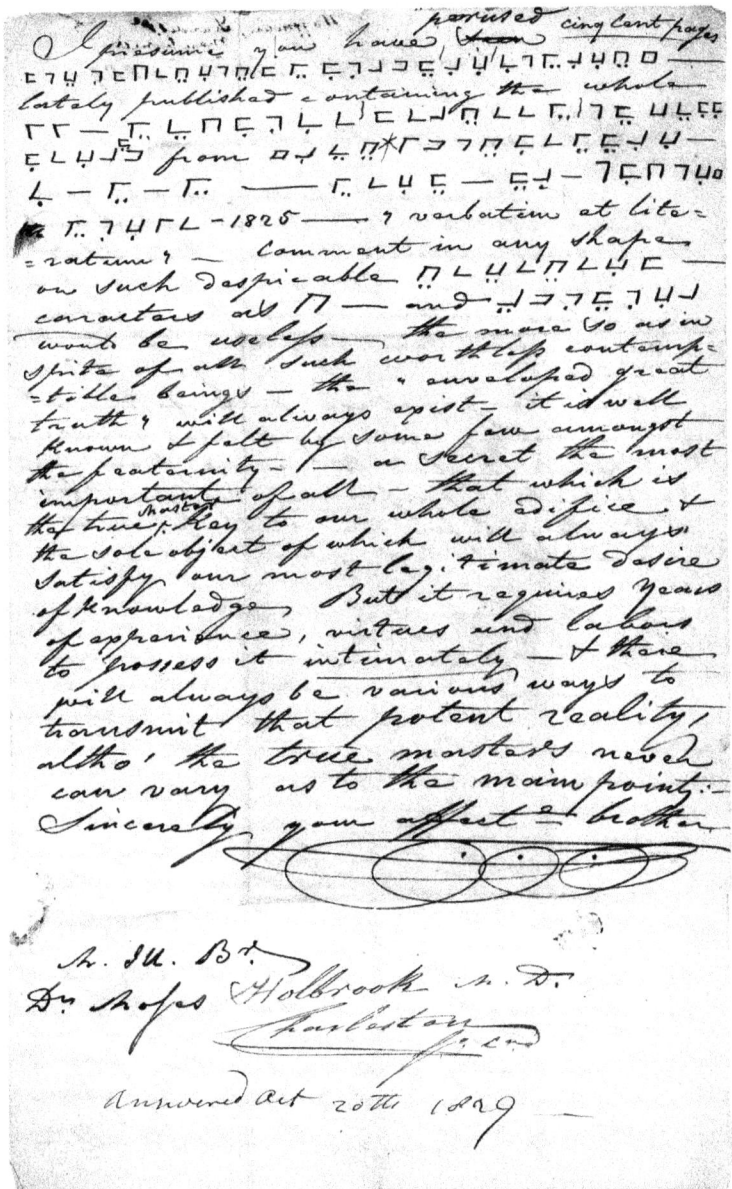

Figure 7. A page from J. J. J. Gourgas's letter of August 6, 1829, to Moses Holbrook. The enciphered text informed Holbrook that the Scottish Rite's rituals had been exposed; Gourgas branded traitors David Bernard and Nathan N. Whiting as "despicable reverend caracters." From the Archives of the Supreme Council, 33°, S.J.

> I think with you that such contemptible persons deserve no notice. I am inclined ^{to think} L[ight on Masonry] has fallen, still-born from the pup —at least comparatively speaking—I shall be pleased to learn that not enough of *"the thing"* has been sold to pay the printer.
>
> A peddler employed by B[ernard] brought some to this place to be sold, ~~but~~ though he remained here nearly a week, he sold only *one*. I was in Albany a few days ago & had the curiosity to look at the shelf ^{of the store} where those books were sold at the time I bought you a copy, and it appeared to me they had not diminished in number, more than a dozen. But it is possible, yet not probable, that the book-seller had received a new supply since I last saw him.[108]

The reader will note that Yates avoids any direct comment on the Degrees unique to the Scottish Rite (Chief of the Tabernacle, Prince of the Tabernacle, etc.). Gourgas was neither dissuaded nor misled by Yates, and he so informed Holbrook, "As to *L[ight on Masonry]*—I cannot change my opinion—it is exactly as I wrote you on 6th August—not withstanding all that Br. Y[ates] may write on the subject. If you have not a copy it is well worth your while & curiosity to possess one more cost $1–50...."[109] Because Holbrook did not know that Whiting was the traitor, his suspicion of John Barker remained. In a December 9, 1829, letter to Gourgas, Holbrook alluded to this, and asked for a copy of the new exposé, "I can get no answer from barker at all—I fear he has been concerned with Bernard in his *Light of Masonry*—Please send me a copy of his *Light*—and I will settle the Bill Send by Packet." In a letter written January 8, 1830, Holbrook acknowledged receiving a copy of *Light on Masonry*. His letter was surprisingly quiet, and it said nothing the Scottish Rite's rituals. After all, what was there to say?

> Your kind favor of 24th ultimo together with the expelled Barnard's light on Masonry—safe—Expelled Masons can say the most against the Order for Elder B. acknowledged in his Preface that he was expelled from the Order—and all his notes are garbled—one sided and unfair.[110]

An Untempered Response

Moses Holbrook's restraint was not shared by other Masons. Within a year a pamphlet was published, *Strictures on Seceding Masons* (1830),[111] which provided some interesting information about Bernard, but was marred by pyrotechnics and *ad hominem* attacks. At this early period most Masons did not know of the Scottish Rite's existence. Thus, when its unfamiliar Degrees were published by Bernard, Masons unwittingly denied the Degrees were even Masonic. In the context presented by Bernard, they were even branded as "villainous."

ELDER DAVID BERNARD

> The active exertions of this man in the cause of anti-masonry, have rendered it incumbent on us to trace again the lamented aberrations, from the

INTRODUCTION.

straight road of christian charity, into the tortuous by-paths, leading unto death, of professed oath-breakers and avowed infidels. We expect to be able to show that the eminence or notoriety, to which this man has attained, by none to be envied, has arisen from perfidy and violation of oaths; which ought to result and, in the minds of all but considerate zealots, would result in the most disgraceful infamy. His volume of pretended disclosures is regarded by many anti-masons as indubitable authority; as the anti-masonic *bible*; and is probably more read, and held in higher estimation, by the men of that party, than is the Bible of the Christian. It is appealed to on all occasions; and its author is held up as the greatest champion in the *cause of the people*: as a martyr to virtue and to the liberties of his country. How far the gentleman's motives are to be respected; what degree of reverence should attach to his character, and what credit there is to be given to the truth of his disclosures, the public will be better able to determine after we shall have done with him. When his character shall be made to appear fully and fairly before them: and when they know the infamy which justly attaches to it, let them weigh and estimate him according to his merits. For the credit of the Church of Christ, we would throw the mantle of charity over the foibles of her communicants: but when her honor is exposed to the depredations of hypocritical knaves and profligate miscreants, honest men and charitable christians, are imperatively called upon to stand forth in her defense, to shield her from the baseness of wretches who have wriggled themselves into her confidence, and who are now sapping the streams of her existence. *Personally* we know nothing of *Elder* Bernard; but *abstractly* we know *too much* of him. Our knowledge of his infamous character is derived from statements publicly made by gentlemen of integrity and honor, in the neighborhoods where he resided. Bernard was *expelled* from the Masonic Institution *before* he commenced his warfare against it; and to this source may be traced the origin of his rancor and deadly enmity to Freemasonry. On this subject, Dr. DANIEL WHITE, of Covington, N.Y. in a letter addressed to Bernard, remarks:—"You state, you requested to be dismissed from the society—that masons were offended at this, and expelled you. Now, sir, you *know* this to be *absolutely and totally false*. You *know*, at the time you was expelled, you said you believed the Institution to be a *good one*, and had *never* spoken against it, except of some errors—the same as you would speak of some errors in the church, to which you belonged. You have used some craft and sophistry, to make people believe the masons did not *speak the truth*, in saying you had *applied* for degrees which you *could not obtain*; and have produced a certificate from Elder N. N. Whiting, &c. Now, Sir, why did you not call on Mr. Allcott, and others, of Rochester? They would have certified that you *applied there for the degrees of Knighthood which were not granted you*. And you requested Col. Stoddard, in case your petition was granted, to accompany you to Rochester, *when you should go to receive the degrees.*—Any person who feels disposed to question this statement, please call on Col. Stoddard, who will give the facts. Now, who has *lied*? Sir, why have you been applying for degrees of Knighthood, if you had, as you say, denounced the Institution as *corrupt, anti-christian, and soul destroying*."

LIGHT ON MASONRY.

It may be proper here also to inquire, if Bernard never received, (which cannot be controverted) any other degrees than those subordinate to the degrees of Knighthood—that is, the first seven degrees in masonry—what authority has he for publishing *forty-eight* degrees, and calling them Masonic? Will the people believe him when he says the impious developments, he has given to the world, are the degrees of Freemasonry? Having been branded in the columns of a public newspaper, as a *liar*, having been invited to a legal investigation of the charge, and having cautiously avoided such an investigation, is his word to be taken, when he deprecates the Masonic Institution?—Is his *book* to be received by this community as *true*, or is it to be hurled into obscurity, with its author, as a budget of *lies*? It is entitled to no weightier consideration. Most of the degrees he has there given were never heard of, even by name, in the history of Masonry. They are the degrees of the Carbonari, and such villanous institutions, which have long since been driven from the earth. *There is no Masonry in them*; and the unworthy compiler knew there was not, when he gave them to the world. To give to them a degree of probability, he has republished the illustrations of Morgan, the Le Roy disclosures, &c. But it requires a more credible name than his to gain for them the credit of honest men; knaves may believe them, and fools may patronize him: honorable men will have nothing to do with either.

A few months since, Bernard procured and published in Chatautaque Phœnix, a "letter of commendation," preparatory to his location in Fredonia, his present place of residence. The manner in which this letter was obtained, and the credit which ought to be attached to it, will appear from the following statement, given by the gentleman already quoted. 'You boast of your letter of commendation from the church in this place. How did you get that letter? Think of the duplicity you practiced; and blush at the deception you have wrought. You told many of the church that the petition, to have the Masonic members renounce Masonry, was merely a request, and nothing more was to be done about it; and then you told, at Deacon Stoddard's, that you meant to present the petition to the masonic brethren, and that would be the first step of labor with them, and would prevent their having a vote in the church, as they would vote against your letter of commendation; and when you had sent the masonic brethren out of the house, you immediately introduced your letter, which you had written yourself, and in that manner you got majority to vote upon the letter; and when you was about to take the vote, and some of the church observed that the masonic brethren *were out*, instead of sending to call them in, *as you say*, you observed that *out of doors was the place for them*. You never sent anyone to call them in, until you closed the meeting. Any one who dispute this, is requested to call on Deacon Glass and Mr. Lewis, who were present, and are as respectable men as belong to any church.' Dr. White also states that Bernard endeavored to obtain retractions for assertions previously made against him, by a person who was supposed to be on his death-bed; which however he failed to obtain, even under such circumstances, for the obvious reason that they were true. Having failed in every attempt to induce Bernard to submit to charges preferred against him, either to legal

INTRODUCTION.

investigation, or to a council of their own choosing, Dr. White then preferred the following charges to the 2d Baptist Church in Le Roy.

    1st. LYING.   3d. DUPLICITY.

    2d. DECEPTION.   4th. PROFANITY,

These charges, or the principal of them, Dr. White pledged himself to prove, if the church before which they were laid, would appoint a council for that purpose. This, under the most frivolous pretexts, they *declined* doing, and it was suspected *from the influence of Bernard himself*; and if justly, then virtually acknowledging that *he dare not abide the issue*. Commenting on the transactions of Bernard, after his removal to Covington, Dr. White says: "Do we not find you, soon after, sowing seeds of discord in families and societies? Have not families in this vicinity, *been on the verge of dissolution;* in consequence of your *kind*, MINISTERIAL *attentions to* WOMEN, *in the absence of their husbands?* Have you not gone from church to church, and from place to place, like an evil genius, blasting the fair fruit, and destroying the peace of society? Are all these things becoming a minister of the Gospel?"

    *   *   *   *   *   *   *   *

Now, Sir, please look and see what a picture you present to the world. All who have witnessed your exertions, and have been acquainted with you for a number of years, know you have been a flaming fanatic; damning all parties but your own—anthematizeing all who would not believe your dictum; and all this while, according to your own story, you have had "Hell's Masterpiece" wrapped up in your bosom.—If you had been thus hypocritical, in the service of your master, no wonder you should practice hypocrisy among your brethren. Do you expect them, who know your heart, will approbate the labors of such a hypocritical servant?

Whiting's Feeble anti-Masonry

Although Bernard was protective of his "source," Whiting gradually became comfortable with his decision to abandon Freemasonry. And, although he never came to the forefront of the anti-Masonic movement or publicly admitted giving the rituals to Bernard, he occasionally lent his support in more subtle ways. As far as I know he delivered his first and only anti-Masonic sermon in January 1830.[112] Contrasted with Bernard's openly zealous aggression, Whiting's anti-Masonry was tame. It is true, however, that he allowed his patents to be reproduced in the anti-Masonic press and would publicly confirm the accuracy of the Masonic exposures. For example, a year and a half after *Light on Masonry*'s publication, Whiting provided Bernard with a letter confirming the accuracy of its Scottish Rite ritual exposure. Whiting's note was reprinted in the *Proceedings of the United States Anti-Masonic Convention, Held at Philadelphia on September 11, 1830*, from which the following copy was transcribed.

LIGHT ON MASONRY.

Vernon, Oneida County, N.Y. September 7, 1830.

ELDER D. BERNARD,

Influenced, as I humbly trust, by a sense of the duty which I owe to the friends of truth and the happiness of mankind, I hereby certify, that the various masonic degrees contained in the list below, and published by you in the work entitled "Light on Masonry," are genuine and authentic, and may be relied on as such by the world. I farther certify, that the degrees from the knight of the East and West, to that of Sublime Prince of the Royal Secret inclusive, were conferred on me and several others informally, that is, without the use of the various ceremonies detailed in those degrees as published; that a simple obligation of secrecy being administered, we were left to learn the nature and tendency of those degrees from the manuscripts in which they were contained; that this mode of conferring the degrees is a regular one, when there is no organized consistory for the Sublime Degrees. I farther certify, that an agent of the Supreme Council of Sovereign Grand Inspectors General, (which Council has its place of meeting in Charleston, S.C.) was employed to communicate the Sublime Degrees to an officer of high masonic rank in the state of New York, and that through *that* officer said degrees have been conferred on various persons residing in said state.

List of Degrees referred to above.

Secret Master,	Illustrious Knight,
Perfect Master,	Grand Master Architect,
Intimate Secretary,	Knight of the 9th Arch,
Provost and Judge,	G. E. and S. Mason,
Intendant of the Buildings,	Knight of the E. and W.
Elected Knights of Nine,	Sov. Prince of Rose-Croix,
Elected Grand Master,	Grand Pontiff.[113]

This letter tells us several interesting things. First, it confirms that the degrees then controlled by the Scottish Rite (17°–32°) were imparted by simple communication, rather than dramatic participation. That this was the regular method at the time is also confirmed in a letter which Yates wrote to Gourgas in 1828.

The obligation administered by Br. J. Barker who established us was a general one as S.P.R.S. & did not go into all the minutiae of the different degrees, which we are now (in case we have any Candidates) bound to administer to such Candidates. You will no doubt say this was doing business in too loose a way.[114]

Whiting's letter explains that the candidates were allowed to study the rituals from manuscript and that an "agent of the Supreme Council" (John Barker) communicated the degrees to an "officer of high masonic rank in the state of New York" (Giles F. Yates), who then conferred the degrees on others. Although Whiting did not publicly assume responsibility for providing the rituals exposed in *Light on Masonry*, the fact must have been as obvious to other Masons as it was to Gourgas;

INTRODUCTION.

for, time and again, it was only Whiting who consistently supported Bernard's exposure of the Scottish Rite's Degrees.

HOMAGE TO WHITING

As he approached the end of his life Bernard made occasional appearances at anti-Masonic conventions—although he failed to attract the size of crowds to which he once lectured during the Morgan Affair. At this late period he reminisced on those earlier days, and on the friendship he shared with Whiting. In an effort to rekindle the fires of anti-Masonry *Light on Masonry* was republished, but without his help. When asked to contribute to new editions, he declined, but sent a note of good wishes to its publisher. In a late publication Bernard shared more details about the source of the Scottish Rite rituals he published.

> It may not be uninteresting to know that the degrees of Freemasonry, as contained in that book, are, as they were received by me (i.e., the first three degrees) in 1822 at Utica, N.Y.; as received by me (i.e., the four chaptoral degrees) at Union Village, Washington County, N.Y.; as received by me (the eleventh ineffable degree) in Schenectady, N.Y.; as received by me through the officers of the 'Lodge of Perfection,' aided by a 'Deputy Sovereign of Sovereigns of Sublime Princes;' and the 'higher degrees,' as written out in full, by the Rev. Dr. Frederick Dalcho, of South Carolina, 'Sovereign Inspector General of Freemasonry of the 33rd degree;' and I gave them *verbatim et literatum*, as *thus given to me* by the highest masonic authority in the world. And what makes the subject particularly interesting to me, is the fact that these degrees were not written out for me, but written out by Dr. Dalcho, for the 'Lodge of Perfection;' and observe, given me, *knowing that I would publish them all to the world*; and I copied these documents, written by the Rev. Dr. Dalcho, as carefully as I would have copied God's pure word which I regard more than all the world besides. And if this is not all true and authentic, I do not know what authenticity means; and if you don't find Freemasonry TRUE and CORRECTLY given in my book called 'Light on Masonry,' you cannot find it anywhere.[115]

There are several errors in this account which will be addressed. Let us first, however, read a more detailed account, made by Bernard in 1874 before the National Christian Association, just two years after Whiting's death.

> In making my arrangements for the publication of "Light on Masonry," at Utica, I called on the Rev. N. N. Whiting, pastor of the Baptist church in Vernon, Oneida Co., N.Y. Prof. Whiting, as he afterward became, was a graduate of Union College, Schenectady, N.Y., in both departments. He graduated in the college proper with honor. He then read law and was admitted at the bar and commenced practice, professed religion and returned to college and went through a theological course. He entered the ministry and was ordained by a large council a pastor of the Baptist church in Sche-

nectady. My acquaintance with Mr. Whiting commenced in 1823, and he was my bosom friend until, in 1872, forty-nine years after our acquaintance and friendship commenced, he passed to the house of many mansions. Prof. Whiting was elected and acted as President of the collegiate institute of Plainfield, N. J. He was a great Bible student; was a profound Greek and Hebrew scholar; and could teach thirteen languages. He was one of the revisers of the American Bible Union....

Prof. Whiting was a very high Mason; one of sixteen, the highest save three in the world. These three are Sovereign Inspectors of Masonry. Masonry has divided the world into sixteen parts, and appoints a Deputy Sovereign of Sovereigns of Sublime Princes over each of these parts, and three are Sovereign Grand Inspectors Generals over the whole earth. These are Sovereign Inspectors General of the 33d degree.

In 1826 the Rev. Dr. Frederick Dalcho, of South Carolina, was one of these three Sovereign Inspector Generals of the order. With him were deposited the written manuscripts of Masonry (all above the Royal Arch are written) of all the higher degrees. When the Lodge of Perfection at Schenectady was installed Dr. Dalcho furnished the manuscripts. He copied them from the original records from that lodge and gave Mr. Yates of Schenectady, the Grand Commander, the eleven degrees for that lodge, and all the rest. Mr. Yates held them in connection with Prof. Whiting for some years. They had them in possession alternately. As Mr. Yates was at the head of the lodge for whom they were written he held them most of the time. But when not in the hands of Yates, they were held by Whiting. When I called on Whiting, Mr. Yates had them in possession; and not until then did I know that any such manuscripts were in existence. I indeed had supposed that my cup was full already, for I had the first three degrees of the Blue Lodge from the pen of Captain Morgan, and sealed with his own blood! And I had the four chaptoral degrees and the degrees of the Cross and Encampment of the Knight Templars from the report of the convention of one hundred and three seceding Masons at Leroy, N.Y., and the eleven Ineffable degrees from the Lodge of Perfection, making twenty-three degrees of pure and unmixed Masonry, and from undoubted authority. I felt well, but little thought I was destined to be the depository or medium through which all the treasures or "Solomon and Hiram the Widow's Son" were to flow to mankind!...

When I entered the house of my friend and brother, Whiting, although knowing his views were all in favor of Masonry, and that he was one of the highest Masons in the world; and remembering that I had taken the higher degrees of Masonry at his suggestion and by his aid; and knowing, too, that he knew as well as I that we were now antipodes on Masonry, and possibly might become violent belligerents, yet I had no misgivings. I knew that he had the intelligence, the learning, the piety, the knowledge of Masonry,—every thing in advance of myself, save truth, common sense, conscience and God. On the great question at issue I knew, I KNEW I was right. No hesitancy, no tremblings. Not a bit of it—but a perfect confidence in the truth and righteousness of my mission.

INTRODUCTION.

> We met in love. The Master was with us. Mr. Whiting knew I was about to publish my "Light on Masonry." I told him all about it. He was not angry; nor was I. We opened the subject, pro and con....
>
> And by this servant of God Mr. Yates was gained, and though not willing to assume any responsibility in the matter, was willing to give up the manuscripts to Mr. Whiting to dispose of as he thought best. And my good brother Whiting thought best to loan them to me, and to me for publication. I copied them as carefully as I could; and I thought best to give them—as I had nothing else to give—and myself for the life of the world; taking my pattern from my glorious Lord.
>
> You can find all the "secrets" of Masonry up to the thirty-third degree as I received them, and as I have here testified, from the hands of the Rev. Dr. Frederick Dalcho, Sovereign Inspector General of the thirty-third degree, through the hands of the Grand Commander, Mr. Yates, of the Lodge of Perfection in Schenectady, N.Y. and Rev. Prof. N. N. Whiting; and if intelligence and learning and piety and official standing as a Mason, and a correct knowledge of Masonry are essential to authenticity and belief, then we have full and reliable evidence from the testimony of the Rev. N. N. Whiting, as given by the testimony of Elder David Bernard, of the truth of the higher degrees of Masonry as reveled in "Light on Masonry," by Elder David Bernard, Grand Elect Perfect and Sublime Mason.
>
> And now is it not a matter of congratulation that this Convention is in possession of Masonry in its details as given in the lodges of this country, from the first to the thirty-third degree, obtained from the highest and purest and most authentic and reliable sources of Masonic authority and knowledge in the world?[116]

As interesting as the above account is relative to his encounter with Whiting, Bernard errs in important details. To begin, Whiting was not one of the sixteen highest Masons in the world. He was only an officer for the local, Schenectady area, bodies of Freemasonry and held the 32°, Sublime Prince of the Royal Secret, as did *scores* of Masons worldwide. In the 1820s there were two Supreme Councils in the United States, each with several *Thirty-third* Degree officers. The Masonic world was never divided "into sixteen parts," although Deputies were indeed appointed over local organizations. The law of the Scottish Rite, known as the *Grand Constitutions*, required not *three,* but rather *nine* Sovereign Grand Inspectors General per Supreme Council. Bernard was confused because only three Sovereign Grand Inspectors General signed the Supreme Council's first printed document, the *Circular throughout two hemispheres* (1802).

The Rev. Frederick Dalcho was Grand Commander from 1801 to 1822, and he remained a member of the Supreme Council at Charleston until his death in 1836. However, when the Lodge of Perfection at Schenectady was installed Rev. Dalcho did not supply its rituals, and neither did the Supreme Council at Charleston.

LIGHT ON MASONRY.

Yates explained in his letter of January 15, 1829 (quoted earlier) that Whiting "took a copy for his own use ... as they came to our hands *previous* to our having any communication with the Charleston Sup[reme]. Council" (emphasis added). I compared the Dalcho ritual collection with the Ineffable Degrees exposed in *Light on Masonry*, and found that the two sets represent completely independent translations. However, several of the higher degrees indeed came from the manuscripts delivered by John Barker to Giles F. Yates in 1825, during Isaac Auld's tenure as Grand Commander.

Bernard states that through the influence of Whiting, "Mr. Yates was gained, and though not willing to assume any responsibility in the matter, was willing to give up the manuscripts to Mr. Whiting to dispose of as he thought best." This implies that Yates knowingly or wittingly surrendered manuscript rituals to Whiting for publication. Because "dead men tell no tales" it is impossible to (dis)prove this assertion. What is known, however, is that Yates remained faithful to Freemasonry throughout his life and became Sovereign Grand Commander of the Supreme Council, 33°, Northern Masonic Jurisdiction in 1851. However, from my study of Yates and by reading his personal correspondence I do not believe Bernard's statement, but rather believe he sought to protect the reputation of his friend, Rev. Nathan N. Whiting.

LIGHT ON MASONRY – AN OVERVIEW OF ITS CONTENTS
(Complete bibliographic information is in the appendix.) *Light on Masonry* opens to two engraved frontispieces based on paintings by "A. Cooley." The first depicts "Wm Morgan," and the second "The Masonic Assassination of Akirop, by Joabert." The latter may have been inspired by a similar illustration in the French exposé, *Le tombeau de Jacques Molai* (1797).[117] Solomon Southwick described Cooley as "not only a self-taught artist, but a native American, whose productions in the way of his profession, do him the highest honor." In August 1828 Cooley exhibited a "Masonic Gallery" in the home of William Hollings in Albany. His exhibition included several paintings, one of which inspired the second frontispiece:

> No. 1 represents the inside of a lodge-room, the candidate kneeling and receiving the obligation, surrounded by the brethren who bring him to light. No. 2, the Craft partaking of refreshment—crackers, brandy &c. substitute for the Bible, square and compasses. While some are indulging in their favorite beverage, others are regaling themselves with eating and smoking—meanwhile the master lectures the new candidate. No 3, the signs and grips from the entered apprentice to the Royal Arch degree. No 4, the death of Akirop, who was killed through Masonic vengeance, as related in Webb's Monitor. A portrait of the patriotic SOLOMON SOUTHWICK, as

INTRODUCTION.

Figure 8. This engraving from *Le tombeau de Jacques Molai* (Paris, 1797) may have inspired the second frontispiece in *Light on Masonry*, "The Masonic Assassination of Akirop, by Joabert."

well as those of the unfortunate widow and children of the martyr MORGAN, are annexed.[118]

The admission price to this exhibit was 12 ½ cents (about $2.50 in today's money). Cooley's amateur portrait of Morgan was repainted by a young artist named Frederick R. Spencer, who would later become a celebrated American portrait painter. Both Spencer's portrait of Morgan and Cooley's "Akirop" painting were engraved on steel by the renowned mapmaker Vistus Balch, who was then employed by Colonel William Williams, the publisher of *Light on Masonry*.

- *Craft Masonry.* At this early period it was not common for American Grand Lodges to have prescribed or "fixed" rituals, so the language could be expected to differ in minor details even within the same jurisdiction. During the 1820s there were two Grand Lodges in New York State. Morgan's exposé represents a ritual of the "Country Grand Lodge," which occupied the western part of the State, while the "City Grand Lodge" had its ritual published in Parker's *Masonic Tablet*. Ritual uniformity was eventually brought about by unification of the two New York Grand Lodges, the frequent use of *Jachin and Boaz* (supplemented with Thomas Smith Webb's *Free-Masons' Monitor*), and the Grand Lodge's appointment of committees. However accurate Morgan's text may have been it did not reflect Masonic practices across America. This proved troublesome in other states, where the ritual differed greatly. The ritual was so different, in fact, that Pennsylvania Masons were able to honestly deny knowledge of many Morgan-style ritual features.

Bernard stated that he republished the Blue Lodge ritual of Morgan's exposé "with the typographical errors all corrected." Both Morgan and Parker err in small details and are sometimes internally inconsistent. In spite of Bernard's comment, I would categorize the typographical errors in the original edition of Morgan's work as trivial.[119] For example, some of the errors corrected by Bernard included *Sheboleth*, *Seboleth*, *Solomons Temple*, *Ja-chihn*, and *Mah hah bon*.

- *Royal Arch Chapter.* The Degrees of Mark Master, Past Master, and Most Excellent Master were transcribed by Morgan and obtained from his presumed widow, Lucinda Pendleton. The text of the catechism of the Royal Arch Degree was purportedly acquired by a "companion" sent by the Le Roy Committee to learn the work of the Jeremy L. Cross, whom they described as "General Grand Lecturer of the United States." However, soon after the publication of *A Revelation of Freemasonry* people objected that the rituals were not accurately transcribed. Bernard and/or his fellow anti-Masons had tampered with the ritual texts prior to publication. "Infamous interpolations" were added to excite further public outrage against Masonry. The most heinous of these changes was in the membership oath or obligation, which was falsely made to say that Royal Arch Masons swore to conceal each other's secrets, *"murder and treason not excepted."* Even honest ex-Masons objected to these lies. For example, in his book *Letters on Masonry and*

INTRODUCTION.

anti-Masonry (1832), seceding Mason William L. Stone wrote, "The obligation has never been so given, within the range of my masonic experience, and is not sanctioned or allowed by the Grand Chapter, having jurisdiction in the premises. Nor have I, as yet, found a Royal Arch Mason who recollects ever to have heard the obligation so given."[120] To the consternation of Jeremy L. Cross the bogus obligation was reprinted in *Light on Masonry*, and quoted elsewhere. Cross's dismay was evident in the following letter that was published in the *Boston Masonic Mirror*.

NEW HAVEN, Feb. 7th, 1831

Mr. C. W. MOORE:

DEAR SIR—Your letter of the 2d instant came safely to hand, informing me that, in the Senate of your commonwealth, on Wednesday, Jan. 26, 1831, the subject of Extra Judicial Oaths being under consideration, the Hon. Moses Thatcher, senator from Norfolk, stated to the honorable Board that, *he had authority for saying that* JEREMY L. CROSS, *Grand Lecturer of the General Grand Chapter of the U.S.A. authorizes the Oaths in chapters so to be given, that the initiated swears to conceal all crimes of a companion R.A. Mason, Murder and Treason not excepted.*

You wish to be informed whether there be any grounds for this declaration? Whether I have ever authorized any oath so to be given? Or if I have ever so given one myself? And whether I was ever Grand Lecturer of the General Grand Chapter of the U.S.A.?

In answer to these inquires, I would state, that during the period that the late Governor De Witt Clinton, was the first officer of the General Grand Chapter, I was sanctioned by him and the other officers of that body, as a Lecturer, who was correct in my mode of work and lecturing as adopted by that body; and under that sanction I visited several States, instructing the Lodges and Chapters in the mode of work and lecturing. In regard to my giving any oath whatever, requiring the initiated to swear to conceal all *crimes* of a companion R. A. Mason, Murder and Treason not excepted, or authorized others so to give it, IS WITHOUT THE LEAST FOUNDATION OF TRUTH. I never gave such an oath, nor have I ever authorized others so to give one; and furthermore, I have never given myself, nor authorized any person to give, any oath in masonry, whereby the person so taking it is required to conceal *any crime whatever*, which may be committed by any mason against the laws of God and his country; and so far from that being the case, every mason is required to keep and obey the moral laws of God; "to be a quiet and peaceable citizen; true to his government, and just to his country." He is *forbid* to countenance disloyalty or rebellion, but is patiently to submit to the legal authority of the country in which he lives."

I can assure you there is nothing *in any oath or regulation in Masonry*, from the first degree to the twelfth, as I understand them, or have taught others to teach them, contrary to the above requirements. I do not impeach the motives or integrity of the Hon. Senator, but I do assure you that his information is *incorrect, and without any shadow of truth for its support.*

LIGHT ON MASONRY.

Should you deem this statement of any value, you are at liberty to make such use of it as will best subserve the cause of TRUTH.
Yours respectfully,
JEREMY L. CROSS.[121]

• **Encampment (Masonic Knighthood).** The Knights of the Red Cross and "Knight Templar and Knight of Malta" (a single degree), were copied from *A Revelation of Free Masonry*. As stated in the report of the publishing committee, "The Degrees of the Encampment are copied directly from the manuscript furnished by the officer sent by the Grand Encampment to install Genesee Encampment, No. 10. This manuscript was left to instruct the officers of the new Encampment in their duties." Only the catechisms of the degrees were exposed, not the full rituals.

• **Order of the Cross.** The "Ancient Council of the Trinity" was operated by James H. C. Miller, a degree peddler, who was chiefly active in the 1820s. The term "Trinity" was not theological, but alluded to the three Degrees conferred by this organization. Although the degrees were a type of Masonic knighthood this organization was condemned by the Grand Encampment of Knights Templar for the State of New York. Anti-Masons, perhaps unaware of this fact, condemned Freemasonry on the basis of passages in Miller's rituals. The Degrees of the Ancient Council of the Trinity published by Bernard were copied from a manuscript left at the formation of a Council in Le Roy. The interested reader can read my study of Miller, along with his full rituals (copied from Moses Holbrook's manuscript copy) in *Heredom*, volume 8 (1999–2000).[122]

• **Scottish Rite.** The Scottish Rite rituals exposed in *Light on Masonry* were composed at various dates and came from several sources (Figure 9).

The 4°–14°, Secret Master through Grand Elect Perfect and Sublime Masons, were *not* those distributed by the Supreme Council at Charleston. As Yates explained in his letter of January 15, 1829, Whiting "took a copy for his own use ... as they came to our hands *previous* to our having any communication with the Charleston Sup[reme]. Council." Neither do they match the ritual used by Yates's Delta Lodge of Perfection, but were likely independently translated, as this was a common practice at the time.

The 15°, Knight of the East was not exposed, although Bernard reproduces a translation of an earlier French version, as a "detached degree."

The 16°, Princes of Jerusalem was likely the ritual of Albany's Grand Council of Princes of Jerusalem, over which Yates presided.

A thorough examination confirms that Bernard's rituals of the 17°–20°, Knight of the East and West through Grand Master of all Symbolic Lodges, ultimately derived from the private ritual collection of Giles F. Yates. This is demonstrated in side-by-side comparisons of ritual texts. The Scottish Rite rituals in *Light on Masonry* include minor deviations from the Charleston rituals as they were given

INTRODUCTION.

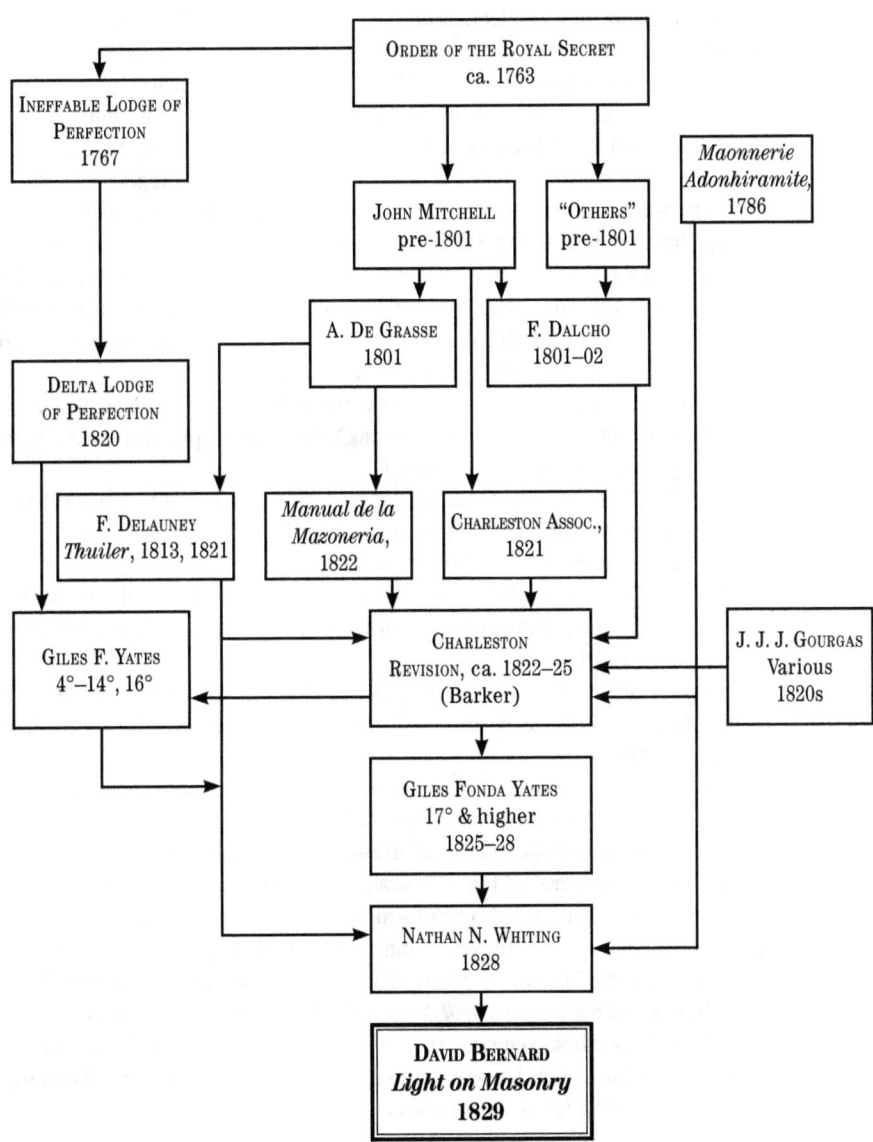

Figure 9. Abbreviated genealogy of the Scottish Rite rituals exposed in *Light on Masonry.*

LIGHT ON MASONRY.

to Yates by John Barker in 1825. These differences are accounted for by examining Yates's surviving ritual collection and noting that the modifications are written *in his own handwriting*. These changes, present in both *Light on Masonry* and Yates's documents, are absent from all other copies of the Charleston rituals.

If we examine the symbols of the Seventeenth Degree, for example, we can see how Yates's editing was carried over into *Light on Masonry*. Bernard's text describes "four lions and four eagles, and between them an angel, or seraphim, with six wings." The Yates manuscript ritual includes alterations which closely match this text, stating that there are "4 Lions ~~or~~ ^& 4 Eagles, and between them ~~an animal of the Human form~~ ^an angel ~~or moving serpent~~ with 6 wings" (Figure 10). Another example from the same Degree reads, "In the east there must be a basin with perfume and a basin of water, and a human skull." Once again, Yates's manuscript closely conforms: "In the East a Bason with perfume—& ^a Basin of water —and a ^human skull." Having compared the entire manuscript collection, line by line, with *Light on Masonry* I am satisfied that the surviving Yates manuscript is a precursor to the document loaned by Whiting to Bernard.

The 21°, Prussian Knight was not exposed in its Scottish Rite form, although Bernard included an earlier French version as a "detached degree." It was similar enough to communicate the substance of the Degree.

The 22°–27°, Knight of the Royal Axe through Grand Commander of the Temple, came from the private collection of Giles F. Yates, who obtained them from Charleston, through Barker.

The 28°, Knight of the Sun, and 30°, Knight Kadosh are slight revisions of the rituals translated by Henry Andrew Francken, who created Albany's Ineffable Lodge of Perfection.

The 29°, Knight of Saint Andrew, and 31°, Grand Inquiring Commander were not exposed, but are reproduced in Appendix 1.

The 32°, Sublime Prince of the Royal Secret was an abbreviation of the ritual.

Bernard's "exposure" of the 33°, Sovereign Grand Inspector General contains no ritual information, but only provides an outline of the Supreme Council's decorations and a hint at the secret words and signs. This sketchy description was translated and extracted from François H. Stanislaus Delaunaye's *Thuileur des Trente-trois Degres de L'Ecossisme du Rit Ancien, dit Accepté* (Paris, 1813, 1821).[123]

• **French Degrees.** The several "Detached Degrees" supposedly conferred in France and in America as honorary degrees, were translated from *Recueil Précieux de la Maçonnerie Adonhiramite* (Paris, 1786).

NEITHER A JOT NOR A TITTLE SHALL PASS

The reader may recollect Giles F. Yates's nervous wish that *Light on Masonry* had fallen "still-born from the pup" and how he would "be pleased to learn that not

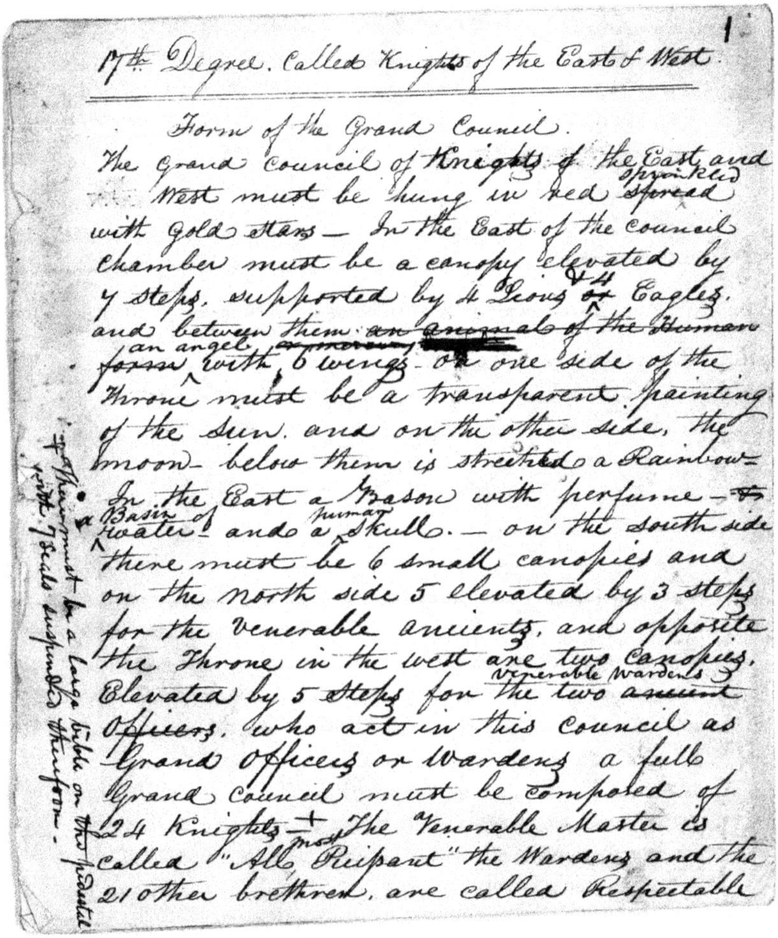

INTRODUCTION.

Figure 10. First page of the 17°, Knight of the East and West, from a ritual of ca. 1825. This manuscript, which once belonged to Giles Fonda Yates, 33°, includes revisions to the text in his handwriting. The revisions help trace the rituals exposed in *Light on Masonry* from David Bernard to his accomplice, N. N. Whiting, and then to the innocent G. F. Yates, who was betrayed by his former deputy.

enough of '*the thing*' has been sold to pay the printer." Sadly, this hope—which was likely shared by other Masons—would not come true. *Light on Masonry* did not fall "still-born," but neither did it emerge fully developed from Rev. Bernard, as Athena did from the head of Zeus. Its improvements did not even appear all at once in each edition, but were introduced somewhat erratically. Between the eight months of April and December 1829 Bernard, endeavoring to produce the *exposé par excellence*, released four improved editions. It is beyond the scope of this introduction to note every change in each edition. However, a few examples will suffice to note some differences and show the kinds of improvements made (most of which would have been very helpful to his readers).

• ***First Edition.*** Although Bernard obtained a large amount of ritual material, he yet lacked several degrees. While the book was being typeset in the offices of Colonel William Williams in Utica, Bernard received some ritual material for the 16°, Prince of Jerusalem, 32°, Sublime Prince of the Royal Secret, and the 33°, Sovereign Grand Inspector General. Also obtained was a list of the Scottish Rite's Thirty-three Degrees, which he said was extracted from the *Circular throughout the two hemispheres* (issued by the Supreme Council at Charleston in December 1802). Actually, the original *Circular* differed slightly from Bernard's version; the differences reveal that he copied his version from a revised list published in Joseph M'Cosh's *Documents upon Sublime Masonry* (1823).[124] Rev. Bernard and Col. Williams decided not to delay publication by resetting the type, but rather opted to place the newly-acquired material toward the back of the book. Although it was set in a smaller typeface, it was no doubt a welcomed addition. The rituals Bernard published in the first edition had many typographical errors, even to the point of erring in the names of the degrees (the 20°, "Venerable Grand Master of All Symbolic Lodges," incorrectly includes "Grand Pontiff" among its titles). Some of the errors were never corrected in any edition ("Alliance, promise, prosecution" [error for *perfection*], "Rivi" [*Kivi*], "Israelites of the perfection" [*protection*], "Silol" [*Siloe*], "Syrentia" [*Sapientia*], etc.).

The reader may recall that on December 5, 1827, the Rev. Nathan N. Whiting certified that he had given Bernard a letter "partly in hieroglyphics, describing the words, pass-words, signs of two or three of the first three degrees" of the Scottish Rite. Although Bernard failed to note its source in *Light on Masonry*, the deciphered secrets were published on pages 210–11 of the first edition. Immediately following Bernard added a note stating that he did not publish all the "Signs, Grips and Words" because he did not want to teach men how to falsely palm themselves off on the Fraternity. The truth, however, is that at the time he wrote this Bernard did not possess the modes of recognition for the other degrees. He soon repaired this deficiency when he obtained a French version of the secrets from Delaunaye's

INTRODUCTION.

Thuileur des Trente-trois Degres, whence he also extracted and translated his brief material relative to the Thirty-third Degree.

• **Second Edition.** In order to accommodate an interpolation of the above-mentioned ritual material the text of the second edition was re-typeset. Another change was to place editorial comments within brackets rather than parentheses. Of greater help to readers was an expansion of material which was abbreviated in the first edition, since the original manuscript rituals were themselves abbreviated. Thus, *S.S.* became *sanctum sanctorum*; *Br.* became *Brother*; *R.W. and R.* became *Right Worshipful and Respectable*; *G.C. of P.* became *Grand Council of Princes*, etc. Some numerical expressions were also spelled out, *4 times 4* became *four times four*, etc. In spite of these changes some inconsistencies remained (the first and second editions used both *Shiboleth* and *Shibboleth*).

Although much of second edition was re-typeset, much was not. This is evinced by printing artifacts and errors seen in the two first editions. Page 201 often includes a printing artifact (a small dot) preceding the last line, "•I know the use...." Another typographical error appearing in both editions is an inverted apostrophe used in place of a period on the third line from the bottom of page 203, "to Solomon and H‚T."

The first edition omitted the passwords, etc., which were supplied in later editions. For example, in the Provost and Judge Degree, Bernard initially wrote, "S. Warden orders him to kneel and say '—,' and puts a naked sword in his hand and on his left shoulder, Master says, '—.'" From the second edition on, these blanks were replaced with the words *Chivi* and *Ky* (though some blanks were left on other pages). For the sake of completion Bernard added a new section, "Remarks on the Signs, Words, &c. of the Ineffable and Sublime Degrees," which translated the modes of recognition from Delaunaye's *Thuileur des Trente-trois Degres*.

Filling in lacunae by using the *Thuileur des Trente-trois Degres* was both helpful and problematic. Although readers were now given the "full" secrets of Masonry, there were actually only provided with an approximate match. The modes of recognition differ regionally. Thus, even when an America ritual appeared similar to a French version, the "secrets" differed in some details. For example, in the first edition of the Knights of the Brazen Serpent Degree the word *Holati* appears, which Bernard subsequently changed to *Hatathi*. The former appears in all authentic manuscript rituals I have studied, and Albert Pike's *Book of the Words* affirms "Holati or Kholatai is correct."[125] It should be understood that the Supreme Council at Charleston introduced intentional changes in the older French degrees, updating their modes of recognition, and making their passwords more "user-friendly" to its English-speaking members (e.g., *jachinai* was changed to *shekinah*).

Some of the changes Bernard made were significant and substantial. For example, the Degree of Knight Kadosh included a ladder of seven steps symbolizing

LIGHT ON MASONRY.

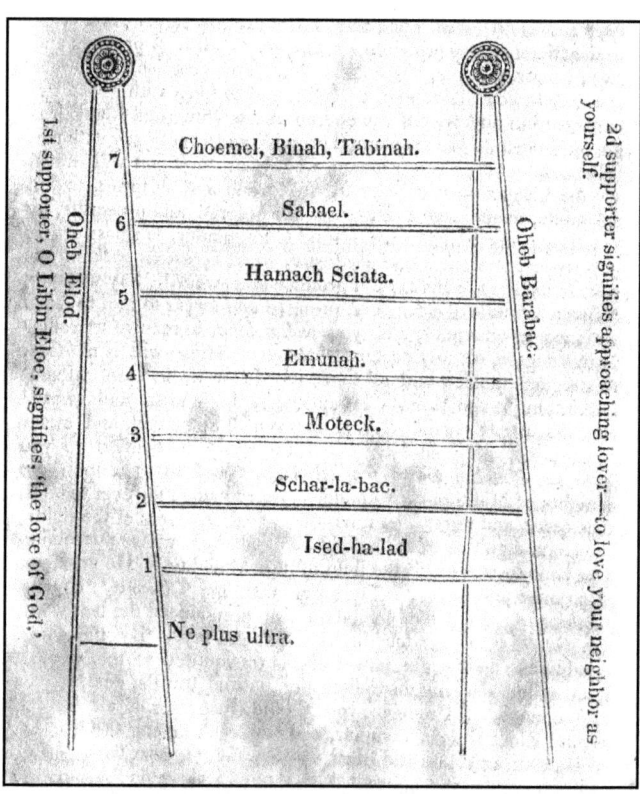

Figure 11. The "mysterious ladder" of the Knight Kadosh Degree, as it appeared in the first edition. Bernard later "corrected" these words in subsequent editions by referring to F. H. S. Delaunaye's *Thuileur des Trente-trois Degres de L'Ecossisme du Rit Ancien, dit Accepté* (Paris, 1813, 1821). Compare with p. 285 of the facsimile.

INTRODUCTION.

the increasing duties and obligations assumed by the initiate. As such, its two sides (or supports) and each of its rungs was given a symbolic name (in broken Hebrew) that expressed these responsibilities. The rituals Whiting obtained from Yates employed words which had appeared in other authentic rituals (such as the *Francken Manuscripts*), even though they were imperfect. Subsequent to the first edition Bernard "improved" the words by substituting words he extracted from the *Thuileur des Trente-trois Degres*.

	FIRST EDITION	SUBSEQUENT EDITIONS
7–	Choemel, Binah, Tabinah	Gemulah, Binah, Tebunah
6–	Sabael	Sabbal
5–	Hamach Sciata	Hamal Saggi
4–	Emunah	Emunah
3–	Moteck	Mathok
2–	Schar-la-bac	Shor-laban
1–	Ised-ha-lad	Tsedakah

After the first edition Bernard further "improved" upon Delaunaye's work by altering the spelling to benefit English-speaking readers; e.g., *Emounah* to *Emunah*; *Sagghi* to *Saggi*; *Gemoulah* to *Gemulah*; *Thebounah* to *Tebunah*.

Large portions of Bernard's later editions were reprinted from the second edition without re-typesetting the pages. Thus, from second edition on the same worn type is seen in the third, fourth, and fifth editions (e.g., on page 285 the first letter *p* in "2d supporter" is worn out).

• ***Third Edition.*** This is the most frequently encountered edition and is physically the smallest in its dimensions. In this edition the numerical expansions continued. For example, although the first two editions read "Master knocks 15," subsequent editions read, "Master knocks fifteen." Some spelling changes were also made, e.g., *vail* becomes *veil*. Other small improvements made the text even more intelligible; e.g., the first two editions read, "the — of the Moors," subsequent editions have "the Juha of the Moors" (Bernard's error, it should read "Juba"), and "the B.g, B.h" becomes "the Burning Bush."

• ***Fourth Edition.*** This is identical to the third edition with three minor exceptions: (1) the words "third edition" are missing from the copyright page; (2) page 421 is mis-numbered 42; and (3) the book is printed on larger paper.

• ***Fifth Edition.*** This is the rarest and most desirable edition. It was printed on high-quality paper and was the largest in its physical dimensions. While other editions were bound in calfskin, the fifth edition is most frequently seen bound in boards, with a cloth spine and red leather spine label. It reprinted all the material of the earlier editions, with an additional revision to the Ineffable Degrees. In his introduction to this new section (facsimile p. 507), Bernard wrote,

> The ineffable degrees have undergone several revisions. The form in which they are exhibited ... is that which has had the most general reception in the United States. In the year 1823, these degrees received their most recent revision, and were brought into a more unexceptional form than those in which they had hitherto existed. In this form they have been propagated in various parts of the eastern, middle, and western sections of this State.

The revision was the work of Giles F. Yates, whose manuscript was most likely copied by N. N. Whiting and given to Bernard. A comparison with an original Yates manuscript (dated 1827) reveals only minor differences on Bernard's part, mostly in regard to the secret words. The revision published by Bernard only included the opening and closing ceremonies of the Ineffable Degrees.

No Honor Among Thieves

Compiling *Light on Masonry* must have been a monumental task, which Rev. Bernard did quite well. In spite of errors, the five editions progressively corrected and improved the text and provided a more coherent presentation of the rituals. Later anti-Masons availed themselves of Bernard's work, sometimes pilfering it piecemeal for its description of the modes of recognition or its membership oaths,[126] or even reprinting it *in toto*[127] without giving the Reverend financial remuneration. The most important of these works are briefly treated below.

• *A Ritual of Freemasonry* (1831).[128] Avery Allyn (1784–1863) was a Connecticut Mason who claimed he "had taken *all* the important *regular* and *honorary* degrees." His book was the chief competitor of *Light on Masonry* because it included several degrees missing from Bernard's collection (i.e., Royal Master, Select Master, Super–Excellent Master, Ark and Dove, Knights of Constantinople, Secret Monitor, Heroine of Jericho, Knights of Three Kings, and Mediterranean Pass). Allyn also provided a superior exposition of the Degrees of Knight of the Red Cross and Knight Templar in that he provided the full ceremonials, rather than just the lectures. However, when Allyn's and Bernard's book are compared side–by–side it becomes evident that Allyn had a copy of *Light on Masonry* opened before him while preparing his work. *A Ritual of Freemasonry* borrows much of its layout, style, and editorial content from *Light on Masonry*. Although many of the degrees were modified to conform with the local practices with which Allyn was familiar, large parts of his text were taken from Bernard. This especially applies to Allyn's brief descriptions of the Scottish Rite Degrees, which are a combination of the material in Webb's *The Freemason's Monitor* and *Light on Masonry*.

• *The Mysteries of Free Masonry* (1852).[129] This work was written by the pseudonymous "George R. Crafts," who falsely claimed he was "formerly Thrice Puissant Grand Master of Manitou Council, New York." The book was cheap paperback abridgement of *Light on Masonry* (fifth edition) set in a small typeface. It substituted Whiting's pre-Supreme Council rituals of the Ineffable Degrees with

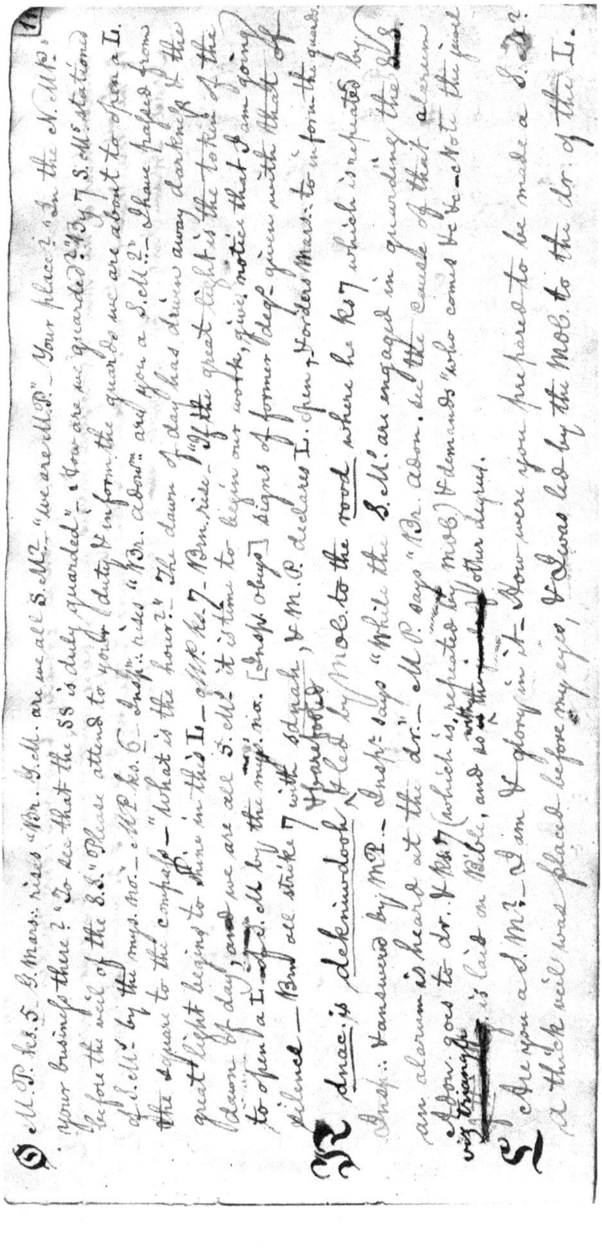

INTRODUCTION.

Figure 12. A portion of the Secret Master Degree, from the ritual revision of Giles F. Yates, manuscript of 1827. Compare with the facsimile of *Light on Masonry*, p. 507.

the ca. 1823 revision of Giles F. Yates. *The Mysteries of Free Masonry* was occasionally reprinted under the title *Morgan's Freemasonry Exposed and Explained*. In both versions the covers depicted lurid, sensational, or surrealistic themes, such as a candidate riding a goat, a set of anthropomorphized working tools lying idly about, or insect-like demons escaping from a book impressed with a human skull. For reasons unknown it omitted some ritual material, including the Rose Croix Degree.

• *Richardson's Monitor of Freemasonry* (1860).[130] Ostensibly written by "Jabez Richardson" this work was actually by the American journalist Benjamin Henry Day, who founded the nation's first penny newspaper, the *New York Sun* in 1833. In the author's preface Day (writing as "Richardson") stated, "I have endeavored to give exact descriptions of the Masonic ceremonies as they are (or should be) performed...." He further claimed that it was an original work (it was not), written with the twofold purpose of satisfying the public's idle curiosity and supplying Freemasons with a guide to their ceremonies. This was a good marketing ploy—evinced by the fact that the book is still in print almost 150 years later. The ceremonies described in *Richardson's Monitor* were never used by Scottish Rite Masons in the form they were presented. By 1860 both Supreme Councils were using rituals differing markedly from the old-style rituals of the Morgan era. The book's text and illustrations had been purloined and amalgamated from various sources, including *Light on Masonry* (fifth edition), Avery Allyn's *A Ritual of Freemasonry* (1831),[131] and sundry Masonic monitors. Its *pièce de résistance* is a wholly spurious ritual of the Thirty-third Degree.

Day did not know enough about Masonic ritual to avoid including errors made by Bernard. For example, in the first edition of *Light on Masonry* the Rose Croix exposé states, "The Senior Warden [I presume it should read, 'The Sovereign Master,'] takes the ribbon..." (p. 229). Bernard inserted his bracketed comments because he wanted to clarify what he believed was an error. Because of this belief he altered subsequent editions and introduced his bracketed comments *as part of the ritual*, "The Sovereign Master takes the ribbon...." Bernard was wrong, however, and *all* authentic manuscript rituals I have seen read, "The Senior Warden takes the ribbon...." As luck would have it *Richardson's Monitor of Free-Masonry* copied Bernard's error.

• *Other Exposures.* Innumerable other publications borrowed from Bernard's text, but most used only brief extracts. These were eclipsed following the publication of Jonathan Blanchard's *Scotch Rite Masonry Illustrated* (1887), which was the first original "Scottish Rite" exposure since *Light on Masonry*. Unknown to most readers of Blanchard's work (which is still in print), its rituals are not those of either of the two authentic Supreme Councils. Rather, Blanchard acquired the rituals used by Henry C. Atwood, and his successor Edmund B. Hays, in their "Supreme Council for the Sovereign and Independent State of New York." This organization was one of the several successive "Cerneau Supreme Councils"—an

INTRODUCTION.

illegitimate form of Freemasonry founded by Joseph Cerneau and chiefly active in the 1800s.[132] Although superficially similar, it differed in both philosophy and ceremony from the legitimate Scottish Rite. A rough analogy is to consider how many self-styled "Christian" Churches are similar in *name* (e.g., the "Church of Christ" vs. the "Church of Christ, Scientist"), or *liturgy* (e.g., Roman Catholicism vs. Anglicanism) yet differ in important aspects. Membership oaths of fealty and other references to the Cerneau "Supreme Council" appear repeatedly throughout Blanchard's exposé,[133] but its rituals continue to be frequently misrepresented by modern anti-Masons, who have found them too convenient to discard.

THE APPENDICES

Appendix 1: The Missing Scottish Rite Degrees. As noted, Bernard was unable to secure copies of some of the Scottish Rite's degrees. Missing from his exposé are the 29°, Knight of Saint Andrew, and 31°, Grand Inquiring Commander. This appendix includes copies of the rituals transcribed from J. J. J. Gourgas's ca. 1827 manuscript, that represents the state of Scottish Rite degrees contemporaneous with *Light on Masonry.*

Appendix 2: The "Missing Degrees" of Avery Allyn. Bernard was apparently unaware of or unable to secure copies of the following degrees that were subsequently published in Avery Allyn's *A Ritual of Freemasonry, Illustrated by Numerous Engravings* (1831): (1) Royal Master, (2) Select Master, (3) Super-Excellent Master, (4) Ark and Dove, (5) Knights of Constantinople, (6) Secret Monitor, or Trading Degree, (7) Heroine of Jericho, (8) Knights of Three Kings, and (9) Mediterranean Pass.

Appendix 3: The Engravings of Avery Allyn's **A Ritual of Freemasonry** **(1831).** Allyn's exposure was accompanied by a series of plates depicting the several modes of recognition. This appendix reproduces his plates, which the reader may compare with Bernard's text.

Appendix 4: Illustrations of the Four First Degrees of Female Masonry, as Practised in Europe. By a Lady (1827). The following little-known degrees were part of the system of "Adoptive Masonry": 1° Entered Apprentice, 2° Fellow Craft, 3° Mistress Mason, and 4° Perfection or Perfect Masoness.

Appendix 5: Bibliography of the 1829 Editions of Light on Masonry. A detailed bibliography of the five original editions.

APPENDIX 1

The Missing Scottish Rite Degrees:
29°, Knight of Saint Andrew;
31°, Grand Inquiring Commander

David Bernard was unable to secure copies of some of the Scottish Rite's Degrees. Missing from his exposé are the 29°, Knight of Saint Andrew, and 31°, Grand Inquiring Commander. The following texts were transcribed from J. J. J. Gourgas's ca. 1827 manuscript copy, which represents the state of the rituals contemporaneous with Light on Masonry.[134] *In transcribing them I have not retained Gourgas's editorial notes as they appear on the manuscript, but rather insert and/or omit the changes indicated. Note that the 29° consists of an obligation only and stands in stark contrast to the much more fully developed ceremonies of the 31°.*

29°, GRAND SCOTTISH MASTER OF ST. ANDREW
PATRIARCH OF THE CRUSADES, KNIGHT OF THE SUN,
GRAND MASTER OF THE SUPREME LIGHT

Obligation

I _____ of my own free will and accord in the presence of Almighty God, and on this holy and sacred book of Christian Faith, hereby most solemnly and sincerely, and without any mental reservation, but in full faith, renew and reassume all and every of the engagements and obligations which I may have heretofore contracted and assumed in relation or appertaining to ancient Sublime Free and Accepted Masonry.

I furthermore do promise and swear true faith and fidelity to Almighty God—allegiance to my Country—respect and subordination to my Superiors, and love and sincerity to my Brethren.

All this I most solemnly promise and swear, with a firm and sincere resolution strictly to observe and perform the same; and should I knowingly violate any part thereof I freely subject myself to the opprobrium of my Brethren and the severest penalty awarded to traitors. And may Almighty God and his Holy Evangelists sustain and help me in the faithful performance hereof. Amen, Amen, Amen.

LIGHT ON MASONRY.

31°, GRAND INSPECTOR INQUISITOR COMMANDER

Decoration of the Sovereign Tribunal

The tenting is all white, and the Canopy of the President also, above his table the two letters J & E—the *altar* which is covered with white, is elevated by three steps, at the end of the draught on the side of the *East*, there must be a stool on which the *box of archives* is to be placed, covered by a white cloth with a large *red cross* of all the length of the cloth; at the *right* of the altar in the corner shall be placed the table of the Chancellor and at the *left* that of the Treasurer: The *Sovereign Tribunal* is decorated by *Eight* columns of Gold, *four* to the *south* and *four* to the *North*, to *each* of these columns is suspended or painted the attributes of the grade, that is to say the *first* column at the *South* an Apprentice's apron, to the *second* the attributes of *Master*, to the *third* those of *Scotch*, to the *fourth* those of R✠—To the *first* of the *North*, the attributes of *Fellow Craft*, to the *second* those of *Elected*, to the *third* those of *Knight of the East*, to the *fourth* those of *Knight Kadosh*. Between the *Eight* columns is placed *six statues*, representing *six virtues* holding *each a cross*, in different attitudes, there shall be *two* statues by the *side* of the *President. Each* column shall be ornamented by *three* wax tapers. In the *middle* of the Sovereign Tribunal, shall be the draught *representing a Cross* surrounded with *all* the attributes of Masonry. To the floor above the table shall be suspended *a pair of scales*, in the *one* at the *right* shall be the *Jewel* of Masonry. The *Grand Inquisitors* are to be *clothed* with *a white Camail* (a kind of short cloak) the *Jewel* to be worn with a *white* apron, to a gold or golden chain, interlaced by the attributes of the *Eight fundamental* grades, or to a *white* favor at the button hole, on the bib of the apron will be embroidered or painted the *Cross*. This clothing is to worn *only* in the Sovereign Tribunal.

Opening of the Sovereign Tribunal

The Tribunal being so decorated, and the Brethren clothed, the *Inspector* opens the Lodges, the *President* enters, holding his *two hands crossed* on the *navel*, the *arms stiff*: which is the sign of query, he is followed by the *Chancellor* and *Treasurer*, as well as by the other *Brethren*, agreeably to the ancientness of initiation, they are all at Sign of Order as the *President*, when they have all entered, the *Inspector* shuts the door, and the *President* says: My dear Brethren, *Grand Inquisitors* arrived in the Tribunal, the Holy of Holies of the Temple of virtue, abode where reigns *Justice* and *Equity*, let us promise to be faithful to the Statutes of this Grade. Then all the Brethren surround the box of archives, extend their hands over it, saying each, "I promise it." They retake their station, and the *President* continues as follows: Work therefore my Brethren for the good of Masonry and help me with your knowledge.

INTRODUCTION.

He makes then the sign of query or order, and the Brethren, that of answer, which is to carry the hands crossed over the head, saying *Justice* and putting themselves back to the sign of order, saying *Equity*, the President answers "so mote it be." The *Chancellor* advances then forwards the box of archives, the *President* gives him the key, and also the *Treasurer*, he takes out the papers, that are wanted, and the *Sovereign Tribunal* proceeds to such business as has offered itself since the last assembly, or of there is a Reception, it is proceeded on in the following manner.

Reception

When a place becomes vacant in a Sovereign Tribunal, either by death or the departure of a Brother, another is to be elected within the first nine days, after the election the *Inspector* is charged to give advice of it to him on whom fate has fallen, without telling him however, the day nor the place of his reception, which takes place as follows.

The *Inspector* brings forward the candidate to the door of the Sovereign Tribunal, decorated with all the attributes of his grades and *strikes as a Kadosh*. The President having heard the knock, says to the brother last received; to see what it is. The *Inspector* answers, it is Brother (such a one) *Apprentice, Fellow Craft, Master, Elected, Illus Scotch, Knight of the East, Sovereign Prince Rose* ✠, and *Knight Kadosh*, who having been elected to fill the place of (such a Brother) ask to present himself so as to be received. This answer being reported to the President, he says: My Brethren so you still consent that this Brother, be introduced among us, all the Brethren having consented—the President says: Let him be introduced. When all the Brethren put sword in hand, and arrange themselves round the box or archives. The Candidate being introduced, the President says to him, "I am well pleased my Brother, that the fate of election has fallen upon you, and I am persuaded that we shall never have any occasion to regret it, but as we shall never have any occasion to regret it, but as we are very scrupulous on this point, you will have to undergo, before you are initiated to our mysteries, an exact examination of the eight grades you already possess." After this the *Inspector* interrogates him on the Apprentice's Degree, the *President* causes him then to be interrogated on the other grades. All this being done, the *President* proposes to him a few questions on the *secret grades of Masonry*, having satisfied the expectation of the Brethren, on this point, *the President continues*, saying: "My Brother, I am well satisfied with your answers, and I believe you worthy to enter into our august Society, come now therefore so as to bind yourself forever to us, by stronger ties." He is then made to advance to the altar, and having made him bend the knee on the cushion, the Chancellor detaches the *scale* which is over the draught, makes him hold it with his *left* hand, his *right* hand on the Statutes, *all* the Brethren cover his head with their left hands, in this position he takes his

LIGHT ON MASONRY.

Obligation

I promise and engage myself, on my word of honor, never to reveal the secrets of the *Grand Inquisitors*, which are going to be confided to me, never to *write, trace, engrave,* or *print them*, under any pretext whatsoever, without having first obtained the permission from the Sovereign Tribunal, I promise besides to observe exactly the Statutes and Regulations of this sublime dignity. If I fail in this my solemn obligation I consent to suffer all the penalties I impose on myself by my first Masonic obligation.

The president says to him, to raise to Heaven the two fingers, and to pronounce with him, "I swear in the presence of the Sovereign Architect of the Universe, never to fail in the obligation I have just been taking. Amen!" At the same time that he pronounces "Amen", the Inspector gives him the light, all the Brethren put back their swords, make the sign or query and that of answer, striking nine times with their hands (4.2.3.) and they all retake their seats. The Inspector raises the Candidate, takes off all his Jewels and hangs them to the columns, when the *President* says to him: "You are divested of these Jewels and attributes because the secret of the grade which you are going to receive, comprehends *all* those you already know, and that being above them all, you no more require them. Brother Inspector, show him the march (stepping) of the Grand Inquisitors, and present the Brother to me."

The Inspector puts him to the Order, in forming a step with the right foot, and advancing with the left, he detaches his hands in forming the three steps with the right foot, he puts him again to the Order and so on nine steps—at the ninth he is to find himself placed before the altar, and the *President* decorates him with the Camail, Jewels and other Clothing saying to him: "Let this clothing and this Cross, make you always remember, that you are a Grand Elect, it orders you exactly to follow the Statutes, these two daggers will serve you; the one to punish perjurers, and other to revenge Masonry, that pair of scales which you see, marks to you the sublimity of this grade, and will cause you to remember *to judge always with Justice*." He then causes him to kneel, putting his two hands on his head and says: "By the power which has been given to me, and with the consent of the Brethren, I make and constitute you—a Grand Inquisitor." After this he gives him the *word* and *token*, seats him next to him for that time only—for the first next assembly after this, he takes and fills the place of Inspector. If there is any cause to be judged, they are then proceeded with, the *Chancellor* reads the verbal process, causes it to be signed by the Brethren, and the *Sovereign Tribunal* is closed in the same manner as it was *opened*.

SIGNS—of query, or order, put the hands in cross on the navel—*answer*—put them in cross on the head.

TOKEN—is given reciprocally with the right hand, a stroke on the right shoulder, taking mutually the left hand, and raising the right arm in cross, foot against foot,

INTRODUCTION.

knee against knee, and give the *Words* in the ear—one says *Justice*, the other answers *Equity*, and both together—"So mote it be."

SACRED WORD—El-Shadday.

KNOCKING—!! – !!!—(five)

The President is called "Most Perfect President"—The Brethren "Most Enlightened." When a Brother visits an inferior Lodge, and announces himself as a "Grand Inquisitor" the Brethren come out to recognize him; which being done they return, make their report to the *ear* of the Venerable, one after the other; the Venerable causes every Brother who is not an Inquisitor to go out, *those that are Inquisitors* surround the draught, he sends the Junior Warden to introduce him, he brings him to the edge of the draught, the Venerable takes the three mallets, puts them on the Bible and on his knees, presents them to the visiting Grand Inquisitor, who accepts them, and returns each to the first and second Wardens, and the Venerable he then seats himself at the place of honor.

The following *second obligation* must be wrote and signed in a book for that special purpose by every Candidate.

"I promise and engage my word of an honest man, exactly to follow the Statutes and Regulations of the Most Perfect and Sovereign Tribunal of the Grand Inquisitors, never to divulge from whom I received that grade, nor the place where I was initiated, finally never to say any thing about this degree, and never to be the direct or indirect cause that any one should have arrived to the grade of Grand Inquisitor: I further more do promise never to give this grade to whomsoever it may be without a written permission from the Sovereign Tribunal of whom I received it. I promise all this, and if I fail in any one of these articles, I consent to pass for a dishonest man, despicable, and unworthy to live among men, deserving to be expulsed from all Lodges, and Assemblies whatsoever, as having dishonored myself towards Society, having consented I have signed the present obligation."

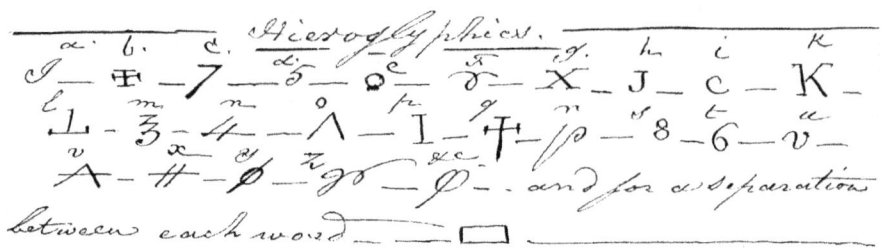

APPENDIX 2

THE "MISSING DEGREES" OF AVERY ALLYN

From A Ritual of Freemasonry, Illustrated by Numerous Engravings. To Which is Added a Key to the Phi Beta Kappa, the Orange, and Odd Fellows Societies. With Notes and Remarks. *(Philadelphia: John Clarke, 1831), pp. 143–83. Transcribed verbatim without use of* sic.

At the time he compiled Light on Masonry, *David Bernard was either unaware of, or unable to secure, copies of some degrees that were later included in Avery Allyn's exposé. This section includes the following "missing degrees": (1) Royal Master, (2) Select Master, (3) Super–Excellent Master, (4) Ark and Dove, (5) Knights of Constantinople, (6) Secret Monitor, or Trading Degree, (7) Heroine of Jericho, (8) Knights of Three Kings, and (9) Mediterranean Pass. Inasmuch as these texts purport to reveal early versions of the rituals, they do not necessarily reflect contemporary practices, but remain of interest for comparative purposes.*

ROYAL MASTER'S DEGREE

The circumstances on which this degree was founded (according to *Masonic tradition,*) originated at the building of King Solomon's Temple; our three ancient grand masters, viz.: Solomon, King of Israel, Hiram, King of Tyre, and Hiram Abiff, at that time formed a resolution to reward all those master Masons who should prove themselves worthy by their fidelity, industry, and skill, by communicating to them the *omnific* word. This being agreed upon, it then became necessary to agree at what time, and under what circumstances it should be first communicated; this was a point not easily determined; several plans were proposed, and found exceptional, insomuch, that their deliberations upon this subject continued until a short time prior to the completion of the Temple; when it was proposed by Hiram Abiff, that the *word* should not be given, until the Temple was completed, and then only in the presence, and by the consent of all three; this plan was adopted, and they bound themselves by solemn oaths to a strict observance of the same. Not long after this agreement, Hiram Abiff went into the sanctum sanctorum, as it was his usual custom at high twelve to offer up his prayers to the Deity, and draw designs upon the trestle-board, and as he was returning, he was accosted at the entrance of the same by Adoniram who in a very friendly manner inquired when he should receive the *omnific* word. Hiram Abiff replied, 'My worthy friend Adoniram, it is uncertain when, or whether you will ever receive it, for, agreeable to arrangements lately entered into by Solomon, King of Israel, Hiram, King of Tyre, and myself, the word cannot be given until the Temple is completed, and then only in the presence of all three.' Adoniram replied, Supposing one of you three be removed hence by death, prior to the completion of the Temple, how then shall I expect to receive it?'

Hiram Abiff, pointing down and tapping the floor three times with his foot, observed in a very solemn tone, 'When I die they'll bury it there.'*

The following passage gives an allusion to what is intended to be represented by this council.

'And he set the *cherubims* within the inner house, and they stretched forth the wings of the cherubims, so that the wing of the one touched the one wall, and the wing of the other touched the other wall, and their wings touched one another, in the midst of the house.'

The ark called the glory of Israel, which was set in the middle of the 'holy place, under the wings of the cherubims, was a small chest, or coffer,' etc. The companions being thus arranged around the altar, the candidate is conducted into the room, or hall; soon after he enters, a companion, in imitation of Hiram Abiff, comes in and kneels at the altar (called sanctum sanctorum) and repeats the following prayer:

'Thou, God, knowest our downsitting and uprising, and understandest our thoughts afar off: shield and defend us from the evil intentions of our enemies, and support us under the trials and afflictions we are destined to endure while travelling in this vale of tears. Man that is born of woman is of few days, aud full of trouble. He cometh forth as a flower, and is cut down: he fleeth also as a shadow, and continueth not; seeing his days are determined, the number of his months are

---

*It is believed by Masons, that Hiram Abiff had been forewarned of his approaching *awful* fate, of which we have a detailed account in the master Mason's degree. This history the author had word for word from the mouth of one Mr. Barney, who styles himself the grand lecturer of Masons; and if the history is merely fiction, probably Mr. B., like the author, was *duped* by some one who made it hit business to peddle falsehoods.

INTRODUCTION.

with thee; thou hast appointed his bounds that he cannot pass; turn from him, that he may rest, till he shall accomplish his day; for there is hope of a tree, if it be cut down, that it will sprout again, and that the tender branch thereof will not cease.

But man dieth and wasteth away: yea, man giveth up the ghost, and where is he? As the waters fall from the sea, and the flood decayeth and drieth up, so man lieth down, and riseth not up till the heavens shall be no more. Yet, O Lord, have compassion on the children of thy creation; administer them comfort in time of trouble, and save them with an everlasting salvation. Amen. So mote it be.'

He rises and passes out of the sanctum sanctorum, under the extended wings of the cherubims. The candidate is directed to walk up to him and accost him as follows: 'Our grand master, Hiram Abiff, when shall I expect to receive the master Mason's word?'

H.A. My worthy companion Adoniram, etc.

The same conversation passes, as related in the history of this degree. The candidate personates Adoniram, and the other companion Hiram Abiff.

The obligation of this degree is given in different ways. When the author received his degree, which was in a regular council, the obligation was thus, viz.: 'Do you promise, upon the oath of a royal arch Mason, to keep the secrets of this degree?' Ans. 'I do.'

LECTURE.

If A and B wish to examine each other on this degree, they will proceed as follows:

A. Taps the floor three times with his toe, and says, 'Do you know anything about this?'

B. I know something about it.

A. What do you know about it?

B. I know something about the beginning of it.

B. Then taps the floor three times, and says, 'Do you know anything about this?'

A. I know something about it.

B. What do you know about it?

A. I know something about the ending of it.

B. What is the beginning?

A. Alpha.

B. What is the ending?

A. Omega.

The grip is given by taking each other by the wrist (as two children do to make a seat for the third), that is, A takes hold of the wrist of his left hand with his right;

LIGHT ON MASONRY.

B does the same, and with the left hand, they each take hold of the other's right wrist, so that the four hands form a square.

The words are given by quitting the hold of your own wrist, extending your left arm downwards at the full length, keeping hold of your companion's right wrist;* at the same time, place your right feet together, toe to heel, so as to form two sides of a triangle; looking down at the feet, each in a low tone says, *Alas, poor Hiram!* [See plate 17, fig. 9.]

The sign of this degree is given by placing the forefinger of the right hand upon the lips. [See plate 17, fig. 1.] It is used as a caution to a companion, when you wish him to keep silence.

The following will serve to cast some *light* on this degree. [See Chart, page 115.]

'This degree cannot legally be conferred on any but royal arch Masons, who have taken all the preceding degrees; and it is preparatory to that of the select master. Although it is short, yet it contains some valuable information, and is intimately connected with the degree of select master. It is also enables us with ease and facility to examine the privileges of others to this degree, while, at the same time, it proves ourselves.'

The following passages of scripture, &c., are considered to be appropriate to this degree. [See Chart, p. 116.]

Rev. xxii. 12—14. 'And behold I come quickly; and my reward is with me, to give every man according as his work shall be. I am Alpha and Omega, the beginning and the end, the first and the last. Blessed are they that do his commandments, that they may have a right to the tree of life, and may enter in through the gates into the city.'

---

*This is said by Masons to represent a broken square, and is emblematical of the untimely death of Hiram Abiff.

INTRODUCTION.

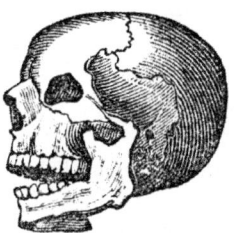

SELECT MASTER'S DEGREE

This degree is the summit and perfection of ancient Masonry: and without which the history of the royal arch degree cannot be complete. It rationally accounts for the concealment and preservation of those essentials of the craft which were brought to light at the erection of the second temple, and which lay concealed from the Masonic eye, four hundred and seventy years. Many particulars relative to those few, who, for their superior skill, were selected to complete an important part of king Solomon's temple, are explained; and here too, is exemplified an instance of *justice* and *mercy*, by our ancient patron towards one of the craft, who was led to disobey his commands, by an over-*zealous* attachment for the institution. It ends with a description of a particular circumstance, which characterizes the degree. [Cross's Chart, p. 118.]

For form of council, see plate 16.

The *first officer* is seated in the east, (council chamber,) under a rich canopy, dressed in royal purple robes, a golden crown on his head, and sceptre in his hand; and a gold trimmed collar on his neck, to which is suspended a gold trowel. He represents king Solomon, and is styled, thrice illustrious grand master.

The *second officer* is on his right, with the same dress and decorations. He represents Hiram, king of Tyre, and is styled deputy illustrious grand master.

The *third* is seated on the left of the first. He is dressed in yellow robes, trimmed with blue, a collar on his neck, and a gold hammer in his hand. He represents Hiram Abiff, and is called Principal conductor of the work.

Before each of the three first officers is a triangular table, upon each angle of which is a burning taper, and in the centre a triangular plate of gold. A *veil* or *curtain* separates them from the rest of the officers and companions, as is represented in plate 16.

The next three officers in rank are seated in the other part of the *hall*, so as to form a *triangle*, in the following order, viz.:

The secretary, who is the fourth officer, in the *south*.

The fifth, treasurer, in the *north*.

The sixth is seated in the *west*, with a drawn sword, represents *Adoniram*, and is styled Captain of the guards.

The seventh officer is called *Ahishar*, the grand steward. He acts as tyler, and is to guard the inside of the door.

The officers being seated, the veil or curtain is drawn aside, which brings them all into one apartment.

The presiding (or first) officer gives notice that he is about to open a council of select masters; and after the necessary precaution to ascertain that there is none present but those of the degree, he proceeds as follows:

K.S. My worthy companion of Tyre, shall we resume our labours and complete the secret work which has been so happily begun?

Hiram, king of Tyre, replies, 'Thrice illustrious grand master, it is my most ardent wish to see it completed, and the sacred treasure therein safely deposited; that I may return to my own country with the satisfaction of having faithfully discharged my duty to the craft.

K.S. Companion conductor, are our numbers complete?

H.A. Thrice illustrious grand master, I find the number of three times nine.

K.S. Companion conductor, you will see that the secret vault is made secure.

Hiram Abiff returns, and says, 'Thrice illustrious, all is in security.'

K.S. Illustrious deputy grand master, what is it o'clock?

H.K.T. Nine at night, thrice illustrious, when all prying eyes are closed in sleep.

K.S. Such being the hour, it is my pleasure that a council of select masters be now opened for the dispatch of business. Companion conductor, you will therefore order the companions to their several stations, and after the regular alarm shall be given, let them proceed to their labours, according to the directions they have received.

H.A. Companions, it is our illustrious grand master's orders that a council of select masters be opened for the dispatch of business; and after the regular alarm of the *mysterious number nine* is given, each will resume his labor.

Solomon then knocks *eight* quick and one slow, and all the officers imitate him in their turn, according to rank.

Then all the companions knock eight quick and one slow with their hands.

Solomon says, 'Attend to giving the signs, companions.'

All the companions rise on their feet and give the signs from entered apprentice to the *royal master*, as before described.

The signs of a select master are as follows: the first is similar to the sign of distress of a master Mason. The fists are both clenched, in allusion to one of the penalties of the obligation, which is to have both hands *chopped off* to the *stumps*. [See plate 17, fig. 7.]

INTRODUCTION.

Another sign is made by crossing the hands and arms, as in plate 17, fig. 4, with a quick motion draw the hands edgewise across the body downwards, as though you were in the act of quartering the body, and let them drop by your sides; this is in imitation of part of the penalty of this degree, which is to have the body *quartered*.

Another sign is given by placing the hands over each eye [as in plate 17, fig. 8] and with a quick motion throw the arms downwards at an angle of forty-five degrees, as though you was 'tearing the eye-balls from the sockets,' and dashing them on the ground, drop the arms by the side; this is a *part* of the penalty of a select master.

Another sign [see plate 17, fig. 6] alludes to that *part* of the penalty of being thrown among the rubbish of the temple; it is made by placing the left hand upon the upper part of the forehead, the palm down, and cover it with the right, the body erect, heels together, step off with the left foot, and plant it about 18 inches in front with a stamp, at the same time dart the hands forward.

The most important signs of this degree among Masons are these, [see plate 17, figs. 2 and 3], they are made in this manner place the palm of the right hand upon the heart, and pronounce the word 'secrecy,' and immediately raise the left hand, and place the palm over the mouth, the first finger against the upper lip, the others a little off, the thumb against the side of the nose, and pronounce the word 'silence,' raise the right hand from the breast, and place it over the eyes, and say *silence* and *darkness*.

Solomon then says, I declare this council of select masters opened in due and ancient form; the companions will govern themselves accordingly. He then gives a heavy rap with his gavel, and his right and left hand companions do the same, and each resumes his seat.

The council being opened, the candidate is conducted to an antechamber, and is told to remain there until he sees the door open, when he must walk into the council.

The tyler (or grand steward Ahishar) takes his post on the inside of the door to guard the same, who, after walking back and forth, he sits down by the door and feigns himself sleeping (this is a very difficult part to act: the *loudest snorers* are always selected and to test this point, each companion *exhibits a specimen* of his talents or skill by laying down the floor or bench near the door, and throws himself into all the attitudes and grimaces of somnolency, by groaning, snoring, grating of teeth, choaking, &c.;); the door is now thrown open and the candidate (Izabud) enters.

Captain of the guards demands, 'Who comes there?'

Izabud replies as directed, 'A zealous brother, who wishes to partake of your labors.'

C.G. Give me the word, sign, and token of your entrance.

I. I have none.

C.G. An intruder! an intruder!

LIGHT ON MASONRY.

Companions all exclaim, Put him to death instantly. For the ceremonies of initiating a companion to this degree see history; the candidate represents *Izabud*, who lived in the days of king Solomon.

HISTORY.

Our three grand masters at building the temple entered into a solemn agreement, by obligation among themselves, not to confer the master's degree until the temple should be completed, and even then only on such as should have rendered themselves worthy by their skill, their virtue, and their inflexible fidelity to the craft; their agreement was such, that all three must be present when it should be conferred, lest partiality for a friend, might occasion the admission of an unworthy member; they also caused their obligation to be such, that if either should be taken away by death prior to the finishing of the temple, the master's degree would of course be lost; they also, in their wisdom, and by the writings of their prophets, possessed a firm belief that if the children of Israel continued not in the belief of the Supreme Judge, to obey his commands, their enemies would be let loose against them, their city and temple would be sacked and destroyed, and themselves carried into captivity, and thus the knowledge of the arts and sciences, together with the patterns and valuable models, which were contained in the temple, and writings of Moses would be for ever lost.

To remedy this great evil, they agreed to build a secret vault under ground, leading from King Solomon's most retired apartment, a due west course, and ending under the sanctum sanctorum, to be divided into nine separate apartments or arches, the ninth to be under the sanctum sanctorum, all of which was to be erected or built by themselves, and such companions as they should select, for the special purpose; the ninth arch was to be the place for holding their grand council, and also a deposit for a true copy of all those things which were contained in the sanctum sanctorum above. There were selected to work in the other eight arches, twenty-three from Gebul, a city in Phenicia, who were Ghiblimites, or stone squarers, who, together with Adoniram, were well skilled in the arts and sciences, particularly sculpture; their hours of labor were from 9 at night to 12, when they retired to rest. During the erection of this secret vault, a circumstance occurred which characterizes this degree.

A particular friend of king Solomon, whose name was Izabud, discovered that a secret work was going on about the temple, of which he was not informed by his friend; he for some time grieved in silence; at length he communicated his suspicions to king Solomon, and begged to know how he had forfeited his confidence; the king told him that his confidence in him remained the same, and desired him to be

INTRODUCTION.

contented for the present, for the time would soon arrive when a door would be left open for his reception (meaning when the temple should be finished and he received the master's degree), this for a time satisfied him, but one evening having some particular business with king Solomon, he went as usual to seek him in his most retired room, and finding the door of the secret vault open and not guarded as usual, by the grand steward Ahishar, he took it for granted that it was left open for his reception, agreeably to the king's promise: he therefore boldly entered, but was soon accosted by Adoniram, the captain of the guard, who sternly demanded, 'Who comes there?'

Izabud replied, 'A zealous brother, who wishes to partake of your labors.'

The captain of the guard demands, 'Give me the word, sign, and token of your entrance.'

Izabud replied, 'I have none.'

The captain of the guard exclaims 'An intruder! an intruder!'

This caused the three grand masters and the rest of the companions to assemble, when king Solomon demanded the cause of alarm. The captain of the guard informed him that 'An intruder has invaded our secret vault.'

King Solomon ordered him to be put to death immediately.

The captain of the guard taking him by the collar, and placing his sword at his breast, was about to execute the order, when he discovered him to be Izabud; and knowing the intimacy subsisting between him and king Solomon, addressed him thus:

'Thrice illustrious king Solomon, consider for a moment on whom you are about to inflict this awful penalty. It is no less than your particular friend Izabud.'

King Solomon said, 'Bind him fast, and see him forthcoming when called for, or your life shall answer for his escape.'

The captain of the guard binds him and conducts him to prison. The three grand masters retire to the ninth arch to consult together; and on examination found that only twenty-seven could be employed in the work; three in each arch; and that those thus employed could not pass beyond that in which they were stationed; nor could any others enter without forfeiting their lives. It was therefore out of the power of the king to pardon his friend. They then returned to the first arch and ordered the offender to be brought before them, when king Solomon thus addressed him:

'Alas, my unfortunate friend Izabud, your disobedience and curiosity have forfeited your life. I have consulted my colleagues, and find them inflexible. My obligation, also, is of such a nature, that I have not the power to pardon you.'

Izabud then fell on his knees, and thus addressed the king: 'Thrice illustrious king Solomon, I pray you to remember how great and sincere my attachment has ever been to your sacred person, to your services and secrets; of late, finding a private work going on, with which I was not made acquainted, I feared I had lost the confidence of my sovereign, and grieved in silence. At length I took the liberty of mentioning the matter to your majesty, and you directed me to rest contented;

for the time would soon arrive when a door would be left open for my reception. This assurance satisfied me; and this evening, having some particular business with your majesty, I sought you in the retired room; and finding the door open and unguarded, I took it for granted it was for my reception, and entered accordingly. But I beg your majesty to believe that it was not a spirit of disobedience or curiosity which prompted me to do it.'

The king of Tyre addressed king Solomon, 'Thrice illustrious, I find your friend is not guilty of the charge alleged against him. His offence is rather owing to some imprudent observation of your own; he must therefore be pardoned, and admitted.'

King Solomon observes, 'My worthy companion of Tyre, how can that be done? is not our number already full?'

Hiram Abiff addresses king Solomon: 'Thrice illustrious, it is true our numbers are full; but Ahishar, the guard, is no longer worthy of our confidence. He was found sleeping at his post, and he alone is guilty. Let him therefore be discharged and immediately executed; and let Izabud be placed in his stead'.

King Solomon observed, 'I thank you, my worthy companion, for your advice: it shall be done. Izabud, are you willing to take a solemn obligation to keep inviolably the secrets of our order?'

Izabud assents.

King Solomon says, 'Free him of his shackles, and conduct him to the altar.'

'I, A.B., in presence of the grand architect of the universe, and before this illustrious assembly, dedicated to the most puissant, most terrible, most merciful Creator, do solemnly swear, that I will never discover the signs, tokens, and words belonging to a select master, nor to any one living, the secret of this royal vault, neither by speaking, writing, engraving, carving, nor painting; or by any dumb sign, or motion, in any unlawful way, whereby the least hint might be taken, that in this place existed a secret work, or that any secrets are deposited here.

'I furthermore swear that I never will penetrate into the secrets of the ninth arch, unless legally authorized by our thrice illustrious grand masters. All this I swear, with a firm and steady resolution, without any mental reservation or self-evasion of mind in me whatever; binding myself under no less penalty, besides all my former penalties, to have my hands chopped off to the stumps, my eyes plucked out from the sockets, my body quartered, and then thrown among the rubbish of the temple; that there may remain no more remembrance of such a vile wretch, if ever I should wilfully violate this my obligation. So help me, God, and keep me steadfast in the same. Amen.'

Kisses the book nine times.

King Solomon took him by the hand, raised him, and observed, 'I now receive you a companion select; therefore, in future, be ever blind and dumb to everything you have seen and heard.'

INTRODUCTION.

The thrice illustrious then gave him all the necessary cautions.

After the ninth arch was completed, the three grand masters deposited therein a true copy of those things which were of importance to the craft and to the Jewish nation; such as the ark of the covenant, the pot of manna, the rod of Aaron, the book of the law, etc.; and that they might be known and duly appreciated, if ever found, by future generations, they agreed to place their names on three of the sides of the ark, and on the fourth side they placed the date of, by whom, and for what purpose they were thus deposited; which was for the good of the craft in general, and the Jewish nation in particular; and that, should the temple be destroyed, and the people carried away into captivity, yet on their release, and rebuilding the house of their God, they might possibly discover these valuable treasures.

After this deposit was made, and prior to the completion of the temple, our grand master, Hiram Abiff, was assassinated in a manner related in a preceding degree; and, by his death, the master's word was lost. The two kings were willing to do all in their power to preserve the sacred word, and as they could not communicate it to any, by reason of the death of their friend Hiram Abiff, they agreed to place it in the secret vault, that if the other treasures were ever brought to light, the word might be found also; they therefore placed it on the top of the ark of the covenant, in the Hebrew, Syriac, and Chaldaic languages; and that it might be known as the true word, when discovered, they placed the three grand masters' jewels, one in each language, well knowing that a description of those jewels would be handed down to the latest posterity, and by these means, the royal arch, or rather the ancient master's word, was finally discovered; being the same which was communicated by God himself to Enoch, and in use 3000 years, when it was lost by the death of Hiram Abiff, and afterwards brought to light at rebuilding the second temple, and has been in use ever since, and will continue to be the same till time shall be no more.

The ceremony of receiving the candidate being through, the officers and companions all resume their seats, as before described, and the *thrice illustrious* reads the following passage from Cross's Chart, p. 120.

Deut. xxxi. 24—26. 'And it came to pass, when Moses had made an end of writing the words of this law in a book, until they were finished, that Moses commanded the Levites which bore the ark of the covenant of the Lord, saying, Take this book of the law, and put it in the side of the ark of the covenant of the Lord your God, that it may be there for a witness against thee.'

When the reading of this chapter is finished, four companions bearing the *ark*, advance to the centre of the council, and place it upon the *altar*, open it, and put the book of the law into it, and return to their seats.

Thrice illustrious reads, Exodus xvi. 33, 34. 'And Moses said unto Aaron, Take a pot, and put an omer full of manna therein, and lay it up before the Lord to keep for your generations. As the Lord commanded Moses, so Aaron laid it up before the testimony to be kept.'

A companion *brings* the *pot of manna*, and puts it into the ark.

Thrice illustrious reads,

Numbers xvii. 10. 'And the Lord said unto Moses, Bring Aaron's rod again before the testimony, to be kept for a token.'

In like manner *Aaron's rod* is deposited.

Thrice illustrious reads,

Numbers vii. 89. 'And when Moses was gone into the tabernacle of the congregation to speak with him, then he heard the voice of one speaking unto him from off the mercy seat, that was upon the ark of the testimony, from between the two cherubims; and he spake unto him.'

The three *grand masters*, viz., Solomon, king of Israel, Hiram, king of Tyre, and Hiram Abiff then places the name of Deity upon the ark, in three languages, in the Hebrew, Chaldaic, and Syriac, and place their three jewels (or squares) in a triangular form upon it. They place on the sides of the ark the time of its deposit, who by, an for what purpose, etc. They also put into the ark a *key* to the *ineffable* characters upon its sides and top. [See plate 13, figs. 7 and 8.]

The ark is then put down through the scuttle or hole through the floor, made for that purpose, and placed in the position in which they are found in the royal arch degree.

The business being through, the companions take their stations, as in opening, and then proceed to close the council, as follows:

K.S. Companion captain of the guards, are you a select master?

C.G. I am acknowledged as such, and have wrought my regular hours in the secret vault.

K.S. What are the regular hours?

C.G. From 9 at night until 12.

K.S. How gained you admission there?

C.G. Through fervency and zeal, which was mistaken for curiosity and disobedience, and had well nigh cost me my life; but justice and mercy prevailed, and I was admitted.

K.S. How so?

C.G. My fervency and zeal led me into a place through a misconstruction of king Solomon's promise, by which I forfeited my life; but mercy triumphed over justice, and I was admitted a member among them.

K.S. What is meant by a select master?

C.G. Those who were selected to build the royal vault. Men whose skill, integrity and secrecy were well known to our grand master.

K.S. How many were there?

INTRODUCTION.

C.G. Twenty-two from Gebal, together with Ahishar, Adoniram, and our three grand masters; making in all twenty-seven, and no more.

K.S. Why but twenty-seven?

C.G. Because there was but nine arches, and three only could be employed in each.

K.S. Where did this royal vault begin?

C.G. At king Solomon's most retired room.

K.S. Where did it end?

C.G. Under the sanctum sanctorum, or holy of holies, of king Solomon's temple.

K.S. When were you to be admitted into the ninth arch?

C.G. When the temple should be completed; but owing to the death of Hiram Abiff, it was then closed from our eyes.

K.C. What countryman are you?

C.G. A Phœnician.

K.S. In what city was you born?

C.G. In Gebal.

K.S. What is your name?

C.G. Giblem, or stone squarer.

K.S. What is it o'clock?

C.G. Low twelve; the usual time to call from labor to refreshment.

K.S. What remains now to be done?

C.G. To retire in peace, practise virtue, and meditate in silence.

K.S. Companion captain of the guard, you will give notice to the companions by the mysterious No. 9, that this council is about to be closed.

The captain of the guards knock eight quick and one slow, which is repeated by Hiram, king of Tyre, and Hiram Abiff.

King Solomon knocks one, and calls to order, and gives the sign of *silence*, with his left hand on his mouth and his right hand on his breast, which is repeated by all the select, and *Ish Soudy* is repeated by all.

K.S. Companions, this council is closed.

'CHARGE. Companion, having attained to this degree, you have passed the *circle of perfection* in ancient Masonry. In the capacity of select master, you must be sensible that your obligations are increased in proportion to your privileges. Let it be your constant care to prove yourself worthy of the confidence reposed in you, and the high honor conferred on you, in admitting you to this select degree. Let uprightness and integrity attend your steps; let *justice* and *mercy* mark your conduct. Let *fervency* and *zeal* stimulate you in the discharge of the various duties incumbent on you, but suffer not an idle, or impertinent *curiosity* to lead you astray, or betray you into danger. Be *deaf* to every insinuation which would have a tendency to weaken your resolution, or tempt you to an act of *disobedience*. Be voluntarily *dumb* and *blind* when the exercise of those faculties would endanger the peace of your mind, or the probity of your conduct; and let *silence* and *secrecy*, those cardinal virtues of a select master, on all necessary occasions, be scrupulously observed. By a steady adherence to the important instructions contained in this degree, you will merit the approbation of the select number with whom you are associated, and will enjoy the high satisfaction of having acted well your part in the important enterprise in which you are engaged; and after having *wrought your regular hours*, may you be admitted to participate in all the privileges of a select master.' [Cross's *Chart*, p. 121]

INTRODUCTION.

SUPER-EXCELLENT MASTER

This degree is said to be founded on circumstances which took place at the destruction of the Temple, by Nebuchadnezzar king of Babylon. The first we heard of it was in 1825; at which time it was annexed to several of the councils of select masters, in Massachusetts. The officers are stationed differently from those of the select master's degree. The *first* officer represents Zedekiah, the last king of Israel. He is seated in the east, and styled most excellent king. The *second* officer represents Gedaliah, is styled companion, and is seated in the west. The *third* officer is called the 1st keeper of the Temple, and is seated on the right of the companion Gedaliah. The *fourth* is called 2d keeper of the Temple, and is seated on the left of the companion Gedaliah. The *fifth* is called the 3d keeper of the Temple, and is seated at the door, within the hall, to guard the sanctuary. There are three officers, called *heralds*, whose stations are without the hall; with bugles in their hands, and whose duty it is to bring intelligence. There are three other officers, called royal guards, whose duty it is to attend upon the king.

Form of Initiation

The candidate is hoodwinked, taken into the hall and seated before opening the council. The king is absent, the business consequently devolves on the second officer, companion Gedaliah, who calls the council to order with one *rap* of the gavel and addresses the first keeper of the Temple as follows:

Com. Ged. Companion 1st keeper of the Temple are all present super excellent masters?

1st K.T. They are.

C.G. As a super-excellent master keeper of the Temple let it be your first duty and last care to see the sanctuary duly guarded.

1st K.T. Companion 3d keeper of the Temple are we duly guarded?

3d K.T. Companion 1st keeper of the Temple we are duly guarded the sanctuary is secure.

1st K.T. Companion Gedaliah the sanctuary is duly guarded.

C.G. Where is the king?

1st K.T. In one of the apartments of the Temple.

C.G. What is the hour?

1st K.T. It is the time of the second watch.

The companion Gedaliah then gives *three raps* with the gavel, the companions all rise and Gedaliah thus speaks—'Companions since it is the time of the second watch let us repair to the holy altar and there offer up our fervent aspirations to Deity that he would be pleased to vouchsafe to us as heretofore his protecting care and favor.' They assemble round the altar kneel on the left knee the right elbow resting on the right knee and the forehead leaning on the right hand in imitation of silent devotion. After remaining in this position a short time companion Gedaliah says, 'Companions let us arise and attend to giving the *signs*.'

The signs are then given, from the entered apprentice degree to the super-excellent master inclusive. After these are given companion Gedalich says;—'Let each repair to his station.'

The first herald sounds.

The 3d keeper of the Temple announces his approach by saying, 'a herald!'

The 1st keeper then exclaims, 'a herald approaches.' The herald then advances and makes the following *proclamation*.

'Nebuchadnezzar, king of Babylon approaches with innumerable forces and fills the city; they are formidable and victorious approaching the king's palace and within a few furlongs of the Temple; and everywhere is unhallowed ravage and devastation.

The 2d herald sounds his approach, and announces, in the same manner, and gives the same intelligence as the first.

The 3d herald sounds.

The 3d keeper of the Temple says, 'a herald!' and this herald is immediately followed by the king with the royal guards, one on each side and one in front.

The 1st keeper announces the approach of the king by saying, 'The king approaches.'

The companion Gedaliah gives *three raps,* and all the companions rise and face the king as he takes his seat in the east Companion Gedaliah then addresses his majesty as follows. 'Most excellent king, the council is assembled, the officers stationed, and we await your order.' The king rises and says, 'I proclaim this council of super-excellent masters duly organized.' The king then inquires of the recorder if there is any business before the council. Recorder replies that a candidate [naming the candidate present,] is desirous of taking the degree of super-excellent master. The 1st herald again sounds; the 3d keeper exclaims, 'a herald!' The 1st keeper exclaims, 'a herald!' The 3d keeper exclaims, 'a herald approaches.' The herald then advances and brings the following intelligence. 'Nebuchadnezzar, king of Babylon, with battering rams assaults the Temple and the courts are filled with carnage.' The king says, 'companion Gedaliah, is there no way of escape?' Gedaliah answers, 'There is none, except by the way of the king's garden, between the walls, by the private entrance, leading out to the plains of Jericho.' The king says, 'Let us make our escape.' At this moment there is great commotion, running and stamping. After the noise has ceased, a herald sounds. His approach is announced, as above described. Companion Gedaliah inquires, 'What tidings from the king?' The herald replies, 'The king, and all the men of war fled by night, by the way of the gate between two walls, which is by the king's garden, and the king went the way

INTRODUCTION.

towards the plain, and the army of the Chaldees pursued after the king and overtook him on the plains of Jericho, and all his army was scattered from him; so they took the king, and brought him up to the king of Babylon, to Riblah, and they gave judgment upon him, and they slew the sons of Zedekiah before his eyes, and they put out the eyes of Zedekiah, and bound him in fetters of brass, and carried him to Babylon.' Then the companion Gedaliah thus addressed the companions; 'The sword of the enemy prevails our young men are captives, and our old men slaves. In this extremity what remains to be done?—Let us repair to the holy altar, and there pledge our faith, and renew our vows.' They then form a circle round the altar; the candidate is caused to kneel at the altar,—both hands on the holy bible, square and compasses,—and take the following obligation.

'I, A.B., of my own free will and accord, in the presence of the most puissant, most holy, and most merciful Creator, and this council of super-excellent masters, dedicated to him, do hereby and hereon, most solemnly and sincerely *promise and swear*, that I will not bow down to other gods, nor pay religious adoration to idols. And I *promise and swear*, that I will not worship the sun, moon, or stars of heaven; but in good faith and conscience to the best of my abilities will serve and worship the only true and living God: And I *promise and swear*, that I will always hail and conceal the secrets of this degree and never reveal them except it be to a true and lawful companion super-excellent master, or in a legally constituted council of such; and neither unto him nor them till first by strict trial and due examination or lawful information I shall have found him, or them, as lawfully entitled to the same as I am, or shall be myself: And I *promise and swear*, that I will give meat, drink, and lodging to a poor unworthy brother in necessity, will defend him in danger, and vindicate his character, so far as honor, justice and good faith may warrant. And I *promise and swear*, that I will not derogate from the character of a super-excellent master now about to be conferred upon me. To all this I do most solemnly *promise and swear*, with a fixed and stedfast resolution to keep and perform the same, without any hesitation, equivocation, or self-evasion of mind in me whatever; binding myself under no less penalty than to have my thumbs cut off, my eyes put out, my body bound in fetters of brass, and conveyed captive to a strange land. So help me God and keep me stedfast in this my solemn oath and obligation of a super excellent-master.

At the close of the obligation a herald sounds. The approach of the enemy is announced. They enter with huzzas and shouting, led by the captain of the guard. They seize the candidate, and thrust him with violence out of the hall. The moment he is out, the bandage is torn from his eyes; he is then introduced to companion Gedaliah, who explains the *pass-word, signs* and *grand-word*. The pass-word is, 'Saul the first king of Israel.' The *first sign* is made by *crossing the arms at right angles in front of the body the right one uppermost the fingers clenched and the thumbs erect.* It alludes to the penalty of the obligation. [See plate 28, fig. 2. *the same as in the degree of sublime knights elected.*] The *second sign* is made by *raising the right hand as high as the eyes, drawing it back over the right shoulder, the elbow raised, and with a quick motion darting it forward in a horizontal direction,* the *two first fingers open, and extended like a fork, the thumb and other fingers being clenched*. It alludes to the penalty of *gouging* out the eyes of a traitor. The *grand-word* is, '*Nahod-Zabod Bone.*'

Closing.—Companion Gedaliah says, Companion 1st keeper of the Temple, where do super-excellent masters convene in council?

1st K.T. In a place representing the sanctuary.

C.G. Their first and last care?

1st K.T. To see the sanctuary duly guarded.

C.G. Please to attend to that part of your duty.

1st K.T. [Addressing the *3d K.T.*] companion 3d keeper, are we duly guarded?

3d K.T. We are duly guarded and the sanctuary is secure.

C.G. Companion 1st keeper, where is the king?

1st K.T. In the prison of Babylon; his thumbs have been cut off, his eyes put out, his body bound in fetters of brass, and conveyed captive to a strange land, as the *penalty of perjury*.

C.G. What is the hour?

1st K.T. It is the time of the third watch.

C.G. Companions, since it is the time of the third watch, let us repair to the holy altar, and offer our fervent aspirations to Deity, for his protecting care and favor. They then assemble round the altar, kneel on the left knee, the right elbow on the right knee, the head bowing on the right hand in imitation of secret prayer. After remaining so a few moments, companion Gedaliah says, 'Let us arise.' They arise, make the signs, from super-excellent master to entered apprentice, companion Gedaliah then raps *ten*, the 1st and 2d keepers do the same, and the council is closed.

INTRODUCTION.

DEGREE OF ARK AND DOVE.

This degree, though short, can boast of as ancient and honorable a pedigree (*if masonic tradition be true*), as any other. It cannot legally be conferred on any but royal arch Masons; upon them (if they are found worthy,) it is conferred as an honorary degree.

THE OBLIGATION. 'Do you solemnly promise, as a royal arch Mason, that you will keep the secrets of this degree?'

Can. I do.

History.

Masonic tradition informs us, that the circumstances upon which this degree was founded took place in the *ark* in which *Noah* and his family were preserved from the deluge. Noah, in order to ascertain if the flood had began to subside, opened the *window* of his ark, and put out a dove, knowing that it would return: and if the flood had subsided, would probably bring back some sign of vegetation.

The dove left the ark, and contrary to Noah's expectations, did not return for many days: he almost despaired seeing it again.

One day, however, as he was standing in the window of his ark, he saw something at a very great distance, moving just above the surface of the water, and as it came nearer to the ark, he discovered it to be the dove; in the great joy of his heart, he raised his hand to an angle of forty-five degrees, and exclaimed, *'Lo, she cometh!'*

If you wish to make yourself known to a brother of this degree, raise the hand as in the plate, and say, *Lo, she cometh!*

LIGHT ON MASONRY.

KNIGHTS OF CONSTANTINOPLE.

This is called an honorary degree, and may be conferred by one Mason on another; but it is generally done in a lodge or chapter, after other regular business is finished.

The presiding officer represents Constantine, and is seated in the east with a crown on his head and a sceptre in his hand. The conductor represents one of Constantine's *noblemen*, the rest of the brethren, or sir knights, represent the *common people*, Constantine's subjects.

The candidate is brought in: each and every one goes at work, in imitation of so many tinkers, shoe-makers, joiners, tailors, &c. The conductor takes the candidate by the arm and opens the door without any ceremony, and both walk up the hall to the east, and introduce themselves to Constantine as follows:

Cond. Your majesty's most humble servants [bowing very low,] we have long observed it has pleased your majesty to show your favor to the *common people*, while we, the *nobility*, have been neglected. We should like to know the reason. If for crimes we may be punished, make amends, and receive your majesty's favor.

Con. None can expect to receive my favor but the knights of Constantinople.

Cond. Ah! the knights of Constantinople.

They turn and walk off. The conductor observes, as he passes the brethren, who are all this time very busily at work, 'These are the *common people*, they are beneath our notice; it would be degrading for us, the *nobility*, to condescend to speak to them.' Our sovereign says, None can receive his favor but the knights of Constantinople. Let us return, and request him to confer that degree on us.

They return, walking arm in arm, to the east.

Cond. Will your majesty confer the degree of knights of Constantinople upon us, your humble servants?

Con. I confer it on no man.

Cond. Where then can we expect to obtain it?

Con. From those laboring people you just *observed* to be your inferiors; the knights of Constantinople.

Cond. Ah! from the knights of Constantinople.

They then go to the brethren who are at work and inquire, Are you the knights of Constantinople?

Com. Peo. We are the knights of Constantinople.

Cond. Will you confer that degree on us?

Com. Peo. O yes, O yes, O yes, (reply three or four voices,) if you are willing to take an obligation.

The candidate is now hood-winked, kneels down, and takes the following oath.

INTRODUCTION.

'I, A. B., in the presence of Almighty God, and these sir knights of Constantinople, do solemnly and sincerely swear, in addition to my former obligations, that I will not confer this degree upon any person, unless he be a worthy master Mason.

'I furthermore promise and swear that I will not confer this degree of knights of Constantinople upon any person, unless he shall acknowledge that all men are equal; to all of which do I solemnly and sincerely promise and swear, without any equivocation, mental reservation, or self-evasion of mind in me whatever; binding myself under no less penalty than to have a dagger thrust through my body, should I violate this my oath and obligation of a knight of Constantinople. So help me, God, and keep me stedfast to keep and perform the same.'

Kisses the book.

As soon as he has received the oath, all the brethren surround him, and strike him in the sides, breast, and back, with the end of the thumb, [see plate 25, fig. 3]asking him *'Are all men equal?'* If the candidate says they are, the bandage is taken off; if he says they are not, they continue to pound him until they have expelled his aristocratical principles.

The sign in plate 25, fig. 3, alludes to the penalty. Hold the hand as though you had a dagger, your thumb against the guard.

History.

According to Masonic tradition, this degree was instituted by Constantine the Great. The circumstances upon which it is founded are as follows:

Constantine saw that the nobility had so completely got the lower of controlling the *common people*, that his kingdom was likely to be endangered; and in order to remedy this very great evil, and bring the nobility to a proper level with the common people, he instituted this degree, and conferred it upon some of his common people: he then engaged that he would not confer it again on any man; but whosoever received it, must receive it from the common people.

He also agreed that he would not associate with, or show his favor to any but the knights of Constantinople. And he gave them orders to put any person to instant death who received the degree, and would not acknowledge all men to be equal. Soon after this arrangement, the nobility saw the sovereign had withdrawn his confidence and favor, and two of them appeared before him and addressed him thus:

Nobility. Your majesty's most humble servants. We have long observed that it has pleased your majesty to show your favor to the common people, while we, the nobility, have been neglected. We should like to know the reason: if for crime, we may be punished, and receive your majesty's favor.

Constantine replied, 'None can expect to receive my favor but the knights of Constantinople.'

The nobility went away; but knowing they could not live without the favor and friendship of their sovereign, returned and requested him to confer that degree on them: he replied, 'I confer it on no man.' 'How,' said they, 'shall we expect to receive it?'

Constantine replied, 'From that class of people you unjustly call your inferiors, the knights of Constantinople.'

They went away and received the degree from the common people, as described in the fore part of this degree.

INTRODUCTION.

SECRET MONITOR, OR TRADING DEGREE.

This degree cannot legally be conferred on any but worthy master Masons. A brother of this degree, who has committed the oath or obligation to memory, has a right to confer it upon a master Mason, in a lodge or private room, or even, in some cases, it is conferred out of doors, providing they are not liable to be discovered by *cowans*, and have a bible to take the oath upon.

The candidate lays his hand upon the book, and takes the following oath.

'I, A. B., in the presence of Almighty God and this witness, do hereby and hereon solemnly and sincerely swear, *in addition to my former obligations*, that I will not confer this degree of secret monitor on any person in the known world, except it be a worthy master Mason.

'I furthermore promise and swear that I will caution a brother secret monitor by *sign*, *word*, or *token*, wherever I see him doing or about to do anything contrary to the true principles of Masonry.

'I furthermore promise and swear that I will caution a brother secret monitor by *sign*, *word*, or *token*, wherever I see him doing or about to do anything contrary to his *interest* in *buying* or *selling*.

'I furthermore promise and swear that when I am so cautioned myself by a brother secret monitor, I will pause and reflect on the course I am pursuing.

'I furthermore promise and swear that I will *assist* a brother secret monitor, in preference to any other person, by introducing him to business, by *sending him custom*, or in *any other manner* in which I can throw a penny in his way.

'I furthermore promise and swear that I will immediately commit this obligation to memory: to all of which do I most solemnly and sincerely promise and swear, without any mental reservation or self-evasion of mind in me whatever; binding myself under no less penalty than that of having my heart thrust through with the arrow of an enemy, and to be without friends in the hour of trouble. So help me, God, and keep me stedfast in this my solemn oath and obligation of a secret monitor.' [Kisses the book.]

The bible is then opened, and the following passages are read:

1 Samuel xx. 16–23, and 35–42. 'So Jonathan made a covenant with the house of David, *saying*, Let the Lord even require it, at the hand of David's enemies. And

Jonathan caused David to swear again, because he loved him: for he loved him as he loved his own soul.

'Then Jonathan said to David, To-morrow is the new moon; and thou shalt be missed, because thy seat will be empty. And when thou hast stayed three days, then thou shalt go down quickly, and come to the place where thou didst hide thyself when the business was *in hand*, and shalt remain by the stone Ezel.

'And I will shoot three arrows on the side *thereof*, as though I shot at a mark.

'And behold, I will send a lad, *saying*, Go, find out the arrows. If I expressly say unto the lad, Behold, the arrows *are* on this side of thee, take them, then come thou, for *there is* peace to thee, and no hurt, as the Lord liveth.

'But if I say thus unto the young man. Behold the arrows are beyond thee, go thy way, for the Lord hath sent thee away. And *as touching* the matter which thou and I have spoken of, behold, the Lord be between me and thee for ever.'

* * * * * *

'And it came to pass in the morning that Jonathan went out into the field at the time appointed with David, and a little lad with him.

'And he said unto his lad. Run, find out now the arrows which I shoot. *And* as the lad ran, he shot an arrow beyond him. And when the lad was come to the place of the arrow which Jonathan had shot, Jonathan cried after the lad, and said, *Is not the arrow beyond thee!*

'And Jonathan cried after the lad, Make speed, haste, stay not. And Jonathan's lad gathered up the arrows, and came to his master.

'But the lad knew not anything: only Jonathan and David knew the matter.

'And Jonathan gave his artillery unto his lad, and said unto him, Go, carry them to the city.

'*And* as soon as the lad was gone David arose out of *a place* towards the south, and fell on his face to the ground, and bowed himself three times; and they kissed one another, and wept one with another, until David exceeded.

'And Jonathan said to David, Go in peace; forasmuch as we have sworn both of us in the name of the Lord, saying, The Lord be between me and thee, and between my seed and thy seed for ever. And he arose and departed, and Jonathan went into the city.'

Lecture.

Brother. I am David.

Can. I am Jonathan.

Brother. David and Jonathan knew the matter.

Can. The lad knew nothing at all.

The *signs*, and also the *words* and *tokens* of this degree, are of two kinds, *negatives* and *affirmatives*.

INTRODUCTION.

The negative *sign* is made by exhibiting two fingers, as in plate 25, fig. 2.

It is given whenever you see a brother doing, or about to do, anything *contrary* to his *interest*, in buying or selling, &c.; it means *desist*; the brother who receives the sign is bound by his oath to pause and reflect.

The sign of approbation is given by holding up one finger, as in plate 25, fig. 1.

It is given whenever you wish secretly to advise a brother in any traffic or dealing to his *profit* and *interest*; it means *proceed*.

Grips are given and received in the same admonishing way. When you take the hand of a brother, if you grip him in the centre of the hand with two fingers, it means *desist;* if you grip with one finger, it means *proceed*.

To caution a brother by *word*. If you see a brother doing anything contrary to his *interest*, in buying or selling, say to him, you had better buy two, *'two is better than one;'* it means *desist*. If you say to him, *'One is as good as two,'* it means *proceed*, and he will directly understand you, and act accordingly.

Thus you can caution a brother, by *sign*, *token*, or *word*, whenever you see him doing anything contrary to the principles of Masonry, or his interest; and he, so cautioned, is bound to pause and reflect before he further goes, under the penalties of having the arrow of an enemy thrust through his heart, etc. There is also another way to caution a brother. If you say to him, *'the arrows are beyond thee,'* it means *desist*. If you say to him, *'the arrows are this side of thee;'* it means proceed.

The due-guard and sign of this degree is given by placing yourself in the attitude of springing a bow; it is in imitation of Jonathan shooting the arrows; it alludes to the penalty of the obligation.

To answer this sign, strike the left side, opposite the heart, with the end of the fore finger of the left hand, the other fingers clenched.

This degree is much in use in the trading part of the fraternity. The following anecdote may serve to illustrate its utility to Masons:

'Brother H****, while in the village of *****, visited a lodge, and in the course of the evening the degree of Secret Monitor was conferred upon a worthy master, to the great edification of all present. At the usual hour, the lodge closed, and each brother repaired to his lodgings, rejoicing in himself that he was *David* or *Jonathan*, as the case might be. In the course of the next day, Mr. H. stepped into a shoe store to treat himself to a new pair of boots. He selected a pair, and was about to pay to the owner (who, unfortunately for himself, was not a Mason) his price: when one of the journeymen of the shoe merchant, who was at work in the store, observed, 'Mr., those boots will do you good service, you had better take two pair, *'two is better than one.'* Mr. H. recognized the friendly journeyman to be a brother Secret Monitor, who he sat in the lodge with the night before. He understood the caution, paused, reflected, and after some excuses, concluded he would not take the boots *then*—he might call again.'

LIGHT ON MASONRY.

David and *Jonathan knew the matter*; the LAD knew nothing about it.

In this case, the journeyman shoemaker felt himself bound to assist a brother Secret Monitor, although a stranger, in preference to his employer, who was not a Mason.

INTRODUCTION.

HEROINE OF JERICHO.

This degree is conferred upon royal arch Masons, their wives and widows; hence it is sometimes called the ladies' degree.

It is generally conferred at parties composed exclusively of royal arch Masons, their wives and widows, convened for that purpose at the house of some royal arch Mason. Those who have taken the degree occupy one room, and those that have not, another. The novices (male or female, as the case may be,) receive the degree one at a time, in the following manner:

The *candidate*, if a female, is conducted into the lodge of heroines, and seated in a chair near the centre of the room, and a male heroine (not her husband,) who is qualified, confers the degree in the following manner:

After a few introductory remarks, he seats himself before the candidate, and requests her to place her hands upon the Holy Bible, which he holds in his lap before her; telling her at the same time that the degree of heroine of Jericho is not at all like Masonry in any of its bearings. That there is an obligation which she must take before she can be made acquainted with the mysteries of this beautiful degree; and she may repeat her name, and say after him. The following oath is then taken:

'I, A. B., of my own free will and accord, in presence of Almighty God, and these heroines of Jericho, do hereby and hereon, solemnly and sincerely promise and swear, that I will not communicate the secrets of heroine of Jericho to any person in the known world, except it be to a true and lawful brother or sister heroine of Jericho.

'I furthermore promise and swear, that I will not confer this degree upon any person in the known world.*

---

*When a man receives the degree, he swears that he 'will not confer *this degree* upon any person except it be a worthy companion royal arch Mason, their wives or widows, and that he will never confer it on his own wife.'

'I furthermore promise and swear, that I will keep the secrets of a brother or sister heroine of Jericho, when they are communicated to me as such, or whenever their interest or safety shall require it.

'I furthermore promise and swear, that I will answer and obey all due signs and summons, handed, sent, or thrown to me from a brother or sister heroine of Jericho.

'I furthermore promise and swear, that I will not give the hailing sign of distress of a heroine of Jericho, unless I am in real distress; and should I see this sign given, I will fly to the relief of the person giving it, and extricate them from difficulty, if in my power.

'I furthermore promise and swear, that I will not speak the word of heroine of Jericho, which I shall hereafter receive, in any manner, except in that in which I shall receive it.

'I furthermore promise and swear, that I will not speak evil of a brother or sister heroine behind their back, or before their face; but will give them due and timely notice of all approaching danger. To all of which do I solemnly and sincerely promise and swear with a firm and steady purpose, to keep and perform the same: binding myself under no less penalty, than to have my head struck off and carried to the highest mountain. So help me. God, and keep me steadfast in the due performance of the same.' Kisses the book.

After the oath is administered, the bible is opened to the second chapter of the book of Joshua, and read as follows:

'And Joshua, the son of Nun, sent out of Shittim two men to spy secretly, saying, Go, view the land, even Jericho. And they went, and came into a harlot's house, named Rahab, and lodged there. And it was told the king of Jericho, saying. Behold, there came in hither to-night of the children of Israel, to search out the country. And the king of Jericho sent unto Rahab, saying, Bring forth the men that are come to thee, which are entered into thy house: for they be come to search out all the country. And the woman took the two men, and hid them, and said thus, There came men unto me, but I wist not whence they *were:* And it came to pass *about the time* of shutting of the gate, when it was dark, that the men went out: whither the men went, I wot not: pursue after them quickly; for ye shall overtake them. But she had brought them up to the roof of the house, and hid them with the stalks of flax, which she had laid in order upon the roof. And the men pursued after them the way to Jordan unto the fords; and as soon as they which pursued after them were gone out, they shut the gate. And before they were laid down, she came up unto them upon the roof: And she said unto the men, I know that the Lord hath given you the land, and that your terror is fallen upon us, and that all the inhabitants of the land faint because of you. For we have heard how the Lord dried up the water of the Red Sea for you, when ye came out of Egypt; and what ye did unto the two kings of the Amorites that *were* on the other side Jordan, Sihon and Og, whom ye utterly destroyed. And as soon as we

INTRODUCTION.

had heard *these things*, our hearts did melt, neither did there remain any more courage in any man, because of you: For the Lord your God, he is God in heaven above, and in earth beneath. Now, therefore, I pray you, swear unto me by the Lord, since I have shewed you kindness, that ye will also shew kindness unto my father's house, and give me a true token: And *that* ye will save alive my father, and my mother, and my brethren, and my sisters, and all that they have, and deliver our lives from death. And the men answered her, Our life for yours, if ye utter not this our business. And it shall be, when the Lord hath given us the land, that we will deal kindly and truly with thee. Then she let them down by a cord through the window: for her house *was* upon the town wall, and she dwelt upon the wall. And she said unto them, Get you to the mountain, lest the pursuers meet you; and hide yourselves there three days, until the pursuers be returned; and afterward may ye go your way. And the men said unto her, We *will be* blameless of this thine oath which thou hast made us swear. Behold, *when* we come into the land, thou shalt bind this line of scarlet thread in the window which thou didst let us down by; and thou shalt bring thy father, and thy mother, and thy brethren, and all thy father's household home unto thee. And it shall be, *that* whosoever shall go out of the doors of thy house into the street, his blood *shall be* upon his head, and we *will be* guiltless: and whosoever shall be with thee in the house, his blood *shall be* on our head, if *any* hand be upon him. And if thou utter this our business, then we will be quit of thine oath which thou hast made us to swear. And she said, According unto your words, so *be* it. And she sent them away, and they departed: and she bound the scarlet line in the window. And they went, and came unto the mountain, and abode there three days, until the pursuers were returned: and the pursuers sought *them* throughout all the way, but found *them* not. So the two men returned, and descended from the mountain, and passed over, and came to Joshua the son of Nun, and told him all *things* that befell them: And they said unto Joshua, Truly the Lord hath delivered into our hands all the land; for even all the inhabitants of the country do faint because of us.'

The candidate is then instructed in the mode or manner of giving the *signs*, and *word*.

The first sign is in imitation of the *scarlet line* that Rahab let down from the window of her father's house to assist the spies to make their escape from the city. [See plate 26, fig. 1.]

The second sign is represented in plate 26, fig. 2.

The *grand hailing sign of distress* is given by raising the right hand and arm to an angle of forty-five degrees, holding between the thumb and fore-finger a handkerchief, which hangs perpendicularly. [See plate 26, fig. 3.]

The *word* is given by placing the right feet together, and A placing his hand upon the shoulder of B, says, '*My life*.' B raises her right hand and places it on A's shoulder and says, '*For yours*.' A then raises and puts his left hand on B's shoulder, and says, '*If ye utter not.*' B places her left hand on A's shoulder, and finishes the sentence, '*This our business.*' The word *Rahab*, is then whispered in the ear of the candidate. [See plate 26, fig. 4.]

The lecture is then given, as follows:

A. It is very dark to-night.

B. Yes, but not so dark but that I can see.

A. What can you see?

B. A scarlet line.

A. Why a scarlet line?

B. Because it saved my life in the hour of danger.

The history of the degree is then related to the candidate as follows:

Tradition informs us that this degree has been known and conferred upon the nobility and royal personages ever since the days of *Rahab*, by whom the degree was founded.* It has been very recently conferred upon royal arch Masons, their wives and widows, as an honorary degree.

Sir William Wallace was a brother heroine of Jericho, and while he was at the head of those noble clans, who so valiantly strove to shake off the yoke of oppression, a circumstance occurred that illustrates the utility of this degree to sister heroine of Jericho.

As he was riding past a house near the enemy's lines, he saw a female standing in a window giving this sign. [See plate 26, fig. 1.] He discovered it to be the sign of a heroine of Jericho, and immediately rode up to the window; and after saluting her as a sister, inquired the cause of her distress, and of giving the *sign;* telling her at the same time, that any service or favor in his power to bestow, should be most cheerfully granted to render her happy. She told him that her husband was a *soldier*, and had joined the army opposed to Wallace., that she feared he was slain, or had been taken prisoner in a late engagement, and in consequence of his absence, she was in want of almost all the necessaries of life. Wallace replied, 'My life for yours, if ye utter not this my business,' and rode off. [Wallace at this time had been to spy out the enemy's camp. She understood him, and acted accordingly.]

Wallace returned to his own camp, and after making strict search he found that the husband of his sister heroine of Jericho was one of his prisoners. He promptly

---

*The reader will understand that this history is the one that the Masons give of this degree to those who receive it. Yet I never have seen a person who received it prior to the abduction of William Morgan, And it is generally believed by those heroines of my acquaintance, that it was 'got up' by those concerned in that Masonic outrage. And by swearing their female relatives to conceal the same crimes, should they come to their knowledge, which they themselves, as royal arch Masons, felt bound to perpetrate, against the law of the land, upon the traitor, Morgan. They expected and hoped to receive the same hospitality from them, in case they were suspected, as did the spies in the house of the harlot, Rahab.

INTRODUCTION.

ordered him to be liberated, which was accordingly done, and he returned to his affectionate wife, to the great joy of all parties.

Not long after this, another circumstance took place no less honorable to Sir William Wallace than the one just related. One day, as he was walking upon the banks of one of those beautiful lakes in Scotland, his attention was suddenly arrested by the upsetting of a sail boat, some distance from the shore; he saw the merciless element engulfing a large number of his fellow beings of both sexes, which (to all human appearance,) defied the frail arm of man to extricate them. One awful shriek of despair was heard—they sunk—and all was silent. He stood, his eyes riveted upon the scene of destruction; already had the tear of sympathy stole down his manly cheek in view of suffering and death. At length he saw a hand rise from the surface of the water, holding a handkerchief and giving the grand hailing sign of distress of a heroine of Jericho [as in plate 26, fig. 3].

He thought of his obligations, and although the undertaking was very dangerous, he plunged into the lake, and swam to the place where he saw the signal, *dove down*, caught hold of the sister heroine of Jericho, and rose with her upon the surface of the waves, like a lion when he shakes the dew from his mane, and being a man of great muscular strength he succeeded in bringing the sister heroine of Jericho to the shore; and she was the only person that was saved.

The secrets and ceremonies of this degree have become extensively known in the State of New York, and in most of the States of New-England, among royal arch Masons, their wives and widows. It was introduced into Connecticut in 1827; and although it was brought by one of the grand dignitaries of the order, it met at first with rather a cold reception; but since that time it has been conferred on many who probably had no connection directly with the Morgan outrage.

LIGHT ON MASONRY.

KNIGHTS OF THREE KINGS.

This degree is generally conferred in a lodge or chapter after other business is finished; all master Masons are entitled to it if they are considered worthy. It is generally conferred by our grand lecturers, as an honorary degree upon their pupils.

Soon after the candidate enters, some brother (best qualified to perform the part) retires from the room, and those that remain proceed to give the degree as follows:

The candidate kneels at the altar, and some one commences administering the following obligations:

'I, A. B., of my own. free will and accord, in the presence of Almighty God, and these witnesses, do hereby and hereon solemnly and sincerely promise and swear, that I will not confer the degree of knights of three kings upon any person except it be a worthy master Mason.

'I furthermore promise and swear, that I will not be offended at any of the ceremonies of this degree.

'I furthermore promise and swear, that I will not confer this degree, unless by the unanimous consent of all present.'

Here an interruption of the ceremonies takes place. The brother who left the lodge returns in a great rage, and very abruptly inquires the cause of conferring the degree, without his consent.

The person administering the oath replies. 'I did not expect that you had any objection to the candidate, and therefore I commenced giving the oath. You should have made your objection known before you left the room.'

The objecting brother replies very vehemently, 'I did make my objection known before I left the room! I stated to you and the rest of the brethren that there was difficulty existing of a very serious nature between the candidate and myself, and unless he gave me satisfaction, I should oppose him.'

All the brethren now interpose in order to settle this affair. They say they are very sorry that two brother Masons should quarrel, especially at this time; it is very wrong to carry their prejudices into the lodge.

The candidate rises from the altar apparently much surprised, says he was not aware until the present moment that brother —— was offended at him; he wishes he would tell wherein he had done him any injury, and if it is in his power he will give him satisfaction.

The offended brother then very gravely relates his aggrievances; he accuses the candidate of slandering him in various ways. You have reported, says he, 'that I am

INTRODUCTION.

a common drunkard,'* [or that I quarrel with my wife, that I am dishonest in deal, that I speak disrespectfully of Masonry, &c. &c.]

The candidate generally promptly denies ever making any such statements, and demands the name of the author.

He is told it came from brother —— (naming some respectable Mason who is not present.)

The candidate says, it is an absolute falsehood, a malicious report circulated to injure him. (Gets in a passion.)

The objecting brother says he believes the candidate has reported the story; it is just like him, he is always meddling with other men's affairs.

A general war of words now ensues, and not unfrequently hard names are called. The candidate by this time being nearly worked up into a passion, and the other brother feigning himself so.

Some brother now makes a proposition that all shall leave the room, and leave them alone to settle their difficulty.

The candidate and his antagonist being left alone, they commence walking the room with rapid strides, and loud and boisterous invectives are exchanged in abundance, each contends with much zeal that he has been misrepresented and abused.

In the course of five or ten minutes one of the brethren returns from the other room and inquires, 'Have you agreed?'

The offending or objecting brother replies, 'The difficulty is not settled, neither is it likely to be.'

They are again left alone for about the same space of time, and the conversation becomes louder and more personal. It is not unfrequent on these occasions that the candidate is worked up to complete madness.

The brother returns to them again and inquires, 'Have you agreed?' Being informed they have not, he retires a third time.

The objecting brother now proposes to the candidate that they submit their case to a third person, and to abide his decision, which being acceded to on the part of the candidate, the rest of the brethren return to the hall and inquire if they have agreed; on being informed they have chosen a referee to settle their differences, the umpire says, '*If you can agree in the dark, you can in the light.*'

---

*I once saw this degree conferred when the candidate assumed quite different ground from what was anticipated. He was one of those candid, prudent men, that never make assertions without satisfactory evidence of their truth.

The brother who made the objection, was a bright Mason of the higher order. He was a man of pretty fair character, yet it was apparent that he had contracted some habits which are characteristic of the art, labor and refreshment. He objected to the candidate on the ground that he had reported stories detrimental to his character, etc., to wit: 'That he was a dissipated character.'

The candidate very honestly replied that he had made such a statement, but he did not recollect who it was to, and he sincerely lamented that he had any occasion for saying or thinking so.

He then takes his seat, and directs the candidate to kneel at the altar and receive the remaining part of the obligation. The candidate kneels again at the altar, and repeats as follows.

'I furthermore promise and swear, that I will not confer this degree upon any person without the *hope of fee or reward*.'*

'To all of which do I solemnly and sincerely promise and swear, with a firm and steady resolution, to keep and perform the same, binding myself under no less penalty than**

*   *   *   *   *   *

So help me, God, and keep me steadfast.' Kisses the book once.

After the candidate has taken the obligation, the person who was chosen judge gives his opinion as follows: 'The candidate and the brother who opposed his taking the degree shall approach each other upon the five points of fellowship, and give the master Mason's word, which balances all difficulties.'

History.

Masonic tradition informs us that the circumstances upon which this degree was founded are briefly these. At the dedication of the Temple, king Solomon invited all the eastern kings and princes to attend and assist in the ceremonies. It happened, however, that two of the kings were at war. Solomon repeatedly attempted to effect a reconciliation between them, but to no purpose, they still persisted in their inveteracy.

Solomon being anxious that all nations should be at peace, determined to effect by force, what he could not by agreement. He therefore invited them into a small apartment in the Temple, locked the door, and left them to meditate in silence, telling them that whenever they settled their difficulties and agreed to live in peace, they would be liberated, and until that time they would be shut up in total darkness, and kept on bread and water.

The next day King Solomon went in to see them, and inquired if they had *agreed*.

They informed him they had not, neither was there a probability they would.

---

*It is believed that this degree was invented by some of our grand lecturers, who make it their business to travel from lodge to lodge and instruct men in the mysteries of ancient Freemasonry.

'They have incorporated in the oath a clause which prohibits them from conferring the degree without pay, and by this means they often replenish the small change.

'After they have conferred the degree, they gravely say: "You see, sir, that I must receive some trifling compensation, just to save the oath." (!!)

"How much is customary?" inquires the brother.

"Oh, any trifling sum, 25 or 50 cents, just to save the oath, merely a matter of form."

**The precise terms of the penalty of this degree has escaped my recollection; yet I have often assisted (some years since) in conferring it.

INTRODUCTION.

King Solomon again left them, and on the next day went in as before, and received a like answer.

On the third day he went in, when they informed him they had agreed.

King Solomon advanced towards them, holding in each hand a lighted taper, said, 'If you can agree in the dark, you can in the light,' bowing at the same time and giving this sign [see plate 25, fig. 4], which is the sign of the degree. The watchword and word of caution of this degree is '*agreed.*'

MEDITERRANEAN PASS.

This is an honorary degree, and is said, by masons, to be of great utility to mariners in passing up the Mediterranean sea. According to Masonic tradition, vessels passing up this sea are often brought to by the guns of the Aborigines, who, in hordes, infest the coast, and narrow passes, so that, unless there is some person on board who has taken this degree, the vessel is detained and not allowed to pass; otherwise it has permission to pass without molestation.

The obligation of this degree is as follows:

I. A.B. in the presence of Almighty God and these witnesses, do hereby and hereon, solemnly and sincerely *promise* and *swear*, in addition to my former obligations, that I will not communicate the secrets of this degree to any person, except it be to a true and lawful companion royal arch mason. I *furthermore* promise and swear, that I will not give the signs of distress, belonging to this degree, unless I am in real distress. I *furthermore* promise and swear, that should I ever see the sign of distress given by a worthy brother of the Mediterranean pass, I will fly to his relief , and extricate him in all cases, even if it certain that I sacrifice my own life in the attempt—to all of which do I solemnly promise and swear, with a firm and steady purpose to keep and perform the same, binding myself under no less penalty, than to be bound hand and foot, and cast into the sea. So help me God, and keep me stedfast in the due performance of the same.

After the candidate has taken the obligation, the following passage of scripture is read to him. Isaiah, chap. viii from the first to the end, beginning thus:—

"Moreover the Lord said unto me, take thee a great roll and write in it with a man's pen concerning Maher-shalal-hash-baz. And I took unto me faithful witnesses to record, Uriah the priest, and Zechariah the son of Jeberechiah. And I went unto the prophetess; and she conceived and bare a son. Then said the Lord to me, Call his name Maher-shalal-hash-baz," &c.

The chapter being read, the *words* and *signs* are explained. The *grand-word is* "*Maher-shalal-hash-baz*;" the *pass-word* is "*Immanuel*."

INTRODUCTION.

Signs.—The first sign is made as follows:—take hold of the collar of your coat with both hands, throw it back as though you was about to strip it off, then raise the hand and interlace the fingers back of the neck. [See plate 25, fig. 5]

Another sign is made by making the motion with your body and arms as though you was *in the act of bailing out a boat*, then partly straighten up, and cross the arms on the back, the right arm resting in the left hand as though your back was in great pain. [See plate 25, fig.6.]

APPENDIX 3

The Engravings from Avery Allyn's

A Ritual of Freemasory (1831)

The following engravings not only supplement Appendix 2, but may be compared with Bernard's text. Note that Plates 6, 8, and 10 are missing, as they apparently were never issued. Kent Walgren lists no examples with the missing plates in his Freemasonry, Anti-Masonry and Illuminism in the United states, 1734–1850: A Bibliography, *2 vols (Worcester, Mass.: American Antiquarian Society, 2003), #3449. The attentive reader can see how Allyn misunderstood many of the the signs and and grips.*

Plate 1, 2, & 3: A Lodge of Entered Apprentices, Fellowcrafts, & Master Masons.
Plate 4: The Craft Degrees.
Plate 5: Degree of Master Mason
Plate 7: Degree of Mark Master
Plate 9: Degree of Past Master
Plate 11: Degree of Most Excellent Maste
Plate 12: A Chapter of Royal Arch Masons
Plate 13: Signs and cipher key of the Degree of Royal Arch Mason
Plate 14: Degree of Royal Arch Mason
Plate 15: Degree of Royal Arch Mason
Plate 16: A Council of Select Masters
Plate 17: Degrees of Royal and Select Masters
Plate 18: A Council of Knights of the Red Cross
Plate 19: Degree of Knights of the Red Cross
Plate 20: Signs of the Degree of Knights of the Red Cross
Plate 21: An Encampment of Knights Templar
Plate 22: Degree of Knight Templar
Plate 23: Degree of Knight Templar
Plate 24: Degree of Knight Templar
Plate 25: Secret Monitor, Knightof Constantinople, & Mediterrean Pass
Plate 26: Degree of Heroine of Jericho
Plate 27: The Ineffable Degrees
Plate 28: The Ineffable Degrees
Plate 1: Penalties of an Entered Apprentice and a Fellowcraft

Plate 2: Penalties of a Master Mason and a Mark Master
Plate 3: Penalties of a Past Master and a Most Excellent Master
Plate 4: Penalties of a Royal Arch Mason and a Select Master
Plate 5: Penalties of a Knight of Red Cross and a Knight Templar
Plate 6: Penalties of a Heroine of Jericho and a Secret Monitor

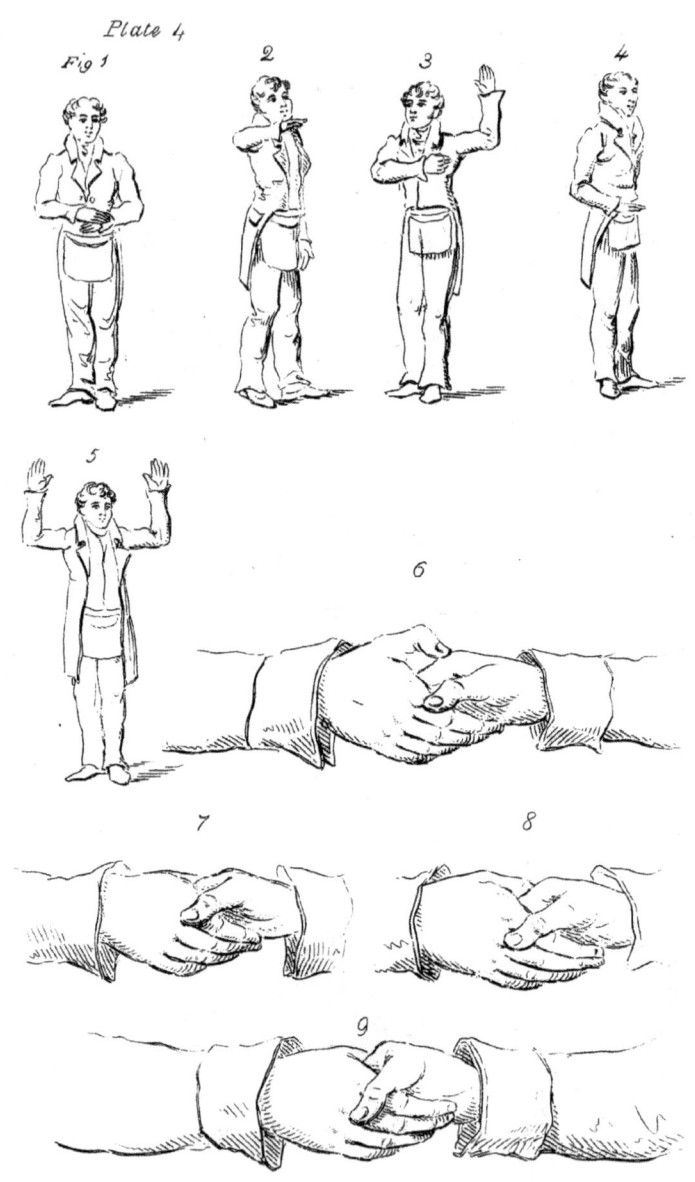

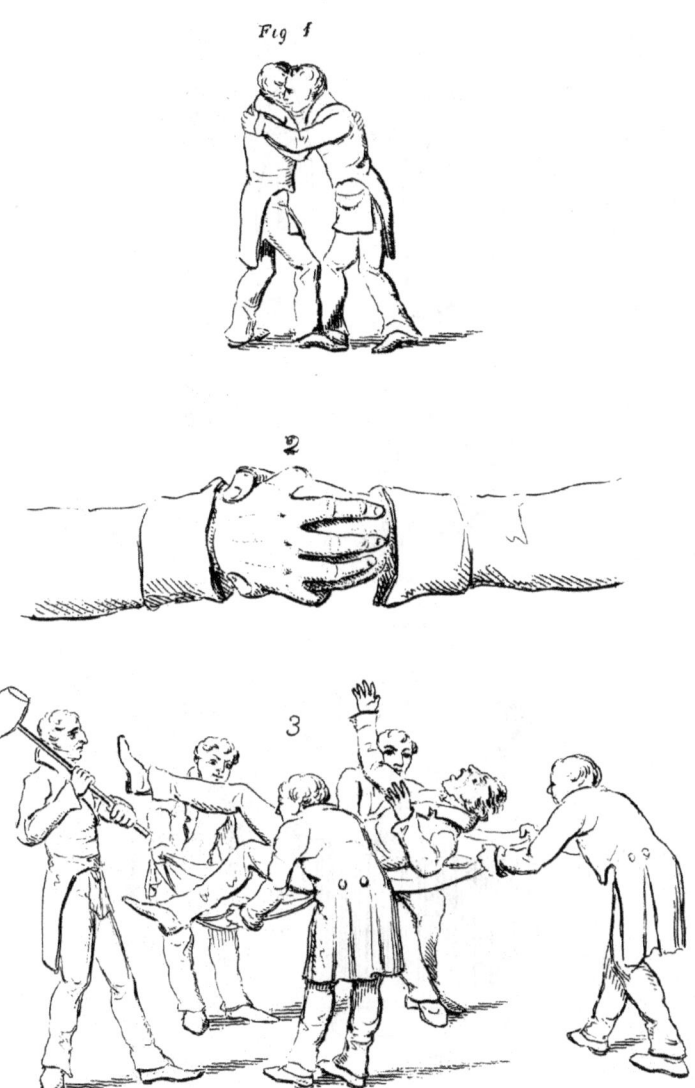

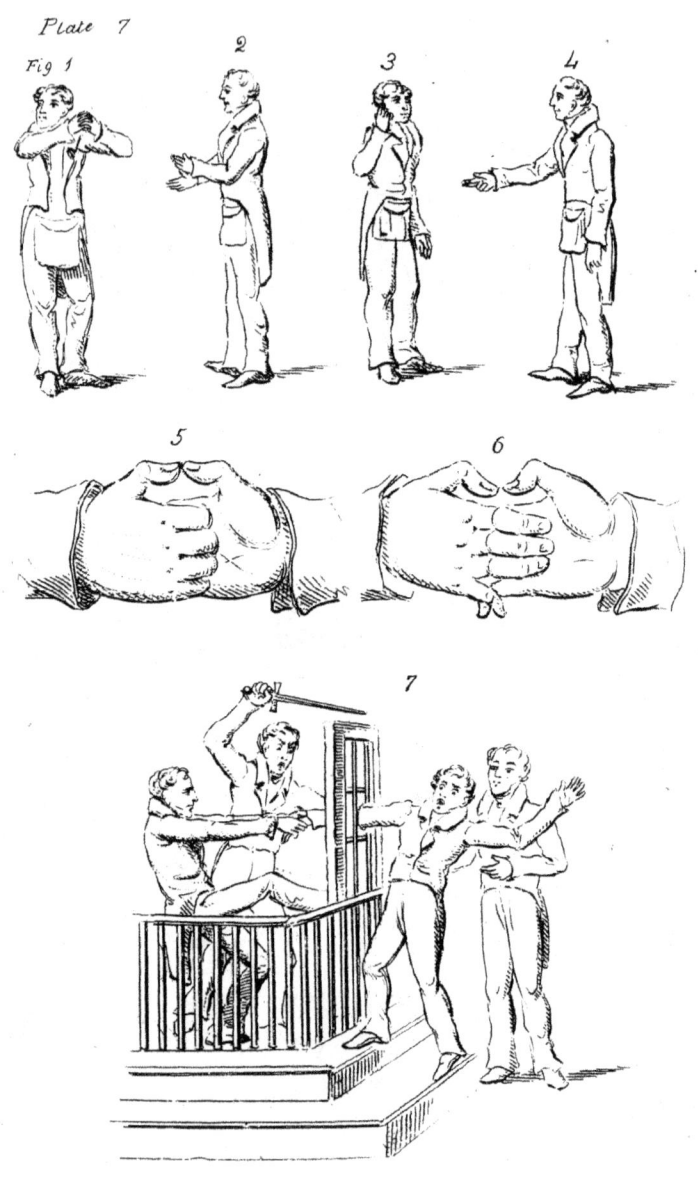

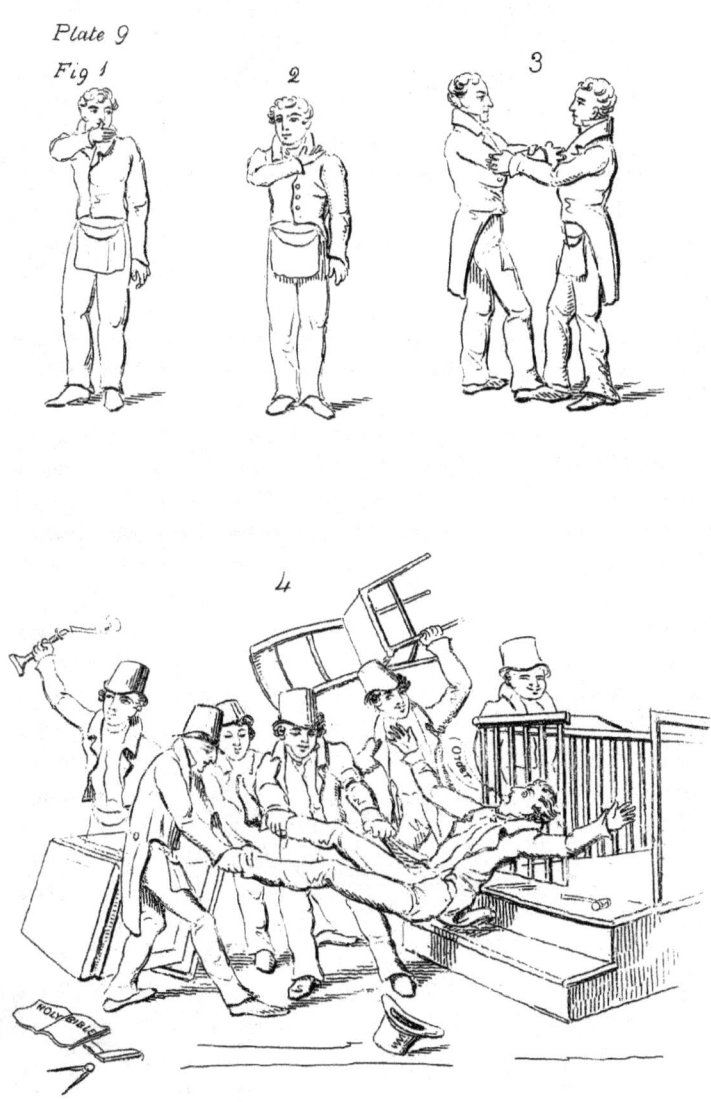

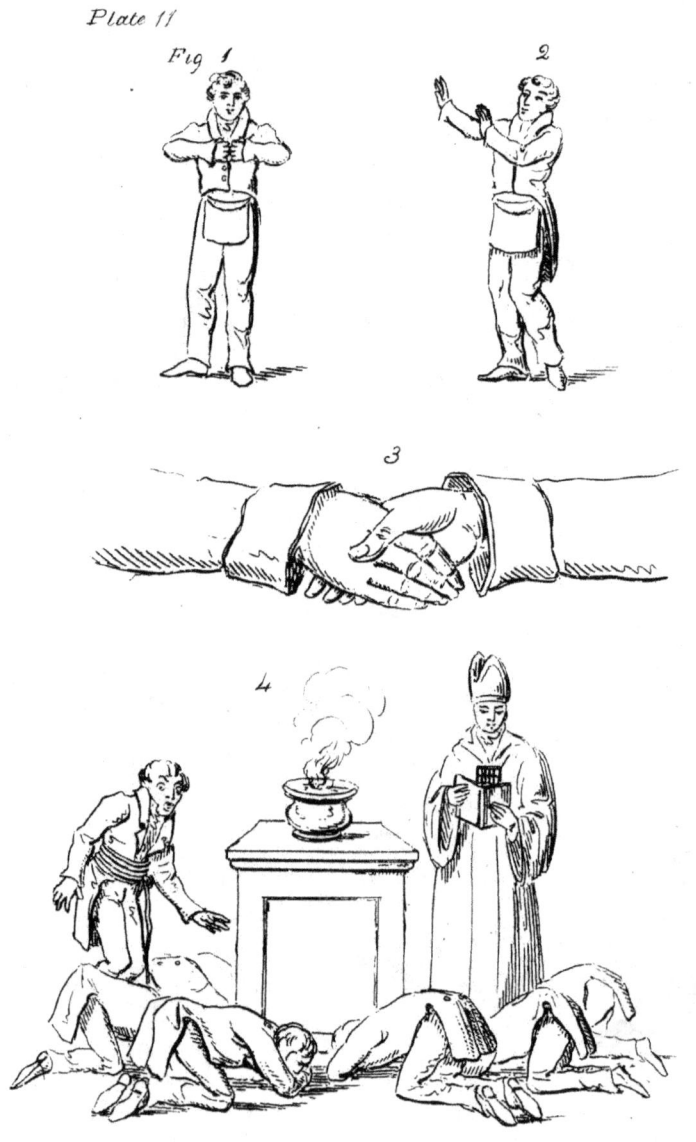

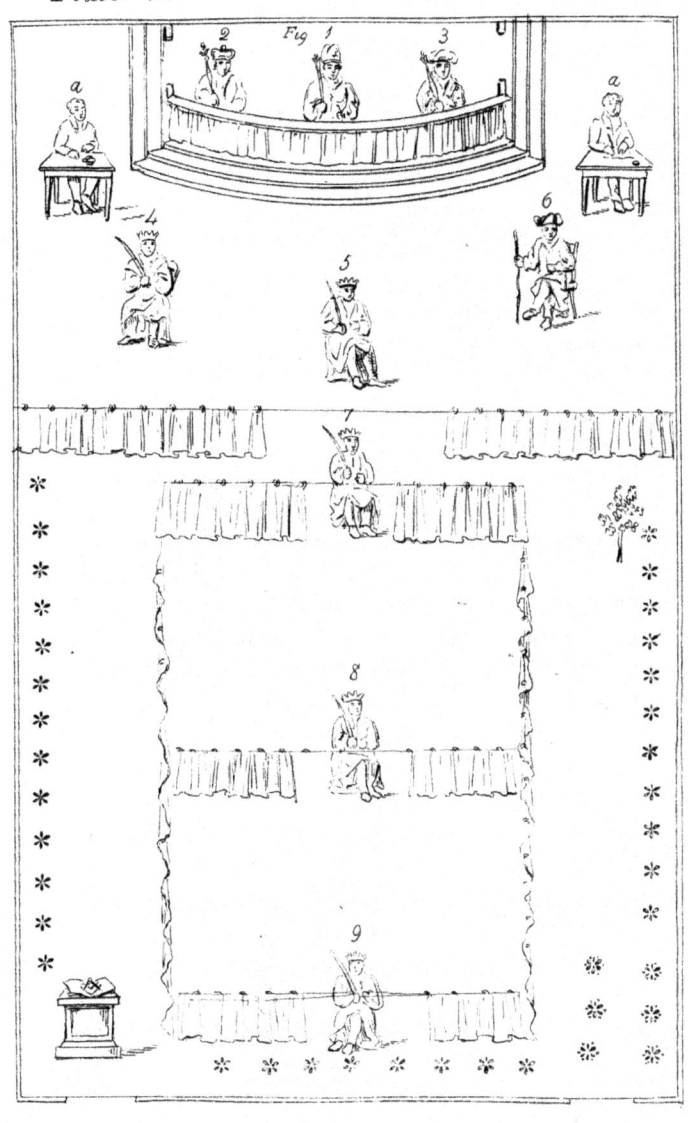

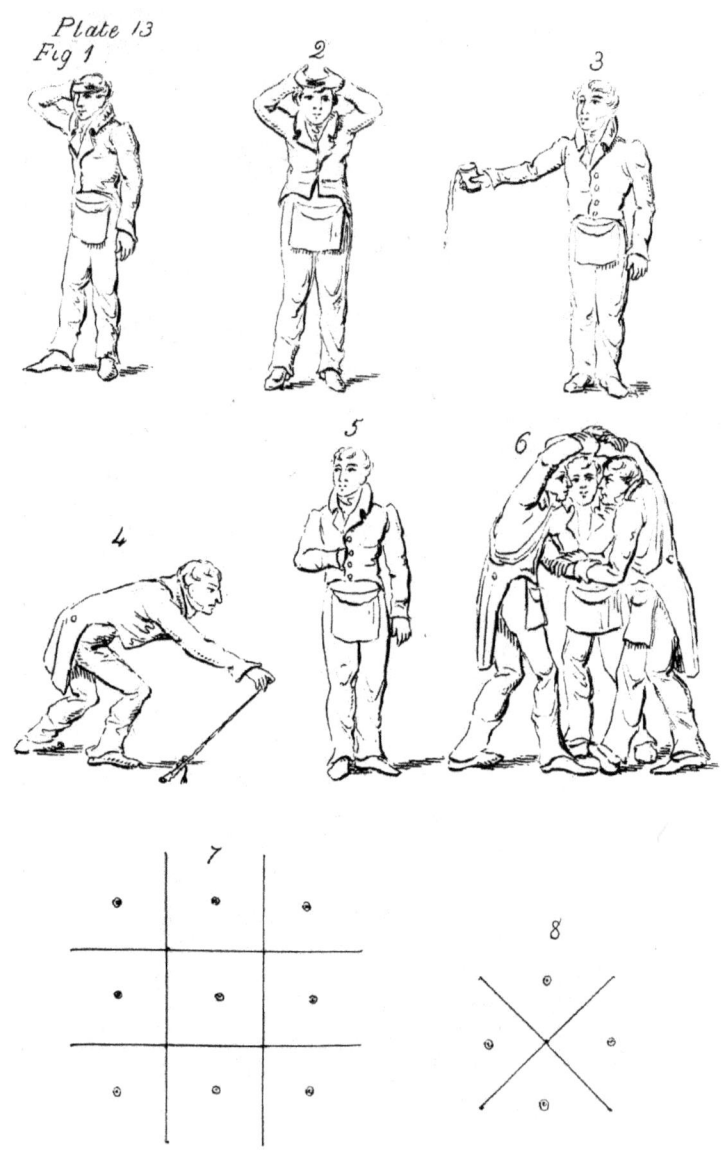

Plate 14

Plate 15

Plate 16

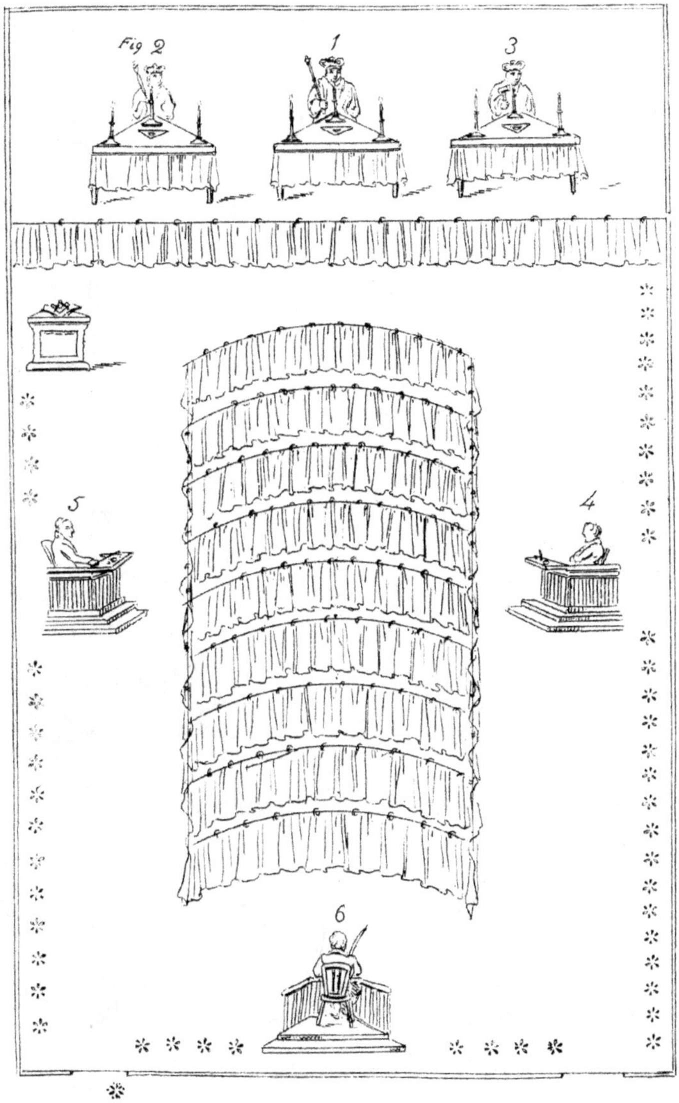

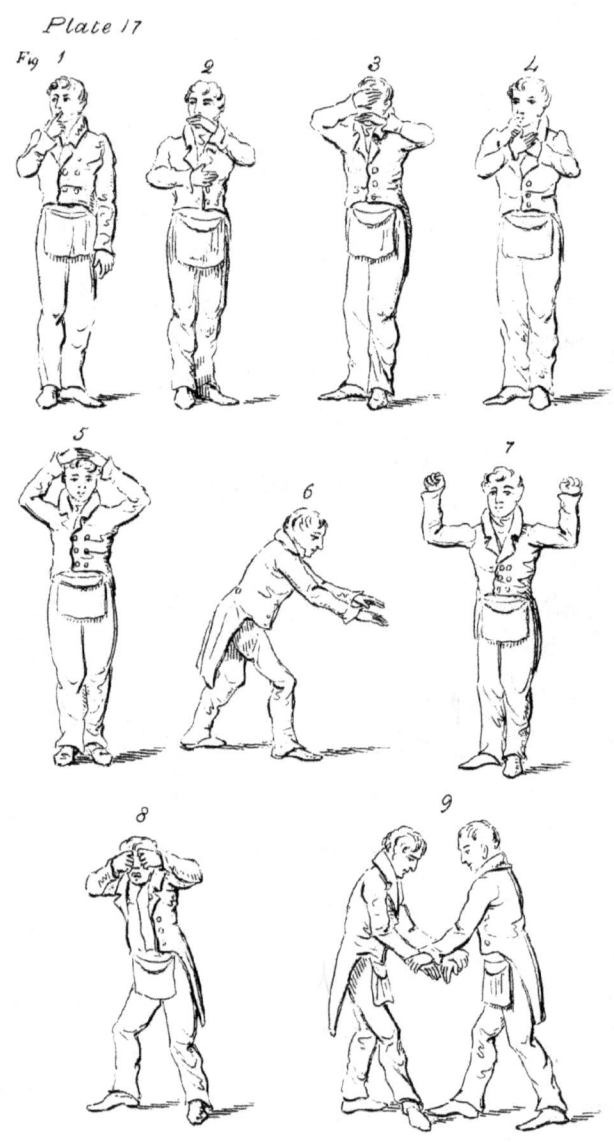

Plate 19

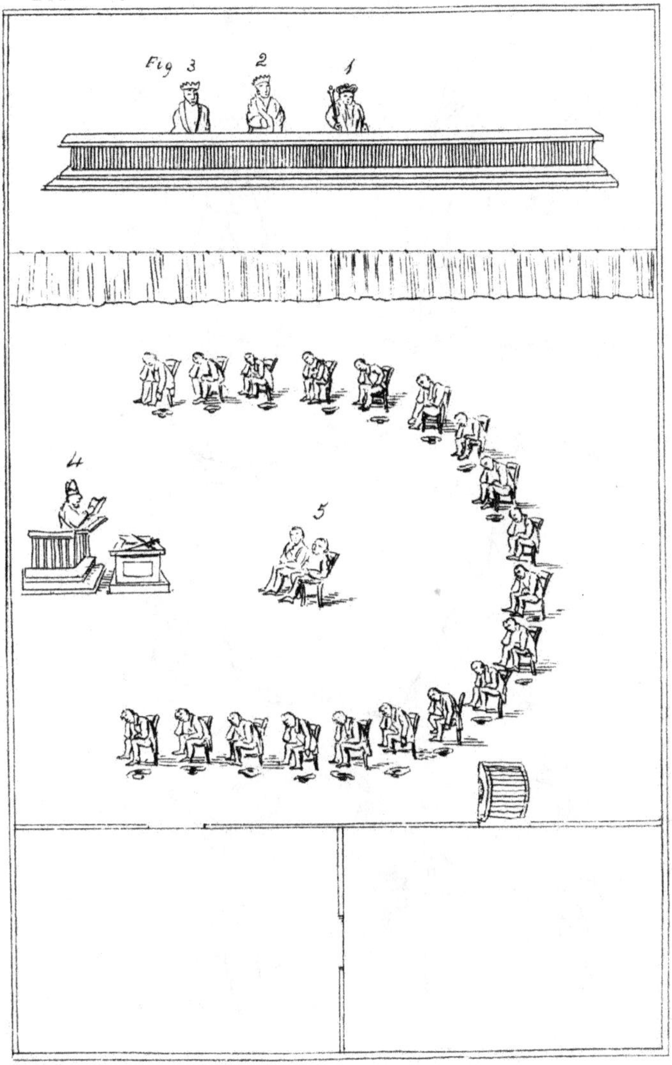

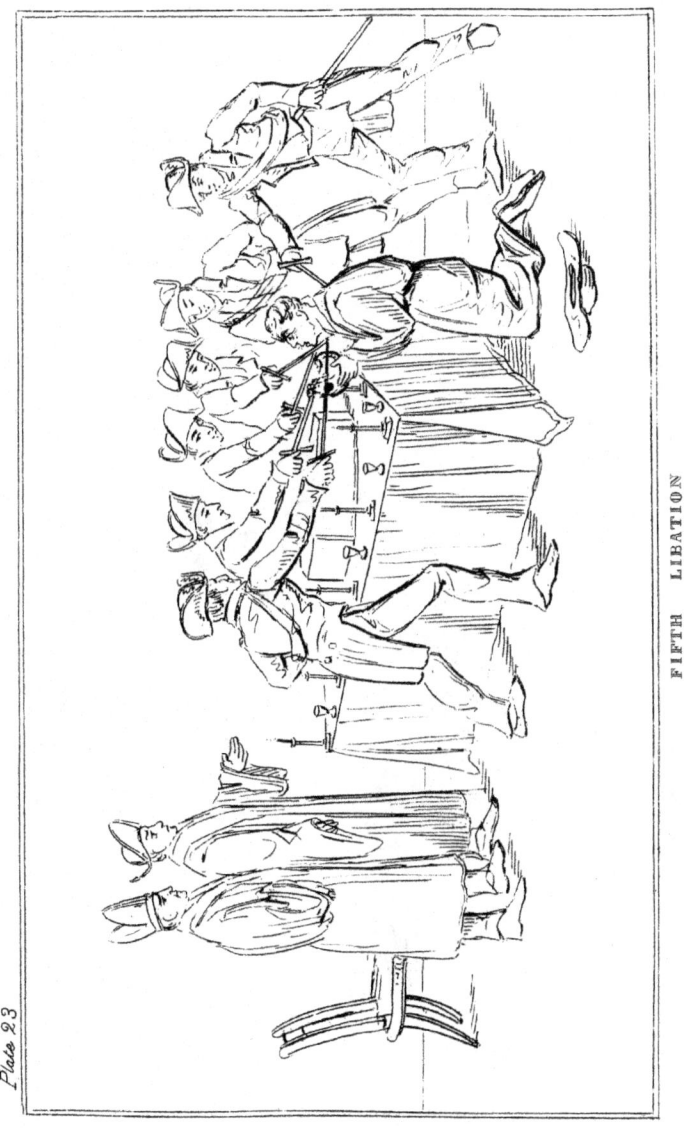

FIFTH LIBATION

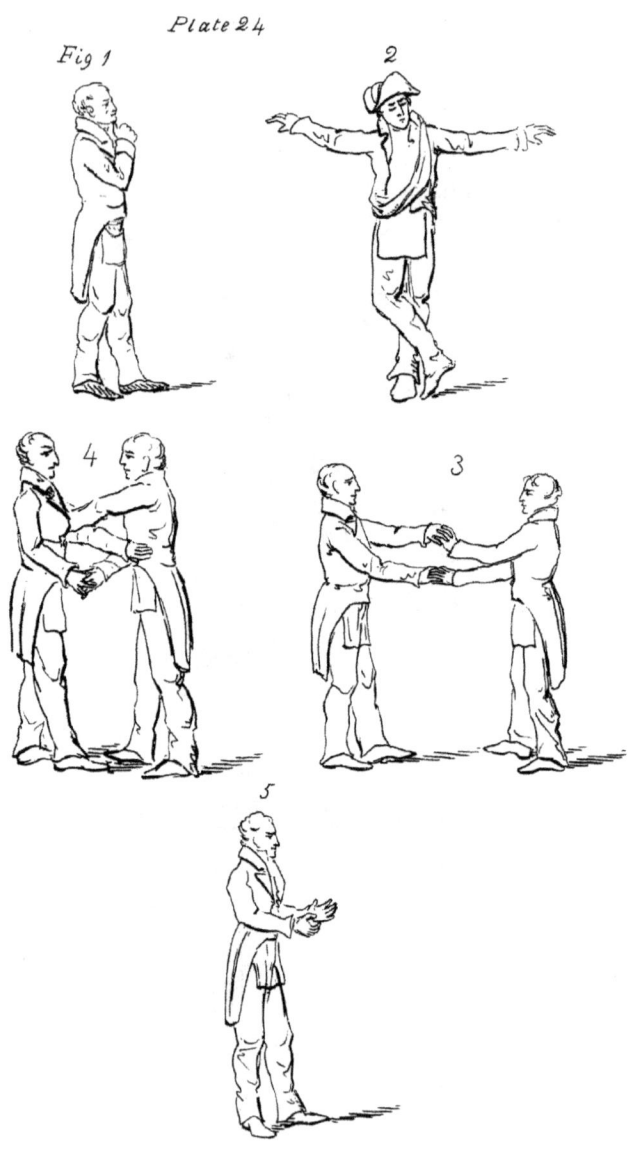

Plate 25 Fig 1

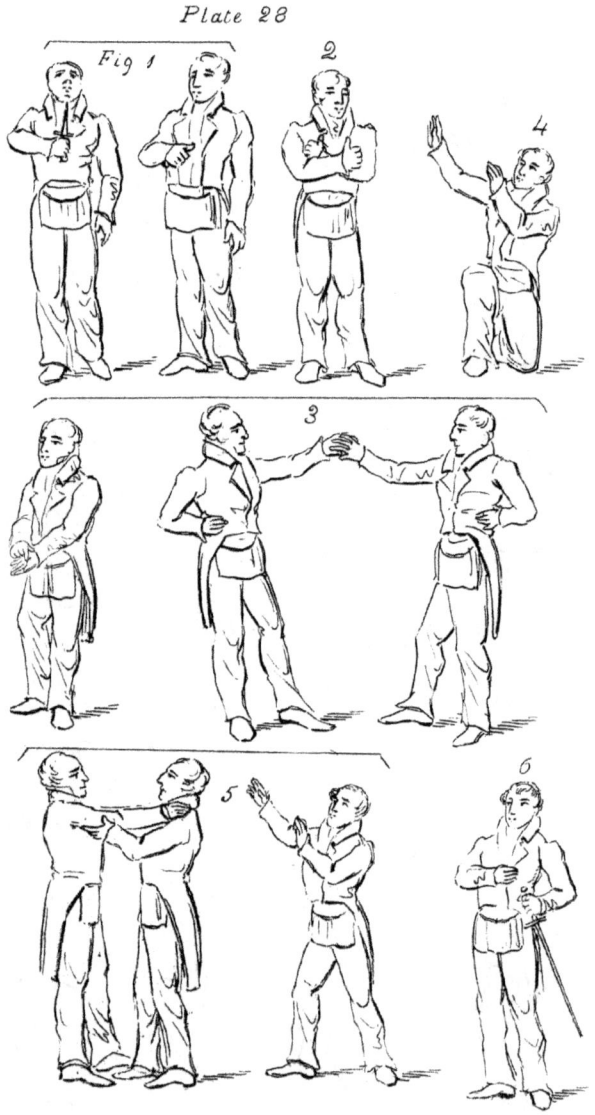

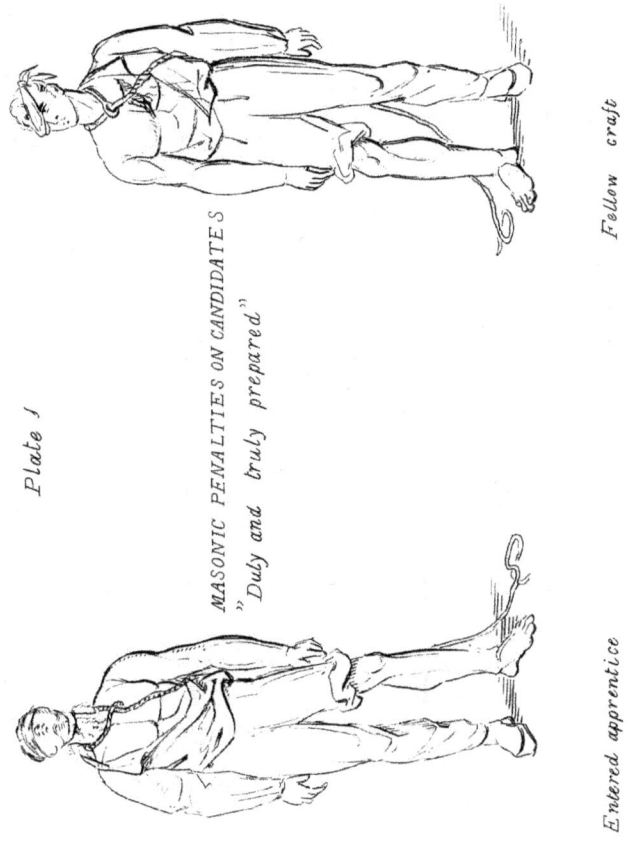

Plate 5

MASONIC PENALTIES ON CANDIDATES
"Duly and truly prepared"

Entered apprentice

Fellow craft

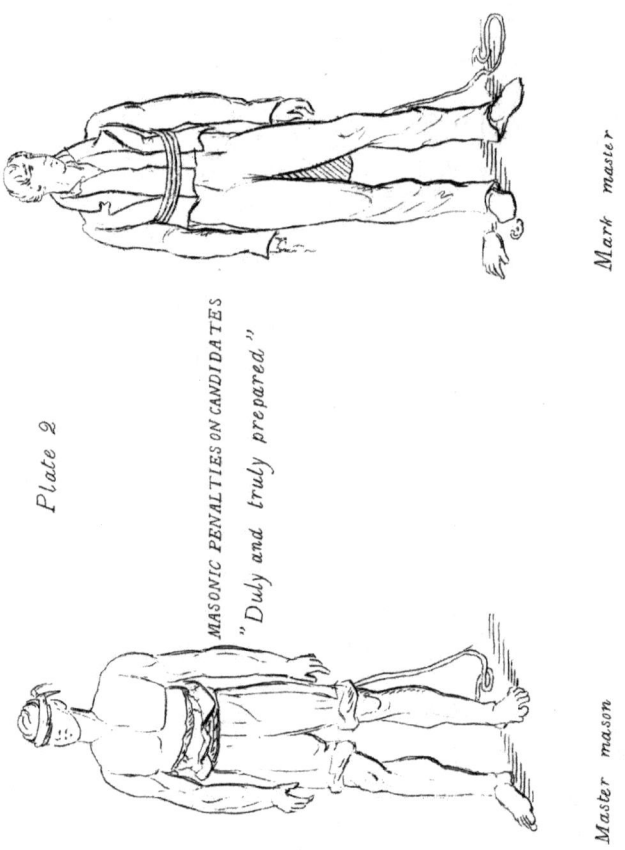

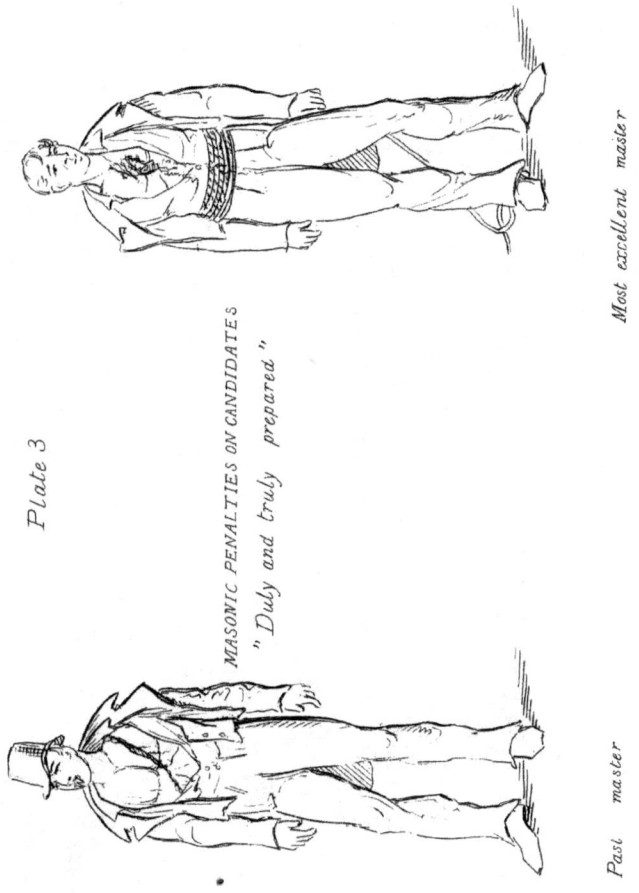

Plate 3

MASONIC PENALTIES ON CANDIDATES
"Duly and truly prepared"

Past master

Most excellent master

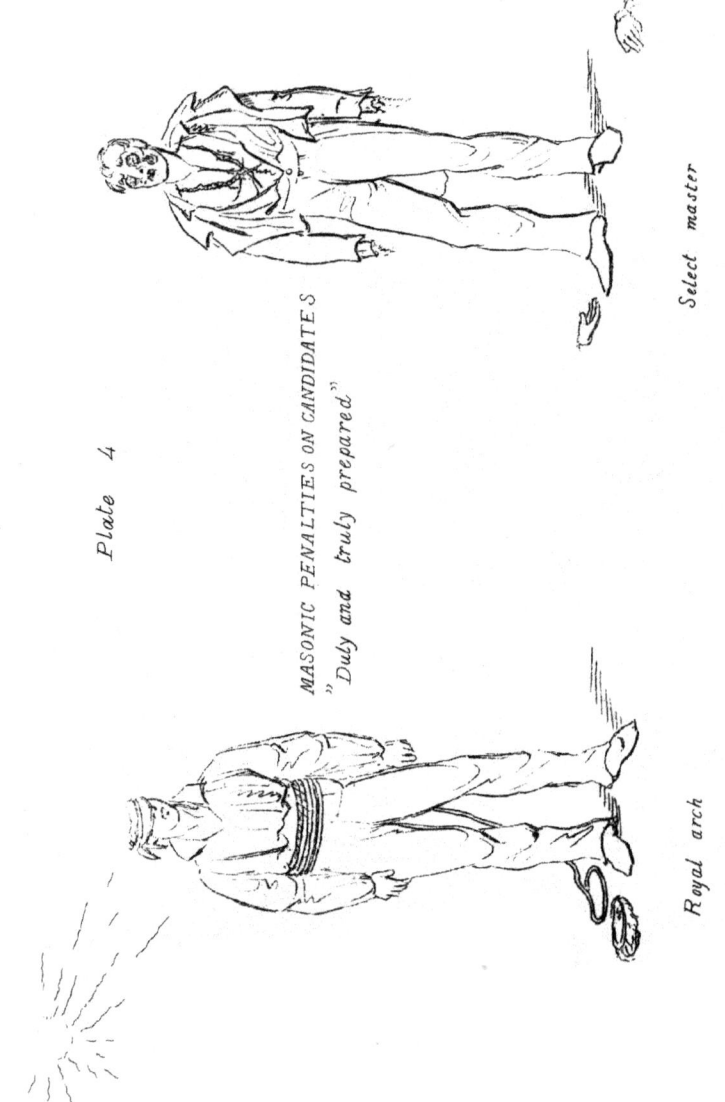

Plate 4

MASONIC PENALTIES ON CANDIDATES
"Duly and truly prepared"

Select master

Royal arch

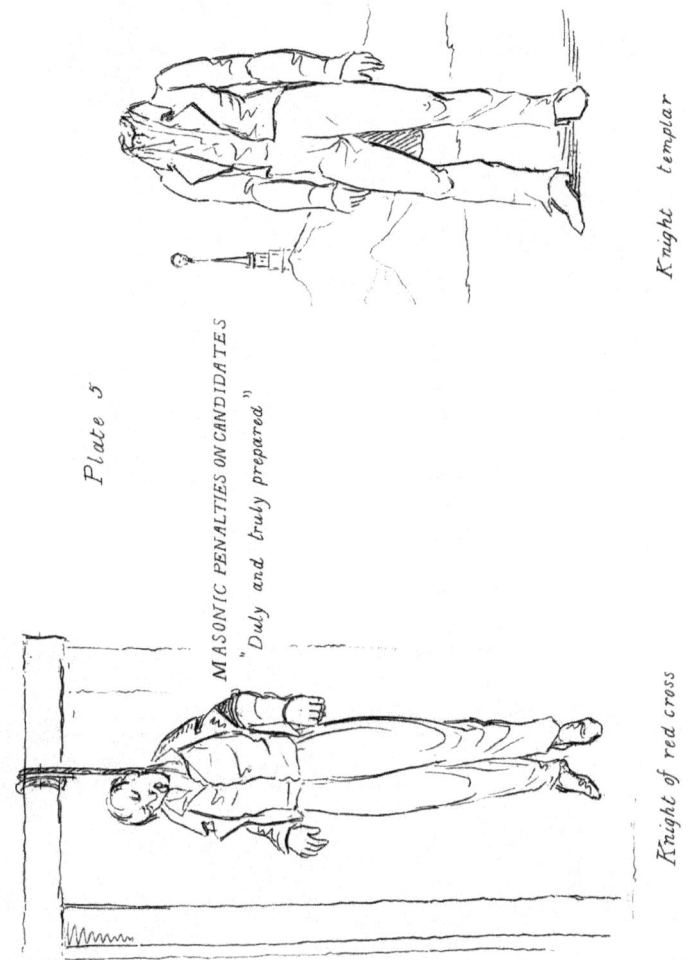

Plate 5

MASONIC PENALTIES ON CANDIDATES
"Duly and truly prepared"

Knight of red cross

Knight templar

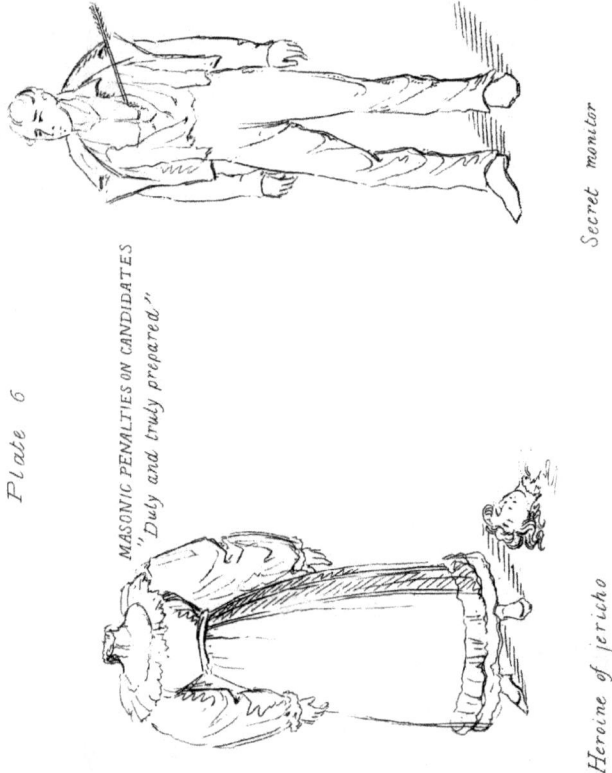

Plate 6

MASONIC PENALTIES ON CANDIDATES
"Duly and truly prepared"

Secret monitor

Heroine of Jericho

APPENDIX 4

THE RITUALS OF "FEMALE MASONRY"

From *Illustrations of the Four First Degrees of Female Masonry, as Practised in Europe. By a Lady* (Boston, 1827). Transcribed verbatim without use of *sic*.

The following text, first published as a catchpenny during the Morgan affair, includes a complete transcript of a little-known exposé of "Adoptive Masonry"—an androgynous system generally unknown to American Masons, but popularized in France by Louis Guillemain de Saint-Victor's book La vraie maçonnerie d'adoption *(1781). According to the* Circular throughout the two hemispheres *(1802), the leaders of the Scottish Rite were in possession of at least six degrees of Adoptive Masonry, and occasionally conferred them upon "those Brethren, who are high enough to understand them." The first four degrees were later revised by Albert Pike, who printed them under the title* The Masonry of Adoption *(1866).*[135] *The identity of our "lady" editor is unknown, but her translation of the original French is uneven, rough, inconsistent, and even ungrammatical. Our transcription retains the format of the original, as well as the many spelling and typographic errors (e.g., "recal," "wortd," "represnntion"), which suggest it was hurriedly typeset. These shortcomings notwithstanding, the rituals themselves remain of interest.*

FEMALE MASONRY,
AS PRACTICED IN ENGLAND, FRANCE, AND GERMANY, &C.

THE FIRST DEGREE OF AN ENTERED APPRENTICE.

The Master is placed at the upper end of the Room in an Elbow Chair under a canopy.

The grand Mistress takes her seat at the right hand of the Grand Master, and are both clothed with plain white aprons; and are decorated with a broad blue ribbon to which hangs the attributes of the order.

At the lower end of the room opposite the Mr. and Mrs. Are placed two elbow chairs, one for the Brother Inspecting Warden, and the other for the sister Inspectrix and Trustee, with the same Ribbon, Jewels and Aprons.

LIGHT ON MASONRY.

The rest of the brethren and Sisters are placed, an equal number on both sides of the room, and are to have white aprons and gloves, as emblems of candour and modesty, they are decorated with a white ribbon and a trowel hanging to it.

The Master holds a mallet and the Mistress a trowel.

At each side of the Master is placed a brother each a naked sabre in their hands and a chain made of tin.

This Lodge ought to be dressed with bows and green verdures, as it represents a forest and is only lighted by five lamps of earth, burning with spirits of wine and salt.

Above the Canopy, behind the Master, must be a transparent Globe. Behind are several tapers fixed to illuminate the lodge.

The draft of the lodge is the Ark of Noah, the tower of Babel, Jacob asleep with the ladder at his head, and several tools of masonry.

The Lodge being thus decorated and illumined and the brethren and Sisters properly arranged, the Master opens the lodge in the following manner:

TO OPEN THE LODGE.

The Questions are asked by the Master and answered by the Brother Inspector.

M.—Brother Inspector advertise the Brethren and Sisters that I am going to open a Lodge of Entered Apprentices.

Br. Insp.—My worthy brethren and sisters, I acquaint you that the Master is going to open the Lodge.

Then the Grand Master says:

Br. and Sister Inspectress, assist me if you please to open this Lodge of Entered Apprentices. Then the Gr. Mrs. Says, brothers and sisters, I beg you to assist me in opening this entered Apprentice Lodge, upon which they all rise from their seats when the Gr. M. knocks 5 times with his Mallet, and the grand Mistress as many with her trowel, and they all make the sign of an entered apprentice, after which the Grand Masters says:

Q. Br. Inspector what are the duties of masons and masonesses?

A. Obedience, Labour and Secrecy—Then the Grand M says, My brethren and sisters the Lodge is open. Let us obey work and be secret.

Then they seat themselves and the minutes of the last Lodge are read, if any thing has remained unsettled, and if any mention is made in their minutes of a princess candidate having been proposed and duly elected, they proceed to the making of her before any other work is taken in hand.

N. B. The fair sex are Mistresses of our hearts, souls, and even our actions. Therefore as soon as they are proposed and admitted they are styled by no other title than Princesses.

INTRODUCTION.

Masons acknowledge no other nobleness in women than virtue, and vice their only blemish, observe further that no man can be admitted in adopted masonry, unless he is at least a M. Mason. Thus it appears that initiating others than women cannot be. It must further be observed that no married lady ca be by any means admitted without the consent of her husband, and he must be a mason, and he must approve of his wife's admittance, verbally or in writing.

An unmarried Lady cannot be initiated under 13 years of age, and must have the full consent of her parents or guardians, which is sufficient if they are no Masons or Masonesses; if an unmarried lady is of age and none that can controul her, there is nothing requisite but her own desire of being initiated; the same is observed with a widow, but none can be conducted but by a Mason or Masoness, as the door of even the first apartment cannot be opened to the Profane.

PREPARATION FOR A RECEPTION.

The princess Candidate waits in the antechamber, a room adjacent, where two brethren are left to keep her company until the brother introductor arrives, and hands her in the preparing room, where he alone remains with her;—he then places her in an elbow chair, and toes a handkerchief over her eyes, and after about a minutes silence, he addresses her thus:

Madam, give me your hand that I may conduct you to the place of your destination, where you desire to arrive. He then leads her to the door of the Lodge, and tells her to knock 5 times with her hand at the door. As soon as the door is opened and she enters, all the brethren and sisters without rising clap their hands on their aprons as hard as they can. Then the brother inspector advances to her, and takes her by her other hand, and then asks her name and age, and what she intends to do in her present situation, she answers that she desires that she might be initiated in the mysteries of masonry and that she may be admitted in the degree of Entered Apprentice, upon which the Grand Mrs. Says: *admit her for she is my particular friend* (although she may not be acquainted with her.

The brothers Inspector and Introductor conduct her to an Elbow chair, which is placed for her Preception, between the brother Insceptor and sister Inspectrix when all the brothers and sisters clap their hands as before; when the grand Mr. holds the following discourse to that purpose.

DISCOURSE BY THE GRAND MASTER:

Madam, we are inclined to believe that curiosity is not the motive that has engaged you to advance to the step you are now making, but that the favourable ideas you have conceived of masonry has been the sole object of your wishes, and the ardent desire, of being admitted by us.

Before I can divulge to you, madam, our mysteries, I am bound to acquaint you with the grandeur the laudable motives and the difficult aim which none can arrive at but masons. the object of masonry is, to arrive to the highest degree of perfection, our labour and sole intentions are, to build in our hearts the Temple of Virtue, where it ought without cessation to be admired, revered and respected, what enables us to destroy those edifices that are by corrupted nature, continually erected to falsehood, deceit, revenge, treachery and numberless their vices, which human nature are inclined to fall into. You may now madam form a small idea of the duties of masons and masonesses to what you are now about engaging yourself. We are fully persuaded Madam, that it will not be a difficult matter for you to fulfill the engagements you are now about contracting, which will strictly unite you to Us. It is necessary before we proceed to your initiation to acquaint you madam, that there is nothing undertaken here that is contrary to the Laws of the state. Religion or morality which I now declare to you by the truth which governs our Lodges. Thus madam by these sentiments, I expect you will declare yourself; Do you still persist in the desire of being initiated into masonry, and do you think that you have courage to undergo the same trial, which all our sisters have done, answer me? After she has given her answer, all the brethren and sisters clap their hands on their aprons together, and then keep a profound silence together. The Mr. then proceeds; Bro. Inspector. Let this lady travel; who takes her by the right hand, raises her from her seat, acquaints her she must salute the Mr. the rest of the company with a respectful courtesy, which is returned by the whole Lodge, with one blow of their aprons, then the brother Inspector travels with her once round the Lodge and when she is returned to her seat again, pays her compliment as before, which is returned also as before. Then the Master addresses himself to her saying, Madam, do you find yourself fatigued, if she replies that she is wary, he returns for answer, Well madam not to abuse of your patience and constancy, the Lodge has consented but one more tour, on which she is led once more round and makes the compliment as before &c. and then every one observes the strictest silence. Then the Grand Master says, *my Brethren and Sisters, are you not struck with the modesty, confidence and constancy of this Lady, do you consent that the light be shown her.* This is answered by the clapping of their hands to their aprons. Then the Mr. says, Brother Inspector, show her the light, and show her to walk as a masoness. Then the handkerchief is taken off her eyes, as soon as she sees the light, they all clap their hands as before, as a token of applause, while she is making a deys courtesy, then the Mr. tells, her come again, come and contract your Obligation, kneel with one knee on that stool, give me your right hand, and give the other to the Grand-misstres; when one of the Brethren [representing the destroying angel] who has a naked sword, which he holds across her arm, in such a manner, as not to touch

INTRODUCTION.

her, and in this position she remains while she repast the Obligation. In the mean time the lamps are extinguished and the light in the sconces and flustres are lighted, which are prepared for that purpose.

OBLIGATION.

"*I A. B. Do in the presence of this worshipful Lodge and assembly, solemnly promise and swear, that I will hail and conceal, faithfully and inviolably keep in my heart, the secrets of Masons and Masonesses, which at this time or hereafter shall be revealed unto me, under the penalty of being disgraced and if I should fail in this my Obligation, I consent that I may be destroyed, by the sword of the destroying Angel. May I thus be guided by a zealous love of virtue, and may that ardour purify my heart, and direct my steps in the most secret paths to perfection.*"

As soon as this Obligation is finished, the chair is immediately taken from her, and she is raised by both the Grand Mr. and Mrs. And they present her the apron, each of them holding one of the strings in their hands, which the Br. Inspector ties behind her, then the guards return to their respective places where they remain standing—when the Gr. Mrs. Presents her two pairs of Gloves, one pair for men: the other for women—then the Grand Master addresses he thus:

You now find yourself my dear sister clothed in the badge of a masoness, the vestment that kings, queens, princes and princesses have preferred to the scepter and crown and have quitted their royal robes for, and accepted the titles of brothers and sisters, in order to satisfy the equality which ought to reign among those who practice virtue.

The Gloves which are for your own use, represent to You the modesty that reigns in our own lodges and those for the men's use, shew you that we are not averse to a tender engagement of the heart, and that we approve and applaud that impulse of tenderness, that endears an amiable lady, to a man of honour, provided the views are legitimate. For this my dear sister you'll make a present of these gloves to him You esteem most worthy of that favour.

He then gives her the mallet and the grand mistress the trowel, and he says: by these and the powers we are invested with, we now make you a free masoness—You now become a sister to kings and queens and are equal to princes and princesses and inferior to none—so saying he kisses her forehead, which the Grand Mistress does also: the Master continues saying, my dear sister, it is in this manner that masons and masonesses salute each other to shew the veneration due to those who have given proofs of virtue, without which no admittance can be obtained in our lodge.

WORD.—The word is FIX or FIAX—and assyrian word which signifies in English 'ACADEMY' or "SCHOOL OF VIRTUE."

LIGHT ON MASONRY.

Sign.—The sign is to slide Your thumb in a serpentine manner from your chest to your waist, as if you were lacing your stays, which is an allusion to the mysterious ladder of Jacob, and denotes the union between perfect virtue, and the just and upright symbols of faith and mercy.

Token.—You give each other reciprocally the right hand and both knock three times with the thumb on the first joint of the forefinger.

The Steps are five made in a square, go my dear sister and give the sign, token and word and salute to the Grand Mistress, after which the Brother Inspector gives her his hand and introduces her to the Brethren and Sisters, who stand in their respective places, after which he hands her to the elbow chair between his and the sister Inspectrix, and when she is seated he receives the sign, token and word with the salute, and after that all the brethren in their turn (one by one) approach her to repeat the same ceremony, which must be performed with noble and graceful air, without her rising from her seat, after which the grand master gives the following instructive history.

Adam the first of masons formed a Lodge with his children—to whom he communicated the knowledge he had received from God. CAIN who succeeded him in the office of Grand M. fixed his settlement at the eastern regions of Eden, where he signalized himself in building a city which he named. Enoch, the son of Gerelds, Virtues were so great, that he merited to be from the communication of men, and restored to the terrestrial Paradise—The spirit of prophecy, which he was endowed with, enabled him to foresee that it would not be long before the wrath of God be manifested by the destruction of the world, he had that the Sciences should be lost, made him erect two large columns, the one of brick and the other of stone, on which he wrote in hierogliphics the Principles and Rules, the one of brick was ruined by the Delude, and of Stone remained to preserve to posterity, that was engraved on it, and his prudent precaution met with the desired effect. *Curon* assures us that this column still remained in *Syria*, at the time of Emperor Vespasian. Men having till this time lived in the worship of the true God, and followed the principle of Virtue, but those that came after, gave themselves up to all manner of Vice.—God in his anger resolved to extirpate this abandoned race, and Noah was the only one who found grace before him. God communicated to him, that he intended to send an Inundation to destroy the earth, and ordered them to build an ARK of five stories high, for his and his family's safety, of which he gave him the plan; it was built of Cedar, a wood by nature, the least liable to decay. Noah having finished the ark, he and his children entered it five days before the *Deluge* began, and by that means they were all preserved, as well as all the Traditions and Secrets communicated by God, and in particular, those concerning Masonry.—When Noah and his family went out of the Ar–, he and his descendants remained for a considerable time, on the highest parts of the mountains, fearing

INTRODUCTION.

a second Deluge might ensue; time after time however they ventured to descend to the plains where they formed different settlements. At this time there was but one language used among men, but still they became rebellious to the orders, and commandments of God; in the apprehensions they had of Gods Vengeance, coming over them—*Nimrod* as valiant, as audacious and the most skilful Mason in his time, assured and offered him his protection, even against God himself, if he should threaten the earth a second time, with a Deluge, and for that purpose he would build a Tower which should reach the heavens—The disappointment this undertaking met with, is known to every body; God having confounded their language, which obliged them to abandon the work and disperse themselves; after this the Grand Mr. explains the draft of the Lodge in the following manner:

EXPLANATION OF THE DRAFT.

My dear sister, You see before you the ARK of *Noah*, tossed about by the waves, which shews you the human mind in agitation by the motions of the passions—Jacobs ladder represents to us the road to happiness by the union of the tow principal virtues, and is represented in the two strait posts, or supporters of the ladder; the one signifies the love of God, and the other the love to our neighbors, (two most excellent precepts) they both together support the different degrees, by which one arrives at happiness, that is the practice of every moral virtue originally springs from the two first principles; the tower of Babel represents to us the variety and ostentation of the children of the earh, which subduing we cannot be warranted as practitioners of the masonick laws the scope of which ism to shew the homage due to the great architect of the Universe, and to dedicate in our hearts a temple to his glory, to love our neighbors as we do ourselves, and to look upon our brethren and sisters as our equals, without distinguishing the state of honor, birth and riches. The masonic tools and utensils are explained to some moral scene, or other according to the capacity of the orator. The instructions my dear sister which the worshipful Mr. will give you before this lodge is closed, will perfectly instruct you in the first degree of masonry, which we now with great joy and pleasure have conferred on you—then the orator makes her compliment and retires to his seat, then the Master resumes the following

DISCOURSE.

My dear sister nothing can be more convincing proof how much our society is devoted to esteem, and how great a confidence they place in you by the entrance in our lodge which we this day have granted you; but that you may be sensible of the price, of that sacrifice, we make of divulging our mysteries to you it is very proper you should conceive the beauties of the secrets we communicated to you, after which you will be sensible of the indispensable necessity of your subjecting yourself to secrecy.—Thus, vulgar always unjust, unpolished and malicious, in their censures, have constantly formed the most disadvantageous ideas of us, and have indefatigably laboured to prepossess the Fair Sex against our assembly and lodge by the most opprobrious aspersions, founded only on the most abominable calumnies—for in short my dear sister, what judgment can an ignorant people form of us, as they are distant from the real light of truth, it is not in their power to be sensible of those benefits that accrue from a perfect knowledge of it. My dear sister, it is us alone that are acquainted with that bright luminary of truth, it is us only that lighten it, in order to follow it, and us also alone to communicate it to you. Oh! Ye Sex, most amiable, who ought to share it with us, and who have for time past been exiled from our lodge.

We have always regretted the loss your absence has occasioned, but having considered that there still remain among your Sex a disposition of a Delilah, a Judith and the accounts of which History furnishes us with, and who have been the cause of your Sexes banishment from our Lodge as a scrupulous thought continued unsatisfied, which is at last conquered by resolution.—In short it is time to recal into our society, such Sisters, who are as discreet as they are amiable, and who are the properest to afford comfort and delight.

It is here you find the Temple of Virtue, which is as ancient as Virtue itself, which, notwithstanding is neglected by the wortd in general, tho' respected by some as much as ever, and the path no less certain, and the only that guides us to morality.—It would be endless my dear Sister for me to undertake giving you a detail of the true pleasure and full extent of our happiness.—True reflection will on one side convince you of it, and practice on the other side will teach you by the good Laws that we are subject to.—You departed from darkness, in order to receive the liveliest and most glorious illuminary—it is that which will light the actions of your life, and guard you from striking on those rocks, where virtue is so liable to be cast away—My dear Sister, You now see the precious treasure we have entrusted you with, it is with joy and pleasure we make you a partaker—Enjoy them Dear Sister, and remember the more they are in danger, the more you ought to defend them.—The secrets of our mysteries, you ought strictly to observe, and maintain them inviolable—may heaven be your guide that you may never forget that sacred Obligation you have here deposited, and let us with pleasure perceive the progress You make in the royal Art, for which reason we are determined to communicate to you a still sublimer degree. Be constant and strict in fulfilling the duties in masonry, as you are amiable and worthy of being beloved—Then all the Brethren and Sisters shew the token of applause, which is answered by the Sisters alone who rise and clap their hands. After this they enter

INTRODUCTION.

upon business to which concerns Masonry in general, or this Lodge in particular, and what may be interesting to the Brethren and Sisters present, or those absent for their benefit or promotion.

GENERAL LECTURE.

N.B. The questions made and answered should be done in the most polite manner and must be preceded with my Dear Sister, or Sister such a one, not using the appellation of Madam or Miss, during the continuation of the Lodge, in default of which they are liable to pay a fine, which is used for the use of the Lodge, or the poor, and must be paid immediately to the Mr. Treasurer, whatever the fines the Sisters are judged to pay, according to the laws of the Lodge, the Brothers are always double as much if they transgress.

LECTURE.

Q. Are you a Masoness's Sister?
A. I believe so.
Q. If you believe, why don't you say you are?
A. Because it is the weakness of my sex, to be doubtful, and that the knowledge of an Entered Apprentice cannot extend far.
Q. Where were you made Masoness?
A. In a place inaccessible to Cowans.
Q. What did you perceive in your entrance into the Lodge?
A. Nothing that I could comprehend.
Q. Are you contented with your fate?
A. All my Brethren and Sisters are convinced that I am.
Q. How do they know that?
A. By the eagerness of being initiated, and by the sufferings I have undergone.
Q. Do you promise to keep our secrets inviolable?
A. That which I deserve shall be my security.
Q. What made you an entered apprentice
A. The Mallet and the Trowel and my virtue.
Q. Of what use is the Mallet?
A. To subdue the obstinacy of my mind, and govern my passions by the example of my Brethren and Sisters.
Q. Of what use is the Trowel?
A. To sir up and firmly fix in my heart the principles of honour and virtue and employ it so that I may be able to erect an edifice worthy of the noblest society.
Q. How does a Masoness travel?

LIGHT ON MASONRY.

A. For the ARK of NOAH.
Q. What does the Ark of Noah represent.
A. The human heart in agitation by the passions, as the Ark was by the waters of the Deluge.
Q. Who was the pilot of the Ark?
A. Noah the Grand Master of Masons in his days.
Q. Who is the pilot of your soul?
A. Reason.
Q. What is the standard?
A. Masonry.
Q. What is the Cargo?
A. Morality.
Q. What does the Tower of Babel represent?
A. Ostentation of the folly of mankind.
Q. What suppresses the Ostentation?
A. The wise laws of Masonry.
Q. Give me the sign?
A. She gives it.
Q. Give me the word?
A. Fix, feix or flax.
Q. What does this word signify?
A. Academy, or school of Virtue; Which is masonry.
Q. What is the signification of that sign?
A. The represnntion of Jacob's ladder.
Q. And where does that carry you?
A. To felicity, which we arrive at with strict Union of Virtue.
Q. What are the duties of a masoness?
A. To obey, to work and keep a secret.

TO CLOSE THE LODGE.

Q. What are the virtues of a Mason and Masoness?
A. Obedience, Labour and Secrecy.
Q. Sister Trustee, what has been done in this Lodge?
A. We have obeyed, we have worked very hard and there remains only to conceal.

Gr. Mr. as we have been hard at work, it is time that we should rest ourselves. I exhort You my Brethren and Sisters to conceal and to preserve inviolable the secrets of Masons and Masonesses. He then addresses himself to the Grand Mr. and says Worshipful Grand Mrs. I crave your assistance in closing this Lodge, he

INTRODUCTION.

then knocks five times with his mallet, and the Grand Mrs. As many times with her trowel, the Brethren and Sisters then all rise and give the sign of this Degree; then the Mr. says, my Brethren and Sisters, this Lodge is closed, the Grand Mrs. Repeats the same, and the Lodge is closed.

DEGREE OF A FELLOW CRAFT.

In the south of the Lodge must be a table covered with a cloth in the form of an Altar, on which is a trough with mortar and the sacred fruit on a dish, and two candlesticks adorned with wax tapers.

At the lower end or west of the Lodge, mnst be a stove, on which is to be an earthen vessel with burning spirits and salt, the Brethren and Sisters form themselves in a circle at the upper end of the Lodge, the R.W. Mr. places himself in the middle, and a Br. opposite to him, holding an Olive Branch.

All the Brothers and Sisters are covered with a white veil and the circumference of the face with a black ribbon, the second Senr. W. wearing black gloves and drawn swords in their hands.

The Br. Introductor (who is chosen amongst the most sedate and skilful) goes to conduct the Apprentice in a preparing room, and asks her is she will consent to snbmit to all those trials which are required for her to undergo, he takes off her right rufle and one of her ear-rings, which he returns to her again, and she puts them on again herself, after which she is hood-wink'd and in this manner she is introduced into the Lodge, leading her twice round and then fixing her back against the Globe of death, or burning spirits, her face towards the W. Mr.—

The Brother Introductor leaves her for a moment and approaching the W. Master telling him this is the Sister which is desirous of being made a fellow Craft, and consents to submit to the necessary trials; See, here is her garter she has given one as a pledge; The W. Mr. asks her is this be true, and forwarns her that by discovering the least dread or feebleness might be a sufficient bar against her gaining admittance—if she is resolved, the Worsh. Mr. orders the Brother Inspector and depositor to let her make the first trial—the Brother Inspector then takes her by the hand and turns her face towards the Globe of Death—the W. Mr. tells the Brother that holds her to shew her all the horrors in his power—the Brother Inspector then takes off the cloth from her eyes, and at that time all the Bretheren clap once on their right knees crying *Eve*, to which the W. Mr. orders the Brother Inspector to let her pass through the trial of the fire of death to life—in consequence of which he turns her towards the Master, and tells her, advance to the stove where the spirits are burning—the R.W. then says, it is sufficient, let her come to me (begining the steps with the right foot, when she is arrived to the Worsh. Mr. he makes her kneel, and then asks her, if she has always faithfully observed the first Obligation, and if she is steadfastly and firmly resolved, to keep inviolable those new secrets, which she will be instructed with, after her answer the Worsh. Mr. makes her repeat the following

OBLIGATION.

"I, A. B. Do in the presence of this venerable assembly promise and oblige myself under the penalties of my former obligation, never to reveal the secrets of a fellow craft, always to retain an effection for my Brethren and Sisters, to protect and succor them on all occasion if in my power, and if they want my assistance, and I promise never to taste the kernel of that apple which may have a similitude to the bud or seed of the forbidden fruit. I further more promise that I will this night of my reception sleep with the garter of the order I now receive, and that I never will these mysteries to any Cowan, or any below this degree, thus I say, as God be my aid."

As soon as this Obligation is taken, the burning spirits are extinguished, and the candles are lighted, the Brother and Sisters clap their hands on their left knees as before, crying EVE, to which the Mr. answers, fear not my brethren the candidate still remaining on her knees—then the Mr. orders the brother depositor to fetch the true and secret fruit, and then bids her rise, telling her the security of Masons still requires this precaution, then places the trowel in the mortar, and passing across her mouth, repeating the same several times, and at last placing it on her lips, says: this is the signal of discretion which I now apply to you, and given her the fruit, receive and maintain the tree in the middle of the garden, which when you have tasted will render you equal to us, in distinguishing the good from the evil—She then eats of the fruit and all the Brethren say, Vivat, Vivat, upon which the W. Mr. goes and gives her the garters of the order, of which he makes her a present—after that she retires in order to put it on, then she is clothed as the Brethren with a Veil and all wish her joy.

She is then instructed by which the mysteries of what she has heard and seen is explained in the following manner.

The approach of death was visible to the state of man after the fall, and the imprudence of your Sex has been the cause of your ruin;—Notwithstanding the day of vengeance is to be succeeded by a day of mercy; which is represented to you by the favour conferred, in introducing you into the dwellings of fidelity, to which you ought to compare the assembly of your Brethren and Sisters here present, among whom you are now admitted and admired, you are come to this as to the terrestrial Paradise, where the nourishment we make use of should be considered as received from the tree of life, and the science of masonry. The picture of draft of the Lodge represents the garden of the terrestrial Paradise.

INTRODUCTION.

THE FIGURES OF ADAM AND EVE.

The tree of knowledge of good and evil, and the serpent twisted round it, sign is: To put the little finger of your right hand to the right ear; and the left hand holding the wrist of the right hand. This sign is answered by applying the 2d and 3d fingers of the left hand to the lips, and the thumb under the chin. The first word is *Belba*, and signifies tower of confusion. The second word is *lamma sabuctami*, which signifies, Lord. I sin on no other account than, because thou hast forsaken me.

There is no token in this Degree.

LECTURE.

Q. Are you a fellew Craft?
A. Give me an apple and you will be able to judge.
Q. How became you a fellow craft?
A. By a fruit and ligament.
Q. What doth the fruit signify?
A. The utility my heart felt of the knowledge of Masonry.
Q. What signifies the ligament?
A. The force of friendship; founded on virtue alone.
Q. What was applied to you on your reception?
A. The seal of masonry.
Q. Why are the fellow crafts forbid to eat the kernel of apples?
A. Because the kernel is the bud and sweet of the forbidden fruit.
Q. What doth the name of fellow craft signify?
A. Peace and concord established among the Brethren by the destruction of the Tower of Babel.
Q. What is the state of Masonry?
A. To be happy.
Q. How do you attain to this happiness?
A. By relief of the tree in the centre of the garden.
Q. Where is that planted?
A. In the garden of Eden or in the garden delightfully besprinkled with flowers.

End of the Lecture.

This fellow Craft's Lodge is opened and closed the same as the entered Apprentice Lodge.

LIGHT ON MASONRY.

THE THIRD DEGREE.

The draft of he Lodge represents:

In the upper part of the Lodge is seen a rainbow of a semicircular figure, nnder which is an altar, whereon is a billet of wood, and on that wood a lamb, consuming by fire from heaven, as the sacrifice which Abraham intended to make of his son Isaac.

In the four corners of the Lodge are placed four figures, representing the four parts of the world, each of them their different attributes.

At the left side is the Ark of Noah resting on a mountains and a Dove entering the ARK with an olive branch in it, bill.

At the right side of the tower of Babel, by the side of which is a trough, a rule and a hammer.

Below at the left is the ladder of Jacob, with angels mounting and descending it, while he is asleep.

Below at the right is a city consuming by fire from heaven, and the wife of LOT represented in the form of a salt pillar facing the city in flames.

Below that in the middle is a well or pit in which Joseph appears—and above said well is seen the sun and moon with eleven stars.

All these above mentioned paintings must be done upon a cloth or board, under which must be his a ladder chalked of 7 steps 8 or 9 inches asonder.

On the right side of the master of the lodge board must be placed 7 candles, and on the left side six, at equal distance according to the length of the board, and no other candles to appear, except two on the table that represents the working place of the Masons, on which must be also a stone made of tin.

TO OPEN THE LODGE.

Q. (By the R.W. Mr.) What are the duties of a Mrs. Masoness?

A. (By the Inspr.) To love, protect and releive the Brethren and Sisters.

Then the W. Mr. says, let us be affectionate, let us mutually protect and succour each other as far as lays in our power.—This Lodge is open.

FORM OF INITIATION.

The candidate of fellow craft must remain in a separate room, and when every thing is ready, the brother Introductor, conducts her to the door of the ledge, on which he knocks five times, having previously mad her some pathetic discourse, concerning the dignity she is now about entering into, and that nothing but merit can recommend her.

INTRODUCTION.

When she enters they make her walk once round the Lodge (being hoodwinked before she enters) and she is placed at the foot of the Ladder under the Lodge board or cloth the brothers and sisters observing a profound silence for some time, after which the W. Mr. questions her in the principal parts of the preceeding degrees, and after she has answered to these questions, he tells the brother Warden depositor: draw that veil which hides the sanctuary from our Sister, and take the cloth from her eyes—then he observes and admonishes her with what perseverance she ought to approach the Altar, then her orders her to take off her shoes and travel about the Lodge board on her stockings and then she kneels before the Altar, on which she lays her right hand in order to take her observation mean while, the Brother Insp. or Depostior, holds a naked sword close to her neck, when she repeats the following

OBLGATION:

"I A. B. Promise and swear at this venerable Altar, and by the sacrifices of Noah, Abraham, and of Jacob, never to reveal any of the secrets of Masons and Masonry, and never even to explain unto any entered apprentice or fellow craft above their degrees, or what I know of the mysterious Ladder, the Ark of Providence and the Tower of Babel, I promise to be affectionate to all my brothers and sisters, and to protect and succour them on all occasions, when I have it in my power—all this I promise on my word of honour: and consent (should I be capable of failing in this my obligation) to incur shame contempt and infamy, which all good and free Masons have reserved for perjuries—as God be my aid."

As soon as she has taken this Obligation, the Inspector withdraws the sword from her neck, and she retires to put on her shoes. Then the W. Mr. orders the Brother Inspector to conduct her to the place for working; and to teach her how to work—then the brother Inspector makes her hold the chisel in her left hand and mallet in her right hand, and bids her to strike 5 knocks with the mallet on the head of the chisel, which is applied to the edge of the stone, immediately after he gives her another mallet, which he tells her to use in the same manner as before, striking with that also five times, after which the Wr. Mr. enquires of the Inspector, what production has the sister to shew from her labour? the Brother Inspector looks at the stone and answers the Wr. Mr. that the sister has produced a heart.—Then the Wr. Mr. explains to the sister that the Art of Masons consists in transforming mankind, and renders the hardest and most cruel hearts docile, soft, human, and civilised after which he bids her mount the ladder as a Mistress Masoness—she places her right foot horizontal mounting the first step, the left foot perpendicular on the 2d steps, then brings up the right foot to the left in a paralel line—then advances the left foot first in a horizontal manner on the 3d step and the right in a perpendicular manner on the 4th step, then moves the left foot on the side of the right in a paralell line, and continue thus unto the top.

When she comes to the last step the Wr. Mr. asks the Brother Inspector where the sister is arrived to, he answers to the summit of felicity the Wr. Mr. then says: Let the sister come to me, that I may reward her for her labour—when the Brother Inspector conducts her to the master, who gives her a trowel of gold, which denotes the Mistress, and this trowel is worn by Mr. Masonnesses round the neck to a blue ribbon when in the Lodge, but otherwise used as a jewel to a watch—then the Wrs. Mr. desires her to be seated at is side, and addresses her thus:

DISCOURSE BY THE WORSH'L MASTER.

You find yourself at last my dear Sister arrived at the door of the Temple of Truth, ridiculous prejudices and gross errors withheld you from it, while you remained ignorant of our mysteries. This began to disappear when you made the first step towards the path of virtue—Let then the object of your happiness never be neglected—it is in the bosom of truth that we enlarge our felicity, and make us envied among the envidious, for tranquility follows us in our troubles and nothing disturbs the sweetness of that amiable delightfulness, which reigns among us without cessation. We take virtue for our guide in all our actions, and never go astray from that road which leads to our happiness, by which supremacy we are formed to withstand the check of conscience, and taste the charms and sweetness thereof.—

The Wr. Mr. then proceeds to the history of *Lot,*

Lot, the son of Haram, the Nephew to Abraham chose Sodom (being a beautiful country) for the place of his abode—after eight years residence there, King *Cader Lahomer*, and his Allies having attracted the inhabitants of Sodom, and the neighboring cities had put them to flight, pillaged *Sodom* and carried numbers captives, and among the rest, *Lot* the nephew of Abraham.

Abraham being informed of this, collected and selected out of his servants three hundred resolute and well armed men, pursued the confederate Kings, and overtook them at the head of Jordon where he defeated them, and put them to flight—when he recovered the booty they had made, and brought back the captives, in the number of which Lot made one.

Some years after that the crimes of the Sodomite and four neighboring cities being arrived to the highest pitch—God sent three Angels, passing by the dwelling of Abraham—this patriarch had the happiness of entertaining them in his tent—and then he escorted them to Sodom, one of them disclosed the purport of this journey—Abraham dreading the danger his Nephew was exposed to, asked him if God mixed the innocent among the guilty, to share the destruction of the

INTRODUCTION.

City? and if he will suffer them to perish suppose thee are seventy righteous and just to be found? the Angel answered him and said, if there be but *ten* just and good to be found, Sodom will not be destroyed.

Abraham returned with that confidence that at least that small number of just would be found in so large a city, among which he did not doubt his Nephew was enclined,

The Angels entered the city in the evening and placed themselves in the public market. Lot knowing that strangers were there, made towards them, and entreated them much to enter his habitation, they entered there, and provided them refreshments—but before they retired to repose themselves, all the inhabitants assembled to besiege the house of Lot, and told him, that they would see those men, who lately had entered his house, and know who they were. Lot went forth and prayed them that they would not commit so abominable an outrage, signifying he had still two virgin daughter, which he rather would deliver unto them, and do with them as they pleased and thought proper, provided they would not insult his guests, who had entered his house as a place of security, and then bid them withdraw—but they answered him, you that arrived as a stranger, do you pretend to act as our Judge? You, yourself shall therefore be treated by us with violence and when they ere on a point of breaking open the door, two of the Angels held forth their hands to *Lot* and made him retire in the house, and then struck those that were about to commit the outrage with blindness, so, that they could not find the door.

The angels then bit lot, make ready and depart from the city with all those that belonged to him, saying, we are commanded to lay it in ashes, for its sins are gone up even before the Lord, and he has sent us to destroy it. *Lot* went and acquainted his sons in low who had married his danghters—saying they must hastily depart the city of *Sodom*, for that the Lord intended to destroy it, but they treated his advice as proceeding from an idle delirium.

The morning following the Angels lead Lot, his wife and daughters out of the city, having by some means got them from their homes, for they were loth to leave it—the Angles then told them to save themselves with all expedition, and never to look back till they gained the mountain for fear they should be envoloped in the misery of the rest.

Lot prayed that the Angels would give him leave to retire to *Zoar*, which was one of the cities condemned to perish by fire, the Angels condescended for his sake and permitted him to seek refuge there—but the wife of *Lot* having looked back (being surprised at the flames and fire that fell from the heavens which overwhelmed the Territories of Sodom) was instantly changed into a pillar of salt.

Lot having seen the miseries of Sodom and it consequences of the neighboring cities, dreaded to remain any longer at *Zoar* in consequence of which he departed from thence and retired to a cave where he took several lodgings to himself and his daughters—the later imaging the world would be at an end, were they not to procure new Inhabitants, they intoxicated their father, and the eldest slept with him without his perceiving it, and she conceived and got a son, which she named *Noah*, and he become the father of the Moabite, the youngest approached herself to him the second night, after having got him also in liquor, and she conceived and got *Amon* of him derived the Amonites.

It is to be seen in the commentaries of — Geneva the 29th chapter, to learn what judgement ought to be formed of the conduct of Lot, his daughters, and his wife.

St. Peter informs us that God delivered *Lot* the righteous from the oppression and vexation of *Sodom*.

Some pretend to say, that *Belbhegor* worshipped by the *Moabites* was no other but *Lot* himself—*Belbhegor* signifies *the naked God and without shame*, which answers to what is said that passed between him and his daughters.

The wife of *Lot* being mentioned among the Rabby's by the name of *Hedith* which signifies a testimony, as if they would say or remark that this woman was an example or witness how God chastised the faithless and imprudence of those who take no notice of his threats, nor believe in his promises.

The greatest part of those who have travelled through Palestine, inform us that they have been shewn the wife of *Lot*, that is to say the rocks in which she was transformed.

THE LECTURE.

Q. Are you an Apprentice.

A. I believe I am.

Q. Are you a fellow craft?

A. Give me an apple and you will be a judge.

Q. Are you a Mistress Mason?

A. I know how to mount the Ladder.

Q. Of what is that ladder composed?

A. Of two upright posts, and the steps.

Q. What are these steps?

A. The different virtues which are grafted one after the other.

Q. How do you reach the first?

A. Through candour, a proper virtue to render a generous soul susceptable of good impressions for Masons and Masonesses.

Q. How do you mount the second?

A. By a lenity and mildness which I show towards my equals, but my brethren in particular.

Q. How do you get to the third step?

INTRODUCTION.

A. By truth, the darling infant of heaven, on of the rays of the sun that great luminary of the Universe.

Q. Which is the great truth?

A. God alone.

Q. How do you arrive to the fourth step?

A. By temperance, which teaches me to curb my passions, and to fly from all excess and irregularities.

Q. Are you able to mount the fifth step?

A. Yes, worshipful, I hope to mount it by practising discretion and secrecy in all the secrets of masonry and of all that in which I may be instructed which concerns masonry.

Q. Which is the last step?

A. Love and charity, which is thus divided: The love of God, and the love towards my neighbors.

Q. Are there no intermediaries?

A. Yes R. Worshipful.

Q. How many?

A. Numberless.

Q. For whom is the knowledge thereof reserved.

A. To all good Masons and Masonesses, who have reached the first step, and have learnt to practice virtue pointed out to them, and who merit by their zeal and discretion to penetrate further in the road of happiness.

Q. Where doth the base of the ladder rest?

A. On the foot stool of the Lord, namely the earth.

Q. How far doth the summit extend?

A. By the justness of his creatures, the source of felicity.

Q. Which was the firtt Mason that merited to be acquainted with this ladder?

A. The Patriarch Jacob, at the time of his mysterious dream.

Q. Do you know the Ark, its property and consrtuction?

A. Yes R. Wrs. I am a Masoness, I work in the Ark, and come to dwell there in order to correct the frailties of human nature.

Q. Who constructed it?

A. *Noah*, the restorer of the new world.

Q. Why did he construct it?

A. To save himself and family from the Universal Deluge, as masons come to the lodge, to withdraw from the inundations of vices, which corrupt nature.

Q. How long was Noah in constructing this Ark?

A. One hundred years to complete it, which teaches me that it requires a long time and great labour to attain to perfect wisdom.

Q. How was it built?

LIGHT ON MASONRY.

A. By command and plan given by the great Architect of the Universe, and by which Masons strive to practise virtue, which is the only means of being delivered from the general corruption, that the tracke of the blackest colour never should ruin their innosence.

Q. How did the Ark receive light?

A. By an only window.

Q. Of what form were the planks?

A. All on an even form and well raised, which shews the perfect equality that reigns among us, in order to extirpate all self love and false prejudices, the destroyers of happiness.

Q. What was the Ark done over with?

A. With a ――― on the inside, and on the outside with a precious cement showing the friendship we possess in our Lodges to preserve the unanimity among the brethren and sisteren.

Q. What bird did Noah send first out of the Ark?

A. A Raven which did not return an unhappy simily to those unhappy Brethren who like this animal has not any other nourishment but by the corrupt allurements of their passions, and afterwards forget those innocent delights of Masonry in order to plunge themselves into the sordid voluptiousness of the age.

Q. What bird did Noah send out after the raven?

A. Two doves—the first being sent out, came back, and 7 days after he send the second, who returned with an olive branch in its bill, a true emblem of all good Masons and Masonesses who support the peace and tranquility of the Lodge.

Q. What represents the tower of Babel?

A. The ostentation of the children of the earth, which cannot be warranted, when they approve the heart which is full of humanity, and the sincerity of a good mason.

Q. Who was it that formed this presumptious project?

A. Nimrod the rebellious grand sire and tyrant of mankind.

Q. What was his reason for so doing?

A. To acquire a great name among men, and aspiring to be equal with God.

Q. What was the foundation of it?

A. Folly.

Q. What was the story?

A. A desire of rnling the Universe.

Q. What was the cement?

A. The poison of discord.

Q. How was it formed?

A. Of a spirit line which shews the knavery and circumvention of a false heart, as well as the vanity of mankind.

Q. What perfection did this monument arrive at?

INTRODUCTION.

A. It went on increasing in height, till God sent a confusion and mixture of languages among the workmen which caused them to leave the work and disperse through the Universe.

Q. What became of this ridiculous edifice?

A. It became the haunt and habitation of the unjust.

Q. What lesson can Masons take from this event?

A. They learn that, to revere the promise of being happy, to form their hopes on that alone, and not on an idle project of honours and fortune, never to build but by the plan of wisdom, and let virtue be the foundation of their edifices.

Q. What further reflections may be drawn from this?

A. That the Tower of Babel represents an ill conducted Lodge, without obedience or concord (which ought always to reign there) will fall into confusion and disregard.

Q. Are you a Mistress Masoness?

A. I know how to mount the ladder.

Q. How did you arrive to that?

A. By application, my zeal and discretion.

Q. What doth the picture of the lodge represent?

A. The sacrifice which Noah offered after he had left the *A*rk, and which was the offering of acknowledgement and gratitude—this teaches us that every true *M*ason, who had escaped from the dangers he has been exposed to, ought to acknowledge, and be thankful to the author of this being, for having supported him in them.

Q. What doth the sacrifice of *A*braham (which he is going to make of his only son) represent?

A. That one cannot be a good *M*ason if he does not conquer those passions which are contrary to the laws of Masonry.

Q. Why is Joseph in the pit represented to us in the picture of this Lodge?

A. To shew us, that if virtue is some times unknown and in obscurity, it is in order, that it may shine forth with more luster, when it comes to light, and receives its just reward.

Q. What represents the Sun, *M*oon and the eleven Stars?

A. The approaching glory of that good son and *M*ason, to whose merit his father and brethren are to render the just homage.

Q. What is further represented in said picture besides Jacob's ladder, Noah's Ark, the Tower of Babel, *A*braham's offer and Joseph's Pit, of which you have already given us the explanation?

A. There is also seen the Rainbow, the covenant of God, Sodom consumed by fire from heaven, Jacob sleeping, and Lot's wife transformed into a pillar of salt.

Q. What doth the rainbow denote?

A. The Union and harmony of *M*asons and *M*asonesses—which resembles the magnifficent colours mixed and blended, that form the Rainbow.

Q. What do we learn from the punishment of Sodom?

A. The horror which all good *M*asons ought to have for the abomniable crimes of these citizens which drew fire from the heavens on this infamous city which destroyed and consumed it. It also serves us, to strengthen our idea which we ought even to form of the corrupted soil on which it stood.

Q. What insptruction can we form or draw from the transformation of Lot's wife?

A. Obedience which is indispensable in a Lodge and that a *M*asoness ought not to vainly search into secrets, which cannot yet be communicated to her.

Q. What doth the sleep of Jacob represent?

A. The peace and tranquility, which a good *M*ason enjoys in this world, and by that tastes the state of immortality.

Q. Why are you deprived of light before you are made a *M*asonness?

A. To shew how much we resemble blindness in indiscretly arguing about *M*asonry.

Q. What is the sign of a *M*istress *M*asoness?

A. They apply the finger of the right hand promiscuously to the left eye sheet.

Q. What is their word?

A. *Avot Fair*.

Q. What is the meaning of that word?

A. The brilliant light of truth has opened my eyes?

Q. What is the token?

A. it is reciprocally to support the right thumb by the joint near the nail between your thumb and finger.

Q. Why do *M*asons apply their token to the 5 senses?

A. It learns us to make no other than good use of them, first on the nose, which shews that the most exquisite perfumes of the most receivable value is nothing to a mason—for it is virtue alone that creates the valuable odour, 2d the ears shews us that all good masons should be deaf to calumny and slander, and never urge a word to give offence to the chaste ear, the 3d on the lips shews that the banquet of the masons are less in order to gratify the appetite, than to repair the exhausted strength by their labor, the 4th on one eye, is to remind us that the external beauty which our sisters might be endued with, ought not to be so much regarded as their virtue, which renders them admirable and nearer approaching the image of the creator; the 5th of feeling, the token which we reciprocally give each other, and by which we are always reminded of our acts of peace and Union and that we always are to be ready to stretch forth a hand to succour a brother and sister in danger and necessity.

INTRODUCTION.

TO CLOSE THE LODGE.

Q. What are the duties of a *M*istress *M*asoness?
A. To love, esteem, protect and releive their brothers and sisters.

The fourth and last degree of Female Masonry,

CALLED PERFECTION.

THE PICTURE OF THE LODGE.

At the top is Joseph seen reconciling himself to his brethren—at the right hand 7 ears of corn that seem to bear plentifully—and on the other side olso 7 ears broken and meagre—Below which are several men represented with aprons on and trowels, who are working the earth on order make bricks.

*M*oses exposed in a basket floating on the river Nile, and the daughter of Pharaoh, rescuing him from the danger of the waters.

*A*t the bottom you see *M*oses and and *A*aron at the head of the Israelites, after having brought them safe over the red sea, which rises and returns on Pharao and his army, in their attempt of passing it.

On the right side of the master is a column made of tin, 5 feet high, with several holes peirced through it, and several stars dispersed all round it promiscuously, so that the light which is placed in the inside of said column might shine through it—this column represents the fiery columns which guided the Israelites in the night during their journey in the desert.

On the left of the master is another column, on which are no stars cut through as the former, and this represents the pillar that guided by day and skreened them from the Egyptians.—Both these columns are on the outside to be furnished with lamps of glass lighted—both these columns are to be encircled and crowned by the rainbow, to which are also to be pendant eleven lamps.

*A*n altar is to be placed under the rainbow and between the two columns, behind which the Wrs. *M*r. sits.

TO OPEN THE LODGE OF PERFECTION.

Q. *W*hat are the duties of perfect *M*asons?
A. To love, instruct and nourish each other in the practice of virtue.
Then the *W*orshipful *M*aster says: *This Lodge of perfection is open.*

LIGHT ON MASONRY.

FORM OF A RECEPTION.

All the brethren and sisters that are in perfection, place themselves in equal numbers on each side of the Lodge, and the moment the candidate enters on each side of the Lodge, and knees, holding a small wand in their left hand, and a sword in the right.—Before this the Candidate is left alone in the preparing room the brother introductory (who is chosen of the most serious turn and who is best instructed in the craft) goes to her when the Lodge is prepared, and after having examined her in the three preceeding degrees, asks her, if it is her ardent desire to arrive to perfection, if she answers accordingly, he briefly demonstrates to her the necessity of strictly concealing the secrets of Masonry, and in future zealously to practise virtue, which is the property peculiar to her present state—having done this he returns and fetches a metal vessel which is not transparent, this is put on a plate or dish reversed under which is put a little live bird, and round the edge of said vessel is put some fine sand about two inches high, and this he so carried to the Candidate acquainting her that it is a precious treasure, with which she is to be intrusted; giving her a strict charge from the worshipful master, who expects that she will not touch it, nor be so curious as to know what it contains. Then he leaves her to her own reflections.

After she has been let alone about two or three minutes, the brother introducter returns to her, and if she has peeped or looked under the vessel, the fine sand which surrounds it will be spread; and the bird undoubtedly flown, and finding it thus he reprimands her very severely for his imprudence, extravagant, curiosity, and the slight regard she paid to her promise—he tells her that she has rendered herself unworthy of being admitted into the sublime degree of perfection, and that she must by her fortune labour and full proof of repentance, hope of soliciting the happiness of being admitted in time, when she is not admitted, and the Lodge closed—and afterwards when a table Lodge is open, the Wrs. Mr. gives her also a severe reprimand and fines her the sum of _____ which must be immediately paid and goes to the poor.

But if the brother introductor finds by the sand that nothing has been touched, he then acquaints her that as a recompence for her discretion and patience, she shall receive the degree of perfection—he then bids her to take the treasure on the plate (after having washed her hands in perfumed water) and conducts her to the door of the Lodge, where he knocks 5 times which is the signal for her introduction, on which the Wrs. Mr. knocks also 5 times—upon which the brother inspector warden depositor &c. opens the door to the Brother Introductor, and asks him if the sister has withstood the temptation? if he answers that she has, he then receives the plate with treasure from her, carries it and places it on the table prepared for that purpose, and immediately returns to the sisters hand, whom

INTRODUCTION.

he hands in the Lodge and places her at he foot of the Lodge, her eyes not being blinded.

When she is placed, the Wrs. Master expounds in a few words concerning the dignity of this degree she is about receiving being the ultimate and last degree—how difficult it is to arrive to that degree, without having given sufficient proof of virtue, of zeal, capacity and discretion.

He then question her in the principal points of the preceeding degrees; he asks her for the sign, token and word of a Wrs. Masoness, which the brother inspector receives and and gives an acct. to the Wr. Mr. who further adds that the sister by a happy inspiration arrived to Masonry; that she has tasted of that mysterious fruit from the tree of knowledge of good and evil, that she has mounted the steps of virtue, and that she desires to enter the promised land of Liberty which flows with milk and honey.

The Wr. Mr. then orders the brother inspector to equip the sister for the voyage, and to let her cross the sea.

The brother inspector then gives her a wand in her hand (after having put the same chain that was used in the first degree round her arms) at which instant the Wr. Mr. knocks five times, a great distance between each knock, at the first knock, all the brethren and sisters rise, at the second they raise the swords in their right hands, in a perpendicular manner and line; at the third they all let the points drop down horizontal in a line; at the fourth they all raise their wands in their left hands perpendicular—and at the 5th knock, they all drop the points of their wands in a horizontal manner, crossing the swords in a diagonal manner on the wands.

As soon as this ceremony is over, the Brother Inspector leads the sister to the foot of the alter —— N. B. The 13 candles used in the degree of Mrs. Masoness are used in the same form of this degree, then the sister cand. Kneels before the Wr. Master who addresses her this: My Dear Sister, it is time you should be received from your chains, and go out of Bondage from which you now come, the Obligation you are now about entering into, requires a complete liberty, he then takes off the chain and she repeats the following Obligation:

"*I. A. B. Promise and swear before the Creator of all Beings and the searcher of the most hidden sentiments, the avenger of Vice, and before my dear brethren and sisters, never to reveal the mysteries of the degree of perfection, which I may be entrusted with, either to an etered apprentice, fellow craft, or Mr. Masoness, and to practice the virtues which shall be thought me under the penalty of being looked upon by every virtuous Mason, as a perjured and infamous Being.*"

After the sister has taken the Obligation, the Wr Mr. desires the brother Inspector to bring forth the charge and treasure, which the sister was entrusted with, in order to convince the brethren and sisters present of her fidelity, and then he bids her rise. The brother Inspector goes for the treasurer and deposits it on the altar.

The Wr. Mr. tells her, in order to begin her new and remarkable race, she must instantly turn the metal vessel, under which the treasure is deposited, as soon as she has obeyed his command the bird that was imprisoned takes its flight—the Wr. Master continues saying: Liberty is the greatest of all Blessings, and that she must patiently support herself in the several misfortunes, for sooner or later the hand of Providence will relieve us in our primitive state.

Then the Brother Inspector conducts the sister to the working place, where he bids her work like a Mrs. Masoness, and makes her further more strike five times on the heard which he takes from from a box.

The Wr. Mr. asks him what are the fruits of our Sisters labour? The Brother Inspector replies:

The first day she laboured in banishing from her, every false prejudice against Masonry.

The 2d day in obtaining strength in her Labour, and in learning the excellence of the order.

The 3d day has produced a heart which shews us, that by the art of free Masonry, the most hard, obdurate, the most cruel and severe heart can be rendered tender and compassionate.

The 4th brings forth the heart of a free Mason, who distributes benevolence among all his fellow creatures, and observes it as a duty to admonish whosoever it be of the brothers and sisters that stay away from the principles of Masonry.

Then the Wr. Mr. tells the brother inspector, hand the sister to me, that I may reward her for her labour. The sister then advances to the Worshipful, who gives her a pair of garters of blue silk, on which are embroidered two hearts in gold, and the following sentence divided among both of them.

La Vertue nour unit
Le ceil nour recompence
　　　　(in english thus)
By virtue we are united,
　By heaven we are requitted

He further more gives her a golden hammer, and a ring of gold and silver, on which is engraved the words (Le secret) the secret—the grand inspector, then teaches her the sign, token and words as will be explained hereafter in the general Lecture of the degree of the perfection of Masonry.

End of the ceremony of a reception.

INTRODUCTION.

HERE FOLLOWS THE GENERAL LECTURE OF THE LAST DEGREE.

LECTURE FOR THE PERFECTION.

Q. Are you a perfect Masoness?

A. By the assistance of the Lord I am delivered out of Bondage.

Q. What do you understand by this Bondage?

A. The captivity we are languishing under in this world represented to us by the Israelites in Egypt—every true Mason ought to consider his state in this world as a stranger languishing in slavery, and breathes only after heaven which ought to be looked upon as the true home.

Q. If you are subject to this frail world, how can you say you are free?

A. My initiation into your mysteries has opened my eyes—I have shook off the yoke of passions, reason has enlightened me, and its torch has pierced through the vail, where vice was covered by voluptuousness.

Q. How are you arrived at the summit of Masonry?

A. By the help and assistance of a brother who became my guide and brought me to the door of the Temple of Virtue, where its glory removed the darkness which covered the Universe.

Q. have you entered in this temple?

A. I have Wr. Master.

Q. How did you enter it?

A. By the vault of steel.

Q. What doth this vault signify?

A. The solidness of a vault depends on the fixing of the stones, which all meet the centrical point in the same manner every member of our order ought to work together in harmony the foundation of our strength, the Key of which is a virtuous and sincere friendship, the true charasterstick of a good Mason,

Q. Why is the vault of iron or Steel?

A. To remind us that we ought to shun the criminal pleasures of the iron age, if we would enjoy the innocent delights of the golden.

Q. How have you re-entered, when turned out of that delightful place?

A. In the Ark built by Noah, after the plan given by the Lord.

Q. To what end was the Ark built?

A. To save Noah and his family, a prophetical choice of the elected.

Q. Why did the rest of mankind not share in this benefit?

A. Because they were blinded by a false light, they divided the work of the Lord, who to punish their ostentation, left them to their hardness of heart and cast them in the abyss.

Q. where was the first Lodge held?

A. By Adam and Eve in the terrestial Paradise—during their state of innocence.

Q. When was the 2d Lodge held?

A. during the Deluge by Noah, who along with the righteous were shut up in the Ark.

Q. When was the 3d held?

A. When God in the shape of three angels visited Abraham and Sarah his wife.

Q. When was the fourth held?

A. When the angels chastised Sodom, and rested in the dwelling of Lott; and rescued the good Masons from the conflagration of that city.

Q. And when was the 5th Lodge?

A. When Joseph had found his Benjamin, and received his brethren at his table.

Q. Did he shew any distinction towards Benjamin.

A. He ordered that Benjamin should be served with five times more than his brethren, he presented him with 5 robes, having only given two to the rest—he introduced 5 of his brethren to Pharaoh, from which period it is that Masons have consecrated the number of 5 and it is become a mark of honour and distinction, the 5 robes signify the five happy degrees which the last merited.

Q. Who can hope to obtain them?

A. All Masons resembling Joseph, after having gone thro' as many dangers, withstood the alurements of voluptuousness, and preserved his purity without dreading the greatest power in the Universe.

Q. How did this Patriarch arrive to such a high degree of glory?

A. Through his Prudence and wisdom, knowing what would fall to his lot—all of us may arrive to the same happiness by following the strict path of virtue.

Q. What was he rewarded with?

A. Pharaoh give him his royal ring, in remembrance of which the Wr. Mr. gives one to the sister in perfection.

Q. What became of the Lodge in which Joseph presided

A. It became numerous and rendered continual services to the King and people of Egypt.

Q. Who distinguished himself after Joseph in the direction of this Lodge?

A. Moses, the elected of God, to shake off the chains of the chosen people.

Q. What doth the picture of the Lodge of perfection represent?

A. Joseph surrounded by all his brethren, and giving them the kiss of peace, which denotes his reconciliation to them—this teaches us that pardoning injuries is the true character of Masons, and that they ought to forget past offences and preserve a sincere and durable friendship.

Seven ears of corn bearing plentifully, and 7 broken and meager ears—the first represents the 7 steps pointed out by the mysterious ladder of Jacob viz: Candour, Meakness, temperance, Clemency, Charity, Humility and Discretion, the practice

INTRODUCTION.

of these virtues leads us with confidence to the enjoyment of plenty, tranquility and hadpiness.

The seven broken and meagre ears, are the image of the opposite vices such as Anger, Hypocricy, Lying, Pride, Vanity, Cruelty and Indiscretion, the practising of every one of them is sufficient to eradicate the luster of those virtues, and make them lose their value, and reduces us to a state of misery which the fall of our first parents has plunged us into.

The men which are seen in the picture in the dress of workmen, shews that we have our origin from Aprons, Trowels, Mallets and other utensils, which points out to us our state, and that men may draw from the captivity of the Israelitesin Egypt, the most striking lesson, in order to regulate our conduct.—We all are exiled from a short space in this perishable world, subjected to the inclemency of the seasons, and at the influence of the heavenly direction we bring with us at our birth, secret inclination to evil, which when cherished leads us into an approaching fall. The reason which providence has endowed us with, is often opposed by folly and unlimited passions, which hurry us into vice, especially when we forget our Bondage. We can never fulful the duty we owe to our State, we ought to make good use of our present time, and we shall have due credit for our labour as thus: To relieve our brethren.—Let us satisfy every one, according to our power, and by our diligence and zeal, that harmony which supports the universe then will be established.

Moses exposed on the waters of the Nile in a basket which is among the bushes, and Pharaohs daughter who comes to save him, the two first objects shews us that it depends on us, to set out in the practice of virtue.—Unhappy for us of we steer our course in that disorderly manner as the torrent which destroyes whatever it meets, we then leave in our passage the monument of horrors, instead of having our memory signalized by our good works.

The daughter of Pharaoh delivering Moses our of the river, teaches us that providence often points out ways to deliver us from our enemies, and oversets the plots they have formed for our destruction.

Moses and Aaron at the head of the Israelites after having crossed the red sea; Pharaoh and his army drowned in the flood, represents those Masons that have thrown off the yoke of passions are in the Lodge like the Israelites in the wilderness sheltered from vice, as is well represented by Pharaoh and his destroyed army.

Q. What doth the Wrs. Mr. in a Lodge of perfection represent?
A. Moses, the chief and conductor of the Israelites?
Q. Whom doth the Brother Inspector represent?
A. Aaron, assistant and companion to Moses.
Q. What do the brethren represent when in the Lodge?
A. The children of Israel, the chosen people of God.
Q. What is the sign of perfection?

A. That, which God ordered Moses to give unto the children of Israel, in order to make himself known to them, as God's deputy.

Q. And what was that?

A. it was done by putting the left hand in the bosom, and after having withdraw it you look at the bosom and hand with an expression of astonishment—then put in your hand a second time, and having withdrawn it, you look at the place and hand with a smiling countenance or expression of joy, which alludes to Moses who by command of God drew his hand from his breast full of leprosy, and returning it again in his breast, drew it out a second time as sound as it was before.

Q. When was it that Moses received this sign?

A. When God appeared to him in the burning bush, represented in the fellow crafts Lodge, by the earthen vessels blazing, around which the person initiated is to pass.

Q. How many words are there in the degree of perfection?

A. There are two.

Q. What is the first?

A. *Achirob* a hebrew word, which signifies a brother rejected.

Q. What is the second?

A. *Beth Abara* also a Hebrew word signifying a house of passage (or an Inn) to remind us that we are no more than passengers in this world, as the Israelites were only for a time in Egypt, which signifies a place of tribulation, having constantly lived in severe captivity.

Q. What is the token?

A. You present the palm of the left hand in making the sign, the brother or sister who is to answer it, stretches the left hand forward then you present it with the palm downwards, the other puts his hand underneath, and finishes the token by sliding his hand as far as the Tips of his fingers.

Q. What is the 6th step of the ladder?

A. *Clemency* which we ought to practice in case of abuses, particularly when it is from one of our brethren.

Q. Name me the 7th step?

A. *Humility* which we ought to shew in the midst of all our actions, and that whatever rank in life we may have or be raised to, this virtue will stifle our self-love aud guards against the poison of flattery.

End of the Lecture.

TO CLOSE THE LODGE.

What are the duties of perfect Masons?

A. To love, instruct and nourish each other in the practice of virtue.

INTRODUCTION.

Then the Wr. Mr. says: my dear brethren and sisters, depart in peace, love, instruct and nourish each other in the practice of virtue which in the end will lead us to everlasting happiness, AMEN, and the Lodge is closed.

The feast of Masons by adoption is celebrated on the 4th day after easter, and they should strive to be as numerous that day as possible; there is generally a gathering made, when the brothers and sisters have an opportunity to shew their charitable disposition, and such gathering is to be carried by the Wr. Mr., the Inspector and two sisters to the most worthy objects among the prisoners for debt, but there is always a preference given to a Brother, if there should be one in that situation.

This is held in remembrance of the feast which God ordered Moses to prescribe for his chosen people to remain as an everlasting monument of the captivity, which he delivered them from.

APPENDIX 5

BIBLIOGRAPHY OF THE 1829 EDITIONS OF

~ LIGHT ON MASONRY ~

The following entries supersede those in Kent L. Walgren's "A Bibliography of Pre–1851 American Scottish Rite Imprints," in *Heredom* vol. 3 (1994), 96–100, while my introduction to the present book corrects his historical information. With due respect to the memory of my very dear and late friend, I assisted him in identifying the various editions and their states, and I note that his bibliography borrowed from my research.

FIRST EDITION

Light on Masonry: a Collection of all the Most Important Documents on the Subject of Speculative Free Masonry: Embracing the Reports of the Western Committees in Relation to the Abduction of William Morgan, Proceedings of Conventions, Orations, Essays, &c &c. with all the Degrees of the Order Conferring in a Master's Lodge, As Written by Captain William Morgan; all the Degrees Conferred in the Royal Arch Chapter and Grand Encampment of Knights Templars, with the Appendant Orders, As published by the Convention of Seceding Masons, held at Le Roy, July 4th and 5th, 1828. Also a Revelation of all the Degrees Conferred in the Lodge of perfection, and Fifteen of a Still Higher Order, with Seven French Degrees: Making Forty-Eight Degrees of Free Masonry. With Notes and Critical Remarks. By Elder David Bernard, of Warsaw, Genesee Co. N.Y. Once an Intimate Secretary in the Lodge of Perfection; and Secretary of the Convention of Seceding Masons, held at Le Roy, July 4th and 5th, 1828. "For there is nothing covered that shall not be revealed, and hid that shall not be known." "And what ye hear in the ear that preach ye upon the house tops." Jesus Christ. (Utica: William Williams, Printer, Genesee–Street, 1829)

[4], x, [2] [13]–552, xxxvi pp., 2 front. plates, one a portrait, illus. 18 x 11cm.

There are three states of the first edition. First state: (a) on p. 246, the digit "2" is upside down; (b) recommendations on p. [xi]; table of contents on p. [xii], the verso [back] of recommendations; Second state: (a) digit "2" on p. 246 is right–side up; (b) recommendations and table of contents as in first state. Third state: (a) digit "2" on p. 246 corrected as in second state; recommendations, p. [xi], and table of contents, p. [xii], each have blank versos. According to p. [xi], the title and prospectus of this book were read to the Antimasonic Convention of Genesee Co. at Bethany on July 23, 1828. The introduction is dated April 1, 1828, and copyright April 13, 1828.

LIGHT ON MASONRY.

Contents: [i]: blank; [ii] engraving of W[illia]m Morgan, by V[istus]. Balch (based on a painting of F[rederick]. R. Spencer, "from an original picture of A. Cooley's"); [iii]: engraving of "The Masonic Assassination of Akirop by Joabert," by V[istus]. Balch (based on a painting of A. Cooley); [iv]: blank; [i]: title page; [ii]: copyright; [iii]–iv: preface; [v]–x: introduction; [xi]: recommendations; [xii]: table of contents; [13]–42: Entered Apprentice; 42–58: Fellow Craft; 58–86: Master Mason; 86: Test–Oath and Word; [*A Revelation of Free Masonry*]: 87–107: Mark Master; 107–14: Past Master; 114–24: Most Excellent Master; 124–44: Royal Arch; 144–54: Knight of the Red Cross; 155–66: Knight Templar and Kt. of Malta; 166–70: Knight of the Christian Mark, and Guard of the Conclave; 170–73: Knight of the Holy Sepulchre; 173–82: The Holy and Thrice Illustrious Order of the Cross; [*The Eleven Ineffable Degrees, Conferred in the Lodge of Perfection*]: 183–86, 210: Secret Master; 186–89, 210: Perfect Master; 189–91, 211: Intimate Secretary; 191–94: Provost and Judge; 194–96: Intendant of the Buildings, or Master in Israel; 196–99: Elected Knight of Nine; 199–200: Elected Grand Master, or Illustrious Elected of Fifteen; 201: Illustrious Knight or Sublime Knight Elected; 201–2: Grand Master Architect; 202–5: Knight of the Ninth Arch; 205–10: Grand Elect Perfect and Sublime Mason; 210–11: Secrets of the Lodge of Perfection; 212–20; Knight of the East and West; 220–33: Knight of the Eagle, and Sovereign Prince of Rose Croix de Heredon; 233–5: Grand Pontiff, or Sublime Scotch Masonry; 235–42: Venerable Grand Master of all Symbolic Lodges, Sover[e]ign Prince of Masonry, Master Advitiam, or Grand Pontiff; 242–3: Knight of the Royal Axe, or Hache (hachet), sometimes called Grand Patriarch; 244–5: Chief of the Tabernacle; 245–8: Prince of the Tabernacle; 248–9: Knight of the Brazen Serpent; 250–1: Prince of Mercy, or Scotch Trinitarian; 251–3: Sovereign Commander or the Temple at Jerusalem; 253–73: The Key of Masonry. Philosophical Lodge. Knight Adept of the Eagle, or Sun; 273–89: Knight of Kadosh; [*Detached Degrees*]: 290–3: Elu de Perignan; 293–7: Le Petit Architect; 298–301: Grand Architect, or Compagnon Ecossois; 302–7: Le Maitre Ecossois; 307–16: Knight of the East, or Chevalier de l'Orient; 317–22: Le Chevalier Rose Croix; 322–7: Noahite or Chevalier Prussien; [*Committee Reports, Convention Proceedings, Orations, Essays, etc.*] 328–36: Proceedings and Result of a Convention of the Saratoga Baptist Convention; 337–72: Narrative of the facts relating to abduction of William Morgan, etc.; 373–413: An address to all honest Masons. In eight numbers; 413–21: Convention of Seceding Masons: held at Le Roy; 421–30: Address to the people of the State of New York; 431–43: Proceedings of the Legislature of the State of New York, March 19, 1828; 433–52: Speech of the Hon. J. Crary in the Senate of the State of N[ew]. York, March 25, 1828, on the proposition for appointing an inquisitor in the case of William Morgan; 542–59: Proceedings of the Adjourned Convention of Seceding Masons: held at Le Roy,

INTRODUCTION.

July 4, 1828; 460–78: Oration of Herbert A. Read, Esq. Pronounced at Le Roy, July 4, 1828, to an assembly of nearly one thousand persons; 478–90: Proceedings of the Anti-Masonic N[ew]. Y[ork]. State Convention., held at Utica, Aug. 4, 5, and 6, 1828; 490–501: Speech of T. F. Talbot, Esq., in the Anti-Masonic New York State Convention, August 4, 5, and 6, 1828; 502–13: Trial of Eli Bruce and Others, for a conspiracy to kidnap and carry off Wm. Morgan; 514–27: Beriah B. Hotchkin, "A Candid Appeal to Professors of Religion, upon the Subject of Speculative Free Masonry"; 527–34: Beriah B. Hotchkin, "The Two Great Questions Answered"; 535–38: Sixteenth Degree, or Prince of Jerusalem; 538–43: Thirty-second Degree, or Prince of the Royal Secret; 543–4: Thirty-third Degree, or Sovereign Grand Inspector General; 544–5: "Circular throughout the two hemispheres"; 547–52: Henry Dana Ward, "History of Freemasonry"; *Appendix*. [i]–xxvi: Depositions of sundry persons and other documents disclosing many important particulars relative to the kidnapping of the unfortunate Morgan; with Government Proclamations, &c. &c. (in 30 Nos.).

SECOND EDITION
——— (same title and imprint)
[4], x, [4] [13]–360, [327]–534, 547–552, xxxvi pp., 2 front. plates, one a portrait, illus. 18 x 10.5cm.
This has parts of the text of both the first and third editions. The first part (through p. 360) is identical to the third edition; the second part (pp. 328–534 of the second series of pagination) is from the first edition. The table of contents is modified to reflect the above changes, including the addition of the secret work for the 4th–11th degrees which is not present in the first edition.
Contents: [i]: blank; [ii] engraving of W[illia]m Morgan, by V[istus]. Balch (based on a painting of F[rederick]. R. Spencer, "from an original picture of A. Cooley's"); [iii]: engraving of "The Masonic Assassination of Akirop by Joabert," by V[istus]. Balch (based on a painting of A. Cooley); [iv]: blank; [i]: title page; [ii]: copyright; [iii]–iv: preface; [v]–x: introduction; [xi]: table of contents; [xii]: blank; [13]–42: Entered Apprentice; 42–58: Fellow Craft; 58–86: Master Mason; 86: Test–Oath and Word; [*A Revelation of Free Masonry*]: 87–107: Mark Master; 107–14: Past Master; 114–24: Most Excellent Master; 124–44: Royal Arch; 144–54: Knight of the Red Cross; 155–66: Knight Templar and Kt. of Malta; 166–70: Knight of the Christian Mark, and Guard of the Conclave; 170–73: Knight of the Holy Sepulchre; 173–82: The Holy and Thrice Illustrious Order of the Cross; [*The Eleven Ineffable Degrees, Conferred in the Lodge of Perfection*]: 183–86, 210, 345: Secret Master; 186–89, 210, 346: Perfect Master; 189–91, 211, 346: Intimate Secretary; 191–94, 346–7: Provost and Judge; 194–96, 347: Intendant of the Buildings, or Master in Israel; 196–99, 347–8: Elected Knight of Nine; 199–200, 348–9: Elected Grand Mas-

ter, or Illustrious Elected of Fifteen; 201, 349: Illustrious Knight or Sublime Knight Elected; 201–2, 349: Grand Master Architect; 202–5, 350–1: Knight of the Ninth Arch; 205–10, 351–2: Grand Elect Perfect and Sublime Mason; 210–11: Secrets of the Lodge of Perfection; 212–6, 353: Prince of Jerusalem; 217–25, 354: Knight of the East and West; 225–38, 354: Knight of the Eagle, and Sovereign Prince of Rose Croix de Heredon; 238–40, 355: Grand Pontiff, or Sublime Scotch Masonry; 240–7, 355: Venerable Grand Master of all Symbolic Lodges, Sover[e]ign Prince of Masonry, Master Advitiam, or Grand Pontiff; 247–8, 356: Knight of the Royal Axe, or Hache (hachet), sometimes called Grand Patriarch; 249–50, 356: Chief of the Tabernacle; 250–2, 357: Prince of the Tabernacle; 253–4, 357: Knight of the Brazen Serpent; 255–6, 357–8: Prince of Mercy, or Scotch Trinitarian; 256–8, 358: Sovereign Commander or the Temple at Jerusalem; 258–78, 358: The Key of Masonry. Philosophical Lodge. Knight Adept of the Eagle, or Sun; 278–94, 359: Knight of Kadosh; 294–301, 360: Prince of the Royal Secret; [Detached Degrees]: 302–5: Elu de Perignan; 305–10: Le Petit Architect; 310–14: Grand Architect, or Compagnon Ecossois; 315–20: Le Maitre Ecossois; 320–30: Knight of the East, or Chevalier de l'Orient; 330–5: Le Chevalier Rose Croix; 335–41: Noahite or Chevalier Prussien; 431–3: Circular Throughout the Two Hemispheres; 343–4: List of Masonic Degrees Conferred in France; 345–60: Remarks on the Signs, Words, &c. of the Ineffable and Sublime Degrees; [Committee Reports, Convention Proceedings, Orations, Essays, etc.] 328–36: Proceedings and Result of a Convention of the Saratoga Baptist Convention; 337–72: Narrative of the facts relating to abduction of William Morgan, etc.; 373–413: An address to all honest Masons. In eight numbers; 413–21: Convention of Seceding Masons: held at Le Roy; 421–30: Address to the people of the State of New York; 431–43: Proceedings of the Legislature of the State of New York, March 19, 1828; 433–52: Speech of the Hon. J. Crary in the Senate of the State of N[ew]. York, March 25, 1828, on the proposition for appointing an inquisitor in the case of William Morgan; 542–59: Proceedings of the Adjourned Convention of Seceding Masons: held at Le Roy, July 4, 1828; 460–78: Oration of Herbert A. Read, Esq. Pronounced at Le Roy, July 4, 1828, to an assembly of nearly one thousand persons; 478–90: Proceedings of the Anti-Masonic N[ew]. Y[ork]. State Convention., held at Utica, Aug. 4, 5, and 6, 1828; 490–501: Speech of T. F. Talbot, Esq., in the Anti-Masonic New York State Convention, August 4, 5, and 6, 1828; 502–13: Trial of Eli Bruce and Others, for a conspiracy to kidnap and carry off Wm. Morgan; 514–27: Beriah B. Hotchkin, "A Candid Appeal to Professors of Religion, upon the Subject of Speculative Free Masonry"; 527–34: Beriah B. Hotchkin, "The Two Great Questions Answered"; 547–52: Henry Dana Ward, "History of Freemasonry"; Appendix. [i]–xxvi: Depositions of sundry persons and other documents disclosing many important particulars relative to the kidnapping of the unfortunate Morgan; with Government Proclamations, &c. &c. (in 30 Nos.).

INTRODUCTION.

THIRD EDITION
——— (same title and imprint)
[4], [xii], 13–506, 55 pp., 2 front. plates, one a portrait, illus. 17.5 x 10.5cm.

The words "Third Edition" are printed below copyright on verso of title page. This and the following entry are the smallest in physical size of any of the 1829 editions. The stated third edition differs from previous editions as follows: (a) the section on Committee Reports, etc. is rearranged to be more chronological; (b) an entry for "History of Freemasonry," p. 501, is added to the table of contents; (c) the Appendix is typeset with smaller type so that it occupies on 26 pp. as opposed to xxxvi pp.; (d) a second appendix is added: "Albany Anti Masonic N.Y. State Convention Proceedings"; (e) the three rules on the title page are separating the author from the imprint and are modified; (f) p. 421 is not misnumbered 42 as in the fourth and fifth editions.

Contents: [i]: blank; [ii] engraving of W[illia]m Morgan, by V[istus]. Balch (based on a painting of F[rederick]. R. Spencer, "from an original picture of A. Cooley's"); [iii]: engraving of "The Masonic Assassination of Akirop by Joabert," by V[istus]. Balch (based on a painting of A. Cooley); [iv]: blank; [i]: title page; [ii]: copyright; [iii]–iv: preface; [v]–x: introduction; [xi]: table of contents; [xii]: blank; [13]–42: Entered Apprentice; 42–58: Fellow Craft; 58–86: Master Mason; 86: Test–Oath and Word; [*A Revelation of Free Masonry*]: 87–107: Mark Master; 107–14: Past Master; 114–24: Most Excellent Master; 124–44: Royal Arch; 144–54: Knight of the Red Cross; 155–66: Knight Templar and Kt. of Malta; 166–70: Knight of the Christian Mark, and Guard of the Conclave; 170–73: Knight of the Holy Sepulchre; 173–82: The Holy and Thrice Illustrious Order of the Cross; [*The Eleven Ineffable Degrees, Conferred in the Lodge of Perfection*]: 183–86, 210, 345: Secret Master; 186–89, 210, 346: Perfect Master; 189–91, 211, 346: Intimate Secretary; 191–94, 346–7: Provost and Judge; 194–96, 347: Intendant of the Buildings, or Master in Israel; 196–99, 347–8: Elected Knight of Nine; 199–200, 348–9: Elected Grand Master, or Illustrious Elected of Fifteen; 201, 349: Illustrious Knight or Sublime Knight Elected; 201–2, 349: Grand Master Architect; 202–5, 350–1: Knight of the Ninth Arch; 205–10, 351–2: Grand Elect Perfect and Sublime Mason; 210–11: Secrets of the Lodge of Perfection; 212–6, 353: Prince of Jerusalem; 217–25, 354: Knight of the East and West; 225–38, 354: Knight of the Eagle, and Sovereign Prince of Rose Croix de Heredon; 238–40, 355: Grand Pontiff, or Sublime Scotch Masonry; 240–7, 355: Venerable Grand Master of all Symbolic Lodges, Sover[e]ign Prince of Masonry, Master Advitiam, or Grand Pontiff; 247–8, 356: Knight of the Royal Axe, or Hache (hachet), sometimes called Grand Patriarch; 249–50, 356: Chief of the Tabernacle; 250–2, 357: Prince of the Tabernacle; 253–4, 357: Knight of the Brazen Serpent; 255–6, 357–8: Prince of Mercy, or Scotch Trinitarian; 256–8, 358: Sovereign Commander or the Temple at Jerusalem; 258–78, 358: The Key of Masonry. Philosophical Lodge. Knight Adept of the Eagle, or Sun; 278–94, 359: Knight of Kadosh; 294–301, 360: Prince of the Royal Secret; [*Detached*

LIGHT ON MASONRY.

Degrees]: 302–5: Elu de Perignan; 305–10: Le Petit Architect; 310–14: Grand Architect, or Compagnon Ecossois; 315–20: Le Maitre Ecossois; 320–30: Knight of the East, or Chevalier de l'Orient; 330–5: Le Chevalier Rose Croix; 335–41: Noahite or Chevalier Prussien; 431–3: Circular Throughout the Two Hemispheres; 343–4: List of Masonic Degrees Conferred in France; 345–60: Remarks on the Signs, Words, &c. of the Ineffable and Sublime Degrees; [*Committee Reports, Convention Proceedings, Orations, Essays, etc.*] 361–66: Proceedings and Result of a Convention of the Saratoga Baptist Convention; 367–91: Narrative of the facts relating to abduction of William Morgan, etc.; 392–418: An address to all honest Masons. In eight numbers; 418–21: Convention of Seceding Masons: held at Le Roy; 421–25: Anti–Masonic Convention of the Twelve Western Councils of N.Y., held at Le Roy, March 6th and 7th, 1828; 425–31: Address to the people of the State of New York; 431–39: Proceedings of the Legislature of the State of New York, March 19, 1828; 439–45: Speech of the Hon. J. Crary in the Senate of the State of N[ew]. York, March 25, 1828, on the proposition for appointing an inquisitor in the case of William Morgan; 445–51: Proceedings of the Adjourned Convention of Seceding Masons: held at Le Roy, July 4, 1828; 451–63: Oration of Herbert A. Read, Esq. Pronounced at Le Roy, July 4, 1828, to an assembly of nearly one thousand persons; 463–71: Proceedings of the Anti-Masonic N[ew]. Y[ork]. State Convention., held at Utica, Aug. 4, 5, and 6, 1828; 471–79: Speech of T. F. Talbot, Esq., in the Anti-Masonic New York State Convention, August 4, 5, and 6, 1828; 479–86: Trial of Eli Bruce and Others, for a conspiracy to kidnap and carry off Wm. Morgan; 487–95: Beriah B. Hotchkin, "A Candid Appeal to Professors of Religion, upon the Subject of Speculative Free Masonry"; 495–500: Beriah B. Hotchkin, "The Two Great Questions Answered"; 501–506: Henry Dana Ward, "History of Freemasonry"; *Appendix No. 1*. [1]–26: Depositions of sundry persons and other documents disclosing many important particulars relative to the kidnapping of the unfortunate Morgan; with Government Proclamations, &c. &c. (in 30 Nos.); *Appendix No. 2*. [27]–55: Proceedings of a Convention of Delegates, from the different Counties of the State of New–York, opposed to Free Masonry. Held at the Capitol in the City of Albany, on the 19th, 20th and 21st days of February, 1829.

FOURTH EDITION
———— (same title and imprint)
[4], [x], [2], [13]–506, 55 pp., 2 front. plates, one a portrait, illus. 17.5 x 10.5cm.

Identical to the stated third edition except: (a) page 421 is misnumbered "42"; (b) the words "Third Edition" do not appear on the copyright page. The fact that page 421 is misnumbered "42" in this and the fifth editions, but not in the third edition, indicates that this edition followed the third.

Contents: Identical to stated third edition.

INTRODUCTION.

Fifth Edition
——— (same title and imprint)
[4], x, [2], [13]–532, 55 pp., 2 front. plates, one a portrait, illus. 19 x 12.5cm.

The words "Fifth Edition" are printed below copyright notice on verso of title page. Fifth edition points: (a) p. 321 unnumbered; (b) p. 341 misnumbered "34"; (c) p. 491 numbered "49"; (d) pp. 507–32 are added material on the Ineffable Degrees not present in other editions; table of contents has entries for added pages. This edition is the largest in content, physical size and is printed on the best quality paper.

Contents: Identical to stated third edition, except with additional revised material on the Ineffable Degrees (see below), which is followed by the Appendices.

507–9: Secret Master; 509–11: Perfect Master; 511–13: Intimate Secretary; 513–15: Provost and Judge; 515–17: Intendant of the Buildings, (or I.B.); 518–19: Elected Knight of Nine; 520–1: Masters Elected of Fifteen; 521–2: Illustrious Knights Elected; 523–4: Grand Master Architects; 524–8: Knights of the Ninth Arch; 528–32: Grand, Elect, Perfect, and Sublime Mason.

LIGHT ON MASONRY.

NOTES

1. The author is pleased to note the influence of an ancient relative, for Cervantes "received the best part of his early training in a school at Madrid conducted by the cleric, Juan Lopez de Hoyos." Charles G. Herbermann, et al., *The Catholic Encyclopedia* (New York: The Encyclopedia Press, Inc., 1913), 3:543. The proverb appears, without credit, in the "Degree of Knight of Kadosh," *Light on Masonry* (1st ed.), 286, (subsequent eds.), 288.

2. [William Morgan], *Illustrations of Masonry by one of the fraternity who has devoted thirty years to the subject* (Batavia, [N.Y.]: Printed for the Author [by David C. Miller], 1826)

3. Kent L. Walgren used some of my research in his masterful *Freemasonry, Anti-Masonry and Illuminism in the United States, 1734–1850: A Bibliography*, 2 vols. (Worcester, Mass.: American Antiquarian Society, 2003), no. 3055. (Note: The Walgren bibliography will hereinafter be designated "Walgren, *Freemasonry ... A Bibliography.*")

4. Arturo de Hoyos, "David Bernard's *Light on Masonry*: An 'Anti-Masonic Bible,'" in *Heredom* (Washington, D.C.: Scottish Rite Research Society, 2004), 12:9–89.

5. David Murray Lyon, *History of the Lodge in Edinburgh (Mary's Chapel), No. 1. Embracing an Account of the Rise and Progress of Freemasonry in Scotland* (Edinburgh: William Blackwood and Sons, 1873; reprint ed.: Gresham Publishing Co., 1900); David Stevenson, *The Origins of Freemasonry: Scotland's Century 1590–1710* (Cambridge: Cambridge University Press, 1988); David Stevenson, *The First Freemasons: Scotland's Early Lodges and Their Members* (Aberdeen: Aberdeen University Press, 1988).

6. Douglas Knoop, G. P. Jones, and D. Hamer, *The Two Earliest Masonic MSS* (Manchester: Manchester University Press, 1938).

7. Douglas Knoop and G. P. Jones, *The Scottish Mason and the Mason Word* (Manchester: Manchester University Press, 1939).

8. In an oft-cited passage, Henry Adamson's *The Muses' Threnodie* (1638) connected Rosicrucianism, Freemasonry, and the occult arts: "For what we do presage is riot in grosse, for we are brethren of the Rosie Crosse; We have the Mason Word and second sight, Things for to come we can foretell aright." No contemporary evidence suggests that Freemasons themselves claimed occult abilities.

9. Frances A. Yates, *Giordano Bruno and the Hermetic Tradition* (Chicago: University of Chicago Press, 1964); Frances A. Yates, *The Art of Memory* (Chicago: University of Chicago Press, 1966).

10. Douglas Knoop, G. P. Jones, and D. Hamer, *Early Masonic Pamphlets* (Manchester: Manchester University Press, 1945), 34–35.

11. Charles Cotton was made a Mason on December 22, 1724, later passed a Fellow Craft (date unspecified), and on May 12, 1725, he and Papillon Ball "Were regularly passed Masters," R. F. Gould, "Philo-Musicæ et Architecturæ Societas Apolloni. [A Review.]," *Ars Quatuor Coronatorum* 16 (1903), pp. 112–28.

12. See Harry Carr, *Samuel Prichard's Masonry Dissected 1730. An Analysis and Commentary* (Bloomington, Ill.: Masonic Book Club, 1977); the text, *sans* commentary, is also

INTRODUCTION.

available in Arturo de Hoyos, ed., *The Symbolism of the Blue Degrees of Freemasonry* (Washington, D.C.: Scottish Rite Research Society, 2005).

13. Harry Carr, *Three Distinct Knocks and Jachin and Boaz* (Bloomington, Ill.: Masonic Book Club, 1981); A. C. F. Jackson, *English Masonic Exposures 1760–1769* (London: Lewis Masonic, 1986).

14. Jackson, *English Masonic Exposures*, 18.

15. Harry Carr, *The Early French Exposures* (London: Quatuor Coronati Lodge No. 2076, 1971).

16. On Scots Masonry and the early high degrees, see J. Fairbairn Smith, "A commentary. D'Assigny's Enquiry–Serious, Impartial," in Fifield D'Assigny, *A Serious and Impartial Enquiry into the Cause of the Present Decay of Free-Masonry in the Kingdom of Ireland* (Bloomington, Ill.: Masonic Book Club, 1974); Alain Bernheim, "Did the Early 'High' or Écossais Degrees Originate in France?," *Heredom* 5 (1996), 87–113.

17. Pierre Mollier, "La première divulgation du ritual des haut grades," in *Renaissance Traditionnelle* 35:138–139–140 (April–July–October, 2004), pp. 79–110. The *Conversations Allégoriques* was not strictly an exposé, because it was printed as an (unauthorized) aid to the memory. It abbreviated and omitted modes of recognition.

18. [Richard Carlile,] *The Republican* vol. 12 (London, 1825). I have not seen the 1845 edition, but have studied several others, beginning with Richard Carlile, *Manual of Freemasonry: In Three Parts. With an Explanatory Introduction to the Science, and a Free Translation of Some of the Sacred Scripture Names* (London: Richard Carlile, 1853). On his works, see S. J. Fenton, "Richard Carlile: His Life and Masonic Writings," in *Ars Quatuor Coronatorum* 49 (1936), 83–121.

19. E. H. Cartwright, *Masonic Ritual: A Commentary on Freemasonic Ritual* 3d ed. (London: Lewis Masonic, 1985). See also F. W. Golby, *A Century of Masonic Working: Being a History of the Stability Lodge of Instruction* (Bath: Herald Press, 1921); C. F. W. Dyer, *Emulation: A Ritual to Remember. Notes on the men and times in the one hundred and fifty years' history of Emulation Lodge of Improvement 1823–1973* (London: A Lewis [for Emulation Lodge of Improvement], 1973).

20. *Antimasonic Pamphlet. No. 4. Portrait of Freemasonry. Facts Worth Reading* (N.p.: n.d. [1832?]), 1.; Walgren, *Freemasonry ... A Bibliography* no. 3608.

21. "The Mystery of Free-Masonry," *The Pennsylvania Gazette. Containing the freshest Advice, Foreign and Domestick.* no. 108 (From Thursday, December 3. to Tuesday, December 8. 1730). My transcript was made from the reduced photographic reproduction in Delmar Duane Darrah, *History and Evolution of Freemasonry* (Bloomington, [Illinois]: Masonic Publishing Company, 1920), 231.

22. For the London edition, see Douglas Knoop, G. P. Jones, and Douglas Hamer, eds., *The Early Masonic Catechisms*, 2d ed. (Manchester: Manchester University Press, 1943, 1963), 152–56.

23. *Masonry Dissected: Being an Universal and Genuine Description of All Its Branches from the Original to This Present Time. As It Is Deliver'd in the Constituted*

LIGHT ON MASONRY.

Regular Lodges Both in City and Country. According to the Several Degrees of Admission; Giving an Impartial Account of Their Regular Proceeding in Initiating Their New Members in the Whole Three Degrees of Masonry; Viz. I. Enter'd Prentice. II. Fellow Craft. III. Master. To Which is Added, the Author's Vindication of Himself. By Samuel Prichard, Late Member of a Constituted Lodge. Reprinted in the Year, M, DCC, XLIX [Newport, Rhode Island?: Anne Franklin], 1749/1750.

24. *Hiram: Or the Grand Master–Key to the Door of Both Ancient and Modern Free–Masonry. Being an Accurate Description of Every Degree of the Brotherhood, as Authorized and Delivered in All Good Lodges. The Whole Comprehending (among an Entertaining variety of Others) the Following the Articles.... With an Appendix, Disclosing the Other Secrets of Free–Masonry, Not Divulged by the Author. Illustrated with Proper Remarks, Necessary to Explain the Whole to the Meanest Capacity, Whether Brethren or Not. And Contains More on the Subject Than Any Book Ever before Published. By a Member of the Royal Arch* (New York: London Printed, New York, Re-printed, and Sold [by] John Holt, 1768). See Walgren, *Freemasonry ... A Bibliography,* no. 24.

25. Walgren, *Freemasonry ... A Bibliography*, 2:993–94.

26. *National Observer* vol. 2 (Albany, May 23, 1828), no. 44—Whole no. 122, [4].

27. Thomas Smith Webb, *The Freemason's Monitor; or, Illustrations of Masonry: In Two Parts. By a Royal Arch Mason, K.T. – K. of M. – &c. &c.* (Printed at Albany, For Spencer and Webb, 1797).

28. Louis Guillemain de Saint Victor, *Recueil Précieux de la Maçonnerie Adonhiramite, Contenant le Catechisme du Premier Grade, l'Ouverture et la Clôture de Cette L∴; l'Instruction de la L∴ de Table; les Santés Générales et Particilières, Ainsi Que les Devoirs des Premiers Officers en Charge; Enrichi de Demandes et de Réponses Symboliques, et de Notes Aussi Curieuses Qu'Utiles: Dédié aux Maçons Instruits, par un Chevalier de Tous les Ordres Maçonniques* (Philadelphia: Chez le F∴, A∴J∴ Blocquesrst, Imprimeur, 5812 [i.e., 1812]). Walgren, *Freemasonry ... A Bibliography*, no. 1250.

29. *4ème Grade sous le Titre de Maître–Parfait, a l'Usage & sous les Auspices du Souv∴ Chap∴ de R∴ †∴ Candeur & Amitié, Annexé a la T∴ Rble∴ L∴ Française, No. 73, sous le Titre Distincif de l'Aménité, Or∴ de Philadelphie* (Philadelphia: Chez le F∴, A∴ J∴ Blocquerst, Imprimeur, 1812) Walgren, *Freemasonry ... A Bibliography*, no. 1275.

30. *The Free Mason's Instructor; or Lectures on the Three First Degrees of Masonry; Being One of the Best Works Ever Published on that Head, and the Only One of the Kind at Present Extent. Carefully Corrected and Revised, with Additions and Alterations, from a London Edition. By John A. Rohr, W[orshipful] M[aster] of P[hiladelphia] U[nion] M[ark] L[odge] No. 1. a H[oly] R[oyal] A[rch] M[ason] K[night] T[emplar] K[night] of M[alta] a K[night] of the R[ed] C[ross] a P[rince] of J[erusalem] and a K[night] of the W[hite] and B[lack] Eagle, &c. Dedicated to all Free and Accepted Masons* (Philadelphia: John A. Rohr, 1812).

31. Philadelphia Union Mark Lodge No. 1 was warranted by the General Grand Royal Arch Chapter of the United States (meeting in Albany, New York), on Dec. 19, 1811. It was not recognized by the Grand Lodge of Pennsylvania. Joshua L. Lyte, *Reprint of the Minutes*

INTRODUCTION.

of the Grand Lodge of Free and Accepted Masons of Pennsylvania Vol. III. 1811 to 1816 (Philadelphia, Pa.: Published by the Grand Lodge, 1897), 174–76.

32. Lyte, *Reprint of the Minutes ... 1811 to 1816*, 188, 201–5, 237–40, 263–64.

33. Walgren, *Freemasonry ... A Bibliography*, Nos. 2038–41.

34. Charles T. McClenachan, *History of the Most Ancient and Honorable Fraternity of Free and Accepted Masons in New York from its Earliest Date*, 2 vols. (New York: Published by the Grand Lodge, 1892), 2:351.

35. *Proceedings of the Grand Chapter of Royal Arch Masons of the State of New York, from its Organization, in 1798, to 1867, Inclusive. Volume I. 1798–1853* (Buffalo: Published by Order of the Grand Chapter, 1871), 208.

36. *Proceedings of the Grand Chapter of ... New York ... 1798, to 1867*, 224–25.

37. *Proceedings of the Grand Chapter of ... New York ... 1798, to 1867*, 239, 257.

38. William L. Stone, *Letters on Masonry and Anti–Masonry, Addressed to the Hon. John Quincy Adams* (New York: O. Halsted, 1832), 80.

39. Stone, *Letters on Masonry and Anti–Masonry*, 130.

40. For a listing of most of the works on the Morgan Affair, see William L. Cummings, *A Bibliography of Anti–Masonry* 2d ed., rev. and enl. (New York: Press of Henry Emmerson, 1963). Subsequent to the works listed in this bibliography, two other books deserve mention: William Preston Vaughn, *The Anti–Masonic Party in the United States 1826–1843* (Lexington, Ky.: University Press of Kentucky, 1983); Paul Goodman, *Towards a Christian Republic. Antimasonry and the Great Transition in New England 1826–1836* (Oxford: Oxford University Press, 1988). For a concise overview, see Stephen Dafoe, "Batavia to Baltimore and Beyond: A Re-examination of the William Morgan Story and Its Efffect on Freemasonry," *Heredom*, vol. 15 (2007).

41. William S. Simons claimed that during the Battle of New Orleans (Jan. 8, 1815) he fought by the side of "Capt. William Morgan." *Anti–Masonic Christian Herald* vol. 1 (Boston, Thursday, Feb. 26, 1829) no. 7, 26. In another publication, it was asserted that Morgan's military commission as a "Capt. in a Militia Regiment, at the battle of New Orleans" was stolen by Masons and never returned. See Edward Giddins, *The Pennsylvania anti–Masonic Almanac, for the Year of our Lord 1830* (Lancaster: Published at the Office of the Anti–Masonic Herald, [1830]), 43.

42. Jeremy L. Cross, *The True Masonic Chart, or Hieroglyphic Monitor; containing all the Emblems Explained in the Degrees of Entered Apprentice, Fellow–Craft, Master Mason, Mark Master, Past Master, Most Excellent Master, Royal Arch, Royal Master, and Select Master* (New Haven, [Conn.]: Flagg & Gray, Printers, 1819).

43. Moses Holbrook, Charleston, S.C., Aug. 21, 1830, to J. J. J. Gourgas, New York, N.Y., copy in the Archives of the Supreme Council, 33°, S.J.

44. Moses Holbrook, Charleston, S.C., May 12, 1828, to J. J. J. Gourgas, New York, N.Y., copy in the Archives of the Supreme Council, 33°, S.J.

45. Arturo de Hoyos, "The Posthumous Success of James H. C. Miller, Degree Peddler," in *Heredom* 8 (1999–2000), 169–217.

LIGHT ON MASONRY.

46. Rob Morris, *William Morgan; or Political Anti–Masonry, its Rise, Growth and Decadence* (New York: Robert Macoy, Masonic Publisher, 1883), 82–84. The cover title of this work is *William Morgan. What the Freemasons Say.*

47. Stone, *Letters on Masonry and Anti–Masonry*, 124, 127, 128, 133.

48. [Richard Carlile,] *The Republican* vol. 12 (London, 1825); Richard Carlile, *Manual of Freemasonry*, 91.

49. The facsimile of Morgan's signature, reproduced as figure 3, appears in Morris, *William Morgan*, 70–1.

50. Stone, *Letters on Masonry and Anti–Masonry,* 129.

51. All nine editions of this work are available on Andrew Prescott's CD–ROM, *Preston's Illustrations of Masonry* (Academy Electronic Publications Ltd., 2001).

52. Morris, *William Morgan; or Political Anti–Masonry*, 166–67.

53. [Martin Smith,] *The Second Part; or, a Key to the Higher Degrees of Freemasonry: Giving a Clear and Correct View of the Way and Manner of Conferring the Degrees of Mark Master, Past Master, Most Excellent Master, and Royal Arch Mason, on a Candidate; as Practised in All Well Governed Lodges and Chapters throughout the Globe: Together with the Means to be Used by Such As Are Not Masons, to gain Admission Therein:—the Whole Intended as a Guide to the Craft, and a Light to the Unenlightened. By a Member of the Craft* (Cincinnati, [Ohio]: Printed for the Proprietor, 1827). See Walgren, *Freemasonry . . . A Bibliography*, no. 2853.

54. *Illustrations of Masonry, by One of the Fraternity, Who has Devoted Thirty Years to the Subject, with an Appendix Containing a Key to the Higher Degrees of Freemasonry by a Member of the Craft* (Cincinnati: Matthew Gardiner [ca. 1850]); *Morgan's Freemasonry Exposed and Explained; Showing the Origin, History and nature of Masonry; it Effects on the Government, and the Christian Religion, and Containing a Key to the Higher Degrees of Freemasonry; Giving a Clear and Correct View of the Way and Manner of Conferring the Different Degrees; as Practiced in All Lodges throughout the Globe; Together with the Means to be Used by Such As Are Not Masons, to Gain Admission Therein. The Whole Intended as a Guide to the Craft and a Light to the Unenlightened. By Captain William Morgan* (New York: William Brisbane, Publisher [ca. 1860]).

55. Mary Hanlon, *Revelations in Masonry, Made by a Late Member of the Craft, in Four Parts. "Try Me, Prove Me." A New Edition, Carefully Revised, and Corrected by the Author* (New York: Printed for the Author, 1827).

56. I provided this information to Kent L. Walgren, who subsequently included it, with credit, in his "A Bibliography of Pre–1851 American Scottish Rite Imprints," *Heredom* vol. 3 (1994), 94–96. It later appeared, without credit, in his *Freemasonry, Anti–Masonry and Illuminism in the United States, 1734–1850. A Bibliography,* 2 vols. (Worcester, Mass.: American Antiquarian Society, 2003).

57. Moses Holbrook, Charleston, S.C., July 23, 1827, to J. J. J. Gourgas, New York, N.Y., copy in the Archives of the Supreme Council, 33°, S.J.

58. *Reminiscences of Masonic Revelations by Elder David Bernard, Author of "Light on Masonry." "In Secret Have I said Nothing," "Ye are my Witnesses, saith*

INTRODUCTION.

the Lord." Published by Special Request of the National Christian Association, at their Sixth Anniversary, held at Syracuse, New York, June 2, 3 and 4, 1874 (Chicago, Ill.: Ezra A. Cook, 1896), 1, 19; "Testimony of David Bernard before the Syracuse Anti–masonic convention...." [Nov. 15, 16, 17, 1870], in Rev. John Levington, *Key to Masonry, and Kindred Secret Combinations* (Dayton, Ohio: United Brethren Publishing House, 1871), 141–46.

59. "Testimony of David Bernard...." 142. Bernard here misspells the name "Ezra S. Cozire"; but see the *Transactions of the Grand Lodge of Free and Accepted Mason of the State of New York 1816–1827* (New York: Masonic Publishing and Furnishing Co., 1880), 421. Cozier, active in numerous Masonic bodies, was President of Utica Village in the mid–1820s, and served on the local Board of Health during Utica's 1832 cholera epidemic.

60. Although I am not sure if he was David Bernard's brother, in 1818 "A. G. Bernard" served on the committee which secured incorporation of the Grand Chapter of New York. If so, one Brother helped build the Grand Chapter, while the other helped destroy it. *Proceedings of the Grand Chapter of ... New York ... 1798, to 1867*, 142.

61. The officers of Schenectady's Delta Lodge of Perfection and Albany's Consistory of Sublime Princes of the Royal Secret are listed in the *Masonic Mirror: and Mechanics Intelligencer* vol. 1 (Boston, [Mass.], Saturday, May 28, 1825), no. 23. The Consistory received a charter (dated Nov. 16, 1824) from the Supreme Council at Charleston (Southern Jurisdiction). The territorial division between the two jurisdictions would not be made until 1827.

62. Giles Fonda Yates, Schenectady, N.Y., Feb. 2, 1828, to J. J. J. Gourgas, New York, N.Y., Archives of the Supreme Council, 33°, S.J.

64. *The Proceedings of the United States Anti–Masonic Convention, Held at Philadelphia, September 11, 1830. Embracing the Journal of Proceedings, the Reports, the Debates, and the Address to the People* (Published by I. Trimble, Philadelphia; Skinner and Dewey, New York; D. Packard, Albany; William Williams, Utica; D. D. Spencer, Ithaca; N. D. Strong, Hartford, Con.; John Marsh and Co. Office of the Boston Christian Herald, and of the Free Press, Boston, Mass.; and at Most of the Bookstores in the United States, 1830), 64.

65. Levington, *Key to Masonry*, 141.

66. Bernard, *Reminiscences of Masonic Revelations*, 31.

67. *Light on Masonry, by Eld. David Bernard. Revised Edition, with an Appendix Revealing the Mysteries of Odd Fellowship By a Member of the Craft*, 11th ed. (Dayton, Ohio: Published by W. J. Shuey, 1870), viii.

68. Arturo de Hoyos and S. Brent Morris, *Is it True What They Say About Freemasonry?* (New York: M. Evans, 2004), 111–31.

69. David Bernard, *Reminiscences of Masonic Revelations*, 6–7.

70. John Glazier Stearns, *An Inquiry into the Nature and Tendency of Speculative Free–Masonry* (Utica, [New York]: Printed for the Author [by William Williams], 1826).

71. *Anti–Masonic Christian Herald* vol. 1 (Boston, Thurs., March 12, 1829) no. 9, 36.

72. David Bernard, *Reminiscences of Masonic Revelations*, 16–17.

LIGHT ON MASONRY.

73. *National Observer* vol. 2 (Albany, [N.Y.,] March 7, 1828), no. 33 – whole no. 111, [1–2].

74. J. J. Gourgas, New York, N.Y., April 10, 1828, to Moses Holbrook, Charleston, S.C., Archives of the Supreme Council, 33°, S.J.

75. Giles Fonda Yates, Schenectady, N.Y., June 9, 1828, to J. J. J. Gourgas, New York, N.Y., copy in the Archives of the Supreme Council, 33°, S.J.

76. *National Observer* vol. 2 (Albany, [N.Y.,] July 18, 1828), no. 52 – whole no. 133, [2].

77. Giles Fonda Yates, Schenectady, N.Y., July 26, 1828, to J. J. J. Gourgas, New York, N.Y., copy in the Archives of the Supreme Council, 33°, S.J.

78. *A Revelation of Free Masonry, as Published to the World by a Convention of Seceding Masons, held at Le Roy, Genesee County, N.Y. on the 4th and 5th of July 1828: Containing a True and Genuine Development of The Mode of Initiation, and also of the Several Degrees: To Wit: in the Chapter, Mark Master, Past Master, Most Excellent Master, and Royal Arch. In the Encampment, Knight of the Red Cross, Knight Templar, Knight of the Christian Mark, and Guards of the Conclave, and Knights of the Holy Sepulcher. In the Ancient Council of the Trinity, Denominated the Holy and Thrice Illustrious Order of the Cross, The Illustrious, Most Illustrious, and Thrice Illustrious Degrees. Published by the Lewiston Committee* (Rochester, N.Y.: Printed by Weed & Heron, 1828).

79. Giles Fonda Yates, Schenectady, N.Y., Nov. 20, 1828, to J. J. J. Gourgas, New York, N.Y., copy in the Archives of the Supreme Council, 33°, S.J.

80. *National Observer* vol. 3 (Albany, [N.Y.,] Aug. 29, 1828), no. 5 – whole no. 135, [2, 3].

81. *Light on Masonry* (1st ed., 544–555; 2d–5th eds., 341–343) reproduces the Supreme Council's degree structure from the *Circular throughout two hemispheres* (1802) as it was reprinted in Joseph M'Cosh's *Documents upon Sublime Masonry* (Charleston, [S.C.: Published by Schenk & Co; Printed by C. C. Sebring],1823), 19. The original version of the *Circular* differed slightly, by listing fewer degrees. For a facsimile of the original, see Ray Baker Harris, History *of the Supreme Council, 33° (Mother Council of the World) Ancient and Accepted Scottish Rite of Freemasonry Southern Jurisdiction U.S.A. 1801–1861* (Washington, D.C.: The Supreme Council, 33°, 1964), 319–25.

82. David Bernard, letter dated Dec. 8, 1828, reprinted in *Anti–Masonic Christian Herald* vol. 1 (Boston, Thurs., Feb. 19, 1829) no. 6, 24.

83. Samuel B. Bradley, Greece, Monroe County, N.Y., Jan. 12, 1829, to Giles Fonda Yates, Schenectady, N.Y., quoted in Giles Fonda Yates, Schenectady, N.Y., Jan. 17, 1829, to J. J. J. Gourgas, New York, N.Y., copy in the Archives of the Supreme Council, 33°, S.J.

84. See Walgren, *Freemasonry ... A Bibliography*, no. 2925.

85. *Anti–Masonic Christian Herald*, vol. 1 (New York, Jan. 17, 1829) no. 1, 4.

86. *Anti–Masonic Christian Herald*, vol. 1 (New York, March 12, 1829) no. 9, [1].

87. *Anti–Masonic Christian Herald*, vol. 1 (New York, March 5, 1829) no. 8, 30.

88. Moses Holbrook, Charleston, S.C., Dec. 24, 1827, to J. J. J. Gourgas, New York, N.Y., copy in the Archives of the Supreme Council, 33°, S.J.

INTRODUCTION.

89. However, in a talk on Aug. 25, 1852, Yates confused names, and credited Joseph M'Cosh with the act, stating, "In 1825 I took my vows as a 'Sovereign Grand Inspector General' 'between the hands' of our Brother JOSEPH M'COSH, he having been specially deputized for that purpose." *Proceedings of the Supreme Council of Sov∴Gr∴ Inspectors General, for the Northern Masonic Jurisdiction of the United States. Gourgas Body, 1813–1851. Raymond Body, 1851–1860. Van Rensselaer Body, 1860–1862* (Portland, [Maine]: Stephen Berry, Printer., 1876), 233–50.

90. Moses Holbrook, Charleston, S.C., Dec. 17, 1828, to J. J. J. Gourgas, New York, N.Y. (Note appended Dec. 19). Copy in the Archives of the Supreme Council, 33°, S.J.

91. J. J. J. Gourgas, New York, N.Y., April 25, 1829, to Moses Holbrook, Charleston, S.C. Copy in the Archives of the Supreme Council, 33°, S.J.

92. *Proceedings of the Grand Chapter of ... New York ... 1798, to 1867*, 176.

93. N. N. Whiting, *The Good News of Our Lord Jesus, the Anointed; From the Critical Greek of Tittman* (Boston, J. V. Himes, 1849)

94. Whiting's participation in the American Bible Union is noted in Thomas Armitage, *A History of the Baptists: Traced by their Vital Principles and Practices, from the Time of Our Lord and Saviour Jesus Christ to the Year 1886* (New York: Bryan, Taylor, & Co.; Chicago: Morningside Publishing Co. 1887), 900, 909.

95. David Bernard, letter quoted "From the Batavia Advocate," in *National Observer* vol. 2 (Albany, Jan. 4, 1828), no. 24, [2].

96. Giles Fonda Yates, Schenectady, N.Y., April 4, 1828, to Rev. N. N. Whiting, Vernon, Oneida County, N.Y., copy in the Archives of the Supreme Council, 33°, S.J.

97. Giles Fonda Yates, Schenectady, N.Y., April 4, 1828, to Rev. N. N. Whiting, Vernon, Oneida County, N.Y., copy in the Archives of the Supreme Council, 33°, S.J.

98. J. J. J. Gourgas, New York, N.Y., April 14, 1828, to Giles Fonda Yates, Schenectady, N.Y., copy in the Archives of the Supreme Council, 33°, S.J.

99. Giles Fonda Yates, Schenectady, N.Y., April 17, 1828, to J. J. J. Gourgas, New York, N.Y., copy in the Archives of the Supreme Council, 33°, S.J.

100. Giles Fonda Yates, Schenectady, N.Y., April 25, 1828, to J. J. J. Gourgas, New York, N.Y., copy in the Archives of the Supreme Council, 33°, S.J.

101. Giles Fonda Yates, Schenectady, N.Y., May 6, 1828, to J. J. J. Gourgas, New York, N.Y., copy in the Archives of the Supreme Council, 33°, S.J.

102. Note dated "Decr 25th" appended to Giles Fonda Yates, Schenectady, N.Y., Dec. 18, 1828, to J. J. J. Gourgas, New York, N.Y., copy in Archives of the Supreme Council, 33°, SJ.

103. Austin A. Yates, *Schenectady County, New York: Its History to the Close of the Nineteenth Century* (New York: New York History Company, 1902), 261–64; 270–77.

104. Giles Fonda Yates, Schenectady, N.Y., Jan 15, 1829, to J. J. J. Gourgas, New York, N.Y., copy in the Archives of the Supreme Council, 33°, S.J.

105. J. J. J. Gourgas, New York, N.Y., April 29, 1829, to Giles Fonda Yates, Schenectady, N.Y., copy in the Archives of the Supreme Council, 33°, S.J.

LIGHT ON MASONRY.

106. Giles Fonda Yates, Schenectady, N.Y., April 23, 1829, to J. J. J. Gourgas, New York, N.Y., copy in the Archives of the Supreme Council, 33°, S.J.

107. J. J. J. Gourgas, New York, N.Y., Aug. 6, 1829, to Moses Holbrook, Charleston, S.C. Archives of the Supreme Council, 33°, S.J.

108. Giles Fonda Yates, Schenectady, N.Y., Sept. 4, 1829, to J. J. J. Gourgas, New York, N.Y., copy in the Archives of the Supreme Council, 33°, S.J.

109. J. J. J. Gourgas, New York, N.Y., Nov. 7, 1829, to Moses Holbrook, Charleston, S.C. Archives of the Supreme Council, 33°, S.J.

110. Moses Holbrook, Charleston, S.C., Jan. 8, 1830, to J. J. J. Gourgas, New York, N.Y., copy in the Archives of the Supreme Council, 33°, S.J.

111. *Strictures on Seceding Masons, with the Reviews of the Anti–Masonic Characters of Pliny Merrick, Esq. of Worcester, Mass.—Rev. Joel Mann, of Suffield, Conn.—Rev. Tho's M. Smith, or Troy, Mass.—and Elder David Bernard, of Fredonia, N.Y. From the Boston Masonic Mirror* (Boston: Carr and Page, 1830).

112. *Proceedings of the Sangerfield Meeting, Held at the Presbyterian Meeting House in the Village of Waterville, January 13, 1830. With and Address of Elder Nathan N. Whiting, on the Subject of Speculative Free Masonry* (Utica, [N.Y.]: Press of William Williams, 1830). Walgren, *Freemasonry ... A Bibliography*, no. 3379.

113. *The Proceedings of the United States Anti–Masonic Convention*, 40.

114. Giles Fonda Yates, Schenectady, N.Y., April 17, 1828, to J. J. J. Gourgas, New York, N.Y., copy in the Archives of the Supreme Council, 33°, S.J.

115. David Bernard, *Appendix to Light on Freemasonry, with Oaths and Penalties* (Rochester, N.Y.: Woodruff Post, Member of E.G. Conf., M.E. Church, 1871), 36–37.

116. *Reminiscences of Masonic Revelations*, 25–31.

117. Charles–Louis Cadet–Gassicourt, *Letombeau de Jacques Molai* (Paris: Desenne, 1797).

118. *National Observer* vol. 3 (Albany, [N.Y.,] Aug. 22, 1828), no. 4 – whole no. 134, [2].

119. Some of the many reprints of Morgan's work include baffling errors. For example, the third edition (Rochester, 1827), has an enigmatic line which reads, "where they join the h&, the word or name is *Tabal Cain*" [*sic*]. If the ampersand, &, meaning "and," is read as a word, "h&" becomes *hand*.

120. Stone, *Letters on Masonry and Anti–Masonry*, 74–75. Additional examples of Bernard's unreliability are cited in *Heredom*, vol. 4 (1995), 23.

121. *Boston Masonic Mirror* vol. 3 (Sat., Jan. 28, 1832), no. 31, 241–42.

122. de Hoyos, "The Posthumous Success of James H. C. Miller," 169–217.

123. [François H. Stanislaus Delaunaye,] *Thuileur des Trente–trois Degres de L'Ecossisme du Rit Ancien, dit Accepté* (Paris: Delaunay, Libraire, Palais–Royal, 1813,1821). Although Delaunay was a non-Mason, his work was both scholarly and widely used by Masons, including Comte de Grasse–Tilly, founder of the Scottish Rite in France. A critical

INTRODUCTION.

text has recently been published which includes a facsimile of the 1821 edition. See Claude Rétat, ed., F. H. S. Delaunaye, *Thuileur de L'Ecossisme. Édition critique, avec presentation et documents inédits* (Paris: Éditions Dervy, 2007).

124. *Light on Masonry* (1st ed., 544–55; 2d–5th eds., 341–343) reproduces the Supreme Council's degree structure from the *Circular throughout two hemispheres* (1802) as it was reprinted in Joseph M'Cosh's *Documents upon Sublime Masonry* (Charleston, [S.C.: Published by Schenk & Co; Printed by C. C. Sebring], 1823), 19. For a facsimile of the original, see Harris, History *of the Supreme Council, 33° ... 1801–1861* (Washington, D.C.: The Supreme Council, 33°, 1964), 319–25.

125. [Albert Pike,] *The Book of the Words. Sephir H'Debarim. A facsimile of the 1879 second edition including pages 92a–92f and "Some Recent Investigations" of 1880. With an introduction by Art deHoyos, 32°, K∴C∴C∴H∴ and an index by Norman D. Peterson, 32°, K∴C∴C∴H∴* (Washington, D.C.: Scottish Rite Research Society, A∴L∴ 5999 [1999]), 157.

126. For example, *Masonic Oaths, with Notes; to Which are Added Practical Proofs of the Character and Tendency of Free–Masonry* (Montpelier: Knapp & Jewett, 1834).

127. For example, David Bernard, *Light on Free Masonry* (Dayton, Ohio: Pub. by a company, and for sale by Vonneida & Sowers, N.d., [ca. 1858]).

128. Avery Allyn, *A Ritual of Freemasonry, Illustrated by Numerous Engravings. To Which is Added a Key to the Phi Beta Kappa, the Orange, and Odd Fellows Societies. With Notes and Remarks*. (Philadelphia: John Clarke, 1831).

129. George R. Crafts [pseud.], *The Mysteries of Free Masonry; Containing all the Degrees of the Order Conferred in a Master's Lodge, as Written by Captain William Morgan. All the Degrees Conferred in the Royal Arch Chapter and Grand Encampment of Knights Templars – Knights of the Red Cross – Of the Christian Mark – and of the Holy Sepulchre. – Also, the Eleven Ineffable Degrees Conferred in the Lodge of Perfection – And the Still Higher Degrees of the Prince of Jerusalem – Knights of the East and West – Venerable Grand Masters of Symbolic Lodges – Knights and Adepts of the Eagle or Sun – Princess of the Royal Secret – Sovereign Inspector General, &c. Revised and Corrected to Correspond with the Most Approved Forms and ceremonies in the various Lodges of Free Masons Throughout the United States* (New York: Wilson and Company, [1852]).

130. Jabez Richardson, [Benjamin Henry Day], *Richardson's Monitor of Free–Masonry; Being a Practical Guide to all the Ceremonies in all the Degrees Conferred in Masonic Lodges, Chapters, Encampments, &c. Explaining the Signs, Tokens and Grips, and Giving all the Words, Pass–Words, Sacred Words, Oaths, and Hieroglyphs used by Masons. The Ineffable and Historical Degrees are also Given in Full* (New York: Dick & Fitzgerald 1860).

131. Allyn, *A Ritual of Freemasonry, Illustrated by Numerous Engravings. To Which is Added a Key to the Phi Beta Kappa, the Orange, and Odd Fellows Societies. With Notes and Remarks.* (Philadelphia: John Clarke, 1831).

132. For a brief historical overview of Cerneauism, and its battle with authentic Freemasonry, see Arturo de Hoyos, "The Union of 1867" in *Heredom*, vol. 4 (1995), 7–46.

133. Jonathan Blanchard, ed., *Scotch Rite Masonry Illustrated*, 2 vols. (Chicago: Ezra A. Cook, 1887), vol. 1, 124, 145, 303, 358, 419, 436; vol. 2, 137, 242, 340, 388, 445, 462, 464, 470, 472, 475.

134. The original manuscript is most likely in the Archives of the Supreme Council, 33°, N.M.J., Lexington, Mass. Our transcription is from a copy in the Archives of the Supreme Council, 33°, S.J., Washington, D.C.

135. The twelve degrees of the Rite were 1° Adoptive Apprentice, 2° Companion, 3° Mistress, 4° Perfect Mistress, 5° Sublime Elect, 6° Dame Ecossais, 7° Grand Elect, or French Dame, 8° Lady of the Dove, 9° Lady of the Rosy Cross, 10° Adonaite Mistress, 11° Perfect Venerable Adonaite Mistress, 12° Crowned Princess, or Sovereign Mistress. The texts of all these rituals were translated by John Yarker and printed in *Collectanea* (Grand College of Rites, USA), vol. 1 (1937), pt. 3.

INTRODUCTION.

THE FACSIMILE

David Bernard, *Light on Masonry*, 5th ed.
(Utica: William Williams, 1829)

Wᴹ MORGAN,

From an original picture of A. Cooley's.

Entered according to Act of Congress, the 17th day of April 1829, by A. Cooley, of the State of N. York.

THE MASONIC ASSASSINATION OF AKIKOP, BY JUABERT.

LIGHT ON MASONRY:

A COLLECTION OF ALL THE

MOST IMPORTANT DOCUMENTS

ON THE SUBJECT OF

SPECULATIVE FREE MASONRY:

EMBRACING

THE REPORTS OF THE WESTERN COMMITTEES

IN RELATION TO THE

ABDUCTION OF WILLIAM MORGAN,

PROCEEDINGS OF CONVENTIONS, ORATIONS, ESSAYS, &c &c.

WITH

ALL THE DEGREES OF THE ORDER CONFERRED IN A MASTER'S LODGE,
As written by Captain William Morgan;

ALL THE DEGREES CONFERRED IN THE ROYAL ARCH CHAPTER AND GRAND EN-
CAMPMENT OF KNIGHTS TEMPLARS, WITH THE APPENDANT ORDERS,
*As published by the Convention of Seceding Masons, held at
Le Roy, July 4th and 5th, 1828.*

ALSO

A REVELATION OF ALL THE DEGREES CONFERRED

IN THE

LODGE OF PERFECTION,

AND

FIFTEEN DEGREES OF A STILL HIGHER ORDER,

WITH

SEVEN FRENCH DEGREES:

MAKING

FORTY-EIGHT DEGREES OF FREE MASONRY.

With Notes and Critical Remarks.

BY ELDER DAVID BERNARD,
OF WARSAW, GENESEE CO. N. Y.
Once an Intimate Secretary in the Lodge of Perfection; and Secretary of the Convention
of Seceding Masons, held at Le Roy, July 4th and 5th, 1828.

" For there is nothing covered that shall not be revealed, and hid that shall not be known.'
" And what ye hear in the ear that preach ye upon the house tops."
Jesus Christ.

UTICA:
WILLIAM WILLIAMS, PRINTER, GENESEE-STREET.

1829.

NORTHERN DISTRICT OF NEW-YORK, TO WIT:

BE IT REMEMBERED, that on the thirteenth day of April, in the fifty-third year of the Independence of the United States of America, A. D. 1829, David Bernard, of the said District, hath deposited in this office the title of a book, the right whereof he claims as author, in the words following, to wit:

"Light on Masonry: a collection of all the most important documents on the subject of Speculative Free Masonry: embracing the Reports of the Western Committees in relation to the abduction of William Morgan, Proceedings of Conventions, Orations, Essays, &c. &c. With all the degrees of the order conferred in a Master's Lodge, as written by Captain William Morgan; all the degrees conferred in the Royal Arch Chapter and Grand Encampment of Knights Templars, with the appendant orders, as published by the convention of Seceding Masons, held at Le Roy, July 4 and 5, 1828. Also, a revelation of all the degrees conferred in the Lodge of Perfection, and fifteen degrees of a still higher order, with seven French degrees: making forty-eight degrees of Free Masonry. With notes and critical remarks. By Elder David Bernard, of Warsaw, Genesee Co. N. Y. once an intimate Secretary in the Lodge of Perfection; and Secretary of the Convention of Seceding Masons, held at Le Roy, July 4 and 5, 1828.

"*For there is nothing covered that shall not be revealed, and hid that shall not be known.*"
"*And what ye hear in the ear that preach ye upon the house tops.*"

Jesus Christ.

IN CONFORMITY to the Act of the Congress of the United States, entitled "An Act for the encouragement of Learning, by securing the copies of Maps, Charts, and Books, to the Authors and Proprietors of such copies, during the times therein mentioned;" and also to the Act entitled "An Act supplementary to an Act entitled 'An Act for the encouragement of Learning, by securing the copies of Maps, Charts, and Books, to the Authors and Proprietors of such copies during the times therein mentioned,' and extending the benefits thereof to the arts of Designing, Engraving, and Etching, historical and other prints."

R. R. LANSING,
Clerk of the District Court of the United States, for the
Northern District of New-York.

FIFTH EDITION.

PREFACE.

The following documents are compiled with the design of securing them from the grasp of Masonic power; advancing the cause of truth and justice; preserving the rights and liberties of our country; promoting the glory of the Redeemer's kingdom; and saving souls from destruction.

During several years the compiler was a member of the Masonic fraternity. While he regarded the ceremonies of the order with disgust, and its oaths with abhorrence, he supposed that there existed principles in the institution which were pure and holy. In the peculiar providence of God, he was led to investigate the subject; he found it *wholly* corrupt; its morality, a shadow; its benevolence, selfishness; its religion, infidelity; and that as a system it was an engine of Satan, calculated to enslave the children of men, and pour contempt on the Most High.

In the immolation of Morgan, he saw the fate of Masonry—

> * * * * 'Its fall
> Determined, and its hapless crew—involved
> In that dark deed of death 'contagion spread
> Both of its crime and punishment:'

He saw the hand of God inscribing on its mystic pillars, 'MENE TEKEL, UPHARSIN;' and

> 'From amidst them forth he pass'd
> Long way through hostile scorn, which he sustain'd
> Superior, nor of violence fear'd ought;
> And with retorted scorn his back he turn'd
> On that proud TEMPLE 'to destruction doom'd!'

Since that event he has been impelled by duty to his country and his God, to hazard his property, character, and life, in exertions to overthrow an institution which has arisen among the nations in power and glory, and like mystic Babylon made them 'drunk with the wine of her fornication!'

> 'Here will he stand and breast him to the shock,
> Till he or Denmark falls.'

iv   PREFACE.

From the unwearied exertions of the brotherhood to suppress the light and impede the progress of truth, in relation to their outrages of September, 1826, and the revelations of Free Masonry made by Capt. Morgan and a Convention of Seceding Masons, he has thought of no way in which he could do so much for the advancement of the cause of liberty and truth, as to embody in one volume all the documents pertaining to the secrets of the institution; the recent violation of our laws and liberties by the Masonic fraternity; the proceedings of Anti-Masonic conventions; essays; orations; and remarks on the principles of the order—all of which are eminently calculated to give light on Masonry. He believes that such a work is important, not only for the present crisis, but for the benefit of posterity. He hopes it will receive that patronage to which it may be entitled. Should he, however, after 'biding the pelting of the pitiless storm,' hear only murmurs of disapprobation from the world, even then he will be cheered in the fulfilment of duty, by the 'still small voice' which whispers 'peace :'

> 'As when a wretch from thick polluted air,
> Darkness, and stench, and suffocating damps,
> And dungeon horrors, by kind fate discharged,
> Climbs some fair eminence, where ether pure
> Surrounds him, and Elysian prospects rise,
> His heart exults, his spirits cast their load;
> As if new born, he triumphs in the change.
> So joys the soul, when from *inglorious aims*,
> And *sordid sweets* from *feculence* and *froth*,
> Of *ties terrestrial*, set at large, she mounts
> To reason's region, her own element,
> Breathes hopes immortal, and affects the skies.'

INTRODUCTION.

In justice to myself, I cannot present this work to the public, without a brief exhibition of the facts which have led to its publication.

Soon after I commenced the service of Christ, Free Masonry was commended to my attention as an institution from heaven; moral, benevolent, of great antiquity, the twin sister of Christianity, possessing the patronage of the wise, the great, and good, and highly important to the ministers of the Lord Jesus. Wishing to avail myself of every auxiliary in promoting the glory of God and the happiness of my fellow men, I readily received the three first degrees. My disappointment none can know but those who have, in similar circumstances, been led in the same path of folly and sin. I silently retired from the institution, and for three years was hardly known as a Mason. I was not, however, without my reflections on the subject. I considered what I had taken as frivolous and wicked; but was unwilling to believe that there existed no substantial good in the order; and this idea was strengthened from the fact that many of my friends of a higher grade in Masonry taught me, that what I had received was not the 'magnum bonum' of the institution, but that this was yet to be attained. Not being able to advocate its cause from the knowledge I had derived of its principles, and supposing that the obligations I had received were morally binding, I could not say 'pro nor con' concerning it, without a violation of my conscience. With these views I embraced an offer to advance into the higher orders of mysticism, and reached forward to attain the desired end. In the reception of the Chaptoral degrees, my embarrassment increased. When I came to the oath of a Royal Arch Mason, which obligates to deliver a companion, '*right or wrong*,' I made a full stop and objected to proceeding. I was then assured in the most positive terms, that all would in the end be explained to my full satisfaction. But no such explanation took place. Thought I—Is this free Masonry? Is this the ancient and honorable institution patronized by thousands of the great and good? Upon my suggesting some queries to a Masonic friend, he gravely informed me, that the first seven degrees were founded on the Old Testament, and were but a shadow of good things to come; that if I wished to arrive at *perfection*, I must proceed to the sublime and ineffable degrees. These assurances, the awful oaths I had taken, with their penalties, and the vengeance of this most powerful institution, combined to deter me from renouncing it as evil. After much deliberation, hoping to find something in the higher orders to redeem the character of the institution in my estimation, I entered the lodge of Perfection and took the ineffable degrees.

About this time I learned that William Morgan was writing Masonry for publication. My informer was *then* a Baptist minister in high standing, and a Royal Arch Mason. He remarked that Morgan's writing Masonry was the greatest piece of depravity he ever knew; that some measures must be taken to stop it; that he would be one of a number to put him out of the way; that God looked upon the institution with so much complacency, he would never bring the perpetrators to light; that there had already been two meetings on the subject; and that he expected there would be another on that day; and finally attempted to justify his murder from Masonry and the word of God!

This conversation took place in Covington, (where I then lived,) five weeks before Morgan was murdered; and I should at this early period have informed him of his danger, had I not understood that he was on his guard and prepared for a defence.

The next week I left home for my health, and was absent some weeks. I returned on the 16th of September, and soon learned that Morgan was kidnapped and probably murdered! I conversed with the Masons on the subject, and they *justified both his abduction and murder!* I now read the first production of Elder Stearns on Masonry with peculiar interest. I also examined the Monitor and other Masonic writings, and reflected deeply on the nature and tendency of the institution. I compared the murder of Morgan and the conduct of the fraternity in relation to his abduction with the oaths and principles of the order, and became fully satisfied that to continue longer with the institution was not my duty. I expressed my opposition to its principles and the recent conduct of the fraternity in a free and open manner, which caused much excitement among the brotherhood. A meeting of the lodge in Covington was soon called, the object of which was to concert measures for an agreement among the fraternity, in what they should say in relation to their outrages, and to attend to members who were disaffected with their proceedings. I attended for the purpose of freeing my mind. When the lodge was duly opened and the subject introduced, I arose and in the most decisive manner disapproved the conduct of the fraternity, in their violation of civil and moral law. The meeting was long and *hor-*

ribly interesting! The true spirit of the institution was peculiarly manifest, especially towards me. For the introduction of Elder Stearns' book, and the honest expression of my sentiments, I was most shamefully abused. The murder of Morgan was justified, and every thing said that was calculated to harrow up the feelings of a patriot or Christian. Elder A****, a Knight Templar, being present, boldly asserted ' that if he should see any man writing Masonry, he should consider it his duty to take measures to stop him; that as cities and churches had their laws, with a right to inflict their penalties, so Masons had their laws, with the right to inflict the penalties to them; and that the *lodge* was the place to try a Mason—that if Morgan had been writing Masonry, and his throat was cut from ear to ear, his tongue torn out by the roots, and his body buried beneath the rough sands of the sea, at low water-mark, where the tide ebbs and flows twice in twenty-four hours, he could not complain in not having justice done him!' Amen, Amen, Amen, was the audible response around the room.

At the next meeting of the lodge, by request of the Master, I attended. Here a scene passed which language cannot describe! Several hours were occupied in abusing and making charges against me, the principal of which were, I had spoken against the institution. Many questions were asked and insults offered me. I told them frankly I had spoken against the principles of the order; that the right of opinion, the freedom of speech, and the liberty of the press, were privileges given to me by God; purchased by the blood of my fathers; that I had inhaled them with my first breath, and I would only lose them with my last; that if they could remove my objections to the institution, which I then exhibited, well—if not, they could expel me; but if they proceeded to farther abuses, they must suffer the consequences. My objections were *not* removed; and I requested permission to withdraw. Soon after I left them they expelled and immediately commenced a most wicked persecution against me. The *professed* ministers of Christ, infidels, and drunkards, from Buffalo to Albany, were united to destroy my character! I was admonished by oral and epistolary communications to be on my guard, to carry arms; and so great was my personal danger, that my friends would not suffer me to ride alone from one town to another.* In short

---

* Let the reader remember that the compiler of this work renounced Masonry in October, 1826—was the first Mason who declared open hostility to the institution subsequent to the abduction of Morgan; and he will not be surprised in learning that his life was in jeopardy!

INTRODUCTION.

they 'opposed my interest, deranged my business, pointed me out as an unworthy and vicious vagabond, an object of contempt,' and ' transferred *this* character after me ;' and it would seem that they intended to do it ' during my natural life !' The united efforts of the fraternity to injure me, have, however, proved unavailing.

I soon became convinced that the peace of society, the salvation of my country, the present and eternal happiness of my fellow men, and the glory of God, required the destruction of the institution. To accomplish this, I was confident but one effectual method could be adopted, and this was to make a full disclosure of its secrets. To this end I then exerted myself. After an interchange of minds with some of the patriots of Batavia and Le Roy, a convention of Masons opposed to the institution was called, to meet on the 19th of February, 1827. This convention was composed of about forty, who after having deliberated upon the principles of the order, and binding nature of its obligations, resolved to make a revelation of its mysteries. They confirmed the 'Illustrations' of William Morgan; published the oaths of twelve degrees of a higher order; appointed a committee to prepare all the degrees which could be obtained for the press; and adjourned to meet on the 4th of July following.

The committee, with much labor and expense, had all the degrees conferred in a Royal Arch Chapter, Encampment of Knight Templars, and orders of the Holy Cross, ready, and presented them to the convention on the 4th and 5th of July, which declared them correct, and ordered them to be published to the world.

The degrees of Mark, Past, and Most Excellent Master, were obtained from Mrs. Morgan, as written by her husband; the Royal Arch, from an agent of the committee, (a Royal Arch Mason,) as given by Jeremy L. Cross, the Grand Lecturer of the United States; and those of the Encampment and Holy Cross, from a Knight of the Thrice Illustrious Order, as transcribed from a copy as given the Encampment at Le Roy, by the Grand Commander at Utica.

In consequence of the zeal manifested by the fraternity to stifle the excitement, I conceived that much good might be done by a compilation of the most important documents in relation to the subject. By the advice of many friends, and under the patronage of a county and state convention, I undertook the work.

While preparing it for the press, I obtained from the *highest authority* thirty-three of the sublime and ineffable degrees, all of which I KNOW TO BE CORRECT, and I give them to the world ' verbatim et literatum.'

But am I justifiable in pursuing this course? Will the law of God approve the violation of such solemn oaths? Passing by the arguments which might be adduced from the fact that the obligations were taken without a previous knowledge of their character—the assurances that they were not to interfere with my political or religious sentiments, when they are diametrically opposite to both—that I swore fealty to a professedly ancient, moral, benevolent, and righteous institution, when it proves to be ' modern, corrupt, selfish, and unholy.' I rest the question upon the principles of moral obligation, by which I expect to be judged, and by which I must stand or fall. Are the oaths of Free Masonry, then, congenial with the duties which I owe to God and my fellow men? If they are, I most certainly am bound to keep them; if not, to break them. By the principles of moral obligation I am required to promote God's glory, and the best good of the universe. My swearing to love God and my neighbor does not enhance the obligation at all; for it says, ' Thou shalt love the Lord thy God with *all* thy heart and with *all* thy soul and with *all* thy strength and with *all* thy mind, and thy neighbor *as* thyself.' It says this to the sinner and the saint—to the man who has sworn and to him who has not sworn, it is alike infinitely binding on all. It cannot be increased nor diminished—it can require no more—it can receive no less. If I swear to love God and keep his commandments, the oath is binding, because moral obligation made these requisitions before I took the oath, and the oath and moral obligation are in perfect harmony. If I swear to violate the command of God; for instance, to kill my neighbor, I am bound to break my oath; for the Divine law says, ' Thou shalt not kill,' and my swearing to violate the command does not, cannot, render the obligation void.—Moral obligation requires me to keep such secrets and such only as are calculated to promote God's glory and the best good of community; and my swearing does not effect the obligation at all. It also requires me to reveal those secrets, the keeping of which have a tendency to mar or prevent His glory and the best good of my neighbor; and my swearing to keep them does not, cannot, render the obligation void; for instance, if I had sworn to keep secret the intention of a highwayman to rob my neighbor's house and murder his family; to keep secret a plot against my country, the government of which is founded upon the principles of truth and justice; to keep secret a grand conspiracy formed by a powerful society, the object of which was, like that of the *Illuminati*, to abolish government and social order and extinguish Christianity—as the keeping of these secrets would be prejudicial to the interests of my neighbor, to the safety of my country, and the glory of God, the principles of moral obligation would require me to reveal them. If I had sworn to assist the robber, to unite in the plot, or conspiracy, my refusing to *act* in either case, *simply*, would not fulfil the duties which I should owe to my neighbor, my country, or my God. So I did not *make known* the intention of the robber, *expose* the plot, or *reveal* the conspiracy, I should be guilty of a violation of moral obligation.

It will not be necessary here to inquire whether the oaths to keep the secrets of a brother, with or without exception, to deliver a companion ' right or wrong,' to ' take vengeance on the traitors of Masonry,' to ' sacrifice all those who reveal the secrets of the order,' are in harmony with the Divine law—but whether the principles of moral obligation require the keeping or revealing of Masonic secrets ?

It will readily be admitted that the *existence* of the institution depends upon the keeping of its secrets inviolate. It will follow, then, that if the existence of the institution is necessary, or has a tendency to promote God's glory and the well being of society, the principles of moral obligations require me to keep its secrets, and by revealing them I am guilty of moral perjury! And on the other hand, if the institution is corrupt, has an evil tendency, is opposed to the order and well being of society and the glory of God, I am under moral obligation to break my oaths, and reveal its secrets to the world, that it may come to an end. My refusing to meet with or support the institution, is not sufficient; I must renounce *fealty* to the order, *reveal* its secrets, *oppose* its influence, and use my exertions to *destroy* it, or I am guilty of a violation of moral obligation.

Let the reader carefully and thoroughly examine the following documents, and he will discover that Free Masonry, as a system, is dark, unfruitful, selfish, demoralizing, blasphemous, murderous, anti-republican, and anti-Christian—opposed to the glory of God and the good of mankind; and hence that the compiler in bursting asunder the bands of the fraternity, and publishing their secrets to the world, is doing no more than is required by the principles of moral obligation—is but fulfilling the duties which he owes to God and his fellow men.

DAVID BERNARD.

Warsaw, April 1, 1829.

RECOMMENDATIONS.

The Baptist Church of Christ in Warsaw, Genesee County, N. Y.,

TO THE CHRISTIAN PUBLIC.

As Elder David Bernard is about publishing a book entitled 'LIGHT ON MASONRY,' which we deem highly important for the purity and advancement of the Redeemer's kingdom; and as we are sensible, from the persecution he has already received, as well as from the nature of the subject, that many aspersions will be thrown upon his character, to impede the righteous influence which the truth should have upon the public mind; we deem it our duty to state, that from the most highly accredited documents, we can vouch for the purity of his moral character from his infancy to the time he professed Christianity—of his moral and Christian conversation from this period, until he became a member of this church; and that during nearly two years he has been the regular and approved pastor among us; that he is a minister of the Genesee Baptist Association, in good standing; and we cheerfully and unanimously recommend him as a man of strict integrity, unblemished moral character, and faithful servant of the Lord Jesus.

Executed by order and in presence of the Church,
this fourteenth day of March, A. D. 1829.

JOHN TRUESDELL, Church Clerk, pro tem.

SAMUEL SALSBURY,
JONATHAN F. HIBBARD, } Deacons of the Church.

RESOLUTION of an Anti-Masonic Convention of Genesee county, held at Bethany, July 23, 1828, in favor of this work. 'WHEREAS the title and prospectus of a book entitled 'LIGHT ON MASONRY,' &c. &c. has been read to this convention—Therefore, *Resolved*, That for the advancement of light and truth in the great and holy cause of Anti-Masonry, and for the good of future generations, we deem it of the highest importance that such a work be published; and from our knowledge of the talents, character, intelligence, and zeal, of Elder *David Bernard*, we believe him to be eminently qualified for such an undertaking; we therefore *solicit* him to persevere in the work without delay, as *such* a work is worthy of the patronage of the friends of liberty and religion throughout the whole civilized world.'

'ROBERT EARLL, jun. President.

CEPHAS A. SMITH, Secretary.'

RESOLUTION of the Anti-Masonic New-York State Convention, held at Utica, August 4, 1828, in favor of this work. 'WHEREAS the title and prospectus of a book entitled 'LIGHT ON MASONRY,' &c. &c. by Elder David Bernard, has been read to the convention, and entertaining the fullest confidence in the integrity, zeal, and ability, of the compiler, and being deeply impressed with the importance of the proposed publication, to the cause of truth and justice—Therefore, *Resolved*, That we recommend the compiler to proceed without delay in the publication of his book; and we recommend it to the attention and patronage of all the friends of truth and the cause of civil liberty throughout the world.'

'JAMES HAWKS, President.

THOS. C. GREEN,
SETH A. ABBEY, } Secretaries,'

TABLE OF CONTENTS.

LIGHT ON MASONRY: Page

DESCRIPTION OF CEREMONIES
USED IN CONFERRING DEGREE OF

Entered Apprentice	13
Fellow Craft	42
Master Mason	58
Mark Master	87
Past Master	107
Most Excellent Master	114
Royal Arch	124
Knight of the Red Cross	144
Knight Templar and Kt. of Malta	155
Knight of the Christian Mark, and Guard of the Conclave	166
Knight of the Holy Sepulchre	170
The Holy and Thrice Illustrious Order of the Cross	173
Secret Master	183,210,345,507
Perfect Master	186,210,346,509
Intimate Secretary	189,211,346,511
Provost and Judge	191,346,513
Intendant of the Buildings, or Master in Israel	194,347,515
Elected Knight of Nine	197,347,518
Elected Grand Master, or Illustrious Elected of Fifteen	199,348,520
Illustrious Knight or Sublime Knight Elected	201,349,521
Grand Master Architect	201,349,523
Knight of the Ninth Arch	202,350,524
Grand Elect Perfect and Sublime Mason	205,351,528
Prince of Jerusalem	212,353
Knight of the East and West	217,352,354
Knight of the Eagle, and Sovereign Prince of Rose Croix de Heroden	225,354
Grand Pontiff	238,355
Venerable Grand Master of all Symbolic Lodges, Sov. Prince of Masonry, Master Advitiam, or Grand Pontiff	240,355
Knight of the Royal Axe, or Hache, (hatchet)	247,356
Chief of the Tabernacle	249,356
Prince of the Tabernacle	250,357
Knight of the Brazen Serpent	253,357
Prince of Mercy, or Scotch Trinitarian	255,357
Sovereign Nommander of the Temple at Jerusalem	256,358
K't. Adept of the Eagle, or Sun	258,358
Knight of Kadosh	278,359
Prince of the Royal Secret	294,360

   Page

Sovereign Grand Inspector General	301
Circular of Grand Inspectors	341

FRENCH DEGREES.

Elu de Perignan	302
Le Petit Architect	305
Grand Architect, or Compagnon Ecossois	310
Le Maitre Ecossois	315
Chevalier de l'Orient	320
Le Chevalier Rose Kroix	330
Chevalier Prussien	335,356

COMMITTEE REPORTS, CONVENTION PROCEEDINGS, ORATIONS, ESSAYS, ETC. ETC.

Saratoga Baptist Convention Proceedings	361
Narrative of facts relating to abduction of William Morgan, &c.	367
Address to honest Masons	392
Le Roy Seceding Masons' Conven.	418
———— Anti-Masonic Convention	421
New York Legislature Proceedings	431
Hon. J. Crary's Speech in Senate	439
Le Roy Adjourned Seced. Masons' Convention—with Declaration	445
Herbert A. Read's, Esq. Oration at Le Roy	451
Utica Anti-Masonic N. York State Convention Proceedings	463
T. F. Talbot's, Esq. Speech at Utica	471
Eli Bruce's (and others) Trial for Conspiracy	479
B. B. Hotchkin's Candid Appeal	487
———— Answer to Two Great Questions	495
History of Freemasonry	501

APPENDIX. NO. I.

Depositions of sundry persons—and other Documents—disclosing many important particulars relative to the kidnapping of the unfortunate Morgan: with Government Proclamations, &c. &c. (In 30 Nos.)	i—xxvi

NO. II.

Albany Anti Masonic N. Y. State Convention Proceedings	xxvii

LIGHT ON MASONRY.

---

* A DESCRIPTION of the ceremonies used in opening a lodge of Entered Apprentice Masons; which is the same in all the upper degrees, with the exception of the difference in the signs, due-guards, grips, pass-grips, words and their several names; all of which will be given and explained in their proper places as the work progresses.

One rap calls the lodge to order; one calls up the Junior and Senior Deacons; two raps calls up the subordinate officers; and three, all the members of the lodge.

The Master having called the lodge to order, and the officers all seated, the Master says to the Junior Warden, 'Brother Junior, are they all Entered Apprentice Masons in the South?' *Ans.* 'They are, Worshipful.' Master to the Senior Warden, 'Brother Senior, are they all Entered Apprentice Masons in the west?' *Ans.* 'They are, Worshipful.' The Master then says, 'They are in the east;' at the same time he gives a rap with the common gavel or mallet, which calls up both Deacons. Master to Junior Deacon, 'Attend to that part of your duty, and inform the Tyler that we are about to open a lodge of Entered Apprentice Masons; and direct him to tyle accordingly.' The Tyler then steps to the door and gives three raps, which are answered by three from without: the Junior Deacon then gives one, which is also answered by the Tyler with one; the door is then partly opened, and the Junior Deacon delivers his message, and resumes his situation, and says, 'the door is tyled, Worshipful,' (at the same time giving the due-guard, which is never omitted when the Master is addressed.) The Master to the Junior Deacon, 'By whom?' *Ans.* 'By a Master Mason without the door, armed with the proper implements of his office.' Master to the Junior Deacon, 'His duty there?' *Ans.* 'To keep off all cowans and eave-droppers, see that none pass or repass without per-

---

* The first three Degrees in Masonry here published, are as written by **Capt. William Morgan**: and as conferred in the Lodges in the western part of the state of New-York.

B

mission from the Master. [Some say without permission from the chair.] Master to Junior Deacon, 'Brother Junior, your place in the lodge?' *Ans.* 'At the right hand of the Senior Warden in the west.' Master to Junior Deacon, 'Your business there, brother Junior?' *Ans.* 'To wait on the Worshipful Master and Wardens, act as their proxy in the active duties of the lodge, and take charge of the door.' Master to Junior Deacon, The Senior Deacon's place in the lodge?' *Ans.* 'At the right hand of the Worshipful Master in the east.' [The Master, while asking the last question, gives two raps, which calls up all the subordinate officers.] Master to Senior Deacon, 'Your duty there, brother Senior?' *Ans.* 'To wait on the Worshipful Master and Wardens, act as their proxy in the active duties of the Lodge, attend to the preparation and introduction of candidates —and welcome and clothe all visiting brethren,' [i. e. furnish them with an apron.] Master to Senior Deacon, 'The Secretary's place in the lodge, brother Senior?' *Ans.* 'At the left hand of the Worshipful Master in the east.' Master to Secretary, 'Your duty there, brother Secretary?' *Ans.* 'The better to observe the Worshipful Master's will and pleasure, record the proceedings of the lodge; transmit a copy of the same to the Grand Lodge, if required; receive all monies and money bills from the hand of the brethren, pay them over to the Treasurer, and take his receipt for the same.' The Master to the Secretary, 'The Treasurer's place in the lodge?' *Ans.* 'At the right hand of the Worshipful Master.' Master to Treasurer, 'Your duty there, brother Treasurer?' *Ans.* 'Duly to observe the Worshipful Master's will and pleasure; receive all monies and money bills from the hands of the Secretary; keep a just and true account of the same; pay them out by order of the Worshipful Master and consent of the brethren.' The Master to the Treasurer, 'The Junior Warden's place in the lodge, brother Treasurer?' *Ans.* 'In the south, Worshipful.' Master to Junior Warden, 'Your business there, brother Junior?' *Ans.* 'As the sun in the south at high meridian, is the beauty and glory of the day, so stands the Junior Warden in the south, the better to observe the time; call the crafts from labour to refreshment; superintend them during the hours thereof; see that none convert the hours of refreshment into that of intemperance or excess; and call them on again in due season, that the Worshipful Master may have honor, and they pleasure and profit thereby.' Master to the Junior Warden, 'The Senior Warden's place in the lodge?' *Ans.* 'In the west, Worshipful.' Master to the Senior Warden, 'Your duty there, brother Senior?' *Ans.* 'As the sun sets in the west, to close the day, so stands the Senior Warden in the west, to assist the Worshipful Master in opening his lodge; take care of the jewels and implements; see that none be lost; pay the craft their wages, if any be due; and see that none go away dissatisfied.' Master to the Senior Warden, 'The Master's place in the lodge?' *Ans.* 'In the east, Worshipful.' Master to the Senior Warden, 'His duty there?' *Ans.* 'As the sun rises in the east to open and adorn the day, so presides the Worshipful Master in the east to open and adorn his lodge; set his crafts to work with good and wholesome laws; or cause the same to be done.' The Master now gives three raps, when all the brethren rise, and the Master, taking off his hat, proceeds as follows: 'In like manner so do I, strictly forbidding all profane language, private committees, or any other disorderly conduct whereby the peace and harmony of this lodge may be interrupted while engaged in its lawful pursuits, under no less penalty than the bye-laws, or such penalty as a majority of the brethren present may see fit to inflict. Brethren, attend to giving the signs.' [Here lodges differ very much. In some they declare the lodge open as follows, before they give the sign.] The Master (all the brethren imitating him) extends his left arm from his body so as to form an angle of about forty-five degrees, and holds his right hand traversely across his left, the palms thereof one inch apart. This is called the first sign of a Mason—is the sign of distress in this degree, and alludes to the position a candidate's hands are placed in when he takes the obligation of an Entered Apprentice Mason. The Master then draws his right hand across his throat, the hand open, with the thumb next to the throat, and drops it down by his side. This is called the due-guard of an Entered Apprentice Mason, (many call it the sign,) and alludes to the penalty of an obligation. (See obligation.) The Master then declares the lodge opened, in the following manner: 'I now declare this lodge of Entered Apprentice Masons duly opened for the despatch of business.' The Senior Warden declares it to the Junior Warden, and he to the brethren. 'Come, brethren, let us pray.' One of the following prayers is used:

Most holy and glorious God! the great Architect of the universe; the giver of all good gifts and graces: Thou hast promised that "Where two or three are gathered together in thy name, thou wilt be in the midst of them, and bless them." In thy name we assemble, most humbly beseeching thee to bless us in all our undertakings; that we may know and serve thee aright, and that all our actions may tend to thy glory, and our advancement in knowledge and virtue. And we beseech thee, O Lord God, to bless our present assembling ; and to illumine our minds through the influence of the Son of Righteousness, that we may walk in the light of thy countenance ; and when the trials of our probationary state are over, be admitted into the temple not made with hands, eternal in the heavens. Amen. So mote it be.

Another prayer, as often used at opening as closing.

Behold how good and how pleasant it is for brethren to dwell together in unity ! It is like the precious ointment upon the head that ran down upon the beard, even Aaron's beard, that went down to the skirts of his garment : as the dew of Hermon, and as the dew that descended upon the mountains of Zion, for there the Lord commanded the blessing, evermore. Amen. So mote it be.

The lodge being now open and ready to proceed to business, the Master directs the Secretary to read the minutes of the last meeting, which naturally brings to view the business of the present.

If there are any candidates to be brought forward, that will be the first business attended to. I will, therefore, proceed with a description of the ceremonies used in the admission and initiation of a candidate in the first degree of Masonry.

A person wishing to become a Mason must get some one who is a Mason to present his petition to a lodge, when, if there are no serious objections, it will be entered on the minutes, and a committee of two or three appointed to inquire into his character, and report to the next regular communication. The following is the form of a petition used by a candidate ; but a worthy candidate will not be rejected for the want of formality in his petition.

To the Worshipful Master, Wardens and Brethren of Lodge No. —, of Free and Accepted Masons.

The subscriber, residing in ———, of lawful age, and by occupation a ———, begs leave to state that, unbiassed by friends, and uninfluenced by mercenary motives, he freely and voluntarily offers himself a candidate for the mysteries of Masonry, and that he is prompt to solicit this privilege by a favourable opinion conceived of the institution, a desire of knowledge and a sincere wish of being serviceable to his fellow creatures. Should his petition be granted, he will cheerfully conform to all the ancient established usages and customs of the fraternity.

(Signed) A. B.

At the next regular communication, (if no very serious objection appears against the candidate,) the ballot-boxes willl be passed; one black ball will reject a candidate. The boxes may be passed three times. The Deacons are the proper persons to pass them; one of the boxes has black and white beans, or balls in it, the other empty; the one with the balls in it goes before, and furnishes each member with a black and white ball; the empty box follows and receives them. There are two holes in the top of his box with a small tube (generally) in each, one of which is black, and the other white, with a partition in the box. The members put both their balls into this box as their feelings dictate; when the balls are received, the box is presented to the Master, Senior, and Junior Wardens, who pronounce clear or not clear, as the case may be. The ballot proving clear, the candidate (if present) is conducted into a small preparation room adjoining the lodge, he is asked the following questions, and gives the following answers. Senior Deacon to candidate, 'Do you sincerely declare, upon your honor before these gentlemen, that, unbiased by friends, uninfluenced by unworthy motives, you freely and voluntarily offer yourself a candidate for the mysteries of Masonry?' *Ans.* 'I do.' Senior Deacon to candidate, 'Do you sincerely declare, upon your honor before these gentlemen, that you are prompt to solicit the privileges of Masonry, by a favorable opinion conceived of the institution, a desire of knowledge, and a sincere wish of being serviceable to your fellow creatures?' *Ans.* 'I do.' Senior Deacon to candidate,* 'Do you sincerely declare, upon your honor before these gentlemen, that you will cheerfully conform to all the ancient established usages and customs of the fraternity?' *Ans.* 'I do.' After the above questions are proposed and answered, and the result reported to the Master, he says, 'Brethren, at the request of Mr. A. B. he has been proposed and accepted in regular form. I therefore recommend him as a proper candidate for the mysteries of Masonry, and worthy to partake of the privileges of the fraternity; and in consequence of a declaration of his intentions, voluntarily made, I believe he will cheerfully conform to the rules of the order.' The candidate, during the time, is divested of all his apparel (shirt excepted) and furnished with a pair of drawers, kept in the lodge for the use of candidates; the candidate is then blindfolded, his left foot bare,

---

* The reader will here learn one reason why those who enter a lodge, never come out, until they have taken a degree. The candidate is made to promise upon his honor that he will " conform to all the ancient established usages and customs of the fraternity;" hence let him be ever so much opposed to the ceremonies of initiation, or the oath of the degree, he cannot go back, for he feels bound by his promise. Should he, however, feel constrained to violate his word, the persuasions, and, if necessary, the threats of the Master and brethren compel him to go forward.

B 2

his right in a slipper, his left breast and arm naked, and a rope called a cable-tow round his neck and left arm, (the rope is not put round the arm in all lodges) in which posture the candidate is conducted to the door where he is caused to give, or the conductor gives, three distinct knocks, which are answered by three from within; the conductor gives one more, which is also answered by one from within. The door is then partly opened and the Junior Deacon generally asks, 'Who comes there? Who comes there? Who comes there?' The conductor, alias the Senior Deacon, answers, 'A poor blind candidate who has long been desirous of having and receiving a part of the rights and benefits of this worshipful lodge, dedicated (some say erected) to God and held forth to the holy order of St. John, as all true fellows and brothers have done, who have gone this way before him.'—The Junior Deacon then asks, 'Is it of his own free will and accord he makes this request? Is he duly and truly prepared? Worthy and well qualified? And properly avouched for?' All of which being answered in the affirmative, the Junior Deacon to Senior Deacon; 'By what further rights does he expect to obtain this benefit?' *Ans.* 'By being a man, free born, of lawful age, and under the tongue of good report.' The Junior Deacon then says, 'Since this is the case you will wait till the Worshipful Master in the east is made acquainted with his request, and his answer returned;' the Junior Deacon repairs to the Master, when the same questions are asked and answers returned as at the door; after which, the Master says, 'Since he comes endowed with all these necessary qualifications, let him enter this worshipful lodge in the name of the Lord and take heed on what he enters.' The candidate then enters, the Junior Deacon at the same time pressing his naked left breast with the point of the compass, and asks the candidate 'Did you feel any thing?' *Ans.* 'I did;' Junior Deacon to candidate, 'What was it?' *Ans.* 'A torture.' The Junior Deacon then says, 'As this is a torture to your flesh, so may it ever be to your mind and conscience, if ever you should attempt to reveal the secrets of Masonry unlawfully.' The candidate is then conducted to the centre of the lodge, where he and the Senior Deacon kneels, and the Deacon says the following prayer.

"Vouchsafe thine aid, Almighty Father of the universe, to this our present convention; and grant that this candidate for Masonry may dedicate and devote his life to thy service, and become a true and faithful brother among us! Endue him with a competency of thy divine wisdom, that by the secrets of our art, he may be the better enabled to display the beauties of holiness, to the honor of thy holy name. So mote it be. Amen!"

The Master then asks the candidate, 'In whom do you put your trust?' *Ans.* 'In God.' The master then takes him by the right hand and says, 'Since in God you put your trust, arise, follow your leader, and fear no danger.' The Senior Deacon then conducts the candidate three times regularly round the lodge, and halts at the Junior Warden in the south, where the same questions are asked and answers returned as at the door.

As the candidate and the conductor are passing round the room, the Master reads the following passage of scripture, and takes the same time to read it, that they do to go round the lodge three times.

"Behold how good and how pleasant it is for brethren to dwell together in unity! It is like the precious ointment upon the head, that ran down upon the beard, even Aaron's beard, that went down to the skirts of his garment: as the dew of Hermon, and as the dew that descended upon the mountains of Zion; for there the Lord commanded the blessing, even life for ever more."

The candidate is then conducted to the Senior Warden in the west, where the same questions are asked and answers returned as before; from thence he is conducted to the Worshipful Master in the east, where the same questions are asked and answers returned as before. The Master likewise demands of him, from whence he came and whither he is travelling. The candidate answers, 'From the west and travelling to the east.' Master inquires: 'Why do you leave the west and travel to the east?' *Ans.* 'In search of light.' Master then says, 'Since the candidate is travelling in search of light, you will please conduct him back to the west from whence he came, and put him in the care of the Senior Warden, who will teach him how to approach the east, the place of light, by advancing upon one upright regular step, to the first step, his feet forming the right angle of an oblong square, his body erect at the altar before the Master, and place him in a proper position to take upon him the solemn oath or obligation of an Entered Apprentice Mason.' The Senior Warden receives the candidate, and instructs him as directed. He first steps off with the left foot and brings up the heel of the right into the hollow thereof; the heel of the right foot against the ancle of the left, will of course form the right angle of an oblong square; the candidate then kneels on his left knee, and places his right foot so as to form a square with the left, he turns his foot round until the ancle bone is as much in front of him as the toes on the left; the candidate's left hand is then put under the Holy Bible, square and compass, and the right hand on them. This is the position in which a candidate is placed when he takes upon him the oath or obligation of an Entered Apprentice Mason. As soon as the candidate is placed in this position, the Worshipful Master approaches him, and says, 'Mr. A. B. you are now placed in a proper position to take upon you the solemn oath or obligation of an Entered Apprentice Mason,* which I assure you is neither to affect your religion nor politics, if you are willing to take it repeat your name and say after me ;' [and although many have refused to take any kind of an obligation, and begged for the privilege of retiring, yet none have made their escape; they have been either coerced, or persuaded to submit. There are thousands who never return to the lodge after they are initiated.] The following obligation is then administered.

"I, A. B. of my own free will and accord, in presence of Almighty God, and this worshipful lodge of Free and Accepted Masons, dedicated to God and held forth to the holy order of St. John, do hereby and hereon most solemnly and sincerely promise and swear, that I will always hail, ever conceal, and never reveal any part, or parts, art, or arts, point, or points of the secrets, arts and mysteries of ancient Free Masonry, which I have received, am about to receive, or may hereafter be instructed in, to any person or persons in the known world, except it be a true and lawful brother Mason, or within the body of a just and lawfully constituted lodge of such, and not unto him, nor unto them whom I shall hear so to be, but unto him and them only whom I shall find so to be, after strict trial and due examination or lawful information. Furthermore, do I promise and swear that I will not write, print, stamp, stain, hew, cut, carve, indent, paint, or engrave it on any thing moveable or immoveable, under the whole canopy of heaven, whereby, or whereon the least letter, figure, character, mark, stain, shadow, or resemblance of the same may become legible or intelligible to myself or any other person in the known world, whereby the secrets of Masonry may be unlawfully obtained through my unworthiness. To all which I do most solemnly and sincerely promise and swear, without the least equivocation, mental reservation, or self evasion of mind in me whatever; binding myself under no less penalty, than to have my throat cut across, my tongue torn out by the roots, and my body buried in the rough

---

* In many lodges this is put in the form of a question, thus: "Are you willing to take an obligation upon you that does not effect your politics or religion?" The promise "to conform," made before entering the lodge, the "assurance that the oath is not to interfere with their political or religious principles," and the manner the obligation is administered,—only two or three words being repeated at a time, consequently not fully understood; are among the reasons which have led many great and good men to take oaths incompatible with the laws of God and our country.

sands of the sea at low water mark, where the tide ebbs and flows twice in twenty-four hours; so help me God, and keep me steadfast in the due performance of the same."*

After the obligation the master addresses the candidate in the following manner: " Brother, to you the secrets of Masonry are about to be unveiled, and a brighter sun never shone lustre on your eyes; while prostrate before this sacred altar, do you not shudder at every crime? have you not confidence in every virtue? May these thoughts ever inspire you with the most noble sentiments; may you ever feel that elevation of soul, that shall scorn a dishonest act. Brother, what do you most desire?' *Ans.* ' Light.' Master to brethren, ' Brethren, stretch forth your hands and assist in bringing this new made brother from darkness to light.' The members having formed a circle round the candidate, the Master says, 'And God said, let there be light, and there was light.' At the same time, all the brethren clap their hands, and stamp on the floor with their right foot as heavy as possible, the bandage dropping from the candidate's eyes at the same instant, which, after having been so long blind, and full of fearful apprehensions all the time, this great and sudden transition from perfect darkness to a light brighter (if possible) than the meridian sun in a midsummer day, sometimes produces an alarming effect. I once knew a man to faint on being brought to light; and his recovery was quite doubtful for some time: however, he did come to, but he never returned to the lodge again. I have often conversed with him on the subject, he is yet living, and will give a certificate in support of the above statement at any time if requested.

After the candidate is brought to light, the Master addresses him as follows: ' Brother, on being brought to light, you first discover three great lights in Masonry by the assistance of three lesser, they are thus explained; the three great lights in Masonry are the Holy Bible, Square and Compass.† The Holy Bible is given

---

* It is frequently said by Masons that the "penalties of Masonic oaths are nothing; that no one is bound to inflict them, and that if Morgan was put to death by Masons it was not done in conformity to Masonic law." But if one part of the oath is nothing, another part is nothing by the same rule. Any Mason, therefore, is at liberty to reveal Masonry without exposing himself any more than he would if the oath was never administered. But if the penalties are not to be inflicted, why did they kill Morgan—and why is a Mason sworn that he will "use his most decided endeavors, by the blessing of God, to bring such person (the person who violates Masonic law) to the most *strict* and CONDIGN PUNISHMENT agreeable to the *ancient rules* and usages of the fraternity?

† The Holy Bible is here said to be given to Masons as a rule and guide for their faith and practice. But I would ask, if Free Masonry is the same among all nations (as is declared by Masonic writers) how this is possible, when it is a well

to us as a rule and guide for our faith and practice; the Square, to square our actions, and the Compass to keep us in due bounds with all mankind, but more especially with the brethren. The three lesser lights are three burning tapers, or candles placed on candlesticks, (some say, or candles on pedestals,) they represent the Sun, Moon, and Master of the lodge, and are thus explained. As the sun rules the day and the moon governs the night, so ought the Worshipful Master with equal regularity to rule and govern his lodge, or cause the same to be done; you next discover me as Master of this lodge, approaching you from the east upon the first step of Masonry, under the sign and due-guard of an Entered Apprentice Mason. (The sign and due-guard has been explained.) This is the manner of giving them, imitate me as near as you can, keeping your position. First. step off with your left foot and bring the heel of the right into the hollow thereof so as to form a square.' [This is the first step in Masonry.] The following is the sign of an Entered Apprentice Mason, and is the sign of distress in this degree; you are not to give it unless in distress. [It is given by holding your two hands traversely across each other, the right hand upwards and one inch from the left.] The following is the due-guard of an Entered Apprentice Mason. [This is given by drawing your right hand across your throat, the thumb next to your throat, your arm as high as the elbow in a horizontal position.] 'Brother, I now present you my right hand in token of brotherly love and esteem, and with it the grip and name of the grip of an Entered Apprentice Mason.' The right hands are joined together, as in shaking hands, and each sticks his thumb nail into the third joint or upper end of the fore finger; the name of the grip is *Boaz*, and is to be given in the following manner and no other; the Master first gives the grip and word, and divides it for the instruction of the candidate; the ques-

---

known fact, that but a small part of the human family are in possession of, or know any thing about, the Bible? And if the Bible is received by Masons as a rule of faith and practice, why do they use a square and compass? Is not the Bible sufficient?

The truth is, Masonry is not the same among all nations, only in some respects, and these are, the fundamental principles of the order. The appendages of the Institution differ according to the peculiar feelings and sentiments of the people among whom it exists. Hence in America, in a religious point of view, it has existed with difficulty: Masonic writers have been at a loss what to say on the subject, and in their extremity, one has called it 'religion,' another the 'hand-maid of religion,' a third the 'twin-sister of Christianity,' and a fourth that it was simply an Institution of 'morality and benevolence.' To please the Christian the Bible is introduced,—to satisfy the infidel, the square and compass are added; the name of Christ is expunged from passages quoted, and the work of the Holy Ghost rejected, and all done in such a manner, that but few see the foul and monstrous imposition.

tions are as follows: The Master and candidate holding each other by the grip as before described, the Master says, 'What is this?' *Ans.* 'A grip.' Q. 'A grip of what?' *Ans.* 'The grip of an Entered Apprentice Mason.' Q. 'Has it a name?' *Ans.* 'It has.' Q. 'Will you give it to me?' *Ans.* 'I did not so receive it, neither can I so impart it.' Q. 'What will you do with it?' *Ans.* 'Letter it or halve it.' Q. 'Halve it and begin.' *Ans.* 'You begin.' Q. 'Begin you.' *Ans.* 'BO. Q. 'AZ.' *Ans.* 'BOAZ.' Master says, 'Right, brother *Boaz*, I greet you. It is the name of the left hand pillar of the porch of king Solomon's Temple—arise, brother Boaz, and salute the Junior and Senior Wardens as such, and convince them that you have been regularly initiated as an Entered Apprentice Mason, and have got the sign, grip, and word.' The Master returns to his seat while the Wardens are examining the candidate, and gets a lamb-skin or white apron, presents it to the candidate and observes, 'Brother, I now present you with a lamb-skin or white apron; it is an emblem of innocence, and the badge of a Mason; it has been worn by kings, princes, and potentates of the earth, who have never been ashamed to wear it; it is more honourable than the diadems of kings, or pearls of princesses, when worthily worn: it is more ancient than the Golden Fleece or Roman Eagle; more honorable than the Star and Garter; or any other order that can be conferred upon you at this, or any other time, except it be in the body of a just and fully constituted lodge; you will carry it to the Senior Warden in the west, who will teach you how to wear it as an Entered Apprentice Mason.' The Senior Warden ties the apron on and turns up the flap instead of letting it fall down in front of the top of the apron. This is the way Entered Apprentice Masons wear, or ought to wear, their aprons until they are advanced. The candidate is now conducted to the Master in the east, who says, 'Brother, as you are dressed, it is necessary you should have tools to work with; I will now present you with the working tools of an Entered Apprentice Mason, which are the twenty-four inch guage and common gavel; they are thus explained:—The twenty-four inch guage is an instrument made use of by operative masons to measure and lay out their work, but we as Free and Accepted Masons, make use of it for the more noble and glorious purpose of dividing our time. The twenty-four inches on the guage, are emblematical of the twenty-four hours in the day, which we are taught to divide into three equal parts, whereby we find eight hours for the service of God, and a worthy distressed brother; eight hours for our usual vocations; and eight for refreshment and sleep; the common gavel is an instrument made use of by operative Masons to break off the corners of rough stones; the better to fit them for the builder's use; but we, as Free and Accepted Masons, use it for the more noble and glorious purpose of divesting our hearts and consciences of all the vices and superfluities of life, thereby fitting our minds as living and lively stones, for that spiritual building, that house not made with hands, eternal in the Heavens.* I also present you with a new name; it is CAUTION; it teaches you, as you are barely instructed in the rudiments of Masonry, that you should be cautious over all your words and actions, particularly when before the enemies of Masonry. I shall next present you with three precious jewels, which are a LISTENING EAR, a SILENT TONGUE, and a FAITHFUL HEART.

' A listening ear teaches you to listen to the instructions of the Worshipful Master; but more especially that you should listen to the cries of a worthy distressed brother. A silent tongue teaches you to be silent while in the lodge, that the peace and harmony thereof may not be disturbed, but more especially, that you should be silent before the enemies of Masonry, that the craft may not be brought into disrepute by your imprudence. A faithful heart teaches you to be faithful to the instructions of the Worshipful Master at all times, but more especially, that you should be faithful and keep and conceal the secrets of Masonry, and those of a brother when given to you in charge as such, that they may remain as secure and inviolable in your breast as in his own, before communicated to you. I further present you with check words two; their names are TRUTH and UNION, and are thus explained. Truth is a divine attribute, and the foundation of every virtue; to be good and true, is the first lesson we are taught in Masonry; on this theme we contemplate, and by its dictates endeavor to regulate our conduct; hence, while influenced by this principle, hypocrisy and deceit are unknown among us, sincerity and plain dealing distinguish us, and the heart and tongue join in promoting each other's welfare, and rejoicing in each other's prosperity.

Union, is that kind of friendship, which ought to appear conspicuous in every Mason's conduct. It is so closely allied to the divine attribute, truth, that he who enjoys the one, is seldom desti-

---

* Let it no longer be said, that "Masonry is not a religious Institution." But while we assert that it inculcates a system of religion, we affirm that it is not the religion of Jesus. There are in the world many religions, but all are false save one, and that is, of the Bible. Any system which professedly teaches a way to Heaven, is a system of religion: but that which points out a path, without a crucified Saviour and the sanctifying influences of the Holy Comforter, is not only false, but in direct hostility to the true God, and the souls of men! Such a religious system is that of Masonry.

tute of the other. Should interest, honor, prejudice, or human depravity, ever induce you to violate any part of the sacred trust we now repose in you, let these two important words, at the earliest insinuation, teach you to put on the check-line of truth, which will infallibly direct you to pursue that straight and narrow path which ends in the full enjoyment of the grand lodge above; where we shall all meet as Masons and members in the same family, in peace, harmony, and love; where all discord on account of politics, religion, or private opinion shall be unknown, and banished from within our walls.'

'Brother, it has been a custom from time immemorial to demand, or ask from a newly made brother something of a metallic kind, not so much on account of its intrinsic value, but that it may be deposited in the archives of the lodge, as a memorial that you was herein made a Mason;—a small trifle will be sufficient;—any thing of a metallic kind will do; if you have no money, any thing of a metallic nature will be sufficient; even a button will do.' [The candidate says he has nothing about him; it is known he has nothing.] 'Search yourself,' the Master replies. He is assisted in searching, nothing is found; 'Perhaps you can borrow a trifle,' says the Master. [He tries to borrow, none will lend him—he proposes to go into the other room where his clothes are; he is not permitted—if a stranger, he is very much embarrassed.] Master to candidate, 'Brother, let this ever be a striking lesson to you, and teach you, if you should ever see a friend, but more especially a brother, in a like pennyless situation, to contribute as liberally to his relief as his situation may require, and your abilities will admit without material injury to yourself or family.' Master to Senior Deacon, 'You will conduct the candidate back from whence he came, and invest him of what he has been divested, and let him return for further instruction. A zealous attachment to these principles will ensure public and private esteem. In the state, you are to be a quiet and peaceable subject, true to your government and just to your country; you are not to countenance disloyalty, but faithfully submit to legal authority, and conform with cheerfulness to the government of the country in which you live. In your outward demeanor be particularly careful to avoid censure or reproach. Although your frequent appearance at our regular meetings is earnestly solicited, yet it is not meant that Masonry should interfere with your necessary vocations; for these are on no account to be neglected: neither are you to suffer your zeal for the institution to lead you into argument with those, who, through ignorance, may ridicule it. At your leisure hours, that you may improve in Masonic knowledge, you are to converse with well informed brethren,

C

who will be always as ready to give, as you will be to receive information. Finally, keep sacred and inviolable the mysteries of the order, as these are to distinguish you from the rest of the community, and mark your consequence among Masons. If, in the circle of your acquaintance, you find a person desirous of being initiated into Masonry, be particularly attentive not to commend him, unless you are convinced he will conform to our rules; that the honor, glory, and reputation of the institution may be firmly established, and the world at large convinced of its good effects.'

The work of the evening being over, I will proceed to give a description of the manner of closing the lodge. It is a very common practice in lodges to close a lodge of Entered Apprentices, and open a lodge of Fellow Crafts, and close that, and open a Master Mason's lodge, all in the same evening.

Some brother generally makes a motion that the lodge be closed; it being seconded and carried:—

The Master to the Junior Deacon—'Brother Junior,' [giving one rap which calls up both Deacons,] 'The first as well as the last care of a Mason?' *Ans.* 'To see the lodge tyled, Worshipful.' Master to the Junior Deacon; 'Attend to that part of your duty, and inform the Tyler that we are about to close this lodge of Entered Apprentice Masons, and direct him to tyle accordingly.' The Junior Deacon steps to the door and gives three raps, which are answered by the Tyler with three more; the Junior Deacon then gives one, which is also answered by the Tyler by one. The Junior Deacon then opens the door, delivers his message, and resumes his place in the lodge, and says, 'The door is tyled, Worshipful.' Master to Junior Deacon, 'By whom?' *Ans.* 'By a Master Mason without the door, armed with the proper implements of his office.' Master to Junior Deacon, 'His business there?' *Ans.* 'To keep off all cowans and eaves-droppers, and see that none pass or repass without permission from the chair.' Master to Junior Deacon, 'Your place in the lodge, Junior? *Ans.* 'At the right hand of the Senior Warden in the west.' Master to Junior Deacon, 'Your duty there?' *Ans.* 'To wait on the Worshipful Master and Wardens, act as their proxy in the active duties of the lodge, and take charge of the door.' Master to the Junior Deacon, 'The Senior Deacon's place in the lodge?' *Ans.* 'At the right hand of the Worshipful Master in the east.' Master to Senior Deacon, 'Your duty there, brother Senior?' *Ans.* 'To wait on the Worshipful Master and Wardens; act as their proxy in the active duties of the lodge; attend to the preparation and introduction of candidates; receive and clothe all visiting brethren.' Master to the Senior Deacon, 'The Secretary's place in the lodge?' *Ans.* 'At your left hand, Worshipful.' Master to Secretary, 'Your duty there, brother Secretary?' *Ans.* 'Duly to observe the Master's will and pleasure; record the proceedings of the lodge; transmit a copy of the same to the Grand Lodge, if required; receive all monies and money bills from the hands of the brethren; pay them over to the Treasurer, and take his receipt for the same.' Master to the Secretary, 'The Treasurer's place in the lodge?' *Ans.* 'At the right hand of the Worshipful Master.' Master to Treasurer, 'Your business there, brother Treasurer?' *Ans.* 'Duly to observe the Worshipful Master's will and pleasure; receive all monies and money bills from the hands of the Secretary; keep a just and accurate account of the same; pay them out by order of the Worshipful Master and consent of the brethren.' Master to the Treasurer, 'The Junior Warden's place in the lodge?' *Ans.* 'In the south, Worshipful.' Master to the Junior Warden, 'Your business there, brother Junior?' *Ans.* 'As the sun in the south, at high meridian, is the beauty and glory of the day, so stands the Junior Warden in the south at high twelve, the better to observe the time; call the crafts from labour to refreshment; superintend them during the hours thereof; see that none convert the purposes of refreshment into that of excess or intemperance; call them on again in due season; that the Worshipful Master may have honor, and they pleasure and profit thereby.' The Master to the Junior Warden, [I wish the reader to take particular notice, that in closing the lodge, the Master asks the Junior Warden as follows:—' The Master's place in the lodge?' and in opening he asks the Senior Warden the same question,] 'The Master's place in the lodge?' *Ans.* 'In the east, Worshipful.' Master to Junior Warden, 'His duty there?' *Ans.* 'As the sun rises in the east to open and adorn the day, so presides the Worshipful Master in the east, to open and adorn his lodge; set his crafts to work with good and wholesome laws, or cause the same to be done.' Master to the Junior Warden, 'The Senior Warden's place in the lodge?' *Ans.* 'In the west, Worshipful.' Master to Senior Warden, 'Your business there, brother Senior?' *Ans.* 'As the sun sets in the west to close the day, so stands the Senior Warden in the west to assist the Worshipful Master in opening and closing the lodge; take care of the jewels and implements; see that none be lost; pay the craft their wages, if any be due; and see that none go away dissatisfied.' The Master now gives three raps, when all the brethren rise, and the Master asks, 'Are you all satisfied?' They answer in the affirmative, by giving the due-guard.

Should the Master discover that any declined giving it, inquiry is immediately made why it is so; and if any member is **dissatisfied** with any part of the proceedings, or with any brother, the subject is immediately investigated. Master to the brethren, 'Attend to giving the signs; as I do, so do you give them downwards;' [which is by giving the last in opening, first in closing. In closing, on this degree, you first draw your right hand across your throat, as herein before described, and then hold your two hands over each other as before described. This is the method pursued through all the degrees; and when opening on any of the upper degrees, all the signs, of all the preceding decrees, are given before you give the signs of the degree on which you are opening.] This being done, the Master proceeds, 'I now declare this lodge of Entered Apprentice Masons regularly closed in due and ancient form. Brother Junior Warden, please inform brother Senior Warden, and request him to inform the brethren that it is my will and pleasure that this lodge of Entered Apprentice Masons be now closed, and stand closed until our next regular communication, unless a case or cases of emergency shall require earlier convention, of which every member shall be notified; during which time it is seriously hoped and expected that every brother will demean himself as becomes a Free and Accepted Mason.' Junior Warden to Senior Warden, 'Brother Senior, it is the Worshipful Master's will and pleasure that this lodge of Entered Apprentice Masons be closed, and stand closed until our next regular communication, unless a case or cases of emergency shall require earlier convention, of which every brother shall be notified; during which time it is seriously hoped and expected that every brother will demean himself as becomes a Free and Accepted Mason.' Senior Warden to the brethren, 'Brethren, you have heard the Worshipful Master's will and pleasure as communicated to me by Brother Junior; so let it be done.' Master to the Junior Warden, 'Brother Junior, how do Masons meet?' *Ans.* 'On the level.' Master to Senior Warden, 'How do Masons part?' *Ans.* 'On the square.' Master to the Junior and Senior Wardens, 'Since we meet on the level, brother Junior, and part on the square, brother Senior, so let us ever meet and part in the name of the Lord.' Here follows a prayer, sometimes used. Master to the brethren, 'Brethren, let us pray.'

'Supreme Architect of the universe! accept our humble praises for the many mercies and blessings which thy bounty has conferred upon us, and especially for this friendly and social intercourse.—Pardon, we beseech thee, whatever thou hast seen amiss in us since we have been together; and continue to us thy presence, protection and blessing. Make us sensible of the renewed obligations we are under to love thee supremely, and to be friendly to each other. May all our irregular passions be subdued, and may we daily increase in faith, hope, and charity; but more especially in that charity which is the bond of peace, and perfection of every virtue. May we so practice thy precepts, that, through the merits of the Redeemer, we may finally obtain thy promises, and find an acceptance through the gates, and into the temple and city of our God. So mote it be. Amen.'

A Benediction, oftener used at closing, than the preceding Prayer.

May the blessings of Heaven rest upon us, and all regular Masons! May brotherly love prevail, and every moral and social virtue cement us. So mote it be. Amen.

After the prayer the following charge ought to be delivered; but it is seldom attended to; in a majority of lodges it is never attended to.

Master to brethren; 'Brethren, we are now about to quit this sacred retreat of friendship and virtue, to mix again with the world. Amidst its concerns and employments, forget not the duties which you have heard so frequently inculcated, and so forcibly recommended in this lodge.—Remember that around this altar you have promised to befriend and relieve every brother who shall need your assistance. You have promised, in the most friendly manner, to remind him of his errors, and aid a reformation. These generous principles are to extend further; every human being has a claim upon your kind offices. Do good unto all. Recommend it more " especially to the household of the faithful." Finally, brethren, be ye all of one mind, live in peace, and may the God of love and peace, delight to dwell with and bless you.'

In some lodges, after the charge is delivered, the Master says, ' Brethren, form on the square.' Then all the brethren form a circle, and the Master, followed by every brother, [except in using the words,] says, ' And God said, let there be light, and there was light.' At the same moment that the last of these words drops from the Master's lips, every member stamps with his right foot on the floor, and at the same instant bring their hands together with equal force, and in such perfect unison with each other, that persons situated so as to hear it, would suppose it the precursor of some dreadful catastrophe. This is called ' *the shock.*'

Having described all the ceremonies and forms appertaining to the opening of a lodge of Entered Apprentice Masons; setting them to work; initiating a candidate, and closing a lodge; I will now proceed to give the lecture on this degree. It is divided into three sections. The lecture is nothing more or less than a recapitulation of the preceding ceremonies and forms by way of question and answer, and fully explains the same. In fact, the

C 2

ceremonies and forms (generally masonically called *the work*) and lecture are so much the same that he who possesses a knowledge of the lectures cannot be destitute of a knowledge of what the ceremonies and forms are. As the ceremonies used in opening and closing are the same in all the degrees, it is thought best to give the whole one insertion; it being the sincere wish of the writer, that every reader should perfectly understand all the formulas of the whole Masonic fabric, as he then will thereby be able to form correct opinions of the propriety or impropriety, advantages or disadvantages of the same.

First Section of the Lecture on the First Degree of Masonry.

Q. From whence came you as an Entered Apprentice Mason?
A. From the holy lodge of St. John at Jerusalem.
Q. What recommendations do you bring?
A. Recommendations from the Worshipful Master, Wardens and brethren of that Right Worshipful lodge, who greet you.
Q. What comest thou hither to do?
A. To learn to subdue my passions, and improve myself in the secret arts and mysteries of ancient Free Masonry.
Q. You are a Mason, then, I presume?
A. I am.
Q. How do you know that you are a Mason?
A. By being often tried, never denied, and willing to be tried again.
Q. How shall I know you to be a Mason?
A. By certain signs, and a token.
Q. What are signs?
A. All right angles, horizontals, and perpendiculars.
Q. What is a token?
A. A certain friendly and brotherly grip whereby one Mason may know another in the dark as well as in the light.
Q. Where was you first prepared to be a Mason?
A. In my heart.
Q. Where secondly?
A. In a room adjacent to the body of a just and lawfully constituted lodge of such.
Q. How was you prepared?
A. By being divested of all metals, neither naked nor clothed, barefoot nor shod, hood-winked, with a cable-tow* about my neck, in which situation I was conducted to the door of the lodge.
Q. You being hood-winked how did you know it to be a door?

---

* Three miles long.

A. By first meeting with resistance and afterwards gaining admission.

Q. How did you gain admission?
A. By three distinct knocks from without, answered by the same from within.

Q. What was said to you from within?
A. Who comes there? Who comes there? Who comes there?

Q. Your answer?
A. A poor blind candidate who has long been desirous of having and receiving a part of the rights and benefits of this Worshipful lodge dedicated to God, and held forth to the holy order of St. John, as all true fellows and brothers have done, who have gone this way before me.

Q. What further was said to you from within?
A. I was asked if it was of my own free will and accord I made this request; if I was duly and truly prepared, worthy and well qualified; all of which being answered in the affirmative, I was asked by what further rights I expected to obtain so great a favor or benefit.

Q. Your answer?
A. By being a man, free born, of lawful age and well recommended.

Q. What was then said to you?
A. I was bid to wait till the Worshipful Master in the east was made acquainted with my request and his answer returned.

Q. After his answer was returned what followed?
A. I was caused to enter the lodge.

Q. How?
A. On the point of some sharp instrument pressing my naked left breast in the name of the Lord.

Q. How was you then disposed of?
A. I was conducted to the centre of the lodge and there caused to kneel for the benefit of a prayer. [See page 18.]

Q. After prayer what was said to you?
A. I was asked in whom I put my trust.

Q. Your answer?
A. God.

Q. What followed?
A. The Worshipful Master took me by the right hand and said, since in God you put your trust, arise, follow your leader, and fear no danger.

Q. How was you then disposed of?
A. I was conducted three times regularly around the lodge,

and halted at the Junior Warden in the south, where the same questions were asked and answers returned as at the door.

Q. How did the Junior Warden dispose of you?

A. He ordered me to be conducted to the Senior Warden in the west, where the same questions were asked and answers returned as before.

Q. How did the Senior Warden dispose of you?

A. He ordered me to be conducted to the Worshipful Master in the east, where the same questions were asked and answers returned as before, who likewise demanded of me from whence I came and whither I was travelling.

Q. Your answer?

A. From the west and travelling to the east.

Q. Why do you leave the west and travel to the east?

A. In search of light.

Q. How did the Worshipful Master then dispose of you?

A. He ordered me to be conducted back to the west from whence I came, and put in care of the Senior Warden, who taught me how to approach the east, the place of light, by advancing upon one upright regular step to the first step, my feet forming the right angle of an oblong square, my body erect at the altar before the Worshipful Master.

Q. What did the Worshipful Master do with you?

A. He made an Entered Apprentice Mason of me.

Q. How?

A. In due form.

Q. What was that due form?

A. My left knee bare and bent, my right forming a square; my left hand supporting the Holy Bible, Square and Compass; I took upon me the solemn oath or obligation of an Entered Apprentice Mason. [See page 20.]

Q. After you had taken your obligation what was said to you?

A. I was asked what I most desired.

Q. Your answer? A. Light.

Q. Was you immediately brought to light?

A. I was. Q. How?

A. By the direction of the Master and assistance of the brethren.

Q. What did you first discover after being brought to light?

A. Three great lights in Masonry, by the assistance of three lesser.

Q. What were those three great lights in Masonry?

A. The Holy Bible, Square, and Compass.

Q. How are they explained?

A. The Holy Bible is given to us as a guide for our faith and practice; the Square to square our actions; and the Compass to keep us in due bounds with all mankind, but more especially with the brethren.

Q. What were those three lesser lights?
A. Three burning tapers, or candles on candle-sticks.
Q. What do they represent?
A. The Sun, Moon, and Master of the lodge.
Q. How are they explained?
A. As the Sun rules the day and the Moon governs the night, so ought the Worshipful Master to use his endeavours to rule and govern his lodge with equal regularity, or cause the same to be done.
Q. What did you next discover?
A. The Worshipful Master approaching me from the east, under the sign and due-guard of an Entered Apprentice Mason, who presented me with his right hand in token of brotherly love and esteem, and proceeded to give me the grip and word of an Entered Apprentice Mason, and bid me arise and salute the Junior and Senior Wardens, and convince them that I had been regularly initiated as an Entered Apprentice Mason, and was in possession of the sign, grip, and word.
Q. What did you next discover?
A. The Worshipful Master a second time approaching me from the east, who presented me with a lamb-skin or white apron, which he said was an emblem of innocence, and the badge of a Mason; that it had been worn by kings, princes, and potentates of the earth, who had never been ashamed to wear it; that it was more honourable than the diadems of kings, or pearls of princesses, when worthily worn; and more ancient than the Golden Fleece, or Roman Eagle; more honourable than the Star or Garter, or any other order that could be conferred upon me at that time, or any time thereafter, except it be in the body of a just and lawfully constituted lodge of Masons; and bid me carry it to the Senior Warden in the west, who taught me how to wear it as an Entered Apprentice Mason.
Q. What was you next presented with?
A. The working tools of an Entered Apprentice Mason.
Q. What were they?
A. The twenty-four inch guage and common gavel.
Q. How were they explained?
A. The twenty-four inch guage is an instrument made use of by operative masons to measure and lay out their work; but we, as Free and Accepted Masons, are taught to make use of it for

the more noble and glorious purpose of dividing our time; the twenty-four inches on the guage are emblematical of the twenty-four hours in the day, which we are taught to divide into three equal parts, whereby we find eight hours for the service of God, and a worthy distressed brother; eight hours for our usual vocation, and eight hours for refreshment and sleep. The common gavel is an instrument made use of by operative masons to break off the corners of rough stones, the better to fit them for the builder's use; but we, as Free and Accepted Masons, are taught to make use of it for the more noble and glorious purpose of divesting our hearts and consciences of all the vices and superfluities of life, thereby fitting our minds as lively and living stones for that spiritual building, that house not made with hands, eternal in the heavens.

Q. What was you next presented with?
A. A new name.
Q. What was that? A. Caution.
Q. What does it teach?
A. It teaches me, as I was barely instructed in the rudiments of Masonry, that I should be cautious over all my words and actions, especially when before its enemies.
Q. What was you next presented with?
A. Three precious jewels.
Q. What were they?
A. A listening ear, a silent tongue, and a faithful heart.
Q. What do they teach?
A. A listening ear teaches me to listen to the instructions of the Worshipful Master, but more especially that I should listen to the calls and cries of a worthy distressed brother. A silent tongue teaches me to be silent in the lodge, that the peace and harmony thereof may not be disturbed; but more especially that I should be silent when before the enemies of Masonry. A faithful heart, that I should be faithful to the instructions of the Worshipful Master at all times; but more especially that I should be faithful and keep and conceal the secrets of Masonry, and those of a brother, when delivered to me in charge as such, that they may remain as secure and inviolable in my breast, as in his own before communicated to me.
Q. What was you next presented with?
A. Check-words two.
Q. What were they?
A. Truth and Union.
Q. How explained?
A. Truth is a divine attribute, and the foundation of every vir-

tue. To be good and true are the first lessons we are taught in Masonry. On this theme we contemplate, and by its dictates endeavor to regulate our conduct: hence, while influenced by this principle, hypocrisy and deceit are unknown amongst us; sincerity and plain dealing distinguishes us; and the heart and tongue join in promoting each other's welfare, and rejoicing in each other's prosperity.

Union is that kind of friendship that ought to appear conspicuous in the conduct of every Mason. It is so closely allied to the divine attribute truth, that he who enjoys the one, is seldom destitute of the other. Should interest, honor, prejudice, or human depravity ever influence you to violate any part of the sacred trust we now repose in you, let these two important words, at the earliest insinuation, teach you to put on the check-line of truth, which will infallibly direct you to pursue that strait and narrow path, which ends in the full enjoyment of the grand lodge above, where we shall all meet as Masons and members of one family; where all discord on account of religion, politics, or private opinion, shall be unknown and banished from within our walls.

Q. What followed?

A. The Worshipful Master in the east made a demand of me of something of a metallic kind, which, he said, was not so much on account of its intrinsic value, as that it might be deposited in the archives of the lodge, as a memorial that I had therein been made a Mason.

Q. How did the Worshipful Master then dispose of you?

A. He ordered me to be conducted out of the lodge and invested of what I had been divested, and return for further instructions.

Q. After you returned how was you disposed of?

A. I was conducted to the north east corner of the lodge, and there caused to stand upright like a man, my feet forming a square, and received a solemn injunction, ever to walk and act uprightly before God and man, and in addition thereto received the following charge. [For this charge see page 25.]

SECOND SECTION.

Q. Why was you divested of all metals when you was made a Mason?

A. Because Masonry regards no man on account of his worldly wealth or honors; it is therefore the internal, and not the external qualifications that recommends a man to Masons.

Q. A second reason?

A. There was neither the sound of an ax, hammer, or any other metal tool heard at the building of king Solomon's temple,

Q. How could so stupendous a fabric be erected without the sound of axe, hammer, or any other metal tool?

A. All the stones were hewed, squared and numbered in the quarries where they were raised, all the timbers felled and prepared in the forests of Lebanon, and carried down to Joppa on floats, and taken from thence up to Jerusalem and set up with wooden malls, prepared for that purpose; which, when completed, every part thereof fitted with that exact nicety, that it had more the resemblance of the handy workmanship of the Supreme Architect of the universe, than of human hands.

Q. Why was you neither naked nor clothed?

A. As I was an object of distress at that time, it was to remind me, if ever I saw a friend, more especially a brother, in a like distressed situation, that I should contribute as liberally to his relief as his situation required, and my abilities would admit, without material injury to myself or family.

Q. Why was you neither barefoot nor shod?

A. It was an ancient Israelitish custom, adopted among Masons; and we read in the book of Ruth concerning their mode and manner of changing and redeeming, and to confirm all things, a brother plucked off his shoe and gave it to his neighbor, and that was testimony in Israel. This then, therefore, we do in confirmation of a token, and as a pledge of our fidelity; thereby signifying that we will renounce our own will in all things, and become obedient to the laws of our ancient institutions.

Q. Why was you hood-winked?

A. That my heart might conceive before my eyes beheld the beauties of masonry.

Q. A second reason?

A. As I was in darkness at that time, it was to remind me that I should keep the whole world so respecting masonry.

Q. Why had you a cable-tow about your neck?

A. In case I had not submitted to the manner and mode of my initiation that I might have been led out of the lodge without seeing the form and beauties thereof.

Q. Why did you give three distinct knocks at the door?

A. To alarm the lodge, and let the Worshipful Master, Wardens and brethren know that a poor blind candidate prayed admission.

Q. What do those three distinct knocks allude to?

A. A certain passage in scripture wherein it says, 'ask and it shall be given, seek and ye shall find, knock and it shall be opened unto you.'

Q. How did you apply this to your then case in Masonry?

A. I asked the recommendations of a friend to become a Mason; I sought admission through his recommendations and knocked, and the door of Masonry opened unto me.

Q. Why was you caused to enter on the point of some sharp instrument pressing your naked left breast in the name of the Lord?

A. As this was a torture to my flesh, so might the recollection of it ever be to my flesh and conscience, if ever I attempted to reveal the secrets of Masonry unlawfully.

Q. Why was you conducted to the centre of the lodge and there caused to kneel for the benefit of a prayer?

A. Before entering on this, or any other great and important undertaking, it is highly necessary to implore a blessing from Deity.

Q. Why was you asked in whom you put your trust?

A. Agreeable to the laws of our ancient institution, no Atheist could be made a Mason; it was therefore necessary that I should believe in Deity; otherwise, no oath or obligation could bind me.

Q. Why did the Worshipful Master take you by the right hand, and bid you rise, follow your leader, and fear no danger?

A. As I was in darkness at that time, and could neither foresee nor avoid danger, it was to remind me that I was in the hands of an affectionate friend, in whose fidelity I might with safety confide.

Q. Why was you conducted three times regularly round the lodge?

A. That the Worshipful Master, Wardens, and brethren might see that I was duly and truly prepared.

Q. Why did you meet with those several obstructions on the way?

A. This, and every other lodge, is, or ought to be, a true representation of king Solomon's temple, which, when completed, had guards stationed at the east, west, and south gates.

Q. Why had they guards stationed at those several gates?

A. To prevent any one from passing or repassing that was not duly qualified.

Q. Why did you kneel on your left knee and not on your right, or both?

A. The left side has ever been considered the weakest part of the body; it was, therefore, to remind me that that part, I was then taking upon me, was the weakest part of Masonry, it being that only of an Entered Apprentice.

Q. Why was your right hand placed on the Holy Bible, Square, and Compass, and not your left, or both?

D

A. The right hand has ever been considered the seat of fidelity, and our ancient brethren worsnipped Deity under the names of FIDES; which has sometimes been represented by two right hands joined together; at others, by two human figures holding each other by the right hand; the right hand, therefore, we use in this great and important undertaking, to signify, in the strongest manner possible, the sincerity of our intentions in the business we are engaged.

Q. Why did the Worshipful Master present you with a lamb-skin, or a white apron?

A. The lamb-skin has, in all ages, been deemed an emblem of innocence; he, therefore, who wears the lamb-skin, as a badge of a Mason, is thereby continually reminded of that purity of life and rectitude of conduct, which is so essentially necessary to our gaining admission into the celestial lodge above, where the Supreme Architect of the universe presides.

Q. Why did the Master make a demand of you of something of a metallic nature?

A. As I was in a poor and pennyless situation at the time, it was to remind me if ever I saw a friend, but more especially a brother, in the like poor and pennyless situation, that I should contribute as liberally to his relief as my abilities would admit and his situation required, without injuring myself or family.

Q. Why was you conducted to the north east corner of the lodge, and there caused to stand upright, like a man, your feet forming a square, receiving, at the same time, a solemn charge to walk and act uprightly before God and man?

A. The first stone, in every Masonic edifice, is, or ought to be, placed at the northeast corner; that being the place where an Entered Apprentice Mason receives his first instructions to build his future Masonic edifice upon.

THIRD SECTION.

Q. We have been saying a good deal about a lodge, I want to know what constitutes a lodge?

A. A certain number of Free and Accepted Masons, duly assembled in a room, or place, with the Holy Bible, Square and Compass, and other Masonic implements, with a charter from the Grand Lodge empowering them to work.

Q. Where did our ancient brethren meet before lodges were erected?

A. On the highest hills, and in the lowest vales.

Q. Why on the highest hills, and in the lowest vales?

A. The better to guard against cowans and enemies either ascending or descending, that the brethren might have timely notice of their approach to prevent being surprised.

Q. What is the form of your lodge?
A. An oblong square.
Q. How long? A. From east to west. Q. How wide?
A. Between north and south.
Q. How high?
A. From the surface of the earth to the highest heavens.
Q. How deep?
A. From the surface to the centre.
Q. What supports your lodge?
A. Three large columns or pillars.
Q. What are their names?
A. Wisdom, Strength, and Beauty.
Q. Why so? A. It is necessary there should be wisdom to contrive, strength to support, and beauty to adorn, all great and important undertakings; but more especially this of ours.
Q. Has your lodge any covering?
A. It has; a clouded canopy, or starry-decked heaven, where all good Masons hope to arrive.
Q. How do you hope to arrive there?
A. By the assistance of Jacob's ladder.*
Q. How many principal rounds has it got? A. Three.
Q. What are their names?
A. Faith, Hope, and Charity.
Q. What do they teach?
A. Faith in God, hope in immortality, and charity to all mankind.
Q. Has your lodge any furniture?
A. It has; the Holy Bible, Square, and Compass.
Q. To whom do they belong?
A. The Bible to God; the Square to the Master; and the Compass to the Craft.
Q. How explained?
A. The Bible to God; it being the inestimable gift of God to man, for his instruction to guide him through the rugged paths of life: the Square to the Master; it being the proper emblem of his office: the Compass to the Craft; by a due attention to which

---

* The ladder which Jacob saw, undoubtedly represented the way of life and salvation through our Lord Jesus Christ. The rounds in that ladder, the several steps He took in the great work of redemption. The angels of God are sent forth, through this medium, to minister unto them who shall be the heirs of salvation; and not upon the principles of faith, hope, and charity, which are graces wrought in the hearts of Christians by the Holy Spirit.

we are taught to limit our desires; curb our ambition; subdue our irregular appetites; and keep our passions and prejudices in due bounds with all mankind; but more especially with the brethren.

Q. Has your lodge any ornaments?

A. It has; the Mosaic, or chequered pavement; the indented tessel; that beautiful tesselated border which surrounds it, with the blazing star in the centre.

Q. What do they represent?

A. The Mosaic, or chequered pavement, represents this world; which, though chequered over with good and evil, yet brethren may walk together thereon and not stumble:—the indented tessel, with the blazing star in the centre, the manifold blessings and comforts with which we are surrounded in this life; but more especially, those which we hope to enjoy hereafter:—the blazing star, that prudence which ought to appear conspicuous in the conduct of every Mason; but more especially, commemorative of the star which appeared in the east, to guide the wise men to Bethlehem, to proclaim the birth and the presence of the Son of God.

Q. Has your lodge any lights? A. It has; three.

Q. How are they situated?

A. East, West, and South.

Q. Has it none in the North? A. It has not. Q. Why so?

A. Because this, and every other lodge, is, or ought to be, a true representation of king Solomon's temple, which was situated north of the ecliptic; the sun and moon, therefore, darting their rays from the south, no light was to be expected from the north; we, therefore, masonically, term the north a place of darkness.

Q. Has your lodge any jewels?

A. It has;—six: three moveable and three immoveable.

Q. What are the three moveable jewels?

A. The Square, Level, and Plumb.

Q. What do they teach?

A. The square, morality; the level, equality; and the plumb, rectitude of life and conduct.

Q. What are the three immoveable jewels?

A. The rough Ashlar, the perfect Ashlar, and the Tressle-Board.

Q. What are they?

A. The rough ashlar is a stone in its rough and natural state; the perfect ashlar is also a stone made ready by the working tools of the Fellow Craft, to be adjusted in the building; and the tressle-board is for the master workman to draw his plans and designs upon.

Q. What do they represent?
A. The rough ashlar represents man in his rude and imperfect state by nature; the perfect ashlar also represents man in that state of perfection to which we all hope to arrive, by means of a virtuous life and education, our own endeavors, and the blessing of God. In erecting our temporal building we pursue the plans and designs laid down by the master workman on his tressle-board; but in erecting our spiritual building we pursue the plans and designs laid down by the Supreme Geometrician of the universe in the book of life; which we, masonically, term our spiritual tressle-board.

Q. Who did you serve? A. My Master.
Q. How long? A. Six days.
Q. What did you serve him with?
A. Freedom, Fervency, and Zeal.
Q. What do they represent?
A. Chalk, Charcoal, and Earth.
Q. Why so? A. There is nothing freer than chalk; the slightest touch of which leaves a trace behind: nothing more fervent than heated charcoal; it will melt the most obdurate metals: nothing more zealous than the earth to bring forth.
Q. How is your lodge situated? A. Due east and west.
Q. Why so?
A. Because the sun rises in the east, and sets in the west.
Q. A second reason?
A. The gospel was first preached in the east, and is spreading to the west.
Q. A third reason?
A. The liberal arts and sciences began in the east, and are extending to the west.
Q. A fourth reason?
A. Because all the churches and chapels are, or ought to be, so situated.
Q. Why are all churches and chapels so situated?
A. Because king Solomon's temple was so situated.
Q. Why was king Solomon's temple so situated?
A. Because Moses, after conducting the children of Israel through the Red Sea, by divine command, erected a tabernacle to God, and placed it due east and west; which was to commemorate, to the latest posterity, that miraculous east wind that wrought their mighty deliverance; and this was an exact model of Solomon's temple: since which time, every well regulated and governed lodge is, or ought to be, so situated.
Q. To whom did our ancient brethren dedicate their lodges?

D 2

A. To king Solomon.   **Q.** Why so?
A. Because king Solomon was our most ancient Grand Master.
Q. To whom do modern Masons dedicate their lodges?
A. To St. John the Baptist, and St. John the Evangelist.
Q. Why so?
A. Because they were the two most ancient christian patrons of Masonry; and, since their time, in every well regulated and governed lodge, there has been a certain point within a circle, which circle is bounded on the east and the west by two perpendicular parallel lines, representing the anniversary of St. John the Baptist, and St. John the Evangelist, who were two perfect parallels, as well in Masonry as Christianity; on the vertex of which rests the book of the holy scriptures, supporting Jacob's ladder, which is said to reach to the watery clouds; and, in passing round this circle, we naturally touch on both these perpendicular paralel lines, as well as the book of the holy scriptures; and while a Mason keeps himself thus circumscribed, he cannot materially err.

Thus ends the first degree of Masonry; and the reader, who has read and paid attention to it, knows more of Masonry than any Entered Apprentice in Christendom, and more of this degree than one hundredth part of the Master Masons, or even Royal Arch Masons; for very few ever attempt to learn the lectures, or even the obligations: they merely receive the degrees, and there stop, with the exception of a few who are fascinated with the idea of holding an office: they sometimes endeavor to qualify themselves to discharge the duties which devolve on them in their respective offices. The offices of Secretary and Treasurer, are, by some, considered the most important in the lodge, particularly where there is much business done.

I will now introduce the reader to the second degree of Masonry. It is generally called passing, as will be seen in the lecture. I shall omit the ceremonies of opening and closing, as they are precisely the same as in the first degree; except two knocks are used in this degree, and the door is entered by the benefit of a pass-word: it is *Shibboleth*. It will be explained in the lecture.

The candidate, as before, it taken into the preparation room, and prepared in the manner following: All his clothing taken off, except his shirt; furnished with a pair of drawers; his right breast bare; his left foot in a slipper; the right bare; a cable-tow twice round his neck; semi-hood-winked; in which situation he is conducted to the door of the lodge, where he gives two knocks, when the Senior Warden rises and says, 'Worshipful, while we are peaceably at work on the second degree of Masonry, under the influence of faith, hope and charity, the door of our lodge is alarmed.' Master to Junior Deacon, ' Brother Junior, inquire the cause of that alarm.' (In many lodges they come to the door, knock, are answered by the Junior Deacon, and come in without being noticed by the Senior Warden or Master.) The Junior Deacon gives two raps on the inside of the door. The candidate gives one without, it is answered by the Junior Deacon with one; when the door is partly opened by the Junior Deacon, who inquires, ' Who comes here ? Who comes here ?' The Senior Deacon, who is, or ought to be, the conductor, answers, ' A worthy brother, who has been regularly initiated as an Entered Apprentice Mason, served a proper time as such, and now wishes for further light in Masonry, by being passed to the degree of Fellow Craft.' Junior Deacon to Senior Deacon, ' Is it of his own free will and accord he makes this request ?' *Ans.* ' It is.' Junior Deacon to Senior Deacon, ' Is he duly and truly prepared ?' *Ans.* ' He is.' Junior Deacon to Senior Deacon, ' Is he worthy and well qualified ?' *Ans.* ' He is.' Junior Deacon to Senior Deacon, ' Has he made suitable proficiency in the preceding degree ?' *Ans.* ' He has.' (Very few know any more than they did the night they were initiated ; have not heard their obligation repeated, nor one section of the lecture ; and, in fact, a very small portion of Masons ever learn either.) Junior Deacon to Senior Deacon, ' By what further rights does he expect to obtain this benefit ?' *Ans.* ' By the benefit of a pass-word.' Junior Deacon to Senior Deacon, ' *Has he a pass-word?*' *Ans.* ' He has not, but I have it for him.' Junior Deacon to Senior Deacon, ' Give it to me.' The Senior Deacon whispers in the Junior Deacon's ear, ' *Shibboleth.*' The Junior Deacon says, ' The pass is right ; since this is the case, you will wait until the Worshipful Master in the east is made acquainted with his request, and his answer returned.' The Junior Deacon then repairs to the Master, and gives two knocks, as at the door, which are answered by two by the Master ; when the same questions are asked, and answers returned, as at the door. After which, the Master says, ' Since he comes endued with all these necessary qualifications, let him enter this Worshipful lodge in the name of the Lord, and take heed on what he enters.' He enters ; the angle of the square is pressed hard against his naked right breast ; at which time, the Junior Deacon says, ' Brother, when you entered this lodge the first time, you entered on the point of the compass pressing your naked left breast, which was then explained to you. You now enter it on the angle of the square, pressing your naked right breast ; which is to teach you to act upon the square with all mankind, but more especially with the brethren.' The candidate is then conducted twice regularly round the lodge, and halted at the Junior Warden in the south, where he gives two raps, and is answered by two, when the same questions are asked, and answers returned as at the door; from thence he is conducted to the Senior Warden, where the same questions are asked and answers returned, as before; he is then conducted to the Master in the east, where the same questions are asked and answers returned, as before; the Master likewise demands of him, from whence he came, and whither he was travelling; he answers, 'From the west, and travelling to the east.' The Master says, 'Why do you leave the west, and travel to the east?' *Ans.* 'In search of more light.' The Master then says to the Senior Deacon, 'Since this is the case, you will please conduct the candidate back to the west, from whence he came, and put him in the care of the Senior Warden, who will teach him how to approach the east, 'the place of light,' by advancing upon two upright regular steps to the second step, (his heel is in the hollow of the right foot, on this degree;) his feet forming the right angle of an oblong square, and his body erect at the altar before the Worshipful Master, and place him in a proper position to take the solemn oath, or obligation of a Fellow Craft Mason.' The Master then leaves his seat, and approaches the kneeling candidate, (the candidate kneels on the right knee; the left forming a square; his left arm, as far as the elbow, in a horizontal position, and the rest of the arm in a vertical position, so as to form a square; his arm supported by the square held under his elbow:) and says, 'Brother, you are now placed in a proper position to take on you the solemn oath, or obligation, of a Fellow Craft Mason, which I assure you, as before, is neither to affect your religion nor politics; if you are willing to take it, repeat your name, and say after me:'—

'I, A. B., of my own free will and accord, in the presence of Almighty God, and this Worshipful lodge of Fellow Craft Masons, dedicated to God, and held forth to the holy order of St. John, do hereby and hereon, most solemnly and sincerely promise and swear, in addition to my former obligation, that I will not give the degree of a Fellow Craft Mason to any one of an inferior degree, nor to any other being in the known world, except it be to a true and lawful brother, or brethren Fellow Craft Masons, or within the body of a just and lawfully constituted lodge of such; and not unto him nor unto them whom I shall hear so to be, but unto him and them only whom I shall find so to be, after strict trial and due examination, or lawful information. Furthermore, do I promise and swear, that I will not wrong this lodge, nor a brother of this degree, to the value of two cents, knowingly, myself, nor suffer it to be done by others, if in my power to prevent it. Furthermore, do I promise and swear, that I will support the constitution of the Grand Lodge of the United States, and of the Grand Lodge of this state, under which this lodge is held, and conform to all the by-laws, rules and regulations of this, or any other lodge, of which I may, at any time hereafter, become a member, as far as in my power. Furthermore, do I promise and swear, that I will obey all regular signs and summons, given, handed, sent, or thrown to me by the hand of a brother Fellow Craft Mason, or from the body of a just and lawfully constituted lodge of such; provided it be within the length of my cable-tow, or a square and angle of my work. Furthermore, do I promise and swear, that I will be aiding and assisting all poor and pennyless brethren Fellow Crafts, their widows and orphans, wheresoever disposed round the globe, they applying to me as such, as far as in my power, without injuring myself or family. To all which I do most solemnly and sincerely promise and swear, without the least hesitation, mental reservation, or self-evasion of mind in me whatever; binding myself under no less penalty than to have my left breast torn open, and my heart and vitals taken from thence, and thrown over my left shoulder, and carried into the valley of Jehosaphat, there to become a prey to the wild beasts of the field, and vultures of the air, if ever I should prove wilfully guilty of violating any part of this my solemn oath or obligation of a Fellow Craft Mason; so keep me God, and keep me steadfast in the due performance of the same.' ' Detach your hands, and kiss the book, which is the Holy Bible, twice.' The bandage is now (by one of the brethren) dropped over the other eye, and the Master says, 'Brother, (at the same time laying his hand on the top of the candidate's head,) what do you most desire ?' The candidate answers after his prompter, ' More light.' The Master says, Brethren, form on the square, and assist in bringing our new made brother from darkness to light; and God said, let there be light, and there was light.' At this instant all the brethren clap their hands, and stamp on the floor, as in the preceding degree. The Master says to the candidate, ' Brother, what do you discover different from before ?' The Master says, after a short pause, ' You now discover one point of the compass elevated above the square, which denotes light in this degree; but as one is yet in obscurity, it is to remind you that you are yet one material point in the dark, respecting Masonry.' The Master steps off from the candidate three or four steps, and says, ' Brother, you now discover me as a Master of this lodge, approaching you from the east, under the sign and due-guard of a Fellow Craft Mason; do as I do, as near as you can, keeping your position.' The sign is given by drawing your right hand flat, with the palm of it next to your breast, across your breast, from the left to the right side, with some quickness, and dropping it down by your side; the due-guard is given by raising the left arm until that part of it between the elbow and shoulder is perfectly horizontal, and raising the rest of the arm in a vertical position, so that that part of the arm below the elbow, and that part above it, forms a square: this is called the due-guard of a Fellow Craft Mason. The two given together, are called the sign and due-guard of a Fellow Craft Mason, and they are never given separately; they would not be recognised by a Mason, if given separately. The Master, by the time he gives his steps, sign, and due-guard, arrives at the candidate, and says, 'Brother, I now present you with my right hand in token of brotherly-love and confidence, and with it the pass-grip and word of a Fellow Craft Mason.' The pass, or more properly the pass-grip, is given by taking each other by the right hand, as though going to shake hands, and each putting his thumb between the fore and second finger, where they join the hand, and pressing the thumb between the joints. This is the pass-grip of a Fellow Craft Mason; the name of it is *Shibboleth*. Its origin will be explained in the lecture—the pass-grip some give without lettering or syllabling, and others give it in the same way they do the real grip. The real grip of a Fellow Craft Mason is given, by putting the thumb on the joint of the second finger, where it joins the hand, and crooking your thumb so that each can stick the nail of his thumb into the joint of the other. This is the real grip of a Fellow Craft Mason; the name of it is *Jachin*; it is given in the following manner: If you wish to examine a person, after having taken each other by the grip, ask him, 'What is this?' *A.* 'A grip.' *Q.* 'A grip of what?' *A.* 'The grip of a Fellow Craft Mason.' *Q.* 'Has it a name?' *A.* 'It has.' *Q.* 'Will you give it to me?' *A.* 'I did not so receive it, neither can I so impart it.' *Q.* 'What will you do with it?' *A.* 'I'll letter it or halve it.' *Q.* 'Halve it, and you begin?' *A.* 'No; begin you.' *Q.* 'You begin?' *A.* 'J A.' *Q.* 'C H I N?' *A.* 'JACHIN.' *Q.* 'Right, brother *Jachin*, I greet you.'

After the Master gives the candidate the pass-grip and grip, and their names, he says, 'Brother, you will rise and salute the Junior and Senior Wardens as such, and convince them that you have been regularly passed to the degree of a Fellow Craft Mason, and have got the sign and pass-grip, real grip, and their names.' [I do not here express it as expressed in lodges generally; the Master generally says, 'You will arise and salute the Wardens, &c.

and convince them, &c. that you have got the sign, pass-grip, and word.' It is obviously wrong; because the first thing he gives is the sign, then the due-guard, then the pass-grip, and their names.] While the Wardens are examining the candidate, the Master gets an apron and returns to the candidate, and says, 'Brother, I now have the honor of presenting you with a lamb-skin, or white apron, as before, which I hope you will continue to wear with honor to yourself, and satisfaction to the brethren; you will please carry it to the Senior Warden in the west, who will teach you how to wear it as a Fellow Craft Mason.' The Senior Warden ties on his apron, and turns up one corner of the lower end of the apron, and tucks it under the apron string. The Senior Deacon then conducts his pupil to the Master, who has, by this time, resumed his seat in the east, where he has, or ought to have, the floor carpet to assist him in his explanations. Master to the candidate, 'Brother, as you are dressed, it is necessary you should have tools to work with; I will, therefore, present you with the tools of a Fellow Craft Mason. They are the plumb, square, and level. The plumb is an instrument made use of by operative Masons to raise perpendiculars; the square, to square their work; and the level, to lay horizontals: but we, as Free and Accepted Masons, are taught to use them for more noble and glorious purposes; the plumb teaches us to walk uprightly, in our several stations, before God and man; squaring our actions by the square of virtue; and remembering that we are travelling on the level of time to that undiscovered country, 'from whose bourne no traveller has returned.' I further present you with three precious jewels; their names are faith, hope, and charity; they teach us to have faith in God, hope in immortality, and charity to all mankind.' The Master to the Senior Deacon, 'You will now conduct the candidate out of this lodge, and invest him with what he has been divested.' After he is clothed, and the necessary arrangements made for his reception, such as placing the columns and floor carpet, if they have any, and the candidate is reconducted back to the lodge, as he enters the door, the Senior Deacon observes, 'We are now about to return to the middle chamber of king Solomon's temple.' When within the door, the Senior Deacon proceeds; 'Brother, we have worked in speculative masonry, but our forefathers wrought both in speculative and operative masonry. They worked at the building of king Solomon's temple, and many other masonic edifices; they wrought six days; they did not work on the seventh, because in six days God created the heavens and the earth, and rested on the seventh day. The seventh, therefore, our ancient brethren consecrated as a day of rest; thereby enjoying more frequent opportunities to contemplate the glorious works of creation, and to adore their great Creator.' Moving a step or two, the Senior Deacon proceeds: 'Brother, the first thing that attracts our attention, are two large columns, or pillars, one on the left hand, and the other on the right; the name of the one on the left hand is *Boaz*, and denotes strength; the name of the one on the right hand is *Jachin*, and denotes establishment; they collectively allude to a passage in scripture, wherein God has declared in his word, ' In strength shall this house be established.' These columns are eighteen cubits high, twelve in circumference, and four in diameter; they are adorned with two large chapiters, one on each, and these chapiters are ornamented with net work, lily work, and pomegranates; they denote unity, peace, and plenty. The net work, from its connexion, denotes union; the lily work, from its whiteness, purity and peace; and the pomegranate, from the exuberance of its seed, denotes plenty. They also have two large globes, or balls, one on each; these globes, or balls, contain, on their convex surfaces, all the maps and charts of the celestial and terrestrial bodies; they are said to be thus extensive, to denote the universality of Masonry, and that a Mason's charity ought to be equally extensive. Their composition is molten, or cast brass; they were cast on the banks of the river Jordan, in the clay-ground between Succoth and Zaradatha, where king Solomon ordered these and all other holy vessels to be cast; they were cast hollow; and were four inches, or a hand's breadth thick; they were cast hollow, the better to withstand inundations and conflagrations; they were the archives of Masonry, and contained the constitution, rolls, and records.' The Senior Deacon having explained the columns, he passes between them, advances a step or two, observing as he advances, 'Brother, we will pursue our travels; the next thing that we come to, is a long, winding staircase, with three, five, seven steps, or more. The three first allude to the three principal supports in Masonry, viz: wisdom, strength, and beauty; the five steps allude to the five orders in architecture, and the five human senses; the five orders in architecture are, the Tuscan, Doric, Ionic, Corinthian, and Composite; the five human senses are, hearing, seeing, feeling, smelling, and tasting; the three first of which, have ever been highly essential among Masons: hearing, to hear the word, seeing, to see the sign, and feeling, to feel the grip, whereby one Mason may know another in the dark as well as in the light. The seven steps allude to the seven sabbatical years; seven years of famine; seven years in building the temple; seven golden candlesticks; seven wonders of the world; seven planets; but, more especially, the several liberal arts and sciences, which are grammar, rhetoric, logic, arithmetic, geometry, music, and astronomy; for this, and many other reasons, the number seven has ever been held in high estimation among Masons.' Advancing a few steps, the Senior Deacon proceeds; 'Brother, the next thing we come to is the outer door of the middle chamber of king Solomon's temple, which is partly open, but closely tyled by the Junior Warden;' [It is the Junior Warden in the south who represents the Tyler, at the outer door of the middle chamber of king Solomon's temple.] who, on the approach of the Senior Deacon and candidate, inquires, 'Who comes here? Who comes here?' The Senior Deacon answers, 'A Fellow Craft Mason.' Junior Warden to Senior Deacon. 'How do you expect to gain admission?' A. 'By a pass, and token of a pass.' Junior Warden to Senior Deacon, 'Will you give them to me?' [The Senior Deacon, or the candidate, (prompted by him,) gives them; this and many other tokens, or grips, are frequently given by strangers, when first introduced to each other. If given to a Mason, he will immediately return it; they can be given in any company unobserved, even by Masons, when shaking hands. *A pass, and token of a pass:* the pass is the word *Shibboleth;* the token, alias, the pass-grip, is given, as before described, by taking each other by the right hand, as if shaking hands, and placing the thumb between the fore finger and second finger, at the third joint, or where they join the hand, and pressing it hard enough to attract attention. In the lecture it is called a token, but generally called the pass-grip. It is an undeniable fact that Masons express themselves so differently, when they mean the same thing, that they frequently wholly misunderstand each other.]

After the Junior Warden has received the pass *Shibboleth*, he inquires, 'What does it denote?' A. 'Plenty.' Junior Warden to Senior Deacon, 'Why so?' A. 'From an ear of corn being placed at the water-ford.' Junior Warden to Senior Deacon, 'Why was this pass instituted?' A. 'In consequence of a quarrel which had long existed between Jephthah, Judge of Israel, and the Ephraimites; the latter of whom had long been a stubborn, rebellious people, whom Jephthah had endeavored to subdue by lenient measures, but to no effect. The Ephraimites being highly incensed against Jephthah, for not being called to fight and share in the rich spoils of the Ammonitish war, assembled a mighty army, and passed over the river Jordan to give Jephthah battle; but he, being apprised of their approach, called together the men of Israel, and gave them battle, and put them to flight; and to make his victory more complete, he ordered

E

guards to be placed at the different passes on the banks of the river Jordan, and commanded, if the Ephraimites passed that way, that they should pronounce the word *Shibboleth;* but they, being of a different tribe, pronounced it *Sibboleth;* which trifling defect proved them spies, and cost them their lives: and there fell that day, at the different passes on the banks of the river Jordan, forty and two thousand. This word was also used by our ancient brethren to distingush a friend from a foe, and has since been adopted as a proper pass-word, to be given before entering any well regulated and governed lodge of Fellow Craft Masons.' Since this is the case, you will pass on to the Senior Warden in the west for further examination. As they approach the Senior Warden in the west, the Senior Deacon says to the candidate, 'Brother, the next thing we come to, is the inner door of the middle chamber of king Solomon's temple, which we find partly open, but more closely tyled by the Senior Warden;' when the Senior Warden inquires, 'Who comes here? Who comes here?' The Senior Deacon answers, 'A Fellow Craft Mason.' Senior Warden to Senior Deacon, 'How do you expect to gain admission?' A. 'By the grip and word.' The Senior Warden to the Senior Deacon, 'Will you give them to me?' They are then given as herein before described. The word is *Jachin.* After they are given, the Senior Warden says, 'They are right; you can pass on to the Worshipful Master in the east.' As they approach the Master, he inquires, 'Who comes here? Who comes here?' Senior Deacon answers, 'A Fellow Craft Mason.' The Master then says to the candidate, 'Brother, you have been admitted into the middle chamber of king Solomon's temple, for the sake of the letter G. It denotes Deity; before whom we all ought to bow with reverence, worship, and adoration. It also denotes geometry, the fifth science; it being that on which this degree was principally founded. By geometry, we may curiously trace nature through her various windings to her most concealed recesses: by it, we may discover the power, the wisdom, and the goodness of the Grand Artificer of the Universe, and view with delight the proportions which connect this vast machine: by it, we may discover how the planets move in their different orbits, and demonstrate their various revolutions: by it, we account for the return of a season, and the variety of scenes which each season displays to the discerning eye. Numberless worlds surround us, all formed by the same Divine Architect, which roll through this vast expanse, and all conducted by the same unerring law of nature. A survey of nature, and the observations of her beautiful proportions, first determined man to imitate the divine plan, and study symmetry and order. The architect began to design; and the plans which he laid down, being improved by experience and time, have produced works which are the admiration of every age. The lapse of time, the ruthless hand of ignorance, and the devastations of war, have laid waste and destroyed many valuable monuments of antiquity, on which the utmost exertions of human genius have been employed. Even the temple of Solomon, so spacious and magnificent, and constructed by so many celebrated artists, escaped not the unsparing ravages of barbarous force. The *attentive ear* received the sound from the *instructive tongue*; and the mysteries of Free Masonry are safely lodged in the repository of *faithful breasts*. Tools and implements of architecture, and symbolic emblems, most expressive, are selected by the fraternity, to imprint on the mind wise and serious truths; and thus, through a succession of ages, are transmitted, unimpaired, the most excellent tenets of our institution.' Here ends the work part of the Fellow Craft's degree. It will be observed that the candidate has received, in this place, the second section of the lecture on this degree. This course is not generally pursued, but it is much the most instructive method; and when it is omitted, I generally conclude that it is for want of a knowledge of the lecture. Monitorial writers, (who are by no means coeval with Masonry,) all write, or copy, very much after each other; and they have all inserted, in their books, all those clauses of the several lectures which are not considered by the wise ones as tending to develope the secrets of Masonry. In some instances, they change the phraseology a little; in others, they are literal extracts from the lectures. This, it is said, is done to facilitate the progress of learners, or young Masons; when, in fact, it has the contrary effect. All lecture teachers, (and there are many travelling about the country, with recommendations from some of their distinguished brethren;) when they come to any of those clauses, will say to their pupils, 'I have not committed that; it is in the Monitor; you can learn it at your leisure.' This course of procedure subjects the learner to the necessity of making his own questions, and, of course, answering monitorially, whether the extracts from the lectures are literal or not. Again, there is not a *perfect* sameness in all the Monitors, or they could not all get copy rights; hence the great diversity in the lectures as well as the work. The following charge is, or ought to be, delivered to the candidate after he has got through the ceremonies; but he is generally told, 'It is in the Monitor, and you can learn it at your leisure.' 'Brother, being advanced to the second degree of Masonry, we congratulate you on your preferment. The internal, and not the external, qualifications of a man, are what Masonry regards. As you increase in knowledge, you will improve in social intercourse. It is unnecessary to recapitulate the duties which, as a Mason, you are bound to discharge; or enlarge on the necessity of a strict adherence to them, as your own experience must have established their value. Our laws and regulations you are strenuously to support; and be always ready to assist in seeing them duly executed. You are not to palliate or aggravate the offences of your brethren; but in the decision of every trespass against our rules, you are to judge with candor, admonish with friendship, and reprehend with justice. The study of the liberal arts, that valuable branch of education, which tends so effectually to polish and adorn the mind, is earnestly recommended to your consideration; especially the science of geometry, which is established as the basis of our art. Geometry, or Masonry, originally synonymous terms, being of a divine moral nature, is enriched with the most useful knowledge; while it proves the wonderful properties of nature, it demonstrates the more important truths of morality. Your past behaviour and regular deportment, have merited the honour which we have now conferred; and, in your new character, it is expected that you will conform to the principles of the order, by steadily persevering in the practice of every commendable virtue. Such is the nature of your engagements as a Fellow Craft, and to these duties you are bound by the most sacred ties.'

I will now proceed with the lecture on this degree; it is divided into two sections.

SECTION FIRST.

Q. Are you a Fellow Craft Mason?
A. I am—try me.
Q. By what will you be tried? A. By the Square.
Q. Why by the Square?
A. Because it is an emblem of virtue.
Q. What is a Square?
A. An angle extending to ninety degrees, or the fourth part of a circle.
Q. Where was you prepared to be made a Fellow Craft Mason?
A. In a room adjacent to the body of a just and lawfully constituted lodge of such, duly assembled in a room, or place, representing the middle chamber of king Solomon's temple.
Q. How was you prepared?
A. By being divested of all metals: neither naked nor clothed; barefooted nor shod; hood-winked; with a cable-tow twice round

my neck; in which situation I was conducted to the door of the lodge, where I gave two distinct knocks.

Q. What did those two distinct knocks allude to?

A. The second degree in Masonry; it being that on which I was about to enter.

Q. What was said to you from within?

A. Who comes there, Who comes there.

Q. Your answer?

A. A worthy brother, who has been regularly initiated as an Entered Apprentice Mason; served a proper time as such; and now wishes for further light in Masonry, by being passed to the degree of a Fellow Craft.

Q. What was then said to you from within?

A. I was asked if it was of my own free will and accord I made this request; if I was duly and truly prepared; worthy and well qualified; and had made suitable proficiency in the preceding degree: all of which being answered in the affirmative, I was asked, by what further rights I expected to obtain so great a benefit.

Q. Your answer?

A. By the benefit of a pass-word.

Q. What is that pass-word? A. *Shibboleth.*

Q. What further was said to you from within?

A. I was bid to wait till the Worshipful Master in the east was made acquainted with my request, and his answer returned.

Q. After his answer was returned, what followed?

A. I was caused to enter the lodge.

Q. How did you enter?

A. On the angle of the square presented to my naked right breast, in the name of the Lord.

Q. How were you then disposed of?

A. I was conducted twice regularly round the lodge and halted at the Junior Warden in the south, where the same questions were asked and answers returned, as at the door.

Q. How did the Junior Warden dispose of you?

A. He ordered me to be conducted to the Senior Warden in the west, where the same questions were asked and answers returned, as before.

Q. How did the Senior Warden dispose of you?

A. He ordered me to be conducted to the Worshipful Master in the east, where the same questions were asked and answers returned, as before; who likewise demanded of me from whence I came, and whither I was travelling.

Q. Your answer?

E 2

A. From the west, and travelling to the east.
Q. Why do you leave the west, and travel to the east?
A. In search of more light.
Q. How did the Worshipful Master then dispose of you?
A. He ordered me to be conducted back to the west, from whence I came, and put in care of the Senior Warden, who taught me how to approach the east, by advancing upon two upright regular steps to the second step, my feet forming the right angle of an oblong square, and my body erect at the altar before the Worshipful Master.
Q. What did the Worshipful Master do with you?
A. He made a Fellow Craft Mason of me.
Q. How? A. In due form.
Q. What was that due form?
A. My right knee bare bent; my left knee forming a square; my right hand on the Holy Bible, Square, and Compass; my left arm forming an angle, supported by the square, and my hand in a vertical position: in which posture I took upon me the solemn oath, or obligation, of a Fellow Craft Mason. [See page 44 for obligation.]
Q. After your oath, or obligation, what was said to you?
A. I was asked what I most desired.
Q. Your answer? A. More light.
Q. On being brought to light, what did you discover different from before?
A. One point of the compass elevated above the square, which denoted light in this degree; but as one point was yet in obscurity, it was to remind me that I was yet one material point in the dark, respecting Masonry.
Q. What did you next discover?
A. The Worshipful Master approaching me from the east, under the sign and due-guard of a Fellow Craft Mason, who presented me with his right hand in token of brotherly love and confidence; and proceeded to give me the pass-grip and word of a Fellow Craft Mason, and bid me rise and salute the Junior and Senior Wardens, and convince them that I had been regularly passed to the degree of a Fellow Craft, and had the sign, grip, and word, of a Fellow Craft Mason.
Q. What next did you discover?
A. The Worshipful Master approaching me a second time from the east, who presented me a lamb-skin, or white apron; which, he said, he hoped I would continue to wear with honor to myself, and satisfaction and advantage to my brethren.
Q. What was you next presented with?

A. The working tools of a Fellow Craft Mason.
Q. What are they?
A. The Plumb, Square, and Level.
Q. What do they teach? [I think this question ought to be, 'How explained?']
A. The plumb is an instrument made use of by operative Masons to raise perpendiculars; the square, to square the work; and the level, to lay horizontals: but we, as Free and Accepted Masons, are taught to make use of them for more noble and glorious purposes. The plumb admonishes us to walk uprightly, in our several stations, before God and man; squaring our actions by the square of virtue; and remembering that we are all travelling, upon the level of time, to that undiscovered country, from whose bourne no traveller returns.
Q. What was you next presented with?
A. Three precious jewels.
Q. What were they?
A. Faith, Hope, and Charity.
Q. What do they teach?
A. Faith in God, hope in immortality, and charity to all mankind.
Q. How was you then disposed of?
A. I was conducted out of the lodge, and invested of what I had been divested.

SECTION SECOND.

Q. Have you ever worked as a Fellow Craft Mason?
A. I have, in speculative; but our forefathers wrought both in speculative and operative Masonry.
Q. Where did they work?
A. At the building of king Solomon's temple, and many other Masonic edifices.
Q. How long did they work? A. Six days.
Q. Did they not work on the seventh?
A. They did not.
Q. Why so? A. Because in six days God created the heavens and the earth, and rested on the seventh day; the seventh day, therefore, our ancient brethren consecrated as a day of rest from their labors; thereby enjoying more frequent opportunities to contemplate the glorious works of creation, and adore their great Creator.
Q. Did you ever return to the sanctum sanctorum, or holy of holies, of king Solomon's temple?
A. I did.

Q. By what way?
A. Through a long porch, or alley.
Q. Did any thing particular strike your attention on your return?
A. There did; viz:—two large columns, or pillars, one on the left hand, and the other on the right.
Q. What was the name of the one on the left hand?
A. *Boaz*, to denote strength.
Q. What was the name of the one on the right hand?
A. *Jachin*, denoting establishment.
Q. What do they collectively allude to?
A. A passage in scripture, wherein God has declared in his word, 'In strength shall this house be established.'
Q. What were their dimensions?
A. Eighteen cubits in height, twelve in circumference, and four in diameter.
Q. Were they adorned with any thing?
A. They were; with two large chapiters, one on each.
Q. Were they ornamented with any thing?
A. They were; with wreaths of net work, lily work, and pomegranates.
Q. What do they denote?
A. Unity, Peace, and Plenty.
Q. Why so? A. Net work, from its connexion, denotes union; lily work, from its whiteness and purity, denotes peace; and pomegranates, from the exuberance of its seed, denotes plenty.
Q. Where those columns adorned with any thing farther?
A. They were; viz:—two large globes, or balls, one on each.
Q. Did they contain any thing?
A. They did; viz:—all the maps and charts of the celestial and terrestial bodies.
Q. Why are they said to be so extensive?
A. To denote the universality of Masonry, and that a Mason's charity ought to be equally extensive.
Q. What was their composition?
A. Molten, or cast brass.
Q. Who cast them?
A. Our Grand Master, Hiram Abiff.
Q. Where were they cast?
A. On the banks of the river Jordan, in the clay ground between Succoth and Zaradatha, where king Solomon ordered these, and all other holy vessels to be cast.
Q. Were they cast solid or hollow? A. Hollow.
Q. What was their thickness?

A. Four inches, or a hand's breadth.

Q. Why were they cast hollow?

A. The better to withstand inundations or conflagrations; were the archives of Masonry, and contained the constitution, rolls, and records.

Q. What did you next come to?

A. A long, winding stair case, with three, five, seven steps, or more.

Q. What does the three steps allude to?

A. The three principal supports in Masonry; viz:—wisdom, strength, and beauty.

Q. What does the five steps allude to?

A. The five orders in architecture, and the five human senses.

Q. What are the five orders in architecture?

A. The Tuscan, Doric, Ionic, Corinthian, and Composite.

Q. What are the five human senses?

A. Hearing, seeing, feeling, smelling, and tasting; the first three of which have ever been deemed highly essential among Masons; hearing, to hear the word, seeing, to see the sign, and feeling, to feel the grip, whereby one Mason may know another in the dark as well as in the light.

Q. What does the seven steps allude to?

A. The seven sabbatical years; seven years of famine; seven years in building the temple; seven golden candlesticks; seven wonders of the world; seven planets; but more especially the seven liberal arts and sciences; which are, grammar, rhetoric, logic, arithmetic, geometry, music, and astronomy. For these, and many other reasons, the number seven has ever been held in high estimation among Masons.

Q. What did you next come to?

A. The outer door of the middle chamber of king Solomon's temple, which I found partly open, but closely tyled by the Junior Warden.

Q. How did you gain admission?

A. By a pass, and token of a pass.

Q. What was the name of the pass? A. *Shibboleth.*

Q. What does it denote? A. Plenty.

Q. Why so?

A. From an ear of corn being placed at the water-ford.

Q. Why was this pass instituted?

A. In consequence of a quarrel which had long existed between Jephthah, Judge of Israel, and the Ephraimites; the latter of whom had long been a stubborn, rebellious people, whom Jephthah had endeavored to subdue by lenient measures, but to no effect. The Ephraimites, being highly incensed against Jephthah for not being called to fight and share in the rich spoils of the Ammonitish war, assembled a mighty army, and passed over the river Jordan to give Jephthah battle; but he, being apprised of their approach, called together the men of Israel, and gave them battle, and put them to flight; and, to make his victory more complete, he ordered guards to be placed at the different passes on the banks of the river Jordan, and commanded, if the Ephraimites passed that way, that they should pronounce the word *Shibboleth*; but they, being of a different tribe, pronounced it *Sibboleth*; which trifling defect proved them spies, and cost them their lives: and there fell that day, at the different passes on the banks of the river Jordan, forty and two thousand. This word was also used by our ancient brethren to distinguish a friend from a foe, and has since been adopted as a proper pass-word, to be given before entering any well regulated and governed lodge of Fellow Craft Masons.

Q. What did you next discover?

A. The inner door of the middle chamber of king Solomon's temple, which I found partly open, but closely tyled by the Senior Warden.

Q. How did you gain admission?

A. By the grip and word.

Q. How did the Senior Warden dispose of you?

A. He ordered me to be conducted to the Worshipful Master in the east, who informed me that I had been admitted into the middle chamber of king Solomon's temple for the sake of the letter G.

Q. Does it denote any thing?

A. It does; DEITY:—before whom we should all bow with reverence, worship, and adoration. It also denotes geometry, the fifth science; it being that on which this degree was principally founded.

Thus ends the second degree of Masonry.

THE THIRD, OR MASTER MASON'S DEGREE.

The traditional account of the death, several burials, and resurrection of Hiram Abiff, the widow's son, (as hereafter narrated,) admitted as facts, this degree is certainly very interesting. The Bible informs us, that there was a person of that name employed at the building of king Solomon's temple; but neither the Bible, the writings of Josephus, nor any other writings, however ancient, of which I have any knowledge, furnish any information respecting his death. It is very singular, that a man, so celebrated as Hiram Abiff was, an arbiter between Solomon, king of Israel, and Hiram, king of Tyre, universally acknowledged as the third most distinguished man then living, and, in many respects, the greatest man in the world, should pass off the stage of action, in the presence of king Solomon, three thousand three hundred grand overseers, and one hundred and fifty thousand workmen, with whom he had spent a number of years, and neither king Solomon, his bosom friend, nor any other among his numerous friends, even recorded his death or any thing about him.

A person, who has received the two preceding degrees, and wishes to be raised to the sublime degree of a Master Mason, is (the lodge being opened as in the preceding degrees,) conducted from the preparation room to the door, (the manner of preparing him is particularly explained in the lecture,) where he gives three distinct knocks, when the Senior Warden rises and says, 'Worshipful, while we are peaceably at work on the third degree of Masonry, under the influence of humanity, brotherly love, and affection, the door of our lodge appears to be alarmed.' The Master to the Junior Deacon, 'Brother Junior, inquire the cause of that alarm.' The Junior Deacon then steps to the door and answers the three knocks that have been given, by three more; (the knocks are much louder than those given on any occasion, other than that of the admission of candidates in the several degrees :) one knock is then given without, and answered by one from within, when the door is partly opened, and the Junior Deacon asks, 'Who comes there? Who comes there? Who comes there?' The Senior Deacon answers, 'A worthy brother who has been regularly initiated as an entered Apprentice Mason, passed to the degree of a Fellow Craft, and now wishes for further light in Masonry, by being raised to the sublime degree of a Master Mason.' Junior Deacon to Senior Deacon, 'Is it of his own free will and accord he makes this request?' A. 'It is.' Junior Deacon to Senior Deacon, 'Is he worthy and well qualified?' A. 'He is.' Junior Deacon to Senior Deacon, 'Has he made suitable proficiency in the preceding degrees?' A. 'He has.' Junior Deacon to Senior Deacon, 'By what further right does he expect to obtain this benefit?' A. 'By the benefit of a password.' Junior Deacon to Senior Deacon, '*Has he a pass-word?*' A. 'He has not, but I have got it for him.' The Junior Deacon to Senior Deacon, 'Will you give it to me?' The Senior Deacon then whispers in the ear of the Junior Deacon, '*Tubal Cain.*' Junior Deacon says, 'The pass is right. Since this is the case you will wait till the Worshipful Master be made acquainted with his request, and his answer returned.' The Junior Deacon then repairs to the Master, and gives three knocks, as at the door; after answering which, the same questions are asked and answers returned, as at the door; when the Master says, 'Since he comes endued with all these necessary qualifications, let him enter this worshipful lodge in the name of the Lord, and take heed on what he enters.' The Junior Deacon returns to the door and says, 'Let him enter this worshipful lodge in the name of the Lord, and take heed on what he enters.' In entering, both points of the compass are pressed against his naked right and left breasts, when the Junior Deacon stops the candidate, and says, ' Brother, when you first entered this lodge, you was received on the point of the compass pressing your naked left breast, which was then explained to you; when you entered it the second time, you was received on the angle of the square, which was also explained to you; on entering it now, you are received on the two extreme points of the compass pressing your naked right and left breasts, which are thus explained: ' As the most vital parts of man are contained between the two breasts, so are the most valuable tenets of Masonry contained betwen the two extreme points of the compass, which are, virtue, morality, and brotherly love.' The Senior Deacon then conducts the candidate three times regularly round the lodge. (I wish the reader to observe, that on this, as well as every other degree, the Junior Warden is the first of the three principal officers that the candidate passes, travelling with the sun, when he starts round the lodge; and as he passes the Junior Warden, Senior Warden, and Master, the first time going round they each give one rap; the second time, two raps; and the third time, three raps. The number of raps given, on those occasions, are the same as the number of the degree, except the first degree, on which three are given, I always thought improperly.) During the time the candidate is travelling round the room, the Master reads the following passage of scripture, the conductor and candidate travelling, and the Master reading, so that the travelling and reading terminates at the same time: ' Remember now thy Creator in the days of thy youth, while the evil days come not, nor the years draw nigh, when thou shalt say, I have no pleasure in them; while the sun, or the moon, or the stars be not darkened, nor the clouds return after the rain; in the day when the keepers of the house shall tremble, and the strong men shall bow themselves, and the grinders cease because they are few, and those that look out of the windows be darkened, and the doors shall be shut in the streets; when the sound of the grinding is low, and he shall rise up at the voice of the bird, and all the daughters of music shall be brought low. Also, when they shall be afraid of that which is high, and fears shall be in the way, and the almond tree shall flourish, and the grasshopper shall be a burthen, and desire shall fail: because man goeth to his long home, and the mourners go about the streets. Or ever the silver cord be loosed, or the golden bowl be broken, or the pitcher be broken at the fountain, or the wheel at the cistern. Then shall the dust return to the earth, as it was; and the spirit return unto God who gave it.' The conductor and candidate halt at the Junior Warden in the south, where the same questions are asked and answers returned, as at the door; he is then conducted to the Senior Warden in the west, where the same questions are asked and answers returned, as before; from thence he is conducted to the Worshipful Master in the east, who asks the same questions and receives the same answers as before; and who likewise asks the candidate, from whence he came, and whither he is travelling? A. 'From the west; and travelling to the east.' Q. 'Why do you leave the west, and travel to the east?' A. 'In search of more light.' The Master then says to the Senior Deacon, 'You will please conduct the candidate back to the west, from whence he came, and put him in care of the Senior Warden, and request him to teach the candidate how to approach the east, by advancing upon three upright regular steps to the third step, his feet forming a square, his body erect at the altar before the Worshipful Master, and place him in a proper position to take upon him the solemn oath, or obligation, of a Master Mason.' The Master then comes to the candidate and says, 'Brother, you are now placed in a proper position, (the lecture explains it,) to take upon you the solemn oath, or obligation, of a Master Mason; which I assure you, as before, is neither to affect your religion nor politics. If you are willing to take it, repeat your name, and say after me :—

'I, A. B., of my own free will and accord, in presence of Almighty God, and this Worshipful Lodge of Master Masons, erected to God, and dedicated to the holy order of St. John, do hereby and hereon, most solemnly and sincerely promise and swear, in addition to my former obligations, that I will not give the degree of a Master Mason to any one of an inferior degree, nor to any other being in the known world, except it be to a true and lawful brother, or brethren, Master Mason, or within the body of a just and lawfully constituted lodge of such; and not unto him, nor unto them, whom I shall hear so to be, but unto him and them only whom I shall find so to be after strict trial and due examination, or lawful information received.—Furthermore, do I promise and swear that I will not give the Master's word, which I shall here-

F

after receive, neither in the lodge, nor out of it, except it be on the five points of fellowship, and then not above my breath. Furthermore, do I promise and swear, that I will not give the grand hailing sign of distress, except I am in real distress, or for the benefit of the craft when at work; and should I ever see that sign given, or the word accompanying it, and the person who gave it appearing to be in distress, I will fly to his relief at the risk of my life, should there be a greater probability of saving his life than of losing my own. Furthermore, do I promise and swear that I will not wrong this lodge, nor a brother of this degree, to the value of one cent, knowingly, myself, nor suffer it to be done by others, if in my power to prevent it. Furthermore, do I promise and swear that I will not be at the initiating, passing, and raising a candidate at one communication, without a regular dispensation from the Grand Lodge for the same. Furthermore, do I promise and swear that I will not be at the initiating, passing, or raising, a candidate in a clandestine lodge, I knowing it to be such. Furthermore, do I promise and swear that I will not be at the initiating of an old man in dotage, a young man in nonage, an atheist, irreligious libertine, idiot, madman, hermaphrodite, nor woman.* Furthermore, do I promise and swear that I will not speak evil of a brother Master Mason, neither behind his back, nor before his face, but will apprize him of all approaching danger if in my power. Furthermore, do I promise and swear that I will not violate the chastity of a Master Mason's wife, mother, sister, or daughter, I knowing them to be such, nor suffer it to be done by others, if in my power to prevent it.† Furthermore, do I promise and swear that I will support the constitution of the Grand Lodge of the State of ——. under which this lodge is held, and conform to all the by-laws, rules, and regulations of this or any other lodge of which I may at any time hereafter become a member. Furthermore, do I promise and swear that I will obey all regular signs, summons, or tokens, given, handed, sent,

---

* Masonry professes to bring men to heaven, and yet it denies its blessings to a large majority of the human family. All the *fair* part of creation, together with the old, young, and poor, are exempted. How unlike the glorious gospel of the Son of God! In *this* there is no restriction of persons; the high and low, rich and poor, bond and free, male and female, are all one in Christ Jesus.

† I ask the candid reader if *this* is morality or benevolence? If a Mason was sworn not to violate the chastity of *any* woman, it would have more the appearance of virtuous principle. But would a Mason's oath restrain a man, who would be guilty of such crimes? If masonry inculcated the *true* principles of morality the fruit would be manifest: I have been acquainted with many Masons, but never knew *one* made better by Masonry; but on the contrary, numbers, who, through its demoralizing influence have been rendered worthless.

or thrown to me, from the hand of a brother Master Mason, or from the body of a just and lawfully constituted lodge of such, provided it be within the length of my cable-tow. Furthermore, do I promise and swear that a Master Mason's secrets, given to me in charge as such, and I knowing them to be such, shall remain as secure and inviolable in my breast as in his own, when communicated to me, murder and treason excepted; and they left to my own election. Furthermore, do I promise and swear that I will go on a Master Mason's errand, whenever required, even should I have to go barefoot, and bareheaded, if within the length of my cable-tow.* Furthermore, do I promise and swear that I will always remember a brother Master Mason, when on my knees, offering up my devotions to Almighty God. Furthermore, do I promise and swear that I will be aiding and assisting all poor indigent Master Masons, their wives and orphans, wheresoever disposed round the globe, as far as in my power, without injuring myself or family materially. Furthermore, do I promise and swear that if any part of this my solemn oath or obligation be omitted at this time, that I will hold myself amenable thereto, whenever informed. To all which I do most solemnly and sincerely promise and swear, with a fixed and steady purpose of mind in me, to keep and perform the same, binding myself under no less penalty than to have my body severed in two in the midst, and divided to the north and south, my bowels burnt to ashes in the centre, and the ashes scattered before the four winds of heaven, that there might not the least tract or trace of remembrance remain among men or Masons of so vile and perjured a wretch as I should be, were I ever to prove wilfully guilty of violating any part of this my solemn oath or obligation of a Master Mason. So help me God, and keep me steadfast in the due performance of the same.'

The Master then asks the candidate, 'What do you most desire?' The candidate answers after his prompter, 'More light.' The bandage which was tied round his head in the preparation room, is, by one of the brethren who stands behind him for that purpose, loosened and put over both eyes, and he is immediately brought to light in the same manner as in the preceding degree, except three stamps on the floor, and three claps of the hands are given in this degree.—On being brought to light, the Master says to the candidate, 'You first discover, as before, three great lights in Masonry, by the assistance of three lesser, with this difference,

---

* Literally a rope several yards in length, but mystically three miles: so that a Master Mason must go on a brother Master Mason's errand whenever required, the distance of three miles; should he have to go barefoot and bareheaded. In the degrees of knighthood the distance is forty miles.

both points of the compass are elevated above the square, which denotes to you that you are about to receive all the light that can be conferred on you in a Master's lodge.' The Master steps back from the candidate and says, 'Brother, you now discover me as Master of this lodge, approaching you from the east, under the sign and due-guard of a Master Mason.' The sign is given by raising both hands and arms to the elbows perpendicularly, one on either side of the head, the elbows forming a square. The words accompanying this sign in case of distress, are, ' O Lord my God, is there no help for the widow's son.' As the last words drop from your lips you let your hands fall in that manner, best calculated to indicate solemnity. King Solomon is said to have made this exclamation on the receipt of the information of the death of Hiram Abiff. Masons are all charged never to give the *words* except in the dark, when the sign cannot be seen. Here Masons differ very much; some contend that Solomon gave this sign, and made this exclamation, when informed of Hiram's death, and work accordingly in their lodges. Others say the sign was given; and the exclamation made at the grave when Solomon went there to raise Hiram, and of course they work accordingly; that is to say, the Master, who governs a lodge, holding the latter opinion, gives the sign, &c. at the grave, when he goes to raise the body, and vice versa. The due-guard is given by putting the right hand to the left side of the bowels, the hand open, with the thumb next to the belly, and drawing it across the belly, and let it fall; this is done tolerably quick. After the Master has given the sign and dueguard, which does not take more than a minute, he says ' Brother, I now present you with my right hand in token of brotherly love and affection, and with it the pass-grip and word.' The pass-grip is given by pressing the thumb between the joints of the second and third fingers, where they join the hand, and the word or name is *Tubal Cain*. It is the pass word to the Master's degree. The Master after giving the candidate the pass-grip and word, bids him rise and salute the Junior and Senior Wardens, and convince them that he is an obligated Master Mason, and is in possession of the pass-grip and word. While the Wardens are examining the candidate, the Master returns to the east and gets an apron, and as he returns to the candidate, one of the Wardens, [sometimes both,] says to the Master, ' Worshipful, we are satisfied that brother —— is an obligated Master Mason.' The Master then says to the candidate, ' Brother, I now have the honor to present you with a lamb-skin, or white apron, as before, which, I hope, you will continue to wear with credit to yourself, and satisfaction and advantage to the brethren; you will please carry it to the Senior Warden in the west, who will teach you how to wear it as a Master Mason.'

The Senior Warden ties on his apron, and lets the flap fall down before in its natural and common situation.

The Master returns to his seat, and the candidate is conducted to him. Master to candidate, 'Brother, I perceive you are dressed, it is, of course, necessary you should have tools to work with; I will now present you with the working tools of a Master Mason, and explain their uses to you. The working tools of a Master Mason are all the implements of Masonry indiscriminately, but more especially the trowel. The trowel is an instrument made use of by operative masons to spread the cement which unites a building into one common mass; but we, as Free and Accepted Masons, are taught to make use of it for the more noble and glorious purpose of spreading the cement of brotherly love and affection; that cement which unites us into one sacred band or society of friends and brothers, among whom no contention should ever exist, but that noble contention, or rather emulation, of who can best work, or best agree. I also present you with three precious jewels; their names are Humanity, Friendship, and Brotherly Love. Brother, you are not yet invested with all the secrets of this degree, nor do I know whether you ever will, until I know how you withstand the amazing trials and dangers that await you.'

'You are now about to travel to give us a specimen of your fortitude, perseverance, and fidelity, in the preservation of what you have already received—Fare you well, and may the Lord be with you, and support you through your trials and difficulties.'— [In some lodges they make him pray before he starts.] The candidate is then conducted out of the lodge, clothed, and returns; as he enters the door, his conductor says to him, 'Brother, we are now in a place representing the *sanctum sanctorum*, or *holy of holies*, of king Solomon's temple. It was the custom of our Grand Master, Hiram Abiff, every day at high twelve, when the crafts were from labour to refreshment, to enter into the *sanctum sanctorum*, and offer up his devotions to the ever living God.— Let us, in imitation of him, kneel and pray.' They then kneel, and the conductor says the following prayer. 'Thou, O God, knowest our down sitting and up rising, and understandest our thoughts afar off; shield and defend us from the evil intentions of our enemies, and support us under the trials and afflictions we are destined to endure, while travelling through this vale of tears. Man that is born of a woman is of few days, and full of trouble. He cometh forth as a flower, and is cut down; he fleeth also as a shadow, and continueth not. Seeing his days are determined, the number of his months are with thee, thou hast appointed his bounds that he cannot pass; turn from him that he may rest, till he shall accomplish his day. For there is hope of a tree if it be cut down, that it will sprout again, and that the tender branch thereof will not cease. But man dieth and wasteth away; yea, man giveth up the ghost, and where is he? As the waters fail from the sea, and flood decayeth and drieth up, so man lieth down, and riseth not up till the heavens shall be no more. Yet, O Lord! have compassion on the children of thy creation; administer unto them comfort in time of trouble, and save them with an everlasting salvation. Amen—so mote it be.' They then rise, and the conductor says to the candidate, 'Brother, in further imitation of our Grand Master, Hiram Abiff, let us retire at the south gate.' They then advance to the Junior Warden, (who represents *Jubela,* one of the ruffians,) who exclaims, 'Who comes here?' [The room is dark, or the candidate hood-winked.] The conductor answers, 'Our Grand Master, Hiram Abiff.' 'Our Grand Master, Hiram Abiff!' exclaims the ruffian, 'he is the very man I wanted to see; (seizing the candidate by the throat at the same time, and jerking him about with violence;) give me the Master Mason's word, or I'll take your life.' The conductor replies, 'I cannot give it now, but if you will wait till the Grand Lodge assembles at Jerusalem, if you are worthy, you shall then receive it, otherwise you cannot.' The ruffian then gives the candidate a blow with the twenty-four inch guage across the throat, on which he fled to the west gate, where he was accosted by the second ruffian, *Jubelo,* with more violence, and on his refusal to comply with his request, he gave him a severe blow with the square across his breast; on which he attempted to make his escape at the east gate, where he was accosted by the third ruffian, *Jubelum,* with still more violence, and refusing to comply with his request, the ruffian gave him a violent blow with the common gavel on the forehead, which brought him to the floor, on which one of them exclaimed, 'What shall we do, we have killed our Grand Master, Hiram Abiff?' Another answers, 'Let us carry him out at the east gate, and bury him in the rubbish till low twelve, and then meet and carry him a westerly course and bury him.' The candidate is then taken up in a blanket, on which he fell, and carried to the west end of the lodge, and covered up and left; by this time the Master has resumed his seat, (king Solomon is supposed to arrive at the temple at this juncture,) and calls to order, and asks the Senior Warden the cause of all that confusion; the Senior Warden answers, 'Our Grand Master, Hiram Abiff, is missing, and there are no plans or designs laid down on the tressle-board for the crafts to pursue their labor.' The Master, alias king Solomon, replies, ' Our Grand Master missing! our Grand Master has always been very punctual in his attendance; I fear he is indisposed; assemble the crafts, and search in and about the temple, and see if he can be found.' They all shuffle about the floor a while, when the Master calls them to order, and asks the Senior Warden, ' What success?' He answers, ' We cannot find our Grand Master, my Lord.' The Master then orders the Secretary to call the roll of workmen, and see whether any of them are missing. The Secretary calls the roll, and says, ' I have called the roll, my Lord, and find that there are three missing, viz: *Jubela, Jubelo,* and *Jubelum.*' His Lordship then observes, ' This brings to my mind a circumstance that took place this morning—twelve Fellow Crafts, clothed in white gloves and aprons, in token of their innocence, came to me, and confessed that they twelve, with three others, had conspired to extort the Master Mason's word from their Grand Master, Hiram Abiff, and in case of refusal to take his life—they twelve had recanted, but feared the other three had been base enough to carry their atrocious designs into execution. Solomon then ordered twelve Fellow-Crafts to be drawn from the bands of the workmen, clothed in white gloves and aprons, in token of their innocence, and sent three east, three west, three north, and three south, in search of the ruffians, and, if found, to bring them forward. Here the members all shuffle about the floor a while, and fall in with a reputed traveller, and inquire of him if he had seen any travelling men that way; he tells them that he had seen three that morning near the coast of Joppa, who from their dress and appearance were Jews, and were workmen from the temple, inquiring for a passage to Ethiopia, but were unable to obtain one, in consequence of an embargo which had recently been laid on all the shipping, and had turned back into the country.

The Master now calls them to order again, and asks the Senior Warden, ' What success.' He answers by relating what had taken place—Solomon observes, ' I had this embargo laid to prevent the ruffians from making their escape;' and adds, ' you will go and search again, and search till you find them, if possible; and if they are not found, the twelve, who confessed, shall be considered as the reputed murderers, and suffer accordingly.' The members all start again, and shuffle about a while, until one of them, as if by accident, finds the body of Hiram Abiff, alias the candidate, and hails his travelling companions, who join him, and while they are humming out something over the candidate, the three reputed ruffians, who are seated in a private corner near the candidate, are heard to exclaim in the following manner—first, *Jubela*, 'O that my throat had been cut across, my tongue torn out, and my body buried in the rough sands of the sea at low water-mark, where the tide ebbs and flows twice in twenty-four hours, ere I had been accessary to the death of so good a man as our Grand Master, Hiram Abiff.'

The second, *Jubelo*, 'O that my left breast had been torn open, and my heart and vitals taken from thence, and thrown over my left shoulder, carried into the valley of Jehoshaphat, and there to become a prey to the wild beasts of the field, and vultures of the air, ere I had conspired the death of so good a man as our Grand Master, Hiram Abiff.'

The third, *Jubelum*, 'O that my body had been severed in two in the midst, and divided to the north and south, my bowels burnt to ashes in the centre, and the ashes scattered by the four winds of heaven, that there might not the least track or trace of remembrance remain among men, or Masons, of so vile and perjured a wretch as I am—Ah, *Jubela* and *Jubelo*, it was I that struck him harder than you both—it was I that gave him the fatal blow—it was I that killed him outright.' The three Fellow Crafts who had stood by the candidate all this time listening to the ruffians, whose voices they recognized, says one to the other, 'What shall we do, there are three of them, and only three of us?' 'It is,' said one, in reply, 'our cause is good, let us seize them;' on which they rush forward, and carry them to the Master, to whom they relate what had passed; the Master then addresses them in the following manner: (They in many lodges kneel, or lie down in token of their guilt and penitence.) 'Well, *Jubela*, what have you got to say for yourself—guilty or not guilty?' A. 'Guilty, my Lord.' '*Jubelo*, guilty or not guilty?' A. 'Guilty, my Lord.' '*Jubelum*, guilty or not guilty?' A. 'Guilty, my Lord.' The Master of the three Fellow Crafts, who took them, 'Take them without the west gate of the Temple, and have them executed according to the several imprecations of their own mouths.' They are then hurried off to the west end of the room. Here this part of the farce ends. The Master then orders fifteen Fellow Crafts to be elected from the bands of the workmen, and sent three east, three west, three north, three south; and three in and about the temple, in search of their Grand Master, Hiram Abiff, [In some lodges they only send twelve, when their own lectures say fifteen were sent,] and charges them if they find the body, to examine carefully on and about it for the Master's word or a key to it. The three that travelled a westerly course, come to the candidate and finger about him a little and are called to order by the Master, when they report that they have found the grave of their Grand Master, Hiram Abiff, and on moving the earth till they came to the body, they involuntarily found their hands raised in this position, [showing it at the same time ; it is the due-guard of this degree ;] to guard their nostrils against the offensive effluvia which arose from the grave ; and that they had searched carefully on and about the body for the Master's word, but had not discovered any thing but a faint resemblance of the letter G on the left breast. The Master, on the receipt of this information, (raising himself,) raises his hands three several times above his head, (as herein before described) and exclaims twice, 'Nothing but a faint resemblance of the letter G ! that is not the Master's word, nor a key to it. I fear the Master's word is forever lost ! (The third exclamation is different from the others—attend to it, it has been described in page 64.) 'Nothing but a faint resemblance of the letter G ! that is not the Master's word nor a key to it,'—' O Lord my God, is there no help for the widow's son !' The Master then orders the Junior Warden to summon a lodge of Entered Apprentice Masons, and repair to the grave to raise the body of their Grand Master, by the Entered Apprentice's grip. They go to the candidate and take hold of his fore finger and pull it, return and tell the Master that they could not raise him by the Entered Apprentice's grip ; that the skin cleaved from the bone. A lodge of Fellow Crafts are then sent, who act as before, except that they pull the candidate's second finger. The Master then directs the Senior Warden [generally] to summon a lodge of Master Masons, and says, ' I will go with them myself in person, and try to raise the body by the Master's grip, or lion's paw.' [Some say by the strong grip, or the lion's paw.] They then all assemble round the candidate, the Master having declared the first word spoken after the body was raised, should be adopted as a substitute for the Master's word, for the government of Master Mason's lodges in all future generations ; he proceeds to raise the candidate, alias, the representative of the dead body of Hiram Abiff. He [the candidate] is raised on what is called the five points of fellowship, which are foot to foot, knee to knee, breast to breast, hand to back, and mouth to ear. This is done by putting the inside of your right foot to the inside of the right foot of the person to whom you are going to give the word, the inside of your knee to his, laying your right breast against his, your left hands on the back of each other, and your mouths to each other's right ear, [in which position you are alone permitted to give the word,] and whisper the word *Mah-hah-bone*. The Master's grip is given by taking hold of each other's right hand, as though you were going to shake hands, and sticking the nails of each of your fingers into the joint of the other's wrist where it unites with the hand. In this position the candidate is raised, he keeping his whole body stiff, as though dead. The Master in raising him is assisted by some of the brethren, who take hold of the candidate by the arms and shoulders; as soon as he is raised to his feet they step back, and the Master whispers the word *Mah-hah-bone* in his ear, and causes the candidate to repeat it, telling him at the same time that he must never give it in any manner other than that which he receives it.—He is also told that *Mah-hah-bone*, signifies marrow in the bone. They then separate, and the Master makes the following explanation, respecting the five points of fellowship. Master to candidate, 'Brother, foot to foot, teaches you that you should, whenever asked, go on a brother's errand, if within the length of your cable-tow, even if you should have to go barefoot and bareheaded. Knee to knee, that you should always remember a Master Mason in your devotion to Almighty God. Breast to breast, that you should keep the Master Mason's secrets, when given to you in charge as such, as secure and inviolable in your breast, as they were in his own, before communicated to you. Hand to back, that you should support a Master Mason behind his back, as well as before his face. Mouth to ear, that you should support his good name, as well behind his back as before his face.'

After the candidate is through with what is called the work part, the Master addresses him in the following manner: 'Brother, you may suppose from the manner you have been dealt with to-night, that we have been fooling with you, or that we have treated you different from others, but I assure you that is not the case. You have, this night, represented one of the greatest men that ever lived, in the tragical catastrophe of his death, burial, and resurrection; I mean Hiram Abiff, the widow's son, who was slain by three ruffians, at the building of king Solomon's temple, and who, in his inflexibility, integrity, and fortitude, never was surpassed by man. The history of that momentous event is thus related. Masonic tradition inform us, that at the building of king Solomon's temple, fifteen Fellow Crafts discovering that the temple was almost finished, and not having the Master Mason's word, became very impatient, and entered into a horrid conspiracy to extort the Master Mason's word from their Grand Master, Hiram Abiff, the first time they met him alone, or take his life, that they might pass as Masters in other countries, and receive wages as such; but before they could accomplish their designs, twelve of them recanted, but the other three were base enough to carry their atrocious designs into execution. Their names were *Jubela, Jubelo,* and *Jubelum.*'

'It was the custom of our Grand Master, Hiram Abiff, every day at high twelve, when the crafts were from labor to refreshment, to enter into the *sanctum sanctorum*, and offer his devotions to the ever living God, and draw out his plans and designs on the tressle-board for the crafts to pursue their labor. On a certain day, [not named in any of our traditional accounts,] *Jubela, Jubelo,* and *Jubelum,* placed themselves at the south, west, and east gates of the temple, and Hiram having finished his devotions and labor, attempted (as was his usual custom,) to retire at the south gate, where he was met by *Jubela,* who demanded of him the Master Mason's word, (some say the secrets of a Master Mason,) and on his refusal to give it, *Jubela* gave him a violent blow with a twenty-four inch guage across the throat; on which Hiram fled to the west gate, where he was accosted in the same manner by *Jubelo,* but with more violence. Hiram told him that he could not give the word then, because Solomon, king of Israel, Hiram, king of Tyre, and himself, had entered into a solemn league, that the word never should be given, unless they three were present; but if he would have patience, till the Grand Lodge assembled at Jerusalem, if he was then found worthy he should then receive it, otherwise he could not; *Jubelo* replied in a very peremptory manner: ' If you do not give me the Master's word, I'll take your life;' and on Hiram's refusing to give it, *Jubelo* gave him a severe blow with the square across the left breast; on which he fled to the east gate, where he was accosted by *Jubelum,* in the same manner, but with still more violence. Here Hiram reasoned as before; *Jubelum* told him that he had heard his cavilling with *Jubela* and *Jubelo* long enough, and that the Master's word had been promised to him from time to time for a long time; that he was still put off, and that the temple was almost finished, and he was determined to have the word or take his life; 'I want it so that I may be able to get wages as a Master Mason, in any country to which I may go for employ, after the temple is finished, and that I may be able to support my wife and children.' Hiram persisting in his refusal; he gave Hiram a violent blow with the gavel, on the forehead, which felled him to the floor and killed him—they took the body and carried it out of the west gate, and buried it in the rubbish, till low twelve at night, (which is twelve o'clock,) when they three met agreeably to appointment, and carried the body a westerly course, and buried it at the brow of a hill, in a grave, dug due east and west six feet perpendicular, and made their escape. King Solomon coming up to the temple at low six in the morning, (as was his usual custom,) found the crafts all in confusion; and on inquiring the cause, was informed that their Grand Master, Hiram Abiff, was missing, and there was no plans and designs laid down on the tressle-board, for the crafts to pursue their labor. Solomon ordered search to be made in and about the temple for him; no discovery being made, he then ordered the secretary to call the roll of workmen to see if any were missing; it appearing that there were three, viz: *Jubela, Jubelo,* and *Jubelum* : Solomon observed, 'This brings to my mind a circumstance that took place this morning. Twelve Fellow Crafts came to me dressed in white gloves and aprons, in token of their innocence, and confessed that they twelve with three others, had conspired to extort the Master Mason's word from their Grand Master, Hiram Abiff, and in case of his refusal, to take his life : they twelve had recanted, but feared the other three had been base enough to carry their atrocious designs into execution.' Solomon immediately ordered twelve Fellow Crafts to be selected from the bands of the workmen, clothed in white gloves and aprons in token of their innocence, and sent three east, three west, three north, and three south, in search of the ruffians, and if found, to bring them up before him. The three that travelled a westerly course, coming near the coast of Joppa, fell in with a way-faring man who informed them that he had seen three men pass that way that morning, who, from their appearance and dress, were workmen from the temple, inquiring for a passage to Ethiopia, but were unable to obtain one in consequence of an embargo which had recently been laid on all the shipping, and had turned back into the country. After making further and more diligent search, and making no further discovery, they returned to the temple and reported to Solomon the result of their pursuit and inquiries. On which Solomon directed them to go again and search until they found their Grand Master, Hiram Abiff, if possible, and if he was not found, the twelve who had confessed, should be considered as the murderers, and suffer accordingly.

They returned again in pursuit of the ruffians, and one of the three that travelled a westerly course, being more weary than the rest, sat down at the brow of a hill to rest and refresh himself; and in attempting to rise, caught hold of a sprig of cassia, which easily gave, and excited his curiosity, and made him suspicious of a deception ; on which he hailed his companions, who immediately assembled, and on examination, found that the earth had been recently moved ; and on moving the rubbish, discovered the appearance of the grave; and while they were confabulating about

LIGHT ON MASONRY. 73

what measures to take, they heard voices issuing from a cavern in the clefts of the rocks, on which, they immediately repaired to the place, where they heard the voice of *Jubela* exclaim, ' O! that my throat had been cut across, my tongue torn out, and my body buried in the rough sands of the sea, at low water-mark, where the tide ebbs and flows twice in twenty-four hours, ere I had been accessary to the death of so good a man as our Grand Master, Hiram Abiff:'—on which they distinctly heard the voice of *Jubelo* exclaim, ' O! that my left breast had been torn open, and my heart and vitals taken from thence, and thrown over my left shoulder, carried into the valley of Jehoshaphat, there to become a prey to the wild beasts of the field, and vultures of the air, ere I had conspired to take the life of so good a man as our Grand Master, Hiram Abiff:'—when they more distinctly heard the voice of *Jubelum* exclaim, ' O! that my body had been severed in two in the midst, and divided to the north and the south, my bowels burnt to ashes in the centre, and the ashes scattered by the four winds of heaven, that there might not remain the least trace of remembrance among men, or Masons, of so vile and perjured a wretch as I am, who wilfully took the life of so good a man as our Grand Master, Hiram Abiff. Ah! *Jubela* and *Jubelo*, it was I that struck him harder than you both! it was I that gave him the fatal blow! it was I that killed him outright!'—on which, they rushed forward, seized, bound, and carried them before king Solomon, who, after hearing the testimony of the three Fellow Crafts, and the three ruffians having plead guilty, ordered them to be taken out at the west gate of the temple, and executed agreeably to the several imprecations of their own mouths. King Solomon then ordered fifteen Fellow Crafts to be selected from the bands of the workmen, clothed with white gloves and aprons, in token of their innocence, and sent three east, three west, three north, three south, and three in and about the temple, in search of the body of our Grand Master, Hiram Abiff; and the three that travelled a westerly course found it under a sprig of cassia, where a worthy brother sat down to rest and refresh himself; and on removing the earth till they came to the coffin, they involuntarily found their hands raised, as herein before described, to guard their nostrils against the offensive effluvia that rose from the grave. It is also said, that the body had lain there fourteen days; some say, fifteen.

The body was raised in the manner herein before described, carried up to the temple, and buried as explained in the closing clauses of the lecture. Not one third part of the preceding his-

G

tory of this degree is ever given to a candidate. A few general, desultory, unconnected remarks are made to him, and he is generally referred to the manner of raising, and to the lecture, for information as to the particulars. Here follows a charge which ought to be, and sometimes is, delivered to the candidate after hearing the history of the degree.

An address to be delivered to the candidate after the history has been given.

'Brother, your zeal for the institution of Masonry, the progress you have made in the mystery, and your conformity to our regulations, have pointed you out as a proper object of our favor and esteem.

'You are bound, by duty, honor, and gratitude, to be faithful to your trust; to support the dignity of your character on every occasion; and to enforce, by precept and example, obedience to the tenets of the order.

'In the character of a Master Mason you are authorized to correct the errors and irregularities of your uninformed brethren, and to guard them against a breach of fidelity.

'To preserve the reputation of the fraternity unsullied, must be your constant care; and, for this purpose, it is your province to recommend to your inferiors, obedience and submission; to your equals, courtesy and affability; to your superiors, kindness and condescension. Universal benevolence you are always to inculcate; and, by the regularity of your own behaviour, afford the best example for the conduct of others less informed. The ancient landmarks of the order, entrusted to your care, you are carefully to preserve; and never suffer them to be infringed, or countenance a deviation from the established usages and customs of the fraternity.

'Your virtue, honor, and reputation are concerned in supporting, with dignity, the character you now bear. Let no motive, therefore, make you swerve from your duty, violate your vow, or betray your trust; but be true and faithful, and imitate the example of that celebrated artist whom you this evening represent; thus you will render yourself deserving the honor which we have conferred, and merit the confidence that we have reposed.'

Here follows the lecture on this degree, which is divided into three sections.

SECTION FIRST.

Q. Are you a Master Mason?
A. I am;—try me, prove me; disprove me if you can.
Q. Where were you prepared to be made a Master Mason?
A. In a room adjacent to the body of a just and lawfully constituted lodge of such, duly assembled in a room, representing the *sanctum sanctorum*, or *holy of holies*, of king Solomon's temple.
Q. How were you prepared?
A. By being divested of all metals; neither naked nor clothed; barefooted nor shod; with a cable-tow three times about my naked body; in which posture I was conducted to the door of the lodge, where I gave three distinct knocks.
Q. What did those three distinct knocks allude to?
A. To the third degree of Masonry; it being that on which I was about to enter.
Q. What was said to you from within?
A. Who comes there, Who comes there, Who comes there.
Q. Your answer?
A. A worthy brother, who has been regularly initiated as an Entered Apprentice Mason, passed to the degree of Fellow Craft, and now wishes for further light in Masonry, by being raised to the sublime degree of a Master Mason.
Q. What further was said to you from within?
A. I was asked if it was of my own free will and accord I made this request; if I was duly and truly prepared; worthy and well qualified; and had made suitable proficiency in the preceding degrees: all of which being answered in the affirmative, I was asked, by what further rights I expected to obtain that benefit.
Q. Your answer?
A. By the benefit of a pass-word.
Q. What was that pass-word? A. *Tubal Cain.*
Q. What next was said to you?
A. I was bid to wait till the Worshipful Master in the east was made acquainted with my request, and his answer returned.
Q. After his answer was returned, what followed?
A. I was caused to enter the lodge on the two extreme points of the compass, pressing my naked right and left breasts, in the name of the Lord.
Q. How were you then disposed of?
A. I was conducted three times regularly round the lodge, and halted at the Junior Warden in the south, where the same questions were asked and answers returned, as at the door.
Q. How did the Junior Warden dispose of you?
A. He ordered me to be conducted to the Senior Warden in

the west, where the same questions were asked and answers returned, as before.

Q. How did the Senior Warden dispose of you?

A. He ordered me to be conducted to the Worshipful Master in the east, where the same questions were asked and answers returned, as before; who likewise demanded of me from whence I came, and whither I was travelling.

Q. Your answer?

A. From the west, and travelling to the east.

Q. Why do you leave the west, and travel to the east?

A. In search of light.

Q. How did the Worshipful Master dispose of you?

A. He ordered me to be conducted back to the west, from whence I came, and put in care of the Senior Warden, who taught me how to approach the east, by advancing upon three upright regular steps to the third step, my feet forming a square, and my body erect at the altar before the Worshipful Master.

Q. What did the Worshipful Master do with you?

A. He made an obligated Master Mason of me.

Q. How?   A. In due form.

Q. What was that due form?

A. Both my knees bare bent, they forming a square; both hands on the Holy Bible, Square, and Compass; in which posture I took upon me the solemn oath, or obligation, of a Master Mason.

Q. After your obligation, what was said to you?

A. What do you most desire.

Q. Your answer?

A. More light. [The bandage round the head, is now dropped over the eyes.]

Q. Did you receive light?   A. I did.

Q. On being brought to light, on this degree, what did you first discover?

A. Three great lights in Masonry, by the assistance of three less, and both points of the Compass elevated above the Square; which denoted to me that I had received, or was about to receive, all the light that could be conferred on me in a Master's lodge.

Q. What did you next discover?

A. The Worshipful Master approaching me from the east, under the sign and due-guard of a Master Mason, who presented me with his right hand in token of brotherly love and confidence, and proceeded to give me the pass-grip and word of a Master Mason, [the word is the name of the pass-grip;] and bid me rise and salute the Junior and Senior Wardens, and convince them that I was an obligated Master Mason, and had the sign, pass-grip, and word. (*Tubal Cain.*)

Q. What did you next discover?
A. The Worshipful Master approaching me, a second time, from the east, who presented me with a lamb-skin, or white apron: which, he said, he hoped I would continue to wear with honor to myself, and satisfaction and advantage to the brethren.

Q. What were you next presented with?
A. The working tools of a Master Mason.

Q. What are they?
A. All the implements of Masonry indiscriminately, but more especially the trowel.

Q. How explained?
A. The trowel is an instrument made use of by operative Masons to spread the cement which unites a building into one common mass; but we, as Free and Accepted Masons, are taught to make use of it for the more noble and glorious purpose of spreading the cement of brotherly love and affection; that cement which unites us into one sacred band, or society, of brothers, among whom no contention should ever exist, but that noble emulation of who can best work, or best agree.

Q. What were you next presented with?
A. Three precious jewels.

Q. What are they?
A. Humanity, Friendship, and Brotherly Love.

Q. How were you then disposed of?
A. I was conducted out of the lodge, and invested of what I had been divested, and returned again in due season.

SECTION SECOND.

Q. Did you ever return to the *sanctum sanctorum*, or *holy of holies*, of king Solomon's temple?
A. I did.

Q. Was there any thing particular took place on your return?
A. There was; viz:—I was accosted by three ruffians, who demanded of me the Master Mason's word.

Q. Did you ever give it to them?
A. I did not, but bid them wait, with time and patience, till the Grand Lodge assembled at Jerusalem; and then, if they were found worthy, they should receive it; otherwise they could not.

Q. In what manner was you accosted?
A. In attempting to retire at the south gate, I was accosted by one of them, who demanded of me the Master Mason's word, and, on my refusing to comply with his request, he gave me a blow

with the twenty-four inch guage, across my breast; on which I fled to the west gate, where I was accosted by the second with more violence, and, on my refusing to comply with his request, he gave me a severe blow, with the square, across my breast; on which I attempted to make my escape at the east gate, where I was accosted by the third with still more violence, and, on my refusing to comply with his request, he gave me a violent blow, with the common gavel, on the forehead, and brought me to the floor.

Q. Whom did you represent at that time?

A. Our Grand Master, Hiram Abiff, who was slain at the building of king Solomon's temple.

Q. Was his death premeditated?

A. It was;—by fifteen Fellow Crafts, who conspired to extort from him the Master Mason's word; twelve of whom recanted; but the other three were base enough to carry their atrocious designs into execution.

Q. What did they do with the body?

A. They carried it out at the west gate of the temple, and buried it till low twelve at night, when they three met agreeably to appointment, and carried it a westerly course from the temple, and buried it under the brow of a hill, in a grave six feet due east and west, six feet perpendicular, and made their escape.

Q. What time was he slain?

A. At high twelve at noon, when the crafts were from labor to refreshment.

Q. How came he to be alone at that time?

A. Because it was the usual custom of our Grand Master, Hiram Abiff, every day, at high twelve, when the crafts were from labor to refreshment, to enter into the *sanctum sanctorum*, or *holy of holies*, and offer up his adorations to the ever living God, and draw out his plans and designs on his tressle-board for the crafts to pursue their labor.

Q. At what time was he missing?

A. At low six in the morning, when king Solomon came up to the temple, as usual, to view the work, and found the crafts all in confusion; and, on inquiring the cause, he was informed that their Grand Master, Hiram Abiff, was missing, and no plans or designs were laid down on the tressle-board for the crafts to pursue their labor.

Q. What observations did king Solomon make at that time?

A. He observed that our Grand Master, Hiram Abiff, had always been very punctual in attending, and feared that he was indisposed, and ordered search to be made in and about the temple, to see if he could be found.

Q. Search being made, and he not found, what further remarks did king Solomon make?

A. He observed he feared some fatal accident had befallen our Grand Master, Hiram Abiff—that morning twelve Fellow Crafts, clothed in white gloves and aprons in token of their innocence, had confessed that they twelve, with three others, had conspired to extort the Master Mason's word from their Grand Master, Hiram Abiff, or take his life; that they twelve had recanted, but feared the other three had been base enough to carry their atrocious designs into execution.

Q. What followed?

A. King Solomon ordered the roll of workmen to be called, to see if there were any missing.

Q. The roll being called, were there any missing?

A. There were three; viz:—*Jubela, Jubelo,* and *Jubelum.*

Q. Were the ruffians ever found?

A. They were.

Q. How? A. By the wisdom of king Solomon, who ordered twelve Fellow Crafts to be selected from the bands of the workmen, clothed in white gloves and aprons, in token of their innocence, and sent three east, three west, three north, and three south, in search of the ruffians, and, if found, to bring them forward.

Q. What success?

A. The three that travelled a westerly course from the temple, coming near the coast of Joppa, were informed, by a wayfaring man, that three men had been seen that way that morning, who, from their appearance and dress, were workmen from the temple, inquiring for a passage to Ethiopia; but were unable to obtain one. in consequence of an embargo which had recently been laid on all the shipping, and had turned back into the country.

Q. What followed?

A. King Solomon ordered them to go and search again, and search till they were found, if possible; and if they were not found, that the twelve, who had confessed, should be considered as the reputed murderers, and suffer accordingly.

Q. What success?

A. One of the three that travelled a westerly course from the temple, being more weary than the rest, sat down under the brow of a hill, to rest and refresh himself; and, in attempting to rise, caught hold of a sprig of cassia, which easily gave way, and excited his curiosity, and made him suspicious of a deception, on which he hailed his companions, who immediately assembled;—and, on examination, found that the earth had recently been moved, and, on moving the rubbish, discovered the appearance of a grave; and while they were confabulating about what measures to take, they heard voices issuing from a cavern in the clefts of the rocks, on which they immediately repaired to the place, where they heard the voice of *Jubela* exclaim, 'O! that my throat had been cut across, my tongue torn out, and my body buried in the rough sands of the sea, at low water-mark, where the tide ebbs and flows twice in twenty-four hours, ere I had been accessary to the death of so good a man as our Grand Master, Hiram Abiff:'—on which they distinctly heard the voice of *Jubelo* exclaim, 'O! that my left breast had been torn open, and my heart and vitals taken from thence, and thrown over my left shoulder, carried to the valley of Jehoshaphat, there to become a prey to the wild beasts of the field, and vultures of the air, ere I had conspired to take the life of so good a man as our Grand Master, Hiram Abiff:'—when they more distinctly heard the voice of *Jubelum* exclaim, 'O! that my body had been severed in two in the midst, and divided to the north and the south, my bowels burnt to ashes in the centre, and the ashes scattered by the four winds of heaven, that there might not remain the least track or trace of remembrance among men or Masons, of so vile and perjured a wretch as I am, who wilfully took the life of so good a man as our Grand Master, Hiram Abiff. Ah! *Jubela* and *Jubelo*, it was I that struck him harder than you both! it was I that gave him the fatal blow! it was I that killed him outright!'—on which they rushed forward, seized, bound, and carried them up before king Solomon.

Q. What did king Solomon do with them?
A. He ordered them to be executed agreeably to the several imprecations of their own mouths.
Q. Was the body of our Grand Master, Hiram Abiff, ever found?
A. It was.
Q. How? A. By the wisdom of king Solomon, who ordered fifteen (in some lodges they say twelve) Fellow Crafts to be selected from the bands of the workmen, and sent three east, three west, three north, three south, and three in and about the temple, in search of the body.
Q. Where was it found?
A. Under that sprig of cassia where a worthy brother sat down to rest and refresh himself.
Q. Was there any thing particular took place on the discovery of the body?

A. There was; viz: on removing the earth till they came to the coffin, they involuntarily found their hands raised in this position, to guard their nostrils against the offensive effluvia that rose from the grave.

Q. How long had the body lain there?
A. Fourteen days.
Q. What did they do with the body?
A. Raised it in a masonic form, and carried it up to the temple for more decent interment.
Q. Where was it buried?
A. Under the *sanctum sanctorum*, or *holy of holies*, of king Solomon's temple, over which they erected a marble monument, with this inscription delineated thereon:—A virgin weeping over a broken column, with a book open before her; in her right hand a sprig of cassia; in her left, an urn:—Time standing behind her, with his hands infolded in the ringlets of her hair.
Q. What do they denote?
A. The weeping virgin denotes the unfinished state of the temple; the broken column, that one of the principal supporters of Masonry had fallen; the book open before her, that his memory was on perpetual record; the sprig of cassia, the timely discovery of his grave; the urn in her left hand, that his ashes were safely deposited under the *sanctum sanctorum*, or *holy of holies*, of king Solomon's temple; and Time, standing behind her with his hands infolded in the ringlets of her hair, that time, patience, and perseverance will accomplish all things.

SECTION THIRD.

Q. What does a Master's lodge represent?
A. The *sanctum sanctorum*, or *holy of holies*, of king Solomon's temple.
Q. How long was the temple building?
A. Seven years; during which it rained not in the day time, that the workmen might not be obstructed in their labor.
Q. What supported the temple?
A. Fourteen hundred and fifty-three columns, and two thousand, nine hundred and six pilasters; all hewn from the finest Parian marble.
Q. What further supported it?
A. Three grand columns, or pillars.
Q. What were they called?
A. Wisdom, Strength, and Beauty.
Q. What did they represent?
A. The pillar of wisdom represented Solomon, king of Israel,

whose wisdom contrived the mighty fabric; the pillar of strength, Hiram, king of Tyre, who strengthened Solomon in his glorious undertaking; the pillar of beauty, Hiram Abiff, the widow's son, whose cunning craft and curious workmanship beautified and adorned the temple.

Q. How many were there employed in the building of king Solomon's temple?

A. Three Grand Masters; three thousand three hundred Masters, or overseers of the work; eighty thousand Fellow Crafts; and seventy thousand Entered Apprentices: all those were classed and arranged in such a manner, by the wisdom of Solomon, that neither envy, discord, nor confusion were suffered to interrupt that universal peace and tranquillity that pervaded the work at that important period.

Q. How many constitutes an Entered Apprentice's lodge?

A. Seven; one Master and six Entered Apprentices.

Q. Where did they usually meet?

A. On the ground floor of king Solomon's temple.

Q. How many constitutes a Fellow Craft's lodge?

A. Five; two Masters and three Fellow Crafts.

Q. Where did they usually meet?

A. In the middle chamber of king Solomon's temple.

Q. How many constitutes a Master's lodge?

A. Three Master Masons.

Q. Where did they usually meet?

A. In the *sanctum sanctorum*, or *holy of holies*, of king Solomon's temple.

Q. Have you any emblems on this degree?

A. We have several, which are divided into two classes.

Q. What are the first class?

A. The pot of incense; the bee-hive; the book of constitutions, guarded by the Tyler's sword; the sword, pointing to a naked heart; the all-seeing eye; the anchor and ark; the forty-seventh problem of Euclid; the hour-glass; the scythe; and the three steps usually delineated on the Master's carpet, which are thus explained:—The pot of *incense* is an emblem of a pure heart, which is always an acceptable sacrifice to the Deity; and as this glows with fervent heat, so should our hearts continually glow with gratitude to the great and beneficent Author of our existence, for the manifold blessings and comforts we enjoy. The *bee-hive* is an emblem of industry, and recommends the practice of that virtue to all created beings, from the highest seraph in heaven to the lowest reptile of the dust. It teaches us, that, as we came into the world rational and intelligent beings, so we should ever be industrious ones; never sitting down contented, while our fellow creatures around us are in want, when it is in our power to relieve them, without inconvenience to ourselves. When we take a survey of nature, we behold man, in his infancy, more helpless and indigent than the brute creation; he lies languishing for days, weeks, months, and years, totally incapable of providing sustenance for himself; of guarding against the attacks of the field, or sheltering himself from the inclemencies of the weather. It might have pleased the great Creator of heaven and earth, to have made man independent of all other beings; but, as dependence is one of the strongest bonds of society, mankind were made dependent on each other for protection and security, as they thereby enjoy better opportunities of fulfilling the duties of reciprocal love and friendship. Thus was man formed for social and active life, the noblest part of the work of God; and he, who will so demean himself as not to be endeavoring to add to the common stock of knowledge and understanding, may be deemed a *drone* in the *hive* of nature, a useless member of society, and unworthy of our protection as Masons. The *book of constitutions, guarded by the Tyler's sword*, reminds us that we should be ever watchful and guarded, in our thoughts, words, and actions, particularly when before the enemies of Masonry; ever bearing in remembrance those truly masonic virtues, *silence* and *circumspection*. The *sword, pointing to a naked heart*, demonstrates that justice will sooner or later overtake us; and, although our thoughts, words, and actions may be hidden from the eyes of men; yet, that *all-seeing eye*, whom the *sun, moon*, and *stars* obey, and under whose watchful care even comets perform their stupendous revolutions, pervades the inmost recesses of the human heart, and will reward us according to our merits. The *anchor* and *ark*, are emblems of a well grounded hope and well spent life. They are emblematical of that divine *ark* which safely wafts us over this tempestuous sea of troubles, and that *anchor* which shall safely moor us in a peaceful harbor, where the wicked cease from troubling, and the weary shall find rest. The *forty-seventh problem of Euclid:* —this was an invention of our ancient friend and brother, the great Pythagoras, who, in his travels through Asia, Africa, and Europe, was initiated into several orders of priesthood, and raised to the sublime degree of a Master Mason.

This wise philosopher enriched his mind abundantly in a general knowledge of things, and more especially in geometry, or Masonry; on this subject he drew out many problems and theorems: and, among the most distinguished, he erected this, which, in the joy of his heart, he called *Eureca* in the Grecian language signifying, *I have found it*; and upon the discovery of which he is said to have sacrificed a hecatomb. It teaches Masons to be general lovers of the arts and sciences. The *hour-glass* is an emblem of human life. Behold!! how swiftly the sands run, and how rapidly our lives are drawing to a close. We cannot without astonishment behold the little particles which are contained in this machine; how they pass away almost imperceptibly, and yet to our surprise, in the short space of an hour they are all exhausted.

Thus wastes man! to-day, he puts forth the tender leaves of hope; to-morrow, blossoms, and bears his blushing honors thick upon him; the next day comes a frost, which nips the shoot, and when he thinks his greatness is still ripening, he falls, like autumn leaves, to enrich our mother earth. The *scythe* is an emblem of time, which cuts the brittle thread of life, and launches us into eternity. Behold! what havoc the scythe of time makes among the human race: if, by chance, we should escape the numerous evils incident to childhood and youth, and, with health and vigor, arrive to the years of manhood, yet withal we must soon be cut down by the all devouring scythe of time, and be gathered into the land where our fathers had gone before us. The *three steps*, usually delineated upon the Master's carpet, are emblematical of the three principal stages of human life; viz:—youth, manhood, and age. In youth, as Entered Apprentices, we ought industriously to occupy our minds in the attainment of useful knowledge; in manhood, as Fellow Crafts, we should apply our knowledge to the discharge of our respective duties to God, our neighbors, and ourselves; so that, in age, as Master Masons, we may enjoy the happy reflections consequent on a well spent life, and die in the hope of a glorious immortality.

Q. What are the second class of emblems?

A. The spade, coffin, death-head, marrow bones, and sprig of cassia, which are thus explained:—The *spade* opens the vault to receive our bodies, where our active limbs will soon moulder to dust. The *coffin*, *death-head*, and *marrow bones*, are emblematical of the death and burial of our Grand Master, Hiram Abiff, and are worthy our serious attention. The *sprig of cassia* is emblematical of that immortal part of man which never dies; and when the cold winter of death shall have passed, and the bright summer's morn of the resurrection appears, the Son of Righteousness shall descend, and send forth his angels to collect our ransomed dust; then, if we are found worthy, by his pass-word, we shall enter into the celestial lodge above, where the Supreme Architect of the universe presides, where we shall see the King in the beauty of holiness, and with him, enter into an endless eternity.

Here ends the three first degrees of Masonry, which constitute a Master Mason's Lodge. A Master Mason's Lodge and a Chapter of Royal Arch Masons, are two distinct bodies, wholly independent of each other. The members of a chapter are privileged to visit all Master Mason's lodges when they please ; and may be, and often are, members of both at the same time : and all the members of a Master Mason's lodge who are Royal Arch Masons, though not members of any chapter, may visit any chapter. I wish the reader to understand that neither all Royal Arch Masons nor Master Masons are members of either lodge or chapter ; there are tens of thousands who are not members, and scarcely ever attend, although privileged to do so.

A very small proportion of Masons, comparatively speaking, ever advance any further than the third degree, and consequently never get the great word which was lost by Hiram's untimely death. Solomon, king of Israel, Hiram, king of Tyre, and Hiram Abiff, the widow's son, having sworn that they, nor neither of them, would ever give the word, except they three were present; (and it is generally believed that there was not another person in the world, at that time, that had it,) consequently the word was lost, and supposed to be for ever ; but the sequel will show it was found after a lapse of four hundred and seventy years ; notwithstanding, the word *Mah-hah-bone*, which was substituted by Solomon, still continues to be used by Master Masons, and no doubt will, as long as Masonry attracts the attention of men ; and the word which was lost, is used in the Royal Arch degree. What was the word of the Royal Arch degree, before they found the Master's word, which was lost at the death of Hiram Abiff, and was not found for four hundred and seventy years ? Were there any Royal Arch Masons before the Master's word was found? I wish some Masonic gentleman would solve these two questions.

The ceremonies, history, and the lecture, in the preceding degree, are so similar, that, perhaps, some one of the three might have been dispensed with, and the subject well understood by most readers, notwithstanding there is a small difference between the work and history, and between the history and the lecture.

I shall now proceed with the Mark Master's degree, which is the first degree in the chapter. The Mark Master's degree, the Past Master's, and the Most Excellent Master's, are lodges of Mark Master Masons, Past Master, and Most Excellent Master; yet, although called lodges, they are called component parts of the chapter. Ask a Mark Master Mason if he belongs to the chapter; he will tell you he does, but that he has only been marked. It is not an uncommon thing, by any means, for a chapter to con-

H

fer all four of the degrees in one night, viz: the Mark Master, Past Master, Most Excellent Master, and Royal Arch degrees.

TEST-OATH AND WORD.

The following "*test-oath* and *word*" were invented and adopted by the "GRAND LODGE" of the State of New-York, at their session in June, 1827, for the purpose of guarding against *book* Masons. They are given in a Master's Lodge.—They were obtained from a gentleman in high standing in society, and among Masons, but a friend to Anti-Masonry. He was a member of the "Grand Lodge," and present when they were adopted.

A person, wishing to be admitted into the lodge, presents himself at the door; the Tyler, (or some brother from within,) demands, or asks, 'Do you wish to visit this lodge?' The candidate for admission says, 'If thought worthy.' *Tyler*, 'By what are you recommended?' *Ans.* 'By fidelity.' *Tyler* says, 'Prove that;' at the same time advances and throws out his hand, or arm, to an angle of about forty-five degrees obliquely forward, the hand open, and thumb upward. The candidate then advances, and places the back of his *left hand* against the *palm* of the Tyler's *right hand*—still extended—puts his mouth to the Tyler's ear, and whispers, L O S, and pronounces LOS.*

TEST-OATH.

'I, A. B., of my own free will and accord, in the presence of Almighty God, solemnly and sincerely promise and swear, that I will not communicate the secret test-word, annexed to this obligation, to any but a true and lawful Master Mason, and that in the body of a lawful lodge of such, in actual session, or at the door of a lodge for the purpose of gaining admission;—under the penalty of being for ever disgraced and dishonoured as a man, and despised, degraded, and expelled as a Mason.'

---

* This word is an inversion of SOL, the Sun, and is very applicable as a Masonic test; the light of Masonry being fast retrograding towards its native darkness!

A REVELATION

OF

FREE MASONRY,

As published to the world by a Convention of Seceding Masons, held at Le Roy, Genesee county, New-York, on the 4th and 5th of July, 1828: containing a true and genuine development of the mode of initiation, and also of the several lectures of the following degrees; to wit :—in the Chapter, Mark Master, Past Master, Most Excellent Master, and Royal Arch.

In the Encampment, Knight of the Red Cross, Knight Templar, Knight of Malta, Knight of the Christian Mark, and Guards of the Conclave, and Knights of the Holy Sepulchre.

In the ancient Council of the Trinity, denominated the Holy and Thrice Illustrious Order of the Cross, the Illustrious, Most Illustrious, and Thrice Illustrious degrees.

FOURTH, OR MARK MASTER'S DEGREE.

Ceremonies used in opening a lodge of Mark Master Masons.— One rap calls the lodge to order; one calls up the Junior and Senior Deacons; two raps call up the subordinate officers; and three, all the members of the lodge. The Right Worshipful Master having called the lodge to order, and all being seated, the Right Worshipful Master says to the Junior Warden, 'Brother Junior, are they all Mark Master Masons in the south?' Junior Warden answers, 'They are, Right Worshipful.' R. W. M. 'I thank you, brother.' R. W. M. 'Brother Senior, are they all Mark Master Masons in the west?' Senior Warden, 'They are, Right Worshipful.' R. W. M. 'They are in the east.' At the same time gives a rap with the mallet, which calls up both Deacons. R. W. M. 'Brother Junior, the first care of a Mason?' 'To see the lodge tyled, Right Worshipful.' R. W. M. 'Attend to that part of your duty, and inform the Tyler that we are about to open a lodge of Mark Master Masons, and direct him to tyle accordingly.' Junior Deacon steps to the door and gives four raps, which are answered by four without by the Tyler—the Junior Deacon then gives one, which is answered by the Tyler with one—the door is then partly opened, and the Junior Deacon then delivers his message, and resumes his station, gives the due-guard of a Mark Master Mason, and says, 'The door is tyled, Right Worshipful.' R. W. M. 'By whom?' J. D. 'By a Mark Master Mason without the door, armed with the proper implements of his office.' R. W. M. 'His duty there?' J. D. 'To keep off all cowards and eaves-droppers, see that none pass or repass without permission from the Right Worshipful Master.' R. W. M. 'Brother Junior, your place in the lodge?' J. D. 'At the right hand of the Senior Warden in the west.' R. W. M. 'Your business there, brother Junior?' J. D. 'To wait on the Right Worshipful Master and Wardens, act as their proxy in the active duties of the lodge, and take care of the door.' R. W. M. 'The Senior Deacon's place in the lodge?' S. D. 'At the right hand of the Right Worshipful Master in the east.' R. W. M. 'I thank you, brother.' He then gives two raps with the mallet, and the subordinate officers rise. R. W. M. 'Your duty there, brother Senior?' S. D. 'To wait on the Right Worshipful Master and Wardens, act as their proxy in the active duties of the lodge, attend to the preparation and introduction of candidates, and welcome and clothe all visiting brethren.' R. W. M. 'The Secretary's place in the lodge, Brother Junior?' J. D. 'At the left hand of the Right Worshipful Master in the east.' R. W. M. 'I thank you, brother. Your duty there, brother Secretary?' Sec. 'The better to observe the Right Worshipful Master's will and pleasure; record the proceedings of the lodge; transmit the same to the Grand Lodge, if required; receive all monies and money bills from the hands of the brethren, pay them over to the Treasurer, and take his receipt for the same.' R. W. M. 'The Treasurer's place in the lodge?' Sec. 'At the right hand of the Right Worshipful Master.' R. W. M. 'I thank you, brother. Your duty there, brother Treasurer?' Treas. 'Duly to observe the Right Worshipful Master's will and pleasure; receive all monies and money bills from the hands of the Secretary; give a receipt for the same; keep a just and true account of the same; pay them out by the order of the Right Worshipful Master and consent of the brethren.*

---

* Supposing that in the United States, there are 500,000 Entered Apprentices, 400,000 Master, and 200,000 Royal Arch Masons; also, 10,000 Knights; and that that they all paid the usual fees, for the degrees; the amount would be the enormous sum of 11,250,000 dollars; the yearly interest of which, at seven per centum, is 787,500 dollars; which sum, (allowing 100 dollars to each individual,) would support 7,875 persons.

Now, I would ask, do Masons, by their charities, support this number of poor in the United States? Do they support one tenth part of that number? Supposing they do, is it necessary to give 10 or 50 dollars, for the privilege of contributing 1, 5, or 50 dollars masonically? Must the privilege of being a charitable man be bought with gold? How many there are who have rendered themselves incompetent to bestow charities, by their paying for, and attendance on, masonic secrets and cere-

R. W. M. 'The Junior Overseer's place in the lodge, brother Treasurer?' Treas. 'At the right hand of the Junior Warden in the south, Right Worshipful.' R. W. M. 'I thank you, brother. Your business there, brother Junior Overseer?' J. O. 'To inspect all materials brought up for the building of the temple; approve or disapprove of the same; and, if approved, pass it on to the Senior Overseer for further inspection.' R. W. M. 'The Senior Overseer's place in the lodge?' J. O. 'At the right hand of the Senior Warden in the west, Right Worshipful.' R. W. M. 'I thank you, brother. Your business there, brother Senior Overseer?' S. O. 'To inspect all materials brought up for the building of the temple; and, if approved, pass it on to the Master Overseer at the east gate for further inspection.' R. W. M. 'The Master Overseer's place in the lodge, brother Senior Overseer?' S. O. 'At the right hand of the Right Worshipful Master in the east.' R. W. M. 'I thank you, brother. Your business there, brother Master Overseer?' M. O. 'To assist in the inspection of all materials brought up for the building of the temple; and, if disapproved, to call a council of my brother Overseers.' R. W. M. 'The Junior Warden's place in the lodge, brother Master Overseer?' M. O. 'In the south, Right Worshipful.' R. W. M. 'I thank you, brother. Your business there, brother Junior?' J. W. 'As the sun in the south, at high meridian, is the beauty and glory of the day; so stands the Junior Warden in the south, the better to observe the time; call the craft from labor to refreshment; superintend them during the hours thereof; see that none convert the hours of refreshment into that of intemperance, or excess; and call them on again in due season, that the Right Worshipful Master may have honor, and they pleasure and profit thereby.' R. W. M. 'The Senior Warden's place in the lodge?' J. W. 'In the west, Right Worshipful.' R. W. M. 'I thank you, brother. Your duty there, brother Senior?' S. W. 'As the sun sets in the west to close the day, so stands the Senior Warden in the west, to assist the

---

monies! If all the money paid for the degrees of Masonry, was applied to charitable purposes, the subject would appear differently; but, it is principally devoted to the erection of Masonic temples,—support of the grand lodges, and for *refreshment* for the crafts; and, I think I may add, for their support in '*kidnapping and murder.*'

(If I had not been informed, from what I believe to be good authority, that the Grand Lodge of this state had recently, since the abduction of Morgan, appropriated 5000 dollars to the wants of the crafts, and had put that sum into the hands of a 'committee,' to be disposed of by them as their judgment should dictate, having a reference to the kidnappers and murderers of Capt. Morgan, I should not have added the last remark.)

Right Worshipful in opening and closing the lodge; take care of the jewels and implements; see that none be lost; pay the craft their wages, if any be due; and see that none go away dissatisfied.' R. W. M. 'The Master's place in the lodge?' S. W. 'In the east, Right Worshipful.' R. W. M. 'His duty there?' S. W. 'As the sun rises in the east, to open and adorn the day; so presides the Right Worshipful Master in the east, to open and adorn his lodge; set his craft to work, and govern them with good and wholesome laws, or cause the same to be done.' R. W. M. 'I thank you, brother.' Gives three raps with the mallet, which calls up all the brethren, takes off his hat, and says, 'In like manner, so do I, strictly prohibiting all profane language, private committees, or any other disorderly conduct, whereby the peace and harmony of this lodge may be interrupted, while engaged in its lawful pursuits; under no less penalty than the by-laws enjoin, or a majority of the brethren present may see cause to inflict. Brethren, attend to giving the signs.' The Right Worshipful Master (all the brethren imitating him,) extends his left arm from his body, so as to form an angle of about forty-five degrees, and holds his right hand transversely across his left, the palms thereof about an inch apart. This is called the first sign of a Mason—is the sign of distress in the first degree, and alludes to the position a candidate's hands are placed, when he takes the obligation of an Entered Apprentice Mason; he then draws his right hand across his throat, the hand open, with his thumb next his throat, drops it down by his side. This is called the due-guard of an Entered Apprentice Mason, and alludes to the penal part of the obligation. Next he places the palm of his open right hand upon his left breast, and, at the same time, throws up his left hand, and so extends his left arm as to form a right angle; from the shoulder to the elbow it is horizontal, from the elbow to the tip of the finger it is perpendicular. This is the sign and due-guard of a Fellow Craft Mason, and also alludes to the penal part of the obligation, which is administered in this degree. After this, the Right Worshipful Master draws his right hand across his bowels, with his hand open, and the thumb next his body, and drops it down by his side. This is the sign, or due-guard, of a Master Mason, and, like the others, allude to the penalty of this degree. He then throws up the grand hailing sign of distress: this is given by raising both hands and arms, to the elbow, perpendicularly, one on each side of the head, the elbows forming a square, his arms then drop by his side; he then clutches the third and little fingers of his right hand; with his thumb extends, at the same time, his middle and fore fingers, brings up his hand in such a manner as to have the side of the middle finger touch the rim of the right ear, then lets it drop, and, as it falls, brings the outward side of the little finger of the left hand across the wrist of the right, then lets them fall by his sides. This is the sign, or due-guard, of a Mark Master Mason, and also alludes to the penal part of the obligation in this degree. Here it is proper to remark, that, in the opening of any lodge of Masons, they commence giving the signs of an Entered Apprentice, and go through all the signs of the different degrees, in regular gradation, until they arrive to the one which they are opening, and commence at the sign of the degree in which they are at work, and descend to the last when closing. After going through all the signs, as above described, the Right Worshipful Master declares the lodge opened, in the following manner:—' I now declare this lodge of Mark Master Masons duly opened for the despatch of business;' the Senior Warden declares it to the Junior Warden, and he to the brethren. The Right Worshipful Master then repeats a charge: ' Wherefore, brethren, lay aside all malice and guile,' &c. &c. (Monitor, page 76.)

The lodge being opened and ready for business, the Right Worshipful Master directs the Secretary to read the minutes of the last meeting, which generally brings to view the business of the present. If there are any candidates to be brought forward, that is generally the first business. A Master Mason, wishing for further light in Masonry, sends a petition to the chapter, and requests to be advanced to the honorary degree of Mark Master Mason; if there is no serious objection to the petition, it is entered on the minutes, and a committee of several appointed to inquire into his character and report to the next regular communication; at that time, if the committee report in his favor, and no serious objection is made against him otherwise, a motion is made that the ballot pass; if carried, the Deacons pass the ballot boxes: these boxes are the same as in the preceding degrees. When the balls are received, the box is presented to the Right Worshipful Master, Senior and Junior Wardens. R. W. M. ' Clear in the west, brother Senior?' S. W. ' Clear, Right Worshipful.' R. W. M. ' Clear in the south, brother Junior?' J. W. ' Clear, Right Worshipful.' Right Worshipful Master says, ' Clear in the east.' This being the case, the candidate is accepted; but if there is one black ball in that end of the box which has the white tube, and the Senior Warden pronouncing ' Not clear,' all stop, and inquiry is made, and the ballot passes again; and, if blacked a third time, the candidate is rejected. It being otherwise, the Senior Deacon, who is the candidate's conductor, passes out of the lodge into the adjoining room, where the candidate is in waiting, and there the conductor is furnished with a small oblong square, six inches long —the candidate is presented with a large white marble key stone, weighing, probably, twenty pounds, and is ordered, by his conductor, to take it by the little end, between his first and second fingers and thumb of his right hand.—The door is then opened without ceremony, and they pass directly to the Junior Overseer's station at the south gate, which is nothing more than the Junior Warden's seat, and the conductor gives four raps, with his block of timber, on a pedestal in front of the Junior Overseer's station. J. O. 'Who comes here?' Cond. 'Two brother Fellow Crafts, with materials for the temple.' J. O. 'Have you a specimen of your labor?' Cond. 'I have.' J. O. 'Present it.' The conductor then presents the piece of timber before described; the Junior Overseer receives it, and applies a small trying square to its different angles, and they agreeing with the angles of the square, he says, 'This is good work, square work, such work as we are authorized to receive.' Returns the block of timber, and turning his eye upon the candidate, asks, 'Who is this you have with you?' Cond. 'A brother Fellow Craft.' J. O. 'Have you a specimen of your labor?' Cand. 'I have.' J. O. 'Present it.' The candidate then presents the key stone; the Junior Overseer receives it, and applies his square to all its angles, and they not agreeing with the angles of the square, he says, 'What have you here, brother? this is neither an oblong nor a square, neither has it the regular mark of the craft upon it, but from its singular form and beauty I am unwilling to reject it; pass on to the Senior Overseer at the west gate, for further inspection.' They then pass on to the Senior Overseer's station at the west gate, which is the Senior Warden's seat, and give four raps, as before, on the pedestal which stands in front of the Senior Overseer. S. O. 'Who comes here?' Cond. 'Two brother Fellow Crafts, with materials for the temple.' S. O. 'Have you a specimen of your labor?' Cond. 'I have.' S. O. 'Present it.' The conductor, as before, presents the block of timber; the Senior Overseer applies his square to it, and finding it agrees with the angles of his square, says, 'This is good work, square work, such work as we are authorized to receive: who is this you have with you?' Cond. 'A brother Fellow Craft.' S. O. 'Have you a specimen of your labor?' Cand. 'I have.' S. O. 'Present it.' The candidate then presents the key stone, and he applies it, but not fitting, he says, 'This is neither an oblong nor a square, neither has it the regular mark of the craft upon it; it is a curious wrought stone, and on account of its singular form and beauty, I am unwilling to reject it: pass on to the Master Overseer at the east gate, for further inspection.' They pass to his station at the east gate, and give four raps. M. O. 'Who comes here?' Cond. 'Two brethren, Fellow Crafts, with their materials for the temple.' M. O. 'Have you a specimen of your labor?' Cond. 'I have.' M. O. 'Present it.' The conductor presents his billet of wood to him, and he applies his square to it, and, like the other Overseers, says, 'This is good work, square work, such work as we are authorized to receive: who is this you have with you?' Cond. 'A brother Fellow Craft.' M. O. 'Have you a specimen of your labor?' Cand. 'I have.' M. O. 'Present it.' [It ought here to be remarked, that, when the candidate is presented with the key stone, and takes it between his thumb and two fingers, it hangs suspended by his side, and he is requested to carry his work plumb; and the conductor taking good care to see that he does it, by the time he arrives at the Master Overseer's station at the east gate, and when the Master Overseer says, 'Present it,' the candidate is extremely willing to hand over the key stone to him for inspection; for, by this time, it becomes very painful to hold any longer the stone which he has in charge.] The Master Overseer having received the key stone, he applies his square to the different angles of it, and, being found not to be square, he, like the other Overseers, says, 'This is neither an oblong nor a square, neither has it the regular mark of the craft upon it.' He then looks sternly upon the candidate, and demands, 'Is this your work?' Cand. 'It is not.' M. O. 'Is this your mark?' Cand. 'It is not.' M. O. 'Where did you get it?' Cand. 'I picked it up in the quarry.' M. O. 'Picked it up in the quarry? this explains the matter: what! been loitering away your time this whole week, and now brought up another man's work to impose upon the Grand Overseers! this deserves the severest punishment. (Motions the candidate to stand aside.) Brothers Junior and Senior Overseers, here is work brought up for inspection which demands a council.' The Junior, Senior, and Master Overseers then assemble in council. M. O., presenting the stone, 'Did a Fellow Craft present this to you for inspection, brother Junior?' J. O. 'A Fellow Craft came to my office and presented this stone for inspection: I examined it, and found it was neither an oblong nor a square, neither had it the regular mark of the craft upon it; but, on account of its singular form and beauty, I was unwilling to reject it, and ordered it to the Senior Overseer at the west gate, for further inspection.' M. O. 'Brother Senior, was this stone presented to you for inspection?' S. O. 'It was: I know of no use for it in the temple: I tried it with the square, and observed it was neither an oblong nor a square, neither had it the regular mark of the craft upon it; but, on account of its singular form and beauty, I was unwilling to reject it, and, therefore, directed it to the Master Overseer at the east gate, for further inspection.' M. O. 'It was also presented to me for inspection; but I do not know of any use which it can be in the building.' S. O. 'I know of no use for it.' J. O. 'I know of no use for it.' M. O. 'Brother Senior, what shall we do with it?' S. O. 'Heave it over among the rubbish.' The Master and Senior Overseers then take the stone between them, and, after waving it backward and forward four times, they heave it over in such a manner that the one letting go while the stone is arriving at the highest point, it brings the stone in a quarterly direction over the other's left shoulder: the Junior Overseer, being stationed in a suitable position, at this moment receives the stone, and carries it away into the preparation room. R. W. M. 'Brother Senior Warden, assemble the craft to receive wages.' At this command the brethren all arise, and form a procession single file; the candidate is placed at the head of the procession, and when stationed, is told, that 'the last shall be first, and the first, last.' The procession being formed, they commence singing the following song; 'Mark Masters all appear,' &c. (see Monitor, page 82;) and, at the same time, commence a circular march (against the course of the sun,) around the room, giving all the signs during their march, beginning with that of Entered Apprentice, and ending at that of Mark Master. They are given in the following manner: the first revolution each brother, when opposite the Right Worshipful Master, gives the first sign in Masonry. The second revolution, when opposite the Master, the second; and so on, until they give all the signs to that of Mark Master. While the ceremony is going on in the lodge, the Senior Grand Warden procures a sufficient number of cents and passes into the preparation room, and opens a lattice window in the door which communicates to the lodge room, and when the craftsmen arrive to the Mark Master Mason's sign, each one of them, in their last revolution, puts his hand through the window in the door and gives a token, (this is given by shutting the third and little fingers, extending the fore and middle fingers, and placing the thumb over them in a suitable manner to receive the penny, or cent;) and receives a penny, or cent, from the Senior Grand Warden. Matters are so timed in the march, that when they come to that part of the song which says, 'Caution them to beware of the right hand,' it comes the turn of the candidate to put his hand through the aperture of the door, and receive his penny; but not being able to give the token, he is detected as an impostor, and the Senior Grand Warden, instead of giving him his penny, seizes him by the hand and draws his arm full length through the door, and holds him securely, exclaiming, at the same time, 'an impostor! an impostor!' Others, who are in the room with the Senior Grand Warden, cry out, 'Chop off his hand! chop off his hand!' At this moment, the conductor steps to the candidate and intercedes warmly in his behalf. Cond. 'Spare him! spare him!' S. G. W. 'He is an impostor. He has attempted to receive wages without being able to give the token. The penalty must be inflicted.' Cond. 'He is a brother Fellow Craft, and on condition that you will release him, I will be responsible that he shall be taken before the Right Worshipful Master, where all the circumstances shall be made known; and, if he condemns him, I will see that the penalty is inflicted.' S. G. W. 'On these conditions, I release him.' The candidate is released, and taken before the Right Worshipful Master. Cond. 'This young Fellow Craft has brought up work for inspection, which was not his own, and has attempted to receive wages for it; he was detected at the Senior Grand Warden's apartment as an impostor, and I became responsible, on condition of his release, that he should appear before the Right Worshipful, and if, after a fair trial, you should pronounce him guilty, that I should see the penalty of an impostor inflicted upon him.' R. W. M. 'Brother Junior Overseer, did this man bring up work to your station for inspection?' J. O. 'He did. I inspected it, and observed that it was neither an oblong nor a square, neither had it the regular mark of the craft upon it; but, on account of its singular form and beauty, I was unwilling to reject it; therefore, I ordered it passed to the Senior Overseer's station at the west gate, for further inspection.' R. W. M. 'Brother Senior Overseer, did this young man bring up work to you for inspection?' S. O. 'He did; and I, for similar reasons offered by brother Junior Overseer, was unwilling to reject it, and ordered it passed on to the Master Overseer at the east gate, for further inspection.' R. W. M. 'Brother Master Overseer, did this young man bring up work to you for inspection?' M. O. 'He did. I inspected the work, and observed that it was neither an oblong nor a square, neither had it the regular mark of the craft upon it: I then asked him if it was his work. He admitted that it was not. I asked him where he got it; he said he picked it up in the quarry. I rebuked him severely for his attempt to impose upon the Grand Overseers, and for loitering away his time, and then bringing up another man's work for inspection. I then called a council of my brother Overseers, and we, knowing no use for the work, hove it over among the rubbish. R. W. M. 'Senior Grand Warden, did the young man attempt to receive wages at your apartment?' S. G. W. 'He did, and I detected him as an impostor, and was about to inflict the penalty, but the conductor becoming responsible, that, if I would release him, he would see the impostor taken before the Right Worshipful, and, if found guilty, that the penalty should be inflicted, I released him.' R. W. M. 'Young man, it appears that you have been loitering away your time this whole week, and have now brought up another man's work for inspection, to impose upon the Grand Overseers, and what is more, you have attempted to receive wages for labor which you never performed; conduct like this deserves prompt punishment. The penalty of an impostor is that of having his right hand chopped off. This young man appears as though he deserved a better fate, and as though he might be serviceable in the building of the temple. Are you a Fellow Craft?' Cand. 'I am.' R. W. M. 'Can you give us any proof of it?' Candidate gives the sign of a Fellow Craft. R. W. M. 'He is a Fellow Craft. Have you ever been taught how to receive wages?' Cand. 'I have not.' R. W. M. 'This serves, in a measure, to mitigate his crime. If you are instructed how to receive wages, will you do better in future, and never again attempt to impose on the Grand Overseers, and, above all, never attempt to receive wages for labor which you never performed?' Cand. 'I will.' R. W. M. 'The penalty is remitted.' The candidate is then taken into the preparation room, and divested of his outward apparel, and all money and valuables; his breast bare, and a cable-tow four times round his body: in which condition he is conducted to the door, when the conductor gives four distinct knocks, upon the hearing of which, the Senior Warden says to the Right Worshipful, 'While we are peaceably at work on the fourth degree of Masonry, the door of our lodge appears to be alarmed.' R. W. M. 'Brother Junior, see the cause of that alarm.' The Junior Warden then steps to the door and answers the alarm by four knocks, the conductor and himself each giving another; the door is then partly opened, and the Junior Warden then asks, 'Who comes there?' Cond. 'A worthy brother, who has been regularly initiated as an Entered Apprentice, served a proper time as such; passed to the degree of Fellow Craft; raised to the sublime degree of a Master Mason; and now wishes further light in Masonry, by being advanced to the more honorable degree of Mark Master Mason.' J. W. 'Is it of his own free will and accord he makes this request?' Cond. 'It is.' J. W. 'Is he duly and truly prepared?' Cond. 'He is.' J. W. 'Has he wrought in the quarry, and exhibited specimens of his skill in the preceding degrees?' Cond. 'He has.' J. W. 'By what further right, or benefit, does he expect to obtain this favor?' Cond. 'By the benefit of a pass word.' J. W.

'Has he a pass word?' Cond. ' He has not, but I have it for him.' J. W. ' Give it me.' Conductor whispers in his ear, ' JOPPA.' J. W. ' The pass word is right. You will let him wait until the Right Worshipful Master is made acquainted with his request, and his answer returned.' The Junior Warden returns him to the Right Worshipful Master, where the same questions are asked, and answers returned, as at the door. The Right Worshipful Master then says, ' Since he comes endowed with the necessary qualifications, let him enter in the name of the Lord, and take heed on what he enters. (Previous to the candidate's entering, one of the brethren, who is best qualified for the station, is selected and furnished with an engraving chisel and mallet, and placed near the door, so that when the candidate enters, it is on the edge of an engraving chisel, under the pressure of the mallet. As this is the business of no particular officer, we have, for convenience, styled him executioner.) Brother, it becomes my duty to put a mark on you, and such a one, too, as you will probably carry to your grave.' Places the edge of the chisel near his left breast, and makes several motions with the mallet, as though he was about to strike upon the head of the chisel. Executioner. ' This is a painful undertaking ; I do not feel able to perform it, Right Worshipful ; (turning to the Right Worshipful Master;) this task is too painful; I feel that I cannot perform it : I wish the Right Worshipful would select some other brother to perform it in my stead.' R. W. M. ' I know the task is unpleasant, and a painful one ; but as you have undertaken to perform it, unless some other brother will volunteer his service and take your place, you must proceed.' Exec. ' Brother, (calling the name,) will you volunteer your service, and take my place ?' Brother. ' I cannot consent to do it ;' (after several solicitations and refusals.) Exec. ' R. W. no brother feels willing to volunteer his services, and I declare I feel unwilling and unable to perform it.' R. W. M. ' As no brother feels disposed to take your station, it becomes your duty to perform it yourself.' Exec. (taking his station,) ' Brethren, support the candidate ; (several take hold of the candidate :) brother, (naming some physician, or surgeon,) will you assist?' Doctor, (stepping up,) ' Brethren, it becomes necessary that we have a bowl, or some other vessel, to receive the blood.' A bowl is presented, having the appearance of blood upon it, and is held in a suitable position to receive the blood ; the surgeon places his fingers on the left breast of the candidate, and gives counsel where it would be adviseable to inflict the wound. The executioner then places the edge of the chisel near the spot, and draws back the mallet, and while making several false motions, says, ' Operative Masons

I

make use of the engraving chisel and mallet to cut, hew, carve, and indent their work; but we, as Free and Accepted Masons, make use of them for a more noble and glorious purpose;—we use them to cut, hew, carve, and indent the mind;' giving, at the instant the last word is pronounced, a severe blow with the mallet upon the head of the chisel, without the least injury to the candidate.* The candidate is then conducted four times round the lodge, and each time, as he passes the station of the Master, Senior and Junior Wardens, they each give one loud rap with their mallet; the Master, in the mean time, reads the following passages of scripture—Psalm cxviii, 22, 'The stone which the builders refused is become the head stone of the corner.' Matt. xxi, 42, 'Did ye never read in the scriptures, the stone which the builders rejected, the same is become the head of the corner?' Luke xx, 17, 'What is this, then, that is written: The stone which the builders rejected, the same is become the head of the corner?' Acts iv, 11, 'This is the stone which was set at nought of you builders, which is become the head of the corner.' The reading of them is so timed, as to be completed just as the candidate arrives at the Junior Warden's post; here he stops, and the same questions are asked and answers returned, as at the door; the same passes at the Senior Warden and Master, who orders the candidate to be conducted back to the Senior Warden in the west, by him to be taught to approach the east, by four upright regular steps, his feet forming a square, and body erect at the altar; the candidate then kneels and receives the obligation, as follows:—

"I, A. B., of my own free will and accord, in presence of Almighty God, and this Right Worshipful Lodge of Mark Master Masons, do hereby and hereon, in addition to my former obligations, most solemnly and sincerely promise and swear, that I will not give the degree of a Mark Master Mason to any one of an inferior degree, nor to any other person in the known world, except it be to a true and lawful brother, or brethren, of this degree; and not unto him nor unto them, whom I shall hear so to be, but unto him and them only, whom I shall find so to be, after strict trial and due examination, or lawful information given: Furthermore, do I promise and swear, that I will support the constitution of the General Grand Royal Arch Chapter of the United States

---

* This is supposed to be the most interesting part of the degree; and is made so, by the pains taken to frighten the candidate. If the floor, bowl, chisel, and mallet are bespattered with blood, or something which resembles it, and the 'executioner' acts his part well, the candidate must necessarily feel very uneasy during the ceremony:—This generally gives great satisfaction to the brotherhood, and is often the subject of their secret discourse for weeks afterwards.

LIGHT ON MASONRY.

of America, also the Grand Royal Arch Chapter of this State, under which this lodge is held, and conform to all the by-laws, rules and regulations of this or any other lodge of Mark Master Masons, of which I may at any time hereafter become a member: Furthermore, do I promise and swear, that I will obey all regular signs and summons given, handed, sent, or thrown to me from the hand of a brother Mark Master Mason, or from the body of a just and legally constituted lodge of such, provided it be within the length of my cable-tow: Furthermore, do I promise and swear, that I will not wrong this lodge, or a brother of this degree, to the value of his wages, (or one penny) myself, knowingly, nor suffer it to be done by others if in my power to prevent it: Furthermore, do I promise and swear, that I will not sell, swap, barter, or exchange my mark, which I shall hereafter choose, nor send it a second time to pledge until it is lawfully redeemed from the first: Furthermore, do I promise and swear, that I will receive a brother's mark when offered to me requesting a favor, and grant him his request if in my power; and if it is not in my power to grant his request, I will return him his mark with the value thereof, which is half a shekel of silver, or quarter of a dollar. To all of which I do most solemnly and sincerely promise and swear, with a fixed and steady purpose of mind in me, to keep and perform the same, binding myself under no less penalty, than to have my right ear smote off, that I may forever be unable to hear the word, and my right hand chopped off, as the penalty as an imposter, if I should ever prove wilfully guilty of violating any part of this my solemn oath, or obligation, of a Mark Master Mason. So help me God, and make me steadfast to keep and perform the same."
" Detach your hand and kiss the book."

The Master then produces the same key stone, concerning which so much has already been said; and says to the candidate, ' We read in a passage of scripture,' Rev. ii, 17, ' to him that overcometh will I give to eat of the hidden manna, and will give him a white stone, and in the stone a new name written, which no man knoweth save him that receiveth it.' He then presents the stone to the candidate and says, ' I now present you with a white stone, on which is written a new name; we give the words that form this circle; (the letters are so engraved on the stone as to form a circle:) the initials are, H. T. W. S. S. T. K. S. Hiram Tyran, Widow's Son, sent to King Solomon. These, placed in this form, were the mark of our Grand Master, Hiram Abiff. At present they are used as the general *mark* of this degree, and in the centre of them each brother places his own individual *mark*.' The stone is then removed, and the candidate still remains on his knees at the altar, the Master then takes the jewel containing his mark from his neck and presents it to the candidate—requests of him some favor, such as the loan of five, ten, or twenty dollars. The candidate having left all his money and valuables in the preparation room, answers, 'I cannot do it; I have no money about me:' and offers to return the *mark* to the Master, but he refuses to take it, and says to the candidate ' Have you not just sworn that you will receive a brother Mark Master's mark when offered to you, requesting a favor, and if not in your power to grant the favor, you would return him his mark with the value of it? Is this the way you mind your obligations? Here I presented my mark with a request for a small favor; you say you cannot grant it, and offer to return my *mark* alone? Where is the quarter of a dollar you have sworn to return with it?' The candidate, much embarrassed, answers, ' I cannot do even that. I have no money about me. It was all taken from me in the preparation room.' The Master asks, ' are you quite sure you have none?' Candidate answers, ' I am; it is all in the other room.' Master, ' you have not examined; perhaps some friend has, in pity to your destitute situation, supplied you with that amount unknown to yourself: feel in all your pockets, and if you find, after a thorough search, that you have really none, we shall have less reason to think that you meant wilfully to violate your obligation.' The candidate examines his pockets and finds a quarter of a dollar, which some brother had slily placed there; this adds not a little to his embarrassment; he protests he had no intention of concealing it; really supposed he had none about him, and hands it to the Master, with his mark. The Master receives it and says to the candidate, ' Brother, let this scene be a striking lesson to you; should you ever hereafter have a mark presented you by a worthy brother, asking a favor, before you deny him, make diligent search, and be quite sure of your inability to serve him; perhaps you will then find, as in the present instance, that some unknown person has befriended you, and you are really in a better situation than you think yourself.' The candidate then rises and is made acquainted with the grips, words, and signs of this degree. The pass-grip of this degree is made by extending the right arms and clasping the fingers of the right hands, as one would naturally do to assist another up a steep ascent; the password is ' Joppa;' the real grip is made by locking the little fingers of the right hand, bringing the knuckles together, placing the ends of the thumbs against each other; the word is, ' Mark well.' The signs have been described. After the grips, words, and signs are given and explained, (see lectures,) the Master says,

'Brother, I now present you with the tools of a Mark Master, (here he points them out in the carpet, or in the chart,) which are the chisel and mallet; they are thus explained; the chisel morally demonstrates the advantages of discipline and education; the mind, like the diamond in its original state, is rude and unpolished, but as the effect of the chisel on the external coat, soon presents to view the latent beauties of the diamond, so education discovers the latent beauties of the mind, and draws them forth to range the large field of matter and space, to display the summit of human knowledge, our duty to God and man. The mallet morally teaches to correct irregularities, and to reduce man to a proper level; so that by quiet deportment, he may, in the school of discipline, learn to be content. What the mallet is to the workmen, enlightened reason is to the passions; it curbs ambition, it depresses envy, it moderates anger, and it encourages good dispositions, whence arises among good Masons that comely order,

> 'Which nothing earthly gives, or can destroy,
> The soul's calm sunshine, and the heartfelt joy.'

The Worshipful Master then delivers the following charge to the candidate, which completes the ceremony of advancement to this degree. (For the charge, see Monitor.)

CEREMONY OF CLOSING A LODGE OF MARK MASONS.

The Worshipful Master says, 'Brother Junior Warden, assemble the brethren, and form a procession for the purpose of closing the lodge.' The brethren then assemble and commence a circular march, singing the song, 'Mark Masters all appear,' (see Webb's Monitor, page 82,) with the same ceremony as described in another part of this degree. After the song is completed, the brethren compare the wages they have received, and finding that all have received alike, (one penny or cent,) they begin to murmur among themselves, some pretending to think they ought to have more, as they have done all the labor—they finally throw down their wages upon the altar, declaring if they cannot be dealt justly with, they will have none. The Worshipful Master calls to order, and demands the cause of the confusion. Some brother answers, 'Worshipful, we are not satisfied with the manner of paying the workmen; for we find those who have done nothing, and even the candidate just received, is paid just as much as we, who have borne the heat and burden of the day.' Master says, 'it is perfectly right.' Brother. 'It cannot be right

—it is very unreasonable.' Master. 'Hear what the law says on this subject.' He then reads the following parable, Mat. xx, 1, 16 : 'For the kingdom of heaven is like unto a man that is a householder, which went out early in the morning to hire laborers into his vineyard. And when he had agreed with the laborers for a penny a day, he sent them into his vineyard. And he went out about the third hour, and saw others standing idle in the market-place, and said unto them, Go ye also into the vineyard; and whatsoever is right, I will give you. And they went their way. Again he went out about the sixth and ninth hour, and did likewise. And about the eleventh hour he went out, and found others standing idle, and saith unto them, Why stand ye here all the day idle? they say unto him, Because no man hath hired us. He saith unto them, Go ye also into the vineyard; and whatsoever is right, that shall ye receive. So when even was come, the lord of the vineyard said unto his steward, call the laborers, and give them their hire, beginning from the last unto the first. And when they came that were hired about the eleventh hour, they received every man a penny. But when the first came, they supposed that they should have received more : and they likewise received every man a penny. And when they had received it, they murmured against the good man of the house, saying, These last have wrought but one hour, and thou hast made them equal unto us, which have borne the burden and heat of the day. But he answered one of them, and said, Friend, I do thee no wrong : didst thou not agree with me for a penny? Take that thine is, and go thy way : I will give unto this last even as unto thee. Is it not lawful for me to do what I will with mine own? Is thine eye evil because I am good? So the last shall be first, and the first last : for many be called, but few chosen.' (We leave it for the public to judge, with what consistency king Solomon in his day, could introduce a passage of the New Testament, written long after, to settle a dispute arising among his workmen. They will observe that many passages of the New Testament are introduced in this and the following degrees, pretended to have been organized at the building of the temple. We make no comments.) The brethren then declare themselves satisfied; the signs are given from Mark Master down to the Entered Apprentice, and the Master declares the lodge closed.

Lecture on the 4th, or Mark Master's degree.
SECTION FIRST.

Question. Are you a Mark Master Mason? *Answer.* I am; try me. Q. By what will you be tried? A. By the engraving chisel and mallet. Q. Why by the engraving chisel and mallet? A. Because they are the proper Masonic implements of this degree. Q. On what was the degree founded? A. On a certain key stone which belonged to the principal arch of king Solomon's temple. Q. Who formed this key stone? A. Our worthy Grand Master, Hiram Abiff. Q. What were the preparatory steps relative to your advancement to this degree? A. I was caused to represent one of the Fellow Craft, at the building of king Solomon's temple, whose custom it was, on the eve of every sixth day, to carry up their work for inspection. Q. Why was you caused to represent these Fellow Crafts? A. Because, our worthy Grand Master, Hiram Abiff, had completed this key stone, agreeable to the original plan, and before he gave orders to have it carried up to the temple, was slain by three ruffians, as already represented in the preceding degrees; and it so happened that on the eve of a certain sixth day, as the craft were carrying up work for inspection, a young Fellow Craft discovered this stone in the quarry, and from its singular form and beauty, supposing it to belong to some part of the temple, carried it up for inspection. Q. Who inspected it? A. The Grand Overseers, placed at the east, west, and south gates. Q. How did they inspect it? A. On its being presented to the Junior Overseer at the south gate, he observed that it was neither an oblong or a square, neither had it the regular mark of a craft upon it; but from its singular form and beauty was unwilling to reject it, therefore ordered it to be passed to the Senior Overseer at the west gate, for further inspection; who, for similar reasons, suffered it to pass to the Master Overseer at the east gate, who held a consultation with his brother Overseers, and they observed, as before, that it was neither an oblong or square, neither had it the regular mark of the craft upon it; and neither of them being Mark Master Masons, supposed it of no use in the building, and hove it over among the rubbish. Q. How many Fellow Crafts were there engaged at the building of the temple? A. Eighty thousand. Q. Were not the Master Overseers liable to be imposed upon by receiving bad work from the hands of such a vast number of workmen? A. They were not. Q. How was this imposition prevented? A. By the wisdom of king Solomon, who wisely ordered, that the craftsman who worked, should choose him a particular mark and place it upon all his work; by which it was known and distinguished when carried up to the building, and if approved, to receive wages. Q. What was the wages of a Fellow Craft? A. A penny a day. Q. Who paid the craftsmen? A. The Senior Grand Warden. Q. Was not the Senior Grand Warden liable to be imposed upon by impostors, in paying off such a vast number of workmen? A. He was not. Q. How was this imposition prevented? A. By the wisdom of king Solomon, who also ordered that every craftsman applying to receive wages, should present his right hand through a lattice window of the door of the Junior Grand Warden's apartment, with a copy of his mark in the palm thereof, at the same time giving a token. Q. What was that token? (This was before explained.) Q. What did it allude to? A. To the manner of receiving wages; it was also to distinguish a true craftsman, from an impostor. Q. What is the penalty on an impostor? A. To have his right hand chopped off.

SECTION SECOND.

Question. Where was you prepared to be made a Mark Master Mason? *Answer.* In the room adjoining the body of a just and lawfully constituted lodge of such, duly assembled in a room, or place, representing a work shop that was erected near the ruins of king Solomon's temple. Q. How was you prepared? A. By being divested of my outward apparel and all money; my breast bare, with a cable-tow four times about my body; in which situation I was conducted to the door of a lodge, where I gave four distinct knocks. Q. What do these four distinct knocks allude to? A. To the fourth degree of Masonry; it being that on which I was about to enter. Q. What was said to you from without? A. Who comes there? Q. Your answer? A. A worthy brother, who has been regularly initiated as an Entered Apprentice, served a proper time as such; passed to the Fellow Craft; raised to the sublime degree of a Master Mason; and now wishes further light in Masonry, by being advanced to the more honorable degree of a Mark Master Mason. Q. What further was said to you from within? A. I was asked if it was of my own free will and accord, I made this request; if I was duly and truly prepared; worthy and well qualified; had wrought in the quarries, and exhibited specimens of my skill and proficiency in the preceding degrees; all of which, being answered in the affirmative, I was asked by what further right, or benefit, I expected to gain this favor. Q. Your answer? A. By the benefit of a pass word. Q. What was that pass word? A. *Joppa.* Q. What did it allude to? A. The city of Joppa, the place where the materials were landed, for building king Solomon's temple, after being prepared in the forest of Lebanon, and carried there on floats, (by sea.) (Masonic tradition informs us, that the banks of this place are so perpendicular, that it was impossible to ascend them without assistance from above, which was effected by brethren stationed there, with this strong grip; [this has been explained,] which, together with the word *Joppa*, has since been adopted as a proper pass to be given before entering any well regulated lodge of Mark Master Masons.) Q. What further was said to you from within? A. I was bid to wait till the Right Worshipful Master in the east, was made acquainted with my request, and his answer returned. Q. When his answer was returned, what followed? A. I was caused to enter the lodge. Q. On what did you enter? A. On the edge of the engraving chisel, under the pressure of the mallet, which was to demonstrate the moral precepts of this degree, and make a deep and lasting impression on my mind and conscience. Q. How was you then disposed of? A. I was conducted four times regularly round the lodge, and halted at the Junior Warden's in the south, where the same questions were asked, and answers returned as at the door. Q. How did the Junior Warden dispose of you? A. He ordered me to be conducted to the Senior Warden in the west, where the same questions were asked and the same answers returned, as before. Q. How did the Senior Warden dispose of you? A. He ordered me to be conducted to the Right Worshipful Master in the east, where the same questions were asked and answers returned, as before; who likewise demanded of me, from whence I came, and whither I was travelling. Q. Your answer? A. From the west, and travelling to the east. Q. Why do you leave the west, and travel to the east. A. In search of light. Q. How did the Right Worshipful Master dispose of you? A. He ordered me to be conducted back to the west, from whence I came, and put in the care of the Senior Warden, who taught me how to approach the east, the place of light; by advancing upon four upright regular steps, to the fourth step, my feet forming a square, and my body erect at the altar, before the Right Worshipful Master. Q. What did the Right Worshipful Master do with you? A. He made a Mark Master Mason of me. Q. How? A. In due form. Q. What was that due form? A. Both knees bent, they forming a square, both my hands on the holy bible, square, and compass, my body being erect; in which posture I took upon me the solemn oath, or obligation of a Mark Master Mason. Q. Have you that oath, or obligation? A. I have. Q. Will you give it me? A. I will, with your assistance. (Here, as in the preceding degree, you repeat, after the Right Worshipful Master, I, A. B., &c. See obligation, page 98.) Q. After your oath, or obligation, what follows? A. Information was brought that the temple was almost completed, but the craft was all in confusion for want of a certain key stone, which none of them had been instrumental to make. Q. What followed? A. King Solomon believing in confidence, that our Worthy Grand Master, Hiram Abiff, had completed this key stone agreeable to the original plan, ordered inquiry to be made among the Master Overseers, if a stone bearing a particular mark had been presented to them for inspection; and on inquiry being made, it was found that there had. Q. What followed? A. King Solomon ordered search to be made for the stone, when it was found, and afterwards applied to its intended use. Q. What color was the stone? A. White. Q. What did it allude to? A. To a passage in scripture, where it says; ' To him that overcometh will I give to eat of the hidden manna, and I will give him a white stone, and in the stone a new name written, which no man knoweth saving him that receiveth.' Q. What was that new name? A. The letters on the stone and the initials of the words for which they stand, viz.—H. T. W. S. S. T. K. S. Q. Of what use is this new name to you in Masonry? A. It was the original mark of our worthy Grand Master, Hiram Abiff, and is the general mark of this degree, and the letters form the circle, in the centre of which, every brother of this degree places his particular mark, to which his obligation alludes. Q. What followed? A. I was more fully instructed with the secrets of this degree. Q. Of what do they consist? A. Of signs and tokens. Q. Have you a sign? A. I have. Q. What is it called? A. Heave over. Q. What does it allude to? A. To the manner of heaving over work that the Overseers said was unfit for the temple; also, the manner the key stone was hove over. Q. Have you any other sign? A. I have, (at the same time giving it.) Q. What is that? A. The due-guard of a Mark Master Mason. Q. What does it allude to? A. To the penalty of my obligation; which is, that my right ear should be smote off, that I might forever be unable to hear the word, and my right hand be chopped off, as the penalty of an impostor, if I should ever prove wilfully guilty of revealing any part of my obligation. Q. Have you any further sign? A. I have. Q. What is that? A. The grand sign, or sign of distress. Q. What does it allude to? A. To the manner the Fellow Crafts carry their work up to the temple for inspection; also the manner I was taught to carry my work, on my advancement to this degree. Q. Have you any other sign? A. I have not; but I have a token, (gives it to him.) Q. What is this? A. The pass-grip of a Mark Master Mason. Q. What is the name of it? A. '*Joppa.*' Q. What does it allude to? A. The city of Joppa. Q. Have you any other token? A. I have. Q. What is this? A. The real grip of a Mark Master Mason. Q. What is the name of it? A. *Mark well.* Q. What does it allude to? A. To a passage of scripture, where it says, ' Then he brought me back the way of the gate of the outward sanctuary, which looketh towards the east, and it was shut; and the Lord said unto me, son of man, mark well, and behold with thine eyes, and hear with thine ears, al that I say unto thee concerning all the ordinances of the house of the Lord, and the laws thereof, and mark well the entering in of the house, with every going forth of the sanctuary? Q. Who founded this degree? A. Our three ancient Grand Masters, viz. — Solomon, king of Israel, Hiram, king of Tyre, and Hiram Abiff. Q. Why was it founded? A. Not only as an honorary reward, to be conferred on all who have proved themselves meritorious in the preceding degrees; but to render it impossible for a brother to suffer for the immediate necessities of life, when the price of his mark will procure them. Q. A brother, pledging his mark, and asking a favor, who does he represent? A. Our worthy Grand Master, Hiram Abiff, who was a poor man, but on account of his great skill and mysterious conduct at the building of king Solomon's temple, was most eminently distinguished. Q. A brother receiving a pledge, and granting a favor, whom does he represent? A. King Solomon, who was a rich man, but renowned for his benevolence.

THE PAST MASTER'S DEGREE.

This degree is very simple, although Monitor writers say much about it. It is necessary that a Master Mason should take this degree, before he can, constitutionally, preside over a lodge of Master Masons, as Master of it; and when a Master Mason is elected Master of a lodge, who has not previously received the Past Master's degree, it is then conferred upon him, often without any other ceremonies than that of administering the obligation.

This lodge is opened and closed, in the same manner that the lodges of the first three degrees are; the candidate petitions, and is ballotted for in the same manner, but he is received into the lodge in a very different manner. He is conducted into the lodge without any previous preparation, when the presiding officer rises and says, 'Brethren, it is inconvenient for me to serve you any longer, as Master of this lodge. I wish you would select some other brother for that purpose.' The candidate is nominated, the usual forms of ballotting for officers are then dispensed with, and a vote of the lodge is taken, by yeas and nays. The candidate is elected, and generally refuses to serve, but he is, eventually, prevailed on to accept; whereupon, the presiding officer addresses the Master elect in the words following, viz: 'Brother, previous to your investiture, it is necessary that you assent to those ancient charges and regulations, which point out the duty of a Master of a lodge.

1. You agree to be a good man, and true, and strictly to obey the moral law.

2. You agree to be a peaceable subject, and cheerfully to conform to the laws of the country in which you reside.

3. You promise not to be concerned in any plots or conspiracies against government; but patiently to submit to the decisions of the supreme legislature.

4. You agree to pay a proper respect to the civil magistrate, to work diligently, live creditably, and act honorably by all men.

5. You agree to hold in veneration the original rules and patrons of Masonry, and their regular successors, supreme and subordinate, according to their stations, and to submit to the awards and resolutions of your brethren, when convened, in every case consistent with the constitution of the order.

6. You agree to avoid private piques and quarrels, and to guard against intemperance and excess.

7. You agree to be cautious in carriage and behavior, cautious to your brethren, and faithful to your lodge.

8. You promise to respect genuine brethren, and discountenance impostors, and all dissenters from the original plan of Masonry.

9. You agree to promote the general good of society, to cultivate the social virtues, and to propagate the knowledge of the arts.

10. You promise to pay homage to the Grand Master, for the time being, and to his officer when duly installed; strictly to conform to every edict of the Grand Lodge or general assembly of Masons, that is not subversive of the principles and ground work of Masonry.

11. You admit that it is not in the power of any man, or body of men, to make innovations in the body of Masonry.

12. You promise a regular attendance on the committees and communications of the Grand Lodge, on receiving proper notice, and to pay attention to all the duties of Masonry on convenient occasions.

13. You admit that no new lodge can be formed without permission of the Grand Lodge, and that no countenance be given to any irregular lodge, or to any person clandestinely initiated therein, being contrary to the ancient charges of the order.

14. You admit that no person can be regularly made a Mason in, or admitted a member of, any regular lodge, without previous notice, and due inquiry into his character.

15. You agree that no visitors shall be received in your lodge without due examination, and producing proper vouchers of their having been initiated into a regular lodge.'

The presiding officer then asks the Master elect (candidate) the following question; which he must answer in the affirmative. Q. 'Do you submit to these charges and promise to support these regulations, as Masters have done, in all ages, before you?' A. 'I do.' The presiding officer then addresses him. 'Brother A. B., in consequence of your cheerful conformity to the charges and regulations of the order, you are now to be installed Master of this degree; in full confidence of your care, skill and capacity, to govern the same. But, previous to your investiture, it is necessary you should take upon yourself the solemn oath, or obligation, appertaining to this degree; if you are willing to take it upon you, you will please to kneel before the altar, when you shall receive the same.' [Here lodges differ very materially, but this is the most prevalent mode of proceeding.] The candidate then kneels on both knees, lays both hands on the Holy Bible, square and compass, and takes the following oath, or obligation:—' I, A B., of my own free will and accord, in presence of Almighty God, and this Worshipful lodge of Past Master Masons, do hereby and hereon, most solemnly and sincerely promise and swear, in addition to my former obligations, that I will not give the degree of Past Master Mason, or any of the secrets pertaining thereto, to any one of an inferior degree, nor to any person in the known world; except it be to a true and lawful brother, or brethren, Past Master Masons, or within the body of a just and lawfully constituted lodge of such; and not unto him or unto them whom I shall hear so to be, but unto him and them only, whom I shall find so to be, after strict trial and examination, or lawful information. Furthermore, do I promise and swear,

K

that I will obey all regular signs and summons, sent, thrown, handed, or given, from the hand of a brother of this degree, or from the body of a just and lawfully constituted lodge of Past Masters, provided it be within the length of my cable-tow. Furthermore, do I promise and swear, that I will support the constitution of the General Grand Royal Arch Chapter of the United States of America, also, that of the Grand Chapter of the State of —— under which this lodge is held, and conform to all the by-laws, rules, and regulations of this, or any other lodge, of which I may at any time hereafter become a member, so far as in my power. Furthermore, do I promise and swear, that I will not assist, or be present at the conferring of this degree upon any person, who has not, to the best of my knowledge and belief, regularly received the degrees of Entered Apprentice, Fellow-Craft, Master Mason, and Mark Master, or been elected Master of a regular lodge of Master Masons. Furthermore, do I promise and swear, that I will aid and assist all poor and indigent Past Master Masons, their widows and orphans, wherever dispersed round the globe, they applying to me as such and I finding them worthy, so far as in my power, without material injury to myself or family. Furthermore, do I promise and swear, that the secrets of a brother of this degree, delivered to me in charge as such, shall remain as secure and inviolable in my breast, as they were in his own, before communicated to me; murder and treason excepted, and those left to my own election. Furthermore, do I promise and swear, that I will not wrong this lodge, nor a brother of this degree, to the value of one cent, knowingly, myself, nor suffer it to be done by others, if in my power to prevent it. Furthermore, do I promise and swear, that I will not govern this lodge, nor any other over which I may be called to preside, in a haughty, arbitrary, or impious manner; but will at all times, use my utmost endeavors to preserve peace and harmony among the brethren. Furthermore, do I promise and swear, that I will never open a lodge of Master Masons, unless there be present three regular Master Masons, besides the Tyler, nor close the same, without giving a lecture, or some section or part of a lecture, for the instruction of the lodge. Furthermore, that I will not, knowingly, set in any lodge where any one presides who has not received the degree of Past Master. [This last point is, in many lodges, entirely omitted. In some, the two last.] All which, I do most solemnly and sincerely promise and swear, with a fixed and steady purpose of mind, to keep and perform the same; binding myself under no less penalty, than to have my tongue split from tip to root: that I might forever thereafter, be unable to pronounce the word, if ever I should prove wilfully guilty of violating any part of this, my solemn oath, or obligation of a Past Master Mason. So help me God, and make me steadfast to keep and perform the same.'

The obligation being administered, the candidate rises,* and the Master proceeds to give the sign, word, and grip of this degree, as follows. The sign (sometimes called the due-guard,) is given by laying the edge of the thumb of the right hand in a vertical position, on the centre of the mouth, high enough to touch the upper lip. The word is given by taking each other by the Master's grip, and pulling the insides of their feet together, when the Master whispers the word, Giblem,† in the ear of the candidate. Then they clap their left hand on each other's right arm, between the wrist and elbow, disengaging, (at the same moment,) their right hand from the Master's grip; they each seize the left arm of the other with their right hands, between the wrist and elbow, and, (almost at the same instant,) yielding their left hand hold on each other's right arm, and moving their left hands with a brisk motion, they clasp each other's right arm with their left hands above the elbow, pressing their finger nails hard against the arms: as they shift their hands from place to place, the Master says, (in union with these movements,) 'From grips to spans, and from spans to grips, a twofold cord is strong, but a threefold cord is not easily broken.' The Master then conducts the candidate to the chair, and, as he ascends the steps, the Master says, 'Brother, I now have the pleasure of conducting you into the oriental chair of king Solomon;' places a large cocked hat on his head, and comes down to the front of the newly installed Master, and addresses him as follows :—'Worshipful brother, I now present you with the furniture and various implements of our profession; they are emblematical of our conduct in life, and will now be enumerated and explained as presented.

'The *Holy Writings*, that great light in Masonry, will guide you to all truth; it will direct your path to the temple of happiness, and point out to you the whole duty of man. The *Square* teaches to regulate our actions by rule and line, and to harmonize our conduct by the principles of morality and virtue. The *Compass* teaches to limit our desires in every station; thus rising

---

* In some lodges, the Master takes the candidate by the Master's grip, and says, 'Brother, you will please rise,' assisting him.

† There is much diversity of opinion, among Masons, respecting this word: some insist that *Giblem* is the right word; others, that *Gibelum* is the right word: —the latter word was rejected because it was used by 'Jachin and Boaz.'

to eminence by merit, we may live respected, and die regretted.' The *Rule* directs, that we should punctually observe our duty; press forward in the path of virtue, and, neither inclining to the right or to the left, in all our actions have *eternity* in view. The *Line* teaches the criterion of moral rectitude; to avoid dissimulation in conversation and action, and to direct our steps to the path that leads to *immortality*. The *book of constitutions* you are to search at all times; cause it to be read in your lodge, that none may pretend ignorance of the excellent precepts it enjoins. Lastly, you receive in charge the by-law of your lodge, which you are to see carefully and punctually executed.

'I will also present you with the mallet: it is an emblem of power. One stroke of the mallet calls to order, and calls up the Junior and Senior Deacons; two strokes call up all the subordinate officers; and three, the whole lodge.' The following charge is then delivered to the newly installed Master, (alias, candidate,) by the former Master.

'Worshipful Master, being appointed Master of this lodge, you cannot be insensible of the obligations which devolve on you, as their head; nor of your responsibility for the faithful discharge of the important duties annexed to your appointment. The honor, usefulness, and reputation of your lodge, will materially depend on the skill and assiduity with which you manage its concerns; while the happiness of its members will be generally promoted, in proportion to the zeal and ability with which you propagate the genuine principles of our institution. For a pattern of information, consider the luminary of nature; which, rising in the east, regularly diffuses light and lustre to all within its circle. In like manner, it is your province to spread and communicate light and instruction to the brethren of your lodge. Forcibly impress upon them the dignity and high importance of Masonry, and seriously admonish them never to disgrace it. Charge them to practice out of the lodge, those duties which they have been taught in it; and, by amiable, discreet, and virtuous conduct, to convince mankind of the goodness of the institution; so that, when any one is said to be a member of it, the world may know that he is one to whom the burdened heart may pour out its sorrows—to whom distress may prefer its suit—whose hand is guided by justice, and his heart expanded by benevolence. In short, by a diligent observance of the by-laws of your lodge, the constitution of Masonry, and, above all, the holy scriptures, which are given as a rule and guide of your faith, you will be enabled to acquit yourself with honor and reputation, and lay up a crown of rejoicing which shall continue when time shall be no more.'* The Master then says to the newly installed Master, ' I now leave you to the government of your lodge.' He then retires to a seat, and, after a moment or two, rises and addresses the candidate, (now in the chair as Master;) ' Worshipful Master, in consequence of my resignation, and the election of a new Master, the seats of the Wardens have become vacant. It is necessary you should have Wardens to assist you in the government of your lodge.— The constitution requires us to elect our officers by ballot, but it is common, on occasions of this kind, to dispense with those formalities, and elect by ayes and noes ; I move we do so on the present occasion. The question is tried and carried in the affirmative.

The Master has a right to nominate one candidate for office, and the brethren one. Here a scene of confusion takes place, which is not easily described. The newly installed *Worshipful* is made the butt for every *worthy* brother to exercise his wit upon. Half a dozen are up at a time, soliciting the Master to nominate them for Wardens, urging their several claims, and decrying the merits of others with much zeal; others crying out,—' Order, Worshipful! keep order !' Others propose to dance, and request the Master to sing for them : others whistle, or sing, or jump about the room ; or scuffle, and knock down chairs or benches. One proposes to call from labor to refreshment; another compliments the Worshipful Master on his dignified appearance, and knocks off his hat, or pulls it down over his face ; another informs him that a lady wishes to enter. If the Master calls to order, every one obeys the signal with the utmost promptness, and drops upon the nearest seat; the next instant, before the Master can utter a word, all are on their feet again, and as noisy as ever : finally, a nominal election is effected, and some prudent member, tired of such a ridiculous confusion, moves that the lodge be closed; which, being done, the poor, (and if a stranger,) much embarrassed candidate, has his big hat taken from him, and is reduced to the ranks ; but, for his consolation, the Worshipful Master informs him that the preceding scene, notwithstanding its apparent confusion, is designed to convey to him, in a striking manner, the important lesson, never to solicit, or accept any office, or station, for which he does not know himself amply qualified.

The LECTURE on the fifth, or Past Master's degree, is divided into five sections. The first section treats of the manner

---

* This charge is frequently omitted, when conferring the degree on a candidate; but never, when really installing a Master of a lodge.

of constituting a lodge of Master Masons. The second, treats of the ceremony of installation, including the manner of receiving candidates to this degree, as given above. The third, treats of the ceremonies observed at laying the foundation stones of public structures. The fourth section, of the ceremony observed at the dedications of Masonic Halls. The fifth, of the ceremony observed at funerals, according to ancient custom, with the service used on the occasion. All the sections of this lecture, are printed in full in Webb's Monitor, from the 83d to the 125th page, Chapter XII; except such part of the second as relates to the induction of candidates, and the ceremony of opening and closing.

It ought to be here remarked, that the statement above is strictly correct. It includes all the ceremonies ever used in conferring the degree of Past Master; but the ceremonies are more frequently shortened by the omission of some part of them; the presenting of the 'various implements of the profession,' and their explanations, are often dispensed with; and still more often, the charge. By comparing this with the 2d section as described by Webb, the reader can see the whole ceremony of installing officers, on all occasions.

MOST EXCELLENT MASTER'S DEGREE.*

A description of the ceremonies used in opening a lodge of Most Excellent Masters.

The lodge being called to order, the Most Excellent Master says, ' Brother Junior, are they all Most Excellent Masters in the south?' J. Warden. ' They are, Most Excellent.' M. E. M. ' Brother Senior, are they all Most Excellent Masters in the west?' S. W. ' They are, Most Excellent.' M. E. M. ' They are in the east; (gives one rap, which calls up both Deacons.) Brother Junior Deacon, the first care of a Mason?' J. D. ' To see the door tyled, Most Excellent.' M. E. M. ' Attend to that part of your duty, and inform the tyler that we are about to open this lodge of Most Excellent Masters, and direct him to tyle accordingly.' Junior Deacon steps to the door and gives six knocks, which the Tyler answers with six more:—

---

* ' Be ye not called Rabbi; (which is Master:) for one is your Master, even Christ, and all ye are brethren.' Mat. xxiii. 8. Do ministers of the gospel, who are ' *Most Worshipful,*' and ' *Most Excellent Masters,*' obey this command?

Junior Deacon gives one more, which the Tyler answers with one;—the door is then partly opened, when the Junior Deacon informs the Tyler that a lodge of Most Excellent Masters is about to be opened, and tells him to tyle accordingly; and then returns to his place in the lodge, and says, 'Most Excellent Master, the lodge is tyled.' M. E. M. 'By whom?' J. D. 'By a Most Excellent Master Mason without the door, armed with the proper implements of his office.' M. E. M. 'His duty there?' J. D. 'To keep off all cowans and eave-droppers; and see that none pass and repass, without permission from the chair.' M. E. M. 'Your place in the lodge, brother Junior?' J. D. 'At the right hand of the Senior Warden in the West, Most Excellent.' M. E. M. 'Your duty there, brother Junior?' J. D. 'To wait on the Most Excellent Master and Wardens, act as their proxy in the active duties of the lodge, and take charge of the door.' M. E. M. 'The Senior Deacon's place in the lodge?' J. D. 'At the right hand of the Most Excellent Master in the east.' M. E. M. 'I thank you, brother. Your duty in the east, brother Senior?' S. D. 'To wait on the Most Excellent Master and Wardens; act as their proxy in the active duties of the lodge; attend to the preparation and introduction of candidates; and receive and welcome all visiting brethren.' M. E. M. 'The Secretary's place in the lodge, brother Senior?' S. D. 'At the left hand of the Most Excellent Master in the east.' M. E. M. 'I thank you, brother. Your business there, brother Secretary?' Sec. 'The better to observe the Most Excellent Master's will and pleasure; record the proceedings of the lodge, and transmit a copy of the same to the grand chapter, if required; receive all monies and money bills from the hands of the brethren; pay them over to the Treasurer, and take his receipt for the same.' M. E. M. 'The Treasurer's place in the lodge?' Sec. 'At your right hand, Most Excellent.' M. E. M. 'I thank you, brother. Your duty there, brother Treasurer?' Treas. 'The better to observe the Most Excellent Master's will and pleasure; receive all monies and money bills from the hands of the Secretary; keep a just and true account of the same; pay them out by the order of the Most Excellent Master, and consent of the brethren.' M. E. M. 'The Junior Warden's place in the lodge?' Treas. 'In the south, Most Excellent.' M. E. M. 'I thank you, brother. Your business in the south, brother Junior?' J. W. 'As the sun in the south, at high meridian, is the beauty and glory of the day; so stands the Junior Warden in the south, the better to observe the time of high twelve; call the craft from labor to refreshment; superintend them during the hours thereof; see that none convert the hours of refreshment into that of intemperance, or excess; call them again in due season; that the Most Excellent Master may have honor, and they profit thereby.' M. E. M. 'The Senior Warden's place in the lodge?' J. W. 'In the west, Most Excellent.' M. E. M. 'I thank you, brother. Your duty in the west, brother Senior?' S. W. 'As the sun sets in the west, to close the day; so stands the Senior Warden in the west, to assist the Most Excellent Master in the opening of his lodge; take care of the jewels and implements; see that none be lost; pay the craft their wages, if any be due; and see that none go away dissatisfied.' M. E. M. 'The Most Excellent Master's place in the lodge?' S. W. 'In the east, Most Excellent.' M. E. M. 'His duty in the east, brother Senior?' S. W. 'As the sun rises in the east, to open and adorn the day; so presides the Most Excellent Master in the east, to open and adorn his lodge; to set his craft to work; govern them with good and wholesome laws, or cause the same to be done.' (In some lodges the foregoing ceremonies are omitted.) M. E. M. 'Brother Senior Warden, assemble the brethren round the altar for the purpose of opening this lodge of Most Excellent Master Masons.' S. W. 'Brethren, please to assemble round the altar for the purpose of opening this lodge of Most Excellent Master Masons.' In pursuance of this request, the brethren assemble round the altar, and form a circle, and stand in such a position as to touch each other, leaving a space for the Most Excellent Master; they then all kneel on their left knee, and join hands, each giving his right hand brother his left hand, and his left hand brother his right hand; their left arms uppermost, and their heads inclining downward: all being thus situated, the Most Excellent Master reads the following portion of scripture: Psalm xxiv.—'The earth is the Lord's, and the fulness thereof; the world, and they that dwell therein. For he hath founded it upon the seas, and established it upon the floods. Who shall ascend into the hill of the Lord? and who shall stand in his holy place? He that hath clean hands, and a pure heart; who hath not lifted up his soul unto vanity, nor sworn deceitfully. He shall receive the blessing from the Lord, and righteousness from the God of his salvation. This is the generation of them that seek him, that seek thy face, O Jacob. Selah. Lift up your heads, O ye gates; and be ye lifted up, ye everlasting doors; and the King of glory shall come in. Who is this King of glory? The Lord, strong and mighty; the Lord, mighty in battle. Lift up your heads, O ye gates; even lift them up, ye everlasting doors; and the King of glory shall come in. Who is this King of glory? The Lord of hosts; he is the King of glory. Selah.' The reading being ended, the Most Excellent Master then kneels, joins hands with the others, which closes the circle; they all lift their hands, as joined together, up and down six times, keeping time with the words as the Most Excellent Master repeats them, one, two, three; one, two, three. This is Masonically called balancing. They then rise, disengage their hands, and lift them up above their heads with a moderate, and somewhat graceful, motion; cast up their eyes, turning, at the same time, to the right, they extend their arms and then suffer them to fall loose and nerveless against their sides. This sign is said, by Masons, to represent the sign of astonishment, made by the queen of Sheba, on first viewing Solomon's temple. The Most Excellent Master now resumes his seat, and says, 'Brethren, attend to giving the signs.' The Most Excellent Master then gives all the signs from an Entered Apprentice Mason, up to the degree of Most Excellent Master; in which they all join and imitate him. M. E. M. 'Brother Senior Warden, you will please to inform brother Junior, and request him to inform the brethren, that it is my will and pleasure that this lodge of Most Excellent Master Masons be now opened for despatch of business, strictly forbidding all private committees, or profane language, whereby the harmony of the same may be interrupted, while engaged in their lawful pursuits, under no less penalty than the by-laws enjoin, or a majority of the brethren may see cause to inflict.' S. W. 'Brother Junior, it is the will and pleasure of the Most Excellent Master, that this lodge of Most Excellent Master Masons be now opened for despatch of business, strictly prohibiting all private committees, or profane language, whereby the harmony of the same may be interrupted, while engaged in their lawful pursuits, under no less penalty than the by-laws enjoin, or a majority of the brethren may see cause to inflict.' J. W. 'Brethren, you have heard the Most Excellent Master's will and pleasure, as communicated to me by brother Senior—so let it be done.'

CEREMONIES OF INITIATION.

The lodge being now opened, and ready for the reception of candidates, the Senior Deacon repairs to the preparation room, where the candidate is in waiting, takes off his coat, puts a cable-tow six times round his body, and, in this situation, conducts him to the door of the lodge; against which he gives six distinct knocks, which are answered, by the same number, by the Junior Deacon from within: the Senior Deacon then gives one knock, and the Junior Deacon answers by giving one more: the door is then partly opened by the Junior Deacon, who says, 'Who comes there?' Senior Deacon. 'A worthy brother, who has been regularly initiated as an Entered Apprentice Mason; passed to the degree of Fellow Craft; raised to the sublime degree of Master Mason; advanced to the honorary degree of a Mark Master Mason; presided in the chair as Past Master; and now wishes for further light in Masonry, by being received and acknowledged as a Most Excellent Master.' Junior Deacon. 'Is it of his own free will and accord he makes this request?' Senior Deacon. 'It is.' J. D. 'Is he duly and truly prepared?' S. D. 'He is.' J. D. 'Is he worthy and well qualified?' S. D. 'He is.' J. D. 'Has he made suitable proficiency in the preceding degrees?' S. D. 'He has.' J. D. 'By what further right, or benefit, does he expect to obtain this favor?' S. D. 'By the benefit of a pass word.' J. D. 'Has he a pass word?' S. D. 'He has not, but I have it for him.' J. D. 'Will you give it to me?' S. D. whispers in the ear of the Junior Deacon the word, 'RABBONI.' (In many lodges, the Past Master's word, 'GIBLEM,' is used as a pass word for this degree, and the word, '*Rabboni*,' as the real word.) J. D. 'The word is right; since this is the case, you will wait until the Most Excellent Master in the east, is made acquainted with your request, and his answer returned.' Junior Deacon repairs to the Most Excellent Master in the east, and gives six raps, as at the door. M. E. M. 'Who comes here?' J. D. 'A worthy brother, who has been regularly initiated as an Entered Apprentice Mason; passed to the degree of Fellow Craft; raised to the sublime degree of a Master Mason; advanced to the honorary degree of Mark Master Mason; presided in the chair as Past Master; and now wishes for further light in Masonry, by being received and acknowledged as a Most Excellent Master.' M. E. M. 'Is it of his own free will and choice he makes this request?' J. D. 'It is.' M. E. M. 'Is he duly and truly prepared?' J. D. 'He is.' M. E. M. 'Is he worthy and well qualified?' J. D. 'He is.' M. E. M. 'Has he made suitable proficiency in the preceding degrees?' J. D. 'He has.' M. E. M. 'By what further right, or benefit, does he expect to obtain this favor?' J. D. 'By the benefit of a pass word.' M. E. M. 'Has he a pass word?' J. D. 'He has not, but I have it for him.' M. E. M. 'Will you give it to me?' Junior Deacon whispers, in the ear of the Most Excellent Master, the word, 'RABBONI.' M. E. M. 'The pass is right; since he comes endowed with all these necessary qualifications, let him enter this lodge of Most Excellent Masters, in the name of the Lord.' The candidate is then conducted six times round the lodge, by the Senior Deacon, moving with the sun. The first time they pass round the lodge, when opposite the Junior Warden, he gives one blow with the gavel; when opposite the Senior Warden he does the same; and likewise when opposite the Most Excellent Master. The second time round, each gives two blows, the third, three; and so on, until they arrive to six. During this time, the Most Excellent Master reads the following passage of scripture:—Psalm cxxii. 'I was glad when they said unto me, Let us go into the house of the Lord. Our feet shall stand within thy gates, O Jerusalem. Jerusalem is builded as a city that is compact together: Whither the tribes go up, the tribes of the Lord, unto the testimony of Israel, to give thanks unto the name of the Lord. For there are set thrones of judgment, the thrones of the house of David. Pray for the peace of Jerusalem: they shall prosper that love thee. Peace be within thy walls, and prosperity within thy palaces. For my brethren and companions' sakes, I will now say, Peace be within thee. Because of the house of the Lord, our God, I will seek thy good.' The reading of the foregoing is so timed, as not to be fully ended until the Senior Deacon and candidate have performed the sixth revolution. Immediately after this, the Senior Deacon and candidate arrive at the Junior Warden's station in the south, when the same questions are asked and the same answers returned, as at the door; (Who comes here? &c.) The Junior Warden then directs the candidate to pass on to the Senior Warden in the west, for further examination; where the same questions are asked and answers returned as before. The Senior Warden directs him to be conducted to the Right Worshipful Master in the east, for further examination. The Right Worshipful Master asks the same questions and receives the same answers, as before. He then says, 'Please to conduct the candidate back to the west, from whence he came, and put him in the care of the Senior Warden, and request him to teach the candidate how to approach the east, by advancing upon six upright regular steps to the sixth step, and place him in a proper position to take upon him the solemn oath, or obligation, of a Most Excellent Master Mason.' The candidate is conducted back to the west, and put in care of the Senior Warden, who informs him how to approach the east, as directed by the Most Excellent Master: The candidate kneels on both knees, and places both hands on the leaves of an opened Bible, square and compass. The Most Excellent Master now comes forward, and says, 'Brother, you are now placed in a proper position to take upon you the solemn oath, or obligation, of a Most Excellent Master Mason; which I assure you, as before, is neither to affect your religion, or politics. If you are willing to take it, repeat your name, and say after me.' The following obligation is then administered.

'I, A B., of my own free will and accord, in presence of Almighty God, and this lodge of Most Excellent Master Masons, do hereby and hereon, in addition to my former obligations, most solemnly and sincerely promise and swear, that I will not give the degree of a Most Excellent Master to any of an inferior degree, nor to any other person, or persons, in the known world, except it be to a true and lawful brother, or brethren, of this degree, and within the body of a just and lawfully constituted lodge of such; and not unto him nor them whom I shall hear so to be, but unto him and them only whom I shall find so to be, after strict trial and due examination, or lawful information. Furthermore, do I promise and swear, that I will obey all regular signs and summons, given, handed, sent, or thrown to me from a brother of this degree, or from the body of a just and lawfully constituted lodge of such, provided it be within the length of my cable-tow, if in my power. Furthermore, do I promise and swear, that I will support the constitution of the General Grand Royal Arch Chapter of the United States of America; also the Grand Royal Arch Chapter of the State of ———————, under which this lodge is held, and conform to all the by-laws, rules, and regulations of this, or any other lodge, of which I may, at any time hereafter, become a member. Furthermore, do I promise and swear, that I will aid and assist all poor and indigent brethren of this degree, their widows and orphans, wheresoever dispersed around the globe, as far as in my power, without injuring myself, or family. Furthermore, do I promise and swear, that the secrets of a brother of this degree, given to me in charge as such, and I knowing them to be such, shall remain as secret and inviolable in my breast as in his own, murder and treason excepted, and the same left to my own free will and choice. Furthermore, do I promise and swear, that I will not wrong this lodge of Most Excellent Master Masons, nor a brother of this degree, to the value of any thing, knowingly, myself, nor suffer it to be done by others, if in my power to prevent it; but will give due and timely notice of all approaches of danger, if in my power. Furthermore, do I promise and swear, that I will dispense light and knowledge to all ignorant and uninformed brethren, at all times, as far as in my power, without material injury to myself, or family. To all which, I do most solemnly swear, with a fixed and steady purpose of mind in me, to keep and perform the same; binding myself under no less penalty than to have my breast torn open, and my heart and vitals taken from thence, and exposed to rot on the dunghill, if ever I violate any part of this my solemn oath, or obligation, of a Most Excellent Master Mason: so help me God, and keep me steadfast in the due performance of the same.' 'Detach your hands and kiss the book.'

The candidate is now requested to rise, and the Most Excellent Master gives him the sign, grip, and word appertaining to this degree. The sign is given by placing your hands one on each breast, the fingers meeting in the centre of the body, and jerking them apart as though you were trying to tear open your breast: it alludes to the penalty of the obligation. The grip is given by taking each other by the right hand, and clasping them so that each compress the third finger of the other with his thumb. (If one hand is large and the other small, they cannot both give the grip at the same time.) It is called the grip of all grips, because it is said to cover all the preceding grips. The Most Excellent holds the candidate by the hand, and puts the inside of his right foot to the inside of the candidate's right foot, and whispers in his ear, 'RABBONI.' In some lodges, the word is not given in a whisper, but in a low voice. After these ceremonies are over, and the members seated, some noise is intentionally made, by shuffling the feet.

M. E. M. 'Brother Senior, what is the cause of this confusion?' S. W. 'Is not this the day set apart for the celebration of the cope-stone, Most Excellent?' M. E. M. 'I will ask brother Secretary. 'Brother Secretary, is this the day set apart for the celebration of the cope-stone?' Secretary, (looking in his book,) 'It is, Most Excellent.' M. E. M. 'Brother Senior Warden, assemble the brethren, and form a procession, for the purpose of celebrating the cope-stone.' The brethren then assemble, (the candidate stands aside, not joining in the procession ;) form a procession double file, and march six times round the lodge, against the course of the sun, singing the following song, and giving all the signs from an Entered Apprentice to that of Most Excellent Master. When opposite the Most Excellent Master, the first time they march round the lodge, each member gives the first sign of an Entered Apprentice, and preserves it until he nearly arrives opposite the Most Excellent a second time, then gives the second sign, and continues it in the same manner, and so of all others, up to that of this degree, saying,

L

'All hail to the morning, that bids us rejoice:
The temple's completed, exalt high each voice.
The cope-stone is finished—our labor is o'er,
The sound of the gavel shall hail us no more.

' To the power Almighty, who ever has guided
　The tribes of old Israel, exalting their fame;
To Him, who hath governed our hearts undivided,
　Let's send forth our vows to praise his great name.

' Companions, assemble on this joyful day,
(The occasion is glorious,) the key-stone to lay;
Fulfilled is the promise, by the ANCIENT of DAYS,
To bring forth the cope-stone with shouting and praise.

(The key-stone is now produced and laid on the altar.)

' There is no more occasion for level or plumb-line,
　For trowel or gavel, for compass or square:*
Our works are completed, the ark safely seated,†
　And we shall be greeted as workmen most rare.

' Names, those that are worthy our tribes, who have shared
And proved themselves faithful, shall meet their reward:
Their virtue and knowledge, industry and skill,
Have our approbation—have gained our good will.

' We accept and receive them,‡ Most Excellent Masters;
　Trusted with honor and power to preside
Among worthy craftsmen, where'er assembled,
　The knowledge of Masons to spread far and wide.

' ALMIGHTY JEHOVAH,‖ descend now and fill
This lodge with thy glory, our hearts with good will:
Preside at our meeting, assist us to find
True pleasure in teaching good will to mankind.

' Thy wisdom inspired the great institution;
　Thy strength shall support it till nature expire:—
And when the creation shall fall into ruin,
　Its beauty shall rise through the midst of the fire.'§

---

　* Here the brethren divest themselves of their jewels, sashes, aprons, &c.
　† The ark, which had been carried by two brethren in the procession, is here placed on the altar.
　‡ At these words the candidate is received into the procession.
　‖ Here all kneel in a circle round the altar.
　§ At the time the ark is placed on the altar, there is also placed on it a pot of incense, to which fire is communicated by the Most Excellent Master, just as the last line of the song is sung: this pot to contain incense, is sometimes an elegant silver urn; but if the lodge is too poor to afford that, a common tea-pot, with spout and handle broken off, answers every purpose:—for incense some pieces of paper are dipped in spirits of turpentine.

The members now all join hands, as in opening; and, while in this attitude, the Most Excellent reads the following passage of scripture:—2 Chron. vii. 1—4. 'Now when Solomon had made an end of praying, the fire came down from heaven, and consumed the burnt-offering and the sacrifices; and the glory of the Lord filled the house. And the priests could not enter into the house of the Lord, because the glory of the Lord had filled the Lord's house. And when all the children of Israel saw how the fire came down, and the glory of the Lord upon the house, they bowed themselves with their faces to the ground upon the pavement, and worshipped, and praised the Lord, saying, FOR HE IS GOOD,* FOR HIS MERCY ENDURETH FOR EVER.' The members now balance six times, as before; in opening, rise and balance six times more, disengaging themselves from each other, and take their seats; the Most Excellent Master then delivers the following charge to the candidate:—

'BROTHER, your admittance to this degree of Masonry, is a proof of the good opinion the brethren of this lodge entertain of your Masonic abilities. Let this consideration induce you to be careful of forfeiting, by misconduct and inattention to our rules, that esteem which has raised you to the rank you now possess.

'It is one of your great duties, as a Most Excellent Master, to dispense light and truth to the uninformed Mason; and I need not remind you of the impossibility of complying with this obligation without possessing an accurate acquaintance with the lectures of each degree.

'If you are not already completely conversant in all the degrees heretofore conferred on you, remember, that an indulgence, prompted by a belief that you will apply yourself with double diligence to make yourself so, has induced the brethren to accept you.

'Let it, therefore, be your unremitting study to acquire such a degree of knowledge and information as shall enable you to discharge with propriety the various duties incumbent on you, and to preserve unsullied the title now conferred upon you of a Most Excellent Master.'

After this a motion is made, by some of the members, to close the lodge. This motion being accepted and received, the Most Excellent says, 'Brother Junior Warden, you will please assem-

---

* At the words "For He is good," the Most Excellent Master, who is High Priest of the chapter, kneels and joins hands with the rest; they all then repeat in concert the words, "For He is good, for his mercy endureth for ever," six times, each time bowing their heads low towards the floor.

ble the brethren round the altar, for the purpose of closing this lodge of Most Excellent Masters.' The brethren immediately assemble round the altar in a circle, and kneel on the right knee, put their left arms over and join hands, as before; while kneeling in this position, the Most Excellent reads the following Psalm:— Psalm cxxxiv. 'Behold, bless ye the Lord, all ye servants of the Lord, which by night stand in the house of the Lord. Lift up your hands in the sanctuary, and bless the Lord. The Lord that made heaven and earth bless thee out of Zion.' The Most Excellent then closes the circle as in opening, when they balance six times, rise and balance six times more, disengage their hands, and give all the signs downwards, and declares the lodge closed.

ROYAL ARCH DEGREE.

All legally constituted bodies of Royal Arch Masons are called chapters, as regular bodies of Masons of the preceding degrees are called lodges. All the degrees from Mark Master to Royal Arch, are given under the sanction of Royal Arch chapters. A person making application to a chapter for admission, is understood as applying for all the degrees, unless he states in his application the particular degree or degrees he wishes to receive. If you ask a Mark Master if he belongs to a chapter, he will answer yes, but has only been marked. If a person make application for all the degrees, and wishes to receive them all at one time, he is frequently ballotted for only on the mark degree, it being understood, that if accepted on that, he is to receive the whole. The members of chapters who have received all the degrees, style each other companions; if they have not received the Royal Arch degree, brothers. It is a point of the Royal Arch degree 'not to assist, or be present, at the conferring of this degree upon more or less than three candidates at one time.' If there are not three candidates present, one or two companions, as the case may be, volunteer to represent candidates, so as to make the requisite number, or a *team*, as it is technically styled, and accompany the candidate or candidates through all the stages of exaltation. Every chapter must consist of a High Priest, King, Scribe, Captain of the Host, Principal Sojourner, Royal Arch Captain, three Grand Masters of the Veils, Treasurer, Secretary, and as many members as may be found convenient for working to advantage. In the lodges for conferring the preparatory degrees, the High Priest presides as Master, the King as Senior Warden, the Scribe as Junior Warden, the Captain of the Host as Marshal, or master of ceremonies, the principal Sojourner, as Senior Deacon ; the Royal Arch Captain, as Junior Deacon ; the Master of the first, second and third Veils, as Junior, Senior and Master Overseers; the Treasurer, Secretary, and Tyler, as officers of corresponding rank. The chapter is authorised to confer the degrees by a charter, or warrant from some Grand Chapter.

The members being assembled, the High Priest calls to order, and demands of the Royal Arch Captain if all present are Royal Arch Masons. The Royal Arch Captain ascertains and answers in the affirmative. The High Priest then directs him to cause the Tyler to be stationed, which being done, the High Priest says, ' Companions Royal Arch Masons, you will please to clothe, and arrange yourselves for the purpose of opening the chapter.' The furniture of the chapter is then arranged, the companions clothed with scarlet sashes and aprons, and the officers invested with the proper insignia of their respective offices, and repair to their proper stations. The High Priest then demands whether the chapter is tyled, and is answered the same as in a lodge. The stations and duties of the officers are then recited, (see lecture, sec. 1st.) After the duties of the officers are recited, the High Priest directs the captain of tne host to assemble the companions of the altar. The companions form a circle about the altar, all kneeling on the right knee, with their arms crossed, right arm uppermost and hands joined, leaving a space for the High Priest, who reads the following passages of scripture, 2d Thess. iii. 6—18. Now we command you, brethren, that ye withdraw yourselves from every brother that walketh disorderly, and not after the tradition that ye have received of us, for yourselves know, how ye ought to follow us, for we behaved not ourselves disorderly among you, neither did we eat any man's bread for nought, but wrought with labor and travail night and day, that we might not be chargeable to any of you ; not because we have not power, but to make ourselves an ensample unto you to follow us. For even when we were with you, this we commanded you, that if any man would not work, neither should he eat. For we hear that there are some, which walk among you disorderly, working not at all, but are busy-bodies. Now them that are such, we command and exhort, that with quietness they work and eat their own bread. But ye, brethren, be not weary in well doing. And if any man obey not our word, note that man and have no company with him, that he may be ashamed. Yet count him not as an enemy but admonish him as a brother. Now the Lord of peace himself, give you peace always. The salutation of Paul, with mine own hand, which is the token, so I write.' (The reader is requested to compare this with the scripture—he will observe that the name of the Saviour is intentionally left out.) The High Priest then takes his place in the circle. The whole circle then balance with their arms three times three, that is, they raise their arms and let them fall upon their knees three times in concert, after a short pause three times more, and after another pause three times more. Then all break into squads of three, and raise the living arch. This is done by each companion's taking his left wrist in his right hand, and with their left hands, the three grasp each other's right wrists, and raise them above their heads. This constitutes the living arch, under which the Grand Omnific Royal Arch word must be given, but it must also be given by three times three. In opening the chapter this is done in the following manner. After the three have joined hands they repeat these lines in concert, and at the close of each line raise them above their heads, and say, ' As we three did agree, the sacred word to keep,' ' And as we three did agree, the sacred word to search,' ' So we three do agree, to raise this Royal Arch.' At the close of the last line they keep their hands raised, while they incline their heads under them, and the first whispers in the ear of the second the syllable J A H, the second to the third, B U H, and the third to the first, L U N. The second then commences, and it goes round again in the same manner, then the third ; so that each companion pronounces each syllable of the word.* They then separate, each repairing to his station, and the High Priest declares the chapter opened.

The LECTURE of the ROYAL ARCH degree is divided into two sections. The first section designates the appellation, number and station, of the several officers, and points out the purpose and duties of their respective stations.

Question. Are you a Royal Arch Mason? *Answer. I am that I am.*† Q. How shall I know you to be a Royal Arch Mason?

---

* There is a great difference in the manner of giving the Royal Arch word in the different chapters. Sometimes it is given at the opening, as above stated, sometimes they commence with the word GOD, each one pronouncing a letter of it in succession, until they have each pronounced every letter of the word, then the word JEHOVAH, a syllable at a time, and then the word JAHBUHLUN, as described. There are also chapters in which the latter word is not known, and there are others in which the word is not given at all at opening.

† 'I AM THAT I AM,' is one of the peculiar names of Deity, and to use it, as above, is, to say the *least*, taking the name of God in vain ! How must the humble disciple of Jesus feel when constrained *thus* to answer the question : ' Are you a Royal Arch Mason.'

A. By three times three. Q. Where was you made a Royal Arch Mason? A. In a just and legally constituted chapter of Royal Arch Masons, consisting of Most Excellent, High Priest, King, and Scribe, Captain of the Host, Principal Sojourner, Royal Arch Captain, and the three Grand Masters of the Veils, assembled in a room or place representing the tabernacle erected by our ancient brethren, near the ruins of king Solomon's temple. Q. Where is the High Priest stationed, and what are his duties? A. He is stationed in the sanctum sanctorum. His duty, with the King and Scribe, to sit in the Grand Council, to form plans and give directions to the workmen. Q. The King's station and duty? A. At the right hand of the High Priest, to aid him by his advice and counsel, and in his absence to preside. Q. The Scribe's station and duty? A. At the left hand of the High Priest, to assist him and the King in the discharge of their duties, and to preside in their absence. Q. The Captain of the Host's station and duty? A. At the right hand of the Grand Council, and to receive their orders, and see them duly executed. Q. The Principal Sojourner's station and duty? A. At the left hand of the Grand Council, to bring the blind, by a way that they know not, to lead them in paths they have not known, to make darkness light before them, and crooked things strait. Q. The Royal Arch Captain's station and duty? A. At the inner veil, or entrance of the sanctum sanctorum, to guard the same, and see that none pass but such as are duly qualified, and have the proper pass words and signets of truth. Q. What is the color of his banner? A. White, and is emblematical of that purity of heart and rectitude of conduct, which is essential to obtain admission into the divine sanctum sanctorum above. Q. The stations and duties of the three Grand Masters of the Veils? A. At the entrance of their respective Veils; to guard the same and see that none pass but such as are duly qualified and in possession of the proper pass words and tokens. Q. What are the colors of their banners? A. That of the third, scarlet, which is emblematical of fervency and zeal, and the appropriate color of the Royal Arch degree. It admonishes us to be fervent in the exercise of our devotions to God, and zealous in our endeavors to promote the happiness of men. Of the second, purple, which being produced by a due mixture of blue and scarlet, the former of which, is the characteristic color of the symbolic, or three first degrees, and the latter, that of the Royal Arch degree, is an emblem of union, and is the characteristic color of the intermediate degrees. It teaches us to cultivate and improve that spirit of harmony between the brethren of the symbolic degrees, and the companions of the sublime degrees, which should ever distinguish the members of a society founded upon the principles of everlasting truth and universal philanthropy. Of the first, blue, the peculiar color of the three ancient or symbolical degrees. It is an emblem of universal friendship and benevolence, and instructs us that in the mind of a Mason, those virtues should be as expansive as the blue arch of heaven itself. Q. The Treasurer's station and duty? A. At the right hand of the Captain of the Host; his duty to keep a just and regular account of all the property and funds of the chapter placed in his hands, and ex*hibit them to the chapter when called upon for that purpose.* Q. The Secretary's place in the chapter? A. At the left of the Principal Sojourner, his duty to issue the orders and notifications of his superior officers, record the proceedings of the chapter proper to be written, to receive all monies due to the chapter, and pay them over to the Treasurer. Q. Tyler's place and duty? A. His station is at the outer avenue of the chapter, his duty to guard against the approach of cowans and eaves-droppers, and suffer none to pass or repass but such as are duly qualified. The second section describes the method of exaltation to this sublime degree, as follows: 'Companion, you informed me, at the commencement of this lecture, that you was made a Royal Arch Mason in a just and legally constituted chapter of Royal Arch Masons.'

Q. Where was you prepared to be made a Royal Arch Mason? A. In a room adjacent to the chapter. Q. How was you prepared? A. In a company of three, I was hoodwinked, with a cable-tow seven times around our bodies; in which condition we were conducted to the door of the chapter, and caused to give seven distinct knocks, which were answered by a like number from within, and we were asked 'Who comes there?' Q. Your answer? A. Three brethren, who have been regularly initiated as Entered Apprentices, passed to the degree of Fellow Craft, raised to the sublime degree of Master Mason, advanced to the more honorable degree of Mark Master, presided as Masters in the chair, accepted and received as Most Excellent Masters, and now wish for further light in Masonry, by being exalted to the more sublime degree of Royal Arch Masons. Q. What was then said to you? A. We were asked if we were duly and truly prepared, worthy and well qualified, had made suitable proficiency in the preceding degrees, and were properly avouched for. All which, being answered in the affirmative, we were asked by what further right or benefit we expected to obtain this favor? Q. Your answer? A. By the benefit of a pass word. Q. Had you that pass word? A. We had not, but our conductor gave it for us. Q. What was then said to you? A. We were directed to wait with patience, till the Grand

Council could be informed of our request and their pleasure known. Q. What answer was returned? A. Let them enter under a living arch, and remember to stoop low, for he that humbleth himself shall be exalted. Q. Did you pass under a living arch? A. We did. Q. How were you then disposed of? A. We were conducted to the altar, caused to kneel, and take upon ourselves the solemn oath, or obligation, of a Royal Arch Mason. Q. Have you that obligation? A. I have. Q. Will you give it me?

A. I, A. B., of my own free will and accord, in the presence of Almighty God, and this chapter of Royal Arch Masons, erected to God, and dedicated to the holy order of St. John,* do hereby and hereon, most solemnly and sincerely promise and swear, in addition to my former obligations, that I will not give the degree of Royal Arch Mason to any one of an inferior degree, nor to any other being in the known world, except it be to a true and lawful companion Royal Arch Mason, or within the body of a just and legally constituted chapter of such, and not unto him or unto them whom I shall hear so to be, but unto him or them only whom I shall find so to be, after strict trial, due examination, or legal information received. Furthermore, do I promise and swear, that I will not give the Grand Omnific Royal Arch word, which I shall hereafter receive, neither in the chapter nor out of it, except there be present two companions Royal Arch Masons, who, with myself, make three, and then by three times three, under a living arch not above my breath. Furthermore, that I will not reveal the ineffable characters belonging to this degree, or retain the key to them in my possession, but destroy it, whenever it comes to my sight. Furthermore, do I promise and swear, that I will not wrong this chapter, nor a companion of this degree, to the value of any thing, knowingly myself, or suffer it to be done by others, if in my power to prevent it. Furthermore, do I promise and swear, that I will not be at the exaltation of a candidate to this degree, at a clandestine chapter, I knowing it to be such. Furthermore, do I promise and swear, that I will not assist or be present at the exaltation of a candidate to this degree, who has not regularly received the degrees of Entered Apprentice, Fellow Craft, Master Mason, Mark Master, Past Master, Most Excellent Master, to the best of my knowledge and belief. Furthermore, that I will not assist or see more or less than three candidates exalted at one and the same time. Furthermore, that I will not assist or be

---

* Or as it is at this time given in some chapters, 'To the honor of our ancient patron Zerubbabel.'

present at the forming or opening of a Royal Arch Chapter, unless there be present nine regular Royal Arch Masons. Furthermore, do I promise and swear, that I will not speak evil of a companion Royal Arch Mason, neither behind his back nor before his face, but will apprise him of approaching danger if in my power. Furthermore, do I promise and swear, that I will not strike a companion Royal Arch Mason in anger, so as to draw his blood. Furthermore, do I promise and swear, that I will support the constitution of the General Grand Royal Arch Chapter of the United States of America, also the constitution of Grand Royal Arch Chapter of the state under which this chapter is held, and conform to all the by-laws, rules and regulations of this, or any other chapter of which I may hereafter become a member. Furthermore, do I promise and swear, that I will obey all regular signs, summons, or tokens given, handed, sent, or thrown to me, from the hand of a companion Royal Arch Mason, or from the body of a just and lawfully constituted chapter of such, provided it be within the length of my cable-tow. Furthermore, do I promise and swear, that I will aid and assist a companion Royal Arch Mason, when engaged in any difficulty; and espouse his cause, so far as to extricate him from the same, if in my power, whether he be right or wrong. Also, that I will promote a companion Royal Arch Mason's political preferment in preference to another of equal qualifications.* Furthermore, do I promise and swear, that a companion Royal Arch Mason's secrets, given me in charge as such, and I knowing them to be such, shall remain as secure and inviolable in my breast as in his own, *murder and treason not excepted.*† Furthermore, do I promise and swear, that I will be aiding and assisting all poor and indigent Royal Arch Masons, their widows and orphans, wherever dispersed around the globe, so far as in my power, without material injury to myself or family. All which I most solemnly and sincerely promise and swear, with a firm and steadfast resolution to perform the same, without any equivocation, mental reservation, or self-evasion of mind in me whatever; binding myself under no less penalty, than that of having my skull smote off, and my brains exposed to the scorching rays of the sun, should I ever knowingly, or wilfully, violate or trangress any part of this my solemn oath, or obligation, of a Royal Arch Ma-

---

* This clause is sometimes made a distinct point in the obligation in the following form, viz: Furthermore, do I promise and swear, that I will vote for a companion Royal Arch Mason, before any other of equal qualifications; and in some chapters, both are left out of the obligation.

† In some chapters this is administered. All the secrets of a companion without exception.

son. So help me God, and keep me steadfast in the performance of the same.

Q. After receiving the obligation, what was said to you? A. We were told that we were now obligated and received as Royal Arch Masons, but as this degree was infinitely more important than any of the preceding, it was necessary for us to pass through many trials, and to travel in rough and rugged ways to prove our fidelity, before we could be entrusted with the more important secrets of this degree. We were further told, that, though we could not discover the path we were to travel, we were under the direction of a faithful guide, who would ' bring the blind by a way they know not, and lead them in paths they had not known; who would make darkness light before them, and crooked things straight; who would do these things, and not forsake them.' (See Isa. xlii. 16.) Q. What followed? A. We were caused to travel three times round the room, when we were again conducted to the altar, caused to kneel and attend to the following prayer. (See this prayer, Monitor, chapter xiv. Sec. 2. p. 134.) Supreme Architect of universal nature, who, by thine Almighty Word, didst speak into being the stupendous arch of heaven! And for the instruction and pleasure of thy rational creatures, didst adorn us with greater and lesser lights, thereby magnifying thy power, and endearing thy goodness unto the sons of men: We humbly adore and worship thine unspeakable perfection! We bless thee, that, when man had fallen from his innocence and his happiness, thou didst leave him the powers of reasoning, and capacity of improvement and of pleasure.* We thank thee, that, amidst the pains and calamities of our present state, so many means of refreshment and satisfaction are reserved to us, while travelling the rugged path of life; especially would we, at this time, render thee our thanksgiving and praise for the institution, as members of which we are, at this time, assembled, and for all the pleasures we have derived from it. We thank thee, that the few here assembled before thee, have been favored with new inducements, and been laid under new and stronger obligations of virtue and holiness.† May these obligations, O blessed Father! have their full effect upon us. Teach us, we pray thee, the true

---

* If Masonry was congenial to christianity, this prayer would read very differently; it would read thus:—' We bless thee, that, when man had fallen from his innocence and happiness,' thou didst send thine only Son, the Lord Jesus Christ, to make a propitiation for our sins;—to renovate our hearts and save us from the wrath to come.

† How stupid must be that man, who supposes that his moral obligations can be increased by taking of Masonic oaths.

reverence of thy great, mighty, and terrible name. Inspire us with a firm and unshaken resolution in our virtuous pursuits. Give us grace diligently to search thy word in the book of nature, wherein the duties of our high vocation are inculcated with divine authority.* May the solemnity of the ceremonies of our institution be duly impressed on our minds, and have a happy and lasting effect on our lives! O thou, who didst aforetime appear unto thy servant Moses *in a flame of fire out of the midst of a bush,* enkindle, we beseech thee, in each of our hearts, a flame of devotion to thee, of love to each other, and of charity to all mankind! May all thy *miracles and mighty works,* fill us with thy dread, and thy goodness impress us with a love of thy holy name! May *Holiness to the Lord,* be engraven upon all our thoughts, words, and actions! May the incense of piety ascend continually unto thee, from the altar of our hearts, and burn day and night, as a sacrifice of a sweet smelling savor, well pleasing unto thee! And since sin has destroyed within us the first temple of purity and innocence, may thy heavenly grace guide and assist us in rebuilding a *second temple* of reformation, and may the glory of this latter house be greater than the glory of the former! Amen, so mote it be.

Q. After the prayer what followed? A. We were again caused to travel three times round the room, during which the following passage of scripture was read, and we were shown a representation of the bush that burned and was not consumed. Exodus iii. 1—6. Now Moses kept the flock of Jethro his father-in-law, the priest of Midian; and he led the flock to the back side of the desert, and came to the mountain of God, even to Horeb. And the angel of the Lord appeared unto him in a flame of fire out of the midst of a bush; and he looked, and, behold, the bush burned with fire, and the bush was not consumed. And Moses said, I will now turn aside, and see this great sight, why the bush is not burned. And when the Lord saw that he turned aside to see, God called unto him out of the midst of the bush, and said, Moses, Moses. And he said, Here am I. And he said, draw not nigh hither: put off thy shoes from off thy feet; for the place whereon thou standest is holy ground. Moreover he said, I am the God of thy father, the God of Abraham, the God of Isaac, and the God of Jacob. And Moses hid his face; for he was afraid to look upon God. Q. What followed? A. We again travelled while the following passage was read.

---

* Here, again, we see the *cloven foot* of the institution! The Bible is rejected, and the '*book of nature*' is received as the rule of faith and practice

2 Chron. xxxvi. 11—20. Zedekiah was one and twenty years old when he began to reign, and reigned eleven years in Jerusalem. And he did *that which was* evil in the sight of the Lord his God, *and* humbled not himself before Jeremiah the prophet *speaking* from the mouth of the Lord. And he also rebelled against king Nebuchadnezzar, and he stiffened his neck, and hardened his heart from turning unto the Lord God of Israel. Moreover, all the chief of the priests and the people, transgressed very much after all the abominations of the heathen; and polluted the house of the Lord which he had hallowed in Jerusalem. And the Lord God of their fathers sent to them by his messengers, rising up betimes and sending; because he had compassion on his people, and on his dwelling place. But they mocked the messengers of God, and despised his words, and misused his prophets, until the wrath of the Lord arose against his people, till *there was* no remedy. Therefore he brought upon him the king of the Chaldees, who slew their young men with the sword in the house of their sanctuary, and had no compassion on young men or maidens, old men, or him that stooped for age; he gave them all into his hand. And all the vessels of the house of God, great and small, and the treasures of the house of the Lord, and the treasures of the king, and of his princes; all *these* he brought to Babylon. And they burnt the house of God, and brake down the wall of Jerusalem, and burnt all the palaces thereof with fire, and destroyed all the goodly vessels thereof. And them that had escaped from the sword carried he away to Babylon; where they were servants to him and his sons, until the reign of the kingdom of Persia. At the close of this there was a representation of the destruction of Jerusalem by Nebuchadnezzar, and the carrying captive of the children of Israel to Babylon. We were seized, bound in chains, and confined in a dungeon.

Q. What followed? A. We heard rejoicing, as of good news; the proclamation of Cyrus, king of Persia, was read in our hearing. [Ezra, i. 1—3.] 'Now in the first year of Cyrus, king of Persia, the Lord stirred up the spirit of Cyrus, king of Persia, that he made a proclamation throughout all his kingdom, and put it also in writing, saying: Thus saith Cyrus, king of Persia, the Lord God of heaven hath given me all the kingdoms of the earth, and he hath charged me to build him an house at Jerusalem, which is in Judah. Who is there among you of all his people? His God be with him, and let him go up to Jerusalem, which is in Judah, and build the house of the Lord God of Israel, which is in Jerusalem.' Q. What was then said to you? A. We were unbound and requested to go up to Jerusalem to

M

assist in rebuilding the temple, but objected, as we had no pass by which to make ourselves known to our brethren. Q. What followed? A. The third chapter of Exodus, 13 and 14 verses, were read to us : ' And Moses said unto God, Behold! when I come unto the children of Israel, and shall say unto them, the God of your fathers hath sent me unto you, and they shall say to me, what is his name? what shall I say to them? And God said unto Moses, I AM THAT I AM : And thus thou shalt say unto the children of Israel, I AM hath sent me unto you.' We were directed to use the words, '*I am that I am,*' as a pass word. Q. What followed? A. We arose to go up to Jerusalem, and travelled over hills and valleys, rough and rugged ways, for many days ; during which time, as we stopped occasionally to rest and refresh ourselves, the following passages from the Psalms, were read in our hearing for our consolation and encouragement. [Psalms cxli. cxlii. cxliii.]

Psalm cxli.—' Lord, I cry unto thee : make haste unto me ; give ear unto my voice. Let my prayer be set forth before thee, as incense : and the lifting up of hands as the evening sacrifice. Set a watch, O Lord, before my mouth ; keep the door of my lips. Incline not my heart to any evil thing, to practice wicked works with men that work iniquity. Let the righteous smite me ; it shall be a kindness : and let him reprove me ; it shall be an excellent oil. Mine eyes are unto thee, O God the Lord ; in thee is my trust ; leave not my soul destitute. Keep me from the snare which they have laid for me, and the gins of the workers of iniquity. Let the wicked fall into their own nets, whilst that I withal escape.

Psalm cxlii.—I cried unto the Lord with my voice ; with my voice unto the Lord did I make my supplication. I poured out my complaint before him ; I showed before him my trouble.— When my spirit was overwhelmed within me, then thou knewest my path. In the way wherein I walked, have they privily laid a snare for me. I looked on my right hand, and beheld, but there was no man that would know me ; refuge failed me : no man cared for my soul. I cried unto thee, O Lord ; I said, Thou art my refuge and my portion in the land of the living. Attend unto my cry, for I am brought very low ; deliver me from my persecutors ; for they are stronger than I. Bring my soul out of prison, that I may praise thy name.

Psalm cxliii.—Hear my prayer, O Lord, give ear to my supplications : in thy faithfulness answer me, and in thy righteousness. And enter not into judgment with thy servant : for in thy sight shall no man living be justified. For the enemy hath persecuted my soul; he hath made me to dwell in darkness. Therefore is my spirit overwhelmed within me; my heart within me is desolate. Hear me speedily, O Lord: my spirit faileth: hide not thy face from me, lest I be like unto them that go down into the pit. Cause me to hear thy loving kindness in the morning; for in thee do I trust: cause me to know the way wherein I should walk, for I lift up my soul unto thee. Bring my soul out of trouble, and of thy mercy cut off mine enemies: for I am thy servant.'

At length we arrived at Jerusalem, and presented ourselves at the first Veil of the Tabernacle.

Q. What was there said to you? A. The Master of the First Veil demanded of us, 'Who comes there? who dares approach this outer Veil of our sacred Tabernacle? who comes here?' Q. Your answer? A. Three weary travellers from Babylon. They then demanded of us who we were, and what were our intentions. Q. Your answer? A. We are your own brethren and kindred, of the tribe of Benjamin; we are the descendants of those noble families of Giblimites, who wrought so hard at the building of the first temple, were present at its destruction by Nebuchadnezzar, by him carried away captive to Babylon, where we remained servants to him and his sons, till the first year of Cyrus, king of Persia, by whose order we were liberated, and are now returned to assist in rebuilding the house of the Lord, without expectation of fee or reward. Q. What further was demanded of you? A. The pass word, 'I am that I am.' After giving which, the Master of the Veil, assured of his full confidence in us as worthy brethren, commended us for our zeal, and gave us the token and words to enable us to pass the second Veil. Q. What are they? A. The token is an imitation of that which Moses was commanded to exhibit to the children of Israel, casting his rod upon the ground it became a serpent, and putting forth his hand and taking it again by the tail, it became a rod in his hand. The words are these, '*Shem, Ham,* and *Japhet.*' Q. What followed? A. We were conducted to the second Veil, where the same questions were asked and answers returned, as before, with the addition of the pass words and token given at the First Veil. Q. What followed? A. The Master of the Second Veil told us that we must be true and lawful brethren to pass thus far, but further we could not go without his pass and token, which he accordingly gave to us. What are they? A. The words are Shem, Japheth, and Adoniram; the token is putting the hand in the bosom, plucking it out again, in imitation of the second sign which Moses was directed to make to the Israelites, when putting his hand into his bosom and taking it out again, it became leprous as snow. Q. How were you then disposed of? A. We were conducted onwards to the Third Veil, when the same questions were asked and answers returned, as before, with the addition of the token and words last received. Q. What followed? A. The Master of the Third Veil then gave us the sign, words, and signet, to enable us to pass the Fourth Veil, to the presence of the Grand Council. Q. What are the words, sign, and signet? A. The words are Japheth, Shem, Noah; the sign, pouring water upon the ground, in imitation of Moses, who poured water upon the ground and it became blood; the signet is called the signet of truth, and is Zerubbabel. It alludes to this passage, 'In that day, I will take thee, O Zerubbabel, my servant, the son of Shealtiel, and will make thee as a signet; for I have chosen thee.' [See Haggai, chap. ii. ver. 23.]

Q. What followed? A. We then passed to the Fourth Veil, where, after answering the same questions, and giving the sign, words, and signet, last received, we were admitted to the presence of the Grand Council, where the High Priest made the same demands as were made at the Veils, and received the same answers. Q. What did the High Priest further demand of you? A. The signs from Entered Apprentice to Most Excellent Master in succession. Q. What did he then say to you? A. He said we were truly three worthy Most Excellent Masters, commended us for our zeal and disinterestedness, and asked what part of the work we were willing to undertake. Q. Your answer? A. That we were willing to undertake any service, however servile or dangerous, for the sake of forwarding so great and noble an undertaking. Q. What followed? A. We were then furnished with a pickaxe, spade, and crow, and were directed to repair to the north west corner of the ruins of the old temple, and commence removing the rubbish, to lay the foundation of the new, and to observe and preserve every thing of importance and report to the Grand Council. We accordingly repaired to the place, and after laboring several days, we discovered what seemed a rock, but on striking it with the crow, it gave a hollow sound, and upon closer examination, we discovered in it an iron ring, by help of which we succeeded in removing it from its place, when we found it to be the key-stone of an arch, and through the aperture there appeared to be an immense vault curiously arched. We then took the stone, and repaired to the Grand Council, and presented it for their inspection. Q. What did the Grand Council then say to you? A. They told us that the stone contained the mark of our ancient Grand Master, Hiram Abiff;

that it was truly a fortunate discovery, and that without doubt the vault contained things of the utmost consequence to the craft. They then directed us to repair again to the place, and continue our researches. Q. What followed? A. We returned again to the place, and agreed that one of our number should descend by means of a rope, the middle of which was fixed firmly around his body, and if he wished to descend, he was to pull the rope in his right hand, if to ascend, that in his left. He accordingly descended, and in groping about, he found what appeared to be some ancient jewels, but the air becoming offensive, he pulled the rope in his left hand, and was immediately drawn out. We then repaired to the Grand Council, made our report, and presented the articles found, which they pronounced the jewels of our three ancient Grand Masters, Solomon, Hiram, and Hiram Abiff. They commended us highly for our zeal and fidelity, assured us that it was a fortunate discovery, that it would probably lead to still more important ones, and that our disinterested perseverance should not go unrewarded. They directed us to repair again to the place, and make what further discoveries lay in our power. Q. What followed? A. We again returned to the place, and let down one of our companions, as before. The sun having now reached its meridian height, darted its rays to the inmost recesses of the vault, and enabled him to discover a small chest, or box, curiously wrought; but the air becoming exceedingly offensive, he gave the sign and was immediately drawn out. We immediately repaired to the Grand Council, and presented our discovery. On examination, the Grand Council pronounced it to be the *ark of the covenant*, which was deposited in the vault by our ancient Grand Master, for safe keeping. On inspecting it more closely, they found a key with which they opened it. The High Priest then took from it a book, which he opened, and read as follows: (Gen. i. 1—3.) 'In the beginning God created the heavens and the earth. And the earth was without form, and void; and darkness was upon the face of the deep: and the Spirit of God moved upon the face of the waters. And God said, Let there be light: and there was light.' [Deut. xxxi. 24—26.] 'And it came to pass, when Moses had made an end of writing the words of this law in a book, until they were finished, that Moses commanded the Levites which bare the ark of the covenant of the Lord, saying, Take this book of the law, and put it in the side of the ark of the covenant of the Lord your God, that it may be there for a witness against thee.' [Ex. xxv. 21.] 'And thou shalt put the mercy-seat above, upon the ark, and in the ark thou shalt put the testimony that I shall give thee.' He then declared it to be the book of the law, upon which the Grand Council, in an ecstasy of joy, exclaimed three times, " Long lost, now found, Holiness to the Lord;" at the same time drawing their hand across their foreheads. Q. What further was found in the ark? A. A small vessel containing a substance, which, after the Council had examined, and the High Priest again read from the book of the law, [Ex. xvi. 32—34,] he pronounced to be manna. ' And Moses said, this is the thing which the Lord commanded: fill an omer of the manna to be kept for your generations, that they may see the bread wherewith I have fed you in the wilderness, when I brought you forth from the land of Egypt. And Moses said unto Aaron, take a pot and put an omer full of manna therein, and lay it up before the Lord, to be kept for your generations. As the Lord commanded Moses, so Aaron laid it up before the testimony, to be kept for a token.' The High Priest then took a rod from the ark, which after he had read the following passage, [Numb. xvii. 10,] ' And the Lord said unto Moses, bring Aaron's rod again before the testimony to be kept for a token,' he pronounced to be Aaron's rod, which budded and blossomed as the rose. Q. Was there any thing further found in the ark? A. There was a key to the ineffable characters belonging to this degree, as follows: ⁻|⁻|⁻ × beginning at top of this diagram at the left hand angle;

A B C D E F G H I J K L M N O P Q R S T U V W X Y Z

⌐ ˙⌐ ⌐˙ ⌐˙⌐ ⌐. ⌐ ⌐⌐ ⌐⌐. ⌐.⌐ ⌐ ⌐. .⌐ .⌐. V V. ≪ ≪. ∧ ∧. ≫ ≫.

The upper left hand angle without a dot is A; the same with a dot is B, &c.

Q. What further was said to you? A. The High Priest read the following passage ; (Exodus vi. 2, 3,) ' And God spake unto Moses, and said unto him, I am the Lord, and I appeared unto Abraham, unto Isaac, and unto Jacob, by the name of God Almighty, but by my name Jehovah was I not known to them.' He then informed us that the name of Deity, the divine Logos, or word, to which reference is had in John, i. 1, 5. ' In the beginning was the word, and the word was with God, and the word was God; the same was in the beginning with God: all things were made by him, and without him was not any thing made that was made: In him was life, and the life was the light of men: And the light shineth in darkness, and the darkness comprehendeth it not.' That this Logos, or word, was anciently written only in these sacred characters, and thus preserved from one generation to another. That this was the true masonic word, which was lost in the death of Hiram Abiff, and was restored at the rebuilding of the temple, in the manner we had at that time assisted to represent. Q. What followed? A. We were reminded of the manner in which we had sworn to give the Royal Arch word; were instructed in the manner and finally invested with the all-important word in due form. Q. What is the Grand Royal Arch word? A. JAH-BUH-LUN.* Q. How is it to be given? A. Under a living arch by three times three, in low breath, (see description of opening a chapter.) Q. What followed? A. We were presented with the signs belonging to this degree. Q. Will you give me those signs? Answered by giving the signs, thus: raise the right hand to the forehead, the hand and arm horizontal; thumb towards the forehead, draw it briskly across the forehead, and drop it perpendicularly by the side. This constitutes the due guard of this degree, and refers to the penalty of the obligation. The grand sign is made by locking the fingers of both hands together, and carrying them to the top of the head, the palms upward, alluding to the manner in which the brother who descended into the vault, and found the ark, found his hands involuntarily placed to protect his head from the potent rays of the meridian sun. Q. What followed? A. The High Priest then placed crowns upon our heads, and told us that we were now invested with all the important secrets of this degree, and crowned and received as worthy companions Royal Arch Masons. He then gives the charge, (see Masonic Chart, p. 113, or Webb's Monitor, chap. xiv. sec. 2, p. 149.)

The second section of the lecture on this degree states minutely the ceremonies and forms of exaltation, (as the conferring of this degree is styled,) but there seems to be some parts which require explanation. The Principal Sojourner conducts the candidate, and is considered as representing Moses conducting the children of Israel through the wilderness. He is usually dressed to represent an old man, bowed with age, with a mask on his face, and long beard hanging down upon his breast; is introduced to the candidate in the preparation room by the name of Moses. On entering the chapter, the candidates are received under a 'living arch;' that is, the companions arrange themselves in a line on each side of the door, and each joins hands with the one opposite to himself. The candidates entering, the conductor says; 'Stoop low, brothers! we are about to enter the arches; remember that he that humbleth himself, shall be exalted: stoop low, brothers, stoop low!' The candidates

---

* This question and answer do not belong to the lecture, but are inserted to show the word plainly and unencumbered with ceremonies.

seldom pass the first pair of hands, or, in other words, the first arch, without being so far humbled as to be very glad to support themselves on all fours. Their progress may well be imagined to be very slow; for, in addition to their humble posture, they are obliged to support on their backs, the whole weight of the living arches above. (Who would not go slow?) The conductor to encourage them, calls out occasionally, 'Stoop low, brothers, stoop low!' If they go too slow to suit the companions, it is not unusual for some one to apply a sharp point to their bodies, to urge them on; the points of the pasteboard crown answers quite well for this purpose. After they have endured this humiliating exercise as long as suits the convenience of the companions, (and if they are not reduced to a more humble posture than all fours, they come off well,) they pass from under the living arches. Surely, after this, they must *stay humbled for life.* The candidates next receive the obligation, travel the room, attend the prayer, travel again, and are shown a representation of the Lord appearing to Moses from the burning bush. This last is done in various ways. Sometimes an earthen pot is filled with earth, and green bushes set round the edge of it, and a candle in the centre; and sometimes a stool is provided with holes about the edge, in which bushes are placed, and a bundle of rags, or tow, saturated with oil of turpentine, placed in the centre, to which fire is communicated. Sometimes a large bush is suspended from the ceiling, around the stem of which tow is wound wet with oil of turpentine. In whatever way the bush is prepared, when the words are read, ' he looked, and behold, the bush burned with fire,' &c. the bandage is removed from the eyes of the candidates, and they see the fire in the bush,* and, at the words, ' Draw not nigh hither; put off thy shoes,' &c. the shoes of the candidates are taken off, and they remain in the same situation while the rest of the passage is read to the words, ' And Moses hid his face; for he was afraid to look upon God.' The bandage is then replaced, and the candidates again travel about the room, while the next passage of scripture is read. [See

---

* This is frequently represented in this manner: When the person reading comes to that part where it says, ' God called to him out of the midst of the bush, and said,' &c. he stops reading, and a person behind the bushes calls out, ' Moses, Moses;' the conductor answers, ' Here am I:' the person behind the bush then says, ' Draw not nigh hither; put off thy shoes from off thy feet; for the place whereon thou standest is holy ground: (his shoes are then slipped off.) Moreover, I am the God of Abraham, the God of Isaac, and the God of Jacob.' The person first reading, then says, ' And Moses hid his face; for he was afraid to look upon God.' At these words the bandage is placed over the candidate's eyes.

Lecture.] At the words, 'and brake down the walls of Jerusalem,' the companions make a tremendous crashing and noise, by firing pistols, overturning chairs, benches, and whatever is at hand; rolling cannon balls across the floor, stamping, &c. &c. and, in the midst of the uproar, the candidates are seized, a chain thrown about them, and they are hurried away to the preparation room. This is the representation of the destruction of Jerusalem, and carrying captive the children of Israel to Babylon.— After a short time the proclamation of Cyrus is read, the candidates are unbound, and start to go up to Jerusalem, to assist in rebuilding the temple. The candidates, still hood-winked, are brought into the chapter, and commence their journey over the rugged and rough paths. They are literally rough paths, sticks of timber framed across the path the candidate must travel, some inches from the floor, make no comfortable travelling for a person blindfolded. But this is not always the way it is prepared; billets of wood singly, or in heaps, ladders, nets of cords, &c. &c. are all put in requisition to form the rough and rugged paths, which are intended as a trial of the *fidelity* of the candidates. If they escape with nothing more than bruised shins they do well. They have been known to faint away under the severity of the discipline, and occasion the *worthy* companions much alarm. After travelling the rugged paths till all are satisfied, they arrive at the first Veil of the Tabernacle, give the pass word, and pass on to the second, give the pass words, and present the sign. This, it will be recollected, is in imitation of the sign which Moses was directed to make to the children of Israel. He threw his rod upon the ground and it became a serpent; he put forth his hand and took it by the tail, and it became a rod in his hand. The conductor is provided with a rod, made in the form of a snake, and painted to resemble one. This he drops upon the floor, and takes up again. They then pass on to the next Veil, give the pass word, and make the sign, (put the right hand in the bosom and pluck it out again;) pass on to the next—give the pass words, and make the sign, (pour water upon the ground;) and are ushered into the presence of the *Grand Council*. The Veils are four in number, and of the same color as the banners of the three Grand Masters of the Veils, and that of the Royal Arch Captain, blue, purple, scarlet, and white, and have the same references and explanations. (See Lecture.) The Grand Council consists of the Most Excellent High Priest, King, and Scribe. The High Priest is dressed in a white robe, with a breastplate of cut glass, consisting of twelve pieces to represent the twelve tribes of Israel, an apron, and a mitre. The King wears a scarlet robe, apron, and crown. The mitre and crown are generally made of pasteboard; sometimes they have them of the most splendid materials, gold and silk velvet; but these are kept for public occasions. The mitre has the words, ' *Holiness to the Lord*' in gold letters across the forehead. The Scribe wears a purple robe, apron, and turban. After having satisfied the Grand Council that they are true brethren, and stated their object in coming to Jerusalem, the candidates are directed to commence the labor of removing the rubbish of the old temple preparatory to laying the foundation of the new. For the purpose of performing this part of the ceremony, there is in or near the chapter a narrow kind of closet, the only entrance to which is through a scuttle at the top; there is placed over this scuttle whatever rubbish is at hand, bits of boards, brick bats, &c. and among them the key stone. After the candidates are furnished with the tools, (pickaxe, spade, and crow,) they are directed to this place, and remove the rubbish till they discover the key stone. This they convey to the Grand Council as stated in the lecture. After the Grand Council have examined it, they pronounce it to be the work of the Grand Master, Hiram Abiff, and direct them to return and prosecute their researches, not doubting they will make many important discoveries. The candidates return and let down one of their number by a rope—he finds three squares, is drawn out, and all proceed with them to the Grand Council.— The Grand Council inspect them and pronounce them to be the three ancient jewels that belonged to the three ancient Grand Masters, Solomon, Hiram, and Hiram Abiff. The candidates then return to the vault and let down another of their number. Here, let it be remarked, some chapters, for the purpose of lightening the labors of the candidates, call in the aid of machinery. A pulley is suspended over the vault, and the candidate is *exalted* from the bottom at the tail of a snatch block, the one last let down finds at the bottom a small chest, or box; upon which he gives the signal to be drawn out : he no sooner discovers the box, than the air in the vault, in the language of the lecture, ' becomes exceedingly offensive.' This is strictly true ; for at the moment he takes up the box and is preparing to ascend, fire is communicated to a quantity of gunpowder at his feet, so that by the time he arrives at the top, he is so completely suffocated with the fumes of the powder, that he is almost deprived of the power of respiration or motion. The box is carried to the Grand Council, and pronounced to be the ark of the covenant. It is opened, and a Bible taken out, and some passages read from it. (See Lecture.) One word respecting the representation of the ark. It ought to be a splendid box covered with gold, and some of them are really elegant; but the chapter must have such as it can afford: if it is too poor to procure splendid furniture, cheap articles are made to answer; for an ark, if the funds are low, a plain cherry or pine box will answer, and sometimes a cigar box is made the humble representation of the splendid ark, made by divine command, of shittim wood, and overlaid with pure gold. The High Priest takes then from the ark a vessel containing something to represent manna. This vessel is of various forms and materials, from an elegant silver urn to a broken earthen mug; and the substance contained is as various as the vessels in which it is deposited; such as a bit of sugar, a piece of cracker, or a few kernels of wheat. Whichever is used, the High Priest takes it out and gravely asks the King and Scribe their opinion of it; they say they think it is manna. The High Priest then looks at it intently and says, 'It looks like manna;' smells it, and says, 'It smells like manna;' and then tastes it, and says, 'It is manna.' The High Priest then takes from the ark a bit of an apple tree sprout, a few inches long, with some withered buds upon it, or a stick of a similar length with some artificial buds upon it, which, after consulting with the King and Scribe, he pronounces Aaron's rod. He then takes out the key to the ineffable characters and explains it. This key is kept in the ark on four distinct pieces of paper. The key is marked on a square piece of paper, and the paper is then divided into four equal parts; thus:—the outside lines represent the dimensions of the paper, the inside ones are the key, and the dotted ones, the section that is made of the whole for the purpose of keeping it secret, should any *graceless cowan* ever get possession of the sacred ark, and attempt to rummage its contents. The other part of the key X is made on the back of the same piece of paper, so that on putting them together, it shows equally plain. It is said that these characters were used by Aaron Burr, in carrying on his treasonable practices, and by that means made public; since which time they have been written and read from left to right. After the ceremonies are ended, the High Priest informs the candidates, in many or few words, according to his ability, that this degree owes its origin to Zerubbabel and his associates, who rebuilt the temple by order of Cyrus, king of Persia. He informs them that the discovery of the secret vault and the inestimable treasures, with the long lost *word*, actually took place in the manner represented in conferring this degree, and that it is the circumstance upon which the degree is principally founded. The ceremony of closing a chapter is precisely the same as at opening, to the raising of the living arch. The companions join hands by threes, in the same manner, and say in concert, with the same ceremony, 'As we three did agree, the sacred word to keep,' 'As we three did agree, the sacred word to search,' 'So we three do agree, to close this royal arch.' They then break without giving the word, as the High Priest reads the following prayer : By the wisdom of the Supreme High Priest may we be directed, by his strength may we be enabled, and by the beauty of virtue may we be incited, to perform the obligations here enjoined upon us, to keep inviolable the mysteries here unfolded to us, and invariably to practice all those duties out of the chapter, which are inculcated in it. (Response.) So mote it be. Amen. The High Priest then declares the chapter closed in due form.

KNIGHTS OF THE RED CROSS.

At the sound of the trumpet the line is formed. Master of Cavalry to the Sir Knight Warden, 'When a council of Knights of the Red Cross is about to be formed and opened, what is the first care?' Warden, 'To see the council chamber duly guarded.' M. C. 'Please to attend to that part of your duty, see that the sentinels are at their respective posts, and inform the captain of the Guards that we are about to open a council of Knights of the Red Cross for the despatch of business.' W. 'The sentinels are at their respective posts, and the council chamber duly guarded.' M. C. 'Are all present Knights of the Red Cross?' W. 'They are.' M. C. 'Attention, Sir Knights, count yourselves from right to left—right files handle sword—draw sword—carry sword—right files to the left double—second division forward, march, halt—right about face.' Sir Knight Master of infantry, accompanied by the sword-bearer and Warden, 'Please inform the Sovereign Master that the lines are formed waiting his pleasure.' At the approach of the council the trumpet sounds. M. C. 'Form avenue : (the council pass :) the Sovereign Master passes uncovered : recover arms, poise arms.' Sovereign Master, 'Attention, Sir Knights ; give your attention to the several signs of Masonry : as I do, so do you.' [The Sir Knights give the sign from the first to the seventh degree.] S. M. 'Draw swords— take care to advance and give the Jewish countersign—recover arms : take care to advance and give the Persian countersign— recover arms.' S. M. to Sir Knight Master of the Palace, 'Advance, and give me the word of a Knight of the Red Cross : the word is right—receive it on your left.' The word is then passed around: When it arrives at the Chancellor, he says, 'Sovereign Master of the Red Cross, word has arrived.' S. M. 'Pass it on to me: [he gives it to the Sovereign Master.] Sir Knight, the word is right.' S. M. to Sir Knight Chancellor, 'Advance, and give me the grand sign, grip, and word of a Knight of the Red Cross: it is right—receive it on your left.' [The word passes around as before, as will hereafter be explained, and when arrived at the Master of the Palace, he says,] 'Sovereign Master, the grand sign, grip, and word have arrived.' S. M. 'Pass them on to me: Sir Knight they are right. Left face—deposit helmets—centre face—reverse arms—to your devotions, [the Sir Knights all kneel and repeat the Lord's prayer:] recover arms—left face—recover helmets—centre face—right about face—to your posts—march.'

FIRST SECTION OF LECTURES.

1st. Q. Are you a Knight of the Red Cross? A. That is my profession. 2d. Q. By what test will you be tried? A. By the test of truth. 3d. Q. Why by the test of truth? A. Because none but the good and true are entitled to the honors and privileges of this illustrious order. 4th. Q. Where did you receive the honors of this illustrious order? A. In a just and regular council of Knights of the Red Cross. 5th. Q. What number compose a council? A. There is an indispensable number and a constitutional number. 6th. Q. What is the indispensable number? A. Three. 7th. Q. Under what circumstances are they authorized to form and open a council of Knights of the Red Cross? A. Three Knights of the Red Cross, being also Knight Templars, and hailing from three different commanderies, may, under the sanction of a legal warrant from some regular Grand Encampment, form and open a council of Knights of the Red Cross for the despatch of business. 8th. Q. What is a constitutional number? A. Five, seven, nine, eleven, or more. 9th. Q. When composed of five, seven, nine, eleven, of whom does it consist? A. Sovereign Master, Chancellor, Master of the Palace, Prelate, Master of Cavalry, Master of Infantry, Master of Finance, Master of Despatches, Standard bearer, Sword bearer, and Warder. 10th. Q. Warder's station in the council? A. On the left of the Standard bearer in the west. 11th. His duty? A. To announce the approach of the Sovereign Master; to see that the sentinels are at their respective posts, and the council chamber duly guarded. 12th. Q. Sword bearer's station in the council? A. On the right of the Standard bearer in the west. 13th. Q. His duty? A. To assist in the protection of the banners of our order: to watch all signals from the Sovereign Master, and see his orders duly executed. 14th. Q. Standard bearer's station? A. In the west. 15th. Q. His duty? A. To display, support, and protect the banners of our order. 16th. Q. Why is the Standard bearer's station in the west? A. That the brilliant rays of the rising sun, shedding their lustre upon the banners of our order, may encourage and animate all true and courteous Knights, and dismay and confound their enemies. 17th. Q. Station of Master of Despatches? A. In front of the Master of the Palace. 18th. Q. His duty? A. To observe with attention the transactions of the council; to keep a just and regular record thereof, collect the revenue, and pay the same over to the Master of Finance. 19th. Q. Station of the Master of Finance? A. In front of the Chancellor. 20th. Q. His duty? A. To receive in charge the funds and property of the council, pay all orders drawn upon the Treasurer, and render a just and regular account when called for. 21st. Q. Station of the Master of infantry? A. On the right of the second division, when separately formed; on the left of the whole when formed in line. 22d. Q. His duty? A. To command the second division or line of infantry, teach them their duty and exercise; also to prepare all candidates, attend them on their journey, answer all questions for them, and finally introduce them into the council chamber. 23d. Q. Station of the Master of Cavalry? A. On the right of the first division when separately formed, and on the right of the whole when formed in line. 24th. Q. His duty? A. To command the first division or line of cavalry, teach them their duty and exercise; to form the avenue at the approach of the Sovereign Master, and prepare the lines for inspection and review. 25th. Q. Prelate's station? A. On the right of the Chancellor. 26th. Q. His duty? A. To preside in the Royal Arch Council; administer at the altar; to offer up prayers and adoration to Deity. 27th. Q. Station of Master of the Palace? A. On the left of the Sovereign Master in the East. 28th. Q. His duty? A. To see that the proper officers make all due preparations for the several meetings of the council; to take special care that the council chamber is in suitable array for the reception of candidates, and the despatch of business; to receive and communicate all orders issued by the Sovereign Master, through the officers of the line. 29th. Q. Chancellor's station? A. On the right of the Sovereign Master. 30th. Q. His duty? A. To receive and communicate all orders and petitions; to assist the Sovereign Master in the discharge of his various duties, and in his absence to preside in the council. 31st. Q. Sovereign Master's station? A. In the east. 32d. Q. His duty? A. To preside in the council; confer this order of Knighthood upon those whom his council may approve; to preserve inviolate the laws and constitution of our order; to dispense justice, reward merit, encourage truth, and diffuse the sublime principles of universal benevolence. S. M. 'Sir Knight Chancellor, it is my will and pleasure that a council of Knights of the Red Cross be now opened, and to stand open for the despatch of such business as may regularly come before it at this time, requiring all Sir Knights now assembled, or who may come at this time, to govern themselves according to the sublime principles of our order. You will communicate this to the Sir Knight Master of the Palace, that the Sir Knights present may have due notice thereof, and govern themselves accordingly.' [The Sir Knight Chancellor communicates it to the Sir Knight Master of the Palace, and he to the Knights.] S. M. 'Return arms; right about face; to your posts; march; centre face; Sir Knights, this Council is now open for the despatch of business.'

SECOND SECTION OF LECTURES.

1st. Q. What were the preparatory circumstances attending your reception to this illustrious order? A. A council of Royal Arch Masons being assembled in a room adjacent to the council chamber, I was conducted to the door, where a regular demand was made by two, three, and two. 2d. Q. What was said to you from within? A. Who comes there. 3d. Q. Your answer? A. Companion A. B., who has regularly received the several degrees of Entered Apprentice, Fellow Craft, Master Mason, Mark Master, Past Master, Most Excellent Master, and Royal Arch degree, and now solicits the honor of being regularly constituted a Knight of the Red Cross. 4th. Q. What was then said to you? A. I was asked if it was of my own free will and accord that I made this request; if I was worthy and well qualified; if I had made suitable proficiency in the foregoing degrees, and was properly vouched for: all of which being answered in the affirmative, I was asked by what further right or benefit I expected to gain admittance. 5th. Q. Your answer? A. By the benefit of a pass word. 6th. Q. Did you give that pass word? A. I did, with the assistance of my companions. [Here the Royal Arch Word is given as described in the Royal Arch degree.] 7th. Q. What was then said to you? A. I was then directed to wait with patience till the Most Excellent Prelate should be informed of my request, and his answer returned. 8th. Q. What was his answer? A. Let him be admitted. 9th. Q. What was you then informed? A. The Most Excellent Prelate observed, that the council there assembled, represented the grand council convened at Jerusalem, in the second year of the reign of Darius, king of Persia, to deliberate on the unhappy state of the fraternity during the reigns of Artaxerxes and Ahasuerus, and to devise some means to obtain favor of the new Sovereign, and to gain his consent to proceed in rebuilding their new city and temple. 10th. Q. What followed? A. The Most Excellent Prelate then informed me that if I was desirous of attending the deliberations of the council at this time, it was necessary that I should assume the name and character of Zerubbabel, a prince of the house of Judah, whose hands laid the foundation of the second temple, and whose hands the Lord had promised should complete it. 11th. Q. What followed? A. The Most Excellent Prelate then read a lesson from the records of the Fathers, stating the impediments with which they were troubled by their adversaries, on the other side of the river, and the grievous accusations which were brought against them before the king. 12th. Q. What followed? A. My conductor then addressed the Most Excellent Prelate thus: Most Excellent Prelate, our Sovereign Lord, Darius the King, having now ascended the throne of Persia, new hopes are inspired of protection and support in the noble and glorious undertaking, which has been so long and so often interrupted by our adversaries on the other side of the river; for while yet a private man, he made a vow to God that should he ever ascend the throne of Persia, he would send all the Holy vessels remaining at Babylon back to Jerusalem.* Our Most Excellent and faithful companion Zerubbabel, who was formerly honored with the favorable notice and friendship of the Sovereign, now offers his services to encounter the hazardous enterprise of traversing the Persian dominions, and seeking admission to the presence of the Sovereign, where the first favorable moment will be seized to remind the King of his vow, and impress on his mind the almighty force and importance of truth; and from his known piety, no doubt can be entertained of gaining his consent, that our enemies be removed far hence, and that we be no longer hindered or impeded in our noble and glorious undertaking. 13th. Q. What was the Most Excellent Prelate's reply? A. Excellent Zerubbabel, the council accept with gratification and joy your noble and generous offer, and will invest you with the necessary passports, by means of which you will be enabled to make yourself known to the favor of one council wherever you may meet them; but in an undertaking of so much importance, it is necessary that you enter into a solemn obligation, to be faithful to the trust reposed in you. 14th. Q. What followed? A. The Most Excellent Prelate then invested me with

---

* This is not found in the scriptures, and is contrary to all probability.—"Add thou not unto his words lest he reprove thee and thou be found a liar." Prov. xxx, 6.

a sword, to enable me to defend myself against my enemies, and said he was ready to administer the obligation. 15th. Q. Did you consent to that obligation ? A. I did in due form. 16th. Q. What was that due form ? A. Kneeling on my left knee, my right foot forming a square, my body erect, my right hand grasping the hilt of my sword, my left hand covering the Holy Bible, Square and Compass, with two cross-swords thereon, in which due form I took upon me the solemn oath and obligation of Knight of the Red Cross. 17th. Q. Repeat the obligation.

'I, A. B., of my own free will and accord, in the presence of the Supreme Architect of the Universe, and these witnesses, do hereby and hereon, most solemnly and sincerely promise and swear, that I will always hail, forever conceal, and never reveal, any of the secret arts, parts or points of the mysteries appertaining to this order of Knight of the Red Cross, unless it be to a true and lawful companion Sir Knight of the order, or within the body of a just and lawful council of such ; and not unto him or them, until by due trial, strict examination or lawful information, I find him or them lawfully entitled to receive the same.—I furthermore promise and swear, that I will answer and obey all due signs and regular summons, which shall be sent to me from a regular council of Knights of the Red Cross, or given to me from the hands of a companion Sir Knight of the Red Cross, if within the distance of forty miles ; natural infirmities and unavoidable accidents only excusing me.—I furthermore promise and swear, that I will not be present at the conferring of this order of Knighthood upon any person, unless he shall have previously regularly received the several degrees of Entered Apprentice, Fellow Craft, Master Mason, Mark Master, Past Master, Most Excellent Master, and Royal Arch degree, to the best of my knowledge and belief.— I furthermore promise and swear, that I will not assist or be present at the forming and opening of a council of Knights of the Red Cross, unless there be present at least five regular Knights of the order, or the representatives of three different Encampments, acting under the sanction of a legal warrant.—I furthermore promise and swear, that I will vindicate the character of a courteous Sir Knight of the Red Cross, when wrongfully traduced : that I will help him on a lawful occasion in preference to any brother of an inferior degree, and so far as truth, honor and justice may warrant.—I furthermore promise and swear, that I will support and maintain the by-laws of the council of which I may hereafter become a member, the laws and regulations of the Grand Encampment under which the same may be holden, together with the constitution and ordinances of the General Grand

Encampment of the United States of America, so far as the same shall come to my knowledge—to all which I do most solemnly promise and swear, binding myself under no less penalty than of having my house torn down, the timbers thereof set up, and I hanged thereon; and when the last trump shall blow, that I be forever excluded from the society of all true and courteous Knights, should I ever wilfully or knowingly violate any part of this solemn obligation of Knight of the Red Cross; so help me God, and keep me steadfast to keep and perform the same.*

18th. Q. What followed? A. The Most excellent Prelate then directed me to rise and be invested with a countersign, which he informed me would enable me to make myself known to the friends of our cause wherever I should meet them, and would ensure me from them, succor, aid and protection. [Here the Master of Infantry, who is the conductor, gives the candidate the Jewish countersign: it is given under the Arch of steel, that is, their swords elevated above their heads, forming a cross, each placing his left hand upon the other's right shoulder, and whispering alternately in each other's ear, the names of Judah and Benjamin.] 19th. Q. What followed? A. The Most Excellent Prelate then invested me with a green sash, as a mark of our particular friendship and esteem: you will wear it as a constant memorial to stimulate you to the faithful performance of every duty, being assured that the memory of him who falls in a just and virtuous cause, shall forever flourish like the green bay tree. 20th. Q. What followed? A. I then commenced my journey, and was frequently accosted by guards, all of which, by means of the countersign I had received, I was enabled to pass in friendship, until I arrived at the bridge, which was represented to be in the Persian dominions: on attempting to pass this bridge, which I found strongly guarded, the Persian countersign was demanded, and being unable to give it, I was attacked, overpowered, and made prisoner. 21st. Q. What followed? A. After remonstrating in vain against their violations, I told them I was a prince of the house of Judah, and demanded an audience with their sovereign. 22d. Q. What was the answer? A. You are a prisoner, and can obtain an audience with the sovereign only in the garb of a captive and slave. 23d. Q. Did you consent to this? A. I did; being firmly persuaded, that could I by any means gain access to the presence of the sovereign, I should be able to accomplish the object of my

---

* By this tremendous imprecation—the candidate of his "own free will and accord" volunteers (in case of a violation,) to come forth to the resurrection of damnation, and receive the sentence, "depart thou accursed into everlasting fire prepared for the devil and his angels."

mission. 24th. Q. What followed? A. They then deprived me of my outward apparel, sash and sword, and having confined my hands and feet in chains, the links thereof were of a triangular form, they put sackcloth and ashes on my head. 25th. Q. Why were the links of the captive's chain of a triangular form? A. The Assyrians having learned that among the Jews the triangle was an emblem of the Eternal, caused the links of their chains to be made of a triangular form, thinking thereby to add to the miseries of their captives. 26th. Q. What followed? A. I was conducted to the door of the council chamber, where the alarm being given by 4×2, the warder appeared and demanded, 'Who comes there?' 27th. Q. What answer was returned? A. A detachment of his majesty's guards having made prisoner of one, who reports himself to be prince of the house of Judah. 28th. Q. What was then said to you? A. I was asked from whence I came. 29th. Q. Your answer? A. From Jerusalem. 30th. Q. What was then demanded of you? A. Who are you. 31st. Q. Your answer? A. The first among my equals, a Mason, and free by rank, but a captive and slave by misfortune. 32d. Q. What was you then asked? A. My name. 33d. Q. Your answer? A. Zerubbabel. 34th. Q. What were you then asked? A. What are your demands. 35th. Q. Your answer? A. To see the Sovereign if possible. 36th. Q. What was then said to you? A. I was then directed to wait with patience until the Sovereign Master should be informed of my request, and his answer returned. 37th. Q. What was that answer? A. That the necessary caution should be taken that I was not armed with any hostile weapons, and that I should then be admitted. 38th. Q. How were you then received? A. The guard being drawn up on the right and left of the throne, swords drawn, two of them placed at the door with swords crossed, under which I was permitted to enter, my face covered with my hands. 39th. Q. How were you then disposed of? A. I was conducted in front of the Sovereign Master, who received me with kindness and attention, and listened with patience to my request. 40th. Q. What did the Sovereign Master then observe to the council? A. That this Zerubbabel was the friend of his youth, that he could neither be an enemy nor a spy. 41st. Q. What followed? A. The Sovereign Master thus addressed me, 'Zerubbabel, having now gained admittance into our presence, we demand that you immediately declare the particular motives which induced you, without our permission, and with force and arms, to pass the lines of our dominions?' 42d. Q. Your answer? A. Sovereign Master, the tears and complaints of my companions at Jerusalem, who have been so long and so often impeded in the noble and glorious undertaking in which they were permitted to engage by our late Sovereign Lord Cyrus the King; but our enemies having made that great work to cease by force and power, I have now come up to implore your majesty's clemency, that you would be pleased to restore me to favor, and grant me employment among the servants of your household. 43d. Q. What was the Sovereign's reply? A. Zerubbabel, I have often reflected with much pleasure upon our early intimacy and friendship, and I have frequently heard, with great satisfaction, of your fame as a wise and accomplished Mason, and having myself a profound veneration for that ancient and honorable institution, and having a sincere desire to become a member of the same. I will this moment grant your request, on condition that you will reveal to me the secrets of Free Masonry. 44th. Q. Did you consent to that? A. I did not. 45th. Q. What was your reply? A. Sovereign Master, when our Grand Master Solomon, King of Israel, first instituted the Fraternity of Free and Accepted Masons, he taught us that truth was a divine attribute, and the foundation of every virtue: to be good and true is the first lesson we are taught in Masonry. My engagements are sacred and inviolable; I cannot reveal our secrets. If I can obtain your Majesty's favor only at the expense of my integrity, I humbly beg leave to decline your royal protection, and will cheerfully submit to an honorable exile. 46th. Q. What was the sovereign's reply? A. Zerubbabel, your virtue and integrity are truly commendable, and your fidelity to your engagements, is worthy of imitation: from this moment you are free—my guards will divest you of those chains and that garb of slavery, and clothe you in suitable habiliments to attend me at the banquet hall. Zerubbabel, you are free: guards, strike off those chains; and may those emblems of slavery never again disgrace the hands of a Mason, more particularly a prince of the house of Judah; Zerubbabel, we assign you a seat of rank and honor among the princes and rulers of our assembly. 47th. Q. What followed? A. The guards being drawn up in the court yard, the warder informed the Sovereign Master that the guards were in readiness, waiting his pleasure. 48th. Q. What followed? A. He then ordered the guards to attend him to the banquet hall. 49th. Q. What occurred there? A. After having participated in a liberal entertainment, the Sovereign Master not being inclined to sleep, and many of the guard having retired, he amused himself by entering into conversation with some of his principal officers and friends, proposing certain questions to them, and offering a princely reward to such as should give the most reasonable and satisfactory answer. 50th. Q. What questions were proposed? A. Among others, 'Which was the strongest, wine, the king, or woman ?"* 51st. Q. What answers were returned ? A. The Chancellor said wine was the strongest; the Master of the Palace said the king was the strongest; but I, being firmly persuaded that the time had arrived in which I could remind the king of his vow, and request the fulfilment of it, replied that women were stronger than either of the former, but above all things truth beareth the victory. 52d. Q. What followed? A. The king being deeply struck with the addition I made to the question, ordered us to be prepared with proper arguments in support of our respective propositions on the day following. 53d. Q. What followed? A. On the day following the council being convened at the sound of the trumpet, the Chancellor was called upon for his answer, and thus replied, (see templar's chart.) 54th. Q. What followed? A. The Master of the Palace thus replied, (see templar's chart.) 55th. Q. What followed ? A. I then being called upon for my defence, answered as follows, (see templar's chart.) 56th. Q. What followed ? A. The king being deeply struck with the force of the arguments I had used, involuntarily exclaimed, 'Great is truth, and mighty above all things: Ask what thou wilt, Zerubbabel, and it shall be granted thee, for thou art found wisest among thy companions.' 57th. Your answer? (See templar's chart.) 58th. Q. What followed ? A. The sovereign Master thus addressed me, Zerubbabel, I will punctually fulfil my vow: letters and passports shall be immediately issued to my officers throughout the realm, and they shall give you, and those who accompany you, safe conveyance to Jerusalem, and you shall be no longer hindered or impeded in rebuilding your city and temple, until they shall be completed.' 59th. Q. What followed? A. The Sovereign Master then invested me with a green sash, and thus addressed me, ' This green sash, of which you were deprived by my guards, I now with pleasure restore to you, and will make it one of the insignia of a new order, calculated to perpetuate the remembrance of the event which caused the renewal of our friendship ; its color will remind you that truth is a divine attribute, and shall prevail, and shall forever flourish in immortal green. I will now confer on you the highest honor, in our power at this time to bestow, and will create you the first Knight of an order, instituted for the express purpose of inculcating the almighty force and importance of truth. 60th. Q. What followed ? A. The Sovereign Master then directed me to kneel, and said, by virtue of the high power in me vested, as the successor and representative of Darius, king of Persia, I now constitute you a Knight of the illus-

---

* See the Apocryphal books, 1, Esdras, chapters iii. and iv.

trious order of the Red Cross—(at the same time laying the blade of his sword, first upon the right shoulder, then upon the head, and then upon the left shoulder of the candidate.) 61st. Q. What followed? A. The Sovereign Master then directed me to arise, and presenting me with a sword, thus addressed me, 'This sword, of which you were deprived by my guards, I now restore in your hands, as a true and courteous Knight : it will be endowed with three most excellent properties—its hilt be faith, its blade be hope, its point be charity : it should teach us this important lesson, that when we draw our swords in a just and virtuous cause, having faith in God, we may reasonably hope for victory, ever remembering to extend the hand of charity to the fallen foe : sheathe it, and sooner may it rust in its scabbard, than be drawn in the cause of injustice or oppression.' 62d. Q. What followed? A. The Sovereign Master then invested me with the Persian countersign. 63d. Q. Give it ? A This countersign is given like the Jewish, excepting this variation, it is given over instead of under the arch of steel. The words are Tatnai Shethar-boznai, Ezra, v. 3. 64th. Q. Who were they ? A. They were governors of Persian provinces, and enemies of the Jews. 65th. Q. What followed? A. The Sovereign Master then invested me with the Red Cross word. 66th. Q. Give it ? A. (Each placing his left hand upon the other's right shoulder, at the same time bringing the point of the swords to each other's left side, in which position the word Libertas is given.) 67th. Q. What followed ? A. The Sovereign Master then invested me with the grand sign, grip and word of Knight of the Red Cross. 68th. Q. Give them.—The grand sign is given by bringing the thumb and finger of the left hand to the mouth, and carrying it off in an oblique direction—the grip is given by interlacing the fingers of the left hands—the word is Veritas. The sign, grip and word is given under the arch of steel. 69th. Q. How do you translate the word ? A. Truth. 70th. Q. To what does the sign allude ? A. To the blowing of the trumpet upon the walls and watch towers of the council, but more particularly to the obligation, ' that when the last trump shall sound, I shall be forever excluded from the society of all true and faithful Sir Knights.' 71st. Q. What is the motto of our order ? A. ' Magna est veritas et prevalebit.*

---

* Great is truth and it will prevail.

KNIGHT TEMPLAR, AND KNIGHT OF MALTA.

1st. Q. Are you a Knight Templar? A. That is my title. 2d. Q. Where were you created a Knight Templar? A. In a just and lawful encampment of Knight Templars. 3d. Q. What number composes a just and lawful encampment of Knight Templars? A. There is an indispensable number, and a constitutional number. 4th. Q. What is an indispensable number. A. Three. 5th. Q. Under what circumstances are they authorised to form and open an encampment of Knight Templars? A. Three Knight Templars, hailing from three different commanderies, may, under the sanction of a charter, or warrant, from some regular Grand Encampment, form and open an encampment for the despatch of business. 6th. Q. What is a constitutional number? A. Seven, nine, eleven, or more. 7th. Q. When composed of eleven, of whom does it consist? A. Warder, Sword Bearer, Standard Bearer, Recorder, Treasurer, Junior Warden, Senior Warden, Prelate, Captain General, Generalissimo, and Grand Commander. 8th. Q. Warder's station? A. On the left of the Standard Bearer in the west, and on the left of the third division. 9th. Q. His duty? A. To observe the orders and directions of the Grand Commander; to see that the sentinels are at their respective posts, and that the encampment is duly guarded. 10th. Q. Sword Bearer's station? A. On the right of the Standard Bearer in the west, and on the right of the third division. 11th. Q. His duty? A. To assist in the protection of the banners of our order; to watch all signals from the Grand Commander, and see his orders duly executed. 12th. Q. Standard Bearer's station in the encampment? A. In the west, and in the centre of the third division. 13th. Q. His duty? A. To display, support, and protect the banners of our order. 14th. Q. Why is the Standard Bearer's station in the west? A. That the brilliant rays of the rising sun, shedding their lustre upon the banners of our order, may encourage and animate all true and courteous Knights, and dismay and confound their enemies. 15th. Q. Recorder's station in the encampment? A. In front of the Captain General. 16th. Q. His duty? A. To observe with attention the order of the encampment; keep a just and regular record of the same; collect the revenue, and pay the same over to the Treasurer. 17th. Q. Treasurer's station in the encampment? A. In front of the Generalissimo. 18th. Q. His duty? A. To receive in charge all funds and property of the encampment; pay all orders drawn upon him, and render a just and faithful account when required. 19th. Q. Station of the Junior Warden in the encampment? A. At the south west angle of the triangle, and on the left of the first division. 20th. Q. His duty? A. To attend to all poor and weary pilgrims travelling from afar; to accompany them on their journey; answer all questions for them, and finally introduce them into the asylum. 21st. Q. Senior Warden's station in the encampment? A. At the north west angle of the triangle, and on the right of the second division. 22d. Q. His duty there? A. To attend on pilgrim warriors, travelling from afar; to comfort and support pilgrims penitent, and, after due trial, to recommend them to the hospitality of the Generalissimo. 23d. Q. Prelate's station in the encampment? A. On the right of the Generalissimo. 24th. Q. His duty there? A. To administer at the altar, and offer up prayers and adorations to the Deity. 25th. Q. Captain General's station? A. On the left of the Grand Commander. 26th. Q. His duty? A. To see that the proper officers make all suitable preparations for the several meetings of the encampment, and take special care that the asylum is in a suitable array for the introduction of candidates and despatch of business; also, to receive and communicate all orders from the Grand Commander to the officers of the line. 27th. Q. Generalissimo's station? A. On the right of the Grand Commander. 28th. Q. His duty? A. To receive and communicate all orders, signals, and petitions, and assist the Grand Commander in the discharge of his various duties, and in his absence to govern the encampment. 29th. Q. Grand Commander's station? A. In the east. 30th. Q. His duty? A. To distribute alms, and protect weary pilgrims, travelling from afar; to encourage pilgrim warriors: to sustain pilgrims penitent; feed the hungry, clothe the naked, bind up the wounds of the afflicted; to inculcate hospitality, and govern his encampment with justice and moderation.

SECOND SECTION OF LECTURES.

1st. Q. What were the preparatory circumstances attending your reception into this Illustrious Order? A. I was conducted to the chamber of reflection, where I was left in silence and solitude, to reflect upon three questions which were left with me in writing. 2d. Q. What were your answers? A. They were satisfactory to the Grand Commander; but, as a trial of my patience and perseverance, he enjoined upon me the performance of seven years' pilgrimage, clothed in pilgrim's weeds. 3d. Q. What followed? A. I was then invested with sandals, staff, and scrip, and commenced my tour of pilgrimage, but was soon accosted by a guard, who demanded of me 'Who comes there?' 4th. Q. Your answer? A. A poor and weary pilgrim, travelling from afar, to join with those who oft have gone before, and offer his devotions at the holy shrine. 5th. Q. What said the guard? A. Pilgrim, I greet thee; gold and silver have

I none, but such as I have give I unto thee. 6th. What followed? After having participated in the refreshments, (which is a glass of water and a cracker,) the guard took me by the hand, and thus addressed me : 'Pilgrim, hearken to a lesson to cheer thee on thy way, and insure thee of success.' 7th. What followed? Lesson read. (See Templar's chart.) The guard then took me by the hand, and said, 'Fare thee well! God speed thee on thy way.' 8th. What followed? I still pursued my pilgrimage, but was often accosted by guards, from whom I received the same friendly treatment, as from the first. 9th. Where did your term of pilgrimage end? At the door of the asylum, where after giving the alarm by 3×3, the Warder appeared and demanded, 'who comes there?' 10th. Your answer? A poor and weary pilgrim, travelling from afar, who, having passed full three long years of pilgrimage, now craves permission, if it shall please the Grand Commander, forthwith to dedicate the remaining four years to deeds of more exalted usefulness, and if found worthy, his strong desire is now to be admitted to those valiant Knights, whose well-earned fame has spread both far and near for deeds of charity and pure beneficence. 11th. What were you then asked? What surety can you offer that you are no impostor. 12th. Your answer? The commendations of a true and courteous Knight, the Junior Warden, who recommends to the Grand Commander the remission of the four remaining years of pilgrimage. 13th. What followed? The Grand Commander then addressed the Most Excellent Prelate :—This being true, Sir Knight, our Prelate, you will conduct this weary pilgrim to the altar, where having taken an obligation always to be faithful to his vow, cause him forthwith to be invested with a sword and buckler, that as a prilgrim warrior, he may perform seven years' warfare, as a trial of his courage and constancy. 14th. What followed? The Senior Warden then detached a party of Knights to escort me to the altar, where, in due form, I took upon me the obligation of a Knight Templar. 15th. What was that due form? Kneeling on both knees upon two cross swords, my body erect, my naked hands covering the Holy Bible, square, and compass, with two cross swords lying thereon ; in which due form I received the solemn obligation of Knight Templar. 16th. Repeat the obligation.

'I, A. B., of my own free will and accord, in the presence of Almighty God, and this Encampment of Knight Templars, do hereby and hereon, most solemnly promise and swear, that I will always hail, forever conceal, and never reveal any of the secret arts, parts, or points appertaining to the mysteries of this order of Knight Templars, unless it be to a true and lawful companion

Knight Templar, or within the body of a just and lawful Encampment of such ; and not unto him or them, until by due trial, strict examination, or lawful information, I find him or them lawfully entitled to receive the same. Furthermore, do I promise and swear, that I will answer and obey all due signs and regular summons, which shall be given or sent to me from regular Encampments of Knight Templars, if within the distance of forty miles— natural infirmities and unavoidable accidents only excusing me. Furthermore, do I promise and swear, that I will help, aid, and assist with my council, my purse, and my sword, all poor and indigent Knight Templars, their widows and orphans, they making application to me as such, and I finding them worthy, so far as I can do it without material injury to myself, and so far as truth, honour, and justice may warrant. Furthermore, do I promise and swear, that I will not assist, or be present, at the forming and opening of an Encampment of Knight Templars, unless there be present seven Knights of the order, or the representatives of three different Encampments, acting under the sanction of a legal warrant. Furthermore, do I promise and swear, that I will go the distance of forty miles, even barefoot and on frosty ground, to save the life and relieve the distresses of a worthy Knight, should I know that his distresses required it, and my abilities permit. Furthermore, do I promise and swear, that I will wield my sword in defence of innocent virgins, destitute widows, helpless orphans, and the Christian religion. Furthermore, do I promise and swear, that I will support and maintain the by-laws of the Encampment of which I may hereafter become a member, the edicts and regulations of the Grand Encampment under which the same may be holden, together with the laws and constitution of the General Grand Encampment of the United States of America, so far as the same shall come to my knowledge.—To all this I most solemnly and sincerely promise and swear, with a firm and steady resolution to perform and keep the same, without any hesitation, equivocation, mental reservation, or self-evasion of mind in me whatever, binding myself under no less penalty than to have my head struck off and placed on the highest spire in Christendom, should I knowingly or wilfully violate any part of this my solemn obligation of a Knight Templar. So help me God, and keep me steadfast to perform and keep the same.'

17th. What followed? The Most Excellent Prelate directed me to arise, and thus addressed me :—' Pilgrim, thou hast craved permission to pass through our solemn ceremonies, and enter the asylum of our encampment ; by thy sandals, scrip, and staff, I judge thee to be a child of humility : charity and hospitality are the grand characteristics of this magnanimous order: in the characters of Knight Templars, you are bound to give alms to poor and weary pilgrims travelling from afar; to succor the needy, feed the hungry, clothe the naked, and bind up the wounds of the afflicted. We here wage war against the enemies of innocent virgins, destitute widows, helpless orphans, and the Christian religion.* If thou art desirous of enlisting in this noble and glorious warfare, lay aside thy staff and take up the sword, fighting manfully thy way, and with valor running thy course; and may the Almighty, who is a strong tower and defence to all those who put their trust and confidence in Him, be now and ever thy defence and thy salvation.' 18th. What followed? Having laid aside my staff and taken up the sword, the Most Excellent Prelate continued:—'Having now taken up the sword, we expect you will make a public declaration of the cause in which you will wield it.' 19th. Your answer? I wield my sword in defence of innocent virgins, destitute widows, helpless orphans, and the Christian religion. 20th. What was the Prelate's reply? With confidence in this profession, our Senior Warden will invest you with the warrior's pass, and under his direction, as a trial of your courage and constancy, we must now assign you seven years of warfare—success and victory attend you. (This pass word is Maher-shalal-hashbaz, and is given under the arch of steel, as has been described.) 21st. What followed? I then commenced my tour of warfare, and made professions of the cause in which I would wield my sword. 22d. Where did your tour of warfare end? At the door of the asylum, where, on giving the alarm by 3×4, the Warder appeared and demanded, 'Who comes there?' 23d. Your reply? A pilgrim warrior, travelling from afar, who, having passed full three long years of warfare, is most desirous now, if it should please the Grand Commander, to be admitted to the honors and rewards that await a valiant Templar. 24th. What was then demanded of you? What surety can you give that you are no impostor. 25th. Your answer? The commendation of a true and courteous Knight, the Senior Warden, who recommends to the Grand Commander the remission of the four remaining years of warfare. 26th. What was then demanded? By what further right or benefit do you expect to gain admittance to the asylum. 27th. Your answer? By the benefit of a pass word. 28th. Give it. (Here the warrior's pass is given, as be-

---

* Says God, 'They that take the *sword*, shall perish with the sword.'
'The *wrath* of man worketh not the righteousness of God.'
'The weapons of our warfare are not carnal.'

fore described.) 29th. What was then said to you? I was directed to wait with courage and constancy, and soon an answer should be returned to my request. 30th. What answer was returned? Let him be admitted. 31st. What did the Grand Commander then observe? Pilgrim, having gained admittance to our asylum, what profession have you now to make in testimony of your fitness to be received a Knight among our number. 32d. Your answer? Most Eminent, I now declare in truth and soberness, that I hold no enmity or hatred against a being on earth, that I would not freely reconcile, should I find in him a corresponding disposition. 33d. What was the Grand Commander's reply? Pilgrim, the sentiments you utter are worthy of the cause in which you are engaged; but still we must require some stronger proofs of your faithfulness: the proofs we demand are, that you participate with us in five libations; this being accomplished, we will receive you a Knight among our number. 34th. What were the ingredients of the libations? Four of them were taken in wine and water, and the fifth in pure wine. 35th. What was the first libation? To the memory of Solomon, king of Israel. 36th. What was the second libation? To the memory of Hiram, king of Tyre. 37th. What was the third? To the memory of Hiram, the widow's son, who lost his life in defence of his integrity. 38th. What followed? The Grand Commander then addressed me: Pilgrim, the order to which you seek to unite yourself, is founded on the Christian religion; let us, then, attend to a lesson from the holy evangelist. 39th. What followed? The Most Excellent Prelate then read a lesson, relative to the apostacy of Judas Iscariot. (See Templar's chart.) 40th. What followed? The Grand Commander then addressed me: 'Pilgrim, the twelve tapers you see around the triangle, correspond in number with the disciples of our Saviour while on earth, one of whom fell by transgression, and betrayed his Lord and Master; and as a constant admonition to you always to persevere in the paths of honor, integrity, and truth, and as a perpetual memorial of the apostacy of Judas Iscariot, you are required, by the rules of our order, to extinguish one of those tapers; and let it ever remind you, that he, who can basely violate his vow and betray his trust, is worthy of no better fate than Judas Iscariot.' (The candidate extinguishes one of the tapers; the triangle is placed in the centre of the room, on which are twelve burning candles; between each candlestick a glass of wine; in the centre of the triangle is placed a coffin, on which are the Bible, scull, and cross-bones.) 41st. What followed? The relics were then uncovered, and the Grand Commander thus addressed me: 'Pilgrim, you here behold an emblem of mortality resting on divinity,—a human scull resting on the holy scriptures; it is to teach us that, among all the trials and vicissitudes which we are destined to endure while passing through the pilgrimage of this life, a firm reliance on divine protection, can alone afford us the consolation and satisfaction which the world can neither give nor take away.' 42d. What followed? The Most Excellent Prelate then read a lesson to me with respect to the bitter cup. 43d. What followed? The Grand Commander took the scull in his hand, and pronounced the following soliloquy: 'How striking is this emblem of mortality, once animated like us, but now it ceases to act or think; its vital energies are extinct, and all the powers of life have ceased their operations; and such, my brethren, is the state to which we are all hastening: let us, therefore, gratefully improve the remaining space of life, that, when our weak and frail bodies, like this memento, shall become cold and inanimate, and mouldering in sepulchral dust and ruins, our disembodied spirits may soar aloft to the blessed regions where dwells light and life eternal.' 44th. What followed? The Most Excellent Prelate then read a lesson relative to the crucifixion. (See Templar's chart.) 45th. What was the fourth libation? To the memory of Simon, of Cyrene, the early friend and disciple of our Saviour, who was compelled to bear his cross, and fell a martyr to his fate.* 46th. What followed? The Grand Commander then addressed me: 'Pilgrim, before you can be permitted to participate in the fifth libation, we must enjoin on you one year's penance as a trial of your faith and humility, which you will perform under the direction of the Junior and Senior Wardens, with the scull in one hand and a lighted taper in the other; which is to teach you that with faith and humility you should cause your light so to shine before men, that they, seeing your good works, may glorify our Father which is in heaven.' 47th. What followed? I then commenced my tour of penance, and passed in a humble posture through the sepulchre, where the fifth lesson was read by the Senior Warden, relative to the resurrection. (Here the ascension of the Saviour is represented on canvass, which the candidate is directed to look at; at the same time the Sir Knights sing a hymn.) After the hymn the Prelate speaks as follows :—

'I am the resurrection and the life, saith the Lord; he that believeth on me, though he were dead, yet shall he be made alive;

---

* There is no evidence in existence that ' Simon, the Cyrenean,' was a *friend* or *disciple* of Jesus, or that he fell a *martyr* to his fate. This 45th answer, then, is absolutely false!

and whosoever liveth and believeth on me, shall never die. Pilgrim, the scene before you represents the splendid conclusion of the hallowed sacrifice, offered by the Redeemer of the world, to propitiate the anger of an offended Deity. This sacred volume informs us that our Saviour, after having suffered the pains of death, descended into the place of departed spirits, and that on the third day, he burst the bands of death, triumphed over the grave, and, in due time, ascended with transcendent majesty to heaven, where he now sits on the right hand of our Heavenly Father, a mediator and intercessor for all those who have faith in him. I now invest you with an emblem of that faith: (at the same time suspends from his neck a black cross:) it is also an emblem of our order, which you will wear as a constant memorial, for you to imitate the virtues of the immaculate Jesus, who died that you might live. Pilgrim, the ceremonies in which you are now engaged, are calculated deeply to impress your mind, and I trust will have a happy and lasting effect upon your character. You were first, as a trial of your faith and humility, enjoined to perform seven years of pilgrimage; it represents the great pilgrimage of life, through which we are all passing: we are all weary pilgrims, anxiously looking forward to that asylum, where we shall rest from our labors, and be at rest for ever. You were then directed, as a trial of your courage and constancy, to perform seven years' warfare; it represents to you the constant warfare with the lying vanities and deceits of this world, in which it is necessary for us always to be engaged. You are now performing a penance as a trial of your humility. Of this our Lord and Saviour has left us a bright example. For though he was the Eternal Son of God, he humbled himself to be born of a woman, to endure the pains and afflictions incident to human nature, and finally to suffer a cruel and ignominious death upon the cross: it is also a trial of that faith which will conduct you safely over the dark gulf of everlasting death, and land your enfranchised spirit in the peaceful abodes of the blessed. Pilgrim, keep ever in your memory this awful truth; you know not how soon you may be called upon to render an account to that Supreme Judge, from whom not even the most minute act of your life is hidden: for although you now stand erect in all the strength of manhood and pride of beauty, in a few short moments you may become a pale and lifeless corpse. This moment, even while I yet speak, the angel of death may receive the fatal mandate to strike you from the roll of existence; and the friends who now surround you, may be called upon to perform the last sad duty of laying you in the earth a banquet for worms, and this fair body become as the relic you now hold in your hand. Man that is born of a woman, is of few days and full of sorrow; he cometh up and is cut down as a flower; he fleeth as a shadow, and continueth not. In the midst of life, we are in death; of whom may we seek for succor but of thee, O Lord, who for our sins art justly displeased. Yet, O God most holy, thou God most mighty, O holy and most merciful Saviour, deliver us from the pains of eternal death :—I heard a voice from heaven, saying unto me, write from henceforth, blessed are the dead that die in the Lord; even so, saith the spirit, for they rest from their labors : be ye also ready, and rest assured that a firm faith in the truths here revealed, will afford you consolation in the gloomy hour of dissolution, and ensure you ineffable and eternal happiness in the world to come—Amen and Amen.

48th. Where did your tour of penance end? It has not yet ended; neither can it end until this mortal shall put on immortality: for all men err, and all error needs repentance. 49th. Were you then permitted to participate in the fifth libation? I was. 50th. Where? Within the asylum. 51st. How gained you admittance there? After having passed my year of penance, I returned to the door of the asylum, where, on giving the alarm, the Warden appeared and demanded, 'Who comes there?' 52d. Your answer? Pilgrim penitent, travelling from afar, who begs your permission here to rest, and at the shrine of our departed Lord, to offer up his prayers and meditations. 53d. What was then demanded of you? What surety can he offer that he is no impostor. 54th. Your answer? The commendation of two true and courteous Knights, the Junior and Senior Wardens. 55th. What was then demanded of you? By what further right or benefit I expected to gain admittance. 56th. Your answer? By the benefit of a pass word. 57th. Did you give that pass word? I did not; my conductor gave it for me. 58th. Give it. Golgotha : (it is given as before described.) 59th. What was then said to you? Wait with faith and humility, and soon an answer shall be returned to your request. 60th. What was the answer of the Grand Commander? That I should be admitted. 61st. What did the Grand Commander then demand? Who have you there in charge, Sir Knight. 62d. What answer was returned? A pilgrim penitent, travelling from afar, who, having passed his term of penance, seeks now to participate in the fifth libation, thereby to seal his fate. 63d. What did the Grand Commander then observe? Pilgrim, in granting your request, and receiving you a Knight among our number, I can only offer you a rough habit, coarse diet, and severe duties: if, on these conditions, you are still desirous of enlisting under our banners, you will advance and kneel at the base of the triangle. 64th. What did the Grand Commander then observe? Pilgrim, the fifth libation is taken in the most solemn and impressive manner; we cannot be too often reminded that we are born to die : and the fifth libation is an emblem of that bitter cup of death, of which we must all sooner or later partake, and from which even the Saviour of the world, notwithstanding his ardent prayers and solicitations, was not exempt. 65th. The Grand Commander asked me if I had any repugnance to participate in the fifth libation. 66th. Your answer? I am willing to conform to the requirements of the order. 67th. What followed? I then took the cup (the upper part of the human skull,) in my hand, and repeated after the Grand Commander, the following obligation: ' This pure wine I now take in testimony of my belief in the mortality of the body and the immortality of the soul,—and may this libation appear as a witness against me, both here and hereafter,—and as the sins of the world were laid upon the head of the Saviour, so may all the sins committed by the person whose scull this was, be heaped upon my head, in addition to my own, should I ever knowingly or wilfully violate or transgress any obligation that I have heretofore taken, take at this time, or shall, at any future period, take, in relation to any degree of Masonry, or order of Knighthood.* So help me God.' 68th. What was this obligation called? The sealed obligation. 69th. Why so? Because any obligation entered into, or promise made in reference to this obligation, is considered by Knight Templars, as more binding and serious than any other special obligation could be. 70th. What followed? The Most Excellent Prelate then read the sixth lesson, relative to the election of Matthias. (See chart.) 71st. What followed? The Generalissimo thus addressed the Grand Commander:—' Most Eminent, by the extinguished taper on the triangle, I perceive there is a vacancy in our Encampment, which I propose should be filled by a choice from among those valiant Knights, who have sustained the trials and performed the ceremonies required by our order.† 72d. What followed? The Grand Commander then

---

* The candidate here not only imprecates the damnation of his own soul, for his own sins, but also for the sins of another, which is a *double damnation ;*—and all this in case of a violation of any oath in Masonry. As, for instance, if he ' speaks *evil* of a brother Master Mason, behind his back or before his face ;' or ' wrongs him out of *one* cent ;' or ' suffers it to be done by others, if in his power to prevent it :—he is to be doubly damned ! ! !

† This lesson is to be found in Acts, chap. i. 21—26. This part of the ceremony there consists in the mockery of electing by lot the candidate, who may

ordered the lots to be given forth, which being done, I was elected, and the Grand Commander thus addressed me: 'In testimony of your election as a companion among us, and of your acceptance of that honor, you will re-light that extinguished taper; and may the Almighty lift upon you the light of his countenance, and preserve you from falling.' 73d. What followed? The Grand Commander then directed me to kneel, and said, by virtue of the high power in me vested, as the successor and representative of Hugh De Paganis, and Geoffrey, of St. Omers, I now dub and create you Knight Templar, Knight of Malta, of the holy order of St. John, of Jerusalem. [This is repeated three times, at the same time laying the blade of his sword first upon the right shoulder, then upon the head, and then upon the left shoulder of the candidate.] 74th. What followed? The Grand Commander then presented me a sword, and thus addressed me: 'This sword in your hand, as a true and courteous Knight, will be endowed with three most excellent qualities; its hilt be justice impartial, its blade be fortitude undaunted, and its point be mercy: and let it teach us this important lesson, that we should ever be assured of the justice of the cause in which we draw our swords, and being thus assured, we should persevere with the most undaunted fortitude, and finally, having subdued our enemies, we should consider them no longer such, but extend to them the most glorious attribute of God's mercy.' 75th. What followed? The Grand Commander then communicated to me the due-guard, the penitent's pass, and the grand sign, grip, and word of Knight Templars. 76th. Give the due-guard. [The sign is given by placing the end of the right thumb under the chin.] 77th. To what does it allude? To the penalty of my obligation; to have my head struck off and placed upon the highest spire in Christendom. 78th. Give the penitent's pass. It is given as before described; the word is Golgotha. 79th. What does this word allude to?

80th. Give the grand sign. This sign is given by placing yourself in a situation, representing the crucifixion of Christ. 81st. To what does this sign allude? To the manner in which the Saviour expired upon the cross, and expiated the sins of the world. 82d. Give the grip and word. The grip is given by interlacing the fingers of the right and left hand, with the fingers of the right and left hands of the candidate, which forms a cross.—

---

be a swearer, drunkard, or Deist, as an apostle of the LORD and Saviour, Jesus Christ!

Diplomas of this degree may be seen, which, 'in the name of the HOLY and UNDIVIDED TRINITY,' recommend the bearer as a true and faithful soldier of Jesus Christ!

83d. What is the word? Immanuel. [This word is given at the time of giving the grip, and is the name of the grip.] 84th. What does the grip teach us? That as our fingers are thus strongly interlaced, so should the hearts of Knight Templars be firmly interlaced in friendship and brotherly love. 85th. What is the motto of our order? Rex regum, et Dominus dominorum. 86th. How do you translate it? King of kings, and Lord of lords.

KNIGHTS OF THE CHRISTIAN MARK,
AND GUARDS OF THE CONCLAVE.

This conclave is governed by an Invincible Knight of the Order of St. John of Jerusalem, a Senior and Junior Knight, six Grand Ministers, Recorder Treasurer, Conductor, and Guard.

Opening.—' Sir Junior Knight, are all convened in a secret place, and secured from the prying eye of the profane?'

' We are, Invincible.'

' Sir Senior Knight, instruct the Sir Knights to assemble in form for the purpose of opening this Invincible order.'

The members kneel on both knees in a circle, each with his right hand on his heart, his left on his forehead.

Prayer.—' Eternal source of life, of light, and perfection, Supreme God and Governor of all things, liberal dispenser of every blessing! We adore and magnify thy holy name for the many blessings we have received from thy hands, and acknowledge our unworthiness to appear before thee; but for the sake and in the name of thy atoning Son, we approach thee as lost and undone children of wrath; but through the blood of sprinkling, and the sanctification of the Holy Ghost, we come imploring a continuation of thy favors, for thou hast said, that he who cometh to thee through faith in the Son of thy love, thou wilt in no wise cast out; therefore, at the foot of the cross we come, supplicating pardon for our past offences, that they may be blotted out from the book of thy remembrance, and be seen no more, and that the remainder of our days may be spent as becometh the followers of the Holy One of Israel; and graciously grant that love, harmony, peace, and unity may reign in this council; that one spirit may animate us—one God reign over us—and one heaven receive us, there to dwell in thine adorable presence, for ever and ever. Amen.'

The Invincible Knight takes the Bible and waves it four times over his head, saying, 'REX REGNANTIUM, ET DOMI-

NUS DOMINANTIUM ;'* kisses it and passes it on his right: it goes around until it come again to the Invincible Knight, who opens and reads, Matthew, v. 3—12, 16.

Always interlace the fingers of the left hand, draw your sword and present it to the heart, and say, 'TAMMUZ TOULIUMETH : I pronounce this convention opened in ample form. Let us repair to our several stations, and strictly observe silence.' *Preparation.*—The candidate is shown into the antichamber by the conductor, who clothes him in a gown of brown stuff, and leads him to the door of the council chamber where he knocks twice, six, and two ;—2, 6, and 2. *Junior Knight.* 'Some one knocks for admission, Invincible Knight.' *Invincible.* 'See who it is, and make report.' J. K. (goes to the door, and reports,) 'One that is faithful in good works, wishes admission here.' Inv. 'What good works hath he performed?' J. K. 'He hath given food to the hungry, drink to the thirsty, and clothed the naked with a garment.' Inv. 'Thus far he hath done well; but there is still much for him to do. To be faithful in my house, saith the Lord of hosts, filled with love for my people. If so, let him enter under the penalties of his symbolic obligation.' He enters, makes signs until he arrives at the altar, there kneels. *Vow.*—'I, A. B., do promise and vow, with this same volume clasped in my hands, that I will keep secret the words, signs, tokens, and grips of this order of Knighthood, from all but those Knights of St. John, of Jerusalem, who have shown a Christian disposition† to their fellow men, are professors of the Christian faith, and have passed through the degrees of symbolic Masonry ; and that I will protect and support, as far as in me lies, the followers of the Lord Jesus Christ: feed them, if hungry ; give them drink, if thirsty ; if naked, clothe them with garments ; teach them, if ignorant, and advise them for their good and their advantage :—All this I promise in the name of the Father, of the Son, and of the Holy Ghost ; and, if I perform it not, *let me be* ANATHEMA MARANATHA ! ANATHEMA MARANATHA ! !'‡

---

* This phrase is probably intended to be translated 'King of kings, and Lord of lords.' We infer this from its being subsequently thus written in plain English, although we know of no rules that would authorize such a translation.—*Ed. Le Roy Gaz.*

† 'Shown a Christian disposition.' Now, reader, remember that this declaration is made under *oath*, often by men, who, so far from being 'professors of the Christian faith,' are Deists, and hesitate not to avow the fact publicly.

‡ *Anathema Maranatha* is a phrase used once in the scriptures ; it signifies, 'accursed at the coming of the Lord.'—*Ed. Le Roy Gaz.*

The Invincible Knight interlaces the fingers of his left hand with those of the candidate, who lays his right hand on his heart. The Invincible Knight draws his sword; the Senior Knight does the same; they cross them on the back of the candidate's neck, and the Invincible Knight says, 'By virtue of the high power in me vested, by a bull of *His Holiness, Pope Sylvester*,* I dub you a Knight of the Christian Mark, member of the Grand Council, and Guard of the Grand Conclave.' The Invincible Knight then whispers in his ear, 'Tammuz Touliumeth.' The Knights come to order; the Senior Knight takes his seat; the candidate continues standing: the conductor brings a white robe; the Senior Knight says, 'Thus saith the Lord, he that believeth and endureth to the end shall overcome, and I will cause his iniquities to pass from him, and he shall dwell in my presence for ever and ever.† Take away his filthy garments from him, and clothe him with a change of raiment. For he that overcometh, the same shall be clothed in white raiment, and his name shall be written in the book of life, and I will confess his name before my father and his holy angels. He that hath an ear to hear, let him hear what the Spirit saith unto the true believer. Set ye a fair mitre upon his head, place a palm in his hand, for he shall go in and out and minister before me, saith the Lord of hosts; and he shall be a disciple of that rod taken from the branch of the stem of Jesse. For a branch has grown out of his root, and the Spirit of the Lord hath rested upon it; the spirit of his wisdom, and might, and righteousness is the girdle of his loins, and faithfulness the girdle of his vine; and he stands as an *Insignia* to the people, and him shall the Gentiles seek, and his rest shall be glorious. Cause them that have charge over the city to draw near, every one with the destroying weapon in his hand.' The six Grand Ministers come forward from the north with swords and shields. The first is clothed in white, and has an inkhorn by his side, and stands before the Invincible Knight, who says, 'Go through the city; run in the midst thereof and smite; let not thine eye spare, neither have pity: for they have not executed my judgments with clean hands, saith the Lord

---

* 'His Holiness, Pope Sylvester.' Must not a Protestant have some qualms of conscience in this recognition of the authority of 'the man of sin.' 2 Thess. iii. 4.

† Let the reader imagine this scene passing before his eyes. 'The candidate continues standing;'—he may regard the LORD Jesus as an impostor, and his religion as a cunningly devised fable;—his face may be marked with intemperance;—yet the Senior Knight puts on him the 'white robe,' and gravely says, in the language of the word of GOD, (Rev. iii. 5; Zech. iii. 1—8; Isa. xi. 1—5; Ezek. ix. :) 'Thus saith the LORD, he that *believeth* and *endureth to the end*,' &c.

of Hosts.' The candidate is instructed to exclaim, 'Wo is me, for I am a man of unclean lips, and my dwelling has been in the tents of Kedar and among the children of Meshec. Then he that has the inkhorn by his side, takes a live coal with the tongs from the altar, and touches the lips of the candidate, and says, 'If ye believe, thine iniquities shall be taken away, thy sins shall be purged: I will that these be clean with the branch that shall be given up before me. All thy sins are removed and thine iniquities blotted out. For I have trodden the wine press alone, and with me was none of my people: For behold, I come with dyed garments from Bozrah, mighty to save. Refuse not, therefore, to hearken; draw not away thy shoulders; shut not thine ear that thou shouldest not hear.' The six ministers now proceed as if they were about to commence the slaughter, when the Senior Knight says to him with the inkhorn, 'Stay thine hand; proceed no further until thou hast set a mark on those that are faithful in the house of the Lord, and trust in the power of his might. Take ye the signet and set a mark on the forehead of my people that have passed through great tribulation, and have washed their robes, and have made them white in the blood of the Lamb, which was slain from the foundation of the world.' The Minister takes the signet and presses it on the candidate's forehead. He leaves the mark in red letters, '*King of kings, and Lord of lords*,'* The Minister opens the scroll, and says, 'Sir Invincible Knight, the number of the sealed are one hundred and forty and four thousand.' The Invincible Knight strikes four, and all the Knights stand before him. He says, 'Salvation belongeth to our God, which sitteth upon the throne, and unto the Lamb.' All the members, fall on their faces, and say, 'Amen. Blessing, honour, glory, wisdom, thanksgiving, and power, might, majesty, and dominion, be unto our God, for ever and ever, Amen.' They all cast down crowns and palm branches, and rise up and say, 'Great and numberless are thy works, thou King of saints. Behold, the star which I laid before Joshua, on which is engraved seven eyes, as the engraving of a signet, shall be set as a seal on thine arm —as a seal on thine heart; for love is stronger than death; many waters cannot quench it: If a man would give all the treasures of his house for love, he cannot obtain it: It is the gift of God through Jesus Christ, our Lord.'

Charge.—'Invincible Knight, I congratulate you on your hav-

---

* The reader is requested to turn to the following passages: Isa. vi. 5—7; Ps. cxx. 5; Isa. xliii. 15, and lxiii. 1—3; Rev. viii. 2—14; xix. 16; v. 13; xv. 3; Zech. iii. 9; Songs of Solomon, viii. 6, 7. The impious perversion of those passages is incapable of defence or excuse.

ing been found worthy to be promoted to this honorable Order of Knighthood. It is highly honorable to all those worthy Knights, who, with good faith and diligence, perform its many important duties. The honorable situation to which you are now advanced, and the illustrious office which you now fill, is one that was much desired by the first noblemen of Italy, but ambition and jealousy caused his Highness, *Pope Alexander*, to call on his ancient friend, the Grand Master of the Knight of St. John, of Jerusalem, to guard his person and the Holy See, as those Knights were known to be well grounded in the faith, and zealous followers of the Lord. The members of the guard were chosen *by their countenances*, for it is believed that a plain countenance is an indication of the heart ; and that no stranger should gain admission and discover the secrets of this august assembly, this Order of the *Christian Mark* was conferred on those who went about doing good, and following the example of their Illustrious Master, Jesus Christ. Go thou and do likewise.

Motto.—' Christus regnat, vincit, triumphat.* Rex regnantium, et Dominus dominantium.'

Israel on the left breast, a triangular plate of gold, seven eyes engraved on one side, on the other the letter G in the five points.

KNIGHTS OF THE HOLY SEPULCHRE.

History.—St. Helena, daughter of Caylus, king of Britain, consort of Constantine, and mother of Constantine the Great, in the year 296, made a journey to the Holy Land in search of the cross of Jesus Christ. After levelling the hillocks and destroying the temple of Venus, three crosses were discovered. It was now difficult to discover which of the three was the one sought for by her. By order of his Holiness, Pope Marcellinus, they were borne to the bed of a woman who had long been visited by sickness, and lay at the point of death ; she placed her hands upon the second cross first, which rendered her no service ; but when she laid her hand upon the third, she was restored to her former health. She instantly arose, giving glory to God, saying, He was wounded for our transgressions, he was bruised for our iniquities, the chastisement of sin was upon him, and with his stripes we are healed, and God hath laid on him all our iniquities. On the spot where the crosses were found, St. Helena erected a stately church,

---

* Christ rules, conquers, triumphs.—*Ed. Le Roy Gaz.*

one hundred paces long and sixty wide ; the east end takes in the place where the crosses stood, and the west of the sepulchre: by levelling the hills, the sepulchre is above the floor of the church, like a grotto which is twenty feet from the floor to the top of the rock : there is a superb cupola over the sepulchre, and in the aisle are the tombs of Godfrey and Baldwin, kings of Jerusalem. In 302, St. Helena instituted the Order of Knights of the Holy Sepulchre of our Lord and Saviour, Jesus Christ. This Order was confirmed in 304, by his Holiness, Pope Marcellinus; they were bound by a sacred vow to guard the Holy Sepulchre, protect pilgrims, and fight infidels, and enemies of the cross of Christ. The city of Jerusalem was rebuilt and ornamented by Ælius Adrian, emperor of Rome, and given to the Christians in 120. The Persians took it from them in 637, and in 1008 it fell into the hands of the Turks, under whose oppressions it long groaned, until Peter the Holy steered the western princes to release the distressed church, and in 1096, Godfrey and Baldwin unfurled the banner of the cross, and expelled the Turks. He was to have been invested with the royal wreath of majesty, but he thought it not meet to wear a crown of laurel when his blessed Saviour had worn a crown of thorns. Yet, for the common good, he suffered himself to be called the king of Palestine.

Description, &c.—The Council must represent a Cathedral Church, the altar covered with black, upon which must be placed three large candles, a cross, and in the centre a scull and cross bones. The Principal stands on the right side of the altar, with a Bible in one hand, and a staff in the other ; soft music plays, and the Veil is drawn up, and discovers the altar ; the choir say :

> ' Hush, hush, the heavenly choir,
> They cleave the air in bright attire:
> See, see, the lute each angel brings,
> And hark divinely thus they sing :—
>
> ' To the power divine,
> All glory be given,
> By man upon earth,
> And angels in heaven.'

The Priest steps before the altar, and says, ' Kyrie Elieson; Christe Elieson; Kyrie Elieson ;* Amen: Gloria Sibi Domino!† I declare this Grand Council opened, and ready to proceed to business.' The Priests and Ministers take their several stations and observe order. The candidates being prepared, he alarms

---

* ' O Lord, have mercy ; O Christ, have mercy ; O Lord, have mercy.'
† ' Glory to the Lord himself.'

at the door by seven raps, and the Prelate says to Verger, 'See the cause of that alarm, and report.' Verger goes to the door, and reports, 'Right Reverend Prelate, there are seven brethren who solicit admission to this Grand Council.' Prelate says, 'On what is their desire founded?' Verger. 'On a true Christian principle, to serve the church and its members, by performing the seven corporeal works of mercy, and to protect and guard the Holy Sepulchre, from the destroying hands of our enemies.' Prelate. 'Admit them that we may know them, if you please.' They are then admitted: Prelate says to them, 'Are you followers of the Captain of our salvation?' Verger says, 'We are, Right Reverend Prelate.' P. 'Attend, then, to the sayings of our Master, Jesus Christ.' Thou shalt love the Lord, thy God, with all thy heart, with all thy mind, with all thy soul, and with all thy might. This is the first great commandment, and the second is like unto it; thou shalt love thy neighbour as thyself: on these two commandments hang all the law and the prophets. The Verger and Beadle hold the Bible on which the candidates place their right hands. *Vow.*—'I, A. B., in the name of the high and undivided Trinity, do promise and vow to keep and conceal the high mysteries of this noble and invincible Order of Knights of the Holy Sepulchre, from all but such as are ready and willing to serve the church of Christ, by acts of valor and charity, and its members, by performing all the corporeal works of mercy; and that, as far as in me lies, I will defend the church of the Holy Sepulchre from pillage and violence, and guard and protect pilgrims on their way to and from the Holy Land; and if I perform not this, my vow, to the best of my abilities, let me become *inanimatus*.'* Interlace your fingers with the candidate, cross your arms, and say, 'De mortuis, nil nisi bonum.'† Prelate says, 'Take the sword, and travel onward—guard the Holy Sepulchre—defeat our enemies—unfurl the banner of our cross—protect the Roman Eagle—return to us with victory and safety.' The candidates depart—go to the south, where they meet a band of Turks—a desperate conflict ensues—the Knights are victorious; they seize the crescent, and return to the cathedral in triumph, and place the banner, eagle, and crescent before the altar, and take their seats. (22d chap. St. John, read by Prelate.) Then the choir sing,—

> 'Creator of the radiant light,
> Dividing day from sable night;
> Who, with the light bright origin,
> The world's creation didst begin.'

Prelate then says, 'Let our prayer come before thee, and let

---

* 'Dead.' † 'Concerning the dead, say nothing but good.'

our exercise be acceptable in thy sight.' The seven candidates kneel at the foot of the altar. The Prelate takes the bread, and says, 'Brethren, eat ye all of this bread in love, that ye may learn to support each other.' He then takes the cup, and says, 'Drink ye all of this cup to ratify the vow that ye have made, and learn to sustain one another.' The Prelate then raises them up by the grip, (interlace the fingers,) and says: '1st, Sir, I greet thee a Knight of the Holy Sepulchre; go feed the hungry: 2d, Give drink to the thirsty: 3d, Clothe the naked with a garment: 4th, Visit and ransom the captives: 5th, Harbor the harborless, give the orphan and widow where to lay their heads: 6th, Visit and relieve the sick: 7th, Go and bury the dead.' All make crosses, and say, 'In nomini patriafilio et spiritus sancto: Amen.' Prelate says, 'Brethren, let us recommend to each other the practice of the four cardinal virtues; prudence, justice, temperance, fortitude.'

Closing.—The Knights all rise, stand in circle, interlace their fingers, and say, 'Sepulchrum.' Prelate then says, 'Gloria patri, et filio, et spiritus sancto.'* Brethren answer, 'Sicut erat in principio, et nunc, et semper et in secula seculorum.† Amen.'

Benediction.—' Blessed be thou, O Lord, our God! Great first cause and Governor of all things! thou createst the world with thy bountiful hand, and sustained it by thy wisdom, by thy goodness, and by thy mercy! It cometh to pass that seed time and harvest never fail! It is thou that givest every good and perfect gift! Blessed be thy name for ever and ever!' To examine a Knight of the Holy Sepulchre; he holds up the first finger of the right hand, Knight holds up the second; you then hold up the third, and he shuts up his first: this signifies three persons in one God.

THE HOLY AND THRICE ILLUSTRIOUS ORDER OF THE CROSS, CALLED A COUNCIL.

Diploma of a Comp. of the Ancient Council of the Trinity.
Anno Cr. seu Covt. 896.

C F	The Ancient Council of the
M C	Trinity, by their succes-
S C	sors in the United States
A O P	of America.

St. Albert, To every Knight Companion of the Holy and Thrice Illustrious ORDER OF THE CROSS: Be it known

---

* 'Glory to the Father, Son, and Holy Spirit.'
† 'As it was in the beginning, is now, and shall be, world without end.'

unto you, that, with regard to unquestionable vouchers, we have confirmed the Induction of the Knight Templar Mason into the Councils of the said Order of Knighthood, and herein do warrant him as a worthy and ILLUSTRIOUS Companion thereof: and hoping and confiding that he will ever so demean himself as to conduct to the glory of I. H. S.,* the Most Holy and Almighty GOD, and to the honor of his MARK, we do recommend and submit him to the confidence of all those throughout the world, who can truly and deservedly say, 'I am a Christian:' and that no unwarrantable benefits shall arise from this Diploma, and we charge all concerned cautiously and prudently to mark the bearer on the mystic letters therein contained, and to regard only the result, in its application and privileges.

Done out of Council, at Le Roy, in the county of Genesee, and state of New-York, of these U. S. A. August 1st. 1827.

Sir ——————————

COMMENDATIONS,	SOVEREIGN PREFECT.
SIR KNIGHTS COMP'NS.	SIR J. H. C. MILLER,
	ACT'G. PREF.

The officers and council all in their places. The Most Illustrious Prefect addresses the Most Worthy Provost thus: 'Most Worshipful Provost, what is the o'clock?' Most Worshipful Provost says, rising and facing the east, at the same time raising his mark in his right hand, 'Most Illustrious Prefect, it is now the first hour of the day, the time when our Lord suffered and the veil of the temple was rent asunder, when darkness and consternation was spread over the earth, when the confusion of the old covenant was made light in the new, in the temple of the cross. It is, Most Illustrious Prefect, the third watch, when the implements of Masonry were broken—when the flame, which led the wise men of the east reappeared—when the cubick stone was broken, and the word was given.' Most Illustrious Prefect says to Worthy Herald, 'It is my will that this house of God be closed, and the remembrance of those solemn and sacred events, be here commemorated: make this, Worthy Herald, known to the Most Worshipful Provost, in due and ancient form.' The Worthy Herald bows and approaches the Most Worshipful Provost, where he bows thrice, faces about and gives a blast with his horn, and after the Knights have filed out by threes without the door, except the Worthy Senior Inductor, he does his errand, viz: 'Most Worshipful Provost, it is the sovereign will of Count Albertus, of Per-

---

* The letters I. H. S. are the initials of the Latin words 'Jesus Hominum Salvator.' (Jesus, Saviour of men.)

gamus, that this house of God be closed, and that those solemn and sacred events in the new covenant be here commemorated: you will observe this.' The Worthy Herald bows, and the Most Worshipful Provost rises and addresses the Worthy Sen. Inductor thus: 'It is the will of the Most Illustrious Prefect that here now be opened a Council of Knights of the Cross: what therein becomes your duty?' Worthy Senior Inductor says, 'To receive the commands of my superiors in the order, and pay obedience thereto—to conduct and instruct my ignorant pass-brethren; and to revere, and inculcate reverence in others, for the Most Holy and Almighty God.' The Most Worshipful Provost rises fiercely and says, 'By what right do you claim this duty?' Worthy S. Inductor says, 'By the right of a sign, and the mark of a sign.' Most Worshipful Provost says, 'Will you give me a sign?' Worthy Sen. 'I could if I should.' The Most Worshipful Provost then partly extends both arms, pointing downwards to an angle of $39°$, with the palms open, and upwards, to show they are not sullied with iniquity and oppression, and says, 'Worthy Sen. Inductor, you may give it.' The Worthy S. Inductor then looks him full in the face, and with his fore finger touches his right temple, and lets fall his hand, and says, 'This is a sign.' Most Worshipful Provost says, 'A sign of what?' Worthy S. Inductor says, 'Aye, a sign of what?' Wor. Pro. says, 'A penal sign.' Wor. S. Inductor says, 'Your sign is——' Most Worthy Pro. says, 'The last sign of my induction.' Most Worthy Pro. says, 'But you have the mark of a sign.' Worthy S. Inductor says, 'The sign whereof my mark is a mark, I hope is in the Council above.' Most Worthy Pro. says, 'But the mark——' Worthy S. Inductor says, 'Is in my bosom.' Thereupon he produces his mark in his left hand, and with the fore finger of his right on the letter S, on the cross, asks, 'What's that?' Most Wor. Pro. says, 'Lisha.' Wor. Pro. puts his finger on the letter H, and asks, 'What is this?' Worthy S. Inductor says, 'Sha.' Worthy S. Inductor then puts his finger on the letter I, and asks, 'What is this?' Most Wor. Pro. says, 'Baal.' 'What, then, is your mark?' Worthy S. Inductor says, 'Baal, Sha-Lisha;* I am the Lord.' The Most Worshipful Provost then says, 'You are my brother, and the duty is yours of ancient right; please announce the Council open.' The Worthy Senior Inductor steps to the door and gives three raps, and is answered by some Knight from without, who is then admitted, and the Worthy S. Inductor gives the *conditional* sign, (which is by partly extending both arms, as before described;) the

---

* 'Lord of the three.'

Knight answering by putting his finger to his right temple, as before. The Worthy S. Inductor then addresses the chair, thus:— ' Most Illustrious Prefect, a professing brother is within the Council by virtue of a sign.' Most Illustrious Prefect says to Worthy Herald, ' Go to this professing brother, and see him marked before the chair of the Most Worshipful Provost; conduct him thither, Worthy Herald.' The Worthy Herald says to the Knight, ' Worthy Sir, know you the sacred cross of our Council?' Knight says, ' I am a Christian.' The Worthy Herald then says, ' Follow me.' When arrived before the Most Wor. Pro. the Worthy Herald says, ' Most Worthy Provost, by order of the Most Illustrious Prefect, I here bring you to be marked a professing brother of the cross.' The Most Wor. Pro. says, ' Worthy Sir, know you the cross of our Council?' Knight says, ' I am a Christian.' The Most Wor. Pro. says, ' No more.'

OBLIGATIONS OF THRICE ILLUSTRIOUS KNIGHTS OF THE CROSS.

FIRST OBLIGATION.

You, Mr. ——, do now, by your honor, and in view of the power and union of the Thrice Illustrious Order of the Cross, now first made known to you, and in the dread presence of the Most Holy and Almighty God, solemnly and sincerely swear and declare, that, to the end of your life, you will not, either in consideration of gain, interest, or honor, nor with good or bad design, ever take any, the least, step or measure, or be instrumental in any such object, to betray or communicate to any person, or being, or number of the same, in the known world, not thereto of cross and craft entitled, any secret or secrets, or ceremony or ceremonies, or any part thereof appertaining to the order and degree known among Masons as the Thrice Illustrious Order of the Cross. That you will not, at any time or times whatever, either now or hereafter, directly or indirectly, by letter, figure, or character, however or by whoever made, ever communicate any of the information and secret mysteries heretofore alluded to. That you will never speak on or upon, or breathe high or low, any ceremony or secret appertaining thereto, out of council, where there shall not be two or more Knights companions of the order present, besides yourself, and that in a safe and sure place, whereby any opinion, even of the nature and general principles of the institution, can be formed by any other person, be he Mason or otherwise, than a true Knight companion of the cross; nothing herein going to interfere with the prudent practice of the duties enjoined by the order, or arrangement for their enforcement.

2. * You further swear, that, should you know another to violate any essential part of this obligation, you will use your most decided endeavors, by the blessing of God, to bring such person to the strictest and most condign punishment, agreeably to the rules and usages of our ancient fraternity; and this by pointing him out to the world as an unworthy vagabond; by opposing his interest, by deranging his business, by transferring his character after him wherever he may go, and by exposing him to the contempt of the whole fraternity and the world, but of our illustrious order more especially, during his whole natural life: nothing herein going to prevent yourself, or any other, when elected to the dignity of Thrice Illustrious, from retaining the ritual of the order, if prudence and caution appear to be the governing principle in so retaining it, such dignity authorizing the elected to be governed by no rule but the dictates of his own judgment, in regard to what will best conduce to the interest of the order; but that he be responsible for the character of those whom he may induct, and for the concealment of the said ritual.

3. Should any Thrice Illustrious Knight or acting officer of any council which may have them in hand, ever require your aid in any emergency in defence of the recovery of his said charge, you swear cheerfully to exercise all assistance in his favor, which the nature of the time and place will admit, even to the sacrifice of life, liberty, and property. To all, and every part thereof, we then bind you, and by ancient usage you bind yourself, under the no less infamous penalty than dying the death of a traitor, by having a spear, or other sharp instrument, like as our divine Master, thrust in your left side, bearing testimony, even in death, of the power and justice of the mark of the holy cross.

SECOND OBLIGATION.

Mr. ——, before you can be admitted to the light and benefit of this Thrice Illustrious order, it becomes my duty, by ancient usage, to propose to you certain questions, not a thing vainly ceremonial; but the companions will expect true answers: they will concern your past life, and resolutions for the future. Have you given me without evasion or addition your baptismal and family names, and those of your parents, your true age as far as

---

* Taking this obligation in connexion with the penalty, it will be seen that the candidate swears by the *blessing of GOD*, to bring one, who shall violate the obligation, to the punishment of 'having a spear, or other sharp instrument, thrust into his left side,' as the Saviour at his crucifixion!

within your knowledge; where you were educated, where you were born, and also where was your last place of residence? or have you not? 'I have.' It is well.

2d. Were your parents free and not slaves? had they right and title in the soil of the earth? were they devoted to the religion of the cross, and did they so educate their family? have you searched the spiritual claims of that religion on your gratitude and your affections? and have you continued steadfast in that faith from choice and a conviction of your duty to heaven, or from education? 'From duty and choice.' This also is right.

3d. Have you ever up to this time lived according to the principles of that religion, by acting upon the square of virtue with all men, nor defrauding any, nor defamed the good name of any, nor indulged sensual appetites unreasonably, but more especially to the dishonor of the matrimonial tie, nor extorted on, or oppressed the poor. 'I have not been guilty of these things.' You have then entitled yourself to our highest confidence, by obeying the injunctions of our Thrice Illustrious Prefect in Heaven, 'of doing to all men even as you would that they should do unto you.' Mr. ——, can you so continue to act, that yearly on the anniversary of St. Albert, you can solemnly swear for the past season you have not been guilty of the crimes enumerated in these questions? 'By the help of God I can.'* Be it so, then, that annually, on the anniversary of St. Albert, you swear to these great questions; and the confidence of the Knights Companions of the order in you, rests on your being able so to do.

4th. For the future, then, you promise to be a good man, and to be governed by the moral laws of God and the rules of the order, in always dealing openly, honorably, and above deceit, especially with the Knights companions of the order. 'I do.'

5th. You promise so to act with all mankind, but especially with the fraternity, as that you shall never be justly called a bad paymaster, ungrateful, a liar, a rake, or a libertine, a man careless in the business of your vocation, a drunkard, or a tyrant. 'I do.'

6th. You promise to lead a life as upright and just in relation to all mankind as you are capable of, but in matters of difference to preserve the interest of a companion of the order; of a companion's friend for whom he pleads, to any mere man of the world. 'I do.'

---

* The word of GOD says, 2 Chron. vi, 36, "There is no man which sinneth not," but each Knight swears annually on the anniversary of St. Albert, that during the past year he has acted on the square of virtue with all men; that he 'has not defrauded any, nor defamed the good name of any,' in short, 'that he has done to all men as he would that they should do unto him.'

7th. You promise never to engage in mean party strife, nor conspiracies against the government or religion of your country, whereby your reputation may suffer, nor ever to associate with dishonorable men even for a moment, except it be to secure the interest of such person, his family or friends, to a companion, whose necessities require this degradation at your hands. 'I do.'

8th. You promise to act honorably in all matters of office or vocation, even to the value of the one third part of a Roman penny, and never to take any advantage therein unworthy the best countenance of your companions, and this, that they shall not, by your unworthiness, be brought into disrepute. 'I do.'

THIRD OBLIGATION.

I do now, by the honor and power of the mark of the Holy and Illustrious order of the Cross, which I do now hold to Heaven in my right hand as the earnest of my faith, and in the dread presence of the most holy and Almighty God, solemnly swear and declare, that I do hereby accept of, and for ever will consider the cross and mark of this order as my only hope :* that I will make it the test of faith and fellowship ; and that I will effect its objects and defend its mysteries to the end of my days, with my life and with my property—and first, that in the state of collision and misunderstanding impiously existing among the princes and pilgrims, defenders and champions of the Holy Cross of Jesus our Lord, now assembled in the land and city of their peace, and considering that the glory of the Most High requires the greatest and strictest unanimity of measures and arms, the most sacred union of sentiment and brotherly love in the soldiers who there thus devote themselves to his cause and banner, I swear strictly to dedicate myself, my life and my property for ever hereafter to his holy name and the purposes of our mark, and to the best interest of all those who thus with me become Knights of the Cross : I swear for ever to give myself to this holy and illustrious order, confiding fully and unreservedly in the purity of their morals and the ardor of their pious enthusiasm, for the recovery of the land of their fathers, and the blessed clime of our Lord's sufferings, and never to renounce the mark of the order nor the claims and welfare of my brethren.

2d. And that the holy and pious enthusiasm of my brethren

---

* 'Consider the cross and mark of this order as my only hope.' The candidate swears then to trust the eternal salvation of his soul, *not* on the death of the Saviour but ' *to the cross and mark of this order !*'

He dedicates himself, his life and his property to his holy name, (Christ,) and the purposes of our mark !' What are those purposes ?

may not have slander or disgrace at my hands, or the order be injured by my unworthiness, I swear for ever to renounce tyranny and oppression in my own person and place, whatever it may be, and to stand forth against it in others, whether public or private ; to become the champion of the cross, to observe the common good ; be the protector of the poor and unfortunate ; and ever to observe the common rights of human nature without encroachment, or permitting encroachment thereon, if in my power to prevent or lessen it. I will, moreover, act in subordination to the laws of my country, and never countenance any change in the government under which I live, without good and answerable reasons for so doing, that ancient usages and immemorial customs be not overturned.

3d. I swear to venerate the mark as the wisdom and decree of Heaven, to unite our hands and hearts in the work of the holy crusade, and as an encouragement to act with zeal and efficacy; and I swear to consider its testimonies as the true and only proper test of an illustrious brother of the cross.

4th. I swear to wear the mark of this order, without any the least addition, except what I shall be legally entitled to by *induction,* for ever, if not without the physical means of doing so, or it being contrary to propriety ; and even then, if possible, to wear the holy cross ; and I swear to put a chief dependence for the said worthy and pious objects therein.

5th. I swear to put confidence unlimited in every illustrious brother of the cross, as a true and worthy follower of the blessed Jesus, who has sought this land, not for private good, but pity, and the glory of the religion of the Most High and Holy God.*

6th. I swear never to permit my political principles nor personal interest to come counter to his, if forbearance and brotherly kindness can operate to prevent it ; and never to meet him if I know it, in war or in peace, under such circumstances that I may not, in justice to myself, my cross, and my country, wish him unqualified success ; and if perchance it should happen without my knowledge, on being informed thereof, that I will use my best endeavors to satisfy him, even to the relinquishing my arms and purpose. I will never shed a brother's blood nor thwart his good fortune, knowing him to be such, nor see it done by others if in my power to prevent it.

7th. I swear to advance my brother's best interest, by always

---

* Here is a stretch of charity altogether unprecedented. It would certainly require the credulity of a child to believe that every man, who has taken this degree, 'is a true and worthy follower of the blessed Jesus ;'—but to swear, in the presence of the great JEHOVAH, to do this, is an act of madness !

supporting his military fame and political preferment in opposition to another; and by employing his arms or his aid in his vocation, under all circumstances where I shall not suffer more by so doing, than he, by my neglecting to do so, but this never to the sacrifice of any vital interest in our holy religion, or in the welfare of my country.

8th. I swear to look on his enemies as my enemies, his friends as my friends, and stand forth to mete out tender kindness or vengeance accordingly; but never to intrude on his social or domestic relations to his hurt or dishonor, by claiming his privileges, or by debauching or defaming his female relations or friends.

9th. I swear never to see calmly nor without earnest desires and decided measures to prevent the ill treatment, slander, or defamation, of any brother Knight, nor ever to view danger or the least shadow of injury about to fall on his head, without well and truly informing him thereof; and, if in my power to prevent it, never to fail, by my sword or counsel, to defend his welfare and good name.

10th. I do swear never to prosecute a brother before those who know not our order, till the remonstrances of a council shall be inadequate to do me justice.

11th. I swear to keep sacred my brother's secrets, both when delivered to me as such, and when the nature of the information is such as to require secrecy for his welfare.

12th. I swear to hold myself bound to him, especially in affliction and adversity, to contribute to his necessities my prayers, my influence, and my purse.

13th. I swear to be under the control of my council, or, if belonging to none, to that which is nearest to me, and never to demur to, or complain at, any decree concerning me, which my brethren, as a council, shall conceive me to deserve, and enforce on my head, to my hurt and dishonor.

14th. I swear to obey all summons sent from any council to me, or from any Most Illustrious Knight, whether Illustrious Consellor for the time being, or by *induction,* and to be governed by the constitution, usages, and customs of the order without variation or change.

15th. I swear never to see nor permit more than two candidates, who, with the Senior Inductor, will make three, to be advanced, at the same time, in any council where I shall be; nor shall any candidate, by suffrage, be inducted without a unanimous vote of the illustrious brethren in council; nor shall any council advance any member, there not being three Illustrious Knights, or one Most Illustrious and four Illustrious Knights of the Cross present, which latter may be substituted by Most Illustrious Induction; nor yet where there shall not be a full and proper mark of the order, such as usage has adopted to our altar, of metal, or other durable and worthy material, contained within the apartment of council, as also the Holy Bible ; nor will I ever see a council opened for business, without the ceremony of testing the mark, exercised on the character of every brother, prayers, and the reading of the 35th Psalm of David ; nor will I ever see, consent to, or countenance, more than two persons of the same business or calling in life, to belong to, or be inducted and advanced in any one council of which I am a member, at the same time ; nothing therein going to exclude members from other parts of the country, or from foreign parts, from joining us, if they consent formally and truly to stand in deference and defence, first, of their special *bar-brethren* in the council, nor to prevent advancements to fill vacancies, occasioned by death or removal. To all this, and every part thereof, I do now, as before, by the honor and power of the mark, as by an honorable and awful oath, which confirmeth all things in the dread presence of the Most Holy and Almighty God, solemnly and in truth, bind and obligate my soul ; and in the earthly penalties, to wit, that, for the violation of the least matter or particle of any of the here taken obligations, I become the silent and mute subject of the displeasure of the Illustrious order, and have their power and wrath turned on my head, to my destruction and dishonor, which, like the *nail of Jael*, may be the sure end of an unworthy wretch, by piercing my temples with a true sense of my ingratitude—and for a breach of silence in case of such an unhappy event, that I shall die the infamous death of a traitor, by having a spear, or other sharp weapon, like as my Lord, thrust in my left side—bearing testimony, even in death, of the power of the mark of the Holy and Illustrious Cross, before I. H. S. our Thrice Illustrious Counsellor in Heaven, the Grand Council of the good.— To this I swear.

(183)

THE ELEVEN INEFFABLE DEGREES,

CONFERRED IN THE

LODGE OF PERFECTION.

SECRET MASTER.

Opening.—*Master.* 'Brother Adoniram, are you a Secret Master?' *Ans.* 'Most Perfect, I have passed from the square to the compass; I have seen the tomb of our Respectful Master, Hiram Abiff, and have, in company with my brethren, shed tears at the same.' M. 'What is the hour?' A. 'The dawn of day has driven away darkness, and the great light begins to shine in this lodge.' M. 'If the great light is the token of the dawn of day, and we are all present Secret Masters, it is high time to begin our labors: give notice that I am about to open a lodge of Secret Masters.' Master claps seven with his hands, which is repeated by the brethren; and then makes sign of admiration, which is answered by the brethren.

Reception.—The candidate is led to the door of the lodge, where the Master of Ceremonies knocks seven times. Adoniram comes and repeats the alarm on the inside, and opens the door, and says, 'Who is there?' *Ans.* 'A brother who is well qualified, wishes to receive the degree of a Secret Master.' Adoniram reports to the Master, and requests that he may be introduced. Master consents, on condition he vouches for his integrity, zeal, and good conduct. He is led in, and advances to the altar; his right knee on the floor; head bound, and a square fastened on his forehead by the bandage; a great light in the right hand.

Obligation.—'1st point, Secrecy. 2. Obey orders and decrees of Council of Princes of Jerusalem, under penalty of all the former degrees.' (The foregoing is the oath in substance.) After the obligation, the Master takes a crown of laurel and olives, and says, 'My brother you are now received as a Secret Master.' [See Monitor.] Sign—that of silence.

After giving the words and signs, the Master says, 'Go, my brother, pass the brethren and then attend to our instruction.'

LECTURE.

Q. Are you a Secret Master? A. I am, and glory in it. Q. How were you received? A. By being passed from the square to the compass. Q. Where were you made? A. Under the laurel and olive tree. Q. In what place were you received? A. In the sanctum sanctorum. Q. Who received you? A. Solomon and Adoniram, the Inspector. Q. In entering the sanctum sanctorum what did you perceive? A. The characteristic of the divinity. Q. What did you see besides? A. The great circle, in the midst of which is enclosed the blazing star, which blinded me with respect and admiration! Q. What signify the Hebrew characters in the triangle? A. Something above the knowledge of a human being, which cannot be pronounced. Q. Why not, since we are in the lodge? A. Because I have seen the great light darting its rays without knowing it myself. Q. What enclosed the great brightness? A. The ineffable name of the Great Architect of the universe. Q. Who was the first that saw it? A. Moses—and he received the pronunciation thereof, from the Supreme Being on the mount, when he appeared unto him; and, by a law of Moses, it was forbidden even to be spoken, unless in a particular manner, by which means it was lost. Q. What did you perceive more? A. Nine other words in Arabic characters. Q. Where were they placed? A. In the nine beams which come from the blazing luminary. Q. What did they signify? A. The nine names which God gave himself, when speaking with Moses on Sinai—He made him hope that his future issue should one day know his real name. Q. give them to me with their significations. A. [Page 345.]
which compose 888 letters, and enclose 72 names, which are taken as names of the Divinity according to the angel's alphabet, or cabalistick tree. Q. What signifies the circle that surrounds the triangle? A. It represents the eternity of the power of God, which hath neither beginning nor ending. Q. What doth the blazing star denote? A. A meteor which ought to guide us to the divine Providence. Q. What is signified by the letter 'G,' in the circle of the blazing star? A. Glory, Grandure, Gornel. By Glory is meant GOD; by Grandure is meant man, who may become great by perfection; and Gornel is a Hebrew word, and signifies thanks to God for his supreme power; it was the first word that was pronounced by our common parent, when, at his raising, he saw Eve. Q. What is signified by the five beams of the blazing star? A. The five orders of architecture, which were used in the construction of the temple. Q. What did you see more in the sanctum sanctorum? A. The ark of alliance;

the golden candlestick of seven branches; the table of bread of proposition. Q. Where was the ark of alliance placed? A. In the middle of the sanctum sanctorum, under the blazing star. Q. What did the ark of alliance, with the blazing star, represent? A. As the ark was the emblem of alliance which God had made with his people, and was put under the shadow of the cherubims' wings, so is the circle which encloses the triangle in the blazing star, an emblem of the alliance of brother Masons. Q. What form was the ark? A. An oblong square. Q. Of what was it made? A. Of shittim wood, covered within and without with pure gold, and covered with a golden crown, and borne with the two cherubims of gold. Q. What was the name of the crown? A. Propitiatory, or the place that served to appease God's anger. Q. What did it contain? A. The tables of laws which God gave to Moses. Q. Of what were they, and what did they contain? A. They were of white marble, and contained the ten commandments in Hebrew characters. Q. What are those commandments? A. The decalogue engraved by the finger of the Almighty. The first table contained the four divine commandments; the second, the six human, which served to regulate all the duties of man to man. Q. What use was made of the table of shew bread? A. To place thereon the twelve loaves of bread of proposition, which ought always to be in the presence of God as he had ordained it to Moses. Q. Of what were the loaves? A. Of pure fine flour. Q. How were they placed? A. Six on the right hand and six on the left, forming two heaps. Q. What was placed over them? A. A very pure and bright ewer. Q. Why so? A. In order that they should remain a monument of the obligations made to God. Q. What was the name of the sanctum sanctorum in Hebrew? A. Dabar. Q. What doth that word signify? A. Speech. Q. Why was it so called? A. Because the DIVINITY, in a peculiar manner, resided there and delivered his oracles. Q. Give the history of the construction of the tabernacle? A. When Moses received the order from GOD to construct the ark, he made choice of Bezaleel, of the tribe of Judah, the son of Aaron and Mary, the sister of Moses, and of Aholiab, the son of Ahisamach, of the tribe of Dan, the most learned of the people; the populace testified so much forwardness in the work, and offered, with so much joy, to carry it on, that Moses gave notice, by the sound of the trumpet, that he did not want any more. They began to work according to the model that God had given to Moses, which also served for the number to be placed in the tabernacle to serve for sacrifices. Q. what is meant by the seven branches of the candlesticks? A. The seven planets. Q. What was on the top of the branches? A. A lamp on each, looking east and south. Q. Of how many parts was the candlesticks of seven branches composed? A. Of seven parts. Q. What is signified by the EYE that is in our lodge? A. An only eye that enlightens us. Q. How did they go up to the gallery of the temple? A. By a spiral staircase, fixed on the wall on the north side. Q. What was the name of that staircase? A Cochleus;—which signifies '*in the form of a screw.*' Q. How many doors were there in the sanctum sanctorum? A. Only one on the east side, which was called '*Zizon,*' which was covered with hangings of purple, azure, hyacinth, and gold, supported by four columns. Q. What did those columns represent? A. The four elements. Q. How old are you? A. three times twenty-seven, and accomplished eighty-one. Q. Give the pass word. A *Zizon.*

Close.—Q. ' Brother Inspector, what's the o'clock?' A. ' The end of day.' Q. ' What doth remain to do?' A. ' To practice virtue, to fly vice, and to remain in silence.' Q. ' Since nothing remains to do but to practice virtue and fly vice, let us enter into silence, that the will of God may be accomplished: it is time to rest. Brother Inspector, give notice that I am about to close this lodge by the mysterious number.' Inspector says, ' The Most Perfect is about to close this lodge by the mysterious number.' All clap seven, as in opening, and the lodge is closed.

PERFECT MASTER.

A table before the Master, covered with black, and strewed with tears.—Adoniram was chosen first of the seven, to replace Hiram Abiff, and he constructed the tomb and urn of Hiram Abiff.—Stokin first found the body of Hiram Abiff.

Opening.—Q. ' Brother Inspector is the lodge well tyled, and are we all Perfect Masters?' A. ' Right Worshipful and Respectable, we are.' Q. 'Give notice that I am going to open a lodge of Perfect Masters,' (done.) Adoniram knocks four, with an iron; Stokin in the west, four; and a brother in the south, four; and a brother in the north, four; and then all make the sign of ' admiration' together! Adoniram says, ' Brother Stokin, what is the o'clock?' Ans. ' It is four.' Adoniram, ' Then it is high time to set the workmen at labor, give notice that a lodge of Perfect Masters is open.' Stokin, ' The lodge is open.'

Reception.—Candidate is ornamented with the dress and jewel of a Secret Master. Master of ceremony knocks four on the shoulder of Inspector and says, ' There is in the antichamber a

Secret Master desirous of being raised to this degree.' The Inspector reports to Master, who says, 'Is he worthy and well qualified to receive this degree?' (Yes.) Mast. 'Let him be introduced according to an ancient due form.' Inspector orders Master of Ceremonies to go and instruct candidate; he goes and examines him on his former degrees, puts on his neck a green cord, and holding it in his left hand, and his sword in his right, leads him to the door and knocks four. Inspector repeats this within, and says to the Master, 'Some one knocks.' Mast. 'See who it is.' Inspector orders Tyler to open the door, and see who knocks, and after the Tyler has repeated to the Master of Ceremonies, he acquaints the Master, who orders him to be introduced and led to the south side of the tomb, at the head of the lodge, where he stands with the sign of a Secret Master. Master says, 'My brother, what do you demand?' Ans. 'To be received to the degree of Perfect Master.' He is then addressed thus: 'It is my,' &c. (see Monitor.) The Inspector then takes him by the cord and leads him four times round the lodge, then makes him kneel during the prayer, after which he passes by the tomb on each side of the two columns; (crossed:) in crossing, he steps from one to the other, still with the sign of a Secret Master he is placed opposite the altar, his right knee a little bent and takes the OBLIGATION. '1st. Secrecy. Penalty:—being *dishonored*, and the penalties of all those of my former obligations, Amen; Amen; Amen; Amen.' Master draws the cord from his neck, saying; 'I now draw,' &c (see Monitor.) Signs are given to the candidate.

History.—Solomon had been informed that the corpse of Hiram Abiff had been already found and deposited in the lower end of the temple, and, pleased to be able at least to gather the precious remains of so good a man, he ordered the noble Adoniram, his Grand Inspector, to make the funeral as pompous as possible, and the brethren to attend in white gloves and aprons; forbidding, at the same time, the marks of blood spilled in the temple to be effaced, until vengeance should be taken.—Adoniram being Grand Master, Architect, and chief of the workmen, presented a plan of a superb monument to be raised to his memory, of black and white marble, which was finished in nine days. The heart of Hiram Abiff was taken enclosed in an urn on the top of an obelisk, which was placed near the west end of the temple a little on the north side, to show that his murderers had first put him under some rubbish in a ditch before they carried him to the place where Stokin found him. The heart in the urn was pierced with a sword, and every person qualified went to testify his grief until vengeance was complete. The heart was enclosed in an obelisk, covered with a triangular stone, on which were the letters, **B. M. I.** engraved in Hebrew characters, with a sprig of cassia on the top; his body was buried in the middle of the great hall, in an apartment separated from the temple, where Solomon used to keep a chapter, and confer with Hiram king of Tyre, and Hiram Abiff on the craft. Three days after the ceremony of burial, Solomon went with his court to the temple, and all the workmen being ranged as at the funeral, he directed his prayer to God, examined the tomb and canopy, repeated the letters on the triangle, and the letters engraved in the centre, then lifting his eyes and his hands towards heaven, he said, with joy in his heart, 'It is accomplished and complete,' and gave the sign of admiration! The brethren also raising their eyes and hands towards heaven, leaning their heads on their shoulders, &c.

LECTURE.

Q. Are you a Perfect Master? A. I have seen the circle and square placed on the top of the two crossed columns. Q. Where are they placed? A. In the place where was deposited the body of our respectable Hiram Abiff. Q. What did they represent? A. The two pillars which I came to when I was made a Perfect Master. Q. What was the design of Solomon in instituting this degree? A. To encourage the brethren with a reverential love, and to excite them to an inquiry who were the bloody assassins of Hiram Abiff. A suspicion being entertained that they were among the workmen, Solomon ordered a general muster of them, when three were found missing and supposed to be the persons. Solomon then ordered a Mason to erect a superb obelisk at the west end of the temple, and to enclose in an urn on the top thereof, the heart of Hiram Abiff, well embalmed, of which none knew except the Perfect Master. This was accordingly done, and was to remain there until vengeance should be taken. A sword appeared to be driven through the urn, as a token of the desire of the brethren to take vengeance on the assassins. The body was found in a place separate from the temple, where Solomon kept his chapter. Q. What is signified by the square stone in the centre of the circle, and also what is signified by the letters on the square stone? A. The secret word of a Perfect Master. Q. Pronounce it. A. '———.' Q. What does it signify? A. The name of God, as known by us. Q. How were you received a Perfect Master? A. On the point of a spear to my heart, and a halter around my neck. Q. Why so? A. *To make me remember*, THEY SHOULD BE INSTRUMENTAL IN MY DEATH *if I revealed any of the secrets!!!!* Q.

How many signs have you? A. One by five. Q. Why so? A. In remembrance of my five points of entrance. Q. Which or what are they? A. The four terms of entrance into the temple, and the fifth of admission? Q. What is represented by the tomb you passed over at your admission? A. The burial of Hiram Abiff in the valley. Q. Why is it situated northeast from the sanctuary? A. To teach us men should be undefiled before they enter the sanctum sanctorum. Q. What is signified by the rope which comes from the tomb to the temple? A. The rope of green with which the brethren raised the body of Hiram Abiff before they put it into the coffin. Q. There is a further reason. A. The virtue of goodness that should link us to the temple. Q. Why were you examined in the former degrees before you were admitted? A. To see if I were perfect in them before I went any further? Q. What is your color? A. Green. Q. Why so? A. To signify, that by flourishing in virtue, I might expect to make progress in my last degrees. Q. What is signified by the two pyramids in the lodge? A. Egypt, from whence the Israelites came. Q. What does the jewel represent? A. That a Perfect Master should measure his conduct by the exact rule of equity.

Close by four times four.

INTIMATE SECRETARY.

Opening.—Solomon knocks three times nine, which is repeated by Hiram of Tyre, and then by all the brethren who are supposed to be Perfect Masters. They kneel, make signs, repeat the 'word' thrice, then rise, take their swords and go out of the lodge.

Solomon having first appointed a captain and lieutenant of the guards, with directions that they take care of the lodge, and see that none approach without permission, and that all the guards observe their duty.

Reception.—Candidate being in the antichamber, the captain of the guards orders two or three of them to take from him his hat, sword, and the decorations of a Perfect Master, and then to place him by the door, (partly open) with his hands across, in the attitude of listening. The guards make a little noise, on which Hiram of Tyre, turning his head, sees the *cowans,* lifts his eyes to heaven and says, 'Oh heavens, there is a listener!' Solomon says, 'It is impossible, as there are guards without.' Hiram of Tyre without reply makes to the door and drags the candidate by the hands into the lodge, crying, 'Here he is!' Solomon, 'What shall we do with him?' Hiram of Tyre, (his hand on his sword,) 'We must kill him!'

Solomon quits his place and lays hold of Hiram of Tyre, and says, 'Stop, my brother:' then knocks on the table, the guards enter and salute the lodge. Solomon, 'Take this prisoner and secure him, and let him be forthcoming when called for!' on which they go out with the prisoner, leaving Solomon and Hiram of Tyre for some time in private and low conversation. Solomon knocks on the table again, and the guards return with the prisoner in the midst. By a signal from Solomon they advance near the foot of the throne and take seats. Solomon then says to candidate, 'I have by my entreaties prevailed on the king of Tyre, my worthy ally, whom your vain curiosity has offended, to remit the sentence of death which he pronounced upon you. I have not only obtained your pardon, but have gained his consent to receive you an Intimate Secretary to the alliance we have contracted. Do you promise to keep inviolate the secrets entrusted to you in this degree, and will you take an obligation for that purpose, in the most solemn manner? (Yes.) Solomon causes him to kneel.

Obligation.—' 1st. Secrecy. 2d. Obey mandates and decrees of the Grand Council of Princes of Jerusalem. Penalty—body dissected, bowels taken out, heart cut in pieces, and the whole thrown to the wild beasts of the field!' Solomon raises the candidate and explains the carpet. ' The window in the clouds represent the vault of the temple, and the letter I, which you see therein, is the initial of the name of the Grand Architect of the Universe. The door represents the great gate, by which they entered from the palace: the tears are emblematical of Solomon's chamber of audience for Masons, in the palace hung with black, and hither he used to retire and lament the unhappy fate of Hiram Abiff, and here he was when Hiram, king of Tyre, came to visit him.' ' I receive you, my brother, an Intimate Secretary, on your promise of being faithful to this order which you have just now entered, as was the great man whose place you are now to supply. The color of your ribbon is intended to remind you of his blood, the last drop of which he chose to spill, rather than betray his secrets; we hope, therefore, that your fidelity will be proof to every trial, and that the sword with which we arm you, will be a weapon of defence, to guard you from the attacks that might be made on you to extort those secrets, which we are now going to confer on you,' &c. &c.

LECTURE.

Q. Are you an Intimate Secretary? A. I am. Q. How were you received? A. By curiosity. Q. What danger did you risk?

A. The loss of life. Q. What was done to you after you were apprehended? A. I had sentence of death pronounced on me, and was delivered into the hands of the guard. Q. Were they Intimate Secretaries or Perfect Masters? A. I was then ignorant thereof, but my resolution and integrity convinced me that I was the first that was made an Intimate Secretary. Q. What are the pass words? A. [See page 346.] Q. What is the grand word? A. * * * *. Q. What were you before you were examined and received an Intimate Secretary? A. A favorite of Solomon. Q. Of what province? A. Copentister. Q. How many cities did Solomon give to Hiram for the materials he supplied him with, in the building of the temple? A. Thirty. Q. Where were you received? A. In Solomon's apartment, lined with black and lighted with twenty-seven lights. Q. What doth the letter I. signify, which you saw in the window? A. * * * *. Q. What does that word signify? A. It is the third name of Deity, and signifies, give thanks to Him, the work is done. Q. What is signified by A and two P's, in the angle? A. Alliance, promise, prosecution. Q. Why is this lodge lighted with twenty-seven lights? A. To represent two thousand seven hundred candlesticks Solomon made for his temple. Q. What doth the great door in the carpet represent? A. The door of Solomon's palace. Q. What is signified by the triple triangle you wear? A. The three theological virtues, faith, hope, and charity. Q. There is another interpretation? A. Solomon, Hiram, and Hiram king of Tyre. Q. What is the hour? A. It is nine. Lodge closed by three times nine, as in opening.

PROVOST AND JUDGE.

Opening.—Master. 'Brother Wardens, are we well tyled?' A. 'Thrice Illustrious, we are.' Master. 'Where is your Master placed?' A. 'Every where.' M. 'Why so?' A. 'To superintend the workmen, direct the work, and render justice to every man.' Q. 'What is the hour?' A. 'Break of day,—eight o'clock,—two and seven.' Master knocks five quick and slow —separate—which is repeated by the Wardens. Master. 'It is break of day,—eight o'clock,—two and seven; it is time to proceed to work.' This is repeated by the Wardens. Brethren clap hands four and one: Master says, 'The lodge is open!'

Reception.—The Master of Ceremonies leads the candidate to the door and knocks four and one, which is repeated by the Wardens and Master from within. Master orders a brother to see who is there; after the brother has inquired, he says, 'A brother who wishes to be passed to the degree of Provost and Judge.' Master sends word to Master of Ceremonies to examine him well and then introduce him in ancient form. Master of Ceremonies leads him, and places him between the Wardens. Senior Warden orders him to kneel and say 'Chivi,' and puts a naked sword in his hand and on his left shoulder, Master says, 'Ky,' and Senior Warden raising candidate, leads him seven times round the lodge, each time he passes the Master he gives a sign, (beginning with Entered Apprentice;) he is then led to the altar, and there addressed by the Master. (See Monitor.) 'I now intrust you with the key of the place, where is kept the body and heart of Hiram Abiff, as also the box in which is kept the plans of the temple; and you are now to give us assurance that you will never discover the place where the body is interred.' (He promises, and takes the following obligation.)

Obligation.—' 1st. Secrecy. 2d. I will justly and impartially regulate all matters of difference between brethren; I will be just and equitable to all the world, as I am constituted by this lodge to render justice. 3d. I will pay due obedience to the mandate of the Grand Council of Princes of Jerusalem, and govern myself by their regulations.' Penalty—that of all the former degrees. Candidate rises, and the Master gives him a blow with the sceptre on each shoulder, saying, 'By the power with which I am invested, I constitute you a Provost and Judge over all the works and workmen of the temple, and I decorate you, in this character, with the golden key, suspended by a red ribbon, which you are to wear in the form of a collar; this apron is trimmed with the same color; the red denotes the order of the Mason, and the pocket in the centre is to carry your plans for the construction of the temple.

LECTURE.

Q. Are you a Provost and Judge? A. I am, and render justice to all the workmen without distinction. Q. How were you introduced into this lodge? A. By four and one distinct knocks. Q. What is signified by four and one, separate? A. The four represents the four fronts of the temple, and the one signifies the temple of God. Q. Whom did you meet with in your road? A. A Warden, who conducted me to the west. Q. What was done with you there? A. The Senior Warden made me kneel on my right knee, and say 'Rivi.' Q. What answer was given to that? A. The Thrice Illustrious, 'said Ky.' Q. What is the signification of these words? A. The first signifies 'kneel,' and the second 'rise.' Q. What was next done? A. He made me a Provost and Judge. Q. What did he deliver to you? A. A golden key to distinguish this degree. Q. For what purpose is this key? A. To open a small ebony box, in which were kept the plans for constructing the temple. Q. What is meant thereby? A. That a Provost and Judge only knows where this box is, as well as where the heart of Hiram Abiff lies. Q. What is the pass word? A. '*Tito.*' Q. What is the signification of that word? A. It is the name of the first Grand Warden, Prince Harodim, and the eldest of the Provosts and Judges, whose care it was to superintend the three hundred architects of the temple. Q. What did you perceive in the lodge? A. A curtain, behind which was suspended a small ebony box enriched with jewels. Q. What did this box contain? A. All the designs. Q. Did you see any thing else? A. I saw a triangle in the centre of the lodge in which was "G. A." Q. What is meant by these two letters? A. " Grand Architect." Q. What more did you see? A. A balance in equilibrio. Q. What is meant thereby? A. That equity of judgment which is our particular duty, being nominated to decide all differences among the workmen. Q. Where was the heart of Hiram Abiff deposited? A. In an urn of gold upon the top of an obelisk. Q. What is signified by the letter X? A. Xinchen, the seat of the soul. Q. What is signified by the letters I. H. S., with the sprig of cassia? A. Juabs, Hiram, Stokin. Q. In what place were you received? A. In the middle chamber. Q. What was your duty? A. To perfect the tomb of Hiram Abiff. Q. What did the Thrice Illustrious invest you with upon your initiation? A. With a white apron, lined with blood red color, and in the centre of which was a pocket with a red and white rose. Q. What was its use? A. To carry the plans in, that they might be laid out on the trestle-board, as regular designs for the workmen. Q. What is signified by the red and white rose? A. The red denotes the blood of Hiram Abiff, and the white, the innocency and truth of the Master. Q. What was the intention of Solomon in forming this degree? A. To preserve order amongst the workmen. Joabert, being honored with the intimate confidence of Solomon, received a new mark of distinction. Solomon first created Tito, Prince Harodim, Adoniram, and Abda, his father, Provosts and Judges, and gave them orders to initiate Joabert, his favorite, into the most sacred mysteries, and to give him the keys of all the buildings, which were inclosed in a small ivory box, suspended in the sanctum sanctorum, under a rich canopy. When Joabert was first admitted into that sacred place, he was struck with admiration and awe, and, falling on his knees, pronounced Chivi. Solomon, see-

R

ing him prostrate, said to him Ky, and gave to him the balance as a badge of his office.

Close.—Q. What is your age? A. Four times sixteen. Q. From whence came you? A. I came and am going every where. Q. What is the o'clock? A. Break of day—eight o'clock—two and seven. Q. How so? A. Because, as Provost and Judge, I must be ready to render justice at all times. The lodge is closed as it is opened.

INTENDANT OF THE BUILDINGS,

OR

MASTER IN ISRAEL.

Solomon is in the east, Tito in the west, and Adoniram in the south.

Opening.—Solomon. 'Tito, are we tyled?' Tito. 'Most Puissant, we are.' Q. 'What is it o'clock?' A. 'Break of day.' Solomon strikes five on the altar with his sceptre, which is repeated by Tito and Adoniram. Solomon. 'As it is break of day, it is time to work.' (The lodge is open.) All the brethren strike five together, and make the sign of surprise and admiration.

Reception.—Master. 'Brother Tito, how shall we repair the loss of our worthy Hiram Abiff? You know he had the ornaments of the secret chamber in charge, which contained the holy ark, which was to assure the Israelites of the perfection of the most Holy God. He is now taken from us by a most horrid crime of our craft, and we are thereby deprived of our most respectable chief; now, my Illustrious Brother, see if you are able to give me advice in this important matter.'

A. 'Most Puissant, the method I would propose would be to create one chief from the five orders of architecture, in order to unite all abilities, and endeavor to finish the work of the secret chamber of the third story.'

M. 'Your advice is good; and to convince you of my readiness to follow it, I appoint you, brethren, to inspect the condition of this business. Excellent brethren, let Adoniram go into the middle chamber, and see if he can find a chief of the five orders of architecture.'

Adoniram goes, and finding Joabert, says, 'Are there here any chiefs of the five orders of architecture?' Joab. 'I am the introductor.' Adon. 'My dear brother, have you zeal to apply yourself with attention to that which the Most Puissant shall request of you?' Joab. 'I have, and will with all pleasure comply with the request of the Most Puissant, and raise this edifice to his honor and glory.' Adon. 'Give me the signs, words, and tokens of the preceding degrees.' Adoniram knocks at the door of the lodge, three, five, and seven. One of the brethren within answers the alarm, and asks what is wanted. A. 'There is one here who is to be employed in the works of the middle chamber.' The door is opened, and Adoniram, griping the candidate by the token of Master, brings him before the altar, and lays him down. Tito stands behind, puts the sprig of cassia in his hand, and he takes the obligation. 1st. Secrecy. 2d. Obedience to the orders and decrees of the Grand Council of Princes of Jerusalem. Penalty.—Body severed in two, and bowels taken out, when the candidate says, 'Amen.' Tito covers his body with a red cloth, and relieves him by the token, and with his hand to his elbow, raises and places him on a stool, when he is thus addressed by the Master :—' My dear brother, Solomon, willing to carry to the highest perfection the work already begun, found it necessary to employ five chiefs of the five orders of architecture ; and he gave command of them to Tito, Adoniram, and Abda ; his father being well assured that their zeal would be exerted to the utmost in bringing to perfection the works of the middle chamber. We, therefore, flatter ourselves, my brother, that you will contribute all in your power to the same end. The situation you have just been in, resembles that of a dead man, and you being relieved from it, signifies our hope that you will repair the loss of our respected Hiram Abiff ; having so bright an example before you, that you will endeavor to show the same firmness and contempt of death, sooner than discover any of the secrets. I will now raise you in the same manner he was raised under the sprig of cassia.' The candidate is raised, and Tito gives him the signs, tokens, and words.

LECTURE.

Q. Are you an Intendant of the Buildings? A. I have made the five steps of exactness ; I have penetrated the inmost part of the temple ; and I have seen the great light, in the middle of which were three mysterious letters, or characters, in Hebrew, without knowing what they meant. Q. How came you to be received? A. By acknowledging my ignorance. Q. Why were you received? A. To point out to me the darkness in which I was, and to procure me a true light to regulate my heart, and regulate my understanding. Q. In what place were you introduced ? A. In a place full of wonder and beauty, where truth and wisdom reside. Q. What was your duty? A. To superintend the work. Q. Why were you made to walk backward and forward in the lodge? A. To show me, that, in advancing to virtue, I should set humanity in opposition to the pride so natural to us. Q. What signify the letters I. I. I. in the centre of the triangle? A. [See page 347.] which are expressive of the wisdom of God. Q. What is meant by the J. in the middle of the blazing star in the lodge? A. It is the initial of that ineffable name. Q. What is signified by the circle in the triangle? A. It teaches the immensity of God, without beginning or ending. Q. What is signified by the four letters J. A. I. N. in the circle? A. The divine attributes of the Deity. Q. What are the principal attributes? A. Beauty, wisdom, mercy, omniscience, eternity, perfection, justice, tenderness, creation, providence;* which together make the square of nine. Q. Why were you barefoot at your admission? A. Because Moses was barefoot when he saw the burning bush. Q. What did the five knocks represent? A. The five points of felicity. Q. What did they produce? A. A Warden, who conducted me five times round the temple, and supported me. Q. What did you see there? A. The holy name in the blazing star. Q. Why had that star no more than five rays? A. To denote the five orders of architecture, made use of in the building of the temple; the five points of fellowship; the five senses, without which a man cannot be perfect; the five lights of Masonry; and the five zones of the world inhabited by Masons. Q. What is the name in the centre of the star? A. * * * * *, or the sacred name. Q. Why is blue and gold so peculiar to this degree? A. That was the color of the clouds in which God appeared to Moses, on the mount. Q. Do you continue still in darkness? A. The morning is light, and the blazing star is my guide. Q. What is your age? A. Twenty-seven. Q. What numbers have you marked? A. Five, seven, and fifteen. Q. Explain them. A. Five points of felicity, seven golden candlesticks, and fifteen Fellow Crafts, who joined Hiram Abiff in the grave.

Close.—Q. 'What's the hour?' A. 'Seven at night.' Q. 'My brethren, after having practised the five points of felicity, it is high time to repose and refresh.' The Master knocks five, which is repeated by the brethren, five, seven, and fifteen, and the lodge is closed.

---

* By numbering the letters of these words, it will be seen they amount to eighty-one.

ELECTED KNIGHTS OF NINE.

For the form of the lodge, see Monitor, and, in addition, the brethren have their knees crossed, and their heads reclining on their right hands. Master. 'Brother Stokin, are you an Elected Knight of Nine?' A. 'One cavern received me, one lamp gave me light, and one spring refreshed me.' Q. 'What is the hour?' A. 'Break of day.' Master knocks eight and one, Stokin repeats it, and then all the brethren, with their poniards; and the Master declares the chapter open.

Reception.—Master of Ceremonies leads the candidate to the door, and knocks eight and one. The Master orders the candidate to be admitted. He is conducted to the west, and placed behind Stokin. M. 'What do you wish?' A. 'To be admitted an Elected Knight.' Q. 'Have you courage enough to revenge the death of your Master, Hiram Abiff?' A. 'I have.' Q. 'If you have, you shall be shown where one of his murderers is concealed—a stranger has shown the place to me, and if you have fortitude, follow the stranger.' The candidate is blinded, led to the cavern, and seated on the stone. The Master of Ceremonies says, 'Be of good courage, I am going to leave you, but shall not be long absent; and after I am gone, you must take the bandage from your eyes, and drink some of the water you will find before I return.' Candidate is left alone, and the door is shut. The Master of Ceremonies returns, and orders him to take the poniard in his right hand, and the head in his left, and he thus goes alone to the door of the lodge, where he knocks eight and one. Master of Ceremonies within, says, 'What do you wish?' A. 'An Intendant of the buildings demands to enter the chapter.' Q. 'Have you finished your time, and satisfied your Master?' A. 'I have had the honor of performing a feat for the honor of the craft, which will, I hope, entitle me to this degree.' Master of Ceremonies repeats to Stockin, who repeats to the Master, and he orders the candidate to be admitted. He advances, by eight quick and one slow steps, holding the poniard elevated, as if to strike. The ninth step brings him to the altar, where he falls on his knees. Master observes him, and says, 'Wretch, what have you done? Do you not know that by this rash act, you have deprived me of the pleasure of devoting the villain to condign punishment? Stokin, let him be put immediately to death.' At this word, all the brethren, falling on their knees, intercede for the candidate, observing to the Master, that his offence arose from zeal, and not from any intention of depriving the Master of the pleasure of punishing the villain. This pacifies him, and he orders Stokin to stop, and tell the candidate, 'that he shall be pardoned this second time, but beware of the third.' Stokin takes the head and poniard from the candidate, and places the poniard at the foot, and the head at the top, of the altar. The candidate is still on his knees, and all the brethren standing round, as if to strike;—he takes the obligation. '1st. I do solemnly swear, in the presence of Almighty God, that I *will revenge* the assassination of our worthy Master, Hiram Abiff, not only on the murderers, but also *on all who may betray the secrets of this degree;* and furthermore, that I will keep and protect this order with all my might, and the brethren, in general, with all my power; and furthermore, that I will obey the decrees of the Grand Council of Princes, of Jerusalem; and, if I violate this, my obligation, *I consent to be struck with the dreadful poniard of vengeance,* now presented to me, and to have my head cut off, and stuck on the highest pole, or pinnacle, in the eastern part of the world, as a monument of my villany! Amen! Amen! Amen! Amen!'

Master raises candidate, and says, 'Some time after the death of Hiram Abiff, and before Solomon had been able to discover the traitors who had murdered him, a great assembly of Masters,' [as in Monitor, to the words] 'who had only time to pronounce Nekam, (vengeance is taken;) immediately after which, Joabert, being thirsty, and perceiving a spring of water, he drank, and then slept until the rest arrived and awoke him. On beholding the bloody scene, they all exclaimed Nekam! Joabert then acquainted them with what had happened, and they *envied* him for having alone avenged the death of Hiram Abiff. After having refreshed themselves at the spring, Joabert *cut off the head,* and divided the body into four quarters, which were burnt, and the ashes scattered in the air, so as that they might be dispersed to the four winds of heaven, and to the corners of the earth. Then, taking the poniard and head, Joabert said Nekam! and returned to Jerusalem.' (See Monitor, part 2d, chapter VI.)

Joabert was afterwards *highly favored* of Solomon, who conferred on him and the others this degree of Elected Knight, and then gave them the following signs: [See p. 347.]

LECTURE.

Q. Are you an elected Knight? A. One cavern I knew, and entered. Q. What did you see there? A. A light, a poniard, and the traitor Akirop. Q. What did you do with them? A. The light to light me, the poniard to revenge, and the spring to refresh me! Q. Where were you admitted? A. In the audience chamber of Solomon. Q. How many were elected? A. Nine, including myself. Q. From what number were they elected? A. Ninety-nine. Q. For what purpose? A. To revenge the death of Hiram Abiff. Q. Where did you find him? A. In the bottom of a cavern, near a burning bush in a cleft, near the coast of Joppa. Q. Who conducted you there? A. A stranger. Q. What way did you travel to the cavern? A. By dark intricate roads. Q. In what manner did the Elected Knights march? A. Darkness often obliged them to put their hands before their eyes, to prevent their being put out; from the difficulty of the roads they were obliged to cross their legs, and this is the reason the Elected Knights sit in that manner in the lodge. Q. What is meant by the dog you see in the carpet of the lodge? A. The sagacity of the stranger who conducted them to the cavern. Q. What does the color of black denote in this degree? A. Grief. Q. What remains to be done? A. Nothing, because every thing is accomplished? Q. Give me the pass word? A. '———,' (all the signs given.) Q. What time did you go in search of the assassins? A. At break of day. Q. When did you return? A. At night. Q. What is your age? A. Eight and one, accomplished.

Close.—Q. What is the time? A. Evening. The Master knocks eight and one, which is repeated by all the brethren. He then gives the sign, which is answered by all. He then says, 'Nekam,' and the rest, 'Vengeance,' and the lodge is closed.

ELECTED GRAND MASTER,

OR

ILLUSTRIOUS ELECTED OF FIFTEEN.

Opening.—Master knocks three times five. The Inspector repeats it, and the Master declares the lodge is open.

Reception.—The candidate has a head in his hand, and is led to the door of the lodge by the Senior Warden, who knocks three times five, and the Inspector goes to the door, and demands, Who is there? Upon which the Senior Warden says, 'An Elected Knight, who is desirous of joining the other Knights in finding the other two assassins, and to be admitted among the elect fifteen.' The Inspector shuts the door and reports to the Master, who gives orders for his admission, and he is taught to make fifteen steps in a triangular form, which brings him to the altar. The brethren all stand round with poniards, and interlacing their hands before their foreheads with the palms presented to view, and they ask pardon for the candidate. M. 'Why do you ask pardon?'

A. 'Because they are not guilty.' M. 'Why do you ask pardon for a person who is not guilty?' A. 'In order to qualify him to become a Grand Master Elect.' M. 'Is he well qualified?' A. 'He is.' M. 'Kneel, brother, the Grand Masters Elect here present desire me to admit you a member of this degree; will you take the solemn obligation to keep the secrets inviolable?' A. 'I will.'

Obligation.—The penalty is, to have the body opened perpendicularly and horizontally, and exposed to the air for eight hours, that the flies may prey on his entrails, also, to have the head cut off and placed on the highest pinnacle in the world, and *to be ready to inflict the same penalty on all who disclose the secrets of this degree!!!* Master raises the candidate and gives the signs, &c. (For history, see Monitor, part 2d, chapter vii.) 'Solomon determined that their punishment should be adequate to their crimes, and when the day of their execution arrived, they were brought forth at 10 o'clock, A. M. and were executed, and were bound, neck and middle, to posts in the most public place, with their arms extended; and their bellies were cut open by the executioner, lengthwise, and across, and in this position they remained until six o'clock in the evening, so that the flies might prey on their entrails; their heads were then cut off and placed on spikes with that of ———— ————, on the east, west, and south pinnacles of the temple, under which they had committed their crime.

LECTURE.

Q. Are you a Grand Master Elect? A. My zeal and works have produced me that honor! Q. How were you received? A. By Solomon himself, in his apartment. Q. When and for what purpose? A. At the time he sent me, together with my companions, to find out the two assassins! Q. How came they to be discovered? A. By the diligence of Bengabee ————, Solomon's intendant, in the province of Cheth. Q. Who carried Solomon's letter to the king Morihah? A. Tabeal. Q. How many did he send on this occasion? A. Fifteen. Q. Give me the sign, token, and word. (Given.) Q. What do they allude to? A. That I *shall always be ready to inflict the same punishment on all who shall betray the secrets of this degree.*

Close.—Q. At what hour did the assassins expire? A. Their execution was at ten o'clock, A. M. and at six in the evening, vengeance was accomplished! Q. *May all traitors meet the same fate!!!* Master knocks fifteen, which is repeated first by the Inspector, then by all the brethren, and the lodge is closed.

ILLUSTRIOUS KNIGHTS,

OR,

SUBLIME KNIGHTS ELECTED.

Opening.—Master knocks twelve times at equal intervals, which is repeated by the Grand Inspector only. M. 'What is the hour?' Grand Inspector. 'Twelve.' M. 'It is time to improve our labors by the greatest of lights; I pronounce the Grand Chapter open.'

Reception.—Candidate is introduced by Master of Ceremonies, who knocks twelve at the door, which is answered by Master within, then by the Grand Inspector, who goes to the door and demands 'Who is there?' Master of Ceremonies. 'A Grand Master Elect of fifteen, who is desirous of being admitted to this Grand Chapter of Illustrious Knights:'—This is repeated to the Master who orders him to be introduced. He must be decorated as a Grand Master Elect of fifteen. He is first led to the Grand Inspector who examines him in all his former degrees. M. 'Companion Grand Inspector, what does this candidate desire?' Grand Inspector. 'To be admitted to the degree of Illustrious Knight.' M. 'As a remembrance of his zeal and labor, I will admit him.' M. (to candidate) 'I suppose, my brother, you only wish to become an Illustrious Knight, from interested motives?' A. 'My first view is, doing my duty, which I have done at my own expense, to punish all traitors; and now I request this honor as a remembrance.' M. 'Advance and take the obligation.'

Obligation.—'1st. Secrecy. 2d. To be charitable.' *Penalty.*—'The body cut in quarters.' The Master raises the candidate and gives the signs, &c.

Close.—M. 'You have this day received pay from the workmen, who have performed well, and you are worthy of the name you bear, from the strict attendance to promote peace and harmony, and to animate the laborers with cheerfulness! Master knocks twelve, which is repeated by the Grand Inspector, and the lodge is closed.

GRAND MASTER ARCHITECTS.

Opening.—Master knocks one and two, which is repeated by the Grand Warden. Q. 'Are you a Grand Master Architect?' A. I know the use of every mathematical instrument.' Q. 'What are they.' A. 'A square, a single compass, a compass with four

202   LIGHT ON MASONRY.

points, a rule, a line, a compass of perfection, a quadrant, a level, and a plumb.' Q. 'Where were you made and received?' A. 'In a white place painted with flames.' Q. 'What do these signify?' A. 'The purity of heart and zeal that should be characteristic of every good Mason Architect.' Q. 'What does the star in the north signify in this degree?' A. 'Virtue, which ought to be a guide to every good Mason, as the north star is to mariners.' Q. 'What is the hour?' A. 'A star appears for break of day.' Master. 'Let us work, I declare this lodge open.'

Reception.—Candidate being introduced by one and two, and led once round the north star, is made to advance three square steps and then takes the same obligation as that of Illustrious Knights; he then rises and is made to recede three steps backward, which brings him between the Wardens, and the Grand Warden gives him the sign, token, and word. (For history, see Monitor.)

Close.—Master knocks one and two, which is followed first by the Grand Warden, then by all the brethren; after this they all salute the Master, and the lodge is closed.

THE DEGREE
OF
KNIGHTS OF THE NINTH ARCH.

Solomon knocks nine, (! ! ! ! ! ! ! ! !) Hiram of Tyre repeats, the Grand Junior Warden calls to order, and then he and the rest of the brethren knock the same. The two kings give signs of admiration, first to each other and then to the brethren, by whom it is repeated. The two kings kneel at the pedestal, Solomon rises, then raises Hiram of Tyre, after which brethren kneel at the pedestal, by order of Solomon.—Solomon says, 'I declare this chapter open.'

Reception.—Previous to the reception the vault and the pedestal are darkened and the trap door is opened, the candidate or candidates, (if more than one,) are introduced into the room over the trap door. Two brethren, at least, being with candidates as guards, one of which demands, 'The favour of being admitted to the degree of 'Knights of the Arch,' on account of his zeal, and his having regularly taken all the foregoing degrees.' He is answered from below that at present it is not possible, but that they must pray to God for permission. The guards retire, and then make the request, to which the same answer is returned. They repeat this the third time. Then the Grand Junior Warden asks if they are willing to descend into the lower abyss in search of great treasure?' (*Ans.* 'Yes.') A rope is then tied round one of the candidates to let him down into the vault. He is told if he sees any thing on being lowered down, he is to shake the rope and he will be raised; he is then twice lowered and raised, the third time they give him a burning taper, and, on his being let down this time, one, who is concealed below, blows out the taper, and one from above throws down some pieces of stone and mortar, and the candidate beholds the pedestal, (uncovered.) He is to fall on his knees, with all below, around the pedestal. Candidate continues in this posture, if there are more than one candidate, until all are let down. The Grand Junior Warden tells him or them that in this posture they are to take that inviolable and secret obligation.

Obligation.—I do promise and vow, in the most solemn manner, and in the presence of the most holy and puissant, and most terrible just and merciful God, that I will double my assiduity zeal and love for my fellow brethren who have taken this degree of K. A. I promise further never to assist at the initiation of any brother into this degree, nor to give my consent that he be initiated, unless he shall regularly have received all the foregoing degrees in a just and regular lodge, and unless he shows a charitable disposition for Masonry, and also obtains a permission from under the hands and seals of the officers of a just and regular lodge, according to ancient laws. I furthermore promise never to give to any number less than three, and those to be well examined, this degree, unless when authorised for that pupose by a particular patent, and with a view of constituting a lodge of K. A. Masons—which I will never consent to be holden within twenty-five leagues of one already regularly constituted. I further promise carefully to observe and pay due obedience to all the laws, rules and regulations, established and appointed by this K. A. Chapter, as also to keep inviolable the secrets communicated in it. I furthermore promise that I *will not debauch any female related to a brother, knowing them to be such.* All this I promise under the penalties of my former obligations, and in case of failure, that my body may be exposed to the beasts of the forest as a prey; so God maintain me in my present obligation. (For history of this degree see Webb's Monitor, 2d part, chapter 10.) 'When the treasure, which had been found in the ground, was produced (to Solomon and Hiram of Tyre) they fell on their knees, gave the sign of admiration, and exclaimed ' Gibulum is a good man!' After Gibulum, Joabert and Stokin were introduced to the second vault, and, receiving all the honors of this degree, Solomon explained to them the sacred word, which was engraved on the golden plate, which was the true name of the Most High, but that it had been already much corrupted as had already been observed. The principle ages of Masonry were three, five, seven, and nine, which by calculation made eighty-one, or the cube of three. I shall give you the different methods of pronouncing the words precious to the Arch we are now treating of, classed according to the above numeral.

3 — All powerful.* 5 — It is what it will be.
3 — Divine light. 5 — God himself.
3 — Striking light. 5 — Eternal God.
7 — O thou who art eternal. 9 — God of mercy.
7 — Sustain us, O God. 9 — My trust is in God.
7 — God of lights. 9 — The grand name.

This last is the application known only to those who have been admitted to the sublime degree of Perfection, which, in due time, will also be communicated to you. From the corruption of the grand word spring the Juha of the Moors, the Jupiter of the Romans, and others of like nature. The true name was visible in the temple, at the time St. Jerome flourished, written in the ancient Samaritan characters, and still preserved in the heart of every good and faithful K. A. Mason. This mysterious word is covered by three signs, three tokens, three covered words, and three pass words, which will all be particularly explained to you in the lodge of Perfection. The *three* now elected took an oath before God, never to pronounce his sacred name, nor even to admit to this sublime degree, any Mason, until he gave sufficient proof of his zeal and attachment, and promise to use the same ceremonies of initiation, in order to commemorate the mysterious history of the divine Delta, and the Burning Bush, and where the Almighty caused the ancient patriarch to promise that he would never fully pronounce his sacred and true name.'

The number of the grand and sublime elect, &c. (as in Monitor, to the word 'Perfection,') where this last mentioned lodge was holden, nine Knights of the Royal Arch, styled the nine arches which led to the sacred vault. The most ancient stood in the arch next to the vault, and so on in regular procession, and none were permitted to pass but those who were qualified, giving the pass of each, viz. [See p. 350.]

And at the sacred vault the pass word of the Fellow Craft pronounced three times. Appertaining to this degree are two signs and one token, besides the before mentioned passes. For charge, see Monitor, and it concludes thus, ' I shall now conclude with exhorting you, my brothers, who have been made acquainted with

---

* The words are omitted, and only the Masonic translation of them is here given.

the mode of contemplating often on the grand mysteries, to endeavour by your zeal and constancy, to receive the ultimate degree of Moral Knowledge.

LECTURE.

Q. In what place are we? A. In the centre of the most holy place on earth. Q. By what means did you gain admission? A. By divine providence. Q. Explain that. A. I wrought in the ruins of the ancient temple of Enoch; I penetrated through nine arches under ground and finally found the Delta, containing the name which God had pronounced to the patriarchs. Q. What is the Delta? A. The triangle of gold, enriched with precious stones and affording great light, and upon which was engraved by Enoch that great and mysterious name, Jehovah. Q. Do you know the true pronunciation of that word? A. I do not, and it is only known to the Grand Elect Perfect and Sublime Masons. Q. Who are you? A. I am what I am: my name is Gibulum. Q. What is your quality? A. A Knight of Royal Arch. Q. How were you received in this quality? A. By the two kings, Solomon, and Hiram king of Tyre, in company with my brethren, Joabert and Stokin, as a reward of my zeal and constancy. Q. Give me the sign, token and words, (given.) Q. Have you any thing else to desire? A. I have, the Ultimate Degree of Masonry, and eternal happiness.

Close.—Q. What is the time, brother Junior Grand Warden? A. It is evening. Q. Acquaint the brethren that I am going to close this Royal Arch Lodge, by the most powerful and mysterious number. Solomon strikes nine, which is repeated by the king of Tyre, by the Grand Junior Warden and officers, and the rest of the brethren. Junior Warden calls to order, on which the two kings, and all the brethren, give the signs, tokens, and words, and Solomon says, 'This Royal Arch Lodge is closed, with all its honors!'

THE DEGREE OF PERFECTION,

OR

GRAND ELECT PERFECT AND SUBLIME MASON.

(*For description of lodge, titles, &c. see Monitor, Part 2d. Book I. chap.* xi.) Delta, and appearance of the burning bush, under which are ruins, and before the Master a broken pedestal, lights are arranged according to the several stages of Masonry, viz. three behind Junior Warden—five behind Senior Warden—seven in the south, and nine behind the Master. When the candidate wishes for admission to the vault he gives the following pass word, viz.—Firstly ———, secondly ———, thirdly; pass word repeated thrice. [See p. 351.]

Opening.—*Master.* 'Most Venerable Wardens, are we well tyled?' *Answer.* 'Right Worshipful and Most Perfect, we are.' M. 'Let us pray.' (See Monitor.) M. 'Venerable brother Senior Warden, what brings you here?' A. 'Right Worshipful and Most Perfect, the love of Masonry, my obligation, and a desire for perfection.' Q. 'What are the properties and qualities for acquiring it?' A. 'The two first lead to the third and are three to happiness.' Q. 'What have you brought here?' A. 'A heart zealous in virtue and friendship.' Q. 'What is the disposition of an Elect Perfect and Sublime Mason?' A. 'To have a heart divested of jealous revenge and iniquity, and always ready to do good and keep his tongue from calumny, and detraction.' Q. 'How are you to behave in this place?' A. 'With the most profound respect.' Q. 'Whence comes it, my brother, that men of all ranks and conditions are in this place, and are termed brethren together, and are all equal?' A. Because that sacred and ineffable name puts us in mind, that there is one Infinity, that is superior to us all.' Q. 'Why is respect paid to that triangle?' A. 'Because it contains the name of the Grand Architect of the universe.' Q. 'What are you?' A. 'I am three times three, the perfect number of eighty-one, according to our mysterious number.' Q. 'Explain that.' A. 'I am a Grand Elect Perfect and Sublime Mason; my trials are finished, and it is now time I should reap the fruit of my labour.' Q. 'What is the hour?' A. 'High twelve.' Q. 'What do you understand by high twelve?' A. 'That the sun has gained its meridian height, and darts its rays with the greatest force on this lodge, which is the time we should avail ourselves of, to profit by his influence.' Q. 'Venerable Senior Warden announce that I am about to open this lodge of Perfect Masons, by the mysterious number of three, five, seven, and nine.' Senior Warden obeys—Junior Warden strikes three, Senior Warden five, and Master seven—silence follows—Master calls to order and gives three strokes, on which the brethren give the first sign; he then gives three other strokes, and the second sign is given; and so on until the third sign is given. M. 'Venerable Brother Senior Warden this lodge of 'Perfect Masons' is open.' Junior Warden announces it to brethren. Master gives sign of admiration, which is first repeated by Junior Warden and Senior Warden, and then by all the brethren. Master salutes the lodge with the first sign, which is answered by brethren. Brethren cover their heads and seat themselves.

Reception.—Candidate is in preparation room separated from the lodge by a long narrow passage, with all the ornaments of his former degrees. Master of Ceremonies directs him to knock three, five, and seven, at the first door of the passage, and to give the first pass word to the first guard, who says, 'Pass;' at the middle door he gives the second pass word to the second guard, who says 'Pass;' at the door of the sacred vault he gives the third pass word, and knocks three, five, seven, and nine, which are answered from within, alternately, by the Junior Warden, Senior Warden, and Master, who says, 'Brother Grand Junior Warden who knocks there in the manner of a Grand Elect Perfect and Sublime Mason?' Junior Warden goes and says, 'Who is there?' Master of Ceremonies answers, 'A Knight of the Royal Arch, who is desirous of arriving at Perfection, and being admitted to the second vault.' Junior Warden reports, and Master says, 'Admit him according to ancient form.' The door is opened, and the Master of Ceremonies and all the brethren presenting swords to his breast, and thus place him between the two Wardens, when he gives the sign of admiration to the Master. Silence follows for two minutes. M. 'What do you want here, my brother?' A. 'Most Royal Grand Perfect I ask the Perfection of Masonry.' M. 'Respectable brethren do you consent that he shall be admitted?' (Affirmative by uplifted hands.) M. 'My brother, before you are initiated into our sacred mysteries, you must answer the following questions, otherwise you must be sent back until you are better qualified.' Q. 'Are you a Mason?' A. 'My brethren all know me as such.' Q. 'Give me the sign, token, and word,' (candidate gives those of an Entered Apprentice.) Q. 'Are you a Fellow Craft?' A. 'I have the letter, —— and know the pass,——.' Q. 'Give me the pass, sign, token, and word.' (Given.) Q. 'Are you a Master Mason?' A. 'I know the sprig of cassia, and what it means.' Q. 'Give me the pass, sign, token, and word.' (Given.) Q. 'Are you a Sublime Mason?' A. 'I have passed from the square to the compass, and have seen the tomb of our respected Hiram Abiff, and have shed tears on his grave.' Q. 'Give me the sign, token, and word.' (Given.) Q. 'Are you a Perfect Master?' A. 'I have seen the two circles and two perfect squares placed on the two columns across.' Q. 'Give me the sign, token, and pass word.' (Given.) Q. 'Are you an Intimate Secretary?' A. 'My curiosity is satisfied, but it nearly cost me my life.' Q. 'Give me the sign, token, and word.' (Given.) Q. 'Are you a

Provost and Judge?' A. 'I render justice to all workmen without distinction.' Q. 'Give me the sign, token, and word.' (Given.) Q. 'Are you an Imtendant of the Buildings?' A. 'I have made the five steps of exactness; I have penetrated the inmost part of the temple; I have seen the great light in which were the three mysterious letters, in Hebrew characters, '———,' the meaning of which is unknown to me.' Q. 'Give me the sign, token, and word.' (Given.) Q. 'Are you an 'Elected Knight?' A. 'One cavern received me, one lamp gave me light, and one fountain refreshed me.' Q. 'Give me the sign, token, and word.' (Given.) Q. 'Are you a Grand Master Elect?' A. 'My zeal and labor have procured me that honor.' Q. 'Give me the sign, token, and word.' (Given.) Q. 'Are you an Illustrious Knight?' A. 'My name will inform you.' Q. 'Give me the sign, token, and word.' (Given.) Q. 'Are you a Grand Master Architect?' A. 'I am skilled in mathematical sciences and know the attributes?' Q. 'Give me the sign, token, and word.' (Given.) Q. 'Are you a Knight of the Royal Arch?' A. 'I have penetrated the bowels of the earth, through nine arches, and have seen the brilliant triangle.' Q. 'Give me the sign, token, and word.' (Given.) Q. 'What do you desire further, my brother?' A. 'To be exalted to the Degree of Perfection!' Master makes a sign of admiration, and says, 'Retire, my brother, God will permit that you receive what you so earnestly desire!' Master orders Master of Ceremonies to take candidate out till he shall be wanted. When he has retired the Most Perfect says, 'Brethren, you are still of the opinion that this Knight of the Royal Arch shall be admitted to the Degree of Perfection?' (The brethren signify their assent by uplifted hands.) The candidate is ordered to be admitted by the mysterious number. The Master of Ceremonies places him below the Wardens, and the Master says, 'Does your conscience, my brother, accuse you of committing any offence against your brethren, which may render you unworthy of this degree?' A. 'It does not.' Several other questions, designed to ascertain his honor and fidelity, are proposed, on which he is informed of the utility and importance of this degree, *which will prepare him for futurity*, &c. &c. The Master requests the Master of Ceremonies to teach the candidate to walk, eight quick and one slow steps, to the Master, with the sign of Elected Master on him, he kneels and takes the obligation. The following are the parts of the obligation.

1st. Secrecy. 2d. To conceal the laws and regulations of this degree. 3d. To assist brethren in sickness with his counsel, purse, and arms. 4th. Not to assist in making a brother of this degree, unless he shall be of good moral character, and who has been an officer of some regular lodge, and to receive him by virtue of a power granted by proper authority. 5th. To endeavor on all occasions to observe strictly, duties to God and community. The Penalty is, 'To have the body cut open, and the bowels torn out and given to the vultures for food!!' The candidate remains on his knees, while the Master of Ceremonies brings the hod and trowel, and the Master anoints his head, lips, and left breast, with the holy oil which anointed David and the wise Solomon. The Master says, 'I stamp you,' &c. (See the Monitor to the charge.) 'The matters which I shall now confer on you will perfect you in the study of Masonry. There are three signs, three guard words, and three pass words, which belong to this degree, besides the mysterious word.' (Master here gives them to candidate.) After this the candidate receives the charge as printed in the Monitor.

LECTURE.

Q. Who are you? A. I am a Grand Elect Perfect and Sublime Mason, and nothing is unknown to me. Q. Where were you admitted to this degree? A. In a place where the light of the sun or moon was not necessary. Q. Where is that place situated? A. Under the holy of holies, in a vault called the sacred vault. Q. Who received you in that sacred place? A. The wisest and most powerful of kings. Q. How did you enter? A. Through nine long arches. Q. How did you gain admission? A. By three knocks. Q. What did they signify? A. The age of the Entered Apprentice, and the number of Elected Knights, who penetrated the bowels of the earth and took from thence the inestimable treasure. Q. What was produced by the three knocks? A. Five other knocks. Q. What is their signification? A. The age of the Fellow Craft, and also the number of the Grand Elect when the treasure was first placed in the arch. Q. What were their names? A. Solomon, Hiram, Gibulum, Joabert and Stokin. Q. What followed these five knocks? A. Seven other knocks. Q. What do they signify? A. The age of the Master Mason, the seven expert brethren chosen to replace one, and the seven years the temple was building. Q. What answer was given to these seven knocks? A. Nine other knocks. Q. What is signified by those nine knocks? A. The age of the Perfect Master. Q. What did they produce? A. The opening of the ninth vault, and I penetrated into the most holy place in the world, where I heard pronounced, the word 'Plenty,' In Hebrew dialect. Q. What is signified by the three lights behind the Mas-

S 2

ter? A. The three Fellow Crafts, who slew Hiram Abiff. Q. Who were they? A. The three brothers of the tribe of Dan. Q. How do you enter the Lodge of Perfection? A. With the character of virtuous firmness and constancy. Q. How do you stand in the lodge of Perfect Masons? A. In an attitude of surprise. Q. Why so? A. Because Moses stood so when he saw God; Solomon and Hiram stood so when the precious treasure was brought before them from the vault of Enoch. Q. What are the tools of Grand Elect Masons? A. The shovel, crow, and pickaxe. Q. How long were the Israelites in bondage in Babylon? A. Seventy years.

Close.—Master. 'Acquaint the Wardens that I am about to close this lodge by three, five, seven, and nine.' This is announced by the Senior and Junior Wardens, who knock three, five, seven, and nine, and give the sign. M. 'Venerable brother Wardens, respectable officers of this lodge of Grand Elect Perfect and Sublime Masons, I charge you to retire in peace to practical virtue, and live always impressed with a just sense of duty, that the Grand Architect of the universe may always be present with us. May he bless us and all our works.'

Lodge is closed by three, five, seven, and nine.

SECRETS OF THE

LODGE OF PERFECTION.

The following are the *Signs*, *Tokens*, and *Words* of the three first ineffable degrees, conferred in the Lodge of Perfection.

SECRET MASTER.

The WORDS in this degree, are 'Shaddai,' 'Adonai,' and 'Juha.' The Pass Word is 'Zizon.'

The SIGN is given by placing the two fore fingers of the right hand on the lips. This is answered by placing the two fore fingers of the left hand on the lips.

The TOKEN, is to join hands as in the Master's Grip, then move hands to the elbows and give a grip, at the same time cross the legs.

PERFECT MASTER.

The Word in this degree is 'Jeva.'

There are three Signs. The *first* is given by placing the palm of the right hand on the right temple, at the same time stepping back with the right foot, after which bring the right foot to its first position. The *second* is that of admiration. Raise the hands and eyes to heaven, then let the arms fall across the belly and look downwards. The *third* is to advance the toes of the right feet, (that is of both persons) until they meet, bring the right knees together, place the hands on the heart, then bring the hand towards the right side.

INTIMATE SECRETARY.

The Grip in this degree is that of a Mark Master, given on the *five points*.

The Pass Words are, ' Joabert' and ' Zerbel.'

The *Mysterious Word* is ' Jova.'

The *first Sign* is to clinch the right hand, then draw it from the left shoulder to the right hip. The *second* is to cross the arms, then let them fall on the right hip.

Grip.—Join right hands, and reverse them thrice, repeating at each time one of these words, ' Berith,' ' Neder,' ' Shelemoth.'

Note.—Should the reader wish to know the reasons why *all* the Signs, Grips, and Words of the higher orders are not published, he may be informed that our object in publishing this work, is not to learn men how they can obtain admittance into the ' Secret Chambers ;' or, should they wish, to palm themselves upon the fraternity as members of the ' Mystic tie,' but to enlighten the community into the ceremonies, oaths, and principles of the institution. It is to these, we would direct their attention, for these are they by which the world must judge of its merits ; and by which, it must stand or fall. They are, however, *all* in possession, and should it be deemed *necessary*, they shall be given to the public, ' without money and without price.'

THE DEGREE OF
PRINCE OF JERUSALEM.

Prerogatives of the Princes.—Princes of Jerusalem have a right to inspect all lodges or councils of an inferior degree, and can revoke and annul all the work done in such councils or lodges, if the same shall be inconsistent with the regulations of Masonry

In countries where there are no Grand Lodges, they have powe to confer the blue degrees. They are the supreme judges of al transactions in the lower degrees; and no appeal can be made to the Supreme Council of the thirty-third degree until an opinion has been given by the Grand Council of Princes of Jerusalem, and the result of their opinion has been made known.

A Prince of Jerusalem who visits an inferior lodge or council, ought to present himself in the dress and ornaments of this degree. When his approach is announced, the presiding officer must send a Prince of Jerusalem to examine him, and if he reports in his favor, the arch of steel is to be formed, and he is conducted beneath it to his seat on the left of the presiding officer. An entry of his name and rank is made on the records, that he may henceforward receive our honors without any examination.

Five Princes are necessary to form a Grand Council.

Duties of Princes.—They are carefully to observe the rules of justice and good order, and to maintain irreproachable lives. It guilty of unmasonic conduct, they are to be punished at the discretion of the Grand Council. Expulsions are to be notified to the Grand Council of the thirty-third degree, and to all inferior Masonic bodies within the district.

If a Prince solicits a vote at an election, he is to be punished with perpetual exclusion.

The annual election is to take place on the twenty-third day of the Jewish month Adar. The meetings of the Councils are termed Conventions.

Apartments used in this degree.—There are two apartments, connected by a long narrow passage. The western represents the court of Zerubbabel, at Jerusalem. The hangings are yellow. Over the throne is a yellow canopy. On a triangular pedestal before the throne, are placed a naked sword, an arrow of justice, a balance, and a shield on which is an equilateral triangle, a sceptre, a chandelier of five branches, which are all lighted in the latter part of the ceremony of reception. The eastern apartment represents the cabinet of Darius. It is hung with red; the canopy is red. Before the throne is a small square pedestal; and in it a drawn sword, a sceptre, paper, pens, &c. The chief Minister of State sits near Darius.

Officers of the Grand Council.—The first officer is styled 'Most Equitable Prince,' and is on the throne. The Senior Warden and Junior Warden are styled 'Most Enlightened;' seated in the west. The other officers and the members are styled 'Valiant Princes.'

Dress.—The 'Most Equitable' wears a yellow robe and turban. The apron is red; on it are painted the temple, a square, a buckler, a triangle, and a hand: the flap is yellow; on it a balance, and the letters D. Z. [Darius and Zerubbabel.] Gloves are red. Sash is yellow, edged with gold, embroidered by a balance, a hand, a poniard, five stars, and two crowns—it is worn from right to left.

Jewel.—A golden medal; on one side a hand holding a balance in equilibris; on the other a two edged sword, with five stars around the point, and the letters D. Z.

Alarm.—The alarm is *three* and *two*. (!!! !!)

Opening.—The 'Most Equitable' strikes *one*, and says, 'Valiant Grand Master of Ceremonies, what is the first business of a Grand Council of Princes of Jerusalem?' Grand Master of Ceremonies. 'To see that the guards are at their proper stations.' M. E. 'Attend to that duty and inform.' &c. G. M. C. 'It is done, Most Equitable.' Most Equitable strikes *two*; the Junior Warden rises. M. E. 'Valiant Junior Warden, what is our next business?' J. W. 'To see that all present are Princes of Jerusalem.' M. E. 'Attend to that duty.' J. W. 'We are all Princes of Jerusalem.' Most Equitable (striking *thrice*) 'Valiant Senior Warden, what is the hour?' S. W. 'The rising of the sun.' M. E. 'What duty remains to be done?' S. W. 'To arrange the Princes in two columns, for the proper discharge of their duties.' M. E. 'Attend to that duty.' S. W. 'Most Equitable, it is done.' M. E. 'Valiant Junior and Senior Wardens, inform your respective columns that I am about to open this Grand Council of Princes of Jerusalem, by *three* and *two*.' (That is done.) M. E. 'Attention, Valiant Princes! (The signs are given; the Most Equitable strikes *three* and *two*: this is repeated by the Wardens.) I declare this Grand Council duly opened and in order for business.'

Reception.—The candidate being hoodwinked, is led by the Master of Ceremonies to the door—the alarm is given—the door is opened without any ceremony, and the candidate is led to the east, and thus addressed :—Most Equitable. 'What is your desire?' Candidate. 'I come to prefer the complaints of the people of Israel against the Samaritans, who have refused to pay the tribute imposed on them for defraying the expense of the sacrifices offered to God in the temple.' M. E. (who represents Zerubbabel) 'I have no power over the Samaritans; they are subject to king Darius, who is at Babylon; it is to him that such complaints must be preferred; but as we are all interested in this thing, I will arm you, and cause you to be accompanied by four Knights, that you may more easily surmount any difficulty which may present itself in your journey to the court of the king of Persia.' The bandage is now removed from the eyes of the candidate; he is armed with a sword and buckler, and decorated as a Knight of the East. The four Knights who accompany him are armed in a similar manner. They commence their journey, and are attacked by some armed ruffians, whom they repulse. They arrive at the door of the cabinet of Darius. The candidate enters with one of the Knights, and thus addresses the king: —'Mighty king! the Samaritans refuse to pay the tribute imposed on them by Cyrus, king of Persia, for defraying the expenses of the sacrifices which are offered in the temple which we have rebuilt: the people of Israel entreat that you will compel the Samaritans to perform their duty.' Darius. 'Your request is just and equitable; I order that the Samaritans shall immediately pay the tribute imposed on them. My Chief Minister shall deliver to you my decree for this purpose. Go in peace!' The candidate retires; the Chief Minister follows, and delivers the decree to him. After surmounting various obstacles, candidate is met on his return by the Knights with lighted torches, and is thus conducted with triumph into the presence of Zerubbabel, and says:—'I deliver to you the decree of Darius, king of Persia, which we have obtained after defeating our enemies, and encountering many dangers in our journey.' Most Equitable reads the decree as follows:—'We Darius, 'King of Kings!' willing to favor and protect our people at Jerusalem, after the example of our illustrious predecessor, king Cyrus, do will and ordain, that the Samaritans, against whom complaints have been made, shall punctually pay the tribute money which they owe for the sacrifices of the temple—otherwise they shall receive the punishment due to their disobedience. Given at Shushan, the palace, this fourth day of the second month, in the year 3534, and of our reign the third, under the seal of our faithful Darius. [L. S.]' M. E. 'The people of Jerusalem are under the greatest obligations to you for the zeal and courage displayed by you in surmounting the obstacles which you encountered in your journey; as a reward we shall confer on you the mysteries of the degree of Prince of Jerusalem. Are you willing to take an obligation, binding you to an exact observance of our laws, and a careful concealment of our mysteries?' Candidate. 'I am.' M. E. 'Kneel before the altar for that purpose.'

Obligation.—I, A. B., do solemnly promise and swear in the presence of Almighty God, the Great Architect of heaven and earth, and of these Valiant Princes of Jerusalem, that I will never reveal the mysteries of the degree of Prince of Jerusalem to any one of an inferior degree, or to any other person whatever. I promise and swear, as a Prince of Jerusalem, to do justice to my brethren, and not to rule them tyrannically, but in love. I promise and swear that I will never, by word or deed, attack the honor of any Prince of Jerusalem; and that I will not assist in conferring this degree except in a lawful Grand Council of Princes of Jerusalem. All this I promise and swear, under the penalty of being *stripped naked*, and having my heart pierced with a poniard. So help me God. Amen! Amen! Amen!

The Most Equitable raises the candidate, and gives him the signs, tokens, and words.

First Sign, ———. *First token,* ———. *Second token,* ———. *Pass word,* ———. *Sacred word,* ———. *The March,* ———. Steps on ———. *Age.*—The age of a Prince of Jerusalem is ———.

Most Equitable. 'I now appoint and constitute you, with your four companions, Princes and Governors of Jerusalem, that you may render justice to all the people. I decorate you with a yellow sash, to which is attached a gold medal. The 'balance' on it is to admonish you to make equity and justice your guides. The 'hand of justice' is a mark of your authority over the people. The 'emblems' of the 'apron' with which I now invest you, have reference to the works and virtues of Masons, and to your duty in the high office with which you are invested. As Princes of Jerusalem, you will assemble in two chambers of the temple. Be *just, merciful,* and *wise.*'

LECTURE.

Question. Are you a Prince of Jerusalem? Answer. I know the road to Babylon. Q. What were you formerly? A. A Knight of the East. Q. How did you arrive at the dignity of a Prince of Jerusalem? A. By the favor of Zerubbabel, and the courage which I manifested in many conflicts. Q. Where did the Prince of Jerusalem travel? A. From Jerusalem to Babylon. Q. Why? A. The Samaritans having refused to pay the tribute imposed on them for defraying the expense of the sacrifices offered to God in the temple, an embassy was despatched to Babylon, to obtain justice of king Darius. Q. How many Knights constituted this embassy? A. Five. Q. Did they encounter any difficulty in their journey? A. They did. The Samaritans, against whom they were to prefer a complaint, armed themselves and attacked the ambassadors, but were defeated. Q. What did they obtain from Darius? A. A decree ordering the Samaritans to pay the tribute, or suffer punishment. Q. How were the ambassadors received on their return to Jerusalem? A. At some distance from the city they were met by the people, who accompanied them to the temple singing songs of joy. On reaching the temple and making their report, and presenting the decree of Darius, they were constituted Princes of Jerusalem. Q. How were they habited as Princes of Jerusalem?. A. In cloth of gold. Q. What were their decorations? A. A yellow sash trimmed with gold from right to left; to which was attached a 'golden medal,' on which was engraved a 'balance,' a 'sword,' 'five stars,' and the letters 'D. Z.' Q. What is signified by the five stars on the sash? A. They are emblematic of the five Knights who journeyed from Jerusalem to Babylon. Q. What is the age of a Prince of Jerusalem? A. Five times fifteen.

Close.—Most Equitable. ' Most Enlightened Junior and Senior Wardens, announce to your respective columns that I am about to close this Grand Council by *five* times *fifteen*.' Each Warden strikes *five*; all rise and the notice is given. M. E. 'Attention, Princes of Jerusalem! (The signs are given. The Most Equitable strikes *five* times *fifteen*, which is repeated by the Wardens.) Be just, merciful, and wise! I declare this Grand Council duly closed.'

(217)

THE DEGREE

CALLED

KNIGHTS OF THE EAST AND WEST.*

Form of the Grand Council.—The Grand Council of Knights of the East and West, must be hung with red and sprinkled with gold stars. In the east of the Council Chamber must be a canopy, elevated by seven steps, supported by four lions and four eagles, and between them an angel, or seraphim, with six wings. On one side of the throne there must be a transparent painting of the sun, and, on the other side, one of the moon; below them is stretched a rainbow. In the east there must be a basin with perfume, and a basin of water, and a human skull. On the south side there must be six small canopies, and on the north side five, elevated by three steps, for the Venerable Ancients, and opposite the throne, in the west, are two canopies, elevated by five steps, for the two Venerable Wardens, who act in this Council as Grand Officers, or Wardens. A full Grand Council must be composed of twenty-four Knights. On the pedestal there must be a large Bible, with seven seals suspended therefrom.

The Venerable Master is called 'Most Puissant;' the Wardens, and the twenty-one other brethren, are called 'Respectable Ancients.' If there are more brethren present, they are styled 'Respectable Knights,' and are placed north and south, behind the small canopies.

The first canopy, at the right side of the Puissant, is always vacant for the candidate. All the brethren are clothed in white, with a zone of gold round the waist, long white beards and golden crowns on their heads. The Knights, in their ordinary habits, wear a broad white ribbon from the right shoulder to the left hip, with the jewel suspended thereto. They also wear a cross of the order, suspended by a black ribbon, round their necks. The 'Most Puissant' has his right hand on the large bible on the

---

* It is an act of justice due to those who have received the higher degrees in the United States, especially those of 'Knights of the East and West,' and that of 'Knight of the Sun,' to observe, that a general obligation was administered, applying to all the highest degrees; and that this, of course, precluded any previous knowledge of the nature and tendency of them.

T

pedestal with seven seals. The draft (or carpet,) of the Council, is an heptagon in a circle—over the angles are these letters, B. D. S. P. H. F. In the centre, a man clothed in a white robe, with a girdle of gold round his waist—his right hand extended, and surrounded with seven stars—he has a long white beard, his head surrounded with a glory, and a two-edged sword in his mouth—with seven candlesticks round him, and over them the following etters; H. D. P. I. P. R. C.

The JEWEL is an heptagon of silver—at each angle, a star of gold and one of these letters, B. D. S. P. H. G. S. in the centre. A lamb on a book with seven seals—on the reverse, the same letters in the angles, and in the centre, a two-edged sword between a balance.

The APRON is white, lined with red, bordered with yellow, or gold; on the *flap* is painted a two-edged sword, surrounded with the seven holy letters—or the apron may have the plan of the draft painted on it.

To open.—The Most Puissant, with his right hand on the bible sealed with seven seals, demands, 'Venerable Knights Princes, what is your duty?' A. 'To know if we are secure.' Most Puissant. 'See that we are so.' A. 'Most Puissant, we are in perfect security.' The Most Puissant strikes seven times, and says, 'Respectable Knights Princes, the Grand Council of Knights of the East and West is open; I claim your attention to the business thereof.' A. 'We promise obedience to the Most Puissant's commands.' They rise and salute him, when he returns the compliment and requests them to be seated.

Reception.—The candidate must be in an antichamber, which must be hung with red and lighted with seven lights, where he is clothed with a white robe, as an emblem of the purity of his life and manners. The Master of Ceremonies brings him barefooted to the Council Chamber door, on which he knocks seven times, which is answered by the Most Puissant, who desires the youngest Knight to go to the door, and demand who knocks. The Master of Ceremonies answers, 'It is a valiant brother and Most Excellent Prince of Jerusalem, who requests to be admitted to the Venerable and Most Puissant.' The Knight reports the same answer to the Most Puissant, who desires the candidate to be introduced. The Most Ancient Respectable Senior Grand Warden then goes to the door, and takes the candidate by the hand, and says, 'Come, my dear brother, I will show you mysteries worthy the contemplation of a sensible man. Give me the sign, token, and word of a Prince of Jerusalem:' after which the candidate kneels on both knees, about six feet from the throne, when the

Most Ancient Respectable Senior Grand Warden says to him, 'Brother, you no doubt have always borne in memory the obligations of your former degrees, and that you have, as far as in the power of human nature, lived agreeably to them?' *Candidate.* 'I have ever made it my study, and, I trust, my actions and life will prove it.' Q. 'Have you particularly regarded your obligations as a 'Sublime Knight of Perfection,' 'Knight of the East and Prince of Jerusalem?' Do you recollect having injured a brother in any respect whatsoever? Or have you seen or known of his being injured by others, without giving him timely notice, as far as was in your power? I pray you answer me with candor.' *Can.* 'I have in all respects done my duty, and acted with integrity to the best of my abilities.' The Most Puissant says, 'You will be pleased to recollect, my brother, that the questions which have now been put to you, are absolutely necessary for us to demand, in order that the purity of our Most Respectable Council may not be sullied; and it behoves you to be particular in your recollection, as the indispensable ties which we are going to lay you under, will, in case of your default, only increase your sins, and serve to hurl you sooner to destruction, should you have deviated from your duty :—answer me, my dear brother.' *Can.* 'I never have.' The Most Puissant says, 'We are happy, my brother, that your declaration coincides with our opinion, and are rejoiced to have it in our power to introduce you into our society. Increase our joy by complying with our rules, and declare if you are willing to be united to us by taking a most solemn obligation.' *Can.* 'I ardently wish to receive it, and to have the honor of being united to so respectable and virtuous a society.' The Most Puissant orders one of the Knights to bring an ewer containing some perfume, a basin of water, and a clean white napkin to the candidate—who washes his hands. The Most Puissant repeats the six first verses of the 24th Psalm. Then the candidate is brought close to the foot of the throne, where he kneels on both knees, and placing his right hand on the Bible, his left hand between the hands of the Most Puissant, in which position he takes the following

Obligation.—I, ———, do promise and solemnly swear and declare, in the awful presence of the only One Most Holy Puissant Almighty and Most Merciful Grand Architect of heaven and earth, who created the universe and myself through his infinite goodness, and conducts it with wisdom and justice—and in the presence of the Most Excellent and upright Princes and Knights of the East and West, here present in convocation and Grand Council, on my sacred word of honor and under every tie, both moral and religious, that I never will reveal to any person whomsoever below me, or to whom the same may not belong, by being legally and lawfully initiated, the secrets of this degree which is now about to be communicated to me, under the penalty of not only being dishonored, but to *consider my life as the immediate forfeiture*, and *that to be taken from me with all the tortures and pains to be inflicted in manner as I have consented to in my preceding degrees.* I further promise and solemnly swear, that I never will fight or combat with my brother Knights, but will, at all times, when he has justice on his side, be ready to draw my sword in his defence, or against such of his enemies who seek the destruction of his person, his honor, peace, or prosperity; that I never will revile a brother, or suffer others to reflect on his character in his absence, without informing him thereof, or noticing it myself, at my option; that I will remember, on all occasions, to observe my former obligations, and be just, upright, and benevolent to all my fellow creatures, as far as in my power. I further solemnly promise and swear, that I will *pay due obedience and submission to all the degrees beyond this,* but particularly to the Princes of the Royal Secret and the Supreme Council of Grand Inspectors General of the 33rd, and regulate myself by their determinations, and that I will do all in my power to support them in all justifiable measures for the good of the craft, and advantage of Masonry, agreeably to the Grand Constitutions.—All this I solemnly swear and sincerely promise, upon my sacred word of honor, under the penalty of the severe wrath of the Almighty Creator of heaven and earth, and may He have mercy on my soul, on the great and awful day of judgment, agreeably to my conformity thereto.—Amen. Amen. Amen.

The Most Puissant then takes the ewer filled with perfumed ointment, and anoints his head, eyes, mouth, heart, the tip of his right ear, hand, and foot, and says, 'You are now, my dear brother, received a member of our society; you will recollect to live up to the precepts of it, and *also remember that those parts of your body, which have the greatest power of assisting you in good or evil, have this day been made holy!*' The Master of Ceremonies then places the candidate between the two Wardens, with the draft before him. The Senior Warden says to him, 'Examine with deliberation and attention every thing which the MOST PUISSANT is going to show you;'—after a short pause, he, the Senior Warden says—'Is there mortal here worthy to open the book with the seven seals?' All the brethren cast their eyes down and sigh. The Senior Warden, hearing their sighs, says to them, 'Venerable and respectable brethren, be not afflicted; here is a victim (pointing to the candidate,) whose courage will give you content.' S. W. to the candidate, 'Do you know the reason why the ancients have a long white beard?' Can. 'I do not, but I presume you do.' S. W. 'They are those who came here, after passing through great tribulation, and having washed their robes in their own blood; will you purchase such robes at so great a price?' Can. 'Yes; I am willing.' The Wardens then conduct him to the basin, and bare both his arms—they place a ligature on each, the same as in performing the operation of blood-letting. Each Warden being armed with a lancet, makes an incision in each of his arms, just deep enough to draw a drop of blood, which is wiped on a napkin, and shown to the brethren. The Senior Warden then says, 'See, my brethren, a man who has spilled his blood to acquire a knowledge of our mysteries, and shrunk not from the trial!' Then the Most Puissant opens the first SEAL of the great book, and takes from thence a *bone quiver*, filled with arrows, and a crown, and gives them to one of the Ancients, and says to him, 'Depart and continue the conquest.' He opens the second SEAL, and takes out a *sword*, and gives it to the next aged, and says, 'Go, and destroy peace among the profane and wicked brethren, that they may never appear in our Council.' He opens the third SEAL, and takes a *balance*, and gives it to the next aged, and says, 'Dispense rigid justice to the profane and wicked brethren.' He opens the fourth SEAL, and takes out a *scull*, and gives it to the next aged, and says, 'Go, and endeavor to convince the wicked that death is the reward of their guilt.' He opens the fifth SEAL, and takes out a *cloth*, stained with blood, and gives it to the next aged, and says, 'When is the time (or, the time will arrive,) that *we shall revenge* and *punish* the profane and wicked, who have destroyed so many of their brethren by false accusations.' He opens the sixth SEAL, and that moment the sun is darkened and the moon stained with blood! He opens the seventh SEAL, and takes out *incense*, which he gives to a brother; and also a *vase*, with seven *trumpets*, and gives one to each of the seven aged brethren. After this, the four *old men*, in the four corners, show their *inflated bladders*, (beeves' bladders, filled with wind under their arms,) representing the four winds: when the Most Puissant says, 'Here is seen the fulfilment of a prophecy; (Rev. vii. 3.) Strike not, nor punish the profane and wicked of our order, until I have selected the true and worthy Masons!'* Then the four winds raise their bladders, and one

---

* Compare the foregoing with the 5th, 6th, and 7th chapters of Revelation, and the reader will discover that the MOST PUISSANT represents Jehovah seated on the throne of heaven—also, the Lamb of God, opening the seven seals. The *Senior Warden* represents the 'Strong Angel' proclaiming, 'Who is worthy

of the trumpets sound, when the two Wardens cover the candidate's arms, and take from him his apron and jewel of the last degree. The second trumpet sounds, when the Junior Warden gives the candidate the apron and jewel of this degree. The third trumpet sounds, when the Senior Warden gives him a long white beard. The fourth trumpet sounds, and the Junior Warden gives him a crown of gold. The fifth trumpet sounds, and the Senior Warden gives him a girdle of gold. The sixth trumpet sounds, and the Junior Warden gives him the sign, token, and words. The seventh trumpet sounds, on which they all sound together, when the Senior Warden conducts the candidate to the vacant canopy. [This canopy, it will be recollected, is at the right side of the Most Puissant, who represents Jehovah. The sounding of the seventh trumpet, and the conducting of the candidate to the canopy, is a representation of the end of the world, and the glorification of true Masons at the right hand of God, having ' passed through the *trials* of Free Masonry,' and ' washed their robes in their *own blood !*'—If this is not antichrist, what is? COMPILER.]

Origin of this degree.—When the Knights and Princes were embodied to conquer the Holy Land, they took a *cross* to distinguish them, as a mark of being under its banners; they also took an oath to spend the last drop of their blood to establish the true religion of the Most High God. Peace being made, they could not fulfil their vows, and, therefore, returning home to their respective countries, they resolved to do in theory what they could not do by practice, and determined never to admit, or initiate, any into their mystic ceremonies, but those who had given proofs of friendship, zeal, and discretion. They took the name of Knights of the East and West, in memory of their homes and the place where the order began; and they have ever since strictly adhered to their ancient customs and forms. In the year 1118, the first Knights, to the number of eleven, took their vows between the hands of Garimout, Patriarch and Prince of Jerusalem, from whence the custom is derived of taking the obligation in the same position.

LECTURE.

Q. Are you a Knight of the East and West? A. I am. Q. What did you see when you were received? A. Things that were

---

to open the book,' &c. The *aged* brethren, and the four old men with bladders, the angels of God with power; and Masonry claiming its faithful adherents as the servants of God, the 144,000 who were sealed in their foreheads, and of whom it is said, ' These are they which were not defiled with women; for they are virgins. These are they which follow the Lamb,' &c. See Rev. 14th chapter.

marvellous. Q. How were you received? A. By water, and the effusion of blood. Q. Explain this to me? A. A Mason *should not hesitate to spill his blood for the support of Masonry*. Q. What are the ornaments of the Grand Council? A. Superb thrones, sun, moon, perfumed ointment, and a basin of water. Q. What is the figure of the draft? A. An heptagon within a circle. Q. What is the representation of it? A. A man vested in a white robe, with a golden girdle round his waist—round his right hand, seven stars—his head surrounded with a glory, a long white beard—a two-edged sword across his mouth, surrounded by seven candlesticks, with these letters; H. D. P. I. P. R. C. Q. What signifies the circle? A. As the circle is finished by a point, so should a lodge be united by brotherly love and affection. Q. What signifies the heptagon? A. Our mystic number, which is enclosed in seven letters. Q. What are the seven letters? A. B. D. W. P. H. G. S.; which signifies Beauty, Divinity, Wisdom, Power, Honor, Glory, and Strength. Q. Give me the explanation of these words? A. *Beauty*—to adorn: *Divinity*—that Masonry is of divine origin: *Wisdom*—a quality to invent: *Power*—to destroy the profane and unworthy brethren: *Honor*—is an indispensable quality in a Mason, that he may support himself in his engagements with respectability: *Glory*—that a good Mason is on an equality with the greatest prince: and *Strength*—is necessary to sustain us. Q. What signifies the seven stars? A. The seven qualities which Masons should be possessed of: Friendship, Union, Submission, Discretion, Fidelity, Prudence, and Temperance. Q. Why should a Mason be possessed of these qualities? A. *Friendship*—is a virtue that should reign among brothers: *Union*—is the foundation of society: *Submission*—to the laws, regulations, and decrees of the lodge, without murmuring: *Discretion*—that a Mason should always be on his guard, and never suffer himself to be surprised: *Fidelity*—in observing strictly our obligations: *Prudence*—to conduct ourselves in such a manner that the profane, though jealous, may never be able to censure our conduct: and *Temperance*—to avoid all excesses that may injure either body or soul. Q. What signifies the seven candlesticks, with their seven letters? A. Seven crimes, which Masons should always avoid; viz: Hatred, Discord, Pride, Indiscretion, Perfidy, Rashness, and Calumny.* Q. What are the reasons that Masons should particularly avoid these crimes? A. Because they are incompatible with the principles

---

* Compare the explanation of the seven stars and seven candlesticks, as given above, with that in the word of God. See Rev. i. 20.

and qualities of a good Mason, who should avoid doing an injury to a brother, even should he be ill treated by him, and to unite in himself all the qualities of a good and upright man. *Discord* is contrary to the very principles of society : *Pride* prevents the exercise of humanity : *Indiscretion* is fatal to Masonry : *Perfidy* should be execrated by every honest man : *Rashness* may lead us into unpleasant and disagreeable dilemmas : and *Calumny*, the worst of all, should be shunned as a vice which saps the very foundation of friendship and society. Q. What signifies the two-edged sword ? A. It expresses the superiority of this degree over all others that precede it. Q. Are there any higher degrees than this ? A. Yes ; there are several. Q. What signifies the book with seven seals, which none but one can open ? A. A lodge, or council, of Masons, which the Most Puissant alone has a right to convene and open. Q. What is enclosed in the first seal ? A. One bow, one arrow, and one crown. Q. What in the second ? A. A two-edged sword. Q. What in the third ? A. A balance. Q. What in the fourth ? A. Death's head. Q. What in the fifth ? A. A cloth stained with blood. Q. What in the sixth ? A. The power to darken the sun, and tinge the moon with blood. Q. What in the seventh ? A. Seven trumpets and perfumes. Q. Explain these things to me. A. The *bow, arrow,* and *crown*, signifies that the orders of this respectable council should be executed with as much quickness, as the arrow flies from the bow, and be received with as much submission as if it came from a crowned head, or the chief of a nation. The *sword,* that the council is always armed to punish the guilty. The *balance* is a symbol of justice. The SKULL *is the image of a brother who is excluded from a lodge, or council ! ! ! This idea must make all tremble, when they recollect the penalties they have imposed on themselves under the most solemn obligations !* [Why tremble, if, as some say, the penalties are not to be inflicted ?— *Compiler.*] The *cloth* stained with blood, that we should not hesitate to spill ours for the good of Masonry. The *power* of obscuring the sun and tinging the moon with blood, is the representation of the power of the superior councils—in interdicting their works, if they are irregular, until they have acknowledged their error and submitted to the rules and regulations of the craft established by the Grand Constitutions. The *seven trumpets*, signify that Masonry is extended over the surface of the earth, on the wings of fame, and supports itself with honor. The *perfumes* denote that the life of a good Mason should be, and is, free from all reproach, and is perfumed by means of good report. Q. What age are you ? A. Very ancient. Q. Who are you ? A.

I am a Patmian : (i. e. of Patmos.) Q. Whence came you? A. From Patmos. End of the Lecture.

To close.—Q. What is the o'clock? A. There is no more time. The Most Puissant strikes seven, and says, 'Venerable Knights Princes, the council is closed.' The two Wardens repeat the same, and the council is closed.

THE DEGREE CALLED KNIGHT OF THE EAGLE, AND SOVEREIGN PRINCE OF ROSE CROIX DE HERODEN.*

Form of admission.—When a brother wishes to receive this high degree, he must produce his certificate of Knight of the East, Prince of Jerusalem, and Knight of the East and West. The following articles must be read to him, to which he must agree before he can be received. 1st. He must present at the door of the chapter the following petition, and must kneel while one of the brethren reads it. 'Brother ——, who is a Knight of the East, Prince of Jerusalem, and Knight of the East and West, begs leave to represent to the Sovereign Chapter the earnest desire he has, to arrive to the Sublime Degree of Rose Croix, the point of Perfection of Masonry, and that you will be pleased (being at present assembled,) to admit him among the number of Knights, if he is found worthy. And your petitioner shall never cease to make vows to Heaven, for the prosperity of the order and the good health of all the brethren.' After the petition is read the candidate must sign it. 2d. The candidate must remain on his knees, at the door of the chapter, until the answer is thrown to him on the floor by a Knight, when he rises and reads it. In the answer he will find the day appointed for his reception, and the name of the Knight, who is to give him the necessary instructions. The Knight who is named in the answer, directs the candidate to procure three pair of gloves, (one pair of which must be women's,) and two sticks of fine sealing wax for the seals. He also directs him to present to each of the brethren, one pair of men's, and one pair of women's gloves, and two sticks of sealing wax. 3d. He must make a donation of at least — dollars to the Superior Lodge, Chapter, or Council of the Sublime Degrees, which must be done before he is received, and may be appropriated either to defray the expenses of the order or be given to the poor. He must also present to the

---

* In this work there are two degrees, entitled 'Knight of the Eagle and Sovereign Prince of Rose Croix.' The above is given as conferred in England, Scotland, and America ; the other is conferred in France.

lodge three white wax candles for the Master, and two to each of the Knights, at his reception, previous to his entering into the third apartment. 4th. He must solemnly engage on his honor, never to reveal the place *where* he was received, *who* received him, nor *those* who were present at his reception. 5th. He solemnly promises to conform to all the ordinances of the chapter, and keep himself uniformly clothed as far as he is able. 6th. He must promise to acknowledge his Master at all times and in all places; never to confer this degree without permission, and to answer for the probity and respectability of those whom he proposes. 7th. That he will be extremely cautious in granting this degree, that it may not be multiplied unnecessarily. If the candidate promises to perform these requisitions he may be admitted.

Title of the Order.—This order being formerly the highest, was termed the *Ne plus ultra*, or ultimatum of Masonry. It has different titles. It is called Rose Croix from the rose on the cross of the jewel, being emblematical of the Son of God, who is compared to a rose by the evangelist. Knight of the Eagle, because of the eagle represented in the jewel. Knight of the Pelican, emblematical of the Son of God, who shed his blood for the great family of mankind. De Heroden, because the first chapter of this degree was held on a mountain of that name, situated between the west and north of Scotland, and where there is at this day the superior lodge and residence of the Sovereign Grand Chapter. They meet in an old castle belonging to the Knights of the Rose Croix.* It is from this circumstance that three fourths of the lodges of England took the name of the Rose Croix de Heroden, and the other fourth the name of Rose Croix, Knights of St. Andrew, because the first Masons of Scotland made a procession every year on the festival of that saint; and because it is the day of their regular constitution, which has induced many to call it St. Andrews, which also is in commemoration of the troubles of that country. The form of the true jewel being lost, they substituted the cross of St. Andrew, though the ceremonies of this degree have no connexion with that jewel. They are yet worn in the lodge of Cologne, suspended to a red ribbon in the form of a collar. In Berlin to a green ribbon; they also wear it to a button hole.

Jewel.—The jewel of this degree is a compass of gold extended to twenty-two and a half degrees. The head of the compass is a covered rose, the stock of which comes to a point. In the middle of the compass is a cross, the foot of which rests on the middle

---

* Our readers should be apprised that this is pure fiction, though firmly believed by many Masons.

of the circle, and the head touches the head of the compass. On one side an eagle, touching a quarter of the circles, the wings and the head reclining. On the other side a pelican picking its breast to nourish its young which must be in a nest under it. On the head of the compass must be a crown. On the circle must be engraved, on one side the name of the Knight in hieroglyphics, on the other side the pass word. The jewel must be of gold ; the eagle and pelican of silver. It is worn to a collar of a bright red color, of at least three inches broad., edged with black ; a rose at the lower end, and a black cross on each side. The Knights must wear this jewel in every lodge, and announce themselves at the door as Knights of Rose Croix, that they may receive the honor due to them.

Aprons.—For the first chamber, white leather lined, and bordered with black, three red roses placed triangularly on the flap ; a human scull with two thigh bones placed across each other, also on the flap. At the bottom of the apron must be a globe, surrounded by a serpent, and on the pocket of the apron a large I.

For the second chamber, red lined and bordered with the same. On the middle of the flap must be embroidered a triple triangle, with three squares within three circles, an I in the middle, which forms the jewel of the second chamber. On each side of this must be embroidered two compasses ; the point of one stands in one square of the circle, and the other stands on a triangle, with the point down.

Jewel and Order.—For the *first* chamber, a broad, black ribbon from the left shoulder to the right hip, (three inches broad.) On the breast a small cross of red ribbon ; below this must be a red rose, and a small rose of black below this, to which must be suspended a gold cross.

For the *second* chamber, the order and jewel of this degree.

Clothing of the Knights, Jewels, and Titles of the Officers.— All the *brethren* must be dressed in black clothes, with their swords on. The *Master* must be decorated with a brilliant *star* of seven points, which he wears on his breast over his heart. In the middle must be a circle, and in its centre the letter G. The following three words must also be engraved within the circle, around the G. ; Faith, Hope, Charity. The Master is called, ' Ever Most Perfect Sovereign.' The Senior Warden wears a triangle, and is called, ' Most Excellent and Perfect.' The Junior Warden wears the square and compasses, one above the other, and is called, ' Most Excellent and Perfect.' The brethren are called, ' Most Respectable Knights Princes of Masons.'

First apartment.—The first apartment is a representation of MOUNT CALVARY. It must be hung with black tapestry, and lighted with thirty-three yellow wax candles, in three candlesticks of eleven branches each. There must be three columns of six feet high, and on the chapiter of each must be wrote one of the following words, in large characters of gold; FAITH, HOPE, CHARITY. These columns may serve as candlesticks. At the east end of the chapter there must be a hill or bank raised to represent Mount Calvary, upon which must be placed three large *crosses*, and upon each a human scull and two thigh bones across. In the front of this must be the altar covered with black, on which must stand a cross and two yellow wax candles, lighted. Behind the altar must be a black curtain to intercept the view of the Mount. It must extend to the top of the chapter, and be made to open in the middle, and be drawn to each side. The *Master* must be seated on the last step of the altar, having a small table before him, on which is a lighted wax candle, a Bible, square and compasses, and triangle. There must be no chairs or benches in the chapter, but all the brethren must be seated on the floor. All the brethren must wear over their black clothes, a white satin chasuble, bordered with black ribbon, two inches in width. A red cross, two incnes in width, must reach from the top to the bottom of it. It must be made as the chasuble of a Catholic priest which he wears over the alb, when celebrating mass.

Second apartment.—The east end of the second apartment must represent, in transparent painting, the resurrection of *Jesus Christ*, the Saviour of mankind; over which must be a brilliant *triangle* surrounded with a *glory*. The hanging must be of transparent painting, representing the light blue ether of the sky, interspersed with glory. The altar must be splendidly decorated and illuminated with transparent lights. There must be no candles in this apartment, as all the light must be received through the transparencies. No other figure must be painted on the hangings but the representation of our Saviour at the resurrection. At the east, and behind the hangings, at some little distance, must be an organ or a band of music.

Third apartment.—On the hangings of the third apartment must be represented, in transparent paintings, *all the horrors which we attach to the idea of* HELL, or of a place formed for the punishment of the worst of crimes; such as human figures and monsters with convulsed muscles, engulfed in flames, &c. &c. On each side of the door a human skeleton, with an arrow in their hands. Each apartment must be separate, only connecting with a narrow door.

To open.—Master, 'My Perfect brothers, Knights Princes of Masons, assist me to open this chapter.' The Wardens repeat the same one after another. The Master then knocks three, four, which is repeated by the Wardens.

M. Most Excellent and Perfect Wardens, what is our care?

S. W. Most Wise Perfect and Sublime Master, it is to ascertain whether the chapter is well covered, and all the brethren present are Knights of the Eagle and Rose Croix.

M. 'Convince yourselves, my Perfect brethren, one from the south and one from the north.' This the Wardens do by demanding from each brother, in rotation the sign, token, and word, after which they give an account to the Master, who says, 'Most Perfect Senior Warden, what is the o'clock?'

S. W. The moment when the vail of the temple was rent; when darkness and consternation covered the earth; when the stars disappeared, and the lamp of day was darkened; when the implements of Masonry were lost, and the cubic stone sweated blood and water; that was the moment when the great Masonic word was lost.

M. Since Masonry, my brethren, has sustained so great a loss, let us employ ourselves, by new works, to recover the word which was lost, for which purpose let us open the chapter of Rose Croix.

S. W. My brethren let us do our duty; the Sovereign Chapter of Rose Croix is open. Junior Warden repeats the same, after which all the Knights bend their right knees to the altar, repeating the same words seven times, a short interval between the sixth and seventh.

M. What is the cause of our assembling here, Most Excellent Senior Warden?

S. W. Ever Most Perfect and Sovereign Master, the propagation of the order and the perfection of the Knight of the East, who demands to be received among us. The brethren then proceed to ballot for the candidate.

Reception.—When the candidate has given satisfactory answers to all the conditions proposed to him, he must be placed in the chamber of REFLECTION, which must be painted black, with a small table in it with a Bible, and several human bones on it. The only light is received from a candle or lamp placed in the scull of a human skeleton. The Master of Ceremonies goes to the candidate and decorates him in the *attributes* of the last degree he has received, and also with his sword and white gloves. He then says to him, 'All the temples are demolished; our tools are destroyed, with our columns; the sacred word is lost, notwithstanding all our precaution ; and we are in ignorance of the means of recovering it, or of knowing each other. The order, in general, is in the greatest consternation! Will you assist us in recovering the word?' The candidate replies, ' Most cheerfully.' The Master of Ceremonies says, ' Follow me, if you please ;' when he conducts him to the door of the chapter, whereon he knocks as a Knight of Rose Croix. The Senior Warden demands, ' What do you want?' Ans. ' It is a brother Knight of the East and West, who is wandering in the woods and mountains, and who, at the destruction of the second temple, lost the word, and humbly solicits your aid and assistance to recover it.' The door is opened and the candidate is introduced. All the brethren are seated on the floor, the right hand on their necks, their left covering their face, their heads down, their elbows on their knees, and their jewels covered with black crape. The Master is in the same position at the table. The Senior Warden knocks as a Rose Croix, and announces him to the Master, who says, ' My brother, confusion has come on our works, and it is no longer in our power to continue them ; you must perceive from our looks, and the consternation which prevails among us, what confusion reigns on the earth. The vail of the temple is rent, [at this moment the black curtain is withdrawn ;] the light is obscured, and darkness spreads over the earth ; the flaming star has disappeared, the cubic stone sweats blood and water, and the sacred word is lost ; therefore it is impossible we can give it to you, nevertheless it is not our intention to remain inactive : we will endeavor to recover it. Are you disposed to follow us?' Ans. ' Yes I am.' Master says, ' Brother Wardens make the candidate travel for thirty-three years, to learn the beauties of the new law,' [which is reduced to seven times round the lodge.] The Wardens lead him slowly round the lodge, and when he passes before the altar he must kneel, and when passing in the west he bends his right knee, they make him observe the columns and repeat the name of each as he passes them. After he has performed this ceremony, the Wardens knock one after the other, and announce him to the Master, who says, ' My brother what have you learned on your journey?' Ans. I have learned three virtues by which to conduct myself in future, *Faith, Hope, Charity ;* inform me if there are any others? M. ' No, my brother, they are the principles and the pillars of our new mystery. Approach near to us and make an engagement never to depart from *that* faith. The brethren rise. The candidate kneels on the last step of the altar and places his hands on the Holy Bible and takes the following obligation.

LIGHT ON MASONRY. 231

Obligation.—I, A, B. do most solemnly and sincerely promise and swear, under the penalty of all my former obligations, which I have taken in the preceding degrees, never to reveal either directly or indirectly, the secrets or mysteries of Knight of the Eagle, Sovereign Prince of Rose Croix, to any brother of an inferior degree, nor to any in the world besides, who is not justly and lawfully entitled to the same, under the penalty of being for ever deprived of the true word, to be perpetually in darkness, my blood continually running from my body, to suffer without intermission the most cruel remorse of soul; that the bitterest gall, mixed with vinegar, be my constant drink; the sharpest thorns for my pillow; and that the death of the cross may complete my punishment, should I ever infringe or violate in any manner or form the laws, and rules which have been, are now, or may be hereafter made known or prescribed to me; and I do furthermore swear, promise and engage on my sacred word of honor, to observe and obey all the decrees which may be transmitted to me by the Grand Inspectors General, in supreme council of the thirty-third degree; that I never will reveal the place where I have been received, nor by whom I was received, nor the ceremony used at my reception, to any person on earth, but to a lawful Prince of Rose Croix; that I never will initiate any person into this degree, but by a lawful patent obtained for that purpose, either from this chapter, or from a superior council : so help me God, and keep me steadfast in this my solemn obligation. Amen. He kisses the bible. The Master says, ' My brethren, all is accomplished !' The brethren all place themselves on the floor and cover their faces with their hands, except the Wardens who continue with the Master, and the candidate whom they deprive of his apron and order. The Master invests him with the chasuble and says, ' This habit, my brother, teaches you the uniformity of our manners, and our belief, and will recall to your recollection the principal points of our mysteries. The black apron with which I invest you, is to mark our sincere repentance of those evils which was the cause of all our misfortunes, and it will also serve to show you those who are in search of the true word; the ribbon is the mark of our constant mourning, till we have found it. Pass to the west and assist us to search for it.' The Wardens conduct him to the west. The Master knocks six and one, as a Knight. The Wardens repeat it. All the brethren rise and place themselves under the sign of the good pastor. The Master demands, ' Brother Master Wardens, what is the motive of our assembling ?' A. The loss of the word, which, with your assistance, we hope to recover. Q. What must we do to obtain it ?

A. To be fully convinced of the three virtues which are the basis of our columns and our principles. Q. What are they? A. Faith, Hope, Charity. Q. How shall we find those three columns? A. By travelling three days in the most profound obscurity. The Master says, 'Let us travel, my brethren, from east to north, and from west to south.' All the brethren travel in silence, bending their knees as they pass the altar in the east, and go seven times round. At the third time of going round the Master passes to the second apartment; at the fourth time, the Wardens; at the fifth time, all the officers; at the sixth time, all the brethren; at the seventh time, the Master of Ceremonies stops the candidate and says, 'You cannot enter unless you give me the word. The candidate answers, 'I am in search of the word, by the help of the new law and the three columns of Masonry.

During this time the brethren in the second apartment take off their black decorations, and put on the red, and also uncover their jewels. The candidate knocks on the door, and the Warden for answer, shuts the door in his face. The master of ceremonies says, 'These marks of indignity are not sufficiently humiliating, you must pass through more rigorous proofs, before you can find it.' He then takes off the candidate the chasuble and black apron, and puts over him a black cloth covered with ashes and dust, and says to him, 'I am going to conduct you into the darkest and most dismal place, from whence the word shall triumphantly come to the glory and advantage of Masonry; place your confidence in me.' He then takes him into the third apartment, and takes from him his covering, and makes him to go three times around, (showing him the representation of the torments of the damned,) when he is led to the door of the chapter and the Master of Ceremonies says to him, '*The horrors which you have just now seen, are but a faint representation of those you shall suffer, if you break through our laws, or infringe the obligation you have taken.** The Master of Ceremonies knocks on the door of the chapter, and the Warden reports to the Master, who orders him to go and see who knocks. The Master of Ceremonies answers, 'It is a Knight, who, after having passed through the most profound and difficult places, hopes to procure the real

---

* This certainly caps the climax, and renders the institution of Masonry complete. The torments of the damned, the awful punishment which the Almighty inflicts on the violators of his righteous law, is but a *faint emblem* of the punishment which Masonry here declares, *shall be inflicted on the violators of Masonic law*, on those who are guilty of an infraction of Masonic obligation!!!

word as a recompense for his labor.' The Wardens give an account to the Master, who says, 'Introduce him to the west of the chapter with his eyes open.' The Wardens bring him in, and then cover him again with his vail. Master. 'From whence came you?' Candidate. 'From Judea.' M. 'By what road have you passed?' C. 'By Nazareth.' M. 'Who conducted you?' C. 'Raphael.' M. 'What tribe are you of?' C. 'Of the tribe of Judah.' M. 'Take the initial letters of each of these words, and tell me what they form?' C. 'J, N, R. J.' M. 'My brethren, what happiness! the word is recovered; give him the light.' The vail is taken off, and all the brethren, striking with their hands seven times, cry, 'Hosanna in the highest; on earth peace, good will towards men!' The music immediately plays the following anthem, which is devoutly sung by all the Knights.

ANTHEM.

Grateful notes and numbers bring,
While the '*name of God*,' we sing:
Holy, holy, holy Lord,
Be thy glorious name adored.
Men on earth and saints above
Sing the great Redeemer's love.
Lord, thy mercies never fail,
Hail, celestial goodness, hail!
While on earth ordained to stay,
Guide our footsteps in thy way:
Mortals raise your voices high,
Till they reach the echoing sky.

After the anthem is sung, the Master says to the candidate, 'Approach, my brother, I will communicate to you our perfect mysteries.' The Wardens conduct him to the Master, who says, 'I congratulate you, my brother, on the recovery of the word, which entitles you to this degree of Perfect Masonry. I shall make no comment or eulogium on it. Its sublimity will, no doubt, be duly appreciated by you. The impression which, no doubt, it has made on your mind, will convince you that you were not deceived when you was informed that the ultimatum of Masonic perfection, was to be acquired by this degree. It certainly will be a source of very considerable satisfaction to you, that *your merit alone* has entitled you to it. And I hope, my brother, that your good conduct, your zeal, your virtue and discretion, may always render you deserving of the high honor which you have received, and I sincerely wish that your life may long be preserved, to enable you to continue an useful

Member, and an ornament to our society.' [Here follow the signs, token, and words.] The Sovereign Master then says, 'Go, my brother, and make yourself known to all the members of the Sovereign Chapter, and return again.' The candidate goes and whispers in the ears of the Knights the pass word; he then returns, and kneels before the altar. All the brethren place their right hands on him. The Sovereign Master takes the ribbon, to which is suspended the true jewel uncovered, and says to him, ' By the power which I have received from the Sovereign Chapter of Rose Croix de Heroden, I receive and constitute you Prince Knight of the Eagle, Perfect Free Mason de Heroden, under the title of the Rose Croix, that you may enjoy, now and for ever, all the privileges, prerogatives and titles attached to that sublime degree, as virtue and humanity are the foundation of it. I hope, my brother, never to see you dishonor the ribbon with which you have been invested, and which a perfect Mason should never quit but at his death.'

LECTURE.

Q. Are you a Knight and Prince of Rose Croix? A. Most Wise and Perfect Sovereign, I have that happiness! Q. Where were you received? A. In a chapter where reigned decency and humility. Q. Who received you? A. The most humble of all. Q. How were you received? A. With all the formalities requisite on that great occasion! Q. How were you presented to the chapter? A. Of my own free will and accord. Q. What have you seen on entering the chapter? A. My soul was in ecstasy at the sight of our ineffable mysteries, and the silence which reigned in the lodge; and the situation of the Knights gave me a high idea of what was going to be communicated to me. Q. What did they do with you afterwards? A. They made me travel for thirty-three years. [This number of years alludes to the age of the Saviour when he was crucified.] Q. What did you learn in your travels? A. I learned the name of the three columns which support our edifice, and as they are three great virtues, they are the foundation of this degree. Q. When your journey was over, was your labor, pains, and work finished? A. The Most Wise ordered me to be conducted to the altar, and there to kneel in the presence of Him before whom all nations bow, and to take a most solemn obligation; which I did with as much respect as possible—my heart was penetrated with what I was saying, with a firm resolution of observing the same. Q. What was done with you after that? A. I was clothed with marks of grief and repentance, and was taught the reason thereof. All the knights then made a journey, by which we passed from misery to happiness ; the dark and obscure road by which we travelled, was overcome with firmness, and we received as a recompense the object of our desire. Q. What were you seeking for in this journey? A. The word which was lost, and which our perseverance enabled us to recover. Q. Who gave it to you? A. It is not permitted to any person to give it ; but having reflected on what I was seeing and hearing, I found it myself with the help of him who is the author of the word. Q. Give it to me. A. I cannot; interrogate me. Q. What country are you of? A. Of *Judea*. Q. Where have you passed ? A. By *Nazareth*. Q. What was the name of your conductor? A. *Raphael*. Q. What tribe are you of? A. The tribe of Judah. Q. I am not better instructed. A. Most Wise, enable me to assemble the initial letters of each word, and you will find the subject of our joy and our mysteries. Q. J. N. R. J. Jesus, Nazareth, Rex, Judaerum. A. It is very just, Most Wise. Q. Did they give you any thing else? A. The pass word, and the signs and tokens to make myself known. Q. Give me the first sign. A. [By giving it.] Q. What do you call it? A. The good pastor or shepherd. Q. After having given you all this, what did they do with you ? A. The Most Wise and the knights constituted me Prince Knight of the Eagle, Perfect Mason, under the title of the Sovereign Knight of Rose Croix, and decorated me with the ribbon and jewel, and gave me the explanation of them ; after which I made myself known to all the Knights, and took my place in the chapter. Q. What was done with you afterwards? A. The Most Wise made an exhortation, after which the business of the chapter was gone through and a convocation made for the next, and the chapter was closed in the usual form.

To close.—The Most Wise knocks seven times on the step of the altar. The Wardens repeat the same. The Knights rise up. The Master asks the following questions :—' Most Excellent brother Senior Warden, what's the o'clock ?' Ans. ' The moment when the word was recovered ; when the cubic stone was changed into a mystic rose ; when the flaming star appeared in all its splendor ; when our altars resumed their ordinary form ; when the true light dispelled darkness, and the new law becomes visible in all our works.' Then the Most Wise takes the charity box to distribute to the ordinary servants, or the brethren, who are in necessity. After which, he demands if any of the Knights have any thing to offer for the good of the order and this chapter, and says, ' Brother Wardens, give notice that this chapter is going to be closed.' This done, they knock the same as the Master, and make the ordinary acclamations. The Master leaves his place, makes his obeisance, embraces all the Knights, and says, '*Profound peace.*' All the brethren do the same. The Most Wise then says, (having first saluted with his mallet,) ' My brethren, this Sovereign Chapter of Rose Croix is closed ; let us do our duty.' They all exclaim, Vivat. The Master says, ' Let us go, my brethren, and make the reflection which our work requires ; let us go, and return in peace.' The brethren take the buckles out of their shoes, and wear their shoes in the form of slippers. The only banquet, or ceremony, of the table, used in the chapters of Rose Croix, is the following, which is indispensably necessary, being in commemoration of the repast of our Saviour, which he gave at Emmaus, when he made himself known to his disciples after his resurrection.

The Most Wise orders the youngest Knight to go and prepare every thing for their repast ; he goes into an apartment appropriated to this purpose, and covers the table with a white cloth, and places thereon a loaf of white bread in a plate in the centre of a triangle, formed with three candlesticks, in which must be candles of white or yellow wax. He then takes to the Master wands of six feet high, who receives them and returns them to the candidate, who presents one to each Knight. They then follow the Master to the banquet, where they place themselves round the table, and standing with their heads uncovered, except the Master, who puts on his hat after prayer.

Prayer.—Sovereign Creator of all things, who provides for all our necessities and wants, bless this food of which we are now going to partake, that we may receive it for thy honor and glory, and for our satisfaction and refreshment. Amen.

The Master breaks the bread and takes a piece, then passes it to the right for the rest ; and when they are all provided, they eat it. The young admitted Knight brings a goblet of wine which he places in the middle of the table. The Master takes it, and makes the sign of the Rose Croix, drinks, and presents the goblet to the brother next to him, who drinks and passes it round till it comes to the Master again, who goes with all the Knights and throws what is left into the fire, being all kneeling on one knee, in the manner of making an offering. They all rise ; when the Master embraces them, and says, ' PEACE BE UNTO YOU ;' they answer, ' *Be it so. Amen.*' They go to the other chamber, where they put their buckles in their shoes and retire.*

---

* The youngest Knight is to clear the table, and, during the whole ceremony of the repast, the most profound silence is to be observed. No servants can be employed in this office, as all the brethren are equal. In some chapters they eat a

The feast of this chapter is on Shrove Tuesday, which cannot be dispensed with; and if there is but one Knight in a place, he must absolutely perform the ceremony of this festival, that he may reunite himself in spirit with his brethren who do the same. If he is travelling on the road and meets a brother, they are obliged to go to some convenient house to celebrate it.

Ordinances.—The Knights of the Rose Croix have the privilege of holding the mallet of the Master in all lodges; but if they do not choose to receive it, they place themselves at the side of the Master, taking rank of all the officers. If the Master, through ignorance of his quality, does not make him that polite offer, he must seat himself on the floor, at the column of the Entered Apprentice. When a Knight signs a Masonic paper, he must affix his rank to his signature, and also seal it with his coat of arms;—

C. S. P. D. R. C.   or K. C. P. of R. C.

Where there is a regular chapter, they must assemble, at least, six times a year, viz: The Annual Feast, Shrove Tuesday, Tuesday after Easter, the Day of Ascension, and All Saints' Day; exclusive of two Grand Festivals of St. John's, which cannot be dispensed with. In a constituted Chapter, there must be, at least, *three*, till the number becomes greater; then the officers are elected as in other lodges. The election is made the Tuesday after Easter, when they enter into their charge, and the former officers are to render an account of their proceedings for the year past.

They are obliged to be charitable to all the poor, particularly to all distressed Masons. They must visit the prisoners. If a Knight falls sick, they are obliged to visit him and pay particular attention that he wants for nothing, which they can supply him with. On the death of a Knight, he shall be decorated with his ribbon and jewel round his neck, and his funeral shall be attended by all the Knights, clothed in all their orders, if it can be done without causing reflection on the order; after which, a chapter shall be opened. The brother who succeeds him, shall wear his jewel, covered with black crape, for three days. In the French Chapters it is usual to keep the anniversary of his death, and pronounce an eulogy on his virtues.

It is forbid, under any pretext whatsoever, for one brother to fight or combat with another. No brother can absent himself

---

roasted lamb, but it must have the head and feet on, which are cut off in the chapter and thrown into the fire, as an offering, before any one eats: Here there must be only one knife and one goblet, but no bottle; but this ceremony has been abolished —the first being only made use of.

from the chapter, unless in case of sickness, or other good and sufficient reasons, of which the chapter must approve. The chapter must only be lighted with wax candles, or sweet oil.—*Finis.*

GRAND PONTIFF,

OR

SUBLIME SCOTCH MASONRY.

Decorations of the lodge, titles, &c.—The hangings of this lodge must be blue, spread with gold stars. The Master of this lodge goes by the title of Thrice Puissant; he is clothed in a white satin robe, and sits on a throne under a blue canopy, behind which, in a niche, is a transparent light, sufficient to light the lodge. The Thrice Puissant holds a sceptre in his hand. There is only one Warden, who sits opposite the Thrice Puissant in the west, and holds a golden staff in his hand. All the rest of the brethren are clothed in white robes, and have the title of Faithful and True Brothers. They all wear a blue satin fillet round their foreheads, with twelve golden stars embroidered thereon.

The draft (or carpet) of the lodge, represents a square city, or celestial Jerusalem, descending on clouds from heaven to crush the remains of the present Jerusalem; or a three headed serpent, or hydra, in chains, representing the wickedness of the infidels yet remaining there. This celestial Jerusalem has twelve gates, three on each side. In the centre of the city is a tree which bears twelve different kinds of fruits. The present Jerusalem underneath seems to be turned upside down, and the celestial Jerusalem appears to crush the three headed serpent. On one side of the draft you see a high mountain.

To open the lodge.—The Thrice Puissant strikes twelve, at equal distances, and then demands the following questions:—Q. 'Brother, what's the o'clock?' A. 'The hour foretold.' M. 'Faithful brethren, the whole is ALPHA, OMEGA, and EMANUEL: Let us work.' Then the Warden knocks twelve, as above, and says,— 'Faithful brethren, the lodge of Grand Pontiff is open.'

Form of reception.—The candidate must be decorated with the attributes of Knight of the East and West, a blue satin fillet with twelve gold stars tied round his forehead, before he enters. He is immediately introduced into the lodge, when the Warden places him on the top of a mountain, and asks him, 'Brother, do you detest what is perfidious ? do you promise that you will break all communications, correspondence, and friendship with those who are so ?' The candidate answers, 'I promise and swear.' Then the Warden leaves the candidate, and comes down the mountain backwards, and goes to the celestial city, and with a surveyor's chain measures the four sides of it; when he goes to the candidate again, and tells him, 'Brother, that city (pointing to it) measures 12,000 furlongs each side.' He then takes the candidate by the hand, and both come down backwards. He places him before the draft, facing the Thrice Puissant. After a minute's silence, he makes him take three square steps towards the chained serpent, then one step on each side of the three heads; he then kneels three times with his right knee, holding, at the same time, his right hand horizontally towards the Thrice Puissant. [This ceremony is instead of an obligation.] The Thrice Puissant orders him to retreat three steps, which again brings him to the bottom of the draft, where the Warden gives him the sign, token, and word. The order is a broad red ribbon, with twelve golden stars embroidered thereon. It is worn from the right shoulder to the left hip.

The Jewel is a square of gold; on one side is engraved ALPHA; on the other, OMEGA.

LECTURE.

Q. What are you? A. I am a Sublime Grand Pontiff. Q. Where have you received this degree? A. In a place where there is neither sun nor moon to light it. Q. Explain this to me? A. As the Grand Pontiff never wants any artificial light, the Faithful and True Brothers, the Sublime Grand Pontiffs, do not want riches or titles to be admitted into the Sublime Degrees, as they prove themselves worthy of admittance by their attachment to Masonry —the faithful discharge of their several obligations—their virtue, and true and sincere friendship for their brethren in general. Q. What does the draft of this lodge represent? A. A square city of four equal sides, with three gates on each side; in the middle of which is a tree, which bears twelve different kinds of fruit. The city is suspended as on clouds, and seems to crush a three headed serpent. Q. Explain this to me. A. The *square city represents ancient Free Masonry, under the title of Grand Pontiff, which comes down from heaven to replace the ancient temple* —represented by the ruins and the three headed serpent underneath. Q. How comes Masonry to have fallen into ruin, since we are bound to support it, and are attached to it by *our obligations, which cannot be equivocal? A. It was so decreed in old times, which we learn from the writings of St. John, whom we know to have been the first Mason who held a Lodge of Perfection.* Q. Where does St. John say this? A. *In his Revelation, where he speaks of Babylon and the celestial Jerusalem.* Q. What signifies the tree with the twelve different fruits, which stands in the centre of the square city? A. The tree of life is placed there *to make us understand where the sweets of life are to be found;* and the twelve fruits signify *that we meet in every month to instruct ourselves mutually, and sustain each other against the attacks of our enemies.* Q. What is the meaning of the satin fillet, with the twelve golden stars, which the candidate wore round his forehead? A. It procures those who wear it an entrance into our lodge, as *it likewise procures the entrance of those who wear it into the celestial Jerusalem, as St. John himself informs us.* Q. What is the meaning of the twelve golden stars on the fillet of the candidate and on those of the brethren? A. They represent the twelve angels who watched at the twelve gates of the celestial Jerusalem. Q. What signifies the blue hangings, with the golden stars thereon? A. The blue is the symbol of lenity, fidelity, and sweetness, which ought to be the share of every faithful and true brother; and *the stars represent those Masons who have given proof of their attachment to the statutes and rules of the order; which, in the end, will make them deserving of entering into the celestial Jerusalem.* Q. What age are you? A. I reckon no more. Q. What remains for you to acquire? A. The sublime truths of the degrees above this. Q. What is your name? A. Faithful and true brother.

To close.—Thrice Puissant. 'What's the o'clock?' *Warden.* 'Thrice Puissant, the hour accomplished.' T. P. 'Alpha and Omega: let us rejoice, my brethren.' He then strikes twelve, which is repeated by the Warden, and the lodge is closed.

VENERABLE GRAND MASTER
OF ALL SYMBOLIC LODGES,
SOVEREIGN PRINCES OF MASONRY,
MASTER ADVITIAM.

Decorations, &c.—This lodge must be decorated with blue and yellow. The Grand Master sits on a throne elevated by nine steps, under a canopy; before it is an altar, on which is a sword, bible, compass, square, mallet, &c. as in the Symbolic Lodges. Between the altar and the south is a candlestick with nine branches, which is always lighted in this lodge. There are two Wardens in the west. The Grand Master represents Cyrus Artaxerxes* wearing his royal ornaments and a large blue and yellow ribbon crossing each other.

To Open.—Grand Master, 'I desire to open the lodge.' He then descends to the lowest step of the throne, and when he is assured that the lodge is tyled, he knocks one and two with his mallet. Each Warden repeats the same, which makes nine. G. M. 'Where is your Master placed?' Warden, 'In the east.' G. M. 'Why in the east?' W. 'Because the glorious sun rises in the east to illumine the world.' G. M. 'As I sit in the east, I open this lodge,' which is repeated by the Wardens. Then all the brethren clap with their hands one and two.

Reception. The candidate represents Zerubbabel, who enters the lodge by himself, without being introduced, decorated with the jewels and badges of the highest degrees he has taken. The Wardens take him by the hand, and place him in a blue elbow chair, opposite to the Grand Master, who demands from him all the words, from an Entered Apprentice up to a Grand Pontiff; and after he has satisfied the Grand Master, and is found worthy to hold a sceptre, they make him travel nine times round the lodge, beginning in the south, and then by nine square steps he advances to the throne, and walks over two drawn swords, laid across. There must be a pot with burning charcoal close by the throne, that the candidate may feel the heat of the fire while taking the obligation; in doing which, he lays his right hand on the bible, which is covered by the Grand Master's right hand, and then takes the following obligation.

Obligation.—I, A. B., do most solemnly and sincerely swear and promise, under the penalties of all my former obligations, to protect the craft and my brethren with all my might, and not to acknowledge any one for a true Mason who was not made in a regularly constituted and lawful lodge. I furthermore do swear, that I will strictly observe and obey all the statutes and regulations of the lodge; and that I never will disclose or discover the secrets of this degree, either directly or indirectly, except by virtue of a full power in writing, given me for that purpose by the Grand Inspector or his deputy, and then to such only as have been Masters of a regular lodge. All this I swear under the penalties of being for ever despised and dishonored by the Craft in general. He then kisses the Bible. Here follow the signs, token and word.

---

* This is the Masonic name of Cambyses.

One word is, * * *, which signifies, 'I am what I am.' This is also the name of the man who found the cavern where the lion hid that kept in his mouth the key of the ark of alliance, which was lost. The second word is * * *, which is the name of him who fought the lion in the cavern. The lion had a gold collar round his neck, on which was engraved the word Jechson. The rest is an enigma to you, as it is only known to the Sublime Princes of the Royal Secret; a degree which you cannot receive unless you crush the serpent of ignorance. The third word is * * *, which was the name of him who laid the first foundation stone of the temple, rebuilt by the Princes of Jerusalem. The JEWEL is a triangle, on which is engraved SECRET, and is suspended by a broad blue and yellow ribbon.

LECTURE.

Q. Are you a Grand Master of all Symbolic Lodges? A. They know me at Jerusalem to be such. Q. How shall I know that you are a Grand Master of all Symbolic Lodges? A. By observing my zeal in rebuilding the temple. Q. Which way did you travel? A. From the south to the east. Q. How often? A. Nine. Q. Why so many? A. In memory of the Grand Masters who travelled to Jerusalem. Q. Can you give me their names? A. Their names are ESDRAS, ZERUBBABEL, PHACHI, JOSHUA, ELIAL, TOYADA, HOMEN, NEHEMIAS, and MALCHIAS. Q. What are the pass words? A. * * * * * * * * * Q. What object engaged your attention most, when you first entered the lodge of Grand Masters? A. The candlestick with nine branches. Q. Why are the nine candles therein always kept burning in this lodge? A. To remind us that there cannot be less than nine Masters to form a Grand Master's lodge. Q. What were your reasons for wishing to be admitted and received in this lodge of Grand Masters? A. That I might receive the benefit of the two lights I was unacquainted with. Q. Have you received those lights, and in what manner? A. In receiving first the small light. Q. Explain this. A. When I was received by steel and fire. Q. What signifies the steel? A. To remind us of the steel by which our Most Respectable Chief, Hiram Abiff, lost his life, and which I am sworn to make use of whenever I can revenge that horrible murder on the traitors of Masonry. Q. What means the fire? A. To put us in mind that our forefathers were purified by fire. Q. By whom were you received? A. By Cyrus. Q. Why by Cyrus? A. Because it was he who ordered Zerubbabel to rebuild the temple. Q. What did you promise and swear to perform when you received this degree? A. I swore that I would see the laws, statutes, and regulations strictly observed in our lodge. Q. What was your name before you received this degree? A. Zerubbabel. Q. What is your name now? A. Cyrus. Q. What means the word Animani? A. 'I am that I am;' and it is also the name of him who found the lion's den. Q. Why is the lodge decorated with blue and yellow? A. To remind us that the ETERNAL appeared to Moses on Mount Sinai, in clouds of gold and azure, when he gave to his people the laws of infinite wisdom. Q. Where do you find the records of our order? A. In the archives of Kilwinning, in the north of Scotland. Q. Why did you travel from the south round to the east? A. In allusion to the power of the Grand Architect of the universe, which extends throughout all the world. Q. Why did you wash your hands in the fourteenth degree? A. To show my innocence. Q. Why is the history of Hiram Abiff so much spoken of? A. To put us always in mind that he chose rather to sacrifice his life than reveal the secrets of Masonry. Q. Why is the triangle, with the word *secret* on it, considered as the most precious jewel in Masonry? A. Because by its justness, equality, and proportion, it represents our redemption. Q. By what mark was the place discovered where Hiram Abiff was buried by his assassins? A. By a sprig of cassia, (say granate.) Q. For what reasons do the Master Masons in the Symbolic Lodges, speak of a sprig of cassia? A. Because the Sublime Grand Elected descendants of the ancient Patriarchs did not think proper to give the real name or truth of Masonry; therefore, they agreed to say that it was a sprig of cassia, because it had a strong smell. Q. What are the reasons for the different knocks at the door to gain admittance? A. To know and be assured that they have passed the different degrees, which number we must understand. Q. For what reasons do we keep our mysteries with such circumspection and secrecy? A. For fear there might be found amongst us some traitorous villains similar to the three Fellow Crafts who murdered our chief, Hiram Abiff. Q. What is the reason that the Grand Masters of all lodges are received with so much honor in the Symbolic Lodges? A. Those homages are due to their virtues as Princes of Masons, whose firmness has been shown on so many occasions, by spilling their blood in support of Masonry and the fraternity. Q. Why do we applaud with our hands? A. In that manner we express our happiness and satisfaction at having done a good action, and rendered justice. Q. What reflections occur, when contemplating the conduct of Solomon? A. That a wise man may err, and when he is sensible of his fault, correct himself by acknowledging that fault, whereby he claims the indulgence of his brethren. Q.

Why do the Symbolic lodges take the name of St. John of Jerusalem? A. Because in the time of the crusades, the Perfect Masons, Knights, and Princes, communicated their mysteries to the Knights of that order; whereupon it was determined to celebrate their festival annually, on St. John's day, being under the same law. Q. Who was the first architect that conducted the works of Solomon's temple? A. Hiram Abiff; which signifies the inspired man. Q. Who laid the first stone? A. Solomon cut and laid the first stone, which afterwards supported the temple. Q. Was there any thing enclosed in that stone? A. Yes; some characters, which were, like the name of the Grand Architect of the universe, only known to Solomon. Q. What stone was it? A. An agate, of a foot square. Q. What was the form of it? A. Cubical. Q. At what time of the day was the stone laid? A. Before sunrise. Q. For what reason? A. To show that we must begin early and work with vigilance and assiduity. Q. What cement did he make use of? A. A cement which was composed of the finest and purest flour, milk, oil, and wine. Q. Is there any meaning in this composition? A. Yes; when the Grand Architect of the universe determined to create the world, he employed his sweetness, bounty, wisdom, and power. Q. What is the reason why the number eighty-one is held in such esteem among Princes of Masons? A. Because that number explains the triple alliance which the Eternal operates by the triple triangle, which was seen at the time Solomon consecrated the temple to God; and also that Hiram Abiff was 81 years of age when he was murdered. Q. Was any thing else perceived at the consecration? A. A perfume which not only filled the temple, but all Jerusalem. Q. Who destroyed the temple? A. Nebuchadnezzar. Q. How many years after it was built? A. Four hundred and seventy years, six months, and ten days, after its foundation? Q. Who built the second temple? A. Zerubbabel, by the grant and aid of Cyrus, king of Persia. It was finished in the reign of Darius, when he was known to be a Prince of Jerusalem. Cyrus not only gave Zerubbabel and the captive Masons their liberty, but ordered all the treasures of the old temple to be restored to them, that they might embellish the second temple, which he had ordered Zerubbabel to build. Q. What signifies the jewel of the Right Worshipful Grand Master of all lodges being a triangle? A. He wears it in remembrance of the presents given by monarchs and the protectors of the order, in recompence for their zeal, fervor, and constancy. Q. What way have you travelled to become a Right Worshipful Grand Master of all Lodges, and Grand Patriarch? A. By the four elements. Q. Why by the four elements? A. To put us in mind of this world, and the troubles in which we live ; to cleanse ourselves from all impurities and thereby render ourselves worthy of perfect virtue. Q. Where was the lodge of Grand Masters first held? A. In the sacred vault, east of the temple. Q. Where is that lodge held at present? A. All over the world, agreeably to the orders of Solomon, when he told us to travel and to spread over the universe, to teach Masonry to those whom we should find worthy of it, but especially to those who should receive us kindly, and who were virtuous men. Q. What did Solomon give you to remember him at your departure? A. He rewarded the merits of all the workmen, and showed to the Chief Master the cubic stone of agate, on which was engraved, on a gold plate, the sacred name of God. Q. How was the agate stone supported? A. On a pedestal of a triangular form, surrounded by three cross pillars, which were also surrounded by a circle of brass. Q. What signifies the three pillars? A. Strength, wisdom, and beauty. Q. What was in the middle of the circle? A. The point of exactness, which teaches us the point of perfection. Q. What else did Solomon give you? A. The great sign of admiration and consternation, by which I am known by a brother. He also put a ring on my finger, in remembrance of my alliance with virtue, and loaded us with kindness. Q. Why have you a sun on the jewel of perfection? A. To show that we have *received the full light, and know Masonry in its perfection.* Q. Who destroyed the second temple which was finished by the Princes of Jerusalem? A. Pompey began its destruction, and king Herodes the Great finished it. Q. Who rebuilt it again? A. King Herodes repenting the action he had unjustly done, recalled all the Masons to Jerusalem who had fled, and directed them to rebuild the temple. Q. Who destroyed the third temple? A. Tito, the son of the emperor Vespasian. The Masons, who with sorrow saw the temple again destroyed, departed from Rome, after having embraced the Catholic religion, and determined never to assist in constructing another. Q. What became of those Masons afterwards? A. They divided themselves into several companies, and went into different parts of Europe, but the greatest part of them went to Scotland, and built a town which they called Kilwinning: at this time there is a lodge there, bearing the same name. Q. What happened to them afterwards? A. Twenty-seven thousand of the Masons in Scotland determined to assist the Christian Princes and Knights, who were at that time at Jerusalem, in a crusade for the purpose of taking the Holy Land and city from the infidels, who were then in possession of it ; and they accordingly obtained leave of the Scottish monarch. Q. What happened most remarkable to them? A. Their bravery and good conduct gained them the esteem and respect of all the Knights of St. John of Jerusalem. The general of that order, and the principal officers, took the resolution of being admitted into the secrets of Masonry, which they accordingly received; and in return they admitted them as Scotch Masons into their order, by the name of ROSE CROIX, or PELICAN. Q. What became of those Masons afterwards? A. After the crusade, they returned and spread Masonry throughout all Europe, which flourished for a long time in France and England; but the Scotch, to their great praise be it spoken, were the only people who kept up the practice of it. Q. How came it again in vogue in France? A. A Scotch nobleman went to France and became a resident at Bordeaux, where he established a Lodge of Perfection, from the members of the lodge in 1744; in which he was assisted by a French gentleman, who took great pleasure in all the Masonic Degrees. This still exists in a most splendid manner. Q. What means the fire in our lodge? A. Submission, purification of morals, and equality among brethren. Q. What signifies the air? A. The purity, virtue, and truth of this degree. Q. What does the sign of the sun mean? A. It signifies that some of us are more enlightened than others in the mysteries of Masonry; and for that reason we are often called Knights of the Sun. Q. How many signs have you in this degree of Grand Pontiff, which is Grand Master of all lodges? A. 1st, The sign of the earth, or Apprentice; 2d, of water—Fellow Craft; 3d, of terror—the Master; 4th, of fire; 5th, of air; 6th, of the point in view; 7th, of the sun; 8th, of astonishment; 9th, of honor; 10th, of stench, or strong smell; 11th, of admiration; 12th, of consternation. End of the lecture.

To close.—The Grand Master says, 'My brother, enter into the cave of SILOL—work with Grand ROFADAM—measure your steps to the sun, and then the great black eagle will cover you with his wings, to the end of what you desire, by the help of the Most Sublime Princes Grand Commanders.' He then strikes four and two, makes the sign of the four squares, which is repeated by the Wardens, and the lodge is closed.

The *examination* of a brother in the foregoing degree, is as follows:

Q. From whence came you? A. From the sacred vault at Jerusalem. Q. What are you come to do here? A. I am come to see and visit your works and show you mine, that we may work together and rectify our morals, and, if possible, sanctify the profane—but only by permission of a Prince Adept, or Prince of the

Royal Secret, (if one is present.) Q. What have you brought? A. Glory, grandeur, and beauty. Q. Why do you give the name of St. John to our lodge? A. Formerly all the lodges were under the name of Solomon's lodge, as the founder of Masonry; but since the crusades we have agreed with the Knights Templars, or Hospitallers, to dedicate them to St. John, as he was the support of the Christians and the new laws. Q. What do you ask more? A. Your will and pleasure as you may find me worthy, obedient, and virtuous.

KNIGHTS OF THE ROYAL AXE OR HACHE, (HATCHET.)

SOMETIMES CALLED

GRAND PATRIARCH, BY THE NAME OF

PRINCE OF LIBANUS.

This meeting is called a College.

To open.—The Chief Prince says, 'To order, brethren;' which is answered by the Senior and Junior Grand Wardens in the same words. After some silence is observed, the Chief Prince holds up both his hands, the fingers and thumbs extended as wide as possible, and says, 'The trees of Libanus are grown up and fit to cut;' on which all the brethren hold up both their hands in the same manner, then let them fall on their thighs, in allusion that they are cut down, in order to be used for holy purposes; viz: 1st. They were used for the building of Noah's ark: 2d. They were used for the construction of the Ark of Alliance: 3d. For the use of Solomon's temple. The Chief Prince then says,

Noah,	The answer to these	Japhet,
Bezaleel,	words are made by the	Eliab,
Sidonians,	Senior Warden.	Libanus.

Origin.—This degree was established on the three abovementioned occasions, the cutting of cedar for holy purposes. The explanation of the letters on the AXE, or JEWEL, will teach you.

L, on one side of the handle, is Lebanon: S, on the top, Solomon: AB, on the same side, Abda: A, on the same side, Adoniram: C, on the same side, Cyrus: D, on the same side, Darius: X, on the same side, Xerxes: Z, on the same side, Zerubbabel: A, on the same side, Ananias.

On the other side of the axe are the following initials:—S, on the blade, Sidonians: N, on the top of the handle, Noah: S, on do. Shem: C, on do. Cham:* I, on do. Japheth: M, on do. Moses: B, on do. Bezaleel: E, on do. Eliab.

The said axe, or jewel, must be crowned, and should be of gold, and must hang on the breast to a ribbon of the colors of the rainbow. It may also be worn from the right shoulder to the left hip.

The Sidonians were always very zealous for holy enterprises : before the deluge they employed themselves in cutting cedars from Mount Lebanon for the construction of Noah's ark, under the conduct of Japheth. The descendants of them likewise cut cedars from Mount Lebanon, that were grown up again, for the construction of the ark of the covenant; and their posterity also cut in the same forest, under the conduct of Prince de Heroden, for the construction of the first temple of God, by the orders of Solomon. The Samaritans assisted in bringing the timbers down from the mount to the seaside, to be transported from thence to Joppa.

Their zealous descendants have since been employed to fell the timbers of the mountain, for the construction of the second temple, by the orders of Cyrus, Darius, and Xerxes, under the direction of Zerubbabel. This celebrated nation formed on the said mountain, Colleges, or meetings, and always in their works adored the Great Architect of the universe. They had the same signs, and their different words were taken from the different inspectors and conductors; as Noah, and his three sons. Noah being the chief, and his sons the conductors and ancient patriarchs, we owe to them the knowledge of these events in succession of time since the deluge.

In the earliest ages of time, Colleges were established on the mountain, for the construction of the ark of the covenant, and in some ages after, the same colleges were held for the construction of Solomon's temple. That wise king ordered a small palace to be built on Mount Lebanon, to which, when finished, he used to go to see what progress the workmen had made in hewing and squaring the cedars. Thus, by their example, we preserve, with the greatest respect, the names of those venerable patriarchs, and also the memory of the Sidonians. The initials of the jewel form an abridgment of this interesting history, as well as the figure of the draft. The College is closed in the same manner as it was opened.

---

* The French spell the name *Ham*, Cham.

CHIEF OF THE TABERNACLE.

Decorations of the lodge.—The hangings are principally white, supported by others of red and black here and there, according to the taste of the architect. At the bottom of this hall is a sanctuary, separated from the upper part by a balustrade, and by a red curtain on every side. In the sanctuary there is placed the throne over a platform, upon which you enter by seven steps. Before the throne is placed a table covered with a red cloth—upon the altar is laid the Holy Bible and a poniard. Beside the throne there is the ARK of ALLIANCE, crowned by a GLORY, in the centre of which is seen God's name, (יהוה) and at the sides the SUN and the MOON. To the right of the first altar, and a little further upwards, is the altar of sacrifices, (Holy Courts.) In front, to the left, is the altar of perfumes. In the west, two chandeliers, of five branches, arrayed in a pyramidal form. In the east, one chandelier, with two branches.

The president is seated on the throne, and the Wardens before the altar. During receptions there is a dark apartment with an altar in the middle, over which is placed a light, and three human skulls. In front of the altar there is a human skeleton.

Titles.—The presiding officer is styled, 'GREAT SOVEREIGN SACRIFICER.' In the French lodge he is styled, 'GRAND COMMANDER.' The Wardens, 'HIGH PRIESTS;' the others, '*Levites.*' The lodge is styled an '*Hierarchy.*' In France it is called, '*Sovereign Council.*' The Chief represents Aaron; the Wardens, his sons, Eleazer and Ithamar. The candidate represents Hamar. He should be introduced covered, hat on, sandals on his feet, and linen small clothes on. Hour of opening is when the descendants of Hiram came to the sacrifices. Of closing—when the sacrifice is consumed, knocking seven blows, by six and one. The candidate knocks, and repeats the following

Obligation.—I, A. B., do promise and swear never to reveal the secrets of this degree to any person in the world, except he has acquired all the preceding degrees, and then, not unless within the body of a Sovereign Council of this degree of Chief of the Tabernacle, regularly holding its authority from some legally established Supreme Council of the thirty-third degree: nor will I be present, or aid, or assist at the communicating them, unless with the above-named authority, regularly obtained. And in case I should violate this my sacred obligation, I perjure myself: I consent that the earth should be opened before my eyes, and that I should be engulfed (swallowed up,) even to my neck, and thus miserably perish. To the fulfilment of which, may God preserve me in my senses. Amen. In token of your sincerity in this obligation you will kiss the Bible. (Nadab and Abihu, Aaron's two sons) were punished in this manner for their crimes. Numbers, chap. 3rd

Dress.—The Chief, or Grand Sacrificer, wears a large red tunic; over which is placed another of yellow, shorter than the first, and without sleeves. Upon his head is a mitre of gold cloth; upon the front is painted or embroidered, a Delta, with the ineffable name. About this dress he puts a black sash with a silver fringe; from which hangs (by a red cockade,) a poniard. This sash is worn from left to right. The two High Priests, or Wardens, have the same dress, with the exception of the Delta upon the mitre, which they do not use. The Levites wear a white tunic, tied with a red belt, with a gold fringe. From this belt, by a black cockade, is suspended a thurible, (censor,) which is the jewel of this degree.

Apron.—The apron is white, lined with deep scarlet, and bordered with red, blue, and purple ribbons. In the middle, it has a gold chandelier of seven branches; and on the flap a myrtle in violet color. The jewel, which is a thurible, is sometimes worn from a broad sash of yellow, purple, blue, and scarlet ribbon, from the left shoulder to the right hip.

PRINCE OF THE TABERNACLE.

Decorations of the lodge rooms.—This lodge consists of two apartments, the first of which proceeds directly into the second, and is called the vestibule, where the brothers clothe themselves. It is ornamented with the different attributes of Free Masonry. The second apartment is made completely circular, by means of the suit of hangings. The decoration of this room varies agreeably to the three points of reception. In its middle, is placed a chandelier with seven branches, and each branch with seven lights; in all forty-nine lights.

Apparel.—A blue silk (taffeta, or sarcenet,) TUNIC; the collar of which is decorated with rays of gold, representing a glory. The surplice is sprinkled with gold stars. Upon the head, a close crown, encompassed by stars and surrounded by a Delta. The sash is a broad watered scarlet ribbon, worn as a collar, or as a sash from right to left.

Apron.—The apron is white bordered with crimson. In the French lodges, white, lined with deep scarlet, and bordered with green. On its middle is painted, or embroidered with red, a representation of the tabernacle. The flap is sky blue.

Titles.—This assemblage is called a 'HIERARCHY.' The Chief Prince is called, 'MOST POWERFUL.' There are three Wardens styled '*Powerful :*'—the first placed in the south—the second, in the west—and the third, in the north. The officers of this Hierarchy represent MOSES, the giver of the law;—AARON, The Chief Priest;—BEZALEEL, the son of URI,—AHOLIAB, the son of AHISAMACH. The candidate represents ELEAZER, who succeeded AARON in the duties of the tabernacle.

To open the Hierarchy.—Moses. 'Powerful, are we well tyled and in perfect security; and are all present, Princes of the Tabernacle?' Aaron. 'We are, Most Powerful, in security; and all present, are regular Princes of the Tabernacle.' M. 'What is the o'clock?' A. 'It is the first hour of the first day of the seven, for building this Hierarchy. It is the first of the day of life, and the sweetness of the seven.' M. 'Since it is so, give notice that I am about to open this Sovereign Council of the Hierarchy.' A. '*Bezaleel* and *Aholiab* repeat.' The Chief Prince gives six equal and one loud raps, and the Wardens all repeat them, one after the other, when Moses says, 'I declare this Sovereign Council duly opened.

Form of reception.—The candidate is first washed in water as in Exodus, xxv. 1—40. He is brought to the altar by six equal and one long steps, when he kneels and takes the following

Obligation.—I, A. B., do promise and swear that I will never reveal to any person in the world whatever, the secrets of this Degree of Prince of the Tabernacle; and that I will never confer them, nor aid, or assist in conferring them on any person or persons, by my presence, or otherwise, except under an authority regularly obtained from some Supreme Council of the thirty-third Degree; which has been constitutionally established, giving full power so to do. That I will stand to, and abide by, all the laws, rules, and regulations which belong to this degree, or may regularly emanate from the Supreme Council of the thirty-third Degree, under which we are now acting; and in case I should violate this sacred obligation, I consent to be stoned to death, (as St. Stephen was;) and that my body be left to rot above ground deprived of burial. For the faithful performance of which, may the Almighty Architect of the universe preserve me. Amen.' In token of your sincerity in this obligation you will kiss the book.

The Chief Prince approaches him (he still kneeling,) with a hod of oil and a trowel, and thus proceeds :—'*I anoint, Eleazer, thy right ear, thy right eye, and thy right thumb, with the holy oil, in token of thy being separated from the foibles of the world, and to set thee apart of well doers in this tabernacle of clay, to be raised at the great and awful day of judgment, as a shining monument of God's glory, in the house not made with hands eternal in the heavens.*'

Jewel.—The jewel of a Prince of the Tabernacle is the letter A, in gold, worn from a collar of broad crimson ribbon.

History.—The history of this degree may be found in the orders which the Almighty gave to Moses and to the children of Israel, to depart from Egypt and go to the promised land, and there to build him a tabernacle. Exodus, chap. xxv.

Table ceremony, observed by the Chiefs and Princes of the Tabernacle.—The table is round, and the *victuals* are not placed on it, but successively presented to the brothers in turn, who are served each to his taste. In the middle of the table is a cluster of inflamed hearts (painted,) and some incense—there must not be but seven lights on the table.

Manner of toasting. First toast: The MASTER says, 'The warm mid-day of our solemnities, invite our inclinations to *new libations.*'

Let us charge.—' Powerful brother Junior Warden, what continuation of success do you announce to us ?' Junior Warden answers according to the ritual. J. W. ' Powerful brothers Wardens, and you Powerful brothers of the Hierarchy, let us celebrate the grandeur of the glorious destiny which associates us. Drink off the cup at one draught.'

Second toast.—The MOST POWERFUL, or Chief Prince, says, ' The warm mid-day of our solemnities invite our inclinations to *new libations.*'

Let us charge.—' Powerful brother Senior Warden, what is the hour ?' Senior Warden, (From the ritual answers.) Chief Prince. 'How do you combine talents?' (Answer by ritual.) C. P. ' Where are your brothers ?' S. W. ' The Sovereign Master of the universe directs them in the lodge, and preserves them in the hierarchy.' C. P. ' Powerful brothers of the Hierarchial Lodge, I give you the health of all Free Masons, elected, or to be elected, for the unity of the seven and of three.

Third toast. The Chief Prince orders to charge the censors agreeably to the ritual, and says, ' Powerful brothers, let us drink to the health of the President of the United States, and to all in authority. May the Sovereign Grand Master of the universe fill them and us with his joy and *property.*' The hour of closing is the day of life and of tranquillity. *March*—six equal, and one long steps ; in all seven.

HIEROGLYPHICS OF THIS DEGREE.

A B C D E F G H I J K L M N O P Q R S T U V X Y Z

KNIGHTS OF THE BRAZEN SERPENT.

Decorations of the lodge.—The hangings are red and blue. Over the throne there is a transparency, on which there is seen a burning bush, and in the middle the name, יהוה In the centre of the lodge there is a mount, elevated by five steps, in the form of a truncated cone. One torch, or great taper, alone enlightens the lodge.

Titles.—The lodge is called the Court of *Sinai;* the Chief Knight is called, ' MOST POWERFUL GRAND MASTER ;' the Wardens, ' *Ministers,* first and second ;' the Orator, ' *Pontiff;*' the Secretary, ' *Grand Inquirer ;*' and the other brothers, ' *Knights.*' There is also an ' *Examiner ;*' and they style the candidate a ' *Traveller,*' &c. He ought to be loaded with chains to the weight of 30 lbs. at least. These heavy chains denote that this degree has reference to the deliverance of the captives. The lodge represents the front of Moses' tent, where he waited upon (gave authority to) the Israelites, who came to prefer their complaints and grievances. The arch over head, sprinkled with stars, and the single light, represents the sun. The officers represent Moses, Aaron, and Joshua, the candidate an Israelite in chains, upon his march.

NOTE. The pleasure of bearing the yoke for our brothers, remembering that they are our equals, and that the same arrow cannot wound us all, should determine us in receiving this degree. We should also be animated by the Divine Spirit, to avenge our country ; to make our mysteries respected, and to carry the law of the Most High to the four quarters of the universe.

Apparel.—A red collar, upon which is painted, or embroidered, the device, *virtue* and *valor.*

Jewel.—The jewel is a serpent entwined upon the environs of a cross pole, in form of a T, about which are the Hebrew characters יהוה, which signify, ' One who shall live.'

This is the image that Moses is said to have erected in the camp of the Israelites ; (Numbers, xxi. 6. &c.) that possessed the virtue to heal the bites of serpents which molested them in the desert. It was afterwards preserved in the temple, with much careful attention ; but as it came in process of time to be an object of idolatry with the Jews, Hezekiah, king of Judea, commanded to take it to pieces, and, full of indignation, called it ' *Ne hush tan,* (Æneus surpens, brazen serpent,) old copper to be melted up,' sordid stuff. The French write the word ' Nechuschthare,' which at the same time signifies, ' *brazen, creeping,*

X

prophecying,' because of the superstition of the Jews in consulting the oracles.

Hours of opening.—The Court is opened at one o'clock, and is closed at four o'clock. *March*—Nine serpentine steps. *Knocks*—Nine blows; five slow, three hurried, and one by itself.

Obligation.—I, A. B., do solemnly promise and swear, in the presence of the Almighty God, the Grand Architect of the universe, that I will never reveal the secrets of this Degree of Knight of the Brazen Serpent; nor, by my presence, aid or assist in revealing them to any person or persons whatsoever, unless the candidate shall have taken all the preceding degrees in a regular manner, nor without a legal authority. I now swear allegiance and true faith. In case I should transgress this my solemn obligation, and *thus perjure myself, I freely consent to have my heart eaten by the most venomous of serpents, and thus to perish most miserably;* from which may the Almighty Creator of the universe guard and defend me! In token of your sincerity you will kiss the Bible.

Apron.—Is white, bound with black tears; upon the flap is a triangle, in a glory; in its centre the Hebrew letter ה Sometimes the JEWEL is embroidered, and on the breast of a broad watered white ribbon, worn from the right shoulder to the left hip.

History.—The history of this degree is drawn from the Bible. Numbers, chap. xxi. When God, to punish the Israelites for their wickedness, sent into their country serpents, which should devour them. They came to Moses with their grievances and confessed their faults. Moses invoked the Almighty for them, and God ordered him to fasten a fiery serpent upon a pole, that all the Israelites who might have been bitten, should turn and look upon it, and be made whole. The signification of the jewel is this; when Moses made a brazen serpent, and placed it upon a pole, as God had ordered him, and it came to pass that every one bitten, looking upon it and pronouncing the word, '*Hatathi*,' (I have sinned) was immediately made whole.

LIGHT ON MASONRY.

PRINCE OF MERCY,
OR
SCOTCH TRINITARIAN.

Decorations of the lodge.—The hangings are green, supported by nine columns, alternately white and red, upon each of which is an arm of a chandelier, sustaining nine lights, forming in all eighty-one lights. The canopy is green, white, and red; under which is a green colored throne. The table before the throne is covered with a cloth of the same color. Instead of a Hiram, the Most Excellent Chief Prince uses an arrow, whose plume is on one side green, and on the other side red, the spear being white and the point gilded. By the altar is a statue which represents " *Truth*," covered with the aforesaid three colors. This statue is the palladium of the order.

Titles.—This Chapter is styled the " *Third Heaven.*" The Chief Prince is called " Most Excellent." Besides the two Wardens and accustomed officers, there is a " *Sacrificer*" and a " *Guard of the Palladium.*"

The Chief Prince represents Moses; Senior Warden, Aaron; Junior Warden, Eleazer; the candidate, Joshua.

Apparel.—The Most Excellent Chief Prince wears a large tricolored tunic, of green, white, and red; and on his head a crown of lace, surmounted with nine points.

Apron.—Red, bordered with white fringe; upon its centre is painted or wrought a white and green triangle. In the centre is a heart, and on it the letter ין. The flap is sky blue, (sometimes green.)

Jewel.—The jewel is an equilateral triangle of gold, and in the centre a gold heart. Upon the heart is engraved the letter ה. It is worn from a broad tricolored ribbon. The collar is green, white, and red.

Age.—Eighty-one years is the age of a *Prince of Mercy.*

March.—Three equal steps beginning with the left foot.

Knocking.—Fifteen blows by three, five, and seven.

Obligation.—I, A, B., do promise and swear, in the presence of the Grand Architect of the universe, and this respectable assembly, and by the most sacred of obligations, that I never will reveal the secrets of this sublime degree of Prince of Mercy to any person or persons whatsoever in the world, except they have received all the degrees below this in a correct manner, and so thereby I shall know him to be regularly entitled to the same. I furthermore promise and swear never to entrust this degree to any person, nor assist at any reception, unless I or they shall have been or are authorized by a particular permission or warrant for that purpose, from some Supreme Council of the thirty-third degree, regularly and constitutionally established, to whose authority, laws, rules, and regulations, I now swear true faith and allegiance ; and in that case I promise and swear, never to give my consent before I have been plainly informed of the life, manners and morals of the candidate. Should I violate or transgress this, my solemn obligation, I consent to be condemned, cast out, and despised by the whole universe. And may the Supreme Architect of heaven and earth, guide, guard, and protect me, to fulfil the same. Amen. Amen. Amen.' In token of your sincerity in this obligation, you will kiss the Bible.

LECTURE.

Q. Are you a Prince of Mercy ? A. I have seen the *great light*, (Delta,) and our MOST EXCELLENT, as well as yourself, in the 'TRIPLE ALLIANCE' of the ' BLOOD OF JESUS CHRIST,' of which you and I have the mark. Q. What is the triple alliance ? A. It is that which the ETERNAL made with Abraham by circumcision; that which He made with his people in the desert, by the intercession of Moses ; and that which He made with mortals, by the death and suffering of our Saviour, Jesus Christ, his dearly beloved son.

HIEROGLYPHICS.

A B C D E F G H I J K L M N O P Q R S T U V X Y Z

SOVEREIGN COMMANDER

OF THE

TEMPLE AT JERUSALEM.

Decorations of the lodge.—The hangings are red, ornamented with black columns ; upon each of which there is an arm (or branch,) holding a light. The canopy and throne are red, sprinkled with black tears. In the centre of the lodge there is a chandelier, with three rows of lights, in all making twenty-seven lights, thus arranged :—twelve on the lowest tier of branches, nine on the second, and six on the third or uppermost tier ; twenty-seven other lights are placed upon a round table, about which the Commanders are seated in council of the Court.

Titles.—This council is styled a COURT. The Grand Commander, 'ALL POWERFUL.' In some Courts he is styled, 'MOST ILLUSTRIOUS,' and 'MOST VALIANT.' The Wardens are called, 'MOST SOVEREIGN COMMANDERS.'

Apparel.—The 'All Powerful' is clad in a white tunic, and over it a Knight's mantle, of red, lined with ermine skin. (In France the robe is blue.) Upon his head he wears a crown of lace.

Apron.—Flesh colored, lined and edged with black. On the *flap* there is a Teutonic cross, (the cross of the order,) encircled by a crown of laurel. Beneath it, upon the flap, there is a key. All these ornaments are done in black. The *gloves* are white, lined and bound with black. (In France with red.) The *sash*, or military scarf, is white, bounded (edged) with red, worn round the neck, from which hangs the jewel. Upon its two sides are embroidered in red, the four crosses of the Commanders. Besides, they wear a red sash, bordered with black, put from the right shoulder to the left hip; from which hangs a cross of a Commander of enamelled gold.

Jewel.—The jewel is a golden triangle, upon which is engraved, in Hebrew, the sacred word יהוה.

Knocks.—Twenty-seven blows with the flat of your sword, by twelve, then by twelve and three. The candidate passes three times round the room. *Hours of opening.*—ten o'clock. *Hours of closing.*—four o'clock.

Obligation.—I, A. B., in the presence of the one Almighty and only true God, the Grand Architect of the universe, and of this Venerable Court of Grand Commanders of the Temple, do, of my own free will and accord, most solemnly and sincerely vow, promise, and swear, never to reveal the secrets of this degree which I am now receiving, to any person or persons below me, except in a court lawfully holden, with a warrant or authority from some regularly established Supreme Council of the thirty-third Degree, empowering me, and them with me, to work in this Sublime Degree. I furthermore promise and swear, that I never will confer, nor assist in conferring this degree, upon any person who has not, in a legal and regular manner, taken all the foregoing degrees of Free Masonry. I furthermore promise and swear, that I will pay due regard and submission to the Supreme Council, under whose authority we are now acting; and that I will always govern myself by their laws, rules, and regulations, so far as the same shall come to my knowledge; and will do all in my power to support them, for the good of the craft and the advantage of Free Masonry, agreeable to the constitutions of the order. To all this I solemnly swear, *under the penalty of having the severe wrath of Almighty God inflicted on me; and may He have mercy on my soul in the day of judgment, agreeably to my performance* of this sacred obligation. Amen. Amen. Amen. In token of your sincerity you will kiss the Bible. Here follow the signs and tokens.

NOTE. It is improper to confound this order of Grand Commander of the temple, thirty-seventh degree of Sublime Free Masonry, with that of the Knights of St. John of Jerusalem, better known by the name of Knights Templars, the immediate successors of the Ancient Knights of the Temple. This military and religious order exists at this day, in spite of the abolishment pronounced by Pope Clement V. It is known, that since that time the *Bull* has been annulled. The Grand Master, James D' Molay, before his death, chose a successor, who has transmitted his powers to the actual Grand Commander, through an uninterrupted series of Chiefs of the order, celebrated for their many titles of respect and valor. Among these Chiefs are recorded many Princes of the house of Bourbon. The Knights of the temple ought not then to be considered as an order of Free Masonry. Nevertheless, from the example of their predecessors they fraternize [hold fellowship with] the Free Masons, and visit them under the title of Brothers of the Order of the East, but they are wanting in the Masonic rites.

THE KEY OF MASONRY.

PHILOSOPHICAL LODGE.

KNIGHTS ADEPTS OF THE EAGLE OR SUN.*

This Council must be illuminated by one single light, and is enlightened by one divine light: because there is one single light that shines among men, who have the happiness of going from the darkness of ignorance and of the vulgar prejudices, to follow the only light that leads to the celestial truth. The light that is in our lodge, is composed of a glass globe filled with water, and a light placed behind it, which renders the light more clear. The glass of reflection, the globe, when it is lighted, is placed in the south.

Robe and sceptre.—The Grand Master or Thrice Puissant, is named 'FATHER ADAM,' who is placed in the east, vested in a robe of pale yellow, like the morning. He has his hat on, and in his right hand a sceptre, on the top of which is a globe of gold. The handle or extremity of the sceptre is gilt. The rea-

---

* This degree should be read by every Christian. It is a dagger aimed at the heart of Christianity! The language in which it is written, is low, and some parts difficult to be understood.

son that Father Adam carries the globe above the sceptre in this Council is, because he was constituted '*Sovereign Master of the world,*' and created '*Sovereign Father of all men.*' He carries a SUN suspended by a chain of gold around his neck; and on the reverse of this jewel of gold is a globe. When this degree is given, no jewel or apron is worn.

There is only one Warden, who sits opposite Father Adam in the west, and is called *Brother Truth.* He is entitled to the same ornaments as Father Adam; and the order that belongs to this degree is a broad white watered ribbon worn as a collar, with an *eye* of gold embroidered thereon, above the gold chain and jewel of the sun. The number of other officers is seven; and are called by the name of the *cherubim* as follows: ZAPHRIEL, ZABRIEL, CAMIEL, URIEL, MICHAEL, ZAPHAEL, and GABRIEL. These ought to be decorated in the same manner as the Thrice Puissant Father Adam. If there are more than that number of the Knights of the Sun, they go by the name of SYLPHS, and are the preparers of the Council, and assistants in all the ceremonies or operations of the lodge. They are entitled to the same jewel, but have a ribbon of a fiery color tied to the third buttonhole of their coats.

To open the Grand Council.—Father Adam says, 'Brother Truth, what time is it on earth?' Brother Truth. 'Mighty Father, it is midnight among the profane, or cowans, but the sun is in its meridian in this lodge.' Father Adam. 'My dear children, profit by the favor of this austere luminary, at present showing its light to us, which will conduct us in the path of virtue, and to follow that law which is eternally to be engraved on our hearts, and the only law by which we cannot fail to come to the knowledge of *pure truth.*' He then makes a sign, by putting his right hand on his left breast; on which all the brethren put up the first finger of the right hand above their heads, the other fingers clenched, showing by that, that there is but *one God*, who is the beginning of all truth; then Father Adam says, 'This lodge is opened.'

Form of reception.—After the Council is opened, the candidate is introduced into an antechamber, where there are a number of *Sylphs*, each with a bellows, blowing a large pot of fire, which the candidate sees, but they take no notice of him. After he is left in this situation two or three minutes, the most ancient of the Sylphs goes to the candidate and covers his face with black crape. He must be without a sword, and is told that he must find the door of the Sanctuary, and when found, to knock on it six times with an open hand. After he finds the door and knocks, Brother Truth goes to the door, and having opened it a little, asks the candidate the following questions, which he answers by the help of the Sylphs. Q. 'What do you desire?' A. 'I desire to go out of darkness to see the true light, and to know the true light in all its purity.' Q. 'What do you desire more?' A. 'To divest myself of original sin, and destroy the juvenile prejudices of error, which all men are liable to, namely, the desires of all worldly attachments and pride.' On which Brother Truth comes to Father Adam, and relates what the candidate has told him; when Father Adam gives orders to introduce the candidate to the true happiness. Then Brother Truth opens the door, and takes the candidate by the hand, and conducts him to the middle of the lodge or sanctuary, which is also covered by a black cloth, when Father Adam addresses him thus: 'My son, seeing by your labor in the royal art, you are now come to the desire of knowledge of the pure and holy truth, we shall lay it open to you without any disguise or covering. But, before we do this, consult your heart, and see in this moment if you feel yourself disposed to obey her, (namely truth,) in all things which she commands. If you are disposed, I am sure she is ready in your heart, and you must feel an emotion that was unknown to you before. This being the case, you must hope that she will not be long to manifest herself to you. But have a care not to defile the sanctuary by a spirit of curiosity; and take care not to increase the number of the vulgar and profane, that have for so long a time ill-treated her, until Truth was obliged to depart the earth, and now can hardly trace any of her footsteps. But she always appears in her greatest glory, without disguise, to the true, good, and honest Free Masons; that is to say, to the zealous extirpaters of superstition and lies. [By a careful perusal of this degree it will be seen, that by '*superstition and lies,*' is meant the true religion.—*Ed.*] I hope, my dear brother, you will be one of her intimate favorites. The proofs that you have given, assure me of every thing I have to expect of your zeal; for as nothing now can be more a secret among us, I shall order brother Truth, that he will instruct you what you are to do in order to come to true happiness.' After this discourse of Father Adam, the candidate is unveiled and shown the form of the lodge or council, without explaining any part thereof. Brother Truth then proceeds thus, 'My dear brother, by my mouth, holy truth speaketh to you; but before she can manifest herself to you, she requires of you proofs in which she is satisfied in your entrance into the Masonic order. She has appeared to you in many things which you could not have apprehended or comprehended without her assistance; but now you have the happiness to arrive at the brilliant day, nothing can be a secret to you. Learn, then, the moral use that is made of the three first parts of the furniture, which you knew after you was received an Entered Apprentice Mason; viz: *Bible, Compass*, and *Square*. By the *Bible*, you are to understand that it is the only law you ought to follow. It is that which Adam received at his creation, and which the Almighty engraved in his heart. *This law is called natural law*, and shows positively that there is but *one God*, and to adore him only without any subdivision or interpolation. The *Compass* gives you the faculty of judging for yourself, that whatever God has created, is well, and he is the sovereign author of every thing. Existing in himself, nothing is either good or evil; because we understand by this expression, an action done which is excellent in itself, is relative, and submits to the human understanding, or judgment, to know the value and price of such action; and that God, with whom every thing is possible, communicates nothing of his will, but such as his great goodness pleases; and every thing in the universe is governed as he has decreed it, with justice, being able to compare it with the attributes of the Divinity. I equally say, that in himself there is no evil; because he has made every thing with exactness, and that *every thing exists according to his will; consequently, as it ought to be.* The distance between good and evil with the Divinity, cannot be more justly and clearly compared than by a circle formed with a compass. From the points being reunited there is formed an entire circumference; and when any point in particular equally approaches or equally separates from its point, it is only a faint resemblance of the distance between good and evil, which we compare by the points of a compass forming a circle, *which circle when completed is God!*

Square.—By the *Square* we discover *that* God who has made every thing *equal*, in the same manner that you are not able to dig a body in a quarry complete, or perfect; thus, the wish of the Eternal in creating the world by a liberal act of his own, well foresaw every matter that could possibly happen in consequence thereof; that is to say, that every thing therein contained at the same time of the creation was good.

Level.—You have also seen a level, a plumb, and a rough stone. By the level you are to learn to be upright and sincere, and not to suffer yourself to be drawn away by the *multitude of the blind and ignorant people;* to be always firm and steady to sustain the right of the *natural law*, and the pure and real knowledge of that truth which it teacheth.

Perpendicular and rough stone.—By these you ought to understand that the *perpendicular man is polished by reason*, and put censure away by the excellence of our Master

Tressle-board.—You have seen the tressle-board, to draw plans on. This represents the man whose whole occupation is the art of thinking, and who employs his reason in that which is just and reasonable.

Cubic stone.—You have seen the cubic stone, the moral of which, and the sense you ought to draw from it, is, to rule your actions, that they might be equally brought to the sovereign good.

Pillars.—The two pillars teacheth you that all Masons ought to attach themselves firmly to become an ornament to the order, as well as to its support; as the pillars of Hercules formerly determined the end of the ancient world.

Blazing star.—You have seen the blazing star, the moral sense of which is, 'a true Mason perfecting himself in the way of truth,' that he may become like a blazing star which shineth equally during the thickest darkness; and it is useful to those that it shineth upon, and who are ready and desirous of profiting by its light.

The *first* instructions have conducted you to the knowledge of Hiram Abiff, and the inquiries that were made in finding him out. You have been informed of the words, signs, and tokens which were substituted for those we feared would have been surprised, but of which they afterwards learnt, that the treacherous villains had not been able to receive any knowledge of; and this ought to be an example and salutary advice to you, to be always on your guard, and well persuaded that it is difficult to escape the snares that ignorance, joined to conceited opinion, lay every day against us, and thereby to overcome us; and the most virtuous men are liable to fall, because their candor renders them unsuspecting. But, in this case, you ought to be firm, as our Respectable Father Hiram, who chose rather to be massacred than to give up what he had obtained.

This will teach you that as soon as truth shall be fixed in your heart, you ought never to consider the resolution you should take; *you must live and die to sustain the light*, by which we acquire the sovereign good. We must never expose ourselves to the conversation of cowans, and must be circumspect even with those with whom we are the most intimate; and not deliver up ourselves to any, excepting those whose character and behaviour have proved them brothers, who are worthy to come and appear in the sacred sanctuary where holy Truth delivers her oracles.

You have passed the '*Secret*' and '*Perfect Master;*' you have been decorated with an 'ivory key,' a symbol of your distinction; you have received the pronunciation of the '*ineffable name*' of the Great Architect of the universe, and have been placed at the first balustrade of the sanctuary; you have had rank among the Levites, after you knew the word 'ZIZON,' which signifies a 'balustrade of the Levites;' where all those are placed, as well as yourself, to expect the knowledge of the most sublime mysteries.

Coffin and rope.—In the degree of Perfect Master they have shown you a grave, a coffin, and a 'withe rope,' to raise and deposit the body in a sepulchre, made in the form of a pyramid, in the top of which was a triangle, within which was the sacred name of the ETERNAL, and on the pavement were the two columns of Jachin and Boaz laid across.

Ivory key.—By the 'ivory key' you are to understand that you cannot open your heart with safety, but at proper times. By the *corpse and grave is represented the state of man, before he had known the happiness of our order!*

Rope.—The rope to which the coffin is tied, in order to raise it, is the symbol of raising *one*, as you have been raised, from the grave of ignorance to the celestial place where truth resides.

Pyramid.—The pyramid *represents the true Mason who raises himself by degrees, till he reaches heaven,* to adore the sacred and unalterable name of the Eternal Supreme.

INTIMATE SECRETARY. This new degree leads you near to Solomon and honor; and after you redoubled your zeal, you gained new honors and favors, having nearly lost your life by curiosity; *which attachment to Masonry gave you the good qualities of your heart,* and which obtained your pardon and led you to the 'Intendant of the buildings;' where you saw a 'blazing star,' a large candlestick with seven branches, with altars, vases, and purification, and a great brazen sea.

Blazing star.—By the expression of '*purification,*' you are to understand that you are to be cleansed from impiety and prejudice before you can acquire more of the sublime knowledge in passing the other degrees, to be able to support the *brilliant light of reason,* enlightened by truth, of which the blazing star is the figure.

Candlestick with seven branches.—By the candlestick with seven branches, you are to remember the mysterious number of the seven Masters who were named to succeed one; and from that time it was resolved that seven Knights of Masonry, united together, were able to initiate into Masonry, and show them the seven gifts of the Eternal, which we shall give you a perfect knowledge of, when you have been purified in the brazen sea.

Brazen sea.—You have passed from the 'Secret' and 'Perfect Master' to the 'Intimate Secretary,' 'Provost and Judge,' and 'Intendant of the Buildings.' In these degrees they have showed you an 'ebony box,' a 'key suspended,' a 'balance,' and an 'inflamed urn.'

Ebony box.—The 'ebony box' shows you with what scrupulous attention you are to keep the secrets that have been confided to you, and which you are to reserve in the closet of your heart, of which the box is an emblem. And were you to reflect on the black color of said box, it would teach you to cover your secrets with a thick veil, in such a manner that the profane cowans cannot possibly have any knowledge thereof.

Key.—The key demonstrates that you have already obtained a key to our knowledge, and part of our mysteries; and if you behave with equity, fervor, and zeal, to your brothers, you will arrive shortly to the knowledge and *meaning of our society*, and this indicates the reason of the balance.

Inflamed urn.—By the 'inflamed urn' you are to understand, that as far as you come to the knowledge of the Royal and Sublime Art, you must, by your behaviour, leave behind you, in the minds of your brethren and the vulgar, a high idea of your virtue, equal to the perfume of the burning urn.

Two kings.—In the degree of 'Intimate Secretary' you have seen and heard two kings who were entering into their new alliance and reciprocal promise, and of the perfection of their grand enterprise. They spoke of the death of Hiram Abiff, our Excellent Master. You saw guards, and a man who was overseen, very near of being put to death for his curiosity of peeping. You also heard of the prospect of a place called the vault, to deposit the precious treasure of Masonry, when the time should be fulfilled, and you afterwards became a brother. The conversation of the two kings is the figure of the coincidence of our laws and the natural law, which forms a perfect agreement with what is expedient, and promises to those who shall have the happiness, to be connected to you in the same manner and perfect alliance that they will afterwards come to the centre of true knowledge.

Tears.—The tears and regret of the two kings are the emblem of the regret you ought to have when you perceive a brother depart from the road of virtue.

The man peeping.—By the man you saw peeping, and who was discovered, and seized, and conducted to death, *is an emblem of those who come to be initiated into our sacred mysteries through a motive of curiosity; and, if so indiscreet as to divulge their obligations,* WE ARE BOUND TO CAUSE THEIR DEATH, AND TAKE VENGEANCE ON THE TREASON BY THE DESTRUCTION OF THE TRAITOR!!!* Let

---

* Since the immolation of William Morgan, and the publication of his 'Illustra-

us pray the Eternal to preserve our order from such an evil you have hereof seen an example, in that degree to which you came, by your zeal, fervor, and constancy. In that degree you have remarked, that from all the favorites that were at that time in the apartment of Solomon, only nine were elected to avenge the death of Hiram Abiff; this makes good, that a great many are often called, but few chosen. To explain this enigma, a great many of the profane have the happiness to divest themselves of that name, to see and obtain the entrance in our sanctuary; but very few are constant, zealous, and fervent, to merit the happiness of coming to the height and knowledge of the sublime truth.

Requisitions to make a good Mason.—If you ask me what are the requisite qualities that a Mason must be possessed of, to come to the centre of truth, I answer you, that you must crush the head of the serpent of ignorance. *You must shake off the yoke of infant prejudice, concerning the mysteries of the reigning religion, which worship has been imaginary, and only founded on the spirit of pride, which envies to command and be distinguished, and to be at the head of the vulgar; in affecting an exterior purity, which characterizes a false piety, joined to a desire of acquiring that which is not its own, and is always the subject of this exterior pride, and unalterable source of many disorders, which being joined to gluttonness, is the daughter of hypocrisy, and employs every matter to satisfy carnal desires, and raises to these predominant passions, altars, upon which she maintains, without ceasing, the light of iniquity, and sacrifices continually offerings to luxury, voluptuousness, hatred, envy, and perjury. Behold, my dear brother, what you must fight against, and destroy, before you can come to the knowledge of the true good and sovereign happiness! Behold this monster which you must conquer—a serpent which* WE *detest as an idol, that is adored by the idiot and vulgar under the name of* RELIGION!!! [Here, indeed, the principles of Masonry are taught with all plainness; and if the reader has heretofore been blind to the nature and tendency of the institution, methinks he can see them now! Here the Christian beholds his blessed Christ rejected—himself charged with the basest crimes—condemned as an idiot—his worship imaginary—his religion founded on the spirit of pride, the daughter of hypocrisy—a serpent, a monster, an idol detested by Masonry!!!] *Editor.*

---

tions,' Masons have boastingly said, ' If the penalty of our laws is death, no one is bound to inflict it.' But Masonry says, ' *We are bound to take vengeance on the treason by the destruction of the traitor;*' ' *we are bound to cause his death!!!*'

Solomon, King Hiram, and St. John the Baptist.—In the degrees of 'Elected of Fifteen, Illustrious Knights, Grand Master Architects, and the Royal Arch,'* you have seen many things which are only a repetition of what you have already examined. You will always find in those degrees, initial letters enclosed in different triangles, or Deltas. You have also seen the planet Mercury, the chamber called 'GABAON,' or the 'THIRD HEAVEN;' the 'winding staircase'—the 'Ark of Alliance'—the 'tomb of Hiram Abiff,' facing the ark and the urn—the precious treasure found by the assiduous travellers—the three zealous brethren Masons—the punishment of the haughty Master Mason in being buried under the ancient ruins of Enoch's temple—and finally you have seen the figures of Solomon, and Hiram king of Tyre, and St. John the Baptist.

3. *I. I. I.*—By the 3. I. I. I. you know the three sacred names of the Eternal and ' Mount Gabaon,' (Third Heaven,) which you came to by seven degrees that compose the winding staircase.

The seven stars represent the seven principal and different degrees to which you must come to attain the height of glory represented by the mount, where they formerly sacrificed to the Most High! When you arrive to that, you are to subdue your passions, in not doing any thing that is not prescribed in our laws.

By the planet Mercury, you are taught continually to mistrust, shun, and run away from those, who, by a false practice, maintain commerce with people of a vicious life, who seem to despise the most sacred mysteries; that is, to depart from those who by the vulgar fear, or a bad understanding, are ready to deny the solemn obligations that they have contracted among us.—When you come to the *foot of our arch* you are to apprehend that you come to the 'SANCTUM SANCTORUM.' You are not to return; but rather to persist in sustaining the glory of our order, and the truth of our laws, principles, and mysteries, in like manner as our Respectable Father Hiram Abiff, who deserved to have been buried there for his constancy and fidelity. We have also another example in the firmness of 'GALAAD,' the son of 'SOPHONIA,' chief of the Levites, under Surnam, the High Priest, as mentioned in the history of perfection. Learn in this moment, my dear brother, what you are to understand by the figures of Solomon, Hiram king of Tyre, and St. John the Baptist. The two first exert you, by their zeal in the royal art, to follow the sublime road of which Solomon was the institutor, and Hiram of Tyre, the 'supporter;' a title legitimately due to that king, who

---

* Knights of the Ninth Arch.

not only protected the order, but contributed with all his might to the construction of the temple (furnishing stone from Tyre, and the cedars of Lebanus) which Solomon built to the honor of the Almighty.

The third, or 'St. John the Baptist,' teaches you to preach marvellous of this order, which is as much as to say, you are to make *secret missions among men*, which you believe to be in a state of entering the road of truth, that they may be able one day to see her virtues and visage uncovered.

Hiram Abiff was the symbol of truth on earth. 'Jubelum Akirop was accused by the serpent of ignorance, which to this day raises altars in the hearts of the profane and fearful. This profaneness, backened by a fanatic zeal, becomes an instrument to the religious power, which struck the first stroke in the heart of our dear Father, Hiram Abiff; which is as much as to say, undermined the foundation of the celestial temple, which the Eternal himself had ordered to be raised to the sublime truth and his glory.

The first age of the world has been witness to what I have advanced. The simple natural law rendered to our first fathers the most uninterrupted happiness. They were in those times more virtuous; but soon as the 'monster of pride' started up in the air and disclosed herself to those unhappy mortals, she promised to them every seat of happiness, and seduced them by her soft and bewitching speeches, viz: That 'they must render to the Eternal Creator of all things an adoration with more testimony, and more extensive, than they had hitherto done,' &c. This HYDRA, with an 'hundred heads,' at that time misled, and continues to this day to mislead men, who are so weak as to submit to her empire; and it will subsist, until the moment that the *true elected* shall appear and destroy her entirely.

The degree of 'Sublime Elected,' that you have passed, gives you the knowledge of those things which conducts you to the true and solid good. The grand circle represents the immensity of the Eternal Supreme, who has neither beginning nor end.

The triangle, or Delta, is the mysterious figure of the Eternal. The three letters which you see, signify as follows:—G, at the top of the triangle, '*the grand cause of the Masons*:' the S, at the left hand, the '*submission to the same order*:' and the U, at the right hand, the '*union that ought to reign among the brethren*:' which altogether make but one body, or equal figure in all its parts. This is the triangle called 'equilateral.' The great letter G, placed in the centre of the triangle, signifies 'Great Architect of the universe,' who is God; and in this ineffable name is found all the divine attributes. This letter being placed in the centre of the triangle, is for us to understand that every true Mason must have it profoundly in his heart.

There is another triangle, on which is engraved, S. B. and N. of which you have had an explanation in a preceding degree. This triangle designs the connexion of the brethren in virtue. The solemn promise they have made to love each other; to help, succor, and keep inviolably secret, their mysteries of the perfection proposed, in all their enterprises. It is said in that degree, that 'You have entered the *Third Heaven*, that means you have entered the place where pure truth resides, since she abandoned the earth to monsters who persecuted her.'

The end of the degree of Perfection, is a preparation to come more clearly to the knowledge of true happiness, in becoming a true Mason, enlightened by the celestial luminary of truth, in renouncing, voluntarily, all adorations but those that are made to *one* God, the Creator of heaven and earth, great, good, and merciful.

The Knights of the East, the Princes of Jerusalem, and Knights of the East and West, are known to us, in our days, to be Masonry renewed, and all of them lead us to the same end of the celestial truth, which is to say, *finished.*

The Knights of the 'White and Black Eagle,' and the 'Sublime Princes of the Royal Secret,' and 'Grand Commander,' are the Chiefs of the great enterprise of the order in general. End of Brother Truth's harangue.

Father Adam then says to the candidate, 'My dear son, what you have heard from the mouth of Truth is an abridgement of all the consequences of all the degrees you have gone through, in order to come to the knowledge of the holy truth, contracted in your last engagements. Do you persist in your demand of coming to the holy brother, and is that what you desire, with a clear heart?—answer me.' The candidate answers, 'I persist.' Then Father Adam says, 'Brother Truth, as the candidate persists, approach with him to the sanctuary, in order that he may take a solemn obligation to follow our laws, principles, and morals, and to attach himself to us forever.' Then the candidate falls on his knees, and father Adam takes his hands between his own, and the candidate repeats the following obligation three times.

Obligation.—I, A. B., promise in the face of God, and between the hands of my Sovereign, and in presence of all the brethren now present, never to take arms against my king,* directly or indirectly, in any conspiracy against him. I promise never to reveal any of the degrees of the Knight of the Sun, which is now on the point of being intrusted to me, to any person or persons whatsoever, without being duly qualified to receive the same; and never to give my consent to any one to be admitted into our mysteries, only after the most scrupulous circumspection, and full knowledge of his life and conversation; and who has given at all times full proof of his zeal and fervent attachment for the order, and a submission at all times to the tribunal of the Sovereign Princes of the Royal Secret. I promise never to confer the degree of the Knights of the Sun, without having a permission in writing from the Grand Council of Princes of the Royal Secret, or from the Grand Inspector or his deputy, known by their titles and authority. I promise also and swear, that I will not assist any, through my means, to form or raise a lodge of the Sublime Orders, in this country 'without proper authority.' I promise and swear to redouble my zeal for all my brethren, Knights, and Princes, that are present or absent; and if I fail in this my obligation, I consent for all my brethren, when they are convinced of my infidelity, to seize me, and thrust my tongue through with a red hot iron; to pluck out both my eyes, and to deprive me of smelling and hearing; to cut off both of my hands, and expose me in that condition in the field, to be devoured by the voracious animals; and if none can be found, I wish the lightning of heaven might execute on me the same vengeance. O GOD, maintain me in right and equity! Amen. Amen. Amen.

After the obligation is three times repeated, Father Adam raises the candidate, and gives him one kiss on his forehead, being the seat of the soul. He then decorates him with the collar and jewel of the order, and gives him the following sign, token, and word. * * * *

After these are given, the candidate goes round and gives them to every one, which brings him back to Father Adam. He then sits down with the rest of the brethren, and then Brother Truth gives the following explanation of the Philosophical Lodge.

Sun.—The sun represents the unity of the Eternal Supreme, the only grand work of philosophy.

3 *S. S. S.*—The 3 S. S. S. signify the *Stiletto, Sidech, Solo*, or the residence of the Sovereign Master of all things.

Three candlesticks.—The three candlesticks show us the three degrees of fire.

---

* In republics this word is changed to " my country."

Four triangles.—The four triangles represent the four elements.

Seven planets.—The seven planets design the seven colors that appear in their original state, from whence we have so many different artificial ones.

Seven cherubims.—The seven cherubims represent the seven metals, viz. gold, silver, copper, iron, lead, tin, and quicksilver.

Conception in the moon.—The conception, or woman, rising in the moon, demonstrates the purity that matter subsists of, in order to remain in its pure state unmixed with any other body, from which must come a new king, and a revolution or fulness of time filled with glory, whose name is ALBRA.

Holy Spirit.—The Holy Spirit, under the symbol of a dove, is the image of the Universal Spirit, that gives light to all in the three states of nature ; and on the ' *animal,*' ' *vegetable,*' and ' *mineral.*'

Entrance of the temple.—The entrance of the temple is represented to you by a body, because the grand work of nature is complete as gold, potable and fixed.

Globe.—The globe represents the matter in the primeval state ; that is to say, complete.

Caduceus.—The caduceus represents the double mercury that you must extract from the matter ; that is to say, the mercury fixed, and from thence is extracted gold and silver.

Stibium.—The word stibium signifies the antimony, from whence, by the philosophical fire, is taken an alkali which we empty in our grand work. End of the philosophical explanation. Then Father Adam explains the

MORAL LODGE.

Sun.—The sun represents the divinity of the Eternal ; for as there is but one sun to light and invigorate the earth, so there is but one God, to whom we ought to pay our greatest adoration.

3 S. S. S.*—The 3 S. S. S. teaches you that science, adorned with wisdom, creates a holy man.

Three candlesticks.—The three candlesticks are the image of the life of man, considered in youth, manhood, and old age, and happy are those that have been enlightened in these ages, by the light of truth.

Four triangles.—The four triangles show us the four principal duties that create our tranquil life, viz : Fraternal love among men in general, and particularly among brethren, and in the same degree with us. 2dly. In not having any thing but for the use

---

* These letters are initials of the words, Scientia, Sapientia, Sanctitas.

and advantage of a brother. 3dly. Doubting of every matter that cannot be demonstrated to you clearly, by which an attempt might be made to insinuate mysteries in matters of religion, and hereby lead you away from the holy truth. 4thly. Never do any thing to another that you would not have done unto you. The last precept, well understood and followed on all occasions, is the true happiness of philosophy.

Seven planets.—The seven planets represent the seven principal passions of man.

Seven cherubims.—The seven cherubims are the images of the delights of the life: namely, by seeing, hearing, tasting, smelling, feeling, tranquillity, and health.

Conception.—The conception in the moon shows the purity of matter, and that nothing can be impure to the eyes of the Supreme.

Holy Spirit.—The Spirit is the figure of our soul, which is only the breath of the Eternal, and which cannot be soiled by the works of the body.

Temple.—The temple represents our body, which we are obliged to preserve by our natural feelings.

Figure of a man.—The figure is in the entrance of the temple, which bears a lamb in his arms, and teaches us to be attentive to our wants, as a shepherd takes care of his sheep; to be charitable, and never let slip the present opportunity of doing good, to labor honestly, and to live in this day as if it were our last.

Columns of Jachin and Boaz.—The columns of J. and B. are the symbols of the strength of our souls in bearing equally misfortunes, as well as success in life.

Seven steps of the temple.—The seven steps of the temple are the figures of the seven degrees which we must pass before we arrive to the knowledge of the true God.

Globe.—The globe represents the world which we inhabit.

Lux ex tenebris.—The device of 'Lux ex tenebris' teacheth, that when man is enlightened by reason, he is able to penetrate the darkness and obscurity which ignorance and superstition spread abroad.

River.—The river across the globe represents the utility of the passions that are necessary to man in the course of his life, as water is requisite to the earth in order to replenish the plants thereof.

Cross surrounded.—The cross surrounded by two serpents signifies that we must watch the vulgar prejudices, to be very prudent in giving any of our knowledge and secrets in matters, especially in religion. *End of the moral explanation.*

PHYSICAL EXPLANATION. (In Lecture.)

LECTURE.

Q. Are you a Knight of the Sun? A. I have mounted the seven principal steps of Masonry; I have penetrated into the bowels of the earth, and among the ancient ruins of Enoch found the most grand and precious treasure of the Masons. I have seen, contemplated, and admired the great, mysterious, and formidable name engraved on the triangle; I have broken the pillar of beauty, and thrown down the two columns that supported it. Q. Pray tell me what is that mysterious and formidable name? A. I cannot unfold the sacred characters in this manner, but substitute in its place the grand word of יהוה. Q. What do you understand by throwing down the columns that sustained the pillar of beauty? A. Two reasons. 1st. When the temple was destroyed by Nebuzaradan, general of the army of Nebuchadnezzar, I was one that helped to defend the Delta on which was engraved the ineffable name; and I broke down the columns of beauty, in order that it should not be profaned by the infidels. 2d. As I have deserved, by my travel and labor, the beauty of the great 'ADONAI,' (Lord,) the mysteries of Masonry, in passing the seven principal degrees. Q. What signify the seven planets? A. The lights of the celestial globe and also their influence, by which every matter exists on the surface of the earth or globe. Q. From what is the terrestrial globe formed? A. From the matter which is formed by the concord of the four elements, designed by the four triangles, that are in regard to them as the four greater planets. Q. What are the names of the seven planets? A. Sun, Moon, Mars, Jupiter, Venus, Mercury, and Saturn. Q. Which are the four elements? A. Air, fire, earth, and water. Q. What influence have the seven planets on the four elements? A. Three general matters of which all bodies are composed—life, spirit, and body; otherwise, salt, sulphur, and mercury. Q. What is life or salt? A. The life given by the Eternal Supreme, or the planets, the agents of nature. Q. What is the spirit or sulphur? A. A fixed matter, subject to several productions. Q. What is the body or mercury? A. Matter conducted or refined to its form by the union of salt and sulphur, or the agreement of the three governors of nature. Q. What are those three governors of nature? A. Animal, vegetable, and mineral. Q. What is animal? A. We understand in this, life—all that is divine and amiable. Q. Which of the elements serve for his productions? A. All the four are necessary, among which, nevertheless, air and fire are predominant; and it is those that render the animal the perfection of the three governments, which man is elevated to by one-fourth of the breath of the Divine Spirit, when he receives his soul. Q. What is the vegetable? A. All that seems attached to the earth reigns on the surface. Q. Of what is it composed? A. Of a generative fire, formed into a body, whilst it remains in the earth, and is purified by its moisture and becomes vegetable, and receives life by air and water; whereby the four elements, though different, co-operate jointly and separately. Q. What is the mineral? A. All that is generated and secreted in the earth. Q. What do we understand by this name? A. That which we call metals and demi-metals and minerals. Q. What is it that composes the minerals? A. The air penetrating by the celestial influence into the earth, meets with a body, which, by its softness, fixes, congeals, and renders the mineral matter more or less perfect. Q. Which are the perfect metals? A. Gold and silver. Q. Which are the imperfect metals? A. Brass, lead, tin, iron, and quicksilver. Q. How come we by the knowledge of these things? A. By frequent observations and the experiments made in natural philosophy, which have decided to a certainty that nature gives a perfection to all things, if she has time to complete her operations. Q. Can art bring metal to perfection so fully as nature? A. Yes; but in order to this, you must have an exact knowledge of nature. Q. What will assist you to bring forth this knowledge? A. A matter brought to perfection; this has been sought for under the name of the *philosopher's stone.* Q. What does the globe represent? A. An information of philosophers, for the benefit of the art in this work. Q. What signify the words, 'Lux ex tenebris?' A. That is the depth of darkness you ought to retire from, in order to gain the true light. Q. What signifies the cross on the globe? A. The cross is the emblem of the true elected. Q. What represent the three candlesticks? A. The three degrees of five, which the artist must have knowledge to give, in order to procure the matters from which it proceeds. Q. What signifies the word '*Stibium?*' A. It signifies antimony, or the first matter of all things. Q. What signify the seven degrees? A. The different effectual degrees of Masonry which you must pass to come to the Sublime Degree of Knights of the Sun. Q. What signify the diverse attributes in those degrees?

A. 1st. The *Bible,* or God's law, which we ought to follow.

2d. The *compass* teaches us to do nothing unjust.

3d. The *square* conducts us equal to the same end.

4th. The *level* demonstrates to us, all that is just and equitable.

5th. The *perpendicular,* to be upright and subdue the veil of prejudice.

[493]

6th. The *tressle-board* is the image of our reason, where the functions are combined to effect, compare, and think.

7th. The *rough-stone* is the resemblance of our vices, which we ought to reform.

8th. The *cubic stone* is our passions, which we ought to surmount.

9th. The *columns* signify strength in all things.

10th. The *blazing star* teaches that our hearts ought to be as a clear sun, among those that are troubled with the things of this life.

11th. The *key* teaches to have a watchful eye over those who are contrary to reason.

12th. The *box* teaches to keep our secrets inviolably.

13th. The *urn* learns us that we ought to be as delicious perfumes.

14th. The *brazen sea* that we ought to purify ourselves, and destroy vice.

15th. The *circles on the triangles* demonstrate the immensity of the divinity under the symbol of truth.

16th. The *poniard* teacheth the step of the elected, many are called, but few are chosen to the sublime knowledge of pure truth.

17th. The word *albra* signifies a king full of glory, and without blot.

18th. The word *Adonai* signifies Sovereign Creator of all things.

19th. The *seven cherubims* are the symbols of the delights of life, known by seeing, hearing, tasting, feeling, smelling, tranquillity, and thought.

Q. What represents the *sun?* A. It is an emblem of Divinity, which we ought to regard as the image of God. This immense body represents the infinity of God's wonderful will, as the only source of light and good. The heat of the sun produces the rule of the seasons, recruits nature, takes darkness from the winter, in order that the deliciousness of spring might succeed. *End of the physical lecture.*

GENERAL LECTURE IN THIS DEGREE.

Q. From whence came you? A. From the centre of the earth. Q. How have you come from thence? A. By reflection, and the study of nature. Q. Who has taught you this? A. Men in general who are blind, and lead others in their blindness. Q. What do you understand by this blindness? A. I do not understand it to be privy to their mysteries; but I understand under the name of blindness, those who cease to be ardent, after they have been privy to the light of the spirit of reason. Q. Who are those? A. Those who, through the prejudices of superstition and fanaticism, render their services to ignorance. Q. What do you understand by fanaticism? A. The *zeal of all particular sects* which are spread over the earth, who commit crimes by making offerings to fraud and falsehood. Q. And do you desire to rise from this darkness? A. My desire is to come to the celestial truth, and to travel by the light of the sun. Q. What represents that body? A. It is the figure of an *only God*, to whom we ought to pay our adoration. The sun being the emblem of God, we ought to regard it as the image of the Divinity; for that immense body represents wonderfully the infinity of God. He invigorates and produces the seasons, and replenishes nature, by taking the horrors from winter, and produces the delights of spring. Q. What does the triangle, with the sun in the centre, represent? A. It represents the immensity of the Supreme. Q. What signifies the three S. S. S. ? A. *Sanctitas, Scientia,* and *Syrentia,* which signify the science accompanied with wisdom, and make men holy. Q. What signifies the three candlesticks? A. It represents the courses of life, considered in youth, manhood, and old age. Q. Has it any other meaning? A. Yes, the triple light that shines among us, in order to take men out of darkness and ignorance into which they are plunged, and to bring them to virtue, truth, and happiness, a symbol of our perfection. Q. What signifies the four triangles that are in the great circles? A. They are the emblems of the four principal views of the life of tranquillity, &c. 1st. Fraternal love to all mankind in general, more particularly for our brethren, who are more attached to us, and who with honor have seen the wretchedness of the vulgar. 2d. To be cautious among us of things, and not to demonstrate them clearly to any who are not proper to receive them; and to be likewise cautious in giving credit to any matter, however artfully it may be disguised, without a self-conviction in the heart. 3d. To cast from us every matter which we perceive we may ever repent of doing, taking care of this moral precept, 'To do to every one of your fellow creatures no more than you would choose to be done to.' 4th. We ought always to confide in our Creator's bounty, and to pray without ceasing, that all our necessities might be relieved as it seems best to him for our advantage; to wait for his blessings patiently in this life; to be persuaded of his sublime decrees, that whatever might fall, contrary to our wishes, will be attended with good consequences; to take his chastisements patiently, and be assured that the end of every thing has been done by him for the best, and will certainly lead us to eternal happiness hereafter. Q. Explain the signification of the seven planets which are enclosed in a triangle, that forms the rays of the exterior circles, and are enclosed in the grand triangle. A. The seven planets, according to philosophy, represent the seven principal passions of the life of man; those passions are very useful when they are used in moderation, for which the Almighty gave them to us, but grow fatal and destroy the body when let loose; and therefore it is our particular duty to subdue them. Q. Explain the seven passions to us. A. 1st. The propagation of species. 2d. Ambition of acquiring riches. 3d. Ambition to acquire glory in the arts and sciences among men in general. 4th. Superiority in civil life. 5th. Joys and pleasures of society. 6th. Amusements and gaieties of life. 7th. RELIGION.*

Q. Which is the greatest sin of all that man can commit, and render him odious to God and man? A. *Suicide* and *Homicide*. Q. What signifies the seven cherubims whose names are written in the circle called the 'First Heaven?' A. They represent the corporeal delights of this life, which the Eternal gave to man when he created him, and are, seeing, hearing, smelling, tasting, feeling, tranquillity, and thought. Q. What signifies the figure in the moon, which we regard as the figure or image of conception? A. The purity of nature, which procures the holiness of the body; and that *there is nothing imperfect in the eyes of the Supreme*. Q. What signifies the figure of the columns? A. They are the emblem of our souls, which is the breath of life proceeding from the All Puissant, and ought not to be soiled by the works of the body, but to be firm as columns. Q. What does the figure in the porch, which carries a lamb in his arms, represent? A. The porch ornamented with the columns of Jachin and Boaz, and surmounted with the grand I, represents our body, over which we ought to have a particular care, in watching our conversation, and also to watch our needs, as the shepherd his flock. Q. What signify the two letters I, and B, at the porch? A. They signify our entrance in the order of Masonry; also the firmness of the soul, which we ought to possess from the hour of our initiation; these we ought to merit, before we can come to the sublime degrees of knowing holy truth, and we ought to preserve them, and be firm in whatever situation we may be in, not knowing whether it may return to our good or evil in the passage of this life. What signifies the large I in the triangle on the crown of the portico? A. That large I, being the initial

---

* Mind this.

of the mysterious name of the Great Architect of the universe, whose greatness we should always have in our minds, and that our labors ought to be employed to please him; which we should always have in our view as the sure and only source of our actions. Q. What signify the seven steps that lead to the entry of the porch? A. They mark the seven degrees in Masonry, which are the principal which we ought to arrive to, in order to come to the knowledge of holy truth. Q. What does the terrestrial globe represent? A. The world which we inhabit, and wherein Masonry is its principal ornament. Q. What is the explanation of the great word, Adonai? A. It is the word which God gave to Adam, for him to pray by; a word which our common father never pronounced without trembling. Q. What signifies *Lux ex tenebris?* A. A man made clear by the light of reason; penetrating this obscurity of ignorance and superstition. Q. What signifies the river across the globe? A. It represents the utility of our passions, which are necessary to man in the course of his life, as water is necessary to render the earth fertile; as the sun draws up the water, which being purified, falls on the earth and gives verdure. Q. What signifies the cross, surrounded by two serpents, on the top of the globe? A. It represents to us *not to repeat the vulgar prejudices;* to be prudent, and to know the bottom of the heart. *In matters of religion to be always prepared; not to be of the sentiments with sots, idiots, and the lovers of the mysteries of religion; to avoid such, and not in the least to hold any conversation with them.* Q. What signifies the book, with the word Bible written in it? A. As the Bible is differently interpreted by the different sects who divide the different parts of the earth: Thus the true sons of light, or children of truth, *ought to doubt of every thing at present,* as mysteries or metaphysics: Thus all the decisions of theology and philosophy, *teach not to admit that, which is not demonstrated as clearly, as that 2 and 2, are equal to 4;* and on the whole to adore God, and him only; to love him better than yourself; and always to have a confidence on the bounties and promises of our Creator, Amen. Amen. Amen.

To close the council. Q. (By Father Adam,) Brother Truth, what progress have men made on earth to come to true happiness? A. (By Brother Truth,) Men have always fallen on the vulgar prejudices, which are nothing but falsehood; very few have struggled, and less have knocked at the door of this holy place, to attain the full light of real truth, which we all ought to acquire.

Then says Father Adam, 'My dear children, depart and go among men, endeavor to inspire them with the desire of knowing holy truth, the pure source of all Perfection. Father Adam then puts his right hand on his left breast ; when all the brethren raise the first finger of the right hand, and then the Council of the Knights of the Sun is closed by seven knocks.

KNIGHT OF KADOSH.

Chapter of the Grand Inspector of lodges, Grand Elected Knight of Kadosh, or the White and Black Eagle. The Chief is the Thrice Illustrious Frederick king of Prussia, under the title of Thrice Illustrious Knight, Grand Commander.

Opening of the Chapter.—The Chapter of the Grand Elected must be composed of five brothers, every one vested in this degree. They must be all dressed in black, with white gloves. The order, a broad black ribbon, worn from the left shoulder to the right hip; to which hangs the attribute of the order, being a red cross ; the same as the Teutonic Knights used to wear, in the middle of two swords, a cross like a St. Andrew's. No aprons are worn.

In this Chapter there are no decorations, nor any emblem, as the curtain is entirely drawn. There is nothing figured on the ground but the mysterious ladder, which must be covered until the candidate has taken his obligation. Observe this well; you are never to admit a person to this eminent degree unless you have full proof of his fidelity. Of the five brothers who compose this Chapter, two must be with the candidate in another apartment, until he is introduced, the other three remain in the Chapter to assist in the reception. In·a distant place a Knight of Kadosh cannot initiate another brother in this eminent degree, unless he has a proper power or patent from an Inspector General or a Deputy Grand Inspector, under his hand and seal ; and when a reception is made, the Grand Commander remains alone in the Chapter with the candidate, and must be so situated that the candidate cannot see him, as he is not to know who initiated him.

Form of opening the Chapter.—Q. Illustrious Knight, are you elected? A. Thrice Illustrious Knight, Grand Commander, I am. Q. How came you to be elected? A. Fortune decided for me. Q. What proof can you give me of your reception? A. A cavern has been witness of it. Q. What did you do in the cavern? A. I executed my commission. Q. Have you penetrated further? A. Yes, Thrice Illustrious Grand Commander.

Q. How shall I believe you? A. My name is Knight of Kadosh; you understand me? Q. What's the o'clock? A. The hour of silence. Q. As it is so, give me the sign, to convince me of your knowledge, ―――― on which they all draw their swords, when the Grand Commander knocks *one*, very hard, on the table before him, and says: Illustrious Knights, the Chapter is open. As soon as the Knights with the candidate in the antechamber have heard the one blow in the Chapter, by which they know the Chapter is open, one of them comes and knocks *one* on the door; one in the Chapter goes and opens the door, and asks what he wants. He replies, that a servant Knight demands to come to the degree of Grand Elected, as he has all the degrees and qualifications of Masonry which are necessary; which being reported to the Thrice Illustrious Commander, who says: Illustrious Knights, can we admit this Free Mason among us, without running any risk of indiscretion from him? The other two Knights then answer, We swear and promise for him. Then the Thrice Illustrious Grand Commander approaches, and they take each other by the hand and take the following obligation to each other: —'We promise and swear, by the living God, always supreme, to revenge the death of our ancestor; and which of us that should in any manner commit the most light indiscretion, touching the secret of our order, *shall suffer death*, and shall have his body buried under the throne of this Illustrious Assembly. So God protect us in our design, and maintain us in equity and right.' Amen.

Form of reception.—A short time after the two Knights with the candidate have heard the loud rap of the Grand Commander to open the Chapter, they both take their hands, and after one of them has been to the door, and when they think the Grand Commander has finished the necessary business, they introduce the candidate and leave him in the hands of the Grand Commander, and all four retire to guard the door of the entrance, and every other door of the adjacent rooms, (if any.) The reason of their leaving the Chapter is, that no person ever assisted at the reception of a Knight Templar. When the candidate enters the Chapter, he prostrates his face to the ground, when the Grand Commander, behind the curtain, reminds him of the principal points of Masonry, from its beginning, to the epoch of the assassination of Hiram Abiff; Solomon's desire of punishing the traitors, in the most exemplary manner; the method he took in disposing the Masters who went in search of the three villains, in order to execute his vengeance; he repeats to him the zeal, constancy, and fervency, of Joabert, Stokin, and Gibulum, who, after the most painful search, (by Solomon's order,) had the happiness of finding among the ruins of Enoch's temple in the Ninth Arch, the precious treasure of the Perfect Masons, &c. &c. &c. He continues to remind him of the firmness of the Grand Elect and Perfect Masons, at the time of the temple's destruction, when they passed through the enemy, at all risks, till they obtained an entrance into the sacred vault, to find the pillar of beauty, that they might, by effacing the ineffable word, hinder its being exposed to the profane. He then reminds him of the seventy-two years' captivity, and the clemency of Cyrus, king of Persia, who, by the request of Zerubbabel, not only gave the Israelites their freedom, but ordered that all the treasure of the temple, taken by Nebuchadnezzar, should be restored to them, in order to decorate the new temple, which he ordered them to build to the infinite God, and created them Knights. Then he repeats the clemency of Darius to Zerubbabel, (at the head of the embassy from Jerusalem to Babylon,) with their complaints against the Samaritans, who refused to contribute to the sacrifices of the new temple, according to the proclamation of his predecessor, Cyrus, in favor of the Knights of the East; when they received Darius' letters to all the governors of Samaria, &c.; how the ambassadors were received on their return to Jerusalem; and elected princes by the people. He then reminds him that, after this, the second temple being destroyed, how the most zealous Masons united under Chiefs, and worked to the reformation of manners, and elevated in their hearts some spiritual edifice, and rendered themselves worthy by their works. They were more particularly esteemed and distinguished in the time of *Manchin*,* who was the most remarkable among them. A great many others embraced Christianity, and communicated their secrets to those Christians, whom they found had the good qualities of it, living in common, and forming themselves as one family; which shows how the brilliant order of Masons sustained themselves until the sixth age, and how it fell into a state of lethargy after that; notwithstanding which, there have been always found some faithful Masons; which is clearly proved by the brilliant manner in which the order of Masonry was received in the year 1118, when eleven Grand Elect and Perfect Masons, the most zealous, presented themselves to *Garinous*, Prince of Jerusalem, Patriarch and Knight Mason, and pronounced their promises between his hands. They taught him the succession of the time, and progress to the time that the princes went to conquer the Holy Land. The alliance and obligations

---

* This word or name is also written Manachem and Manahen.

that were formed between those princes, was, that they would spill the last drop of their blood, in order to establish in Jerusalem the worship of the Most High. He informs him, that the peace which took place after these wars, hindered them from accomplishing their design, and therefore have continued in theory what they had sworn to do practically, never admitting in their order only those who had given proofs of friendship, constancy, and discretion. In fine, the Illustrious Grand Commander gives a general history, in chronological order, of the Masonic order, its progress, its decline, and the manner how it was sustained, till the epoch of the crusades, and until the historical circumstances that have given occasion to the degree which the candidate expects; a degree that will give him a perfect knowledge of the precedent degrees, and the manner how Masonry has come to us; after which, the candidate takes the following obligation, his right hand on the Bible, his left hand between the hands of the Grand Commander.

Obligation.—I promise and swear, never to reveal the secrets of the Grand Elected Knights of Kadosh, or White and Black Eagle, to any person. *I swear to take revenge on the traitors of Masonry;* and never to receive in this degree, none but a brother who has come to the degrees of Prince of Jerusalem and Knight of the Sun, and then only by an authority given to me by a Grand Commander or Deputy Inspector, under his hand and seal. I promise to be ready at all times to conquer the Holy Land, when I shall be summoned to appear; to pay due obedience at all times to the Princes of the Royal Secret; and if I fail in this my obligation, I desire that all the penalties of my former obligations may be inflicted on me. Amen. He kisses the Bible, and rises. Then the Grand Commander proceeds and says, ' My dear brother, he who has bestowed this degree on you, which you have now aspired to, and who is described in this place as Grand Commander, and Grand Inspector of all lodges, and Grand Elected, is sensible of the importance of the secret already confided in you; it is, therefore, necessary to recommend a circumspection, and also to observe to those who take the name of Knights of the White and Black Eagle, and Kadosh, to be always attentive, and not to give the least suspicion relative to our mysteries, order, progress, and end of Masonry. The imprudence and indiscretion of many brothers have given knowledge to the world of many of our emblems, by which Masonry has greatly suffered, and will be repaired with difficulty. Their indiscretion has caused the loss and retreat of many Puissant brothers, who would have been an ornament and support of our lodge. Such indiscretion in this degree, my dear brother, would be without any recovery, as there are no more emblems; when every matter shall be discovered and disclosed to you, that will give room for some events of which you will see the consequences when you shall have heard all my instructions. The word which our brothers place at the end of their obligations, viz. *Amen*, signifies *this is no more*, that *shall be no more; if this shall be again*. This ought no longer to be a secret to you, who are going to have an explanation of the origin of Masonry, and what has occasioned the society.

Truth penetrates the cloud and the shade, which we can leave to come to the knowledge of what we were before in quality of Knights of Kadosh, White and Black Eagle, and what we are as Symbolic Masons, and what we can be by the destruction of our enemies. Let us pray. *Prayer*.—O most eternal, beneficial and all gracious, great Architect of the universe; we from the secret depths of our hearts offer thee a living sacrifice. We beseech thee to inspire our enemies with a just sense of the evil they have done us, and from their having a conviction of their wrongs, they might atone for their manifold injuries, which do not belong to us thy servants to redress ourselves, but by their eyes being opened we might be reconciled, and by a hearty union take possession of those blessed lands where the original temple was first established, where we might be gathered into one band, there to celebrate thy holy praises once more on the holy mount, in whose bowels was deposited thy ever glorious, respectable, ever blessed, and awful name. Amen. Then the veil is taken from the floor, and he continues, ' Learn that the slightest indiscretion will infallibly undermine us and throw us into an horrible abyss, where we should see buried the whole order of Masonry, the remains of an illustrious and glorious order. By its heroism in favor of the unfortunate, how great it has been in the time when its power, authority and riches were arrived to the highest pitch, when the distinguished birth of those who were members of it, celebrated its glory. It was not less so in its tragic end, when by the noble firmness of these Knights who appeared in the middle of irons, frames and torments. What can we think of the prophecy of James DeMolay, and which was verified according to his prediction. What respect ought we not to have for the courageous zeal of those who have kept the precious remains of an order which the blackest treason, envy, and the most atrocious malignity have not been able to extinguish! What hatred ought we not to have, to those usurpers who occupy the wealth and dignity of this order! They cannot be regarded but only as a powerful enemy, the ashes of which ought to renew that unfortunate period when the members of the Knights shall be increased, so that they shall be able, under the auspices and conduct of a Grand and Powerful Commander, to retake the possession of all the wealth and dignity which did belong to them formerly, and is now held by those who have no other title this day but injustice and malignity.

This is not said, my dear brother, to intimidate those who have, as well as yourself, aspired to this degree which we are going to confer on you this day, or to inspire them with an ardor or indiscreet zeal, for they ought every one to wait the time in silence, to become essential; and if the trust is the more authentic mark of sincere friendship, they ought to wish to augment the number of the Knights, and fear to confer this degree, with too much confidence, on an ordinary friend, lest his discretion should not be so sure as your own. You remember, my dear brother, the obligation you have taken between my hands, at the beginning of the ceremony—and to render you the justice you deserve, I have too good an opinion of you to fear the least indiscretion in you concerning the first notions I have given you of *this last degree of Masonry*. If in this discourse you have made any remark that would keep you from pronouncing the obligation or vow we are obliged to take from you, before we can give you greater knowledge of the degree of 'Grand Elected Knights of Kadosh,' consult yourself and see if you are disposed to penetrate farther, and fulfil exactly all the points of the obligation you are going to pronounce with me, *in order to link you to us for ever.*' There is a pause for some time.

NOTE.—If the candidate is afraid to engage in, or hesitates to pronounce the further obligations, the Illustrious Grand Commander, without going further, sends him out, and closes the Chapter. In regard to the notions which the candidate might have already, *the obligation which he has already taken* will assure us of his discretion. If, on the contrary, he persists in going further, and will take the obligation, the Grand Commander continues the ceremony in the following manner :

The candidate kneels at the feet of the Grand Commander, puts his right hand on the Bible, and his left between the hands of the Grand Commander—when in this posture, the Grand Commander says, 'You swear and promise to me, on that you hold most dear and sacred, 1st. To practise the works of corporeal mercy, *to live and die in your religion,** and never declare

---

* Suppose the religion of the candidate is *false,* and he becomes convinced of his error, what shall he do ? He must either live and die contending for that he knows to be a lie, or break his Masonic oath!

to any man who received you, or assisted at your reception in this sublime degree.' The candidate answers, 'I promise and swear;' then the Grand Commander says, 'Say with me, '*Tsedakah,*' (righteousness,) which he repeats. 2dly. 'You promise and swear to have candor in all your actions, in consequence never to receive in this degree any brother who is not your most intimate friend, and then by the consent of two Grand Elected Inspectors, if to be met with, or by a patent given you for that purpose;' the candidate answers, 'I promise and swear.' He then repeats '*Shorlaban,*' (white ox, figuratively.) 3dly. 'You promise and swear at all times to possess a sweetness of mind, as much as you are capable, to love and cherish your brothers as yourself, to help them in their necessities, to visit and assist them when they are sick, and never draw arms against them on any pretence whatsoever.' *Ans.* 'I promise and swear.' Say with me, '*Mathok,*' (sweetness.) 4th. 'You promise and swear to regulate your discourse by truth, and to keep with great circumspection and regard the degree of the White and Black Eagle or Kadosh.' He answers, 'I promise and swear.' Say with me, '*Emunah.*' 5th. 'You promise and swear that you will travel for the advancement of heaven, and to follow at all times, and in all points, every matter that you are ordered and prescribed by the Illustrious Knights, and Grand Commander, *to whose orders you swear submission and obedience, on all occasions, without any restrictions.*' He answers, 'I promise and swear.' Say with me, '*Hamal saggi,*' (great labor.) 6th. 'You promise and swear to me, to have patience in adversity, and you swear never to receive a brother in this degree, on any pretext whatsoever, whose will is not free, as religious monks and all those who have made vows without restriction to superiors.' He answers, 'I promise and swear.' Say with me, '*Sabbal,*' (a burden, or patience.) 7th. 'You promise, in the end, and swear to keep inviolably secret, what I am going to confide to you—*to sacrifice the traitors of Masonry,* and to look upon the Knights of Malta, as our enemies—to renounce for ever to be in that order, and regard them as the unjust usurpers of the rights, titles, and dignities, of the Knights Templars, in whose possession you hope to enter with the help of the Almighty.' He answers, 'I promise and swear.' Then say with me '*Gemulah, Benah, Tebunah,*' (retribution, intelligence, prudence.) After the candidate has pronounced the last word, the Grand Commander relieves him, and says, 'By the seven conditions, and by the power that is transmitted to me, which I have acquired by my discretion, my untired travels, zeal, fervor, and constancy, I receive you Grand Inspector of all lodges, Grand Elect Knight Templar, and take rank among the Knights of Kadosh, or White and Black Eagle, which we bear the name of; I desire you not to forget it. It is indispensable for you, my brother, to mount the *mysterious ladder*, which you see there; it will serve to instruct you in the mysteries of our order, and it is absolutely necessary that you should have a true knowledge of it. The candidate then ascends the ladder. When he is on the seventh or highest step, and has pronounced the three last words, the ladder is lowered, and the candidate passes over it, because he cannot retire the same way, as he would in such a case be obliged to go back, against which he has taken an obligation, not to retire by the interests and views of the order, which is the reason that the ladder is lowered and he passes over it. He then reads the words at the bottom of the ladder, '*Ne plus ultra.*'

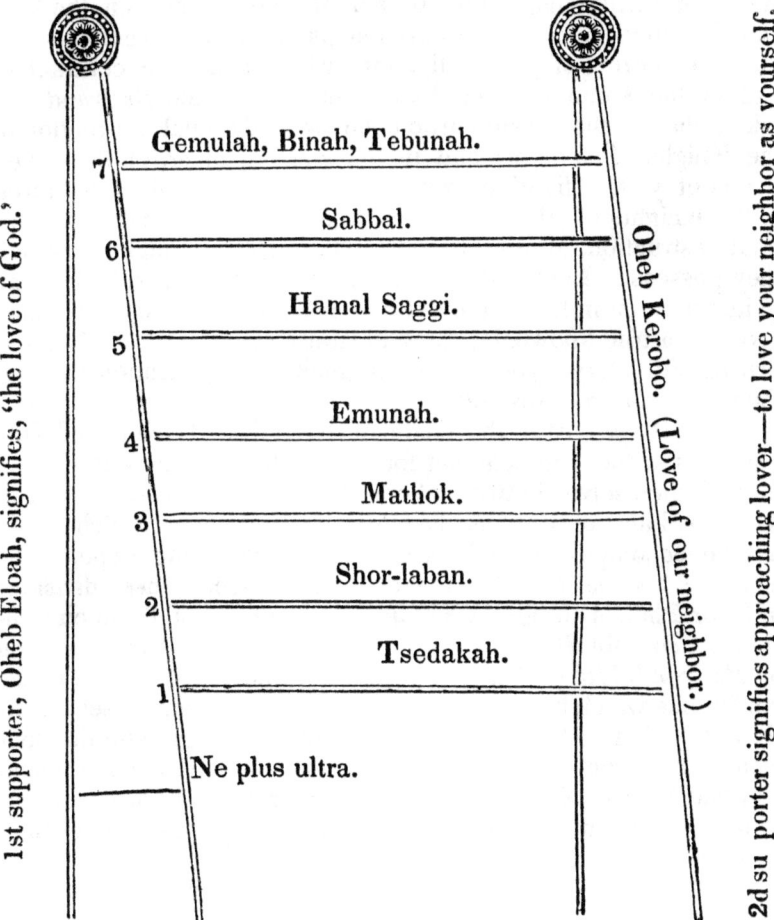

Then the Grand Commander embraces the candidate, and says to him, 'My dear brother, I am going to give you the sign, token, and word, with the pass word of the Grand Elected and Grand Inspectors, after I have given you the explanation of the mysterious ladder which you have ascended and passed over, without knowing the reason thereof. This ladder, my dear brother, is the most essential and analagous to the history which I shall recite to you. Like a ladder she is composed of two supporters, which will give you a just idea of the strength which *Philip Le Belle*, (or the fair,) king of France, had, in his union with *Pope Clement* V. The reunion of the second supporters, by the seven steps, gives you a just idea of the seven conditions, that *Philip*, the Fair, imposed on the archbishop, *Bertrand Got*, to make him pope, and the two supporters being united by the seven steps, or conditions, are the base of the union between the king and this pope elect. The seven steps are also a resemblance of the seven points of your obligation, which you have contracted, and in the same manner *Philip*, the Fair, made *Bertrand Got* take; that by the seventh article, he swore the final destruction of the Knights Templars; and in the same manner, of the seven points of your obligation, you swear to bear an implacable hatred to the Knights of Malta,* and engage yourself to endeavor their total destruction, in order to reclaim the rights and dignities which they possess. Lastly, this moment, my dear brother, is the time to instruct you in full in the degree of Grand Elected, and which gives us a true knowledge how Masonry came to us. Attend to that painful story—you will easily make the application yourself the more you are instructed.

The history.—After the death of Benedict XI. who died July 13th, 1304, the cardinals met for the election of a new Pope, and formed themselves in two factions, French and Italians; *Philip*, the Fair, king of France, had then several views which could not be accomplished without the assistance of the Pope, to be elected; and his party in the conclave fomented these divisions to favor Philip's design, who taking advantage of these circumstances, sent for *Bertrand Got*, then archbishop of Bordeaux, son of *Bertrand*, lord of Villandran, in the same diocese, and in the conference which he had with him at a pleasant country seat, near St. John of Angels, he informed him of his design, and the division in the conclave, which put it in his power to elect a pope, and that he was disposed to favor him, provided he would swear to perform seven articles, the seventh of which was to be even a

---

* Not the Masonic Knights of Malta, but the Catholic Military of that name

secret to him until the time for the execution of it should be ripe. Accordingly he revealed the six first articles which are foreign to our history, but the seventh, for the exact performance of which they both took the sacrament to each others promise; and *Philip*, the Fair, took the brother and nephew of *Bertrand Le Got*, as hostages for the seventh article. This king having found a man fit for his purpose to be the agent of his revenge, caused him to be elected pope, and promoted to St. Peter's chair, in the year 1305, under the name of *Clement* V. This pope after his election established his see at the city of Lyons, where his first care was to execute the six first conditions which Philip had imposed upon him. The time of declaring the seventh being arrived, Philip did not delay in declaring to the pope, that, by his oath, he was to join him to entirely destroy and exterminate the Knights Templars, to the extent of Christendom. Here is what attracted the hatred of Philip the Fair, and what made him take the barbarous resolution against them all.

Some time before the death of Benoit XI. there was a sedition in Paris, occasioned by Philip, who had coined some money, which was light, mixed with base metal, on which the populace were mutinous, and plundered and demolished the house of Stephen Beribet, master of the mint. They went afterwards to the king's dwelling, and committed a great deal of indecency, so that every matter conspired an insurrection. The Knights Templars (against whom envy had raised many powerful enemies) were suspected to have been at the bottom of these outrages, although without any foundation, and their ruin was determined by the king; for which purpose he sought the means of obtaining assistance, when the most favorable opportunity offered itself by the death of *Benoit* XI. In order to put in his stead a pope, on certain conditions, that should be imposed on him, nothing was now wanting but a pretence, for when force and authority are in hand, every matter becomes easy; for which purpose they prevailed on two abandoned men, with money, whose names were *Gerard Labe* and *Benoit Mehuy*. They proposed to them to get admission among the Knights Templars, and when admitted into their mysteries, to accuse the whole order of the greatest crimes, which these two villians executed exactly. They desired to be received into the order, which was an easy matter, as they had an honest exterior, titles, and apparent qualities, besides a supposed credit at court. Every one was in their favour, and they were received; but it was not long before the Templars repented heartily of having lighted the fire brand, which was the cause of the deplorable and tragic scene in which most all of the

Templars were involved in one common destruction; for these two wretches, soon after their admission, accused the whole order of the most dreadful and most execrable crimes, demanding to be separated from them, for the unheard of terrible things which were suggested. The treason is good, but the traitor is detestable, and they suffered the same lot that was intended for the Templars, for they for their treachery received the most dreadful torments, and were not suffered to live. They had been the instruments, or the cause of vengeance to the Templars, by their false accusations. Upon their reports, the king, (who had lately an interview with the pope at Portier,) took the surest measures to arrest all the Templars in his dominions in one day. This was done on the 13th of October, 1307, two years after the accusation of these two villains was made. They seized on all their papers, titles, and treasures, and most of their wealth, over which were placed overseers and stewards. King Charles, of Naples, in like manner, ordered all the Templars in his province to be arrested. Those taken in France were locked up in the Castile of Melun, to wait for their trials. The pope, at the same time, sent for their Grand Master, 'James De Molay,' a native of Burgundy. Soon as he received the orders of the pope, he came to Paris with sixty Knights of the order, among which was one *Guy,* brother of the dauphin, *Devienois Hugues de Peraldes,* and *Theodore Bazillede Monancoart.* They were all arrested and made to suffer the most dreadful torments, in order to draw from them a confession of the crimes they were accused of, though without effect, as they bore bravely every torment, rather than accuse themselves of things of which they were innocent. So that on no other proof than that of two infamous suborned witnesses, their trials were concluded, (it being impossible to obtain the least evidence against them, as never any person assisted at the making of a Templar.) They executed and burnt alive fifty-seven in one day; on the next fifty-nine, and so on, until they had completed almost their total destruction. They pardoned none, not even those that served them in accusing the whole order, for as Templars they were included in the general sentence, and burnt alive with the others!

Let the end of these unhappy wretches serve as a lesson to us, that we are not in future to be seduced by fine promises, and initiate any but those who have given us, by a long train of service, proofs of the most solid worthiness, lest we might, by their indiscretion, be dragged again with all the Knights of the Black Eagle, or Kadosh, in a common fate. The Grand Master and the three above mentioned brethren, were nevertheless not comprehended in the first execution. The pope, for reasons which no historian has mentioned, kept the judgment to himself. Most or all of the Templars at the time of this prosecution (which lasted till 1314,) were arrested in all Christian states, but were not all put to death. Philip the fair, was continually hurrying the Pope to make an end of James De Molay, the Grand Master of his companions, (after having groaned nearly seven years in prison, overloaded with irons,) which was at last executed, when they were burnt alive, the 11th March, 1314, in the isle of Paris, which moved to pity and tears the numerous spectators who were present. They were steady, heroic, constant, and made the most solemn vows of their innocence, which was afterwards apparent, supported by an event extremely memorable. Jacques or James De Molay, the Grand Master, seeing himself on the scaffold ready to end his life in the flames, (after having lingered in irons for several years, death in any manner was now a relief to him, rather than to linger in prison in this uncertain world,) with great composure turned himself and directed to God the following prayer.—'Oh, Almighty and Everlasting God, who knows the innocence of the victims who have been sacrificed for several years, permit us to reflect on the approach and infamous torments which you permitted J. C. to be covered with at his death, to redeem us from the slavery of our sins, to give an example to the innocent, in teaching them, by his mildness, to suffer without murmuring, the persecution and torments, which injustice and blindness prepare for them. Forgive, O God, the false accusations and imputations which have caused the destruction of the whole order, of which your Divine Providence had established me chief; and if you are pleased to accept the prayer which we now humbly offer you, permit, O God, that one day these people may know the innocence of those who have endeavored to live in thy holy fear and love: we wait your bounty and compassion, *the reward of the torments and death we suffer, which we offer to you in order to enjoy your divine presence in everlasting happiness.*' Then addressing himself to the people, he said, 'Good people, who see us ready to perish in the flames, you will be able to judge of our innocence, for *I now summon Pope Clement V. in forty days, and Philip, the Fair, in twelve months, to appear before the awful and tremendous throne of the ever living God, to render an account of the blood they have wickedly shed!*' after which they were hurried to execution, fearing a rescue from the populace. The prediction of James De Molay was accomplished, as Pope Clement V. died the 19th of April, the same year, at '*Rocque Mowe,*' on

A a

the Rhone, and Philip the Fair, within twelve months at *Fontainbleau.* The news of the persecution of the Knights Templars had already reached the Knights which were left in Cyprus, and who, in the absence of their Grand Master, had been overpowered by the Turks, when they lost *Acre*, with several other strong places in that island, and were obliged to retire to the isle of Rhodes and the adjacent islands. The prosecutions against them in open council at Vienna, ended the 1st of October, 1311, when their order was banished, their estates confiscated, and left at the Pope's disposal, who in the year 1312, gave a part to the Knights of St. John at Jerusalem, who at this day possess the greatest part of their estates. To this confiscation of their estates reference is made to this day in a part of the obligations of the Grand Elect and Knight Templars. As the number of them who escaped was very small, it rendered their enmity to their oppressors the more powerful, they sought to increase their order by admitting persons whom they believed and thought worthy of keeping the most important secret. Such they found among the good and virtuous Masons whom Solomon had distinguished and favored after the construction of the temple. The candor and intrepidity which appeared among them in the greatest dangers; their wisdom, union, charity, love, impartiality, firmness, discretion, and zeal, all led them to believe they could do no better than to unite themselves to them. Their fathers, protectors, and supporters, sought the favor to be admitted into their society, and initiated into their mysteries. Those who were newly initiated into their mysteries were informed by the Masons, who they were, and the barbarous events they had escaped, and the resolutions they had taken, secretly to increase their numbers, re-establish their order, and take possession again of their estates. The Templars then offered their brethren, the Masons, their assistance, in taking their revenge, and as a common cause to accept the tribute from them of the most just gratitude and thankfulness. The Grand Elected Knights, and Princes Masons approved their designs, accepted their offers, and agreed among themselves, instead of the character of their order, which was a cross, to use the sign, token, and word of Masons, and by the conformity of several analogies, (events in their history,) persuaded them that the different signs of Masons would put them entirely under cover against the maliciousness of such as, '*Gerard Labe*,' or '*Benoit Mehuy*,' should they undertake to be admitted into the order, and that they should not entrust the true secret to any but those whom they had tried, and of whom they had the utmost confidence. After having made them pass through the different degrees which we know in Masonry, the birth of which was taken from the construction of Solomon's temple, until its destruction; characterised by the most remarkable events, and by an event entirely analogous to the destruction of the Knights Templars, who, as elects of Masonry, cry only to revenge the death of their Illustrious Grand Master, and retake their possession. My dear brother, from the degree of Master Mason that you have received, and from your having learned to shed tears at the tomb of Hiram Abiff, have you not been disposed to take vengeance? Did they not show you the traitor, Jubelum Akirop, (or Abiram,) in the most dreadful colors. Would it be exaggerating to compare the conduct of Philip the Fair, with his? and to compare the two infamous informers, '*Gerard Labe*,' and '*Benoit Mehuy*,' to the two villains who joined Akirop to murder Hiram Abiff? Do they not kindle in your heart the same revenge which those fellow Crafts deserved, and was executed on them?

The trials you have gone through, to learn the historical facts of the ancient Bible, do they not serve to make an impression on your heart, and enable you to make a just application of the death of Hiram Abiff, in comparing it with that of James De Molay? By the degree of 'Elected Knights of Nine,' where your heart was disposed to revenge, you have been prepared to the implacable hatred that you have sworn to the Knights of Malta, on whom you ought to revenge the death of James De Molay. As a Grand Elected, you have acquired, by your proved discretion in symbolic Masonry, the light which leaves nothing more for you to desire, than your submission to the degree of the Sublime Princes of the Royal Secret, our Chief and Grand Elected of the Order, who have bestowed on you this singular favor. Thus you learn, my Most Illustrious brother, how, and by whom, Masonry has been transmitted to us. You ought to see what it is, to enter to our lawful rights, which leads us to associate with men to whom merit, bravery, and good manners, give titles, which only birthright grants to the ancestors of the Templars. You are now a Knight, and on a level with them; you have the same hazards to run, as much from the side of envy as persecution, which you may escape by keeping carefully your obligation, and secreting from the vulgar your rank and what you are.

Having attained to this degree of light by your merit, and the knowledge we have of your manners, we are persuaded that our confidence towards you will be sufficient to make you apprehend how important it is to you, not to be the cause of our repenting your initiation. We know you too well to have the least doubt of you. We therefore did not hesitate to enlighten you into the true interests of the order, and that by your uniting yourself to us, with a sincere submission, you will acquire that perfection your zeal deserves. You are now in the rank of those who shall be elected to the grand work. When once your name is in the urn of your election, the delicious perfumes of your actions will bring you to the true happiness of your desire, which I wish you. Amen. Amen. Amen.

After this discourse the Grand Commander knocks one great blow on the table, in order to call the four Knights to enter into the Chapter who were out. After which the Grand Commander finishes the reception, and gives the new Knight the sign, token, and word. He arms him, and decorates him with the attributes, and communicates the name he must take in future, which is uncommon to all others, and is *Knight Kadosh*, or Knight of the White and Black Eagle, instead of Knight Templars.

The JEWEL is a red cross, as before described, but in the room of that now it is a black spread eagle with two heads, suspended by a broad order of fiery bloody color, worn from the left shoulder to the right hip. The eagle, as if going to fly, with a naked sword in his claws.

The brother who desires to be better acquainted with the foregoing interesting history of the Knights Templars, may consult the following authors, viz. Villancus' History; History of all Orders, by Mathai, (in Paris;) History of Malta, by Verto; and an essay on Paris, by St. Foix.

LECTURE.

Q. Are you a Grand Elected? A. I am, Thrice Illustrious Knight. Q. Who received you in this degree. A. A worthy Deputy Grand Inspector, by the consent of two others. Q. What was done with you? A. He created me Knight. Q. How can I believe you? A. My name, which I leave, will convince you. Q. What is your name? A. Kadosh, or Knight of the Black Eagle. Q. Was any thing else done to you? A. The Deputy Inspector adorned me with the habit, ribbon, and jewel of the order. Q. Where have you received the prize of your election? A. I have received it in a very deep grotto, and in the silence of the night. Q. To what do you apply? A. I work with all my might and strength to raise an edifice worthy my brothers. Q. What progress have you made? A. I have conquered the knowledge of the mysterious *ladder*. Q. Of what is that ladder composed? A. Two supporters and steps. Q. What are the names of the two supporters. A. *Oheb, Elvah, Oheb Kerobo.* Q. What design have these two supporters? A.

The first is the love of God, and the other the love of our neighbors. Q. What are the seven steps of the mysterious ladder? A. The virtues which I must practice, conformable to my obligations. Q. Name them to me. A. *Tsedakah*, (righteousness) practice or works of mercy. 2nd. *Shor laban*, (*White ox*, figuratively,) candor of our actions. 3rd. *Mathok*, (sweetness) sweetness of character, which all brethren must follow. 4th. *Emunah*, truth in discourse. 5th. *Hamal saggi*, (great labor) advancement to the practice of Heaven. 6th. *Sabbal*, (a burden, or patience) patience in adversity. 7th. *Gemulah, Binah, Tebunah*, (retribution, intelligence, prudence.) Signifies that we must be prudent to keep secret every matter confided to us. Q. What are your ordinary pass words? A. *Manchin*, a name of the Grand Master most renowned among the Solitaries, known by the name of Kadosh. Q. What signifies that name? A. Solitary or separate. Q. What was the answer of the solitaries, when they were asked to what they pretended? A. *Abarekah, eth Adonai becol heth, thamid tehillatho bepi*, (see Psalm xxxiv, 1.) which is, I will bless God at all times, and will praise him with my mouth. Q. Do they never say any thing else? A. Yes, they say also, *Baahabah achullek him heani*; which is, I will assist the poor, and always sustain them with all my might and power. Q. How comes the cross surmounted with the eagle and the sword? A. That is that it shall remember to employ my sword, in the fulness of time, under the banner of the black eagle, to support the order. Q. Where did you work? A. In a place of security, to reestablish secretly the edifice ruined by the traitors. Q. What success do you expect from it? A. The right of virtue, the accord of brothers, and the possessions of our forefathers, and *everlasting happiness*. Q. Have you shed tears? A. I have. Q. Have you wore mourning? A. Yes, I wear it still. Q. Why do you wear it? A. Because virtue is despised, and as long as vice reigns innocence will be oppressed, and crimes will be left unpunished. Q. What is it that will punish vice and reward virtue? A. The Great Architect of the Universe alone. Q. How so. A. To favour our designs and desires. [Here every brother says three times, 'God favor our designs.'] Q. Have you any other name than *Kadosh*, or Knight of the Black Eagle? A. I have still the name of Adam to teach me, that from the most low I must go to the most high. Q. Give me the sign of knowledge against surprise. A. Here it is, [and he gives it in the following manner. He puts his right hand on the heart of a brother, in the same manner as with the poniard in the degree of 'Nine Elected,'—then give the token of the 'Grand Elected,' and then

A a 2

both strike the right knee.] Q. How came you to carry your fingers extended on your heart? A. That my trust is in God. Q. How came you after that to extend your hand? A. To show to my brother that he is welcome to all in my power, and *to encourage him to vengeance!** Q. How came you to let your hand fall on your right knee? A. To show we must bend our knees to adore God. Amen. *End of the lecture.*

To close.—Q. What's the o'clock? A. The break of day demonstrates. *Grand Commander.* 'If the break of day demonstrates, let us depart *for revenge.*' After which the Grand Commander puts his hand on his heart; then lets it fall on his right knee, which is answered by all; then the Grand Commander embraces each, and each other all around, and then the Chapter is closed.

PRINCE OF THE ROYAL SECRET.†

The Assembly of Princes is termed a '*Consistory.*'

Officers.—The first officer represents Frederick II. king of Prussia; he is styled 'Sovereign of Sovereigns,' 'Grand Prince,' 'Illustrious Commander in Chief.' The two next officers are styled 'Lieutenant Commanders.' The fourth officer is the 'Minister of State,' who acts as the *orator.* The fifth officer is the 'Grand Chancellor.' Then the 'Grand Secretary;' the 'Grand Treasurer;' the 'Grand Captain of the Guards;' a 'Standard Bearer;' a 'Grand Master Architect;' and two 'Tylers.'

Place of meeting.—This is to be a building at least two stories in height, situated on elevated ground, in the open country.

---

* 'Vengeance is *mine;* I will repay, saith the Lord.'

† It will be recollected, that in calling this the thirty-second degree, the degrees conferred in a Royal Arch Chapter and Grand Encampment, with those of the Thrice Illustrious Order of the Holy Cross, are not numbered.

The *ostensible* object of this degree is the invasion of the Holy Land, and its deliverance from the infidels. This is to be effected by uniting all the Masons, ancient and modern, under one commander, and directing them '*en masse*' upon the Mahometans, who have wickedly established themselves in that sacred region. Hence the complexion of this degree is military. The draft or carpet contains the plan of the camp of this 'Masonic Army!' The watchwords are to serve the purposes of countersigns. It is believed that the ceremonies of initiation have never been committed to writing, or practised in North America; hence, though many have received the obligation, words, signs, &c. *formally,* they remain like the rest of the world *ignorant* of the peculiar rites of the degree. It may be proper to apprise the reader that this degree, which is now numbered as the thirty-second, was fifty years ago (or less) the twenty-fifth. All those degrees which intervene between the K——H, or Kadosh, and this degree, have been interpolated, and probably manufactured within that period.

Three apartments on the second floor are necessary in this degree. In the first of these the guards are stationed. The second is used as a preparation room. The third is occupied by the members of the Consistory. This last apartment is hung with black, sprinkled with tears, 'death's heads,' 'cross bones,' and 'skeletons.' The throne is in the east, elevated by seven steps. On the throne is the chair of state, lined with black satin, flamed with red. Before the chair is a table covered with black satin, strewed with tears. On this cloth, in front, is a 'death's head' and 'cross bones;' over the 'death's head', is the letter I; and under the 'cross bones' is the letter M. On the table is placed a naked sword, a buckler, a sceptre, a balance, and a book containing the statutes of the order. In the west is placed another table covered with crimson, bordered with black, and strewed with tears; on the front of this cloth are the letters N. K. M. K. in gold.

Dress and stations of officers.—The 'Sovereign of Sovereigns' is dressed in royal robes, and seated in the chair of state. The Lieutenant Commanders dressed like the modern princes of Europe, and seated at the table in the west; their swords are crossed on the table. The Minister of State is placed at the Sovereign's right hand. The Grand Chancellor stands on the left hand of the Sovereign. Next to the Minister of State is placed the Grand Secretary. Next to the Grand Chancellor is placed the Grand Treasurer. Below the last named officers are placed on one side the Standard Bearer, the Grand Master Architect, and the Captain of the Guards. Below these officers are placed six members dressed in red, without aprons, wearing the jewel of the order, suspended on the breast by a black ribbon.

Collar of the order.—The collar is black, and edged with silver. On its point is embroidered in red a Teutonic cross. On the middle of the cross is a double headed eagle in silver. The collar is lined with scarlet, on which is embroidered a black Teutonic cross. Around the waist is girded a black sash, embroidered with silver. The cross is embroidered on that part of the girdle which is in front.

Jewel.—The jewel is a golden Teutonic cross.

Qualifications of candidate.—The candidate who receives this degree must be faithfully examined in that of 'Kadosh,' previous to admission. The Master of Ceremonies will acquaint him with the 'pass word,' which he is to give to the Lieutenant Commander. The Master of Ceremonies will then lead him to the 'Sovereign of Sovereigns.'

Opening and closing.—The Sovereign of Sovereigns says, '*Sal ix.*' The Lieute reply, '*Noni.*' They then together say,

'*Tengu.*' All give the sign. The Sovereign of Sovereigns says —Let us imitate our Grand Master Jacques De Molay, Hiram Abiff,* who to the last placed all his hopes in the Great Architect of the universe; and pronounced the following words just as he passed from this transient life into eternal bliss:—' Spes mea in Deo est,' (My hope is in God.)

Description of the carpet representing the camp.—On the carpet is drawn an ' enneagen,' in which is inscribed a pentagon; within this is an equilateral triangle, and in the triangle a circle, Between the heptagon and pentagon, upon the sides of the latter, are placed the standards of the five Standard Bearers, and the pavilions inscribed by the letters **T. E. N. G. U.** The emblems on the standard **T.** are the ' ark of the covenant,' an ' olive tree,' and a ' lighted candlestick,' on each side. The ground color of this standard is purple. On the ark is written the motto ' Laus Deo.' The standard **E.** bears a golden lion, holding in his mouth a 'golden key;' wearing around his neck a golden collar, on which is engraved '515.' The ground is azure; the motto 'Admajorem Dei gloriam.' On the standard **N.** is an ' inflamed heart,' in red, with two wings, surrounded by a laurel crown. The ground is white. The flag **G.** bears a double headed eagle, crowned, holding a sword in his right claw, and in his left a bloody heart. Ground is sea green. The flag **U.** has an ox, sable, (black,) on a golden ground. On the sides of the enneagen are nine tents, and on its angles nine pendants, each belonging to its appropriate tent. The pendants are distinguished by numerals, and the tents by the letters **I. N. O. N. X. I. L. A. S.**, disposed from right to left. These tents signify the different grades of Masonry. Thus:

Tents.	Names of Tents.	Pendants.	Represents,
S.	Malachi,	White, spotted with red,	Knights of Rose Croix Kts. of East & West, and Pr's of Jerus'm.
A.	Zerubbabel,	Light green,	Knights of the East.
L.	Neamiah.	Red,	Grand Elect, Perfect, and Sublime Masons.
I.	Hobben or Johaben	Black and red,	Sublime Elect, and Elect of fifteen.
X.	Peleg,	Black,	Elect of Nine, or Gr. Master Architect.
N.	Joiada,	Red & black in lozenges,	Provost and Judges.
O.	Aholiab,	Red and green,	Intendant of the buildings and Intimate Secretary.
N.	Joshua	Green,	Perfect Master.
I.	Ezra,	Blue,	Master, Fellow Craft. and Enter'd Appren.

* In the sublime degrees Hiram Abiff is considered merely as an allegorical personage.

The equilateral triangle in the middle represents the centre of the army, and shows where the Knights of Malta are to be placed who have been admitted to our mysteries, and have proved themselves faithful guardians. They are to be joined with the Knights of Kadosh. The corps in the centre is to be commanded by five Princes, who command jointly or in rotation according to their degrees, and receive their orders immediately from the Sovereign of Sovereigns. These five Princes must place their standards in the five angles of the pentagon, as above described. These Princes, who are Standard Bearers, have the following names, viz.

Standard. $\begin{cases} \text{T.} \text{ -------- Bezaleel,} \\ \text{E.} \text{ -------- Aholiab,} \\ \text{N.} \text{ -------- Mahuzen,} \\ \text{G.} \text{ -------- Garimont,} \\ \text{U.} \text{ -------- Amariah,} \end{cases}$ *Names.*

The heptagon points out the Encampment destined for the Princes of Libanus, Jerusalem, &c.; and these are to receive their orders from the five Princes. The enneagen shows the general order of Masons of all degrees.

Instructions for the reunion of the brethren, Knights, Princes, and Commanders, of the Royal Secret or Kadosh, which really signifies, '*Holy brethren of all degrees separated.*'

Frederick III. king of Prussia, Grand Master and Commander in Chief, Sovereign of Sovereigns, with an army composed of the Knights, Princes of the White and Black Eagle, including Prussian, English, and French; likewise joined by the Knights Adepts of the Sun, Princes of Libanus or the Royal Axe, the Knights of the Rose Croix or St. Andrew, Knights of the East and West, the Princes of Jerusalem, Knights of the East or Sword, the Grand Elect Perfect and Sublime Masons, the Knights of the Royal Arch, (ninth Arch,) Sublime Knights Elected, &c. &c.

The hour for the departure or march of the army is the fifth after the setting of the sun; and is to be made known by the firing of five great guns in the following order (0)—(0 0 0 0)—that is, with an interval between the first and second. The first rendezvous is to be the port of Naples—from Naples to the port of Rhodes—from Rhodes to Cyprus and Malta, whence the whole naval force of all nations is to assemble. The second rendezvous is to be at Cyprus, &c. The third rendezvous is to be at Jerusalem, where they will be joined by our faithful guardians. The watchwords for every day of the week are as follows; and they are not to be changed but by express order from the king of Prussia:

Protectors of Masonry.		*Prophets.*
Sunday — Cyrus,	⎫	Ezekiel.
Monday — Darius,	⎪	Daniel,
Tuesday — Xerxes,	⎪	Habakkuk,
Wednesday — Alexander,	⎬ Answer.	Zephaniah,
Thursday — Philadelphus,	⎪	Haggai,
Friday — Herod,	⎪	Zechariah,
Saturday — Hezekiah,	⎭	Malachi.

Sign. * * *, * * *, * * *. *Sacred words.* One says '* * *;' to which the other replies '* * *;' both then repeat the word, '* * *.' *Pass words.* '* * *,' '* * *,' which signifies ' separated;' '* * *,' '* * *,' which signifies, ' reunited;' '* * *,' '* * *,' '* * *,' which signifies, ' to avenge.' ' Each then letters the word '* * *;' which signifies, ' Omnipotent.'

Charge addressed to the candidate.—My dear brother: The Saracens having taken possession of the Holy Land, those who were engaged in the Crusades not being able to expel them, agreed with Godfrey De Bouillon, the conductor and chief of the Crusaders, to veil the mysteries of religion under emblems by which they would be able to maintain the devotion of the soldier, and protect themselves from the incursion of those who were their enemies, after the example of the scriptures, the style of which is figurative. Those zealous brethren chose Solomon's temple for their model. This building has strong allusions to the Christian church. Since that period they (Masons) have been known by the name of Master Architect; and they have employed themselves in improving the law of that admirable Master. From hence it appears that the mysteries of the craft are the mysteries of religion. Those brethren were careful not to entrust this important secret to any whose discretion they had not proved. For this reason they invented different degrees to try those who entered among them; and only gave them symbolic secrets, without explanation, to prevent treachery, and to make themselves known only to each other. For this purpose it was resolved to use different signs, words, and tokens, in every degree, by which they would be secured against cowans and Saracens. The different degrees were fixed first to the number of seven by the example of the Grand Architect of the universe, who built all things in six days and rested on the seventh. This is distinguished by the seven points of reception in the Master's degree. Enoch employed six days to construct the arches, and on the seventh, having deposited the secret treasure in the lowest arch, was translated to the abodes of the blessed. Solomon employed six years in constructing his temple; and celebrated its dedication on the seventh, with all the solemnity worthy of the divinity himself. This sacred edifice we choose to make the basis of figurative Masonry. In the first degree are three symbols to be applied. First, the first of the creation, which was only chaos, is figured by the candidate's coming out of the black chamber, neither naked nor clothed, deprived, &c.; and his suffering the painful trial at his reception, &c. The candidate sees nothing before he is brought to light; and his powers of imagination relative to what he is to go through are suspended, which alludes to the figure of the creation of that vast luminous body confused among the other parts of creation before it was extracted from darkness and fixed by the Almighty FIAT. Secondly, the candidate approaches the footstool of the Master, and there renounces all cowans; he promises to subdue his passions, by which means he is united to virtue, and, by his regularity of life, demonstrates what he proposes. This is figured to him by the steps that he takes in approaching the altar; the symbolic meaning of which is the separation of the firmament from the earth and water on the second day of creation. (The charge proceeds by giving a figurative interpretation of the ceremonies, &c. of the first and second part of the third degree, which I pass over as uninteresting to my readers, and commence with an interpretation which will be as novel to the Craft of the lower grades as to the Cowans.'*)

In the Master's degree is represented the assassination of Hiram by false brethren. This ought to put us in mind of the fate of Adam, occasioned by perverseness in his disobeying his great and awful Creator. The symbolic mystery of the death of Hiram Abiff represents to us that of the Messiah; for the three blows which were given to Hiram Abiff, at the three gates of the temple, allude to the three points of condemnation against Christ, at the High Priest's Caiphas, Herod, and Pilate. It was from the last that he was led to that most violent and excruciating death. The said three blows with the square, guage, and gavel, are symbols of the blow on the cheek, the flagellation, and the crown of thorns. The brethren assembled around the tomb of Hiram, is a representation of the disciples lamenting the death of Christ on the cross. The Master's word, which is said to be lost, since the

---

* I have consulted a number of authors and many Masons of high rank to learn the origin and definite meaning of this word; but have obtained no satisfactory information on the subject. However, from the manner in which it is used, I should suppose that it referred to the 'non-initiated.'

death of Hiram Abiff, is the same that Christ pronounced on the cross, and which the Jews did not comprehend, 'Eli, Eli, lama sabachthani,' 'my God, my God, why hast thou forsaken me! have pity on and forgive my enemies'—Instead of which words are substituted, M. B. N. (Mac-be-nac,) which, in Arabian, signifies, 'The son of the widow is dead.' The false brethren represent Judas Iscariot, who sold Christ. The red collar worn by the Grand Elect Perfect and Sublime Masons, calls to remembrance the blood of Christ. The sprig of cassia is the figure of the cross, because of this wood was the cross made. The captivity of the Grand Elect and Sublime Masons, (i. e. by the Chaldeans,) shows us the persecution of the Christian religion under the Roman emperors, and its liberty under Constantine the Great. It also calls to our remembrance the persecution of the Templars, and the situation of Jacques De Molay, who lying in irons nearly seven years, at the end of which our worthy Grand Master was burnt alive with his four companions, on the eleventh of March, 1314, creating pity and tears in the people, who saw him die with firmness and heroic constancy, sealing his innocence with his blood. My dear brother, in passing to the degree of Perfect Master, in which you shed tears at the tomb of Hiram Abiff, and in some other degrees, has not your heart been led to revenge? has not the crime of Jubelum Akirop been represented in the most hideous light? Would it be unjust to compare the conduct of Philip the Fair to his, and the infamous accusers of the Templars, to the two ruffians who were accomplices with Akirop? Do they not kindle in your heart an equal aversion? The different stages you have travelled, and the time you have taken in learning these historical events, no doubt, will lead you to make the proper applications; and by the degree of Master Elect and Kadosh, you are properly disposed to fulfil all your engagements, and to bear an implacable hatred to the Knights of Malta,* and to avenge the death of Jacques De Molay. Your extensive acquaintance with symbolic Masonry, which you have attained by your discretion, leaves you nothing more to desire here. You see, my dear brother, how, and by whom, Masonry has come to us. You are to endeavor by every just means to regain our rights, and to remember that we are joined by a society of men, whose courage, merit, and good conduct, hold out to us that rank that birth alone gave to our ancestors. You are now on

---

* The reader must not suppose that the Masonic Knights of Malta are here intended; the reference is to the ancient order of that name, which, when the order of Templars was suppressed, received their estates.

the same level with them. Avoid every evil by carefully keeping your obligations, and carefully conceal from the vulgar what you are, and wait that happy moment when we all shall be reunited under the same Sovereign in the mansions of eternal bliss. Let us imitate the example of our Grand Master, Jacques De Molay, who to the end put his hope in God, and at his last dying moments ended his life saying, 'Spes mea in DEO est!'

Obligation.—I do, of my own free will and accord, in the presence of the Grand Architect of the universe, and this Consistory of Sovereign Princes of the Royal Secret, or Knights of St. Andrew, faithful guardians of the faithful treasure; most solemnly vow and swear, under all the different penalties of my former obligations, that I will never directly or indirectly reveal or make known to any person or persons whatsoever, any or the least part of this Royal degree, unless to one duly qualified in the body of a regularly constituted Consistory of the same, or to him or them whom I shall find such after strict and due trial. I furthermore vow and swear, under the above penalties, to always abide and regulate myself agreeably to the statutes and regulations now before me; and when in a Consistory to behave and demean myself as one worthy of being honored with so high a degree, that no part of my conduct may in the least reflect discredit on this Royal Consistory, or disgrace myself. So may God maintain me in equity and justice! Amen! Amen! Amen! Amen! Amen!

SOVEREIGN GRAND INSPECTOR GENERAL.

The number of Inspectors in a kingdom or republic is not to exceed nine. They claim jurisdiction over all the ineffable and sublime degrees, and in reality form an *aristocratic body*, with power to appoint their own successors, and act as 'Sovereigns of Masonry.'

Decorations of the place of meeting.—The hangings are purple, embroidered with 'skeletons,' 'death's heads,' and 'cross bones.' Before the canopy is a transparent delta, (equilateral triangle.) In the middle of the room is a grand triangular pedestal, near which is seen a skeleton holding in his left hand the standard of the order, and in his right hand a poniard in the attitude of striking. Above the door, or place of entrance, is the motto of the order, 'Deus meumque jus.' In the east is a chandelier of five branches; in the south one of two branches; in the west one of three; and in the north a single one.

B b

Officers and titles.—The assembly is termed 'Supreme Council.' The first officer 'Thrice Puissant Sovereign Grand Master.' He represents Frederick II. The second officer is termed 'Sovereign Lieutenant Commander.' Besides these there is a 'Treasurer of the Holy Empire;' an 'Illustrious Grand Secretary of the Holy Empire;' an 'Illustrious Master of the Ceremonies;' and an 'Illustrious Captain of the Guards'—in all seven officers.

Dress.—The Thrice Puissant Sovereign wears a crimson satin robe, bordered with white—a crown on his head, and a sword in his hand. The Lieutenant Commander wears a ducal crown.

Sash.—The sash is black, edged with gold, from left to right; at the bottom a rose of red, white, and green. On the part crossing the breast is a *delta* with rays traversed by a poinard, and in the midst the figure '33.'

Jewel.—A black double headed eagle holding a sword. His beak, claws, and the sword, are of gold.

Signs.—First sign, '* * *. Second sign, '* * *.' Alarm.—Five, three, one, two.

Sacred words. '* * *,' '* * *,' '* * *,' '* * *,' signifying, 'Who is like unto thee among the mighty, O Lord!'

Pass words.—Question. 'D * * * y?' Answer. 'H * * * i.' Question. 'F * * * c?' Answer. 'D * * * c.'

DETACHED DEGREES.

The following degrees, with some others, are conferred in France and in this country as honorary degrees. The reader, perhaps, may not have been apprised that the Masonic systems of different countries vary much after the Master's Degree.

THE DEGREE OF
"ELU* DE PERIGNAN."

Description of the lodge.—The room represents the cabinet of Solomon, hung with many colors, lighted by twenty-seven lamps, distributed by three times nine. *Solomon*, dressed in royal robes, sits in the east—holds a blue sceptre, gilt, with a luminous triangle at the top, emblematical of his wisdom, power, and benevolence. *Solomon* wears gloves, adorned with a black

---

* Elu means 'elect.'

fringe, and his apron (white) trimmed with silver lace. *Hiram, king of Tyre,* is dressed like *Solomon,* and holds a large poniard in his hand.

Dress.—The brethren are clad in black, and wear a small breastplate on the left side, on which is embroidered in silver a death's head, a bone, and a dagger *across,* surrounded by these words, 'Vaincre ou mourir :' (Victory or death.) They wear a black sash four fingers wide, from right to left, with the same words on it. On the bottom is a black rose, from which is suspended a poniard. The apron is of white lambskin, lined and trimmed with black. On the flap is a '*death's head,*' with a bone and a sword *across.* On the upper part of the *apron* is represented a large drop, or tear, and on the sides and below eight smaller tears; at the bottom is a branch of cassia; the gloves are white, bordered with black.

Officers.—The Master is styled '*Most Respectable,*' and sits in the east. The Wardens are styled '*Venerable;*' one in the south, the other in the north.

Ceremony of opening.—*Master.* 'Brother Senior Warden, are we well tyled?' S. W. 'Most Respectable we are.' M. 'Venerable Senior Warden, as an 'Elu de Perignan,' do you know any thing besides the letters N. N.?' S. W. 'I know the letter P.' M. 'At what hour is a lodge of this degree to be opened?' S. W. 'At the commencement of night, or the end of day.' M. 'What is the hour?' S. W. 'The end of day.' Master knocks three times nine, gives the sign, and says, 'Give notice, brother Wardens in the south and north, that the lodge is opened.' (This is done.) After the brethren are seated, Master says, 'Venerable brothers Senior and Junior Wardens, is there any thing to be proposed?' Master of Ceremonies rises and says, 'There is an 'Elect of Nine,' who wishes to learn the mysteries of this degree.' M. 'Brother Master of Ceremonies go to the candidate, examine him on his former degrees, and introduce him in due and ancient form.'

Reception.—The candidate should be led through rough, bushy places to the cavern, where is a burning bush; after viewing *this,* he is led into the lodge, dressed as an 'Elect of Nine,' (which is in black,) and placed in the west, between the two Wardens. M. 'What is your desire?' *Candidate.* 'To receive the degree of 'Elu de Perignan.'' M. 'My brethren, do you believe this candidate to be worthy?' The Junior Warden and Master of Ceremonies reply, 'We do.' M. 'Brother Master of Ceremonies cause the candidate to travel.' Candidate passes to the east, by the way of the south, and returns again to the west; he then goes directly to the east, and returns to the west twice; he goes to the east, by the way of the north, and returns again to the west, and then goes directly to the altar in the east, to take the obligation.

Obligation.—I swear and promise on my word of honor, on the faith of an honest man, in the presence of the Grand Architect of the universe, and before this assembly, to guard and preserve the mysteries of this degree which has been conferred on me, not only from the profane, but from all of an inferior degree, under the penalties of all my former obligations; and I consent, if I violate this obligation, to have my tongue torn out by the roots. May God keep me in this, &c. Amen.

LECTURE.

Master. Do you, as an 'Elu de Perignan,' know any thing besides the letters N. N.? Senior Warden. Yes; I know the letter P. M. What does that letter signify? S. W. It is the initial of the name of the stranger who discovered to Solomon where the ruffian Akirop, otherwise called Abiram, was concealed. M. Pronounce the name. S. W. Perignan. M. How were you introduced into the lodge? S. W. By three times nine. M. What do these signify? S. W. The first nine signifies that I was one of the nine elect, who were chosen to search for the assassin of our Respectable Master, Hiram Abiff: the second nine, the number of Masons who searched for the body of Hiram Abiff; and the last nine, the three gates of the temple, the first Grand Masters, and the three blows struck by the three assassins on the body of Hiram Abiff. M. What do the letters A. K. and G. on the carpet signify? S. W. The names of the assassins of our Respectable Master, Hiram Abiff. M. What were their names? S. W. Akirop, or Abiram, Kumuvil, and Gravolet. M. How did they station themselves to accomplish their design? S. W. Kumuvil was at the south gate, armed with the twenty-four inch guage—Gravolet at the west gate, armed with the square, and Akirop at the east gate, armed with the gavel. M. How did the stranger Perignan discover that Akirop was concealed in the cavern? S. W. Perignan was at work by the light of a burning bush, near which was a cavern. His dog suddenly began to bark, and looking towards the mouth of the cavern, he saw a man, who appeared terrified, suddenly look out and immediately retire. Moved by curiosity, Perignan entered the cavern. Akirop, finding himself discovered, threw himself at his feet, confessed his guilt, and entreated him to keep it secret, kissed his hand, and besought him to procure him some food. M. Why did the stranger inform Solomon of this? S. W. In obedience to a proclamation issued by Solomon, and that justice might be done. M. How long did Perignan furnish Akirop with food, before he gave information to Solomon? S. W. Seven days. M. Why did he not inform the king sooner? S. W. He was ignorant of the existence of the proclamation until he saw it at a village, where he went to purchase food for Akirop and himself. M. What is the word of this degree? S. W. '*Maobon;*' which signifies, 'Thanks to God, the criminal is punished!' M. What is the sign? S. W. To make the motion of tearing out the tongue, with the hands extended. M. What is the answer to this sign? S. W. To lift the eyes and hands to heaven, as if imploring mercy! M. From what are these signs taken? S. W. Partly from my obligation, and partly from the surprise which Akirop manifested when he was discovered. M. What is the token? S. W. To present the hand to a brother, who kisses it. M. To what does this token relate? S. W. To the fact that Akirop kissed the hand of Perignan, that he might induce him to be silent respecting his discovery. M. What is the pass word? S. W. '*Abiram;*' which signifies, '*assassin,*' or '*murderer.*' M. What was done with the head of this ruffian? S. W. Solomon caused it to be embalmed and placed on the east pinnacle of the temple, with a poniard just below it, that it might be seen that the crime had been punished. M. What was signified by the nine journeys which you made before taking the obligation? S. W. The nine days Akirop remained concealed in the cavern.

The lodge is closed by three times nine; that is, twenty-seven knocks by the Master.

THE DEGREE OF

"LE PETIT* ARCHITECT."

Description, &c.—The carpet or floor, is an oblong square, drawn east and west; at the west end is a triangle, containing a blazing star, in which is the letter G. On the corner of the triangle, are the letters S. U. G. The triangle is enclosed in a circle. The lodge is hung with black, and lighted by twenty-one candles, eighteen of which are placed by nine, in two chandeliers. The throne is elevated on three steps, on one side is an altar, on which

---

*Minor Architect.

is placed a Bible, compass, square, triangle, and a chandelier, with the three remaining lights, and an urn, containing a golden trowel, and a paste made of flour, milk, oil, and wine. The brethren wear an apron, lined and trimmed with crimson. The Master and brethren, wear a broad crimson ribbon around the neck, at the bottom of which the jewel is attached by a blue rose. [The jewel is a triangle.] The jewels of the officers are worn within the triangle. The brethren are armed with swords, and are covered. On the hat is a crimson cockade. The Master represents 'SOLOMON.' and is called 'POWERFUL MASTER.' The Wardens are called 'Respectable,' and the brethren, 'Venerable.'

Opening.—Master knocks seven; (!!! !!!!) the Wardens repeat it. *Master.* 'Respectable brother Wardens, assist me in opening this lodge of 'Petit Architect.' Wardens give notice that the Master is about to open the lodge. M. 'Are we well tyled?' S. W. 'We are, Powerful Master.' M. 'Respectable Wardens, to prevent discovery, receive from each brother the sign, word, and token, of this degree, and give them to me.' The Wardens do this and say, 'The brethren are all Petit Architects.' M. 'Brother Senior Warden what is the hour?' S. W. 'The first instant, the first hour, the first day, which the Grand Architect employed in the creation of the universe.' M. 'My brethren, it is the first instant, the first hour, the first day, in which the Grand Architect employed in the creation of the universe. It is the first hour, the first day, the first year, when Solomon commenced the temple. The first day, the first hour, the first instant, for opening this lodge. It is time to commence our labors.' S. W. 'My brethren it is the first day, the first hour, and the first instant, when our Powerful Master opens this lodge of Petit Architect. The lodge of Petit Architect is open.' The Junior Warden repeats the same words.

Reception.—The candidate is placed in a room lighted by a little lamp placed on the floor. The Master of Ceremonies leaves him, and, entering the lodge, gives the key of the preparation room to the Secretary and Treasurer, who go to the candidate and receive his dues for the degree. The Master of Ceremonies returns, and divests the candidate of all weapons, which are carried into the lodge. He blindfolds the candidate, and ties a rope with a slip noose on his wrist, and leads him into the lodge, giving the alarm, &c. as usual: he places him between the Wardens, one of whom says, 'Powerful Master, the candidate is present with us.' Master. 'My brother, this degree cannot be obtained, unless you give us satisfactory proof that you have not been an accomplice in the death of our Master, Hiram Abiff

To assure us of this, we require you to participate in a symbolic offering of the portion of the heart of our Respectable Master, Hiram, which we have preserved since his assassination. You are to swallow the portion which we shall present to you. Every faithful Mason of this degree may receive it, but it cannot remain in the body of one who is perjured. Are you disposed to submit to this proof?' Ans. 'Yes.' Master. 'Respectable Wardens, cause the candidate to advance by three steps to the place where the urn is deposited, containing what is to be presented to him!' [The urn is placed on the *altar*.] The candidate is brought by three steps to the altar—he kneels on one knee—his right hand resting on the triangle placed on the Bible. M. 'Before we admit you to this august participation, you must give us an assurance of your fidelity. Are you willing to take upon you an obligation belonging to this degree?' Ans. 'Yes.'

Obligation.—I promise, under the same obligations which I have already contracted, and in the presence of this august assembly, to hold, guard, and conceal the secrets of this degree of Petit Architect, and never to reveal them to any one of an inferior degree, or to any other person, under the penalty of being deprived of that honorable burial which was given to our Honorable Master. Finally, I promise to support Masonry with all my power, and to assist my brethren, as far as lies in my power. So mote it be.

The Master, taking the trowel, presents with it a portion of the paste to the candidate, who swallows it. Master. 'This mystic oblation, which we partake with you, forms henceforth a tie so indissoluble that nothing can break it; say with me, and with all the brethren—Wo to him who shall disunite us!' Master raises the candidate, and the Wardens conduct him to the west by three steps backwards. M. 'My brother, one thing which you come here to learn is, that you ought never to refuse to confess your faults; obstinacy ought to be banished from the heart of every good Mason.'

The Wardens seize the candidate and place him on his hands and knees, his face towards the floor, nearly touching the 'blazing star,' and his mouth on the letter G. In this position the Junior Warden removes the bandage from his eyes, and the Senior Warden covers his body with a black cloth; (covering his head so that he sees nothing except the star.) M. 'My brother what do you see?' Candidate. 'The letter G, in a blazing star.' M. 'What does that letter signify?' C. 'Glory, Grandeur, and Geometry.' M. 'Does it signify any thing else?' C. 'Yes;— God.' M. 'My brother that is the name of the Grand Architect of the universe! Your position represents that in which our Respectable Master was buried; that is, his face towards the blazing star, his mouth on the letter G. engraved on a golden plate of a triangular form, which is emblematic of three mystic angles united in one. The circle represents the immensity of space, and also the space enclosed in the third part of the temple, called the 'Holy of Holies,' and in Hebrew, '*Hekal.*' Do you promise us, that if, during the journey you are about to make through the forests and mountains, you should discover any accomplices in the death of Hiram, you will arrest them at the hazard of your life?' Ans. 'Yes.' The Master knocks one, as a signal to the Wardens to raise the candidate, to remove his bonds and cause him to make the tour of the lodge eighteen times, [these are reduced usually to three, six, or nine;] by the way of the north, south, and east. When this is done, the Senior Warden announces it to the Master. M. 'Have you met with no obstacles in your journey?' C. 'No.' Master. 'It is with much joy I proceed to recompense your zeal for Masonry, by conferring on you the rank of '*Petit Architect*,' with the direction of the works of the temple: Approach and learn the mysteries of this degree.' The Senior Warden takes off the apron of the candidate, which he throws on the floor, and causes the candidate to advance to the throne by three steps, (of a Master Mason.) Master gives the candidate the apron of this degree, saying, 'Your business hereafter consists in architecture, and in completing the ornaments of the temple.' Master gives the candidate the *cordon, jewel,* and *gloves*, and says, 'We have in this degree one *word*, a *token*, and two *signs*—one of which is called the '*pass sign*,' because none can enter the lodge without giving it. It is given thus: One says, 'Are you an Architect?' at the same time placing his right hand on his right hip, the *thumb* and *fore finger* being *closed*, raising his eyes to heaven, and making a motion as though to retreat backwards. The other answers by doing the same thing on his left hip, with his left hand, and saying, 'I am.'

The other sign in demanding, is made by carrying the right hand to the heart, then carrying the hand diagonally to the top of the forehead, the thumb touching the forehead, forming a triangle, and then placing the arm across the belly. The answer is to carry the right hand open to the right side, and making a movement as if to retire, and placing the right foot behind the left so as to form a square. The '*token*' is that of giving the 'Past Master's' '*token*' *thrice*, pronouncing each time one syllable of the word, 'Ga-ba-on,' (French;) Gib-e-on, (English.) 'Go salute your brethren, and return to me.' After he has done so, Master says, 'My brother, after the death of 'Hiram,' the labors were lighter. Solomon, willing to gratify the desires of the Masters, resolved o choose another new Architect for the work. For this purpose ne assembled the most worthy Masters, distinguished by their genius, capacity, and virtues, in the hall of his palace. By the plans which were presented to him, he ascertained that the first part of the building was perfected. He named some of these Masters 'Petit Architects.' Their engagements were the same which you have taken, and which entitle you to their rank. Long may you enjoy this rank with honor to yourself and advantage to us!'

LECTURE.

The Master, giving the '*pass sign*,' says, Respectable brother Senior Warden are you a Petit Architect? S. W. Powerful Master, I am. M. In what place were you received? S. W. In the circle of the square, and the holy of holies. M. What does that circle signify? S. W. The eternity of the Grand Architect, who has neither beginning nor end. M. What does the square signify? S. W. The oblong square of the tomb of Hiram. M. What is signified by the holy of holies? S. W. The space within the triangle, where the name of the Grand Architect is engraved. M. By what means were you received as a Petit Architect? S. W. By the cement which was employed in laying the stones of the temple. M. What cement was employed? S. W. A mystic cement, composed of flour, milk, wine, and oil. M. What does this represent? S. W. The flour represents goodness; the milk, gentleness; the wine, strength; the oil, wisdom:—qualities which distinguished our Respectable Master. M. How was he buried? S. W. His face to the centre, his mouth on the letter G. engraved within the blazing star. M. In what place? S. W. Behind the sanctuary. M. Did Solomon suffer the death of Hiram to remain unpunished? S. W. No. He named those Architects who were willing to engage themselves by new promises, to pursue his murderers. M. How did the Architects pursue them? S. W. They travelled round mount Lebanon three times seven, visited the neighboring mountains, and the most secret places, until they were discovered. M. What was he called, who killed Hiram? S. W. Akirop, or Abiram; which signifies assassin, or murderer. M. How did you come to this degree? S. W. By three steps forward and three backward. M. In what have you been employed? S. W. In perfect architecture, in composing and in forming the triangle, placed in the tomb of Hiram. M. Describe that work. S. W. The middle contains the letter G. and the corners the letters S. U. G. M. What do those letters signify? S. W. The G. is the initial of the word ' GOD;' the S. of the word ' *Submission ;*' the U. of ' *Union ;*' and the G. of the word ' *Gomez ;*'—the grand word said to be the first word pronounced by the first man. M. Have you no other letters in your lodge? S. W. We have the letters M. B. which signify the word which we do not pronounce *aloud,* and which was uttered in raising the body of our Respectable Master; and three other letters of brass, incrusted on the border of his tomb. M. Give me those letters, with their signification. S. W. They are M. A. S. The M. signifies ' *Moriah,*' the name of the mountain where the temple stood; the A. ' *Adoniram,*' or Hiram, the Master; and the S. ' *Stokin.*' M. Were your labors confined to the temple alone? S. W. No; I have traced a circle by its circumference, upon a space which we term the holy of holies. M. What does that circumference signify? S. W. The eternity of the Supreme Being, which geometry represents to us under that emblem. M. What are your marks? S. W. Two signs, a word, a token. M. What do you call the token? S. W. The double arch. M. Give me the ' pass word.' S. W. Ga-ba-on. (Gibeon, according to the English Bible.) M. Give me the grand word. S. W. ' GOMEZ.'

Closing.—M. ' My brethren, it is the last instant, the last hour, the last day which the Master of the universe employed in the creation; it is the last instant, the last hour, and the last day when Solomon wrought in building the temple; and the last instant when Architects ought to labor. It is time for us to repose.' He knocks seven, which is repeated by the Wardens, and the Master says, ' My brethren, the lodge is closed !'

THE DEGREE OF
"GRAND ARCHITECT,"
OR
COMPAGNON ECOSSOIS.*

The lodge is divided into two parts, by a black curtain behind the throne. Near the throne is the altar, on which is the Bible, a double triangle, a square, a compass, and a plan of the temple

---

* Scotch Fellow Craft.

finished, as far as the third story. The whole lodge is hung with red, adorned with hyacinth flowers, but the hangings of the first apartment should be covered with a black drapery, which may be removed when the proper time arrives. This first apartment is illuminated by twenty-seven lights, distributed by three times nine. The titles of the officers are the same as in the preceding degree. The carpet, or flooring, only differs in having the triangle *double*. The jewel is a double triangle formed with a compass and level, and contained within a golden circle. The head of the compass has a golden sun, whose rays touch the head of the level. This jewel is worn by a large red cordon* from left to right. In the first apartment, when hung with black, the cordon of the jewel is black; but the instant the hangings are changed, the cordon is changed also.

Second Apartment.—(used in the next degree.) Behind the black curtain is an ' *altar*,' with Masonic emblems painted on it. It is erected on seven steps, and lighted with eighty-one candles, placed in a triangular form. Above it is a transparent painting representing a ' *glory*,' surrounded by seven celestial intelligences. In the middle a luminous ' triangle' in which is written יהוה'; on the edge of the cloud appear seven angel's heads. The ark of alliance supported by two cherubims, covering it with their wings. Before the ark is a lamb, reposing on a book sealed with seven seals. Before the ark, on the right, is the brazen sea. On each side of the room are placed five urns, in the middle is the altar of burnt offerings, the golden candlestick, and table of shew-bread.

Opening.—The Powerful Master, seated on a moveable throne, knocks one, which is repeated by the Wardens, and Master says, ' Most Respectable Wardens, before the opening of this lodge of Grand Architects, examine the brethren, and see if all the avenues of the temple are guarded.' This is done, and Junior Warden says, ' Powerful Master, all the brethren present are Grand Architects, and all the avenues of the temple are guarded.'

Master.—' Most Respectable Wardens, assist me in opening this lodge of Grand Architects. Respectable Senior Warden, what is the hour?' The response and the residue of the ceremony of opening, is the same as in the degree of Petit Architect.

Reception.—The candidate being divested of all weapons, and blinded and led to the door, the Master of Ceremonies gives the alarm of the Petit Architect. The Junior Warden knocks the

---

* Collar.

alarm of this degree, which is repeated by the Senior Warden, and then by the Master. Junior Warden says 'Respectable Brother Senior Warden some one knocks at the door after the manner of a Petit Architect!' S. W. 'Powerful Master, some one knocks at the door,' &c. M. 'Venerable brother Senior Warden see who knocks.' Junior Warden goes to the door, gives the alarm of a Petit Architect which is answered from without, and he asks, 'What is your desire?' Master of Ceremonies. 'Here is a brother Petit Architect who wishes to be examined, that he may receive the degree of Grand Architect. The Junior Warden shuts the door and repeats to the Senior Warden, who repeats to the Master. M. 'Respectable brother Junior Warden demand his name, if he is properly prepared, and has resolution to undergo the severe trials as all Grand Architects have done, who have gone this way before him.' The Junior Warden does this, and repeats the answers of candidate to Senior Warden, who reports to Master. Brethren all rise, and Master says, 'My brethren, the second story of the temple accords to the Supreme orders—It is necessary that it should be elevated another story, which will be the height which it ought to have according to the designs given by the Grand Architect of the universe. The direction of this part of our work has been reserved for the Grand Architect who is to replace Hiram. The work ought to be deferred no longer; it must be completed before our next meeting. It is necessary that the Architect who presents himself, should make us acquainted with the justice of his plans, since none but skilful Grand Architects can bring the temple to perfection. Is it your wish, my brethren, that we should admit and examine him who is at the door?' Brethren assent by clapping hands three times. M. 'Brother Junior Warden cause 'Moabon' to be introduced in due form.' Candidate is led in, and placed in the west, his feet or toes on the points of the square. Master knocks one for order; Junior Warden knocks seven, (alarm of Grand Architect) this is repeated by Senior Warden and by Master. Junior Warden says, 'Powerful Master, you behold 'Moabon' who desires to obtain the degree of Grand Architect.' M. 'My brother, the degree which you desire to obtain, is one of high rank, the perfecting of the temple is a work of such importance, that we fear you will not submit to the trials to which we subject those whom we admit. Yet the necessity of finding a worthy successor to Hiram, renders it necessary to prove those who think themselves capable of filling his place. It is necessary to make the tour of the temple twenty-seven times, which I have reduced to nine for the purpose of examining the work. It is also necessary to produce a plan drawn with exactness. You will present this to the

Grand Architect, who will judge whether you are worthy to replace Hiram, whom we have lost!' Master knocks one, as a signal for the Junior Warden to lead the candidate round the lodge; he also puts the plan in the hands of the candidate; he travels as in the degree of Petit Architect. Junior Warden knocks one, and says, 'Respectable brother Senior Warden, 'Moabon' has finished his mysterious travels.' Senior Warden repeats this to the Master. M. 'My brother, what are the fruits of your travels?' Candidate. 'Powerful Master, I have brought a plan of the works of the temple, which I am ready to present for inspection.' M. 'My brother, present it to me by three steps.' Candidate makes three steps, and falls on one knee at the foot of the throne. Master receives it, and, after examining it, hands it to the brother next to him, who passes it on; thus it returns again to the Master in the east, who, receiving it, places the hand of the candidate on the square and double triangle placed on the altar. The compass on his wrist, a sword is held above, and he takes the obligation.

Obligation.—'I promise, under the same obligations which I have already taken, never to reveal the secrets of this degree of Grand Architect to any one of an inferior degree, or to any other person, under the penalty of being expelled from all our lodges. Amen.'

Master. 'Brother Senior Warden conduct the candidate backward by three steps.' In the west he is turned with his back to the east, and is seated on a stool before the table, and then turned again towards the east. M. 'Do you persist in your determination to keep our secrets inviolably?' Ans. 'Yes.' Master. 'Brother Senior Warden remove the veil of obscurity; 'Moabon' is worthy to behold our labors.' (The bandage is removed from his eyes at the stroke of the mallet.) M. 'My brother, it is with pleasure we have seen you fulfil the conditions prescribed to you. The exactness of your plan induces us to admit you among our number, that with us you may complete this vast and sublime edifice. Approach, my brother, and receive the marks of distinction to which your constancy entitles you!' 'We have, in this degree, a sign of demand, a response, a token, and two words. The sign of demand is made by placing the hands on the stomach so as to form a triangle with the thumbs and fore fingers. This is termed the 'summoning sign;' and the sign of response is made by carrying the two hands in the same form above the head. This is the sign of distress, and is only to be used in danger. The token is made by joining right hands and reversing them three times. The word is 'Moabon,' given by pronouncing a syllable each time the hands are reversed in the token. Pass word, the same as the pass word of Fellow Craft. Go, my brother, salute the brethren, and return to me.' When the candidate has done this, he takes his seat in the west, and hears the lecture.

LECTURE.

M. Most Respectable Senior Warden, are you a Grand Architect? S. W. Powerful Master, I have wrought in the third story of the temple. M. Where were you received? S. W. In the middle chamber. M. What is that chamber? S. W. The place where king Solomon completed the plan of the temple with the Grand Architects. M. How were you employed in the degree of Grand Architect? S. W. In building the third story, which was the top of the temple. M. How did you merit this degree? S. W. By the perfection of the designs which I presented to Solomon. M. What was your reward? S. W. Two signs, a token, and two words. M. Give them to me. S. W. Powerful Master, give me the first and I will give you the second. M. What are these signs called? S. W. The first the sign of demand, and the second the sign of distress. M. What does the first sign show, and why does it bear that name? S. W. That a good Mason in distress, may depend on the assistance of his brethren; also, that it is only to be given in the lodge or in danger. M. Give the token to your nearest brother. (Given, saying Moabon.) M. What is the word you cannot pronounce? S. W. The word given me by Solomon. M. What is the other word? S. W. (Repeating the pass word of the Fellow Craft,) which is the pass word. M. What is your age? S. W. Twenty-seven years.

Closing.—Master. Respectable brethren, Senior Warden, and Junior Warden, give notice that I am about to close this lodge of Grand Architect. (They do it.) M. What is the hour, brother Senior Warden? S. W. The last instant, the last hour, the last day in which the Grand Architect of the universe was employed in creating the world; the last instant, the last hour, the last day which Solomon employed in constructing the temple. M. Therefore it ought to be the last instant of holding this lodge; it is time to close, and repose ourselves. Wardens repeat this. Master knocks twenty-seven, and says, ' My brethren, the lodge is closed!

NOTE. The apartment behind the black curtain is not used in this degree, but in that of ' Le Maitre Ecossois.'

THE DEGREE OF
LE MAITRE ECOSSOIS.*

Description, &c.—The two apartments mentioned in the last degree, are those used in this, except that in the first apartment the altar is placed in the west between the Wardens, and, in the place of the first plan, one is used which represents the temple complete, but destitute of any ornaments. Below the temple are represented many working tools, and on the back is written the names of those who have taken the degree, in the lodge; below these names the word ' *excluded*' is written, for the purpose of being filled up with the names of those who may have refused to undergo the trials hereafter mentioned. Such a refusal excludes the person for ever from all lodges of ' Maitre Ecossois,' and consequently from all the degrees above it. Before the altar is a stool, on which the candidate is made to sit, leaning his head on the altar, at the time the hangings of the lodge are changed from black to red.

Titles.—Master, ' *Most Puissant ;*' Wardens, ' *Most Respectable ;*' and brethren ' *Most honorable.*'

Opening.—Like that of the last degree.

Reception.—Candidate is prepared as in the degree of Grand Architect, except that he is not blinded. ' Master of Ceremonies' causes him to sign his name on the back of the plan, without letting him see the other side, and tells him that, if he wants resolution to undergo the trials, he had better go no further; since, if he shows any weakness, he will be for ever excluded. If he persists, the Master of Ceremonies knocks at the door the alarm of a Grand Architect, which is answered within by the alarm of this degree. He is led in and placed in the west, facing the east, between the Wardens. The Wardens give the alarm, which the Master answers, and says, ' Most Respectable Wardens, what do you desire ?' S. W. ' Most Puissant, here is ' Moabon,' who, full of zeal, strength, and courage, wishes to submit to all the trials which you may impose on him, to obtain the ' Puissant degree' of ' Superintendent Maitre Ecossois.' '
M. ' My Brother, we approve the zeal which induces you to make this request, but you know not the sublimity of the degree which you solicit. The temple is finished, and it only remains to complete the ' altars' and ' tabernacles' which Hiram left unfinished, and of which he has furnished the designs. He is no more : it is neces-

---

*Scotch Master.

sary to have a successor who will with honor and skill pursue and finish his designs. Are you capable of doing this?' Candidate. 'Most Powerful, if zeal, labor, and constancy claim any right, condescend to prove me.' M. 'Most Respectable Junior Warden, cause the candidate to make the usual journey by three times twenty-seven, and if the designs which he shall submit to us are worthy of being pursued, we will proceed to the trials necessary to enable him to see the brilliant light!' Junior Warden gives the plan to the candidate, causes him to travel, and then the Wardens knock, and the Senior Warden says, Most Powerful, Moabon has fulfilled your orders, and wishes to present his designs to you.' M. 'Most Respectable Junior Warden cause him to advance by three steps:' he does this—the Master examines the plan, and passes it to the brethren. M. 'My brother, this alone is not sufficient; there are other trials to be submitted to. Do you persist in your first demand?' C. 'Yes, Most Powerful. M. 'Most Respectable Junior Warden, cause the candidate to return to the west, by three steps backward, that he may see his duty to be firm in the path of virtue, notwithstanding the humiliations which will be required of him!' When the candidate is placed in the west, Master says, ' My brother, it is necessary to examine you on the degrees which you have already taken.' This is done, and Master says, ' My brother, though you have passed through all these degrees, you are not yet one of the most perfect. It remains for you to behold the brilliant light, which is submitted to the view of those only, who have been well tried. It is necessary that you should take an obligation, which is contained in the paper which I present to you; read to yourself, and afterwards, if you are willing to take it, read it aloud.'

Obligation.—' In the name of the Host High, who has created, sustained, and guided me thus far in my life, I promise and swear that I will keep inviolably all the secrets, signs, and mysteries of this degree, except it shall be in a just and regular lodge of the same; and if I shall violate this obligation, I consent that the veins of my temples and throat shall be opened, and my body exposed on the highest pyramid, in the open air, to the rigor of the winds, the heat of the sun, the dews of the night, until the blood flowing gradually from my veins, my life shall be extinct through loss of blood and famine. May the Grand Architect of the universe keep me in this obligation. Amen.'

Master says, ' My brother, have you resolution to pronounce this obligation from your heart, in a loud voice, before this august assembly?' If the candidate refuses, the Wardens, placing the points of their swords in his back, cause him to make the twenty-seven tours of the Grand Architect, and the eighteen of the Petit Archirect round the room, and then drive him out of the room. If the candidate consents, he reads the obligation with a loud voice, and the Junior Warden then burns it in one of the lights. When it is consumed, they all clap hands thrice.

Master. 'My brother, since your zeal has induced you to persevere, we recognize you as 'Superintendent of the Tabernacles' we are about to raise. You will succeed our Respectable Master, Hiram; but before your honor is proclaimed in the east of the temple, let us render a tribute of respect to the memory of him whose loss we deplore in profound silence.' Master says, '*Civi,*' and knocks one; all the brethren place one knee on the floor, and resting the head on one hand, remain silent. Master knocks one, and the Wardens place the candidate on his knees before the table, his face covered with his hands and placed on the open Bible, so that he sees nothing. The Wardens cross their swords on his neck. While he is in this posture, the black drapery of the first apartment is removed, and the black curtain of the second drawn, and all the brethren put on the red cordon; when the change is made the Master knocks one for silence. He knocks again, and says, 'Caki.' (rise.) Brethren all rise, and the Wardens raise the candidate; as he rises, Master knocks one, and all the brethren say, 'Hiram is dead, and 'Moabon' supplies his place.'

After a moment's silence, Master says, 'It is with pleasure, my brother, that we have proclaimed you a 'Superintendant Maitre Ecossois!' Approach and learn the mysteries of this degree.' He is caused to advance to the brazen sea, from which the Master takes water with an urn, and, throwing some drops on the left side of the candidate, says, 'Be purified!' He is then placed at the foot of the throne, and the Master, giving him the cordon and jewel, says, 'This cordon and jewel gives you the command over all other Masons of inferior degrees. (Giving the gloves,) These gloves belong to this degree. We have in this degree two signs, a token, and four words. The two first words are '*Urim*' and '*Thummim.*' The secret and incommunicable word is יהוה, (JEHOVAH;) the word of Ancient Masters, which had been lost! The pass word is '*Zedidiac.*' The sign is to present the hands, forming a triangle, at the top of the forehead, saying, 'The triangle on the forehead is my support!' The answer to this sign is made by placing the right hand on the eyes, inclining the head, and bending the knee. The token is to take the right hand (as in the degree of Grand Architect but in place of reversing them;) three times, and giving mutually three light blows with the four fingers joined, placing the left hand on the

C c 2

right shoulder, saying, 'Virtue unites two hearts, two bodies, and two hands; and the whole make but one!' Go, my brother, salute the Wardens, and return to the east for further instruction.'

LECTURE.

M. Most Respectable brother Senior Warden what do you know as a Maitre Ecossois? S. W. Most Puissant, I know the grand light of the third apartment. M. Where were you received? S. W. In the high place. M. What road did you travel? S. W. By that of the middle chamber, to the third apartment. M. Has not this third apartment another name? S. W. It is named 'Gibeon,' and is the high place where David and Solomon offered their burnt offerings, before the building of the temple. M. In what were you occupied as a 'Maitre Ecossois?' S. W. In furnishing the altars and tabernacles, and in completing the precious ornaments. M. What are those ornaments? S. W. the ark of alliance and cherubims, the brazen table, the table of shew-bread, the altar of burnt offerings, and the candlestick of seven branches. M. What was above the ark of alliance? S. W. The 'SHEKINAH,' between the cherubim's wings. M. Under what form is the 'Shekinah' represented? S. W. Under that of a lamb reposing on a book sealed with seven seals. M. Of what wood was the ark made? S. W. Of shittim wood, which is incorruptible, and it was covered with gold. M. What was its size? S. W. Two cubits and a half long, one cubit and a half broad, and one cubit and a half high. M. What did the ark contain? S. W. The tables of the law, Aaron's rod, and the pot of manna. M. Give me the sign of that law. S. W. It is given by placing the two hands on the head, the fingers extended, which represents the ten commandments. M. In what place was the ark made, and by whom? S. W. It was made at Horeb by Bezaleel and Aholiab. It was carried from Horeb to Moab, from Moab to Shechem, afterwards to Shilo, from Shilo to the temple of Dagon, from thence to the house of Aminadab, then to the house of Obed Edom, afterwards to Kirjath Jearim, thence to Jerusalem, and placed on Mount Zion, and afterwards to the temple on Mount Moriah. M. Where were the ornaments placed? S. W. The altar of burnt offerings was placed before the door of the tent of the congregation. The altar of incense was at the west end of the holy place of the tabernacle. The table of shew-bread on the north, and the golden candlestick of seven branches on the south. The ark itself was placed in the west end of the most holy place. M. What is represented by the candlestick of seven branches? S. W. The seven days of creation, including the day of rest. S. W. How did you become acquainted with all these things? S. W. By the designs which I presented to Solomon after a dangerous journey. M. What was that? S. W. I made the tour of all the works of the temple, three times twenty-seven. M. Was a sight of the brilliant light the reward of this labor? S. W. No, Most Puissant; I was subjected to three trials. M. What were those? S. W. The first, to make three steps backward, to teach me firmness in the path of virtue under humiliations. The second, to give an exact account of the progress which I had made in Masonry, and in the practice of virtue. The third, to make a voluntary engagement which my heart approved, and my lips avowed. M. What did this engagement produce? S. W. A tribute of respect to the memory of Hiram. M. What followed? S. W. The word 'Civi,' which signifies kneel. M. Did the grief for the death of Hiram continue long? S. W. After seven minutes the word, 'Caki,' was pronounced, which signifies rise. M. What followed that word? S. W. A surprise, splendor, the brilliant light, and a proclamation. M. What was the surprise? S. W. My sight was struck with the view of scarlet and hyacinth. M. What was the splendor and brilliant light? S. W. The Shekinah, and the glory of the Grand Architect. M. What was the use of the proclamation? S. W. To show that all my brethren had selected me to replace Hiram, and had declared me Superintendent of all the works of the temple by the name of Moabon. M. What does the luminous triangle represent? S. W. The glory of the Grand Architect of the universe, and his three divine attributes, eternity, wisdom, and power. What do the letters within signify? S. W. The name of 'GOD,' the sacred word of 'Maitre Ecossois.' It shows us that GOD is the centre and source of all light, and the only one who is able to know all things. M. Why do the Maitre Ecossois wear the triangle? S. W. Because it is an emblem of the triple unity. M. What does the circle, enclosing the triangle, represent? S. W. That GOD has neither beginning nor end. M. Why is this jewel suspended by a flame colored ribbon? S. W. To teach us the order with which we should endeavor to destroy vice. M. In what place was your first lodge holden? S. W. Between three mountains inaccessable to the profane, in a deep valley, where peace, virtue, and union reign. M. What are those three mountains? S. W. Mount Moriah, Mount Sinai, and Mount Heroden. M. Where is Mount Heroden situated? S. W. Between the west and north of Scotland, at the end of the Sun's course, where the highest Masonic lodge is holden in that country, which has given a name to this degree. M. What do you mean by a deep valley? S. W. The tranquillity which reigns in our lodges. M. What produces this tranquillity? S. W. The preservation of our marks unchanged. M. What are the marks of a Maitre Ecossois? S. W. Two signs, a token, and four words, of which one is incommunicable. M. Give me the sign. (That of response is given.) M. Give the token to your nearest brother. (It is given.) M. What do you call that token? S. W. 'The perfect proof.' M. Give me the grand word. S. W. I will letter it with you. (Done.) M. What does that word signify? S. W. The name of the Grand Architect. M. Give me the two first words. (Given.) M. Give me the pass word. (Zedidiac.) M. Why is the lodge purified before labor begins? S. W. After the construction of the temple, the Grand Architect caused fire to descend from Heaven to purify it, and to consume the burnt offering. M. What is your age? S. W. As an Apprentice, three years; as a Fellow Craft, five; as a Master, nine; as a Petit Architect, twenty-one; as a Grand Architect, twenty-seven; as a Maitre Ecossois, eighty-one.

Close.—Same as in degree of Grand Architect.

THE DEGREE OF
KNIGHT OF THE EAST,
OR
'CHEVALIER DE L'ORIENT.'

Description of the lodge.—For this degree two apartments are necessary, situated on the same floor.

First apartment.—Is hung with green on the east, west, and north sides, so as to leave a space of six feet between the hangings and the wall. The space enclosed is an oblong square. It represents the apartment of Cyrus, king of Assyria; the throne is in the east, two arm chairs in the west, and the seats for the members in the south. Behind the throne is a transparency, representing the dream of Cyrus, (mentioned hereafter,) and above, near the ceiling, is a triangular glory, and in it 'יהוה,' (Jehovah.) The glory rests on a luminous cloud, from which an eagle is issuing, with a label in its beak, and on it the words, '*Give liberty to the captives.*' Below appear Nebuchadnezzar and Belshazzar, loaded with chains. No carpet is placed in this apartment, but that which supplies its place is a long square, formed by a little wall of wood or painted cloth, one foot round, and half a foot high. This little wall, commencing at the two sides of the throne, passes by the feet of the brethren in the south, and extends to the hanging in the west, so that the two chairs may be within the long square; it is then continued the whole length of the north side until it reaches the east. At the four corners of this wall, and also in the middle of the south and north, is a little tower, one and a half feet higher than the wall. In the west is the seventh tower, which divides both the wall and the hangings. This tower should be seven feet high, and large enough to contain a man. It has two doors, one within the lodge and one without. At this last door are two centinels, armed with spears and swords. They are in the six feet of space before named. The residue of this space, from the north to the east, (where the door of the second apartment is placed,) is occupied by a bridge lighted by a lantern. At the entrance of the bridge it is guarded by many armed men. The other end reaches to the door of the second apartment. Water so placed as to be agitated, is beneath the bridge, and represents the river Staburzania, (or Euphrates.)

Second Apartment.—Represents the court of the temple, hung with red. The carpet represents the furniture of the holy and most holy places. Above the ark, the Shekinah, (symbol of the presence of Jehovah,) represented by a lamb reposing on a book sealed with seven seals. At the corner of the temple is the column Boaz, broken. The carpet is covered with black, which is removed at the proper time for its being uncovered.

Titles, ornaments and jewels of the first apartment.—Master—Cyrus, called Sovereign; Senior Warden—Nebuzaradan, called First General; Junior Warden—Mithridates, called Second General; Secretary—Chancellor; Master of Ceremonies—Grand Master; Brethren—Knights.

The Sovereign carries a sceptre. All the officers wear a broad green ribbon, crossed, round the neck without any jewel. The Wardens and brethren have naked swords in their hands, and wear a single ribbon (green) from right to left, without any jewel. Apron, white, lined and bordered with green, without any emblems.

Titles, ornaments, and jewels of the second apartment.—Master is called Most Excellent; Wardens Most Powerful; Brethren, Most Venerable; and candidate, Zerubbabel. In passing from the first apartment to the second they change the color green for red. The cordon is red, and at the bottom are rosets marking the color of the preceding degrees, with one of green, for Knight of the East, and one of black for Knight of the Eagle. The brethren wear a girdle of water colored silk, embroidered with gold fringe, sprinkled with 'death heads' and 'cross bones,' and in the middle a representation, in gold, of a bridge, on which are the letters, L. D. P.* The Master and officers wear their jewels suspended from the neck, and the brethren from the bottom of the cordon. The jewel of the Master is a triple triangle enclosed in a circle. The Senior Warden wears a 'square,' and the Junior Warden, a 'level,' within the triple triangle. The other officers wear the usual jewel in a triple triangle. The brethren wear the triple triangle, crossed by two swords, the hilts resting on the level. The jewels are of gold; each brother has a trowel suspended from the string of his apron.

Preparation.—The candidate is to be clothed as a Maitre Ecossois; his hands bound with a chain, whose links are triangular. This chain must be so long that he may use his hands. He is informed that he represents Zerubbabel, and is to assume the air of a captive. He is unarmed, and puts his hands over his face, at the door of the tower, where the guards search him (for weapons,) before he is admitted.

Opening.—Sovereign. 'My brethren, assist me to open a lodge of Knights of the sword.'† The Generals repeat this. The Sovereign knocks seven, (! ! ! ! ! ! !) The Generals repeat this. Sov. 'Senior General, see if we are well guarded, and it we are all Knights of the Sword.' The General obeys, and says, 'Sovereign Master, we are well guarded from the view of the profane, and are all Knights of the Sword.' Sov. 'What is the time?' Senior General. 'This day completes the seventy years of captivity.' Sov. 'Generals, Princes, and Knights, I have long since resolved to liberate the Jews who are in captivity: I am wearied with seeing them in chains; but before I liberate them I wish to consult you respecting a dream which I have had this night, and which requires an interpretation. I imagined I saw a ferocious lion about to throw himself on me and devour me—his appearance terrified me, and I hastily looked for some shelter from his fury; but at that instant I saw my two predecessors, habited as slaves, beneath a glory, which Masons designate by the name of the Grand Architect of the universe. I was made to understand two words which I saw issuing from a blazing star: they signified '*Liberate the captives;*' and I understood if I did not do this my crown would pass from me to strangers. I remained speechless and confused, and suddenly awoke. From that instant my tranquillity fled. It remains for you Princes to assist me with your advice on this occasion.'

---

* Liberte de passer.
† This degree is called 'Knight of the Sword,' and 'Knight of the Eagle,' as well as 'Knight of the East.'

During this relation the brethren look downwards, but when it is ended they look at the Senior General, and imitate him. The Senior General draws his sword, elevates the point, his arm being extended before him. He then points it down, to signify his agreement in the opinion of the Sovereign; he then directs its point upwards, to signify liberty, and remains in that position. Sov. 'Let the captivity be finished; Generals, Princes, and Knights, this lodge of Knights of the Sword is open.' The Generals, each in his place, repeat these words.

Reception.—The Master of Ceremonies leads the candidate to the door of the tower, where he is thus interrogated by the guards. Gen. 'What do you wish?' Can. 'I wish, if possible, to speak with your Sovereign.' Gen. 'Who are you?' Can. 'The first among my equals, by rank a Mason, by misfortune a captive.' Gen. 'What is your name?' Can. 'Zerubbabel.' Gen. 'What is your age?' Can. 'Seventy years.' Gen. 'What is the cause of this application?' Can. 'The tears and misery of my brethren.' Gen. 'We will endeavor to make your request known to the Sovereign.' The guard knocks (! ! ! ! ! ! !) at the door of the tower. This alarm is repeated; one by the Junior General, two by the Senior General, and three by the Sovereign. The Junior General says, 'The guard knocks at the door of the tower, in the manner of a Knight of the Sword.' S. Gen. 'Sovereign Master, the guard knocks,' &c. Sovereign says, 'Senior General, some one is to be introduced. Be prudent.' ———— 'In my present embarrassed state the least advice is not to be disregarded.' The Junior General goes to the door of the tower, knocks, and it is opened. The guard lays aside his spear, comes before the Sovereign, crosses his arms, bows, and says, 'The first among Masons, his equals, aged seventy years, wishes to appear before you.' Sov. 'When he shall have been introduced into the tower of the palace, we will examine him.' The guard bows, retires, and makes the candidate enter the tower, which is closed on him. The Sovereign questions the candidate through the door, which is shut. Sov. 'What is the cause of this application?' Can. 'I come to implore the justice and benevolence of the Sovereign.' Sov. 'For what purpose?' Can. 'That mercy may be shown to my brethren, who have been in captivity seventy years!' Sov. 'What is your name?' Can. 'Zerubbabel; the first among my equals, by rank a Mason, by misfortune a captive.' Sov. 'What is that mercy which you demand of me?' Can. 'That, under the protection of the Grand Architect of the universe, the king will restore our liberty and allow us to return and rebuild the temple of our God.' Sov.

' Since motives so just have conducted you hither, you are permitted to appear in our presence.' The guards open the door of the tower, and cause the captive to prostrate himself in the west. (done.) Sov. ' Zerubbabel, I have, like you, lamented the severity of your captivity. I promise to grant you liberty instantly, if you will communicate to me the secrets of Masonry, for which I have always entertained the greatest veneration.' Can. ' Sovereign Master, when Solomon communicated to us the first principles of Masonry, he informed us that equality was its foundation. Equality does not reign here; and your rank, your titles, and your court, are not admissible in the place where instruction is given in our mysteries. Besides, our exterior *marks* are unknown to you; my engagements are inviolable; I am unable to reveal our secrets, and if liberty is to be obtained at this price, I prefer captivity.' Sov. ' I admire the discretion and the virtue of Zerubbabel; he deserves liberty as a reward for his firmness.' The brethren assent, by pointing their swords downwards, and then upwards. Sov. ' Junior General, cause Zerubbabel to undergo the seventy trials, which I reduce to three, viz. 1st. That of the body; 2d. That of his courage; 3d. That of his mind; after which, perhaps, he may merit the favor which he demands.' The Junior General causes him to go round the lodge three times; —the first time, a small ' *shell*' is exploded; the second time, he is examined to ascertain whether he persists in his demand; the third time, he holds his hands at the top of his forehead. After this, the Junior General knocks seven, and the Senior General says, 'What do you wish?' J. Gen. ' The candidate has submitted to his trials with firmness and constancy.' Sov. ' Zerubbabel, I grant to you the favor which you solicit, and consent that you shall be set at liberty.' Sovereign knocks seven, which is the signal at which the Generals divest Zerubbabel of his chains. Sov. ' Return to your own country; I permit you to rebuild the temple, destroyed by my ancestors; its treasures shall be sent to you before the setting of the sun; you shall be acknowledged chief over your brethren. I ordain that all shall obey you in the country through which you shall pass; that they shall render you assistance as though it were to myself; I will only exact a tribute from you of three lambs, five sheep, and seven rams, which I will receive under the porch of the new temple; if I demand this, it is rather in remembrance of the friendship which I have promised you, than as a reward. Approach, my friend.' The Generals place him at the foot of the throne. Sov. ' I arm you with this sword, as a mark of your superiority over your equals; I am persuaded you will employ it only in their defence, and I create you a 'Knight of the Sword.'' In saying these last words, the Sovereign strikes with his sword on the shoulders, and then raises him. He gives the candidate the apron, and green cordon, which passes from left to right, and says, 'As a mark of my esteem, I decorate you with an apron and sash, which I have adopted in imitation of the workmen of your temple. Though these decorations are not accompanied with any mysteries, yet I confer them on the princes of my court as marks of honor; henceforth you enjoy the same honor. I now commit you to the care of Nebuzaradan, who will give you guides to conduct you in safety to your brethren, in the place where you will found the new temple—Thus I decree!' The Senior General leads the candidate and places him in the tower, where he remains while the brethren silently pass into the second apartment. After they are in order, the candidate is led behind the hangings to the bridge. At its entrance he is opposed by guards, who rob him of his apron and sash, and endeavor to prevent his passage; he attacks, drives them off, and arrives at the door of the second apartment. The Master of Ceremonies knocks seven at the door: [Master of Ceremonies accompanies candidate.] When the brethren hear the alarm, they detach the trowel from their aprons, and hold it in the left hand, and the sword in the right. The Junior General knocks seven. This is repeated by Senior General. Junior General. 'I hear a knocking at the door of the lodge, in the manner of Knights of the Sword.' Senior General. 'Most Excellent Master, some one knocks at the door of the lodge, in the manner of Knights of the Sword.' Master. 'Most Powerful brother Junior Warden, see who knocks.' The Junior Warden goes, knocks, and opening the door, says, 'What do you wish?' Candidate. 'I wish to see my brethren, that I may inform them of my deliverance from Babylon, and that of the unhappy remnant of the fraternity, which has been freed from captivity.' Junior Warden shuts the door and reports to Master. Master says, 'The news which the captive brings is true. The seventy years are expired, and the day has arrived for rebuilding the temple. Ask the captive his name, his age, and country, for fear of surprise.' Junior Warden knocks seven, and is answered; he opens the door, and says, 'What is your name?' Can. 'Zerubbabel.' J. W. 'What is your age?' Can. 'Seventy years.' J. W. 'Where is your country?' Can. 'On this side of the river Staburzania, to the west of Assyria.' Junior Warden shuts the door, reports to Senior Warden, who reports to the Master. Master says, 'His name is Zerubbabel, his country lies on this side of the river Staburzania, his age seventy years; yes, my

D d

brethren, the captivity is ended! The captive is truly the Prince of the sovereign tribe which is to rebuild the temple. Let him be admitted among us and acknowledged as the one who is to direct and assist our labors.' Junior Warden knocks, opens the door, and conducts the captive to the west. S. W. 'Most Excellent Master, behold Zerubbabel, who demands to be admitted into the bosom of our fraternity!' M. 'Zerubbabel, give us an exact relation of your deliverance!' Can. 'Cyrus gave me permission to approach the foot of his throne, he was touched with the miseries of the fraternity, he armed me with this sword, for the defence of my brethren, and honored me with the title of brother among his companions. He finally granted me my freedom, and committed me to the care of his faithful subjects, who conducted me on my journey, and assisted me in conquering our enemies at the passage of the river Staburzania, where, notwithstanding our victory, we lost the marks of distinction, which had been given to us by the king, our deliverer.' M. 'My brother, the loss which you have met with shows that the justice of our fraternity would not endure the triumph of pomp and grandeur. In decorating you with these honors, Cyrus was not guided by that spirit of equality, which has always characterized you. By this loss, all the marks of distinction received from that prince have disappeared, but you have preserved those of true Masonry; but before I can communicate to you those secrets, which, since our captivity have been preserved among the remnant of our fraternity, we must require of you assurances that you have not lost the sentiments, or the knowledge of Masonry, during your servitude.' Can. 'Examine me; I am prepared to answer.' M. 'What degree have you received in Masonry?' Can. 'That of Most Excellent Master.' M. 'Give me the signs.' (Given.) M. 'Give me the grip.' (Given.) M. 'My brethren Knights, I believe Zerubbabel is worthy to participate in our new mysteries.' The brethren assent by elevating their swords. M. 'Most Powerful Senior Warden cause the candidate to advance by three steps; and at the third, let him kneel at the foot of the throne of the Grand and Sublime Architect, where he will make the engagements which we require.'

Obligation.—I promise, under the same obligations which I have contracted in the different degrees of Masonry, never to reveal the secrets of the 'Knights of the Sword,' or Free Masons, to any one of an inferior degree, or to any one who is not a Mason, under the penalty of enduring a captivity so rigorous that my chains shall never be broken, and that my body be exposed to the beasts of the forest, and that a thunderbolt may dash me to atoms, as an example to others who are indiscreet. So mote it be.

The Master raises the candidate, and (while he and the brethren are sheathing their swords) says, ' My brethren, the destruction of the temple subjected Masons to such severe calamities, we have feared lest their captivity and dispersion might have impaired their fidelity to their engagements ; for this reason, we have been obliged, while rebuilding the temple, to remain in a secret and retired place, where we carefully preserve some ruins of the ancient temple. We do not introduce any to that place, unless we know them to be true and worthy Masons, not alone by their signs, words, and grips, but also by their conduct ; to such we communicate our new secrets with pleasure, but we require, as a pledge, that they should bring with them some remains or monuments of the ancient temple ; those which Cyrus has given to you are sufficient.' (While these last words are pronounced, the captive is uncovered.) M. ' Most powerful Senior Warden, cause the candidate to recede three steps, that he may learn that we esteem perfect resignation as a masonic virtue.' Candidate stands in the west, and Master says, ' My brother, the object of our labors is to rebuild the temple of the Grand Architect of the universe ; this sublime work has been reserved for Zerubbabel. The engagements into which you with us have entered under that name, require you to aid us in rebuilding the temple in its splendor. The sword which Cyrus has given you, is to be used in defending your brethren, and punishing those who would profane the august temple which we raise to the glory of the Holy One of Israel. It is on these conditions you participate in our secrets.' The pass word is * *. Go give the brethren of this lodge the signs, grips, and words, and return to me.' He goes by the north, and returns by the south. M. ' My brother, after your deliverance Cyrus had you created a Masonic Knight, and I now present you with the trowel, the symbol of your new dignity, that hereafter you may labor with the trowel in one hand, and use the sword with the other, if the temple should ever be destroyed, for it is in that manner we have proceeded to rebuild it.' (Master gives the girdle, and says,) ' This scarf ought always to accompany you in all lodges ; you will have a mark of true Knighthood, which you acquired at the river Staburzania, by the victory obtained over those who opposed your passage !' (Gives the green rosette, saying) ' Though we do not admit among our ceremonies any of the decorations given you by Cyrus, yet we are willing to preserve their remembrance by a rosette of that color, which he had chosen, and we affix it to your cordon.' (Gives the jewel.) ' This jewel is a badge of the Knights of the Sword; may justice and equity, represented by the sword, be your guides!' (Gives the gloves.) 'We proceed to proclaim you a Knight of the Sword. My brethren, see that Zerubbabel shall hereafter rule the labors of Masonry!' They assent by saluting with swords. Candidate is then conducted to a chair designed for him, the Master saying 'My brother ascend the throne of the Sovereigns of our lodges; preserve the triangular stone of this edifice, and rule the laborers as Solomon, Hiram of Tyre, and Joabert have done before you!' When the candidate is seated the brethren sheath their swords, clap their hands three times, crying Zerubbabel each time, and then commence the

LECTURE.

Master. Brother Senior Warden, how did you arrive at the eminent dignity of the Knights of the Sword? S. W. By humility, patience, and frequent solicitations. M. To whom did you apply? S. W. To the great king. M. What is your name? S. W. Zerubbabel. M. What is your country? S. W. Judea; I was born of noble parents, of the tribe of Judah. M. What art do you profess? S. W. Masonry. M. What buildings have you erected? S. W. Temples and tabernacles. M. Where have you constructed them? S. W. For want of ground, we build them in our hearts. M. What is the name of a Masonic Knight? S. W. A Mason, perfectly free. M. Why perfectly free? S. W. Because the Masons selected by Solomon for the work of the temple, were for themselves and their descendants, declared free from all tributes. They also possessed the privilege of carrying arms. When the temple was destroyed by Nebuchadnezzar, they were led captive with the rest of the Jews; but king Cyrus kindly gave them permission to build the second temple, under Zerubbabel, and declared them free; since that epoch we bear the name of Free Masons. M. Was the ancient temple distinguished for its beauty? S. W. It was the first edifice in the world for its richness and grandeur. The court would contain two hundred thousand persons. M. Who was the principal Architect of this building? S. W. GOD was the first, Solomon the second, and Hiram the third. M. Who laid the first stone? S. W. Solomon. M. At what hour? S. W. Before the rising of the sun. M. Why at that hour? S. W. To teach us that in the service of the Grand Architect of the universe, we should exercise vigilance. M. What cement was employed? S. W. A mystic cement composed of flour, of milk, of oil, and of wine. M. Explain the mystic signification of this. S. W. In forming the first man, GOD employed his kindness, his wisdom, his power, and his benevolence. M. Where was the first stone of the temple placed? S. W. In the middle of the chamber designed for the sanctuary. M. How many gates had the ancient temple? S. W. Three; one at the east, one at the south, and one at the north. M. How long did that temple stand? S. W. Four hundred and seventy years, six months, and ten days. M. Under what king of Israel was it destroyed? S. W. Zedekiah, the last of the family of David. M. What is signified by the column Boaz, which you see broken? S. W. The confusion and injury arising from the reception of an unworthy Mason. M. Why is the number 81 held in veneration among Masons? S. W. That number is symbolic of the three persons of the Divine Being, represented by the triple triangle, by the square of nine, and the number three. M. Why were the chains of the Jewish captives of a triangular form? S. W. The Chaldeans knew that the triangle was, with the Jewish Masons, an emblem of the name of GOD; they therefore made their chains of that form to inflict greater pain upon the captives. M. Why were Masons forbidden to work in erecting profane edifices? S. W. To make us remember that we are not to frequent irregular lodges. M. What was the plan given by Cyrus, for the new temple? S. W. One hundred cubits in length, sixty in breadth, and sixty in height. M. Why did Cyrus order timber to be cut, in the forest of Lebanon, and stones to be taken from the quarries of Tyre, for the construction of the new temple? S. W. Because it was necessary that the second temple should be entirely like the first. M. Give me the name of the principal architect of the second temple. S. W. 'Bibot.' M. Why do the workmen carry a sword when they labor? S. W. Because, while they wrought with one hand in bringing materials for building the temple, being subject to invasion from their enemies, they held their swords in the other to defend their labors and their brethren. M. Why is this lodge enlightened by seventy tapers? S. W. In memory of the seventy years of the Babylonish captivity. M. Are you a Knight of the Sword? S. W. Look! (places his hand on his sword.) M. Give me the sign. (Gives the second sign.) M. Give me the words and the pass word. S. W. 'Judah,' 'Benjamin,' and 'Libertas.' M. Give the grip to the Junior Warden. (Given.) M. Where have you labored? S. W. At the rebuilding of the temple. M. What hour is it? S. W. The hour of commencing that work. M. My brethren, since we have sufficient time to rebuild the temple of the LORD, let us remember these things in silence. It is time to repose.—Brothers Senior Warden and Junior Warden,

D d 2

announce in the south and in the north, that I am about to close this lodge of Knights of the Sword.' It is announced. Master knocks seven, and the two Wardens repeat.

M. 'The lodge is closed; retire in peace.' The Wardens repeat this, and the lodge is closed.

[N. B. The letters on the girdle, L. D. P.; Liberte de passer.]

'LE CHEVALIER ROSE CROIX.'*

Titles and jewels.—The lodge is called '*Sovereign Chapter;*' The Master, '*Most Wise;*' Senior Warden, '*Most Respectable first Knight Warden;*' Junior Warden, '*Most respectable second Knight Warden;*' the other officers are called, '*Most Respectable.*'

The jewel is a kind of quadrant, formed by a compass and a quarter circle. In the middle is a cross, on which is a rose, and at the foot a pelican feeding its young with blood. The jewel is suspended from the neck, or from right to left, by a red watered ribbon. This jewel is worn in all lodges, except in that called 'the first point of the Red Cross,' where the ribbon is black.

Observations on the degree.—Though this lodge is the '*Ne plus ultra*' of Masonry, and when one has received it he has a right to assist in all others without being subjected to an examination, yet he ought to attend lodges which are free from all suspicion, as such will only admit those who are well known and vouched for. It is necessary for receiving this degree, to have taken those of the 'Elu,' the 'Ecossois,' and the 'Knight of the East.' There are three points, or parts in this degree; two for reception, and the third called the 'Mystic Sacrament,' which is only used at quarterly communications, or on festivals.

Lodge room—Is hung with red. In the east, in place of a throne, is a triangular altar, one side of which faces the west. This is elevated on seven steps. On this is placed a transparency, representing 'Calvary.' The two side crosses are plain, but that in the middle has a rose and drapery interlaced and above the letters I. N. R. I. Below, before the transparency, are broken columns, on the ruins of which guards are sleeping; and in their midst is seen a tomb, the stone of which is removed, and at its mouth grave clothes are seen. There are three triangular tables, with a light on each. One is placed at the right of the

---

* Knights of the Rose Cross.

altar in the east at the foot of the steps. The two others facing each other in the west. All this decoration in necessary whenever a Chapter is opened. But the time of reception the lodge is hung with black, &c. No furniture is used except that in 'the second point;' except three triangular columns, placed east, west, and south, with a transparent inscription on each; that is in the east, 'Faith;' in the south, 'Hope;' and in the west, 'Charity.' Two preparation rooms are necessary, one containing a table and chair, the other is entirely dark.

Opening. The 'Most Wise' is seated on the third step of the altar, his head leaning on one hand; he knocks four (!! !!) on the triangular table near him, and says, 'Most Respectable first and second Knight Wardens, what is the hour? S. W. The first hour of the day. M. It is time to commence our labors, Most Respectable first and second Knight Wardens; request our respectable Knights to assist me in opening this 'Sovereign Chapter of Rose Croix.' They obey. M. 'Most Respectable first and second Knights Wardens, are all the Knights in order?' (The Knights are uncovered, and ranged in two columns.) S. W. 'They are, Most Wise.' M. 'My brethren, I am overwhelmed with distress, all is changed, the veil of the temple is rent, the columns of Masonry are broken, the cubic stone is sprinkled with blood, the word is lost, and 'consummatum est.'' Most Respectable first and second Knight Wardens, examine each of your columns, and see if by the aid of these Knights some remedy for our distress may not be found, and report to me.' The Wardens go one to the north column and one to the south, and in a whisper demand the word of each Knight. It is given in a whisper without any sign; they begin with the west wing of each column, and proceeding eastward, give the word to the Master. They return to their places, and Master says, 'Most respectable first knight Warden, now the word is discovered, what remains for us to do?' S. W. 'Most Wise, to respect the decrees of the Most High, to render homage to the Supreme Architect, and always to humble ourselves before him, who is able to reinstamp his image upon us!' M. 'Respectable Knights, you see the object of our labors: my brethren, let us bend our knees before him who has given us our existence!' All rise; each one faces the east, makes the sign, bows and kneels on one knee, afterwards the Master and all rise. Master and all clap hands seven times, saying three times 'Amlu.' M. 'Respectable Knights, the Sovereign Chapter is open.' The Wardens repeat this.

Reception.—While in the press room, the candidate writes his name, profession, and the names of the degrees which he has received; and also states that his age is thirty-three years. The Master of Ceremonies leads him to the lodge door, and gives the alarm of a Knight of the East. The Grand Marshall within answers it by that of the Rose Cross, and informs the Junior Warden that an alarm is heard at the door of the Sovereign Chapter. The Junior Warden repeats it to the Senior Warden, who reports to the Master. The Master orders the Junior Warden to see who knocks, when the report is made. The Master puts the question as to the admission of Candidate. The brethren assent by clapping hands seven times, and crying 'Houze,' thrice. After this, Master orders Grand Marshall to admit him. In the mean time the Master of Ceremonies takes from him the decorations of his former degrees, puts a sword by his side, and takes him by the hand. He is introduced, and placed between the two Wardens. (The Master and brethren assume an appearance of sorrow.) The two Wardens knock, and Master answers it. S. W. 'Most Wise, you behold a worthy Knight of the East, who presents himself before the Sovereign Chapter, that he may obtain the favor of being admitted to the most sublime degree of 'Rose Cross!' M. 'Worthy Knight, who are you?' Can. 'I am descended from noble parents, of the tribe of Judah.' M. 'What is your country?' Can. 'Judea.' M. 'What art do you profess?' Can. 'Masonry.' M. 'Worthy Knight, you inspire me with esteem, but you see us overwhelmed with sorrow. All is changed, the great support of Masonry is gone, the veil of the temple is rent in twain, the columns are broken, the most precious ornaments are removed, and the word is lost, and we have no other hope of recovering it, than what rests on your courage. Will you employ it to aid us?' Can. 'I will.' M. 'Will you give us an assurance by taking an obligation that you will keep all our mysteries profoundly secret?' Can. 'I will.' Candidate kneels on one knee at the triangular table, near the Master, right hand on the Bible—a sword and compass are laid on the same hand.

Obligation.—' In the presence of these Respectable Knights, I swear and promise on my word as an honest man and Mason, that I will not reveal any of the secrets of this degree of Rose Cross, under the penalty of being dishonored and banished from all lodges, as unworthy to associate with virtuous Masons. I pray God to keep me steadfast. Master raises candidate, and says, ' My brother, you understand the importance of your obligation, it remains for you to travel a dangerous journey. The brother Knight Master of Ceremonies will make you know how you are to conduct yourself. Brother Knight Master of Ceremonies, show this worthy Knight the means by which the word may be recovered.' The Master of Ceremonies causes the candidate to walk round the Chapter, showing him successively the columns of 'Faith,' 'Hope,' and 'Charity.' After this the Master of Ceremonies apprises the Master through the Wardens, that the candidate has been properly instructed. M. 'Worthy Knight, remember what you have learned, and recollect we await your return with anxiety. May you be prospered and restore peace and happiness to our minds!' The Master of Ceremonies leads out the candidate, and conducts him to the dark room, and makes him go round it seven times. In the mean time the black drapery of the lodge (which covers the red) is removed, and the decorations appear. Master of Ceremonies brings candidate to the door of the Chapter, gives the alarm as before; he enters, and is thus questioned by the Master.

Master. 'My brother, from whence do you come?' Candidate. 'From the land of Judea.' M. 'Through what place have you passed?' Can. 'Nazareth.' M. 'Who conducted you?' Can. 'Raphael.' M. 'Of what tribe are you?' Can. 'Of the tribe of Judah.' M. 'Pronounce the initial letters of these four words,' (above the cross, 'Jesus Nazaremus Rex Judacorum.') M. 'What word do they form?' Can. 'I. N. R. I.' M. 'My dear brother, this is the inscription which you see above the cross, it is the word which we had lost, and which your zeal has recovered. Approach the foot of this altar and receive the reward due to you.' Candidate kneels, and the Master, laying his naked sword on his head, says, 'In virtue of the power which I have received from the Grand Lodge of Heroden, before this august assembly of Knights, my brethren, my equals, I admit, receive, and constitute you, now and from henceforth, a Knight and Prince of the Eagle and Pelican, Perfect Free Mason of Heroden, under the title of Sovereign of the Rose Cross, to enjoy the titles and prerogatives of '*Princes of Perfect Masons*,' wherever they are, with power to hold a lodge in lodges regularly assembled, and to confer the different degrees.'

Master raises candidate and gives him the cordon, word, sign, and grip. The word '*Inri*,' is given by lettering it. The sign is to cross arms on the breast, and incline the body as if to kneel on one knee. *Grip*. The two brethren mutually place the right hand on each other's right shoulders, and the left hand on the left shoulder, the arms crossing and interlaced; one says 'Emanuel,' the other 'Pax vobiscum.' (Peace be with you.) The candidate gives the *sign*, *grip*, and *word* to the Wardens; he is then placed in the south, where he makes an offering of mercy, for the use of the poor brethren, and then hears the lecture.

LECTURE.

M. Most respectable Knight Wardens, whence do you come? S. W. Most Wise, from Judea. M. Through what place have you passed? S. W. Through Nazareth. M. Who conducted you? S. W. Raphel. M. Of what tribe are you? S. W. Of the tribe of Judah. M. Pronounce the initial letters of those four words. S. W. Most Wise, I cannot do it without your assistance. M.—'I.' S. W.—'N.' M.—'R.' S. W.—'I.' M. What do those letters spell? S. W. 'Inri,' the sealed word of the Knights of the Rose Cross. M. How were you admitted to this degree? S. W. By the three theological virtues, Faith, Hope, and Charity. M. What can you give besides the word? S. W. A sign and a token. M. Give me the sign; (Given.) M. Give the token to one of our Respectable Knights; (Given.) M. Do you know the 'Pelican?' S. W. I do. M. What does it signify? S. W. Among us it is a symbol of the Saviour of the world, and of his perfect humanity.* M. What is the object of the degree of Knights of the Rose Cross. S. W. To lead us to respect the decrees of the Most High, to render homage to the Supreme Architect, and always to humble us before him who is able to reinstamp his image on us. M. My brother Knight, that is the object of every true Mason. My brethren, let us kneel before him who has given us existence. Knights kneel and rise as in opening.

Close.—Master. 'Most Respectable first Knight Warden, what is the hour?' S. W. 'The last hour of the day.' M. 'If it is so, Most Respectable first and second Knight Wardens, inform our brother Knights that it is time to close this Sovereign Chapter, and to retire in peace.'

The Wardens give notice. Master knocks seven; this is repeated by the Wardens. All rise and face the Master, who gives the sign; they do the same. All clap hands seven times, and cry 'Houze,' thrice. M. 'Most Respectable first and second Knight Wardens, the Sovereign Chapter is closed!'

[N. B. The *instant* when the Sovereign Chapter is hung with black, for a reception, is called the 'first point,' the *instant* when the decoration is changed or hung with red, is the 'second point,' of this degree.]

Third point of Rose Cross.—It is after having held a Chapter, as above described, that this ceremony is practical. On occasions

---

* Why do they not also admit his perfect Divinity.

when this is to be done, the Master does not close the Chapter, but only suspends the demand of 'What is the hour?' The decorations in the same state. A table covered with white, on which is a loaf, and a cup of wine, stands in the middle of the room. On the table is placed a small paper, on which is 'I. N. R. I.' Each Knight holds a staff in his hand. They are ranged in two lines from north to south; the Wardens are at the head and the Master between them. Master knocks and gives notice that the Chapter resumes its power; the Wardens repeat this. The Master, followed by the rest, passes seven times around the lodge, and then stops, facing the east, and makes the sign; he breaks a small piece from the loaf and gives it to the Senior Warden at his right hand, who breaks a piece and passes it to his brother at the right hand, and in this manner it is passed on until it reaches, at last, the Junior Warden, who eats it. The Master takes the wine, drinks, and passes it as he did the bread. Senior Warden turns to the Master, who gives him the token, saying 'Emanuel.' The Senior Warden replies 'Pax vobiscum.' When the cup has reached the Junior Warden he gives it and the token to the Master. The Master shows the brethren that nothing remains in the cup. He advances to the table, takes the paper, sets it on fire, and casts it into the cup, where it is consumed;* he makes the sign, and says, 'Consummatum est:' (It is finished.) After this, all the Knights repeat the sign, and the Chapter is closed as before described.

* Let the friend of Jesus read this again, and then answer the question, 'Can you fellowship Masonry?'

THE DEGREE OF "NOACHITE."

OR

"CHEVALIER PRUSSIEN."*

Origin and dignities.—The Grand Master, General of the order, whose title is 'Chevalier Grand Commander,' is Frederic William, King of Prussia. His ancestors, for three hundred years, have been protectors, of this order. The Knights were formerly known by the name of 'Noachites,' or descendants of Noah. By the Pagans they were called the 'Titans,' who were said to have attempted to scale the heavens for the purpose of dethroning

* Prussian Knight.

Jupiter. But the Prussians, who acknowledge no other GOD but the Supreme Architect of the universe, each year, on the night of the full moon of the month, March, celebrate the confusion of languages and the dispersion of the builders of the tower of Babel, one of the miracles of the Creator. That time is the anniversary of that day of his vengeance.

It is for this reason, these Knights assemble on the night of the full moon, in a secret place, to hold their lodges; and they cannot initiate a candidate into the mysteries of this degree unless by the light of the moon.

The Master of the lodge is called 'Chevalier Lieutenant Grand Commander;' the officers are a Deputy Lieutenant Grand Commander, Chevalier Master of Ceremonies, Chevalier of Eloquence, (orator,) Chevalier of the guard, Chevalier Chancellor, Chevalier of the Finances. The title, Chevalier Prussian Mason, is given to ordinary Masons. The three officers, viz. 1st. Lieutenant Grand Commander, 2nd. Deputy Grand Commander, and 3rd. Master of Ceremonies, must always be present when a lodge is opened.

The 'Noachites' now called 'Prussian Chevaliers,' are descended from 'Peleg,' the Grand Architect of the tower of Babel, their origin being much more ancient than that of the Masons descended from Hiram. In the time of the crusades, when the different orders of European Knighthood were established by the Christain Princes leagued for the conquest of Palestine, the Masons descended from Hiram through their respect for the 'Noachites,' who were in high esteem, wished to be made acquainted with their mysteries. The Prussian Chevaliers were persuaded none could be found to whom they could more properly confide their mysteries than to these descendants of Hiram. Since that period the 'Noachites' always require, therefore, that their candidates should be Masters of the Order of Hiram. In the statutes of this order, preserved among the archives of the king of Prussia, it is expressly forbidden to any Prussian Chevalier, to receive any candidate, unless he has given proofs of his zeal and capacity in the order of Masters descended from Hiram. It is also necessary that he should prove that he has discharged the duties of an office in some regular lodge.

Disposition of the lodge. —The Commander is placed opposite to the moon; the next four officers before him, that they may better attend to his orders. They have no fixed place, as a sign that a Chevalier has renounced pride and glories in the practice of humility, at all times. The room is enlightened by a large window, so made as to receive a feeble light from the moon. According to the statutes of the order, it is forbidden that the lodge should be enlightened by the rays of the sun, or those of any artificial light.

Opening.—Commander knocks *three* gentle blows, at equal distances. The Deputy Commander answers by a single blow on the hilt of his sword. Com. ' Order, Chevaliers !' He lifts his arms extended towards heaven, his face turned to the east, where the moon appears. The others do the same, and the Commander, after asking some questions from the lecture, says to the Deputy Commander, ' Announce to all the Chevaliers that the lodge is enlightened.' This is done, and all resume their natural attitudes. The Chevaliers remain looking at the firmament until the candidate arrives.

Reception.—The candidate unarmed, his head uncovered, in his ordinary clothing, has on the white apron and gloves of Master Masons. The Master of Ceremonies, who is with him, gives three light blows, at equal distances, at the door. The Chevalier of the Guard replies by a single blow ; in a whisper repeats the alarm to the Commander, and by his order goes to the door, opens it, and in a whisper demands of the Master of Ceremonies the sign, token, word, and pass word. He then closes the door, and whispers his report to the Deputy Commander, saying, ' The Chevalier Master of Ceremonies has answered well and demands to enter.' The Deputy Commander repeats this aloud to the Commander, who orders him to tell the Master of Ceremonies he may enter if he is alone. Deputy Commander. ' He is accompanied by a Master descended from Hiram, who has on a ' white apron,' and ' white gloves.' ' Com. ' In this case inquire of the Master of Ceremonies, what this Mason, descended from Hiram, wants.' Deputy Commander goes to the door, knocks one, which Master of Ceremonies answers by three light, equal blows. The Chevalier of the Guard opens it, and the Deputy Commander says to the Master of Ceremonies, ' What is your desire?' M. of C. ' Here is a Master descended from Hiram, who wishes, if it is according to the pleasure of the Chevalier Lieutenant Commander, to be received a Prussian Chevalier.' Deputy Commander reports this to the Commander, who orders him to let the Master enter, after he has given the Master's pass word. When this is given, the Master of Ceremonies leads the candidate into the lodge, and causes him to go to the other door, within the lodge, by three Master's steps. Com. ' Chevalier Master of Ceremonies, will you vouch for the Master whom you present to me ?' M. of C. ' I vouch for him that he is a Master descended from Hiram.' The Commander quits his place, goes to the Candidate, and demands the Master's word ; it is given as

E e

usual. Com. 'Chevaliers, I announce to you a Master Mason descended from Hiram, who wishes to be received a 'Chevalier Prussian,' do you consent?' The brethren, without saying a word, draw their swords, and present their points to the body of the candidate. Through the Master of Ceremonies, he replies, 'I continue my request, if it shall be according to the pleasure of the Chevalier Lieutenant Commander, and the Chevaliers of this lodge.' Com. 'These brave Chevaliers, with me, consent to your request, provided you renounce all pride for the remainder of your life. Commence, then, by performing an act of humiliation.' The Master of Ceremonies and Deputy Commander conduct the candidate to the feet of the Commander, by three genefluctions of the left knee; having arrived there, he prostrates himself before the Commander, who orders him to kiss the hilt of his sword. The Chevalier of Eloquence pronounces a discourse on the pride of the sons of Noah, and upon the humility of him who was sensible of his fault. (Peleg.) During all this the candidate is kneeling on one knee. He rises, and the Commander and all the brethren, with their swords, give the sign of a Master Mason. Commander says to candidate, 'Do you promise on the faith of a Master Mason descended from Hiram, to keep the secrets which I shall confide to you under these three conditions:—1st. That you will never reveal any of our mysteries to any descendant of Adam, unless you know him to be a Mason; 2nd. That you will be obliging and kind to the charities of this order; 3rd. That you will suffer no one, even at the hazard of your life, to wear the jewel of our order, unless he shall have made himself known to you as a 'Chevalier Prussian.'' Candidate says, I swear and engage under these conditions!'

Commander then gives a history of the order, and at its close says, 'You see, Chevalier, the grand secret of our order, which is unknown to all but Chevaliers. I confer it on you with pleasure; but wo to you should you violate your engagements! Be circumspect, and on every occasion practice humility after the example of our Grand Architect.' The brethren sheath swords, and the Commander gives one to the candidate, and fastens to the third buttonhole of his vest, with a black ribbon, the jewel, which is of silver, and orders him to lay aside the decorations of a Master descended from Hiram, and he gives him those belonging to this order. He wears the apron like a Fellow Craft. The Master of Ceremonies directs the candidate to offer the gloves to the Commander, who, having received them, gives him the sign, token, word, and pass word, which the candidate gives to each of the brethren on their presenting him with their gloves

It being contrary to the statutes of this order, to hold a Table Lodge, (i. e. one for lecturing and refreshment,) and as the candidate cannot be instructed without the aid of some light, besides that of the moon, the Chevalier Lieutenant Commander, who is the sole depository of the lecture, is authorized to hold a Fellow Craft's table lodge; in which, however, only a frugal collation can be introduced, but no liquors.

Close.—Commander strikes three, which Deputy Commander answers by one blow. Commander. ' Chevaliers Deputy Lieutenant Commander and Master of Ceremonies, give notice to all the Chevaliers present, that the lodge is darkened and it is time to retire!' All the Chevaliers, standing in order, repeat thrice, in a melancholy tone, ' * * * ,' and the lodge is closed.

Dress and jewel.—The apron and gloves are yellow. The jewel is an equilateral triangle, traversed by an arrow pointing downward. It should be of gold, attached to a large black ribbon, passing from the right shoulder to the left, unless one wears it at the button-hole, then it is of silver.

Coat of arms.—1st. Azure, moon of silver, and golden stars. 2nd. Sable, triangle, and arrow of gold.

LECTURE.

Question. Who are you? Answer. Inform me who you are, and I will tell you who I am. Q. Do you know the sons of Noah? A. I know three. Q. Who are they? A. Shem, Ham, and Japhet. Q. What do these names signify? A. The initial letters are the sacred word. Q. Give me the token. A. Behold! (embracing three times.) Q. Give me the sign. A. I will. (Given.) Q. Give me the pass word. A. ' * * * ,' Q. Do you know the Grand Architect of the tower of Babel? A. His name was ' Peleg.' Q. Who gave you his history? A. The Chevalier Lieutenant Commander of Chevaliers Prussian. Q. In what lodge? A. In a lodge where the moon gave light. Q. Was no other light allowed? A. No. Q. Was that edifice a commendable one? A. No; it was impossible to complete it. Q. Why was it impossible to complete it? A. Because pride was its first foundation. Q. Do you remember the sons of Noah to imitate them? A. No; but to avoid their fault, by having it before my eyes. Q. Where does the body of Peleg repose? A. In a tomb. Q. Was he rejected for his guilt? A. No; the agate stone declares that God had mercy on him, because he humbled himself. Q. How were you received a Chevalier Prussian? A. By three genuflections, after I had kissed the sword hilt of the Chevalier Lieutenant Commander. Q. Why were you caused to make these genuflections? A. To make me remember, that during my whole life I ought to practice humility. Q. Why do Chevaliers wear a triangle? A. In memory of the temple of Peleg. Q. Why is the arrow represented as inverted? A. In memory of the ruin which came upon the tower of Babel. The apron and gloves are in memory of the laborers of the tower. The black ribbon is a mark of grief. Q. Did the laborers work day and night? A. Yes; in the day by the light of the sun, and in the night by the light of the moon.

History.—The descendants of Noah, notwithstanding God had appointed the bow in the clouds a sign of the covenant which he had made, that he would not again destroy men by a universal deluge, resolved to build a tower sufficiently elevated to shelter them from the Divine vengeance. They selected for this purpose a plain called Shinar, in Asia. Ten years after they had laid the foundation of this edifice, God, according to the scriptures, cast his eyes upon the earth and saw the pride of the sons of men. He came down to confound their rash designs and their language. It was for this reason the tower was called Babel, which signifies confusion. Some time after, Nimrod, who first established distinctions of rank among men, and arrogated to himself the reverence and worship due to God, built a city called after the tower, Babylon; that is, the 'Court of confusion.' It was on the night of the full moon of March that God wrought this miracle. The Noachites held their grand meeting on the night of the full moon of March. Their ordinary meetings were in all the rest of the months, only however, when the moon was full; no light but that of the moon was admitted in their lodges. After their language was confounded, the workmen, being obliged to separate, each pursued his own course. Peleg, who had suggested the plan of this tower, and had been Grand Architect, was the most culpable. He condemned himself to a rigorous penance. He retired to the north of Germany, where he arrived after having suffered great fatigue and pain in the desert countries through which he passed, where no articles of food could be found except roots and wild fruits.

In that part which is now called Prussia, he constructed some huts to shelter himself from the inclemency of the weather; and he also built a temple in the form of a triangle, where he enclosed himself that he might implore from God the forgiveness of his sin.

In digging in the salt mines of Prussia, in the year 553, there was found among the rubbish, at the depth of fifteen cubits, a triangular foundation of an edifice, in which was a marble column, on which the whole history was inscribed in Hebrew. At the side of this column was a tomb of free-stone, in which was found a quantity of dust—and an agate stone, on which was this epitaph: 'Here repose the ashes of our Grand Architect of the tower of Babel. God showed him mercy because he humbled himself.'

These monuments are in the possession of the king of Prussia. The epitaph does not declare that Peleg was the Architect of the tower of Babel; but the history, which was on the base of the column, informs us that 'Peleg was the son of Eber, whose father, Salah, was the son of Arphaxad, who was the son of Shem, the youngest son of Noah.'

[The Grand Inspectors of the United States of America, issued and published on the 4th day of December, 1802, a circular, from which the following extracts are made.

CIRCULAR

THROUGHOUT THE TWO HEMISPHERES.

Universi terrarum orbis Architectonis per Gloriam Ingentis.

DEUS MEUMQUE JUS.

ORDO AB CHAO.

From the east of the Grand and Supreme Council of the Most Puissant Sovereigns, Grand Inspectors General, under the celestial canopy of the Zenith, which answers to the 32nd degree, 45 minutes N. L.

To our Illustrious, Most Valiant, and Sublime Princes of the Royal Secret, Knights of K———H, Illustrious Princes and Knights, Grand, Ineffable, and Sublime, Free and Accepted Masons of all degrees, ancient and modern, over the two hemispheres.

To all whom these letters shall come:

HEALTH, STABILITY, AND POWER.

At a meeting of Sovereign Grand Inspectors General in Supreme Council of the thirty-third degree, duly and lawfully established and congregated, held at the Grand Council chamber, on the 14th day of the seventh month, called Tisri, 5563, Amno. Lucis, 5802, and of the Christian era the 10th day of October, 1802:

UNION, CONTENTMENT, WISDOM.

The Grand Commander informed the Inspectors that they were convened for the purpose of taking into consideration the propriety of addressing circular letters to the different Symbolic Grand Lodges, and Sublime Grand Lodges and Councils throughout the two hemispheres, explanatory of the sublime degrees of Masonry and their establishment in South Carolina: when a resolution to that effect was immediately adopted, and a committee consisting of the illustrious brethren Dr. Frederick Dalcho, Dr. Isaac Auld, and Emanuel De La Motta, Esq., Grand Inspectors General, was appointed to draft and submit such letter to the Council at their next meeting.

At a meeting of the Sovereign Grand Inspectors General, in Supreme Council of the thirty-third degree, &c. &c. on the 10th day of the eighth month, called Chisleu, 5563, A. L. 5802, and of the Christian era this 4th day of December, 1802, the committee to whom was referred the foregoing resolve, respectfully submitted, &c. &c.

* * * * * * * * *

The names of the Masonic degrees are as follows, viz:

1st degree called Entered Apprentice,
2nd — — Fellow Craft,
3rd — — Master Mason.
} Given in the Symbolic Lodge.

4th — — Secret Master,
5th — — Perfect Master,
6th — — Intimate Secretary,
7th — — Provost and Judge,
8th — — Intendant of the building,
9th — — Elected Knights of Nine.
10th — — Illustrious Elected of Fifteen,
11th — — Sublime Knight Elected.
12th — — Grand Master Architect.
13th — — Royal Arch, [Knights of the Ninth Arch,]
14th — — Perfection.
} Given in the Sublime Grand Lodge.

15th — — Knight of the East,
16th — — Prince of Jerusalem.
} Given by the Princes of Jerusalem, which is a governing council.

LIGHT ON MASONRY. 343

17th — — Knight of the East and West,
18th — — Sovereign Prince of Rose Croix de Heredon,
19th — — Grand Pontiff,
20th — — Grand Master of all Symbolic Lodges,
21st — — Patriarch Noachite, or Chevalier Prussian,
22nd — — Prince of Libanus,
23rd — — Chief of the Tabernacle,
24th — — Prince of the Tabernacle,
25th — — Prince of Mercy,
26th — — Knight of the Brazen Serpent,
27th — — Commander of the Temple,
28th — — Knight of the Sun,
29th — — Knight of St. Andrew,
30th — — K——H, [Holy,]
31st — — Grand Inq. Commander,
32d — — Sublime Prince of the Royal Secret, Prince of Masons,
33d — — Sovereign Grand Inspectors General; Officers appointed for life.

Given by the Council of Grand Inspectors, who are Sovereigns of Masonry.

* * * * * * * * *

Charleston, South Carolina, the 10th day of the eighth month, called Chisleu, 5563, A. L. 5802, and of the Christian era this 4th day of December, 1802.
FREDERICK DALCHO.
K——H, Sovereign Grand Inspector General of the thirty-third, and Lieutenant Grand Commander in the United States of America.
ISAAC AULD.
K——H, P. R. S., Sovereign Grand Inspector General of the thirty-third.
E. DE LA MOTTA.
K——H, Sovereign Grand Inspector General of the thirty-third, and Illustrious Treasurer General of the H. empire.

List of Masonic degrees conferred in France in the year 1796, according to the work entitled ' Maconnerie Adonhiramique.

1st degree called Apprenti - - Apprentice,
2d   —   — Compagnon - Fellow Craft, } Symbolic degrees.
3d   —   — Maitre - - - Master.

[563]

4th	—	—	Maitre Parfaite, - - -	Perfect Master,
5th	—	—	Elu des Neuf, - - -	Elect of Nine,
6th	—	—	Elu de Perignan, - -	Elect of Perignan,
7th	—	—	Petit Architect - - -	Sub Architect,
8th	—	—	Grand Architect - -	Grand Architect,
9th	—	—	Maitre Ecossois, - - -	Scotch Master,
10th	—	—	Chevalier de l'Orient,	Knight of the East,
11th	—	—	Chevalier de Rose Croix,	Knight of the Rose Cross.
12th	—	—	Chevalier Prussien, - -	Prussian Knight,

} Sublime degree.

List of degrees acknowledged and conferred under the sanction of the Grand Orient of France, in the year 1804.

1st degree called Apprenti,
2nd   —   —   Compagnon, } Symbolic degrees.
3rd   —   —   Maitre.
4th   —   —   Elu Secret   - - - -   Secret Elect.
5th   —   —   Grand Elu Ecossois, - Grand Scotch Elect.
6th   —   —   Chevalier de l'Orient, - Knight of the East.
7th   —   —   Rose Croix, - - - -   Rosy Cross.

REMARKS

ON THE SIGNS, WORDS, &c. OF THE

INEFFABLE AND SUBLIME DEGREES.

The note which will be found in page 211 of this work was written at a time when a disclosure of the signs, words, &c. of the ineffable and sublime degrees, was deemed inexpedient. Subsequent reflection has convinced us that a full and satisfactory exhibition of all the secrets of those degrees will enable those who wish for "light," more fully to understand and appreciate the merits or demerits of Masonry. The reader should be apprised that as these degrees are preserved in manuscripts, many of which have been translations from different European languages, and some copies of such translations, a diversity in the words has been gradually introduced. Different Masonic bodies have attempted to correct these mistakes, sometimes with success. Often, however, greater confusion has been the result of attempts at amendment. The signs and words which follow, have the highest claims to correctness and authenticity, of any in existence.

SECRET MASTER.

In addition to the signs, tokens, and words of this degree, as given in page 210, the following words are given in many Lodges of Secret Masters:—JOD, ADONAI, JEVAH. This last word is a contraction of Jehovah.

In page 184, the question, or rather demand, "Give them to me, with their significations," receives the following answer: " A. Jevuh, Adonai, Jehovah, Javha, Jov, Alion, Oheb, Asem, Jesays."

In page 186, the demand, "Give the pass word," is to be answered, " Zizon," or according to some, " Ziza."

PERFECT MASTER.

Instead of the word "*Jeva*," given in page 210, some Lodges use the word "*Jehovah*," and, as a pass-word, "*Acacia.*"

INTIMATE SECRETARY.

In page 191, the question, "What are the pass-words?" is to be answered "*Joabert*" and "*Zerbal.*" In some Lodges, "*Jehaoben,*" and "*Shereb-Jah,*" are used as pass-words.

The question in the same page, "What is the grand word?" is to be answered, "*Jova,*" or in some Lodges, "*Jevah* or *Ivah,*" a contraction of the word "*Jehovah.*"

In the same page, the question, "What doth the letter (I.) signify, which you saw in the window?" is to be answered, "*Jova.*"

The question, "What is signified by *A*. and two *P's*. in the angle?" is to be answered, "Alliance, Promise, Perfection."

NOTE.—These three words form the translation of the words given in the grip "*Berith, Neder, Shelemoth*" See page 211.

PROVOST AND JUDGE.

The reader will turn to page 193, and fill the blank with the following word, viz:—"*Tito.*"

The following are the signs, words, &c. of this degree.

Sign.—Place the two first fingers of the right hand on the side of the nose. The answer to this sign is made by placing the first finger of the right hand on the tip of the nose, and the thumb of the same hand under the chin.

Token.—Lock the little fingers of right hands, and give seven light blows with the thumbs of right hands, on the palms of the same.

Pass-word.—Tito. Ordinary words, Geometros, Xinchen, Ky, Civi, Jova, Hiram, Stokin, Architect. In some Lodges, the following words are used, viz:—Geometros, Xinchen, Yzirie, Ivah, Hiram, Stolkin.

Those who pretend to be best acquainted with Masonic *lore*

adopt the following, viz :—Izrachiah, Jehovah, Hiram, Stolkin, Geometry, Architect.
Sacred word—Jakinai.

INTENDANT OF THE BUILDINGS.

The 1st blank, page 196, is to be filled with the words "*Jakinai, Junaka, Jua.*"

The 2d blank, page 196, is to be filled with the word "*Jakanai.*"

Signs, Words, &c.—First sign, viz. : that of surprise. Place the thumbs on the temples, the hands opened and resting on the forehead, so as to form a square—step backward two paces—step forward two paces—lower the hands till they touch the eyelids, and say, "Benchorim." In some Lodges, the sign of surprise very nearly coincides with one of the same name which is given in the Most Excellent Master's degree.

Second Sign.—That of admiration. Interlace the fingers, turn the palms upward above the head, let the hands fall on the wrist, (being still interlaced,) look upward and say, "Achard," (or Hakar.)

Third Sign.—That of grief, (as given by two at the same time.) Place the right hand on the heart, the left on the left hip, balance thrice with the knees—one says, "*Ky,*" the other replies, "*Jea.*" Instead of these words, the *learned* substitute the words "Chai," and "Jah," (signifying *the* LORD *liveth.*)

Token.—The brethren strike a light blow with the right hand over the heart, pass hands to the middle of the fore-arm, placing left hands on the elbow; this is repeated thrice, one saying *Jakinai*, and the other "*Judah.*"

NOTE.—This token has variations in different Lodges.

Pass-word, "Judah." *Sacred word,* "Jakinai."

ELECTED KNIGHTS OF NINE.

Signs, Words, &c.—The sign given by two is as follows, viz : One raises his poniard and makes the motion of striking the other, first in the head, and then in the heart. The second, claps his right hand first to his heart, and then to his head, as if wounded.

The following method of giving the sign is considered by well instructed Masons, as more correct than the above.

Strike at the forehead with the poniard—the brother will answer by carrying his hands to his forehead, as if to examine the supposed wound, plunge the poniard at the breast, crying "Nekum," (i. e. vengeance)—the brother replies by carrying his hand to his heart, saying, " Necar."

Token.—The first clenches the fingers of his right hand, at the same time elevating and extending his thumb ; the second seizes that thumb with his right hand and extends the thumb of his own hand ; the eight fingers which are thus closed, represent the eight companions of Joabert, and the thumb which is extended, represents Joabert himself.

Pass-word.—In some Lodges, the pass-word is, " Bagulhal," in others, the words " Nekum" and " Joabert" are used, and often " *Abiram* and *Akirop.*"

Sacred words.—In some Lodges, "*Nekum*" and "*Necar*," in others, " *Begalkul.*"

ELECTED GRAND MASTER, OR, ILLUSTRIOUS ELECTED OF FIFTEEN.

Fill blank in page 200 thus :—" *Jubulum Akirop.*"

Signs, Words, &c.—Sign.—Place the point of the poniard under your chin, and draw it downwards to the waist, as if in the act of ripping open the body. The brother will answer by giving the sign of the Entered Apprentice, with the fingers clenched, and thumb extended.

The following mode of giving the sign has been used in some Lodges, viz :

Clench the fingers of the right hand, extend the thumb, place it on the abdomen, move the hand upward to the chin ; the motion of the thumb as it glides upward, is designed to represent that of the knife with which the penalty of this degree is to be executed. The answer is the sign of the Entered Apprentice, the fist being clenched during the motion.

Token.—Give the sign.—One says " Zerbal," the other replies, " Eleham."

Pass-word.—In some Lodges, " Eliham," or " Eleham," in others, " Zerbal."

Sacred words.—In some Lodges, " Zerbal," in some, " Beniah," in some, " Benhakar," or " Bendaka," and in others, " Eleham."

ILLUSTRIOUS KNIGHTS, OR SUBLIME KNIGHTS ELECTED.

Signs, Words, &c.—*Signs.*—Cross the arms on the stomach, the fingers clenched, and thumbs elevated. In addition to this, in some Chapters of this degree, the eyes are raised to heaven in giving the sign.

Token.—That of the Intimate Secretary.—In some Chapters there is a second or responsive token, viz : take the right hand of the brother, and with the thumb strike thrice on the last joint of the middle finger.

Pass-word.—*Stolkin* or *Stokin.* Some Chapters use " *Emerh,*" or more correctly, " *Emeth.*" Others, " *Amariah.*"

Sacred word—" Adonai."

GRAND MASTER ARCHITECT.

Sign.—Slide the right hand into the palm of the left, pause a moment, clench the fingers of the right hand, extend the thumb, and with it make the motion of tracing a plan in the palm of the left, directing your eyes to the brother as if drawing from his dictation. This sign is varied in some Chapters, by using the fore finger in place of the thumb.

Token.—Join right hand to the brother's left, interlacing the fingers, place the left hand on your hip, the brother will do the same with his right hand.

Some give the following token, viz : join right hands, interlacing the three last fingers, and fixing them so as to form a square; place the left hand on your brother's shoulder.

Pass-word.—" Rabacim," or correctly, " Rab-banaim."

Sacred word.—" Adonai."

F f

KNIGHT OF THE NINTH ARCH, OR, MORE CORRECTLY, KNIGHT OF THE ROYAL ARCH.

The table in page 204 is completed, and explained as follows:

3. *Juh.* All Powerful.
3. *Jeo.* Divine light.
3. *Jua.* Striking light.
7. *Adonai.* O thou who art eternal.
7. *Jakinai.* Sustain us, O God.
7. *Jehavah.* God of light.
5. *Havah.* It is what it will be.
5. *Gotha.* God himself.
5. *Jevah.* Eternal God.
9. *Elchannan.* God of Mercy.
9. *Jehaburlum.* My trust is in God.
9. יהוה. The grand name.

The proper *Masonic* pronunciation of this last (יהוה) is not made known to the candidate, until he reaches the degree of perfection. The reader will observe that the figures above given in the table, indicate the number of letters in each word. It is pretended that the above words are Hebrew, and that the English phrases placed against them, (with the exception of the last,) are translations. Let Hebrew scholars determine the point.

Fill the blank in page 204, which follows the words "giving the pass of each," with the words, "Juh, Jeo, Jua, Adonai, Jakinai, Jehavah, Havah, Gotha, Jevah, Elchannan, Jehaburlum."

Signs, Token, and Words.—First sign—That of admiration—raise the hands to heaven, the hand inclined to the left shoulder, one knee touching the ground.

Second sign—That of Adoration—fall on the knees.

Token.—Place your hands beneath the brother's arm-pits as if to raise him up, and at the same time repeat the words "*Tob, Banai, Amalabec.*" The brother returns the token, saying, "*Jubulum*" or "*Gibulum.*" The *Masonic* translation of these words is, "Jubulum (or Gibulum) is a good Mason." Some of the "*knowing ones*" maintain that the words should be "Tub, Bahani, Hamal, Abel," and "Zebulun."

Sacred word—"*Jehovah.*"

Some Chapters of Knights adopt the following Signs, Token, and Words.

First Sign.—Fall on the left knee, with the right hand behind the back. The answer to this, (used as a token,) consists in raising the brother from the posture after the first sign, by placing your hand behind his back.

Words.—"Gibulum Hamaluheek," which is translated, "Gibulum is a good man."

Some Chapters use the following as the pass-words, one of which is to be given at each end, viz:

Jod.—The beginning.
Juho.—Existing.
Juh.—God.
Ehjeh.—I Am.
Elion.—Strong.

Juheb.—Conceding.
Adonai.—Lord.
Elhannan.—Merciful.
Jobel.—Praising.

THE DEGREE OF PERFECTION, OR, GRAND ELECT PERFECT AND SUBLIME MASON.

Fill the blanks on page 206, thus : first, "Mahabon," second, "Eleneham," third, "Fellow-Craft's."

The blanks on pages 207 and 208, may be easily filled by referring to the Signs, Tokens, and Words, of the degrees which have been given in these remarks.

Signs, Tokens, and Words.—*First sign*, that of the Obligation. Place the right hand on the left side of the abdomen, and draw it horizontally across the body, to the right side.

First token.—Join right hands, reverse them thrice ; the first brother says, "Berith ;" the second says, "Neder ;" the first again says, "Shelemoth."

First covered word.—"Jibulum, or Jabulum."

First pass-word.—"Shibboleth."

Second sign.—That of Fire ; (probably in allusion to the burning bush.) Carry the right hand open to the left cheek, the palm outwards, as if to guard the face from the heat ; at the same time grasping the right elbow with the left hand.

Second token.—Give the Master Mason's grip ; one then says, "*Can you go farther ?*" the other slips his hand to the middle of the brother's arm, and then to his elbow, each places his left hand on his brother's right shoulder; they balance thrice, their right legs crossed. (This *attitude* of the legs bears a close resemblance to what wrestlers term, "*the inside lock.*")

Second covered word.—"Mahabin" or "Mahabon."

Second pass-word. "Eleanam" or "Elhanan."

Third sign.—That of admiration and silence. Raise the arms to heaven, the hands opened, the head inclined, the eyes directed upwards ; afterwards place the two first fingers of the right hand upon the lips.

Third token.—Seize your brother's right hand, grasp his right shoulder with your left hand, pass your left hand behind his back, as if to raise or support him.

Third covered word.—" Adonai."
Sacred word.—" Jehovah."
Grand pass-word.—" Mac-maha, Rababack." Some adopt the following words: " Makeh, Meharah, Beha."

The following Signs, Words, &c. are more generally used by Perfect Masons in North America.

First sign.—Same as the one guard of a Master Mason.

Second sign.—Bring your right hand to your left cheek, extending it as though to guard that side of the face; your left is to support the right elbow—apply the left hand in the same manner to the right cheek, supporting the left elbow with the right hand. It is pretended that Moses placed himself in these attitudes when he saw the burning bush.

Third sign.—Give the sign of admiration, and then place three fingers of the right hand on the lips.

First token.—Same as that of the Entered Apprentice.

Second token.—Same as the Master's grip; having giving it, say " Can you go farther?" he will slip his hand above your wrist, to the middle of the arm, and so to the elbow, he then puts his left hand to your shoulder and thus passes thrice.

Third token.—Seize each other's elbows with the left hand, and put the right hand on each other's neck, as if in the act of raising one up.

First pass-word.—" Shibboleth," repeated thrice.
Second pass-word.—" Heleniham."
Third pass-word.—" Mahak-makar-a-bak." This is translated, *Masonically,* " God be praised, we have finished it."
First covered word.—" Gibulum."
Second covered word.—" Mahabin."
Third covered word.—" Adonai."
Grand word.—" Jehovah." This word is given by repeating alternately, the names of the Hebrew letters used in the word Jehovah, (יהוה) thus, " Jod," " He," " Vau," " He."

KNIGHT OF THE EAST.

Sign.—Carry the right hand to the left shoulder, and move it downwards to the right hip with a serpentine motion; this represents the motion of waves. Draw your sword and bring it to the guard.

Token.—Seize mutually the left hand, the arm lifted and extended as if to repulse each other. Point the sword to the heart; one says, "Judah," the other, "Benjamin."

Sacred word.—"Raphodon," or, more correctly, "Rephidim."

Pass-word.—"Ya-vaurum-hamen," or, as some say, "Yaver-on-hammaim," or, according to others, "Yahaboru Hammaim," "they will pass the waters."

Grand word.—"Shilo, Shalom, Abi," or, more correctly, "Shalal, Shallum, Abi."

Some Chapters of Knights of the East, have adopted the following signs, words, &c.

Sign.—Carry the right hand to the left shoulder, and bring it down diagonally to the right hip, as if to quarter the body. The answer is made by carrying the right hand from the left hip across the body to the right hip.

Token.—Place the right hand on the sword, as though to draw it; throw the weight of the body on the left foot, draw back the right foot, raise the left hand, as if to repulse an enemy; interlace right hands; place the left arm behind the back.

Pass word.—"Libertas."

Words.—"Judah and Benjamin."

PRINCE OF JERUSALEM.

First sign.—Extend the right arm horizontally at the height of the shoulder. This is termed *the sign* of command.

First token.—Each places his left hand on his left hip, and the right hand on his brother's left shoulder.

Second token.—Join left hands, placing the thumb on the second joint of the little finger; with the thumb strike five times on that joint.

Pass-word.—"Tebeth." The name of the Jewish month in which the Ambassadors entered Jerusalem.

Sacred word.—"Adar."—The name of the month in which thanks were given to God for the completion of the Temple.

In some Councils the following sign is given, viz:

Present yourself before your brother with your sword advanced, and your left hand resting on your hip, as if to commence a combat. He will answer the sign by extending his arm at the height of the shoulder, the right foot forming a square with the toe of the left.

The march.—Five steps on the diagonal of the square towards the throne.

Age.—The age of a Prince of Jerusalem, is 5 times 15.

KNIGHT OF THE EAST AND WEST.

Sign.—Look at your right shoulder; it will be answered by looking at the left shoulder. One says, "Abaddon," the other, "Jubulum."

First token.—Place your left hand in the right hand of your brother, who will cover it with his left; both at the same time look over their right shoulders.

Second token.—Touch your brother's left shoulder with your left hand; he replies by touching your right shoulder with his right hand.

Sign for entering the Lodge.—Place your right hand on the brother's forehead, (i. e. the Tyler's,) he will do the same.

Pass-word.—"Jubulum," or according to some, "Perignan" and "Gadaon."

Sacred word.—"Abaddon." This name will be found in Rev. ix. 11.

SOVEREIGN PRINCE OF ROSE CROIX D'HERODEN.

First sign.—Termed the sign of the good Shepherd. Cross the arms on the breast, hands extended and eyes raised to heaven.

Second sign.—That of recollection. Raise the right hand, and with the fore finger point to heaven. It is answered by pointing to the earth with the fore finger. This sign and answer are given alternately.

Third sign.—That of help. Cross the legs, the right behind the left. Answer; cross the legs, the left behind the right.

Token.—Give the sign of the good Pastor; face each other; bow; place reciprocally the hands on the breast crossed; give the fraternal kiss, pronouncing at the same time the pass-word.

Pass-word.—"Emmanuel."

Sacred word.—"I. N. R. I." This is given by pronouncing its letters alternately. They are initials of the words Jesus, Nazarenus, Rex, Judæorum. Jesus of Nazareth, King of the Jews.

GRAND PONTIFF.

Sign.—Elevate the right hand horizontally, fingers extended; cross the three last fingers perpendicularly.

Token.—Each places the palm of the right hand on his forehead,—one says "Hallelujah," the other, "Praise the Lord." The first says "Emmanuel," the second, "God bless you."

Pass-word.—"Emmanuel."

Sacred word.—"Hallelujah," or "Alleluia."

VENERABLE GRAND MASTER OF ALL SYMBOLIC LODGES.

In this degree the variations in the signs, words, &c. which may be discovered in the MSS. used by different Lodges, is more striking than in any other sublime degree.

The following, though not corresponding with those referred to in page 241, are still sanctioned by very high Masonic authority

First sign.—Form *four squares* thus; with the fingers joined, and the thumb elevated, place your right hand on your heart—(this forms two squares.) Place the left hand on the lips, the thumb elevated so as to form a third square; place the heels so as to form a square with the feet.

Second sign.—Place yourself on your knees, elbows on the ground, the head inclined toward the left.

Third sign.—Cross the hands on the breast, the right over the left, fingers extended, thumbs elevated, and the feet forming a square.

Token.—Take reciprocally the right elbow with the right hand, the thumb on the outside, the fingers joined, and on the inside; press the elbow thus four times, slip the hands down to the wrists, raise the three last fingers, and press the index on the wrist.

Sacred word.—"Razabassi," or "Razah Betzi-Yah."

Pass-words.—"Jechson," "Jubellum," "Zanabosan;" some however give "Jehovah" as the sacred word, and "Belshazzar" as the pass word.

CHEVALIER PRUSSIAN.

Sign.—Point with the three fingers of the right hand—(the brother does the same)—he takes the fingers of the first and says, "Fredeiu."

II. You reply by taking the fingers of the brother, and saying, "Noah."

Sign used in opening Lodge.—Lift your arms to heaven, looking at the East, where the moon rises.

Token.—Grasp between the thumb and the index, the fore finger of your brother; press it and say, "Shem;" he will do the same, and say "Ham;" you will repeat the motion and say "Japhet."

Pass word.—"Peleg," or "Phaleg," repeated thrice in a melancholy tone.

Sacred words.—"Shem," "Ham," "Japhet."

KNIGHT OF THE ROYAL AXE, OR, PRINCE OF LIBANUS.

Sign.—Raise both hands toward the right shoulder, let them fall on the left thigh, (indicating the fall of the cedars of Libanus by the blows of the axe.)

Token.—As a sign of fidelity, cross and join hands.

Pass-words.—"Japhet, Aholiab, Libanus."

Sacred words.—"Noah, Bezaleel, Sidonius."

CHIEF OF THE TABERNACLE.

Sign.—Advance the right foot, make the motion of taking a censer with the right hand.

Token.—Seize mutually the left elbow with the right hand, bending the arm so as to form a kind of circle.

Sacred word.—"Jehovah."

Pass-word.—"Uriel." The answer to this is, "The tabernacle of revealed truth."

PRINCE OF THE TABERNACLE.

Sign of recognizance.—Raise the eyes to heaven, cover them with right hand, place left hand on the stomach, incline the head, place right hand on left shoulder, bring the right hand down diagonally to the right side.

Grand sign.—Place the hands open upon the head, join the thumbs and fore fingers, (by their extremities,) forming a triangle.

The word, and pass word, and token, are the same as in the preceding degree.

KNIGHT OF THE BRAZEN SERPENT.

Sign.—As that of the Rose-Croix.

Order, or entering sign.—Point to the earth, as if showing a plant.

Token.—Place yourself on the right of the brother—take his left wrist with your right hand.—He answers by taking your right wrist with his right hand.

Covered word.—" *John Ralp,*" the founder of this degree ! !

Sacred word.—" Moses."

Pass-word.—I. N. R. I. given as in the degree of Rose-Croix.

PRINCE OF MERCY.

First Sign.—That of entrance. Place the right hand above the eyes so as to form a triangle with the forehead.

Second sign.—Form a triangle with the thumbs and the two fore fingers, and place them on the abdomen.

Third sign.—That of help. Place the arms on the head, the hands open, the palms outward, and say, " With me are the children of truth."

Token.—Take your brother's shoulders with your hands—press them slightly, saying, " Gomel."

Sacred words.—" Jehovah, Jakin." Masons of this degree tell us these words signify, " one only God, eternal, the Sovereign Master of all things."

Common words.—" Ghiblim," " Gabaon." The first word is said to signify, " Excellent Master;" and the last, " the Chamber of the third heavens."

Pass-word.—" Gomel," or according to others, " Magacacia," or as others say, " Abi," and these last use " Jakinai," as the pass-word.

SOVEREIGN COMMANDER OF THE TEMPLE.

Sign, used only in the Court,—(i. e. Lodge.) Form a cross on the forehead of your brother with the thumb of the right hand. The answer consists in kissing the forehead on the place where the cross was made.

Ordinary sign.—Place the two first fingers of the right hand on the mouth, the others closed and towards the examiner.

Token.—Give three blows with the right hand upon the left shoulder of the brother—he will answer by taking your right hand and giving it three light shakes.

Pass-word.—" Solomon."

Sacred word.—I. N. R. I.

KNIGHT OF THE SUN, OR, PRINCE ADEPT.

Sign.—Place the right hand flat upon the heart, the thumb forming a square. The answer; raise the hand, and with the index, point to heaven. This is to show that there is but one God, the source of all truth.

Token.—Take in your hands those of your brother, and press them gently. Some Knights in addition to this, kiss the forehead of the brother, saying, " Alpha," to which he answers, " Omega."

Sacred word.—" Adonai." This word is answered by " Albra," or, " Abbraak," which is rendered " a king without reproach." Some contend that this word should be written, " Abrah."

Pass-word.—" Stibium," (antimony.) By this is intended as among the Hermetic Philosophers, *the primitive matter whence all things are formed.* To this pass-word some add the following: " Helios," " Mene," " Tetragrammaton."

KNIGHT OF KADOSH.

Sign.—Place the right hand on the heart, the fingers separated, let the hand fall on the right thigh, bend the knee, seize the poniard, raise it to the height of the shoulder, as if to strike, and say, " Nekam Adonai." Another sign used in some chapters : Place the right hand on the heart, and afterwards on the right knee, which you then grasp with that hand.

Order or Saluting Sign.—Hold the sword in the left hand, place the right hand on the red cross which covers the heart.

Token.—Place right foot to right foot, and knee to knee, present the right fist, the thumb elevated ; he takes the fist. He will then present his own, which you will seize in the same manner ; each steps back a pace and lifts his left arm as though to strike, one says, " Nekamah Bealim" the other replies, " Pharas Kol."

Some chapters use the token of Elect of Nine. Another token used by some Knights : One says, " are you Kadosh ?" He answers by placing his right hand on his forehead, and saying, " Yes I am." He presents his right fist thrice, with the thumb elevated ; at the third time, the other seizes the thumb and they embrace thrice.

WORDS AND PASS-WORDS.

The degree of Kadosh is divided into two, and sometimes into three points, each has its peculiar pass-words and words.

First Point word, " Jabamiah" or " Habamah." Pass-word, " Eliel" or " Manchen." Answer, " Nemehaniack" or " Menachem" and "Nechemiah." Others use the words " Nika-Maka," or properly " Nekam Makkah." The following word is also given with the token, viz : Kiries, or properly " Kyrie."

In the second point of this degree, the words of the mysterious are used. (See page 280.)

Sacred Word.—" Nekam Adonai."

Other Sacred words.—"Nekamah Baelim." Answer, "Begoal Kol" " Pharas Kol." After repeating these words, they embrace repeating the word "Adonai."

Pass-Word for Entry.—" Nekam." Answer " Menachem."

For retiring.—" Phual Kol." Answer " Pharas Kol "
The following is used as the examining form or lecture :
Q. At what hour is the Chapter opened ?
A. The commencement of night.
Q. Whom do you know ?
A. Two wretches.
Q. Name them.
A. Philip the Fair, and Bertrand the Goth. (Clement V.)

PRINCE OF THE ROYAL SECRET.

Sign.—Place the right hand on the heart ; extend it forward, the palm downwards ; let it fall by the right side.

Sacred words.—Those of the Carpet, which are to be read backward around the circle from right to left, thus : One says " Salix," and the other " Noni ;" both then repeat (by letters) the word " Tengu."

Pass-words.—" Phual Kol," " Pharas Kol," " Nekam Makah," both pronounce (by lettering) the word " Shaddai."

(361)

PROCEEDINGS AND RESULT

OF A

CONVENTION OF THE SARATOGA BAPTIST ASSOCIATION,

CONTAINING FIFTEEN REASONS FOR THEIR DISFELLOWSHIPPING FREE MASONRY.

Held at Milton, Sept. 12*th and* 13*th,* 1827.

Wednesday, September 12, 1827.

Agreeably to the vote of the Saratoga Association, in June, 1827, delegates from various churches composing the same, assembled at Milton, to confer on certain grievances in reference to active Free Masonry, intimated to the association, by the churches at Battenkill, and Milton.

Elder Seamans opened the meeting by prayer.

Deacon Child called upon the delegates to signify what churches were represented at this convention—which furnished the following result.

Amsterdam.—Timothy Crane, Waterman Sweet.

Battenkill.—Elder Edward Barber, Richard Parker, Samuel Hale, James Teft, Eber Crandell, William Henry.

Broadalbin.—Elder William Groom, John Tanner, Amos C. Cornwell, James H. Sumner.

Burnthills.—Nathaniel Jennings, David Schauber, Bradley Morehouse.

Corinth.—Elder Benjamin St. John, Ira Heath, John Eggleston, Zira H. Coles.

Edinburgh.—Elias Manning, Eli Manning, Daniel Corey.

1st Galway.—Alpheus Moore, Daniel Ludlow, Ira Barberry.

2d Galway.—Elder William E. Waterbury, Eli Smith, Asa Cornell, Edmond Hewitt, Peter Wright, David Benedict, Samuel Cook.

Kingsbury.—Chester Cook, Samuel Cole.

Kingsborough.—Elder John Lathrop, Alexander Gloss.

Milton.—Elder Thomas Powell, Gilbert Waring, Salmon Child, Silas Adams, Increase W. Child, Adam Swan.

Northampton.—Elder Aaron Seamans.

Saratoga Springs.—William Wait, John C. Whitford, John A. Waterbury.

Stillwater.—Samuel Moore, David Newland, Daniel Munger.

Saratoga.—Elder Jonathan Finch, William I. Smith, Reuben Perry.

Moreau.—Pardon Elms, John W. Angle, Nathan Kingsley.

Total of the Saratoga Association—16 churches, 55 delegates.

The convention being thus organized, Elder Seamans was chosen moderator, Elder Powell, clerk.

Invited delegates from other churches and associations to share in our deliberations—Accordingly, Elder David Bernard read credentials of appointment as a delegate to this convention, from five churches,—Elba, Le Roy, York, Middlebury, and Warsaw, and took his seat; together with John Ford, John D. Lindsey, and Peter I. Warndell, delegates from the church at Northumberland.

Invited the brethren generally present to share in all the privileges of the meeting, voting excepted.

The delegates from the church at Milton, expressed a desire that a spirit of Christian wisdom and moderation might characterize this meeting; and stated that their investigation of Masonry arose from complying with the vote of

G g

the association in 1826, in relation to Battenkill church—that they utterly disclaimed any hostility to Masons, and condemned that proscription of them in general, which had prevailed in some parts of our state—and that as men holding property by the same tenure, and possessing similar unalienable rights with others, Masons were entitled to respect, and fully qualified, when possessing integrity and talents, to hold all civil offices of power and trust.

Adjourned for 30 minutes. Prayer by Elder Finch.

Met pursuant to adjournment. Elder Wayland opened by prayer.

Written communications were read from the churches at Battenkill, and Milton.

Elder Bernard made some statements illustrative of his views, and opposition to Masonry.

Brother Increase W. Child read to the convention, touching a part of the tendency of Masonry, the 8th chapter of Town's treatise on that subject.

One of the Brethren read several decided renunciations of Free Masonry, made by persons formerly members of that fraternity, and testimonies to the correctness of William Morgan's book—and likewise letters addressed to the convention from sundry churches in the western parts of the state. In answer to an inquiry from the chair, it appeared that nine of the churches here represented, (belonging to this association,) had expressed decisions approbatory of the views of the churches at Battenkill and Milton, on the subject of Masonry.

Appointed a committee consisting of Elders Finch, Groom, and Waterbury; and brethren Increase W. Child, and James Teft, to draft an instrument expressive of the views and decisions of this convention and present it for consideration to-morrow.

Adjourned until 9 o'clock to-morrow morning, requesting Elder Herrick to deliver a sermon at that hour. Prayer by Elder Bernard.

Thursday, September 13th.

Elder Herrick preached from Isa. liv, 17.

The minutes of yesterday were read and approved.

The committee appointed to draft an instrument expressive of the views and decisions of the convention, brought in the following report; which, after a second reading by sections, with the authorities quoted in it, was adopted.

Resolved, That this convention hereby approve of the conduct pursued by the churches at Battenkill, and Milton, and further declare—as we trust in the fear of God, and in accordance with his revealed will—to the association, sister churches, and brethren in general—that we have no fellowship for or with the institution of Free Masonry. We thus declare :—

1. Because Free Masonry professes to have its origin in, and from God. ' This supreme and *divine* knowledge being derived from the *Almighty Creator*, to Adam, its principles ever since have been, and still are, most sacredly preserved, and inviolably concealed. They (Masons) have the art of finding new arts, which art the first Masons received from God.' Vide Calcotty Disquisition, Boston ed. 1772, pp. 89—90.

' It is no secret that Masonry is of divine origin. In view, therefore, of the divine origin of ancient Masonry,' &c. Town's Speculative Masonry, ed. 1818, pp. 37—175.

2. Because it professes to correspond with and bears an affinity to the ancient Egyptian philosophy. ' Our records informs us that the ways and customs of Masonry have ever corresponded with those of the Egyptian philosophers, to which they bear a near affinity.' Bradley, Albany ed. 1821, p. 60. Monitor, 1805 ed. p. 38.

3. Because it adopts a novel and unscriptural manner of instructing men in the doctrines, promises, and consolations of the gospel, and draws its lessons of morality from stone hammers, mallets, chisels, and other working tools. ' The first degree in Masonry naturally suggests that state of moral

darkness which begloomed our world. On the apostacy of our first common parent, not a gleam of light was left to cheer his desponding mind. Soon, however, the first kind promise was made. Adam was, therefore, in a comparative sense, still in darkness. Such is the very nature of the first degree, that every observing candidate is led to view his moral blindness, and deplorable state by nature. Under these impressions he enters on the second degree, which, in view of his moral blindness, he is to consider emblematical of a state of imprisonment and trial. Such was the second state of Adam. Hence arises the idea of probationary ground. A due observance of all former requisitions, and a sincere desire to make advances in knowledge and virtue, open the way for the reception of more light. Having diligently persevered in the use of appointed means, the third degree prefigures the life of the good man in his pilgrimage state. Although the true light has shined into his heart, and he has experienced much consolation, yet he sometimes wanders into devious and forbidden paths. In the midst of such trials, he resolves to be faithful, and manfully to withstand temptations. He determines to pursue that sacred trust committed to his care, and therefore endeavors to escape with his life to the great Ark of his salvation. In advancing to the fourth degree, the good man is greatly encouraged to persevere in the ways of well doing, even to the end. He has a name which no man knoweth save he that receiveth it. If, therefore, he be rejected, and cast forth amongst the rubbish of the world, he knows full well, the great Master Builder of the universe, having chosen and prepared him as a lively stone in that spiritual building in the heavens, will bring him forth with triumph, while shouting grace, grace, to his Divine Redeemer. Hence opens the fifth degree, where he discovers his election to, and his glorified station in the kingdom of his Father. Here he is taught how much the chosen ones are honored and esteemed by those on earth, who discover and appreciate the image of their common Lord. This image being engraven on his heart, he may look forward to those mansions above, where a higher and more exalted seat has been prepared for the faithful from the foundations of the world. With these views the sixth degree is conferred, where the riches of divine grace are opened in boundless prospect. Every substantial good is clearly seen to be conferred through the great atoning sacrifice. In the seventh degree the good man is truly filled with heartfelt gratitude to his heavenly Benefactor, for all those wonderful deliverances wrought out for him, while journeying through the rugged paths of human life. Great has been his redemption from the Egypt and Babylon of this world. He beholds in the eighth degree, that all the heavenly sojourners will be admitted within the veil of God's presence; where they will become kings and priests before the throne of his glory for ever and ever. Such, my brethren, in brief, is the moral and religious instruction derived merely from the order of Masonic degrees.' Town's Speculative Masonry, whole of 8th chapter.

'The twenty-four inch guage—Free and accepted Masons are taught to make use of it, for the noble and glorious purpose of dividing our time. The common gavel—We, as Free and Acepted Masons, are taught to make use of it, for the more noble and glorious purpose of divesting our minds and censciences of all the vices and superfluities of life; thereby fitting our bodies as living stones for that spiritual building, that house not made with hands, eternal in the heavens. The chisel morally demonstrates the advantages of discipline and education. The mallet morally teaches to correct irregularities, and to reduce man to a proper level.' Free Mason's Monitor, 1805 ed. pp. 36—87.

4. Because it publishes to the world songs, &c. of such a contrariety of character, as to serve the purposes of profanity, revelry, the worship of the true God, and heathen deities.

"Then from their high windows the heavens did pour,
  Forty days and nights one continual shower,
Till nought could be seen but the waters around;
  And in this great deluge most mortals were drown'd.
                    Derry down, down, derry down.

"Sure ne'er was beheld so dreadful a sight,
  As the old world in such a very odd plight;
For there were to be seen all animals swimming,
  Men, monkeys, priests, lawyers, cats, lapdogs, and women.
                    Derry down, down, derry down."
Vide Ahiman Rezon, p. 166.

"Glory to God on high,
  Let earth and skies reply,
        Worthy the Lamb."
Vide Masonic Minstrel, ed. 1816, p. 316, &c. Also, see Monitor.

5. Because it pretends that its religion and morality are the same as those taught in the Bible. 'Our principles being drawn *from revelation* do not require us to make the secrets of Masonry known.' Bradley, ed. 1821. p. 12.

'The principles of speculative Free Masonry have the same co-eternal and unshaken foundation—contain and inculcate in substance the same truths—and propose the same ultimate end, as the doctrines of Christianity taught by Divine *revelation*. This is a position of very high import; yet the truth of it is not doubted by those who are thoroughly versed in Masonic knowledge. If we would give universal celebrity to our institution, the world must be convinced that the foundation is laid in evangelical truth.' Town, ed. 1822, pp. 13, 14.

6. Because the ancient Egyptian philosophy, with its hieroglyphics and mysteries, and the religion of Christ, cannot correspond or bear affinity to each other. 'Beware, lest any man spoil you through philosophy and vain deceit, after the tradition of men, after the rudiments of the world, and not after Christ.' Col. ii. 8. 'And have no fellowship with the unfruitful works of darkness; but rather reprove them. For it is a shame even to speak of those things which are done of them in secret.' Eph. v. 11, 12.

'Besides the public worship of the heathen deities—the Greeks, the Egyptians, the Indians, and some others had recourse to a dark and concealed species of worship, under the name of mysteries. None were admitted but such as had approved themselves by perseverance in initiatory forms. The votaries were enjoined on peril of instant death to observe the most profound secrecy respecting every thing that passed. These mysteries were first invented in Egypt; from whence they spread into most countries of Europe and Asia. The most noted, were the Eleusinian. Bishop Warburton, who contends for high honor in this primary institution, acknowledges that the mysteries of those deities being performed during nocturnal darkness, or in gloomy recesses, and under the seal of the greatest secrecy, the initiated indulged themselves on these occasions in all the abominations with which the object of their worship was supposed to be delighted. In fact, the enormities committed became so intolerable, that their rites were proscribed in various countries. In proportion, therefore, as the gospel made its progress in the world, the mysteries fell into disrepute, and, together with all the other pagan solemnities were at length suppressed.' Jones' Church History, Cone's ed. pp. 10—13.

7. Because it perverts and degrades the meaning of Scripture passages, and by their use and application to Masonic ceremonies, dishonors God the Son. 'In the honorable character of Mark Master—while such is your conduct, should misfortunes assail you, friends forsake you, envy traduce your good

name—yet may you have confidence among Mark Master Masons—ever bearing in mind as a consolation and encouragement to hope for better prospects, that the stone which the builders rejected (possessing merit, to them unknown) became the chief stone of the corner.' Bradley, ed. 1821, p. 181.

'On the order of High Priest—of a Royal Arch Chapter—the following passages of scripture are made use of during the ceremonies. 'And Melchisedec, king of Salem, brought forth bread and wine, and he was the priest of the Most High God. Thou art a priest for ever after the order of Melchisedec. And inasmuch as not without an *oath*, he was made priest.' Bradley, pp. 232, 233.

'Laying the foundation stone of a monument in memory of Washington, in Baltimore, the Grand Chaplain read the following passages from the holy writings: 'Thus saith the Lord God, Behold I lay in Zion, for a foundation, a stone, a tried stone, a precious corner stone, a sure foundation. Judgment also will I lay to the line, and righteousness to the plummet. For behold the stone which I have laid before Joshua, upon one stone shall be seven eyes. Behold I will engrave the engraving thereof, saith the Lord of hosts.' Appendix to Masonic Minstrel, by Veriton, p. 432.

8. Because it unwarrantably and irreverently employs the name of Jehovah, in the dedication of Masonic halls.

'In the name of the *Great Jehovah*, to whom be all honor and glory, I do solemnly dedicate this hall to Masonry.' Masonic Chart, ed. 1824, p. 79. Monitor, ed. 1825, p. 130.

9. Because it dedicates lodges, chapters, &c. to St. John and Zerubbabel.

'To the memory of holy St. John, we dedicate this lodge.' Monitor, ed. 1825, p. 164. 'To our Most Excellent Patron, Zerubbabel, we solemnly dedicate this chapter.' Masonic Chart, ed. 1824, pp. 60, 130.

10. Because it authorizes the practice of religious rites, ceremonies and observances, not commanded or countenanced in the New Testament—such as observing St. John's days; wearing garments in imitation of those worn by the Jewish High Priests; making, and carrying in procession, a mimic representation of the ark of the covenant; making and wearing similar representations of the breast plate; inscribing on mitres, 'Holiness to the Lord;' and sundry other ceremonies and observances.

In confirmation of these facts, we appeal to all who have witnessed the celebration of St. John's days, Masonic funerals, laying foundation stones in Masonic order, &c.

11. Because it imposes obligations of a moral and religious nature, which cannot be communicated to any other than Masons or candidates of the order —not even to brethren in the church of Christ. 'Such is the importance of our secrecy, were no other ties upon our affections or consciences, than merely the sense of the injury we should do to the poor and the wretched. By a transgression of *this rule*, we are persuaded it would be sufficient to lock up the tongue of every Mason, and lead him solemnly to look in the heavens and say, 'Set a watch, O Lord, before my mouth; keep thou the door of my lips.' Every candidate for admission may be informed, that the obligation which he is to take is perfectly moral, and compatible with the principles of Christianity. It cannot be criminal that we make every candidate promise to keep the secrets of Masonry.' Bradley, pp. 11—15; and Cabests's Disquisitions, Boston ed. 1772, pp. 46—54.

12. Because it affixes new names and appellations to both God the Father, and God the Son, and those which are immoral and irreligious to men. 'The Great Architect of the universe, Great Architect in heaven, Supreme Architect, Grand Overseer, Supreme High Priest.' Bradley, pp. 157—186. 'Supreme Grand Master.' Cabest's Disquisitions, ed. 1772, p. 156. 'Most Excellent, Most Worshipful, Prince of Mercy,' &c. Vide Monitor, Bradley, &c.

13. Because it amalgamates in its societies, men of all religions, professing

to believe the existence of a Supreme Being of any description; thereby defeating all its pretensions to the morality and religion of the Bible, and sapping the foundation of Christian fellowship. 'There is *one body* and *one spirit*, even as ye are called in one hope of your calling; one Lord, one faith, one baptism, *one God* and Father of all, who is above all, and through all, and in you all.' Eph. iv. 5, 6. 'Masonry becomes an universal language;... the distant Chinese, the wild Arab, and the American savage, will embrace a brother Briton.' Monitor, Albany ed. 1797, pp. 8, 9. 'Into the merciless hands of unrelenting Turks, the shackles of slavery are broken, through the interposition of a brother.' Town, ed. 1818, p. 160.

14. Because it authorizes forms of prayer, accommodated to the prejudices of the Jews, thus rejecting the only Mediator and way of access to the Father. 'O Lord, enlighten us, we beseech thee, in the true knowledge of Masonry, by the sorrows of Adam, thy first made man; by the blood of Abel, the holy one; by the righteousness of Seth, in whom thou art well pleased; and by thy covenant with Noah, in whose architecture thou wast pleased to save the seed of thy beloved, number us not among those that keep not thy statutes, nor the divine mysteries of the secret Cabala; but grant the ruler of this lodge may be endued with knowledge to explain to us his secret mysteries as Moses did (in his lodge,) to Aaron, to Eleazer, and Ithamar, and the seventy elders of Israel, Amen, Lord.' Ahiman Rezon, New-York ed. 1825, p. 93.

15. Because it receives and adopts orders of knighthood from Popery. 'Masonic degrees conferred in the Sublime Grand Lodges in Charleston, S. C.; in the city of New-York; and in Newport, R. I.: Knight of the Red Cross, Knight of Malta, Knight of the Holy Sepulchre, Knight of the Christian Mark, Knight Templar, Grand Pontiff, Knight of the Brazen Serpent, Knight of the Sun, Knight of the Holy Ghost.' Masonic Minstrel, ed. 1826, p. 421.

And, whereas, we cannot fellowship Free Masonry for the reasons assigned:

Resolved, That we do not fellowship our Baptist brethren, unless they completely abstain from the same.

We commit our doings in this matter, to Him who is head over all things, blessed for ever: praying him to correct and restore us, (if we have erred,) to the paths of truth, and (if we have not erred) to give us wisdom and strength to maintain the truth as it is in Him.

We commend our brethren and sister churches to the word of His grace, which is able to build them up, and give them an inheritance among the sanctified.

The delegates from the churches in Battenkill, Broadalbin, Edinburgh, 1st Galway, Kingsborough, Milton, Northampton, Saratoga, Northumberland, 2d Elba, 2d Le Roy, 1st York, 1st Middlebury, and Warsaw, voted to accept the report.

Those from Amsterdam, Burnthills, Corinth, 2d Galway, Kingsbury, Saratoga Springs, Stillwater, and Moreau, concluded to waive expressing a decision, and to lay before their respective churches the proceedings of the convention, in order to have their voice on the same, prior to the next association.

Resolved, That the clerk prepare and forward the minutes and report of this convention, for insertion in the New-York Baptist Register; and procure a number of extra copies for distribution amongst our churches, reserving *one*, to be read at the next association.

Elder Herrick closed the convention with prayer.

AARON SEAMANS, *Moderator.*

THOMAS POWELL, *Clerk.*

A NARRATIVE

Of the facts and circumstances relating to the Kidnapping and presumed murder of William Morgan, and of the attempt to carry off David C. Miller, and to burn, or destroy, the printing office of the latter, for the purpose of preventing the printing and publishing of a book entitled, " Illustrations of Masonry." Prepared under the direction of the several Committees appointed at meetings of the citizens of the counties of Genesee, Livingston, Ontario, Monroe, and Niagara, in the State of New-York: with an appendix, containing most of the depositions and other documents, to substantiate the statements made, and disclosing many particulars of the transactions, not included in the narrative.

ADVERTISEMENT.

The committees, upon whom their fellow citizens in different counties and towns imposed the duty of investigating the transactions detailed in the subjoined narrative, were soon convinced that it would be their duty to publish, as soon as should be practicable, an account of them. They were anxious to use all possible precaution to avoid errors in the statements. For that purpose, three of their number visited Lewiston and Niagara in March last, by which some unimportant mistakes were corrected, and some further important information was elicited. It should be noticed by the reader, that the transactions detailed, extended over a distance of 170 miles ; that the information is drawn from various and distant sources; that the character of the conspiracy is entirely new ; that the committees have no means of acquiring information but persuasion, which often fails of success ; that their investigation encountered almost every kind of opposition from the parties concerned, and the numerous friends of those implicated in the conspiracy. Under all these embarrassments, they trust that the candid part of their fellow citizens will attribute the delay in the publication of this account, to the causes assigned, and not to negligence or improper motives. Good faith, and a due regard to the course of public justice, require them, even now, to withhold many facts and circumstances, until legal investigations are instituted and finished.

INTRODUCTION.

The following narrative has been compiled with as much care and accuracy as the circumstances would admit. It has been frequently called for, and, as many may think, has been too long kept back; but the causes of delay were such as the committees could not prevent or obviate. We trust that it will be found to contain a plain and unvarnished statement, and that we have used no harsh terms or extravagant expressions. The committees have considered the duty of preparing it as one, the performance of which they could not neglect, without disappointing the reasonable expectations of a large number of their respectable fellow citizens. The transactions detailed in the narrative, have, in themselves, a character of such enormous wickedness—they exhibit such utter disregard of all those principles and rules of conduct, which have, heretofore, been held sacred in all civilized communities—their consequences seem to us so entirely subversive of the principles of our government, and so destructive of our rights, that any attempt, on our part, to comment upon them appeared superfluous.

The general voice of the community has been heard already. The free and enlightened citizens of our country have not been unmindful of the duty they owed to themselves, their country, and their offspring.

We have not been left to act alone and unsupported. Whatever apprehensions some of us might at first have entertained, as to the extent of the enmity and violence we might be called upon to encounter, in the prosecution of objects we had in view, we were not long left in doubt or apprehensions whether we should receive the support of the virtuous part of our countrymen.

Those objects were, 1st.—To aid in re-establishing the authority of the laws, by the restoration of William Morgan to his country, his liberty, and his family.

2d. To aid in the discovery, exposure, and punishment of those who had, by violence and fraud, deprived him of his liberty, and, as we now believe, of his life.

3d. The discovery and disclosure of the extent of the conspiracy, which, it was manifest to us, had been formed to effect the unlawful objects of the conspirators. And,

4th. The making known to the public, the principles and motives which appeared to have governed the conspirators, so far as those principles seem to us in direct hostility to our civil rights, and so far as those motives are calculated to prompt persons, under their influence, to actions destructive of, and inconsistent with, our free institutions.

The first of these declared objects, we deeply regret to say, we have failed to accomplish, and scarcely a ray of hope enlightens the dark cloud of guilt and mystery which impends over the fate of our fellow citizen.

The probability that several hundred of our fellow citizens, most of whom had, heretofore, maintained a good character, had conspired to effect the *murder* of a helpless man, seemed to us so shocking, so at war with that reverence for the life of our fellow creatures, which God himself has impressed upon the human mind, so decidedly in opposition to that general benevolence of feeling which has distinguished our countrymen in particular, that for many months, we resisted the supposition, of the bare possibility of such a crime, with disgust and horror. We were unwilling to believe that respectable men would, directly or indirectly, suggest or aid the commission of a crime which seldom escapes punishment, or expose themselves to the disgrace which any attempts, on their part, to baffle investigation by secrecy or silence, could not fail eventually to bring upon them. But we have been compelled to feel the justice of the remark made to us by one well versed in the operations of the human mind :—" *That when the demon of fanaticism is at work, there is no knowing to what extent of mischief and turpitude he may lead his disciples.*"

The second object has been, in part, effected by the influence of that high and holy regard to official duty, which has operated upon the public *officers*, and *grand jury of Ontario county*, and which is still manifesting itself by a faithful application of the powers vested in them by their country. How far their honorable example will be imitated in other counties remains to be seen.

The third and fourth objects, it is not intended to prosecute in the following statement, excepting so far as they may be of necessity brought into view, in the detail of facts which we purpose to make.

We do not feel qualified, nor have we time, for the proper performance of a duty in which our fellow citizens, and those who shall succeed us, are so deeply interested. Time, the test of truth, which brings to light the hidden works of iniquity, and exposes the unhallowed designs of the guilty, will contribute to unfold the principles and motives which have prompted the crimes of fraudulent arrests, by the abuse of civil process, riot, kidnapping, and perhaps murder, and which have induced so many to sanction them openly.

Those who have more leisure and more ability than ourselves, may, and we have no doubt will, hereafter call the attention of our fellow citizens to the questions, how far these principles are in conformity with our republican maxims—how far their influence is calculated to corrupt and destroy the integrity of the human mind—and how far the existence of the source from which they are believed to emanate, is reconcilable with the stability and preservation of the constitution, and the enjoyments of our rights and liberties.

We trust we have no desire to give to the transactions we have detailed, a consequence which they do not deserve. Those actions cannot be unimportant, in which so large a portion of our countrymen have taken so deep an interest. That they have done so, we think is honorable to themselves, useful to their country, and has been gratifying to us.

We have studiously, and we hope conscientiously, avoided throwing the slightest imputations upon any one, however humble his situation in life, when a correct statement of facts did not require it ; and we have not refused to disclose the names of the actors, when we had unexceptionable evidence of the parts they have performed. We have disclosed things truly as they have come to our knowledge, without fear or favor.

A NARRATIVE, &c.

William Morgan was a native of the state of Virginia, born in Culpepper county, in the year 1775 or 6, and a mason by trade. Having by his industry accumulated a fund sufficient for the purpose, he commenced business as a trader, or merchant, in Richmond, in that state.

During his residence there, in October 1819, he married Lucinda Pendleton, the oldest daughter of the Rev. Joseph Pendleton, of the Methodist connexion, and a respectable planter, residing in Washington county. He removed from the state of Virginia in the fall of 1821, and commenced the business of a brewer, near York, in Upper Canada. The destruction of his establishment by fire, reduced him from a comfortable situation to poverty, and rendered it necessary for him to resume his trade of a mason: with that intention he removed to Rochester in this state, where he laboured at that business for some time. From Rochester he removed to Batavia, in Genesee county where he worked at his trade until a short time before he was carried away from his home and his family. Sometime in the year 1826, rumors were heard, that Morgan, in connexion with other persons, was preparing and intended to publish a book which would reveal the secrets of Free Masonry, and that David C. Miller, a printer in the village of Batavia, was engaged in putting the work to press. This rumor, like all others in which the community at large feel no interest, excited no attention from the respectable part of it, who supposed that the publication, whatever it might be, was intended as a catchpenny production, for the supply of pedlers and hawkers. It was at last noticed by some of the citizens, that an excitement of some kind, existed among certain persons in the village, in relation to the publication of the book, which it was said Morgan was engaged in compiling; and it was at length openly avowed by a number of persons, who were understood to be members of the Masonic fraternity, that the suppression of the work was determined on at all hazards. A large number of the subscribers to Mr. Miller's paper suddenly withdrew their subscriptions, numerous suits were commenced against him, to enforce the payment of small debts, and their collection was prosecuted in the manner most calculated to distress and embarrass him.

On the ninth day of August, 1826, an advertisement was inserted in a paper printed in Canandaigua, of which the following is an exact copy:

'NOTICE AND CAUTION.

'If a man calling himself William Morgan, should intrude himself on the community, they should be on their guard, particularly the MASONIC FRATERNITY. Morgan was in this village in May last, and his conduct while here and elsewhere, calls forth this notice. Any information in relation to Morgan, can be obtained by calling at the MASONIC HALL, in this village. *Brethren* and *Companions* are particularly requested to *observe, mark,* and *govern* themselves accordingly.

' ☞ Morgan is considered a swindler and a dangerous man.

' ☞ There are people in this village, who would be happy to see this Capt. Morgan.

'Canandaigua, August 9th, 1826.'

This notice and caution was immediately copied into the 'Spirit of the Times,' and the 'People's Press,' two newspapers printed in the village of

Batavia, and, as we are well assured, it was inserted in many other public papers, printed in the western counties of this state.

We are assured also, and to some of the committee it is personally known, that about the same time that this notice appeared, Morgan and Miller were industriously slandered, and abusive epithets heaped upon them, by a number of individuals, who alleged no particular crimes against them, and with whom they were not known to have had any recent connexions or collisions whatever, that were apparent to the public at large.

Miller declared to his particular friends that he was alarmed for his personal safety, and feared an attack upon his office, and he took measures to defend himself against secret or open violence. What reasons he had for his apprehensions we do not think it necessary or proper to state in this place, but the most careless observer took notice that the reputed members of the Masonic fraternity had frequent assemblages, and very many strangers appeared in, and disappeared from the village of Batavia, without openly assigning any object for their visit, or appearing to have any ostensible business to transact, and most of whom seemed desirous of avoiding observation. About the middle of August, a man calling himself Daniel Johns, suddenly appeared in Batavia and took up his lodgings at one of the public houses; he soon proposed associating himself with Miller in the publication of Morgan's book, and offered to advance any sum of money that might be wanted; he was accepted and received into their confidence.

His history, and the object of his visit, were thus detailed by James Ganson, of Le Roy, formerly a member of the legislature from the county of Genesee, and a Knight Templar, to a person whose affidavit of that statement is now in our possession. That he was sent for from thirty miles beyond Kingston, to cheat or take in Miller; that he was a Knight Templar, and a cunning fellow, and had answered the purpose he was sent to accomplish: for he had got away part of the papers and cut the work into two parts, so that Miller could not go on with it.*

On the 25th day of July, 1826, Morgan was committed to the custody of the sheriff of the county of Genesee, at the suit of Nathan Follett, and gave bail for the jail limits. He had been sued sometime before in the Supreme Court, for a considerable debt due to a gentleman of Rochester, and two of his then friends had become his special bail, to wit: Nahum Loring and Orange Allen. During the month of August, his family and himself boarded at Mr. Stewart's in the crowded part of the village, but for the purpose of security and to avoid interruption, he himself spent most of his time in the upper room of Mr. John Davids' house, some distance from his lodgings, and separated by the Tonawanda creek from the business part of the town. On the 19th of August, 1826, Johnson Goodwill, Kelsey Stone, and John Wilson, residents of the village, but holding no official station, accompanied by one Daniel H. Dana, a constable residing at Pembroke, about fourteen miles distant from the village of Batavia, went together to Davids' house. They first inquired for Davids and Towsley, the two men who were heads of the two families that occupied the house, and being told they were not at home, without asking for Morgan, or giving any previous notice to the families, they rushed at once up the stairway into the room where he was writing, seized his person and all the papers which he was then busied in arranging for the press, and took him at once to the county jail, without allowing him time or opportunity to procure other bail.

We pretend not to state how far the sheriff was a party in this transaction. He was observed to be in the company of the four, and went with them to the bridge, where he appeared to stay on the look out until they returned with Morgan, when he accompanied them to jail. Morgan remained in close con-

---

* See Appendix, No. 1, end of the volume.

finement from Saturday afternoon until Monday morning, during which time he received numerous visits from the persons who had interested themselves in the suppression of the book. As soon as Morgan's imprisonment was known to his friends, which was not more than an hour after his capture, three of them made diligent search for the sheriff in all the usual places of his resort, for the purpose of offering themselves as bail for him. They went three times to his dwelling house, without being able to see him; they inquired at the jail and sheriff's office for the jailer: neither sheriff or jailer was to be found until after 12 o'clock at night, when, of course, it was too late to procure his release until Monday morning. On the evening of the same Saturday, about sunset, the same Johnson Goodwill, and Daniel H. Dana, with Thomas McCully, repaired to the dwelling house of Mr. Stewart, where Morgan boarded. They alleged, and we presume they had an execution, in which McCully was plaintiff, and Morgan defendant. McCully inquired of Mrs. Morgan, whether Morgan had any property, who answered, 'You know we have none; we have got nothing since we came from your house.' To a similar inquiry addressed to Miss Stewart, she answered, 'She knew of none, but that they lodged in an upper chamber.' Goodwill and Dana passed into the chamber, leaving McCully below, and proceeded to rummage, without permission or ceremony, among the trunks, boxes, drawers, and every other place where it was probable that papers could be found: they examined such letters as they found, and seized a small trunk of Morgan's which had a few papers in it, saying they would examine, and if they were of consequence to Morgan they would return them. While Goodwill and Dana were thus employed above stairs, McCully observed to Miss Stewart, who remained with him below, 'That he should like to find property to satisfy his execution, but that was not his principal object, he did not care so much about that, as he did to get some papers belonging to Morgan.' One of the chests or trunks was found locked. It belonged to a lodger in the house. His name was mentioned, and McCully declared 'He did not wish to examine that, as he was a Royal Arch Mason.' After remaining in the house about half an hour, they departed; and as they were leaving the house, McCully or Goodwill said to Mrs. Morgan, 'We have just conducted your husband to jail, and shall keep him there until we find his papers.' That numerous individuals, in different and distant parts of our country, took a deep interest in the suppression of the book, we are not at liberty to doubt in the slightest degree; and the intenseness of their anxiety, betrayed them, in very many instances, into the avowal of intentions and feelings which manifested how little they were disposed to regard the laws of the land, and the lives of their fellow citizens, if the violation of the first, and the destruction of the second, should become necessary to effect that object. Some of the particular declarations of individuals from which we have drawn these conclusions, will be found in an appendix, with some of the authorities upon which they are published.*

After Morgan was taken away, the sheriff of the county of Genesee avowed to Mrs. Morgan his belief that the real object of taking him away, was to coerce the surrender of his papers; and he opened a negociation with her, by the aid of Nathan Follett and George Ketchum, for the restoration of her husband, upon condition of surrendering his papers to the Masons; and if any doubts could have existed in our minds of the anxiety to suppress this work, and the determination to effect it at all hazards, they would have been set at rest by the affidavits of Nicholas G. Chesebro, and Edward Sawyer, read before the court which sentenced them, of which copies will be found in the appendix.†

On the 8th day of September, 1826, Nathan Follett, an active member of the Masonic fraternity, residing at Batavia, desired James Ganson, who then

---

* Appendix, No. 30.   † Appendix, Nos. 8 and 9.

kept a tavern at the village of Stafford, six miles east of Batavia, to prepare a cold supper, or refreshment, for between forty and fifty men, who, he said, would be there that night. They accordingly assembled, and were headed or commanded by a Col. Edward Sawyer, residing at Canandaigua. From the affidavit of Green, and other information received, it appears that this mob, which was to act under the direction of Sawyer, was to have been composed of persons from several different and distant places, and some of them even from Upper Canada. At a late hour of the night, the conspirators, conducted by Sawyer, departed from Ganson's, and proceeded to Batavia, for the purpose, as was avowed, of procuring the manuscript papers, and printed sheets, and suppressing the publication of Morgan's book, by breaking into the printing office, and, if necessary to effect their object, carry off Morgan and Miller. What circumstances or occurrences deterred them from proceeding to extremities, are not known, further than have been derived from their own statements since, and the affidavit of Green.* They received information, it is supposed, of the fact, that Miller knew of their intention, and had prepared to defend the office with fire arms, and of course concluded that their project could not be carried into effect, without the risk and probable loss of some of their lives; and however anxious to prevent the disclosure of the secrets of Masonry, they seem to have been unwilling to sacrifice their limbs or lives in its service. At day dawn they separated, and retreated from the village, without having effected any thing. Part of them re-assembled at Ganson's house, in Stafford, where Sawyer was branded as a coward for not effecting the object for which he had started.†

Miller occupied, as printing offices, the second story of two wooden buildings in the compact part of the village of Batavia, nearly all of which consists of wooden buildings—the two offices were separated by an alley about twelve feet wide. A family of ten persons occupied the lower part of one of the buildings, and Miller's assistants, six in number, always slept in the upper rooms. On the night of Sunday, the 10th of September, 1826, the inhabitants of the village were alarmed by the cry of fire, which proceeded from these offices, but was soon extinguished; the fire was first discovered by bright flames bursting from under the outside stairways, leading into the printing offices. On examination it was evident that the attempt had been made with very minute preparations. Remains of straw, and cotton balls, saturated with spirits of turpentine, were found under the stairs: a short brush was found, which had evidently been dipped in turpentine; and the sidings of the houses were smeared with that liquid. A short distance from the building a dark lantern was found. It will be manifest to every person who sees the situation of the offices, and adjacent buildings, that if the fire had gotten much headway, a considerable portion of the village would have been consumed. For some other information relating to the different attempts on Miller's office, the reader is referred to the affidavits of John Mann, and Thomas G. Green, contained in the appendix. (No. 16, and 17.)

In March, 1827, the committee, on the affidavit of John Mann, (to which the reader has been referred,) obtained a warrant for the apprehension of Richard Howard, as the incendiary, and despatched a messenger to Buffalo for the purpose of arresting him. That no step should be taken without due caution, they requested a friend in Buffalo to examine into the affair, and instructed him, that, if satisfactory proof existed that Howard was at Buffalo, on Monday morning early, engaged in his usual occupations, he was authorized to withhold the precept. The friend to whom they had written, chose to call in to his aid four others, who, after much reflection, say they 'felt it to be

---

* Appendix, No. 16.

† Sawyer, and some others, have been indicted for this attempt, but their trials have not yet taken place.

right to advise the officers not to arrest Howard, and had taken their measures with such prudence as they thought would prevent all knowledge of the complaint from coming to his ears; that they had felt the more confidence in that course, from the belief that Howard would not leave the place, but would be found to answer the charge, if such proof should thereafter be produced, as should warrant the pursuit of criminal proceedings against him.' A few days after receiving the letter of these gentlemen, the committee obtained satisfactory proof that, about the time the attempt was made, Howard had been at Batavia, in secret consultation with a member of the fraternity. A second officer was despatched, with positive directions to arrest him for examination. But the officer, on his arrival at Buffalo, was informed, by one of the gentlemen who had written the letter, that the night after its date, (March 9th,) Howard had absconded, though they could not ascertain by what means he had been alarmed. He has never since been heard of by any member of the committee. The secrecy and celerity of his departure—the active part he took in the conspiracy—and the facts detailed in the second affidavit of John Mann, will leave not much doubt on the minds of the readers, that he feared an arrest on a much higher charge than that of attempting to set fire to the printing offices of Miller.*

On Sunday morning, the tenth day of Sept. 1826, Nicholas G. Chesebro, of the village of Canandaigua, a hatter by trade, and Master of the Masonic Lodge in that place, and one of the coroners of Ontario county, applied for, and obtained from Jeffrey Chipman, a justice of the peace, a warrant for the apprehension of William Morgan, on a charge of stealing a shirt and cravat, in May previous, from an innkeeper named Kingsley, who afterwards deposed that he had no intention of entering a complaint against Morgan, until he was prompted to it by Chesebro and his associates. Having obtained the warrant, which was directed to him as coroner, he called upon Holloway Hayward, a constable, who, with Chesebro, Henry Howard, a merchant of Canandaigua, Harris Seymour, Moses Roberts, and one Joseph Scofield, took their departure from Canandaigua, on the morning of the same day, in an extra stage, hired for the occasion by Chesebro.

At Avon, the party were joined by Asa Nowlen, an innkeeper; at Caledonia, by John Butterfield, a store keeper; and at Le Roy, by Ella G. Smith: all of whom, as Hayward has since deposed, seemed to know that he had a warrant against Morgan. The party proceeded to the village of Stafford, where they stopped to take supper at a public house then kept by James Ganson. Immediately after their arrival at Stafford, on Sunday evening, Samuel S. Butler, a physician residing there, was introduced to some of the party, and informed that they, or the officer, had a warrant for Morgan, and he was requested to mention that circumstance to Nathan Follett and William Seaver, then Master of the Batavia Lodge, both residents of Batavia village, for which he immediately started. The party having finished their supper were now joined by Ganson, and started for Batavia. About two miles from that place they were met by Dr. Butler, who had some conversation, in a low voice, with Ganson, and communicated to him the answer of Follett, which was, that they should *not come on*. Some of the party said they would proceed; they had come for the purpose, and would go on. They concluded, however, that it was not adviseable to proceed in the carriage, and most of the party left it about a mile and a half east of the village, and proceeded on foot to Batavia, and the remainder returned with the carriage. The next morning early, Morgan was arrested and taken to the public house where the party had slept. An extra stage was procured for the return of the party, in which they left the village with Morgan. Just as they were about to start, Miller came up and insisted that Morgan should not be taken away, as he was in

---
* Appendix, No. 25.

custody of the sheriff of the county for debt, and he, Miller, was one of his bail. Miller, however, was immediately pushed aside by Danolds, the tavern keeper, who closed the door, and Chesebro, having seated himself on the outside with the driver, urged him to drive fast until he should get out of the county. But the driver became uneasy, and stopped about eighty rods from Danolds, refusing to proceed. He was, however, persuaded to go as far as Stafford, where he was assured Ganson would become his surety against all responsibility; and on his arriving at Stafford, Ganson accordingly gave him such assurances as induced him to proceed. At Le Roy, Hayward, who held the process, offered, as he afterwards said, to take Morgan before the justice of the peace, who had endorsed the warrant, that he might give bail if he chose. No such offer was made to him in Batavia, where he might have found bail, and there was no reason to suppose that he could have friends in Le Roy, to whom he could apply in such an emergency. He accordingly declined, saying, that when he got to Canandaigua, he could convince Mr. Kingsley, the apparent prosecutor, that he did not intend to steal the shirt and cravat. The party arrived at Canandaigua, fifty miles east of Batavia, about sunset, and Morgan was examined by the magistrate. Loton Lawson appeared as a witness on his behalf, and made such statements as induced the discharge of Morgan. To have procured his imprisonment for a larceny, would, of course, have defeated the real object of the conspirators, because his person would have been out of their control. As soon as Morgan was thus discharged from arrest under the criminal process, Chesebro produced a claim against him for a debt of two dollars, due to one Aaron Ackley, an innkeeper in Canandaigua, with an authority to collect the debt on his own account. Morgan admitted the debt, confessed judgment, and, seemingly aware of the determination to detain him, pulled off his coat, and desired the constable to levy on it, or take it as security for the debt. Hayward, the constable, refused to take it, and conducted Morgan to jail, where he was left about ten o'clock in the evening.

On Tuesday, the 12th day of September, about noon, a crowd of men suddenly appeared in the village of Batavia, nearly all of whom carried with them clubs, or sticks, newly cut, and resembling one another, and, to all appearance, provided for the occasion. The crowd assembled themselves at the house of Danolds, an innkeeper. To the oldest inhabitants of the village, almost all of them were strangers, and to this day the names of very few have been distinctly ascertained by us, although the whole number thus equipped was sixty or seventy. They were manifestly selected for the occasion, because their names and persons were not known to the inhabitants of the village generally. No motive for their sudden appearance was assigned. Immediately after this assemblage, *Jesse French*, one of the constables of the county, repaired to Miller's printing office, and, in a rude and violent manner, arrested him, alleging that he had a criminal process, or a process in behalf of the people. After detaining him in a room at Danolds' tavern about two hours, they put him into an open wagon. Seven men, exclusive of the driver, all armed with clubs, took their seats in the wagon, all of whom were unknown to him. French, the constable, having mounted his horse, the whole mob proceeded to Stafford, a village about six miles east from Batavia. On arriving there, Miller was seized by two men, and conducted to a room in the third story of a stone building, ordinarily used as a Masonic lodge room. In this room he was guarded by five men, who said they were acting as assistants to French, and under his orders. While thus secluded and guarded, his counsel, with four or five of his friends, arrived, and the former, after some short detention, was permitted by French to see him. The constable was then asked for a sight, or description of the warrant, by virtue of which he held Miller in custody; but he steadily refused to exhibit or describe it; but still left no doubt on the mind of Miller or his counsel, that the warrant was in a criminal proceeding, and at length avowed that it had been issued by a magistrate at Le

Roy. It should here be stated, that, about three days before the successive arrests of Morgan and Miller, Daniel Johns, whose sudden appearance at Batavia has been mentioned, suddenly disappeared from that place. A short time after Miller's introduction to the lodge room at Stafford, this same Daniel Johns entered the room, holding in his hand a drawn sword, and walked, with large and quick steps, across the room, and, as Miller describes it, seemed anxious to inspire terror into the captive. Miller, however, ventured to remonstrate with him; having learned, in some way which he cannot recollect, that Johns was his prosecutor. Johns, however, answered in a voice that faltered a little, 'Miller, I am only doing what I have been ordered to do.' During his detention in the room, one of the guards told him, in language loud enough to be heard by all in the room, that he was not to be tried at Le Roy, nor to stop there, nor to be tried by an ordinary tribunal; but was going where Morgan was. Miller asked what tribunal; he replied, you will see. The others made no remarks in denial or explanation, but he heard one man say to another, Miller is nothing but *an Entered Apprentice.* To detail all the evasive falsehoods and idle assertions, by which French and his coadjutors endeavored to excuse themselves from proceeding with Miller to the justice's office at Le Roy, would be a useless waste of our own time, and the patience of the reader.

It was manifest that the conspirators wished to consume the time, until night should favor the completion of their projects, and that to proceed to Le Roy was no part of their plan; if it could be avoided. But in the course of the afternoon, French, seemingly by inadvertence, admitted that the process he had against Miller, was, in fact, a process in a civil suit; and from that time his resolution seemed somewhat shaken. About dusk the whole crowd proceeded, with much nose and tumult, to Le Roy, four miles, and, after many efforts on the part of French to prevent him from so doing, Miller got himself placed before the justice, who had issued the warrant. French then gave directions to two of his assistants, and disappeared. Miller staid in the office about half an hour, during which time the justice called for the constable and warrant, but neither constable, warrant, or plaintiff appeared, and the justice informed Mr. Miller that he was at liberty to go where he pleased. This was about nine o'clock in the evening. It appeared from the docket of the magistrate that a warrant had been issued against Miller, and one John Davids, on the oath, and at the request of Daniel Johns. John Davids had been also arrested by the directions of French, but the sheriff of the county informed them that he was in his custody on the jail limits, upon which he was discharged from the arrest.—Miller having thus obtained permission to return, was making the best of his way to a public house, when French and Johns suddenly appeared again: The former endeavoured to seize Miller by the collar, and called loudly for help to retake the prisoner; Johns asked if there was no person there who would help to secure that man. But although attempts were made to regain possession of Miller, he succeeded in reaching a public house; and after another ineffectual attempt by French, and his associates, to prevent him, he returned late at night to Batavia, and relieved his family from terror and alarm. That this lawless assemblage of men took place for the purpose of securing the arrest of Miller, by virtue of a process never intended to be acted upon, we shall take no trouble to show to the public. We have conclusive proof from the express declarations of those who led the troop, and from various other sources, that one of the objects they had in view was to pull down the office of Miller, if that should be necessary for the purpose of getting possession of the printed sheets and manuscripts of the expected book.

We are satisfied that their visit was expected by many decent men in the village of Batavia, and their intention to pull down the printing office of Miller, if such a step should become necessary to get possession of the printed sheets and manuscripts of Morgan's book, has been repeatedly proved: and we are also bound to declare, that some of those who were in the secret, disapproved of the design, and endeavored, by the exertion of their personal influence, to prevent them from coming. We are not, however, able to state, what it would give us satisfaction to state, that any information was given to the magistrates, or other public officers, or to any other respectable inhabitants of the village, which would have apprised them of the intended outrage, and justified them in requiring the interference of the civil or military authority. It was a singular circumstance, that on the day when the visit of this mob took place, all the magistrates of the village were called upon to attend as witnesses before a justice of the peace, in an adjoining town, and were actually absent when they arrived, and continued so, absent, until they had departed. We are satisfied that they were regularly summoned to attend as witnesses; and if the circumstance was not accidental, it must of course have been known to the leaders of the mob that their operations on that day would not probably be interrupted by any interference on the part of the official conservators of the peace. At the October sessions of the county court, James Ganson, Jesse French, Roswell Wilcox, and James Hurlburt, were indicted for a riot, and for assaulting and falsely imprisoning David C. Miller. Their trial took place at the court of Oyer und Terminer, held in April before Judge Birdsall, in Genesee county. French, Wilcox, and Hurlburt, were found guilty, and sentenced to close confinement in the county jail for different periods—viz: French for one year, Wilcox for six months, and Hurlburt for three: Ganson was acquitted: two other indictments were found against him—one for a conspiracy with Daniel Johns, and George Ketchum, to obtain Morgan's manuscripts or printed sheets; the other, for a conspiracy, with sixteen others, to destroy Miller's office. On these he has not yet been tried.

On the trial, above mentioned, it was proved, that on the morning of the 12th, before the party came to Batavia, at Stafford, and in the lodge room, Ganson was appointed the leader or captain of the expedition against Miller's office.

Supposing the reader to have perused the affidavit of Mrs. Morgan, contained in the Appendix, we proceed to mention that immediately after her return, (i. e. not more than a few hours,) from her useless visit to Canandaigua, to her desolate home, the same Thomas M'Cully, whom we have mentioned before, called on her, and said 'that he had been appointed by the lodge to provide for the support of herself and her children, and had provided board for them at a public tavern in the village;' the same in which her husband had been detained after his arrest on Monday morning, before he was put into the carriage and taken away. The unfortunate woman promptly answered, 'that she should accept no assistance from 'the Masons,' for she attributed to them, without any hesitation, the afflictions she was suffering.'

It will be seen by her statement that, on her way home, James Ganson got into the stage at Le Roy, and assured her that he was then on his way to Batavia '*to make arrangements for her support.*' He told her 'That her husband had not been killed, but that she must not be surprised if she did not see him again in a year: and if she never saw him again she should be well provided for, and her children sent to school as soon as they were old enough.'*

Her distress of mind, and unprotected situation, did not fail to excite the sympathy, and call forth the kind offices of those whose sensibilities were not

---

* About the first of March, 1827, Henry Brown, Esquire, of Batavia, said to be the Grand Commander of the Knight Templars encamped at Le Roy, called at Mrs. Morgan's lodgings, and exhibited to the woman with whom she boarded, a bag containing, as he said, silver dollars, which he professed great anxiety to give to her without delay. Mrs. Morgan never sent for the dollars, and they were taken away by Mr. Brown, but it is not known to what use they were subsequently appropriated.

blunted by vice or hatred to her husband. To compel her, by dire necessity, to cast herself upon the bounty of those who had almost avowed their agency in producing the sudden calamity which had come upon her, and had declared their certain knowledge that there was no probability that she would again have the support and protection of her husband until after the lapse of a year, if ever, could not be tolerated. Her immediate wants were provided for, and an agent sent to Canandaigua to make inquiries into the fate of her husband. He procured the information contained in the depositions, No. 2, 3, 4, 5, 6, and 7, which gave such an extraordinary aspect to the transactions, that it was deemed absolutely necessary to lay them at once before the public, at a meeting called for that purpose, in the village of Batavia. The committee appointed at that meeting, published the notice contained in the Appendix, No. 12; and sent an agent to make inquiries along the road from Rochester to Lewiston and Fort Niagara.

Hopes were for many weeks entertained that he was merely detained in confinement until the suppression of his book could be effected by terror or negociation: but week after week passed away, and no correct information of him was received. In this state of suspense and anxiety, circumstances occurred which in a great degree destroyed all hopes of his being discovered, and created the most unpleasant feelings in the community. It soon became manifest to the committee of Genesee county, that several hundred men had been actually concerned in different parts of the transactions which had ended in his disappearance. Many of them were men of high standing, and good general characters. Numbers of them, without hesitation, openly declared that Morgan would never be seen again; men, who had frequently asked for, and obtained, the confidence of their fellow citizens, unreservedly justified the conduct of those by whom he had been kidnapped, and laughed at the efforts that were making to discover his fate. The distress of his wife was spoken of with contemptuous levity in the streets.

Chesebro had assured the keeper of the jail in Canandaigua, that Morgan 'had gone where Miller would never see him *again*.' James Ganson exultingly told a member of the Genesee committee, whom he met in the streets of Rochester, that Morgan could not have been rescued if he had been closely followed by his friends—that if the committee 'could hang, draw, and quarter all the Masons that had a hand in it, they could not get him back—that he *was not dead, but was put where he would stay put, until God Almighty should call for him.*' Similar, and well authenticated, declarations reached us from the neighboring towns, and from distant places; and a large number of citizens, who were understood to be members of lodges, spoke of the occurrence with a visible air of triumph. The members of the committee, as they walked the streets, were several times asked by men, who had openly justified the conduct of his kidnappers, 'Well, have you found Morgan yet?'

Various efforts were made to deter some of them from acting, by friendly remonstrances, by hints of the great disadvantage it would be to them, by saying they would raise up numerous and powerful enemies. Many decent men of the order of Masons declared, 'that efforts to learn the fate of Morgan would be useless—that if we could discover the guilty, we could not get them punished; that they had acted according to their orders, and would be borne out—that their body had a right to deal with their own members according to their own laws—that if they had done any thing with him, it was no one's business but their own.'* They said, that the men who had determined to

---

* A similar declaration, in relation to the destruction of Miller's office, should not be omitted. Two of the justices of the peace, residing in the village of Batavia, are active members of the Masonic society. On the day when Miller was taken away, they were, as before related, attending as witnesses before a magistrate in Bethany.

suppress the book, acted in a body, and in concert; were well organized, and could act with effect, and possessed the offices, talents and wealth of the country; that they understood one another, and would pursue with their vengeance all who should interfere with them.

Far from affecting to think that Morgan had disappeared voluntarily, and for sinister purposes, or was colluding with his kidnappers to deceive the public, and excite attention to his book, (the first part of which was not then published, and did not appear for some weeks afterwards,) we heard not the slightest insinuation of the kind. On the contrary, his abduction was spoken of as having defeated the publication; and we believe they, in general, supposed that its suppression was accomplished; and were extremely mortified and disappointed when it made its appearance, with assurances from the publisher that the other parts of the work had been finished by Morgan, and would certainly be published.*

We now resume our narrative in relation to the fate of Morgan, after he had, as before related, been imprisoned at the jail at Canandaigua.

The next evening after Morgan's imprisonment for the small debt, soon after dusk, Loton Lawson called at the jail, and desired to see Morgan, which, after some objections from the keeper, he was permitted to do. He proposed paying the debt, and taking Morgan with him to his house, a short distance from the village; Morgan seemed willing to be relieved, but expressed an inclination to wait in jail until the next morning, and retired to his bed. After a short absence Lawson returned again; and having procured a carriage, and the assistance of a sufficient number of men, he eventually obtained the consent of the jailer's wife, who was acting in the absence of her husband, to the discharge of Morgan, and he accordingly left the apartment in which he had been confined, (Lawson holding him by the arm,) at about nine o'clock in the evening. Almost directly in front of the jail he was seized by his supposed friend Lawson, and some other person, and notwithstanding his struggles and cries of *murder*, he was gagged, and led away from the jail. The cry of murder, and the appearance of a struggle in the street, excited a momentary attention from the people living in the vicinity of the jail, and a man ran out to ascertain what was the cause. The first person he came up with was Col. Edward Sawyer, who, with Nicholas G. Chesebro, was standing near by, spectators of the scene.—When asked what was the matter, Col. Sawyer answered him promptly, 'Nothing, only a man has been let out of jail, and has been

---

One of them declared to a member of the Genesee committee, in the presence of the other, that 'he need not be surprised if, when he returned to Batavia, he found Miller's office levelled with the ground.' He asked them, 'if they, being justices of the peace, thought such proceedings right.' 'Why,' said one of them, 'if you found a man abusing your marriage bed, would you have recourse to law, or take a club and beat his brains out?' This person still holds the office which renders it his peculiar duty to preserve the peace of the county, and secure by recognizance or imprisonment the persons of those who may threaten to break it.

* The reader will readily perceive that their confidence in having suppressed the work, was not without plausible foundations. Ketchum had obtained from Mrs. Morgan the original manuscripts of the three first degrees: (see her affidavit:) they were delivered to her by Miller for the purpose of negotiating with the fraternity for the restoration of her husband, after he had no further use for them. Goodwill, Stone, and others, had surreptitiously gotten several of the sheets into their possession, when they broke into Morgan's room; and they, the same evening, had ransacked every place at his lodgings, where they could hope to find the manuscripts. Such parts of the unprinted work as were then completed, and had not been delivered to Miller, were at the time concealed in a straw bed, in the room from which Morgan was taken.

taken on a warrant, and is going to be tried.' Receiving this answer from a person of good character, whom he knew, the man turned about and declined to interfere. Sawyer's own account of the transactions, and the part he took in it, will be seen by the copy of his affidavit in the Appendix, No. 9. The carriage, after having left Canandaigua, was next noticed at the village of Victor: it was first driven into the open shed of a tavern, kept by Dr. Thomas Beach, from thence into the yard of one Enos Gillis, back of the barn, and out of sight of the road, about forty rods from the tavern of Beach. James Gillis here took from his brother's stable a horse, which he mounted, and proceeded on. The ostler was called on to get a horse for Lawson, whom he knew. James Gillis, who then resided at Montmorency, in Pennsylvania, a brother of Enos Gillis, was recognized at Victor by several persons who knew him well, and was seen the next day on horseback in the vicinity: his participation in the transaction will account for the assertion of George Ketchum, as stated in Mrs. Morgan's affidavit, ' That a man had come from Pennsylvania, and had taken him away in a private carriage.' A comparison of these assertions and circumstances will enable the reader to form some opinion of the extent of the conspiracy, the ample preparations that had been made to effect the object of it, and the accuracy of the information possessed by all concerned in it, as to who were the principal managers. Gillis disappeared immediately, and has not since been seen in this state. He was included in the first indictment found against Lawson, Sawyer, Chesebro, and others, but as yet has not been arrested or tried. Enos Gillis also soon afterwards left the country, and has lately moved his family away, and, since he was examined before the jury in November, 1826, has always been absent from the county at such times as it was probable he would be called on to testify. After leaving Victor, the party drove to Rochester, twenty-eight miles north westerly from Canandaigua, and reached Hanford's tavern, about three miles below that place, a little after day light, with horses very much fatigued. Hubbard, who owned and drove the carriage, when applied to for information in relation to his employers, and his journey, gave the extraordinary and incredible account detailin the affidavit of Mr. Fitch;* and when afterwards examined on oath before the grand jury, his account was entirely the same: he has, however, been since indicted as a conspirator, but has not yet been tried. Before the Canandaigua carriage arrived at Rochester, a carriage belonging to Ezra Platt, a Royal Arch Mason, and a livery-stable keeper in that place, was procured, and sent forward in advance of the Canandaigua carriage, and stopt at some sequestered place, while it was yet dark, in the vicinity of Hanford's tavern. The Canandaigua carriage, on its arrival at Hanford's tavern, was driven under a shed, opposite the house, before any of the party alighted. Two men then got out of it, went into the tavern, and requested some grain for their horses, and something to drink for themselves: they drank at the bar, and took a bottle of gin and a glass to the carriage. One of them remarked to the other, while standing on the steps of the house, ' He was damned glad to get out of jail.' This observation attracted Mrs. Handford's attention, as she suspected from it that a person, for whom one of her neighbors was bail, had been spirited away from the limits, and she feared her neighbor might be injured by it. The men came in soon, and said they had not time to feed their horses, and did not want the grain. All that had alighted returned to the carriage, except one, who remained walking the piazza. This tavern stands at the intersection of the Lewiston ridge road and the Genesee river road; and the carriage drove out upon the ridge with the curtains all down: it was absent nearly an hour, and returned with the curtains up, and a man on a horse, (also belonging to the same Ezra Platt,) riding before it. This man was recognized as being the person who had came to the tavern and made inquiries for a car-

---

* Appendix, No. 7.

riage of such description, and the direction it had taken, and who, upon being informed, had immediately rode in the direction which he was told the carriage had taken; and the informant has declared that he recognised the rider in the person of Edward Doyle, of Rochester, a merchant.* Hubbard deposed before the grand jury, that the persons whom he took from Canandaigua left his carriage in a secluded place, a short distance from Hanford's, and entered into the Rochester carriage, which proceeded along the ridge road. It was next noticed at Clarkson, fifteen miles further west, about nine o'clock in the morning. It was an extremely warm day, and the singularity of the circumstance, that the curtains were all closed in a warm morning, attracted attention—the carriage made a short stop in the middle of the street, which also attracted some notice. No person alighted, except the driver, who went into Baldwin's tavern, and then immediately proceeded onward.

The horses were exchanged about two and a half miles west of Clarkson, at the house of one Allen, whose horses were taken from the field for that purpose. Here, too, the carriage remained closed, and no one alighted while the horses were changed. The person who drove the carriage from Rochester to this place, as soon as inquiries in relation to the transaction were set on foot, left the country, and has not yet returned. The carriage arrived at the village of Gaines, about twelve o'clock, closed in the same manner as at Clarkson; passed through the village without stopping, and proceeded about one mile west of the village, where it stopped in the road at a short distance from any house. Elihu Mather, of that place, took a pair of horses belonging to his brother, James Mather, and overtook the carriage, about one mile from Gaines, where the horses were exchanged in the middle of the road, and at a distance from any house. Mather himself then mounted the box, and drove on, which circumstance excited observation, as he is a man of property, at the head of a large tanning establishment, and of course not accustomed to be seen in such employment. On his return, he stopped at Hughes' tavern—said he had driven the carriage for his brother to Morehouse's tavern, and added, 'I think I make a good stage driver, do I not?' At Ridgeway, one Jeremiah Brown, supervisor of that town, and lately a member of the legislature, suddenly took his horses from the field, where they were hitched to a harrow, led them to the nearest public house, where they were fed, and then harnessed them to the carriage, and mounted the box himself, and drove on.†
About, or shortly before sundown, the carriage arrived at Wright's tavern, nearly north of the village of Lockport, and, instead of driving up to the door

---

* On the trial of Chesebro, Sawyer, Lawson, and Sheldon, for kidnapping William Morgan, Burrage Smith and John Whitney were called as witnesses. Both of them objected to answering any questions, because to do so would criminate themselves: after being well instructed by the court as to the nature of this privilege, they in substance deposed—That they were at Lewiston on the 14th of September; that two or three days before that day, they went together from Rochester, (where they lived, and had families,) to Canandaigua, where they arrived about three o'clock, P. M.; that they heard that Morgan was in jail at that place; that they saw Lawson in the evening; that they heard Lawson converse that night about the taking away of Morgan, in company with three or four others. Smith admitted that he left Canandaigua the night Morgan was taken away, and as he said, probably about eight o'clock. Whitney refused to say at what time he had left Canandaigua, because it would criminate him, and the court decided that he was not bound to answer the question. A few days after the trial, these two men absconded, leaving their families at Rochester, where they were both engaged in regular business. They had before enjoyed a respectable standing in that place, and were generally considered as thriving men.

† See note in the Appendix, No. 30.

of the house, it was driven into the barn, and out of sight. The persons who came with it, guarded the barn and carriage in such a manner as to keep off all persons from seeing the carriage.* A large number of men were seen assembled at Wright's, some of whom appeared to be armed with clubs, and the horse of Wright was kept standing all night at the post, saddled. Much whispering and clustering was observed, and it was rumored or given out that they were collected for the purpose of preventing the escape or rescue of a prisoner, under the charge of the people in the carriage. The next day a niece of the innkeeper told one of the neighbors, that they had prepared supper for a number of Masons, and had received previous notice to be ready for them. About ten o'clock at night, the gate keeper heard a carriage pass the toll house, distant a few rods from Wright's tavern, very quietly, and supposing it was intended to pass without paying toll, he went hastily to the door. On opening it, he found Brown standing in front of it, holding the toll money in his hand, but the carriage had passed on a short distance. Being well acquainted with Brown, he asked him familiarly, 'What is the great hurry.' Brown answered nothing, and immediately went to the carriage, which drove off with great speed.

About sunrise, the next morning, the same carriage repassed the gate, driven by Mather, the curtains up, and Brown, the only passenger, asleep, or pretending to be so. Maxwell, the gate keeper, asked the person driving, 'How far did you go last night; did you go to Lewiston?' He answered, with a little hesitation, ' No, not so far.' This, as relates to the carriage, was a falsehood, as will be seen by the subsequent narration. The distance from Wright's to Mollineux's tavern, in Cambria, is about six miles, and from thence to Lewiston, is thirteen miles. About eleven o'clock at night, of the same 13th of September, Eli Bruce, then and now the high sheriff of Niagara county, who resides at Lockport, about four miles from the ridge road, arrived at Mollineux's tavern, in company with the carriage driven by Brown.† It stopped in front of the house, the curtains being closed quite round. Bruce went into the house and inquired for the landlord, who was in bed. He was shown to his room by a hired girl, the only person up. After a short conversation in private with the landlord, Bruce called up his son, and desired him to put a pair of horses before the carriage, to go as far as Lewiston. The son expressed to Bruce his desire to drive himself, as the horses were young, and he did not like to trust them with other persons: Bruce objected to his doing so, and said he had a careful driver, pointing to a man who he (young Mollineux) knew to be Jeremiah Brown. The apparent hurry, and the circumstance that Bruce was sheriff of the county, induced the girl to inquire of Bruce what was the matter. He answered, 'You cannot know at present.' The carriage soon afterwards started for Lewiston, driven by Brown, and Mather remained at Mollineux's. Brown returned with the same carriage before day light, having travelled a distance of twenty-six miles in about five hours. The horses were so much jaded that young Mollineux was very angry at their

---

* Between the house and barn there was a large open shed, amply sufficient to cover many carriages and horses.

† A few minutes before Bruce arrived with the carriage, a man rode up, on horseback, to the same tavern, and inquired for Col. Mollineux, a son of the tavern keeper, and a member of the fraternity; and being told that he had gone to Lewiston, rode off at a quick rate eastward, and returned with the carriage. From this, and similar inquiries and occurrences at Hanford's, and other places, the reader will observe how accurate was the information possessed by the conspirators, as to the time when the carriage would arrive at places sixty miles distant from each other, and he may form some opinion of the extent of the conspiracy, and the number concerned in it.

usage, and declared to a relation 'That Bruce should never have his horses again to drive in that fashion.'

Sometime in the night of the same 13th of September, the carriage arrived at Lewiston, seventy miles westerly from Rochester. Bruce, and Samuel Barton of Lewiston, one of the stage proprietors, went together into the stage office at Lewiston, and Barton inquired of Joshua Fairbanks, (who kept the stage books, and usually slept in the office,) what drivers were at home. Fairbanks answered him, none but Fox, who was asleep in an adjoining room. Barton immediately called up Fox, and soon left the office, followed by Bruce. When Fox went out, Barton told him to get up a carriage, and drive some gentlemen to Youngstown. The carriage was accordingly got ready by Fox, who drove it up to the front door of the tavern, called the Frontier House, where he found Bruce waiting, who immediately got into it, and told him to drive round the house into a back street, where he drove accordingly, and found a carriage standing in the middle of the street, in front of Samuel Barton's dwelling house. The horses had been taken from it, and the curtains were all closed: he drove along side of that carriage, but remained on his seat. Here Bruce got out, and Fox then saw him and another man assist a third man to get out of one carriage into the other;* they then both entered the carriage, and Bruce told Fox to drive on. During all this time, as Fox deposed, not a word was said: not even a whisper heard from any one of the three men. The carriage then proceeded to Youngstown, a distance of six miles, during all which time the same profound silence seemed to be preserved by those in the carriage. At Youngstown, the carriage stopped by order of Bruce, in the street in front of the house occupied by Col. William King; then Bruce got out, and knocked at the door, and called up Col. King; the door was soon opened, and a light soon after seen in the house, where Bruce remained about fifteen minutes. During that time, the driver heard something said by a person in the carriage, which appeared to him a call for water; Bruce appeared to hear the voice, and replied 'Yes, yes, you shall have some:' no water, however, was brought to the carriage. King came out of the door, and with Bruce got into the carriage; and Bruce directed the driver to go on, when the carriage proceeded towards Fort Niagara, which is about one mile distant from Youngstown. About eighty rods from the Fort, near the grave yard, Bruce ordered him to stop, which he did; but (as he said) still did not leave his seat—when four persons left the carriage, and walked from it in a huddle (as he expressed it) towards the Fort. When they had proceeded a short distance from the carriage, Bruce told him he might go back about his business; and he (Fox) returned with the carriage to Lewiston, empty.

The next day Fox mentioned the singularity of the circumstances attending his jaunt to Paul Mosher, a Mason; and told him, he (Fox) thought he heard King say, as he came to the carriage, 'What, Morgan, are you here!' Mosher being struck with the strangeness of the transaction, asked another member of the lodge what it meant? who told him 'He believed it was Morgan.' He made similar inquiries of another Mason, who told him 'It was

---

* Another witness deposed, that on the morning of the 14th September, 1826, he was up taking care of a sick person about one or two o'clock; that he looked towards Samuel Barton's stage barn; saw a carriage and horses driven near a carriage without horses; saw three men go from the standing carriage, to the one with horses; one of the men appeared to have a handkerchief around his head, and to be intoxicated, and was helped by the other two. Sometime afterwards he saw a man in Lewiston, whom he believed was the same he saw at the carriage: asked who he was, and was told it was Eli Bruce: knew the driver at the time—it was Corydon Fox: he stood about one hundred feet from the carriage; it was a bright moonlight night.

Morgan, for Bruce told him so.' In the forenoon of the same day, September 14th, Mosher saw Bruce at Lewiston, and asked him why he was so imprudent as to have the driver he did, for he was not a Mason, Bruce answered that *Sam* (meaning *Samuel Barton,*) was more in fault than he was, for he told him to send a Mason. Mosher asked Bruce, if he actually had Morgan, who answered that he *had*. On the same day, Samuel Barton asked Mosher if Fox mistrusted that Morgan was in the carriage, Mosher told him that Fox was telling the circumstance about the village. Barton then told him to say to Fox, if he knew any thing he must keep it to himself, and hold his tongue, or he would discharge him; and at the same time remarked to Mosher that there must be another man smuggled away, to blind that transaction; that Mosher being a Mason, ought to have been sent, but having been called up in the night, in his hurry he did not think.*

Thus far we have positive testimony, sufficient, we think, to prove most satisfactorily that William Morgan was, in the manner we have related, conducted to the vicinity of Fort Niagara; and here our direct and positive proof ends: but the facts and circumstances hereafter detailed, are authenticated by unquestionable testimony, and will be submitted to the reader, that he may draw such conclusions as he shall think they warrant.

The fort at that time was unoccupied, except by the keeper and his wife; and there is no dwelling house near it excepting a small ferry house, directly on the bank of the river, occupied by Mr. Giddins, who then occasionally entertained travellers, and has had charge of the fort from May, 1826, when the troops left it, until August 1st, 1826, when he surrendered it to the care of the person who still has charge of it. The magazine is a very strong building, the entrance to which is secured by two doors: the first or outside door is usually fastened by an iron bolt, secured from being slipped by a padlock; the inside door is made of white oak plank, cased on the outside with sheet iron, and was originally fastened by a large stock lock, nailed to a large piece of white oak plank, which had been nailed to the inner side of the door, with wrought nails of a large size. Directly opposite to the inside door is a thick stone wall, forming one side of a stone portico, built around the inner door which opens into the portico, and is furnished with a large wooden handle, spiked on, to facilitate the pulling of it open. No light can enter the building except from two very small windows, very near the ridge of the roof, elevated about fifteen feet from the floor. The keys have usually hung in the open entry of the mess room, a very large building occupied by the keeper. It will be seen by the affidavit of Giddins,† (who is a member of the Masonic society,) that he surrendered the building to the present keeper on the first of August, in perfect order. That the empty ammunition boxes were ranged along the walls at the distance of about a foot from them. That he recollects of no loose door being inside of the building, when he delivered it up to the present keeper, and should not have considered it proper to leave that, or any other thing there, which did not properly belong to it. That it was as usual, white washed on the inside, about the first of May. In the month of January last, (1827,) this building was visited by a number of gentlemen from different counties, who were members of the committees appointed at meetings of the citizens; and in March, 1827, it was again examined by three of those who have signed this narrative, for the express purpose of re-examination, and to ascertain as far as possible, the accuracy of the opinion formed, and the facts stated, by the persons who first visited it for investigation. It was found that one of the floor planks had been broken up; that part of the floor was covered with the loose door, mentioned in the affidavit of Mr. Giddins, on which were piled a number of the empty ammunition boxes. The large stock

---

* See Appendix, for extracts from other depositions.
† Appendix, No. 26.

lock, and the block to which it was nailed, were found knocked off, and marks on the door showed that they had been forced off by striking on the upper edge of them; this was also evidenced by the bend of the wrought nails, and the appearances of the holes from which the nails had been forced : this lock and block had manifestly been thrown with great force, and very many times, against the door, at the upper corners; and the blows had been so continually repeated, that the door was bruised in two places, so as to make it easy to pick splinters from the oak plank, which was done by one of the visiters : a corresponding bruise was found on one corner of the lock and block. Outside of the inner door was found a piece of wide pine board, one end of which had been recently sawed in an irregular line across to a length which made it reach exactly from under the large handle on the outside of the inner door, to the bottom of the stone wall opposite, and when placed in that position it effectually prevented the inner door from being pushed open from the inside, after the lock was forced off. The rust of the sheet iron was found on the edge of the board; and corresponding marks were distinctly observed on the door directly under the handle.

Neither Mr. Giddins, or the then keeper, could give any account of the manner in which the lock had been taken off, or the bruises on the door, or why the board had been used; and neither of them recollected ever to have noticed these appearances before they were pointed out at that time. Outside of the door, and very near it, was found an ammunition box, which was seen there in October previous, and the bottom of which was covered almost two inches thick with a substance that two persons who then saw it supposed to be human excrements. When seen in March, the bottom was clean, but one of the sides was still stained. From these circumstances, the persons who visited the place in March were perfectly satisfied that after Giddins had surrendered the care of the fort, in August, some person had been confined in the magazine, who had made violent and reiterated efforts to force his way out; and that these efforts must have been attended with much noise. How far these appearances will account for the declaration of Barton, made on the 14th of September, that there was trouble at the fort, the reader must conjecture for himself.

Mr. Giddins was distinctly asked by one of the visiters in March, whether he had not, on the night of the 13th of September, seen Bruce and King, and was not called up by them. He declined answering the question, saying that when legally called on, he would attest to all he knew. He was then told that his declining to answer so plain a question left on the mind of the person who asked him the inevitable impression that he *had seen them*, and would probably make the same impressions on the minds of others—to which he made no answer or observation.

On the morning of the 14th of September, a party of ladies and gentlemen went into the steam boat Martha Ogden, from Youngstown to Lewiston, to attend the installation of a Chapter, which was to take place that day. On board the boat was Bruce, King, Mrs. Giddins, and other ladies. During the voyage, one of the ladies familiarly asked Bruce what he meant by going about at nights, and disturbing people, and calling up her husband. Yes, observed Mrs. Giddins, they came too and routed up my poor husband.

The certificate of the magistrate, and the affidavit of Mosher, were transmitted by the Genesee committee to the Governor, for the purpose of obtaining his proclamation, offering a reward for the discovery of Morgan, or his murderers. On the suggestion of His Excellency, a regular complaint was made against Bruce, and laid before him. To obviate the charge, Bruce transmitted to him affidavits, impeaching the character of Mosher, and his motives of action; but did not attempt to deny or explain by his own depositions, or that of any other person, the part attributed to him; nor did he produce the

I i

deposition of Barton, or Mollineux, or any other person, to show what was the occasion of the extraordinary course he had pursued.*

A reverend clergyman, residing in the village of Lewiston, and a member of the Masonic lodge, or society, declared in Batavia to the gentleman, at whose house he lodged, while attending the synod in the month of September, 1826, that Morgan had passed through Lewiston on his way to Canada. When requested by a member of the Genesee committee to give what information he possessed on the subject, he declared, that on the morning of the 14th of September, about ten o'clock, P. M. he was going to the house where the lodge was to meet, and heard some person in the crowd assembled in front of the house say, that Morgan had passed on the night before to Canada; but he declined saying, or did not recollect, who had made the assertion.†

On the night of the 14th of September, 1826, nine persons ordered supper at the house of Mr. Giddins, five of whom were known to him. They all left his house at about eleven o'clock at night; and he could not tell where they had spent the rest of the night. They did not lodge and were not seen that night at either of the taverns in the village of Youngstown. The next morning before day light, and between the hours of three and four o'clock, four of the five men designated by Giddins, and another man, were seen by Josiah Tryon, whose deposition will be found in the Appendix, travelling on foot about two miles from Lewiston, and about five miles from the house of Giddins, walking towards Lewiston, where three of them resided. One of the other two resided at the Falls of Niagara, and one at Black Rock.

On the afternoon of September the 14th, Samuel Barton told Mosher, who was then in his employment, to borrow a saddle and bridle, and put them on a horse as soon as possible, and hitch him beside another horse then standing under the shed. He did as directed, and found that the latter horse appeared to have been ridden very fast. Barton said to Mosher that 'he had heard from the fort, and must send a man down, for he was afraid there would be trouble yet.' The two horses were rode off the same afternoon; one by a Mason resident at Lewiston, the other by a person whom he did not know. Next morning Mosher asked Barton if there was any trouble at the fort, to which Barton answered, 'I guess it is still enough now.'

It is known to many persons, that, in a letter written by one of the gentlemen who visited Niagara in January last, it was stated that Morgan had been taken to the house of a member of parliament, residing in the village of Newark, or Niagara, in Upper Canada. This assertion was erroneous, and it occurred in part from haste, or want of care, in writing a confidential letter, and in part from misapprehension of the information given by William Terry, of that place, who had received his information from one Stocking, a respectable hatter living in that town. The information intended to be given by Mr. Terry, will be seen by reading his deposition contained in the Appendix. The Mason, before whom Morgan was said to have been taken, is now understood to have been a Mr. M'Bride, a member of the provincial parliament. His letter, purporting to be a contradiction, or denial of the facts stated in the letter first mentioned, will be found in the Appendix. Since the publication of these letters, M'Bride and Stocking called upon Mr. Terry, in company with Dr. Chapin, and in presence of a large number of respectable inhabitants of Nia-

---

* We are officially informed that His Excellency has told the counsel of Bruce that he shall expect a satisfactory account of his proceedings on the 13th and 14th of September, before he pronounces his acquittal.

† How could such a report have gotten about in that place a few hours after the mysterious carriage left the front of Barton's house, unless some person knew the fact, or some circumstances were known which created that belief among some of those who had assembled there. Burrage Smith, John Whitney, Loton Lawson, and Eli Bruce, were all at Lewiston on that day.

gara, for the purpose of explanation. At this meeting Terry distinctly declared, 'Stocking you said that M'Bride saw the man; that he was here on this side the water, and he saw him.' Stocking then acknowledged that he had named M'Bride. M'Bride appeared to drop his head and eyes, and said, 'He did not see what right any man under heavens had to say that;' but did not deny that he said any thing of the kind to Stocking, nor declare in any other way that he did not see Morgan, or that he knew nothing of the transaction. We have been informed by those whose veracity we have no reason to question, that the worthy and respectable gentleman alluded to in the letter of M'Bride, as having slept that night at his house, has distinctly declared, that late in the night alluded to, M'Bride was called up by a loud rap on the door, which awoke the lodgers, who, with his wife, arose from bed, and looked out of the window; they saw two men near the house. M'Bride dressed himself, and went away with them, and was gone about half an hour, perhaps more; that on the next morning he did not mention or explain the circumstance.

That after M'Bride had prepared his letter, and before its publication, he submitted it to the perusal of the same gentleman to whom he alluded. After looking it over, his friend observed in substance to M'Bride, 'Your letter does not amount to a full denial; you do not say you did not see Morgan.' M'Bride replied, intimating that it was full enough.

It will be readily perceived that the assertions of M'Bride in his letter, 'that Morgan was not, on the night of the 14th of September, 1826, at his *house;* that Morgan is to him an utter stranger; that he never exchanged a word with him in his life; and would not know him from the greatest stranger in existence;' may all be perfectly true, and yet are perfectly reconcilable with the facts that Morgan was taken to the British side of the river, and was seen by M'Bride; and his omission to declare in his letter, (and that, too, after the observation of his friend,) and before Mr. Terry, and his townsman, that he never saw Morgan, and had no knowledge of his abduction on the night of the 13th of September, (not the 14th,) or any other night, or day, or was applied to to assist in disposing of him, like the silence of Giddins, amounts to very strong presumptive proof that, in fact, he did, on the night of the 13th of September, or morning of the 14th, have an interview with some persons whom he knew had Morgan under their control, and, in fact, that he did see him.

About the 1st of November, and before the publication of the Governor's first proclamation offering a reward for the discovery of Morgan, and the conviction of his kidnappers, and before serious apprehensions of his murder were entertained, and before any investigations had been made along the Ridge road, a respectable inhabitant of Niagara county, Sylvester R. Hathaway, called upon a member of the Genesee committee, whom he met at Lockport, and informed him 'that he had been for some time past working on the Welland Canal. That a friend who resided in Canada, near the canal, had a few days before called on him, and exacted a promise from him to go to Batavia, and communicate to the committee that Morgan had been taken to Fort Niagara in the night—put into the fort, and detained there three or four days. That they tried to get the Masons on the Canada side to take him, but they refused. That afterwards, two ruffians had taken him out, and cut his throat, and tied his body to a rope and stone, and threw it into the lake. That he had been told so by Masons, of which society he was a member, and that he conscientiously believed it. That his name must not be used, or given in, for if it was known that he had informed, he should fare no better.' The messenger assured us that his informant was a grave respectable man of the society of Friends, and not inclined to confide in, or to repeat idle tales, or improbable stories. This communication was not made known even to the other members of the committees, nor any other person, excepting the Governor of the state, until some time after the examination took place in January, and after two other accounts were distinctly stated to us from other sources, which did not differ from it in any essential particulars.

A physician, residing at or near Niagara, U. C., informed one of his friends, that during the sitting of the court of that province in September, a person called on him at the court house, and requested him to attend as one of the counsel on Morgan: he said to his friend, 'I did not go, and I am glad of it; for if I had gone, I should have gotten into a d———d pretty scrape, for they murdered Morgan afterwards.' This communication was obtained in writing, in March, 1827, from the physician's friend, who is a professional gentleman of high standing at Niagara.

The communications made to Dr. Terry, and the letter of M'Bride, (affecting to deny their correctness,) will be found in the Appendix,* upon the contents of which some comments have already been submitted.

Let the reader connect the various accounts received from distinct and entirely separate quarters and persons, with the corresponding and authenticated facts detailed in this narrative, or in the Appendix, and form, if he can, any other conclusion than that which both parties of the visiters to Niagara for examination did form, and do not hesitate to declare; to wit: That the persons who had Morgan under their conduct at Lewiston and Youngstown, on the night of September the 13th, 1826, took him over the Niagara river. That some persons on that side knew he was brought over, and had an interview with his conductors. That he was taken back and confined in the magazine at Fort Niagara; and that a court or council of some kind was held on him, under a pretext of Masonic authority. Those of us who did make investigations at that place in January and March, think that no person of common candor, whose mind is not blinded by prejudice, or under the influence of strong delusion, can visit there, and examine for himself, without forming similar conclusions.

But, again, it will be seen by the reader, that at the court of Oyer and Terminer, held at Canandaigua, in January, 1827, before Judge Throop, Lawson, Sawyer, and Chesebro, withdrew their pleas of not guilty, which they had at a previous court interposed, and plead guilty, and that Sheldon was convicted after a trial. The indictments against all these men charged them with having kidnapped William Morgan, and taken him out of the state of New-York, and out of the United States, and *to places unknown.* They were, beyond any doubt, informed by the able counsellors who defended them, that the uncertainty as to Morgan's fate, and the probability of his having been murdered, would greatly enhance their punishment, unless they could show that they had not participated in the murder of their victim, or been concerned in the latter part of the transaction. Three of them, Sawyer, Chesebro, and Sheldon, accordingly produced their depositions, to show how far they had acted. If these depositions can be relied upon, both Chesebro and Sawyer, by their confession of guilty to the charges contained in the indictments, voluntarily exposed themselves to punishment for the most heinous part of the crime alleged against them; when, in fact, they had not participated in that part of the crime charged. The court, however, seem to have given credit to their depositions, and apportioned their punishment accordingly. But Lawson, it will be seen, gave no account whatever of the part he had performed, and left the court and the public at liberty to form no other opinion than, '*that he had been guilty of all that the indictment charged on him:*' and gave them not even his naked assertions to show '*that Morgan had not been immolated as a victim to their rage, or was then in the land of the living.*'† We know that he was at Lewiston and Youngstown late in the night of the 14th of 'Septem-

---

* Appendix, Nos. 24 and 27.
† See the sentence of Judge Throop, in the Appendix, No. 11.

ber;' and that on his return he stopped at Wright's tavern, and left a message for a relation who then resided a short distance from that place.

If Lawson had dared to depose that he had handed Morgan over to the care or custody of other persons, of whose subsequent action he (Lawson) had no knowledge, (as Chesebro had done,) that he had voluntarily absented himself, (as Sawyer pretended to think;) that he had left him well, and knew not where he had gone, that he was then residing at any place, or that he was then alive—can it be believed that he would not have offered such a deposition, and thus entitled himself to the lenity of the court, from which Chesebro and Sawyer reaped such substantial fruits? Did not these men, who were so anxious to reduce the measure of their punishment, and so well informed as to the mode of effecting that object—did not they (unless they knew that Morgan was dead) importune Lawson to depose to that effect in their behalf, even if he was indifferent about exonerating himself from the crime of being accessary (at least) to murder, which he must have known his silence could not fail to make the community impute to him? Nay, would they not have all gladly given to the court, and to their fellow citizens, any evidence in their power to have shown that Morgan was *probably* alive, or that none of them had been concerned in his death? If Morgan was then living, could not Lawson have given a clue by which to trace him? If no motive whatever, neither the desire to serve his associates in guilt, nor the wish to diminish the measure of his own punishment, nor a decent regard to the opinion of his fellow citizens, and feelings of his family, could induce him to venture on a declaration under oath that Morgan was then alive, or might be for aught he knew, who can doubt that he knew of his death? If he choose to set down quietly under such overwhelming suspicions of his being an accessary to murder, who can suppose that Morgan was then living?

We have now laid before our fellow citizens the detail, or report, which has been so often called for. If it has not been as interesting as they had been led to expect, they must remember that we did not undertake to gratify curiosity, or give our own speculations. We have given, as we promised, 'A narrative of facts and circumstances,' relating to transactions which have excited the earnest attention of the community. Those facts and circumstances are evidenced by the depositions of credible witnesses, or vouched for by the distinct allegations (most of them in writing) of men entitled to our entire confidence for veracity and integrity; to whom we can resort for legal proof, if called for. Whether the conclusions which we have drawn are the legitimate results of those facts and circumstances, our readers must of course decide for themselves. Let them recollect that our exertions (which have not been feeble ones) to trace Morgan beyond Fort Niagara, have been unavailing; that the pecuniary rewards offered by the governor of the state of New York, and Governor of Upper Canada, have not elicited the slightest information on the subject; that the Governor's offer of pardon, promised in his proclamation at our request, has produced no effect; that no attempt has been made, that we know of, by those so directly implicated to explain or deny the extraordinary conduct and occurrences which have fastened such strong and well founded suspicions upon them; that they have thus long set public opinion at defiance, and relinquished their claim to the good opinion of their fellow citizens, without a struggle to retain it; that five of them have absconded, viz. James Gillis, Joseph Scofield, Burrage Smith, John Whitney, and Richard Howard; that others have absented themselves from their families, and the state, and continue absent with a full knowledge of the suspicions which rest upon them; that many of the witnesses have suddenly disappeared, and cannot be traced; that two of those who were called as witnesses before the grand jury of Monroe county, at Rochester, to wit. Edward Doyle, merchant, and Simon B. Jewet, attorney at law, refused to testify, because, as they alleged, *they could not do so truly, without criminating them-*

selves; that others have related stories on oath, which are utterly incredible; and what inference can be drawn from all this but that Morgan has been murdered, and that great numbers of men, heretofore respectable, have been accessaries to his murder? Whether ALL who were concerned in his kidnapping have been accessaries, or consented to his death, we undertake not to decide: But, whatever were the *original designs or motives* of those who were concerned in his disappearance, all of them who have not fully, frankly, and promptly explained the part they are known to have performed, have, we think, no right to complain, if their fellow citizens in general regard them as accessaries to the murder of William Morgan, and shall hereafter treat them accordingly.

COMMITTEE.

GENESEE COMMITTEE.

T. F. TALBOT,
TRUMBULL CARY,
TIMOTHY FITCH,
JAMES P. SMITH,
LYMAN D. PRINDLE,
ELEAZER SOUTHWORTH,
WILLIAM KEYES,
JONATHAN LAY,
WILLIAM DAVIS,
HINMAN HOLDEN.

ROCHESTER COMMITTEE.

JOSIAH BISSELL, JR.
F. F. BACKUS,
HEMAN NORTON,
FREDERICK WHITTLESEY,
THURLOW WEED,
SAMUEL WORKS.

VICTOR COMMITTEE.

SAMUEL RAWSON,
ELIJAH SEDGWICK,
SAMUEL EWING,
NATHAN JENKS,
JAMES M. WHEELER,
THOMAS WRIGHT,
JOHN SARGEANT.

CHILI COMMITTEE.

ISAAC LACY,
WILLIAM PIXLEY,
BENJAMIN BOWEN,
SAMUEL LACY.

WHEATLAND COMMITTEE.

JOHN GARBUT,
TRUMAN EDSON,
CLARK HALL.

BLOOMFIELD COMMITTEE.

RALPH WILCOX,
HEMAN CHAPIN,
BANI BRADLEY,
JOSIAH PORTER,
ORSON BENJAMIN,
JONATHAN BUELL.

LEWISTON COMMITTEE.

BATES COOK,
JOHN PHILIPS.

POSTSCRIPT.

We had long expected to receive a statement, or deposition, from an eye witness, which, we had good reason to suppose, would put an end to all conjectures, as to the course that had been pursued, in disposing of William Morgan, after his arrival at Fort Niagara. After the narrative had been put to the press we received the following statement, made to two members of one of the committees, by a credible witness, a man of good character and standing, a Royal Arch Mason, as from his own knowledge, but who has as yet declined giving his deposition, because he has been called upon as a witness, and expects to testify in court his knowledge of the matter. The statement is as follows:

"After Morgan left the carriage at the grave yard, he was taken to the bottom of the hill at the fort. The ferryman was called up by those who had the charge of him. Here Morgan received some water, which he had called for in front of Col. King's at Youngstown. When taken to the boat he was supported by two men; he was pinioned and hoodwinked; and in that condition placed in the boat and carried to the Canada shore. On reaching that shore two of the keepers left the boat; Morgan and two others remained on the beach, while they (i. e. the two first,) went into the town. Those who were left with the boat, were directed to leave the shore in the boat, if any person should approach it without giving a signal which had been agreed upon. There was, however, no intrusion. The two who had gone into the town, returned, after an absence which might have been one and a half, or two hours. The time of their absence seemed long to the informant, who waited with the boat. Two other persons came to the shore with them on their return: they came near the boat, and held a consultation in a low tone of voice, which the informant did not hear. When it broke up, all who had crossed from the United States' shore, returned in the boat to the fort. Morgan, as before, was supported from the shore by two men, taken into the fort, and put into the magazine. This place had been fixed upon one or two days previous, as one where Morgan could be lodged in case of necessity. This took place in the morning of the 14th of September.

"During that day Morgan made much noise; and in the course of the day two messengers were sent to Lewiston, where a Chapter was that day installed, to procure aid to silence the noise. Some persons came down to the fort from Lewiston, and produced stillness. On the evening of the 14th of September, twenty or thirty persons came to the fort in the steam boat, or otherwise, all of whom soon disappeared, excepting about eleven; after a time several of those last went away.

"During the night several persons were together in the vicinity of the fort, among whom the fate or disposition of Morgan was discussed. This discussion ended sometime after midnight, and nothing was decided upon. The next evening a small number debated the same subject with great animation, but came to no decision. Morgan was still in the magazine on the seventeenth, when our informant left the place and did not return until the twenty-first day of the same month, when he found that Morgan had been disposed of. Those who had Morgan in their custody when he left the place, gave him, on his return, to understand that Morgan had been put to death. That the interior of the magazine was put in order and as our informant was told, had been examined by one or more persons from Lewiston, who visited the fort for that purpose, and all things were pronounced to be in order. That the walls were closely looked over to see if Morgan had left any writings upon them. After all which, a man, or perhaps two, were requested to traverse the shore of the lake, to see if any body should float ashore."

AN ADDRESS TO ALL HONEST MASONS.

IN EIGHT NUMBERS.

NO. I.

To all honest Masons:

BRETHREN, when our institution, assailed by its enemies as containing principles derogatory to the laws of our country, stands tottering to its base, an inquiry into the principles of the institution becomes of vital importance. If I mistake not, we have taken too much for granted, and, charmed with its high sounding titles, have not scrutinized the fundamental principles which have kept it in existence thus long with that caution which the importance of the case demands. When I speak of principles, I mean not those published to the world in the Monitor and Chart, for no society, however base, but exhibits to the world some degree of decency: but I mean by principles, the obligations, and their tendency upon the members, and also inquire whether the occurrences, which have made a blot on our society which ages cannot obliterate, and all the waters of the Atlantic can never wash away, were not performed in strict observance of those obligations. A free people, very justly alarmed at seeing the majesty of the law trampled upon, have commenced an inquiry into the causes; and I repeat, we must examine before the pillars of the temple fall and bury us in its ruins.

According to Masonic tradition, our society was formed at a very early age of the world, when there were no laws to protect the weak against the assaults of the strong, but violence and outrage were the predominant features of the day; the arts and sciences were very imperfectly known to any, and not known to the great mass of the people. At such a time, it might have been necessary that a society be formed with a strong bond of union for the protection of its members, and a repository for the very imperfect arts and sciences. For such purposes a selfish society, which should bind its members to aid and assist each other in preference to mankind generally, might have been as good as any that could have been devised. We need not rest upon Masonic tradition alone, to support the antiquity of our order. Our forms and ceremonies point conclusively to what is now emphatically called the dark ages. The Masonic society is, beyond dispute, a selfish one; having exclusively in view the advantage of the few who have bound themselves together for mutual benefits. That this society should be useful to its members, it was necessary that some method of communication should be devised; hence our signs, grips, and pass words: and to preserve its selfish purposes, its own peculiar method of communication must be kept secret from the world; hence those barbarous oaths which bind us to protect one another whether 'right or wrong,' and to infuse more deeply the minds of the new members, those degrading scenes which we pass through, previous to our taking those obligations, were invented. I do not deny but such a society was necessary, where the only law was that of power. Thus we see it was well adapted to the day of its birth.

But we live in a brighter and better day: mankind, emerging by degrees from darkness and doubt, have arrived at a period when all rights of citizens are well known and secured. If, in the Roman government, the exclamation, 'I am a Roman citizen,' was a good protection, is not 'I am an American citizen,' a pass word which will admit us into the 'inner temple' of freedom, or the 'sanctum sanctorum' of liberty, where equal rights and privileges are administered to all this American people, whether high or low, rich or poor? Can you point me to a single privilege our society guarantees to us, which, as good citizens, ought to be granted, that the laws of the republic does not? Any protection that we may lawfully claim, which is not secured to us by the constitution and laws of our country? Not one, my brethren, in the whole catalogue of our boasted privileges, which we can lawfully claim, but what is secured to the lowest citizen of this country. There is, indeed, a protection granted which our laws do not give; but it is a protection which we, as good citizens, do not wish. It is a protection (as I shall in some future number show) to the designing, and, in too many cases, to those who have become amenable to the laws of their country.

What then, I ask, is the institution in this country? Millions of dollars have been paid to support it in all its gaudy splendor. It has, indeed, attracted the attention of people; yet no substantial good, but much real evil has resulted from it. I have seen the poor man, in his eagerness to become a member of our society, part with his last cow to pay the initiation fee: I have seen the society in their meetings, devote the hard earned money of their members to purposes worse than useless. Does not the frequent meetings of the society addict its members to idleness? I fear the Junior Warden's too frequent call 'from labor to refreshment,' has created dissipation in many members, which will end in wretchedness and despair. Brethren, when you consider the enormous amount of money which has been expended to support it—the many evils that have resulted from it—the corruption which is embosomed within it—will you not say its day of usefulness is past, and you are contented to be nothing more than plain American citizens, and look for no support but what the inestimable laws of this republic grant to every one of its citizens?   A MASON.

NO. II.

To all honest Masons:

Brethren, in my first number I attempted to show that our society was adapted to the dark ages, and consequently could not apply to the present age; and also, if it did apply, it had become perfectly useless. I shall, in this number, show that the titles given to the officers of our institution, have a very bad effect upon republican principles. Our ancestors, oppressed by the aristocratical principles of Europe, having endured, for a long series of years, the oppression of kings, lords, and dukes, and no choice left them but slavery or flight, resolutely chose the latter, and breaking asunder the bonds which bind friends together, and suffering the hardships of a tempestuous passage, sat themselves quietly down in the savage wilds of North America. No lords or dukes, no grand high priests, nor grand kings were there, to extort the hard earnings of the laboring poor; bound together by mutual wants, and asking no privilege from others which they were unwilling to bestow, they here sowed the first seeds of equal rights and privileges, which has sprung up and yielded an abundant harvest; they here taught their sons to prefer death to slavery. After the struggle of the revolution, and no enemy near to disturb their deliberations, a government was founded on plain, simple, republican principles. No high sounding titles found a place in the government; no high priests were exacting tythes; no grand kings, with their royal robes, were demanding the adoration of the people. All were reduced to a common level, and the man that held the highest and most enviable station mortal ever held, was simply styled, President of the United States. Such was the government founded by a Washington, a Franklin, a Jefferson, and the patriots of the revolution. Now let us examine our own institution, and clearly ascertain whether it is established on as pure a basis as that of our common country. If it is as pure and well adapted to our circumstances, we had better ingraft with it our political government ; if not, and it does have a tendency to inculcate aristocratical principles, then abandon Masonry and adhere to the government established by our ancestors ; for it is true, that in the various requirements of life we cannot fulfil our duty to both at the same time. The government was founded in open day with all the light of heaven shining upon it, its principles open and equal to all men. Masonry is the child of darkness, and nothing but secrecy can sustain it. Its principles are partial, and its ultimate aim is the benefit of the few at the expense of the many. All its ceremonies are anti-social and anti-republican ; the titles given to its officers, I do not believe, are very republican. I will rehearse them, that you may, with a single glance, see the bearing they may have on the pure republican.

In the Grand Lodge they have their Grand Lecturer, Grand Junior and Senior Deacons, Grand Master of Ceremonies, Grand Marshal, Grand Secretary, Grand Treasurer, Grand Chaplain, Worshipful Grand Junior and Senior Wardens, Right Worshipful Deputy Grand Master, Most Worshipful Grand Master.

In the General Grand Royal Arch Chapter there is an Excellent General Grand Marshal, Excellent General Grand Chaplain, Excellent General Grand Treasurer, Excellent General Grand Secretary, Most Excellent General Grand Scribe, Most Excellent General Grand King, Most Excellent General Grand High Priest.

The titles in the Grand Encampment are, Worshipful Grand Sword Bearer, Worshipful Grand Standard Bearer, Worshipful Grand Marshal, Worshipful Grand Recorder, Worshipful Grand Treasurer, Worshipful Grand Wardens, Worshipful Grand Captain General, Worshipful Grand Generalissimo, Worshipful General Grand Master.

What titles the Knights of Tutons, the Knights of Calatrava, Kings of Alcantara, Knights of Redemption, Knights of Christ, Knights of the Mother of Christ, Knights of Lazarus, Knights of the Star, Knights of the Band, Knights of the Annunciation of the Virgin Mary, Knights of St. Michael, Knights of St. Stephen, and Knights of the Holy Ghost, gave to their officers I do not know ; but thus much I do know, that every officer in the long catalogue of titles, had some emblem of royalty affixed to him. This being the case, my brethren, and it being equally true that the great end and aim of Masonry, is to create distinctions among mankind, and secure to the few the rights of the many, will any of you blindly adhere to Masonry when it comes in contact with the least of those equal laws which were secured to you by the blood of your fathers ? If you will, then I must bid farewell to you and Masonry ; but before we part let me ask you, if, when you were young and your minds unsullied with the aristocratic trappings of Masonry, when your playful spirits were buoyant, and your consciences void of offence ; if then, when you heard recounted the many attempts of the tyrants of the Old World, to chain down and enslave your fathers, and to enforce their unholy system of distinctions and divine rights of kings upon them, and had heard enumerated the long sufferings and manly firmness of your sires, in not only driving those tyrants from their shores, but also their unequal and accursed principles with them ; did not, I say, your bosoms burn with a pure patriotism which made you swear, that should the enemies of civil liberty and equal rights, ever assail the fair fabric of freedom, your blood should flow as freely in maintaining it, as your fathers did to achieve it : if so, then for heaven's sake abandon an institution which has a direct tendency to contaminate the minds of almost all who unite themselves with it, and insensibly steals away that purity of sentiment, which alone can support a free, and equal, and happy government.

A Mason.

NO. III.

To all honest Masons:

Brethren, as a general thing, secret associations are formed for the purpose of evading the laws, or for the overthrow of the government; ever since our government was formed, the people have regarded them with jealousy. The patriots of the revolution, after our liberty was established, entered their solemn protest against secret associations of every kind. All lawful purposes need not the covering of mystery or secrecy to sustain them. Their views, principles and purposes being honest, are open and can be examined by every freeman. No midnight meetings are necessary for societies who have nothing but honest and honorable objects to effect. But, on the other hand, if a society has unlawful purposes to effect, how can they effect them if their designs are exposed? No band bound together for unlawful purposes, but have their domes covered with the mantle of secrecy, and the darkness of midnight protects their nefarious purposes. It is not surprising that a free people, ever jealous of their rights, should look with suspicion upon a society like ours, whose meetings are held in secret and at the late hour of midnight. No one of the people are allowed to enter within. Nothing but mysteries attend them in their whole progress; they acknowledge they are bound by solemn oaths not to discover the nature of the institution; and no one can but discover that the greatest facilities are offered for unlawful purposes. If there had been no wrongs committed by such a society, an independent and free people whose freedom had been purchased by the blood of their fathers, and transmitted to them under solemn instructions to preserve it, even at the expense of life, ought to lift their voice against it, when they find it extending through the Union, embracing all the officers of the land, and possessing every means of crushing, at one blow, the proud and elevated title of freemen. But if a secret society of itself will cause suspicion when combined with the actual evils which have been the result of such societies, we cannot expect this free people will any longer suffer it to exist in this country.

It is well known to all 'active Masons' and to persons generally, that in the dark conclave and secret meetings of Masons, have been planned conspiracies that have caused convulsions which have been felt in every part of the government under which they were bound to live as good citizens. There has been planned and executed deeds by them in their midnight conspiracies, (I cannot call such meetings by a more gentle term,) at which humanity has revolted. In France all was thrown into confusion, and anarchy came near ruling a people striving for liberty, by the society of Free Masons. At one time, considering they had all power, they threw off all disguise and discovered their real object. The candidate for the degree of Master Mason had the following questions put to him, 'Brother, are you disposed to execute *all* the orders of the Grand Master, though you were to receive contrary orders from a king, emperor, or any other sovereign whatever?' In one instance, receiving a candidate not as much infatuated as the others, they were answered 'No!' 'What, No!' replies the venerable, 'are you only entered amongst us to betray our secrets? Would you hesitate between the interests of Masonry and those of the profane? You are not aware then that there is not one of our swords but is ready to pierce the heart of a traitor!' Comment on such language is not necessary. I need not say more on the dangerous tendency of Free Masonry. In France it is too well known to be soon forgot by that people. But France is not alone in having her liberties invaded by Masons. It at one time came near overthrowing the government of Germany, and those that were honest Masons among them separated and forsook the institution. The following is the language of a venerable master of a lodge in Germany, pronounced at the dissolution of the lodge, and closing it up forever.

'However holy our mysteries may have been, the lodges are now profaned and sullied. Brethren and companions, attired in your mourning robes, attend and let us seal up the gates of our temple, for the profane have found means of penetrating into them—they have converted them into retreats for their impiety, into dens of conspirators. Within the sacred walls they have planned the horrid deeds and the ruin of nations. Lodges which serve as hiding places for these conspirators, must remain for ever shut both to us and every good citizen.' Brethren, ought we not to adopt the language and actions of this venerable man? Masonry was considered in Spain, Portugal, and Russia, of such a dangerous tendency, that it was put down by the strong arm of the law. It is now disturbing the tranquillity of our brethren in South America. In England, the king being Grand Master of all the lodges, and all being sworn to obey his mandate, it is made subservient to his own purposes, and consequently he suffers it to exist in his government. But we need not go abroad for proof that secret associations are dangerous; the proof is nigh, *even at the door.* Passing by all the smaller transactions of the fraternity, and making no mention of the perversion of justice by it in our courts, and its intrigue at elections, another and blacker transaction stares us in the face. A deed has been committed in this country, on this sacred ground of liberty, which ought to stamp with 'everlasting infamy and disgrace,' the society by whose mandate the damning deed was committed. A free citizen has been deprived of his liberty and life! And by whom? Did the light of day shine upon the meeting which plotted the hellish deed? Was it the great body of a free people which sanctioned a deed without a parallel, except on Masonic record? No, my brethren, it was in the dark, mysterious, secret, and midnight meeting of the ancient and honorable fraternity of Free Masons, the damning deed was planned; it was the Great Grand Worshipful members which justified the 'deep damnation of his taking off!' Not by a few individuals of the order, but by them as a body, assembled in their lodges for the purpose of learning his fate and planning the destruction of others, and by their vote were the murderers of Morgan justified. Do you expect that our society will be supported by a free and independent people? Were the causes which produced a separation of the then colonies and mother country, more alarming than our society in this republic, at this time, and under the present circumstances? The great body of freemen have been insulted for attempting to put it down; but there have been no transactions which are to be so much feared, as overthrowing the government of the United States, as the transactions of the fraternity for the last six months. The impressment of seamen, which was a very just cause for the declaration of war against Great Britain, bears no comparison with this. In that case they were impressed by a rival nation, and we could defend manfully our rights. The cause was open, and an enemy met us in open day. On the other hand, the late outrages were committed by citizens of our common country, connected by oaths not to betray each other; members of a society, whose meetings were in secret, and whose ramifications extended through the union, holding all the offices of power, and impiously saying the people could not help themselves; they would do what they pleased to their members, who were wolves in sheep's clothing. Such a deed strikes the very foundation of our liberty. If our society considers itself powerful enough to deprive one citizen of his liberty and life, you will soon see it take great strides and claim all power. Can it be possible, my brethren, that you will longer attempt to support a society, which has not only become obsolete and useless, and savors of aristocracy, but is stained with the blood of a free citizen: Rather come out like good citizens and say it is worse than useless; and inasmuch as nine or ten millions of people say they do not wish it to exist in this republic, magnanimously say you will desert it and be good citizens in common with all. This people will never suffer the institution to exist in this republic; if they do permit it to assume all its former power and grandeur, then indeed, are they slaves, and fit only for vassalage. A Mason.

NO. IV.

To all honest Masons:

Brethren, in all countries and under all governments where secret societies nave existed, they have never failed to create distrust among the uninitiated, and eventually to overturn all fair principles. But the greater part of them have long since gone to their graves; and all that have gone, sleep in disgrace. In this country, no secret society has an existence, except that of Masonry; and with regard to this, an inquiry has gone forth, and you might as well place your hands against the sun of a summer's morning and stop its rising, as to stop the inquiry, or prevent the downfall of the order. Some of you may believe, that, from the many ties which bind Masons together, and from their almost united exertions to smother crime and distract public opinion, that the cause of the people will ultimately go down, and you rise triumphant. If any of you who are honest, have fallen into this error at this time, I sincerely pity you. You must be sensible, at this late day, that all fair and honorable members of the institution; men who were not concerned in the late disgraceful transactions, in their incipient stages, nor parties to their succeeding crimes; men who since have not done all in their power to palliate and smother them, and paralyze the strength of the law, will leave their hiding places and endeavor again to deserve the confidence of their country. No matter how many kings and emperors you enroll on your tablets: no matter how many governors and judges are found in your halls, and are now exercising the power of the country: no matter how many servile and contemptible editors are, either publicly justifying kidnapping and murder, or are palliating Masonic crimes, or are, in the most degrading condition, peddling their silly gingerbread stories: all in this country, who support the Monster, must give place to others, and your dark temple of crime and iniquity, tumble to the ground.

Turn your attention to old Peter, the hermit, and under him trace your different orders of knighthood to their respective founders. Follow them through their mad career of bloodshed and slaughter to the walls of Jerusalem, and there prepare to weep over a scene of carnage and crime which beggars all description. Neither arms defended the valiant, nor submission the timorous. No age or sex was spared: infants on the breasts were pierced by the same blow with their mothers who implored for mercy: even a multitude to the number of ten thousand persons, who had surrendered themselves prisoners, and were promised quarter, were butchered in cool blood by the magnanimous founders of your illustrious orders. Long shall the friends of humanity bemoan this unhallowed and blood-stained day; and long shall the warm and smoking blood of murdered innocence cry from the ground for vengeance.

Next, behold these holy and blood-stained hypocrites, in dark conclave, plotting another feast of blood in the heart of Germany! See wretched France groan beneath their dark designs, and bleeding at every pore. And, even now, and while I am writing, behold our sister republic (Mexico) reel to its base, beneath a wretched conspiracy of York and Scotch Masons. When you have done this, and when you have clearly sketched in ' the mind's eye' the general outlines of this pretty picture, then sit down and calmly ask yourselves, Where is the author of Jachin and Boaz? Where is Smith, of Vermont? Where is Murdock, of Rensselaerville? Where is Morgan, and where are his lonely widow and orphan children? Alas! my brethren, this is a sorry and blood-stained picture, and you, who are not satisfied with what Masons have already done, let your distorted eyeballs glare upon it, until your carniverous appetites are glutted with blood for once, and after that return to your dens of carnage and plot more mischef. But to you, my honest brethren, who have seen enough of Satan's kingdom already displayed; and you, who love your country more than Masonry, arise from this den of conspirators, and, with minds unalloyed, feast your eyes on the effulgent morn of our rising REPUBLIC, and I will vouchsafe to my country that you will never return again. A MASON.

NO. V.

To all honest Masons:

Brethren, having in my former numbers touched upon the general principles of the order, I now shall ask you to candidly traverse with me, a more particular charge against the Masonic order; which is that the LAWS OF MASONRY IN AND OF THEMSELVES, DO AUTHORIZE THE TAKING OF THE LIFE OF A MEMBER OF THE FRATERNITY GUILTY OF DIVULGING THE SECRETS OF MASONRY. Startle not, my brethren, at this appalling charge, but candidly follow me through my observations and proof. I must here remark, that I could satisfy the most scrupulous of the order, were I at liberty to write some of the hidden mysteries of the different degrees, but shackled as I am with these absurd ties, enough can be shown, without violating any of our principles, to convince that part of my brethren whom I now address. Now then to the subject. It is not denied, I believe, by any Masons, that the penalty of their obligations is death. [I shall not, at present, refer to Morgan's illustrations, for I neither deny nor acknowledge that book.] Almost all Masons admitted this in their assertions for three months after the abduction of Morgan, by saying, that he (Morgan) had submitted himself to the punishment of death, by revealing the secrets of Masonry. I believe that the most careful do not pretend to deny that such is the penalty. But it is useless to remark further on this point, for *we do know* that the penalty in that case is *death*, in the most shocking and barbarous manner. If then such is the penalty, was it never intended to inflict that penalty? It is absurd in the extreme, to suppose that a society, ranking among its members such illustrious personages, as we pretend ours does, with all that pomp and parade attached to it, with all our monarchical titles of Kings, Grand and Sublime Masters, would attempt to make a mockery of laws which they call sublime and useful, tell a candidate if he divulges the secrets he shall be put to death, and after the *solemn* ceremonies are over, tell him we never intended to *inflict that penalty, but only meant to scare you.* Such a course would very soon sink the institution into merited contempt. Why then bind our members under penalty of death, to keep inviolate our secrets, if we never intended to inflict that penalty? What has kept thousands from divulging the secrets long before now? Would simply expelling them from the lodge have deterred them from it? No! It was the well known fact that the *laws and principles of Masonry* were such that they would be barbarously murdered, or in the Masonic phrase *executed.* There are many of the craft, who have long since wished them known to the whole world, and care not for expulsion, knowing full well that revealing the iniquities of our dark conclaves would justify them in the minds of an enlightened people. There is another class who have been expelled from the lodge, and out of revenge would, if they dare, write, print, stamp, &c. all the secrets of the order.

I repeat, then, it was a fact, which recent events fully prove, that their lives would pay the forfeiture of such an act. The only question that can possibly be raised, is, that there is no person designated in our statutes to execute the *traitor.* But I think a little reflection and examination will obviate this difficulty. Precedents of long standing in all well established societies and governments, constitute law. Hence, in all legal proceedings, where there is no statute direct to the point, they refer to former decisions, and what has been done under similar circumstances. In this case, then, if we have no express statute appointing the executive officer, (the manner of execution is pointed out explicitly in the obligation,) when a traitor, if found, we must refer to what has been done under similar circumstances by our society; and as all former decisions of law are more or less binding, by the wisdom or ignorance of the persons giving those decisions, so in this case, we ought to examine carefully the precedents, and see if they were given by persons who were well informed as to the laws and principles of our order. I will now refer you to some of those precedents which do show conclusively that we are authorized to execute any member of the fraternity who so far loses sight of his safety as to divulge the secrets of the craft. These precedents may be found in the 'Free Masons' Monitor,' published by Thomas S. Webb; and that no one may say the book is not good authority, I will give you the vote of the Grand Royal Arch Chapter, which is as follows:

Resolved unanimously, That this Grand Chapter recommend the Free Masons' Monitor to the attention and study of all the members of the fraternity to whom the same may come. *Amos T. Jenks, Grand Secy.*

The first precedent I shall give, may be found at page 242* of Webb's Free Mason's Monitor. It appears that several of the craft became, in the language of Masons, traitors.—Six had fled Jerusalem. Solomon published a particular description of all those who had made their escape: shortly after, he received information that several persons answering his description had arrived in the country of Cheth, and believing themselves perfectly secure, had began to work in the quarry of Bendaca. As soon as Solomon was made acquainted with this circumstance, he wrote to Maacha, king of Cheth, to assist in apprehending them, and cause them to be delivered over to persons he should appoint to secure them, and have them brought to Jerusalem to receive the punishment due their crimes. Solomon then elected fifteen Masters in whom he could place the highest confidence, and among whom were those who had been in the cavern, and sent them in quest of the villains, and gave them an escort of troops. Five days were spent in the search, when Tirbal discovered them cutting stone in the quarry; they immediately seized them and bound them in chains. When they arrived at Jerusalem, they were imprisoned in the tower of Achizer, and the next morning a punishment was *inflicted on them adequate to their crimes.*

The next precedent which I shall cite, is found at page 239,† and is styled, 'Observations on the degree of Elected Knights, called a Chapter.' This case is so striking, and in many parts, so similar to that of the Morgan case, I shall be more minute in description, and more profuse in extracts. That you may realize it in its full force, I here will remark that this degree was instituted by Solomon after the execution of the traitor, to reward the zeal of the persons engaged in his execution; and to give more weight to their offices, and impress the minds of the fraternity with the great danger of divulging the secrets of Masonry, the furniture and dress of the Chapter, and members, were of the bloodiest kind imaginable. I shall, therefore, give a description of the dress and furniture.

This Chapter represents the audience chamber of Solomon, and is to be decorated with white and red hangings; the red with white flames. There are nine lights in the east and eight in the west. The Master represents Solomon seated in the east, with a table before him covered with black, and is styled Most Potent. There is only one Warden in the west, who represents Stokin, (one of the executioners,) with seven brethren around him. All the brethren *must* be dressed in black, and their hats *flapped* (surely a suitable dress for assassins) with a broad black ribbon from the left shoulder to the right hip, on the lower part of which are nine red roses, (an emblem that Masonic murderers shall be highly valued and protected,) four on each side and one at the bottom, to which is suspended a poniard. The aprons are white, lined with black, speckled with BLOOD; on the flap, A BLOODY ARM

---

* Salem ed. p. 265; Part second, chap. vii.   † Ib. p. 264; Part second, chap vi.

WITH PONIARD; and on the area, A BLOODY ARM HOLDING BY THE HAIR A BLOODY HEAD. Near to the lodge is a small dark place representing a cavern, in which is placed a lamp; a place representing a spring, with a basin to hold water; and a table, on which is laid a PONIARD, and the representation of a BLOODY HEAD AS JUST SEVERED FROM THE BODY. Near the table a large stone to sit on, and below the lamp, in capital letters is written, VENGEANCE.

The history of this degree is as follows :—In the reign of Solomon, several of the workmen had been guilty of some crime of an enormous nature, [What more enormous crime can there be than to expose their impious ceremonies and bring to light their internal deeds?] and made their escape from Jerusalem. A great assembly of Masters had sat in consultation, [It has been sworn to, that seventy or eighty met at Stafford to consult on the Morgan case] on the best means of discovering and apprehending them. Their deliberations were interrupted by the entrance of a stranger, [Daniel Johns, the Canadian spy, suddenly made his appearance at Stafford,] who demanded to speak to the king in private. Upon being admitted, he acquainted Solomon that he had discovered where Akirop, one of the traitors, lay concealed, and offered to conduct whom the king should please to appoint to go with him. This being communicated to the brethren, ONE AND ALL requested to be partakers in the vengeance due the villain. Solomon checked their ardor, declaring that only nine should undertake the task ; and to avoid giving any offence, ordered all their names to be put into an urn, and that the first nine that should be drawn should be the persons to accompany the stranger. [They departed from this rule in the Batavia cases : for between one and two hundred went for Miller.] At break of day, Joabert, Stokin, and seven others, conducted by the stranger, travelled through a dreary country. On the way, Joabert found means to learn from the stranger, that the villain they were in quest of had hidden himself in a cavern not far from the place they then were ; he soon found the cavern, and entered it alone, where, by the light of the lamp, he discovered the villain asleep, with a poniard at his feet. Inflamed at the sight, and actuated by an impatient zeal, he immediately seized the poniard and stabbed him first in the head and then in the heart ; he had only time to cry, *Vengeance is taken*—and expired. When the other eight arrived, and had refreshed themselves at the spring, Joabert severed the head from the body, and *taking it in one hand*, and his poniard in the other, he, with his brothers, returned to Jerusalem. Solomon was at first very much offended that Joabert had put it out of *his* power to take vengeance *himself* in PRESENCE of and as a *warning to the rest of the workmen to be faithful to their trust;* (not their work) but by *proper intercession* was again *reconciled*. Joabert became *highly favored* of Solomon, who conferred upon him and his eight companions the title of ' *Elected Knights*.' Ought not the Grand Lodge to confer upon the murderers of Morgan some new and sublime degree of Masonry, with still more bloody emblems ? To show you, beyond the possibility of a doubt, that this transaction was in strict conformity with the principles of the order, I will quote once more from page 243, where you will find the history of the *Illustrious Knights*, which is as follows :—' After vengeance had been fully taken on the traitors mentioned in the foregoing degrees, Solomon instituted this, both as a REWARD FOR THE ZEAL AND INTEGRITY of the Grand Masters elect of fifteen, (the persons who took vengeance on the traitors,) and also by their preferment to make room for other WORTHY brethren (*murderers*) from the lower degrees to that of Grand Masters elect of fifteen. He accordingly appointed twelve of the fifteen to constitute a Grand Chapter of *Illustrious Knights*, and gave them command over the twelve tribes. He expressed a *particular regard* for this *order*, and showed them the precious things of the tabernacle. Here follow the names of the twelve ' *Illustrious Knights :*' Joabert, the man who assassinated Akirop, and Stokin and the other zealous assassins, head the list. Here, my brethren, I must ask you to pause, ponder, and deeply reflect on the history here given, and fate of Akirop; compare it, with all its bearings, with the fate of Morgan, and then say, if you dare say it, that Morgan was not executed according to the laws,—yes, the infernal laws of *Masonry*. Why has a degree, instituted to keep in remembrance the execution of a traitor, been kept in existence ever since, if not to stimulate the brethren to a similar act, should a similar circumstance ever arise? Such a degree is in existence at this day in the United States—yes, in the state of New-York—and it is preposterous to suppose, that the members of that degree, assembled in their bloody dens, with bloody aprons, and representations of the bloody head of a traitor before them, and seeing vengeance written in capital letters upon the walls of their dark cavern, and knowing Morgan was writing the secrets of Masonry, that they would not, one and all, with all the zeal of Joabert and Stokin, arise in their wrath and strike the villain to the heart. If they were active members and believed their obligations binding, it was their duty to strike the deadly blow, deep, and to the heart, even as Murdock was so struck. I have heard Masons blame those concerned in the recent transactions: some have even said the murderers of Morgan ought to be hung. This my brethren is wrong. If there is a blame to be attached any where, it is to the institution. If these men were firm supporters of the order, they acted right. They expected the laws of the institution to support them in such an act, and that the members (except the recreants) would justify them; and they had good grounds for so supposing. On the contrary, any member of the institution, being fully satisfied that Morgan was writing the secrets of Masonry, and did not immediately proceed to apprehend the villain, 'that he might have a punishment inflicted adequate to his crime,' neglected the laws of Masonry, and ought, in strict conformity to those laws, to be expelled as an unworthy member. Blame not those who acted in strict conformity to the laws of the institution, but cast the blame where it is richly deserved, namely, upon an institution which required of them such an act. These men expected our support; and when their trouble comes upon them it is cowardly to say, punish them, the institution did not require such an act. Thus, my brethren, we have gone through this subject, and do see that those engaged in the late outrages had ancient authority for so acting. No one who candidly examines the cases here cited, but will say that *murder is authorized* by the Masonic institution, under particular circumstances. I now ask you again, will you longer support such an institution? A MASON.

NO. VI.

To all honest Masons:

Brethren—The great subject which agitates the people at present, seems every day of its existence to draw nearer to the point which is to decide the destiny of the Masonic institution. On the one hand it is contended that Morgan was carried off and murdered by a few Masonic stragglers and outlaws; and that the usages and customs of the order in no way encourage or sanction such acts; while on the other hand it is asserted, that those concerned in the outrages were some of the first men of the order, and that the ancient usages and customs of the institution required such acts at their hands. If this be true, it requires no great discernment to discover that we have a government within a government; and that either the constitution and laws of our country, or those of ancient Free Masonry must give way; and that if our government is triumphant in the present conflict, Masonry must go down for ever.

Again, if the men concerned in the outrages were in no way authorized or encouraged by the usages and customs of Free Masonry, to kidnap and execute the traitor, and the principles of the order in no way come in contact with the constitution and laws of our country, and are otherwise pure and wholesome, then indeed Free Masonry may stand for ages. In order, therefore, to investigate this subject, it is necessary we should touch in a slight degree upon some of the mysteries and principles of ancient and modern Free Masonry.

And first, my brethren, I shall have the hardihood to assert, that before any of you ever entered a lodge, you pledged your honor cheerfully to conform to all the ancient usages and customs of the order.

After this you went farther—you entered the lodge and there solemnly made oath not only to adhere to the ancient usages and customs of the order, but to have your throat cut across, your tongue torn out, and your body buried in the rough sands of the sea, should you ever be wilfully guilty of divulging any of the secrets of Free Masonry; and so on, from an Entered Apprentice, in every degree up to that of the Thrice Illustious Order of Knights of the Cross, you have solemnly sworn to suffer some penalty to be inflicted on your body, which if inflicted would take life, should you ever be wilfully guilty of revealing any of the secrets of either or all their degrees. Surely, the good Mason says, we have sworn to suffer all these penalties, if we betray our trust. But the traitor will not inflict them upon himself, and there is no one authorized to inflict them upon him. If this be true, then, indeed, those concerned in the Morgan case were nothing but a Masonic banditti and murderers, and the institution in no way to blame. But I shall not, as readily as some do, stop exactly here. I shall go a little further and inquire what the ancient usages and customs are, which our honors and oaths are pledged to support. It is a fact I believe well known to all Masons, that Solomon was the great founder and pattern of ancient Free Masonry, and that all the Grand Masters from his day down to this time, have, one after another in regular succession, been considered the successors and representatives of Solomon; and all the laws, usages and customs, which were established in his day, all Masons ever since, of both low and high degree, have most religiously pledged their honors, and their solemn oaths and obligations, always to observe and maintain. To illustrate my ideas more familiarly on this subject, suppose one of you were elected to preside over the Masonic institution of the United States for seven years; that in all the degrees from Entered Apprentice up to the higher and sublimer station which you fill, and that all the ancient laws, usages and customs of the order, were enforced upon the mind with all the power and ingenuity which man could invent, as the only means of preserving the institution from ruin and destruction. Suppose, at your installation, it was required of you as the presiding officer of the institution, to deviate in no instance from the ancient landmarks and customs, but to preside with that promptness and decision of character which will carry down to future ages the secrets of the order, as pure and unimpaired as they were given to you; and suppose, under all of these circumstances, and while you were at the head of the institution, and in the place of Solomon, a messenger should arrive and inform you that Morgan, a Royal Arch Mason, was writing the secrets of Masonry; and Miller, an Entered Apprentice Mason, was absolutely about to publish them, even up to the Royal Arch; and unless measures were immediately taken to bring the traitors to condign punishment, the small streams which cause the money, for quarterly dues, initiations, and for the sale of charters, to flow in such profusion from a thousand ways to the fountain head, would dry up; that in short they would publish the real and genuine secrets of Free Masonry, up to the Arch, to the world, and Masonry be ruined and undone for ever. What would you do? Would you disregard your honor, your solemn oaths, and all your admonitions at your installation; suffer the traitors under your administration to publish the sacred and holy secrets of ancient Free Masonry to the world, and the institution be ruined for ever? Or would you rather have some little regard to your honor, your solemn oaths and admonitions? Look about you and inquire what are the ancient laws usages and customs of the order which are every where so rigorously enforced upon the candidate? What did Solomon do in the case of Jubela, Jubelo, and Jubelum, where the ruffians attempted to extort the Master's word from our worthy Grand Master, Hiram Abiff? How was it in the case of the seven traitors that fled from Jerusalem? And how was it in the case of Akirop? Surely in all these cases Solomon appointed discreet Masons to seize the villains and traitors, and to bring them before him; and he ordered punishments to be inflicted on them proportionate to their crimes, except in the case of Akirop, and there the Mason, whom Solomon appointed, took the power into his own hands, and executed the traitor himself. Solomon approved of this, and conferred on the executive officer new and lasting honors. How has it been with all succeeding Grand Masters in cases of treachery, from Solomon down to this day? Surely Masonic traitors have every where had those penalties inflicted upon them, which they had sworn might be inflicted, were they ever wilfully guilty of revealing any of the secret and hidden mysteries of Masonry. Would you not say, Sovereign Master, these are the laws, usages and customs of the order which we have all pledged all that is sacred on earth or holy in heaven cheerfully to conform to—therefore, I will do in the Morgan and Miller case, as is required of me to do by the order. I will do as all former Grand Masters have done in similar cases. I will appoint discreet and subtle Masons to inflict upon Morgan and Miller, those penalties which they have sworn to suffer should they ever be wilfully guilty of revealing the secrets of the order, and thereby save the institution of Masonry from everlasting disgrace and absolute ruin. Daniel Johns is a discreet and subtle Mason, and what is more, he is a stranger in the country where the traitors reside: I will select him as my chief executive officer; and as all my Masonic subjects have every where solemnly sworn, with their hands on the Holy Bible, and in the presence of Almighty God, to obey all due signs and regular summons, given, handed, sent or thrown to them by the hand of a Master Mason,—I will furnish him with some regular summonses, requiring of them to obey him in whatever he may direct with regard to the traitors, and send him away to the place where they reside; and I have no doubt a punishment will be inflicted on them 'adequate to their crimes.' When you have gone thus far, Most Sovereign Grand Master Elect, you have done your duty, and the remainder is left to the subtlety and cunning of Daniel Johns and all those to whom he may give, hand, or send summons to assist him. Thus, my brethren, the conclusion is irresistibly forced upon us, that the institution of Free Masonry does hold its members in the strong bonds of life and death; that our Sovereign Grand Master, as far as regards the revealing of the secrets of the order, is absolute in power, and all that are under him are bound to obey. This accounts in the most satisfactory manner for what we have witnessed in this part of the country fourteen months past; and this, in my humble opinion, Masonically justifies all those who were concerned in the abduction of Morgan, and the attempt on the life of Miller.

Such being the facts, my brethren, do you not discover that the 'Ancient laws, usages and customs of Free Masonry' are diametrically opposed to the constitution and laws of our country? If so, (and on this point there can be no doubt, for if the Sovereign Master had not been absolute in power, the traitors long since would have swarmed like the locusts in Egypt,) ought we not as honest men and good citizens, with one accord, to rise in the dignity of *freemen*, and like our fathers, tear asunder those bonds which make us slaves, and tend to entail misery upon our children? Our fathers were under solemn obligations to be faithful to the crown of Great Britain; but when they discovered that an observance of their oaths and obligations which they had taken, were detrimental to freedom and the rights of man, they with a manliness of spirit which all future ages will admire, tore their bonds asunder, fought the monarch whom they were sworn to protect; established freedom for themselves, and as they fondly hoped, had entailed it upon their children. Why not we then, when we become convinced that our obligations jeopardize our lives, and make slaves of us, and endanger the liberties of our children—why not we, I say, like our fathers, rend our bonds asunder; open the bowels of the beast, and expose to the scorn and contempt of all mankind, the selfishness and sin that has there been smothered so long.

Do you think this would be unmasonic, and therefore we had better withdraw and say nothing about it, if we are displeased with it. Such advice I know is given every day in the streets, but this was not the course pursued by our fathers—they not only withdrew their oath and allegiance from the crown of Great Britain, but they turned about and fought her with a firmness of purpose which always ensures success. Therefore, my brethren, if you agree with me, that under existing circumstances it is proper and necessary so far to disregard the Masonic obligations as to make open and honorable war upon the monster,—then I beseech you, by all the fondness you ever bore for the purity of our government and the rights of mankind, to come out of that dark, absolute, and bloody government of Free Masonry, which was established in the dark and bloody ages of the world, and is handed down unimpaired, with all its horrid rites and ceremonies. And then, my brethren, when you have done this, instead of retreating into some dark garret, with a Tyler at the door with an old rusty sword in his hand to guard it, and there under the black flag of iniquity and crime marching around the room and singing,

> Mark Masters all appear
> Before your Grand Overseer,—

we in open day will hoist high in the air the star spangled banner of our country, that floated over the bloody field of our fathers, and shout aloud in presence of the universe,

> Hail Columbia, happy land,
> Hail ye heroes, heaven born band;

and then march on, conquering and to conquer, (the mind only I mean,) until every dark and wicked right and ceremony of ancient FREE MASONRY, be driven far away beyond the borders of our country.   A MASON.

NO. VII.

To all honest Masons:

Brethren—I again ask you to examine the charge made in No. 5; for the reported attempts to clear the institution of Masonry, at the expense of the individuals engaged in the kidnapping and murder of Morgan, calls for the serious attention of every person who wishes to fix the blame where it deservedly belongs. That the institution required those acts of its members, is as evident as any proposition; and one would suppose, that, at this day, there are none who would have the effrontery to deny it. But, strange as this may appear, there are some who deny that the laws and customs of Masonry do authorize the abduction and murder of a Masonic traitor. They say, it is true I have sworn to have my throat cut across, &c.; but I, nor no one else, have sworn or promised to perform the execution: it is merely an imprecation without meaning. Once more, I ask you to *candidly* examine the laws of the order, and I am satisfied, unless you allow your prejudices to influence you, you will be fully satisfied on the point. In the Free Mason's Monitor, at page 31,* the candidate is requested to answer the following questions:—'Do you seriously declare, upon your honor, before these gentlemen, (members of the lodge, who conduct him through the ceremonies) that you will cheerfully conform

---
* Salem ed. p. 30.

to ALL THE ANCIENT ESTABLISHED USAGES AND CUSTOMS OF THE FRATERNITY?'—and not until he has answered this in the affirmative, is he allowed to observe *even the form of the lodge.* At page 46 * is the first charge a Mason ever receives; it is a charge to a newly initiated Entered Apprentice: he is there solemnly charged—' If, in the circle of your acquaintance, you find a person desirous of being initiated into Masonry, be *particularly careful not to recommend him* UNLESS HE WILL CONFORM TO OUR RULES.' No matter how fair a character he may sustain; you need not inquire whether he be a believer in the sublime doctrines of Christianity—no matter if he be the veriest infidel —the only question is, will he conform ' *to our rules.*'

In the charge to a Fellow Craft, at page 65,† they thus address the candidate:—' OUR LAWS AND REGULATIONS YOU ARE STRENUOUSLY TO SUPPORT, AND BE ALWAYS READY TO ASSIST IN SEEING THEM DULY EXECUTED.' In the charge to a Master Mason, at page 74,‡ the Worshipful Master thus addresses the new made Master Mason:—' You are now bound, by *honor and gratitude to be faithful to your trust;* to support the dignity of your character on every occasion; and *to enforce, by precept and example, obedience to the tenets of our order.* The ANCIENT LANDMARKS OF THE ORDER *intrusted to your care, you are carefully to preserve, and never suffer them to be infringed, or countenance a deviation from the* ESTABLISHED USAGES AND CUSTOMS *of the fraternity.*' Before a lodge can do any business, there must be granted to them a charter; and the Master, in a solemn manner, is instructed what are the duties of his office, by the Grand Master, or some person representing the Grand Master. You will find all these instructions at page 96 § of the Monitor. The Master thus addresses him: (the Master elect)—'Previous to your investiture, it is necessary that you should signify your assent to those ANCIENT CHARGES AND REGULATIONS, which point out the duties of a Master of a lodge.' Among other charges is the following;—' You agree to hold in *veneration the original rules and patrons of the order of Masonry, and their regular successors, supreme and subordinate, according to their stations.*' Page 100 ‖ —The Grand Master then addresses the Master elect in the following manner: ' Do you submit to these charges, and promise to support these regulations, *as Masters have done in all ages before you?*' And not until he, in the most solemn manner, in the presence of all his brethren and the officers of the Grand Lodge, pledged himself to do it, can he be vested with authority to govern a lodge. At page 152,¶ you find the same doctrine insisted upon, earnestly, in a charge to a newly exalted Royal Arch Mason.

' We expect you will never recommend any candidate to this chapter, whose abilities and *knowledge of the foregoing degrees you cannot fully vouch for, and whom you do not firmly and confidently believe will conform to the principles of our order, and fulfil the obligations of a Royal Arch Mason.*' Thus, my brethren, we find insisted upon, with an earnestness which nothing but a case of desperation can urge, that we support ' *all the ancient usages and customs of*' ancient Free Masonry. I wish you to examine these instructions with care and candor, for I do consider there is a meaning cloaked under them, which, in the hurried manner the degrees are usually given, do not meet our view at first sight. Why do they so earnestly urge us, from the time we step into the preparation room to prepare to be initiated into the sublime mysteries of an Entered Apprentice, up to the time we are exalted to the degree of a Royal Arch Mason, to support ' *all the ancient usages and customs of the Fraternity?*' I will now show you what are some of the laws of Masonry, and then most conclusively prove that the ' *ancient usage and custom*' of our ancient brethren was, to inflict on a Masonic traitor punishment adequate to his crime.

---

* Salem ed. p. 44. † Ib. p. 62. ‡ Ib. p. 72. § Ib. p. 93. ‖ Ib. p. 97.
¶ Ib. p. 146.

The first law of Masonry which I shall give you, may be found at page 20 of the 'Illustrations of Masonry,' as given by Morgan: how near it is to the obligations which you actually took upon you in the lodge, I will leave you to judge. 'Furthermore, I do promise and swear, that I will not write, print, stamp, stain, hew, cut, carve, indent, paint, or engrave (the secrets of Masonry,) on any thing moveable or immoveable, under the whole canopy of heaven, whereby or whereon the least letter, &c. may become legible or intelligible to myself, or any person in the known world, whereby the secrets of Masonry may become unlawfully obtained through my unworthiness: binding myself under no less penalty, than to have my *throat cut across, my tongue torn out by the roots, and my body buried in the rough sands of the sea, at low watermark, where the tide ebbs and flows twice in twenty-four hours.*' One would suppose, if true, this was a *powerful* law; I should wish for no greater punishment, than the penalty of this law to be inflicted on me. The next Masonic law I shall cite, may be found at page 49 of the same work:—' Furthermore, do I promise and swear, that I will support the constitution of the Grand Lodge of the United States, and the Grand Lodge of this state, under which this is held, and conform to all the *by-laws, rules, and regulations of this, or any other lodge,* of which I may at any time hereafter become a member, as far as in my power. Furthermore, do *I promise and swear*, THAT I WILL OBEY ALL (no exceptions) REGULAR SIGNS AND SUMMONS, GIVEN, HANDED, SENT, OR THROWN, *to me by the hand of a brother Fellow Craft Mason, or from the body of a just and lawfully constituted lodge of such*: binding myself under no less penalty, than to have my *left breast torn open, and my heart and vitals taken from thence and thrown over my left shoulder, and carried into the valley of Jehosaphat, there to become a prey to wild beasts of the field and vultures of the air,* if ever I should be wilfully guilty, &c. Stronger still, page 71, same work, obligation of a Master Mason:—' Furthermore, do I promise and swear, that I will support the constitution of the Grand Lodge of the state of ———, under which this lodge is held, and conform to all the *by-laws, rules, and regulations of this, or any other lodge, of which I may hereafter become a member.* Furthermore, do I promise and swear, that I will OBEY ALL THE REGULAR SIGNS, SUMMONS, OR TOKENS, HANDED, SENT, OR THROWN, *to me from the hand of a brother Master Mason, or from the body of a just and lawfully constituted lodge of such.* Furthermore, do I promise and swear, that *I will go on a Master Mason's errand, whenever required, even should I have to go barefoot and bareheaded:* binding myself under no less penalty than *to have my body severed in the midst and divided to the north and south, my bowels burnt to ashes in the centre, and the ashes scattered before the four winds of heaven, that there might not the least track or trace of remembrance remain among men or Masons, of so vile and perjured a wretch as I should be, were I ever to prove wilfully guilty,*' &c. Stronger and stronger, and thus they continue to increase in all important parts, up to the degree of Knights of the Holy and Thrice Illustrious Order of the Cross, as many of us full well know. I have given authority sufficient to satisfy any one, beyond the bare possibility of a doubt, that every Mason, from the days of our founder, Solomon, down to that of the murdered Morgan, who has 'received a part of the rights and benefits of a Worshipful Lodge,' have been bound by their honor, and the strongest obligations which man could invent, to support ' *all the ancient usages and customs*,' as well as laws of ancient Free Masonry. One point only is wanted to establish the charge made in number five, that the ancient usages and customs of our ancient brethren, was to execute any Masonic traitor found among them. On this point proof is abundant. As we all know, in the different degrees we have taken, Masonic tradition inform us of a number of instances of the kind. No Fellow Craft Mason can forget the slaying of forty and two thousand of the Ephraimites in one day; and that our ancient brethren adopted the pass word used on that occasion, as a proper pass word to be given before entering any well regulated lodge of Fellow Crafts. Every Master Mason must remember the execution of the three Fellow Crafts, executed by order of king Solomon. I will now, my brethren, show conclusively, that the ancient usages and customs of our brethren, was to inflict on the Masonic traitor a punishment due his crimes. Before entering on that point I would remark, that in all the ancient ceremonies we allow the Master of a lodge full and complete power; no one can direct, but all must obey his mandate; and thus of the Grand Master: all the subordinate officers are under his control, and must execute whatever he directs; equally so is it with the presiding officer of the Chapter and Grand Chapter and General Grand Chapter, who represents king Solomon, and according to 'ancient usage and custom,' gives orders for the apprehension and execution of Masonic traitors. I do not wish to be misunderstood, for I well know that in all minor concerns, such as disposing of the funds, &c. he is under control of the members of his lodge; but I speak expressly of his power as derived from 'ancient usages and customs.' Thus, for example, all the subordinate officers say:—' You will wait until the Worshipful Master can be informed and his order given—It is the *order* of the Worshipful Master— The Worshipful Master *ordered me*, &c. ;' showing conclusively that the Master in all cases which refer to ' ancient usages and customs of the fraternity' is absolute, and all the brethren are sworn to ' *obey all signs, summons, or tokens, given, handed, sent, or thrown, to them.*'

I shall first quote from page 49 of the ' Illustrations,' where the Junior Warden inquires of the considerate, why was this pass instituted? Answer. In consequence of a quarrel which had long existed between Jephthah, judge of Israel, and the Ephraimites, the latter of whom had been a stubborn and rebellious people, whom Jephthah had endeavored to subdue by lenient measures, but to no effect. The Ephraimites being highly incensed against Jephthah, for not being called to fight and share in the rich spoils of the Ammonitish war, assembled a mighty army and passed over the river Jordan to give Jephthah battle; but he being apprised of their approach, called together the men of Israel and gave them battle and put them to flight; and to make his victory more complete he ordered guards to be placed at the different passes of the river Jordan, and commanded if the Ephramites passed that way, that they should pronounce the word Shibboleth; but they being of a different tribe, pronounced it Siboleth; which *trifling* defect proved them spies and cost them their lives; and there fell that day, at the different passes on the banks of the river Jordan, forty and two thousand. This word was also used by our ancient brethren, to distinguish a friend from a foe, and has since been adopted as a *proper pass word*, to be given before entering any well regulated and governed lodge of Fellow Craft Masons.

I am well aware you will say this is not directly to the point; but a very little reflection will show you that it has an important bearing on this question. It is said to be a proper pass word. It is so truly; the candidate hears of the slaughter of forty and two thousand of the Ephraimites, to impress his mind of the great danger of being an enemy to Free Masonry. It has another still more important bearing, and is in substance the same as to tell the candidate, should you, or any number of you, turn traitors, and expose the true pass word, we can invent a new ' check word,' and armed with the dirks of the Knights, can require of you, ' Say now our new check word ;' and every man of you not having the new check word shall be slain; and the day may arrive when we shall make as great slaughter among our enemies as did Jephthah among the Ephraimites.

This, my brethren, is no trifling subject; the Grand Lodge has seen fit, in the plenitude of their wisdom, to invent a new pass word, and no man can be admitted into any lodge under their jurisdiction without he can distinctly pronounce this new *Shibboleth*, (FIDELITY, the new pass word;) and when the time may come when those who cannot pronounce it may receive the deadly thrust, no one can tell. It carries also one other important lesson with it:

as Jephthah had full power to command the forces of Israel to fight his battles, and invent a new pass word to detect his enemies; so has our Grand Master an undoubted right to call upon every Mason under his jurisdiction, to turn out at his command and fight for the cause of Masonry, and give the deadly thrust to every one who cannot distinctly pronounce, *Fidelity*.

The next instance of Masonic execution I shall give, may be found from page 80 to 82, and is a history of the death of our Worthy Master, Hiram Abiff, and the execution of the three Fellow Crafts who murdered him. I am aware that some of the brotherhood, like drowning men catching at straws, will say this was for murder, and did not relate to the revealing the secrets of Masonry. I only answer that my object now is to show that if a person is found guilty of a crime deserving death in the Masonic order, our 'ancient usages and customs' give sufficient power to execute him, and it is left to the successors of king Solomon to determine whether he be worthy of death or not; and still farther, if the 'ancient usages and customs' were to execute a member for doing an act which he had not sworn to refrain from, surely those same 'ancient usages and customs' would not allow a member to escape punishment who by his oath had submitted himself to be executed should he commit certain acts: then if our 'ancient usages and customs' are such that a person can be executed when the representative of king Solomon supposes he has committed a crime worthy of death, they most assuredly will authorize the inflicting a penalty which the member has subjected himself to, should he reveal the secrets of Masonry. I would farther remark, they were executed 'agreeably to the imprecations of their own mouths:' then certainly any member according to the same rule can be executed according to the 'several imprecations' they take upon themselves in their obligations, when they swear in the presence of Almighty God and this Worshipful Lodge erected to him,' that they will never reveal the secrets of Masonry.

The substance of that history is as follows:—A number of the workmen of the temple became dissatisfied, because they had wrought long on the temple, and had not received the grand and sublime word of a Master Mason; wishing to obtain it, that they might travel in foreign parts and obtain better wages, they accosted Hiram and demanded the word from him. He told them he could not give it, unless there were three present to wit, Solomon, Hiram, king of Tyre, and himself; but to wait with patience until they were assembled in the Grand Lodge at Jerusalem, and if found worthy they should receive it. But they wished not to wait; and in their attempts to get it, they killed our Grand Master, Hiram Abiff. Solomon coming to the temple, as was his usual custom, found the workmen in confusion, and on inquiring the cause was told there were no designs drawn on the tressle board. After considerable ceremony it was found Hiram was missing. He then orders twelve of them to go in search of him. They returned with no distinct tidings, but related some suspicious circumstances. He then orders them to go a second time, and return with the murderers. After some search, the murderers are heard lamenting the act, and asking certain punishments inflicted on their heads for the murderous deed. They were seized and brought before king Solomon, 'who after hearing the testimony of the three Fellow Crafts, and the three ruffians having pleaded guilty, orders them to be taken out at the west gate of the temple, and there EXECUTED ACCORDING TO THE SEVERAL IMPRECATIONS OF THEIR OWN MOUTHS.' It is true that is not direct in point, so far as the revealing the secrets was the crime, but conclusively shows the power of punishing was vested in king Solomon. The history of Akirop and the other six traitors, as given in No. 5, comes directly to the point in question. Here were six persons executed by king Solomon, for some enormous crime; and from the circumstances as recorded, there is no reason to doubt it was for revealing some of the secrets of the order. Indeed, some who have taken that degree, do not deny such to be the fact. The execution of Akirop is no common execution: found resting secure as he supposed, the executioner entered the cave; 'inflamed at the sight, he seized the poniard and plunged it first in the head, then in the heart;' not satisfied with this, he severs the head from the body, and taking his poniard in one hand, and the bloody head in the other, he proceeds back with his bloody trophies to king Solomon. Do you hear him condemning Joabert for his bloody act? Does he mourn the loss of Akirop? It is true he was at first displeased because he put it out of his power to take vengeance himself, in presence of all the craft, as a warning to them against such an act; but so easily is he reconciled, that Joabert is soon received into favor, and new and distinguished honors conferred upon him, to reward his zeal in an act at which humanity would shudder; and the bloody deed is to be kept in remembrance, and transmitted down to the latest posterity, by instituting a new degree of Masonry, and having the emblems and furniture of it represent this same bloody act. The halls of their dark cavern, to strike fear to the heart of those who would otherwise become traitors, and to stimulate the zeal of those who are determined to stick to the order at all hazards, are painted to represent the execution of Akirop in its full force. The candidate, on entering this Chapter, by the feeble light of one lamp has represented the cavern where Akirop reposed. He sees the bloody poniard which struck the fatal blow; he sees the representation of Akirop's bloody head, as just severed from the body, held by a bloody arm in an attitude of exultation at the death of a traitor; and some kind brother, with his apron sprinkled with blood, points to him, VENGEANCE, written in capital letters upon the walls of the cavern. Should any person caught in the street be blindfolded and carried into this Chapter, and when brought to light, see the bloody trophies scattered about the cave, and the members should crowd around him with their bloody dress,—instead of supposing he had been introduced to the society of honest men, he would rather conclude that demons of darkness had dragged him down to the regions of despair. All things considered, my brethren, it is not surprising that this society has existed thus long; for who, under any government, where personal liberty is not as safely secured as in this republic, would dare divulge the secrets of Masonry. In the foregoing cases we see clearly what were the 'ancient usages and customs of the fraternity' which we have all pledged our honor, and have solemnly sworn to support.

There is one case more which I shall here cite, and, I trust, show plainly, was performed in strict accordance with the 'ancient usages and customs of ancient Free Masonry.' I shall refer you to no book for this instance, for it is not written on perishable materials, but with imperishable characters, on the memory of every true patriot in the United States; and the bloody tale will be told to their children, and transmitted down to all posterity, as a convincing proof of the bloody character of this *ancient and honorable society*. I speak now of the Morgan case, the tragical scenes of which are too well known in this section of the country to need a full description. I shall only show the similarity between this case and those I have quoted.

I am well aware, that from the difference of the government under which the Morgan case was performed, and that under which the other Masonic executions were performed, that an exact similarity could not exist, but where it was possible to follow; the 'ancient usages and customs of the ancient Fraternity' have been copied so nearly as to show that those engaged in the Morgan case 'did carefully preseve the ancient landmarks of the order, committed to their care, and did not suffer them to be infringed upon, nor suffer a deviation from the established usages and customs of the Fraternity,' more than was possible. In the case of the murderers of our Grand Master, Hiram Abiff, as soon as Solomon had learned the case, he despatched a number of the craft to apprehend the villains, that they might receive a punishment adequate to their crimes: they did find the murderers, and he ordered them

L l

to be punished 'agreeably to the several imprecations of their own mouths.' In the case of Akirop a great assemblage of Masters was held, to consult on the best means of apprehending the traitor ; and after the consultation, Solomon ordered nine of the craft to apprehend the traitor, and bring him to a punishment due his crimes : they did find the traitor, but instead of bringing him back, they only returned with such bloody evidence as convinced all that the traitor had been executed. In the case of the six traitors, who had fled from Jerusalem, Solomon elected fifteen persons, in whom he could place the highest confidence,' and sent them in quest of the villains, and gave them letters to different persons on their way, ' to assist them in apprehending the villains.' Not knowing the complete history of the Morgan case, we cannot follow it with that minuteness we can the other cases, but we can discover a most striking similarity between the cases ; from which we may suppose, with confidence, they followed those cases in almost every particular. Agreeably to the 'ancient usages and customs' of the fraternity, the person representing Solomon, our former Master, should, upon hearing Morgan was publishing, and Miller printing, the secrets of Masonry, appoint some judicious person or persons, in whose discretion and prudence he ' could place implicit confidence,' to ascertain the fact, and give him a ' *summons*;' and should such be the fact, to call for such assistance as the case should require. It is not in my power to say that the person representing Solomon, in the United States, did thus appoint a person, thus qualified ; but I well know that a person calling his name Daniel Johns, and unknown to any one in this section, ' suddenly' made his appearance in Batavia, and by his cunning and prudence, (which are well worthy the 'implicit confidence,' of the representatives of Solomon,) gained admittance into the printing office of D. C. Miller, and learned the fact that Morgan had written, and Miller was publishing the secrets of Masonry, and did actually call upon many Masons to ' assist him in apprehending the villains ;' and some of our brethren have said, (how true it is, I do not say,) that he had written orders to that effect. It has also been sworn to, that some of the leaders in that transaction said he had been sent here expressly for that purpose ; but who sent him I cannot tell.

In the case of Akirop and the other six traitors, 'a great assembly of Masters was held, in consultation on the best means of apprehending the villains.' It has been fully proved that a large assemblage of Masons was held in Stafford, on the 8th of September, and Dr. Butler has testified, to consult on the best means of stopping the publication of Morgan's book ; and others have said, if no means could effect it, to devise means to carry off Morgan. What means were actually devised, can only be drawn from what transpired after the meeting : on the next Monday, Morgan was taken from Batavia ; on the next day, Miller was violently torn from his family, and brought to this place, where, by the timely assistance of his friends, he was saved from the fate allotted to Morgan, who was amidst the cries of murder taken from Canandaigua and carried to the magazine of Fort Niagara, a place as nearly representing the cave in which Akirop was executed, as any that could conveniently be found, and there probably murdered; but his murderers did not dare return with the bloody trophies of their vengeance to the person authorizing the transaction. I cannot positively state that Daniel Johns carried with him such a summons as we have all sworn to obey, whether given, handed, sent, or thrown, unto us ; but we all know that many obeyed some summons or sign, by neglecting their common avocations and assisting in transporting him beyond the reach of his friends ; others, when called upon, took their horses from their plough, to aid, and in other ways assisted in getting him through a large tract of country, which nothing can reconcile, unless they had a ' sign, summons, or token, given, handed, sent, or thrown to them,' which they had sworn to obey. I give one more reason for supposing the Morgan case to be in strict conformity to the 'ancient usages of ancient Free Masonry.' On the morning they were going on this infernal errand, many of them said they had sworn never to suffer the secrets of Masonry to be published, if in their power to prevent it, and *they could prevent it by going to Batavia that day;* others said they had ancient authority for this conduct in the Morgan case; and one of the captains of the band, when asked for a reason, took his Monitor and read the case of Akirop and the other six traitors, as given in No. 5, supposing that would suppress any further inquiry on that point. Whether Morgan suffered a fate similar to that of Akirop, or whether, according to the several imprecations of his own mouth, he had his throat cut, 'left breast torn open, body severed in two, bowels *burnt to ashes, those ashes scattered to the four winds of heaven, that there might be no more trace or remembrance among men or Masons, of so vile and perjured a wretch as he was,*' as well as those who were actually his murderers,—it is true, remains somewhat in doubt. But should Masonry survive this tremendous shock, and assume all its former power and glory in some after age, our Monitor would disclose to future generations the manner of his murder, and his murderers occupy as conspicuous a place in it as does Joabert in the execution of Akirop; but should it be left until that time, I fear it will never be known, for Masonry is now in the last convulsive agonies of death. Let us now, my brethren, candidly review this subject, for it is of great importance. It is fully proved from unquestionable authority, that before entering a lodge we are required to pledge our honor, and after entering it we are repeatedly charged to support all the ancient usages and customs of ancient Free Masonry, and never suffer the least deviation from the established rules and customs of the fraternity. Morgan, in his illustration, informs us that all Masons solemnly swear to obey all signs, summons or tokens, given, handed, sent or thrown, to them by a Fellow Craft or Master Mason, thereby establishing a sure way to carry into effect the ' ancient usages and customs' of our ancient brethren; also that should we divulge any of the secrets of Masonry, we will suffer death in the most cruel and barbarous manner; establishing clearly that the law of Masonry is to execute any member who shall divulge the secrets of Masonry. It is most conclusively shown, from unquestionable authority, that the usages and customs of our ancient brethren were to execute a Masonic traitor according to the 'several imprecations of his own mouth,' or inflict a punishment upon him adequate to his crimes. It is also clearly shown, that in almost every particular, so far as the facts have come to light, that Morgan was dealt with agreeably to the ancient usages and customs of the fraternity; therefore I do consider the charge made in No. 5 proved beyond the bare possibility of a doubt. One doubt however, has been raised, and as it comes from a source I highly respect, I will answer it. It is said that the Masons of the present age are under no more obligations to obey the laws of Solomon, than they are those of Moses; thereby admitting fully that the laws of Solomon were such as have been given.

In answer, it might be said we are bound to obey all laws which we have pledged our honors and oaths to support, and never suffer a deviation from. I admit Masons are not bound in their Masonic capacity to obey all the laws and advice Solomon has given in the sacred writings, any more than they are those which Moses has so given; but I do contend that all the Masonic laws which Solomon, as Grand Master of the lodge, gave, are as binding upon us, if we adhere to the Masonic institution, as the laws of Moses are binding upon the Jews as firm believers in the Mosaic dispensation, and who suppose that all the customs of the ancient Jews under Moses, their leader, are binding upon them. But I will not pretend to say, that for following the ancient usages and customs of our ancient brethren, as given to them by Solomon, the wrath of heaven will be as severely poured upon our heads as it is upon the Jews; so that we be scattered among all the nations of the earth, and become a byword and reproach among men.

I will make a few more observations, and close this part of the subject. I have addressed my numbers to all honest Masons. Such I wish to examine this subject with care and attention. To those who are dupes to the designing part of the fraternity, and are blindly determined to adhere to the institution through 'thick and thin;' or to those who adhere to it because it has shielded them from merited punishment, or expect it will still aid them to commit crime with impunity; or those who expect still to defraud the lodges and Chapters of their funds, I have nothing to say—I wish to address those who are honest, and who have honestly supported, from the many borrowed morals which have been added to Masonry to deceive the world, and not having frequently attended the meetings of their brethren, and heard the obligations administered, and seen the ceremonies of Masonry, that no evils have or can arise from Masonry, when its members performed all that is required of them by its principles. Such I would earnestly request to examine this subject with all the care and attention the importance of it deserves; we have slumbered too long upon our posts; but let the cries of the murdered Morgan arouse us from our slumber, and inquire by whom, for what, and by what, laws was he murdered? After thus examining the case, let us honestly and fearlessly cast the blame of this murderous transaction where it actually belongs. Some of those men engaged in the late outrages are well known to all of us to be men, in other respects, of good character, who would shudder at the commission of any crime. Then if they are murderers, what, I ask, has made them so? Shall we, to save an institution groaning under the blackest of crimes, make them *common* murderers and vagabonds of the land? They adhered closely to the ancient usages and customs which we have all of us pledged our honor, and have solemnly sworn in presence of Almighty God to support. I beseech you then, my brethren, come out manfully and show some sympathy for them and their families; acknowledge it was for adhering to an institution which has become not only useless, but dangerous, that has produced this disasterous transaction which has thrown this section of country in such confusion. A Mason.

NO. VIII.

To all Honest Masons:

Brethren—In my former numbers I have fully shown that our society was not only useless, but dangerous, in a republican government—that the laws of Masonry authorized the murder of a Masonic traitor who should divulge their secrets; I have also shown that Morgan was executed in the same way all other Masonic traitors have been, as laid down by our best Masonic writers. *I now assert, and will prove, that the obligations which are given in our Masonic lodges to their members, are not binding, morally, religiously, or legally —but on the contrary, it is a duty from which no honest Mason will shrink, to absolve himself from all allegiance to Masonry, and expose to the scorn and contempt of all mankind their unlawful and blasphemous obligations.* To ascertain this point, let us inquire what is the nature of these obligations. They are not oaths in a legal sense; for to constitute a lawful oath it is necessary that the person administering it should be legally authorized to do thus, and the person receiving should swear to things within his knowledge; but in this case the person administering our obligations derives no authority for it by any law—the person swearing to perform the promise knows nothing what will be required of him; therefore, they cannot be called legal oaths. If not legal oaths, they cannot be any thing more than mere simple conditional promises. I am ready to grant that a promise made, (the maker of it knowing the subject matter of the promise,) and the performance of the same being lawful, that the promise is morally binding. On the contrary, however, not knowing at the time of making it the subject matter of the promise, and the performance of it being unlawful, we are in no manner bound to perform the promise. The manner of administering the obligation is such that we cannot conceive even the nature of the promises until after we have taken them, and time is afforded to examine them. After going through a scene of nonsense and fright, well calculated to confuse our ideas, we are required to kneel and say after the person administering the obligations—only a few words are said at a time, and this in broken sentences, in a manner in which no one can obtain a correct knowledge, even after hearing them administered: for example, the master says, requiring the candidate to repeat:—I, A. B., of my own free will and accord, in presence of Almighty God and this Worshipful Lodge, &c. No person can possibly tell the bearing which the obligations may have on his conscience or duty to his country, until he has had sufficient time to peruse and reflect upon it. If, after the ceremonies are performed—and in his cooler moments, he can deliberately examine the nature and actual promise—he is satisfied that it does interfere with either his 'religion or his politics,' most assuredly he cannot be bound to perform the same; and he only can determine for himself whether it does interfere with his own individual duty to his God or his country. We ought not therefore to judge too severely those who, considering them thus to interfere, throw them aside as null and void; for men will construe the same passages differently; and in this land of freedom the inestimable privilege of thinking for ourselves, provided it does not interfere with the laws of our country, is fully and perfectly secured to every citizen. That you may fully understand the subject, and not rest on my individual assertion, I will give you the opinion of moral and religious writers on this subject. Paley, a great Theologian, and one of the best moral writers of our age, says, 'Promises are not binding when the performance is unlawful. There are two cases of this: one where the unlawfulness is known at the time of making the promise; the other case [which is even stronger and more applicable to Masonic promises] is when the unlawfulness did not exist, or was unknown in the making of the promise. When the promise is understood to proceed upon a certain supposition, and that promise turns out to be false, the promise is not binding.' Thus, when we are about to receive the obligation, we are told it does not interfere with our 'religion or politics.' Should they interfere with either they certainly cannot be binding upon any man receiving them. The examples which Paley gives in his Moral Philosophy, it is useless to quote, as they are familiar with all of you. The Rev. Thomas Scott has written upon the subject of oaths, and describes the nature of Herod's. He says, 'Herod's oath was rash and profane in the extreme; and when it was found to involve such consequences, it became absolutely unlawful to observe it. He ought to have repented of his impiety, and with abhorrence have rejected Salome's application. Rash oaths are above all things to be be avoided; but if men *are entangled by them,* they ought rather to infringe the sinful oaths than add sin to sin and ruin to their own souls.' It is unnecessary to quote from other authors on this subject; for every one must at once perceive the only crime there can be is in taking the obligations. Are the obligations which are administered in our different lodges, Chapters, Councils, and Encampments, of the nature of those described by Paley, Scott, and others, as not binding? I shall give a part of the different obligations; and should any Mason in the United States dare deny that the quotations from these obligations are not substantially correct, I pledge myself to prove them so by competent witnesses, if such person will give his name to the editors of the Le Roy Gazette, he proving that he has taken the degree the obligation of which he disputes. In the Master Mason's obligation, as given by Morgan in his 'Illustrations'—and no Mason who regards his veracity dare deny the correctness of that book—is the following:—' Furthermore, do I promise and swear, that I will not give the grand hailing sign of distress except I am in real distress, or for the benefit of the craft when at work; and should I ever see that sign given, or the word accompanying it, and the person who gave it appearing to be in distress, I will fly to his relief at the risk of my life, should there be a greater probability of saving his life than losing my own. Furthermore, do I promise and swear, that a Master Mason's secrets given to me in charge as such, and I knowing him to be such, shall remain as secure and inviolable in my breast as in his own, when communicated to me as such, murder and treason excepted, and they left to my own elicitation.' Thus, under the solemnity of an oath, should we ever see a brother giving the grand hailing sign of distress, we are bound to fly to his relief, should there be a greater probability of saving his life than losing our own. We are here sworn without any reservation; neither are there any distinguished marks drawn about the kind of distress; the only question is, does he appear in any kind of danger? Should he flee from the punishment due his crimes, we are sworn to protect him, so long as there is more probability of saving his life than losing our own—a lawful promise, truly, in a government where the only safety of our property consists in affording our aid in the execution of the laws. To show fully the force of this part of the obligation, I will put a case which has too often been realized since the establishment of our ORDER. A Master Mason commits arson—is seen or suspected —the necessary steps are taken—an officer attempts to arrest him—a Master Mason gives him 'timely notice'—(the reason for his so doing I will presently explain)—and he attempts to flee—the officer closely pursues—perceiving a probability of receiving his just deserts, he, at venture, gives the grand hailing sign of distress—you, standing perhaps in the door of your house, see him 'give the sign,' or it being dark, 'hear the words accompanying the same,' you are bound (if the oath is obligatory) to fly to his relief, rescue him from the officer, and receive him into your house, and there defend him so long as there is a 'greater probability of saving his life than losing your own.' You do thus defend your criminal brother; and the officer seeing he cannot execute the laws of his country without endangering his life, at length desists and leaves you in possession of your criminal brother. After the officer has withdrawn from the contest, your criminal brother confesses the crime, and tells you when, where, and how, it was committed, and you become in possession of all the facts concerning it. At length, supposing all is safe, you admit your brother to escape from your house—the officer waiting without to execute his duty, seizes the criminal, and he is brought to the trial—from the circumstances it is supposed he has entrusted you with all the facts. You are called upon the stand and legally sworn to tell the 'truth, the whole truth, and nothing but the truth.' The question is—Did your brother Mason tell you he committed the crime he is charged with? What a situation are you placed in? Your criminal brother gave the secret to you 'in charge as such, and you knew him to be as such,' and you are sworn 'that they shall remain as secure and inviolable in your breast as in his own.' Should you consider your Masonic obligation as binding, you must necessarily perjure yourself: should you be a true patriot and supporter of the laws of your country, it is true you will break your Masonic promise; but there should be no promise, especially on oath, which is in contradiction to the obligations we are under to our country. I ask—Is it lawful to protect a criminal, and screen him from the punishment due his crime?—Is it lawful to conceal a crime committed against the laws of your country?—Should you do it, do you not become accessary after the fact? and as such are you not liable by law to be punished? The promise made in the Master Mason's obligation is there unlawful, and no one can for a moment suppose he is bound by such obligation. In the same obligation is the following:—Furthermore, do I promise and swear, that I will not speak evil of a brother Master Mason, &c.; but *will apprize him of all approaching danger*, if in my power. I have before said that some Mason would give a criminal brother timely notice—the reason has been explained; he has sworn to apprize him of approaching danger. Should, therefore, any Mason know his brother guilty of any crime, and there is a probability of his being arrested, he is sworn to apprize him of his danger. The same material points are kept in view through the other degrees. Having reached the Royal Arch, they suppose you are prepared in full to assist them in their purposes. You are then required to swear in the following manner :—' Furthermore, do I promise and swear, that I will protect a companion Royal Arch Mason, whether right or wrong.' Throwing off all reserve, they here tell us at once we must ' go the whole load,' and protect them in any villany whatever, and however guilty they may be. Can any Royal Arch Mason, if he has any regard for his Masonic promise, sit on a jury where a Royal Arch Mason is to be tried for any crime, and bring in a verdict of guilty, when he has sworn to protect a companion, 'whether right or wrong—under the no less penalty than to have his scull smote off, and his brains exposed to the scorching rays of the sun ?' Can he do justice to a man who knows not our order, when his antagonist is a Royal Arch Mason? Most assuredly he cannot! for he has sworn to 'protect a companion of this exalted degree, whether right or wrong.' It is absurd in the extreme, to urge such obligations upon a person. We are all bound by every tie which binds societies together, to dispense justice and equity whenever we are called upon, either by the laws of our country, or as disinterested persons, to decide any dispute which may arise in a government founded upon equal rights. There should be no distinction in any *case whatever*. We are all, both by nature and law entitled to every privilege which can be granted to any person ; and to mark outlines of distinction, and afford protection to one man in preference to another, because he may belong to an order we are unacquainted with, and can scientifically draw his hand across his forehead in allusion to the penalty of this obligation, is contrary to every principle of virtue, morality, religion, or law ; and no obligation which requires us to do so, can possibly be binding. The following outrageous and unlawful promise is contained in the same oath :—*Furthermore, do I promise and swear, that a companion Royal Arch Mason's secrets, given me in charge as such, and I knowing him to be such, shall remain as secure and inviolable in my breast as in his own, when communicated to me,* MURDER AND TREASON NOT EXCEPTED.

Paley says, ' Promises are not binding, where there is a prior obligation to the contrary.' Every citizen of the United States is under a natural and paramount obligation to support the government which affords him protection. As good citizens we are bound to afford every assistance to preserve the good order of society, and aid in the execution of the laws. Therefore, we must communicate to the proper authorities, all crimes which come within our knowledge. Should we, *by any means whatever,* know murder to have been committed, humanity, the laws of God and man, all require us to communicate the same immediately, that the murderer may receive a punishment 'due his crime,' and the majesty of our laws be not trampled upon with impunity. But as Royal Arch Masons, we are sworn to conceal the horrid crime of murder, provided the person committing it should be a companion Royal Arch Mason! What security have we, if crimes of the deepest dye are to be committed and concealed ? The cries of murder may arouse us from our sleep at the silent hour of night—our villages may be wrapt in flames—our property stolen and destroyed—and the person committing these flagrant crimes may escape punishment, if he is so fortunate as to be a ' companion Royal Arch Mason!' Should it, however, be suspected by 'those who know not our order,' that a ' companion of this exalted degree' had performed these diabolical acts, and he should be brought to trial, a Royal Arch Mason sitting on the jury is bound by all they call sacred to clear him, 'right or wrong,' and he will of course escape punishment. But, should he be so *unfortunate,* however, as to have no ' companion Royal Arch Mason' on the jury, and he is found guilty of this crime by his lawful peers, he sues a *Royal Arch Governor* for pardon ; and the said Royal Arch Governor, if he supposes his Masonic oath binding, must, and will grant his petition. We have no security for our lives or property, while such obligations are administered and adhered to. We have had a full demonstration of this fact, in the unhappy fate of Capt. William Morgan. A free citizen may be torn from his family and his friends —deprived of his liberty and life—and no punishment awarded to the villains performing so hellish an act, (should they be Royal Arch Masons who committed the same)—and none but Royal Arch Masons be privy to the circumstance; or a Royal Arch Mason who regards his Masonic obligation as binding, may sit upon the jury to try the criminals. But if so dangerous in the case of individual property, or the safety of individuals themselves, how is their dangerous tendency magnified, when even treason is not excepted in their obligations? We live under the best organized government ever formed; a government dispensing its salutary influence equally upon all—all partaking, when administered in its purity, of its equal rights and protection. But it may be overthrown and destroyed at any time; and should none but Royal Arch Masons know the existence of the treasonable purposes, there can be no remedy.

There is, perhaps, from three to five hundred thousand Royal Arch Masons scattered over the United States, possessing means of communicating their laws and objects over any other society. No member of that degree hazards any thing by disclosing his treasonable purposes to them all in their meetings; holding out inducements of different kinds to each, there may be no such number of them who will conspire with him to overthrow the only republican government in the world. Should they thus agree what means do they possess to carry their designs into effect? Possessing a key which has for ever (until of late) been unknown to any but Royal Arch Masons, they can communicate without danger; for should their letters be intercepted, none but 'companions of this exalted degree' can know its contents; and they are sworn to protect them right or wrong; and 'murder and treason' are not excepted in their oath of secrecy. That this may not seem too much like fiction, I would remark, that in the celebrated conspiracy of Aaron Burr, this same Royal Arch key was used, and their characters, in his letters to his coadjutors. How can they be punished? None but 'companions of this exalted degree,' have any knowledge of their purposes, and they are sworn not to divulge it; and should any of them not enter the conspiracy, they are sworn to protect those who may, 'right or wrong.' I again ask, what safety have we for our lives, or liberties, or government, if such obligations are administered and adhered to? But so far from these obligations being binding, we are bound by our prior obligations to the government, to absolve ourselves from all allegiance to an institution administering them; and to expose them to the world.

I will now ask you to examine the obligation of the Holy and Thrice Illustrious Order of the Cross:—'YOU FURTHER SWEAR, THAT SHOULD YOU EVER KNOW A COMPANION VIOLATE ANY ESSENTIAL PART OF THIS OBLIGATION YOU WILL USE YOUR MOST DECIDED ENDEAVORS, BY THE BLESSING OF GOD, TO BRING SUCH PERSON TO THE MOST STRICT AND CONDIGN PUNISHMENT, AGREEABLY TO THE RULES AND USAGES OF OUR ANCIENT FRATERNITY; (See No. 7;) *and thus, by pointing him out to the world as an unworthy and vicious vagabond; by opposing his interest; by disarranging his business; by transferring his character after him, wherever he may go; by exposing him to the contempt of the whole fraternity and the world, but of our Illustrious Order more especially, during his whole natural life.*' That masterpiece of men, the declaration of independence, declares that man possesses certain inestimable rights: such as life, liberty, and the pursuits of happiness. The laws of our country guarantee to us the privilege of following such pursuits as we please, in safety; and declares it a misdemeanor for any number of men to conspire to destroy the lawful pursuits of any person. Slander is punishable by heavy fines. Morality, religion, and the best interest of society, forbids us to destroy the reputation of any person whatever. But it has come to this, that a set of men are combined to bring to strict and condign punishment citizens of a free republic, for no offence against the law of the land—for no offence of the law of God—for no offence against the equal rights of mankind ? What offence is recognisable by this band, worse than a banditti, who attack not only the property, but the reputation of a man ? It is the heinous offence of telling the world, here are a horde of villains, self-created, bound together by oaths to protect each other, 'right or wrong;' and that an honest man who disbelieves in their infernal principles, must be branded with infamy. Is it lawful to punish 'strictly, and with condign punishment,' a man who has violated no law ? And how punish ? '*By pointing him out to the world as an unworthy and vicious vagabond.*' We can here exclaim with emphasis, 'Tell it not in Gath—publish it not in the streets of Askelon'—that in this land of liberty, where we are daily boasting of our superior advantages of equal rights, we are fostering in our bosom a set of men possessing the spirit of demons ; who are sworn to make a vagabond of a man who does not subscribe to their hellish tenets. No matter how fair a character he may have sustained ; no matter if the 'frost of seventy winters' has whitened his head in the cause of his Redeemer ; no matter if his whole life has been one continued act of benevolence and good will to mankind ; still he must be pointed out to the world, by the fingers of scorn, as an 'unworthy and vicious vagabond.' Again, '*By opposing his interest.*' Not satisfied with destroying his reputation, they must even oppose his interest in society. I had ever supposed that any individual had an undoubted right to advance his political or worldly interest by all lawful means. Has he talent and honesty sufficient, he may aim at filling any office under the government which he lives.

But this blood-stained few say, that if he has violated any essential part of our law, we will not allow him the privilege of gaining any interest whatever with his fellow citizens ; however capable he may be, he shall gain no influence in society, but shall be forced to submit to become an outcast of society ; and to carry this into full effect, the most palpable falsehoods are circulated. This has been verified for sometime past ; but of this more anon. Again, '*By destroying his business.*' Not satisfied with destroying his reputation, the brightest jewel in his possession ; not satisfied with opposing his best interest in the world ; but should he after this be pursuing some lawful vocation—perhaps the only support for himself and family—they swear to derange even this, and turn him out upon the world, as a vagabond both in property and reputation. Freedom and equality indeed ! Boast no more of our wholesome laws, and of the equality of our government ; boast no more of the 'land of the brave, and the home of the free,' where every citizen can pursue his vocation in peace, if the combination is yet in the bosom of our country, pretending to be the most honorable and respected part of community, and sworn to take the bread from the mouth of honest industry, and to turn a man destitute and dependent upon the cold charity of the world. Should he be found in the street, sustaining the 'peltings of the pitiless storm' and asking the charities of the world which are given to the meanest vagabond, for some scanty provision, even the 'crumbs which fall from the rich man's table,' to support for a short time a destitute but unfortunate family,—they are sworn to represent him in such a view, that even this scanty provision cannot be given him. What awful crime has he been guilty of, that the common acts of charity cannot be administered to him? None: no offence against the laws of his country whatever, has he been guilty of ; but on the contrary, he has ever sustained a good character ; but he supposed, and *rightly too*, that the obligations imposed upon him in the lodges, chapters, &c. were at variance with the best interests of society ; and he boldly steps forward, and fearless of consequences, tells the world what are truly the Masonic principles. For this he must be deprived of every privilege of citizenship ; made an outcast from society; and his business destroyed; while many a dishonest man, guilty o. crimes which, if strictly punished, would gain him a residence at state prison, is applauded and held out to the world as deserving their patronage; and too often do they receive the patronage and good wishes of community, through the influence of this dark, mysterious, midnight, and hellish banditti. 'O shame, where is thy blush.'

But still farther—' *By transferring his character* [that is, the character which they give him] *after him wherever he may go.*' The unhappy sufferer, satisfied that *Masonic vengeance* will destroy every hope of gaining a subsistence for himself and those dependent upon him, unless he becomes dishonest, seeks some distant part of the community, and there hopes to avoid the fiend-like malice of the *brotherhood*, and pursue his avocation in peace; but alas! even this consolation is not left him. They swear 'to transfer his character after him wherever he may go.' Not satisfied with traducing his character, destroying his business, and opposing his interest in the immediate vicinity where he has ever supported the character of an honest and respectable citizen; but he must be utterly destroyed. With malice well becoming the infernal spirits, they pursue their Masonic victim to the 'uttermost parts of the earth,' and destroy every vestige of hope. To carry this into full and complete effect, the council which receive him require him to give his name, the names of his parents, the place where he was born, where he was educated—in fact, a description of every circumstance of his life by which he may be traced through the world, is registered in their bloody annals. No hope is left the unhappy fugitive, even in flight! He must be pursued and ruined in reputation, and become a vagabond and an outcast of society, and a mark put upon him as indelible as that put upon Cain by the hand of Omnipotence, through the influence of an *ancient and honorable society*. Finally, ' *By exposing him to the contempt of the whole fraternity and the world, but of our Illustrious* [illustrious indeed!] *Order, more especially, during his whole natural life.*' If he has committed an error and becomes convinced of it, (no matter if he repent of his frailties in sincerity,) no pardon can be granted him; he must be held out to the scorn and contempt of the ' whole world, during the whole of his natural life.' No consolation or inducement of reform can be found, no mitigation of *Masonic vengeance* can be realized, neither in flight or repentance. Conduct worthy, indeed, of a society styling themselves 'ancient, honorable, and the handmaid of religion.'   A MASON.

NOTE. The foregoing eight numbers of 'A MASON' were originally published in 1828, in the *Le Roy Gazette*, Genesee county, N. Y.

CONVENTION OF SECEDING MASONS,

Held at LE ROY, *February 19th and 20th, and July 4th and 5th,* 1828.

AT a convention of Free Masons opposed to secret societies, held at Le Roy, in the county of Genesee, New-York, on Tuesday, February 19th, 1828—

The convention organized at one o'clock, P. M. and Elder David Bernard, of Warsaw, addressed the Throne of Grace. Leonard B. Rose, Esq. of Castile, was called to the chair, and Elder David Bernard appointed secretary. Voted, That the Rev. James Cochrane, of Batavia, be requested to deliver an address to the convention upon the subject of its present meeting.*

---

* Nearly one year and a half had elapsed, after the abduction and murder of William Morgan, before this convention was called; during which period but few had the moral courage to openly dissent from the Masonic institution, and denounce

Mr. Cochrane then rose and delivered an address.

The object of the meeting having been stated, it was agreed that the principles and obligations of Free Masonry be freely discussed :—Therefore,

Voted, That the first obligation in Masonry be read. Mr. H. A. Read read the obligations of an 'Entered Apprentice,' as published by Capt. William Morgan. The chairman addressed the meeting on the binding nature of Masonic obligations. Mr. S. D. Green of Batavia, followed him on the same subject. Mr. H. A. Read, of Le Roy, spoke largely on the principles and obligations of the order ; he was followed by J. Hascall, Esquire, on the same subject. The secretary then addressed the convention on the *antiquity* of the institution, showing that it was not *ancient;* on the *morality* of the institution, showing that it did not promote morality ; on the benevolence of the institution, showing that it was not *benevolent;* on the *ceremonies* of the institution, as far as the Royal Arch degree, showing that they were not only degrading to human nature but blasphemous; on the principles of the institution, showing that they were opposed to *Christianity;* and gave his reasons for believing it the duty of honest Masons to expose the secrets and obligations to the world.

Voted, That the second and third obligations in Masonry be read. They were according read, as published by Morgan.

Voted, That the fourth, fifth, sixth, and seventh obligations be read, as submitted to the convention, in manuscript. They were accordingly read by Mr. Read.

Mr. Read then spoke very extensively upon the obligations of Masonry—showing that they were diametrically opposed to good government, and subversive of the principles of justice and good order.

The convention then adjourned until seven o'clock, P. M.

During the adjournment, Solomon Southwick, Esq, of Albany, who had been invited to attend the convention, arrived to take his seat as a member.

A large and respectable concourse of citizens having convened, and being anxious to see the man whom they considered the champion of their liberties, were admitted into the convention chamber, when Mr. Southwick was introduced by Elder Bernard. He briefly addressed them upon the subject of self-created societies in any government, particularly a republican government ; reminded them with what jealousy the people of these United States had watched the introduction of societies and combinations anti-republican in their tendencies ; and instanced the decline of the Cincinnatti society, composed of many of the veterans of the revolution ; and the opposition to that article of our federal constitution which authorizes secret sessions of Congress, although they had not until lately become suspicious that the Masonic institution had been all this while growing up amidst them, with their indulgence, to subvert their liberties. He remarked that he had not the least anticipation of being called upon to address his fellow citizens ; that he was wholly unprepared, and completely exhausted with his journey.

---

it as wicked and dangerous. Those who dared to stand in defence of their country's rights, at the hazard of Masonic vengeance, stepped forth and united with their fellow citizens in their noble attempts to kill the BEAST ! But the 'MONSTER,' by his cunning devices, foiled every attempt to take his life. At length a few became convinced that it was their duty, at the hazard of every thing dear on earth, to publish *all* the secrets of the order to the world ;—that this was the *only* way in which this institution of darkness could be destroyed, and our country saved from ruin ! Though they were few in number—though they had a secret, midnight, and powerful foe to encounter ; yet, with 'TRUTH and JUSTICE' inscribed on their shield, and the God of battles to lead them on, they moved forward undaunted to the mighty conflict—they bravely fought—they nobly conquered ! !

The citizens then departed, and the convention then re-organized. The following resolution was then passed *unanimously.*

Resolved, That the book written by Capt. William Morgan and published by Col. David C. Miller, entitled 'Illustrations of Masonry,' is a fair and full exhibition of the three first degrees of speculative Free Masonry; that we solemnly and unequivocally testify to the above, we cheerfully subscribe our names thereto. We certify according to the degrees we have taken.

Entered Apprentices—Platt S. Beech, Henry Peck, David C. Miller.

Fellow Craft—George W. Blodgett.

Master Masons—Leonard B. Rose, George W. Harris, James Cochrane, Jonathan Foster, Edmund Badger, Orasmus Bowers, Jason Gratton, James Gray, Benjamin Cooley, Enos Bachelder, A. E. Hutchins, John Tomlinson, Samuel D. Green, Pelatiah Dewy, Adam Richmond, David Webb, John Ammock, James Taylor, William W. Phelps, B. Bliss.

Mark Master—Solomon Southwick.

Royal Arch Masons—Miles P. Lampson, David Bernard.

Knight of the Red Cross—Richard Hollister.

Knights Templars and Illustrious Knights of the Cross—Anthony Cooley, Cephas A. Smith, Augustus P. Hascall, Hollis Pratt, Herbert A. Read, James Ballard, John Hascall.

The obligations of Mark Master, Past Master, Most Excellent Master, and the Royal Arch degrees, were again read. [See the obligations in the degrees conferred in the chapter.]

The political, moral, and religious nature and tendency of the foregoing obligations, were again freely discussed; whereupon it was resolved by all the Royal Arch Masons, that the foregoing obligations are, according to our best recollections, substantially true—and by the convention unanimously, that they are neither legally, morally, or religiously binding; and that they be published to the world.

The obligation of the Knights of the Red Cross, Knights Templar, the sealed obligation and obligations of the Thrice Illustrious Order of the Cross, were then read. [See the obligations in the degrees conferred in the Encampment.]

After another short discussion, the knights present then unanimously resolved, That the foregoing obligations are substantially correct—and by this convention unanimously, that they are neither legally, morally, or religiously binding; and that they be published to the world.

The convention then adjourned to nine o'clock of the next day.

LEONARD B. ROSE, *Chairman.*

DAVID BERNARD, *Secretary.*

Wednesday, Feb. 20, 1828.

The convention met pursuant to adjournment.

In the absence of Messrs. Rose and Bernard, Solomon Southwick, Esq. of Albany, was unanimously chosen chairman. Mr. Richard Hollister was then unanimously appointed secretary.

The chairman addressed the meeting briefly to the following effect:

Gentlemen—I have a proposition to make, which is demanded by what we owe to the character of our country, and the cause in which we are engaged. If it be true, as has been stated, that William Morgan was incarcerated in the magazine of the fortress of Niagara, it was a prostitution of that bulwark of our freedom and independence unparalleled in the history of our country, or in that of any other country pretending to the possession of civil liberty. If done, it must have been done by or through the tacit permission or direct agency of the person or persons having charge of that fortress, as servants of the people of these U. States; and hence both the government and people owe it to their own dignity of character and the cause of civil liberty, to discharge the guilty from their service, if true; or to wipe off, both from the accused and themselves, the foul stain, if the report be false. For myself I know nothing of the facts; but I have seen them stated under sanction of such names as command my full confidence. I allude, gentlemen, to what is called the Lewiston Convention; authors of which, though greatly abused, I believe to have been actuated by the purest of motives, and to deserve the gratitude of their country. They have made the report on testimony satisfactory to themselves; and it is now due to the character of our country and its government, that the charge be investigated by those whose (if not exclusive) province it was in the first place.

The chairman then moved the following resolutions, which were unanimously adopted:

Resolved, That a committee be appointed to draft a memorial to Congress, on the subject of the prostitution of the fortress of Niagara to the incarceration of William Morgan, a free citizen of the United States, by persons calling themselves Free Masons, and without any legal authority for such a violence and coercion.

Resolved, That Solomon Southwick, James Ballard, John Hascall, Herbert A. Read, Anthony Cooley, W. W. Phelps, and Edward Badger, compose said committee; and that they sign the memorial in behalf of this convention. On motion,

Resolved, That a committee of fifteen be appointed to prepare the degrees of Free Masonry above that of Master, for publication; and Elder David Bernard, Elder John G. Stearns, Solomon Southwick, Rev. Reuben Sanborn, David C. Miller, John Hascall, Herbert A. Read, Richard Hollister, Samuel D. Green, Oliver Forward, Edward Giddins, Judge Hinman, (of Pike, Allegany county,) William Perry, and W. W. Phelps, (of the state of Vermont,) compose the said committee. On motion,

Resolved, That a committee of seven be appointed to draft a circular invitation to all Free Masons who are opposed to the institution of Masonry, and to secret associations in general in the United States, to meet at this place on the 4th of July next; that they prepare an address to be delivered on the occasion; and that Solomon Southwick, John Hascall, John Tomlinson, Herbert A. Read, David C. Miller, W. W. Phelps, and A. P. Hascall, compose said committee.

Resolved, That the editors of the following papers be, and they are hereby requested to publish the proceedings of this convention, to wit—Republican Advocate, Western Advertiser, Buffalo Patriot, Jamestown Journal, Western Star, Le Roy Gazette, Livingston Register, Anti-Masonic Inquirer, Seneca Farmer, Lake Light, Cazenovia Monitor, National Observer, Sandy Hill Sun, Palladium of Liberty, New Jersey Union Telegraph, Indiana and Jefferson Whig, National Intelligencer, and Georgetown Columbian, and all others who are willing to give the public information upon this subject.

S. SOUTHWICK, *Chairman*

RICHARD HOLLISTER, *Secretary.*

ANTI-MASONIC CONVENTION

Of the twelve western counties of N. Y., held at LE ROY, *March 6th and 7th,* 1828.

AT a convention of delegates from twelve counties, at the village of Le Roy, on the 6th of March, General WILLIAM WADSWORTH, of the county of Livingston, was appointed president, and Doct. MATTHEW BROWN, jun. of the county of Monroe, and the Hon. ROBERT FLEMING, of the county of Niagara, appointed secretaries.

M m

The president took the chair, and the following delegates presented credentials and took their seats.

From the county of Chautauque.—Joseph White, jun., Abner Hazeltine.

Erie.—Thomas C. Love, H. Rutgers Stagg, Willard Filmore, Henry E. Davies, Calvin Bishop, Benjamin O. Bivens, Aaron Parker.

Niagara.—George H. Boughton, Bates Cooke, Robert Fleming, Asher Saxton, Asher Freeman.

Genesee.—Samuel Warner, Amos Tyrell, Calvin P. Bayley, Timothy Fitch, Andrew Dibble, David C. Miller, Edmund Barnes, Luther A. Baker, John Haskall, Shubael Dunham, Daniel Woodward, Chauncey P. Smith, Martin C. Coe, George W. Lay, Moses Taggart, Harvey Putnam, James Lathrop, Leverett Seward, Amos W. Muzzy.

Orleans.—Benjamin W. Van Dyke, Chauncey Robinson.

Monroe.—Matthew Brown, jun., William Groves, John G. Crandall, Zolved Stephens, William B. Brown, Simeon M. Coe, Joseph Randall, William Garbutt, Joshua Howell, Thomas Bingham, Milton Sheldon, Frederick Whittlesey, James K. Livingston, Thurlow Weed.

Livingston.—William Wadsworth, Andrew Arnold, Halloway Long, Tabor Ward, S. M. Smith, Levi Sadler.

Wayne.—Israel J. Richardson, Robert Luze, Henry S. Gilbert, William P. Richardson, Loammi Beadle, Charles S. Williams.

Ontario.—James Watson, J. Mason, Elisha Peck, Isaac Lapham, Oliver Heartwell, John Crandal.

Yates.—Alexander Parkman.

Seneca.—William Child, Aaron Davis, William Thompson, Charles Starret, Allyn Boardman, Elnathan Winans, Jacob B. Farr, John Goltry.

Tompkins.—H. Jerome, Jonathan Owen.

The objects of the meeting being explained by T. Fitch, Esq., it was, on motion of Mr. Love, of Buffalo, resolved, That a committee of one from each county represented, be appointed to digest and report to the convention proper questions for its deliberations; and the following persons were appointed said committee:—Messrs. Hazeltine, Love, Cooke, Fitch, Van Dyke, Whittlesey, Ward, W. P. Richardson, Heartwell, Parkman, Child, and Jerome.

The committee appointed to report the subjects that ought to claim the consideration of this convention, report:

That it is expedient to present an address from this convention to the people of the state of New-York, expressive of the views of this convention upon the subject of Free Masonry; and that a committee of five be appointed to draft the same.

That it is expedient that resolutions be adopted by this convention, expressive of their views; and that a committee of five be appointed to draft the same.

That it is expedient to present a memorial to Congress upon the subject of the incarceration of a citizen in a fortress of the United States, praying for an inquiry into the same.

That it is expedient to appoint a General Central Committee.

That it is expedient to raise means for the publication and dissemination of light and truth, relating to the character and principles of Free Masonry.

That it is expedient that this convention recommend a State Convention to be held at a suitable time and place, for the purpose of adopting more general and efficient means for the destruction of the Masonic institution.

The report of the committee was accepted, and the following gentlemen appointed to carry its recommendations into effect.

Committee to draft an address to the people of this state.—Bates Cooke, Thurlow Weed, William Thompson, Timothy Fitch, Horace Jerome.

To draft resolutions.—Frederick Whittlesey, George W. Lay, A. Hazeltine, I. J. Richardson, Jonathan Mason.

To draft a memorial to the legislature.—Thomas C. Love, B. W. Van Dyke, John Haskall, Oliver Heartwell.

To draft a memorial to Congress.—James K. Livingston, William Groves, Joseph White, jun., Edmund Barnes.

Mr. Whittlesey, from the committee to draft resolutions, reported the following, which were unanimously adopted:

Resolved, That it is a peculiar feature of our free government, that all measures should be open and amenable to public opinion ; and that the existence of any society in this country, whose objects, principles, and measures are secret and concealed, is not merely useless but hostile to the spirit of our free institutions.

Resolved, That the bare existence of secret societies in these United States, justify fears, jealousies, and suspicions as to their objects, in the breasts of the uninitiated, which have a tendency to distract society and sow ill will and dissentions in community.

Resolved, That the disclosures which have been made of the principles and obligations of speculative Free Masonry, prove it to be an institution of dangerous tendency—liable to be used by the ambitious and designing as an engine for exalting unworthy men, and effecting improper measures—placing the citizen in a situation in which his duty to his country must in many instances conflict with his obligations to the fraternity—and weakening the sanctions of morality and religion by the multiplication of profane oaths, and an irreverent familiarity with religious forms and sacred things.

Resolved, That we discover in the ceremonies and obligations of the higher degrees of Masonry, principles which deluged France in blood, and which tend directly to the subversion of all religion and government.

Resolved, That the obligation in one of the degrees of Free Masonry to protect a brother, 'right or wrong,' and to preserve his secrets inviolate, even in cases of murder and treason, has a tendency to unnerve the arm of justice, and to afford protection to the vicious and profligate from the punishment due to their crimes.

Resolved, That the tendency of such obligations is to weaken the sanction of virtue in the minds of the recipients, by making bad men bold and unblushing to trust the history of their crimes to the ears of a brother, and thus making them familiar with iniquity, to the destruction of all correct moral principles.

Resolved, That we view the impious personification of the Deity, and the irreverent introduction of the name of our blessed Saviour, and the Holy Trinity, in Masonic meetings and ceremonies, with mingled pain and abhorrence ; and that we regard the unhallowed substitution of the profane orgies of Free Masonry for the Christian religion, as fraught with more danger to the peace of society and the truths of revelation, than open Deism or avowed infidelity.

Resolved, That the outrages upon the liberty of one citizen, and upon the liberty and life of another, committed by Masons in these western counties, afford horrible proof of the sanguinary nature of Masonic oaths.

Resolved, That the wide spread conspiracies of numerous Masons to plot these outrages—their attempts to stifle investigation after they had been committed—and to screen the actual offenders from the justice due their crimes—sufficiently identifies the institution with these enormities, and justifies us in holding it and its supporters responsible for the same.

Resolved, That an institution whose rites are impious—whose obligations are blasphemous—and, if observed in the spirit of their horrid import, must necessarily lead to perjury and murder—an institution in one instance at least stained with the blood of one of its members, by a crime which has in an unequivocal manner received the sanction of the order, is unworthy to exist in a free government ; and that we pledge ourselves to each other and to the world, that we will use all lawful and constitutional means to banish entirely from our country that bloody relic of barbarism.

Resolved, That those Masons who have disclosed the horrid obligations which bind the fraternity together, deserve the warmest gratitude of their fellow citizens ; and that we will do every thing in our power to sustain them against those persecutions which the nature of those obligations and the vindictive character of the institution teach us to fear will be their lot.

Resolved, That this convention are satisfied, from the evidence adduced before them, of the substantial truths of the Masonic obligations recently published—and that the same be published to the world in connection with the proceedings of this convention.

Resolved, That we regard the public press as the sentinel of freedom, and cannot but lament its entire subjugation throughout the Union to the control of Free Masonry.

Resolved, That we earnestly recommend to the citizens of the several counties of this state to procure the establishment of free presses, whose editors will fearlessly vindicate the rights of its citizens and laws of the land.

Resolved, That a state Convention, to be composed of delegates from the several counties of the state of New-York, equal to double the number of their representatives in the Assembly, be called to meet at the village of Utica, on the fourth day of August next, to take measures for the destruction of the Masonic institution ; for sustaining the liberty of the press, and asserting the supremacy of the laws ; for protecting the rights and privileges of the citizens against the vindictive persecutions of members of the Masonic society ; and to take into consideration such other business as the said convention shall deem expedient in furtherance of such objects—and that it be and is hereby recommended to the different counties in this state to send delegates to the same.

Resolved, That a General Central Committee, consisting of five members, be appointed by this convention ; and that it be and is hereby recommended to the different counties to appoint Committees of Correspondence, and report their names to the General Central Committee at Rochester.

Resolved, That the several towns in the county that have not already done so, be requested to appoint town Committees of Correspondence, and forward their names to the Central Corresponding Committee.

Resolved, That it be and is hereby recommended to the several counties to raise funds for defraying the expenses of publishing the proceedings of this convention, and such other publications as the General Central Committee may think proper to make ; and to defray the expenses heretofore incurred by the different committees in the investigation of the late outrages ; and that such funds be transmitted to the General Central Committee.

Resolved, That the proceedings of this convention be signed by the chairman and secretaries—and that five thousand copies be published in a pamphlet form for distribution, under the direction of a General Central Commitee.

Resolved, That SAMUEL WORKS, HARVEY ELY, FREDERICK F. BACKUS, FREDERICK WHITTLESEY, and THURLOW WEED, of the village of Rochester, be appointed a General Central Committee of Correspondence and Publication.

Mr. Davies, from the committee to whom was referred the subject of the charges made by Masons against the Morgan committee, made the following report, which was read and adopted unanimously:

Whereas reports of the most malignant and scandalous nature have been circulated by the Masonic fraternity, in relation to the members of the several committees commonly denominated the Lewiston Committee, charging them with having misrepresented facts in their possession, and with having from sinister views created an unjust excitement :

And whereas this convention have had adduced to them the most satisfactory and conclusive evidence that the said committee have fairly and impartially conducted all their inquiries—therefore,

Resolved, That the said Lewiston Committee are entitled to the thanks of this convention for their patriotic and praiseworthy exertions in exposing to the world the extensive Masonic conspiracy formed in this country, which seemed to threaten the civil liberty of this nation; and that they merit, and we trust will receive, the countenance and gratitude of every well wisher to the perpetuity of our free institutions.

Resolved, That all the newspapers in the Union friendly to the cause of civil liberty, be requested to publish these proceedings.

Mr. Love, from the committee to draft a memorial to the legislature on the subject of unlawful oaths, made a report, which was read and adopted by the convention.

Mr. Livingston, from the committee appointed to draft a memorial to Congress, reported the same, which was read and adopted.

Bates Cooke, Esq., from the committee appointed for that purpose, reported an address to the people of the state, which was read and adopted.

ADDRESS

TO THE PEOPLE OF THE STATE OF NEW YORK.

Fellow citizens—The institution of speculative Free Masonry has existed in these United States, ever since the formation of our government. Assuming to be the patron of science, the protector of morality, and the handmaid of religion, it has been suffered to exist without question or suspicion. Its votaries have ever been enthusiastic and extravagant in praise of its character, principles, and tendency. It is, in their own language, a system not only beautiful, but *divine*—whose principles are the purest morality; whose objects are to inculcate universal benevolence and good will among the brethren; and whose operations have been an extended system of holy and healing charity. It is calculated, they say, to enlighten the ignorant—to reform the bad—to protect the weak—and to relieve the necessitous. We have seen many good men, venerable sages, worthy patriots, and pious divines, belonging to this institution; and have suffered ourselves to be lulled into security by the impression that such men could not lend their countenance to an association whose principles were dangerous to society, government, or religion. Their principles have thus been taken upon trust, and the institution has been suffered to exist in a community prone to suspect that where all is not open all is not honest. It is, perhaps, a singular fact, that in a free government like ours, a government of opinion, operating upon a people jealous of their rights and peculiarly suspicious and jealous of any secret influence, and of any thing that could bear the semblance of an insidious encroachment upon their liberties,—such an institution should have been permitted to grow and increase in strength, without subjecting itself to those investigations which the nature and spirit of our government are so well calculated to encourage. Other secret societies have, after a brief existence, been frowned into oblivion, as dangerous to a free government. It is owing, doubtless, to the circumstances above set forth, and to the fact that many whom we esteem as our fathers, brothers, and connexions, are members of this institution, that speculative Free Masonry has not shared the fate of other secret societies. Some weight too may be attached to the fact that most men of influence and political eminence—those who are wont to take the lead in affairs that concern the government—have themselves been high officials in the institution, and of course interested in its support. But whatever the cause may have been, it is certain that Free Masonry has been suffered to exist and to extend itself in this free government, and that without question or inquiry. Addressing itself to the cupidity, the ambition, the vanity, or the curiosity of individuals, it has gone on increasing like the fame of the classic poet, until it has become wide spread in its influence, extended in its operations; and in its multiplied mystic ramifications, it has become interwoven with the very frame and fabric of society, and secretly connected with all our institutions. A cool observer cannot but look back with astonishment and see how secretly and covertly, and at the same time how *rapidly*, it has spread itself through this Union—how speciously it has insinuated and connected itself with almost every interest, either of a private or public nature. In the foundation of every public building we have beheld the interference of these mystic artisans with their symbolic insignia; in every public procession we have seen their flaunting banners, their muslin robes, and mimic crowns. In the executive of the state we have beheld a man holding the highest office in the order bound to his brethren by secret ties, of whose nature, strength, and character, we knew nothing. We have seen our legislature controlled by majorities bound to the fraternity by the same ties. The ermine of justice we have seen worn by men whose brows were decorated with the gilded mitre of the order in their midnight and secret meetings. We have seen others of this mystic tie empanneled as jurors to hold the balance of justice between a brother and a stranger to the order, and that brother capable of communicating with such, his judges, by a mystic and symbolic language unintelligible to his adversary. We cannot now but be astonished that so much should have passed, and that no danger should have been apprehended. Perhaps it may have occasionally occurred to some minds more than ordinarily watchful, that some designing men may have made use of the order as a ladder to their ambition; that more than an ordinary share of official patronage was distributed among the brethren; that the even balance of justice may, in some instances, have been made to incline its scale in favor of a brother; that her descending sword may have been averted from the head of a guilty member by the broad shield of the order. But these suspicions, if any such have been entertained, were partial, and the institution has felt itself so strong, that it has been supposed that it might safely set at defiance every effort to pull it down.

The year 1826, however, introduced a new era in the history of Masonry and of our country. From that year to the present time, enough has transpired to show in a broad and fearful light the danger of secret institutions. That citizen who will close his eyes to this light, is criminally negligent to his own rights and the safety of this government. The order has been bold enough to assume to itself powers which belong only to the government of the land; and in the exercise of these assumed powers has violated the liberty of one citizen, and taken the life of another, for an alleged breach of obligations which our laws do not recognize.

In September, 1826, Capt. William Morgan, a citizen of this state, was seized under feigned process of the law, in the day time, in the village of Batavia, and forcibly carried to Canandaigua in another county. Capt. Morgan was engaged in the publication of a book which purported to reveal the secrets of Free Masonry. This contemplated publication excited the alarm of the fraternity, and numbers of its members were heard to say that it should be suppressed at all events. It is known that meetings of delegates from the different lodges in the western counties were held to devise means for most effectually preventing the publication. It is known that the matter was a subject of anxious discussion in many and distant lodges. It is known that the zealous members of the fraternity were angry, excited, and alarmed, and occasionally individuals threw out dark and desperate threats. It is known that an incendiary attempt was made to fire the office of Col. Miller, the publisher of the book. That this attempt was plotted by Masons, and attempted to be carried into execution by Masons. The gang who seized Morgan at Batavia were Masons. They took him to Canandaigua ; after a mock trial he was discharged, but was immediately arrested and committed to prison on a stale or fictitious demand. The next night, in the absence of the jailer, he was released from prison by the pretended friendship of a false and hollow hearted brother Mason. Upon leaving the prison door he was again seized in the streets of Canandaigua, and notwithstanding his cries of murder, he was thrust with ruffian violence into a carriage prepared for that purpose. At Batavia he had been torn from his home—from his amiable wife and infant children. At Canandaigua he had been falsely beguiled from the safe custody of the law, and was forcibly carried, by relays of horses, through a thickly populated country, in the space of little more than twenty-four hours, to the distance of one hundred and fifteen miles, and secured as a prisoner in the magazine of Fort Niagara. This outrage necessarily required many agents—and to the shame of our country enough Masons were found, and of these, too, many who were bound by their official oaths to protect the liberty of the citizen and prevent the violation of the laws—who readily lent their personal assistance, and the aid of their carriages and horses, in the transportation of this hapless man to the place of his confinement and subsequent death.

This was not their only outrage. About the same time Col. David C. Miller was also seized in Batavia, under like color of legal process, and taken to Le Roy. He was also seized by Masons, and accompanied to Le Roy by a ferocious band of Masons armed with clubs. He was discharged from the process under which he was arrested, and with lawless violence they attempted to seize him again ; but to the praise of the citizens of Le Roy, and to some who were members of the Masonic fraternity too, be it spoken, he was rescued, and suffered to return to Batavia. The avowed intention of Col. Miller's seizure was to take him where Morgan was—and where that was may be best gathered from the impious declaration of one of the conspirators, James Ganson, for several years a member of our legislature—that ' *he was put where he would stay put until God should call for him.*'

These acts of outrage and violence at length became the subject of inquiry, and excited the honest indignation of a community always alive to the rights of the citizen and the violation of the laws. Committees of investigation were appointed in the different counties which were the scenes of this violence, with instructions to do every thing in their power to ferret out this crime and trace it to the perpetrators. It was, however, perpetrated under the cover of so much secrecy, that it was long before even the course which had been taken with Morgan could be traced. Certainly the committees did not commence their investigations under the impressions that they should find the fraternity implicated in the transaction. They were slow to believe, as the public have generally and very properly been slow to believe, that a society which embraces among its members so many worthy and pious men, could have ever connived at so foul a crime. It was considered as a blot upon the escutcheon of Masonry ; and Masons were publicly called upon to assist in the investigation of this transaction, for the honor of the order, and to wipe out the stain. The committees soon discovered, with no little surprise, that they could expect no assistance from members of the fraternity. On the contrary, every obstacle and impediment was thrown in the way. They found the fraternity in a hostile attitude. They found that they were made the objects of ridicule, threats and detraction—that their motives were impugned, and their characters vilified. Defeat, disgrace, and ruin, were confidently predicted to them ; and certainly no means were spared to give to these predictions the character of prophecy. These acts of violence were made a jest of—the excited feeling of the public was ridiculed—their honest indignation was defied. The courts have been appealed to for justice ; but in very few instances has justice been visited upon the heads of the offenders. The Masonic oath was soon found to be a shackle upon the officers and ministers of the law—the lips of witnesses were sealed by a mysterious and invisible influence, or opened only in the utterance of falsehoods. Jurors were influenced in their verdicts by an obligation more powerful than their oaths as jurors. Many of the chief offenders fled the country; and the crime yet remains in a great measure unpunished, and the violated laws unavenged. When it was found that the laws were too weak to vindicate their offended majesty, the committees appealed to the legislature of this state to institute an inquiry into these outrages. Here, too, it was found that the obligations which bound members to the fraternity were stronger than their oaths to support the constitution and the laws—and here too they were baffled and left to seek such redress as a few men could obtain against the united influence, wealth, and the determined and persevering hostility of a powerful combination.

When it came to be ascertained that great numbers of the fraternity had been long engaged in devising means for suppressing Morgan's book—when it became known that the subject was a matter of discussion in many different and distant lodges—when it was also known that many individuals, all members of the fraternity, and some high in civil office, were implicated as accomplices in the actual outrages—when the course pursued by members of the fraternity generally, in relation to the investigation, was marked—all cool thinking people began to look further for the origin of the crime, and felt fully justified in identifying the Masonic institution with these outrages, and holding that responsible for it.

The matter began to assume a new complexion: the dangers of secret societies began to flash across the minds of the reflecting: here was a bloody text which afforded matter for fearful comment. The conviction became general that the safety of government and religion, the rights of the citizen, and the impartial administration of justice, required that this institution should be banished from our soil. The freedom and boldness with which the principles and tendency of the Masonic institution began now to be discussed, encouraged many honest and conscientious members of the fraternity, who had heretofore been shackled by fear, to renounce their connexion with the society, and to disclose the nature of these secret obligations which bound them together. Taking upon themselves those horrid obligations as they do, ignorant of their nature and import, there rests no obligation upon them, either legal, moral, or honorable, to consider them of any binding force. On the contrary, the duty which they owe to society and their country, as citizens—the duty which they owe to God and his church—loudly call upon them to divulge the principles of an institution so hostile to government and religion. This class of men are entitled to the gratitude of the public for their disclosures, and have deserved and should receive the countenance and support of every patriotic citizen, to sustain them against every attempt to injure them, or defame their characters. These obligations have been published to the world, and furnished farther and weighty evidence of the dangers of the Masonic institution: with the substantial truth of these obligations—and that they are such as are actually taken, we have every reason to be satisfied; and it encourages us in the pledge which we have mutually given to each other and to the world —that we will use our best endeavors to banish this relic of barbarism from our land. It is upon the subject of the dangers of the Masonic institution, fellow citizens, that we desire to address you; and we are anxious that you should give the subject that consideration which its importance demands. This is not an ordinary topic. It is not a question whether this or that man shall be president or governor—it is not a question whether this or that line of measures shall be pursued—but it is a question of immeasurably greater importance—a question whether the rights of the citizen shall be held sacred —whether the laws shall be impartially administered—whether religion shall be duly reverenced.

It may be safely said that secret societies, in their best shape, are useless in a free government; calculated to excite jealousies and suspicions in the breasts of the uninitiated, which may lay the foundation of dissentions and ill will. If their objects are honest and praiseworthy, there is no need of secrecy: honesty needs no cloak, and deeds of charity seek not the cover of darkness. Secrecy and concealment ever afford grounds of suspicion. If, however, Masonry is only what it has ever been professed to be, perhaps it might be safely left to the amusement of full grown children; perhaps they might be safely left to the enjoyment of their mock dignities—their muslin robes—their pasteboard crowns—and their gilded mitres. But when the obligations which bind them '*to vote for a brother before any other person of equal qualifications*'—to always support his '*military fame and political preferment in opposition to another*'—to aid and assist a brother in difficulty, so far as to extricate from the same, '*whether he be right or wrong*'—to keep his secrets in all cases inviolably, '*murder and treason not excepted,*' and these under no less penalties than a torturing and ignominious death—then it becomes a question of serious import, whether such an institution can be tolerated in our free government. By the force of these obligations a member can claim the vote of a brother for any elective office, in derogation of that equality guaranteed to us by our constitution; and the brethren thus elected, gradually obtaining the control of the executive, legislative, and judicial departments of the government, can, and must, dispense their patronage in strict consonance with the obligations of this mysterious fraternal tie: so that soon the government, in all its branches, must be controlled by the members of the order. What guarantee is there for the impartial discharge of official duties, when the officer is shackled by such obligations? What hold have we upon the conscience, the integrity or justice of such a man? Is it his oath to support the constitution of this state and the United States? Is it his oath to faithfully discharge the duties of the office which he fills? He has taken a previous oath of more horrid import, and of paramount obligation, to which all other oaths, all other ties, all other duties, must yield. He is not a free man. He stands shackled and bound by invisible and mysterious chains. He cannot do his duty to his country if he would—he has a duty to perform to the fraternity, under the severest penalties of Masonic vengeance. What guarantee have we for the impartial administration of justice? A felon communicates the mystic sign to a brother on the grand inquest—the juror's oath to screen no man from fear, favor, or affection, must yield to the obligation to extricate a brother, '*whether he be right or wrong.*' If he escapes not here, there is the same facility of communication with the jurors who are to try him—and strange would it be if some of the brethren who have found means to insinuate themselves into every station, should not be found upon the panel —and in a panel where one stout and persevering negative prevents his conviction—or the judge who tries him may receive the '*grand hailing sign,*' and the purity of the ermine may be sullied by the contamination of Masonic iniquity. If all this is not sufficient, the mystic signal may avail with the executive, and the avenging sword of the law may be turned aside from the execution of justice. Where is the security for justice between man and man? Can a Masonic judge or Masonic jurors hold the scales even between adverse parties, when one can appeal for assistance through the medium of mysterious signals? This is not all. Witnesses who solemnly appeal to God to tell the truth, the whole truth, and nothing but the truth, in what they shall be called upon to relate, may be bound under obligations more awful, and under penalties more severe, not to disclose the secrets of a brother. No! though it extend to the *murder* of a fellow being, or to *treason* to the state. Is there then, fellow citizens, any safety in trusting those persons who have taken such obligations and believe in their binding sanction, with any office in our government? Is there any safety in committing our lives, our liberty, our property, or our reputation to them, as judges or jurors? Is any confidence to be placed in witnesses who have bound themselves under such awful obligations to keep the secrets of a brother? These obligations strike at the very existence of our government—at the very foundation of our rights—and at the impartial administration of our laws.

This institution threatens not only danger to government and the cause of justice, but strikes at the basis of all morality and religion. The obligation not to disclose the secrets of a brother, even in cases of murder and treason, has a tendency to invite the confidence of a brother Mason. Under the sanction of this oath, a bold bad man will not fear to disclose the history of his crimes to the ears of the virtuous, to the ears of even a minister of the holy gospel, and, secure against detection, make an imprudent boast of his iniquities. This will make virtuous men familiar with the detail of crimes, and confidants in criminal secrets—and vice is of a character so contagious, that one cannot even listen to its history, or be familiar with its secrets, without some danger of contamination—and that nice, delicate, moral sense, which characterizes a virtuous man, must be gradually effaced, and his principles of virtue must be in a great measure rendered unsettled. Is Free Masonry the handmaid of religion? That institution in whose rites and ceremonies the most touching portions of that Holy Book, which holds out to us the promise of eternal life, are introduced in solemn mockery, and represented in the shape of a miserable theatrical farce!—where a weak, sinful mortal undertakes to personify the Almighty God!—where the name of our blessed Saviour and the Holy Trinity are introduced in a vain and irreverent manner!—where the belief of the immortality of the soul is pledged in a libation from the skull of a Masonic traitor!—where the life eternal in the heavens is represented only as one great lodge, and the Almighty is blasphemously typified as Grand Master thereof! Is such an institution the handmaid of religion! We think we are safe in saying that the frequent use of profane oaths, the irreverent familiarity with religious forms and sacred things, the blasphemous mockery of the name of the Triune God, in the recesses of the lodge room, are more dangerous to the cause of the benign religion of Jesus than open and avowed infidelity. It is to be feared that many substitute and rely on the religion of Masonry instead of the religion of Him who died to atone for our sins; or if not, they come to the belief that all religion is only the farce which their impious ceremonies represent it to be. It is time these delusions were dispelled. Masonry now stands before us in its naked deformity, stripped of its tinsel ornaments and solemn mummery. It behoves us to take warning from the past, and receive instruction from the school of experience. We see in these disclosures the same principles which deluged France in blood, and were the cause of the dark crimes which stained that distracted country during the period of her sanguinary revolution. We see the same principles which governed Illuminism in the last century, and lighted her path in that foul plot which would have substituted anarchy for government and civil rule, and Atheism for the religion of the Cross. It is from the bosom of Free Masonry that this dark conspiracy originated. To the bosom of Free Masonry, every revolution and conspiracy which has agitated Europe for the last fifty years, may be distinctly traced, and the secret workings of this all pervading order can be clearly seen. The governments of the world are beginning to be awake to the danger. Russia has suppressed the order in her own dominions: Spain has suppressed it; and our sister republic of Mexico is exerting herself to crush one of its hydra heads. Shall we alone look tamely on and use no endeavors to check the spread of its contaminating principles? You ask how it is to be suppressed in this free government. They confidently boast that it is not in the power of man to suppress it—that even this *government itself,* with all its power, cannot do it. This may be true. But there is a power in this free land, superior even to our government, and which guides, controls, and directs it; and that power is *public opinion*. The laws we have found too weak. Government may be too weak; but there is a moral force in *public opinion* which must in this free country crush every thing, however powerful, which is arrayed against it. This opinion speaks in our public meetings—it speaks from the sacred desk—it speaks through the organ of the press—it speaks through the ballot boxes, when Masons appeal to you in this manner for support and countenance. This power, fellow citizens, you have under your control. It is the only legitimate and proper force that can be put in operation in this emergency and in this country. This is a power for you to wield—and in its exercise remember the warning voice of the father of his country: to '*beware of all secret societies.*'

As the convention was about to adjourn, Mr. Thompson offered the following resolution, which was unanimously adopted:

Resolved, That the thanks of this convention be presented to our highly respected fellow citizen, Gen. William Wadsworth, the president of this convention, for his patriotic and able discharge of the duties of the chair; and also to Doctor Brown and Col. Fleming, as secretaries on this interesting occasion.

WILLIAM WADSWORTH, *President.*

MATTHEW BROWN,
ROBERT FLEMING, } *Secretaries.*

PROCEEDINGS

Of the Legislature of the State of New-York, March 19th, 1828.

IN SENATE.—A message from his honor the Lieutenant Governor was received and read as follows:

To the Senate.

Gentlemen—Among the duties devolved by the constitution upon the person administering the government, that of 'taking care that the laws are faithfully executed,' is perhaps, the most important. A large portion of the inhabitants of the state has been for more than a year highly excited by the alleged forcible and clandestine removal of a citizen, and by the uncertainty of his fate. It is believed by many that he has been murdered, and it is certain that if alive, he is held in captivity. The outrage upon our laws has justly alarmed our fellow citizens in that part of the state, and has produced exertions such as might have been expected from freemen conscious of their rights, and determined to maintain them, to develope the mysterious transaction, and to bring the offenders to justice. As yet their efforts have failed. The rewards and inducements heretofore proffered for a discovery have been unavailing. The trials and convictions that have taken place, have rather increased the mystery of the transaction. The efforts of individual citizens, stimulated by a patriotic zeal, have not always been guided by discretion; and there is reason to fear that they have sometimes tended rather to prevent than to promote a judicial developement of the truth. It is publicly stated that a witness, while on his way to attend the trial of some of the persons charged with a participation in the original outrage, has suddenly and unaccountably disappeared, and advertisements offering rewards for his discovery have been extensively circulated. If there be any foundation for this suggestion, it affords a strong reason for the adoption of proper measures to quiet the alarms of our fellow citizens. Under these circumstances, it has appeared to me important that such constitutional measures as may be within the power of the legislature, should be adopted, in order to facilitate the discovery and punishment of the offenders. It is equally due to the violated majesty of the laws, to the apprehension of our fellow citizens, which never can or ought to be satisfied until justice is obtained, and to those who have been or may be included in the general and vague suspicions which are always produced by such transactions. It is an imperative duty to the innocent, that those really guilty should be detected and punished.

Without intending to encroach upon the particular duties of the legislature, I respectfully recommend, in accordance with these views, that a law be passed authorizing the appointment of a competent person for the special purpose of investigating the alledged criminal transactions in relation to the removal of William Morgan, and all the incidents connected therewith; that the power of district attornies be also vested in him; that it be made his duty to repair to the places where the offences were committed; to examine witnesses; to enter complaints; to cause witnesses and parties implicated to be bound over to appear; to conduct all criminal prosecutions which may be instituted; and to perform all other acts and duties which shall be necessary to a full and fair judicial investigation and determination of the alleged offences.

That our government is adequate to the punishment of crimes, and the protection of innocence, is the belief of all who are best acquainted with its principles. Hitherto, justice has been administered without any arbitrary stretch of power, or any violation of constitutional principles by the constitutional authorities, and without the interference of any private citizens not clothed with public authority. By exerting the power of the government in a constitutional manner, we can show that the present instance need not form an exception to the general course of justice. All experience teaches us, that designing men will be found ready always to avail themselves of a strong and honest public feeling to pervert it to their own selfish purposes. Any such attempts will be most effectually prevented by the interposition of the government; because it will then be perceived that all individual interference will be unnecessary—then the public mind will be preserved from unnecessary agitation and prejudice; fair and impartial trials will be secured to those who may be accused; and the course of justice will be uniform, steady, and effectual. Calm inquiry will succeed feverish conjecture; deliberate decision will take the place of impatient prejudice; and the impartial, unbiassed judgment of independent juries will vindicate the law, and establish the vigor and efficacy of our institutions.

Albany, March 18th, 1828. NATHANIEL PITCHER.

March 21.—Mr. Spencer, from the committee on the judiciary to whom was referred the message from the Lieutenant Governor recommending the adoption of legislative measures to ensure the detection and punishment of persons concerned in the forcible removal of William Morgan, reported:

That from the facts and circumstances stated in the message referred to the committee, and from general information, it appears that the transactions connected with the abduction of William Morgan, took place in the several different counties. The testimony in relation to it must therefore necessarily be scattered over those different counties, and over an extensive region of country. Under such circumstances it is obvious that the District Attorney of any one county, from the limited scope of his authority, would be incapable of connecting the various ramifications of the offence, and of collecting the scattered and disjointed testimony, so as to bring it to bear in any one case. The necessity of the employment of some competent person, whose authority would extend over all the counties which formed the scene of the alledged offences; whose whole time and attention would be devoted to the investigation; and who would concentrate the necessary information, seems manifest. The very circumstance, that hitherto no judicial developement of the facts has taken place, affords strong reasons to believe that it has arisen from the want of united and connected efforts. The committee concur with the Lieutenant

Governor in the opinion expressed by him, that it is due 'to the violated majesty of the laws, and to the apprehensions of our fellow citizens,' that all proper measures within the constitutional power of the legislature should be adopted to secure a full investigation of the high-handed offence committed on the person of William Morgan ; a fair and impartial trial of the persons implicated; the detection and punishment of the guilty ; and the acquittal and exoneration of the innocent—and they know of no means so effectual as those recommended by him. The employment of the Attorney General for this purpose would be wholly incompatible with the duties of that officer at the seat of government, and with that attention which is requisite to the civil business of the state. The committee have accordingly prepared a bill providing for the temporary employment of competent counsel; according to the recommendation of the Lieutenant Governor which is herewith reported.

AN ACT *to provide for the employment of counsel for the purposes therein mentioned.*

The people of the state of New-York represented in Senate and Assembly, do enact as follows :

SEC. 1. The person administering the government of this state is hereby authorized to employ and appoint a competent person of the degree of counsel in the Supreme Court, whose special duty it shall be,

1. To institute inquiries concerning the abduction of William Morgan, and his fate subsequently, and all the incidents connected therewith.

2. To ascertain the witnesses whose testimony can establish the commission of any crime against the laws of this state, in and of the said transactions.

3. To cause such witnesses to be examined before the proper magistrates, and to be bound over to appear before the proper courts, in order to testify.

4. To cause the necessary process to be issued for the apprehension of the persons implicated.

5. To assist in preparing any indictments that may be found against such persons, and to prepare for the trial thereof.

6. To attend the trials of persons indicted at any court of Oyer and Terminer or General Sessions of the Peace ; and to superintend and conduct such trials, with the like authority and in the same manner as the Attorney General of this state: and

7. To perform all other acts and duties which shall be necessary to a full and fair judicial investigation and determination of the offences alleged to have been committed by the persons so indicted.

SEC. 2. The person so appointed is hereby vested with powers and authority of District Attornies, in the several counties in which any such accusations shall be made ; and shall be authorized to attend any grand jury for the purpose of examining witnesses before them, but not to be present at their deliberations ; he shall have authority to issue subpœnas signed by himself, to compel the attendance of any witness at any court of Oyer and Terminer, or court of General Sessions of the Peace; which subpœnas shall have the same force and effect as if issued by the clerks of such courts respectively, under the seal thereof.

SEC. 3. The expenses attending the execution of the duties hereby imposed, shall be paid out of the treasury, on the order of the person administering the government of this state, after being audited by the comptroller.

SEC. 4. This act shall be in force until the first of May, one thousand eight hundred and twenty-nine, and no longer.

March 25.—A part of the day was spent in committee of the whole, on the bill for the employment of counsel to investigate the facts in relation to the abduction and supposed murder of William Morgan. The bill was opposed by Messrs. Livingston, and Crary, and supported by Messrs. Spencer, Viele, Wilkeson, and Allen; and was passed by the committee. On the question of agreeing to the report, Mr. Crary offered an amendment, which was previously lost in committee of the whole: that all the expenses heretofore incurred by any person to effect the objects contemplated by this bill, shall be paid out of the treasury. Lost, ayes 3, noes 23. The ayes were, Messrs. Crary, M'Martin, and Porter.

The report of the committee was then agreed to, ayes 23, noes 3, as follows:

Ayes.—Messrs. Allen, Benton, Dayan, Elsworth, Enos, Hager, Hart, Lake, M'Carty, M'Martin, Oliver, Porter, Schenck, Spencer, Stebbins, Todd, Throop, Tyson, Viele, Warron, Wheeler, Wilkeson, and Woodward: 23.

Noes.—Messrs. Crary, Livingston, M'Michael: 3. Adjourned.

March 26.—Bill read the third time and passed: for the employment of counsel to investigate the facts relative to the abduction and supposed murder of William Morgan, ayes 24, noes 3. (The noes were, Messrs. Crary, Livingston, and M'Michael.)

IN ASSEMBLY, *March* 19.—Mr. Childs presented a memorial from delegates from several western counties, assembled in convention at Le Roy to take into consideration the effects, &c. of Free Masonry, They say the oaths of that society are impious and profane, &c. They pray that a law may be passed, declaring that oaths administered by other than public officers under the laws, are illegal; and that their administration may be forbid under a penalty. After the memorial was read, it was referred to a select committee, consisting of Messrs. Childs, Granger, and Wardwell.

April 2.—Mr. Childs, from the select committee to which was referred the memorial of the delegates from twelve of the western counties of the state, on the subject of *Free Masonry*, reported and asked leave to bring in a bill to prevent the administration of extra judicial oaths. Leave was granted and a bill brought in accordingly, subjecting every person taking or administering an extra judicial oath to fine and imprisonment—fine not to exceed $200, and imprisonment not to exceed six months. [The following is the report of this committee:]

The select committee to which was referred the memorial of the counties of Chautauque, Erie, Niagara, Orleans, Genesee, Monroe, Livingston, Wayne, Yates, Seneca, and Tompkins, on the subject of extra judicial and Masonic oaths.

Report—That they have devoted to the subject of the memorial, that diligent examination which was demanded by its intrinsic importance, magnified as it is by acts set forth in the memorial. In deliberating upon this subject, your committee have directed their attention to the general character and consequences of all oaths unsanctioned by the laws, as well as the particular nature and policy of those set forth in the papers referred to in the memorial. Under every form and character which human government has at any time assumed, the principle of responsibility to higher power, however modified or perverted, has been appealed to as furnishing the foundation of the highest obligations which could be imposed upon human nature. Most civilized governments have approved the wisdom of resorting to an oath as a security for the faithful discharge of official duty; and all have deemed it indispensable in the administration of justice. The most sacred rights of society and individuals are subjected to its disposal, and no vice could be regarded as more alarming than a practice which in any degree should have the effect to weaken the obligation, or impair the confidence, which, not less by the law than the authority of the human heart, is reposed in an oath. The right to exact it belongs to the sovereign power of the state; and, in most instances, its efficacy is attempted to be increased by inflicting the severest penalties upon its violations. The duties it imposes must be the same, whatever may be the form of its administration; but it is entirely obvious that reverence to the being whose attention is invoked, not less than a regard to its influence upon the mind, demand that the occasion should be important, and the ceremony solemn. The unfrequent, unauthorised and irreverent administration of oaths, has a powerful influence, in the judgment of your committee, to destroy that religious sensibility to their nature, and that scrupulous and conscientious regard to all their requirements, which alone entitle them to confidence. Great and enlightened men have, with one accord, condemned the multiplication of oaths, with or without the sanction of law, as immoral and impolitic.

If these very general considerations were not entirely satisfactory to your committee, the most unanswerable reasons for abolishing extra judicial oaths, would be found in the character and consequences of a certain description of oaths as stated and set forth in the memorial. The memorial has called the attention of the legislature specifically to the abuse of the practice of administering oaths, as it is alledged to exist in Masonic societies; and subjoined the forms of obligations, as they are said to be administered in the different stages of advancement in that society. When it is recollected that these oaths have been communicated to the public by members of that society highly elevated, and maintaining a fair character and respectable standing in community, it is not perhaps unjust to believe those annexed to the memorial are substantially correct. They exhibit a perversion of the appropriate office of an oath, which strongly recommends the policy of a law prohibiting the administration of any extra judicial oath. These oaths could, by no possibility, enjoin the practice of a virtue not already commanded by religion and morality; and a literal observance of them would bind the sworn individual, under the severest penalties, to the performance of acts forbidden by both. The efficacy of these oaths is illustrated by the petitioners, by ascribing to their injunctions the outrage committed within a recent period upon two of our citizens, followed by what is now generally admitted to be the murder of one.

Whether the oaths referred to would authorize the commission of the crime, when rightly understood, is deemed by your committee altogether immaterial. The petitioners represent, that persons upon whom these oaths have been imposed, acting under a belief of their controlling power, have committed violence upon the liberty of one citizen, and upon the life of another; and that no doubt can exist upon that subject in the mind of any person who has attentively examined and weighed the testimony disclosed upon the trial of the several indictments which have grown out of the abduction of William Morgan, an unoffending citizen of this state. If there is reasonable ground for this belief—and the circumstances which have been developed leave little doubt—it is the duty of government to adopt such measures as may be best calculated to prevent the recurrence of an outrage so flagrant as that to which the petitioners have referred, and which so anxiously and painfully occupies the public mind.

The possibility that the obligations imposed by an extra judicial oath may conflict with the duty which a citizen may be called upon to discharge, is conclusive in the minds of your committee, in favor of granting the prayer of the memorialists. Although the law would pronounce an extra judicial oath, and all its obligations, nugatory, when in collision with a legally administered oath; yet, having done so, it is apparent that the individual must judge for himself of the relative power of conflicting obligations. There is danger then that justice may be perverted, and truth falsified, in courts created to develope truth and administer justice. The suspicion that such may be the consequence, is sufficient, in the judgment of your committee, to induce the legislature to remove the possibility of it by a statute prohibiting all oaths not authorized by law. The committee have therefore directed their chairman to ask leave to introduce a bill. T. CHILDS, *Chairman.*

April 4.—The house resolved itself into a committee of the whole on the bill from the Senate for the appointment of a commissioner to investigate the transactions relative to the abduction of *William Morgan*—Mr. Ruggles in the chair.

Mr. Gross moved to strike out the first section, or in other words to reject the bill. He avowed himself a Mason; but warned the house against partaking of the excitement which was felt on this subject in the western part of the state, and under its influence to pass a law which would hereafter, when the passions of men become cool, subject the legislature to contempt. The powers with which it was proposed to clothe this officer to be appointed by the executive, were enormous; it would, in fact, be establishing an inquisition in our state which would violate the principles of our institutions, and involve the innocent with the guilty in one common ruin. He believed Morgan was murdered and murdered by Masons, but he would consider the conferring of this inquisitorial power an infinitely greater evil, and more to be deprecated than even the murder of Morgan by deluded and wicked men. He was not disposed to condemn the excitement which existed on this subject in the western part of the state; on the contrary, he was proud of it, for the honor of human nature; for a deed of the darkest dye had been perpetrated, and that by Masons, by members of a numerous fraternity; and it was honorable to the character of our citizens that they should deeply interest themselves on the occasion; but it became the legislature of the state of New-York to act with caution and deliberation—to free themselves from the contagion of this excitement—boldly to stem the current of popular feeling—and to save unimpaired the principles of liberty, by refusing to violate the principles of sound jurisprudence, and refraining from setting a precedent of the most dangerous character.

Mr. Skinner hoped the motion to strike out would not prevail. He urged that two years had now elapsed since the perpetration of this horrid crime; and all the ordinary means to bring to justice the actors of this dark scene had proved unavailing. He contended that this bill did not propose to erect a new tribunal unknown to our laws, but simply provided the means of investigation which do not now exist. Nor was the precedent of sending a public officer to attend to those duties novel; as the Attorney General was frequently required to attend in particular counties the prosecution of criminal offences, either at the requisition of the executive or one of the judges of the Supreme Court. He thought this an occasion which demanded extraordinary efforts for the detection and punishment of offenders, to which the ordinary course of judicial proceedings was totally inadequate.

The speaker, Root, addressed the house in support of the motion to reject the bill. He alluded to various instances in the history of England, to show the effect of popular excitement and the injurious effect flowing from it. Admitting that Morgan was murdered, he asked whether it was right to change our course of judicial proceedings on that account. If our laws were defective, they should be amended; but when amended they should be made to bear upon all offenders alike. He asked whether Morgan, though murdered by Free Masons, was entitled to more commiseration than if he had been destroyed by a highwayman?

Mr. Granger said that the excitement in the western section of the state on this subject was as much, if not more, attributable to Free Masons, than to those who were charged with carrying on a crusade against Free Masonry. If Free Masons, and those, too, distinguished men, had done their duty, this excitement might have been checked. As to the delusion which is supposed to prevail on this subject, he could say that amongst those who felt a deep interest on this question, there were men second to none in the United States, as the list of the names of the delegation who attended the convention from whom emanated the memorial to the legislature would show. He could not perceive the evil which was apprehended from sending a public agent to investigate this affair, to collect testimony, and drag offenders to justice. He was not conscious how such a proceeding encroached upon the fundamental principles of government. The comptroller had been vested with similar powers to investigate frauds upon the canal. He regretted that the proposition made last winter to send a special commissioner of the legislature into the section of the state where the outrage had been committed, had not been adopted. If much good might not result from this measure, it would have a tendency to produce something like quiet and harmony, when the people saw that the legislature did not turn a deaf ear to their prayers. The people at the west were not exactly crazy ; but there is abroad in the community a feeling, a deep toned feeling, which is not to be trifled with—it is not to be scouted or laughed at, but must be soothed and not aggravated.

Mr. Brinckerhoof said he had hoped that the bill would have passed without debate. Whatever excitement existed elsewhere, it ought not to be brought into action here ; and to prevent every thing like feeling in the house, he called for the question.

Mr. Emmet said he was a Mason, and as yet he had no cause to regret it. He was decidedly in favor of the bill. If a crime had been committed, whether by Masons or others, and the ordinary process of the law is not sufficient to bring the offenders to punishment, it was the duty of the legislature to afford every facility to accomplish the end. He was inclined to believe that this measure would have a tendency to allay excitement. As a Mason, he could not perceive any objection to the bill ; on the contrary, the very principles of Free Masonry bound him to do all in his power to bring the perpetrators of the crime to punishment.

Mr. Wardwell also acknowledged himself a Mason, and said, when he first heard of this tragedy he was disposed to laugh at the stories which were told, deeming them unworthy of notice, and believing that there was not a Mason in this country so deluded and wicked as to commit so great a crime. He however had changed his opinion, and now believed that Morgan had been murdered, and murdered by Free Masons ; and could he believe that all Masons could act under similar delusions, he would not only abolish all extra judicial oaths, as proposed by a bill brought in on this subject, but he would abolish all Free Masonry, by making it penal to attend a lodge. This was not an ordinary case of murder. It was perpetrated by members of a numerous fraternity ; and it is said and believed that many Masons were engaged in the transaction, and that several in different counties combined and acted together in bringing about the destruction of the individual. If men under a mistaken sense of duty had committed the crime, others under a similar delusion might be guilty of similar offences. A high degree of excited feeling existed on this subject in the western part of this state ; he therefore thought that a public officer should be sent to make the necessary inquiries on the spot, to elicit all the evidence that could be obtained, and to bring the offenders to public punishment. The commission of the crime was without excuse or palliation. There were no principles of Free Masonry which require a man to act contrary to the dictates of morality and religion, and to run counter to the principles of good order.

The question was taken on striking out the first section, and lost, only seven rising in favor of it.

Mr. Williams, after adverting to the forms which the bill proposed to confer on this special Attorney General, observed that he was not prepared to give the bill his assent ; he wished time to examine it ; and with that view moved that the committee rise and report, which motion prevailed, ayes 49, noes 21. Then the house adjourned.

April 9.—Mr. Childs made the same motion as to the bill to appoint a commissioner to make inquiries in relation to the abduction of Morgan, and the bill to prevent extra judicial oaths. Carried, ayes 36, noes 35.

The house then went into the committee of the whole, Mr. Ruggles in the chair, on the said bills. The first section of the former bill passed, when Mr. Gross moved an amendment directing the payment of all expenses heretofore incurred by individuals in investigating this business. Mr. G. spoke some time in opposition to the bill; but if it must pass, he hoped this amendment would be adopted. So far as he could learn, the western people did not want this bill to pass. Southwick's paper, and some western papers, had condemned it. Mr. Southwick was opposed to the bill in principle; and he believed it would be inefficacious in its ends.

Mr. Childs said the people of the west had not called for this bill—it was the offspring of the Lieutenant Governor; but the people wanted further investigation.

Mr. Bryan said no body asked for compensation; wait till the people who have endeavored to ferret out this business ask for pay, before it is offered to them.

Mr. Sackett spoke against the bill. If the law was insufficient, let it be altered; but he was opposed to making a provision for a particular case. The almost inquisitorial powers given to this commissioner, he disapproved of.

Mr. Chever spoke in favor of the bill.

Mr. Speaker asked wherefore was this disposition to change the whole course of law. Is it because Free Masons have killed Morgan; (that is, admitting that he is killed, which is not certain, though conjectures fasten strongly on the belief that he is;) and because by persecuting them it is hoped to get into power? He spoke of the jury of inquest which determined that the body found at Oak Orchard creek was that of Morgan. When fanaticism, whether political or religious, rages, we often find men of private worth hurried away by it, and doing acts of which in moments of reflection they would be ashamed. He did not wish to derogate from the respectability of the western people; but they could be led away by fanaticism as well as others. The times of 1817, 1824, and 1825, sufficiently elucidate the truth of this. He alluded to the cry raised against secret societies in Europe, about the time of the French revolution, when so much feeling was excited without cause. He adverted to the inquisition in Spain, where all Free Masons were considered as devils, and were put to the torture and made to confess that they were guilty of crime whether they were or not—where a trial was made of the mathematical question: strength of nerve and sensibility of muscle given, required to know what degree of torture is necessary to make man confess himself guilty of crime. He said that this tirading about secret societies and extra judicial oaths, did not become sensible men; and they would not pursue it, unless they were driven by political fanaticism. He did not care whether Masonry were put down by legislative enactment or not; but if it were put up or down by such enactment, it would be acting foolishly. All this cry is to get power or to retain it. Some of the members were elected on the Anti-Masonic ticket; and they came here and were compelled to cry, Morganize Masons! Morganize Masons! Away with him! Crucify him! Crucify him! The excitement has been got up and fostered and fanned to get into power. We did not make so much fuss in Delaware county, a few years ago, when an Irishman killed two Scotchmen, we caught him, and hanged him.

This is made a political question. It is said that one of the presidential candidates is a Mason, and that the other is not, and therefore the excitement must be kept up: that is all there is to harp on. The six militiamen and ebony and topaz are worn out. One of the political parties—and I don't know how many political parties there are in the state—but one of the parties desire to keep up the excitement, in order to induce votes in favor of the candidate who is said not to be a Free Mason. And how do they work it on the other side, in the party to which I belong, but which party sometimes acts a little too silly. Why they show themselves eager to hunt down Free Masons, in the hopes that they will get votes by it. They cry, we don't approve of Masons murdering Morgan; we are as eager to find them as the other party. They mean to be first in the chase; and I dont know but they will be first in at the death. Why should we perform such a foolish, silly act, to get votes next November, when many of us do not much care which side we go on.

Mr. Johnson made some remarks against Mr. Gross's amendment, and it was lost.

The whole bill then passed. When the committee rose, their report was agreed to 82 to 17.

The committee of the whole then took up the bill to prevent extra judicial oaths.

Mr. Speaker then moved to rise and report. Lost.

A motion to rise prevailed.

Mr. Emmet hoped that leave to sit again would be refused. He wished to get rid of this ridiculous subject, for it was ridiculous in the extreme, if not something worse. We have important business before us; and a thing like this, of not a particle of merit, should not be suffered to interfere with it.

Mr. Bucklin was willing leave should be given to sit again. This bill was, he supposed, a part of the crusade against Free Masonry. But they were ignorant of the institution who supposed it would touch it; but it would touch a more important portion of society; it would interfere with a long established practice of Christian churches; and if gentlemen were willing to go on with it they might. Adjourned.

April 12.—The bill authorizing the employment of counsel for the investigation of facts relative to the abduction of *William Morgan*, and the incidents connected with that transaction, was read a third time: a discussion ensued, in which several gentlemen took a part, and which occupied a greater part of the morning session. The bill was passed by a vote of 66 to 44.

SPEECH OF THE HON. JOHN CRARY,

In the Senate of the State of New-York, March 25th, 1828.

On the proposition for appointing an inquisitor in the case of William Morgan.

Mr. Chairman—The complaint is, that a citizen has been forcibly taken and held in captivity, or inhumanly murdered. This awful act of violence was committed in September, 1826, upon the person of William Morgan. He was seized by ruffian hands, and taken against his will, in the village of Batavia, and carried from thence to Fort Niagara; beyond which he has not been traced; nor has he been heard of since that time.

The cause assigned for his abduction and murder is, that he was a Free Mason, and as such had disclosed the secrets of Masonry; and when we consider that the persons concerned in the acts of violence committed upon him, were Free Masons—and for such acts there is no other assignable reason, than that he had published the secrets of Masonry—the conclusion is, that for such publication he has suffered death.

The ostensible object of the bill under consideration is, to provide for detecting the offenders; and the question is, will it be likely to have the effect?

It will be recollected that Morgan is considered a victim of Masonic vengeance, and a martyr in the cause of liberty and his country. This is a reproach to the Masonic fraternity; and as such they have tried to get rid of it, while the people have endeavored to fix it upon them.

A war thus waged, is not likely to terminate short of the political extermination of one of the parties. Is it then probable, that this voluntary Masonic measure, at this very late day, will restore harmony between them? Will it not rather be considered as tantalizing the feelings of the people—especially as it is not called for by them—and more particularly so, as the offenders have already escaped to parts unknown, and the fraternity are charged with facilitating the escape?

Assistance was prayed for last year, but refused by the legislature; and now, when a law to abolish extra judicial oaths is prayed, instead of granting it, we give that which is not called for, and refuse that which is. Thus treating the people like children that do not know what is good for themselves.

All attempts to bring the perpetrators of the crime to justice, have hitherto proved abortive. Repeated trials have been had, but no convictions have followed; and a general belief is now entertained, that the offenders have in more than one instance been borne off by the perjured testimony of their brethren. As the means of discovering and punishing the offenders, the bill authorizes the person administering the government of this state to appoint some person, of the degree of counsellor in the Supreme Court, to repair to the west and institute inquiries concerning the abduction of William Morgan. This is adding one to the number who have for the last eighteen months been engaged in performing that service and duty. And is it any thing more? Can the person thus authorized do any thing that has not already been done without effect?

Is it not then time to change the manner of proceeding, and if we cannot punish for the crime committed, prevent the future repetition of it? It would seem from the petition in the house, that such is the conclusion of the people of the west: and when we consider that the Free Masons of that region have met in convention at Le Roy; disclosed the secrets of the higher orders of Masonry, not known to Morgan; and publicly renounced Masonry; and that a subsequent Anti-Masonic convention have, by their memorial in the other house, suggested the remedy of prohibiting extra judicial oaths as the most effectual; it is difficult to conceive on what principle we are proceeding on the bill under consideration. Will it not be considered the contrivance of Masonry to perpetuate the order; and thus, instead of allaying the excitement, tend to increase it. The people will suspect rather than confide in this state commissioner, after they have, both separately and collectively, exhausted all the means which by this bill is placed in his power. It is insulting to suppose that a single individual with the mandate of the legislature, can do what the great body of the people have not been able to perform. The people of the west are laboring under a deep-toned sense of injury; and any profferred redress which is evasive, will be considered as sporting with their feelings. Whatever is done should be to soothe, and not to aggravate, sufferings which are the most excruciating, the most tormenting.

Hitherto I have considered this question as between the Free Masons who were concerned either directly or indirectly in the abduction and murder of William Morgan, on the one hand; and the people contiguous to the place where the catastrophe happened, striving to bring the offenders to justice, on the other: But there is another view of the subject, compared to which the fate of William Morgan dwindles into a point. His cause has become that of the constitution and the law; and in that view I shall now proceed to consider it.

When the future historian shall relate the fate of William Morgan, he will pause and inquire for the persons concerned; but when he is told the abduction was perpetrated in open day, in the populous yet peaceful village of Batavia; and above all, when he is also told the persons concerned have escaped detection; he cannot but exclaim, how impotent are human laws, and how inefficient the administration of justice, even in the most civilized part of the world! It cannot be denied but that our system of jurisprudence is defective; there is a power among us: it is a secret invisible power, exerted by Free Masons, which is above the law. While the order of Free Masons did not pervert public justice, or interfere to prevent the apprehension and conviction of offenders, their pretended mysteries, though they sought concealment excited no alarm.

The attribute of secrecy was accorded to the order, as a prerogative handed down from high antiquity and always claimed and exercised; the pretence for continuing and perpetuating Free Masonry has been the security, protection, and advantage, which it afforded to the traveller and the stranger; while it has been supposed the order did not interfere with the duties of the citizen, the politician, the statesman. Under such pretences, not contradicted by appearances, it has hitherto been viewed with complacency; its members respected and esteemed. And it was not until it was found that the obligations of the order had alienated those belonging to it from their allegiance to the constitution and the law, and the community began to suspect the imposition which had been practiced upon them, and exert the supremacy of their power to bring the kidnappers and murderers of Morgan to justice. On this occasion the people soon found their own impotence and that of the laws when exerted against Free Masons for the abduction and murder by them of one belonging to the order. It is this secret invisible power to which I am opposed; a power exerted in the midst of us, from the horrible and tragical effects of which, neither friends nor foes, not even the wandering stranger can escape.

By the common consent of mankind, each individual has certain absolute and unalienable rights: these are the right of personal liberty, the right of personal security, and the right of private property. The great end and object of government should be to protect each individual in the enjoyment of these rights: when that is not done, the government must be defective either in the form or in the administration. Public sentiment is the only test to determine whether it be done or not; and every thing depending on public sentiment must be open and exposed to public scrutiny and observation. Publicity, then, is and must be the redeeming principle of every system; without it the most perfect government will be found in practice to permit every thing that is wrong, and afford no security for any thing that is right. That the order of Free Masons has always required secrecy from those belonging to it, is a fact that cannot be questioned. If for that they ought to be condemned, they will not complain that it is done without testimony. Let us then test the order by one of its cardinal principles, and see whether it is at variance with truth and justice.

Openness and honesty form the criterion by which the character of every transaction relating to the affairs of men is investigated and determined. Vice has always shunned the light.

The concealment of the fact is evidence that the fact itself, if it appeared, would disclose something that is wrong. Thus if a man be found with stolen goods in his possession, and he has concealed or attempts to conceal them, it is evidence that he received the goods knowing that they were stolen. A person is examined on a charge of felony and conceals the facts and states what is not true: the conclusion is that he is guilty. A party in a suit secretes a paper: the conclusion is, that if it were produced it would disclose some facts against him which without it do not appear; and thus it is that secrecy and concealment have always been considered as tantamount to deceit and falsehood. It was so at the beginning; for after eating the forbidden fruit our first parents hid themselves from the presence of God.

If I have succeeded in showing that the first principle of the order is wrong, it is not to be expected in practice that it can ever become right; when the principle on which it is founded is erroneous, it will practically proceed on the same wrong ground. If we take the wrong road at the commencement of our journey, the longer we travel it the farther we are from the place of destination.

The ostensible objects of Free Masonry are *benevolence* and *kindness*, but if it should appear that the real objects are *selfishness* and *cruelty* in disguise, no one not of the order will hesitate to admit that it is time the veil was torn off, and the society exhibited in all its deformity. Names can never alter things; but care should be taken, that things have their proper names. The appropriate use of names is to represent things truly, but that they do so, should never be taken for granted: For as often as the despot has intended to lead the multitude captive at his will, he has done it by the delusion of a name. If vigilance is the price of liberty, the point at which it should first be exerted, is to distinguish between names and things. To do so we must become familiar with the thing itself, which we never can if it is to us invisible; and that I understand to be the precise character of the order of Free Masonry: and why is it so? men never act without a motive. Is it not then fair to conclude that these stolen abuses are secret pleasures enjoyed at the expense of others not belonging to the order?

Unity of action and design has always enabled those belonging to the combination not only to protect themselves, but to oppress others; hence it is that an act done by a conspirator is more heinous in the eye of the law, and alarming to the community, than if done by an isolated individual. But when impunity is added to secrecy of design, it is then that we realize in imagination the horrors which William Morgan must have endured when the midnight assassin stalked forth before his swimming eyes.

The entering of a dwelling house against the will of the occupant, in the day time, is a simple trespass; but when the same act is done in the silent watches of the night, it is felony. Why is it so? Can there be any other reason for it, than the helpless condition of the tenant at that season destined by nature for silence and repose?

Hence it is obvious that no other relation among men can be just but that which places them on a footing of equality. That which is not known to us can never be guarded against by us. It is by deceit or falsehood that distress and misery have been communicated and extended far and wide among the human race; and if deceit and falsehood be not descriptive of Free Masonry, they are of its effect and operation upon the rest of mankind.

To illustrate: A witness that is interested is incompetent to testify: a juror that has a bias upon his mind is disqualified from sitting in judgment. But how can the one or the other be excluded, when the fact of such interest or bias is not known to the parties? It may be said that the bias which one Free Mason has in favor of another is slight and trifling; admitted, and what follows? Do we not know that when all other things are equal the least item inclines the scale? and it is by the influence of these imperceptible trifles that every doubtful question is decided.

It has been said, that a man might as well be suspected, because he belonged to another church. But on what principle does the argument rest? It must be upon the assumption that there is no difference between Christianity and Free Masonry; and will that be pretended by the most devoted friend of the order? It is sufficient for my purpose to mention one particular about which there is no controversy. The obligation of secrecy is enjoined according to the order of Free Masonry; while the Saviour, at parting with his disciples, said unto them, " *Go ye into all the world and preach the gospel to every creature.*"

The charge against Free Masons is not that they are all bad men, or that they ought to be condemned because there are some bad men among them : But it is, that the order justifies individuals belonging to it, who could not be justified by the laws of society. The conclusion, therefore, is against the order, not the individuals belonging to it. The individuals may be good or bad, like other men; their character must depend upon their walk and conversation. It will not be pretended that individuals belonging to any society are for that reason to be justified for any thing they may do. The objection is, that the members of the Masonic society are not made amenable to justice like other men. It is not that every Free Mason shall be condemned because he is a Free Mason; but that the order screens men from punishment because they are members of it. No matter who subverts public justice, it is an offence which deserves reprehension and punishment.

But it may be asked, what have the order done?

I answer, *they have justified the* KIDNAPPERS *and* MURDERERS *of* WILLIAM MORGAN.

This is a serious charge; but it is believed to be supported by the best evidence the nature of the case will admit. When the conduct of men cannot be reconciled with their innocence, the conclusion is that they are guilty.

The sense of right and wrong is impressed by the Deity himself upon the heart of man. The effect of this impression will naturally appear at the recital of wrongs; and when it does not, the conclusion is that natural feelings are suppressed.

The story of William Morgan is the most tragical, and calculated the most effectually to harrow up all our feelings and excite all our sensibilities; and even to impel us by an impulse not our own, to seek the place of our martyr's sufferings and death, and there avenge this most foul and unnatural murder.

But has the story had that effect upon those belonging to the Masonic order? Will it be denied that as often as it has been related in the presence and hearing of Free Masons, one has inquired, if the facts stated by Morgan in his book were true, did not he deserve the fate he was supposed to have suffered! Another has said, he has gone off and keeps out of the way to give value to his book, and will return when his fortune is made! Others, though silent, have given a smile of approbation, while with inverted looks the countenance of all have indicated mystery and concealment! And when a numerous body of men, both separately and collectively, can suppress the strongest natural emotions, is it not fair to conclude that such suppression is the effect of design? Thus much for the evidence of observation; and for the correction of it, I appeal to the most superficial observer.

But the evidence against Free Masonry does not rest entirely upon the unnatural looks and actions of individuals belonging to the order, when Morgan's case is mentioned. There is another fact imputing moral guilt to the order itself, unless the maxim that a man is known by the company he keeps, can be controverted. It is this: that three persons belonging to the order have confessed themselves guilty, and admitted they were concerned in the abduction of William Morgan. We have occasionally seen notices of expulsion, from which we are to conclude that it is according to the discipline of the order to expel for some offences; but we have seen no notice of the expulsion of those three persons; hence we are to conclude that the abduction of William Morgan is not an offence according to the order of Free Masonry!

It is not my object here to dilate upon the enormity of this offence: It must be obvious to all, that the right of personal liberty is of all others the most invaluable; and if the fate of William Morgan had been less tragical, and instead of being put to death he had obtained his liberty after a short interval, and had been restored to his family and friends; yet the offence would remain; and all those accessary to it, whether before or after the fact, must be considered among the offenders.

Can the order escape from this conclusion; and if they cannot, what does it prove? Surely this, that the malignant pleasure of Free Masons is, with the order itself, a consideration paramount to the rights of individuals, or the observance of the laws: and are we not only to countenance in the midst of us their invisible power, but the unjust and cruel exercise of it?

But that is a question I need not ask; for the power exists and has thus far been exercised, without our opposition; and it remains to be seen whether it shall continue and triumph in spite of it. Although the aggregate number of Free Masons bears but a small proportion to the great body of the community, yet it is not to be controverted that they enjoy the offices of honor and profit, while at the same time they profess to take no part in politics. The places occupied by Free Masons in all parties, show how their professions are to be understood; apparently they belong to no party, that thereby they may be the better enabled to control the whole. Hence it is that they are to be found at the head of every party; that whatever party prevails, the affairs of government may be conducted by Free Masons; which would not be the case, if they were known to belong to any particular party. It is against this gigantic power with all its trappings, that we are to contend. It is true, we are neither armed nor disciplined for the battle; but let us not despair; we have with us the moral courage, the physical power, and the force of principle; and it is with pleasure that I add, the best men are every day renouncing Free Masonry and rallying around our standard. With such aid, although the contest may be long, the victory must be certain.

Let us not deceive ourselves: it is with rank and fashion, with power and wealth, that we have to contend; and in such a contest it is not to be expected that the selfish, the sycophantic, the slavish, will ever embark; yet the cause is worthy of freemen impelled by the force of principle and the sense of injury; and such only will engage. The exclusive privilege of individuals with the prerogative of power, has held millions in bondage. Men not knowing that they were born free, and possessed of certain equal and unalienable rights, might content themselves to linger out a miserable existence in servitude and chains. If we were of that degraded and degenerate race, Free Masonry might triumph here as it has done in the old world and in the darkest ages. But as we are free men, with the gift of reason, and a knowledge of our rights, can our friends expect, or our enemies require, that we should countenance an institution founded in error? But the question still recurs, is it so.

As we hold the affirmative, let us advert for a moment to the mode of initiation, and the manner of conferring degrees, both of which have now become public.

The candidate presents himself blindfolded and naked, with the cable-tow about his neck, without any previous knowledge of what he is to do, or what is to be required of him; and in this helpless condition the dreadful oath is administered and taken. If the candidate should falter or hesitate, the ruffians on each side of him holding the cable-tow which is about his neck, can in a moment tighten the cord and extinguish him and his complaints: And how many noble spirits preferring death to degradation have been thus despatched, the world can never know! Is this true? If it is not, it can be shown to be false by disclosing the fact. If it should be said that this would destroy the order, by revealing the mystery, then it follows that the secrets of Free Masonry were with the order itself a consideration paramount to the reputation of those belonging to it. If then they can live by Free Masonry, we must try to live without it, and judge of it, as we do of other things, from **what we know.**

It is not to be questioned that worthy men have thus by duresse and imprisonment become Free Masons; and from the fact that many have withdrawn themselves and for years declined associating with the order, it is evident that Free Masonry is held in derision by many and the better part of those belonging to the order. Hence it is that the most corrupt institution is kept up and continued by the worst of men. And from such continuance, what is to be expected? Surely if there be any antidote it must be poison; if any remedy it must be death.

For the violation of the Masonic oath, the most dreadful pnnishment is invoked; and every subsequent degree not only imposes new and additional obligations, but is a repetition of all the preceding ones. Hence it is that the compunctious visitings of conscience, if any, are stifled by the vile oath of profanity taken by every member of the order: they cannot repent because they dare not confess. Whatever crimes are perpetrated, the conclusion is and must be by the perpetrators, that they had better go on than to go back. Thus poor human nature is perverted and left without the power of repentance or hope of redemption.

If I am right in the view I have taken of Free Masonry, it is wrong in principle as well as in practice. Various other views might be suggested; but I forbear. If I am right, enough has been said; if I am wrong, nothing that I could add would be of any avail. But I cannot close these remarks without adverting to those of my friend from Genesee, (Gen. Allen,) with whom I have so long and so pleasantly travelled; and I must say it is with sincere regret that I differ with him on this occasion; but I have high authority for saying that every difference of opinion is not a difference of principle.

PROCEEDINGS

Of the Adjourned Convention of Seceding Masons: held at Le Roy, July 4th, 1828.

At an adjourned meeting of the convention of Seceding Masons, held at Le Roy, July 4th, 1828. Solomon Southwick, President, and David Bernard, Clerk.

On motion, it was resolved, that the committee appointed to draft a declaration of independence from the Masonic institution, be requested to report. A. P. Hascall, from the said committee, then reported the declaration.

On motion, it was unanimously resolved, that the declaration be adopted and signed.

DECLARATION.

When men attempt to dissolve a system which has influenced and governed a part of community, and by its pretentions to antiquity, usefulness, and virtue, would demand the respect of all, it is proper to submit to the consideration of a candid and impartial world, the causes which impel them to such a course. We, seceders from the Masonic institution, availing ourselves of our natural and unalienable rights, and the privileges guaranteed to us by our constitution freely to discuss the principles of our government and laws, and to expose whatever may endanger the one or impede the due administration of the other, do offer the following reasons for endeavoring to abolish the order of Free Masonry, and destroy its influence in our government.

In all arbitrary governments free inquiry has been restricted as fatal to the principles upon which they were based. In all ages of the world tyrants have found it necessary to shackle the minds of their subjects, to enable them to control their actions; for experience ever taught that the free mind ever exerts a moral power that resists all attempts to enslave it. However forms of government heretofore have varied, the right to act and speak without a controlling power has never been permitted. Our ancestors who imbibed principles of civil and religious liberty, fled to America to escape persecution; and when Britain attempted to encroach upon the free exercise of those principles, our fathers hesitated not to dissolve their oaths of allegiance to the mother country, and declare themselves free and independent; and exulting millions of freemen yet bless their memories for the deed. A new theory of government was reduced to practice in the formation of the American republic. It involved in its structure principles of equal rights and equal privileges; and was based on the eternal foundation of public good. It protects the weak, restrains the powerful, and extends its honors and emoluments to the meritorious of every condition. It should have been the pride of every citizen to preserve this noble structure in all its beautiful symmetry and proportions. But the principle of self aggrandizement, the desire to control the destinies of others, and luxuriate in their spoils, unhappily still inhabits the human breast. Many attempts have already been made to impair the freedom of our institutions and subvert our government. But they have been met by the irresistible power of public opinion and indignation, and crushed. In the mean time the Masonic society has been silently growing among us, whose principles and operations are calculated to subvert and destroy the great and important principles of the commonwealth. Before and during the revolutionary struggle, Masonry was but little known and practised in this country. It was lost amid the changes and confusion of the conflicting nations, and was reserved for a time of profound peace, to wind and insinuate itself into every department of government, and influence the result of almost every proceeding. Like many other attempts to overturn government and destroy the liberties of the people, it has chosen a time when the suspicions of men were asleep; and with a noiseless tread, in the darkness and silence of the night, has increased its strength and extended its power. Not yet content with its original powers and influence, it has of late received the aid of foreign and more arbitrary systems. With this accumulation of strength, it arrived at that formidable crisis when it bid open defiance to the laws of our country in the abduction and murder of an unoffending citizen of the republic. So wicked was this transaction, so extensive its preparation, and so openly justified, that it aroused the energies of an insulted people, whose exertions have opened the hidden recesses of this abode of darkness and mystery; and mankind may now view its power, its wickedness, and folly.

That it is opposed to the genius and design of this government, the spirit and precepts of our holy religion, and the welfare of society generally, will appear from the following considerations:

It exercises jurisdiction over the persons and lives of citizens of the republic.

It arrogates to itself the right of punishing its members for offences unknown to the laws of this or any other nation.

It requires the concealment of crime, and protects the guilty from punishment.

It encourages the commission of crime, by affording to the guilty facilities of escape.

It affords opportunities for the corrupt and designing to form plans against the government, and the lives and characters of individuals.

It assumes titles and dignities incompatible with a republican form of government, and enjoins an obedience to them derogatory to republican principles.

It destroys all principles of equality, by bestowing favors on its own members to the exclusion of others equally meritorious and deserving.

It creates odious aristocracies by its obligations to support the interests of its members, in preference to others of equal qualifications.

It blasphemes the name, and attempts a personification of the Great Jehovah.

It prostitutes the Sacred Scriptures to unholy purposes, to subserve its own secular and trifling concerns.

It weakens the sanctions of morality and religion, by the multiplication of profane oaths, and an immoral familiarity with religious forms and ceremonies.

It discovers in its ceremonies an unholy commingling of divine truth with impious human inventions.

It destroys a veneration for religion and religious ordinances, by the profane use of religious forms.

It substitutes the self righteousness and ceremonies of Masonry for the vital religion and ordinances of the Gospel.

It promotes habits of idleness and intemperance, by its members neglecting their business to attend its meetings and drink its libations.

It accumulates funds at the expense of indigent persons, and to the distress of their families, too often to be dissipated in rioting and pleasure and its senseless ceremonies and exhibitions.

It contracts the sympathies of the human heart for all the unfortunate, by confining its charities to its own members; and promotes the interests of a few at the expense of the many.

An institution thus fraught with so many and great evils, is dangerous to our government and the safety of our citizens, and is unfit to exist among a free people: We, therefore, believing it a duty we owe to God, our country, and to posterity, resolve to expose its mystery, wickedness, and tendency, to public view—and we exhort all citizens who have a love of country, and a veneration for its laws, a spirit of our holy religion, and a regard for the welfare of mankind, to aid us in the cause which we have espoused—and appealing to Almighty God for the rectitude of our motives, we solemnly absolve ourselves from all allegiance to the Masonic institution, and declare ourselves free and independent: and in support of these resolutions, our government and laws, and the safety of individuals, against the usurpations of all secret societies and open force, and against the 'vengeance' of the Masonic institution, 'with a firm reliance on the protection of Divine Providence, we mutually pledge to each other, our lives, our fortunes, and our sacred honor.'

July 4th, 1828.

Signers of the Declaration of Independence from the Masonic Institution, adopted at Le Roy, July 4th, 1828.

NAMES.	RESIDENCE.	NO. OF DEGREES.
Solomon Southwick,	Albany,	Four
David Bernard,	Warsaw,	Intimate Secretary
W. W. Phelps,	Canandaigua,	three
Isaac B. Barnum,	Perrington,	four
Cephas A. Smith,	Le Roy, twenty-one or	Thrice Illustrious Order of the Cross
J. Van Valkenburgh,	Prattsburgh,	three
Platt S. Beach,	Stafford,	one
Elam Badger,	Cazenovia,	three
Joseph Hart,	Albion,	four
Kneeland Townsend, jun.	Lewiston,	three
Anthony Cooley,	Le Roy,	Thrice Illustrious Order of the Cross
John G. Stearns,	Paris,	three
Reuben Winchell,	Lockport,	three
Augustus P. Hascall,	Le Roy,	Thrice Illustrious Order of the Cross

NAMES.	RESIDENCE.	NO. OF DEGREES.
Noble D. Strong,	Auburn,	seven
John Hascall,	Le Roy,	Thrice Illustrious Order of the Cross
Robert Earl, jun.	Attica,	one
James Ballard,	Le Roy,	Thrice Illustrious Order of the Cross
Leonard B. Rose,	Castile,	three
Timothy C. Strong,	Albion,	four
William Waggoner,	Lebanon,	three
John Aumock,	Le Roy,	four
Herbert A. Read,	Le Roy,	Thrice Illustrious Order of the Cross
W. Robinson,	Springwater,	three
Jesse Badcock,	Springwater,	two
Lemuel Cook,	Lewiston,	three
James Gray,	Le Roy,	three
Elijah Gray,	Le Roy,	four
William Howe,	Gorham,	seven
Samuel Pierce,	Ridgeway,	three
Adam Richmond,	Le Roy,	seven
George W. Harris,	Batavia,	three
Benjamin Cooley,	Stafford,	three
John Joslen,	Wheatland,	three
A. F. Albright,	Wheatland,	three
Fayette Cross,	Wheatland,	three
Elias Cooley,	Le Roy,	three
Olney F. Rice,	Gorham,	three
Warren Kneeland,	Sempronius,	three
Jabez A. Beebe,	Hinsdale,	three regular and three honorary
Burroughs Holmes,	Clarendon,	seven
Noah B. Denton,	Covington,	three
Truman J. Wield,	Covington,	four
Edward Giddins,	Rochester,	seven
Abram Cherry,	Rochester,	six
Richard Hollister,	Le Roy,	fourteen
Amos E. Hutchins	Le Roy,	three
Henry Conkling,	Covington,	three
Pascall D. Webb,	Le Roy,	three
Daniel Rowley,		six
Jonathan K. Barlow,	Bethany,	seven
Mills Averill,	Bethany,	three
Noah Ingersoll,	Albion,	three
Chapman Hawley,	Niagara co.	
Auren Dabell,	Prattsburgh,	ten
Frederick C. Farnam,	Attica,	three
Joel Bradner,	Barre,	three
Robert Shadders,	Barre,	two
Jonathan K. Foster,	Batavia,	three
Seth M. Gates,	Le Roy,	three
David Reed,	Hopewell,	three
Willard Smith,	Adams, Jefferson co.	twelve
Solomon Barker,	Gates,	three
Orson Nichoson,	Albion, Orleans co.	three
J. K. Brown,	Barre,	seven
Enos Bachelder,	Le Roy,	three

NAMES.	RESIDENCE.	NO. OF DEGREES.
Stephen Robinson,	Springwater,	three
Robert McKely,	Clarence,	two
John Law,	Le Roy,	four
Isaac S. Fitch,	Jamestown,	
Hiram Cornell,	Jamestown, Chautauque co.	
Asa Turner,	Jamestown, Chautauque co.	
Samuel Ledyard,	Pultneyville,	three
John Smith,	Prattsburgh,	three
Benjamin F. Welles,	Pultney,	three
Anson Hinman,	Pike, Allegany co	three
Samuel D. Greene,	Batavia,	three
Chester Coe,	Bennington,	three
Theodore Hooker,	Duchess co.	ten
Elijah Northup,	Pine Plains, Duchess co.	five
Reuben Sanborn,	Painted Post,	seven
Jarvis Swift,	Auburn,	three
David Snow,	Covington,	three
John Tomlinson,	Stafford,	three
Nathan M. Mann,	Wales, Erie co.	seven
Nathan Townsend,	Batavia,	seven
Andrew Couse,	Cazenovia,	three
Russel Waters,	Cazenovia,	
Phlegmoncy Horton,	Cazenzovia,	
W. J. Edson,	Batavia,	two
David C. Miller,	Batavia,	one
James Rolfe,	Elba,	three
George W. Blodgett,	Le Roy,	two
Uriah Slayton,	Le Roy,	three
Martin Flint,	Vermont,	
Darius Sprague,	Vermont,	
Joseph Cochran,	Vermont,	
Orcutt Hyde,	Vermont,	
William Hyde,	Vermont,	
Phinehas Smith,	Vermont,	
Lund Tarbox,	Vermont,	
Hollis Platt,	Le Roy,	{ Thrice Illustrious Order of the Cross
Norman Bently,	Guilford,	seven.

The convention then adjourned until four o'clock, P. M., to meet at the Presbyterian meeting house.

Met according to adjournment: Elder Bernard addressed the Throne of Grace. Solomon Southwick then delivered an address in pursuance of previous appointment.

The convention then adjourned to meet at the same place on the next morning, at eight o'clock; at which time and place the convention was opened by prayer.

A number of communications was received by the convention, from persons residing in different parts of this state, and also in the states of Vermont, Connecticut, Pennsylvania, New Jersey, and Maryland, stating that it was inconvenient attending at this season of the year, and from so great a distance, and requesting copies of the new declaration of independence, and other proceedings, forwarded to them for their sanction. Delegates from ten counties in this state, attended the convention and signed the declaration. The number of persons attending the convention was about eight thousand.

On motion it was then resolved, That the committee of fifteen, appointed at the last sitting of the convention, to prepare the upper degrees of Masonry, be requested to report.

The committee then reported the degrees from the Master's to the Royal Arch, and including the Royal Arch, which were read: Whereupon, it was resolved by the Masons present who had received these several degrees, that they are substantially correct. It was then resolved by the convention, that the report of the committee be accepted, and the said degrees published to the world. [See the degrees in this book.]

The convention then adjourned for one hour.

Met pursuant to adjournment, and received the further report of the committee of fifteen, as follows—The degrees of knighthood, to wit, Knight of the Red Cross, Knight Templar, Knight of Malta, Knight of the Christian Mark and Guard of the Conclave, Knight of the Holy Sepulchre, and the order of Illustrious, Most Illustrious, and Thrice Illustrious Council of the Knights of the Holy Cross. They were then read and resolved by the Knights present, numbers of whom had received these several degrees, to be substantially correct: Whereupon it was

Resolved by the convention, That the degrees be published to the world. [See the degrees in this book.]

Resolved, That Solomon Southwick, David Bernard, Richard Hollister, Willard Smith, Herbert A. Read, John Hascall, and Samuel D. Greene, be a committee to prepare a preface to, and superintend the publication of the degrees adopted by this convention.

Miles B. Lampson, Seth M. Gates, and A. P. Hascall, were then appointed a committee to draft resolutions expressive of the sentiments of this convention.

The committee retired a short time, when Mr. Gates from said committee reported the following:

Resolved, That however beneficial secret societies may have been considered in the dark ages of the world, as bonds of union and shields of protection to the members against the violence of the times; yet in this enlightened age and country, where the private rights and the civil liberty of our citizens are guaranteed by a free constitution, and an impartial administration of justice, they became not only useless to their members, but dangerous to the government.

Resolved, That the order of Free Masonry is a system of slavish despotism, calculated to break down the pride and spirit of freemen, and thus render them fit subjects of despotic power.

Resolved, That whatever may be our predilections for the prominent candidates for the presidency, and whatever part we as individuals may see fit to take in national politics, we consider the overthrow and destruction of the Masonic institution as wholly disconnected therewith, and of vastly paramount importance—that this convention would view with the most undissembled feelings of regret, any attempt to render the honest indignation existing against the institution subservient to the views of any of the political parties of the day—that we unhesitatingly disclaim all intention of promoting party views or political purposes.

Resolved, That the Masonic obligations, especially those of the Knight of the Christian Mark and Guard of the Conclave, and the Knight of the Holy Sepulchre, are of the most blasphemous nature; and we cannot but deliver our sentiments in unqualified terms against them.

Resolved, That the Committee of Publication be also a Central Corresponding Committee; and be authorized to convoke the Convention of Seceding Masons, if at any time it shall be deemed expedient.

Resolved unanimously, That the thanks of this convention be presented to Solomon Southwick, for the masterly and eloquent address delivered yesterday by appointment of this convention—and that to prevent the work from being garbled by the fraternity, or its agents, he be requested to secure a copy right and publish the same.

Resolved, That the thanks of this convention be tendered to the president and secretary thereof, for the assiduous and able manner in which they have performed the duties devolving upon them during the sitting of the convention.

The same being severally read and considered, were unanimously adopted—when the convention adjourned *sine die*.

NOTE.—The artillery of the fraternity has been unceasingly discharged upon the members of this convention. Mr. Child, the editor of the Albany Masonic Record, 'the only hebdomadal paper devoted to the cause of Masonry in the United States,' has more than intimated that they were a set of vagabond book Masons, who would run together with no better views than to get a good dinner free of expense, and get decently drunk to boot, by renouncing what they knew nothing about. The same gentleman, with his usual regard for truth, politeness, and elegance of diction, mentions them as a set of political demagogues assembled to make or adopt a mock imitation of the original declaration of independence. The day, however, has happily passed when such graceless calumniators can gain credence.

Those men formed a convention, which, for talents and respectability, for real worth and standing in community, is rarely equalled in conventional or deliberative bodies. There are of those whose names appear above, three judges of county courts, seven ministers of the Gospel in regular standing in their respective churches, three practising attorneys at law, two physicians, and four editors of newspapers, besides several justices of the peace and postmasters. They are scattered through the western part of the state of New York, and many of them are extensively known. They need not even this feeble tribute of respect of the compiler, to establish or promulgate their characters. The beneficial effects of the doings of that convention will be experienced, and duly appreciated, when their calumniators shall quietly repose with the institution of Free Masonry in the tomb of forgetfulness.

ORATION OF HERBERT A. READ, ESQ.

Pronounced at Le Roy, July 4, 1828, to an assembly of nearly ten thousand persons.

WE are assembled for no ordinary purpose, and to celebrate no common event in the history of the world. The object is no less than to destroy an institution which has secretly fastened itself upon the republic; whose principles are at variance with the first and unalienable rights of man. An institution, which, under the garb of morality, teaches and encourages the grossest immoralities. An institution professing to be the handmaid of religion, whose ceremonies are blasphemies and impiety, and which has been emphatically the school of infidelity. An institution professing to teach its members subjection to the laws of our country; but which has set at defiance the laws both of God and of man—destroyed the sanctity of domestic life—torn asunder the tender ties of humanity—in a word, sacrilegiously trampled upon the dearest rights of American freemen; and to conceal its own impious principles and blasphemous ceremonies, has stained its kingly robes with the blood of a free citizen. Such, fellow citizens, is the object of our meeting. The event we celebrate is the birthday of a nation—the first dawn of the polar star which shall guide all nations to the harbor of pure and legitimate freedom—the redemption of a patriotic people from bondage: an event unparalleled in the history of the world. To contemplate the conduct of a brave and magnanimous people, who, at a time when monarchy and despotism were the only governments in existence, and the strong arm of power was exerted against them—in defiance of all the powers of kings and emperors threw off all allegiance to tyrants: declaring that they were, and of right ought to be, free and independent; and sealed the declaration with their blood; and thus, upon the firm and immutable basis of equal rights, established a free government. We are assembled to contemplate this stupendous work, and lay the foundation for the entire overthrow of the Masonic institution. Heretofore the object has been merely to celebrate it as a day in which our fathers emancipated themselves from foreign power; but we this day have the twofold purpose of reverting back to that period, and to overthrow all internal enemies, that we may, in very deed, be disenthralled and redeemed from all things which impede the grand and triumphant march of liberty. Who, among us, whose heart beats not high at such prospects? Who that has witnessed the surrounding gloom which has overspread this western section, but now rejoice at the dispelling of the clouds, and the bright prospect before us? As freemen jealous of your liberties, rejoice in the anticipation of that day when the institution which has proudly bid defiance to the public opinion—which has exulted in its own damning deeds, and insulted the majesty of the laws, shall be swept from our land, and leave not a wreck behind. The book of her mysteries will be opened—her hidden abominations exposed—her profane altars will be overthrown—her noisy revels will no longer greet our ears—her covers will be opened to the gaze of the uninitiated: for her iniquities have called for retributive justice. The voice has not been in vain. Freemen have asserted their dear bought rights, and Masonry vanished like mist before the sun.

A brief history of the eventful period we now celebrate, and of the characters engaged in our revolutionary struggles, may not be unnecessary to nerve our arms in defence of those principles which our fathers so manfully established by their sufferings and privations. They were men stamped with the principles of liberty by the God of nature. Driven from their homes and their land of nativity by those who should have been their protectors, after suffering from the hardships of a long tempestuous voyage, they established themselves in this western world for the enjoyment of civil and religious liberty, the natural birthright of man. Many were the sufferings and great the privations they were destined to experience; but men who for the enjoyment of rational liberty had deserted their former residence, and broken asunder the endearing ties of relationship, were not to be driven from their purpose, nor baffled in their attempts by such trials. They saw in prospective the blessings which their labors would purchase, if not for them, for future generations. This supported them in all their trials, and stimulated to greater exertions. Their labors were crowned with success. A new world sprang into existence, and that liberty they had so ardently toiled for, richly compensated them for their suffering. Such characters as the settlers of North America, are worthy our highest admiration. Amidst the hardships and sufferings of that period, they were not unmindful of their descendants and the future inhabitants of the new world. While struggling against the rigor of a new climate, engaged in repelling the attacks of their savage enemies, they laid a broad and deep foundation for the future civil and religious liberty of this western continent. But soon the colonies had new difficulties to encounter. After the savage fires were extinguished, and the war whoop had ceased to arouse them, and after subduing the wilderness, agriculture, manufacturers, and commerce, steadily advanced. The colonies were in an unparalleled state of improvement, and exhibited a determination of actual independence. The suspicion and jealousy of the mother country was aroused, and such acts were enacted as tended to paralyze the efforts of this enterprising country; burdens were imposed, tyranical laws enforced, and a course was pursued, by the mother country, which had a direct tendency to bring the colonies into actual dependence upon and subjection to her authority. But that spirit which had subdued the wilderness, repelled the savage foe, which had in fact suffered all the difficulties of the new settlement for the enjoyment of civil and religious liberty, was not to be crushed, even in infancy, without an effort for preservation. Although not all the actual settlers of this new world, yet the sufferings of their fathers were fresh in their memory, and they exhibited a determination not to disgrace their noble sires. Long they suffered from the oppression heaped upon them, before even a murmur of complaint was heard. Encouraged by such compliance, new acts of oppression were enacted, and the old ones enforced with new rigor. Yet still such was the deference they paid to England, instead of repelling it with force and asserting their rights at the mouth of the cannon, a remonstrance against those acts, and a petition for redress of grievance, were the only measures pursued by the colonies.

Supposing this deference to be servile submission—that in their destitute situation, without arms, without an army, or a revenue to raise or support one, they were incapable of resisting their superior force: without the least regard for the welfare of their lawful subjects, the mother country persevered in her course, and attempted to subject the colonies at all hazards and make them subservient to her interest alone. In this they reckoned without their host. The spirit of liberty had not forsaken the western world. Although they were willing to be dutiful subjects, they were unwilling to be slaves. The toils, sufferings, privations, and conflicts which they had already encountered and overcome, were not forgotten; neither were they to be in vain. After remonstrance and petition had failed, then was aroused the spirit of their sires; then were they willing to hazard their all in defence of that freedom which they had so anxiously sought. On the memorable 4th of July, 1776, appealing to the author of their existence and the God of armies for the rectitude of their conduct, they declared themselves free and independent; pledging their lives, their fortunes, and their sacred honor, to support that declaration. What an eventful period was that when men, bearing the impress of the heavenly gift of liberty, threw off all allegiance to the mother country, declaring the most powerful nation in the world, in war, enemies; in peace, friends. The history is to well known to require from me a minute detail.

A colony destitute of every means to carry on a warfare, without an army, arms, or ammunition, yet trusting to the righteousness of her cause, unfurls the banners of freedom, and invites her votaries to rally round her standard and be free, or sacrifice their lives in the conflict. The call was not in vain: the angel of liberty had not taken his flight from the world. The patriotic sons of America hear the call, and leave all other concerns and fly to the battle-field. The conflict for independence was long and arduous; but liberty, civil and religious, was the reward of their labors. The proud empire who refused to hear the remonstrance of her children, was compelled to acknowledge them of age, and capable of governing themselves. The conflict over, and the din of battle no more heard within our borders, with rapid strides America emerged from her former obscurity, and took her stand among the nations of the earth. Although scattering clouds at times obscured the political horizon, they were soon dispelled, and liberty with its cheering rays dispensed its blessings upon this patriotic people. The arts and sciences dispensed their rich blessings. Manufactures were encouraged; the fruits of the soil amply repaid the husbandman for his labors, and every sea was soon visited with the banner of the United States. Her settlements were extended, and the wilderness 'budded and blossomed like the rose;' our country grew in strength and foretold her future greatness. England, retaining her former jealousy—justly fearing she might diminish the lustre of her crown—saw the example she already set to other nations to throw off allegiance to sovereigns and be free—basely insulted our flag and infringed upon the dearest rights of Americans. The impressment of American seamen into the service of a foreign power was, and justly too, considered a sufficient cause to again appeal to arms for the protection of our privileges. The din of battle again resounded through our land. The horrors of war were again experienced; but the proud monarch was again compelled to acknowledge the supremacy of American arms, and to respect the American flag. The honor of America was advanced by this appeal to arms, and the just rights of the United States was recognized. Our star spangled banner was waved in triumph, and all nations of the world compelled to respect it. Peace was again restored, and the visible prosperity of the republic advanced with increased rapidity.

While the patriots of the revolution and the sages of America were resting in security, proud of the triumphant march of free principles and equal rights, supposing the free institutions of America were fixed upon those inimitable principles, which the revolution of empires could never effect, a secret society was slowly, but with a steady and determined step, possessing itself with all the power and danger of monarchs. Although proverbially jealous of their liberty, and ever watchful of open enemies and foreign powers, still they suffered a secret combination to increase in strength, numbers, and power, until it had become the most powerful combination in the world. The Inquisition of Spain, with all its terrors and power, possesses less means to carry into execution its designs. Secret societies, of different kinds, have, at various periods attempted to arise; but the powerful voice of public opinion has stopped their progress on the very threshold of their existence. A society composed of the veterans of the revolution, whose professed object was to continue those offices of kindness which had been so often administered in their struggle for independence, and keep in remembrance those trying scenes, created such jealousy, and called forth the energies of the sages to such an extent, that the society soon dwindled away. Although public opinion was so strong as to stop the progress of such a society, composed of members who had been tried in the hour of adversity, and had not been found wanting—men of sterling integrity and unyielding patriotism; yet the Masonic institution has so artfully concealed its real principles, that it has extended itself over the Union, increased its members to an alarming number, accumulated funds to an enormous amount, possessing means to learn its enemies, and power to punish them. Although the production of a foreign power, and deriving its authority from foreign lords, still the American republic has suffered it to increase to its present gigantic size, until they openly boast of possessing sufficient power of choosing the officers, and directing the government of the United States. So powerful does this society consider itself, that its members unblushingly tell the citizens of America, 'You have a secret society existing among you, whose power and influence is so great that the government itself cannot put it down; nay, the world in arms, cannot suppress it.' This is no picture of fancy; neither are the shades too highly colored. It is their own insulting language to freemen, openly declared and published to the world. To show distinctly, what they conceive to be the power and influence of their society, permit me to extract from a public address delivered by one of their devoted subjects on one of their festive days. After describing its pretended origin and its vast increase of number, he exclaims—'What is Masonry now? It is powerful! It comprises men of rank, wealth, office, and talent, in power and out of power, and that in almost every place where power is of any importance; and it comprises among the other class of community to the lowest, in large numbers, and capable of being directed by the efforts of others, so as to have the force of concert throughout the civilized world. They are distributed, too, with the means of knowing each other, and the means of keeping secret, and the means of co-operating—in the desk, in the legislative hall, on the bench, in every gathering of men of business, in every party of pleasure, in every enterprise of government, in every domestic circle, in peace and in war, among its enemies and friends, in one place as well as another; so powerful indeed is it at this time, that it fears nothing from violence, either public or private; for it has every means to learn it in season; to counteract, defeat, and punish it. The power of the Pope has been sometimes friendly, and sometimes hostile. Suppose now, the opposition of either should arouse Masons to redress its grievances. The Jesuits with their cunning might call on the holy brotherhood, and the holy brotherhood on the holy alliance, and they might all come, too, and in vain. For it is too late to talk of the propriety of continuing or suppressing Masonry, after the time to do so has gone by; so, good or bad, the world must take it as it is. Think of it, laugh at it, hate it, or despise it, still it is not only what I have told you, but it will continue to be—and the world in arms cannot stop it—a powerful institution.*

Such, fellow citizens, is the description of the influence and power of the Masonic institution, by one of its orators, and published to a public of freemen. An institution whose members have been supported and protected by the laws of this republic, until it assumes its present enormous power, and now bids defiance to the government which has fostered them in its bosom, and attempts to give the deadly sting. Shall it be said that in a free government which professes to distribute justice equally upon all, whether high or low, rich or poor, we have an institution which, in the language of a bravado, boasts that its strength is so great that even the government itself is unable to put it down; that it is too late to talk of the propriety of continuing or suppressing Masonry; so, good or bad, the world must take it as it is? Yes, fellow citizens, we have an institution within our borders, and in the midst of us, composed of citizens of a free government, which proudly boast that the jesuits, with all their cunning, the Pope, the combined force of European monarchs, all concentrated, nay, the world in arms, cannot stop its progress; that it will continue to be what it now is, a powerful institution.

Freemen of America! have you been faithful guardians of your liberties, to permit this institution to assume such powers? Are you now faithful sentinels, and will you allow this society to make farther progress? This boast of theirs was not an idle tale, told to amuse a few fanatical hearers, but was a true and faithful portrait of the power Masons actually believed their institution to possess. This declaration was made and published to the world in 1825, when it was unknown their force would require concentration to possess the force of concert throughout the civilized world, to their proud institution. The disastrous events of September, 1826, show conclusively this was not the fancy of one wild brained member, but the opinion of the whole Masonic body. They learned its enemy, and exercised the power to counteract, defeat, and punish it. The magazine of Niagara tells the tale of their punishment; but may Heaven avert the disastrous event of their counteracting all its enemies. A brief history of this institution, together with its professed objects, and a delineation of its true principles, may not at this time be unappropriate. To deceive its votaries and allure the unsuspecting into its snares, this institution attempts to trace its origin to the earliest period of existence; that it was the gift of God to man; that its regular organization was executed by men inspired of heaven to ameliorate the condition of man, and smooth his path through his probationary existence. Some assert it to be the handmaid of religion, given as an assistant to point man to his duty here, and a sure way of gaining admittance to the abode of happiness, or Masonically speaking, to the Grand Lodge above. They have heaped a mountain of pretensions upon it, and offer no proofs to support their assertions but Masonic traditions, which are too absurd to be listened to in mo-

---

* Oration of Brainard, before Union Lodge, New London, Connecticut, June 24th, 1825.

ments of reflection. Nay, so absurd are many of their traditional histories, that the greatest devotee* to Masonry has been compelled in his public addresses to pronounce them as absurd, contradictory, and ridiculous; so much so, that the candidate can, from that Holy Book upon which she requires her members to swear allegiance, prove them to be deceptions of the basest kind. As well, says he, might we believe that the sun travels round the earth instead of the earth round the sun, as to believe in all the incongruities which are taught in the lodges, [symbolic degrees.] Yet so successfully has she trumpeted forth her own praise, so completely has she shrouded herself in mystery, that a majority of her subjects have been last to ascertain her real origin; and for that very reason suppose she must be ancient, and have claimed as her supporters the kings of Israel, the prophets, saints, and apostles, for no other possible reason than Masonry has so instructed them. Masonry, it is true, is ancient, as the laying of brick and stone to form a habitation for man; but the supporters of speculative Free Masonry despise so humble an origin for their mistress, and assert the word from which their institution derives its name, means those initiated into the sacred mysteries.† The true history of Masonry is this:—A society of honest mechanics was formed with established rules to govern themselves in contracting for work, and also for governing their apprentices and journeymen, or Fellow Crafts. Every symbol and article of clothing of the present day show this conclusively. Whence do they derive the origin of their apron, trowels, plumblines, gavel, &c. if not from operative masons? What do thousands of their members know of the technical terms of this laboring class of men, such as the entablature, the plinth, the die, and surbase? In the mouth of operative masons they have an important meaning; but in the mouth of a member of speculative Free Masonry who is initiated into the sacred mystery, they mean nothing.

In the years 1716 and 1717 an attempt was successfully made to convert this system into speculative Free Masonry; and when at length many of different trades were admitted, they raised it above its *vulgar* origin and attempted to load it with pretensions of honor and antiquity; the records and constitution were committed to the flames that they might not give a lie to their assertions. Three degrees only were then invented, and these were in 1720 passed into the different nations having communication with Great Britain. At this time her historians are capable of giving the name of the Grand Master, the date of the warrant to a year, and the place where it was sent. Do they give the dates of warrants, or the operation of this society, previous to this? They are as silent as the grave from the days of king Solomon down to 1717. Could they not have given the history with the same accuracy, previous? The first introduction of Masonry into America was by a warrant granted by the Right Honorable and Most Worshipful Anthony Lord Viscount Montague, Grand Master, &c., dated April 30, 1733; and the first lodge ever held in America was in Boston, July, 1733. This lodge granted ten warrants for other lodges in different parts of the colonies. Although Masonic history was careful to give the days in which the lodges met in after years, yet her historians give no account of her progress for a number of years. In 1755 a grant was given by another individual to hold a lodge in the same place as the former; so much was the society in its infancy at this time that no established rule or organization was formed, and an infringement was here made upon their established customs. The next meeting of the society which they give an account of was in December, 1769, when, the historian asserts, was celebrated the festival of the Evangelist in due form. A period of thirty-six years has elapsed since the formation in America of the society claiming relationship with the apostles, ere they thought of commemorating the birth-

---

* See Dalcha's Oration, p. 43, Sovereign Inspector General.
† Smith, p. 35. Hale's Speculative Masonry, p. 15.

day of their Christian patron. This is the first celebration of that day, within my knowledge, on record. Little or no mention is made of the progress of light until 1777, when a new lodge was formed. In so little repute was the society held in that day, that it fell into disrepute: once, no less than three regular formations are mentioned. But in 1783 a committee was appointed to draft resolutions explanatory of the power and authority of the Grand Lodge. Thus we find, five thousand seven hundred and thirty-three years after its pretended existence, a society claiming Solomon, king of Israel, for their Grand Master—and under whose patronage a regular organization was formed—a society which they pretend has continued the same in every age, whose regular or constitutional powers were not defined—its powers were now established, and Masonry slowly extended itself.

Until the nineteenth century Masonry made but little progress in America, but then is recorded its rapid spread over the United States. Not a village could make its appearance in the wilderness, but some Mason would establish a lodge, to give himself and brethren an undue advantage over the common citizens. Although the Masonic historians with minuteness relate the particulars of the formation of the first lodge in America, giving the date of the first warrant and the name of the individual granting the same, with all his Masonic and civil titles, he gives the name of no one who stands as godfather to a chapter. No warrant was ever granted by any power to hold a chapter in America. The Masonic history of this degree in this country is very short. It commences by saying, 'Previous to 1797 no Grand Chapter of Royal Arch Masons was ever organized in America; previously a competent number of companions under the sanction of a Master's warrant, exercised the right of Royal Arch Masons.

It cannot be unknown to the public that a Master's warrant cannot authorize work, (as Masons may say) beyond three degrees. Yet, a number of men, under the sanction of such a warrant, exercise the authority of conferring four more degrees than their warrant authorizes. Can it be possible that degrees founded in the days of Solomon, which in its tradition traces events which occurred at the building of the temple, which contains important secrets hid from the world for the period of seven hundred years, had no regular form of government, no proper manner of conferring its favors? The whole truth is, these degrees are an innovation on what Masons call ancient Free Masonry. Its introduction called forth animadversions from the warmest supporters of Masonry. The first formation, I believe, was of Horodim Chapter, in 1787. Mr. Preston in his first editions makes no mention of any degrees above the Master, but in his later he mentions the formation of this chapter, and expresses fears for the consequences of some modern innovations in Masonry.—Huchinson's spirit of Free Masonry, published in 1794 treats of three degrees only; Ahimon Rezon, published in London, 1764, treats, of three degrees; Jachin and Boaz, published 1770, gives a true history of all Masonry then in existence, but is silent concerning any degrees above the Master's. The book of constitutions of Massachusetts, edition of 1792, which professes to give a complete history of Free Masonry both in England and Massachusetts, makes no mention of any degree in either country above the lodge of Master Masons; Laurie's history of Free Masonry gives no degree above the Master's, but says in the constitution of the Grand Lodge of Scotland that all ancient St. John Masonry is contained within the three degrees; Smith's use and abuse of Masonry declares the same thing; the union of the Grand Lodge of England with the dissenters, ratified in London, 1803, delares all ancient Free Masonry contained within the lodges of Master Masons; the Free Mason's Library, written since, declares there are but four degrees of Masonry; Mr. Cole, the writer, says, 'This opinion accords not only with the sentiments of the oldest but best informed Masons with whom I have conversed, but is agreeable to written and printed documents in my

P p

possession. The following degrees which have been manufactured within a few years past are merely elucidatory of the second, third, and fourth degrees.' He then enumerates all the degrees conferred by a chapter.

At the time these authors wrote, Masonry was so much in its infancy, the most unblushing writers on Masonry dare not claim the degrees conferred in a chapter as belonging to Free Masonry; but as they had deceived the world in the origin of the three degrees, their writers soon had the effrontery to claim the highest degrees as ancient. We soon found them enumerating the degrees of Masonry as high as thirty-three, and in 1816 they have increased as high as forty-three, and at this day they attempt to claim ninety-six regular degrees in Masonry, and all them founded in the days of Solomon; and some of them go back to the antideluvian days without finding any mention of them until 1786, or acknowledged as belonging to their system until 1797. The truth is, too many of what they call the vulgar, and European Princes, and American aristocrats, could not meet upon a level with the vulgar crowd; and in later days the managers have found it to increase the Masonic funds, and consequently, their own interest. Such, fellow citizens, is the brief but correct history of Free Masonry.

If this society has been presumptuous in claiming for herself antiquity, no less effrontery has she exhibited in her professed objects and avowed privileges. Her members state that the principles of speculative Free Masonry have the same co-eternal and unshaken foundation; contain and inculcate the same truth; and propose the same ultimate end as the doctrines of Christianity taught by Divine Revelation. 'The pious will embrace it as an auxiliary to human happiness, and a guide to a blessed immortality.' 'Here [that is, in speculative Free Masonry] we view the coincidence of principle and design between the Christian scheme and speculative Free Masonry, with that pleasing admiration which satisfies inquiry, and clearly proves our system based on the rock of eternal ages.' 'Here [in a lodge room] we are taught all the combined and unspeakable excellencies of the Omnipotent Creator. To adore that Divinity whose goodness and mercy are so astonishingly displayed in the salvation of man.' 'No moral character is regarded by the *Divine Being with greater complaisance than a Mason.*' 'Masonry preaches the eternal word manifested in the flesh.' 'Masonry embraces the subject matter of Divine economy.' 'Masonry presents to the mind the co-equal and co-eternal existence of the adorable Trinity.' Such are the principles and avowed objects of Free Masonry. It is by such palpable falsehoods and great pretensions she has allured thousands into her deceitful snare. If such are indeed its principles, who would not be a Mason? Who would not belong to a society whose members are regarded by the Divine Being with the greatest complacency? It is with such pretensions as these she has deceived the public, and been permitted to extend her dominions. So powerful have been her bonds, and such influence has she exerted, that few in any former period of her existence have dared to deny her authority or lay naked her hidden enormities. An opposition to Masonry by any number of her members would have proved their inevitable ruin. She arrogated to herself the privilege of publishing her enemies to the world as unworthy and vicious vagabonds; of deranging their business; and her influence has been so great that she has been able to do it effectually. Some few have attempted to divulge her true character—to disrobe the harlot and expose her native ugliness to the common gaze; but dearly have they paid for their temerity. But the strong bonds which bound them to this moloch are broken. Men, trusting to the free institutions of their country for support, have dared to brave Masonic vengeance, and expose the secret enormities of this dark conspiracy against the liberties of man; she has filled the measures of her iniquities; her crimes are of a scarlet die; they have aroused insulted freemen to investigate her principles; she must pass the ordeal of public opinion: if her principles are compatible with our free institutions, she can still exist; but should she prove to be a hypocrite, a base dissembler—if in her secret places she generates the principles of discord, sanctions the crimes of her votaries, exercises an undue influence in the councils of the nation, she must fall, and receive the contempt of an insulted and much abused public.

That Free Masonry inculcates such principles as have been quoted, the most credulous cannot but believe, should they investigate one single moment. The same authors who so shamefully say she ' is in body and substance the whole duty of man as a moral being, and its precepts equally sacred and equally precious with Christianity;' that it inculcates the deep mysteries of the Divine Word, in whom all the fulness of the Godhead dwelt bodily;' say, ' the wandering Arab, the civilized Chinese, and the native American; the rigid observer of the Mosaic law, the followers of Mahomet, and professors of Christianity, are all connected by the mystic union in one indissoluble band of affection.' How absurd that the Jew should meet in good fellowship with a society which teaches that in Christ the fulness of the Godhead dwelt bodily, that the wandering Arab should unite with men in precepts equally sacred and precious with Christianity; and how delighted must the native of the forest be with all these Heavenly principles taught in the Holy Bible, which has been to him a sealed book, whose pages of inspiration he never understood, and in whose precepts he never was instructed. Masonry becomes all things to all men, says a late author. ' This is the true character of the harlot: she loves every body dearly, and him with whom she cohabits, supremely; she also reveres the Bible in America, the Koran in Turkey, and the Shaster in India, as equally worthy of acceptation, and revealing the whole duty of man: she possesses the remarkable quality of being the same thing and its opposite to any extent required.' Instead of hearing within the lodge the warning voice and the duty of man explained, often is heard the noisy bacchanalian revels, occasioned by too frequent calls from labor to refreshment. The true principles of Free Masonry are not found in her Monitor, neither are they published by her orators. These are prepared for the public, who are never admitted behind the scenes to view the actors in their common apparel. They consist solely in her senseless ceremonies and unhallowed obligations. To these, then, we appeal. Secret societies of any description should awaken the suspicion of freemen living under a government whose acts are open to the scrutiny of all its subjects; no society, however limited it may be, should be suffered to be regularly organized with regular and stated meetings, whose objects are unknown. Such societies are not the product of republican soil. They are the legitimate offsprings of tyranny. The former reign of darkness and despotism were effected by means of secret societies. To secret societies can be distinctly traced the conspiracies which have convulsed Europe. When a society becomes so regularly organized as to defy the scrutiny of government, the public should demand an investigation of its principles. The Masonic society has become regularly organized, possessing one grand governing power which extends over the whole United States, with stated periods of meeting; has elected its officers, who hold them for seven years; and its real object is unknown to the public. It is also divided into smaller governments whose authority extends over every part of the state in which the same is held, and again subdivided into lesser or auxiliary societies who exercise authority over its own immediate members, but all subject to the controlling power of the general grand society. Thus there is one grand connecting link existing from a simple lodge to a Grand Chapter, Encampment, and Consistory; all pursuing one grand object, and that object unknown to all but those initiated into their sublime mysteries. The members of this society are found in every important station in the Union. In the legislative hall, on the bench, in all the executive departments: in fact, distributing among and commingling with us in all the scenes of life, and all of them, in their own language, 'capable of being directed by the efforts of others.' With such an organization, its officers regularly chosen, from the 'Most Puissant Sovereign Inspector General,' 'Deputy Sovereign of Sovereigns,' down to the simple 'Worshipful Master and Wardens,' they possess to an alarming degree the power to destroy any government, however pure or well fortified. Although a small minority, yet with such a powerful combination, such facilities to concert its plans of operation, no power could stop the progress of such a conspiracy. In their own language, the 'Jesuits with all their cunning might call on the Holy Brotherhood, and the Holy Brotherhood on the Holy Alliance, and they all might come too, and in vain, for the world in arms cannot stop it.'

Such is the power of the Masonic institution, unassisted by other means than the regular distribution of power. But the danger increases ten fold, when, in addition to her secret meetings, she binds her members to silence, under no less penalty than an ignominious and inhuman death, to forever conceal her dark conspiracies from the world. She possesses a mystic language by which she can communicate all her wants, and make known her objects, unknown to and unperceived by those unacquainted with her mysteries. Whence the necessity of an unknown language, in a government providing for all the honest wants of its subjects? Knaves and villains only need a mystic language. Honest men need them not. But Masonry possesses them; and it is one of her grand principles and most powerful engine to carry into effect her secret and unwarrantable acts. She also requires her subjects to swear they will obey all regular signs or summons, given, handed, sent, or thrown them by the hand of a brother, or from the body of a lodge or chapter; and conform to all her rules and regulations: should she require her summons sent, she binds her members to perform this duty, should they in its performance have to do it bareheaded, barefooted, and on frosty ground. Thus distributed, and possessing such powers, no government can be safe, should they arise and unite their strength to overthrow it. Should her plans be concerted and require the aid of her subjects, they must obey all her summons, no matter what may be its import, and arouse the energies of the brethren to bring them to the field of battle, or act as occasion might require. They are sworn to sound the alarm, to notify all, should they do it barefoot and on frosty ground. Provision is made in their code for the most extreme case that can possibly arise. So distributed are her members that her whole force can receive the summons and concentrate before the government can receive the alarm. But to cap the climax of Masonic government, she requires her subjects to solemnly swear to conceal the secrets of a companion, murder and treason not excepted. What facilities are here offered to the ambitious! What safeguard can avert the impending tempest? Without the least danger, a member of this infernal institution can propose to citizens of this free government schemes of treason, should he do it with a charge of secrecy; for however disposed to support our free institutions, his hearers must remain for ever silent, their lips must be forever hermetically sealed. No punishment can be awarded to so daring villains, should they confide the secrets only to worthy companions. No government was ever formed, so powerful and well organized for plans of operation. Possessing such means, well may she bid defiance to the 'world in arms!'

In this society can be distinctly traced the spirit of the Illuminati; and from her were lighted those fire brands of discord which ravaged France in her revolution, and extinguished all rational liberty. What security can we possibly possess in our government with such a society? Should she be suffered to increase in the same ratio for a few more years that she has for the last ten or fifteen, from her dark caverns and midnight conclaves would issue some despotic and ambitious Cæsar, who, with wide spread desolation, would destroy the labor of our fathers; and our country, instead of the land of Li-

liberty and happiness, would become the oppressed land of Masonic tyranny. If such are not her objects, why does she guard herself with such impenetrable barriers? Does the benign Gospel, whose handmaid she stiles herself, require such secrecy, and such impious oaths? Does the dispensation of charity require such regulations? Does the propagation of morality require such aid? No: the only reason for her shrouding herself in such impenetrable darkness and mystery, is because her 'deeds are evil, therefore she chooses darkness rather than light.' The only safety we can possess consists in the patriotism of her leading members, and this has been the great bulwark of her defence. But has she not ambitious aspirants registered in the archives of her lodge? Have we not seen the man who has been elected to the second office in the gift of a free people, attempt the overthrow of our government? What security then is this? In some desperate moment, smarting under wounded defeat, some powerful and ambitious man may survey the materials, and concentrate the force of the institution to obtain the object of his ambition. It is too powerful an engine to be left in the hands of any man or set of men; and our own safety, our allegiance to our common country, the experience of past ages, all unite in one loud appeal to the freemen of America for the total annihilation of speculative Free Masonry. Should our country, however, escape the alarming danger of overthrow from this society, she inculcates those of a lesser grade which effectually infringe upon our dearest rights as citizens of the elective franchise. By requiring her members to swear, as she does in some chapters, to 'vote for a companion before any other of equal qualifications;' to require under the sanction of a barbarous oath, to always 'support his political preferment in opposition to any other;' she places her own chosen children in every station of our government; and they, after obtaining complete control of the executive, legislative, and judicial departments, must and will dispense their patronage upon the members of the institution, which forms a complete Masonic government—a government within a government. This secret influence exercised in our elections is a source of great corruption, and attended with great danger to the government itself. The firm support, the main pillar of a republican government, is the free choice of its rulers given to the electors. But if our rulers are to be made in a lodge room, and all the brotherhood bound on oath to support such candidates, then indeed is the choice taken from the people, and eventually the overthrow of the free institutions will be the inevitable consequence. When her obligations require her subjects to assist each other so far as to extricate them from any difficulty, whether 'right or wrong,' then are the fountains of justice polluted, and the crime becomes sullied by Masonic influence. We have no security for the faithful administration of justice, while such obligations are administered and adhered to. A felon may be arraigned for an offence against the laws of his country; should he belong to this society, no punishment can be awarded him adequate to his crime. Such has been the influence of Masonry that few jurors have been empannelled without finding at least one Mason among them. No matter if a Masonic juror has taken an oath a 'true verdict to find, according to evidence,' he has taken a Masonic obligation paramount to his civil one, and of much more horrid import, to shield the culprit whether right or wrong; but should this fail him, he gives the grand hailing sign to the executive, and the sword of justice is averted. Neither have we any security for the impartial administration of justice between man and man. A Masonic juror is bound to aid a brother whether right or wrong; and the sanctity of a witness' oath to tell the 'truth, the whole truth, and nothing but the truth,' is lost in his previous oath to conceal the secrets of a companion, '*murder and treason not excepted.*' Such obligations have a direct tendency to promote crimes of the deepest dye. It emboldens the criminal to commit greater crimes by the facilities afforded him in this oath of secrecy. Few persons individually commit crimes of great magnitude; and fear of exposure in ordinary cases would deter him from communicating his designs: but in the present case he runs no risk. Should he require an accomplice, he finds a Master Mason—he confides his intended crime to him ; with perfect knowledge he is bound by an oath to conceal the same, should it be less than murder and treason. Should it exceed these, he seeks a companion Royal Arch Mason. He communicates his intended purpose to him, requires his aid: perhaps he finds a companion who will not stoop to commit such acts : he readily answers, Do as you choose, but recollect you are bound to keep the secrets of a companion, 'murder and treason not excepted.' It necessarily familiarizes the young noviciate with the relation of the most horrid crimes; and however honest he may be when first caught in her snares, from the recital of actual crimes, he is impressed with a belief that his oath of secrecy forbids his communicating the same. It emboldens *him* to commit crimes. Is it uncharitable to suppose that many of the corruptions which have been committed by our lawgivers have been done by the members of this society, under the sanction of Masonic obligations? The same facilities are offered for her subjects to effect their purposes in the legislative hall, as in the commission of crime; and there are but too many who are ready to accept of the inducements she holds forth. In ordinary cases, the offer or acceptance of a bribe would be attended with the fear of detection; but in this case there is none, unless some members should consider their obligation to their country paramount to all others. An account of this kind is now registered on the journals of Congress, when a bribe was offered a member to assist in some monied concerns. This bribe was offered under the sanction of Masonry. The words were as follows:—' I give it you as a man and a Mason, and hope you belong to that society.' If one case can be found where the exposition was made because the person was not a Mason, or considered his duty to his country of more consequence than that to Masonry, have we not reason to fear that too many of the mysterious acts of our lawgivers spring from the same corrupt source? Too much facility is offered for bribery and corruption in so important a branch of our government. Fellow citizens! these are the true principles of Masonry, disrobed of all her pretensions. Is not a society, bound by such ties, and possessing such power, which has exercised such influence, of great danger to our republican institutions ? Are you not bound by your love of country, and by the blood of martyrs who fell in our glorious revolution, to take decided measures to stop the progress, and entirely overthrow the society of speculative Free Masonry ? Should you need other facts to stimulate you to such a glorious act, review the bloody scenes of September, 1826. If you are deaf to the voice of reason, let those transactions, added to the conduct of this society since that period, arouse you to exterminate this hydra-headed monster. You have seen the crime of kidnapping, arson, and murder, committed by members of this society, and under such circumstances as leave no doubt they were the legitimate productions of their laws. You have seen the public press, the palladium of liberty, silent as the grave on these important subjects. You have seen those guilty of such acts screened from punishment through Masonic influence. You have seen your fellow citizens who attempted to investigate this transaction, and raised their voice against them, visited with vindictive and malevolent persecution by this society. All this you have seen ; and are you not prepared to act on such an occasion ? A fearful gloom has indeed been spread around, but the prospects are brightened. Freemen have aroused to assert their rights. They have indeed boasted that the government, the world in arms, is unable to suppress Masonry. This may be so; but public opinion, stronger than the government itself, is able to accomplish this glorious work. We wish not to array the world in arms against them. It must be a bloodless victory. Their principles are now divulged. This day commences a revelation of all their unhallowed orgies. Men, trusting to the protection of an intelligent community, have commenced, and will disclose the utmost secrets of that blood stained institution. To secure victory, it is necessary that these revelations be promulgated to the uttermost bounds of our country. A knowledge of the facts is all that is requisite to assert the rights of freemen.

Finally, fellow citizens, in view of all that you have seen, in view of the scenes of violence and iniquity, and of the lawless usurpation of your rights, which have passed before your eyes or come to your knowledge, act as freemen; fulfil your duties as the possessors of this soil, which was once drenched with the blood of your patriotic sires. Look upon the remnant of this invincible band now before you, whose hands, once nerved with almost superhuman strength, are now trembling with age; whose heads, now whitened with years, yet blooming with honors, are fit objects of your veneration. Look upon them, and read in their wrinkled brows, as well as in the history of their bravery, the monition to act as becomes their offspring; to conduct in such a manner, that ere their bones are laid by the side of their compatriots, they may behold the joyful earnest of their country's greatness. Reflect that not their eyes alone, but those who have gone before them, are upon you. Go to your homes; behold the companions of your bosoms and the offspring of your affections, and remember that they too are involved in the welfare of our land; and let a father's care and a husband's love inspire your devotion to your country's cause. Thus let us reflect—thus let us act—and heaven will bless our endeavors—shall crown our land with blessing—and earth shall know no nobler clime than ours.

ANTI-MASONIC STATE CONVENTION.

PROCEEDINGS

Of the Anti-Masonic N. Y. State Convention, held at Utica, August 4th, 5th, and 6th, 1828.

At a convention of Anti-Masonic delegates from the different counties of the state, held at the Baptist church in the village of Utica, on the 4th of August, 1828, prayer by Deacon Jonathan Olmstead, the following proceedings were had: The Hon. James Hawkes, of the county of Otsego, was chosen president, and Thomas C. Green, of Saratoga county, and Seth Abbey, of Jefferson county, were chosen Secretaries.

The resolutions adopted by the Le Roy convention in March last were then read. The following resolutions were adopted:

1. *Resolved*, That a committee of five be appointed to draft resolutions expressive of the sense of this meeting in relation to Free Masonry.

2. *Resolved*, That a committee of one from each county represented be appointed to report what measures ought to be adopted to counteract the influence, and destroy the existence, of Masonic societies.

3. *Resolved*, That a committee of five be appointed to prepare an address to the people of this state.

On the first resolution, the following persons were appointed: Theodore F. Talbot, T. Fitch, J. C. Morris, Alexander Sheldon, James Dean.

On the second resolution, the following persons were appointed: Samuel Humphrey, Henry Parsoll, jun., Laban Hazeltine, Russell Waters, Thomas C. Love, H. A. Read, Alfred Guthrie, James Percival, Thomas Beekman, Timothy Childs, George Davis, Bates Cook, A. McAllister, Calvin Peck, Nathan Pierce, Gideon Hard, William Hawks, William Utter, Thomas C. Green, Ansel Bascom, Thomas Lewis, Israel J. Richardson, Morris F. Sheppard.

On the third resolution, the following persons were appointed: Timothy Childs, John C. Morris, Herbert A. Read, Frederick Whittlesey, Bates Cooke.

The following preamble and resolution were then adopted: Whereas the title and prospectus of a book entitled ' *Light on Masonry*, &c. &c.' compiled by David Bernard, has been read to this convention; and entertaining the fullest confidence in the integrity, zeal, and ability of the compiler; and being deeply impressed with the importance of the proposed publication to the cause of truth and justice, therefore

Resolved, That we recommend the compiler to proceed without delay in the publication of his work ; and we recommend it to the attention and patronage of all the friends of truth, and the cause of civil liberty, throughout the world.

The convention adjourned till nine o'clock the next day.

Met pursuant to adjournment.

The reading of the Royal Arch degree being called for, it was requested that Mr. H. A. Read perform that duty, which was done by him in a plain, clear, and distinct manner: also the Knights of the Christian Mark and Guards of the Conclave.

Mr. Love, as chairman for the second resolution, reported as follows; which report was adopted by the convention.

The committee appointed to consider and report what measures ought to be adopted to counteract the influence and destroy the existence of Masonic societies, in addition to the measures already adopted, report,

1. That it is expedient to recommend to the people of the several counties of this state to establish free presses in their respective counties, and to place the same under the control of discreet and competent persons who will fearlessly publish the whole truth, in violation to the principles, obligations, and tendency of speculative Masonry.

2. That it is expedient to appoint an Anti-Masonic General Committee for the state of New-York, to whom the Anti-Masonic Central Committees for the several counties may report themselves.

3. That it is expedient to recommend to the people of the several counties of this state, who have not already appointed a Central Committee, to appoint such and report themselves to the General Committee.

4. That it is expedient to recommend to the people of the several towns of this state to raise money by contribution, and transmit the same through their respective county committees to the General Committee, for the purpose of defraying the expense that has already been incurred, and that it may become necessary to expend in the publication and distribution of facts and documents exposing the outrages and iniquities of the Masonic institution.

5. That it is expedient to petition the legislature of this state to prohibit the use or administration of extra judicial oaths.

6. That it is expedient for this convention in pursuit of the good objects to be accomplished, wholly to disregard the two great political parties that at this time distract this state of the Union, in the choice of candidates for office; and to nominate Anti-Masonic candidates for Governor and Lieutenant Governor.

7. That it is expedient to publish in a pamphlet form the proceedings ot this convention, together with such disclosures of the secret ceremonies and blasphemous rites of the Masonic institution, as have been made to this convention.

Resolved, That the following persons compose the General Central Committee of the state of New-York:—Samuel Works, Harvey Ely, Frederick F. Backus, Frederick Whittlesey, Thurlow Weed.

Resolved, That the address this day delivered by T. F. Talbot, Esq. be published.

Adjourned until to-morrow, at eight o'clock.
Met pursuant to adjournment.

Resolved, That this convention nominate FRANCIS GRANGER, of Ontario, as candidate for the office of Governor of this state; and JOHN CRARY, of the county of Washington, for the office of Lieutenant Governor of this state.

Resolved, That the General Central Committee shall have authority to notify the meeting of a state Anti-Masonic Convention, to meet hereafter at such time and place as the committee in the exercise of a sound discretion shall designate.

Resolved, That this convention recommend the publication and circulation of a book entitled Free Masonry, by a Master Mason, &c.

Resolved, That the thanks of the convention be presented to the Second Baptist Church and Society of Utica, for the kind and generous offer of their house of public worship for the purpose of this convention.

Resolved, That the thanks of this convention be presented to the president, for the able and impartial manner in which he has presided over the deliberations of this convention.

Resolved, That the proceedings of this convention be signed by the president and secretaries, and published under the direction of the General Central Committee.

Resolutions and Address adopted by the Anti-Masonic State Convention, held at Utica the 4th, 5th, and 6th of August, 1828.

Resolved, That in a republican government the existence of an institution exercising a secret and irresistible control over public opinion, is dangerous to the rights, and may be fatal to the liberties of the people.

Resolved, That it is the right and the duty of the citizens of these United States to use all lawful means to annihilate an institution which has shown itself capable of contriving, effecting, and in a great degree concealing the crimes of kidnapping and murder.

Resolved, That we will not give our suffrages to any member of the Masonic fraternity who adheres to the institution, or acknowledges the binding force of their wicked and blasphemous obligations; nor in any manner directly or indirectly promote their election to any office or place of public trust.

Resolved, That those members of the institution who have courageously broken the shackles of Masonry, and thus restored themselves to the full enjoyment of the rights of freemen, have set an example highly worthy of imitation, and have entitled themselves to the approbation of their fellow citizens.

Resolved, That this convention feel a deep sense of the gratitude due to those resolute men who have torn the covering from Free Masonry, and exposed her deformity and vileness.

Resolved, That the control which Free Masonry has heretofore exerted, and still does exert, over the liberty of the press, is conclusive proof that her existence and influence is irreconcilable with the full possession and enjoyment of our civil rights.

Resolved, That the power which for nearly two years past has baffled every effort to discover and bring to justice the perpetrators of outrage and murder, is fearfully and alarmingly great: it cannot be suffered to exist without the utmost danger to the personal safety of every citizen; and must be destroyed, or it will destroy the government.

Mr. Whittlesey, from the committee appointed for that purpose, reported the following address, which was read and unanimously adopted·

ADDRESS

TO THE CITIZENS OF THE STATE OF NEW-YORK.

Fellow citizens—The principles and obligations of the institution of Free Masonry have, for more than a year past, been the subject of deep and interesting investigation by citizens in certain portions of the state. This institution has existed in this country ever since the foundation of the government. Professing to support morality and religion, to aid the government, and to be the almoners of an extended system of charity, it was suffered to gain footing on our soil. With these high pretensions it was admirably calculated to gain proselytes. The seal of secrecy, which was wisely placed upon the lips of the uninitiated, prevented any exposure of the hollowness of these pretensions to the world; and the piety, the public reputation, or private worth of every novice, were made to add to the character of an institution which he had ignorantly joined. With the rapid and unparalleled growth of our country this institution extended itself, and its numbers increased. The young and thriving settlements of the west have been made the theatre of its extension; and not a village in our fair and flourishing country has grown into any kind of importance, but the enterprize of the brethren of the mystic tie have established the secret empire of the lodge within it. They have endeavored to identify themselves as much as possible with every thing of a public or imposing character. At the foundations of our public buildings; at the commencement of our great projects of internal improvement; in the celebration of our festal days, they have come forth with flaunting banners, their gilded insignia, their pasteboard crowns, and mimic mitres, to catch the breeze of popular favor—to impress respect for their almost divine character, or a salutary awe of their invisible power.

The curiosity, the cupidity, the vanity, and ambition of man, have added to their numbers new and numerous votaries, until this institution has spread itself throughout our whole country; has established a lodge in every village and town in our wide and flourishing state; has extended its ramifications into every shape of society; and has interwoven itself in all our institutions. Its adepts may be found in the executive chair, in the legislative hall, on the bench of justice, in every civil office down to the very lowest and least influential known to our laws; yea, and even in the sacred desk, and among those who minister at the holy altar. Their members had become a host; their influence had increased to a boundless extent; and in the wantonness of their invisible power they had dared to boast that the laws were too weak, that the government was too feeble to check them; and this society, so strong in numbers, so boundless in influence, and so boastful of power, and bound together by secret ties of whose nature we know nothing, hold their meetings under cover of night, and, in this free land, guard the entrance of their secret conclave with naked swords. The citizens of these United States should be jealous of their liberties, for they were bought with the blood of their fathers; (and we are but the immediate offspring of those who paid so dear a price;) they should watch every insidious encroachment upon their rights in whatever covert manner they are assailed, for those rights are the rich legacy from sainted sires, entrusted to us to hand down unimpaired to posterity. And they are wont to be jealous and watchful of such dear privileges, and to resist promptly and firmly every encroachment, whether open or covert, upon their rights; and it is surpassing strange that an institution like Free Masonry, whose principles are unknown, whose obligations are secret, and whose meetings are held under the cover of darkness, should have been suffered to extend itself into such multiplied ramifications without even suspicion or enquiry. The very genius and spirit of our government are essentially opposed to the existence of such institutions. Our fellow citizens desire to see every thing publicly discussed, and openly submitted to the ordeal of public opinion; and are prone to suspect that when all is not open all is not honest.

Other secret societies after a brief existence have been frowned into disgrace by public opinion; but the Masonic institution has grown with the growth of our country until it has become so wanton in its strength that it has dared to set at defiance every effort to pull it down. It might have gone on to this day, still increasing in strength, had they not ventured to inflict the penalties of their secret obligations upon the person of a citizen of our country. The history of the outrage upon William Morgan, it is not important for us to detail at length. If not known to you now, it may be found duly authenticated in the documents within your reach. Suffice it to say, that in September, 1826, he was seized under color of legal process at Batavia, carried to Canandaigua, confined in jail, released by a pretended friend, seized at the very threshold of the prison, and with ruffian violence thrust into a carriage, and transported by relays of horses to the frontiers of the United States, and confined in the magazine of Fort Niagara; that he was there after cool and mature deliberation, inhumanly put to death. Numerous individuals, and all of them Free Masons, were engaged in planning this outrage; numbers in different and distant lodges were concerned and aided in it. Men of respectability and character, some of them high in civil and military office, assisted in the execution of this plan; and the outrage and murder was perpetrated to pay the penalty of the Masonic oath. The rumor of these outrages alarmed the free citizens of the west. A freeman had been torn from his family and his home. The liberties of the country had been violated in his person; and however insignificant that individual may have been, that violation must be atoned. Investigations and inquiries were instituted, and then it is found that the whole Masonic fraternity were disturbed. The characters of those investigating it were abused and vilified; their motives impugned; and vengeance denounced against them. Every impediment that they could throw in the way of investigation was done; every obstacle which ingenuity could contrive was opposed to the inquiry. The public press was overawed; its editors were threatened and denounced if they ventured to breathe the least word in relation to those outrages. This course shed a broad and fearful light upon the transaction; it exposed Masonry in its true colors, and taught all who were not wilfully blind to look to the institution and not to a few misguided men, as the authors of the outrage, and to hold that and its principles responsible for it.

The whole matter began to assume a new complexion. The enormity of the individual outrage, great as it was, began to be overlooked in the fearful dangers which the reflecting began to see were concealed beneath the mantle of secret societies. The principles of an institution which had been heretofore thought to contain something too sacred and venerated to be lightly approached, began now to be discussed with openness and boldness. Its dangerous principles began now to be commented upon, and its evil tendency pointed out: many of the honest and virtuous of its members, emboldened by this freedom of discussion, made further disclosures of the secret obligations; and the oaths which bound the higher degrees together were made public. This was a further and fearful cause of alarm. The citizens looked about them and shuddered at the progress of that dreadful poison which had so nearly approached the vitals of our liberties. Fellow citizens, we owe these men very much who have laid open this institution in its bare and naked deformity to the gaze of the world. The truth of these disclosures has been avouched by so many names whose characters are above reproach for private worth and virtue, and whose motives are above suspicion, that on this subject we are not at liberty to entertain a doubt. The persecutions and vindictive malice with which the business, the prospects, the reputations and characters of these men have been assailed, furnish other evidence, if other were wanting, of the truth of the obligation which inculcates the 'pointing him out to the world as an unworthy and vicious vagabond, by opposing his interest, by deranging his business, and transferring his character after him wherever he may go, by exposing him to the contempt of the world during his whole natural life.' It should be our duty to see that these denunciations fall harmless. These obligations are now before the world; and the whole method of proceeding in the higher degrees will soon be. These contain the principles and essence of Free Masonry. It is to this subject, fellow citizens, we wish to draw your attention. This is not a common occasion or a common topic. We have enlisted ourselves in support of no individual, and of no political party. We have convened to take measures which shall secure the rights of citizens sacred; an impartial administration of the laws; and a due reverence for religion. We honestly conceive the spirit of Free Masonry is essentially opposed to these; and we wish to give you timely warning of the dangers. It cannot be necessary to go into a detail of these dangers to convince you that they are real and not imaginary. It would require but slight reasoning, one would think, to convince you that *secret societies* in a free government are in their best shape useless, if not positively dangerous. But when you are told that the obligations which Free Masons take upon themselves bind them 'to vote for a companion before any other person of equal qualifications;' to always support his 'military fame and political preferment in opposition to another;' to aid and assist a brother in difficulty so far as to extricate him from the same 'whether he be right or wrong;' to keep his secrets in all cases inviolably, 'murder and treason not excepted;' and this under the denunciation of the most horrid penalties which human ingenuity could invent—you need no argument to convince your reason that such an institution is at war with the very genius and spirit of our free government; that it is hostile to all equal rights; that it is a barrier to the impartial administration of justice; that it is fatal to the blood-bought liberty which has descended to us from our sainted fathers. How easy is it for them, under these obligations, to obtain the control of every department of government, and to dispense their patronage so that the whole constituted authorities of the land, from the president's chair to the constable's staff, shall be vested in these brethren of the mystic tie? and will they discharge their official duties faithfully? will they regard their oaths to support the constitution? will they regard their oaths of office? They cannot if they would: they are bound by invisible chains; they are shackled by oaths of more horrible import; with sanctions more highly penal than any obligations which bind a man to his country, or to the due observance of her laws. And what security have we for the impartial administration of justice? The ermine of the bench is sullied by Masonic contamination. The juror's oath is but a rope of sand in comparison with his obligation to extricate a brother '*whether he be right or wrong.*' The avenging sword of justice is stayed in the hands of the executioner; and the pardoning power, in strict consonance with the secret oath, must be interposed to snatch a guilty brother from the punishment due by the laws to his crimes. The witness too, who lays his hand upon the Holy Evangelist, and swears in the presence of God and his fellow men, to tell the truth, the whole truth, and nothing but the truth, cannot and dare not disclose the secrets of a brother, even though his hands have been imbrued in his own father's blood, or madly plotted the ruin of the country of his birth. Fellow citizens is this picture overdrawn? Have you not under your own observation seen members of the fraternity elevated to office in an inexplicable manner? have you not seen the course of justice stayed, the guilty felon escape by means for which you cannot account? It is time at least that the principles of Free Masonry should be understood, if they lead to the above results, as they strike at the very existence of government, at the very foundation of our rights, and at the impartial administration of our laws.

The institution is not more hostile to government and the cause of justice, than it is opposed to morality and religion. That institution cannot be moral which encourages a criminal confidence, and which protects by her obligations bad men, and inculcates the concealment of crime. The landmarks between virtue and vice are thus broken down, and that nice delicate moral sense which distinguishes a virtuous man, is thus in a great measure effaced.

Free Masonry too claims connexion with the family of the Cross, as a handmaid. She claims the Bible a principal light of the lodge, placing it next above the square and compass. She claims to be a guide to a blessed immortality, but seems shocked at the imputation of substituting her darkness for the gospel light. Our most dangerous foes are those who are clad in our own livery; and such a foe is Free Masonry to Christianity. In her ceremonies she personates the Deity, seemingly to honor, but actually to mock the Most High. She ordains High Priests of Jehovah for ever after the order of Melchisedek, in contempt of the Son of God, to whom alone inspiration applies this mysterious title. She clothes her officers in the regalia appointed by the Most High for the house of Aaron, exhibiting with her aprons the holy garments of the ancient priesthood, the ephod, the breast plate, the robe, and the mitre with its inscription, HOLINESS TO THE LORD. She makes the ark of the covenant, the consecrated utensils, and the treasures of the Holy of Holies, common among the emblems of her pretended mysteries. The sacred symbols of man's regeneration through the Holy Spirit—of Him who laid down his life to save sinners—are introduced in solemn mockery at her midnight orgies. She claims some of the apostles to have been patrons of her mysteries; and celebrates their anniversaries. She lifts up her voice in unhallowed prayer for a blessing on her assemblies, refusing to acknowledge the name of the only Mediator. She teaches her pupils that walking on the square, and worthily wearing the white apron, the emblem of innocence, they shall have admission into the Grand Lodge above. She teaches to circumscribe our passions with the compass; and she does not, like Christianity, regard the heart. She teaches a selfish love for the brethren instead of an enlarged philanthrophy to the human race; and in her higher degrees, hatred to her enemies is inculcated, which is a doctrine not of Christ. She places the Koran and the Shaster upon a level with the Bible; but most of all, in all her ceremonies and rights slights the name of the Lord Jesus Christ. Is this then the boasted handmaid of religion? This institution in whose rites and ceremonies the most touching and sublime portions of the Holy Book which holds out to us the promise of eternal life, are represented in the shape of a miserable theatrical farce, and the Almighty God and his holy angels, and the spirits of the blessed made perfect, are personified by weak and sinful mortals? where the touching rites of our blessed religion are mocked by vain men? where the name of our sanctified Redeemer is omitted or introduced in an irreverent manner? where the immortality of the soul is only alluded to by a foul libation from the skull of a traitor? where the life eternal in the heavens is represented as one Grand Lodge, and the Almighty blasphemously typified as the Grand Master thereof? This is surely admirably calculated to cheapen religion, and to teach us to rely upon Masonry instead thereof; or that all religion is only the farce which their ceremonies represent it to be. These are delusions, and it is time they were dispelled. We have now the lights upon which to act. Masonry stands now before us in the deformity of her nakedness. Her ridiculous pretensions, her tinsel ornaments and solemn mummery are now duly appreciated. It is now time to arouse ourselves, and give a check to the spread of her principles before she becomes too powerful for restraint. You ask what is to be done with all the power, the wealth, the talents, and the influence of the fraternity. You ask how can we successfully resist it. There is one engine, and one only, which can be successfully arrayed against her, and that is *public opinion*. Public opinion is the law of this land. Government exists only by this opinion. Public men flourish only by this opinion ; public measures are sustained by this opinion. We are not yet so reduced and enslaved, that public opinion will not bear down every thing opposed to it. It is like the resistless wave of the ocean, and will sweep away every barrier, however secured, which shall oppose itself to it. This opinion speaks through the people ; it speaks in their meetings ; it speaks for a time here ; it speaks through the press, however shackled it may be ; and above all, it speaks through the ballot boxes. This is the only legitimate and effectual expression of opinion in this land : these are the instruments by which the people correct all evils. These means are in our power, and they are the only constitutional means we can use. It is idle to talk about any other expression of opinion than the ballot boxes. Our public meetings, our resolutions, our indignant expressions of disapprobation, will be only ridiculed and mocked at, if we do not use the means of enforcing it which the laws have put into our hands. Do you startle at a resolution not to support any member of the Masonic fraternity for any office whatever ? Reflect that they are bound 'to vote for a brother before any other person of equal qualifications,' and to support his 'military fame and political preferment in opposition to another ;' that with them we have not those equal rights which the constitution guarantees to us. We cannot shut our eyes to the fact that ambitious and designing men have attached themselves to this institution to obtain thereby that preferment to which their merits might not attain in any other way. Let this no longer be a passport to office, and the institution has received its death blow, and it will finally crumble into ruin, and sink into oblivion.

This is a measure which takes from them a large portion of their power, their influence, and their consequence ; and if we do not deceive ourselves, will be found to be one of the most effective measures for the entire destruction of the order. Does this measure look like proscription ? Then is the conduct of every party which has ever existed proscription, and all party politics unjust and proscriptive. If it is considered fair and honorable to shut out from office those who are in favor or opposed to us in any particular measures, then it cannot be deemed unfair or dishonorable to attempt to shut out from office those who are sworn to assist their brethren, to vote for them or aid them, 'whether right or wrong,' and who have it by that means in their power to trample upon our rights, and to impede the impartial administration of justice. Have the members of the fraternity enjoyed our highest offices so long that they can claim any prescriptive right to them ? or is it the people who shall say whom they will elevate to their offices of honor and trust ? We are not, however, embarked in a cause which seeks the elevation of one man or the depression of another. Neither is it individuals with whom we war. Our battle is with the institution and its principles ; and we should rejoice if those who were attached to it would come out from among them, and abandon the institution which we hold dangerous to our liberties.

We address you, fellow citizens, as a body intrusted especially to devise measures for the destruction of this order, and to suggest the means to be used to effect its entire banishment from our free soil. Among the most efficient means are free presses. We have seen, known, and felt how the press has been shackled and overawed, nay, almost literally bound in servitude to the will and wishes of this grasping fraternity. This slavish subserviency of the press has been one of the many means by which they have attempted to control and direct public opinion, and perpetuate the influence of their dangerous principles. By means of the secret and invisible influence which they have exercised over this mighty engine, investigation has been stifled, and the spread of information checked ; and, worse than all, falsehoods the most gross have been planted upon the public, and deceptions the most base have been practised to sustain the tottering empire of their falling order. This evil should be remedied, and those faithless sentinels should meet their punishment in the just indignation of an insulted and deceived community. We earnestly advise that means should be provided in every portion of the state, for the communication of facts and correct information to the public. It certainly cannot be dangerous in this land to intrust an intelligent people with a knowledge of facts sufficient to enable them to decide with judgment upon the great question now at issue. It is important also that an unity of action as well as community of feeling should be established among the friends of our cause, which we cannot doubt will be one great mean in effecting the object we are desirous of accomplishing. For this purpose we have deemed it advisable to erect a common standard, around which all may rally, and by nominating candidates for the two highest offices within the gift of the electors of this state, to appeal to them to say, through the ballot boxes, whether they will sanction an institution whose principles are so fatal to our rights. In selecting candidates for these distinguished stations, it was all important that those should be taken who have shown by their acts that they esteem our cause—a higher and holier cause than any of the mere party contests of the day. In presenting you FRANCIS GRANGER, of Ontario, as a candidate for Governor, and JOHN CRARY, of Washington, as a candidate for Lieutenant Governor, we think we have selected such men. They have both of them, from the earliest investigations of the principles of Free Masonry, shown themselves the friends of our true rights; and both of them have dared to stand forth fearlessly and boldly, at a period when such a course was attended with no little hazard, the champions of civil liberty, and the avowed foes of secret societies. The zeal, ability, and fearlessness with which they have respectively advocated our cause in the halls of the house and the Senate of this state, should embalm them in our hearts, and endear them to our memories. Public sentiment has pointed to these gentlemen as our ablest champions; and we take pride in presenting them to you as candidates for your suffrages, to fill the highest offices within your gift as citizens of this state. Go to the polls then, fellow citizens; exercise that power for the destruction of the Masonic institution which the constitution and laws have put into your hands; and in the performance of that duty remember the solemn warning of the father of our country, to '*beware of all secret self-created societies.*'

JAMES HAWKES, President.

THOMAS C. GREEN, } Secretaries.
SETH A. ABBEY,

SPEECH OF T. F. TALBOT, ESQ.

In the Anti-Masonic New-York State Convention, August 4th, 5th, and 6th, 1828.

Mr. Chairman—The opinions advanced in the resolutions which I have offered on behalf of the committee appointed to prepare them, although long entertained by a large portion of our fellow citizens, may still, however, seem to others harsh and perhaps not well founded. It becomes me, therefore, to lay before the convention some of the reasons which have conducted our minds to the conclusions we have formed. A due respect for my fellow citizens engaged in the same cause to which I have devoted much of my time, has induced me to present these reasons in a more formal shape than is usual, that I may not be supposed to advance without due consideration, the crude and ill digested suggestions of a heated imagination; and that what shall be said may not be mistaken or misrepresented without the power to correct it.

It is not yet two years since a large portion of our state was suddenly aroused from the peace and harmony in which they had long reposed, by the high handed and daring outrages of a body of men whose objects and motives we were for some time entirely unable to ascertain. It was readily perceived that no slight cause nor ordinary inducements could have so entirely subdued that reverence for the laws of our country which had heretofore so uniformly distinguished our countrymen. To discover the powerful motives which impelled them on, has been the work of time and perseverance. In this, as in most other cases, the discovery of truth has been slow and progressive. Like the approach of day to the traveller on the mountain, slight indications of light are discerned long before objects can be distinctly seen—and thus it should be. The mind requires time to accommodate its powers to the full perception of new and unexpected truths. We are sometimes mortified and surprised at our own dulness, in not having sooner discerned what now appears sufficiently plain to our understanding; and we can with difficulty discover the reasons why we have so long been ignorant, when the means of knowledge were at our command.

But if the discovery of truth in this instance has been slow, it has at last been complete and full. Doubts and obscurities have vanished like the mists of the morning before the rising sun. What at first was conjecture, is now certainty. Did we at first suspect that the influence of Masonry was not friendly to the true interests of our country? we now know that it is directly hostile to our dearest rights. Did we at first entertain doubts whether the existence of this secret association was compatible with our republican institutions? we now know that where it flourishes true liberty cannot dwell. Did we at first merely fear that the obligations of the members to each other might not always harmonize with their obligations to their fellow citizens at large? we now know that those obligations are utterly inconsistent with their duty to themselves, their country, and their God. Did we at first suspect that the claims of this society to be the friends of truth were not well founded? we now know that she is the fruitful mother of delusion and of error. If we then felt reluctant to admit her pretensions to be the handmaid of Christianity; we now know that her votaries (of the higher order at least) regard not the precepts, reverence not the ordinances of Christianity, and blaspheme the God whom Christians worship. If at first we suspected her purity; we now know that she is filthy, disgusting, and full of unsoundness—stripped by her own votaries of all her borrowed vestments of pretended holiness, she at last stands before us naked and exposed, in all her native pollution and deformity.

Thus, fellow citizens, reversing the order of nature, and the hitherto progress of knowledge, we trust *light* has arisen in the west which shall soon spread its rays over our whole country. A fire has been kindled which shall not be soon extinguished, but will rapidly, we hope, spread through the fields of error, delusion, and prejudice; consuming the rubbish of Masonic folly, and pouring a flood of light upon the dark recesses of the lodge rooms; exposing the mystery of iniquity which has so long been shrouded in night; sweeping away the receptacles of folly, the haunts of idleness, and drying up the sources of mischief to the weak and ignorant—as the devouring element, when it rages in a great city, is often beneficial, by consuming the receptacles of vice, the hiding places of crime, and making way for the erection of useful edifices and comfortable dwellings. But, fellow citizens, these good effects cannot be produced without your aid, and perhaps your unceasing exertions. It is an important truth which we must never lose sight of, that our civil and political rights and privileges can be preserved unimpaired only by constant vigilance. We owe it to our fathers, and shall disgrace their memory, if we do not try all the means in our power to transmit those rights and privileges unimpaired to our posterity. It will be in vain that any of the conspirators have been, or that any of them shall be, exposed and punished, if the motives which actuated them still continue to operate in full force upon others. It is in vain that we have ascertained those motives to be corrupt, if they are to operate unresisted, and are not counteracted by examining and exposing their pernicious tendency.

But our civil and political rights are not the only proper objects of our regard and watchfulness. Dear to us as they are, and highly as we do and ought to prize them, their value will be diminished to ourselves and our offspring, if their influence of moral principles shall be gradually relaxed and finally destroyed, and the still more important influence of Christianity shall be continually counteracted by constant efforts to connect its institution with one to which it can bear no affinity whatever—an institution which counts among its active supporters and warmest advocates, a large number of men, who, both by their words and their actions, not only manifest an entire disregard of the injunctions of Christianity, but openly deny the divinity of its origin, and make a mock of its most sacred mysteries.

Without intending to occupy your time by unnecessary details, let me barely say, that no two institutions can be selected whose distinguishing characters are so entirely dissimilar. The one delights in parade and show; the other in simplicity and retirement. The benefits of the one are freely offered to all 'without money and without price.' From the advantages of the other, (if any there be,) all are excluded who cannot open her doors by keys of silver or gold. One drawing eagerly to itself the poor and despised of this world; the other courting the rich and the great. One rigidly excluding the most amiable part of our species; the other peculiarly adapted to their natural sensibilities and best feelings, and calculated to promote their importance in society, their comfort in this world, and their happiness in eternity. Away, then, with this and all other vain pretensions and idle claims of Masonry to our regard or reverence. The more they are examined the less will they be valued. They cannot bear the test of truth; they shrink from it, like the sensitive plant from the rude touch of the incautious examiner, and when exposed to its full influence, will wither like the sickly plants when first brought from the obscure light of the hothouse, and exposed to the full power of the meridian sun.

To counteract and destroy the baneful influence so opposed to morality and religion, is a duty not less sacred than to preserve our civil and political institutions from the secret attacks which we believe are constantly aimed at them. Nor let it be said that these apprehensions are unfounded; that these fears are the mere chimeras of distempered minds; that Masonry has no means of injuring our rights or undermining our institutions. It is most manifest that the influence of this association has already been extensively exercised in our country, although the manner of its operation has not always been visible. That it has been exerted for the purpose of giving authority and consequence to men who were not fairly entitled to them. That bad men have from this source found support and countenance, which they ought not to enjoy, and could not receive, from any other source. That the influence of good men is diminished, and their attention withdrawn from those objects most worthy of regard. That by promoting, and in a good degree requiring, the promiscuous assemblage of the wicked and the good, the profane and the pious, the infidel and the Christian, the profligate and moral, the sober and the intemperate—it is calculated to weaken the influence and diminish the respect which is due to virtue. That it promotes useless expense among those who are least able to bear it, and incites to vicious excesses by the seeming necessity of assemblages at the houses of entertainment. That it erects a false standard of excellence, by substituting a useless knowledge of absurd customs and ridiculous legends, for true wisdom and valuable acquirements. That it diverts the attention of its votaries from objects of real and permanent utility, by placing it on objects too frivolous to deserve the regard of reasonable and enlightened minds. That far from being the handmaid of religion, her progress is impeded by it, because it deludes by its supposed morality; diverts the mind from examining and attending to the precepts and sanctions of the Divine law; and because in truth it subtitutes the words of man for the words of God. Nor can we now entertain any doubts that the relative obligations which Masonry imposes upon its members are inconsistent with the obligations of men to society at large, to their country, and their Creator. That their alleged duties to each other are inconsistent with the higher duties which they owe to the laws of their country, and the obligations of charity and humanity to all their fellow creatures. Let me add, that the peculiar structure of the institution qualifies it to effectuate designs and accomplish plans, such as to its members may seem good, however hostile those designs may be to the rights of others.

If these evils, or any of them, may, and in fact do, arise from that source, it will be readily granted that while the fountain remains the impure streams will not cease to flow from it. That while the corrupt tree is permitted to grow, it will continue to produce corrupt fruit. That as the vigor of its growth is increased, its mischievous effects will be more extensively felt. If even one of these evils do in truth originate in that source, its pernicious tendency is abundantly evident. The words of unerring wisdom have assured us, that the same spring cannot send forth bitter and sweet waters.

Let it not be urged, that imperfection is the characteristic of all human institutions. The most zealous advocate of Masonry has not dared to attempt proving, even by the semblance of argument, that she can claim a right to our favor or regard, by the benefits she confers on mankind at large. But, say they, her excellence is concealed from vulgar eyes; her beauties can be seen only by the initiated; her virtues are not blazoned forth to the world: all these are hid by the veil of secrecy. They are indeed secret. 'For eye hath not seen, nor man heard, neither hath it entered into the heart of man to imagine,' their loud assertions, pompous eulogiums, and swelling declamations. Bold claims are indeed made on her behalf. But the time for these to avail her has passed by. Her pretensions will be brought to the test of truth. They can no longer escape rigorous investigation; and if they are found false, they will be pronounced so, by the intelligent people of these United States. It may be matter of just pride to Americans, that it has been reserved for them to destroy the influence of an institution which has continually boasted of its ability to withstand all the power of kings—which proudly asserts that no human force can weaken or destroy her. Let not her votaries deceive themselves by these idle suppositions. She has now a different force to contend with. She may have evaded the power of kings by taking refuge in the ignorance of their subjects. Her vainglorious boastings may have imposed upon those who had no means of investigating their truth, and no interest in exposing their falsehood. What matters it to the poor peasant of Germany, who exercises the authority by which he is not protected, but oppressed. He has no hopes of avoiding the misery which he endures, if indeed his moral susceptibilities are not so deadened by tyranny that he feels not his wretchedness. What interest has the ignorant serf of Russia in the question, whether the secret recesses of the lodge can be, or ever are, used to conceal the conspiracies and cabals by which one military despot is strangled, and another elevated to his place. He is still to remain a slave, and, like the beasts of the field, be bought and sold with the land which he cultivates. Why should the oppressed Spaniard endeavor to expose the dark designs and treasonable projects of Free Masonry. They may sometimes shield him from the power of a detestable tyrant, or save him for a time from the torture of the inquisition.

Shall we be told that no such influence is claimed or can be exerted by Free Masonry in America? What then is American Free Masonry? For what purpose have *two thousand lodges* been organized in these United States? To what use is their vast annual income applied?*

Why are six hundred thousand men united together by mysterious ties, the nature of which are studiously concealed from their countrymen. Studiously concealed, did I say? Nay, they are concealed at the peril of life itself; and recent events have proved that these perils are by no means imaginary. But Free Masonry vauntingly points us to the names of distinguished men whom she has enrolled among her members. It is so, fellow citizens. And are all these lodges organized merely for the purpose of private charity? Is all this income exhausted in deeds of benevolence? Are all these men united so closely, merely to promote conviviality and provide cheer? Are their lives subject to be sacrificed for the preservation of secrets in which the community at large have no interest? Have the great men of our country sought for her highest honors, merely to bear a part in her gaudy shows and pompous processions? Does the statesman of the north and the warrior of the south become rival candidates for the highest office that Free Masonry can bestow, merely that one may wear a higher cap, or broader sash, than the other? Do republicans condescend to receive the empty title of kings and high priests, illustrious knights and princes, for no purpose but to gratify a corrupt taste for insignificant distinctions? Are all these the mere puerile amusements of full aged children? Is it for mere amusement that so many who desire to enjoy the esteem and respect of their countrymen—who claim and obtain the offices and honors she has to bestow—bear a part in the idle parades of Masonry—partake of her profane ceremonies, and load their conscience with her blasphemous obligations? Rather let me ask, is there no secret and well organized influence which can readily make itself felt from one end of the Union to the other? No method of writing to effect a common object, by means which will not bear investigation. No secret obligations to aid one another in projects which are not known to the world. No plan of action which subjects not the agents to that responsibility for their actions, attached to all who are not initiated into the order.

It is our duty and our privilege faithfully to examine these questions; and enough, I trust, has been said to show that they are worthy the grave attention of intelligent freemen. It may, indeed, be true that correct opinions on these subjects do now prevail in a large portion of our state; but the work is not therefore finished—our duty is not therefore performed. We are bound by every tie that connects us with our country and our fellow citizens, not to limit our exertions to the district we dwell in. Such selfishness finds no place in the breasts of freemen. If our own minds have been disenthralled from these delusions—if light has arisen upon us—we cannot contentedly see our fellow citizens groping in darkness. It will, I trust, be our delight to keep alive the sacred flame, and guard it cautiously, as the Roman vestals watched the sacred fire. It may indeed be entering upon an arduous task, and to accomplish it may require patience, fortitude, industry, and zeal. Those who engage in it must be prepared to encounter difficulties not now foreseen. Their motives may and probably will be misrepresented; their objects misstated; their efforts impugned; but in the end they will reap the fruits of their exertions—secure the applause of their own consciences, and the commendation of the good. The period in which we live is favorable to the discovery of truth, and unfriendly to the endurance of error. The various systems of superstition and delusion seem to have had their day; their influence is declining rapidly, and they are daily giving evidence of their tendency to moral dissolution. All

---

* The author of 'Free Masonry,' lately published in the city of New-York, who is a Master Mason, computes from well founded *data*, that their income is not less than 120,000 dollars a year. This volume should be read by every citizen of the United States who regards the welfare of his country.

false lights are fast extinguishing to make way for the true light that 'lighteth every man that cometh into the world.' The dark clouds of superstition and ignorance are rolling away. The clear and beautiful atmosphere of religious knowledge is occupying their place; and the words of the Saviour himself hath assured us, that 'there is nothing hidden that shall not be revealed.'

Let it not be said that in promoting these investigations—in attempting to dispel this moral darkness—we persecute our fellow citizens. It is not so. We war with the abominations of Masonry. We will not that an authority exists among us, which elevates itself above the laws of our country; which can with impunity trample upon those, and which violates without remorse the principles of humanity. We mourn over the delusion which prevails in the minds of so many whom we regard with kindness and esteem. We long to see them freed from the chains of darkness by which they have been bound. We rejoice that they shall soon be free. We would say to them in the language of inspiration, 'Come out of her, that ye be not partakers of her sin.' As well might the benighted Indian cry oppression against the humble missionary who labors to infuse into his mind the light of the gospel. As well might the Hindoo widow cry oppression, because she is urged to descend from the funeral pile which is to consume the body of her deceased husband. As well might the deluded worshipper of Juggernaut cry oppression, because he is withheld from being mangled under the bloody wheels of the idol god.

We may indeed offend the pride of some who have chosen to give a consequence to Free Masonry which she does not possess. And perhaps the blush of shame may suffuse the cheeks of some who see her folly and her nothingness exposed. But the emotion will be salutary, and be succeeded by self congratulation at their removal from a sickly delirium.

But, fellow citizens, we have heard much of excitement, and we have been accused of keeping up an *excitement* in relation to Masonry. The advocates of Masonry who reprobate *excitement* so violently, seem to have forgotten that excitement is not fanaticism. And what great moral benefit, let me ask, was ever conferred upon mankind which was not produced by *excitement*? How was the Christian religion itself propagated but by *excitement*? Are we not assured in the volume of inspiration, that it is good to be zealously affected in a good cause? What but excitement to ameliorate the condition of mankind has sent the missionary of the Cross to the frozen shores of Greenland and the burning sands of Africa? What but excitement has roused the Christian world from the lethargy of centuries, and prompted them to send the Bible to the natives that still set in darkness, to rejoice their hearts with the glad news of salvation—to cheer the lonely Laplander with the blessed hope that his long night may at last end in an effulgent day of never ending happiness—to guide the roving Indian along the true road to the residence of the Great Spirit—to revive the saddened heart of the poor West Indian slave, and teach him that at last he shall be free. What but excitement against tyranny and oppression prompted our fathers to resist the exactions of Great Britain, to risque their lives in the conflict, and finally resolve on liberty or death.

What! shall a free citizen of these United States, in the full enjoyment of life and liberty, be seized upon in open day—torn from his wife and family—carried in unholy triumph through our country—be incarcerated in the very edifice which was erected to defend the liberty of his country—be secretly tried and secretly executed, without even the forms of law? Shall the guilty participators in these foul crimes justle us in the streets—sneer at our reproof—laugh at our efforts to produce legal proof of their guilt, and defy our attempt to bring them before the country; and shall this be passed by in silence lest some should cry out excitement? Shall all these enormities be fairly and distinctly traced to the dark recesses of the lodge rooms—shall we know, from testimony delivered in courts of justice, that the practicability and the proper means of sacrificing lives and destroying the liberty of the press, were coldly discussed in Masonic lodges, and deliberately resolved on—that all this was done to prevent bringing the institution of Masonry into disgrace by publishing a true account of them. And shall no excitement arise in our breast—no swelling of the heart—no heaving of the bosom. Wo be to our country when all these things can take place without being followed by excitement. Shall we see all these rank corruptions boil and bubble in this caldron of abominations, and shall we make no effort to extinguish them.

I would not, sir, have it supposed that I advocate harsh or severe measures to effect even this holy purpose. None such are justifiable—none such ought to be used—none such will be used. We may confidently assert that our fellow citizens who have engaged in this investigation cannot be made instrumental in effecting any unjust measures towards their fellow citizens, however elevated or humble may be their station. Their object has been the discovery and the publication of truth; and if such discoveries have convinced that secret associations ought not to exist in a republic, and have diminished their respect for the adherents of such societies, these effects have necessarily resulted from their causes. No excitements have been used to produce such convictions. They have been the productions of right reason deliberately exercised. The facts fairly presented to them, they failed not to draw from them legitimate conclusions; and Free Masonry must abide the consequences. We see nothing sacred in her which should exempt her from these. With much difficulty she has at length been brought to the bar of truth; and let her not hope to return from it until all her pretensions to excellence, and all her capabilities for crime, have been thoroughly investigated. Neither the shameless falsehoods and swollen verbiage of St. John's day orators, nor the pompous eulogiums of schoolboy declaimers, can any longer save her. Her borrowed plumes will be plucked from her shameless front, and her silken vestments can no longer conceal her impurities. She will be weighed in the balance, and if found wanting she will be consigned to merited destruction. Those who have undertaken the task cannot be driven from it by fear nor by favor. They believe the investigation to be connected with the substantial good of their country, and they will not recede; they have put their hands to the plough, and they will not look back. No motive of self interest prompted them to action, and no fear of loss will deter them from proceeding. They are not seekers for honors or offices, and no fears of such accusations will deter them from inquiring and deciding for themselves how far the influence of Free Masonry may disqualify their fellow citizens for fulfilling the duties of office—how far a secret and constant intercourse with a small body of men distinguished from their fellow citizens at large as a separate society, governed by separate laws and bound to each other by peculiar obligations, may, and of necessity will, influence their minds in the distribution of official favors, or warp their judgments from the straight path of integrity. How far those secret obligations may fetter their minds, and be paramount to or inconsistent with their known obligations to their country in general, they know, and they will remember when called upon to give their suffrages; that the mere habit of frequent and intimate intercourse with a select body of men using the imposing, however abused, name of brother, is not without its influence even upon strong minds; that it improperly contracts the feelings of the heart, and limits the extension of that good will which a true patriot and a wise statesman will desire to feel towards ALL his countrymen, unfettered and unrestrained by opposing influences. I repeat, sir, the men with whom we act in this matter are not needy office seekers. We can point with pride and with pleasure to the great body of our most efficient friends, as men who never have and never will desire office. We can number among them many whose elevation of mind and self respect have never permitted them to use the ordinary and most successful methods of procuring offices, however well they were qualified to perform their duties; who will not sacrifice their independence at the shrine of party, though they are willing to serve their country.

It may perhaps be expected that I should, in the course of my remarks, take notice of an attempt made by some of those venders of falsehoods and tools of party who disgrace our country, to create an impression that this impulse, which has roused a whole community to action, can be used for mere party purposes; and that an eminent statesman had made an attempt to buy it for his own purposes. I cannot consent to occupy your attention by a serious effort to refute a calumny so absurd in itself—so contemptible by the source from which it originated—and so insulting to the patriotism, integrity, and understanding, of many thousands of my countrymen. Be it known to those who have made the assertion and those who have pretended to repel it, that the freemen who have been influenced by this excitement can neither be bought or sold. They aim not to elevate one man or depress another—to aid one political party or injure another. They have higher and holier objects in view, from which they cannot be terrified or diverted by such insignificant accusations. They aim to rid their country of a noxious pestilence which walks in darkness through the land—to take from all parties the power to wield this ' black engine of night'—to dispel the moral darkness in which so many of their countrymen have so long groped—to strike off the base chains which have so long held in ignoble bondage the minds of many thousands of their fellow citizens, and restore them to the full enjoyment of those privileges purchased by the blood of their fathers—to seize this many headed monster by the throat, drag it forth from the murky den in which she has so long concealed herself, and strangle it in open day before its venom had been scattered over the land to corrupt the very fountain of all that is good and valuable in our civil and religious institutions. We may not indeed live to see these objects completely effected; but they are worthy to employ the energies of every generous mind; and he who shall assist to accomplish them will not have lived without benefit to his country.

But, sir, will it be seriously contended, or can it be expected, that all who have aided to lay the foundation for accomplishing these glorious objects, are therefore to be excluded from the service of their country? By what means shall they know that their exertions are appreciated and favored by their fellow citizens? How shall the dishonest or deluded advocates of this system of error and deception be convinced that they can no longer uphold it with impunity? Do you expect aid from the timid, the selfish, or the wilfully ignorant? Will the profane altars of Free Masonry be overthrown by the hands of her General Grand High Priest? Think you that those who have contributed to erect her idle temples will themselves assist to tumble them into ruins? Such is not the usual course of action. What we have cherished as valuable, we are unwilling to believe has at last become worthless. Even the useless bauble which has long hung about us we reluctantly part with.

There are indeed some, and not a few, among us, whose clear perceptions and strong minds have enabled them to discover their true situation—who have nobly dared to be free, and to throw off by one vigorous effort the fetters which have so long bound them to an institution to whose iniquities they could not be blind. With such men we can cheerfully and gladly co-operate in the good work we have engaged in. We feel that for ourselves and our country we owe them much, and we shall not be reluctant to discharge the debt to our utmost ability. We know, in part, what they have encountered, and how they have overcome.

Away then, sir, with all your poor attempts to deter us from the performance of the sacred duties which circumstances have imposed upon us. Let not our opponents amuse themselves with such hopes. They are vain. We trust that we have counted the cost, and that we shall not shrink from the consequences. Our cause is good: we will not abandon it. Our motives are pure: we fear not to have them investigated. Let us be united, and we shall be strong. Let us be prudent and firm, and we shall be successful. May HE who has the hearts of us all in his hands, guide and direct us in all our deliberations, and so control all our exertions, that they may be productive of lasting benefits to our beloved country.

TRIAL OF ELI BRUCE AND OTHERS,

FOR A CONSPIRACY TO KIDNAP AND CARRY OFF WM. MORGAN.

[From the Ontario Messenger.]

THE following report comprises all the material testimony taken on this ininteresting and important trial. It is proper to state, that Willis Turner was called after Mrs. Hall had testified, but not being then in court, other witnesses were sworn before him; and that his testimony has been introduced next to her's because it relates to the same part of the case.

ONTARIO GENERAL SESSIONS—AUG. 20th, 1828.

Present Hon. Nathaniel W. Howell, Hon. Chester Loomis, Hon. John Price, and Hon. Samuel Rawson, judges of the county courts of Ontario county.

The indictment against *Eli Bruce, Orsamus Turner,* and *Jared Darrow,* for a conspiracy to kidnap and carry away *William Morgan* from the county of Ontario to parts unknown, was brought on for trial at the opening of the court in the afternoon.

Counsel for the people, Daniel Mosley, Esq., special commissioner; Bowen Whiting, district attorney of Ontario county; and Charles Butler, Esq.

Counsel for the defendants, Hon. Dudley Marvin, and Mark H. Sibley, Esq., of Canandaigua; William H. Adams, Esq., of Lyons; and Vincent Matthews, and Ebenezer Griffin, Esqrs., of Rochester.

The following persons were sworn as jurors:—Hiram Anson, Nathan Cary, Jasper W. Peet, Levi Smith, Amasa Spencer, John Stults, Everet Green, Abraham Dodge, Henry Lincoln, Daniel Short, John Pennal, jun., and Samuel Reed.

Mr. Whiting having opened the case to the jury, on behalf the people, the following testimony was introduced.

Israel R. Hall, sworn.—The witness was jailer of Ontario county in 1826. He knew William Morgan who was committed to the jail of said county, on the tenth of September, in that year, and discharged on the twelfth of the same month, as this witness has been informed. Witness was absent from the jail at the time of Morgan's commitment and discharge.

Jeffrey Chipman, sworn.—Witness was a justice of the peace in Canandaigua, in September 1826. On the morning of the tenth of that month, it being Sunday, Nicholas G. Chesebro came to the witness' house and requested him to go to his office. He did so. Chesebro came in soon, and, shortly after him, Ebenezer C. Kingsley, who made a complaint against William Morgan, for larceny: Chesebro stated that Morgan had come from Batavia, and was, at that time, about six miles west of Canandaigua. Witness issued a warrant against Morgan, directed to the sheriff or either of the constables of Ontario county, or to Nicholas G. Chesebro, one of the coroners thereof; by virtue of which he was apprehended, brought before witness on Monday evening, and by him discharged for want of sufficient proof to convict him. Chesebro then requested of witness a warrant against Morgan, on a demand which he held against him as assignee of Aaron Ackley. A warrant was accordingly issued, Morgan arrested, judgment entered up against him by his consent, execution thereon taken out and given to Holloway Hayward, then being a constable in Canandaigua.

Holloway Hayward, sworn.—The witness was a constable of the town of Canandaigua in 1826. He received the warrant issued against Morgan on the charge of larceny; went to Batavia with five others, of whom Chesebro was one, arrested Morgan at that place, brought him before Mr. Chipman on Monday, was present during a part of his examination, received the execution against Morgan, arrested him by virtue of it, and committed him to the jail of Ontario county, between eight and nine o'clock in the evening of the eleventh of September.

Mary W. Hall, sworn.—She is the wife of the jailer. She was not at home when Morgan was committed; but came home on Tuesday the twelfth of September, and found him in jail. Mr. Hall went out about dark on the evening of that day. A person came to the jail and inquired for Mr. Hall; she told him he had gone from home. The person then wished to go into Morgan's room, which she refused. He then asked permission to have a private conversation with Morgan, which was also refused. He then insisted on paying the debt for which he was imprisoned, and taking him away; this too was refused. The person then went in search of Mr. Hall, and soon returned without finding him, and again urged witness to permit him to pay the debt and take Morgan away; to which she would not consent. He then asked her whether she would discharge him if Col. Sawyer would say it was right; witness did not say she would or would not. The person went away, and soon came back with Col. Sawyer. Chesebro advised witness to let Morgan go. Lawson paid the amount for which Morgan was imprisoned, which was a little more than three dollars. Stranger went to the door and whistled. Witness unlocked the door of Morgan's room, and Lawson went in and led Morgan into the hall of the jail by the arm. After they went out of the door, and before it was shut, she heard the cry of Murder. She went to the door and saw three men taking Morgan east; he was struggling, his hat fell off, and one of them took it up. She saw no other person about the jail. An unknown person rapped on the well curb, and a carriage soon passed by the jail from the west. It went east, and shortly returned, driven with great rapidity. This took place about nine in the evening of the twelfth of September. She has not seen Morgan since.

Willis Turner sworn.—In September 1826, witness lived with Mr. Freeman Atwater, in the street on which the jail is situated, a little west of it, and on the same side of the road. As he came out of Atwater's gate one evening, he met Chesebro and Sawyer going west. Saw Sawyer pick up a stick. They turned about and went to the west corner of the jail, and were there whispering together. Witness went to Mr. Hall's well, which is in the street, a little west of the jail, for water; and as he was turning the water into his pail he heard the cry of murder. He saw three men coming down the jail steps with their arms locked. Heard the cry of murder once while they were coming down the steps, and twice after they had left them. Mrs. Hall was standing in the door. Some one, he believes Chesebro, stopped the mouth of the man who cried murder. When they had gone a little distance from the steps, the middle man of the three appeared to hang back; his hat fell off, and a Mr. Osborn took it up and gave it to Sawyer. Asked Sawyer what the rumpus was, who replied that a man had been arrested for debt, and was unwilling to go. Saw Sawyer rap on the well curb. Hubbard's carriage soon drove by rapidly to the east, with Hubbard driving: the horses were gray, and the curtains down. The carriage went a little beyond the pound, east of the jail, and turned about. A man was put in by four others, who then got in, and the carriage drove west and went round the corner of th tavern then kept by Mr. Kingsley. Witness followed the men as they went east, and was near the pound when they got into the carriage. It turned round before they got in. As the carriage was returning west, some one in it cried out, 'Hubbard, why don't you drive faster; damn you, why don't you drive faster.' Hubbard then cracked his whip. Had seen Morgan, but did not know whether he was the man taken from the jail. Did not know those who came down the steps. The moon shone bright.

Hiram Hubbard, sworn.—In September, 1826, the witness kept a livery stable in Canandaigua. He was applied to by Mr. Chauncey H. Coe to take a party to Rochester on the twelfth of September, and was paid for it last summer or fall by Mr. Nicholas G. Chesebro. His was a yellow two-horse carriage. His horses were gray. They were at the barn near Mr. Kingsley's tavern, west of the jail. About the time he was ready, some person on the side walk, then and now unknown to the witness, told him to go on the Palmyra road when he was ready, for the party had gone on. This was the only direction he had as to setting out. He did not hear a rap on the well curb. He started about nine o'clock in the evening. It was pleasant, and the moon shone. No one was in the carriage when he left the barn. He went beyond the jail east fifty or sixty rods, and stopped opposite the long house. His party, supposed to be five in number, there opened the carriage and got in. He heard no noise. He presumed the people in the road were his party. He knew none of them then, nor where they came from, and has not known them since. He cannot say whether he saw them get into the carriage. He was not very particular in noticing them. After the party had got in, he turned round. On his way to Rochester he first stopped at Brace's, six miles from Canandaigua, to water; the people had not gone to bed; some of the company went in; he don't know but he saw them by candle light; he don't know how many went in. He stopped again at Bacon's, in Victor, or at the house beyond; people had gone to bed. Stopped also at Mendon; nobody was up. Did not feed his horses at either of these places. He stopped at Stone's, in Pittsford, long enough to water. The bar keeper was up waiting the return of some young men belonging to the house. Don't remember whether any of his party got out beyond Brace's. He stopped in Rochester, at the large watering place in Main street, ten or twelve minutes; it was just at twilight. Some of the party got out here, but he don't know whether any went from the carriage; he saw no one of them then that he knew, and has seen none since to recognize them. The party desired him to go on beyond Rochester. He consented to go; he took the Lewiston road. On arriving at Hanford's, which was then a tavern, one of the party got out. He called for feed for his horses, but got none; he went about eighty or one hundred rods beyond the house and stopped near a place of woods. It was not a usual stopping place; the party got out before he turned his carriage; he thinks he must have seen them, but he saw no one that he knew, and has seen no one of them since. He don't know why he stopped at that place, but presumes his party told him to do so. Returning he stopped at Hanford's and endeavoured to get feed for his horses, but could not. He saw two or three carriages going out of Rochester when he did, which turned round and went back. One was a small carriage; its color he cannot recollect. After he had turned round he met a hack with two horses, near the house; thinks it was green; did not see it stop, nor hear it hailed; thinks it was not the hack he saw going out of Rochester. He heard nothing from his party about carriages coming from Rochester. Knows Mr. Platt, who kept a livery stable in Rochester, but not his carriages. No one returned in his carriage to Rochester except two transcient persons whom he took in on the road, neither of whom was known to him. An unknown man on horseback passed his carriage between Canandaigua and Rochester.

Ezra Platt, sworn.—In September, 1826, the witness kept a livery stable at Rochester. He is a Mason, and a member of a Chapter. A lodge had previously been established at Lewiston. A Chapter was expected to be installed

R r

in that place, and the Rochester Chapter had been authorised to install it. It is usual for the Grand Chapter to issue to suitable persons a special commission for such a purpose. The first officers of a Chapter would be proper commissioners. After the fact of the Rochester Chapter having received a commission to install one at Lewiston had been for some time known, and about ten days before the installation, the witness was asked if he could furnish carriages to take the commissioners to Lewiston; and he said that he could, but advised that he should take the stage. He stated he could not go himself by reason of ill health. About four or five o'clock in the morning of the day, or day but one, before the Lewiston installation, some person called at his front door and said he wanted a carriage to go to Lewiston, and desired it might be sent to Ensworth's where the company was. He then went away immediately. The witness called up his driver, whose name was Parker. The driver had been in witness' employ several months, but left him a month or two afterwards on account of sore eyes. He don't know where he lives now. The carriage was sent soon after it was called for. The witness did not see it start. He had two carriages, one of a cinnamon color, or yellow, and the other green. He thinks the first was taken. The horses were black, or of a brown bay color. They were gone several days. He supposed the carriage was for the commissioners, and had no intimation that Morgan was going in it. He did not see the person that called for the carriage, and has never been able to ascertain who he is. The only charge he made was on the paper in his wallet, in these words, 'Grand Chapter pro tempore, to carriage to Lewiston.' He supposed the carriage was for the Chapter, and expected some one, in its behalf, would pay him; but he has never been paid, and has never asked any person to pay him. He has heard that some of the Chapter went in a steam boat to Lewiston. He knows Hiram Hubbard, but did not see him or a carriage with gray horses that day. He let to George Ketchum a carriage and horses to go to Batavia, the day before Morgan went to that place. If the installation was the fourteenth, his carriage must have gone the eleventh, or twelfth. It was not engaged on Sunday evening, nor any thing then said about it. Reuben Leonard kept tavern in Rochester at that time. Don't know that any persons were at Leonard's in relation to carriages to go to Lewiston. Was not there himself. He knows nothing of a carriage and horses being employed, on the Friday evening previous, to go to Batavia.

Harry Olmstead, sworn.—He resided at Greece, near Handford's landing, in September, 1826. One morning of that month, just at daylight, he saw a carriage with a pair of gray horses in the road south of Handford's. The horses were very sweaty and appeared to be much fatigued. The curtains of the carriage were drawn. There were two men on the box. He did not know either of them. Does not know how far it went beyond Handford's. About fifteen minutes afterwards he saw the carriage standing under Handford's shed opposite his house. About an hour after sunrise he saw the same carriage come on the Ridge road, take the River road, and proceed towards Rochester. Its curtains were up, and five or six men in it. He was standing in the road. He saw no other carriage that morning coming from Rochester. The end of the Ridge road is a few rods from Handford's house. A person passed on a brown mare, whom he has since ascertained to be Edward Doyle.

Silas Walker, sworn.—Witness lives on the River road, directly opposite the point where the Ridge road intersects it. On the morning of the twelfth of September, 1826, while talking with Mr. Olmstead, he saw a yellow carriage with gray horses pass by. When it returned the curtains were up, and three, four, or five persons in it, one of whom he knew to be Burrage Smith. A person on Mr. Platt's brown mare was forward of the carriage. He saw no other carriage that morning, having been from home most of the time.

Silas Walbridge, sworn.—He lived, in 1826, in Clarkson, about fifteen miles from the River road. Near the time of the races, which commenced that year on the fourteenth day of September, he was applied to by a gentleman for a pair of horses to go before a hack, which he stated would arrive between eight and ten o'clock in the morning. The gentleman said he did not want a driver. Witness at first declined letting his horses go without a driver, but finally consented, harnessed his horses about eight o'clock, and tied them under his shed. The hack came along between eight and nine o'clock, and when it approached his house the gentleman went along by the side of it and had some conversation with the driver who soon drove on. He then said he did not want the horses. A person, since dead, told witness what was to take place, and when the hack came in sight, pointed it out to him. The hack was of a dark color, and the horses dark bay.

Sarah Wilder, sworn.—The witness lived, in September, 1826, with Capt. Isaac Allen, about five miles east from Clarkson. Allen does not keep tavern, and there are no houses near him. About the eleventh or twelfth of September in that year, at ten or eleven o'clock in the forenoon, Mr. ——— came and inquired for Capt. Allen. Did not know where he was. Mr. ——— went hastily in pursuit of him, hallooed for him, soon found him, and returned after the hack. The hack came up before the house in about fifteen minutes. It was brown, and the horses were brown; the curtains were down, and the day was very warm. Did not know the driver. Capt. Allen's horses were brought up, and Capt. Allen and Mr. ——— changed the horses; those that came with the hack were put in Capt. Allen's barn. The hack went west, and Mr. ——— with it, and returned about an hour before sunset the next day. The curtains were up and no one in it. Capt. Allen had gone to Clarkson, but had told witness where the horses that came with the hack the preceding day might be found. They were put to it again, and the hack returned to the east. Don't know who was with it when it returned.

William Cooper, sworn.—Witness lives in Clarkson. About the middle of September, 1826, coming from the west he passed a carriage and two pair of horses in the road about four miles west of Clarkson, and about one third of the distance from Capt. Allen's to Mr. Spencer's. It was between eleven and twelve o'clock in the forenoon. Does not recollect the day of the month, but it was near the time of the races that year. They were then training horses on the race grounds. He cannot say whether the horses were attached to the carriage or not; they appeared to be changing them. A man on the box, whom he had never seen before, was holding the lines; one span of horses was Capt. Allen's, the other he did not know. The weather was very warm, and the curtains of the carriage were down. There were four or five men in a lot south of the Ridge road conversing; two about fifteen rods from the carriage, the others nearer. Two of them were sitting, the others standing. Witness knew several of the men: Capt. Allen, Mr. Spencer, and Mr. ———. He afterwards thought that another's name was Augur, but is not positive of it. The carriage did not start while he saw it.

Solomon C. Wright, sworn.—He kept a public house in Niagara county, in September, 1826. His house is on the north side of the Ridge road, at the point of its intersection by the Lockport road, six miles east of Col. Mollieux's, and three and a half miles north of Lockport. In the month of September in that year, on the day before the installation at Lewiston, just at night, a two-horse pleasure carriage or hack drove under his shed, and afterwards into his barn, which is a few rods farther from his house. The barn doors are usually shut. The feeding troughs in the shed were broken down, and the carriage was driven into the barn to feed the horses, and they ate from boxes placed before them on the floor where the carriage stood, in the farther end of the barn. Don't know whether they were taken from the carriage. The horses were not changed. Did not see those who came in the carriage get out or in. Don't know where they got out, nor how many there were. Did not know any of them or the driver. Has never seen the driver since. All who came in the carriage, including the driver, took supper at his house, and each paid his own bill to him. His bar keeper was gone, and he tended bar. Was in the bar when they first came in, and saw them go through the bar room to supper. The driver obtained food for the horses. Witness does not know that any persons came in the carriage. Did not see the door open. Don't know whether the curtains were down or not. Don't know that any one was in the carriage during supper. Saw no one go to the carriage during supper, and did not go himself. He once went into the barn to find a servant while the carriage was there. Neither saw nor heard any person. Passed the shed in going to the barn. There were horses under it. It was dark when they finished supper. After supper they proceeded west. Did not see them get into the carriage. His house, shed, and barn, are on the same side of the road. The installation was talked of. Don't know how many went in the carriage. There were less in his house after the carriage had gone than before. Did not see it start. Nothing mysterious about it that attracted particular attention. There were persons at his house who did not come in the carriage. He did not know them or their business. Isaac Farewell came to witness' well to get water about the time the carriage came. Had no conversation with him. He has since moved to Canada. Witness knew Eli Bruce at that time. Did not see him at his house that evening. He knows Elisha Mather, did not see him that night. He was at witness' house about that time. Thinks it was before. Saw him the next day, or next day but one. The next day a carriage passed his house from the west to the east. Don't know whether it stopped, nor whether it was the same that was at his house the preceding night. A hack stopped at his house the next day. It is usual for carriages to stop there.

William Mollineux, sworn.—In September, 1826, witness lived in Fleming, Niagara county, on the Ridge road, at a point where it is intersected by the road from Lockport; a little more than twelve miles from Lewiston, six from Solomon C. Wright's, and six or seven from Lockport. On the night before or the night after the installation, about twelve o'clock, Eli Bruce, who then lived at Lockport, came to witness' house with two strangers. Bruce came up stairs where witness was in bed, and said some of his friends were going to Lewiston, and asked him for a change of horses. Bruce told witness that they should be used carefully. Witness called up his son, and after consulting with him concluded to let Bruce have his horses. Bruce and witness' son got up the horses. Does not know from what place the carriage came, nor whether Bruce went on with it. One of Bruce's companions staid over night at witness' house, and took care of the horses that were with the carriage, and helped change them when it returned. Does not know who drove. Bruce spoke of Brown as the driver. The horses returned the next morning a little before sunrise, in the charge of Brown. The carriage was large and of a dark brown or black color. He saw no persons but Bruce and the two strangers that came with him. Can't say which road the carriage took in the morning, nor how many were in it. Did not see Bruce again till next winter. Brown said Bruce would pay for the horses. Witness has not been paid. Has an account with Bruce.

Corydon Fox, sworn.—In September, 1826, the witness lived at Lewiston, with Mr. Barton, in the capacity of a stage driver. The night before or night after the installation, between ten and twelve o'clock, Mr. Barton called witness up and told him to get his hack and horses ready to go to Youngstown. When he was ready Bruce got on the box with him and directed him to drive into a back street to a carriage which he found standing there without any horses attached to it. He drove by the carriage in the back street. Some persons were standing near it. One or two got out of it, and after they and Bruce had got in his hack, Bruce told him to drive to Col. King's, about six miles distant. He would have noticed violence if there had been any, but he saw none. Saw nothing brought from the carriage in the road to his hack. On arriving at King's he stopped, by direction of Bruce, who got out and called to King, who came down into the hall, where he and Bruce conversed together. While they were conversing, some one in the carriage asked for water in a whining voice, to which Bruce answered, 'You shall have some in a moment.' King and Bruce then got in, and he drove to the burying ground, about three quarters of a mile from King's, and a half a mile from the fort, where he stopped, by Bruce's direction. There were no houses near. The party, four in number, got out, and proceeded side by side towards the fort, and witness, by Bruce's orders, returned to Lewiston, where he arrived before daylight. The witness was often called up late at night, and frequently drove passengers whom he did not know; but it is not usual to take up a party in the back street; and he never before left a party at the burying ground, which is not an ordinary stopping place. The next day he saw Bruce at the Frontier House, in Lewiston. Knows not what became of the carriage in the road. Saw nothing unusual in the manner of getting in and out of his hack.

The witness was asked whether he was taken into the lodge soon after this occurrence; but the court said the question was improper, and it was not answered.

Ebenezer Perry, sworn.—Lives in Lewiston, on Back or Ridge street. On the night following, the 13th of September, 1826, after twelve o'clock, he saw a person harnessing a carriage at Barton's stable; heard it start, and went to the door. Saw a carriage coming, which went a little distance beyond another standing in the street without horses, and stopped. Two men were on the box. One of them he knew to be Corydon Fox, and the other he recognized at an examination at Lockport about two months afterwards, and ascertained to be Eli Bruce. Witness thought something strange was going on and went into his garden near his house, where he had a view of what took place in the road. Saw a man go from the box of the carriage which had driven by, to the one standing in the street, and opened the door. Some one got out backwards by the assistance of two in the carriage. He had no hat, but a handkerchief on his head, and appeared intoxicated and helpless. They went to Fox's carriage and got in. The man he supposed to be drunk was helped in. One went back and took something from the carriage they had left; he thinks a jug; returned, got in, they drove off, and he saw no more of them. Witness saw no person in the unharnessed carriage, the curtains being down. Said nothing about what he had seen for four or five months.

[The prosecution then called Edward Giddins, but the defendant's counsel objected to his being sworn because he had no religious belief whatever. After hearing the testimony respecting his religious opinions, and the arguments of counsel on both sides, the court unanimously decided that he was not a competent witness. The evidence in relation to Mr. Giddins is subjoined. It is not introduced in its order as given in court, because it has no direct bearing upon the main question.]

Elisha Adams, sworn.—He lived in Porter, Niagara county, in 1826, about two miles down the lake from the village of Youngstown. The troops left the fort in June, except one old soldier who died there soon after they had gone. About the middle of September Giddins went to York. Was absent three or four days, and witness took charge of the ferry and his house during his absence. Giddins' house was on the flat below the fort, twenty or thirty rods distant from it. That part of the fort nearest to his house is the magazine, which forms part of the wall. There was ammunition, quarter master's stores, &c. in the fort. He went away the day before Giddins came home, Was frequently at the fort in September. Giddins had charge of the fort and public property there. Don't know where the key of the magazine was while Giddins was absent. Supposed it was in the mess house, which is to the left of the magazine as viewed from Giddins' house. Heard no one in the magazine while tending ferry. Don't know that any one was there. Heard, about the time of Giddins' return, of Morgan's having been brought there. Never heard so from either of the defendants. Don't know that food or drink was carried to the magazine while Giddins was absent. Was in it both before and since the troops left the fort. About the time the public property was sold, he was employed to put things in order at the fort. Witness went to Giddin's house at his request, but at what time he cannot tell, and saw there Col. King. Dr. Maxwell and Obed Smith had nothing to do with them. Giddins said he had some work for him to do; showed it to him. Went home without doing it, having no tools with him.

John Jackson, sworn.—In the fall of 1826 he lived in Lockport. The night before the installation he stayed at Giddins', his brother in law. Went to installation. Don't know whether Giddins went. Before going to the installation he went with Giddins to the magazine. Twenty or thirty minutes previously to setting out, Giddins had a pistol. Requested witness to take it; he declined. Did not see Giddins lay it aside. Did not see it after they left the house. Giddins carried something with him. Don't know what. Witness approached within about two rods of the magazine. Giddins went up to the door. Don't know whether it was opened by Giddins or not. Something was said inside of the door. He heard a man's voice not uncommonly loud, and supposed a man was in the magazine. Don't know what was said, nor whether he heard the voice before or after Giddins reached the door. Thought he had better be missing, and immediately retreated. Giddins soon followed him. Witness started in ten or twelve minutes for Lewiston. Giddins informed witness whose pistol it was that he showed him, but the defendants' counsel objected to his repeating what Giddins had told him. He never had any conversation with either of the defendants respecting their participation in the abduction of Morgan.

William Hotchkiss, sworn.—Three or four days after the installation, went to the fort to make inquiries respecting a man's being confined there—found out nothing. Did not go to the magazine—nor did Giddins while witness was there.

The testimony on the part of the people closed here.

Mr. Whiting stated that the bill against Turner and Darrow, two of the defendants, had been found on the testimony of Giddins alone, and that he having been excluded, the prosecution has no evidence whatever against them.

Mr. Adams addressed the jury in behalf of Bruce, and Mr. Mosley for the people. The jury retired at nine o'clock on Friday evening, after receiving a charge from his honor Judge Howell; and having been absent about three hours, returned a verdict of GUILTY against *Bruce*, and NOT GUILTY in favor of *Turner* and *Darrow*.

The court suspended their judgment against Bruce in order to take the advice of the Supreme Court on some important questions of law which were raised during the trial.

A CANDID APPEAL TO PROFESSORS OF RELIGION,

UPON THE SUBJECT OF

SPECULATIVE FREE MASONRY.

By BERIAH B. HOTCHKIN, *Ruling Elder in the First Presbyterian Church of Le Roy, New-York.*

THE Christian religion has ever been marked for its plainness and simplicity; and if there be any difference in the degree of the excellence of the characteristics which are attached to it, the comprehensiveness of the doctrines which it inculcates, and the reasonableness of the demands which it makes upon the services of its votaries, hold a prominent place among these characteristics. The church which is founded upon this religion has, in fulfilment of prophecies long since uttered respecting her, been called to pass through the fires of persecution, and has been almost overwhelmed by the billows of affliction; to which truth many a ransomed soul that now mingles with the glorified throng of 'the just made perfect' can bear testimony. But there are evils to which the religion of the gospel is subject which can bear no comparison with these. For these outward tribulations can affect only its temporal condition, and they ultimately produce good rather than evil. They serve as fuel to feed the flame of its spirituality, and to enliven that fire which is to purify it and purge it from the dross of error and hypocrisy. The days of Zion's prosperity are the days of her danger; and when foes are fewest from without, it becomes her friends to watch with the most assiduous care over her purity, and to guard her, with the strictest scrutiny, from the innovations of those heresies and delusions which, if fostered, will render her odious to God, with whom all other foes, whether in heaven, on earth, or in hell, are not to be compared. Not that the vigilance of her members alone is to preserve her from such contaminations, for it is the province of her Guardian above to preserve her internal as well as outward prosperity, and speed her march from triumph to triumph, until all the glorious things that are spoken in her behalf shall be consummated. But it is the privilege as well as the duty of all the true disciples of the Cross, to endeavor to seek out and unveil every latent iniquity that lurks within her bosom and pollutes her sacredness; and happy are we all, if this privilege of co-operating with our covenant God in fulfilling his will, be ours.

It is not my present design to comment upon all the evils of this description which at the present day exist in the church, and claim and receive admission into her sanctuaries. To make a few passing remarks upon one of them, which has long lain unmolested within her embrace, deadening the spiritual vitality, estranging the hearts and alienating the affections of her members, is the business to which I have now assigned myself. This evil is the institution of *speculative Free Masonry;* and it has been so long upheld by the charities and the countenance of professing Christians, that to undo the evils which it has hitherto created, and is still creating, in the religious world, will require no ordinary degree of Christian exertion. The public mind is already somewhat awake to its dangerous tendency upon our civil liberties, and my voice has been mingled with that of many of my fellow citizens in opposing it upon patriotic principles; but in attempting to expose its gross impiety, I am well aware that I am touching another and more delicate chord which may vibrate in tones of opposition that have never yet been awakened. But it would be a poor fulfilment of the duties which, as a patriot and a professing

Christian, I owe to my country and my God, were I to confine my feeble energies to commenting upon the anti-republicanism of Masonry, when I have so much reason to fear that it is wresting from very many of my fellow creatures their inheritance to those incorruptible joys which shall endure when earthly dynasties and temporal kingdoms shall be for ever forgotten. It is the principles of Masonry alone that I combat; for in them do I believe the great evil consists, and nothing but their entire eradication can arrest its fearful progress. The rights and benefits they confer are sordid and temporal alone. They foster crime, feed avarice, and promote social divisions. Beyond the grave they hold forth no rational hope, nor can the utmost extent of their power impart a single ray of peace to the departing soul. If any of its former votaries are now enjoying the rewards of the blessed, (and such I trust and believe there are,) it can only be accounted for upon the presumption that although they were Masons in name, they were not such *in reality*. Masonry itself could never have sped their course thither, nor are they now exalted above those who never bowed at its shrine. But that these remarks may not seem rash or uncandid, I shall subjoin a few of the reasons which have induced me to believe them correct.

My first reason why I consider Masonry as warring against religion, is, that it prostitutes the Holy Scriptures to unholy purposes. Instead of receiving them as the simple and unadulterated 'man of our counsel and rule of our guide,' it has mingled them with a mass of fables; and upon this impure and motley collection it has founded a series of ceremonies, which, to say the least, are not Divine institutions, and no others should claim their origin and their warrant from that Holy Word. Of this character is the building of Solomon's temple, and the fabled story of the death of Hiram Abiff; and upon these the foundation of a ceremony amounting in fine to the discovery of an all-important word, which probably was never articulated until long after Solomon and Hiram were laid with their fathers, and the fair structure they had reared crumbled to ruins. The improbability of this story will appear from the circumstance that the murderers of Hiram Abiff wished to obtain the Master's word, that, by its aid, they might obtain employment in foreign countries, while the word was not known abroad, and therefore could be of no service to them whatever. Also that Solomon, upon finding the work in confusion, then, and not till then, remembered that certain men had appeared before him and confessed themselves conspirators in the transaction. Also that but twelve men were despatched to make a thorough search throughout the whole land of Israel. In going from the Master's to the upper degrees, the investigation of this point is still more painful to the feelings of the Christian. In the Mark Master's, the parable of the laborers in the vineyard (See Matthew xx, 1—16) is coupled with the story of the rejection of a *stone* presented by the candidate in the building of the temple. The absurdity of this will be apparent to every sacred chronologer. In the Most Excellent Master's or sixth degree, we find to our astonishment that the offering of sacrifices and oblations are not yet done away, although our *only* Great High Priest has long since made the last propitiatory sacrifice, and has left his word that none other are now well pleasing in his sight. This degree is chiefly founded upon 2d Chronicles, vii. 1—4; and in imitation of the solemnity of the scene there described, the incense is laid before the Lord; but no fire comes down from heaven to consume it, nor are the priests unable to enter the room because it is filled with the glory of the Lord. In the Royal Arch degree, the wanton levity with which the sacred names of *Jah, Jehovah,* and *God,* are introduced and used, is truly trying to Christian sensibility; and in the degrees of Knighthood, where the interesting scenes of the New Testament are burlesqued with the same thoughtlessness and indecorum, we see still more to deplore and condemn. It ought certainly to be a serious question with every devout Christian, in what light he ought to view this prostration of the original and holy design of the Scriptures of his salvation, and what degree of crime he ought to affix to such an unholy commingling of Divine truth with human invention.

The second reason that I shall name is the unchristian nature of Masonic oaths. Upon this point my remarks will be very few, because the most, if not all of those who will read this, have perused the remarks of an abler pen upon the same subject.* But I cannot forbear appealing to the conscience of every Christian, whether in the face of the Divine mandate to ' hold no fellowship with the unfruitful works of darkness,' he can swear to fulfil the desires and follow the leadings of those whose deeds are, for ought he knows, works of darkness and impiety. And though his Christian brethren may tell him to the contrary, where, I would ask, is his warrant to take their declarations upon trust, when his Spiritual directory informs him that he needs no other 'light to his feet and lamp to his path' than that 'sure word of prophecy,' in taking heed to which he does well! What authority has he from the word of God, to bind himself to co-operate with those who are then his associates, or may afterwards become so, in fulfilling the mandates of their Masonic ruler, and keeping all the secrets of his brethren, murder and high treason alone excepted, and not even that in the upper degrees? But, if the promissory part of the obligations are inconsistent with Christian character and Christian duty, how much more criminal must be those awful imprecations which constitute their penalty. With what feelings of abhorrence should we view a legal contract where life was a penalty of the failure in its fulfilment; or would a church be fellowshipped in the Christian community, whose members were required to covenant, upon pain of the most barbarous and inhuman death from the hands of their brethren, that they would faithfully observe all its commands and ordinances! Yet the moral guilt, in these cases, as heinous as it would be, would not be commensurate with the crime of invoking the same penalty, for the promiser's failing to fulfil, he knows not what. In this particular, like every other, the higher we ascend in the scale of Masonic wisdom, the more we see that it is inconsistent with gospel piety, as well as degrading to humanity. The imprecations become more and more awful as the candidate's conscience becomes less and less susceptible of their horrors, until he has the temerity to add to his temporal death, THE EVERLASTING PERDITION OF HIS SOUL! Let every Christian, before he extends his charity to such an institution, examine whether such an imprecation as this is warranted in the Holy Scriptures, or whether God can smile with complacence upon the administration of such oaths as claim in their penalty the disposition of 'the life that now is, and that which is to come.'

My third reason is the sacrilegious nature of Masonic ceremonies. And here it will not be consistent with the limits to which I must confine myself, to follow the institution through all its senseless mummeries, and point out their bearing upon the Christian character, or their inconsistency with the Christian religion. Suffice it to say that they are all, as was before remarked, founded in part upon Scripture scenes, and in part upon ' old wives' fables.' Witness the representation of God in the burning bush, in the Royal Arch degree, where a frail mortal is made to represent the immortal Jehovah, and in his presence the trembling candidate is commanded by this would-be deity, 'put off thy shoes from off thy feet, for the place wheron thou standest is holy ground;' and, as a reason why he should pay such deference to his divinity, he adds, 'I AM THE GOD OF THY FATHER, THE GOD OF ABRAHAM, THE GOD OF ISAAC, AND THE GOD OF JACOB.' How many of these mortal gods, would, at such a moment, shrink to meet the Being whom they attempt to personate, is known only to the searcher of all hearts; but I am safe in saying, that the number of Christians who would choose such a time and

* Rev. John G. Stearns.

place to exchange worlds, is few indeed. The same remarks will apply to the ceremony of *three times three*, in the same degree, where the most solemn appellation by which the Supreme Being is known, that word which the Jews dared not to speak but with the deepest reverence, is used to give a zest to one of the most fulsome ceremonies in the whole catalogue. In the degrees of Knighthood the candidate is brought before a triangular table, on which is laid something that is not exposed to him, and the whole is covered with a black cloth. He then drinks four libations of wine, the first to Solomon, King of Israel, the second to Hiram Abiff, the third to Hiram, King of Tyre, the fourth to Simon of Cyrene, who was compelled to bear the Saviour's cross. Previous to drinking the fifth, the cloth is removed, and he is startled by the sight of a COFFIN upon which lies a *human skull* and *thigh bones*. After some preliminary ceremony, among which is a mock exhibition of the Saviour rising, the wine for this libation is presented him in another skull, which he kneeling takes and says, 'This pure wine I now take in testimony of my belief in the mortality of the body and immortality of the soul; and may this libation appear as a witness against me, both here and hereafter; and as the sins of the whole world were laid upon the head of the Saviour, so may all the sins committed by the person whose skull this once was, be heaped upon my head, in addition to my own, should I ever knowingly or wilfully violate or transgress any obligation that I have heretofore taken, take at this time, or shall at any future period take, in relation to any degree of Masonry or order of Knighthood.' After this, the candidate still kneeling, the Sovereign Master puts wine upon his head in the form of baptism, and says, 'I now dedicate thee to the service of God, in support of truth, honor, and justice, in defence of innocent virgins, destitute widows, helpless orphans, and the Christian religion.' If there can be any piety in scenes like these, I have yet to learn where it is evinced, or to entertain entirely different notions respecting the sacredness of the gospel, from what I now possess. On the contrary, I see much that is calculated to excite the abhorrence of all who have a holy jealousy for the sanctity of the institutions of the Christian religion. The path of Christian duty is given so plain that 'the wayfaring man, though a fool, need not err therein;' and this path will lead to all the needful privileges of life, and to ultimate glory, without wandering through the dark mazes of Masonic mysticism. No offering of incense, no adoration of a pretended deity who shows his naked back through a burning bush, no invocation of temporal and eternal wretchedness over a skull filled with wine, and in a style at which humanity revolts, is required in the simple word of Divine truth. There the plain system of moral duty is given in all its length and breadth; and let the man who adds thereto beware lest its author add unto him the plagues which it denounces against such a sacrilege.

My fourth reason for denouncing Masonry is, its religious assumption o titles to which it has no claim, and its confounding knight errantry with Christianity. The objection naturally divides itself into two paragraphs.

1st. With regard to the irreligious assumption of titles, we find but little to condemn until we arrive to the third or Master's degree. To the appellation of 'Worthy,' which I believe is all that is claimed before this, I shall not at this time demur. Whether it is, or is not, in most cases well applied, I shall not take it upon me to say, my present business being with the principles and not the individual members of the Masonic fraternity. In the third degree we find ourselves introduced to the *Worshipful Master;* and with a few ignoble exceptions, it is upon the records of Masonry alone that we find so bold and so sacrilegious an assumption. The proud king of Egypt, the splendid ruler of Persia, the haughty monarch of Babylon, the impious Herod of Judea, never laid this claim to the adulation of their dependants; nor do all the annals of sacred or profane history furnish a corresponding example, save those instances where men arrogated to themselves super-humanity. We read indeed of those who worshipped they knew not what; but only in idolatrous nations do we find that children of mortality are esteemed worthy of adoration. From the word of God we have the most indubitable evidence that worship is due to *One alone;* and sure I am that no true Christian will attempt to compete with the Sovereign of the universe for the praise of the creatures of his power. Next this worm of the dust is presented to us as not only Worshipful, but *Most Excellent;* superlative in excellence, without a superior, *without a parallel!* Well may we tremble for the purity of our holy religion when its supporters can hear, and especially can receive, such expressions of unqualified devotion, without a blush of shame for the utter unworthiness of the object upon whom it is bestowed. But the saddening picture ends not here. Though modesty has already fled from the exhibition, and Christianity weeps at this wanton violation of her sacredness, yet we have only to turn a little farther to behold greater evils than these. Else what means those pomegranates and bonnets and robes of olden time? What means that mitre and breast plate, upon which is inscribed, 'HOLINESS TO THE LORD,' with all the other insignia of Jewish High Priesthood. Yes, it is even so. Though the blood of bulls and of goats is no longer an expiation of sin, though the altars of sacrifice are broken down, and the Priesthood abolished by the great sacrifice of the last High Priest, yet here we find it revived with threefold pomp, and with an ostentation which Aaron and his sons never displayed. And has the ministration of Jesus, our Great High Priest, who for ever abolished the order, become insufficient to accomplish the great object for which it was designed? Tremble, Christian, lest thou 'limit the Holy One of Israel,' by giving to another that High Priesthood which is for ever done away. Upon this point, like every other I have touched upon, I have only given two or three instances as specimens of the whole. I know not but there may be some who will attempt an apology for the assuming of such sacred titles, but for myself I can conceive of none. If one was smitten with a most signal judgment from the hand of the Almighty for even listening with complacency to the responce of the multitude to his words, 'It is the voice of a God,' what must be the measure of their guilt who bear these titles which are little less assuming in name, and perhaps none in reality.

2d. With regard to its confounding Knight errantry with Christianity, I need say but very few words. In the degrees of Knighthood the Saviour is for the first time brought into view, and reference is often made to his life, sufferings, and death; indeed scenes taken from the New Testament form their most prominent features. Hence its pretensions to Christianity are not to be called in question, and I am not aware that they have ever been denied. Its affinity to the chivalrous spirit of knight errantry is equally obvious, as the protection of females at the hazard of life and limbs, and upon the penalty of temporal death and eternal perdition, forms a conspicuous part of the obligations. There is no impiety nor impropriety in risking life to protect the weak and defenceless, and it is certainly suitable that the fair part of creation should receive such protection from 'the sterner sex;' but that chivalrous gallantry upon which the ancient, and I may add, the *modern* knights built their renown, was far from being a kindness to the objects of its professed care; and no true Christian could wish to see it identified with the religion he professes, or claiming patronage from that holy name whereby he is called.

My fifth reason is that Masonry is considered as a saving institution, and makes a religion of the performance of outward duties. This reason also divides itself into two parts.

1st. It is regarded as a saving institution. No where in their whole catalogue of duties enjoined, or doctrines inculcated, is there the least reference to any thing but the observance of Masonic rules as necessary to a preparation for eternal glory; nor is there any other way or any other hope of salvation held forth to the trembling sinner, but that which leads through the Lodge, the Chapter, and the Encampment. In accordance with this, the Almighty is styled the *Great Architect of the universe* and the *Grand Master above ;* and the abode of the blessed is denominated the *Grand Lodge above,* and the attainment of its joys is often spoken of as the *perfection of Masonic wisdom.* Hence it is evident that whatever may be the external professions of its members, its true principles, when divested of that ostentatious show of gospel religion which gives the genius of Masonry its semblance to an ' angel of light,' do recognize ' no other way given under heaven, among men, whereby any can be saved,' but that which is displayed within the pale of the *Masonic church,* and embraced by *Masonic charity.* The Grand Lodge above, according to their doctrine, is designed for the eventual reward of *worthy brethren ;* hence the expulsion of a brother from the lodge on account of unworthy and unmasonic conduct, implies a declaration of his unworthiness of that glorious reward ; and hence it amounts, in reality, to a *religious excommunication.* To decide respecting the piety or impiety of all this, we need only refer to the perfect law of God, and see whether the Lord of Glory has chosen the appellation of *Grand Master of a Masonic society* to magnify his honor, or whether the celestial paradise is nothing more than a Lodge of worthy Masons. No such representations of the character or name of the Almighty are there made ; ' I AM,' is his name, and the redeemed will sum up his character and his most glorious title in ' *Alleluia, for the* LORD GOD OMNIPOTENT *reigneth !*' Nor are the gates of the New Jerusalem guarded by ' a tyler with a drawn sword ;' nor do the pillars of Jachin and Boaz, the square and compass, the level, the plumb line, or the gavel, adorn the celestial city. In all things, but, above all, in regard to the way of salvation and the true character of the God he worships, does it become the Christian to take heed how he believes.

2d. It makes a religion of the performance of outward duties. It is already shown that it is regarded as a means of salvation, and hence the inference is plain that it makes a religion of something. The question then arises, is it of free and undeserved grace, or the performance of external duties ? It is not to be denied that after arriving to the degrees of Knighthood, (to which very few arrive,) we find the Saviour introduced, and his sufferings and death typified, or rather burlesqued. But he is not exhibited as the vicarious sacrifice for sin. Else why is not the entire depravity of the human heart, and the utter helplessness of human nature, made the first lesson of Masonic instruction and the foundation of the whole system ? Why is the Mason made to fulfil the duties of the Entered Apprentice, the Fellow Craft, the Master Mason, the Mark Master, the Past Master, the Most Excellent Master, and finally to ' tread through the rough way' of the Royal Arch, before he is permitted to hear the glad tidings of salvation through the Redeemer ? And even then, why is he not taught that lesson of deep humility and of his native and entire thraldom to sin, without which he needs no such redeeming sacrifice ! Why is he not made to deplore those sins which were visited upon the head of the Saviour, ' *in sackcloth and ashes,*' instead of carelessly reciting the interesting truth over a skull bone filled with pure wine ? These are important questions in deciding upon the nature of the Masonic religion; and a moment's reflection upon them cannot fail to convince every candid mind that is not founded upon the doctrine of grace; hence, I need offer no further proof that it is of works. The inconsistency of this with the Scripture is a truth which is, or ought to be, familiar with every Christian. That entire dependence upon the Saviour, which excludes all boasting and gives all glory to that grace which begins the work of sanctification, and forwards it until ' the topmost stone is brought in with shouting, crying *grace, grace unto it,*' finds no place in this self-sufficing system ; but it is allied to that spirit which the Chaldean king evinced when in the fulness of his pride he said, ' Is not this great **Babylon** that I have built ?'

My sixth reason is, that the institution is blasphemous. In proof of this I shall only extract a diploma which has recently met my eyes, and which is here given correct, *word for word*, the signature alone excepted.

'*Anno Cr. seu Covt.* 896.

<table>
<tr><td>S</td><td>M
A O P</td><td>C F
C</td><td>C</td><td>'THE ANCIENT COUNCIL OF THE TRINITY,
BY THEIR SUCCESSORS
IN THE UNITED STATES OF AMERICA.</td></tr>
</table>

'St. Albert—To every Knight Companion of the Holy and Thrice Illustrious Order of the Cross : Be it known unto you, that, with regard to unquestionable vouchers, we have confirmed the induction of the Knight Templar Mason into the Councils of the said order of Knighthood, and herein do warrant him as a worthy and Illustrious Companion thereof: and hoping and confiding that he will ever so demean himself as to conduct to the glory of I. H. S., the Most Holy and Almighty God, and the honor of his mark, we do recommend and submit him to the confidence of all those throughout the world who can truly and deservedly say, ' I am a Christian ;' and that no unwarrantable benefits shall arise from this diploma, we charge all concerned, cautiously and prudently to mark the bearer on the mystic letters therein contained, and to regard only the result, in its application and privileges.

' Done in Council at Le Roy, in the county of Genesee and state of New-York of these U. S. A., August 1st, 1827.

' Sir ——— ———,
Sovereign Prefect.

' Commendations
Sir Knights Companions.'

' Sir ——— ———,
Act'g Prefect.

I did not see the above document until after I had finished the preceding reasons ; and although from many things there related, I felt perfectly satisfied of the blasphemous nature of the institution, yet had I not perused this degree of the 'Ancient Council of the Trinity, *by their successors in the United States of America,*' I should not have made against it this direct and heavy charge of blasphemy. And I can hardly say whether I am gratified with this exposure of such daring and impious presumption, since it does really exist ; or whether I could have wished that my Christian friends might be spared from the trial of contemplating this awful wickedness. At all events, its language is plain and unequivocal, and every heart possessed of true Christian sensibility, will shudder at its repetition. Let these successors of the 'Ancient Council of the Trinity' show me their order from the Triune God to issue decrees in his name, and then, nor until then, will I acknowledge the falsity of my charge.

In addition to the charge of blasphemy which this document most abundantly substantiates, I might, had I seen it in season, have brought it forward in support of some of the declarations before made, particularly in support of the charge made in the first part of my fifth reason for considering the institution of Masonry as opposed to the Christian religion. It will be noticed that the bearer is recommended and submitted ' to the confidence of all those throughout the world who can truly and deservedly say, '*I am a Christian.*' It will not be denied that Masonry, with respect to the privileges it confers upon its members, is entirely a selfish institution, and that Masonic recommendations, diplomas, &c. are designed to avail the bearer among his brethren only, and cannot be considered as addressed to any others. The one before us is addressed to *every individual* who can *truly* and *deservedly* say, ' I am a Christian,' while from its very nature it can be addressed to *none* but brethren of the order. Hence the inference is plain, that *none others* ' can

S s

truly and *deservedly* say, 'I AM A CHRISTIAN.' But upon this point, as well as all the others, I consider the proof as having been sufficiently positive; and I cannot but believe that those to whose consciences these remarks are addressed, will acknowledge the reasoning to be conclusive.

I have now done, for this time, with my reasons for regarding the Masonic institution as I do, upon religious principles. Those I have mentioned, although some of the most prominent, are very far from being all that have influenced my belief respecting it. But I do not wish to burden the subject with any thing more than is necessary to exhibit it in its true and unadorned light, believing that such an exhibition, in its simplest form, will be sufficient for my Christian brethren, for whose benefit these remarks are especially designed. For the same reason I have avoided all unnecessary comment upon the reasons mentioned, and have satisfied myself by simply laying down the propositions and then establishing their correctness. If those to whom my appeal is made are indeed what their professions indicate, it will not be necessary for me to meet them upon the ground that I should such as are disposed to quibble and prevaricate. The unsophisticated truth is all that they ought to require, and I submit it to their Christian candor whether such is not here given.

Before taking leave of this part of the subject, I ought, perhaps, to anticipate an inquiry respecting the correctness of my extracts from the upper degrees which have never been published. For the entire satisfaction of all who may have the least misgivings on this point, I will add, in addition to my solemn declaration, that from the most unquestionable evidence *I do* KNOW *them to be true*, I believe I can satisfy any candid inquirer who will communicate to me his incredulity, that I do indeed possess this knowledge.

It may now be proper to introduce a few words in answer to the objection. 'If the institution of Masonry be so awfully wicked, why are so many good men connected with it?' Should such a remark be introduced as a conclusive evidence of the purity of Masonry, I should not feel myself obligated to pay any regard to it; for no point can be more self-evident than that the virtue of the members of any society cannot be *conclusive* proof that its principles are equally virtuous. But if it be offered as *circumstantial* evidence against the correctness of my remarks, I admit its plausibility and notice it accordingly. The institution of Masonry, though fraught with absurdities which falsify its pretensions to antiquity, does nevertheless evince in its design and establishment no ordinary degree of cunning and witchery. With respect to the means by which good men are allured into it, nothing need be said, its external professions and ostentatious display of piety being notorious. Upon the first induction of the candidate, he finds to his disappointment, that he has made no remarkable discovery, but the good still lies before him. He sees some things to condemn, but is disposed to believe that when he shall attain the great object of his search, these apparent improprieties may be reconciled with his ideas of propriety; and on the whole, an impetus is given to his curiosity. In the third degree he finds still more to disgust his feelings, but having already advanced to the dimensions of his mantle of charity, he is the more ready to widen it still farther. But here he finds himself no nearer the object of his wish, while the thing is so devised that his curiosity is vastly increased. Thus onward from degree to degree until the last, which is attained by very few, (probably not one in two thousand,) whose perseverance in attaining this summit of Masonic greatness evinces that they have made Masonry their great concern; and they doubtless find sufficient charms in the honors which attend their attainment, to deter them from informing the deluded aspirants for that station that their labors and expense will end in mere nothing; or else they have too much shame to confess the fruitlessness of their tedious labors. But by far the greater part of Christians become disgusted long before this, and are contented to leave the wisdom of Masonry to those who choose to search for it, and for themselves to seek that which cometh from above, and rest satisfied with the simple knowledge of 'Christ and him crucified.' There may be other causes which lure Christians into this abode of darkness, but the above is certainly a very probable one, and it accords with the experience of some whom I esteem for their apparent piety. The reason why those who have become disgusted with the institution have not until recently exposed its abominations, is doubtless their apprehensions respecting the result; and after taking a Masonic oath and learning the nature of Masonic principles, it is not to be wondered that they should fear Masonic 'VENGEANCE.'

The foregoing objection is the only one which I anticipate to my remarks; and having endeavored to answer it, I shall dismiss the argumentative part of this subject. As my address is to the candid inquirer for truth, I have endeavored to manifest an appropriate coolness and candor. My investigation has been confined to the principles of the institution alone; and all reference to *bad members* or *Masonic outrages* has been studiously avoided. These things might have added to the force of many of my arguments; but I chose rather to expose the corruptions of the fountain, that others might be spared the trouble of philosophizing upon the impurity of its streams. I have aimed to give a fair portrait of Masonry itself, and without visiting upon its head the sins of its devotees, to display it in its unclad moral deformity, that no Christian reader who may be beguiled by its external embellishments to worship at its idolatrous shrine, may hereafter charge his sad delusion to my account. And in doing this I am conscious of entire purity of motives. Had I looked no farther forward than the many frowns which I shall doubtless receive from those who are esteemed good and great, I should probably never have raised my warning voice against the dark catalogue of Masonic impieties. But I remember that the time is short in which I shall be awed by the frowns or flattered by the smiles of the good and the great of this world, and that at its expiration their bed will be as narrow and as low as mine. I recollect also that it is the mandate of him whom we are forwarned to fear, 'In the morning sow thy seed, and in the evening withhold not thy hand,' and after the performance of this duty to commit the event and the consequences to him 'who is a faithful keeper.' And while I call for the candid and impartial attention of every reader to this momentous subject, I would impress upon his mind also the same great truth, that in deciding upon it he is acting for eternity. If the order of Masonry be indeed so blasphemous against the God of Heaven, and so destructive to the immortal soul, let him beware of smiling with complacency upon an institution which lies beneath the frowns of the Almighty; and since he has the unerring declaration of Him 'who cannot lie,' that 'he will not give his glory to another, nor his worship to graven images,' let him not, upon the peril of his soul, dare to worship a mortal or ascribe Divinity to a worm of the dust.

THE TWO GREAT QUESTIONS ANSWERED.

If the Masonic institution be so great an evil, why have good men united with, and continued to countenance it so long? and,

Are Masons justifiable in breaking their Masonic oaths, and publishing the secrets of the order to the world?

By Beriah B. Hotchkin.

PART I. If the Masonic institution be so great an evil, why have good men united with, and continued to countenance it so long?

The above question is based upon the supposition that the Masonic institution is charged with being a *great evil*. It also supposes that it has attracted the favorable attention of *good men* who have united with it, and some of whom still continue its supporters. Both of these positions are matters of so common remark, that little more need be said than that they are facts granted by all. In attempting to answer one of the chief objections against the charge entertained in the first, I, of course, stand committed among the opposers of Masonry. But I trust that I shall ever exercise a mildness and forbearance, and address myself to the heart rather than the passions of men, both at this time, and whenever else I shall have occasion to remark upon the subject. But to the matter before us.

It is an unsafe rule to make the general virtue of the members of any association the test of its merits, although it is not to be denied that it may be a circumstance in its favor. But are Masons really willing that the question should be tried upon this ground?—that the institution should be judged by the qualities of its members as a whole? For if they flee to this resort, they certainly cannot expect us to set aside any whom they hold in good fellowship; they cannot place before us the good, the great, the profound, the erudite, and the exemplary, and say these are the materials of our fair fabric, while the *mixed multitude*—the impious, the ignoble, the superficial, the ignorant, and the licentious, are, for a brief moment, disclaimed, to be again received with open arms when the ordeal shall have been passed. Unless I am much mistaken, the welkin has already rung with loud complaints of the institution's having been condemned for the acts of its members, and that must be a poor rule which is unequal in its application to different sides of the same subject. For the sake of the order, then, as well as our own, be it repeated, that it is unsafe to make the general virtue of the members of any association the test of its merits. True, we do not 'gather grapes from thorns, nor figs from thistles,' but we frequently see men of honest hearts and exemplary lives ensnared in toils laid by some evil hand; and, what is still more to be deplored, we sometimes discover the show of virtue where there is a heart of guile. I will not, therefore, condemn the institution for the waywardness of some of its devotees, nor will I laud it for the praiseworthy qualities of others. I judge Masonry, not Masons; let the principles of the institution determine its moral worth or profligacy, and as for the members, abstracted therefrom, '*honor to whom honor is due.*'

However, as the question noticed at the head of this article has been, and doubtless will continue to be, pressed hard and displayed in triumph upon the banner whose streaming colors wave above 'the outer wall,' it may perhaps be worth the while to give it a passing notice.

Why, then, have good men united with the institution?

It is one of the most prominent characteristics of the mind, to be dissatisfied with its present condition, unsatiated with knowledge, and incessantly upon the alert for new food for its propensities. Its quality determines the nature of the object of its ambition. If vicious, it will devise new plots of wickedness; if sordid, it searches for some new and hitherto untrodden road for wealth; if virtuous, it studies the most effectual method of putting its most noble principles into active operation; if heavenly minded, 'its being's end and aim' is to learn how it may most rapidly grow in grace, and ripen for the fruition of its hopes—'the general assembly of the church of the first born'—the New Jerusalem and the society of those who dwell therein. The good man is, in some degree, aware that many unholy feelings hold their sway over him, he earnestly desires deliverance therefrom, and seizes with avidity upon whatever bids fair to speed his conquest over his direct foes, 'the world, the flesh, and the devil.' While pondering in sadness upon his present infirmities, and looking for somewhat to infuse vigor into his spiritual strength, his attention is arrested by an institution claiming to be the handmaid of the religion he professes—to point out new beauties in the God he adores—beauties too vivid for the gaze of the *unenlightened* eye—to open the avenues and direct the pilgrim steps of the novitiate to a sublimer field for benevolence and a more refined state of morality: and display over its portals a wily allurement for a heart like his—'FAITH, HOPE, CHARITY.' Already hungering for a repast like that promised in such a bill of fare, forgetting for the moment the history of our mother Eve, which is set forth as a timely warning to all her offspring, and perhaps, too, unmindful of the monition to seek counsel from above, he looks wistfully; he sees among the inmates some with whom he has erst taken sweet counsel and walked to the house of God in company; and though commingled in the same group are those whom his soul abhors, yet there he may peradventure approach, conciliate, and reform them; and full of brilliant expectations, and keenly set for new and richer consolations, he enters, he bows before the altar reared within, and immolates himself in the strange abode. Now is he grappled to the car of that deity he had thought to clasp with unimpelled and fond adoration; instead of the live coal from God's own altar, the seal of silence is put upon his lips, and however sickening his thraldom may be to his heart, it is only in the silence of his closet he dare say, 'Wo is me, for I am a man of unclean lips, and my dwelling has been in the tents of Kedar, and among the children of Meshec.'

Why have good men, after having had an opportunity to discover the nature of the institution, continued their connexion with it? Various circumstance may have contributed to produce such a result; some may have been swayed by one influence, others by another, and others still by the combination of a part or all that do exist. The great objection that by some is made against Masonry is that it is frivolous and obscene. Such is doubtless the case, and, although it is reprehensible, yet, in our estimation, it comes far, very far, short of the extent of the evils embodied in that society. Still, however, as the faults of greater magnitude are so warily arranged that, at the first view, they do not strike the mind so forcibly as those of the lesser kind, it is not to be wondered that the first impression of the new made votary should be formed by the frivolity, &c. of the scenes which transpire before him, rather than by the deeper laid, but more crying sins; and experience proves that men are prone to make up their judgment from first impressions, and ever afterwards to rest satisfied therewith, unless some extraordinary circumstance should perchance warn them to renew their examination. The novitiate is awake to a sense of the foolishness of many things that he beholds in this his new sphere, and could wish that they were not there; but the natural aversion of the heart to being taken in error, the boasted renown that is emblazoned on the escutcheons of the order, and the retribution that is held *in terrorem* over the head of the disquiet member, one or all prey like a canker upon his resolution, and induce him to content himself with the solecism that the institution is trivial in its nature, and therefore unworthy of the labor of a careful examination. Hence he deems it wise, so far as personal considerations are concerned, to continue a nominal patron of the society, without taking any active part except on days of festivals, funerals, &c.: at the same time contriving to compute with his better judgment by his Masonic laxity. There is a still more crafty feature of the institution, which has led on another class from one step to another, until they have advanced well nigh to the summit of Masonic knowledge. Masonry pretends to teach some new and valuable science. A thirst for knowledge has induced many to swallow the bait; and the degrees are so constructed, that each one foils their expectation, but, at the same time, sharpens their appetite for the promised feast which is ever held before them, inviting them onward. They pursue until they become convinced that they are chasing an illusion; they turn to retrace their steps, but now, for the first time, they bethink themselves of the vows, which, in the ardor of their curiosity, they heedlessly made, nor do they forget that a penalty was annexed thereto. They see that they are in fault, and that it

S s 2

would have been better for them to have been satisfied, at the first, with the simple knowledge of 'CHRIST AND HIM CRUCIFIED.' Of these, some continue their heartless attachment to the order on account of a mistaken apprehension of the nature of their obligations; others, half convinced of their nullity, neglect to attend to the 'customs and usages' prescribed for them, and become the silent, but hearty enemies of the institution. I can conceive of another reason which may induce the Christian to continue his connexion with the fraternity, viz. a feeling of *shame* which prevents him from publishing openly (or by a silent renunciation, virtually) his folly and delusion to the world. I say, I can *conceive* of such a reason; but I dismiss it without any further remark, hoping and trusting that the world does not furnish a solitary case in which it is applicable.

And I dismiss this subject by commending one simple, but important question to the reflection of those whom I have thus far patiently heard and answered, viz. If the Masonic institution be pure in its principles and congenial to the nature of our holy religion, why do so many men of sound judgment, and whose piety has never been questioned, renounce and denounce it?

Part II. Are Masons justifiable in breaking their Masonic oaths, and publishing the secrets of the order to the world?

The Masonic institution has long stood the pride and glory of its followers, the wonder of the curious, and the admiration of the superficial observer. The curtain of mystery which has been thrown around its *sanctum sanctorum*, the drawn sword which has warned the unbidden to beware that they enter not therein, and the seal of everlasting secrecy that has been put upon the lips of its members, that its principles, and the practices of its secret conclaves, might never meet the scrutiny of the world, have only served to render it more imposing. Its novitiates, from the moment they crossed its threshold, seemed bound by a magic spell. The witchery of gold, the splendor of courtly favor, the threats of punishment, the monitions of conscience, and the most abject profligacy of principle, were alike unable to break their bonds, or draw from them a single developement. Was this steadfastness a virtue? If their cherished secrets were immaculate in their nature, it might not have been an offence of the grossest kind, although the established principles of general benevolence forbid us to commend aught that excludes any one from participating in what is calculated to promote temporal enjoyment, or fit the soul for heaven. If otherwise, no sanctity or grandeur which the patronage of the good and the great may have attached to it, should for a moment deter us from answering, No.

But that strange enchantment is now broken; that spell is dissolved; the acts, the principles of Masonry have ceased to be *secrets*; the veil of *mystery* is rent in twain, not by the ruthless hands of a stranger, but by those who have been cherished inmates, who have bowed before its altar, and paid their vows at its shrine. For this act the *unprivileged commonalty* have spontaneously given them their thanks, and lauded their patriotism. For this act, many of their brethren have heaped the stores of their wrath upon their heads, and ascribed to them guilt of the deepest dye. Here, then, are conflicting opinions—not a difference of feeling with regard to non-essentials, but sentiments as widely distant as the east from the west—not touching matters of trivial moment, but involving consequences of unspeakable importance. Who, then, is right, and who wrong? Or in other words,

Are Masons justifiable in breaking their obligations, and publishing the secrets of the order to the world? And, first of all, be it remarked, that the truth of their expositions is a *settled preliminary*. I am not under the necessity of asking any one to grant me that point; it is gratuitously done in the very charge made against the offending members, and which is now under consideration.

It appears that Masons have sworn, under the most horrid penalties, to perform a variety of duties, and to keep certain secrets. It is an established and undisputed principle in moral philosophy, that promissory oaths are not binding, unless the promise itself is so. A promise is generally deemed, and perhaps actually is, more sacred, and the breach thereof a more glaring crime, when it has been sealed by an oath; but it cannot change its nature or render it valid, when it would otherwise be unlawful. So that the case rests entirely upon the claims of the promise to fulfilment. Promises are not binding where the performance is unlawful. The Mason swears to conform to all the customs and usages of the order; and of the nature of these he must be entirely ignorant at the time, as he cannot be entrusted with them until he has made this oath. Without waiting to inquire into the nature of these customs and usages, I will here ask whether such a transaction as this can commend itself to the judgment of any reflecting man? whether an obligation of unqualified observance, and adoption of rules and principles yet to be unfolded, can be other than nugatory? They may, perhaps, embrace nothing that is nefarious, but in that case they must be the opposite, and consequently among the common obligations of life—obligations which the receiver was ever most sacredly bound to fulfil, and hence, in fulfilling them, is only discharging a common duty, without rendering any credit to the interference of Masonry in the matter; and she would doubtless be clear enough of sharing any part of the blame, in case of the profligacy of her follower. If Masonry enforced all that is pure in morality—all that is lovely in virtue—all that is holy in religion—no man could dispute the obligations of her followers to conform to her regulations in the practice of these virtues; but what constitutes this obligation? and when was it first laid upon him in its full strength? and what is his duty in the case, more than that of the man who never knelt and laid the offering of his services upon the altar of midnight sacrifice?

But if the circumstances under which the Mason received his obligation nullify, how much more completely does its nature absolve him from all obligation to fulfil it. The reader will not here interrupt me with the inquiry, 'What, is this its nature?' He has, doubtless, ere this perused it, and he would rather avoid than court so horrid a recital here. Respecting its import, let every man be his own umpire; I wish not to judge for any one. At present, I can only say that the violators have honestly judged it unlawful to conform to them. They, after a careful examination of the subject, in all its bearings, have come to the conclusion that a strict adherence to Masonry, would involve them in legal or moral transgression; and if such be the case, every patriotic moral or principle warns them to absolve themselves from so unnatural an allegiance. I do not mean by such a remark, that their private opinions constitute the propriety of such a course, but from all circumstances, I give credence to the correctness of their views, and draw the conclusion accordingly.

Promises are not binding, when a fulfilment of them would constitute a breach of prior and lawful engagements: so says the learned Dr. Paley, and so say we all. I should be paying but a sorry compliment to my fellow citizens, were I to spend a moment in proving that they are under the most sacred obligations to support the institutions of the country whose fostering care they enjoy. If there be aught in Masonry which comes in competition with our common duty to the regulations and laws of the land, then no promise of fealty to its mandates can cancel the prior engagement. Seceding Masons judge that such is the fact, and have acted under the influence of that opinion. If their views respecting the tendency of the laws of the order be correct, then their conduct, so far from being censurable, is worthy of all praise.

Promises are not binding, which are obtained by means of misrepresentation on the part of the promisee. I promise a man my vote on his professing himself favorable to the passage of an act which I have much at heart; but before the day of election I discover that he was insincere, and will, if elected, oppose such an act. He obtained my promise fraudulently, and I am certainly under no obligation to fulfil it. The Mason is assured, previous to taking his oath, that it will not interfere with his religion, or his duty to his country. Whenever he becomes satisfied that such is not the case—that this assurance was only an allurement to entrap him and secure his devotion to an extra-legal or irreligious power, then so far from being bound by a promise thus extorted from him, it is his privilege, his most sacred duty, to disentangle himself from the evil snare into which he has fallen, and to denounce the lawless power which cast upon his neck the iron yoke of its unnatural thraldom.

This subject might furnish a theme for more remarks, and perhaps more to the purpose ; but I have not set myself down to *write a book*, but to record a few of the most prominent arguments in defence of the course which has met with so free and unmerited censure. For those that have been brought forward, I am indebted to others ; indeed they are nothing more than long established and indisputable principles applied to the case before us ; and as fast as the public shall be made acquainted with facts that are before the world, they will be better enabled to judge of the appropriateness of the application. I ask them not to take any of my conclusions upon trust ; I would rather that they would stay their decision, until they shall be in possession of all the information they need to enable them to form their judgment. Truth, not my simple assertions, but disrobed and unadorned TRUTH, fresh from the fountain, has been given to the world—genuine Masonry has been presented to their view; let them read that, and then judge whether I am guiltless in attempting to open the door and bid the inmates of the dark abodes of mysticism flee, and yet bear off the triumphs of honor and the meed of their fellow freeman's praise with their escape. But let no man say that, in attempting to render Masonic oaths void, I am introducing a dangerous precedent, breaking asunder the bonds which, in this depraved world, hold men to fidelity, hurling contempt at the sacredness of that ' which confirmeth all things,' and ' with one fell swoop,' razing one of the surest safeguards of our peace, and disannulling pledges of whatever name or nature. Such a charge, if made, I shall throw back upon the institution that first estranged the hearts of our citizens from their duty. My object is to restore, not to devastate ; to build up what has been laid waste ; to arrest the ruthless hand of the spoiler ; and to re-stake the landmarks that have been removed.

(501)

HISTORY OF FREE MASONRY:

Being the substance of remarks made in the State Convention, at Albany, and reduced to form for the Anti-Masonic Review and Monthly Magazine.

BY HENRY DANA WARD, A. M.

THE early history of Free Masonry, like that of Rome, is involved in obscurity. The conquerors of the world were not satisfied with the plain truth of their national origin. To have sprung from a band of lawless marauders, stained the pride of the Cæsars. They taught that the 'Eternal City' was founded and first ruled by the son of Mars, whose name was Romulus; who was taken to the gods in a tempest of lightning, and became *Quirinus*, the patron saint of the heathen city, and one of the chief gods of Rome. This was lofty, and sonorous, and unexceptionable, had it been true.

Our modern *power*, which seeks with Roman ambition to lord it over the whole habitable earth, also styles itself *eternal*, as did Rome; deduces its origin from heaven; claims the wisest man for its lawgiver, and some mighty thing in the nature of the philosopher's stone for its secret—all which is equally credible, and as well attested, as that Romulus was nursed by a wolf, or Jupiter was a god that could save. And these Masonic fables are likewise told to cover the meanness of Free Masonry's origin: for she too sprung from a confederacy of lawless plunderers; and it mortifies the pride of the High Priests, it tops the vanity of the Grand Masters, and it makes the Puissant Sovereigns of Free Masonry to tremble for the security of their thrones, to be told that their boasted order sprung from the mire of the Rosicrucians, and spread abroad over the face of the earth, upon the licentious cupidity of its speculative fathers; that it originated within the eighteenth century, among men capable of the most atrocious falsehoods, and base enough to sell their reputation for money, and to barter a good conscience for the delusion of a lodge room; men who sold Masonic charters for an appearance of mystery, but of a truth for gold.

Stone Masons, in common with ninety-one other crafts and trades, in the city of London, have been in the habit, for centuries, of meeting in club for the purpose of improving in the elements of their business, and craft. Each craft has its public hall, its admission fee, its coat of arms, and its charity fund. The companies are given by name, in the order of their rank, in Rees' Encyclopedia, art. Company. And out of eighteen only whose form of government is particularly mentioned, sixteen are governed by a *Master, two Wardens*, and a various number of other assistants. So Free Mason lodges are governed; and the titles *Worshipful*, and *Most Worshipful*, now peculiar to Free Masonry, were common to gentlemen of the sixteenth and seventeenth centuries, as Esquire, and Honorable, are at the present day.

The Lord Mayor of London, at his election, makes himself *free*, that is, becomes a member of one of the twelve principal societies, (if he were not a member of one of them before;) 'for these twelve,' says the Cyclopedia, 'are not only the oldest, but the richest; many of them having had the honor of kings and princes to be their members; and the apartments of their halls being fit to entertain a monarch.' But *Masons* are not among the first twelve. Their rank is No. 31, Hall in Basinghall street; charter, A. D. 1677, in the reign of Charles II.

Some of these companies meet by prescriptive right. The oldest charter is that of the Parish Clerks, A. D. 1233, in the reign of Henry III. The Bakers A. D. 1307, Edward II. Six others were chartered in the fourteenth century; eighteen in the fifteenth century; twelve in the sixteenth century; forty, and among them the stone masons, in the seventeenth century; and some in the eighteenth century.

Handicraft Masonry is an ancient *trade*, and has ever received the fostering attention of distinguished princes. Both in France and in Scotland, the craft were allowed a peculiar jurisdiction over all disputes growing out of the exercise of their trade. (Lawrie's history of Masonry, p. 110, and 297.) This was granted in France, A. D. 1645; and in Scotland near two hundred years earlier, to real builders.

In the rude times, when men, ignorant of chirography, impressed the seal of their parchments with the tooth in their head for their signature, it was usual for Master Masons to give their apprentice *a grip or sign*, by which he should make himself known to any Mason as a regularly entered apprentice to the trade; and another when he had completed his apprenticeship, and passed to the rank of a journeyman, or fellow-craft; and a third, when by assiduity, experience, and skill, he had become himself a master of work, took buildings to rear, hired fellow-crafts or journeymen, and received apprentices. The *word*, the *sign*, and the *grip*, in those unlettered ages, were the certificate of the craft to its regularly taught members; and in Germany were common before *Free Masonry* was imported from England. (*See Prof. Robison's Proofs,* p. 54.)

Masonic historians claim the men to be Free Masons, against whom a statute was passed in the 25th of Edward III.; and again, in the reign of Henry VI., forbidding them to assemble in congregations and chapters. (See *Free Mason's Library,* p. 25.; *Hardie's Monitor,* p. 20.; *Lawrie's History of Masonry,* p. 94. ; *Encyclopedia Brittanica,* art. Masonry, sec. 62. et alias.) Now Edward III. dealt with Englishmen of that day, as George III. would have dealt with Americans in his day—as if they had been slaves. A plague had swept away a fearful portion of the English population; and the scarcity of laborers caused all classes of mechanics to demand an increase of wages. Edward had several castles and magnificent edifices in building; and to make his money hold out, must compel the Masons and mechanics to work at the old rates. To effect this, he issued an ordinance, and enforced it by his sheriffs, who returned masons for the king's buildings, as they are wont to return jurors for the king's courts. (See *Hume's History of England, reign of Edward* III.) This was equally agreeable to the lords of Parliament as to himself; and accordingly it was enacted, A. D. 1350, that 'as servants, not willing after the pestilence to serve without taking excessive wages, had been required to serve in their accustomed places at the rate they had received in the 20th year of Edward III.; and as it is given the king to understand, in this present parliament, that the servants have paid no regard to the said ordinance, but to their ease do withdraw from the service of great men and others, unless they have livery and wages to the double or triple of that they were wont to take in the said 20th year, and before, to the great damage of the great men, &c.; be ordained and established the things underwritten.'

Chap. 1. Fixes the day and year wages of *farm servants.*

Chap. 2. Fixes the price of threshing all sorts of grain, by the quarter.

Chap. 3. Prescribes the wages of several sorts of artificers, and laborers; among whom ' *Carpenters and Masons*' are particularly specified.

Chap. 4. Requires artificers to make oath that they will use their crafts, as they had done in the 20th year of the same Edward III.

See *Ruffhead's English Statutes,* vol. I. p. 251.

Seventy-four years after the enactment of this statute, which plainly is applicable only to handicraftsmen and servants, Henry VI., in parliament, at Westminster, ordained that 'no confederacies and congregations shall be made by masons in their general chapters and assemblies, whereby the good course and effects of the statute of laborers (25th Edward III.) are violated and broken in subversion of law; and if any be, they that cause such chapters and congregations to be assembled and holden, shall be adjudged felons.' (*Coke's 3rd. Ins.* p. 99.)

The common pretence of Free Masons, that these statutes were levelled particularly against their mystic order, by the influence of bigoted priests, because the *secret* was not betrayed in the office of *auricular* confession, is too shallow after once reading these statutes, to cover the nakedness of the falsehood, or to conceal the evident duplicity of its first publishers. But one thing these statutes conclusively show, with the aid of the Masonic historians, viz. That in the reign of Edward III. and Henry VI. there were no *Free Masons* in England, but stone Masons, who met in general chapters and assemblies, not to cultivate the knowledge of a wonderful mystery, but to impede the execution of the laws, and to violate the statutes of their country.

With this view faithful history fully concurs. That a society, claiming the glories of Free Masonry, should have existed for ages unnoticed by any writer, noble or contemptible, foolish or learned, is wholly incredible and unworthy of belief. The Puritans and the Presbyterians, the Cabalists and the Rosicrucians, the Gypsies and the Necromancers, the Alchymists and the Jesuits, are each liberally noticed in the works of various authors during the sixteenth and seventeenth centuries; but Free Masonry has not so much as a name until the eighteenth century. To any historical scholar, this fact alone is enough. We read of the *fraternitas lathomorum*, or company of bricklayers; but it requires not a lawyer to discern that these are the men against whom the statute of laborers was directed, in the 25th year of Edward III., and are *not* the men who have at this day in their lodges the language of Eden, and the mysteries of the antediluvian world. This is irresistible truth; and I challenge any man to turn its edge, or to break its point, or to show one particle of evidence to the contrary, except it proceed from the vainglorious boastings of the mystic order itself, which is not evidence, the witness being confessedly interested, and standing publicly convicted of shameless duplicity, and of atrocious falsehood. (See Illustrations of Masonry by WM. MORGAN, compared with the standard works and authorised pretensions of the order.)

Of the same tenor is the fact that Papacy and Free Masonry cannot dwell together in peace; but we hear not a word of their disagreement until the eighteenth century. Certainly Papacy is older than one hundred years; and if Free Masonry be much above that, how did it previously escape a conflict which has never ceased since first it commenced, A. D. 1730 to 1740? The canons of the church require full and free confession to the priests from every good Catholic. The oaths of Free Masonry require absolute secrecy upon the transactions of the brethren, and of the lodge room, from every good Mason. *Now*, these canons and oaths nowhere abide together without discord, and a deprivation of church privileges, and they could never harmonize for one moment. Therefore the time when they first fell out and contradicted each other, must have been near the beginning of one or both of them. That time is determined by the Pope's bulls, A. D. 1738, and 1739. Wring and twist the brother Mason may, but there is no escape; the date is correctly stated—*seventeen hundred and thirty eight*, issued by Clement XII. (See *Lawrie's History of Masonry*, p. 122. *Encyclopedia Brittanica*, art. Masonry, last edition.)

What has been said is proof, not only that the account which Free Masonry gives of itself is erroneous, but is grossly erroneous; not only that the order was not organized by Solomon, and patronized by St. John, but that it had no existence in the days of Edward III. and of Henry VI. of England. The question becomes interesting: Whence did it originate? and who first promulgated its falsehoods?

The Rosicrucian mania sprung up in Germany, A. D. 1610, nearly; and overspread Christendom. This puff of indefinable extravagance originated from the writings of John Valentine Andrea, a celebrated theologian of Wurtemburg; (See *London Magazine*, 1824, vol. 9, p. 143.)—who amused himself with tales of spiritual wonder, and of mystical glory, *as a literary hoax*, in the style of Baron Munchausen's wonderful adventures, in his memoirs. The visionary minds of that day took his work in earnest. They claimed for the Rosy Cross philosophy in general, whatever is now particularly claimed for Free Masonry—a heavenly origin, a magic influence, a wonderful secret, and unbounded excellence. The universal medicine, and the philosopher's stone, were gravely professed for the glory of its mystical laboratory; and to so great a pitch of extravagance did its vain professors run, that modern Free Masons are sober men in the comparison. This folly was greatly admired in England, by some men of a strange fancy, and of great learning; and by others publicly professing the black art. Among the former, the name of *Elias Ashmole*, the antiquary, stands conspicuous; and among the latter, *William Lilly*, the astrologer; and somewhere between them is *Robert Fludd*. This Ashmole is greatly accounted of as a brother, by Masonic historians; and is the first *accepted* Free Mason, claimed by Professor Robison. (See *Proofs of a Conspiracy*.) Ashmole himself says, 'I was *elected* in Mason's hall, Basinghall street, A. D. 1646.' (See *Biog. Britt.*) This is the hall of the Stone Mason's company, London; chartered A. D. 1677, thirty-one years after Ashmole's admission into its livery, and remaining to this day, as it ever has been, in the possession of Stone Masons, a society distinct from, and independent of, the modern Free Masons; and it is evident that Ashmole was only made *free* of the Mason's company, as his friend Lilly was made *free* of the Salter's company; and as the Lord Mayor is usually made *free* of some one of the twelve principal companies of tradesmen or mechanics, in the city of London; and that Ashmole was *not* initiated, passed, and raised to the sublime degree of a Master Mason, as in a modern lodge of Free Masons. Therefore the record must be *wrong* which makes Ashmole a Free Mason of the modern type. But Ashmole was made *free* of the Mason's company; and was a Rosicrucian, and a famous zealot for the philosopher's stone, which, in his own words, 'is to convert the basest metals into perfect gold and silver, and flints into rubies, sapphires, emeralds, and diamonds.' He further treats copiously upon 'the vegetable, magical, and angelic stones, with which Adam and the fathers before the flood, with Abraham, Moses, and Solomon, doubtless wrought many wonders; yet the utmost of their virtues they never understood.' (*Biog. Britt.*) This Mr. Ashmole is honorably mentioned in the biographical dictionaries, and was a very learned man. He wrote a tremendous folio history of the order of the Garter; and founded the celebrated museum at Oxford. It is an undeniable fact, that the conceited mystery of the Rosicrucians, and their vainglorious pretences to every thing good, and great, and magical, or holy, are united with the emblems and working tools of a handicraft mason, the trowel and level, square and compasses, and leather apron, to form this lying wonder of the nineteenth century, commonly called Free Masonry. This union did not take place in one day, nor until the false philosophy of the Rosicrucians fell into merited disgrace, and the sect run out. Ashmole died A. D. 1692, and with him the last of the Rosy Cross philosophers; but the spirit of this order, after lingering a few years among men of less note, passed by a species of metempsychosis into a new body, the company of handicraft Masons, with whom it first appears in the early part of the eighteenth century.

At the time of Ashmole's death, Sir *Christopher Wren* was at the head of the English architects; holding the office of Deputy Surveyor of the king's buildings. In 1698, he was made by William III. Surveyor General of the public works; and in 1714 to 1718, for political considerations, he was removed from office by George I. All Masonic historians call Wren, Deputy Grand Master, at the time when he was Deputy Surveyor; and *Grand Master* of the Free Masons, at the time when he was Surveyor General to the throne. But in doing this they make a very short rope to hang themselves; for, by their own showing, the first Grand Lodge was formed A. D. 1717. Then how could Wren be Grand Master, A. D. 1698, nineteen years before there was a Grand Lodge? (See any Masonic history of the year 1717, *Preston, Dermott, Lawrie,* et alias.)

During this period, the Rosicrucian pretensions were seeking, like a troubled spirit, for some resting place. The age was one of the most extravagant speculation; and moved by a strange desire of fame, and money, and conviviality, four companies of stone masons, who were left of those who had been associated in building the proud edifices of London, after the fire of 1666, met, the lodge that had worked on St. Paul's church being at the head, and formed the Grand Lodge of London, in February, and elected their officers June 24, A. D. 1717. With a view to fill up their ranks and to increase their importance, they voted to *accept* men of other trades and professions, as members of the society. (See *Preston, Lawrie, Hardie, Tannehill,* et alias; and particularly the *Ahiman Rezon* of *Lawrence Dermott*, quoted in the 4th No. of the Anti-Masonic Review, and Monthly Magazine.)

Three years they struggled, accommodating the Rosicrucian pretensions to the emblems of a handicraft mason; and then, in 1720, burnt their papers for the benefit of the mystery. (See each of the above writers.) They give out that this bonfire was made '*by some too scrupulous brethren*,' who feared that the secrets of Masonry would be exposed in the Book of Constitutions about to be published. But the smoke of that fire was not thick enough to envelope the origin of their mystic order in impenetrable obscurity. No doubt they hoped by burning their pretended parchments, to destroy all evidence disproving their claim to immemorial customs, and to imprescriptible rights; which claim was in a course of preparation for the public, in the dreaded Book of Constitutions.

After three years more the volume came forth from the hands of *Anderson* and *Desaguilliers*, or *Desaguliers*, and blew the first strain of Masonic vainglory, and unearthly mystery, which is heard from any book, or printed treatise! *Anderson* and *Desaguilliers*, a Scotchman and a Frenchman, in London, were the men who first published to the world the high pretensions of Free Masonry—men of a low character and of a base spirit; whose book of Constitutions of Masonry was ushered from the press, A. D. 1723, and is hardly older than our grandfathers! For the mean repute of the men and of their works, see *Prof. Robison's Proofs of a Conspiracy*, pp. 19 and 20, N. York edition; and *Lawrie*, p. 92. This volume of mock *constitutions* is the basis of all Masonic history; and its delusive statements have been servilely copied, and greatly magnified, until the mystic wonder has grown beyond the size and power of the fabled monsters of antiquity.

Now the false spirit of the Rosy Cross philosophy was fairly embodied with the emblems of a mechanic's society, and was brought forth by the Book of Constitutions in the form of Free Masonry. From the time of its birth the lying wonder began to run to and fro in the earth, wherever British commerce could convey it; and charters for holding Masonic lodges, were every where sold at a cash price, and an annual stipend by the Grand Lodge of London. To that Grand Lodge the inhabitants of the most part of continental Europe, of the East and West Indies, of Africa, and of America, paid an

T t

annual tribute for the right to confer the three degrees of *Morgan's* Masonry! The date, and the Grand Master who issued the warrant, are carefully recorded in Preston, Smith, Lawrie, Tannehill, and others, for holding lodges in all quarters of the earth. A. D. 1729, Free Masonry was first introduced into the East Indies; 1730 the Grand Lodge of Ireland was formed; 1731 a patent was sent from England to erect a lodge at the Hague; 1733 Free Masonry established itself in North America, at Boston; 1736 at Cape Coast, in Africa, and at Geneva, in Europe; in Scotland the same year the first Grand Master was elected; and so the triple headed monster went round the world, while in its *teens.*

The higher degrees began to be added in France; the first notice of them is near A. D. 1740, in connexion with the enthusiastic and learned chevalier *Ramsay.* (See *Robison's Proofs of a Conspiracy.*) They were received and modified under the hand of Frederick of Prussia, and by the school of Voltaire were introduced from France into the United States, through the channel of Jews, A. D. 1760, and afterward. (See the grand circular of the Sublime Sovereigns of Masonry, *A. M. Review*, No. 4.) They first appear in a distinct shape in the United States A. D. 1796, and 1797; and already, in thirty years, the *Grand* High Priests, and *Most Excellent* Kings, and *General Grand Commanders* of the Order are as plenty as blackberries, and are in their own estimation superior, as an order, to the legal authorities of the country.

The unlawful seizure, the violent abduction, and the felonious murder, of Captain William Morgan, for publishing the pretended mysteries of the order, A. D. 1826, brings both the life and the history, with the influence of Free Masonry in this country, suddenly to an end.

This is the nucleus of the history of Free Masonry.—Around it we shall gather distinct dissertations upon the Rosicrucians, upon the Scotch Masons, upon the York Masons, and upon the ancient and Modern Masons. We shall hereafter, if life is spared, trace upon it the rise of the degrees of Knighthood, the Chapters, the Councils, and the Sublime Sovereignties of Sublime Freemasonry, even to that lying "*under the celestial canopy of the zenith*, 32° 45′ *North Latitude.*" We will unravel the labyrinth of this boasted mystery; we will expose the falsehood of its appearances, and put the light of truth in the place of its misty darkness; that all the world may know how utterly worthless in its history is this modern Bethaven, this house of vanity; and how despicably false it is in its divine importance and assumed antiquity.

[Many of our readers have heard the epithet *ineffable* applied to certain degrees in Masonry. It may possibly interest them to learn the origin of that application. These degrees, eleven in number, commence with that of Secret Master, and end with that of Perfection. In each of these degrees some name of God is used, as the distinguishing word. Each name, however, is only a mode of pronouncing the Hebrew word Jehovah. The later Jews have a superstitious fear of pronouncing that name. Whenever it occurs in the Hebrew Text, they substitute the word Adonai in its place. To those who read the original language of the Old Testament, it is well known, that while the consonants of a Hebrew word remain, the vowel points may be so changed as to afford several different pronunciations. In the different degrees of Ineffable Masonry, the four consonants (Jod, He, Vau, He,) of the name Jehovah are differently pointed, so as to furnish a word for each degree. In the degree of Perfection, the candidate is sworn not to pronounce the word but once during his life, hence it is termed *ineffable*, or unutterable. The ordinary mode of giving it in that degree consists in simply repeating the names of it's letters, "Jod, He, Vau, He." On receiving that degree, the candidate is told that he is to become acquainted with the true pronunciation of the ineffable name of God, as it was revealed to Enoch. He is then taught to pronounce the word "Ya-ho"—sounding the *a* like *a* in wall. When written in Masonic manuscripts, this word is spelled "Ja-hoh."

The ineffable degrees have undergone several revisions. The form in which they are exhibited, (see page 183, &c.) is that which has had the most general reception in the United States. In the year 1823, these degrees received their most recent revision, and were brought into a more unexceptionable form than those in which they had hitherto existed. In this form they have been propagated in various parts of the eastern, middle, and western sections of this State. The following is the ceremony of opening the Lodge of Secret Masters, according to the revised ritual.—EDITOR.]

SECRET MASTER.

OPENING.

The Master strikes *five*. At this signal the Grand Marshal rises, and the Master addresses him:

Master. "Your place in the Lodge? *Answer.* In the north, Most Powerful.—*M.* Your business there? *A.* To see that the Sanctum Sanctorum is duly guarded.—*M.* Please to attend to your duty, and inform the guards that we are about to open a Lodge of Secret Masters by the *mysterious number*. *A.* It is done.—*M.* How are we guarded? *A.* By seven Secret Masters stationed before the veil of the Sanctum Sanctorum."

The Master strikes *six*. The Inspector rises.

Master. "Brother Adoniram, are you a Secret Master? *Inspector.* I have passed from the square to the compass.—*M.* What is the hour? *I.* The dawn of day has driven away darkness, and the great light begins to shine in this Lodge."

The Master strikes *seven*. The brethren rise.

M. "If the great light is the token of the dawn of day, and we are all Secret Masters, it is time to begin our labours; give notice that I am about to open a Lodge of Secret Masters by the mysterious number."

The Inspector obeys. The signs of the degrees from Entered Apprentice to Royal Arch, inclusive, are given with that of silence, which belongs to this degree. The Master places the two fore fingers of his *right* hand on his lips. This is answered by the brethren with the two fore fingers of the *left.* All clap hands seven times.

M. I declare this Lodge of Secret Masters open, and in order for business. Brother Grand Marshal, please to inform the guards.

SECTION II.

Q. What did you see in the Sanctum Sanctorum when the thick veil was removed? *A.* I saw the great circle, in which was enclosed the blazing star, which filled me with awe and reverence.—Q. What do the Hebrew characters in the triangle signify? *A.* Something above my knowledge, which I cannot pronounce.—Q. What word did those Hebrew characters compose? *A.* The ineffable name of the Great Architect of the Universe.—Q. To whom was that name revealed? *A.* To Moses; he received the pronunciation thereof from the Almighty on the mount, when he appeared to him, and by a law of Moses it was forbidden ever after to be pronounced unless in a certain manner, so that in process of time the true pronunciation was lost.— Q. What more did you perceive?—*A.* Nine other words.—Q. Where were they placed? *A.* In the nine beams of the blazing luminary.—Q. What did they signify? *A.* The nine names which God gave himself when speaking to Moses on Mount Sinai, and the promise that his posterity should one day discover his real name.—Q. Give them to me, with their significations? *A.* "Eloah," The strong. "Hayah," He is. "Shaddai," The Almighty. "Elyon," The Most High. "Adonai," The Lord. "Ahad Kodesh," The Holy One. "Riba," The Mighty. "Mahar," Merciful. "Eloham," Merciful God.—Q. What doth the circle which surrounds the delta signify? *A.* The eternity of the power of God, which hath neither beginning nor end.—Q. What doth the blazing star denote? *A.* That light which should guide us to the Divine Providence.—Q. What is signified by the letter G in centre of the blazing star? *A.* Glory, Grandeur and Gomez, or Gibber Hodihu.—Q. What is meant by these? *A.* By glory is meant God, by Grandeur, man who may be great by perfection; and Gibber Hodihu, is a Hebrew word signifying thanks to God. It is said to have been the first word spoken by the first man.—Q. What else did you see in the Sanctum Sanctorum? *A.* The ark of alliance or covenant.—Q. Where was the ark of alliance placed? *A.* In the west end of the Sanctum Sanctorum, under the blazing star.—Q. What did the ark with the blazing star represent? *A.* As the ark was the emblem of the alliance which God had made with his people, so is the circle which surrounds the delta in the blazing star, the emblem of the alliance of Brother Masons.—Q. Of what form was the ark? *A.* A solid oblong square.—Q. Of what was it made? *A.* Of shittim wood covered within and without with pure gold, surmounted with a golden crown and two cherubims of gold.—Q. What was the covering of the ark called? *A.* Propitiatory.—Q. Why so? *A.* Because God's anger was there appeased.—Q. What did the ark contain? *A.* The tables of the law which God gave to Moses.—Q. Of what were they made? *A.* Of white marble.—Q. Who constructed the ark? *A.* Bezeleel of the Tribe of Judah, and Aholiab of the Tribe of Dan, who were filled with the spirit of God in wisdom and understanding, and in knowledge and in all manner of workmanship.—Q. What was the name of the Sanctum Sanctorum in Hebrew? *A.* "Dabir."—Q. What does that word signify? *A.* Speech.—Q. Why was it so called? *A.* Because the Divinity resided there in a peculiar manner, and delivered his oracles. —Q. How many doors were there in the Sanctum Sanctorum? *A.* Only one on the east side called "Zizon," or Balustrade. It was covered with hangings of purple, scarlet, blue, and fine twined linen of cunning work, embroidered with cherubims, and suspended from four columns.—Q. What did these columns represent? *A.* The four cardinal points.—Q. Your duty as a Secret Master? *A.* To guard the Sanctum Sanctorum, and sacred furniture of the holy place.—Q. What was that furniture? *A.* The altar of incense, the two tables of shew-bread, and the golden candlesticks.—Q. How were they placed? *A.* The altar of incense stood nearest the Sanctum Sanctorum, and the tables and candlesticks were placed five on the north and five on the south side of the holy place.—Q. What is meant by the *eye* in our Lodge? *A.* That Secret Masters should keep a careful watch over the conduct of the craft in general.—Q. What is your age? *A.* Three times twenty-seven, and accomplished eighty-one.

CLOSING LODGE OF SECRET MASTER.

The Master strikes *five.*—The Grand Marshal rises.
Master. "Brother Grand Marshal, what is the last as well as the first care of a Lodge of Secret Masters? *Answer.* To see that the Sanctum Sanctorum is duly guarded.—*Master.* Please attend to your duty, and inform the guards that we are about to close this Lodge of Secret Masters by the mysterious number." The Grand Marshal obeys, and repeats, "It is done Most Powerful!" Master strikes *six.*—Adoniram rises. *Master.* Brother Adoniram, what is the hour? *Answer.* The end of day.—*Master.* "What remains to do?" *Adoniram.* To practice virtue, fly vice, and remain in silence.—*Master.* Since there remains nothing to do but to practice virtue and fly vice, let us enter again into silence, that the will of God may be accomplished." The signs are given, and *seven* blows struck as at opening. *Master.* "I declare this Lodge duly closed."

DEGREE OF PERFECT MASTER.

OPENING.

Right Worshipful and Respectable Master strikes *two*—upon which Grand Marshal rises, and Master says, "Brother Grand Marshal, are we all Perfect Masters?" *Answer.* We are, Right Worshipful and Respectable. Q. Your place in the Lodge? *A.* In the north, Right Worshipful and Respectable.—Q. Your business there? *A.* To see that the Lodge is duly tiled. Q. Please to attend to your duty and inform the Tiler that we are about to open a Lodge of Perfect Masters. (Grand Marshal reports.) Right Worshipful and Respectable Master knocks *three,* upon which the Warden and the Master of Ceremonies in the south rise. Master says, "Brother Stokin, are you a Perfect Master? *A.* I have seen the tomb of our respectable Master Hiram Abiff, and have in company with my brethren shed tears at the same.—Q. What is the hour? *A.* It is four.

Master then knocks *four,* upon which all the brethren rise. Master says, "If it is four, it is time to set the workmen to labor. Give notice that I am going to open a Lodge of Perfect Masters by four times four." (Senior Warden reports to brethren.) Sign's given of former degrees, together with those of this degree.

Master knocks *four,* Stokin four, Master of Ceremonies four, and Grand Marshal four—then all the brethren strike four times four with their hands. Then Master declares the Lodge open, and orders the Marshal to inform the Tiler.

RECEPTION.

The candidate has a green cord put round his neck and is led by the Master of Ceremonies to the door, who knocks *four,* which is repeated by the Warden and answered by the Master. Then Senior Warden says, "While the craft are engaged in lamenting the death of our Grand Master, Hiram Abiff," an alarm is heard at the inner door of the Lodge.

LECTURE.

Q. Are you a Perfect Master? *A*. I have seen the tomb of Hiram Abiff, and have in company with my brethren, shed tears at the same.—*Q*. How were you prepared to be made a Perfect Master? *A*. A sprig of cassia was placed in my left hand, and a green cord about my neck.—*Q*. Why was the sprig of cassia placed in your left hand? *A*. That I might deposit it in the grave of Hiram Abiff.—*Q*. Why was a rope of green color put round your neck? *A*. Because the body of Hiram Abiff was lowered into the grave by the brethren, at his second interment, by a rope of that color. There is another reason, to signify thereby that a Perfect Master by flourishing in virtue, might hope for immortality.—*Q*. How did you gain admission? *A*. By four distinct knocks.—*Q*. What did they denote? *A*. Life, virtue, death, and immortality.—*Q*. How were they answered? *A*. By four from within.—*Q*. What was then said to you? *A*. Who comes there?—*Q*. Your answer? *A*. A Secret Master who is well qualified, &c.—*Q*. What was then said to you? *A*. I was then asked by what further right, &c.—*Q*. Your answer? *A*. By the right, &c.—*Q*. What was then said to you? *A*. Wait until the Right Worshipful and Respectable Master has been informed of your request and his answer returned.—*Q*. What was his answer? *A*. Introduce him in due and ancient form.—*Q*. What was that form? *A*. I was conducted to the west by the Master of Ceremonies and interrogated by the Master, "What is your request?"—*Q*. Your answer? *A*. To receive the degree of Perfect Master.—*Q*. What was then said to you by the Master? *A*. Before you can be admitted to this privilege, it will be necessary for you to join the funeral procession of Hiram Abiff.—*Q*. What followed? *A*. I joined in the procession, which moved four times round the Lodge, the brethren singing a funeral ode; when we arrived at the grave, the procession moved in an inverted order—the coffin was lowered with a green rope, and the sprigs of cassia thrown into the grave.—*Q*. What followed? *A*. The Master resumed his station, and the procession moved to the east.—*Q*. What followed? *A*. When he directed the Grand Marshal to inform King Solomon that the tomb of Hiram Abiff was completed, and request him to examine the same.—*Q*. What followed? *A*. Solomon entered and proceeded with the procession to the tomb of Hiram Abiff, and having examined the same and read the inscription J. M. B. he made a sign of admiration, and said in the joy of his heart, "It is accomplished and complete;" the brethren all making the same sign.—*Q*. What followed? *A*. The brethren resumed their places, and the Master directed the Master of Ceremonies to cause me to approach the east by four times four steps from the compass extended from an angle of seven to that of sixty degrees, and take the obligation of a Perfect Master.—*Q*. Repeat that obligation, (same as Secret Master, see p. 183.) *A*. Under penalty of being smitten on the right temple, with a common gavel or setting maul, so help, &c.—*Q*. What did the Master then communicate to you? *A*. He said, "It is my desire to draw you," &c. (as in the Monitor,) and then gave me the signs, words, tokens and history of this degree.—*Q*. Give me the signs. *A*. 1st sign—Place the palm of the right hand on the right temple, at the same time stepping back with the right foot, then bring up the right foot to its first position and let the right arm fall perpendicularly on the right side; (alluding to the penalty.) Second sign is that of admiration.—Raise the hands and eyes to heaven, let the arms fall crossed upon the belly, looking downwards.—*Q*. Give me the pass word. *A*. (Accassia.)—*Q*. To what does the word allude, &c. Give me the token and mysterious word? *A.* (Token is that of the Mark Master, given on the five points of fellowship; the mysterious word Jeva, (pron. Je-vau.)—Q. What was then done? *A.* The Master invested me with the jewel and apron of this degree, and informed me that my jewel was designed to remind me, that, as a Perfect Master, I should measure my conduct by the exact rule of equity.—Q. Give me the history of this degree. *A.* After the body of Hiram Abiff had been found, Solomon, pleased with having an opportunity of paying a tribute of respect to the memory of so great and good a man, ordered the noble Adoniram, his Grand Inspector, to make the suitable arrangements for his interment; the brethren were ordered to attend with white aprons and gloves, and he forbade that the marks of blood which had been spilled in the temple, should be effaced until the assassins had been punished. In the mean time, Adoniram furnished a plan for a superb tomb and obelisk of white and black marble, which were finished in nine days. The tomb was entered by passing between two pillars, supporting a square stone surrounded by three circles;—on the stone, was engraved the letter J. On the tomb, was a device representing a virgin, &c. (as in third degree.) The heart of Hiram Abiff was enclosed in a golden urn, which was pierced with a sword to denote the desire of the brethren to punish the assassins. A triangular stone was affixed to the side of the urn, and on it were the letters J. M. B. surrounded by a wreath of cassia. This urn was placed on the top of the obelisk which was erected on the tomb. Three days after the interment, Solomon repaired with his court to the temple, and all the brethren being arranged as at the funeral, he directed his prayer to heaven, examined the tomb and the inscription on the urn: struck with admiration, he raised his hands and eyes to heaven, and said in the joy of his heart, "It is accomplished and complete." —Q. Where was this monument situated? *A.* Near the west end of the temple.—Q. What is meant by the letter J. on the square stone? *A.* Jeva. The ineffable name as known by us.—Q. What is meant by the letters J. M. B. on the triangular stone? *A.* They are the initials of the three Hebrew words, Joshagn, Mawkoms, Bawheer—signifying "the elect sleeps in his place."—Q. What is signified by the pyramids in the Lodge? *A.* Pyramids were used by our Egyptian brethren, for Masonic purposes. Being built on rocks, they shadow forth the durability of Masonry. Their bases were four cornered, their external surfaces equilateral triangles, pointing to the four cardinal points. The pyramidical form is also intended to remind us of our mortality. Its broad base represents the commencement, and its termination in a point, the end of human life.

CLOSING.

Master strikes *two.*—Marshal rises. Master says, "The last as well as the first care," &c. as in opening.

INTIMATE SECRETARY

OPENING.

Most Illustrious Master knocks *nine.*—Marshal rises.
Master says, "Are we all Intimate Secretaries?" *A.* We are, Most Illustrious.—Q. Your place? *A.* In the antichamber, at the head of the guards. —Q. Your business there? *A.* To see that the hall of audience is duly guarded.—Q. How are we guarded? *A.* By Perfect Masters.
The Most Illustrious says, "I appoint Brother ———, Lieutenant of the

Guards, to aid you in the execution of your duty. Repair to your station and see that none approach without permission." The guards then fall on their right knees, cross their hands in such a manner that their thumbs touch their temples, and repeat in a low voice, Jeva (pron. Je-vau,) thrice, and then retire. Solomon then strikes twice nine, upon which Hiram rises; they make signs of former degrees with twenty signs of this degree. Most Illustrious strikes three times nine and declares Lodge open. A triple triangle is placed on a Bible.

LECTURE.

Q. Are you an Intimate Secretary? *A.* I am.—*Q.* How were you received? *A.* By curiosity.—*Q.* Explain that. *A.* Being placed among the guards in the antichamber, a brother, representing the King of Tyre, hastily made his way through the guards, with a countenance expressive of anger, and entered the hall of audience, leaving the door partly open; curiosity led me to the door to observe what passed within.—*Q.* Was you perceived by them? *A.* I was. Hiram, King of Tyre hearing the noise I made, suddenly turned his head and discovered me. He exclaimed to Solomon, "My brother, there is a listener." Solomon replied, "It is impossible, since the guards are without."—*Q.* What followed? *A.* Hiram, without replying, rushed to the door, and dragging me into the Lodge, exclaimed, "Here he is." Solomon inquired, "What shall we do with him?" Hiram laid his hand on his sword, and answered, "Let him be delivered into the custody of the guards, that we may determine what punishment we shall inflict upon him, for this offence." Solomon then struck on the table which stood before him, whereupon the guards entered, and saluting the Lodge, received this order from him: "Take this prisoner, secure him, and let him be forthcoming when called for."—*Q.* Were those guards Intimate Secretaries or Perfect Masters? *A.* Of that I was then ignorant, but I am now convinced that I was the first that was made an Intimate Secretary.—*Q.* What followed? *A.* I was conducted out of the hall of audience, and detained in the custody of the guards, until a second alarum from within caused them to return with me into the hall. When the guards taking their seats around me, I was thus addressed by Solomon: "I have, by my entreaties, prevailed upon my worthy ally, Hiram, King of Tyre, whom your vain curiosity had offended, to pardon you, and receive you into favor, &c. (as in Monitor,) are you willing to take an obligation to that effect? which question I answered in the affirmative, and then received at the altar, the obligation of his degree.—*Q.* Repeat that obligation, (same as Secret Master.) *A.* Under penalty of having my body quartered, so help, &c.—*Q.* What did the Master then communicate to you? *A.* He addressed me thus: "My brother, I receive you an Intimate Secretary, on your having promised to be faithful, (as in Monitor,) and then gave me the signs, words, and token of this degree.—*Q.* Give me the signs. *A.* The first alludes to the penalty made by clenching the right hand, and drawing it from the left shoulder, to the right hip. The second is the one made at opening by guards.—*Q.* Give me the token. *A.* Made by joining right hands, and turning them downwards thrice, saying, the first time, Berith—the second time, Nedir—and the third time, Shelemoth. —*Q.* Give me the pass words? *A.* Joabert, response Terbal. The first is the name of the listener; the second, of the captain of the guards.—*Q.* Give me the mysterious word? *A.* Jeva, (pron. Je-vau.)—*Q.* What was then done to you? *A.* I was invested with the jewel and apron of this degree, and was thus addressed by the Master: "The color of your ribbon, is intended to remind you of the blood of Hiram Abiff, the last drop of which he chose to spill, rather than betray his trust; may you be equally faithful. The triple triangle is emblematical of the three theological virtues, faith, hope, and charity; it is also emblematical of the three masons who were present at the opening of the first Lodge of Intimate Secretaries, to wit: Solomon, King of Israel, Hiram, King of Tyre, and Joabert, a favorite of King Solomon.—Q. What then followed? *A.* I was ordered to salute the King of Tyre, as an Intimate Secretary, and attend to the instruction of this degree.—Q. To what does the three times nine allude in this degree? *A.* To the twenty-seven lamps with which the hall of audience was enlightened.—Q. What is signified by the letter J. which you perceive in the clouds? *A.* It is the initial of the ineffable name as known by us.—Q. What is represented by the door? *A.* The door by which they entered from the palace.—Q. Why was the hall of audience furnished with black hangings strewed with tears? *A.* To represent the grief of Solomon, for the unhappy fate of Hiram Abiff.—Q. What is meant by the A. and the two P's in the triangle? *A.* Alliance, promise and perfection.—Q. Give me the history of this degree? *A.* Hiram gave Solomon cedar trees, and fir trees, &c. (as in Monitor.)

CLOSING.

Master knocks *nine.*—Marshal rises, and says, " Brother Grand Marshal, the last as well as the first care of an Intimate Secretary? To see that the hall of audience is duly guarded. Your place, &c. How are we guarded, &c. Brother Captain of the guards, we are about to close this Lodge of Intimate Secretaries, repair to your station," &c. (Upon this, guards all make sign as at opening, and leave the room.) Then Solomon strikes twice nine, and Hiram rises—signs reversed. Solomon knocks three times nine, and declares Lodge closed.

PROVOST AND JUDGE.

OPENING.

Thrice Illustrious knocks *three.* Marshal rises. Thrice Illustrious says, "Brother Grand Marshal, are we all Provosts and Judges?" *Marshal.* We are.—Thrice Illustrious. Your place? *M.* In the north.—Thrice Illustrious. Your business there? *M.* To see that the middle chamber is duly tiled. Thrice Illustrious says, " Attend to your duty, and inform the Tiler that we are about to open this Lodge of Provost and Judge." (Grand Marshal obeys.) Thrice Illustrious strikes *four.*—Wardens rise. " Brother Junior Warden, where is the Master placed? *A.* Every where.—Q. Why so? *A.* To superintend the workmen, direct the work, and render justice to every man.—Q. What is the hour? *A.* Break of day, eight, two and seven. Thrice Illustrious strikes *five.*—Brethren rise. Thrice Illustrious says, " It is then time to begin our labors; give notice that I am going to open a Lodge of Provost and Judge, by four and one." (Signs given, Master strikes four and one—Senior Warden, four and one—Junior Warden, four and one, and Marshal, four and one; the brethren all strike four and one, with their hands, and the Master declares the Lodge open.)

RECEPTION.

Master of Ceremonies conducts candidate to the door, and knocks *four* and *one,* which is answered from within by Senior Warden, and Thrice Illustrious and Senior Warden says, "While the Provosts and Judges are engaged in right, an alarum is heard at the inner door of the Lodge," &c. a golden key is placed on the Bible.

LECTURE.—Section I.

Q. Are you a Provost and Judge? *A.* I am, and render justice to all men without distinction.—*Q.* Where were you received? *A.* In the middle chamber.—*Q.* How did you gain admission there? *A.* By *four* and *one* distinct knocks.—*Q.* To what do they allude? *A.* To the qualifications of a Provost and Judge, to wit: impartiality, justice, prudence, discretion, and mercy; of which the five lights in the middle chamber are also emblematical.—*Q.* How were these knocks answered? *A.* By *four* and *one* from within.—*Q.* What was then said to you? *A.* I was asked by what further right, &c.—*Q.* Your answer. *A.* By the right of a pass.—*Q.* What was then said to you? *A.* Wait until the Thrice Illustrious is informed of your request, and his answer returned.—*Q.* What was his answer? *A.* Introduce him in due and ancient form.—*Q.* What was that form? *A.* I was conducted by the Master of Ceremonies to the south-west corner of the middle chamber, between the Wardens, and caused to kneel on my right knee, and say Beroke. —*Q.* What answer was given to that? *A.* The Thrice Illustrious said Kumi. —*Q.* What do these words signify? *A.* The first signifies to kneel, the last, to rise.—*Q.* What followed? *A.* I was conducted three times round the Lodge, giving the signs of the ineffable degrees, and led to the altar, and caused to kneel and take the obligation of this degree.—*Q.* Repeat that obligation. *A.* Same as Secret Master, with the addition, that I will justly and impartially decide all matters of difference between brethren of this degree, if in my power so to do, under penalty of being punished as an unjust Judge, by having my nose severed from my face. So help, &c.—*Q.* What followed? *A.* The Thrice Illustrious gave me the signs, tokens, and words of this degree.—*Q.* Give me the signs? *A.* (Put the two first fingers of your right hand to the right side of your nose, the thumb under the chin, forming a square.)—*Q.* Give me the token? *A.* (Clench the three first fingers of the right hand over the thumb, and join hands by interlacing the little fingers.)—*Q.* Give me the password? *A.* Jev. (pron. Jo.)—*Q.* What was then done to you? *A.* I was invested with the jewel, apron, and gloves of this degree, and was thus addressed, "Respectable Brother, it gives me joy, that I am now about to recompense, &c. (as in Mon.) this key opens a small ebony box, in which are contained the plans for the building of the Temple, and this key opens a small ivory box containing all the keys of the Temple. I clothe you with a white apron, lined with red, having a pocket in its centre, and in which you are intended to carry the plan for the building of the Temple, that they may be laid out on the tressel board for the use of the workmen when wanted. I also give you a balance in equilibrio, as a badge of your office. Let it remind you of that equity of judgment which should characterise your decisions."—*Q.* What was next done? *A.* He made me a Provost and Judge. —*Q.* In what manner? *A.* He gave me a blow on each shoulder, and said, "By the power with which I am invested, I constitute you Provost and Judge over all the works and workmen of the Temple. Be impartial, just, prudent, discreet, and merciful. Go salute the Junior and Senior Warden as a Provost and Judge, and return to the Lodge for further instruction.

SECTION II.

Q. What did you perceive in the middle chamber? *A.* A curtain, behind which was suspended a small ebony box containing the plans for the construction of the Temple.—*Q.* What else did you see? *A.* A triangle enclosing the letters G. A.—*Q.* What is their meaning and use? *A.* Grand Architect, and are designed to make us remember him in all our decisions and actions.—*Q.* Did you perceive any thing more? *A.* I saw the letters

I. H. S. with the sprig of cassia.—Q. What is meant thereby? *A.* Imitate Hiram's Silence, and Justice, Humanity and Secrecy, which are designed to teach Provost and Judge, that while their decisions are just, they should be tempered with humanity, or mercy, and that all differences which may arise among the craft, should be kept secret from the world.—Q. What was the intention of Solomon in instituting this degree? *A.* To strengthen the means of preserving order among such a vast number of workmen; the duty of Provosts and Judges, being to decide all differences that might arise among the brethren.—Q. Who was the first that was made Provost and Judge? *A.* Joabert being honored with the intimate confidence of King Solomon, received this new mark of distinction. Solomon first created Tito, Adoniram, and Abda, his father, Provosts and Judges, and gave them orders to initiate Joabert into the mysteries of this degree, and to give him all the keys of the Temple, which were inclosed in a small ivory box suspended in the Sanctum Sanctorum, under a rich canopy. When Joabert was first admitted into this sacred place, he was struck with awe, and involuntarily found himself in a kneeling posture, and said Beroke, Solomon observing him, said Kuni, which signifies to rise.—Q. Whence came you as a Provost and Judge? *A.* I came and am going every where.

CLOSING.

Thrice Illustrious Master knocks *three*, (Marshal rises,) and says, "Brother Grand Marshal, the last as well as the first care of Provost and Judge?" *A.* To see that the middle chamber is duly tiled.—"Attend to your duty, and inform the Tiler that we are about to close this Lodge of Provosts and Judges by *four* and *one.*" Marshal reports. Thrice Illustrious strikes *four.*—Wardens rise, and Master says, "Brother Senior Warden, what is the hour?" *A.* Break of day, 8, 2, and 7.—Q. "Brother Junior Warden, how so?" *A.* Because Provosts and Judges should be ready at all times to render justice. Thrice Illustrious knocks *four* and *one*, and brethren all rise. Signs reversed given. Thrice Illustrious strikes *four* and *one*, Marshal *four* and *one*, Junior Warden *four* and *one*, and Senior Warden *four* and *one*, and then all the brethren strike *four* and *one* with their hands, and Thrice Illustrious declares Lodge duly closed.

INTENDANT OF THE BUILDINGS, (OR I. B.)

OPENING.

Most Puissant knocks *three*, (Marshal rises,) and says, "Brother Grand Marshal, are we all I. B.?" *A.* We are, Most Puissant.—Q. Your place? *A.* In the North.—Q. Your business there? *A.* To see that the Lodge is duly tiled. "Attend to your duty, and inform the Lodge that we are about to open a Lodge of I. B. by the number *five.*" Marshal obeys. Most Puissant knocks *four*, and Wardens rise.—Q. "Brother Senior Warden, what is the hour?" *A.* Break of day. Most Puissant knocks *five*, and brethren all rise. Most Puissant says, "If it is break of day, it is time to begin our labors; give notice that I am going to open a Lodge of I. B." Senior Warden obeys. All make signs. Most Puissant knocks *five*, Senior Warden *five*, Junior Warden *five*, and brethren *five*, with their hands; and Most Puissant declares Lodge open.

RECEPTION.

Most Puissant knocks *seven*, and Senior Warden rises. Most Puissant says, "My excellent Brother, how shall we repair the loss of our worthy

Hiram Abiff, he is now removed from us, and we are thereby deprived of his counsel and services: can you give me any advice in this important matter?" Senior Warden answers, "The method I would propose, would be to select a chief from the five orders of architecture, upon whom we may confer the degree of I. B. and by his assistance fill the secret chamber of the third story." Most Puissant says, "I approve of your advice, and to convince you of my readiness to follow it, I appoint you and brothers Adoniram and Abda to carry the same into execution. Excellent brothers, let Adoniram go into the middle chamber and see if he can find a chief of the five orders of architecture." Junior Warden goes out of the lodge into the antechamber, and finding the candidate, addresses him as in the Lecture.

NOTE. When the alarum of *five* is given, Senior Warden rises and says, "Most Puissant, we are disturbed in our deliberations by an alarum at the inner door of the secret chamber." Most Puissant says, "Brother Senior Warden, see the cause of that alarum."

LECTURE.

Q. Are you an Intendant of the Buildings? A. I have made the five steps of exactness; I have penetrated the inmost part of the Temple, and have seen the great light, in which were three mysterious characters, J. J. J. —Q. How were you received? A. Being in the middle chamber, in company with the Master of Ceremonies, Adoniram entered and inquired, "Is there here a chief of the five orders of architecture?"—Q. Your answer. A. I am one.—Q. What followed? A. I was then asked, "My dear brother, have you zeal to apply yourself with attention to that which the Most Puissant shall request of you."—Q. Your answer. A. I have, and will comply with the request of the Most Puissant, and raise this edifice to his honor and glory.—Q. What followed? A. Adoniram demanded of me the signs, words, and tokens of my former degrees, which being given, the Master of Ceremonies conducted me to the door of the Lodge, where he gave five distinct knocks.—Q. To what did they allude? A. To the five orders of architecture.—Q. How were they answered? A. By five from within.—Q. What was then said to you? A. I was asked, "Who comes there?"—Q. Your answer? A. A chief of the five orders of architecture, who is to be employed in the works of the secret chamber.—Q. What was then said to you? A. I was then asked by what further right, &c.—Q. Your answer? A. By the right of a pass-word.—Q. Give me that pass-word? A. Bonahim, (pron. Bo-nau-heem.)—Q. What was then said to you? A. Wait until the Most Puissant is informed, &c.—Q. What was his answer? A. Let him be introduced in due form.—Q. What followed? A. I was conducted to the altar and caused to recede five steps, and then to advance to the altar by five steps of regular exactness.—Q. What is meant thereby? A. That I should recede from vice, and advance to virtue, before I was qualified to supply the place of so good a man as the lamented Hiram Abiff.—Q. What followed? A. I was laid prostrate before the altar, with a sprig of cassia in my right hand, and my left upon the first great light of Masonry, in which posture I took the obligation of this degree.—Q. Repeat that obligation. A. (Same as Secret Master,) under penalty of being deprived of my sight. So help, &c.—Q. What then followed? A. I was thus addressed by the Most Puissant, "Your present posture is that of a dead man, and is designed to remind you of the fate of our worthy Hiram Abiff. I shall now raise you in the same manner he was raised, under the sprig of cassia." I was then raised by the Master's grip, and further addressed, "By your being raised, our hope is signified, that in some measure you will repair his loss, by imitating his bright example."—Q. What followed? A. I received the signs, tokens, and words of this degree.—Q. Give me the signs? A. (Interlace the fingers, and place the hands over the eyes, alluding to penalty; second sign is that of grief, made like Fellow-Craft's, with left hand on the left hip.)—Q. Give me the token? A. (Take hold of each other by the right wrists with the right hand.)—Q. Give me the pass-word? A. Bonahim.—Q. What does that word signify? A. Builders.—Q. Give me the words? A. Achard, jenok, (pron. yo-kayn.)—Q. Give me the mysterious word? A. Jah, (pron. yaw.)—Q. What was next done? A. I was invested with the apron, gloves, and jewels of this degree, and was thus addressed, "I decorate you with a red ribbon, to be worn crossing the breast from the right shoulder to the left hip, to which is suspended a triangle fastened by a green ribbon. I also present you with a white apron, lined with red, and bordered with green. The red is emblematical of that zeal which should characterize you as an I. of B., and the green, of the hope we entertain that you will supply the place of our lamented Hiram Abiff. My brother, King Solomon willing to carry," &c. (as in Monitor.)—Q. What is meant by the letters B. A. J. on the triangle which you wear? A. They are the initials of the pass word and words of this degree.—Q. What followed? A. I was directed to salute the Senior Warden as an Intendant of the Buildings, and return to the east for further instruction.

SECTION II.

Q. What did you see in the Lodge? A. A triangle enclosing a circle, having on its circumference the letters J. A. I. N. and in its centre the letters J. J. J.—Q. What is signified by the circle in the triangle? A. The eternity of the powers of God, which hath neither beginning nor end.—Q. What is signified by the letters J. A. I. N.? A. They are the initials of the four Hebrew words, Jad, Ail, Jotsare, and Nogah, which are expressive of four attributes of the Deity; power, omnipresence, creation, and splendor.—Q. What is signified by the letters J. J. J.? A. Jah, Jokayn, and Jireh, signifying "The Lord, the Creator seeth."—Q. What else did you see? A. A blazing star with five beams, in the centre of which appeared the letter J.—Q. What is signified by the five beams? A. The five equal lights of Masonry, the Bible, the square, the compass, the key, and the triangle.—Q. What is signified by the letter J.? A. It is the initial of the ineffable name, as known by us.—Q. Are you in darkness? A. No, the blazing star is my guide.—Q. What is your age? A. 27, or 5, 7, and 15.—Q. To what do those three numbers allude? A. To the five chiefs of the five orders of architecture, to seven cubits, which was the breadth of the golden candlestick, and the fifteen Fellow-Crafts, who conspired against the life of our Grand Master, Hiram Abiff.

CLOSING.

Most Puissant knocks *three*, (and Grand Marshal rises,) and says "Brother Grand Marshal, the last as well as the first care of I. of B.? A. To see that the Lodge is duly tiled.—" Attend to your duty," &c. Most Puissant knocks *four*, and Wardens rise, "Brother Senior Warden, what is the hour?" A. Seven at night. Most Puissant strikes *five*—all brethren rise. Most Puissant says, "As it is seven at night, it is time to retire: Brother Junior Warden, give notice that I am going to close this Lodge of Intendants of the Buildings." Signs reversed. Most Puissant knocks *five*, Junior Warden *seven*, and Senior Warden *fifteen*, then the brethren *five*, *seven*, and *fifteen*, with their hands, and the Most Puissant declares the Lodge closed.

ELECTED KNIGHTS OF NINE.

OPENING.

Form of Lodge, (see Monitor.) The brethren sit cross-legged, and lean their heads on their right hands. Most Potent knocks *seven*—(Grand Marshal rises,) "Brother Grand Marshal, are we all Elected Knights of Nine?" *A.* We are.—*Q.* Your place? *A.* In the north, Most Potent.—*Q.* Your business there? *A.* To see that the Chapter is duly guarded.—" Please attend to your duty, and inform the Sentinel that we are about to open this chapter of E. K. and charge him," &c. Marshal obeys. Most Potent knocks *eight*, and the Warden rises, and Master says, " Brother Stokin, are you an E. K.?" *A.* One cavern received me, one lamp gave me light, and one fountain refreshed me.—*Q.* What is the hour? *A.* Break of day. Most Potent knocks *eight* quick and *one* slow strokes, and companies all arise. Most Potent says, " If it is break of day it is time to open a Chapter of E. K's. Inform the companies," &c. Warden obeys. Signs given. Most Potent knocks eight and one, and Warden eight and one, and companies eight and one, with their hands; and Most Potent declares the Chapter open.

LECTURE.

Q. Are you an E. K.? *A.* One cavern received me, one lamp gave me light, and one fountain refreshed me.—*Q.* Where were you received? *A.* In the audience chamber of Solomon.—*Q.* How were you received? *A.* I was hoodwinked and conducted by the Master of Ceremonies to the door of the Chapter, where he gave eight and one distinct knocks?—*Q.* To what do those knocks allude? *A.* To the number of the nine elect.—*Q.* How were those knocks answered? *A.* By eight and one from within.—*Q.* What followed? *A.* I was asked " Who comes there?"—*Q.* Your answer? *A.* A companion, to whose lot it has fallen to accompany the stranger in search of the assassins of Hiram Abiff.—*Q.* What followed? *A.* I was conducted by the hand to the West, and asked by the Most Potent, what I wanted.—*Q.* Your answer? *A.* To be made an Elected Knight.—*Q.* What then followed? *A.* I was asked if I had courage to go in pursuit of the assassins of Hiram Abiff, which question I answered in the affirmative, and was addressed by the Most Potent in the following manner; " If you have, you shall be shown the place where one of his murderers lies concealed, a stranger has discovered it to me, and if you have resolution, follow this stranger."—*Q.* What was then done to you? *A.* The Master of Ceremonies led me out of the Chapter, by intricate roads, and at last seated me on a stone, and thus addressed me; "I am going to leave you, but be of good cheer, I shall not be long absent; when I am gone you must take the bandage off your eyes, and drink some water from the fountain beside you, that you may be refreshed after so fatiguing a journey.—*Q.* What followed? *A.* I removed the bandage and found myself alone in a cavern, in which was a lamp, a fountain, and a head just severed from the body. In a short time the Master of Ceremonies returned, and directed me to take a poniard in my right hand, and the head in my left, and then conducted me to the door of the Chapter, where I knocked eight and one with my foot, which was answered from within, and I was asked, "What do you want?"—*Q.* Your answer? *A.* To enter this Chapter of Elected Knights.—*Q.* What followed? *A.* I was asked by what right I claimed this privilege.—*Q.* Your answer? *A.* I have performed a feat for the honor of the craft, which I hope will entitle me to this degree.—*Q.* What followed? *A.* I was admitted, and directed to approach the altar by eight quick and one slow steps, still holding the head in my left hand, and the poniard in my right, as if in the act of striking, the ninth step brought me to the altar, where the Most Potent addressed me in an angry tone, "Wretch, what have you done, do you not know that by this rash act you have deprived me of an opportunity of inflicting condign punishment on the assassin?"—*Q.* What followed? *A.* The companies made earnest intercession for me, observing that my offence had doubtless arisen from the warmth of my zeal, and not from any bad intention. Upon this the Most Potent was reconciled, and he administered to me the obligation of this degree, the companies all standing round me with their poniards as if going to stab me.—*Q.* Repeat that obligation? *A.* (Same as in Secret Master.) Under penalty of being stabbed in my head and in my heart, so help, &c.—*Q.* What followed? *A.* The Most Potent gave me the sign, token, and words of this degree.—*Q.* Give me the sign? *A.* (Clap your right hand first to your head and then to your heart.)—*Q.* Give me the token. *A.* (Grasp the thumb of your brother's right hand, both clenching the fingers and extending the thumb of the hand that is uppermost.)—*Q.* To what does that token allude? *A.* The eight fingers and extended thumb allude to the eight and one elect; the one to Joabert, who left his eight companions, and went alone in search of, &c.—*Q.* Give me the pass-words? *A.* Rawkam and Akirop.—*Q.* What is the word? *A.* Bugelkal, who was chief of the tabernacle.—*Q.* Give me the mysterious word? *A.* Jeva, (pron. Je-vau.)—*Q.* What was then done to you? *A.* I was invested with the apron, gloves, and jewel of this degree, and ordered to salute the Warden, and to return to the east for further instruction.

SECTION II.

Q. Give me the history of this degree? *A.* After the death of Hiram Abiff, the three ruffians who had been apprehended, having made their escape, a great assembly of Masters had sat, &c. (as in Monitor, to the words,) he had only time to pronounce Naukam, which signifies, "vengeance is taken," and expired. Joabert being extremely fatigued, refreshed himself at the spring, which he found in the cavern, and then slept until he was awakened by the other eight, who arrived shortly after. On beholding what Joabert had done, they all exclaimed Naukam. Joabert then severed the head from the body, divided the body into four quarters which were burnt to ashes, and the ashes scattered to the four winds of heaven. Joabert then taking the head, &c. (as in Monitor, to the words,) again reconciled. Solomon then ordered the head to be placed on the east pinnacle of the temple.—*Q.* What was the name of the assassin? *A.* Jubelum Akirop.—*Q.* From what number were the nine elect chosen? *A.* Ninety-nine.—*Q.* Where was the assassin found? *A.* In a cavern, near the coast of Joppa.—*Q.* How did the nine elect travel? *A.* By dark and intricate roads, which often obliged them to cross their legs, and this is the reason why the nine elect sit in this manner in the Chapter.—*Q.* What is meant by the dog you saw on the carpet, in the Lodge? *A.* The dog of the stranger, through whose sagacity Akirop was discovered.—*Q.* What does the color, black, denote in this degree? *A.* Grief.—*Q.* What is your age? *A.* Eight and one, accomplished.

CLOSING.

Most Potent knocks *seven*, (Grand Marshal rises,) and says, "The last as well as the first care of a Chapter of E. K." *A.* To see that the Chapter is duly guarded. Please attend to your duty, and inform the Sentinel, &c. Most Potent knocks *eight*, and Warden rises. *Q.* "What is the hour?" *A.* Evening. Most Potent knocks *eight* and *one*.—Companies all rise. (Companion Stokin gives notice, &c.) Most Potent knocks *eight* and *one*, Warden, *eight* and *one*, Companions, *eight* and *one*, and the Chapter is declared duly closed.

520   LIGHT ON MASONRY.

MASTERS ELECTED OF FIFTEEN.

OPENING.

Most Potent knocks *five*, (Grand Marshal rises,) "Brother Grand Marshal, are we all Masters Elected of Fifteen?" *A*. We are, Most Potent.—*Q*. Your place? &c. Your business? &c. Please inform the Tiler, that we are about to open a Lodge of Masters Elected of Fifteen. Most Potent knocks *twice five*.—Senior Warden rises. Most Potent knocks *three times five*.—Brethren rise. Most Potent, says, "Brother Inspector, give notice that I am going to open a Lodge of Masters Elected of Fifteen, by three times five." Inspector obeys. Most Potent knocks *three times five*, Senior Warden, *three times five*, Junior Warden, *three times five*, and the Brethren the same, and the Lodge is declared open.

LECTURE.

Q. Are you a Master Elected of Fifteen? *A*. My zeal and works have prepared me that honor.—*Q*. How were you prepared? *A*. A head was placed in my hands, and I was conducted to the door of the Lodge by the Master of Ceremonies, who knocked three times five.—*Q*. How were those knocks answered? *A*. By three times five from within.—*Q*. To what do they allude? *A*. The fifteen elected Masters.—*Q*. What followed? *A*. I was asked, "Who comes there?"—*Q*. Your answer? *A*. An elected Knight, who is desirous of joining the other Knights, for the purpose of discovering the other assassins.—*Q*. What was then said to you? *A*. I was told to wait until the Most Potent had been informed of my request, and his answer returned.—*Q*. What was his answer? *A*. Let him be introduced in due form.—*Q*. What was that due form? *A*. I was conducted to the altar, and caused to make fifteen steps in a triangular form, which brought me again to the altar, when the Most Potent ordered me to kneel, and thus addressed me: "My Brother, the Elected Masters here present, wish me to admit you to this degree; will you take the obligation appertaining to the same?" Which being answered in the affirmative, I took the obligation.—*Q*. Repeat that obligation? *A*. (Same as Secret Master.) Under penalty of having my body cut open perpendicularly, and my head cut off and placed on the highest pinnacle in the world, so help me, &c.—*Q*. What did the Most Potent then communicate to you? *A*. He gave me the signs, words, and token of this degree.—*Q*. Give me the signs? *A*. (Hold the thumb of the right hand at the bottom of the belly, and move it perpendicularly upwards.) The second sign, (that of the entered apprentice, with the fingers clenched.)—*Q*. Give me the token? *A*. (Join left hands.)—*Q*. Give me the pass word? *A*. Eleham.—*Q*. Give me the mysterious word? *A*. Jevah, (pron. Je-vau.)—*Q*. What then followed? *A*. I was invested with the apron, gloves, and jewels of this degree, and directed to salute the Senior Warden as a Master Elected of Fifteen, and return to the east for further instruction.

SECTION II.

Q. Give me the history of this degree? *A*. Not long after the execution, &c. (as in Monitor, to words,) they were discovered cutting stone, in a quarry. They were immediately seized and carried to Jerusalem, and imprisoned in the tower of Achizer, and at ten o'clock on the ensuing morning, they were brought forth for execution. They were bound neck and middle, to posts, with their arms extended, and their bellies were cut open by the executioner, lengthways and across, and thus they remained until six in the evening, their entrails exposed to flies and other insects; their tongues and entrails were afterwards taken out for the beasts of the field and the birds of the air to prey upon, and their heads were cut off and placed upon spikes, like that of Akirop, on the west and south pinnacles of the temple. Thus we see that although corruption, perjury, and treason, assisted our ancient Knights, their quarters were discovered by the unerring eye of justice, and they were doomed to suffer penalty tantamount to their crimes.—Q. What were the names of the two assassins? *A.* Jubela Kurmavil, and Jubelo Gravolet.—Q. At what hour did the assassins expire? *A.* At six in the evening.

CLOSING.

Most Potent knocks *five,* (Grand Marshal rises.) Most Potent says, "Brother Grand Marshal, the last as well as the first care of a Lodge of Masters Elected of Fifteen. *A.* To see that the Lodge is duly tiled. "Please attend," &c. Most Potent knocks *twice five.*—Senior Warden rises. Signs reversed. Most Potent knocks *three times five,* which is repeated by Wardens, and then by Brethren, with their hands, &c.

ILLUSTRIOUS KNIGHTS ELECTED.

OPENING.

Most Potent knocks *ten,* (Grand Marshal rises.) "Are we all Illustrious Knights Elected?" *A.* We are, Most Potent. "Your place? &c. Your duty?" *A.* To see that the Chapter is duly guarded. "Please attend," &c. Most Potent knocks *eleven,* (Grand Inspector rises.) "Companion Inspector, what is the hour? *A.* It is twelve. Most Potent knocks *twelve,* (Companions rise.) "If it is twelve, it is time to labor by the greatest of lights." (Signs given.) Most Potent knocks *twelve,* Inspector, *twelve,* and Companions, *twelve,* with their hands, &c.

LECTURE.

Q. Are you an Illustrious Knight Elected? *A.* My name will inform you. —Q. What is that name? *A.* Payrawsh, Baw-heer, (or Illustrious Knight Elected.)—Q. How were you admitted? *A.* I was hoodwinked and conducted by the Master of Ceremonies, to the door of the Chapter, where he gave twelve distinct knocks.—Q. To what did they allude? *A.* To the twelve tribes of Israel.—Q. How were they answered? *A.* By twelve from within.—Q. What was then said to you? *A.* "Who comes there?" —Q. Your answer? *A.* A Master Elected of Fifteen wishes to receive the degree of Illustrious Knight.—Q. What was then said to you? *A.* I was asked by what further right, &c. and I was told to wait until the Most Potent was informed of my request and his answer returned.—Q. What was that answer? *A.* Let him be introduced in due form.—Q. What then followed? *A.* I was conducted to the west, and the Most Potent inquired what I wanted?—Q. Your answer? *A.* To receive the degree of Illustrious Knight, as a reward for my zeal and labor.—Q. What did the Most Potent say to you then? *A.* My Brother, you cannot receive this degree, until you have given us satisfactory proof that you have not been an accomplice in the death of our Grand Master, Hiram Abiff; to assure us of this, we require you to participate in a symbolic offering, of a portion of the heart of our Respectable Master, Hiram Abiff, which we have preserved since his assassination. You are to swallow the portion we present to you. Every faithful Mason may receive it without injury, but it cannot remain in the body of one who is perjured. Are you disposed to submit to this trial? Q. What was your answer? A. I am.—Q. What followed? A. The Most Potent directed the Master of Ceremonies to cause me to advance to the altar, by twelve upright regular steps, where the Most Potent, with the trowel, presented to me the symbolic offering which I swallowed, and was thus addressed by the Most Potent: "This mystic oblation, which, like you, we have received, forms a tie so strong that nothing can break it; wo to him who attempts to disunite us." I then received the obligation of this degree. —Q. Repeat that obligation. A. (Same as Secret Master.) Under penalty of having my hands nailed to my breast, so help, &c.—Q. What was then communicated to you? A. The Most Potent removed the bandage, and gave me the sign. (Cross hands on breast,) it alludes to penalty.—Q. Give me the token? A. (Token of Intimate Secretary, with left hand on Brother's heart.)—Q. Give me the pass-word. A. Emun.—Q. What does that word signify? A. Truth.—Q. Give me the mysterious word. A. Johe, (pron. Yo-hay.)—Q. What followed? A. I was invested with the apron, gloves, and jewel of this degree, and was told that the device on my sash and apron, and also the color of the latter, was an emblem of a heart inflamed with gratitude for the honors and rewards conferred on me, and the sword of that justice, which overtook and punished the assassins, and was designed to admonish me that perjury and treason will never escape the sword of justice, and I was directed to go and salute the Inspector, and return to the east for further instruction.

SECTION II.

Q. Of what was the symbolic offering presented to you, at your initiation composed? A. Of flour, milk, wine, and oil.—Q. What did they represent? A. Flour represents goodness, the milk, gentleness, the wine, strength or fortitude, and the oil, light and wisdom, qualities which distinguished Hiram Abiff, and should distinguish every Illustrious Knight.—Q. How were the Illustrious Knights employed at the erection of the temple? A. They had command over the twelve tribes, and by their strict attention, promoted peace and harmony, and animated the laborers with cheerfulness.—Q. What was the intention of Solomon, in instituting this degree? A. To reward the zeal, &c. and also by their preferment to make more.

CLOSING.

Most Potent knocks *ten*, (Grand Marshal rises.) "The last as well as the first care of a Chapter of Illustrious Knights." A. To see that the Chapter is duly guarded. "Attend to your duty, and inform the Sentinel," &c. Most Potent knocks *eleven*, (Senior Warden rises.) "Brother Inspector, what is the hour?" A. Low six. Most Potent knocks *twelve*, (Brethren rise.) "Brother Inspector, give notice," &c. Signs. Most Potent knocks *twelve*, Inspector, *twelve*, Brethren, *twelve*, with their hands, and Most Potent declares the Chapter duly closed.

GRAND MASTER ARCHITECTS.

OPENING.

Most Potent knocks *one*. (Grand Marshal rises.) "Are we all," &c. Your place? &c. Your duty? *A.* To see that the Chapter is duly guarded. "Attend," &c. Most Potent knocks *two*.—Warden rises. Most Potent says, "What is the hour?" *A.* A star indicates the first instant, the first hour, and the first day, in which the Grand Architect commenced the creation of the universe. Most Potent knocks *one* and *two*.—Companions rise. Most Potent says, "Companions, it is the first instant, the first hour, the first day, in which the Grand Architect commenced the creation of the universe; it is the first hour, the first day, the first year, when Solomon commenced the Temple; the first day, the first hour, the first instant for opening this Chapter. It is time to commence our labors. Give notice," &c. Signs. Most Potent knocks *one* and *two*, Senior Warden, *one* and *two*, Companions, *one* and *two*, and Most Potent declares Chapter open, &c.

LECTURE.

Q. Are you a Grand Master Architect? *A.* I know the use of every mathematical instrument.—*Q.* What are they? *A.* A square, a single compass, a compass with four points, a rule, a line, a compass of perfection, a quadrant, a level and plumb.—*Q.* Where were you received? *A.* In a white place, painted with flames.—*Q.* What does that signify? *A.* That purity of heart, and that zeal which should characterize every Grand Master Architect.—*Q.* How were you admitted? *A.* I was conducted by the Master of Ceremonies to the door of the Chapter, where he gave one and two distinct knocks.—*Q.* How were those knocks answered? *A.* By one and two from within.—*Q.* What followed? *A.* I was asked, "Who comes there?"—*Q.* Your answer? *A.* An Illustrious Knight, who wishes to receive the degree of Grand Architect.—*Q.* What then followed? *A.* I was conducted by the Master of Ceremonies, to the west, and thus addressed: "It has become necessary to form a school of Architecture for the instruction of the brethren employed in the Temple, as none but skilful Architects can bring the same to perfection. In order to prevent some brethren from receiving the honors and rewards due only to brethren of talents, we have deemed it expedient to prove and test all those who present themselves as candidates for this degree. We therefore require you to make the tour of the Temple, for the purpose of examining the work, and to produce a plan drawn with exactness which you must present for inspection, that we may judge whether you are entitled to this degree."—*Q.* What followed? *A.* I was conducted through the antechamber and round the Lodge, when the Master of Ceremonies again stationed me in the west, and where I drew a plan according to his direction. When the same was finished, the Master of Ceremonies informed the Most Potent that I had obeyed his directions. Most Potent inquired, "My brother, what are the fruits of your travels?"—*Q.* Your answer? *A.* "Most Potent, I have brought a plan of the works of the Temple, which I am ready to present for inspection."—*Q.* What followed? *A.* I was directed to approach the east, and present the plan to the Most Potent, which I accordingly did, and the Most Potent examined the same, and then passed it on to the other companions, who, after examining, returned it with expressions of approbation, and then the Most Potent addressed me thus: "It is with pleasure we witness the skill you have manifested in fulfilling the conditions prescribed to you, but we require further proof before you can be admitted among us. We again require you to travel."—*Q.* What followed? *A.* I was conducted once round the Lodge, to the north, where I stopped to view the north star, and was told, that as the north star was a guide to mariners, so ought virtue to be a guide to every Grand Master Architect, and was again conducted to the west and directed to approach the east by one and two steps, which brought me to the altar, when the Most Potent inquired, "What have you learnt in your travels?"—*Q.* Your answer? *A.* That virtue as well as talents should be possessed by every one who is admitted to this degree.—*Q.* What followed? *A.* I received the obligation of a Grand Master Architect.—*Q.* Repeat that obligation? *A.* (Same as Secret Master.) Under the penalty of having my left hand cut in twain, so help, &c.—*Q.* What then followed? *A.* I was then addressed by the Most Potent.—*Q.* What then followed? *A.* The Most Potent gave me the signs, words, and token of this degree.—*Q.* Give me the sign? *A.* (Make the motion of writing in the left hand,) also alluding to penalty.—*Q.* Give me the token? *A.* (Interlace the last finger of the right hand, so as to form a square, and place the left hand on each other's right shoulder.)—*Q.* Give me the pass-word? *A.* Rab-kuam.—*Q.* What does that word signify? *A.* Grand Master Architect.—*Q.* Give me the mysterious word? *A.* Jehovah, (pron. Ye-ho-wah.)—*Q.* What was then done to you? *A.* The Most Potent invested me with the jewel, apron, and gloves of this degree, and thus addressed me: "I have elevated," &c.—*Q.* What then followed? *A.* I was directed to salute the Senior Warden, as a Grand Architect, and return to the east for further instruction.—*Q.* Give me the history? *A.* Solomon established this degree for the purpose, &c.—*Q.* What do the seven small   round the north star, signify? *A.* Seven liberal arts and sciences.

CLOSING.

Most Potent knocks *one*. (Grand Marshal rises.) Most Potent says, "The last as well as the first care," &c. Most Potent knocks *two*, (Senior Warden rises.) Most Potent says, "What is the hour?" *A.* The last instant, the last hour, the last day, in which the Grand Architect completed the creation of the universe. Most Potent knocks *one* and *two*.—Companions rise. Most Potent says, "It is the last instant, &c.; it is the last hour, the last day, the last year, in which Solomon completed the Temple, the last instant for closing this Chapter. Give notice," &c. Signs. Most Potent knocks *one* and *two*, Senior Warden, *one* and *two*, and Companions *one* and *two*, with their hands.

KNIGHTS OF THE NINTH ARCH.

OPENING.

Most Potent knocks *seven*. (Grand Marshal rises.) "Are we all Knights of the Ninth Arch?" *A.* We are, Most Potent.—*Q.* Your place? &c. &c. Most Potent knocks *eight*. (Junior Warden rises.) *Q.* What is the hour? *A.* The rising of the sun. Most Potent knocks *three times three*.—Companions rise. Most Potent says, "If it is the rising of the sun, it is time to commence our labors. Give notice," &c. Signs of former degrees. Then two kings kneel at the pedestal, as in the first sign, and raise each other by the token. Companions do the same. Most Potent knocks *three times three*, Senior Warden, same, Junior Warden, same, and Companions, same, and Most Potent says, "I declare this Chapter open."

LECTURE.

Q. Are you a Knight of the Ninth Arch? *A.* I have penetrated the bowels of the earth, through nine arches, and have seen the brilliant triangle.—*Q.* In what place were you admitted? *A.* In the audience chamber of King Solomon.—*Q.* How did you gain admittance there? *A.* In company with some Intendants of the Building, Illustrious Knights, and Grand Master Architects. I was conducted by the Master of Ceremonies to the door of the audience chamber, where he gave three times three distinct knocks.—*Q.* To what did they allude? *A.* To the nine arches which led from the palace of Solomon to the secret vault, and the nine arches of the Temple of Enoch.—*Q.* How were they answered? *A.* By three times three from within.—*Q.* What followed? *A.* I was asked, "Who comes there?"—*Q.* Your answer? *A.* Several I. of B's, I. K's, and Grand Master Architects solicit the honor of being admitted into the secret vault under the Sanctum Sanctorum.—*Q.* What was then said to you? *A.* I was told to wait until the Most Potent had been informed of my request, and his answer returned. *Q.* What was his answer? *A.* My brethren, your request cannot now be granted.—*Q.* What followed? *A.* We were conducted back to the antechamber, when the nine Masters entered and thus addressed us: "My brethren, our Most Potent Master requests Grand Master Architects, Joabert, Stokin, and Gibulum, to attend in the audience chamber," whereupon, we were introduced into the presence of Solomon, who thus addressed us: "My brethren, you know that in digging for a foundation for the Temple, we found the ruins of an ancient edifice. Among the ruins, we have already discovered much treasure which has been deposited in the secret vault. Are you willing to make farther researches among the ancient ruins, and report to us your discoveries?"—*Q.* What was your answer? *A.* We are.—*Q.* What followed? *A.* We were conducted to the ruins, and commenced our labors. Among the rubbish, we discovered a large iron ring fixed in a cubic stone, which we raised with much difficulty. Upon examining the same, we discovered an inscription, of the meaning of which we were ignorant. Beneath the stone, a deep and dismal cavern appeared.—*Q.* Did you enter that cavern? *A.* I did.—*Q.* In what manner? *A.* A rope was fastened round my body, and descending, I found myself in an arched vault, in the floor of which was a secret opening, through which I also descended, and in like manner through a third; being in the third vault, I found there was an opening for descending still farther, but being afraid of pursuing my search, I gave a signal and was hoisted by my two companions. I then recounted to them what I had seen, and proposed to them to descend by turns, which they refused; upon this I determined to descend again, and told them that through every arch I passed, I would gently shake the rope. In this manner I descended from arch to arch, until I was lowered into the sixth arch, when finding there was still another opening, my heart failed me, and giving the signal, I was again pulled up. I acquainted my two companions with the particulars of my second descent, and now earnestly urged that one of them should go down, as I was very much fatigued; but terrified at my relation, they both refused. I then received fresh courage, went down a third time, taking a lighted flambeau in my hand. When I had descended into the ninth arch, a parcel of stone and mortar suddenly fell in and extinguished my light, and I immediately saw a triangular plate of gold, richly adorned with precious stones, the brilliancy of which struck me with admiration and astonishment. Again I gave the signal and was assisted in reascending. Having related to my two companions the scene which I had witnessed, they expressed a desire to witness the same; they also concluded to go down together, by means of a ladder of ropes, which they did, and shortly after returned with the golden plate, upon which we saw certain characters, of the meaning of which we were then ignorant.—*Q*. What followed? *A*. We repaired to the apartment of King Solomon, the King of Tyre with him, and said, "Most Potent, we have obeyed your commands and present you with the fruits of our labors, and solicit the honor of being made acquainted with the inscription on this cubic stone and this golden triangle." Upon beholding it, the two Kings raised their hands, and exclaimed "Gibulum ishtov." The Kings then examined the sacred characters with attention, and Solomon thus addressed us: "My brethren, your request cannot now be granted. God has bestowed upon you a particular favor, in permitting you to discover the most precious jewel of Masonry. The promise which God made to some of the ancient patriarchs, that in fulness of time his name should be discovered, is now accomplished. As a reward for your zeal, constancy, and fidelity, I should now constitute you Knights of the Ninth Arch, and I promise you an explanation of the mysterious characters on the golden plate, when it is fixed in the place designed for it, and I will then confer on you the most sublime and mysterious degree of Perfection."—*Q*. What followed? *A*. The Most Potent directed the Master of Ceremonies, to conduct us to the south-west, in the west, and from thence to approach the altar, by three times three steps, and there to take upon ourselves the obligation of this degree.—*Q*. Repeat that obligation? *A*. (Same as in Secret Master.) I further promise never to be concerned in the initiation of any brother in this degree, unless he manifests a charitable disposition for Masonry, and a zeal for the brethren, and also obtains permission under the hands and seal of the first regular officers of the Lodge of Perfection. I further promise that I will not debauch any female related to a companion of this degree, either by blood or marriage, knowing her to be such, under penalty of being crushed under the ruins of a subterraneous Temple, so help, &c.—*Q*. What followed? *A*. The Most Potent gave me the signs, token, and words of this degree.—*Q*. Give me the sign. *A*. (Made by kneeling on the left knee, the right hand on the back, the left raised above the head, the palm upward, the body leaning forward, alluding to penalty.)—*Q*. Give me the token? *A*. (Being in the last mentioned position, token is made by raising each other from the same, by interlacing the fingers of the left hand.)—*Q*. How many pass-words are there? *A*. One for each arch.—*Q*. Give them to me? *A*. 1st, Jov; 2d, Jeho; 3d, Juha; 4th, Havah; 5th, Elgibbor; 6th, Adonai; 7th, Joken, 8th, Eloah; 9th, Elzeboath.—*Q*. Give me the grand word. *A*. Gibulum ishtov.—*Q*. What does that signify? *A*. Gibulum, is a good man.—*Q*. What was then done to you? *A*. I was invested with the jewel, apron, and gloves of this degree, and directed to salute the Senior Warden as a Knight of the Ninth Arch, and return to the east for further instruction.

SECTION II.

Q. Give me the history and charge of this degree? *A*. My worthy brother, it is my intention, at this time, to give you a clearer account of certain historical traditions, &c. (to the words "favored with a mystical vision,") when the Almighty thus deigned to speak to him, as thou art desirous to know my name, attend, and it shall be revealed unto thee. Upon this a mountain seemed to rise to the heavens, and Enoch was transferred to the top thereof, where he beheld a triangular plate of gold most brilliantly enlightened, and upon which were some characters which he received a strict injunction never to pronounce. Presently he seemed to be lowered perpendicularly into the bowels of the earth through nine arches, in the ninth or deepest of which he saw the same brilliant plate which was shown to him in the mountain. Enoch being inspired, &c. (as in Monitor, to the words,) "You, as a Knight of the Ninth Arch, are entitled to receive." In digging for a foundation they discovered an ancient edifice, among which they found a considerable quantity of treasure, such as vases of gold and silver, urns, marble, jasper, and agate columns, and precious stones. All these treasures were collected and carried to Solomon, who upon deliberation concluded that they were the ruins of some ancient temple, erected before the flood, and possibly to the service of Idolatry. He therefore determined to build the Temple in another place, lest it should be polluted. Solomon caused a cavern to be constructed under the Temple, to which he gave the name of secret vault. He erected in this vault a large pillar of white marble, to support the Sanctum Sanctorum, and which, by inspiration, he called the pillar of beauty, from the beauty of the ark which it sustained. There was a long narrow descent through nine arches from the palace of Solomon to this vault. To this place he was accustomed to retire with Hiram of Tyre, and Hiram Abiff, when he had occasion to enter upon important business. There were none else, then living, qualified to enter this vault. One of their number being removed, disordered their business for a time, as the two kings were on one occasion consulting on business of the craft, application was made to them by several I's of B. I. K's. and Grand Master Architects, soliciting the honor of being admitted to the secret vault, to whom Solomon replied, "My brethren, your request cannot now be granted." Some days afterwards, Solomon sent for the three Grand Master Architects, Gibulum, Joabert, and Stokin, and directed them to go and search among the ancient ruins, in hopes of discovering more treasure. They departed, and one of them, viz: Gibulum, in working with a pickaxe among the rubbish, discovered a large iron ring fixed in a cubic stone. On removing this stone, a cavern was discovered. Gibulum offered to descend. A rope being fastened round his body, and in this manner he descended thrice, and discovered the golden triangle of Enoch, as was represented in the ceremony of your initiation. They then carried the stone and triangle to King Solomon, when the same circumstances occurred, which took place when you presented the same to us. The two Kings then informed the three Knights that they were ignorant of the true pronunciation of the mysterious word until that time, and that this word being handed down through a succession of ages, had been much corrupted. The two Kings accompanied by the three Knights, descended with the sacred treasure into the secret vault. They encrusted the golden plate upon the pedestal of the pillar of beauty, and the brilliancy of the plate was sufficient to enlighten the place. The secret vault was afterwards called the sacred vault, &c. (as in the Monitor, to the words, "which is the cube of three.") Whenever the Lodge of Perfection was holden, nine Knights of the Ninth Arch, tiled the nine arches which led to the sacred vault; the most ancient stood in the arch next to the antechamber of the vault, and so on in regular progression, the youngest taking his station in the first arch, which was near the apartment of Solomon. We were suffered to pass without giving the pass words of the different arches. There were living at that time several ancient masters, who, excited by jealousy at the honors conferred upon the twenty-five brethren, deputed some of their number to wait upon Solomon, and request that they might participate in those honors. The King answered that the twenty-five masters were justly entitled to the honors conferred on them, for their zeal and fidelity. Go, said he, in peace, you may one day be rewarded according to your merits. Upon this, one of the deputies with an unbecoming warmth, observed to his companions, "What occasion have we for a higher degree? We know the word has been changed, we can travel as masters and receive pay as such." Solomon mildly replied, "Those whom I have advanced to the degree of perfection, have wrought in the ancient ruins, and though the undertaking was difficult and dangerous, they penetrated the bowels of the earth, and brought thence treasure to enrich and adorn the Temple of God. "Go in peace, wait with patience, and aspire to perfection by good works." The deputies returned and reported their reception to the masters. These masters, vexed at the refusal, unanimously determined to go to the ancient ruins, and search under ground, with a view of arrogating the merit necessary for the accomplishment of their desires. They departed the next morning, and raising the cubic stone, descended into the cavern with a ladder of ropes, by the light of torches, where no sooner had the last descended, than the nine arches fell in upon them. Solomon hearing of this accident, sent Gibulum, Joabert and Stokin to inform themselves more particularly of the matter. They departed at break of day, and upon their arrival at the place, could discover no remains of the arches, nor could they learn, that one single one of all those who had descended, escaped the destruction. They examined the place with diligence, but found nothing except a few pieces of marble, on which were inscribed certain hieroglyphics; these they carried to Solomon, and related what they had seen. King Solomon examining these hieroglyphics, discovered that these pieces of marble were part of one of the pillars of Enoch. Solomon ordered these pieces of marble to be carefully put together and deposited in the sacred vault.—Q. What followed? *A.* The Most Potent gave me the mysterious characters of this degree, which were engraved on the triangle of Enoch.

CLOSING.

Most Potent knocks *seven*, (Grand Marshal rises,) "The last as well as the first care," &c. Most Potent knocks *eight*, and Junior Warden rises. "Brother Junior Warden, what is the hour?" *A.* "The setting of the sun." Most Potent knocks *three times three*, and Companions all rise. "Brother Junior Warden, give notice," &c. (Signs.) Most Potent knocks *three times three*, Hiram of Tyre, *three times three*, Junior Warden, *three times three*, and Companions, *three times three*, with their hands, and Most Potent declares Chapter closed.

GRAND ELECT, PERFECT, AND SUBLIME MASON.

OPENING.

Most Perfect knocks *three*, (Grand Marshal rises,) "Are we all," &c. Most Perfect knocks *five*, and Junior Warden rises. Most Perfect says, "Brother Junior Warden, what is the hour?" *A.* "High twelve." Q. What do you understand by high twelve? *A.* That the sun has gained its meridian heighth, and darts its rays with greatest force on this Lodge. Most Perfect says, "It is then time that we should profit by its light." Most Perfect knocks *seven*, and Senior Warden rises, and Most Perfect says, "Venerable Brother Senior Warden, what brings you here?" *A.* My love of Masonry, my obligation, and a desire for perfection.—Q. What are the proper qualities for acquiring it? *A.* Frequent innocence and benevolence. —Q. How are you to conduct in this place? *A.* With the most profound respect.—Q. Why is it that men of all conditions assemble in this place, are termed brethren, and are all equal? *A.* Because the ineffable name puts us in mind that there is one being superior to us all.—Q. Why is respect paid to the triangle? *A.* Because it contains the name of the Grand Architect of the universe. Most Perfect knocks *nine*, and Brethren all rise. Most Perfect says, "Brother Senior Warden, give notice that I am going to open a Lodge of Perfect Grand Elect and Sublime Masons, by the mysterious number 3, 5, 7 and 9. Senior Warden obeys. Signs of former degrees given, then the Most Perfect knocks *three*, and all the Brethren give the first sign of this degree. Most Perfect knocks *three*, and second sign is given. Most Perfect knocks *three*, and then third sign. Most Perfect knocks *three, five, seven* and *nine*, Senior Warden, the same, Junior Warden, the same, and then all the Brethren with their hands, and Most Perfect declares Lodge open.

Note.—Behind the Master, is the burning bush, in which is a transparent triangle with the letters יהוה placed therein. In the west, is the pillar of beauty. The pedestal appearing to be broken, is a part of the pillar of Enoch, the pieces of which were found among the ruins, and carefully put together. The Lodge is adorned with vases of gold and silver, urns, &c. which were found among the ruins. The lights are thus arranged: three in the west, behind the Junior Warden; five in the west, behind the Senior Warden; seven in the south, and nine behind the Master. The Brethren are seated in a triangular form around the altar.

LECTURE.

Q. What are you? A. I am three times three, the Perfect's number of eighty-one, according to our mysterious numbers.—Q. Explain that? A. I am a Perfect Grand Elect and Sublime Mason; my trials are finished, and it is now time I should reap the fruits of my labor.—Q. Where were you made a Grand Elect Mason? A. In a place not enlightened by the sun nor moon.—Q. Where was that place situated? A. Under the Sanctum Sanctorum.—Q. How did you gain admission? A. By the nine pass-words of Knights of the Ninth Arch, which brought me to the door of the antechamber leading to the sacred vaults, where I gave three distinct knocks.—Q. How were they answered? A. By three from within.—Q. What was said to you? A. Who comes there?—Q. Your answer? A. A Knight of the Ninth Arch, who wishes to be admitted into the sacred vault.—Q. What was then said to you? A. I was directed to give the pass; when I did, I was permitted to pass to the second door of the antechamber, where I gave *three*, and *five* knocks, which were answered by *three*, and *five*, and *seven* from within, and the pass-word demanded as before, which I gave and was permitted to pass to the door of the sacred vault, where I gave *three, five,* and *seven* and *nine* distinct knocks. (Note. These knocks are answered from within, by the Junior Warden, and Senior Warden, and Most Perfect; and Most Perfect says, "Brother Junior Warden, see who knocks there in the manner of a Perfect Grand Elect and Sublime Mason.")—Q. To what do these knocks allude? A. The three knocks signify the age of the Entered Apprentice, and the number of the Grand Master Architects who penetrated the bowels of the earth. The five allude to the age of the Fellow Craft and the number of the Grand Elect Perfect and Sublime Masters who placed the sacred treasure upon the pedestal of beauty.—Q. What are their names? A. Solomon, Hiram, King of Tyre, Gibulum, Joabert, and Stokin. The seven allude to the age of the Master Mason, and to Enoch who was the seventh from Adam. The nine represent the age of the Perfect Grand Elect and Sublime Mason, and the nine guards of the arches.—Q. How were these knocks answered? A. By three, five, seven and nine from within.—Q. What followed? A. I was asked, "Who comes there?"—Q. Your answer? A. A Knight of the Ninth Arch, who is desirous of being admitted into the sacred vault and arriving at perfection.—Q. What followed? A. The pass was demanded, which I gave and was ordered to wait until the Most Perfect in the east had been informed of my request and his answer returned.—Q. What was his answer? A. Let him be introduced in ancient form.—Q. What was that form? A. I was conducted to the west and placed between the Wardens, and having made the sign of admiration, was thus interrogated by the Most Perfect: "My Brother, what is your desire?" A. "To

be made a Perfect Grand Elect and Sublime Mason."—*Q*. What followed?
A. The Most Perfect said, "Before I can initiate you, you must satisfy us that you are well skilled in Masonry, otherwise you must be sent back until you are better qualified," whereupon I was thus examined:—*Q*. Are you a Mason? *A*. My brethren all know me as such.—*Q*. Give me the sign, token and word? *A*. (Given.)—*Q*. Are you a Fellow Craft? *A*. I have seen the letter G. and know the pass.—*Q*. Give me the sign, token and words? *A*. (Given.)—*Q*. Are you a Master Mason? *A*. I have seen the sprig of cassia and know what it means.—*Q*. Give me the sign, token and words? *A*. (Given.)—*Q*. Are you a Secret Master? *A*. I have passed from the square to the compass opened to seven degrees.—*Q*. Give me the sign, token and words. *A*. (Given.)—*Q*. Are you a Perfect Master? *A*. I have seen the tomb of our respectable Master Hiram Abiff, and have in company with my brethren, shed tears at the same.—*Q*. Give me the sign, token and words? *A*. (Given.)—*Q*. Are you an Intimate Secretary? *A*. My curiosity is satisfied, but it nearly cost me my life.—*Q*. Give me the sign, token and words? *A*. (Given.)—*Q*. Are you a Provost and Judge? *A*. I am, and render justice to all men, without distinction.—*Q*. Give me the sign, token and words? *A*. (Given.)—*Q*. Are you an Intendant of the Buildings? *A*. I have made the five steps of exactness, I penetrated the inmost part of the Temple, and have seen the great light in which was three mysterious characters, J. J. J.—*Q*. Give me the sign, token and words? *A*. (Given.)—*Q*. Are you an Elected Knight? *A*. One cavern received me, one lamp gave me light, and one fountain refreshed me.—*Q*. Give me the sign, token and words. *A*. (Given.)—*Q*. Are you a Master Elected of Fifteen? *A*. My zeal and works have procured me that honor.—*Q*. Give me? &c. Are you an Illustrious Knight? *A*. My name will inform you.—*Q*. Give me, &c. Are you a Grand Master Architect? *A*. I know the use of the mathematical instruments.—*Q*. Give me, &c. Are you a Knight of the Ninth Arch? *A*. I have penetrated through the bowels of the earth, through nine arches, and have seen the brilliant triangle.—*Q*. Give me, &c. What then followed? *A*. The Most Perfect inquired of the brethren whether they consented that I should be exalted to the sublime and mysterious degree of Perfection, whereupon one of the brethren rose and said, "I have objections to this candidate." The Most Perfect inquired what these objections were, to which this brother answered, "I will communicate them if the candidate retires." I was then ordered to retire, which I did.—*Q*. What then followed? *A*. Shortly after, the Master of Ceremonies conducted me again into the Lodge, and placing me in the west, I was asked the following questions: viz.—1st, Have you never wilfully revealed any of the secrets of Masonry? 2d, Have you always been charitable towards your brethren? 3d, Have you never defrauded a brother? 4th, Are you in the habit of using the name of God profanely? 5th, Does your conscience accuse you of having committed any offence against your brethren, which ought to debar you from receiving this degree? Be sincere and answer me. Which questions being answered, the Most Perfect said, "Brethren, do you consent that this candidate be admitted among us? If you do, raise your right hands." Which being done, I was directed to approach the altar, by three, five, seven and nine steps, which I did and took upon me the obligation of a Perfect Grand Elect and Sublime Mason.—*Q*. Repeat that obligation? *A*. (Same as Secret Master.) I further promise that I will aid all my worthy brethren in distress and sickness, as far forth, &c. with my counsel as well as my purse. I further promise, &c. that I will not be concerned in conferring this degree upon any Mason whose character and knowledge I disapprove, nor unless he has been elected and installed as an officer in some regular Lodge, Chapter, Encampment, or Council. I further promise that I will never fully pronounce more than once in my life the mysterious word of this degree,

under penalty of having my body cut in twain, so help, &c. Amen, Amen, Amen.—Q. What followed? *A.* While I was still in a kneeling posture, the Most Perfect said, "Let us pray," which was done, and the Master of Ceremonies then presented the hod and trowel to the Most Perfect, who said, "My brother, I shall now proceed to anoint you with the holy oil wherewith Aaron, David, and the wise Solomon were anointed." And then anointing my head, lips, and heart, at the same time, said, "Behold how good and pleasant," &c. (as in Monitor to the words,) "shall not break my head;" and then placing his hand upon me, said, "I impress you," &c. (as in Monitor.)—Q. What followed? *A.* The Most Perfect presented me with the bread and wine, and rising, said, "Eat of this bread," &c. (as in Monitor to the words,) "nearest friend." When this part of the ceremony was ended, the brethren made a libation according to ancient usage.—Q. What followed? *A.* The Most Perfect raised me and said, "That which I shall now communicate to you, will make you accomplished in Masonry." He then gave me three signs, three tokens, the three pass-words, and the three grand words of this degree.—Q. Give me the signs? [First sign made like Master Mason's, with hands clenched.]—Q. To what does that sign allude? *A.* To the penalty of my obligation. [Second sign: bring your right hand upright, the palm outwards to guard your left cheek, your left hand supporting your elbow, then guard your right cheek with left hand, &c.]—Q. To what does that sign allude? *A.* To the manner in which Moses guarded his eyes from the light of the burning bush, from which the Almighty revealed to him his true name. [Third sign is that of surprise: raise both hands as high as the shoulders, and step back with the right foot.]—Q. To what does this sign allude? *A.* To the attitude of Solomon and Hiram, when the sacred treasure was first produced.—Q. Give me the first token? [First token, same as Intimate Secretary, giving words Berith, Neder, Shelemoth.]—Q. What do those signify? *A.* Alliance, Promise and Protection.—Q. To what do they allude? *A.* To the alliance of Moses and Aaron, of Solomon and Hiram, King of Tyre. The promise made by the Almighty, to the ancient patriarchs that the true pronunciation of his name should be revealed to their posterity, and the perfection attained when this promise was fulfilled.—Q. Give me the second token? [Pass from Master's grip, and seize his right arm above the elbow and place your left hand on his right shoulder.]—Q. Give me the third token? [With your left hand seize your brother's right elbow, and with your right hand, his right shoulder.]—Q. Give me the three pass-words? *A.* First, Master Masons; second, Elhanon; third, Fellow-Craft's repeated thrice.—Q. Give me the the three grand words? *A.* First, Gibulum; second, Eh-yeh-asher-eh-yeh.—Q. What does that word signify? *A.* I am what I am, Third, El-hod-dihu-kaw-lu. —Q. What does that word signify? *A.* God be praised, we have finished it.—Q. What followed? *A.* The Most Perfect caused me to pronounce the mysterious word of this degree.—Q. Pronounce it? *A.* I cannot but once in my life.—Q. How will you then give it? *A.* ——————— יהוה
Q. What followed? *A.* The Most Perfect thus addressed me: "You are already acquainted with the fact, that the true pronunciation of the name of God was revealed to Enoch, and that he engraved the letters composing that name on a triangular plate of gold. The name was represented by the four Hebrew consonants, *Jod,* ` *He,* ה *Vau,* ו and *He,* ה. The vowel sounds of this language being represented by points placed about the consonants, and being frequently omitted in writing, the consonants, composing the mysterious word, at different ages received different pronunciations. Hence, though the method of writing this word remained uniform, its pronunciation underwent many changes. These changes constitute what are termed the different ages of Masonry. These are 3, 5, 7 and 9. These are the three

ages of Masonry, and are thus estimated. After the death of **Enoch**, the ineffable name was pronounced by

3 { Methuselah, Lamech, and Noah,	Juha, (Yu-haw.)	5 { Shem, Arphaxed, Salah, Eber, and Peleg,	Jeva, (Ye-waw.)	5 ages.	
7 { Reu, Serug, Nahor, Terah, Abraham, Isaac, Judah,	Jova, (Yo-waw.)	7 ages.	9 { Hezron, Ram, Aminadab, Nasshou, Salmon, Boaz, Obed, Jesse, David,	(Yay-wo.) Jevo. Jevah, (Ye-way.) Johe, (Yo-hay.) Jehovah, (Ye-ho-waw.)	9 ages.

The true pronunciation of the name was revealed to Enoch, Jacob, and Moses, and on that account are not named in this enumeration. The perfect number is thus formed: The number of corrupted words is 9. The ages of Masonry, 3, 5, 7, 9+24 multiplied by 3, the number gotten who discovered Tunsune, (noticed in the degree of Knight of the Ninth Arch,) gives the product 72, to this add 9, the number of corrupted words, the amount is 81. The mysterious words which you received in the preceding degrees, are all so many corruptions of the true name (of God) which was engraved on the triangle of Enoch. In this engraving, the vowel points are so arranged as to give the pronunciation which you have just received, (Yow-ho.) This word when thus pronounced, is called the ineffable word, which cannot be altered as other words are, and the degrees which you have received, are called, on this account, "*ineffable degrees.*" This word you will recollect was not found until after the death of Hiram Abiff, consequently the word engraved by him on the ark, is not the true name of God."
—Q. What then followed? A. The Most Perfect gave me the secret characters of this degree, and then invested me with the jewels, apron and girdle of this degree, and I was again addressed: "I now with the greatest pleasure salute you," &c. (as in Monitor,) "thus my brother," &c. (as in Monitor.)

CLOSING.

Most Perfect knocks *three*, (Grand Marshal rises,) "The last," &c. &c. Most Perfect knocks *five*, and Junior Warden rises. "Brother Junior Warden, what is the hour?" Most Perfect knocks *seven*, and Senior Warden rises. Most Perfect says, "Venerable brother Senior Warden, how should the Grand Elect, Perfect and Sublime Mason part?" A. "They should part in peace, love and unity." Most Perfect knocks *nine*, all Brethren rise. (Signs.) Most Perfect knocks *three*, *five*, *seven* and *nine*, Junior Warden, the same, Senior Warden, the same, and Brethren the same, with their hands, &c.

APPENDIX.

NO. 1.

Genesee County, *ss:* LUCINDA MORGAN, aged twenty-three, the wife of William Morgan, of Batavia, in said county, being duly sworn, deposeth and saith—that on Monday last, about, or a short time before, sunrise, her said husband left his house, and went into the street of the village: that finding he did not come home to his breakfast as usual, she made inquiries for him, and was told that he had been forcibly taken away by six men, and put into a carriage and taken to Canandaigua. That during the whole of Monday she remained in ignorance of which way he had been taken, or who had taken him, excepting by loose information, that an officer from Canandaigua had taken him. That on Tuesday morning soon after breakfast she sent for William R. Thompson, the sheriff, and requested to know of him if he knew on what pretext her husband had been taken away. Said Thompson told her he understood he had been taken under a charge of having stolen a shirt and cravat, and that he presumed it was merely a pretext to get him away, or carry him away; that thereupon this deponent asked him if he thought Mr. Morgan could be got back, or brought back, if she gave up to the Masons the papers she had in possession; said Thompson answered that he thought it was very likely that Mr. Morgan would be brought back if she would give them up; but he would not obligate himself, or undertake to say that he should be brought back. That thereupon said Thompson proposed that this deponent should go to Canandaigua, and take the papers, and give them to Morgan, or to them, or give them up; and deponent agreed to go and take the papers accordingly. Thompson then asked this deponent if there was any person or friend whom she would like to have go with her. She mentioned Mr. Gibbs, (meaning Horace Gibbs,) and asked if it would do for him to go; said Thompson said it would not do for him to go, as he was not a Mason, and added, it would not do for any person to carry her there but a Mason. She asked him twice if Mr. Gibbs was not a Mason, and he said he was not, and then asked deponent if she was acquainted with Mr. Follett; deponent said she was not. Thompson said he was a nice man, and a gentleman with whom she could safely trust herself. Said Thompson departed, and soon returned, and told deponent that Mr. Follet was not willing to go, unless she would let him (Follet,) and Mr. Ketchum see the papers; he did not want to go on a Tom fool's errand. This deponent then objected to the papers being seen by them; Thompson then said it was useless; he should do no more, and he could not send her out there unless they could see the papers. Deponent then, with great reluctance, finally consented to let them see the papers, if they would take her to see her husband. This second visit lasted about twenty minutes, during which time Thompson urged the deponent to let the papers be seen. Deponent told him she was afraid they would take the papers away from her, if she let them see them. Thompson said they would not. She offered to let Mr. Thompson see the papers; he said that would not answer, they would not take his word. Thompson then told her he would go to Humphrey's and stay until she had got the papers, and she must then make a sign to him when she was ready. Accordingly, a short time afterwards she made a sign to Mr. Thompson, then standing on Humphrey's stoop, and immediately after, he, with Mr. Follet, and Mr. Ketchum, came to her apartment, when Thompson introduced Follet and Ketchum, and said they had come to see the papers, which this deponent then handed to them. They all looked at them a short time, and Thompson then asked her if she was ready

APPENDIX.

to go, saying, Mr. Follet was ready to take her. Follet then said he would go home with the papers, and look them over, and told Ketchum to stop for him at his gate. Accordingly, about four o'clock in the afternoon of Tuesday, deponent started with said Follett and Ketchum in a small wagon, and proceeded to Stafford, where they stopped at a house, where she was conducted into a back room, into which Follett and Ketchum came, and were joined by one Daniel Johns, and by James Ganson; all of whom immediately proceeded to examine the papers with much earnestness, and held much low conversation with themselves in under voices. Ganson appeared to speak the most. One of them then asked Johns if those were the papers that were in the office when he was there. Johns answered there was one degree back, and then took a piece of paper, and folding it up, said the papers that were back were folded so. They then held considerable more conversation in voices too low to be heard. Follett then turned to deponent, and told her he did not see that he could go with her; that Mr. Ketchum was going to Rochester, and would be willing to take her to Canandaigua to see Mr. Morgan; said he was not much acquainted with him, (Ketchum,) but took him to be a gentleman,—and Ketchum then said he called himself a gentleman, and she need not be afraid to trust herself with him. Ketchum then took the papers, and tied them up in his pocket handkerchief, and took them with him into the wagon in which they rode. Johns then got into the wagon, and rode to Le Roy, when he got out, and bid Ketchum good-bye, saying, I hope I shall see you day after to-morrow. They then proceeded to Avon, and staid all night. The next day they again started for Canandaigua, when Ketchum put the papers into this deponent's trunk. They arrived at Canandaigua about twelve at noon, and stopped at a tavern at the corner of the main street. After being there some time, this deponent asked Ketchum if he had heard of Mr. Morgan. Ketchum said he had not; that the Masons could not talk to him; he could not see them; they seemed jealous of him; thought him a friend of Mr. Morgan, and was afraid he had come to get him away from that place. Then asked her where the papers were; he took them, and said he would go and make further inquiries for Mr. Morgan; and if he could find him, or where he was, or where they had taken him, he would let her know all he could find out. This was about dinner time. He returned again a short time before night, and told her he had heard Mr. Morgan had been there; had been tried for stealing a shirt, and cleared, had been then put in jail for a debt of two dollars; and that Tuesday night a man had come from Pennsylvania, who said he had a warrant against him for a debt he owed there; that he, the man, had paid the two dollars, and had taken him away in a private carriage on Tuesday night, and he had no doubt he was gone; and asked this deponent when she would go home again. The deponent then expressed her anxiety to return speedily on account of having left her child of two year's old, and having with her a baby of two months old. Ketchum then went out, as he said, to take a passage in the stage, and returned after candle light. This deponent was then walking the room in great distress, and in tears. She asked him if he could hear nothing of Mr. Morgan. He then seemed to pity deponent, and told her not to be uneasy, and after looking at her a short time, told her to come and sit down by him, and asked her if she would feel any better if he told her what he knew. Being answered yes, he then said that Mr. Morgan would not be killed—that he would be kept concealed until they could get the rest of the papers. She asked him what papers were back. He said there was some sheets on the Mark Master's degree back; and they wanted also to get the printed sheets that Miller had printed on the three degrees. He then said he wanted to take the papers he had received from this deponent to Rochester, and he thought through the means of them he could find out where Mr. Morgan was; it was a secret where he was. Said he had paid her passage, and

APPENDIX. 3

then gave her two dollars to bear her expenses home. He then wrote his name with a pencil on a scrap of paper, hereto annexed, as follows: 'George Ketchum, Rochester,' and promised to write to her if he could hear of Mr. Morgan: he then told her if she would, by any means, get hold of the papers that Miller had, or find out where they were deposited, so that he could get hold of them, he would give her $25 out of his own pocket, and he had no doubt the lodge would give her one hundred if she could get what Miller had now. Deponent told him she would not try to get the papers that Miller had, and would take no money, and would not let him have the papers she had delivered to him, but on condition he would try and find out where Mr. Morgan was, and let her see him. He then repeated his promise to try and find out, and said he would write to her as soon as he got to Rochester, and urged her to write to him immediately on her return, and let him know about the papers, and what the people were doing generally in Batavia, and whether they were making a great rumpus about Mr. Morgan. Deponent then expressed her fears, that if she did give him any information about the papers, he would not keep his promise about letting her see him, but would keep him concealed until they got all the papers, and finally kill him. Ketchum then said, 'I promise before my God that I will not deceive you, but will do all I can to find out where he is, and let you see him. I have no doubt when I get back to Rochester I can find out more, and I think I can find out where he is.' He then again urged her to find out where the papers were, and let him know. In the course of his conversation he said, that if Mr. Morgan had managed rightly he could have made a million of dollars, if the work had been published. Ketchum then departed for Rochester, leaving this deponent at the tavern—she, the same day, started for Batavia. The papers taken away by the said Ketchum were numerous, and formed a very large bundle—they were written in the hand writing of her husband, excepting a few, which were written by a person who sometimes assisted her husband by copying, or taking down, as he dictated to him. The deponent further says she has no knowledge of the place where her husband now is, or what is his situation, and feels the most anxious fears for his life—that she was born in Virginia, and is a stranger, without any intimate friends or relations in this country, and is left with two infant children, without any money, except what is left of that given to her by said Ketchum, and has no property nor any means of supporting herself and her children, her constitution being very feeble, and her health being bad most of the time. L. MORGAN.
 Sworn the twenty-second day of September, 1826, before me,
 DANIEL H. CHANDLER, J. P.

NO. 2.

State of New-York, Ontario } MARY W. HALL, of Canandaigua, in said
 County, ss. } county, being duly sworn, deposeth and saith—
that she is the wife of Israel R. Hall, keeper of the common jail of said county; that she, this deponent, the said keeper, her husband, and family, reside in the jail of said county; that she, this deponent, and her husband, had been absent, and returned home on the twelfth of September instant, in the afternoon; that in the early part of the evening of the said twelfth day of September, her husband went out from the jail; that soon after her husband left the jail, and about seven o'clock in the evening, or a little past, a man, who afterwards and during the same evening said his name was Lawson, called at the jail and inquired for Mr. Hall, the keeper, and she, this deponent, informed the said Lawson that Mr. Hall was not at home, and that she did not know where he was; that the said Lawson then said that he wanted to see Morgan, alluding, as this deponent supposed, to a man in prison by the name of William Morgan; that this deponent then went to the door of the room in which the said Morgan was confined; that the said Lawson requested to go into the

APPENDIX.

room where Morgan was, but this deponent told him he could not, for it was against the rules of the prison; that the said Lawson said he wished to have a few moments private conversation with Morgan, but this deponent told Lawson he could not say any thing to Morgan but what this deponent should hear; that the said Lawson then spoke to Morgan through the grates of the door, and said he wished to have some private conversation with him, the said Morgan, but this woman, alluding to this deponent, would not let him; that this deponent said to Lawson, who be you? do you live in the village? to which the said Lawson made no reply, but the said Morgan said he is a neighbor; that the said Lawson told Morgan he had come to pay the debt for which the said Morgan was committed; and Lawson asked Morgan if he would go home with him; to which Morgan answered, yes; that Lawson then said, when Mr. Hall, meaning the said keeper, came in, he (Lawson) would satisfy the execution, and take him, the said Morgan, out, and carry him home; that the said Morgan answered it was no matter about it that night; he could wait till morning; that Lawson said no, he would rather take him, the said Morgan, out, and carry him home with him that night, for he had been running all day for him, and he was so tired he could hardly stand on his feet; that the said Lawson then went away, and said he would look for Mr. Hall, the said keeper; that in about half an hour the said Lawson returned, and said he had been to the hotel, conference room, and every other place in which he thought he should be likely to find Mr. Hall, but he could not find him; that the said Lawson then requested that this deponent should receive the amount of the execution on which Morgan was committed, and discharge him; but this deponent refused to do this, and told Lawson she did not know the amount; that Lawson told her it was a small sum, and he (Lawson) would leave five dollars, which he knew was more than sufficient; that this deponent then told Lawson that she, this deponent, had understood that Morgan was a rogue, and that she did not like to liberate a rogue; that she, this deponent, understood great pains had been taken to secure Morgan, and that the public or individuals were interested in having him kept secure; that what she (this deponent) should do would be considered the same as if it had been done by her husband, the said keeper; and if she (this deponent) should discharge Morgan, she was afraid her husband would be blamed; that Lawson said no, Mr. Hall would not be blamed, and represented to this deponent that Mr. Hall understood it perfectly, and if he was at home would discharge Morgan; and further, he, Lawson, said he would pledge himself that Mr. Hall should not be injured or blamed; that he, Lawson, would pledge himself to the amount of fifty or an hundred dollars that Mr. Hall should not be injured if this deponent would discharge Morgan; but this deponent refused, and told Lawson she valued public opinion more than money; that Lawson then asked this deponent if she would discharge Morgan if Col. Sawyer (meaning, as this deponent supposes, one Edward Sawyer, of Canandaigua aforesaid) would say she could safely do it, and that it would be right, or if he would pledge himself that Mr. Hall should not be injured, or would run no risk in discharging Morgan; that she, this deponent, answered that she did not know Col. Sawyer any better than she did him, (Lawson,) and that Col. Sawyer was not plaintiff in the execution upon which Morgan was committed, and that he, Col. Sawyer, had nothing to do with it; that, however, Lawson then went away, and said he would go and see Col. Sawyer; that Lawson then went away, and was gone but a few minutes when he (Lawson) returned, and Col. Sawyer with him; that Col. Sawyer requested that this deponent would discharge Morgan, and said there could be no kind of risk in doing so; that Mr. Hall should not be injured; that Lawson would pay the debt, and there could be no harm in discharging the prisoner when that was done; that this deponent said she did not wish to keep a man in jail who ought to be let out, but she did not wish to liberate a rogue, as she understood Morgan was one; that nearly the same conversation

APPENDIX.

again took place as had before passed between this deponent and Lawson; that Col. Sawyer and Lawson appeared to be offended; that this deponent would not discharge Morgan; that Lawson said the debt for which Morgan was committed was assigned to Chesebro; (meaning, as this deponent supposed, and afterwards learned, Nicholas G. Chesebro) that Lawson said to Sawyer, 'Let us go and find Chesebro;' that they both went to the door, and this deponent also, and saw two men a few rods from the jail coming towards it ; that this deponent observed that, perhaps, one of them might be Mr. Hall, upon which Lawson went towards them, and directly one of the said men came to the door of the jail where this deponent and Col. Sawyer were standing ; that this deponent asked if it was Mr. Chesebro, to which the man answered yes ; and this deponent immediately recognised him to be the said Nicholas G. Chesebro ; that this deponent said to Chesebro, there is a man in jail that these men (meaning Lawson and Col. Sawyer) want me to liberate, and they say you are interested, or that you have bought the debt; that Chesebro said let him go ; these men will pay the execution ; I don't want to see him ; I have no demands upon him ; that this deponent in the early part of the evening, and before Mr. Hall left the jail, had observed Mr. Hall and Chesebro in low conversation, and supposed that probably it was understood between them : she, this deponent, then consented to receive the amount of the execution, and discharge Morgan ; that during the evening a man had been to the jail with Lawson ; that Lawson called Foster, but unknown to this deponent ; that Lawson, after this deponent consented to receive the amount of the execution, and discharge Morgan, paid to this deponent the said amount of execution, or laid it on the table ; that then this deponent took the keys and was going to liberate Morgan; that Lawson spoke to this deponent and said, ' Wait, and I will go with you ;' that Lawson then stepped to the door and whistled, and then followed this deponent ; that when they came to the outer door of the prison; Lawson said to this deponent, ' You need not fasten this door after us ;' but this deponent said she should, for there were other prisoners in the room ; that this deponent and Lawson went into the hall adjoining the room where Morgan was, and Lawson spoke in a low voice to Morgan through the grates, ' Get yourself ready to go with me—dress yourself quick :' that Morgan was soon ready, and this deponent let him out, and Lawson took Morgan by the arm and went out of the prison to the outer door ; that while this deponent was fastening the prison door she heard, at or near the outer door of the jail, a most distressing cry of murder; that this deponent ran to the door, and saw Lawson and the man that he called Foster, one on each side of Morgan, having hold of Morgan's arms ; that Morgan continued to scream or cry in the most distressing manner, at the same time struggling with all his strength, apparently, to get loose from Lawson and Foster ; that the cry of Morgan continued till his voice appeared to be suppressed by something put over his mouth ; that during the time that Morgan was struggling, and crying murder, the said Col. Sawyer, and the said Chesebro, were standing at a short distance from the jail door, near the well, and in full view and hearing of all that passed, but offered no assistance to Morgan, nor did they attempt to release him from Lawson and Foster ; but one of them struck with a stick a violent blow upon the well curb, or a tub, standing near ; that soon after this deponent saw a carriage pass the jail in the direction that Lawson and Foster took Morgan ; that the evening was quite light in consequence of its being about the full of the moon ; that she, this deponent, could distinguish from the jail door the horses in the carriage which passed to be gray ; that, this deponent supposed the striking upon the well curb, or tub, by Chesebro or Col. Sawyer, was a signal for the carriage to come, as it came immediately after : that when the carriage passed, Lawson and Foster could not have got but a few rods with Morgan ; that immediately after the striking upon the well curb, or tub, Col. Sawyer, and, as this deponent thinks, Chesebro also,

1*

APPENDIX.

passed the jail door in the direction that Lawson and Foster took Morgan, but not apparently to render Morgan any assistance towards being released from Lawson and Foster; but Col. Sawyer, however, picked up Morgan's hat, which had fallen off in the struggle; that when Morgan was taken from the jail it was about nine o'clock in the evening, or a little past: that this deponent has since been informed that Lawson lives about two or three miles from the jail; that this deponent has never seen Morgan since he was taken from the jail as aforesaid, and knows nothing about where he was taken to, or where he now is, and further saith not. MARY W. HALL.

Subscribed and sworn to, this twenty-third day of September, 1826, before me,
JEFFREY CHIPMAN, J. P.

NO. 3.

State of New-York, } DANIEL TALLMADGE, being duly sworn, deposeth and
Ontario County, ss. } saith—that he now is, and on the eleventh day of September instant, was, a prisoner in the jail of said county, at Canandaigua; that on the evening of the said eleventh day of September, a man, whose name this deponent learned was William Morgan, was committed to said jail, and put into the room with this deponent; that during the following day Morgan asked this deponent whether Mr. Hall, the jailor, was a Mason, and said if he was, he (Morgan) would fare hard, as he was suspected of an intention to reveal the secrets of Masonry; that early in the evening of the same day, being the twelfth, Mrs. Hall, the wife of the said jailer, together with a man whose name this deponent understood to be Lawson, came to the door of the prison room, in which this deponent and Morgan were; that Lawson said he came to pay the debt on which Morgan was committed, and let him out; to which Morgan consented; that after Lawson went away, as this deponent understood, to find Mr. Hall, the jailer, Morgan said to this deponent, if that man (Lawson) was a traitor to him, (Morgan) he would not give much for his life; that Morgan had some doubts about trusting himself with Lawson, but upon the whole concluded he would; that some time after, during the same evening, Lawson came again to the room where this deponent and Morgan were, and Mrs. Hall, the wife of the jailer, let Morgan out, and Lawson went out with Morgan; that, in a moment after, this deponent heard a cry of murder, which appeared to be near or at the outer door of the jail; that the said cry of murder, was repeated two or three times till it appeared to be suppressed, and further this deponent saith not. DANIEL TALLMADGE.

Subscribed and sworn to, this twenty-third day of September, 1826, before me,
JEFFREY CHIPMAN, J. P.

NO. 4.

State of New-York, } MARTHA DAVIS, wife of Nathan Davis, of Canandai-
Ontario County, ss. } gua, in said county, being duly sworn, deposeth and saith—that she resides nearly opposite the jail, in Canandaigua; that on the evening of the twelfth day of September, instant, she, this deponent, saw a number of men walking, standing, and sitting in the street, and by the fence by the side of the street, about and near the jail; that this deponent could recognise but three of the men, to wit: Col. Edward Sawyer, Nicholas G. Chesebro, and Chauncey Coe, all of Canandaigua aforesaid; that at one time this deponent was out at the door, and spoke to said Chesebro, but he made no answer; that there were in all about eight or ten men; that they seemed to be consulting together in an under tone, as this deponent thought, and she expressed her fears to her husband that something was going on about the jail which was not right; that about nine o'clock in the evening this deponent heard the fastenings of the prison doors, as she frequently does when the doors are opened; that at the same time this deponent discovered two men near the jail door, and also, two men on the opposite side of the street from the jail,

APPENDIX. 7

and but a little distance from the house of this deponent; that immediately after, this deponent heard a cry of murder near the jail door, and discovered men apparently in a scuffle; that at the same time she heard a violent rap, apparently upon the well curb, near the jail door, and one of the men who were seated near the house of this deponent, immediately ran past the house of this deponent, and in a direction from the place from which the cry of murder proceeded; that the cry of murder seemed to be suppressed as by a hand, or something similar, upon the mouth, which appeared at times to be partly removed in the struggle, and then this deponent could hear an inarticulate sound, indicating great distress; that immediately after the rap upon the well curb, this deponent discovered a carriage, which she supposed to be the carriage of Mr. Hubbard, who keeps horses and carriages to let, with two grey horses, coming down the street very rapidly, but could not discover any one in the carriage; but the carriage passed the house of this deponent towards the place where this deponent had heard the last cries of distress, as aforesaid; that the carriage was gone a few minutes, and then returned with men in it, and passed back again by the house of this deponent; and further this deponent saith not. MARTHA DAVIS.

Subscribed and sworn to, this twenty-third day of September, 1826, before me,
JEFFREY CHIPMAN, J. P.

NO. 5.

State of New-York, } LASIRA I. OSBORN, daughter of Seth Osborn, of Ca-
Ontario County, ss. } nandaigua, in said county, aged about twenty-four years, being duly sworn, deposeth and saith—that on the evening of the twelfth of September, instant, about nine o'clock in the evening, she, this deponent, was in the chamber of her father's house, which is but a few feet from the jail in Canandaigua; that this deponent heard some bustle about the house, apparently near the jail door; that this deponent then heard a cry of murder, apparently about in front of her father's house, in the street, and but a few feet from the house; that the distinct cry of murder, which this deponent first heard, was soon suppressed into an inarticulate sound of distress, and soon ceased; that just before the time that this deponent heard the said cry of murder, she heard some one whistle, and then, or soon after, a loud rap upon the well curb, as this deponent supposes, as it appeared to be at the well, a few rods from the jail door; that this deponent then heard a carriage pass in the street; that this deponent soon after came down from the chamber, and a carriage passed the other way, having two grey horses before the carriage; and further this deponent saith not. LASIRA I. OSBORN.

Subscribed and sworn to, this twenty-third day of September, 1826, before me,
JEFFREY CHIPMAN, J. P.

NO. 6.

State of New-York, } SETH OSBORN, of Canandaigua, in said county, being
Ontario County, ss. } duly sworn, deposeth and saith—that on the evening of the twelfth of September, instant, about nine o'clock, or between nine and ten o'clock, he, this deponent, went to the door of his house, which is near the jail in Canandaigua; that he saw some men a few rods from his door; that one of the men appeared to be partly down and struggling, and making a faint noise of distress; that this deponent went towards the men, one of whom was a little behind the rest, and this deponent asked him what was the matter? to which the man, whom this deponent understood and believes to have been Col. Sawyer, of Canandaigua, aforesaid, answered, 'nothing, only a man who has been let out of jail, and been taken on a warrant, and is going to be tried, or to have his trial,' upon which this deponent went back into his house, and further saith not. SETH OSBORN.

Subscribed and sworn to, this twenty-third day of September, 1826, before me,
JEFFREY CHIPMAN, J. P.

APPENDIX.

NO. 7.

Genesee County, } ss. { TIMOTHY FITCH, of Batavia, in said county, being duly sworn, deposeth and saith—that on the twenty-third day of September, instant, he, this deponent, was at Canandaigua, and saw Hiram Hubbard, and this deponent asked Hubbard if he knew any thing about William Morgan being taken away from Canandaigua, and Hubbard said he did not, but on the evening that it was said Morgan was taken away, he, Hubbard, was applied to, to carry some men to Rochester, and he agreed to go with his carriage, as he did frequently ; but he did not know who applied to him on this occasion ; that he expected they would get into his carriage at Mr. Kingsley's tavern, in Canandaigua ; but in the evening, about nine o'clock, a man whom he did not know, came to him, and said the party had gone down the road towards Palmyra, and wished him to come along, and they would get into the carriage when he overtook them ; that he, Hubbard, then drove down the road as he was requested, passed the jail a few rods, until he saw some men in the road, who told him to stop, and five or six men got into the carriage, but he did not know one of them ; that they then told him to turn about and go to Rochester, which he did ; that he stopped twice on the road, and passed through Rochester about day light, and continued on to Hanford's Landing, about three miles below Rochester, where the men said they wanted to take a vessel ; that he then left them, and returned home to Canandaigua ; that he did not know one of the men whom he carried, though he saw them on the road when they stopped, and also when they got out of the carriage at Hanford's Landing ; that he had never been paid any thing for going with said party to Hanford's Landing ; and did not know who to look to for pay ; that one of the men said to him he would see him another day and pay him, but he did not know who it was, nor had he ever seen him since, or any one of the party ; that he, Hubbard, kept a livery stable, and horses and carriages, and frequently carried people to different places. And this deponent further saith, that he asked Hubbard to make affidavit of what he had said, but Hubbard said he had rather not, and finally declined. And this deponent further saith, that the place described by Hubbard where he took the party into his carriage, was but a few rods from the jail, and near the place where Mrs. Hall, and Miss Osborn deposed they saw Morgan last, on the evening he was taken from the jail, and further saith not.

TIMOTHY FITCH.

Subscribed and sworn to, this twenty-ninth day of September, 1826, before me,
C. CARPENTER, J. P.

NO. 8.
ONTARIO OYER AND TERMINER.

NICHOLAS G. CHESEBRO, Edward Sawyer, Loton Lawson, John Sheldon, ads.
The People.

NICHOLAS G. CHESEBRO, being duly sworn, deposeth and saith—that since the finding of the indictment in the above entitled cause, and in the course of last week, this deponent has been served with a *capias ad respondendum*, issued out of the Supreme Court, of the state of New-York, at the suit of *William Morgan*, for assault and battery, and false imprisonment, to the damage to the said William Morgan, of ten thousand dollars ; and this deponent has been held to bail in virtue of said writ, and an allowance of bail thereon endorsed, for fifteen hundred dollars ; that this deponent doth verily believe that the said *capias* was issued against this deponent, as the commencement of a suit by the said William Morgan against this deponent, for his private damages sustained, by reason of the facts disclosed in the indictment, in the above entitled cause ; and this deponent further saith, that he saw the said William Morgan in the office of J. Chipman, Esq. a justice of the peace, in the village of Canandaigua, on the evening of the 11th Sept. last, during his examination

APPENDIX.

before the said justice, and that he has not seen him since that time :—this deponent knew that it was intended to release the said Morgan from jail, and was informed, and verily believed, that the said Morgan had consented to go away ; and that the only object of this deponent, in assisting to get said Morgan out of jail, was to keep him from falling into the hands, or under the influence of one David C. Miller, of Batavia ; that he, this deponent, had been informed, and believed, that said William Morgan was compiling a book on the subject of Masonry, at the instigation, or with the concurrence, of said Miller, who was to print the same, with a view to pecuniary profit; in which book the said Morgan pretended to disclose secrets which he averred that he had most solemnly engaged never to reveal ; that deeming such publication calculated to degrade the institution of Masonry, and to bring disgrace on the members thereof, this deponent was desirous to remove the said Morgan to some place beyond the reach of said Miller, where his friends and acquaintance might endeavour to convince him of the impropriety of his conduct, and prevent the consequence before mentioned. That this deponent was not concerned, directly or indirectly, in using any force in the removal of the said Morgan from the said jail ; that he has had no concern whatever, in any transactions concerning the said Morgan since that time. That all he knows of said removal is, that he has been informed that the said Morgan was carried into the county of Monroe ; and that this deponent does not know where said Morgan now is. And this deponent further saith, that he is somewhat in debt, has but little property, a family to provide for, and feels, in common with his fellow citizens, the pressure of the times : and further saith not.

N. G. CHESEBRO.

Sworn this fifth day of January, 1827, before me,
RALPH LESTER, Clerk of Ontario County.

NO. 9.

Ontario County, ss. EDWARD SAWYER, of Canandaigua, one of the above named defendants, being duly sworn, deposes and says, that he never to his knowledge saw William Morgan, mentioned in the indictment in this cause, until the evening of the eleventh day of September last past, when he saw him at the office of Jeffrey Chipman, Esq. in the village of Canandaigua, under examination on a complaint against him, as this deponent was informed, for larceny. And this deponent further says, that he had no knowledge or intimation, in any manner whatever, that any person or persons were to go for the said Morgan, or that they had gone for the said Morgan, to bring him to Canandaigua, until he was informed that he was at the Office of the said Chipman on the said examination. And this deponent further says, that he took no part, either directly or indirectly, in the said examination, or in any subsequent proceedings by which the said Morgan was committed, as this deponent has been informed, to the jail of Ontario county. And this deponent further says, that he had no knowledge or intimation of any design or intention to liberate or remove the said Morgan from the said jail in any manner whatever, until the evening of the 12th day of September last, when Loton Lawson met this deponent in the street near the dwelling of this deponent, and informed this deponent that Morgan had agreed to go away with him, and that he was about to be discharged from the jail, and would voluntarily leave the place with the said Lawson. And some time after that, in the course of the same evening, the said Lawson called on this deponent and informed him that he had been to the jail, and that Mr. Hall, the jailor, was not at home ; and that Mrs. Hall was not acquainted with him, Lawson, and was not willing to let Morgan go on his application; that he had asked her if she would discharge him provided this deponent would come to the jail and say it was proper ; and that she said on that condition she would let him go. And the said Lawson requested this deponent to go to the jail for that purpose. And this deponent believing the statement of the said Lawson to be true, did accompany him to the jail for the purpose above expressed, and for no other, and at the jail stated to Mrs. Hall that in his opinion there would be no harm in discharging Morgan, provided the debt for which he was committed was paid. And this deponent further says, that he verily believed that the said Morgan was voluntarily going away with Lawson. And this deponent had no knowledge or intimation of any design or intention on the part of any one to use any force or violence in carrying away Morgan; nor should this deponent have gone to the jail aforesaid except on the solicitation above mentioned. And this deponent further says, that when Morgan came to the outer door of the jail, and had descended the steps, to the great surprise of this deponent, he, Morgan, as appeared from his exclamations, made resistance, and was taken down the street east from the jail; but what kind of resistance he made, or what force was used to compel him to go, this deponent does not know, for he was not near enough to Morgan at any time after he came out of the jail to see or know what was done to him. But this deponent freely and without any reserve acknowledges that he was near enough to hear the noise, and might have interfered to endeavour to prevent any abuse of Morgan; and that he did follow at a distance of some rods behind Morgan and the persons with him, until the carriage came up, and he, Morgan, and the persons with him, got into the carriage. And this deponent then verily believed, and still does believe, that Morgan got into the carriage without any force whatever. And this deponent was at no time nearer than within several rods of Morgan on that evening, before he got into the carriage. And this deponent further says, that this omission to interfere and assist Morgan, was the first and only act or omission of this deponent in which he was conscious of having been guilty of any criminal or improper conduct, or participation in the matters contained in the indictment in this case. And this deponent says, that he was taken wholly by surprise, and had no time for reflection; that he did not expect, and had no reason to expect, any such occurrence; and he did sincerely and deeply regret that he had been guilty of any such improper conduct as soon as he saw what had been done; and he still does with deep and unfeigned regret acknowledge and lament the part which he so took in said transaction. And this deponent further says, that at the time aforesaid he understood and believed that Morgan was voluntarily going away with Lawson to some place in this or the adjoining county, but to what place he did not know, for the purpose of being out of the reach and influence of David C. Miller, who, as this deponent was informed, was engaged with said Morgan in publishing a book, which, as this deponent considered, would be calculated to bring the institutions of Masonry into disrepute, by professing to reveal secrets which he was bound by solemn obligations not to disclose. And this deponent was desirous to prevent the publication of such book, provided Morgan could be persuaded to keep out of the way of said Miller, and not to permit himself to be influenced by him or his friends; and it was with this view, and no other, that this deponent was desirous to have Morgan depart with Lawson. And this deponent further says, that he has never seen Morgan since he got into the carriage as aforesaid; nor does he know where he is at present; nor has he known any thing of him since the time he so got into the carriage. And this deponent further says, that in going down the street, after Morgan and those with him had passed from the jail, he met a man who was, as he supposed, a Mr. Osborn, who asked this deponent what was the matter; to which this deponent replied, that a man had been released from jail, and he believed they had another precept for him, or words to that effect. And this deponent also picked up a hat which he found in the street there. And this deponent further says, that the foregoing is a true and impartial account of all the participation of this deponent in the matters contained in the said indictment, and of the motives which influenced him in the same, according to the best of his knowledge and belief.

And this deponent further says, that an action of assault and battery and false imprisonment has been commenced in the Supreme Court of the State of New-York, in the name of William Morgan, plaintiff, against this deponent. And this deponent has been arrested on a capias issued in the same, in which the damages are laid at ten thousand dollars, and on which this deponent is held to bail in the sum of fifteen hundred dollars, by order of judge Birdsall.

And this deponent further says, that he has a family of four children, and is in moderate circumstances as to property; and the situation of his pecuniary affairs is such as to require his constant and unremitted attention to business to meet the engagements and responsibilities into which he has entered.

And this deponent further says, that he never knew, nor has he any reason to believe, that the said John Sheldon, the above named defendant, had any part or concern whatever, either directly or indirectly, in any of the transactions above referred to. And this deponent has been well acquainted with the said John Sheldon for several years. And further this deponent says not. EDWARD SAWYER.

Sworn and subscribed this sixth day of January, A. D. 1827, before me,
RALPH LESTER, Clerk of Ontario County.

NO. 10.

Ontario County, } *ss.* LOTON LAWSON, being duly sworn, says that he has no knowledge of any agency or participation by John Sheldon in the matter or acts charged in the foregoing entitled indictment; that he never had any conversation with him in relation thereto before the said Sheldon was arrested on the said charge; that he does not know, or believe, that said John Sheldon was at Batavia in the month of September last.
LOTON LAWSON.

Sworn this sixth day of January, 1827, before me,
JEFFREY CHIPMAN, Commissioner, &c.

NO. 11.

The following is the address of judge Throop, upon his sentencing the prisoners:

You have been convicted of a daring, wicked, and presumptuous crime—such an one as we did hope would not, in our day, have polluted this land. You have robbed the state of a citizen; a citizen of his liberty; a wife of her husband; and a family of helpless children of the endearments and protecting care of a parent. And whether the unfortunate victim of your rage has been immolated, or is in the land of the living, we are ignorant, and even you do not pretend to know. It is admitted in this case, and stands proved, that Morgan was, by a hypocritical pretence of friendship and charity—and that, too, in the imposing shape of pecuniary relief to a distressed and poverty bound prisoner—beguiled to entrust himself to one of your number, who seized him, as soon as a confederate arrived to his aid, almost at his prison door, and in the night time hurried him into a carriage, and forcibly transported him out of the state. But, great as are the individual wrongs which you have inflicted on these helpless and wretched human beings, they are not the heaviest part of your crime. You have disturbed the public peace; you have dared to raise your parricidal arms against the laws and constitution of your government; you have assumed a power which is incompatible with a due subordination to the laws and public authority of your state. He was a citizen, under the protection of our laws; you were citizens, and owed obedience to them. What hardihood and wickedness then prompted you to steel your hearts against the claims of humanity, and to dare set at defiance those laws to which you owed submission, and which cannot suffer a citizen's liberty to be restrained with impunity, without violating its duties of protection assured to every individual under the social compact? Will you plead ignorance? Some of you, at least, have had the advantage of education, and moral instruction, and hold respectable and responsible stations in society; and all of you have learned what every school boy in this happy land, this free and intelligent community, knows; that the unrestrained enjoyment of life, liberty, and property, is guaranteed to every individual living obediently under our laws. Our constitution shows it; and the declaration of our independence declares, that the unmolested enjoyment of liberty, and the pursuit of happiness, are the unalienable rights of man. So sacred do we hold personal liberty, that even the impressment of a seamen from one of our ships, has been considered a sufficient cause for national war: man here is not like men in other countries, a submissive vassal, but every citizen is a sovereign; and I am happy to say that here he posesses that intelligence and high sense of feeling which befits his elevated station. Our laws will resent such attacks as you have made upon their sovereignty. Your conduct has created, in the people of this section of the country, a strong feeling of virtuous indignation. The court rejoices to witness it—and to be made sure that a citizen's person cannot be invaded by lawless violence, without its being felt by every individual in the community. It is a blessed spirit, and we do hope that it will not subside; that it will be accompanied by a ceaseless vigilance and untiring activity, until every actor in this profligate conspiracy is hunted from his hiding place, and brought before the tribunals of the country to receive the punishment merited by his crime. We think that we see in this public sensation the spirit which brought us into existence as a nation, and a pledge that our rights and liberties are destined to endure. But this is not all; your offence was not the result of passion suddenly excited, nor the deed of one individual. It was preconcerted, deliberated upon, and carried into effect, by the dictates of the secret councils and conclave of many actors. It takes its deepest hues of guilt from a conspiracy—a crime most dreaded from the depravity of heart it evinces, the power for unlawful purposes which it combines, and from its ability to defy the power of the law, and ultimate danger to the public peace. Hence it is, that the crime is considered full, when the wicked purpose is proved to have been formed; and the subsequent carrying into effect the object of the conspiracy, does not in the eye of the law, elevate the degree of the crime.

The legislature have not seen fit, perhaps, from the supposed improbability that the crime would be attempted, to make your offence a felony. Its grade and punishment has been left to the provisions of the common law, which treats it as a misdemeanor, and punishes it with fine and imprisonment in the common jail. The court are of opinion that your liberty ought to be made to answer for the liberty of Morgan: his person was restrained by force; and the court, in the exercise of its lawful powers, ought not to be more tender of your liberty, than you, in the plenitude of lawless force, were of his.

With regard to you, *Lawson*—It appeared, in proof, that you was an active agent in this affair; you went forward and took this man from the jail, and delivered him over to those who stood waiting with a carriage to receive him. Whether you accompanied that carriage or not, is not in proof. But in your excusatory affidavit you say nothing about it, leaving it to fair inference that you did accompany him in that carriage. There is nothing, either in your affidavit, or your proof to the court, which does much to mitigate your offence, except so far as they show that your poverty has not been accompanied by idleness, and your character has not been stained by other transgressions. Under all the circumstances of your case, the court feel it their duty to sentence you to two years imprisonment in the common jail of this county.

As to you, *Chesebro*—It appears, by your affidavit, that you did not lay your hands upon this man, to carry into effect the conspiracy; and it appears by unquestionable proof that you did not leave this village with the carriage. But you admit, at least tacitly, in your affidavit, that you were one of the conspirators; and your language to the jailer, when he called upon you the next day to account for your conduct, and warned you that the public would demand an explanation, showed an unsubdued spirit. It has been satisfactorily proved to us that you are a thriving mechanic—that you have a respectable standing in the community; and up to the period of this transaction your character for industry, honesty, quiet and moral deportment, was without reproach. Under the circumstances of your case, the court sentence you to one year imprisonment in the common jail of this county.

As to you, *Sawyer*—Your affidavit, which, from the uniform good character you have proved, we fully believe to be true, states, that you had no knowledge of this conspiracy, and took no active part in it. But your accompanying Lawson, at his request, to the jail, to inform the jailer's wife that she would be safe in receiving the amount of Morgan's debt from Lawson and letting him go, with the other circumstances, were sufficient to have convicted you, if you had stood trial; and you acted wisely in pleading guilty. You state that you had no idea that he was under restraint, until you saw him enter the carriage, a short distance from you, and you did not suspect that he was forced into it, until, in the progress of your walk, you picked up his hat; that you were then surprised and confounded, and did not therefore give the alarm; but you spent the rest of the evening at a public house, and gave no intimation of what you had seen. This, then, was your offence:—You should have given the alarm; you should have raised the hue and cry, and endeavored to effect a rescue. You, however, expressed in your affidavit, and have always evinced, a feeling of remorse. The court, therefore, sentence you to one month imprisonment in the common jail of this county.

As to you, *Sheldon*—You denied any participation in the conspiracy, and put yourself upon trial. As to all the acts proved against you, there was mystery; and I doubt whether you were the man. You were at the time confined on the limits of the jail—you were most strongly identified in an appearance at Batavia; and although your proof of an *alibi* was not complete, there was much in it to shake our faith in the fact that you were the mysterious stranger whom the witness saw. Your confessions of guilt, however, were clear and indisputable, and fully warranted the verdict; and the only explanation of them you offered was the ungracious one, that your confessions were the vainglorious boastings of a drunkard and a liar. Taking all things into consideration, the court have adjudged you to three months imprisonment in the common jail of the county.

NO. 12.

TO THE PUBLIC.—On the 11th day of September, William Morgan, a native of Virginia, who had for about three years past resided in this village, was under pretext of a justice's warrant hurried from his home and family and carried to Canandaigua. The same night he was examined on the charge of petit larceny, and discharged by the justice. One of the persons who took him away immediately obtained a warrant against him, in a civil suit, for an alleged debt of two dollars, on which he was committed to the jail of Ontario county. On the night of the 12th of September he was released by a person pretending to be his friend; but directly in front of the jail, notwithstanding his cries of *murder*, he was gagged and secured and put into a carriage, and after travelling all night, he was left (as the driver of the carriage says) at Hanford's landing, about sunrise on the 13th; since which he has not been heard of. His distressed wife and two infant children are left dependent on charity for their sustenance. The circumstances of the transaction have given rise to the most violent fears that he has been murdered. It is however hoped by his wife and friends, that he may be now kept concealed and imprisoned in Canada. All persons who are willing to serve the cause of humanity, and assist to remove the distressing apprehensions of his unfortunate wife, are earnestly requested to communicate to one of the committee named below, directed to this place, any facts or circumstances which have come to their knowledge, and are calculated to lead to the discovery of his present situation, or the particulars of his fate, if he has been murdered.

Batavia, October 4, 1826.

T. F. TALBOT,   JON. LAY,
D. E. EVANS,   T. FITCH,
T. CARY,   L. D. PRINDLE,   } Committee.
WM. KEYES,   E. SOUTHWORTH,
WM. DAVIS,   JAS. P. SMITH,

N. B. It is hoped that printers throughout the state, in Canada, and elsewhere, will give the above a few insertions, and thus serve the cause of justice and humanity.

NO. 13.

State of New-York, } JOHN K. LARKIN, of the town of Byron, in said *Genesee County, ss.* county, being duly sworn, deposeth and saith, that on the morning that William Morgan was carried off from the village of Batavia, he, this deponent, went to Andrew Adams to borrow a saddle; before the said deponent had got far off, said Adams called to him and said he must have his saddle, for he, Adams, was notified to attend a special meeting of the Masons at Le Roy, at 10 o'clock, same morning—Adams also understood to be a Free Mason. And this deponent asked Dr. Taylor what the fuss was; to which Dr. Taylor replied, they, the Masons, had orders from the Grand Lodge to notify a special meeting. And this deponent further saith not.

JOHN K. LARKIN.

Subscribed and sworn to, this ninth day of March, 1827, before me,
ANDREW DIBBLE, J. P

(COPY.)

State of New-York, } JOHN SOUTHWORTH and LUTHER WILDER, of the *Genesee County, ss.* town of Byron, in said county, being duly sworn, depose and say, that some time after the abduction of William Morgan from the village of Batavia, in the month of September last, they, the deponents, with others, had a conversation with Dr. Samuel Taggart of said town, (who is reputed and understood to be a Free Mason,) about the carrying off said Morgan; in which Dr. Taggart said there had been a rumpus at Batavia; that Morgan was taken away; and Miller's office (meaning as the deponents understood, the printing office of David C. Miller, a printer, in Batavia) had been set on fire: and on some person present saying he had not heard any thing of the affair, Dr. Taggart said he had known it for a length of time. Dr. Taggart further stated that he should not be afraid to bet a thousand dollars that Morgan was not in the land of the living: that he had taken a voyage on lake Ontario without float or boat, and would never be seen again by any human being. And further saith not.

JOHN SOUTHWORTH,
LUTHER WILDER.

Subscribed and sworn to, this ninth day of March, 1827, before me,
ANDREW DIBBLE, J. P.

(COPY.)

State of New-York, } ELIAS WILDER, of the town of Elba, in said coun-
Genesee County, ss. ty, being duly sworn, deposeth and saith, that about

two or three weeks before William Morgan was carried from Batavia, he, this deponent, had a conversation with one Cyrus Grout, (whom this deponent understands and verily believes to be a Free Mason,) on the subject of said Morgan's attempt to publish the secrets of Masonry; and that the said Cyrus Grout told this deponent that the Masons had sent to the Grand Lodge for instructions, and when they got word from them, (meaning said Grand Lodge, as this deponent understood,) there would be something done. And this deponent further saith, that after the abduction of said Morgan, he, this deponent, had another conversation with said Cyrus Grout, and others, on the subject of what had become of said Morgan; and Grout said he, Morgan, was gone a fishing on the Niagara river of lake Ontario. And further saith not.
ELIAS WILDER.
Subscribed and sworn to, this ninth day of March, 1827, before me,
ANDREW DIBBLE, J. P.

NO. 14.

Genesee County, } ss.   LYMAN D. PRINDLE, being duly sworn, saith, that on the 4th day of October last he met with James Ganson at Rochester, who beckoned to him to come to him, Ganson; he entered into conversation with him, this deponent, relating to the disturbances at Batavia, about the taking away of William Morgan. This deponent expressed his opinion that he could have rescued Morgan if he had known it. Ganson said, 'Let me tell you, you know nothing about it. Suppose there had been carriages ready at every road leading into Canandaigua ready to receive Morgan, in case he had been pursued he could have been shifted; and let me tell you it was the case; or let me tell you it is likely that was the case. Let me tell you, if you could hang, draw, and quarter or gibbet the Masons, (them that had a hand in it,) it would not fetch Morgan back. He is not dead; but he is put where he will stay put until God Almighty calls for him.' And further saith not.
LYMAN D. PRINDLE.
Sworn the eleventh day of October, 1826, before me,
C. CARPENTER, J. P.

NO. 15.
LETTER FROM GEORGE KETCHUM TO MRS. MORGAN.
'Rochester, September 14, 1826.
' *Mrs. Morgan*—Make yourself contented: I have learned your husband is well, but cannot learn where or which way he went: when I can learn, I will give you the earliest information. Be faithful to what I said to you, and you will find friends: keep your own council, and communicate to me through the postoffice. When I write to you it will be handed to you by the person I deliver it to—you must not pass a word with him; but write all the information you can obtain by following what I advised. If you want money, write to me, and I will send it. Commit this to the flames as soon as you read it.
'Your friend, ———— ————.
'You have the name on a small paper I gave you.'
N. B. A line was run through the postscript as above, but the words are perfectly legible.

NO. 16.

Genesee County, } ss.   JOHN MANN, of Buffalo, blacksmith by trade, deposeth and saith, that in the latter part of August last, or early in September, and very shortly before he heard that an attempt had been made to burn the printing office of David C. Miller, at Batavia, he was riding with one Richard Howard, of Buffalo, a book binder, who then worked with Mr. Haskins; and in the course of the ride he, said Howard, asked deponent to purchase or procure a keg of spirits of turpentine, (as he thinks,) saying he wanted to switch Miller's office with it, avowing at the same time his object to be to destroy the building for the purpose of suppressing a publication, which he said Morgan and Miller were about making, relating to Free Masonry. This deponent declined to assist in the act, intimating to him (as he believes) that he had no money to do it with. After he heard that such attempt had been made on the office of Miller, said Howard told this deponent that he had, with others who aided and assisted him, attempted to burn said office—that he had called at a store west of Batavia and bought a broom or brush to spread the turpentine with, and with his dark lanthorn had set fire to it; that the fire was lighted up, and he ran off; that some person ran after him, and he supposed was about to overtake him, when he turned and dashed his dark lanthorn into his face, which stopped the pursuit. That upon reflection since he concluded that it was a friend who ran after him, but had never found out. He believed then, and still does believe, that said Howard's object was to implicate him in the transaction.   JOHN MANN.

Sworn the twenty-first day of February, 1827, *before me*,
WM. H. TISDALE, First Judge of Genesee.

NO. 17.

State of New-York, }   THOMAS G. GREEN, late of the town of Henrietta, in *Genesee County, ss.* } the county of Monroe, and state aforesaid, carpenter, being duly sworn, deposeth and saith, that during the summer and until November in the fall of the year 1826, this deponent resided in the village of Buffalo. Sometime between the twentieth day of August and the seventh day of September last, he, this deponent, was requested by Richard Howard of Buffalo, aforesaid, to attend the lodge of Free Masons in that place; but Howard did not state to this deponent for what purpose the lodge was requested to meet—said there would be but a few there. In the evening this deponent started to go to the lodge, and on the way fell in with said Howard and went to the lodge with him. After the lodge was organized and had proceeded to business, it being then understood that William Morgan and David C. Miller, of Batavia, were about to publish at that place a book purporting to be a disclosure of Masonic secrets. This deponent was in the chair and presided for the time. Howard proposed that something should be done to prevent the publication of said book. B. Wilcox, of Buffalo, who was present, opposed the use of any rash or violent means for that purpose. Wilcox wished to know what measures it was intended should be adopted. Howard proposed that he and one other person, not now recollected by this deponent, should be a committe to attend to the business; and that they should be left to use such measures as they should think proper, so that the book should be suppressed. Wilcox proposed that they should be restricted from the use of any violent measures; and it was so concluded at that time that no rash or violent measures should be used to suppress the book.

A short time afterwards Howard requested that this deponent should go to the lodge room with him that evening—that a few were to meet there. In the evening this deponent started to go to the lodge room, and on the way fell in with Howard, but did not go to the lodge room. They walked together as far as the Franklin House, thence to the terrace back of the village, where Howard and this deponent had the following conversation:—Howard asked this deponent if he was willing to aid him in suppressing the book above alluded to. This deponent said he was willing to assist as far as was reasonable and proper, or according to what was proposed by Wilcox. Howard said he wanted a decisive answer one way or the other—he wanted to know whether he, this deponent, was for them, the Masons, as this deponent supposed, or against them. This deponent said he was for them, and was willing to aid in suppressing the book, if it were to promote the interests of the Masonic institution; and asked Howard what plan he intended to pursue. Howard said they intended to go to Batavia and get the papers; which this deponent understood to mean the manuscript papers of the book; and they were to get them peaceably if they could—if not, by force; and if they could not get them without, they would take Morgan and Miller, and carry them off too. This deponent finally consented to join the party and go to Batavia, for the purpose of getting the papers as aforesaid. The time for this expedition was not agreed upon at this time; but Howard afterwards informed this deponent that it was arranged to be in Batavia, for the above purpose, on the Friday evening following, being the eighth day of September last. This deponent does not recollect how many were going from Buffalo. This deponent accordingly got into the stage at Buffalo on Thursday evening, the seventh of September, for Batavia, and arrived in Batavia on Friday morning. During the day this deponent remained in and about Batavia, but conversed with none on the subject of his being at that place, except James B. Towsley, to whom he communicated the plan of attacking Miller's office. In the early part of the evening this deponent was informed that Towsley had told George W. Harris of the contemplated attack upon Miller's office; and that this deponent was the author of this information. This threw many obstructions in the way of the expedition, and was a principal cause of its total failure; and for which Howard blamed this deponent. In the evening a number of men were assembled in the village of Batavia—how many this deponent cannot say—there might have been forty or fifty, and perhaps more; but they were mostly strangers to this deponent; nor did he know where they came from. This deponent understood from some of them that it was expected that there would have been twenty-five from fort George and its vicinity; but as he understood, they did not come. Eight or ten were put under the immediate direction of this deponent, and the remainder were in different parts of the village, and directed by different persons. The whole party did not get into the village till nearly two o'clock in the morning of Saturday; and they remained about two hours and till the western stage came in, when the whole company dispersed in different directions. This was about four o'clock in the morning. During the time they were in the village no attack was made upon Miller's office. It was understood that Miller and Morgan, in consequence of the information communicated to them by way of Towsley, had been alarmed, and were on the watch; which caused some consultation and consequent delay, until the stage came in. When the party dispersed, this deponent made his best way to Buffalo—went west to the brick tavern, about fourteen miles; thence south to what is called the south Pembroke road, and pursued his way to Monroe's tavern, about five miles from Buffalo. At this place this deponent saw Col. Joseph Shaw, who spoke to this deponent, and asked him what he was doing there. This deponent then took Shaw one side and requested that he would not call him, this deponent, by name again, or mention to any one that he had seen him at that place; for he, this deponent, had been in a bad scrape, and wished him not to speak of it. Shaw asked this deponent what it was; but this deponent refused to tell him, but said he would at some future time, and that Shaw would hear about it. From this place this deponent went to Buffalo, where he arrived the same evening. And this deponent further saith, that he has never been personally concerned otherwise than above stated, in any measures to suppress the publication of the book, or for the carrying away or disposing of Morgan. And further saith not. THOMAS G. GREEN.

Subscribed and sworn to, this sixteenth day of July, 1827, *before me*,
C. CARPENTER,
One of the Justices of the Peace in and for Genesee Co.

APPENDIX.

NO. 19.

Niagara County, ss. } DAVID MAXWELL, being sworn, saith that in the night of the thirteenth day of September last he was at home attending to the keeping of the turnpike gate on the Ridge road, so called, about nineteen miles distant from Lewiston. About eleven o'clock, P. M. he was sitting in the toll house, and heard a carriage pass through the gate very slowly; and upon opening the door he saw Jeremiah Brown, of Ridgeway, standing directly in front of the door, and saw the carriage standing in the road, about three rods west of the house. He, Brown, had a shilling in his hand, which he handed to him, being the exact amount of the toll on the carriage. Deponent said, ' How do you do, captain Brown?' he made no answer and turned away quickly and went towards the carriage. Deponent called to him quite loudly, and said, ' What is the matter?' Brown answered, ' Nothing.' Deponent took notice of the carriage because he had never known Brown to have any thing to do with a coach before; and it struck him as a thing out of the usual course. He thinks the curtains were closed. Brown joined the carriage ; but whether he got into it, or got on to the driver's seat, deponent cannot say. The carriage drove off quickly, when deponent entered into the house : himself and his wife had a conversation, and expressed to each other their wonder as to the cause that should take captain Brown west with a coach so late at night. He, Brown, is a farmer, in good circumstances, residing about thirteen miles east of the gate, and well known to deponent and his wife, and passing the gate frequently, and never to the knowledge and recollection of deponent with any other carriage than a common two-horse farm wagon. They eventually concluded, that he perhaps had gone on to Lewiston to an installation. The next morning before breakfast, and not far from sunrise, the same carriage, as he thinks, arrived at the gate, driven by a person he did not then know. The middle curtains were then up, and deponent distinctly saw the said Jeremiah Brown sitting on the back seat of the carriage, appearing to be asleep and leaning back ; he saw no other person in the carriage. Deponent said to the driver, 'How far did you go out; did you go to Lewiston?' He hesitated a little and said, ' No, we did not go to Lewiston.' The deponent and his wife then observed to each other, that they had not gone to the installation. Deponent took notice that the coach was a chocolate color ; it appeared to be a hack carriage that had been much used.

DAVID MAXWELL.

Sworn the twenty-second day of March, 1827, before me,
DANIEL SEAMAN, J. P.

NO. 20.

Niagara County, ss. } PAUL MOSHER, of Lewiston, in said county, being duly sworn, doth on his oath declare that previous to the month of December last past this deponent had been in the employ of the stage proprietors at Lewiston, (his special business being to regulate and superintend the arrival and departure of the stages,) for more than one year. That while in such employ, on the morning of the fourteenth day of September last, (about four o'clock, A. M.) one of the drivers informed him that he had just returned from Youngstown. This driver was Corydon Fox, who further stated that Samuel Barton, one of the stage proprietors, had called him up sometime that night, and directed him to get up a carriage and drive it to Youngstown. Fox also stated that Eli Bruce, (Sheriff of Niagara county,) or as he called him, Bruce, came with Mr. Barton, when he was called up—that after the getting the carriage ready, Bruce told him (Fox) to drive round to a back street. He did so, and found a carriage in the street without horses—that there was something curious about it; he thought there was a man in the carriage who was gagged and bound. That there were two persons who came out of the carriage standing in the street ; and both, with Bruce, got into the one he was driving. Bruce told him to go or drive on : he was directed to stop at the residence of Col. King. He halted accordingly in front of the door or house at Youngstown. Bruce got out and called up King. Bruce and King both got into the carriage. That he heard a man in the carriage call for water, and Bruce said he should have some ; he also thought he heard King say, 'Morgan, are you here.' That he (Fox) was directed to drive on ; and when about half way from Youngstown to the fort, Bruce told him to stop : he did so, and they all got out, and he returned to Lewiston. Fox has more recently stated that it was near the grave yard where he stopped. This deponent thinking it strange that passengers should leave the carriage distant from a house, in the night, was led to inquire of a Mason present (this deponent being also one) the reason of it : he answered that he believed it was Morgan. The deponent inquired of another Mason, and was told it was Morgan, for Bruce told him so. In the forenoon of the same day (14th September) the deponent saw Bruce and asked why he was so imprudent as to have the driver he did, for he was not a Mason ; to which Bruce replied that Sam (meaning Samuel Barton) was more in the fault than himself, for he told him to send a Mason. The deponent then asked Bruce if he actually had Morgan ; he said he had. And the conversation ended here. Samuel Barton asked this deponent the same day if Fox mistrusted Morgan was in the carriage : the deponent told him that Fox was telling about the village the circumstances of his having driven the carriage, &c.; which led this deponent to believe and probably would others, that it was Morgan. Barton then told the deponent to go and say to Fox that if he knew any thing to keep it to himself and hold his tongue, or he would discharge him ; and further stated that there must be another man smuggled away to blind that transaction ; he further said that the deponent being a Mason, was the man who ought to have been sent as a driver, but being called up in the night in a hurry, he did not think. In the afternoon of the same day said Barton came to the deponent, and directed him to borrow a saddle and bridle and put them on a horse as soon as possible, and hitch it by another horse standing under the shed, pointing that way, and which horse appeared as if he had been rode fast ; he added that he had heard from the fort, and must send a man down, for he was afraid there would be trouble yet. He did as directed, and the two horses were rode off soon after ; the one put there by this deponent, by a Mason resident in Lewiston ; the other by a person not known to this deponent. Next morning the deponent asked said Barton if there was any trouble at the fort; to which he replied, 'I guess it is still enough.' Fox, the driver before mentioned, within say three or four weeks afterwards, joined the lodge in Lewiston, at a special meeting called for that purpose ; and on being solicited so to do by a Mason who was sent to Fox to induce him to join, and who, pursuant to instructions, told Fox that if he wanted funds, meaning for his admittance, he should have them. This deponent further saith, that in relating the above facts and circumstances, which he heard from several individuals at different times and places, he has not pretended to give the exact words in all cases ; but verily believes the substance is truly and correctly set forth. And further saith not. PAUL MOSHER.

Subscribed and sworn to, at Youngstown, Niagara County, the twenty-second of March, 1827, *before me,* A. G. HINMAN.

NO. 21.

State of New-York, }
Niagara County, ss. } JOSIAH TRYON, of said county, being sworn, saith, that on the evening of the fourteenth of September last past he attended a dance or ball at Lewiston, there having been on that day a considerable collection of ladies and gentlemen at Lewiston on the occasion, of what was called the installation of a chapter, (so called.) That at the same ball were present a Mr. Edwin Scrantom, a friend of deponent's,

who wished to leave town in time to get on board of the steam boat for York, U. C.; and to induce him to remain at the ball, this deponent had promised to take him there: as soon as the ball closed he would start right off with him to Youngstown, that he might be in time for the boat. Accordingly he started from Lewiston with his friend in a one horse wagon. That the night was clear, and the moon was remarkably bright. That about two miles from Lewiston, he met five men walking towards Lewiston, of whom he then distinctly recognized and believed to be Timothy Shaw, Samuel Chubbuck, and General Parkhurst Whitney, who keeps what is called the Eagle Hotel, at the falls of Niagara; and he has since been informed, and has ascertained to his own perfect satisfaction, that the other two were James L. Barton, of Black Rock, and Noah Beach, of Lewiston. It was, as he thinks, between the hours of three and four of the clock, in the morning of the fifteenth of said September. The deponent drew up his horse, and said to one of them who was a little behind the rest, '*What are you here this time of night for?*'—or words to that purport. He answered, as I think, '*We have had a set down at Youngstown*—and passed on. That this deponent mentioned the circumstances to others in the village of Lewiston, and the story soon enlarged by report, so as to implicate the above named men in the extraordinary disappearance of William Morgan. And three of them have had conversation with him in relation thereto; and one of them requested him to correct erroneous reports of what he had said. But in none of those conversations did either of them attempt to say where they had spent the night, or how it happened that they were on their way to Lewiston on foot at that time of the morning. He further says, that all of the said men are men having families, and following business with ordinary regularity, and of ordinary good habits. He further says, that according to his recollection and belief, none of the above named persons have given to him any explanation of the above circumstances.

JOSIAH TRYON.

Sworn the twenty-second day of March, 1827, *before me,*

A. G. HINMAN, J. P.

NO. 23.

Niagara County, ss. I, A. G. HINMAN, one of the justices of the peace, of said county, do hereby certify, that on the 29th of last December, complaint was made on oath before me, setting forth in substance that there was full cause to suspect that Eli Bruce, sheriff of the said county, had, on or about the thirteenth or fourteenth of last September, forcibly and without due process of law, held William Morgan in duress for some time, within the said county, and had secretly and illegally conveyed him thence to parts unknown. Whereupon I issued a warrant against the said Eli Bruce, who was brought before me, for examination, on the thirtieth of said December. And I do further certify that the information taken on such examination was substantially as follows, to wit, that the said Eli Bruce came to Molineaux's tavern, about twelve miles East of Lewiston, on the Ridge road, on the night of the thirteenth of said September, at about ten or eleven o'clock, in a hack or coach, the curtains of which were closed quite around. He went in and inquired for the landlord, who was in bed; was shown into his room; afterwards called up the landlord's son, who was also in bed, and requested him to put a pair of horses before his carriage, to relieve those that came with it, to go as far as Lewiston; which was done. The son asked if he should drive; Bruce replied he had a driver who was a careful man, pointing to a man whom the witness knew to be Jeremiah Brown. Bruce was also asked by a hired girl, what the matter was; he answered, you cannot know at present. He soon left there with the carriage, driven by Brown towards Lewiston. At Lewiston the same night, but the hour not ascertained, the said Bruce went with Samuel Barton, a stage proprietor, to the stage office to ascertain what driver could be had to go to Youngstown. On being informed by Joshua Fairbanks who slept there, that none but Fox was there, Fox was called up and directed to harness a carriage, which he did, and drove up to the Frontier House, where said Bruce got in, and ordered the carriage driven to a back street. On arriving there, in front of said Barton's dwelling house, a carriage was found in the street without any horses attached to it, and two men, either one or both of whom were in it, got out, and went into the other: one was helped in by the arm—nothing was said. When, together with said Bruce, being seated, the driver was ordered by Bruce to drive to Youngstown. Witness heard no conversation from the passengers that he could distinguish. On arriving at Youngstown, Bruce directed him to stop in front of Col. King's house in Youngstown. He did so, and Bruce got out and called up Col. King; went in, and in a few minutes, say fifteen, came out, together with King, and both got into the carriage, when Bruce told the driver to go on. While at this house the driver heard a strange kind of sound from one of the persons in the carriage, which he thought was a call for water, though he could not say that the articulation was sufficiently distinct to be understood; Bruce answered he should have some presently—none was, however, given or brought. The carriage proceeded to within a short distance of Fort Niagara, near the grave yard, when the driver was directed to stop, and the persons within, four in number, he thought, got out—one was assisted as before—and they proceeded off from the side of the carriage, closely together, towards the fort. Bruce told the driver to go back; and he immediately returned. The next morning (the fourteenth).the said Eli Bruce being at Lewiston, he was asked if he went to Youngstown the night before; he said he did. He was then asked if he took Morgan down; he replied he did, and observed that Sam., meaning said Barton, was very imprudent in sending Fox—that he told him his business, and that he had not ought to have sent any but a Mason.

There were five witnesses sworn, whose testimony is included in the above statement. No attempt was made to impeach either of them, nor was there any evidence offered on the part of Mr. Bruce.

As there was no proof adduced on this examination, that a William Morgan had been forcibly seized and carried away from Canandaigua, or elsewhere; nor that force, violence, or restraint, had been exercised upon the person of any individual in the carriage, the said Bruce was discharged.

Given under my hand, at Youngstown, in the said county, the twenty-first day of March, 1827. A. G. HINMAN, J. P.

NO. 24.

State of *New-York*, } WILLIAM TERRY, of Niagara, province of Upper
Niagara County, ss. } Canada, druggist, being duly sworn, doth depose and say, that in the month of September or October last this deponent was in ill health and confined to his dwelling, and had been so some time. That about this time a neighbor of this deponent informed him that a man had engaged, in some part of the state of New-York, in publishing a book concerning Masonry, or disclosing the secrets of Masonry, or words to that effect. This deponent does not recollect the name mentioned at this time by his informant, but has now no doubt that it related to the abduction of William Morgan. This deponent was further informed at the same time, by the same person, that the person so taken and carried away had been killed, and sunk in lake Ontario. This deponent's informant was of the fraternity of Free Masons, as is also this deponent, which this deponent believes was the reason why this story was related to him. That this deponent at the time disbelieved the facts related, and told his informant that it could not be possible, but was assured it was a fact, and said he (the informant) would relate more about it at another time. Some few weeks afterwards, when this deponent was recovering, the same informant added, or further related, that Morgan had been brought to

Fort Niagara, or to the other side of the river opposite this, (meaning the town of Niagara,) and was there put to death. This deponent again expressed doubts of the truth of the relation, and expressed himself in warm terms of disapprobation, denying the right of the society of Masons, or any members of the fraternity, to commit such a deed. The relator was, however, of a different opinion, and said it was right.

Some time in the month of December last, this deponent was further informed by another member of the society aforesaid, who also resides in the same town with this deponent, that Morgan had been taken at Batavia, was brought to Fort Niagara, and from thence to the town of Niagara, and was taken before another Mason of the same place—that the Masons in Canada refused to receive Morgan, or to have any thing to do with him—and that Morgan was returned to Fort Niagara—that after, Morgan was tried by some sort of a council, or tribunal, which sentenced him to death—that he was executed by having his throat cut; his tongue was torn out, and buried in the sands of the lakes or lake; and that his body was also sunk in the lake or deep water opposite, off, from, or near the fort; which is as near the substance of what was said as this deponent can recollect. The relator further added that Morgan did not know where he was—that he was blinded—that the boat was rowed about the river for the purpose of deranging the man—that while at Fort Niagara, Morgan asked permission for a Bible, and a short time in the light, in order that he might peruse it. This deponent asked what was the result of the request; to which the relator added, that he was soon despatched. This deponent asked how those who had been engaged in the affair felt about it; the relator observed that they felt bad, and some had expressed so much contrition as to say that they would have given all they were worth if the affair had not happened, or if Morgan could be produced again. And this deponent further saith, that the relator added that one of the persons concerned was sick and delirious in consequence of it, and had to have watches, according to the best belief of this deponent. Further, the relator stated that those engaged at Canandaigua, and there indicted, were to be kept harmless by the General Grand Chapter of the state of New-York; and that all expense requisite to pay any fines that might be imposed was to be defrayed by the said chapter; and that the actors in the affair of the abduction of Morgan so acted in obedience to the order, (or by the consent or knowledge,) or directions, of the said Grand Chapter. The relator also stated that it was the intention of those who had Morgan to have taken Miller also. This deponent, at the time he heard the last relation, did believe the substantial part of it, and still does most firmly believe it.

This deponent further saith, that another member of the Masonic society also related the same facts substantially, and said he derived his information from a gentleman of Buffalo, (a Mason,) now deceased. This latter part is intended to be restricted to the fact of the death of Morgan, and the place of depositing the body. This deponent further saith, that the foregoing was prepared and signed (though not sworn to) some time since. Subsequent to that period further information has been received by this deponent, which has induced him to believe that the manner of putting Morgan to death was different from the relation of *Stocking*. WILLIAM TERRY.

Sworn before me, at *Niagara, Upper Canada*, this twentieth day of March, 1827.
J. B. CLENCH, J. P.

NO. 25.

Genesee County, } ss.   JOHN MANN, being sworn, deposeth and saith, that about the time that he heard and understood that William Morgan had been taken away from Batavia, he had a conversation with Richard Howard, of Buffalo, bookbinder, (who works, or did work, with Mr. Haskins,) who then informed this deponent that Morgan was confined in Fort Niagara

And he believes, in the same conversation with said Howard, he informed him that five persons had drawn lots to see who it would fall upon to execute the laws of Masonry upon Morgan: that the lot fell upon him. He seemed much distressed, and clasped his hands together and exclaimed, My God! must it be done! or some words to that effect. He appeared to be under an impression that his Masonic obligations placed him under a necessity of submitting to do an act which seemed abhorrent to his natural feelings. In subsequent conversations said Howard gave this deponent to understand that the execution had been performed, but said nothing more as to his own agency in the transaction. This deponent further saith, that until within a few days past his mind has been very unsettled as to the course which he ought to have pursued in relation to the communications so made to him; and he has been operated upon in some degree by fears for his personal safety, and doubts as to the extent of his obligations to observe secrecy in respect to the statements so communicated to him. That a few days ago he held a consultation with a friend, as to the general duties of a person so situated; and he at last determined to communicate the facts to some person who might feel bound to act upon them as public good should seem to require.   JOHN MANN.

Sworn, the twenty-first day of February, 1827, before me,
           WILLIAM H. TINSDALE, First Judge of Genesee.

NO. 26.

Niagara County, ss. } EDWARD GIDDINS, of the county aforesaid, being duly sworn, saith, that he has resided at Fort Niagara from the year eighteen hundred and fifteen till the present time, with the exception of about eight months. That from the year sixteen to the year twenty, this deponent had charge of the building, called the magazine, the greater part of the time. That when the United States' troops left the fort in the month of May last, this deponent again took charge of the building, and continued so in charge until about the first of August, when he gave up the keys to Col. E. Jewett, who yet retains the care of it. This building stands on the southerly side of the fort—is built of stone, about the height of a common two story building, and measures about fifty by thirty feet on the ground—is arched over—the side and end walls are about four feet thick—the wall over the top is about eight feet thick, and is considered bomb proof—covered with a shingle roof. There is but one door, around which there is a small entry, to which there is a door also. There are no windows or apertures in the walls, except a small ventilator for the admission of air, and one small window in each end about ten feet from the ground—they are usually kept closed, and locked on the outside with a padlock—these shutters are made of plank, covered with sheet iron—the floor is laid with plank, pinned to the sleepers with wood pins. That at the time certain persons were at the fort in January last, Col. Jewett being unwell, this deponent was requested to visit the magazine, which they wished to examine. That on entering and examining the said building, one of the floor planks, supposed to be one and an half inches thick, was observed by some of the committee to have been newly broken, directly on one of the sleepers, and about six feet from one end; and this deponent was inquired of by some of the committee how that plank became broken. This deponent told them he did not know: farther, he has now no recollection of its being broken when he gave up the keys, and believes it was not. This deponent has also been inquired of whether a loose door, which the committee saw in the building, belonged there, or was there, when he gave up possession; to which this deponent answered that it did not belong to the building, nor did he recollect of its being there at the time he surrendered the key. Farther, whether it has been usual to admit any liquid within the building; to which this deponent answered that he never admitted any while he had charge, nor was it usual, so far as his knowledge extends; and he should suppose it one of the last things to be admitted to such a place. The chief aim ought to be to keep it dry; the utmost care has always been taken, and the key of the building only intrusted with particular persons. On entering the building it has been usual to remove or leave the shoes at the door, or else draw on woollen socks over them. There is, nearly in the middle of the floor, frame pieces upon which to lay fixed ammunition. The usual arrangement of the boxes, kegs, &c. containing powder, is to place them round the building on the floor, so far distant from the wall as to prevent them contracting dampness, say from one to two feet, unless empty, when they are set next the wall.

EDWARD GIDDINS.

Subscribed and sworn to, at Porter, in the county of Niagara, the nineteenth day of March, 1827, before me, A. G. HINMAN.

NO. 27.

Niagara, U. C. March 3, 1827.

Gentlemen—On my return from my parliamentary duties at York, I observed in the Albany Observer a letter dated 'Lewiston, N. Y. January 12, 1827,' in which I perceived some indirect allusions to the name of ' M'******, a member of Parliament,' to whose house, it is stated, a William Morgan, of Batavia, was brought, 'blindfolded and tied.'

Now, gentlemen, I beg leave to declare through the medium of your paper, to your readers and to the world at large, that no such occurrence ever took place—that on the night of the 14th of September, 1826, nor at any other time, was Morgan in my house to my knowledge. And I further declare the said Morgan is to me an utter stranger, except as to report; and I never exchanged a word with the man in my life, and would not know him from the greatest stranger in existence.

In justice to my own reputation, as well as to that of my family and friends, I hereby most solemnly assert the whole statement to be utterly false and unfounded. And further, that I never conversed with the brother of S******* (Stocking,) of Buffalo, on the affair of Morgan, as to his abduction, till after the appearance of the letters alluded to in that paper, when I called on him for that purpose; and he then most explicitly declared that he had never given me as his author to Dr. *****, and admitted that I never had the slightest conversation with him on the subject previous. I could add to the foregoing declarations and assertions, my own affidavit, if necessary, as well as that of my family, consisting of three persons, and a worthy and respectable gentleman and lady who slept that night at my house. I cannot refrain from expressing my belief, before I close this letter, that *malice, envy,* and foul *revenge,* are at the bottom of the heart of him, whoever he may be, that would thus villainously attempt to assassinate the character of any man in society. I mean to cast no reflection on the characters of the gentlemen who formed the committee of vigilance, but on him to whom it justly belongs. *And from declarations made even on the* BED OF DEATH, *that he, the Dr. ******, would be revenged of me, for assisting to destroy a den of rogues and coiners, with whom he was implicated, has been his only inducement thus to do.*

As, gentlemen, I am the only member of Parliament residing in Niagara whose name commences with the letter M, I have come to the conclusion that I am particularly referred to; and beg you will insert in your paper this refutation of the infamous and foul charges.

I am, with respect, your obedient servant,

EDW. M'BRIDE, M. P. P.

APPENDIX. 25

NO. 29.
First Proclamation of the Governor.

De Witt Clinton, Governor of the state of New-York, to state officers
and ministers of justice in the said state, and particulary in the
L. S.   county of Genesee and the neighboring counties: *Greeting.*

Whereas information, under oath, has been transmitted to me by Theodore F. Talbot, Esq. and other citizens of the county of Genesee, acting as a committee in behalf of the people of that county, representing that divers outrages and oppressions have been committed on the rights of persons residing in the village of Batavia; and that disturbances have ensued which are injurious, and may prove destructive to peace and good order in that quarter:—Now, therefore, I enjoin it upon you, and each of you, to pursue all proper and efficient measures for the apprehension of the offenders, and the prevention of future outrages. And I do also request the good citizens of this state to co-operate with the civil authorities in maintaining the ascendancy of law and good order.

Second Proclamation of the Governor.

Whereas, it has been represented to me that *William Morgan*, who was unlawfully conveyed from the jail of the county of Ontario some time in the month of September last, has not been found; and that it might have a beneficial effect in restoring him to his family, and in promoting the detection and punishment of the perpetrators of this violent outrage, if, in addition to the proceedings heretofore adopted by me, a proclamation was issued offering a specific reward for these purposes:—*Now, therefore*, in order that the offenders may be brought to condign punishment, and the violated majesty of the laws thereby effectually vindicated, I do hereby offer, in addition to the assurances of compensation heretofore given, a reward of *three hundred dollars* for the discovery of the offenders, and a reward of *one hundred dollars* for the discovery of any and every one of them—to be paid on conviction; and also a further reward of *two hundred dollars* for authentic information of the place where the said William Morgan has been conveyed. And I do enjoin it upon all sheriffs, magistrates, and other officers and ministers of justice, to be vigilant and active in the discharge of their duties on this occasion.

In witness whereof, I have hereunto set my hand and the
L. S.   privy seal, at the city of Albany, this 26th day of October, Anno
Domini 1826.   De Witt Clinton.

Third Proclamation of the Governor.

Whereas, the measures adopted for the discovery of *William Morgan*, after his unlawful abduction from Canandaigua in September last, have not been attended with success; and whereas many of the good citizens of this state are under an impression, from the lapse of time and other circumstances, that he has been murdered:—*Now, therefore*, to the end that, if living, he may be restored to his family; and if murdered, that the perpetrators may be brought to condign punishment, I have thought fit to issue this proclamation, promising a reward of one thousand dollars for the discovery of the said William Morgan, if alive; and, if murdered, a reward of two thousand dollars for the discovery of the offender or offenders: to be paid on conviction, and on the certificate of the attorney general, or officer prosecuting on the part of the state, that the person or persons claiming the said last mentioned reward is or are justly entitled to the same, under this proclamation. And I further promise a free pardon, so far as I am authorized under the constitution of this state, to any accomplice or co-operator who shall make a full discovery of the offender or offenders. And I do enjoin it upon all officers and ministers of justice, and all other persons, to be vigilant and active in bringing to justice

3

the perpetrators of a crime so abhorrent to humanity, and so derogatory to the ascendancy of law and good order.

IN witness whereof, I have hereunto set my hand and the privy seal, at the city of Albany, this 19th day of March, Anno Domini 1827.

L. S.

DE WITT CLINTON.

NO. 30. [Referred to in page 258.]

The only passenger who went in the stage from Rochester to Lewiston, on the 13th of September, 1826, the day, of course, after Morgan was taken away from Canandaigua, and the day on which he was carried from Rochester to Lewiston, was a reverend clergyman of Rochester, who officiated in some capacity at the Lewiston installation on the 14th. The stage stopped at Murdock's tavern, near the residence of Brown. A boy was immediately despatched on horseback with a note from this gentleman to Brown, and a request that he would come without any delay on the same horse which the boy had ridden. Brown came accordingly, and had a private interview with the reverend gentleman. This was but a short time before he brought his horses to the same tavern, where he fed them, and waited for the carriage.

At Buffalo, a man, high in office, declared that he was astonished that Miller had been permitted to go so far in printing the book; and that if Morgan should come there, there were twenty men who would take his life in less than half an hour.

In Attica, a former member of the legislature declared as follows:—'If they are publishing the true secrets of Masonry, I should not think the lives of half a dozen such men as Morgan and Miller of any consequence in suppressing the work.'

In Le Roy, a physician, formerly sheriff of the county, declared at a public table, 'That the book should be suppressed if it cost every one of them their lives.'

In Batavia, a person holding a respectable office declared to another officer—'That Miller's office would not stand there long.'

A justice of the peace in Le Roy said—'If he could catch Morgan on the bridge in the night, he would find the bottom of that mill pond.'

A judge of the county court of Genesee said—'That whatever Morgan's fate might have been, he deserved it—he had forfeited his life.'

A high priest of the order at Le Roy said—'That Morgan deserved death—he hoped he had received it—a common death was too good for him.'

A justice of the peace in Middlebury, a sober respectable man, said, publicly—'That a man had a right to pledge his life;' and then observed to those who answered him—'What can you do? what can a rat do with a lion? who are your judges? who are your sheriffs? and who will be your jurymen?'

APPENDIX, NO. II.

Proceedings of a Convention of Delegates, from the different Counties in the state of New-York, opposed to Free Masonry. Held at the Capitol in the City of Albany, on the 19th, 20th and 21st days of February, 1829.

THE CONVENTION,

Of whose proceedings the following sheets furnish a history, was called by the following notice :—

ANTI-MASONIC STATE CONVENTION.

In pursuance of a resolution passed by the Anti-Masonic State Convention which met at Utica on the 4th day of August last, authorising the General Corresponding Committee to call future Conventions, when, in their judgment, the cause required it, notice is hereby given that a STATE CONVENTION of Delegates opposed to the Institution of Free Masonry will be holden at the city of Albany on the 19th day of February next, to deliberate upon and adopt such measures as may be deemed best calculated to vindicate the laws of the land from Masonic violence, and to redeem the principles of civil and political liberty from Masonic encroachments. The citizens of the several counties in the state are requested to appoint a number of Delegates corresponding with their respective representations in the House of Assembly, to attend this Convention.

SAMUEL WORKS,
HARVEY ELY,
F. F. BACKUS,
FR'K. WHITTLESEY,
THURLOW WEED.

} GENERAL CENTRAL COMMITTEE.

ROCHESTER, DEC. 30, 1828.

PROCEEDINGS, &c.

The Delegates met in the Assembly Chamber of the Capitol at the City of Albany, on the 19th day of February, 1829, at four o'clock, P. M., and were called to order by *Samuel M. Hopkins*, delegate from Albany County, and on his motion, WILLIAM FINN, of Orange county, was chosen President of the Convention—and JAMES HAWKS, of Otsego, and ALEXANDER SHELDON of Montgomery, were chosen Vice Presidents. NICHOLAS DEVEREAUX, of Oneida, and FREDERICK WHITTLESEY, of Monroe, were duly appointed Secretaries.

After an address from Mr. Southwick, delegates from the following counties answered to their names.

Albany.—Solomon Southwick, Samuel M. Hopkins, Albany; Thomas Helmes, Guilderland.

Cataraugus.—Russell Hubbard, Farmersville P. O.

Cayuga.—William Bruce, Auburn; John A. Taylor, Mentz; Aaron Watson, North Scipio; William H. Seward, Auburn; Samuel Phelps, Ira.

Chautauque.—Abner Hazeltine, Jamestown; Nathan Nixen, Forestville.

Chenango.—Joel Hendrix, Coventry; Jethro Hatch, Otselic; James Thompson, Sherburne.

Columbia.—David Wager, Ghent; Isaac B. Bassett, Hudson; John Hoes, Stuyvesant.

Cortland.—Alanson Carley, Harrison; Eli Carpenter, Homer.

Delaware.—Ebenezer Penfield, Hapersfield Center, Joel Parks, Delhi.

Dutchess.—Cornelius Husted, Rolend Hoag, Pine Plains; Thomas H. Rickey, Fishkill; Abraham Van Keezer, Rhinebeck-Flatts.

Erie.—Thaddeus Joy, Albert H. Tracy, Buffalo; Israel P. Trimble, [removed to Derby, Penn.]

Essex.—Franklin Stone, Jay.

Greene.—Joseph Carman, Cairo; Knight Bennett, Freehold.

Genessee.—Timothy Fitch, George W. Lay, Batavia; Augustus P. Hascall, Le Roy.

Herkimer.—Abraham Randall, jr. German Flatts; Hiram Nolton, Fairfield.

Jefferson.—A. W. Stow, Sackets Harbor; S. M. Sweet, Adams; Albert Guthrie, Hounsfield.

Livingston.—James Percival, Geneseo; Halloway Long, York.

Madison.—John F. Fairchild, Cazenovia; Francis Whitmore, Lebanon; Thomas Beekman, Peterborough.

Monroe.—Brooks Mason, Penfield; William Groves, Clarkson; Frederick Whittlesey, Thurlow Weed, delegate from Central Committee, Rochester.

Montgomery.—John Merrill, Glen; Tiffany Brockway, Broadalban; Alexander Sheldon, Charleston.

New-York.—Henry Dana Ward, S. B. Griswald, B. J. Seward.

Niagara.—Bates Cooke, Lewiston; John Phillips, Lockport.

Oneida.—Thomas R. Palmer, New-Hartford; William Williams, Richard R. Lansing, Nicholas Devereaux, Satterlee Clark, Utica.

Onondaga.—Parley Howlett, Onondaga West Hill P. O.; John Myres, Fabius, Delphi P. O.; Parson G. Shipman, Pompey, Delphi P. O.

Ontario.—Ralph Wilcox, East Bloomfield; Irving Metcalf, Gorham; Francis Granger, Canandaigua.

APPENDIX.

Orange.—William Finn, Walkill, P. O. Phillipsburgh.
Oswego.—Arvin Rice, Hannibal.
Otsego.—Erastus Crafts, Laurens; James Hawks, Richfield; Richard P. Marvin, Cherry Valley; John C. Morris, Butternuts.
Putnam.—Harrison Hopkins, Patterson, Mill Town P. O.
Renssalaer.—Welcome Whittaker, Troy; Ambrose Mosley, Hoosick Falls; Lewis Buffit, David Green, Jonathan Nichols, Holden Sweet, Berlin.
Saratoga.—Caleb Greene, Mechanicville; James Mott, Saratoga; David Garnsey, Clifton.
Schenectady.—Solomon Kelly, Schenectady.
Schoharie.—J. W. Throop, Schoharie Court House; Jacob H. Hagar, Blenheim P. O.
Seneca.—Enoch Chamberlain, Waterloo; David Scott, Ovid.
Steuben.—Henry A. Townsend, Urbanna.
Tioga.—Stephen L. Pert, Spencer.
Tompkins.—Hiram Cobb, Groton; Robert Swartwout, Hector; John Haxton, Ulyssis.
Ulster.—Jonathan Dubois, Newport; Jesse P. Conklin, Milton.
Washington.—John Crary, Salem; Chauncey Whitney, White Creek, Cambridge P. O.; Benjamin Ferris, Sandy Hill.
Wayne.—Myron Holley, Lyons.
Yates.—Morris F. Shepard, Penn Yan.
On motion of Mr. Whittlesey.
Resolved, That Thurlow Weed be admitted to a seat in this Convention, as a delegate from the General Central Anti-Masonic Committee.
On motion of Mr. Morris,
Resolved, That the delegations from the several counties whose members are deficient, shall have power to supply such deficiences, and the persons thus selected shall be entitled to seats in this Convention, as delegates from such counties.
On motion of Mr. Granger,
Resolved, That Mr. Maynard of the Senate and Mr. Williams of the House, be admitted members of this Convention.
On motion of Mr. Southwick,
Resolved, That Martin Flint, of Vermont, Mr. Pratt, of Connecticut, and Mr. Merrick, of Massachusetts, be admitted honorary members of this Convention.
Mr. Whittlesey explained the objects for which the Convention was called.
On motion of Mr. Tracy,
Resolved, That the report of the General Central Committee, be submitted to the Convention.
Mr. Weed, the delegate from the Central Committee of the state, submitted the following report of the Committee, on the progress and present state of the Anti-Masonic cause.

The General Central Corresponding Committee embrace what they deem a proper occasion to make a brief Report upon the progress and condition of the Anti-Masonic cause.
In rendering our grateful acknowledgments to the Dispenser of all good, and congratulating our fellow-citizens upon the "*signs of the times*" which indicate a great moral and political revolution, in the coming overthrow of Free Masonry, it may not be unprofitable to glance backwards over the relationship which that Institution bore to the people and the country, at the period when the overt acts were committed, which are leading the American Republic to re-assert and confirm its Independence.
The Masonic Society, by its arrogation of all the Science, wisdom, patriotism and virtues, which illumine the age, endow and sustain the Institutions of

the country, and adorn the human character, had conciliated the esteem and won the confidence of public opinion. It had grown under these genial influences, unsuspected of other motives than those which it professed, into enormous wealth and gigantic power. Professing strict obedience to the laws, and a wedded affinity to the religion of the country, it had implanted its roots, extended its arms, and established its laws all over the land. The suspicions and apprehensions that had watched and overcome all other secret associations, by the soothing pretensions and specious bearing of Free Masonry, were quieted and disarmed.

At this crisis of popular credulity, the Masonic conspiracies and outrages which have aroused the moral energies of this state, and promise to interest the whole nation, were matured and perpetrated. Voluntary investigations were speedily undertaken, but the people were slow to entertain evil thoughts of an ancient and honorable Institution. The great, the wise, and the good, of every age and country, were claimed to be among its votaries and patrons. Investigations, embarrassed and crippled by the influence and stratagems of the fraternity, proceeded with slow and uncertain steps. The laws were relaxed, and the ministers of justice lingered in their course. The constitutional reliances of the people, for protection and safety, were soon found too weak to discharge their functions. And the public press, which, on all other occasions of existing evil or approaching danger, had asserted its high prerogative, was now awed into silence.

A general alarm spread through the western counties. The people met and appointed committees of investigation. It was soon discovered that the outrages had not been unadvisedly perpetrated by irresponsible members of the fraternity, but were authorised by the Institution, and impelled by its principles. The conspiracy, from its origin to its conclusion, embraced a period of more than four months, and the knowledge of it extended from the immediate actors in it, to the highest authorities pertaining to the Order.

The results of the first six months investigation were embodied in a Narrative, and published by the Lewiston Committee. The facts and developments therein set forth, have withstood the " *test of truth and the scrutiny of time.*" With a view to possess the people of information which so deeply concerned their individual rights and the public safety, the committee caused five thousand copies of this narrative to be gratuitously circulated through this and the adjoining states.

Finding the ordinary tribunals of justice, in some instances, disinclined to discharge their duties, and, in all cases, too feeble to resist the mysteriously powerful influence of Free Masonry, the people memorialized their Representatives for relief. Their Petition, respectfully detailing the alarming facts now so well known to all, and earnestly praying that the arm of the law might be strengthened, scarcely received the decent forms of Legislative interment. The same irresistible power which had misruled our public officers, sealed the lips of witnesses, tampered with the consciences of Jurors, and suspended the sword of justice, now closed the Halls of Legislature upon the people.

Turned out of Court, and repulsed by their Representatives, the people of the western counties, appealed, not to the " weapons which God and nature had put into their hands," as would have been the case in a less enlightened country, but to public opinion, lawfully and understandingly expressed, through the Ballot Boxes, for protection and redress. Every other avenue was closed. This was the only *constitutional* last resort. Truly auspicious results and salutary influences, are vindicating the wisdom of this appeal, and all coming experience will sanction its justice.

Meantime, the public eye, and the committees more especially, turned inquiringly from individual offenders, towards the Institution itself. A keen desire was manifest to know the real character of Free Masonry, and the true tendency of its principles. Morgan had made a full revelation of the three first degrees, the truth of which was attested by his abduction, and sealed with his blood. Masonry, however, professed to be a "*progressive science*," and further developements were necessary to the formation of a correct estimate of its character. These were not long withheld. An Encampment of Knights Templars at Le Roy, after a violent and protracted struggle with that portion of their companions which approved of the outrages, resolved to restore themselves to society and their country, by renouncing the principles, and exposing the secrets, of the Institution. This solemn duty was discharged, in Convention, at Le Roy, on the 19th of February, 1828. The horrid oaths, unearthly penalties, profane orgies, and blasphemous rites, of the higher degrees, were there made public. Free Masonry, stripped of her seeming vestal garments and gorgeous attire, now stood bald and naked, exposed to the scorn and abhorrence of a long deluded, but finally disabused people.

The committee continued their investigations, and were in constant attendance upon the several courts, where indictments were pending, vainly endeavouring to aecelerate the tardy and fettered footsteps of justice.

Near the close of the winter session of 1828, the Executive and Legislative departments of the Government, became suddenly impressed with the propriety and necessity of according the relief which was so promptly denied the preceding session. An act was passed, authorising the appointment of special counsel, to prosecute the investigation of the Masonic outrages. The then acting Governor appointed Daniel Moseley, Esq. to discharge this responsible duty. That gentleman entered immediately into the investigation, which he continued to prosecute, diligently, until he was called from the discharge of those duties, to a seat upon the Bench, in the 7th Judicial District.

Mr. Moseley has collected and arranged an important mass of complicated testimony, evidencing a wide-spread conspiracy, and an accumulation of crime, fearfully dark and atrocious. This fulfilling measure of guilt grows out of the necessity, from which the Institution cannot escape, of protecting those, who, in obeying its mandates, violated the laws of the land. The Masonic conspirators acted under the advice of their chapters, the principles of which, in letter and spirit, cover the whole ground—Even the murderers of Morgan, can open their Free Masons' Monitor, and demand the reward for executing the traitor!

If any thing were wanting to prove that these outrages were the natural offspring of Masonic principles, we would refer to the fact, that the persons notoriously concerned in them, not merely stand fair with their lodges and chapters, but have been elevated to their highest honors and offices! Those too who fled from justice, have been protected and supported by the fraternity. And we have strong reasons to believe, though unsupported by positive testimony, that monies have been furnished by the Grand Chapter for the relief and defence of the conspirators, who are distinguished by the mystic brotherhood, as the "*Western Sufferers.*"

The time and manner of Morgan's murder have been ascertained by those who were immediately connected with the investigations—Most, if not all of the persons by whom the foul deed was perpetrated, are satisfactorily known —but when, and by whose agency, their guilt will be judicially established, remains with the great disposer of all human events.

Edward Giddins, whose testimony would go very far in developing the *finale* of this extended conspiracy and foul murder, has been rejected as a witness, in the Ontario court of common pleas, by a rule, in relation to the soundness of which, the most distinguished jurists entertain conflicting opinions. Had the objection went to Mr. Giddins' *credibility*, he would have been fully sustained—for few men have passed through life with a more blameless reputation.

Elisha Adams, into whose charge Morgan passed from Mr. Giddins, and who continued to feed and guard him until the night of the murder, was sent by the confederates to Vermont, from whence he was demanded as a fugitive from justice. Adams was a reluctant agent of the conspirators, and during his seclusion, had determined, if brought to the bar as a witness, as he himself repeatedly averred, to "*make a clean breast of it*," by telling the truth. He continued in this wholesome frame of mind, until he found himself surrounded by his guilty Royal Arch Companions, who soon succeeded in re-establishing their mysterious influence over his conscience; and subjecting him to that obligation of their peculiar code, which, under the most fearful penalties, enjoins the keeping of a companion's secret in all cases, "murder and treason not excepted." William King, who professed to have returned to Niagara county, for the purpose of confronting his accusers, swore off his trial, and has retraced his steps to Arkansas. Howard, of Buffalo, who applied the torch to Miller's office, fled to Europe, and has not since been heard of. John Whitney, of Rochester, who, following the councils of more wary conspirators, went fearful lengths, after hiding in distant states for nearly two years, has returned and awaits his trial. Loton Lawson, who pleaded guilty to the conspiracy indictments, to prevent the production of testimony, that would inculpate him for a higher offence, has completed his two years' imprisonment, and taken up his abode in the state of Pennsylvania. It is known that a Masonic friend of Lawson's preceded him, on his route from Canandaigua to his destined residence, summoning the Chapters to meet—but for what purpose, we are left to conjecture.

The case of Eli Bruce, late Sheriff of Niagara county, who was convicted in Ontario of receiving and confining Morgan in Fort Niagara, was referred, on a question of form, to the supreme court, and has been decided in his favor. Eighteen other persons, concerned in the outrages, have been indicted, but the public prosecutor has not been able to bring on their trials.

Nothing but the intelligence and virtue of a great proportion of its members, had so long restrained Free Masonry from open misrule and violence. Its signs, grips and obligations afford every facility for the protection and escape of Masonic offenders. And these facilities are far from having been unimproved. Depredations to a greater amount, and conspiracies of a more formidable character, have been committed and concealed under the ripening influences of Free Masonry, than the public, aided by recent developements, would be willing to believe. The Institution exerts a mysterious and pernicious influence over all the relations of life. The obligation which binds Masons to warn their brethren of all approaching danger, and to keep, inviolable, their guilty secrets, is a direct bribe to the vicious propensities of our nature. And that obligation which compels a Mason to assist a mystic brother out of difficulty, "right or wrong," furnishes the widest latitude to crime.

It is not unknown to those who have given the subject their attention, that the numerous gangs of counterfeiters who have so frequently flooded the state with spurious notes, and base coin, were almost wholly composed of Free Masons. With this knowledge, it is no longer a mystery how they so frequently eluded the ministers of justice, or escaped through the meshes of the law.

But there is an evil of a more alarming nature, to which we feel constrained to draw the public attention. Free-Masonry has cast her broadest mantle over legislative corruption and bribery. The attempt of John Anderson, to bribe the Hon. Lewis Williams, chairman of the committee of claims, in the House of Representatives, has led to a brief examination of transactions of a similar character in our state legislature. Col. Anderson attempted to bribe Mr. Williams as a "*man and a Mason*," but being no Mason, Mr. W. was at liberty, not only to reject the bribe, but to expose the culprit. This incident is full of instruction. Had Mr. Williams been a Mason, though promptly rejecting the bribe, he was not at liberty to expose a mystic brother to shame and punishment. A Free Mason approaches his legislative brother with the wages of iniquity in his hand, in the full assurance that, if his bribe is rejected, his guilty secret will be inviolably kept. This reasoning is fortified by an extended train of facts. The history of all the known corruptions practised in our legislature, from the briberies committed with the Merchants' Bank in 1804, to those of the Fulton and Chemical Charters in 1824, is pregnant with testimony against Free Masonry. The fact that almost every man known to have been disreputably concerned in those transactions, was a Free Mason, admonishes the people to guard these avenues against the corrupting influence of that Institution. And that ancient, if not honorable fraternity, the Lobby, which still infest the seat of government, and beleaguer the capital, stands conspicuous in the lists of Free Masonry. Of all the horde of mercenaries who hang year after year upon the legislature, let even one be named who is not a bright Free Mason. These assertions are not brought upon slight or insufficient testimony. The evidence of their entire truth may be obtained by all who make proper enquiries.

But the Institution puts forth on all occasions, as a shield and defence against the accusations brought against her, the names of eminently virtuous men, who in their youth, misled by her false pretensions to science and wisdom, "*took her for better or for worse.*" The sainted name of WASHINGTON, though his recorded admonitions, to "*beware of all secret, self-created associations, under what specious garb soever they appeared,*" forbid the profanation, is impudently used to patch up the tattered vestments with which a detected impostor still seeks to cover her deformities. The stainless reputation of a contemporary, whose boundless charities have engraven his name upon the hearts of thousands, and whose munificence is even now unfolding the treasures of knowledge to the humblest citizen, and extending the boundaries of science to the remotest sections of the state, is daily pressed into the service of Free Masonry, to give false lustre to its character, and posthumous currency to its principles. It is due to this distinguished gentleman to state, that although the swelling titles and empty honors of the Fraternity have been continuously lavished upon him, he never could be pressed beyond the third degree of speculative Free Masonry. And a confiding hope is entertained, based upon our knowledge of his virtues and patriotism, that ere long, he will feel constrained to inhibit the use of his bright name in beguiling the footsteps of our youth into the dark and devious recesses of the Lodge Room. More than four hundred initiates, within our own state, including Members of every Degree, from an Entered Apprentice to the Thrice Illustrious Knights of the Holy Trinity, have publicly renounced the Institution. Thousands have silently withdrawn, and it cannot be presumed that any good man, who received it upon trust, will continue his connexion with the Fraternity after he has thoroughly examined the tendency of its principles.

Free Masonry is deeply anxious to conceal the truth in relation to herself and her fast votaries. It will require much zeal and labor to expose and dissipate the falsehoods and delusions which the fraternity have so industriously spread abroad. Time and truth, however, will ultimately encompass these ends. All there is of Free Masonry, pertaining to the Lodges, Chapters and Encampments, may be gathered from Morgan's Illustrations, and the Le Roy Revelations. But the inquirer for real Free Masonry, divested of its gaudy trappings, and its traditionary fables, must seek out other sources of information. The work of the Abbe Barruel and Professor Robison's Proofs of a conspiracy to overthow all Religion and Government, present faithful and alarming pictures of Free Masonry, and commend themselves to the deliberate consideration of the American people. Of the various writers who are now developing, with fearless pens and surpassing powers, the legitimate tendency and aims of Free Masonry, Henry Dana Ward, of New-York, and Elder John Stearns, of Oneida county, have attained a proud eminence, from which they are dispensing floods of light and knowledge. These gifted and enlightened men were members of the Masonic Fraternity. They had, however, sifted its pretensions and eschewed its principles, previous to the murder of Morgan. The writings of these gentlemen ought to be speedily procured and extensively circulated through every town in the state. We hazard nothing in saying that no intelligent man or Mason, can read Mr. Ward's volume entitled Free Masonry, without being convinced that the Institution is a rank imposture and dangerous cheat.

Perhaps we cannot convey a bolder or more comprehensive view out of fancied power and unchastened ambition of Free Masonry, than is found in the Oration of the late W. F. Brainard, at New-London, Ct. before the Union Lodge, June 24, 1825, on the recurrence of one of her fabulous Anniversaries. Mr. Brainard says:—

"What is Masonry now? IT IS POWERFUL. It comprises men of RANK, wealth, office and talent, in power and out of power; and that in almost every place where POWER IS OF ANY IMPORTANCE; and it comprises among other CLASSES of the community, to the lowest, in large numbers, active men, united together, *and capable of being directed by the efforts of others*, so as to have the FORCE OF CONCERT *throughout the civilized world!* They are distributed too, with the means of knowing one another, and the means of keeping secret, and the means of co-operating, in the DESK—in the LEGISLATIVE HALL—on the BENCH—in every GATHERING OF BUSINESS—in every PARTY OF PLEASURE—IN EVERY ENTERPRISE OF GOVERNMENT—in every DOMESTIC CIRCLE—in PEACE and in WAR—among ENEMIES and FRIENDS—in ONE PLACE as well as in ANOTHER! SO POWERFUL indeed, is it at this time, [June 24th, 1825] that it fears nothing from VIOLENCE, either PUBLIC or PRIVATE; FOR IT HAS EVERY MEANS, TO LEARN IT IN SEASON TO COUNTERACT, DEFEAT AND PUNISH IT!"

Such were the views and aims entertained and cherished by distinguished Free Masons, of the extent and power of their institution. The issue of the moral conflict in which we are engaged, must determine how well or ill these extravagant opinions were founded.

At the period when the Masonic outrages were perpetrated, only three papers [the Republican Advocate, the Cazenovia Monitor, and National Observer] had the moral courage to raise their voice against those high-handed infractions of the laws. Their contemporaries, either maintained a studied silence, labored to quiet the apprehensions and misdirect the investigations of the people, or treated the whole subject with ridicule and levity. Soon, however, a Press, avowedly Anti-Masonic, was established at Rochester. Simultaneously, the Livingston Register, Le Roy Gazette, Seneca Farmer, Trumansburgh Lake Light, and Sangersfield Intelligencer, devoted their columns to the cause of civil and political liberty.—Other papers, in defiance of the wealth and influence of "All-powerful Free Masonry," soon followed in the path of duty, and Free-Presses are now established in the counties of Chautauque, Erie, Niagara, Genesee, Orleans, Monroe, Livingston, Ontario, Wayne, Seneca, Yates, Cayuga, Oswego, Madison, Oneida, Jefferson, Tompkins and Ulster, and in the cities of Albany and New-York. Hopes, which we confidently believe will not be disappointed, are entertained, that faithful public sentinels will soon be stationed in all, or nearly all the other counties.

Free Presses constitute the means upon which the country must rely to uproot and overthrow Free Masonry. They enlighten and stimulate public opinion. All the counties in this and the neighboring states, in which Free

APPENDIX. 35

Presses have been established, are now contributing their best efforts to exterminate the Institution. They are multiplying with considerable alacrity, and the Committee deem the continued augmentation of their members, an object of primary and paramount importance.

The Presidential election seriously embarrassed our cause during its pendency. That question settled, the people are giving their attention to a subject of immensely greater moment than the success or defeat of any mere political party. The citizens of Vermont, Connecticut, Massachusetts and Rhode-Island, are deeply imbued with our sentiments. The counties of Indiana, Lancaster and Union, in the state of Pennsylvania, and the county of Morris, in the state of New-Jersey, have shorn Free Masonry of her strength. The inhabitants of Michigan are laboring with praise-worthy firmness, to drive the monster from their flourishing Territory. Ohio is shaking off the incubus, and an earnest spirit of inquiry is rapidly spreading all over the Union.

Entirely erroneous opinions have been propagated, far and wide, in relation to the views and conduct of Anti-Masons. We are represented as persecuting and oppressing all the members of the Masonic society, thereby confounding the innocent with the guilty. Nothing, but Free Masonry itself, is more fallacious than this accusation. Free Masons have violated the laws of the state, and taken the life of an unoffending citizen. The influence of the Fraternity has impeded, and continues to impede, the course of justice, and the offenders stalk abroad in the community, cherished and supported by the Institution, unmolested and unpunished. The secrets and principles of the Institution, which have been fully exposed, are positively and undeniably bad and dangerous. We therefore ask Free Masons to renounce them. If they refuse to accede to a request so reasonable, are we made obnoxious to the charge of persecution for withholding our support from them? How are the people to redeem their Halls of Legislation, to purify their temples of justice, or to re-establish the ascendancy of their laws, if the supporters of Free Masonry are not dispossessed of place and power?

The progress of truth and the developments of time, have refuted many of the fictions, and turned back some of the calumnies, with which the Fraternity so long held public opinion in suspense. It is no longer gravely asserted that Morgan is selling his books, that he has retired beyond the Rocky Mountains, or that he has joined the standard of the false prophet, at Smyrna. All who do not egregiously undervalue the intelligence of the people, are constrained to admit that this citizen, blameless of all offence to the laws of the land, after five days confinement, was deliberately murdered at Fort Niagara, and cast into Lake Ontario. The idle calumny which represented the just indignation of freemen, as an excitement, got up for the temporary purpose of aiding a particular party, has spent its impotent malice, and passes, with the mass of falsehoods which that fruitful occasion for private and public defamation provoked. The deep sensibility and awakened interest which ten free states are manifesting, by unequivocal demonstrations of hostility to the Masonic Institution, repels the accusation of the Fraternity which confined their belligerents to an infected district of madmen and fanatics in the western part of the state of New-York.

But we turn from the past to contemplate the future—where hope is unfolding her bright visions to the eye of patriotism, and promising her treasured rewards to the aspirations of piety. The quiet, but resistless power of public opinion is accomplishing a great moral and political revolution. This work, which moved forward with cautious and faultering steps, through its incipient stages, is now rapidly spreading all over this and the neighboring states. We cannot yet fix its boundaries, or estimate the time that it will require to accomplish its high purposes. But one thing is certain—the fire will burn while the fuel lasts; and the disenthralling spirit which has gone abroad, will not return until the Republic is effectually redeemed from the unhallowed grasp of Speculative Free Masonry.

SAMUEL WORKS,
HARVEY ELY,
F. F. BACKUS,
FR'K. WHITTLESEY,
THURLOW WEED.

ROCHESTER, FEB. 15th, 1829.

Mr. J. C. Morris addressed the Convention, and submitted the following resolution, which, on his motion, was adopted.

Resolved, That a Committee of one from each Senatorial District, be appointed to prepare and submit to this Convention the subjects proper to be taken into consideration by this Convention.

Mr. Fitch addressed the Convention and submitted the following resolutions, which, on his motion, were adopted.

Resolved, That a committee of five be appointed to draft an address to the people of this state, on the subject of the late Masonic outrages committed in this state, and the principles of Masonry and Anti-Masonry.

Resolved, That a committee of five be appointed to draft resolutions expressive of the views and feelings of this Convention, in reference to the principles of the Masonic society and their effect upon the civil and religious institutions of our country.

Resolved, That a committee of five be appointed to enquire whether the ceremonials, obligations and secrets of the Masonic order, as disclosed by the late William Morgan before his abduction and murder, and the Convention of Seceding Masons at Le Roy on the 4th and 5th of July last, are substantially correct and true.

Resolved, That a committee of five be appointed to enquire whether there exists in this state, any private or public act or acts of the legislature, in reference to the order of Free Masonry, and if so, the nature, objects and effects of such acts, and whether it is expedient to memorialize the legislature for a modification or repeal of the same.

Resolved, That a committee of five be appointed to enquire whether it is expedient to memorialize the legislature on the subject of extra judicial oaths, and more particularly when administered in secret, the object, nature and tendency of which are concealed from the government and the community at large.

Resolved, That a committee of five be appointed to enquire whether it is expedient for this convention to recommend a convention of delegates from the several United States, to be held at some future time and suitable place, to deliberate on the subject which has called this Convention together, and if so, whether it is expedient for this Convention to designate the time and place and also the suitable number of delegates from each state.

Resolved, That a committee of five be appointed to enquire whether Mrs. Lucinda Morgan, widow of the late Capt. William Morgan, is provided with the pecuniary means for supporting herself and her orphan children, and if not, whether it is expedient and proper for this convention to adopt any measures for her relief.

On motion of Mr. Sweet

Resolved, That a committee of five be appointed, whose duty it shall be to enquire into the expediency of erecting some honorable and durable monument to the memory of Wm. Morgan.

Resolved, That the foregoing committees be appointed by the President and Vice Presidents.

Resolved, That the Convention adjourn until 9 o'clock to-morrow morning, to meet at the Mayor's Court room.

Friday, Feb. 20th. The Convention met, pursuant to adjournment, in the Mayor's Court room.

The appointment of the following Committees were announced from the chair.

Committee to present subjects for consideration of Convention: Messrs. Morris of the 6th District, Lansing 5th, Fitch 8th, Griswold 1st, Dubois 2d, Bennet 3d, Merrill 4th, and Wilcox 7th.

Committee to draft Address: Messrs. Holley, Ward, Tracy, Conklin, Groves.

Committee to draft resolutions:—Messrs. Hopkins of Albany, Whittlesey, Weed, Hazeltine, Percival.

Committee to ascertain the truth of the Masonic revelations:
Messrs. Cook, Hascall, Fairchild, Williams of Oneida, and Southwick.

Committee on legislative acts in relation to Free Masonry
Messrs. Beekman, Long, Penfield, Nolton and Crafts.

Committee on memorial relative to extra judicial oaths:
Messrs. Crary, Stow, Howlett, Moseley, Townsend.

Committee on National Convention:—Messrs. Granger, Seward, Robinson, Lay, Green.

Committee relative to Mrs. Morgan.—Messrs. Fitch, Thompson, Rice, Nolton, Shipman.

Committee on monument to Wm. Morgan—Messrs. Sweet, Southwick, Throop, Hopkins of Putnam, and Rickey.

A communication from Dr. C. C. Blatchley, a delegate elect from the city of New-York, accompanied by 100 tracts was read:

On motion of Mr. Whittlesey,

Resolved, That the same, together with the tracts, be referred to the committee on the subject of memorializing the legislature in relation to extra judicial oaths.

On motion of Mr. Weed,

Resolved, That the convention adjourn to half past 3 o'clock, P. M. to meet in the assembly chamber.

Afternoon Session—Convention met, pursuant to adjournment.

The convention was opened with prayer by Elder Green, delegate from Saratoga.

A communication from the Hon. Moses Hayden of the Senate, was read:

On motion of Mr. Cooke,

Resolved, That the same be printed with the proceedings of this convention.

To the President of the Anti-Masonic Convention, held at the Capitol on Thursday the 19th of Feb. 1829.

Sir,—Having to acknowledge the honor of an election as delegate to your Convention by the inhabitants of the county of Allegany—I enclose herewith the proceedings of the Convention, appointing me, that you may be apprized of their desire to co-operate with you in the great work of reform, which now engrosses your attention. But entertaining serious doubts, whether my attendance upon the Anti-Masonic Convention is compatible with the public duties with which I am already charged, I beg to be excused from serving as a delegate.

With the expectation that your patriotic efforts will be distinguished by their temperance, prudence and firmness,

I am very respectfully,
Your obedient servant,
M. HAYDEN.

Senate Chamber, Feb. 19, 1829.

APPENDIX.

On motion of Mr. Lansing,

Resolved, That Maj. Satterlee C'ark be admitted to a seat in this Convention, as a delegate from Oneida county.

Henry F. Yates, Esq., of Montgomery county, read a document renouncing all connexion with the Institution of Free Masonry.

Maj. Satterlee Clark, delegate from Oneida, publicly renounced all connexion with Free Masonry, and stated his reasons for so doing.

On motion of Mr. Seward, of New-York,

Resolved, That the members of the Senate and Assembly, elected on Anti-Masonic principles be invited to take seats in this convention as honorary members.

Mr. Granger, chairman of the committee on the subject of calling a National Anti-Masonic Convention, submitted the following Report and Resolution, which, after the Convention was addressed by Messrs. Granger, Seward, Green, and Cooke, were adopted.

The committee appointed to enquire into the propriety of recommending a National Convention to deliberate upon the dangerous tendency of Masonic Institutions, and devise such means as may be necessary to secure our people from their encroachment upon their freedom,

REPORT:

That, in considering this question, your committee have naturally been led to enquire, what are the feelings of our sister states upon this subject, and whether it is probable that the lights which have been shed from this state upon other sections of our confederacy, have been such as to have roused to action any considerable portion of their citizens. In pursuing this enquiry, they have been gratified to learn, that, although but comparatively few states have as yet taken prominent measures to arrest the progress, and to eradicate the existence of the evils of which we complain, there is a spirit abroad in the land which gives sure promise of future action and the strongest hopes of ultimate success.

From public journals, from a free correspondence with men of intelligence, and from information furnished by gentlemen now with us, and whose moral worth and character is a sure guarantee for their assertions, we learn that in Vermont, Massachusetts, Connecticut, and Rhode Island, measures are already concerted, and operations are already commenced, which will submit this question to the decision of the descendants of those who lit the first torch of liberty upon their hills, and through whose vallies was sounded the first alarm for freedom. To this decision your committee look with unwavering confidence, not only as to its result upon the states already mentioned, but as to its moral effect upon the neighboring states of New-Hampshire and Maine.

From Pennsylvania, the intelligence is of a character that leaves no doubt of final victory, and that her tried democracy will be found in the ranks of the conflict. Ohio, early took part in this contest, and although intelligence on this subject has not there spread with the rapidity which marked its progress among our people, there is ample proof, that the flame so early kindled, though slowly, is safely and surely extending throughout that whole state. From the states of New-Jersey, Alabama and Kentucky, and from the Territory of Michigan, we learn that meetings have been held and measures taken to produce a general diffusion of knowledge upon this subject.

Your committee have thus briefly stated for the information of the Convention, what they believe to be the true condition of Anti-Masonry throughout the several states, so far as the same has been developed through public channels. Private letters would carry the belief, that in several other states investigations are about commencing, which, though they may be smothered for a ne, will ere long break forth with a resistless force. The spirit of enquiry so natural to freemen, and the indulgence of which is secured by the intelligence of our citizens, will soon fix the public attention in every state in the Union, and no reflecting man can doubt the result of a free inquiry.

Upon a full examination of this subject, your committee are unanimously of the opinion, that the period has arrived, when measures should be taken to form a general national Convention, for the purposes for which we have assembled.

Although your committee are well aware, that the right of our people to assemble in their representative capacity in any manner that may be deemed most advisable, is amply secured by the Constitution and laws of our country, yet a view of the past cannot leave a doubt, that there will be those ready to sound the alarm, and to endeavor to create the belief, that the call for such a Convention, must proceed from men of wicked design, and can be the result only of arrogance and presumption. Should such objections arise, your committee would remark, that it is their intention to constitute not a secret, but an open organization, co-extensive with the evils which they would correct.

It will be recollected by all who are conversant with the journals of the day, that in 1826, a General Grand Chapter, and a General Grand Encampment of Masonic Delegates from the several States of the Union were assembled in the city of New-York.

Although, if Free Masonry be as is claimed, a mere charitable Institution, it is difficult to perceive how it can be necessary for the good government of its members to bring delegates from the remotest verge of a confederacy, within which are recognised, neither governmental pensioners, nor national recipients, of even Masonic charity, your committee are not disposed to comment upon these circumstances, nor to cavil at these assemblages, and only ask that the same charity may be extended to them, that is demanded by those from whom unjust imputations would probably emanate.

The Grand Chapter and Encampment were secret conclaves, consisting of delegates from the same states, whose representation we seek; their deliberations, whatever they may have been, were veiled by the deepest mystery, and no evidence of their existence was presented to the public gaze, but in the display of their robes, and the gorgeous exhibition of the pageantry of their power. The Convention we propose, would consist of delegates coming directly and publicly from the people; its deliberations like those of this Convention, would be open to all; and the measures it should propose would be freely but fearlessly submitted to the approbation or rejection of a nation of freemen.

If there be danger to our Republican Institutions in either of the cases here stated, let a discerning people determine in which it would be most likely to exist.

Your committee therefore recommended the adoption of the following resolution.

Resolved, That in order to concentrate public opinion, correct error, and diffuse more general information as to the true character and nature of the Institution of Speculative Free Masonry, and the principles for which we are contending: We recommend to the citizens of these United States, to meet in Convention at the City of Philadelphia, on the 11th day of September, 1830, by delegates from each state, equal in number to their respective representatives in the Senate and House of Representatives in Congress, and to be elected in such manner as the several states shall deem most advisable. The objects of which Convention, when assembled, shall be to adopt such measures, as to them, in their deliberate wisdom, shall appear to be most effectual to annihilate the Masonic Institution, and all other secret societies which claim to be paramount to our Laws, and are hostile to the genius and spirit of the Constitution.

Mr. Morris, Chairman of the Committee to submit to the Convention, the subjects for its consideration, submitted the following—which, after some remarks from Mr. Morris, were adopted.

The Committee appointed to prepare and submit to the Convention the subjects proper to be taken into consideration by the Convention, respectfully

REPORT:

That it is, in their opinion, proper for the Convention to appoint a State Central Corresponding Committee, to consist of five members residing in the village of Rochester, and to authorise that committee to call a State Convention, whenever, in their judgment, the public interest shall require it.

That in order to provide the necessary funds to enable Anti-Masonry to wage a successful contest against an Institution, embracing a large proportion of the intelligence and wealth of the community, and whose means of operating upon, and influencing the public mind, are fearfully great, the Convention recommend to the corresponding committees of the several counties in the state, to raise and transmit to the Central Committee, such monies as they may be enabled to collect in their respective counties.

That the Convention recommend to the corresponding committees of the different counties, to transmit to the State Committee the names and places of residence of their members, and that in those counties in which committees have not been chosen, it be recommended to Anti-Masons to choose them, and transmit their names and places of residence to the State Committee.

That the Secretaries be instructed to prepare and publish with the proceedings of the Convention, a list of the names and places of residence of the delegates comprising the Convention.

By Order of the Committee,
JOHN C. MORRIS, *Chairman.*

Mr. Stow, from the Committee on the subject of memorializing the Legislature in relation to extra judicial oaths, submitted the following report and resolution, which, after the Convention had been addressed by Messrs. Fitch, Whittlesey and Ward, were adopted.

The Committee appointed to enquire into the expediency of memorializing the Legislature on the subject of extra judicial oaths,

REPORT:

That the Institution of Speculative Free Masonry, as it exists in this country, is, in the opinion of the Committee, an embarrassment to the administration of justice and the government. That its principles are at variance with the doctrines of democracy and morality, and its practices hostile to the safety and welfare of community.

Whatever may have been the merits of this Institution at its inception, it cannot be rationally supposed that a secret combination, originating under a monarchial government, can be adapted, for any virtuous purpose, to a country of intelligence and liberty. The only utility pretended in this Institution by its most zealous votaries, is that of its being charitable. Even this claim the committee are not disposed to allow. In their opinion it is totally unfounded, and a mere pretence devised by designing men for the purpose of deceiving the public, and literally " covering a multitude of sins." So far from charity being its characteristic, it is directly the reverse—like all corporations, it is a body without a soul—selfish and monopolizing, and directs all its views to its own aggrandizement. Though it be admitted that in some instances it may extend a helping hand to a distressed member, we ask, what benefit this can be to the great body of community? And is not the civilization of the age and the doctrines of christianity a sufficient guaranty of the exercise of all rational benevolence, without the aid of Masonic obligations.

But the great objection to Free Masonry is not the negative one of its being useless. Were this the case, this Convention would never have been assembled. There are objections of a more positive nature, and such as every member of society is interested in exposing. It is a fact, which it is folly for its votaries longer to attempt to disguise, that its practices are pernicious and its doctrines at war with christianity and the laws of the country.

Its practices are pernicious in withdrawing a certain portion of community from the great body of society, thereby weakening the social compact in rendering a part independent of the whole ; and in the administration of extra judicial and blasphemous oaths, whose inevitable tendency is to demoralize society, and bring into contempt and disrepute the solemnity of judicial proceedings. Though the recipients of these oaths should not in many instances believe them to be obligatory, still they have a pernicious effect in familiarizing the mind to blasphemy and falsehood ; but when believed by those who have received them to be obligatory, the evil becomes insufferable—the government and judiciary become corrupted, and the great bulwark of liberty and the rights of the citizen, the trial by jury, is prostituted to the basest purposes. That such is the effect of oaths thus administered every man can bear witness who is familiar with our courts of justice ; he must often have observed how little importance men accustomed to the foolery of an extra judicial attach to the sanctity of a judical oath.

The doctrines of Free Masonry are at war with Christianity and the laws, in inculcating a spirit of revenge, in imposing a duty on its members of shielding each other in the perpetration of crimes, and in assuming the right of punishing, even with death, the commission of imaginary offences. These evils are not merely ideal ; the murder of William Morgan (and his murder the committee feel authorised to assume as a fact) shows that the right of punishing for pretended offences is not only claimed by the Institution, but exercised with demoniac vengeance ; and the ineffectual attempts which have hitherto been made to expose and bring to justice his murderers, alarmingly demonstrate how weak are the obligations of morality, religion and law, when brought in competition with Masonic ties and terrors.

To abate these evils as they now exist, and to prevent their extension, is, in the opinion of the committee, a duty which the Legislature owes to the state. The most effectual means of accomplishing this great purpose will be, in the opinion of the committee, the enactment of a law rendering penal the administration and reception of all extra judicial oaths, and declaring all such oaths totally void and in no respect obligatory upon the recipients. With regard to the latter suggestion, the committee beg leave to remark, that, although extra judicial oaths are not recognized by the common law, and are well known by professional men to be entirely nugatory, yet many persons suppose them obligatory, and the committee believe that a declaratory law, such as they have suggested, will have a happy effect in disabusing the minds of many well meaning men of error, and be attended with the most salutary consequences.

Such being the views of the committee, they beg leave to introduce the accompanying resolution :

Resolved, That a committee be appointed to prepare and present to the Legislature of this state, a memorial in behalf of this convention, praying legislative enactment against the administering, or receiving, any Masonic oath or obligation, or any oath or obligation imposed by any other secret society whatever.

Resolved, That a committee of five be appointed to enquire whether there exists, in this state, any private or public act or acts of the legislature in reference to the order of Free Masonry, and if so, the nature, object, and effect of such acts, and whether it is expedient to memorialize the legislature for a modification or revival of the same.

Members of the above committee—Messrs. Beekman, Long, Penfield, Nolton and Crafts.

Mr. Beekman, chairman of the committee to ascertain what legislative acts have been passed in this state, in relation to Free Masonry, submitted the following report and resolution, which, after some remarks from Mr. Beekman, were adopted.

The committee, to whom the foregoing resolution was referred, have the honor to report to the convention; that they have given all the attention to the subject, which the short period allotted to them, has enabled them to bestow—and they would preliminarily remark, that the subject of the resolution was entirely new to them, and had not, previously to its submission, occupied any portion of their attention, and it will not, therefore, be expected, that your committee have, in the course of a few hours, been enabled to give the subject so minute an examination, as its importance certainly requires.

In examining the statute book, your committee have ascertained that there exist two public acts of the legislature on the subject—The first, entitled " An act to incorporate the Grand Chapter of the State of New-York, passed 31st March, 1818;" and the other, is entitled " An act to enable Masonic lodges to take and hold real estate, for certain purposes therein mentioned, passed April 16, 1825,"—both of which, are extraordinary in their nature, and could have been procured by no less powerful an influence than that which the institution it incorporates, has long possessed, and it is believed, exercises, as well in our Legislative Halls, as in our courts of justice.

The preamble to the act of 1818, contains this extraordinary recital:—
" Whereas it is represented to the Legislature, by the Grand Chapter of Free Masons of the State of New-York, that they experience great difficulties in vesting and securing their funds, which are chiefly intended for charitable purposes."—Your Committee are at some loss to understand this language, unless, they are to infer, that the funds of this Grand Chapter had accumulated upon their hands to such an amount, that there were not objects of benevolence, sufficient in number and importance, upon which to expend such a portion of this fund, as to reduce it to a sum, which might be invested profitably, in the ordinary mode resorted to for a fair investment of capital. That their load had become so great, and their monied operations so extensive and complicated, that no one man was competent to its proper management, but it required that congregated wisdom of a body of men to reduce it to order, and explain, and ascertain a new and profitable mode in which to dispose of it, for the future use of this society. If such is the truth, (and of this perhaps there is no doubt,) can it be reconciled with the further declaration, that the funds of this institution were chiefly intended for charitable purposes? Is it indeed true that we have reached that state of prosperity, that there does not exist among us a sufficient number of objects, upon which we may properly expend our charities, and is there any difficulty in disposing of that small portion of his estate, which the heart of selfish man prompts him to set apart for that purpose? The daily experience of every man teaches him the contrary—and the mind will, therefore, be compelled to adopt the conclusion, that it is the selfish and contracted charity of Free Masonry only—that is here intended—that which says to the imploring voice of want and poverty, " depart in peace, be ye warmed, and be ye filled," rather than that which, with open hand and heart, giveth liberally and withholdeth not from the naked and destitute.

Some of the avowed objects of this act are to create the said chapter a body politic and corporate, to enable them to hold and convey real estate to the value of $50,000, and to grant to it, all the privileges and immunities

APPENDIX. 43

severally conferred on corporate bodies—but for what end is not declared.—In other incorporations created by acts of our legislature, the distinct objects for which they receive their charters are enumerated, and their powers clearly specified, and when they transcend them, or are directed from their legitimate objects, the remedy is at hand, and is quickly applied, to stop them, or impede their course—not so with this incorporation—its purposes and ends being a profound secret to the world, who can charge it with a violation of its charter? —Its immense resources may be applied to the affecting the most pernicious and dangerous consequences, to individuals, and the very government which created it, without fear of detection.—It is true, that the power of the trustees, who are to be created, according to the provisions of this act, for the purposes of managing the affairs of this institution, so far as concerns its personal estate only, are declared to be confined to the " vesting and securing their funds, and the transfer and distribution thereof, for the ordinary and usual purposes of the said Chapter." But who can tell what are the ordinary and usual purposes of the said Chapter. They are not declared by the legislature, the public do not know them, and the initiated dare not reveal them.

The act of April, 1825, is an extension of the principle of the act of 1818, and the remarks upon the latter, apply with equal force to the former—It confers on lodges, throughout the state, powers very similar to those granted to the Grand Chapter, and the objections to the one, apply with equal force to the other. They are irresponsible bodies, controlled only by their own interest, and in effect answerable to no tribunal—Their objects not ascertained, and their powers not enumerated.

Of the effects of these acts, your committee are at no loss to express an opinion—It is natural to man to abuse the powers that are entrusted to him, and to make encroachments on the rights of others. It is the knowledge of the existence of this principle, which has produced the codes of laws, which all nations have found it necessary to enact, distinctly defining the rights and duties of man to his brother, and to such tribunals, where the weak may be protected against the strong.—If this is true of individuals under such circumstances, how much more strongly does the remark apply to a collection of men, incorporated for objects known only to themselves, and which none, until lately, dared to reveal. The effect has been as it always will be in such cases—that the power has created the disposition to do wrong, and inflict injury upon all whom it deems hostile to its interests—and we have at least one instance upon record, where the blood of the victim has been required by it, as an atonement for his offence.

As to the expediency of memorializing the legislature, for a modification or repeal of these acts, at present, your committee are in some doubt—That they ought to be repealed, so far as constitutionally they may be, this we do not hesitate to say—but they believe that this cannot be now effected.—That the axe, instead of being applied to the root, would be either entirely withheld or only used to cut off some small branches, deemed superfluous by the institution itself, and of small consequence in extirpating the evil—and they would prefer to await the period, which cannot be far distant, when this whole people will rise in their strength, and imperiously demand of their servants, that this abomination shall no longer defile our Statute Books. All which is respectfully submitted.

Resolved, That in the opinion of this convention, it is inexpedient at this time to memorialize the legislature to repeal or modify the charters, incorporating the Masonic Institutions of this State.

Mr. Sweet, chairman of the committee, on the erection of a Monument to the memory of William Morgan, submitted the following Report, which was adopted.

The committee appointed to enquire into the expediency of erecting some honorable and durable Monument to the memory of Capt. William Morgan, would respectfully

REPORT:

That, in the opinion of your committee, Capt. William Morgan is entitled to Eulogy and Monument, arising from the consideration that he fell a martyr to the liberties of his country.

He was a son of Virginia, a citizen of this state, the defender of liberty, who met the invaders of his country at New-Orleans—The revealer of Masonic secrets, for which he was torn from his family at Batavia, incarcerated in the fortress of Fort Niagara, and finally murdered by Masons in pursuance of their penalties, and buried at midnight in the bosom of the cataract.

We are the more indignant at this outrage, because it is sought to be concealed in the disguise of liberty. When the imagination dwells at Fort Niagara, on the forlorn husband, and the weeping father, the feelings which agitated the breast, and the tears which flowed down his cheeks, while he mourned alone in the darkened cell, under the chilling fear of insecurity and death. When we remember that the cold blooded assassins, led him forth like a lamb to the slaughter,* and all to sustain their system of self interest, impiety and blasphemy. What ought to be the feeling of the country, at so gross and unparalleled a violation of its laws and liberties. It ought undoubtedly to be in unison with the design to erect a monument to the memory of the man who has thus suffered, thus fallen, in a virtuous attempt to preserve those laws and liberties, unsullied and unimpaired. But your committee nevertheless believe, that the time has not yet arrived, when such a mark of distinction can be conferred upon his memory with any probability of its remaining undisturbed.

It would, no doubt, be mutilated, if not destroyed, by those who have sworn, that "no trace or memorial of such an apostate, as they term William Morgan, shall remain among men." In the mean time, the memory of the man, and the patriot, must, and will live in the affectionate remembrance of all faithful Americans.

He perished, as we hope, and trust, to rise in a brighter and better world, and to be numbered among the Army of the Martyrs. The committee however believe, that we cannot in any better manner, at present, evince our respect for his name, and gratitude for his services, than by making some effectual provision for the maintenance of his Widow, and the education of his Orphan children.

But, as this subject has been referred to gentlemen who are amply qualified for the duty assigned them, this committee forbear any further remarks upon it.

On motion of Mr. Weed,

Resolved, That the convention adjourn until half past 3 o'clock to-morrow afternoon.

Saturday, February 21st.—Convention met, pursuant to adjournment.

Mr. Hopkins, chairman of the committee to draft and report resolutions for adoption by the convention, submitted the following, which after some remarks from Mr. Hopkins, on motion of Mr. Tracy, were adopted.

Resolved, That it is a peculiar feature of our Free Government, that all measures should be open and amenable to public opinion; and that the existence of any society in this country, whose objects, principles and measures, are secret and concealed, is not merely useless, but hostile to the spirit of our free Institutions.

Resolved, That the bare existence of Secret Societies in these United States, justifies fears, jealousy, and suspicion, as to their objects, in the breasts of the uninitiated, which have a tendency to distract society, and sow ill will and dissentions in community.

APPENDIX. 45

Resolved, That the disclosures which have been made of the principles and obligations of Speculative Free Masonry, prove it to be an Institution of dangerous tendency—liable to be used by the ambitious and designing as an engine for exalting unworthy men, and effecting improper measures—placing the citizen in a situation in which his duty to his country must, in many instances, conflict with his obligations to the Fraternity—and weakening the sanctions of morality and religion by the multiplication of profane oaths, and an irreverent familiarity with religious forms and sacred things.

Resolved, That we discover in the ceremonies and obligations of the higher Degrees of Masonry, principles which tend directly to the subversion of all religion and government.

Resolved, That the obligations in one of the Degrees of Free Masonry to protect a brother "right or wrong," and to preserve his secret inviolate, even in cases of murder and treason, have a tendency to unnerve the arm of justice, and to afford protection to the vicious and profligate from the punishment due to their crimes.

Resolved, That the tendency of such obligations is to weaken the sanction of virtue in the minds of the recipients, by making bad men bold and unblushing, to trust the history of their crimes to the ears of a brother, and thus making them familiar with iniquity, to the destruction of all correct moral principles.

Resolved, That Free Masonry, instead of being the boasted "hand maid of religion," is its most dangerous foe; and that we view the impious personification of the Deity, and the irreverent introduction of the name of the blessed Saviour, and the Holy Trinity, in Masonic meetings and ceremonies, with pain and abhorrence; and that we regard the unhallowed substitution of the profane orgies of Free Masonry for the Christian Religion, as fraught with more danger to the peace of society and the truths of revelation, than open Deism or avowed Infidelity.

Resolved, That an Institution whose rites are impious—whose obligations are blasphemous—and, if observed in the spirit of their horrid import, must necessarily lead to perjury and murder—an Institution, in one instance at least, stained with the blood of one of its members, by a crime which has in an unequivocal manner received the sanction of the Order, is unworthy to exist in a free government; and that we pledge ourselves to each other and to the world, that we will use all lawful and constitutional means to banish entirely from our country that bloody relict of barbarism.

Resolved, That those Masons who have disclosed the horrid obligations which bind the Fraternity together, deserve the warmest gratitude of their fellow citizens; and that we will do every thing in our power to sustain them against those persecutions which the nature of those obligations, and the vindictive character of the Institution, teach us to fear will be their lot.

Resolved, In order to leave no doubt what are the objects of Anti-Masonic Conventions, that the same are intended to oppose those usurpations of Masonry which are inconsistent with the safety and equal rights of the citizen; that a secret and self formed society, avowedly acting so as to control the operations of government, is an insult to a free people, and incompatible with liberty;—that when such a society can, by hidden and unsuspected machinery, control the elections, it shows us that our liberty is but a phantom. And the power of enforcing its laws by the highest penalty, proves that under this tyranny, life, property, and liberty, are alike insecure. The object therefore of Anti-Masonic measures, is the restoration of private safety and public right.

Resolved, That the means to be used for these purposes ought to be an open appeal to public opinion every where—and to the source of power at the elections; that at every election, whether local or general, a ticket should be formed on the distinct principle of opposition to Masonry: that the pursuit of this principle ought to be undeviating and uncompromising; that meetings and conventions should be universally called; the public should be aroused to a sense of the public danger, and that these efforts ought not to cease until our country is completely rescued from the domination of Masonry.

Resolved, That while this Convention avows its settled and deliberate purpose to annihilate the Institution of Free Masonry, it cherishes every feeling of good will and personal respect for those of its unoffending members, who have been incautiously drawn into the society, or yielded their assent to its principles, without fully investigating their character and tendency.

On motion of Maj. S. Clark, the following resolution was adopted:

Resolved, That we, the members of this Convention, disavow all connexion between Anti-Masons and any political party which has heretofore existed in the United States.

On motion of Mr. Tracy,

Resolved, That this Convention do most respectfully present their thanks to the Honorable Assembly for the use of their Hall, for the sittings of this Convention; and that a copy of this resolution be signed by the President and Vice Presidents and Secretaries, and enclosed to the Honorable Speaker of the House.

On motion of Mr. Fitch.

Resolved, That the thanks of this Convention be presented to Dr. C. C. Blatchly for his excellent Anti-Masonic Tracts, so kindly forwarded and presented to this Convention.

Mr. Cooke, chairman of the committee on the truth of the Masonic disclosures, submitted the following Report and Resolution, which, after the Convention had been addressed by Messrs Cook, Williams of Oneida, and Ward, on motion of Mr. Weed, were adopted.

The committee appointed to enquire whether the ceremonials, obligations and secrets of the Masonic order, as disclosed by the late William Morgan, before his abduction and murder, and the convention of seceding Masons at Le Roy, on the 4th and 5th of July last, are substantially correct and true, &c., respectfully

REPORT:

That the subject of inquiry allotted to your committee, has received that mature deliberation, which its importance seemed to demand—your committee are of opinion, that in the exercise of their legitimate powers, it does not appear proper to introduce in their report animadversions upon Masonry, and they therefore confine the report strictly to the evidences, in relation to the disclosures, reference to which has been had.

In regard to the correctness and truth of the three first degrees as disclosed by the late William Morgan before his abduction and murder, your committee deem it unnecessary to multiply proofs—no further evidence would seemingly be necessary on that point, than what has been heretofore laid before the public. The murder of the author has effectually and conclusively impressed the seal of authenticity upon his revelations. But, if further proof be required by any, it may be found in the clearly expressed concurring testimony borne by some hundreds of seceding Masons—and also, by the ready admission of many of the order, who still adhere to the precepts and principles of Masonry, and who, not only admit the truth of the degrees published, but likewise the murder of the author for a violation of his obligations in writing those degrees.

In relation to the truth of the disclosures made at Le Roy, at the period stated in the resolution, your committee have been enabled to receive from the lips of three persons of high reputation, who have taken all the degrees, such a statement of attendant facts and circumstances, as that none can doubt the general correctness and truth of the disclosure—your committee in preparing

APPENDIX. 47

their report, have studied to make it as brief as the nature of the subject, and the mass of information obtained would admit. They respectfully submit the following as a statement of facts authenticated to the entire satisfaction of your committee. The Royal Arch degree as published, was obtained through an authentic source, directly from Jeremy L. Cross, Grand Lecturer of the United States.—That differences in the manner of work, and in the lectures, had sprung up among the Lodges and Chapters, to check which, and produce uniformity, this Mr. Cross was appointed to the office he now holds—that in administering the obligation of the Royal Arch Degree, as he instructs, the words "*murder and treason not excepted*," are expressly used, while some chapters before had only required a companion's secret to be kept "in all cases without exception"—that instances have often occurred where the recipients of the Royal Arch obligation have refused to attest to certain parts of it, and that such parts, after fruitless and artful attempts to explain them to the satisfaction of the candidate, have been omitted. That on the trial of S. D. Green of Batavia, before an ecclesiastical tribunal, three witnesses, on oath, stated that the degrees as disclosed by the Le Roy Convention of the 4th and 5th July last, were substantially true—that affidavits of some ten or twelve persons to the same effect, were made and attested to, for the purpose of being used at a meeting of the Presbyterian order held in Bergen, Genesee county, in December last—five of which deponents had received all the degrees—that on numerous occasions during the pendency of trials in courts of justice, some of the seceding Masons at Le Roy, were subpœnaed to attend such trials as witnesses, to sustain objections against Masonic jurors, when called in a cause where a Brother or companion was a party—that they did attend, that objections were interposed on the ground of the existing obligation between the juror and party, and that the objected jurors have uniformly been dispensed with, rather than submit to a trial of the objection.

With respect to the correctness and truth of the degrees of Knights of the Red Cross—Knights Templars, and Knights of Malta—Knights of the Christian Mark—and Knights of the Holy Sepulchre, the evidence is written, and a reasonable doubt cannot be entertained. A ritual of these degrees in manuscript was left with those who made the disclosure by a high Masonic officer, known to have been authorized to confer those degrees.

This ritual formed the basis on which the publication was made, and still remains in their possession. There has been also a ritual in manuscript left by a high and authorized Mason, who came among them to establish a council, called "The Holy and Thrice Illustrious order of the Cross, called a council," and grant diplomas, headed "The Ancient council of the Trinity, by their successors in the United States of America"—from these rituals were the degrees of Knighthood taken and published. Your committee therefore are of opinion, that the evidence in relation to these latter degrees is conclusive.

The progress in Masonry, of one of the informants, was thus given Masonically.

Regularly *initiated* into the degree of Entered Apprentice Mason.
Passed to the degree of Fellow Craft.
Raised to the *sublime* degree of Master.
Advanced to the Honorary degree of Mark Master.
Presided in the chair.
Acknowledged and received as most Excellent Master, and *Exalted* to the sublime degree of Royal Arch.
Degrees in the Encampment.
Knight of the Red Cross.
Knight Templar, and Knight of Malta.
Knight of the Christian Mark, and
Knight of the Holy Sepulchre.

APPENDIX.

In the council he received the degree of Illustrious, Most Illustrious, and Thrice Illustrious Order of the Cross.

The offices he held were, Worshipful Master.

Secretary of the Chapter, and Generalissimo of the Genesee Encampment.

That, in addition to the three degrees of Masonry revealed by William Morgan, and the twelve degrees disclosed by the convention of seceding Masons at Le Roy, on the 4th and 5th of July last, your committee would beg leave to state that Elder David Bernard, late Intimate Secretary of the Lodge of Perfection, and one of the seceding Masons at Le Roy, is about to publish the "*Eleven Ineffable Degrees*" conferred in the Lodge of Perfection, and also, Seven French Degrees of a still higher order of Masonry: the authenticity of which your committee think cannot reasonably be doubted; that in one of these degrees now revealed, namely, the " *Knights and Adepts of the Eagle, or Sun !*" Deism is plainly avowed, and a dagger aimed at the Christian Religion.

BATES COOKE, *Chairman.*

Resolved, That in the opinion of this convention, the authenticity of the thirty-three degrees of Free Masonry revealed, is satisfactorily established.

Mr. Morris read the following Circular, which, on motion of Mr. Percival, was ordered to be printed:

CIRCULAR.

To the Worshipful Master, Wardens, and Brethren of Lodge No.

NEW-YORK, July 16, 1825.

Brethren—As a Member of our ancient and Honorable Fraternity, I take the liberty to transmit to you the Prospectus of a Charter for a BANKING COMPANY, and to announce to you, that I intend to make application to the Legislature of this state, at their next Session, for an Act of incorporation of the same, under the style of "THE MASONIC BANK OF THE STATE OF NEW-YORK," for the purpose of allowing an interest on all deposits which may be made therein, by Masons and their Widows, and for the benefit of the children of Masons; and to execute all trusts in their behalf, &c. with a capital of $300,000, and the privilege of increasing the same whenever it should be deemed expedient by the Directors, to $600,000, and of establishing a Branch or Branches in one or more of the Senatorial Districts of this State.

The advantages to be derived to the Fraternity from such an Institution, to be under the direction of respectable Master Masons, *and guarded by the solemnity of Masonic Obligation,* must be too obvious to you to require from me any comment or elucidation. Should the plan, of which a Prospectus is herewith respectfully submitted for your consideration, meet with your concurrence, I beg that you will as early as convenient, adopt such measures as you may deem the most expedient and effectual, to aid me in obtaining a Charter from the Legislature. With sentiments of fraternal regard and consideration, I have the favor to be,

My Respected Brethren,
Your Devoted Brother,
AARON H. PALMER,
Past Master of Holland Lodge, No. 16.

Mr. Fitch, Chairman of the Committee on the subject of providing for the support of Mrs. Lucinda Morgan, submitted the following Report and Resolutions—which, after some remarks from Mr. Fitch, were adopted.

The committee " appointed to enquire whether Mrs. Lucinda Morgan, widow of the late Capt. William Morgan, is provided with the necessary means of supporting herself and her orphan children, and if not, whether it is expedient and proper for this Convention to adopt any measures for her relief," beg leave to

APPENDIX.

REPORT:

That Mrs. Morgan is the daughter of Joseph Pendleton, a respectable Methodist Clergyman residing in the county of Richmond, in the state of Virginia; she is now about twenty-seven years old, and was married to Capt. Morgan in 1819. He was at that time a man of respectable character and standing in society and worth considerable property. He soon after removed to York, in the province of Upper Canada, where he established himself in business with a fair prospect of success, which, however, was soon blasted. His whole establishment, and all his property to the amount of several thousand dollars, was destroyed by fire, and he was reduced to absolute poverty, and compelled to resort to manual labor for the support of his wife and children. He then removed to the state of New-York, and soon after took up his residence in Batavia, Genesee county, where, by honest industry, he was enabled to procure a comfortable support for his family. He continued to reside at that place till September 1826, when he was kidnapped and murdered, through the instrumentality and in obedience to the laws and principles of the order of Free Masonry. By this bold and unparalleled outrage upon the public laws of the land and the private rights of the citizen, Mrs. Morgan was deprived of the protecting care of a tender husband, and left with two small children, one about two years and the other only two months old, totally destitute of all means necessary for procuring the actual necessaries of life, and dependent upon private charity alone, which is still her only resource. Your committee, however, do not wish it to be understood as saying that Mrs. Morgan, widow of the late Capt. William Morgan, who was immolated upon the altar of Masonic vengeance—sacrificed as a martyr to his country's liberty, among a generous and hospitable people—in a land of plenty and even abundance, is permitted to want the common necessaries and comforts of life. No—the conduct of such base ingratitude lies not at the door of our western brethren. A grateful people have promptly extended a liberal hand for her relief; but still this source of sustenance is humiliating and painful to the recipient, precarious in its nature, and unjust in its operation.

Mrs. Morgan is a woman of feeble constitution, and consequently unable, by her personal exertions, to procure the means of support, and if the sources of private charity should be dried up, or their channels be diverted or obstructed, she must become the tenant of a poor house.—Until the breath of Masonic calumny assailed her character, it was fair and unblemished, and for ought that she has done to tarnish it, is still fair. Immediately after the abduction and murder of her husband, the authors and abettors of that atrocious outrage, without the slightest foundation in truth, assailed her character with every species of calumny, whether from motives of revenge on her husband, whose blood was still reeking upon their hands, or with a view to divert public sympathy from her relief, your committee will not undertake to say—but certain it is that a system of persevering and cruel slander has in some instances withheld the hand of charity, and chilled the heart of benevolence. Your committee, therefore, think it due to Mrs. Morgan, as well as to the cause of Anti-Masonry and the character of those who sustain it, that this Convention adopt the most efficient measures for her relief, and to produce so desirable a result, they beg leave to recommend the adoption of the accompanying resolutions.

Resolved, That it be recommended to the state central committee to appoint five suitable persons of the village of Utica, as trustees, whose duty it shall be to receive in trust, all donations and contributions which may be made for the future support of Mrs. Morgan, and the support and education of her two children, Lucinda and Thomas, and to vest all such monies in such manner as in their judgment will be most productive, and to receive and pay over the income thereof, for the foregoing objects.

Resolved, That it be recommended to the central committees of each county, already appointed, or hereafter to be appointed, throughout this state, to appoint in each county a suitable person to receive in trust, all donations and contributions, which may be made in such county, for the foregoing objects, whose duty it shall be to pay over the same to the trustees above mentioned.

Resolved, That the central committees of each county also appoint three persons in each town of their respective counties, whose duty it shall be to appoint one suitable person in each school district, in their respective towns, and in the wards of the several cities and villages, to collect and receive monies therein.

Resolved, That the persons thus appointed in the respective school districts, shall circulate therein, subscription papers, and to collect and receive such sums of money as the people will voluntarily contribute for the foregoing objects, and to pay the same over to the county receiver.

Resolved, That the state central committee draw up a subscription paper, with a suitable appeal to the people of this state, and cause a sufficient number thereof to be printed and forwarded to the central committees of their respective counties, as occasion may require to be, by the said committees, distributed in the several towns of their respective counties, to be circulated as aforesaid.

Resolved, That all such monies when collected and vested as aforesaid, shall remain unimpaired, and the income thereof only shall be appropriated for the support of Mrs. Morgan and her children, until her youngest child shall arrive at the age of twenty-one years, when it shall be divided into three equal parts, the one part to be paid to Mrs. Morgan, and one part to each of her children.

Resolved, That in case of the death of Mrs. Morgan or either of her children, before the youngest shall arrive at the age of twenty-one years, then the said monies so collected and vested as aforesaid, shall be equally divided among the survivors or paid to the survivor as the case may be.

Resolved, That in case of the death of Mrs. Morgan and both her children before the youngest shall arrive at the age of twenty-one years, that then and in said case, the monies so collected and vested as aforesaid, shall be appropriated under the direction of the Trustees aforesaid, to the erection of a suitable monument, commemorative of the events connected with the abduction and murder of Capt. William Morgan.

Resolved, That in case of the death, removal, inability, or refusal to act of any of the said Trustees, or any of the persons appointed in pursuance of the foregoing resolutions, that such vacancy shall be supplied by the authorities herein respectively designated to make the appointment.

Resolved, That the citizens of other states be earnestly solicited to co-operate with the people of this state, to promote the objects mentioned in these resolutions.

Mr. Holley, from the committee appointed to prepare an address, reported the following, which was read and adopted.

ADDRESS

TO THE PEOPLE OF THE STATE OF NEW-YORK.

FELLOW-CITIZENS—A great crisis has occurred in our social condition. The peace of this community has been extensively disturbed, the domestic security of the citizens openly violated, their property unlawfully invaded, and the life of one of them, without doubt, feloniously destroyed. And these calamitous events have proceeded from a source which threatens our most valuable institutions, and all those possessions which make life desirable. With these facts deeply impressed upon our hearts, we have been delegated to assemble here, to consult together, and advise upon the proper course to be pursued, in so momentous an emergency.

We will not disguise the painful conviction of our minds, and we cannot suppress it, that we are commencing a course of action which will necessarily bring with it, much disquietude and distress. The intercourse of business will be obstructed, the laudable associations of neighbourhoods will be convulsed, and many of the best sympathies of our nature will be violently turned away from their customary channels. Such a course of action should not be commenced for slight or transient causes. Nothing which does not affect the essence of our freedom, and which does not manifest itself in the most decisive and solemn forms, can justify it. But, when the public peace, our domestic safety, our property, our life, our reputation, our equal rights as citizens, are all assailed, by the concerted action of numerous, wealthy, intelligent, and powerful bodies of men; and the regular operations of our constituted authorities is found unable to protect us, then, it is equally becoming to our minds and hearts, to our self-respect, and the most cherished interests of human liberty, that we should protect ourselves whatever evils may ensue.

The following facts are well established:

In the summer of 1826, a peaceable citizen was lawfully engaged in preparing for publication, a pamphlet, in which he discloses the secrets of the first degrees of Free Masonry.

It was known to many Free Masons, that this publication was preparing, and numerous meetings of Free Masons were held, at different places and times, to consider the subject of this publication. At these meetings it was resolved, with the universal approbation of those present, to destroy the intended publication, against the known will, and the lawful rights, of its author.

In pursuance of this resolve;

On the 19th of August, 1826, the private papers of the author were unlawfully seized, by Free Masons.

On the 8th of September next following, formidable preparations were made, by Free Masons, to assault the private lodgings of a peaceful citizen engaged in printing the said publication.

On the 10th of the same month, a felonious attempt was made, by Free Masons, to burn the printing office, where the said publication was supposed to be, and the dwelling house of the printer.

On the 11th of the same month, the dwelling house of a fellow-citizen was maliciously invaded by Free Masons, he seized under the forms of law, forced from his family, transported to a foreign county, and there confined in jail.

On the 12th of the same month, another fellow-citizen was maliciously seized, in his domestic residence, by Free Masons, under the forms of law, and transported against his will, to a lodge room, where he was forcibly and unlawfully detained a prisoner.

On the night of the day last mentioned, a fellow-citizen, under false pretences, was unlawfully seized by Free Masons, who bound, gagged, and blindfolded him, and thereafter transported him, against his will, more than one hundred miles, to the borders of our national territory, and there confined him, for several days.

During these outrages, the citizens against whom they were more immediately committed, were repeatedly assaulted, and threatened with death, and otherwise most inhumanly treated by Free Masons. Subsequently, one of them has never been seen, by his family or friends, and many Free Masons have declared, that he was murdered, and many more, that he deserved to be

APPENDIX.

so, for having violated his Masonic obligations, by the lawful publication of the pamphlet aforesaid.

The unlawful seizure and transportation of one of these citizens having been accidentally discovered, by some intelligent and public spirited persons, three Free Masons were indicted, before one of our courts, for a conspiracy to effect those objects ; and being guilty, and to prevent the disclosure of the names of their accomplices, if possible, and the discovery of a much more aggravated crime perpetrated by one of them, in case of examination of witnesses summoned to sustain the indictment, they confessed themselves guilty of the conspiracy, and were thereupon sentenced to imprisonment, in the jail of the county were they were convicted, for different periods of time. Notwithstanding their conviction and punishment as infamous criminals, these Free Masons, since the expiration of their different periods of imprisonment, have maintained a good standing with the fraternity, of which they were members, and been objects of its peculiar sympathy and favor.

Many other exertions have been made, by respectable citizens, to establish, with legal formality, facts, as they are too well known to exist, relating to these outrages ; and to bring to punishment those who were concerned in perpetrating them. All these exertions have been resisted by Free Masons, and that successfully, with few and unimportant exceptions. Masonic witnesses have refused to testify, when brought upon the stand, because they could not do so, without criminating themselves. And leading members of the fraternity have been known to persuade their brethren not to testify what they knew, against the persons who might be called before courts to answer for these outrages, by reminding them of their Masonic obligations to protect their brethren, and alleging that the violation of these obligations constituted a self-crimination, which was a lawful reason for their declining to testify. Gross irregularities have been practised by Grand Jurors, and higher ministers of the law, during the pendency of legal proceedings instituted for the ascertainment of truth and the promotion of justice, in respect to these outrages. Masonic witnesses have perjured themselves, and when witnesses not of the Fraternity have established guilt, by their testimony, their characters have been impeached by Masonic witnesses, who had previously conspired together for that purpose. These exertions, in behalf of truth and justice, have continued, for more than two years, and they have, hitherto, even with aid of extraordinary official appointment, done little more than make known the vigilance, address, and power, with which the institution of Free Masonry is able to protect its members.

The commission of these crimes afforded serious causes of alarm ; the designed, systematic, persevering, and effectual prevention of their disclosures, before the tribunals legally authorised for their investigation and punishment, by a particular description of men, greatly aggravated those causes ; this description of men acting, in this prevention, as the agents, and in conformity with the solemn requirements, of the most secret, most extensive, and most craftily concerted combination of active, intelligent, and powerful persons, both fellow citizens and aliens, that has ever existed in the world ; gives to these causes the most frightful and protentous aspect.

The most interesting facts, therefore, respecting these crimes, are those, which have been incidently developed, in the course of enquiry and examination into them. These facts are included in the revelation of the extraordinary oaths and penalties, extent, funds, means of secret and universal concert, and power, of Free Masonry. In this state alone, there are near 30,000 Free Masons, who meet, frequently, in about 500 different lodges, 100 chapters, and several councils and encampments.

A more minute and extended specification of facts seems to be unnecessary here, since it may be found, in the numerous and able newspapers, magazines, and other well conducted publications, which the awakened fears and indignation of an abused community, have recently originated.

In our country the people are the only legitimate source of civil power. It is the will of the people, by which laws are enacted, and applied to the various rights and pursuits of life. This will calls into employment, elective, legislative, judicial, and executive bodies, which are only the instruments by which it is brought into visible and useful action. But the will of a state, or nation, like the will of an individual, depends upon opinion,—the opinion of a majority of the people of a state, or nation; and the opinion of such majority is PUBLIC OPINION.—Public opinion, therefore, controlling the will of the people, in every free country, must govern every thing, which is properly subject to governmental power. This is the theory of our government. It is clearly the only theory consistent with the rights of man. And among us, it has been so well applied in practice, heretofore, as to ensure the good anticipated by the framers of our government.

But we have recently witnessed an alarming change. The machinery of our government has become obviously disordered.—Free Masonry has come into violent collision with it; and its healthful operations are either suspended, or rendered ineffectual. And the great question is now presented to the people of this state, what shall be done to restore it to its salutary and effectual operation.

Our fathers gave this government the holiest name that can be applied to civil institutions; they called it FREE. And we recollect, with admiration and pride, the wisdom, the firmness, the toils, the dangers, the sufferings, the heroic and disinterested virtues, through the exercise of which, it was established. Under its protecting and paternal power, we have grown up to be a great nation. A question affecting, vitally, all the beneficent objects, and prosperous results of such a government, must be regarded, by the freemen whom it has fostered in all their honorable avocations, and most interesting ties, with the deepest solicitude. Every one of them, when such a question is brought home to his understanding and his interests, will apply his best faculties to its thorough examination, and deliberately settle it for himself; and if he finds it pregnant with evil, beyond all power of description, he will, with a high heart, and unswerving constancy, pursue the most prudent measures to remove the evil.

Free Masonry is a distinct, peculiar, independent government. It acknowledges no allegiance to civil government, nor alliance with it. It has departments of its own, titles of its own, officers of its own, laws of its own, revenues of its own, oaths of its own, penalties of its own, sympathies of its own, and purposes of its own. All the nations of the earth, however diverse their forms of government, or distant their territories, are but its provinces. It has no jurisdictional limits but the habitable globe. Throughout its whole extent, it secures the loyalty of its subjects, by cords most ingeniously twisted, and of surpassing strength. In its injunction by oath, upon its higher members, to protect a brother, right or wrong, in all cases whatsoever, even at the risk of life, it inculcates treasonable resistance to civil authority, as well as every subordinate crime against the public, whenever the protection of an offending brother, from the just animadversions of the law, shall require a resort to them. And this inculcation is enforced by such penalties, that we have seen, in our state, men of mature years, in good business, and of respectable standing in society, while they were under the strongest hindrances offered by the ties of nature and of patriotism, yield to the enforcement.

A single exhibition of such an evil, is enough for men watchful for their liberties, and determined to maintain them. The possibility of its existence is dangerous; its actual occurrence demands instant, resolute, continued, and united, though prudent, exertion, till it shall become impossible. What, then, are the prudent means, by the application of which, such an evil can be effectually and for ever precluded? This can be only by the annihilation of the source from which it springs. Free Masonry must be utterly suppressed. And it is the peculiar duty, and will be the peculiar honor of this land of free principles, of free thoughts, and of free communications, to suppress it.

One very important means of its suppression is, the renunciation and exposure of it by the virtuous men who have heedlessly fallen into its embrace. Many such men have already separated themselves from its polluting folds. And this Convention cannot but indulge the hope, that every good man, upon whom a single one of its guilty obligations remains, will soon discard it altogether, and contribute his utmost to redeem the land of his fathers, the inheritance of his children, and the sacred rights of the human race, from its blighting influences.

But to the far more numerous class of good men among us, who are not Free Masons, belong the highest responsibilities of this mighty work. They are under no imaginary ties to the institution, they can be restrained by none of its horrible oaths, its terrible penalties, or its mysterious sympathies, while they array themselves for war against it. Looking more exclusively upon the all absorbing mischiefs which it threatens, under an equal sense of all their civil and social duties, and equally impelled by love of country and every honorable affection, they must prescribe the course to be pursued, and be chiefly answerable for its success. If they at all indulge the spirit of individual persecution; if they engage in the conflict with any trait of selfish or sinister purposes; or if they waver in the course prescribed by prudence; they will deserve all the odium of defeat, and all the infamy of betraying the highest earthly hopes of man.

Free Masonry can be suppressed by no common power. Claiming a peculiar sovereignty, it contemplates, with lofty contempt, or manifest indifference, all other human sovereignties. Its legislators, its expounders, and its orators profess to believe that its existence, its safety, even its immunities and privileges are beyond the reach of either peace or war, from the nations of the earth. Have our fathers been so mistaken? Are we so deluded? In our country is not Free Masonry subject to the mighty sovereignty of public opinion? Must it not surrender all its strong holds to the enlightened, determined, repeated, and plainly expressed will of the majority? Let us subject it to the trial. Let us ascertain whether the glorious temple of our liberties is founded on the sand, to be subverted by the storms of Free Masonry, or rests on the rock of human rights, in the protection of Him who built the earth and the heavens.

There is but one way in which the power of public opinion can be fully applied to Free Masonry. A part of this power exists in our executive offices, a part in our legislatures, a part in our courts of justice. In all these parts Free Masonry has been in conflict with it, for two years, and with appalling success. By its secret poisons, and its concentrated efforts, it has wonderfully and fearfully prevailed. But the whole power of public opinion is to be found in the BALLOT-BOXES. And these are the depositories, as we humbly trust, of the mightiest earthly power which the Divine wisdom has ever permitted man to control. If we would effectually destroy Free Masonry, then, we have no alternative; we must call to our aid, and persist in the uses of our elective rights. We must unite, as a party, at the polls. We must select for all elective offices, the best men opposed to Free Masonry, whether they are those who have renounced it, or otherwise; and we must select them *because they are opposed to it.* And these men we must support, uniformly, constantly, zealously, always, till Free Masonry, with all its fantastical pageantry, its false pretensions, its unhallowed means, its alarming power, and its monstrous crimes, shall be numbered with the past misfortunes of our country.

To this resort we are summoned, by every fear and every hope which can affect the souls of Freemen. Our country appeals to us, to make this effort, in a cause as high and as sacred as any that ever was promoted by human means; by all the sorrows and joys, by all the prevalent blessings, venerated recollections, and exulting anticipations of our social condition. And let us not fear the charge of too much "*excitement.*" In such a cause, excitement brings blame only to those with whom it is weak or wavering. What individual has ever satisfied himself, in a good cause, without excitement? What nation has ever wrested its liberties, from the grasp of tyranny, without excitement? What great reformation in religion has ever been effected, without excitement? Whence originate the purest virtues, and the most exalted achievements of created intelligences, but from powerful excitement? The strongest love of justice, the quickest indignation at wrong, and the most impassioned admiration of beneficence, are the appropriate signatures of a *superior* nature; but these are only other names for high excitement. And such excitement the cause we are engaged in both requires and sanctifies.

On motion of Mr. Weed,

Resolved, That the delegates from each county be called to state whether the sheriffs of their respective counties were Masons in the year 1826—the time of Morgan's abduction.

The result of the information thus obtained was, that of 43 counties, concerning which information was submitted to the convention, the sheriffs of 33 counties were known to be Masons in 1826—the sheriffs of 7 counties were known not to be Masons, and from three counties the information received was not positive.

On motion of Mr. Tracy,

Resolved, That HARVEY ELY, SAMUEL WORKS, FREDERICK WHITTLESEY, FREDERICK F. BACKUS, and THURLOW WEED, constitute the general central state committee.

Resolved, That BATES COOKE, of Lewiston, and TIMOTHY FITCH, of Batavia, be added to the above committee.

Resolved, That 10,000 copies of the proceedings of this convention be published under the direction of the central committee, and that the expense be defrayed by voluntary contribution from members of this convention.

The convention then closed its session with prayer by Elder Green.

Resolved, That the convention adjourn without delay.

WILLIAM FINN, *President.*
JAMES HAWKS,
ALEX'R. SHELDON. } *V. Presidents.*

NICHOLAS DEVERAUX,
FREDERICK WHITTLESEY, } *Secretaries.*

ROCHESTER, March 15, 1829.

At a meeting of the State Central Committee, NICHOLAS DEVEREAUX, APOLLAS COOPER, WILLIAM WILLIAMS, THOMAS F. FIELD, and CHARLES MORRISS, were appointed, pursuant to a resolution of the State Convention, Trustees of the Fund for the relief of Mrs. Lucinda Morgan, and her infant children.

By Order of the Committee,
F. WHITTLESEY, Sec'y

Designed by Elizabeth A. W. McCarthy and Arturo de Hoyos.
Layout by Elizabeth A. W. McCarthy and S. Brent Morris.

Composed with InDesign CS2 using Adobe Jenson Pro, ITC Century Std. Book
Condensed, Symbol, Wingdings, and Zapf Dingbats.

Related Titles from Westphalia Press

Ancient Mysteries and Modern Masonry: The Collected Writings of Jewel P. Lightfoot, Edited by Billy J. Hamilton Jr.

Jewel P. Lightfoot. Former Attorney General of the State of Texas. Past Grand Master of the Masonic Grand Lodge of Texas. From humble beginnings in rural Arkansas, he worked to become an educated man who excelled in law and Freemasonry. He was a gentleman of his time, well-known as a scholar, public speaker, and Masonic philosopher.

Essay on The Mysteries and the True Object of The Brotherhood of Freemasons
by Jason Williams

This isn't a reprint of a classic. It's a new rendition with new life breathed into it, to be enjoyed both by the layperson trying to understand the Craft and Masonic scholars taking a deeper dive into the fraternity's golden years—when the concepts of liberty and equality were still fresh.

Female Emancipation and Masonic Membership:
An Essential Collection
By Guillermo De Los Reyes Heredia

Female Emancipation and Masonic Membership: An Essential Combination is a collection of essays on Freemasonry and gender that promotes a transatlantic discussion of the study of the history of women and Freemasonry and their contribution in different countries.

Freemasonry, Heir to the Enlightenment
by Cécile Révauger

Modern Freemasonry may have mythical roots in Solomon's time but is really the heir to the Enlightenment. Ever since the early eighteenth century freemasons have endeavored to convey the values of the Enlightenment in the cultural, political and religious fields, in Europe, the American colonies and the emerging United States.

Freemasonry: A French View
by Roger Dachez and Alain Bauer

Perhaps one should speak not of Freemasonry but of Freemasonries in the plural. In each country Masonic historiography has developed uniqueness. Two of the best known French Masonic scholars present their own view of the worldwide evolution and challenging mysteries of the fraternity over the centuries.

Worlds of Print: The Moral Imagination of an Informed Citizenry, 1734 to 1839
by John Slifko

John Slifko argues that freemasonry was representative and played an important role in a larger cultural transformation of literacy and helped articulate the moral imagination of an informed democratic citizenry via fast emerging worlds of print.

Why Thirty-Three?: Searching for Masonic Origins
by S. Brent Morris, PhD

What "high degrees" were in the United States before 1830? What were the activities of the Order of the Royal Secret, the precursor of the Scottish Rite? A complex organization with a lengthy pedigree like Freemasonry has many basic foundational questions waiting to be answered, and that's what this book does: answers questions.

The Great Transformation: Scottish Freemasonry 1725-1810
by Dr. Mark C. Wallace

This book examines Scottish Freemasonry in its wider British and European contexts between the years 1725 and 1810. The Enlightenment effectively crafted the modern mason and propelled Freemasonry into a new era marked by growing membership and the creation of the Grand Lodge of Scotland.

Getting the Third Degree: Fraternalism, Freemasonry and History
Edited by Guillermo De Los Reyes and Paul Rich

As this engaging collection demonstrates, the doors being opened on the subject range from art history to political science to anthropology, as well as gender studies, sociology and more. The organizations discussed may insist on secrecy, but the research into them belies that.

The Great Transformation: Scottish Freemasonry 1725-1810
by Dr. Mark C. Wallace

This book examines Scottish Freemasonry in its wider British and European contexts between the years 1725 and 1810. The Enlightenment effectively crafted the modern mason and propelled Freemasonry into a new era marked by growing membership and the creation of the Grand Lodge of Scotland.

Getting the Third Degree: Fraternalism, Freemasonry and History
Edited by Guillermo De Los Reyes and Paul Rich

As this engaging collection demonstrates, the doors being opened on the subject range from art history to political science to anthropology, as well as gender studies, sociology and more. The organizations discussed may insist on secrecy, but the research into them belies that.

Freemasonry: A French View
by Roger Dachez and Alain Bauer

Perhaps one should speak not of Freemasonry but of Freemasonries in the plural. In each country Masonic historiography has developed uniqueness. Two of the best known French Masonic scholars present their own view of the worldwide evolution and challenging mysteries of the fraternity over the centuries.

Worlds of Print: The Moral Imagination of an Informed Citizenry, 1734 to 1839
by John Slifko

John Slifko argues that freemasonry was representative and played an important role in a larger cultural transformation of literacy and helped articulate the moral imagination of an informed democratic citizenry via fast emerging worlds of print.

Why Thirty-Three?: Searching for Masonic Origins
by S. Brent Morris, PhD

What "high degrees" were in the United States before 1830? What were the activities of the Order of the Royal Secret, the precursor of the Scottish Rite? A complex organization with a lengthy pedigree like Freemasonry has many basic foundational questions waiting to be answered, and that's what this book does: answers questions.

A Place in the Lodge: Dr. Rob Morris, Freemasonry and the Order of the Eastern Star
by Nancy Stearns Theiss, PhD

Ridiculed as "petticoat masonry," critics of the Order of the Eastern Star did not deter Rob Morris' goal to establish a Masonic organization that included women as members. Morris carried the ideals of Freemasonry through a despairing time of American history.

Brought to Light: The Mysterious George Washington Masonic Cave
by Jason Williams MD

The George Washington Masonic Cave near Charles Town, West Virginia, contains a signature carving of George Washington dated 1748. This book painstakingly pieces together the chronicled events and real estate archives related to the cavern in order to sort out fact from fiction.

Dudley Wright: Writer, Truthseeker & Freemason
by John Belton

Dudley Wright (1868-1950) was an Englishman and professional journalist who took a universalist approach to the various great Truths of Life. He travelled though many religions in his life and wrote about them all, but was probably most at home with Islam.

History of the Grand Orient of Italy
Emanuela Locci, Editor

No book in Masonic literature upon the history of Italian Freemasonry has been edited in English up to now. This work consists of eight studies, covering a span from the Eighteenth Century to the end of the WWII, tracing through the story, the events and pursuits related to the Grand Orient of Italy.

westphaliapress.org

www.ingramcontent.com/pod-product-compliance
Lightning Source LLC
Chambersburg PA
CBHW071213040426
42333CB00068B/1727